J. M. AND M. J. COHEN

THE PENGUIN
DICTIONARY OF
MODERN
QUOTATIONS

SECOND EDITION

ALLEN LANE

ALLEN LANE

Penguin Books Ltd
536 King's Road
London SW10 0UH

First published in Penguin Books 1971
Second edition first published simultaneously
by Allen Lane and Penguin Books 1980

Copyright © J. M. and M. J. Cohen, 1971, 1980

ISBN 0 7139 1092 5

Set in Monotype Times
Printed in Great Britain by
Richard Clay (The Chaucer Press) Ltd,
Bungay, Suffolk

FOREWORD TO THE FIRST EDITION

This dictionary contains what we hope will be remembered in the year 2000 of the things said and written in the first two thirds of the century. It no doubt contains also a great deal that will have been forgotten by then, and perhaps a good deal that has already been forgotten, but which has amused, impressed or exasperated us at some time in the three years of the sixties in which we have been collecting these four thousand-odd quotations from poets, politicians, novelists, lawyers, comedians and others who somehow get into print or on the air. The bias is predominantly English; translations are given for all sayings in foreign languages. We have set the year 1900 as our starting point, and though we may inadvertently have filched one or two things from the nineties, we have tried to keep strictly to our date.

As we found in compiling the *Penguin Dictionary of Quotations*, it is not always the great who make the best remarks. We are very conscious that some of the finest minds of the century are almost unrepresented. Scientists are seldom brief. Politicians are especially disappointing in their failure to provide the sparks for which we searched the dull embers of their biographies. The great criminal lawyers and judges seldom say anything that seems either impressive or funny out of court. Radio programmes like *Itma* and *The Goon Show*, on the other hand, offer far more good lines than we can include. Books and the theatre provide the bulk of our offerings; advertisement slogans, music-hall lyrics and remarks on public occasions supply the rest. We have been careful not to include anything that appeared in the *Penguin Dictionary of Quotations* itself. This may inconvenience a reader in search of a line of Shaw or a saying of Churchill's, who has to use two books to find it. But to serve up perhaps a thousand quotations from the first book in the second seemed to us like delivering short weight.

Difficulties in compiling this *Dictionary of Modern Quotations* have been far greater than in making our original dictionary, for which we had every age and many works of reference to draw on. Here we have had to rely on our own judgements and a brief seventy years of history. We have not given dates of birth for our authors (as in so many instances it was not possible to do so), and most of them have fortunately as yet no dates of death. Nor can we be as certain of our accuracy in this book except when using printed sources. Many sayings have had to be marked 'attributed', and many others circulate in more than one form; two newspaper accounts of a speech seldom entirely agree. Many readers will consequently be in the position to correct us in one respect or another. We hope they will do so.

We have had much help in collecting our quotations both from friends and public institutions. It is possible only to name our principal helpers. The BBC allowed us to check our memories of various radio programmes; the *Observer* put its files of *Sayings of the Week* at our disposal, and we have drawn very profitably on them. The *Observer*, the *Sunday Times* and *New Society* published our letters of request for memorable sayings, which produced some interesting suggestions. Among our friends perhaps fifty have contributed a quotation or two or put us on the track of something good. John Gloag, G. M. Lee and Geoffrey Strachan and Peter Ford have been particularly generous in drawing on their reading and memory. We thank everyone who has helped us.

In order to save space, lines of verse are run on and the divisions between lines are indicated by oblique strokes.

We hope that this book will instruct, amuse and entertain, and that the very full index will enable readers to find what they want under the key word that they most clearly remember; also that when they look up a familiar word they will find something unknown and impressive that has been said on the subject.

October, 1970   J. M. and M. J. C.

FOREWORD TO THE SECOND EDITION

Ten years have passed since the first edition of *The Penguin Dictionary of Modern Quotations*, and much that is memorable has been said, sung and written since President Nixon's somewhat over-emphatic reaction to the first moon-landing – the latest entry in our first edition. We have taken advantage of this new edition to cut out entries which now strike us as dated, forgettable or unfunny; to improve details in ascription or reference; and to make good our worst omissions. We gave unduly short measure to science, the cinema, television, popular song and graffiti. These subject areas we have expanded. Many authors now provide additional entries, many others contribute quotations for the first time.

The help we have received on the new edition has been still more significant than when first preparing our dictionary. Letters appealing for help appeared in many papers and periodicals, including *Books and Bookmen*, *Gay News*, *Guardian*, *Irish Times*, *New Society*, *New Statesman*, *Observer*, *Private Eye*, *Radio Times*, *Times Educational Supplement* and *Time Out*. Many hundreds of people were kind enough to ransack their memories, and their common-place- and note-books, and our collection and selection has been immeasurably helped by this response.

We should like to thank in particular: Sally Adams, Brian W. Aldiss, Sydney D. Bailey, Philippa Bignell, Henry Blyth, Ivan Brown, John Brunner, Dr and Mrs O. Buchan, G. M. Byrne, Victor Cappaert, J. L. Carr, Martin Childs, Margaret Coombs, Design and Art Directors Association of London, Vince Dowd, Wanda Ealing, T. Eldridge, Valerie Ferguson, M. Fores, Jonathon Green, Colin Greenland, Frank Hancock, R. D. Hill, Arthur Koestler, Tony Lacey, Phyllis M. Lee, Claire L'Enfant, Ellie Ling, T. J. Lustig, Kevin McDermott, Malcolm McEachran, John Major, G. Miller, Ken Mullen, Christopher Murphy, Eric Partridge, R. D. Pearce, Nigel Price, B. Ramsay, James Reeves, B. Rochester, John M. Ross, Ronald Searle, Finbarr Slattery, Per Skjaeveland, R. Stanton, Geoffrey Strachan, W. J. Thaxter, Vera Thomas, Richard Walters, Jon Wynne-Tyson.

Four friends have provided constant help and advice in the preparation of this new edition; sieving, suggesting, augmenting. Without the contributions from Ingrid von Essen, Brian Thompson and Elizabeth Teague (who also performed, with Judith Wardman, the massive task of renewing the index) and Peter Ford (who also carried out the final preparation of the text for the press) the book would be greatly the poorer.

January, 1980   J. M. and M. J. C.

It is a good thing for an uneducated man to read books of quotations.
Winston Churchill, *My Early Life*

She said she didn't care a jot
If people quoted her or not.
Noël Coward, *Sigh No More*

Sometimes it seems the only accomplishment my education ever bestowed on me, the ability to think in quotations.
Margaret Drabble, *A Summer Bird-Cage*

I imagine we're going to find this *full* of quotations!
Ruth Draper, *The Italian Lesson*

I might repeat to myself, slowly and soothingly, a list of quotations beautiful from minds profound; if I can remember any of the damn things.
Dorothy Parker, *The Little Hours*

It seems pointless to be quoted if one isn't going to be quotable ... It's better to be quotable than honest.
Tom Stoppard, in the *Guardian*, 21 March 1973

Someone, some spokesman on education, I assume in the Labour Party, only I somehow have a hunch that it *wasn't* someone in the Labour Party, that it was someone more surprising than that, or possibly not, possibly it was someone quite obvious, said, or perhaps wrote, but I think said, about two years ago, but it may have been three or four, or further back still ... said *something* to the effect that even corporal punishment was better than selection, because selection something like made as it were brothers and sisters, or some such categories of close blood relationship, into as it were enemies, or something equally undesirable ...
  ... I just want to know who said it. And also when he said it, and where he said it, and what it was he said, and whether he said it at all or whether I've merely imagined it ... (see page 372)

A

MARK ABRAMS

1 We continue to overlook the fact that work has become a leisure activity. [*Observer*, 'Sayings of the Week', 3 Jun. 1962]

DANNIE ABSE

2 So in the simple blessing of a rainbow, / in the bevelled edge of a sunlit mirror, / I have seen, visible, Death's artifact / like a soldier's ribbon on a tunic tacked. [*The Pathology of Colours*]

GOODMAN ACE

3 TV – a clever contraction derived from the words Terrible Vaudeville. However, it is our latest medium – we call it a medium because nothing's well done . . . It has already revolutionized social grace by cutting down parlour conversation to two sentences: 'What's on television?' and 'Good night.' [Letter to Groucho Marx, quoted in *The Groucho Letters*, n.d.]

4 I would have answered your letter sooner, but you didn't send one. [Quoted in *ib*. 'Sunday 1950']

5 All I can say is that if you read these routines and you like them, then you're the easiest guy to write for since Moses wrote the Ten Commandments after that Short Story Conference with God. [Quoted in *ib*. 23 Jun. 1953]

6 Every time a gun goes off in a have-not country another Communist is born. [*Saturday Review*, 12 Jun. 1965]

DEAN ACHESON

7 Great Britain has lost an Empire and not yet found a role. [Speech, 6 Dec. 1972]

8 [Of America's involvement in Vietnam] It is worse than immoral, it's a mistake.

[Quoted by Alistair Cooke in a *Letter from America* broadcast]

J. R. ACKERLEY

9 There was so much sculpture that I should certainly have missed the indecencies if Major Pomby had not been considerate enough to mention them. [*Hindoo Holiday*, Pt I, 28 Dec. 1923]

LORD ACTON

10 The atmosphere of accredited mendacity. [*The Study of History*]

ARTHUR ADAMOV

11 The reason why Absurdist plays take place in No Man's Land with only two characters is primarily financial. [Edinburgh International Drama Conference, 13 Sep. 1963]

RICHARD ADAMS

12 Many human beings say that they enjoy the winter, but what they really enjoy is feeling proof against it. [*Watership Down*, Ch. 50]

W. ADAMS and T. HOWARD

13 I Wonder Who's Kissing Her Now. [Title of song in musical, *Prince of Thought*]

HAROLD ADAMSON

14 Comin' in on a Wing and a Prayer. [Title of song]

ALISON ADBURGHAM

15 It was not that she herself [Queen Victoria] was a fashion leader. Probably the most notable garment she ever wore was the nightdress in which she received,

9

that early morning at Kensington Palace, the news of her uncle's death – the nightdress in which she became Queen. [*A Punch History of Manners and Modes*]

SIR FRANK ADCOCK

1 That typically English characteristic for which there is no English name – *esprit de corps*. [Presidential address]

GEORGE ADE

2 'Whom are you?' said he, for he had been to night school. [*Bang! Bang!: The Steel Box*]

3 Anyone can win, unless there happens to be a second entry. [Quoted in E. Esar and N. Bentley, *Treasury of Humorous Quotations*]

4 The house was more covered with mortgages than with paint. [Quoted in *ib.*]

5 The music teacher came twice each week to bridge the awful gap between Dorothy and Chopin. [Quoted in *ib.*]

ZOE ADKINS

6 The Greeks Had a Word For It. [Title of play]

ALFRED ADLER

7 When he heard that an egocentric had fallen in love, he [Adler] said: 'Against whom?' [Quoted in J. Bishop, *Some of my Best Friends*, 'Exponent of the Soul']

LARRY ADLER

8 Vasectomy means not ever having to say you're sorry. [Parody of line from E. Segal, *Love Story* (see 300:19). Contributed to B B C programme, *Quote … Unquote*, and recorded in book of selections from the programme, ed. N. Rees]

ADVERTISEMENTS

9 Be a real he-man and wear a Tarzan chest-wig. [Bogus advertisement in *Ballyhoo*, 1930s]

10 Beanz Meanz Heinz. [Ascribed to Ruth Watson of Young & Rubicam agency]

11 Body Odour. [Advertising slogan for Lifebuoy soap]

12 Born 1820 – Still Going Strong ['Johnny Walker' advertisement]

13 Drinka pinta milka day.

14 Even your best friends won't tell you. [American advertisement for Listerine, a deodorant]

15 Every picture tells a story. [Advertisement for Sloane's Backache and Kidney Pills, *c.* 1907]

16 Go to work on an egg. [Ascribed to Fay Weldon in the *Sunday Times*, 12 Jan. 1975]

17 He's a big shot in steel, but he's a dental cripple all the same. [American insurance advertisement, *c.* 1934]

18 Heineken. Refreshes the parts other beers cannot reach. [Ascribed to Terry Lovelock *et al.* of Collett, Dickenson, Pearce & Partners in *Design and Art Direction* '78, ed. E. Booth-Clibborn]

19 His hands are insured for thousands, but he suffers from athlete's foot. [American insurance advertisement, *c.* 1934]

20 I've never tried it because I don't like it. [Of *Guinness*. Ascribed to Jeremy Bullmore and Tom Rayfield of J. Walter Thompson, in *Design and Art Direction* '78, ed. E. Booth-Clibborn]

21 The man from the Pru. [Used from 1950, but phrase of far earlier origin]

22 Say it with Flowers. [Advertising slogan of American florists, 1920s. *See* Fleeson, 117:23]

23 That's Shell, that was.

24 Things happen when you take a Badedas bath. [Ascribed to Ogilvy, Benson & Mather agency]

25 We take you in so that the boys will take you out. [Notice in New York corsetière's, 1964]

26 Which Twin has the Toni?

1 We're number two. We try harder. [Avis car rental slogan. Ascribed to Doyle, Dane & Bernbach agency]

2 Whiter than white. [Detergent advertisement]

ADVERTISING COPYWRITER

3 *The Times* is read by the people who run the country.
The *Guardian* is read by the people who would like to run the country.
The *Financial Times* is read by the people who own the country.
The *Daily Telegraph* is read by the people who remember the country as it used to be.
The *Daily Express* is read by the people who think the country is still like that.
The *Daily Mail* is read by the wives of the men who run the country.
The *Daily Mirror* (which once tried to run the country) is read by the people who think they run the country.
The *Morning Star* is read by the people who would like another country to run the country.
The *Sun* – well, Murdoch has found a gap in the market – the oldest gap in the world.
[Quoted on the cover of F. Hirsch and D. Gordon, *Newspaper Money*]

H. AGAR

4 The truth that makes men free is for the most part the truth which men prefer not to hear. [*A Time for Greatness*]

JAMES AGATE

5 The leader-writer in a great Northern daily said on the morning after King Edward died that if he had not been a king he would have been the best type of sporting publican. [*Ego I*, 1935]

6 But I warn the Revenue and my creditors generally that I am nearing the end of my patience. It is a long worm that has no turning, and the turn this worm will take if not left reasonably alone is Carey Street ... They have had eightpence out of every shilling the worm has made. At ninepence it gets restive

and at tenpence it turns. [*Ego 4*, 3 Jun. 1940]

7 Is the Pathetic Fallacy less fallacious than we think? [*Ib.* 10 Jun. 1940]

8 Long experience has taught me that in England nobody goes to the theatre unless he or she has bronchitis. [*Ego 6*. See also Schnabel, 299:12]

9 I like listening to it [Tchaikovsky's 5th] just as I like looking at a fuchsia drenched with rain. [*Ego 8*, 1947]

10 A schoolgirl answered the question 'In what countries are elephants found?' Elephants are very large and intelligent animals, and are seldom lost. [*Ego 9*. Quoted in Edward Marsh *Ambrosia and Small Beer*, 'Envoi']

JAMES AGEE

11 If music be the breakfast food of love, kindly do not disturb until lunch time. [On Hollywood musicals, *Age of Film*]

SPIRO T. AGNEW

12 To some extent, if you've seen one city slum you've seen them all. [Speech during election campaign at Detroit, 18 Oct. 1968]

ANNA AKHMATOVA

13 Only the dusty flowers, / the clank of censers, and tracks / leading from somewhere to nowhere. [*Requiem 1935–1940*, v, trans. Richard McKane]

14 But in the room of the banished poet / Fear and the Muse stand watch by turn, and the night falls, / without the hope of dawn. [*Voronezh* (written after her visit to the banished Osip Mandelstam there), trans. S. Kunitz and M. Hayward]

'ALAIN'

(pseudonym of Émile Auguste Chartier)

15 What is fictitious in a novel is not so much the story but the method by which thought develops into action, a method which never occurs in daily life. [Quoted in E. M. Forster, *Aspects of the Novel*, III]

11

EDWARD ALBEE

1 Who's Afraid of Virginia Woolf? [Title of play]

2 Musical beds is the faculty sport around here. [*Who's Afraid of Virginia Woolf?*, Act I]

3 Martha is the only true pagan on the eastern seaboard. [*Ib.*]

4 I have a fine sense of the ridiculous, but no sense of humour. [*Ib.*]

5 Until you start ploughing pertinent wives, you really aren't working. The way to a man's heart is through his wife's belly and don't you forget it. [*Ib.* II]

6 You gotta have a swine to show you where the truffles are. [*Ib.*]

7 You just gird your blue-veined loins, girl. [*Ib.* III]

G. S. ALBEE

8 'I don't like to sleep with anybody,' replied Myrthis. 'I wouldn't sleep with my own mother.' [*By the Sea, By the Sea*, Ch. 5]

RICHARD ALDINGTON

9 Wearily the sentry moves / Muttering the one word: 'Peace'. [*Picket*]

10 Kill winter with your cannon, / Hold back Orion with your bayonets / And crush the spring leaf with your armies. [*In the Trenches*]

BRIAN ALDISS

11 Hubris clobbered by Nemesis. [Shortest definition of science fiction, *Science Fiction Art*, Introduction]

12 Science fiction is no more written for scientists than ghost stories are written for ghosts. [*Penguin Science Fiction*, editor's introduction]

13 Keep violence in the mind where it belongs. [*Barefoot in the Head*]

VICENTE ALEIXANDRE

14 Poetry must be human. If it is not human, it is not poetry. [Interview on receiving the Nobel Prize. *Observer*, 'Sayings of the Week', 9 Oct. 1977]

TSARINA ALEKSANDRA

15 They accuse Rasputin of kissing women etc. Read the Apostles; they kissed everybody as a form of greeting. [Letter to the Tsar, quoted in Leon Trotsky, *History of the Russian Revolution*, Vol. I, Ch. 4]

SAMUEL ALEXANDER

16 Evil is not ... wholly evil; it is misplaced good. [*Space, Time and Deity*]

NELSON ALGREN

17 He [Algren] shunts aside all rules, regulations, and dicta, except for three laws he says a nice old Negro lady once taught him: Never play cards with any man named 'Doc'. Never eat at any place called 'Mom's'. And never, ever, no matter what else you do in your whole life, *never* sleep with anyone whose troubles are worse than your own. [H. E. F. Donohue, *Conversations with Nelson Algren*, Foreword]

FRED ALLEN

18 A celebrity is a person who works hard all his life to become known, then wears dark glasses to avoid being recognized. [*Treadmill to Oblivion*]

19 A gentleman is any man who wouldn't hit a woman with his hat on. [Quoted in Laurence J. Peter, *Peter's Quotations*]

HERVEY ALLEN

20 Religions change; beer and wine remain. [*Anthony Adverse*, Pt I, Ch. 3, sect. xx]

WOODY ALLEN

21 Is sex dirty? Only if it's done right. [From film, *All You've Ever Wanted to Know About Sex*]

22 [On sex] It was the most fun I ever had without laughing. [From film, *Annie Hall*, scripted with Marshall Brickman]

1 [Of masturbation] Don't knock it, it's sex with someone you love. [From *ib.*]

2 The food in this place is really terrible. Yes, and such small portions.
That's essentially how I feel about life. [From *ib.*]

3 And if it turns out that there is a God, I don't believe that he is evil. The worst that can be said is that he's an under-achiever. [From film, *Love and Death*]

4 I'm short enough and ugly enough to succeed on my own. [From film, *Play It Again Sam*]

5 I'm really a timid person – I was beaten up by Quakers. [From film, *Sleeper*, scripted with Marshall Brickman]

6 My brain: it's my second favourite organ. [From *ib.*]

7 Q. Have you ever taken a serious political stand on anything?
A. Yes, for twenty-four hours I refused to eat grapes. [From *ib.*]

8 Eternal nothingness is OK if you're dressed for it. [*Getting Even*, 'My Philosophy']

9 Not only is there no God, but try getting a plumber on weekends. [*Ib.*]

10 Then Job fell to his knees and cried to the Lord, 'Thine is the kingdom and the power and the glory. Thou hast a good job. Don't blow it.' [*Without Feathers*, 'The Scrolls']

11 The lion and the calf shall lie down together but the calf won't get much sleep. [*Ib.*]

12 It's not that I'm afraid to die. I just don't want to be there when it happens. [*Ib.* 'Death (A Play)']

13 The thing to remember is that each time of life has its appropriate rewards, whereas when you're dead it's hard to find the light switch The chief problem about death, incidentally, is the fear that there may be no afterlife – a depressing thought, particularly for those who have bothered to shave. Also, there is the fear that there is an afterlife but no one will know where it's being held. On the plus side, death is one of the few things that can be done as easily lying down. [*Ib.* 'The Early Essays']

14 Money is better than poverty, if only for financial reasons. [*Ib.*]

15 I was thrown out of college for cheating on the metaphysics exam: I looked into the soul of another boy. [Quoted in Adler and Feinman, *Woody Allen: Clown Prince of American Humor*, Ch. 1 (used in film, *Annie Hall*)]

16 My parents were very old world. They come from Brooklyn, which is the heart of the Old World. Their values in life are God and carpeting. [Quoted in *ib.* 2]

17 I am an only child. I have one sister. [Quoted in *ib.*]

18 I want to tell you a terrific story about oral contraception. I asked this girl to sleep with me and she said 'no'. [Quoted in *ib.*]

19 I am at two with nature. [Quoted in *ib.* 3]

20 Some guy hit my fender the other day, and I said unto him, 'Be fruitful, and multiply.' But not in those words. [Quoted in *ib.*]

21 I wanted to be an arch-criminal as a child, before I discovered I was too short. [Quoted in *ib.* 4]

22 I asked the girl if she could bring a sister for me. She did. Sister Maria Teresa. It was a very slow evening. We discussed the New Testament. We agreed that He was very well adjusted for an only child. [Quoted in *ib.* 5]

23 And my parents finally realize that I'm kidnapped and they snap into action immediately: they rent out my room. [Quoted in E. Lax, *Woody Allen and His Comedy*]

24 My one regret in life is that I am not someone else. [Epigraph *ib.*]

25 Death is an acquired trait. [Quoted in *ib.* Ch. 11]

26 I don't want to achieve immortality through my work . . . I want to achieve it through not dying. [Quoted in *ib.* 12]

27 I took a course in speed reading, learning to read straight down the middle of the page, and was able to read *War and Peace* in twenty minutes. It's about Russia. [Quoted in Peter and Josie Holton, *Quote and Unquote*]

LISA ALTHER

1 If this was adulthood, the only improvement she could detect in her situation was that now she could eat dessert without eating her vegetables. [*Kinflicks*, Ch. 2]

2 People knew a man by the company he kept, but they generally knew a woman by the man who kept her. [*Ib.*]

3 There was nothing wrong with her that a vasectomy of the vocal chords wouldn't fix. [*Ib.* 4]

4 I've always felt that a person's intelligence is directly reflected by the number of conflicting points of view he can entertain simultaneously on the same topic. [*Ib.* 7]

5 She had learnt . . . that it was impossible to discuss issues civilly with a person who insisted on referring to himself as 'we'. [*Ib.* 8]

LEO AMERY

6 Speak for England. [Said to Arthur Greenwood, spokesman for the Labour Party, in the House of Commons, 2 Sep. 1939, but Harold Nicolson, in his diary, attributes the words to Robert Boothby]

7 You have sat too long here for any good you have been doing. Depart, I say, and let us have done with you. In the name of God, *go*! [Speech, repeating Cromwell's words, addressed to Neville Chamberlain's government, House of Commons, May 1940]

FISHER AMES

8 Monarchy is like a splendid ship, with all sails set; it moves majestically on, then it hits a rock and sinks forever. Democracy is like a raft. It never sinks, but, damn it, your feet are always in the water. [Quoted in D. W. Brogan, *The Free State*]

PRESIDENT IDI AMIN OF UGANDA

9 I myself consider myself to be the most important figure in the world. [Interview on BBC Radio, 11 Aug. 1976]

KINGSLEY AMIS

10 Outside every fat man there is an even fatter man trying to close in. [*One Fat Englishman*, Ch. 3. See also 84:20; 254:14; 347:13]

11 He was of the faith chiefly in the sense that the church he currently did not attend was Catholic. [*Ib.* 8]

12 It was no wonder that people were so horrible when they started life as children. [*Ib.* 14]

13 Work was like cats were supposed to be: if you disliked and feared it and tried to keep out of its way, it knew at once and sought you out and jumped on your lap and climbed all over you to show how much it loved you. Please God, he thought, don't let me die in harness. [*Take A Girl Like You*, Ch. 5]

14 The point about white burgundies is that I hate them myself . . . so closely resembling a cold chalk soap and alum cordial with an additive or two to bring it to the colour of children's pee. [*The Green Man*, 'The Red-haired Woman']

15 They were mad about hell – it was going to be just like their public school, where they'd had the only really intense emotional experiences they were capable of. Caning and flogging and fagging and cold baths and rowing and slip-practice and a terrifying all-powerful old man always telling you what an utter shit you were and how you were polluting yourself. [*Ib.* 'The Young Man']

16 Rural life is a mystery until one realizes that nearly all of it, everywhere in the world, is spent in preparing for and recovering from short but punishing bouts of the tedium inseparable from the tasks of the land, or rather their failure to give the least sense of achievement, as it might be a lifetime spent washing up out of doors. I have never understood why anybody agreed to go on being a rustic after about 1400. [*Ib.* 'Dr Thomas Underhill']

17 In the old days a lot of people, men as well as women, didn't know quite what to expect of sex so they didn't worry when it didn't work too well. Now everybody knows exactly what's required of them and exactly how much

they've fallen short down to the last millimetre and second and drop, which is frightfully relaxing for them. [*Jake's Thing*, Ch. 25]

1 The pseudo-light it [Welch's article] threw on non-problems. [*Lucky Jim*, Ch. 1]

2 In the field of evasion-technique, verbal division, and in the physical division of the same field this chap had Welch whacked from the start: self-removal to South America was the traditional climax of an evasive career. [*Ib*. 19]

3 He thought what a pity it was that all his faces were designed to express rage or loathing. Now that something had happened that really deserved a face, he'd none to celebrate it with. As a kind of token, he made his Sex Life in Ancient Rome face. [*Ib*. 25]

4 Tapped untalent. [Remark on the *Robbins Report on Higher Education*, which suggested that higher education should cater for 'the untapped talent']

HARRY ANDERSON

5 Beer, beer, glorious beer, / Fill yourself right up to here. [*Beer*]

SHERWOOD ANDERSON

6 The beaten, ignorant, Bible-ridden, white South. [A. M. Schlesinger Jr, *The Politics of Upheaval*, Pt I, Ch. 4, sect. v]

ANNA

7 The diffrense from a person and an angel is easy: Most of an angel is in the inside and most of a person on the outside. [Fynn, *Mister God, This Is Anna*, Ch. 1]

PRINCESS ANNE

8 When I appear in public people expect me to neigh, grind my teeth, paw the ground and swish my tail – none of which is easy. [*Observer*, 'Sayings of the Week', 22 May 1977]

ANON

9 American women like quiet men: they think they're listening.

10 And not / to spot / the purer / Führer. [Continuation of W. N. Ewer's: 'How odd / Of God / To choose / The Jews'. See *Penguin Dictionary of Quotations*, 156:8, for original lines]

11 An Arab is only a Jew on horseback.

12 As Romeo he [Irving] reminds me of a pig who has been taught to play the fiddle. He does it cleverly but he would be better employed in squealing. [Quoted in Ellen Terry, *The Story of My Life*, Ch. 9]

13 All is not queer that titters. [Proverbial in Bayswater, 1964]

14 A bachelor is a cagey guy / And he has loads of fun: / He sizes all the cuties up / And never Mrs one. [Quoted in Bennett Cerf, *A Treasury of Atrocious Puns*, Ch. 8]

15 A bayonet is a weapon with a worker at each end. [British pacifist slogan, 1940]

16 Be like Dad, keep Mum. [Ministry of Information slogan, 1941]

17 The best contraceptive is a glass of cold water: not before or after, but instead. [Pakistan delegate at International Planned Parenthood Federation Conference]

18 Bigamy is having one husband too many. Monogamy is the same. [A woman. Epigraph to Erica Jong, *Fear of Flying*, Ch. 1]

19 Black is beautiful. [Black Power slogan]

20 Clean-limbed American boys are not like any others / Only clean-limbed American boys have mothers. [Said by an anonymous American, quoted in review, *Times Literary Supplement*, 1964]

21 Dancing is a perpendicular expression of a horizontal desire.

22 Dear Sir, your astonishment's odd, / I am always about in the quad, / And that's why the tree / Continues to be / As observed by yours faithfully, God. [Limerick riposte to earlier limerick by Ronald Knox. See *Penguin Dictionary of Quotations*, 225:27]

23 Delightfully simple. It is refreshing to meet a man who has played the piano

for twenty years in a brothel. [On Attlee and the Lynskey Enquiry quoted in O. Brown, *The Extended Tongue*]

1 The English treat the commonplace as if it were remarkable and the Americans as if it were commonplace. [Quoted by James Thurber in Malcolm Cowley (ed.), *Writers at Work, First Series*]

2 Every government carries a health warning. [Badge slogan, 1976]

3 The future is not what it was. [Attr. to an anonymous professor of economics by Bernard Levin in the *Sunday Times*, 22 May 1977]

4 Frankie and Albert were lovers, O Lordy, how they could love. / Swore to be true to each other, true as the stars above. / He was her man, and he did her wrong. [Song: *Frankie and Albert*. Original version, based on a St Louis murder, later went through many variants as *Frankie and Johnny*.]

5 God don't come when you want Him but He's right on time. [Jazz historian. Quoted in Tennessee Williams, *Memoirs*]

6 The god-men say when die go sky / Through Pearly Gates where river flow, / The god-men say when die we fly / Just like eagle-hawk and crow – / Might be, might be; but I don't know. [North Australian aborigine version of Christianity]

7 Half of Christendom worships a Jew, and the other half a Jewess. [Quoted in H. L. Mencken, *A New Dictionary of Quotations*]

8 Hark the Herald Angels sing, / Mrs Simpson's pinched our king. [Children's street rhyme widely current during the Abdication crisis of 1936. Quoted in Iona and Peter Opie, *The Lore and Language of Schoolchildren*, Ch. 1]

9 Have you heard? The Prime Minister [Lloyd George] has resigned and North-cliffe has sent for the King. [Popular saying, 1919. Quoted in Hamilton Fyfe, *Northcliffe, an Intimate Biography*, Ch. 16]

10 He is a real pessimist – he could look at a doughnut and only see the hole in it. [Quoted in P. and J. Holton, *Quote and Unquote*]

11 He is like the woman in an Elinor Glyn novel who describes another by saying 'she is like a figure in an Elinor Glyn novel'. [Quoted in Daniel Boorstin, *The Image*, Ch. 2]

12 Henry's the sort that keeps you guessing as to whether he's going to deliver a sermon or wet the bed. [Said of Henry Wallace by an anonymous American politician. Quoted in A. M. Schlesinger Jr, *The Coming of the New Deal*, Pt I, Ch. 2, sect. v]

13 Hollywood buys a good story about a bad girl and has to change it to a bad story about a good girl.

14 Horsepower was wonderful when only horses had it. [Quoted in *Dramatists' Guild Bulletin*, 1963]

15 [Of Harold Wilson] How can you tell when he's lying? When his lips are moving. [From a late-night TV programme. Quoted in Bernard Levin, *The Pendulum Years*, Ch. 19]

16 I don't like the family Stein! / There is Gert, there is Ep, there is Ein. / Gert's writings are punk, / Ep's statues are junk, / Nor can anyone understand Ein. [Quoted in Robe.t Graves and Alan Hodge, *The Long Weekend*, Ch. 12]

17 If she were cast as Lady Godiva the horse would steal the act. [Of a certain actress]

18 If the sergeant steals your rum, / Never mind! [Soldiers' song of the First World War]

19 If you're not a rogue you should take a libel action against your face.

20 I'm backing Britain. [Slogan of 1968]

21 I'm sixty-one today, / A year beyond the barrier, / And what was once a Magic Flute / Is now a Water Carrier.

22 The Irish don't know what they want and won't be happy till they get it. [Unknown infantry officer, 1975]

23 It isn't the wild ecstatic leap across I deplore. It's the weary trudge home. [On Double Beds versus Single Beds]

24 [Of the philosophy of Hugh Hefner] It would not impress anyone with as much

knowledge of the subject as can be gained by catching sight of a copy of a popular philosophical digest in a bookcase on the other side of a fairly large room. [Quoted in Bernard Levin, *The Pendulum Years*, Ch. 1]

1 Join the Army, see the world, meet interesting people and kill them. [Pacifist slogan, 1970s]

2 Keep on trucking.

3 [Of Oxford] The Latin quarter of Cowley.

4 Little nips of whisky, little drops of gin, / Make a lady wonder where on earth she's bin.

5 Living in the past has one thing in its favour – it's cheaper. [Quoted in *Dramatists' Guild Bulletin*, 1963]

6 Logic is the art of going wrong with confidence. [Quoted in W. H. Auden, *A Certain World*]

7 Loose talk can cost lives. [American Second World War poster. The British version was 'Careless talk costs lives']

8 Lousy but loyal. [East End slogan at King George V's Jubilee, 1935]

9 Make love not war. [Hippie slogan]

10 Marriage is an attempt to change a night owl into a homing pigeon.

11 May all the saints be praised! Hell's full at last! [Said by an Irishman when the trapdoor failed to engulf Don Giovanni at a performance of the opera. Story told by Sir Compton Mackenzie]

12 Military justice is to justice as military music is to music. [Quoted in Max Ophuls's film, *The Memory of Justice*]

13 Montezuma's revenge. [Proverbial nickname for digestive complaint suffered by European visitors to Mexico]

14 Mrs Thatcher may be a woman, but she isn't a sister. [Feminist writer at the time of 1979 General Election. Quoted in the *Observer*, 7 Oct. 1979]

15 My brother's a slum missionary / Saving young virgins from sin: / He'll save you a blonde for a shilling – / By God, how the money rolls in. [Song quoted in T. R. Ritchie, *The Singing Street*]

16 ADMIRING FRIEND: 'My, that's a beautiful baby you have there!'
MOTHER: 'Oh, that's nothing – you should see his photograph!' [Quoted in Daniel Boorstin, *The Image*, Ch. 1]

17 The Navy's here! [Call on boarding German commerce destroyer *Altmark* carrying British prisoners. Quoted in Winston S. Churchill, *The Gathering Storm*, Ch. 31]

18 Never put a hot baby on a cold slab.

19 The new definition of psychiatry is the care of the id by the odd. [Quoted in M. B. Strauss, *Familiar Medical Quotations*]

20 A New York actress has just got back to Broadway after a year in Hollywood. She says that she has been so long among the false fronts and papier-mâché mansions on the set that nowadays she finds herself sneaking a look at her husband to see if he goes all the way round or is just a profile. [Quoted in P. G. Wodehouse, *Performing Flea*]

21 Nice one, Cyril. / Nice one, son! / Nice one, Cyril. / Let's have another one! [Football chant at Tottenham Hotspur, prompted by Cyril Knowles]

22 [Of Louis B. Mayer, the movie mogul] The only reason so many people attended his funeral was they wanted to make sure he was dead. [Quoted in Leslie Halliwell, *The Filmgoer's Book of Quotes;* some attrib. to S. Goldwyn]

23 The other one [Pope Pius XII] was nearer to God, but this one [John XXIII] is nearer to us. [Italian]

24 A pessimist is a man who is never happy unless he is miserable; even then he is not pleased. [Quoted in C. Hunt, *The Best Howlers*]

25 A pessimist is just a well-informed optimist. [Quoted by Robert Mackenzie on the BBC TV programme, *24 Hours*, 18 Mar. 1968, as current Czech aphorism on Dubček's government]

26 A politician is an animal who can sit on a fence and yet keep both ears to the ground. [Quoted in H. L. Mencken, *A New Dictionary of Quotations*]

27 A poor aviator lay dying / At the end of a bright summer's day; / And his com-

rades were gathered around him / To carry his fragments away. [*A Poor Aviator*, sung in Korea, 1954, but dates from 1st World War. Quoted in Alan Lomax, *Folk Songs of North America* (No. 234)]

1 Take the manifolds out of my larynx / And the cylinders out of my brain, / Take the piston rods out of my kidneys, / And assemble the engine again. [*Ib.*]

2 The R A F do not have traditions, they only have habits. [Petty officer on HMS *Daedalus* writing to *The Times*, 1977]

3 Regret cannot come today; have not yet got home yesterday. [Telegram attributed to employee during traffic crisis]

4 Say it loud, we're gay and we're proud ... Two, four, six, eight, gay is just as good as straight ... Three, five, seven, nine, lesbians are mighty fine. [Gay Liberation Front slogans. Quoted in Jeffrey Weeks, *Coming Out, Homosexual Politics in Britain from the Nineteenth Century to the Present*]

5 Sire, four virgins wait without.
Without what?
Without food and clothing.
Give them food and bring them in. [Quoted in Katharine Whitehorn, *Only On Sundays*, Ch. 33]

6 Take up your cross and relax. [Alleged American slogan of the 1960s. Quoted by Elizabeth Hardwick in radio interview with A. Alvarez, 14 Jun. 1964]

7 *Teppichfresser!* – Animal that chews the carpet! [Unknown German editor of Adolf Hitler, quoted in W. L. Shirer, *The Rise and Fall of the Third Reich*, Ch. 12]

8 Their faces are so sad, but their bottoms are so gay. [Comment by French diplomat on modern dancing (1918). Quoted in Sir Thomas Beecham, *A Mingled Chime*]

9 There are three arts – painting, music and ornamental pastry-making; of which last architecture is a subdivision. [Pastry cook. Quoted in F. and V. Meynell, *The Week-End Book*]

10 [An Italian immigrant, when asked to say what forty years of American life had taught him] There is no free lunch. [Quoted in Alistair Cooke, *America*, 'Epilogue']

11 There's nothing quite like it [hanggliding]. Nothing. Sex is the nearest, but this lasts longer. [*Observer*, 4 Sep. 1977]

12 There was a dachshund, once so long / He hadn't any notion / How long it took to notify / His tail of his emotion; / And so it happened, while his eyes / Were filled with woe and sadness, / His little tail went wagging on / Because of previous gladness. [Quoted in John F. Kennedy, *Profiles in Courage*]

13 The trains run to time. [Common remark in praise of Italian Fascism]

14 [Of unsuccessful actors] To change agents is like changing deckchairs on the *Titanic*.

15 *Vencéremos!* [We shall overcome: Republican chant in Spanish Civil War. See also 158:16]

16 What is the difference between Capitalism and Communism? Capitalism is the exploitation of man by man; Communism is the reverse. [Polish joke. Quoted in R. T. Tripp, *International Thesaurus of Quotations*]

17 When I [an old Oklahoma farmer] was a young man we had ten cows and we did very well. When I was thirty we had twenty cows and we did no better. When I was forty we had forty cows and we were barely making it. Now I'm seventy and we have seventy cows, we are not making it at all, and it's all the fault of the Agricultural Extension Service. [Quoted in D. A. Schon, *Change and Industrial Society*]

18 When Lady Jane became a tart, / It almost broke her father's heart. / But blood is blood, and race is race, / And so, to mitigate disgrace, / He bought a most expensive beat / From Asprey's up to Oxford Street. [Quoted in Seymour Hicks, *Vintage Years*]

19 Wot, no Watneys? [Said by Chad, a long-nosed character peering over a wall, used in wartime propaganda, and on poster]

20 A year ago Gerald Ford was unknown throughout America, now he's unknown throughout the world. [On his appointment as Vice-President of the United

States. Quoted in the *Guardian*, Aug. 1974]

1 You don't have to be a Marxist to see that history repeats itself, first as tragedy, then as farce. [An American wit. Quoted in the *Sunday Times*, 14 Sep. 1975]

2 Your King and Country need you. ['Kitchener' recruiting poster, 1914]

JEAN ANOUILH

3 Love is, above all, the gift of oneself. [*Ardèle*, Act II]

4 The object of art is to give life a shape. [*The Rehearsal*, Act I, sc. ii]

5 What fun it would be to be poor, as long as one was *excessively* poor! Anything in excess is most exhilarating. [*Ring Round the Moon*, Act II]

MICHELANGELO ANTONIONI

6 Hollywood is like being nowhere and talking to nobody about nothing. [Quoted in the *Sunday Times*, 20 Jun. 1971]

GUILLAUME APOLLINAIRE

7 *Ah Dieu! que la guerre est jolie | Avec ses chants ses longs loisirs* – Ah God, how pretty war is with its songs, its long rests! [*L'Adieu du Cavalier*]

8 *Voie lactée ô sœur lumineuse | Des blancs ruisseaux de Chanaan | Et des corps blancs des amoureuses | Nageurs morts suivrons-nous d'ahan | Ton cours vers d'autres nébuleuses* – Milky Way, O shining sister of the white streams of Canaan and the white bodies of women in love, shall we follow your track towards other nebulae, panting like dead swimmers? [*La Chanson du mal-aimé*]

9 *Les souvenirs sont cors de chasse | Dont meurt le bruit parmi le vent.* – Memories are hunting-horns, whose noise dies away in the wind. [*Cors de Chasse*]

10 *Bergère ô tour Eiffel le troupeau des ponts bêle ce matin.* – Shepherdess O Eiffel Tower the herd of bridges is bleating this morning. [*Zone*]

SIR EDWARD APPLETON

11 I do not mind what language an opera is sung in so long as it is a language I don't understand. [*Observer*, 'Sayings of the Week', 28 Aug. 1955]

LOUIS ARAGON

12 *Ô mois des floraisons mois des métamorphoses | Mai qui fut sans nuage et Juin poignardé | Je n'oublierai jamais les lilas ni les roses | Ni ceux que le printemps dans ses plis a gardés.* – O month of flowerings, month of metamorphoses, May without cloud and June that was stabbed, I shall never forget the lilac and the roses, nor those whom the spring has kept in its folds. [*Les lilas et les roses*]

13 *Le démenti des fleurs au vent de la panique | Aux soldats qui passaient sur l'aile de la peur | Aux vélos délirants aux canons ironiques | Au pitoyable accoutrement des faux campeurs.* – The flowers' contradiction of the wind of panic, of the soldiers who passed on the wings of fear, of the delirious bicycles, of the ironic guns, of the pitiable equipment of the bogus campers. [*Ib.*]

14 *Fuyez les bois et les fontaines | Taisez-vous oiseaux querelleurs | Vos chants sont mis en quarantaine | C'est le règne de l'oiseleur | Je reste roi de mes douleurs.* – Flee the woods and the springs. Be silent, wrangling birds. Your songs are sent to Coventry. It is the reign of the bird-catcher. I remain king of my griefs. [*Richard II quarante*]

15 *J'ai bu l'été comme un vin doux.* – I drank summer like a sweet wine. [*Zone libre*]

ELIZABETH ARDEN
(Florence Nightingale Graham)

16 To be Catholic or Jewish isn't chic. Chic is Episcopalian. [Quoted in John Julius Norwich, *A Christmas Cracker*]

HANNAH ARENDT

17 The banality of evil. [Referring to the revelations of the Eichmann trial in Jerusalem in her book, *Eichmann in Jerusalem*]

1 Under conditions of tyranny it is far easier to act than to think. [Quoted in W. H. Auden, *A Certain World*]

2 There exist labour songs but no work songs. The songs of the craftsman are social; they are sung after work. [Quoted in W. H. Auden and L. Kronenberger, *The Faber Book of Aphorisms*]

DUKE OF ARGYLL

3 As far as I'm concerned there are only two kinds of people in the world. Those who are nice to their servants and those who aren't. [Attr. by Art Buchwald in *I Chose Caviar*]

MICHAEL ARLEN

4 It is a sorry business to inquire into what men think, when we are every day only too uncomfortably confronted with what they do. [*The Three Cornered Moon*]

5 Nothing is so generally destructive as the spiritual vanity of men who refuse to store up goods in this world. Remember Jesus said he came bringing a sword. But he was so detached from the goods of this world that he left it behind him. [*Man's Mortality*]

6 Well, emotionally she was unimportant, like a play by Mr Noël Coward, but her construction was faultless, like a play by Mr Noël Coward. [*Short Stories*, 'Portrait of a Lady on Park Avenue']

7 My forbears were successful crooks living on the slopes of Mount Ararat. [*Conversation*]

8 She not only expects the worst, but makes the worst of it when it happens. [Quoted in A. Andrews, *Quotations for Speakers and Writers*]

GEORGE ARLISS

9 [After describing himself in a court of law as the greatest living actor, excused his boastfulness with] You see, I am on oath.

NICHOLAS ARMFELT

10 There's a rumour going round in theological circles that the powers who arrange all these matters have done away with Hell now that Heaven has gone comprehensive! [*Smudge*]

ANN ARMSTRONG

11 In the space age the most important space is between the ears. [Quoted in the *Guardian*, 30 Jan. 1974]

NEIL ARMSTRONG

12 That's one small step for a man, one giant step for mankind. [On first setting foot on the moon, 20 Jun. 1969. Quoted with slight variants in various sources]

PETER ARNO

13 I consider your conduct unethical and lousy. [Caption for cartoon]

14 Wake up, you mut. We're going to be married today. [Caption for cartoon]

15 Have you read any good books lately? [Caption to cartoon of lovers in a clinch]

'DAISY ASHFORD'

16 Oh Bernard muttered Ethel this is so sudden. No no cried Bernard and taking the bull by both horns he kissed her violently on her dainty face. My bride to be he murmered several times. [*The Young Visiters*, Ch. 9]

ISAAC ASIMOV

17 The Laws of Robotics:

(1) A robot may not injure a human being, or through inaction allow a human being to come to harm.
(2) A robot must obey the orders given it by human beings, except where such orders would conflict with the First Law.
(3) A robot must protect its own existence as long as such protection does not conflict with the First and Second Laws. [*I, Robot*, 'Runaround']

20

ARTHUR ASKEY

1 Hullo playmates! [*Passim* in radio programmes before and during the Second World War]

2 Ay thang yew! [Recurrent tag in radio comedy routine. Quoted in Eric Partridge, *A Dictionary of Catch-Phrases*]

EARL ASQUITH

3 One to mislead the public, another to mislead the Cabinet, and the third to mislead itself. [On the War Office's keeping three sets of figures. Quoted in Alastair Horne, *The Price of Glory*, Ch. 2]

4 Elizabeth told me of an American girl who spoke scoffingly of the Ten Commandments: 'They don't tell you what you ought to do and only put ideas into your head.' [*Letters to a Friend*. Quoted in Samuel, *A Book of Quotations*]

5 It is fitting that we should have buried the Unknown Prime Minister by the side of the Unknown Soldier. [Attr. remark at the funeral of Bonar Law, 5 Nov. 1923]

6 Youth would be an ideal state if it came a little later in life. [Quoted in P. and J. Holton, *Quote and Unquote*]

MARGOT ASQUITH

7 He [Lloyd George] could not see a belt without hitting below it. [Quoted in Mark Bonham Carter, introduction to reprint of her *Autobiography*, 1962]

8 Mr Balfour was difficult to understand ... because of his formidable detachment. The most that many of us could hope for was that he had a taste in us as one might have in clocks or china. [*Ib.* 11]

9 Lord Birkenhead is very clever, but sometimes his brains go to his head. [Quoted in the *Listener*, 15 Aug. 1974]

10 Jean Harlow [Hollywood's sexy actress] kept calling Margot Asquith by her first name, or kept trying to: she pronounced it Mar*got*. Finally Margot set her right. 'No, no, Jean. The *t* is silent as in Harlow.' [Quoted in T. S. Matthews, *Great Tom*]

FRED ASTAIRE

11 Can't act. Can't sing. Slightly bald. Can dance a little. [*Anon.* Talent scout's judgement on F.A. Quoted in Leslie Halliwell, *The Filmgoer's Book of Quotes*]

JOHN JACOB ASTOR III

12 A man who has a million dollars is as well off as if he were rich. [Attr.]

NANCY, VISCOUNTESS ASTOR

13 [To Winston Churchill]: Winston, if I were married to you, I'd put poison in your coffee.
CHURCHILL: Nancy, if you were my wife, I'd drink it. [At Blenheim Palace, *c.* 1912. Quoted in E. Langthorne, *Nancy Astor and Her Friends*]

14 Grass is growing on the Front Bench. [*Observer*, 'Sayings of the Week', 17 Mar. 1940]

CLEMENT ATTLEE

15 Democracy means government by discussion but it is only effective if you can stop people talking. [Quoted in Anthony Sampson, *Anatomy of Britain*]

W. H. AUDEN

16 Yet no one hears his own remarks as prose. [*At a Party*]

17 But each ear / Is listening to its hearing, so none hear. [*Ib.*]

18 ... hinting at the forbidden like a wicked uncle, / Night after night to the farmer's children you beckon. [*The Capital*]

19 Speechless Evil / Borrowed the language of Good / And reduced it to noise. [*The Cave of Making*, Postscript]

20 Let us honour if we can / The vertical man / Though we value none / But the horizontal one. [*Epigraph*]

21 Within these breakwaters English is spoken; without / Is the immense, improbable atlas. [*Dover*]

21

1 He knew human folly like the back of his hand, / And was greatly interested in armies and fleets; / When he laughed, respectable senators burst with laughter, / And when he cried the little children died in the streets. [*Epitaph on a Tyrant*]

2 One tapped my shoulder and asked me 'How did you fall, sir?' / Whereat I awakened. [*1st January 1931*]

3 Makers' lives are spent / Striving in their chosen / Medium to create a / De-narcissus-ized en- / during excrement. [*The Geography of the House*]

4 To us he is no more a person / Now but a climate of opinion. [*In Memory of Sigmund Freud*]

5 In the nightmare of the dark / All the dogs of Europe bark, / And the living nations wait, / Each sequestered in its hate. [*In Memory of W. B. Yeats*]

6 Intellectual disgrace / Stares from every human face, / And the seas of pity lie / Locked and frozen in each eye. [*Ib.*]

7 When I try to imagine a faultless love / Or the life to come, what I hear is the murmur / Of underground streams, what I see a limestone landscape. [*In Praise of Limestone*]

8 And on the issue of their charm depended / A land laid waste, with all its young men slain, / Its women weeping, and its towns in terror. [*In Times of War*]

9 To throw away the key and walk away, / Not abrupt exile, the neighbours asking why / But following a line with left and right, / An altered gradient at another rate. [*The Journey*]

10 To rule was a pleasure when / One wrote a death-sentence / On the back of the Ace of Spades and played on / With a new deck of Honours. [*The Managers*]

11 Private faces in public places / Are wiser and nicer / Than public faces in private places. [*Marginalia*]

12 Five minutes on even the nicest mountain / Is awfully long. [*Mountains*]

13 About suffering they were never wrong, / The Old Masters. [*Musée des Beaux Arts*]

14 ... even the dreadful martyrdom must run its course / Anyhow in a corner, some untidy spot / Where the dogs go on with their doggy life. [*Ib.*]

15 To the man-in-the-street, who, I'm sorry to say, / Is a keen observer of life, / The word 'Intellectual' suggests straight away / A man who's untrue to his wife. [*New Year Letter*, note to line 1277]

16 God bless the USA, so large, / So friendly, and so rich. [*On the Circuit*]

17 The glacier knocks in the cupboard, / The desert sighs in the bed, / And the crack in the tea-cup opens / A lane to the land of the dead. [*One Evening*]

18 Attractions for their coming week / Are Masters Wet, Dim, Drip and Bleak. [*The Orators*, Ode, 'Roar Gloucestershire']

19 The Oxford Don: 'I don't feel quite happy about pleasure.' [*Ib.* 'Journal of an Airman']

20 Three kinds of enemy face – the June bride – the favourite puss – the stone in the rain. [*Ib.*]

21 Only those in the last stage of disease could believe that children are true judges of character. [*Ib.*]

22 But Tennyson, remember, thought trains ran in grooves; / The Queen believed cigars were all one price. [*Ib.*]

23 To ask the hard question is simple. [*The Question*]

24 Verse was a special illness of the ear; / Integrity was not enough. [*Rimbaud*]

25 His truth acceptable to lying men. [*Ib.*]

26 Over the heather the west wind blows, / I've lice in my tunic and a cold in my nose. / The rain comes pattering out of the sky, / I'm a Wall soldier and I don't know why. [*Roman Wall Blues*]

27 At Dirty Dick's and Sloppy Joe's / We drank our liquor straight, / Some went upstairs with Margery, / And some, alas, with Kate. [*The Sea and the Mirror*, 'Song of the Master and the Boatswain']

28 The nightingales are singing in / The orchards of our mothers, / And hearts that we broke long ago / Have long been breaking others. [*Ib.*]

1 Embrace me, belly, like a bride. [*Ib.*, 'Stephano's Song']

2 Out of the air a voice without a face / Proved by statistics that some cause was just. [*The Shield of Achilles*]

3 No hero is mortal till he dies. [*A Short Ode to a Philologist*]

4 O for doors to be open and an invite with gilded edges / To dine with Lord Lobcock and Count Asthma. [*Song*]

5 So take your proper share, man, of / Dope and drink · / Aren't you the Chairman of / Ego, Inc? [*Song of the Devil*]

6 Noises at dawn will bring / Freedom for some, but not this peace / No bird can contradict. [*Taller Today*]

7 He is not that returning conqueror, / Nor ever the poles' circumnavigator. / But poised between shocking falls on razor-edge / Has taught himself this balancing subterfuge / Of the accosting profile, the erect carriage. [*Watch Any Day*]

8 This great society is going smash; / They cannot fool us with how fast they go, / How much they cost each other and the gods! / A culture is no better than its woods. [*Winds*]

9 Be clean, be tidy, oil the lock, / Weed the garden, wind the clock; / Remember the Two. [*The Witnesses*]

10 Of course, Behaviourism 'works'. So does torture. Give me a no-nonsense, down-to-earth behaviourist, a few drugs, and simple electrical appliances, and in six months I will have him reciting the Athanasian creed in public. [*A Certain World*, 'Behaviourism']

11 Good can imagine Evil, but Evil cannot imagine Good. [*Ib.* 'Imagination']

12 All sin tends to be addictive, and the terminal point of addiction is what is called damnation. [*Ib.* 'Hell']

13 When I find myself in the company of scientists, I feel like a shabby curate who has strayed by mistake into a drawing-room full of dukes. [*The Dyer's Hand*]

14 The true men of action in our time, those who transform the world, are not the politicians and statesmen, but the scientists. Unfortunately, poetry cannot celebrate them, because their deeds are concerned with things, not persons and are, therefore, speechless. [*Ib.*]

15 Few writers have less journalistic talent than [Henry] James, and this is his defect, for the supreme masters have one trait in common with the childish scribbling mass, the vulgar curiosity of a police-court reporter. [*Ib.*]

16 Man is a history-making creature who can neither repeat his past nor leave it behind. [*Ib.* 'D. H. Lawrence']

17 The ear tends to be lazy, craves the familiar and is shocked by the unexpected: the eye, on the other hand, tends to be impatient, craves the novel and is bored by repetition. [*Ib.* 'Hic et Ille']

18 Some books are undeservedly forgotten; none are undeservedly remembered. [*Ib.* 'Reading']

19 No poet or novelist wishes he were the only one who ever lived, but most of them wish they were the only one alive, and quite a number fondly believe their wish has been granted. [*Ib.* 'Writing']

20 Geniuses are the luckiest of mortals because what they must do is the same as what they most want to do. [Foreword to Dag Hammarskjöld, *Markings*]

21 A verbal art like poetry is reflective; it stops to think. Music is immediate; it goes on to become. [Quoted in Aaron Copland, *Music and Imagination*]

22 Music is the best means we have of digesting time. [Quoted in Robert Craft, *Stravinsky: The Chronicle of a Friendship*]

W. H. AUDEN and J. GARRETT

23 Poetry, in fact, bears the same kind of relation to Prose, using prose simply in the sense of all those uses of words that are not poetry, that algebra bears to arithmetic. [*The Poet's Tongue*, Introduction]

24 Poetry is not concerned with telling people what to do, but with extending our knowledge of good and evil, perhaps making the necessity for action more urgent and its nature more clear, but only leading us to the point where

23

it is possible for us to make a rational and moral choice. [*Ib.*]

W. H. AUDEN and CHRISTOPHER ISHERWOOD

1 Acts of injustice done / Between the setting and the rising sun / In history lie like bones, each one. [*The Ascent of F6*, Act II, sc. v]

ALAN AYCKBOURN

2 If S-E-X ever rears its ugly head, close your eyes before you see the rest of it. [*Bedroom Farce*, Act II]

3 Few women care to be laughed at and men not at all, except for large sums of money. [*The Norman Conquests*, Preface]

4 If you gave Ruth a rose, she'd peel all the petals off to make sure there weren't any greenfly. And when she'd done that, she'd turn round and say, do you call that a rose? Look at it, it's all in bits. [*Ib. Table Manners*, Act I, sc. ii]

5 I – don't dislike you. You're like – mild athlete's foot. You make me irritable. [*Ib. Round and Round the Garden*, Act I, sc. ii]

6 Anyway, Hyde Park's not country. It's just an underground car park with a grass roof. [*Ib.* Act II, sc. ii]

7 I was brought up to believe it was very insulting to sleep with your wife or any lady. A gentleman stays eagerly awake. He sleeps at his work. [*Ib.*]

8 Comedy is tragedy interrupted. [From an interview]

A. J. AYER

9 No morality can be founded on authority, even if the authority were divine. [*Essay on Humanism*]

10 The principles of logic and metaphysics are true simply because we never allow them to be anything else. [*Language, Truth and Logic*]

PAM AYRES

11 I am a cunnin' vending machine, / Lurkin' in the hall, / So you can't kick

24

me delicate parts, / I'm bolted to the wall, / Come on! Drop in your money, / Don't let's hang about, / I'll do my level best to see / You don't get nothing out. [*Some More of Me Poetry*, 'I Am a Cunning Vending Machine']

12 And when at last I'm seated by / The great typewriter in the sky, / Let me type the letters right, / In the morning and at night, / Let the Snopake grow on trees, / Let man's hands stay off me knees, / Let it be a place harmonic, / With no need for gin and tonic, / Thank you in anticipation / Of a favourable reply, / Craving your indulgence, / Yours sincerely. / Goodbye. [*Ib.* 'The Secretary's Song']

13 I might have been a farmyard hen, / Scratchin' in the sun, / There might have been a crowd of chicks, / After me to run, / There might have been a cockerel fine, / To pay us his respects, / Instead of sittin' here, / Till someone comes and wrings our necks. [*Some of Me Poetry*, 'The Battery Hen']

14 I see the Time and Motion clock, / Is sayin' nearly noon, / I 'spec me squirt of water / Will come flyin' at me soon, / And then me spray of pellets, / Will nearly break me leg, / And I'll bite the wire nettin' / And lay one more bloody egg. [*Ib.*]

15 Oh, I wish I'd looked after me teeth, / And spotted the perils beneath, / All the toffees I chewed, / And the sweet sticky food, / Oh, I wish I'd looked after me teeth. [*Ib.* 'Oh, I Wish I'd Looked After Me Teeth']

16 Medicinal discovery, / It moves in mighty leaps, / It leapt straight past the common cold / And gave it us for keeps. [*Ib.* 'Oh, No, I Got a Cold']

17 I had a lovely boyfriend, / Knit one, purl one. / Had him for a long time, / Cast on for the back, / Had him all the summer, / Loved him, cuddled him, / Push it up the knitting pin / And gather up the slack. [*Thoughts of a Late-Night Knitter*, title poem]

18 Our home's a railway carriage / And it cannot be denied / That you might describe our dwelling / As a little bit on the side. [*Ib.* 'The Railway Carriage Couple']

B

ISAAC BABEL

1 No iron can stab the heart with such force as a full stop put just at the right place. [*Guy de Maupassant*]

LAUREN BACALL

2 He [Humphrey Bogart] cried at all his own weddings – and with reason. [Quoted in Nathaniel Benchley, *Humphrey Bogart*]

3 But Jesus, you can't start worrying about what's *going* to happen. You get spastic enough worrying about what's happening now. [Quoted in A. Spiegelman and B. Schneider, *Whole Grains*]

FRANCIS BACON

4 How can I take an interest in my work when I don't like it? [Quoted by Sir John Rothenstein in his introduction to *Francis Bacon*]

BUGS BAER

5 It was as helpful as throwing a drowning man both ends of a rope. [Quoted in A. Andrews, *Quotations for Speakers and Writers*]

ENID BAGNOLD

6 It's not the party of life in the end that's important. It's the comment in the bedroom. [*The Loved and the Envied*]

S. D. BAILEY

7 [The party system] is merely a convenient device to enable the majority to have their way and the minority to have their say. [*The British Party System*]

8 [Regarding the Lord Privy Seal] It has been said that this Minister is neither a Lord, nor a privy, nor a seal. [*British Parliamentary Democracy*]

BERYL BAINBRIDGE

9 Being constantly with children was like wearing a pair of shoes that were expensive and too small. She couldn't bear to throw them out, but they gave her blisters. [*Injury Time*, Ch. 4]

10 It was astonishing how fashionable it was to be unfaithful. He often wondered if it had anything to do with going without a hat. No sooner had the homburgs and the bowlers disappeared from the City than everyone grew their hair longer, and after that nothing was sacred. [*Ib.*]

11 It amazed Ann that Mrs Kershaw, who held such strong views, should send her children to a Parochial school with a vicar coming in twice a week to take morning prayers. You'd have thought she might have preferred one of those progressive places where the teachers were called by their christian names and told to shut up. [*Sweet William*, Ch, 1]

12 Old soldiers, she knew, never died; in her father's case she felt it was not so much that he was fading away, as that he had never been there in the first place. [*Ib.*]

13 He is, after all, the reflection of the tenderness I bear for myself. It is always ourselves we love. [*A Weekend with Claud*, 'Maggie']

14 He liked touching people – it was due to him being a foreigner. [*Young Adolf*, Ch.2]

15 We are essentially fragile. We don't have to to wait for the sword or some other equally sensational weapon to strike us down. One may go just as easily with the measles or diphtheria, meningitis, colic, influenza or mere hunger. There are so many ways of us dying it's astonishing any of us choose old age. [*Ib.* 12]

25

KENNETH BAINBRIDGE

1 Now we are all sons of bitches. [After first atomic test, of which he was in charge. *The Decision to Drop the Bomb*]

JANET BAKER

2 Singing lieder is like putting a piece of music under a microscope. [Interview in *Opera News*, Jul. 1977]

3 We are all influenced by it [criticism]. The responsibility of the critic to us as performers is important and necessary and vital. How important it is, and how the critic weighs his responsibility to the profession against his responsibility as a journalist, is where the two things divide and worry us all, I'm sure [BBC interview, quoted in the *Gramophone*, Oct. 1977]

GEORGES BALANDIER

4 *Le Tiers Monde* – the Third World. [Based on *Le Tiers État*. Attr.]

NIGEL BALCHIN

5 Seldom have so many babies been poured out with so little bath water. [Of the philosophy of this age. *Lord, I Was Afraid*]

JAMES BALDWIN

6 The future is ... black. [*Observer*, 'Sayings of the Week', 25 Aug. 1963]

7 White people in this country will have quite enough to do in learning how to accept and love themselves and each other, and when they have achieved this – which will not be tomorrow and may very well be never – the Negro problem will no longer exist, for it will no longer be needed. [*The Fire Next Time*, 'Down at the Cross']

8 If the concept of God has any validity or use, it can only be to make us larger, freer, and more loving. If God cannot do this, then it is time we got rid of Him. [*Ib.*]

9 Consider the history of labour in a country [USA] in which, spiritually speaking, there are no workers, only candidates for the hand of the boss's daughter. [*Ib.*]

10 If they take you in the morning, they will be coming for us that night. [Epigraph to Angela Davis, *If They Come in the Morning*]

11 It is a great shock at the age of five or six to find that in a world of Gary Coopers you are the Indian. [Speech at Cambridge Union, 17 Feb. 1965]

STANLEY, EARL BALDWIN

12 One morning they [the millions of un-attached voters] opened their papers and read that Lloyd George had said of Bonar Law that he was 'honest to the verge of simplicity'. And they said, 'By God, that is what we have been looking for.' [Speech at an Oxford dinner, quoted in G. M. Young, *Stanley Baldwin*, Ch. 2]

13 Then comes Winston with his hundred-horse-power mind and what can I do? [*Ib.* 11]

14 The only defence is in offence, which means that you have to kill more women and children more quickly than the enemy if you want to save yourselves. [Speech, Nov. 1932. *Ib.* 17]

15 Supposing I had gone to the country and said that Germany was rearming and we must rearm ... I cannot think of anything that would have made the loss of the election from my point of view more certain. [Speech, 12 Nov. 1936. *Ib.* 23]

16 My lips are not yet unsealed. Were those troubles over I would make a case, and I guarantee that not a man would go into the Lobby against us. [Speech on the Abyssinia crisis, quoted in Mac-Neill Weir, *The Tragedy of Ramsay MacDonald*, Ch. 61]

17 What the proprietorship of these papers [referring to Beaverbrook and Rother-mere] is aiming at is power, and power without responsibility – the prerogative of the harlot through the ages. [By-election speech, 18 Mar. 1931. Quoted in D. Butler and A. Sloman, *British Political Facts*. Lord Birkenhead claims in his biography of Kipling that the

26

phrase originated with Kipling and was borrowed by his cousin, Stanley Baldwin. See also 97:13; 320:26]

1 I met Curzon in Downing Street, from whom I got the sort of greeting a corpse would give to an undertaker. [Attr. said in 1933 on Baldwin becoming prime minister, a job coveted by Curzon. Quoted in J. Wintle and R. Kenin, *Dictionary of Biographical Quotation*]

2 I would rather be an opportunist and float than go to the bottom with my principles round my neck. [Attr.]

3 The difference between a man of intellect and an intellectual is the same as the difference between a gentleman and a gent. [Attr.]

4 There are three groups that no British Prime Minister should provoke: the Vatican, the Treasury and the miners. [Attr.]

ARTHUR, LORD BALFOUR

5 FRIEND: I hear you are going to marry Margot Tennant.
A.J.B.: No, that is not so. I rather think of having a career of my own. [Quoted in Margot Asquith, *Autobiography*, Ch. 9]

6 Christianity naturally, but why journalism? [Said to Frank Harris who claimed that the two greatest curses of civilization were Christianity and journalism. Quoted in *ib.* 10]

7 Nothing matters very much, and very few things matter at all. [Attr.]

LORD BALFOUR OF BURLEIGH

8 London is a splendid place to live in for those who can get out of it. [*Observer*, 'Sayings of the Week', 1 Oct. 1944]

PIERRE BALMAIN

9 The trick of wearing mink is to look as though you are wearing a cloth coat. The trick of wearing a cloth coat is to look as though you are wearing a mink. [*Observer*, 'Sayings of the Week', 13 Feb. 1955]

DR HASTINGS BANDA

10 I wish I could bring Stonehenge to Nyasaland to show there was a time when Britain had a savage culture. [*Observer*, 'Sayings of the Week', 10 Mar. 1963]

TALLULAH BANKHEAD

11 There is less in this than meets the eye. [Said at the revival of a Maeterlinck play, quoted in Alexander Woollcott, *Shouts and Murmurs*, 'Capsule Criticism']

12 I'm as pure as the driven slush. [*Observer*, 'Sayings of the Week', 24 Feb. 1957]

13 The only thing I regret about my past is the length of it. If I had to live my life again I'd make all the same mistakes – only sooner. [Quoted in L. and M. Cowan, *The Wit of Women*]

14 Cocaine isn't habit-forming. I should know – I've been using it for years. [Quoted in Lillian Hellman, *Pentimento*, 'Theatre']

15 They used to photograph Shirley Temple through gauze. They should photograph me through linoleum. [Quoted in Leslie Halliwell, *The Filmgoer's Book of Quotes*]

16 Only good girls keep diaries. Bad girls don't have the time. [Attr.]

NANCY BANKS-SMITH

17 The most formidable headmaster I ever knew was a headmistress ... She had X-ray pince-nez and that undivided bust popularized by Queen Mary. I think she was God in drag. [*Guardian*, 8 Jan. 1977]

18 In my experience, if you have to keep the lavatory door shut by extending your left leg, it's modern architecture. [*Guardian*, 20 Feb. 1979]

SIR HENRY CAMPBELL BANNERMAN

19 This is not the end of me. [Dying words quoted in H. H. Asquith, *Memoirs*]

27

HENRI BARBUSSE

1 I see too deep and too much. [*L'Enfer* (*Hell*), trans. John Rodker]

WILKIE BARD

2 She cost me seven and sixpence. / I wish I'd bought a dog! [Song: *She Cost Me Seven and Sixpence*]

MAURICE BARING

3 We see the contrast between the genius which does what it must and the talent which does what it can. [On Pushkin's *Mozart and Salieri, Russian Literature*]

4 He was forbidden to mention ginger beer or warm affection between a man and woman or the execution of Charles the First. [Describing E. Gosse's dealings with Swinburne's family in letter to E. Marsh, 1917]

5 If you would know what the Lord God thinks of money, you have only to look at those to whom He gives it. [Quoted by Dorothy Parker, in Malcolm Cowley (ed.), *Writers at Work, First Series*]

H. GRANVILLE BARKER

6 Do you notice how near the Crystal Palace seems? That means rain. [*The Madras House*, Ch. 1]

7 Some of 'em want to be kissed and some want you to talk politics . . . but the principle's the same. [*Ib.* 2]

8 Let us cling to our legends, sir . . . they are the spiritual side of facts. [*Ib.* 3]

9 Rightly thought of there is poetry in peaches . . . even when they are canned. [*Ib.*]

10 The middle-class woman of England, as of America . . . think of her in bulk . . . is potentially the greatest money-spending machine in the world. [*Ib.*]

11 But oh, the farmyard world of sex! [*Ib.* 4]

12 There's a longer lease for the old gang in letting the youngsters in than in keeping them out, isn't there? [*The Secret Life*, II, i]

13 For you have never found that the whole world's turmoil is but a reflection of the anarchy in your own heart? [*Ib.* II, iii]

14 What is the prose for God? [*Waste*, Act II]

15 MOORE: The fame of the actress is transitory.
GRANVILLE BARKER: Not so transitory as the fame of the authors she represents; their works remain to decry them. The actress is more fortunate: she leaves only a name and a legend. [Quoted in George Moore, *Conversations in Ebury Street*, Ch. 18]

RONNIE BARKER

16 The marvellous thing about a joke with a double meaning is that it can only mean one thing. [*Sauce*, 'Daddie's Sauce']

DJUNA BARNES

17 When she smiled the smile was only in the mouth, and a little bitter: the face of an incurable yet to be stricken with its malady. [*Nightwood*, Ch. 2]

18 When she fell in love it was with a perfect fury of accumulated dishonesty; she became instantly a dealer in second-hand and therefore incalculable emotions. [*Ib.* 4]

J. M. BARRIE

19 Has it ever struck you that the trouts bite best on the Sabbath? God's critters tempting decent men. [*The Little Minister*, Ch. 8]

20 'It's a kid or a coffin,' he said sharply, knowing that only birth or death brought a doctor here. [*Sentimental Tommy*, Ch. 1]

21 A boy does not put his hand into his pocket until every other means of gaining his end has failed. [*Ib.*]

22 'God's gift!' Tommy shuddered, but he said sourly, 'I wish he would take her back.' [*Ib.* 2]

23 It might be said of these two boys that Shovel knew everything but Tommy knew other things. [*Ib.* 3]

1 'Oh, God, if I was sure I were to die tonight I would repent at once.' It is the commonest prayer in all languages. [*Quality Street*, Act II]

2 Oh, that weary Latin, I wish I had the whipping of the man who invented it. [*Quality Street*, Act II]

3 What is algebra exactly; is it those three-cornered things? [*Ib.*]

4 He had the most atrocious bow-wow public park manner [*What Every Woman Knows*, Act III]

5 I have always found that the man whose second thoughts are good is worth watching. [*Ib.*]

6 Every man who is high up likes to feel that he has done it all himself; and the wife smiles, and lets it go at that. It's our only joke. Every woman knows that. [*Ib.* IV]

7 That is ever the way. 'Tis all jealousy to the bride and good wishes to the corpse. [Quoted in Sagittarius and George, *The Perpetual Pessimist*]

8 He was the most brilliant of our company, recently notable in debate at Oxford, where he was runner-up for the presidentship of the Union and only lost it because the other man was less brilliant. [*Dear Brutus*, Act I (stage direction)]

9 They say that in the wood you get what nearly everybody here is longing for – a second chance. [*Ib.*]

10 Fame is rot; daughters are the thing. [*Ib.* II]

11 The same kind, beaming smile that children could warm their hands at. [*Ib.* III]

KARL BARTH

12 Men have never been good, they are not good, they never will be good. [Quoted in *Time*, 12 Apr. 1954]

13 Whether the angels play only Bach in praising God I am not quite sure: I am sure, however, that *en famille* they play Mozart. [Quoted in obituary, *New York Times*, 11 Dec. 1968]

DONALD BARTHELMÉ

14 The first problem in finding a lost father is to lose him decisively. [*The Dead Father*]

ROLAND BARTHES

15 What I claim is to live to the full the contradiction of my time, which may well make sarcasm the condition of truth. [*Mythologies*, Preface]

16 I think that cars today are almost the exact equivalent of the great Gothic cathedrals: I mean the supreme creation of an era, conceived with passion by unknown artists, and consumed in image if not in usage by a whole population which appropriates them as a purely magical object. [*Ib.* 'The New Citroën']

17 *Myth is a type of speech* ... Innumerable other meanings of the word 'myth' can be cited against this. But I have tried to define things not words. [*Ib.* 'Myth Today']

BERNARD BARUCH

18 The cold war. [Said on 16 Apr. 1947, South Carolina. Quoted in *Boston Globe*, 1 Apr. 1949. In fact, Baruch gave credit for the phrase to his speechwriter, H. Swope]

19 I will never be an old man. To me, old age is always fifteen years older than I am. [*Observer*, 'Sayings of the Week', 21 Aug. 1955]

20 A political leader must keep looking over his shoulder all the time to see if the boys are still there. If they aren't still there, he's no longer a political leader. [Quoted in his obituary, *New York Times*, 21 Jun. 1965]

JACQUES BARZUN

21 Intellect deteriorates after every surrender as folly, unless we consciously resist, the nonsense does not pass by but into us. [*The House of Intellect*]

L. FRANK BAUM

22 The road to the City of Emeralds is paved with yellow brick. [*The Wonderful*

29

Wizard of Oz, Ch. 2. This became 'Follow the yellow brick road' in the musical version.]

ARNOLD BAX

1 One should try everything once, except incest and folk-dancing. [*Farewell to My Youth*]

'BEACHCOMBER'
See Morton, J. B.

DITTA BEARD

2 I don't put anything in writing. If it's important enough, you shouldn't, and if it is not important enough, why bother? [Quoted in Anthony Sampson, *The Sovereign State*, Ch. 9]

CECIL BEATON

3 Mrs [Elinor] Glyn achieved the paradox of bringing not only 'good taste' to the colony [Hollywood] but also 'sex appeal'. She coined the word 'It' . . . [*Three Weeks*, Introduction]

VICE-ADMIRAL BEATTY

4 There seems to be something wrong with our bloody ships today. [Attr. On sinking of battle-cruisers at Battle of Jutland, 30 May 1916]

GEORGE BEAUCHAMP

5 She was one of the early birds, / And I was one of the worms. [Song: *She was a Sweet Little Dickie Bird*]

SIMONE DE BEAUVOIR

6 One is not born a woman, one becomes one. [*The Second Sex*, Ch. 2]

LORD BEAVERBROOK

7 With the publication of his [Earl Haig's] Private Papers in 1952, he committed suicide twenty-five years after his death. [*Men of Power*]

8 He [Lloyd George] did not care in which direction the car was travelling, so long as he remained in the driver's seat. [Quoted in the *New Statesman*, 14 Jun. 1963]

9 This is my final word. It is time for me to become an apprentice once more. I have not settled in which direction. But somewhere, sometime, soon. [Speech on 25 May 1964, his 85th birthday; his last public statement]

SAMUEL BECKETT

10 It is suicide to be abroad. But what is it to be at home . . . what is it to be at home? A lingering dissolution. [*All that Fall*]

11 What sky! What light! Ah in spite of all it is a blessed thing to be alive in such weather, and out of hospital. [*Ib.*]

12 This dust will not settle in our time. And when it does some great roaring machine will come and whirl it all sky-high again. [*Ib.*]

13 We could have saved sixpence. We have saved fivepence. [*Pause*] But at what cost? [*Ib.*]

14 That's what hell must be like, small chat to the babbling of Lethe about the good old days when we wished we were dead. [*Embers*]

15 CLOV: Do you believe in the life to come?
HAMM: Mine was always that. [*Endgame*]

16 But we breathe, we change! We lose our hair, our teeth! Our bloom! Our ideas! [*Ib.*]

17 No better, no worse, no change. [*Happy Days*, Act I]

18 Nothing to be done. [*Waiting for Godot*, Act I]

19 ESTRAGON: . . . Let's go.
VLADIMIR: We can't.
ESTRAGON: Why not?
VLADIMIR: We're waiting for Godot. [*Ib.*]

20 We should have thought of it when the world was young, in the nineties. [*Ib.*]

21 He can't think without his hat. [*Ib.*]

1 We are all born mad. Some remain so. [*Ib.*]

2 Personally I have no bone to pick with graveyards. [*First Love*]

3 One is no longer oneself, on such occasions, and it is painful to be no longer oneself, even more painful if possible than when one is. For when one is one knows what to do to be less so, whereas when one is not one is any old one irredeemably. What goes by the name of love is banishment, with now and then a postcard from the homeland. [*Ib.*]

4 To be buried in lava and not turn a hair, it is then a man shows what stuff he is made of. To know he can do better next time, unrecognizably better, and that there is no next time, and that it is a blessing there is not, there is a thought to be going on with. [*Malone Dies*]

5 My photograph. It is not a photograph of me, but I am perhaps at hand. It is an ass, taken from in front and close up, at the edge of the ocean, it is not the ocean, but for me it is the ocean. [*Ib.*]

6 For why be discouraged, one of the thieves was saved, that is a generous percentage. [*Ib.*]

7 Death must take me for someone else. [*Ib.*]

8 There is no returning game between a man and his stars. [*Murphy*]

9 I have my faults, but changing my tune is not one of them. [*The Unnameable*]

10 If anyone should have a smell, it is I. [*Ib.*]

11 UPTHEREPUBLIC! [Expressing support for the republican side in the Spanish Civil War. Quoted in Hugh Thomas, *The Spanish Civil War*, Ch. 25]

12 A very fair scholar I was too; no thought but a great memory. [Quoted in *The Times Educational Supplement*, 2 Jun. 1978]

WILLIAM BEEBE

13 The isness of things is well worth studying; but it is their whyness that makes life worth living. [Quoted in Konrad Lorenz, *On Aggression*, Ch. 2]

SIR THOMAS BEECHAM

14 Musicians did not like the piece [Strauss's *Elektra*] at all. One eminent British composer on leaving the theatre was asked what he thought of it. 'Words fail me,' he replied, 'and I'm going home at once to play the chord of C major twenty times over to satisfy myself that it still exists.' [*A Mingled Chime*, Ch. 18]

15 The plain fact is that music *per se* means nothing; it is sheer sound, and the interpreter can do no more with it than his own capacities, mental and spiritual, will allow, and the same applies to the listener. [*Ib.* 33]

16 A musicologist is a man who can read music but can't hear it. [Quoted in H. Procter-Gregg, *Beecham Remembered*, 'Beecham's Obiter Dicta']

17 The English may not like music – but they absolutely love the noise it makes. [Quoted in L. Ayre, *The Wit of Music*]

18 Why do we have to have all these third-rate foreign conductors around – when we have so many second-rate ones of our own? [Quoted in *ib.*]

19 The sound of the harpsichord resembles that of a bird-cage played with toasting-forks. [Attr.]

MAX BEERBOHM

20 There is disrespect in setting up a dead man's effigy and then not unveiling it. But there would be no disrespect, and there would be no violence, if the bad statues familiar to London were ceremoniously veiled, and their inscribed pedestals left just as they are. [*And Even Now*, 'Mobled King']

21 There is always something rather absurd about the past. [*1880*]

22 To give an accurate and exhaustive account of that period would need a far less brilliant pen than mine. [*Ib.*]

23 The only tribute a French translator can pay Shakespeare is not to translate him – even to please Sarah [Bernhardt]. [*Around Theatres*, 'Hamlet, Prince of Denmark']

1 He [Henry Irving] did not, of course, invent the 'star' system. But he carried it as far as it could be carried. [*Ib.* 'Henry Irving']

2 He cannot see beyond his own nose. Even the fingers he outstretches from it to the world are (as I shall suggest) often invisible to him. [*Ib.* 'A Conspectus of G.B.S.']

3 Humour undiluted is the most depressing of all phenomena. Humour must have its background of seriousness. Without this contrast there comes none of that incongruity which is the mainspring of laughter. [*Ib.*]

4 As a teacher, as a propagandist, Mr Shaw is no good at all, even in his own generation. But as a personality he is immortal. [*Ib.*]

5 The Mote in the Middle Distance by H*nry J*m*s. [Story title in *A Christmas Garland*]

6 It is doubtful whether the people of Southern England have even yet realized how much introspection there is going on all the time in the Five Towns. [*Ib.*]

7 I looked out for what the metropolitan reviewers would have to say. They seemed to fall into two classes: those who had little to say and those who had nothing. [*Seven Men*, 'Enoch Soames']

8 A hundred eyes were fixed on her, and half as many hearts lost to her. [*Zuleika Dobson*, Ch. 1]

9 She had the air of a born unpacker – swift and firm, yet withal tender . . . She was one of those born to make chaos cosmic. [*Ib.* 2]

10 The Duke had an intense horror of unmarried girls. [*Ib.* 3]

11 She was hardly more affable than a cameo. [*Ib.*]

12 It was but a few weeks since he had taken his seat in the Lords; and this afternoon, for want of anything better to do, he strayed in. [*Ib.*]

13 It needs no dictionary of quotations to remind me that the eyes are the windows of the soul. [*Ib.* 4]

14 Women who love the same man have a kind of bitter freemasonry. [*Ib.*]

15 You will find that the woman who is really kind to dogs is always one who has failed to inspire sympathy in men. [*Ib.* 6]

16 Beauty and the lust for learning have yet to be allied. [*Ib.* 7]

17 You will think me lamentably crude: my experience of life has been drawn from life itself. [*Ib.*]

18 He held, too, in his enlightened way, that Americans have a perfect right to exist. But he did often find himself wishing Mr Rhodes had not enabled them to exercise that right in Oxford. [*Ib.* 8]

19 You cannot make a man by standing a sheep on its hind legs. But by standing a flock of sheep in that position you can make a crowd of men. [*Ib.* 9]

20 She had the sensitiveness, though no other quality whatsoever, of the true artist. [*Ib.* 10]

21 Ever since I can remember I have been beset by a recurring doubt as to whether I be or be not quite a gentleman. [*Ib.* 11]

22 Death knocks, as we know, at the door of the cottage and of the castle. He stalks up the front-garden and the steep steps of the semi-detached villa, and plies the ornamental knocker so imperiously that the panels of imitation stained glass quiver in the thin front-door. [*Ib.* 13]

23 There he adjusted his hat with care, and regarded himself very seriously, very sternly, from various angles, like a man invited to paint his own portrait for the Uffizi. [*Ib.* 14]

24 The Socratic manner is not a game at which two can play. Please answer my question to the best of your ability. [*Ib.* 15]

25 And love levels all, doesn't it? Love and the Board school. [*Ib.* 17]

26 Byron! – he would be all forgotten today if he had lived to be a florid old gentleman with iron-grey whiskers, writing very long, very able letters to

The Times about the Repeal of the Corn Laws. [*Ib.* 18]

1 As for you, little Sir Lily Liver, leaning out there, and, I frankly tell you, looking like nothing so much as a gargoyle hewn by a drunken stonemason for the adornment of a Methodist Chapel in one of the vilest suburbs of Leeds or Wigan ... [*Ib.* 22]

2 Lytton Strachey ... had, like the rest of us, imperfect sympathies. [*Lytton Strachey*, Rede Lecture, 1943]

3 What were they going to do with the Grail when they found it, Mr Rossetti? [Caption to a cartoon]

4 Of course we all know that [William] Morris was a wonderful all-round man, but the act of walking round him has always tired me. [Quoted in S. N. Behrman, *Conversations with Max*]

5 [On subscribing a shilling to W. G. Grace's Testimonial] It's not in support of cricket but as an earnest protest against golf. [Quoted in *Carr's Dictionary of Extraordinary English Cricketers*]

BRENDAN BEHAN

6 He was born an Englishman and remained one for years. [*The Hostage*, Act I]

7 PAT: He was an Anglo-Irishman.
MEG: In the blessed name of God, what's that?
PAT: A Protestant with a horse. [*Ib.*]

8 Meanwhile I'll sing that famous old song, 'The Hound that caught the Pubic Hare'. [*Ib.*]

9 When I came back to Dublin, I was courtmartialled in my absence and sentenced to death in my absence, so I said they could shoot me in my absence. [*Ib.*]

10 I wish I'd been a mixed infant. [*Ib.* II]

11 I met with a Gaelic pawnbroker, / From Killarney's waterfalls, / In sobs he cried, 'I wish I'd died, / The Saxons have stolen my balls.' [*Ib.*]

12 I am a sociable worker. [*Ib.*]

13 Go on, abuse me – your own husband that took you off the streets on a Sunday morning, when there wasn't a pub open in the city. [*Ib.* III]

14 How dare you! Men of good taste have complicated me on that carpet. [*Ib.*]

15 We're here because we're queer / Because we're queer because we're here. [*Ib.*]

16 I think weddings is sadder than funerals, because they remind you of your own wedding. You can't be reminded of your own funeral because it hasn't happened. But weddings always make me cry. [*Richard's Cork Leg*, Act I]

17 Other people have a nationality. The Irish and the Jews have a psychosis. [*Ib.*]

18 The English and Americans dislike only *some* Irish – the same Irish that the Irish themselves detest, Irish writers – the ones that *think*. [*Ib.*]

19 It was my belief that they bought the books for the prison by weight. I once got a *Chums* annual for 1917 and a Selfridge's furniture catalogue for my non-fiction or education book. [*Borstal Boy*]

20 [To the nun nursing him on his deathbed] Thank you, sister. May you be the mother of a bishop! [Quoted in *The Wit of Brendan Behan*]

DOMINIC BEHAN

21 Then one day they opened a Catholic chapel, which was quickly followed by a pub, a block of shops and eventually a school. The school went up last because there was no profit in it. [*Teems of Times and Happy Returns*, 'The Christian and My Brother']

CLIVE BELL

22 It would follow that 'significant form' was form behind which we catch a sense of ultimate reality. [*Art*, Pt I, Ch. 3]

23 One account ... given me by a good artist, is that what he tries to express in a picture is 'a passionate apprehension of form'. [*Ib.*]

1 Art and Religion are, then, two roads by which men escape from circumstance to ecstasy. [*Ib*. II. 1]

2 I will try to account for the degree of my aesthetic emotion. That, I conceive, is the function of the critic. [*Ib*. II. 3]

3 We are in the age of names and catalogues and genius-worship. Now, genius-worship is the infallible sign of an uncreative age. [*Ib*. III. 2]

4 Let the artist have just enough to eat, and the tools of his trade: ask nothing of him. Materially make the life of the artist sufficiently miserable to be unattractive, and no one will take to art save those in whom the divine daemon is absolute. [*Ib*. V. 1]

5 Culture is far more dangerous than Philistinism, because it is more intelligent and more pliant. It has a specious air of being on the side of the artist. [*Ib*.]

6 Comfort came in with the middle classes. [*Civilization*, Ch. 4]

7 Only reason can convince us of those three fundamental truths without a recognition of which there can be no effective liberty: that what we believe is not necessarily true; that what we like is not necessarily good; and that all questions are open. [*Ib*. 5]

H. E. BELL

8 Parents are the very last people who ought to be allowed to have children. [Speech at University of Reading, Mar. 1977]

JAMES WARNER BELLAH and WILLIS GOLDBECK

9 When the legend becomes fact, print the legend. [From the film, *Who Shot Liberty Valance?*]

GUY BELLAMY

10 I'm in the last eight of the world celibacy championships. Meet the Pope in the quarter finals. [*The Secret Lemonade Drinker*, Ch. 1]

11 THE WORLD ENDED YESTERDAY. TODAY IS AN ACTION REPLAY. [*Ib*.]

12 If all Englishmen were like him we wouldn't have colonized the Isle of Wight. [*Ib*. 2]

13 The nearest I've been to a sexual experience lately is finding lipstick on a café cup. [*Ib*. 3]

14 The man has a high mendacity quotient. If his lips move, he's lying. [*Ib*. See also anon. entry about Harold Wilson, 16:15]

15 Can you also tell me how anyone can reach my age with so little sense of direction? I'm the rake that never made any progress. [*Ib*. 4]

HILAIRE BELLOC

16 Prince of the Empire, Prince of Timbuctoo, / Prince eight foot round and nearly four foot wide, / Do try to run a little faster, do. / – The ice is breaking up on every side. [*Ballade of Genuine Concern*]

17 Pale Ebenezer thought it wrong to fight, / But Roaring Bill (who killed him) thought it right. [*Epigrams*, 'The Pacifist']

18 I'm tired of Love: I'm still more tired of Rhyme. / But Money gives me pleasure all the time. [*Epigrams*, 'Fatigue']

19 Compact of ancient tales, and port / And sleep – and learning of a sort. [*Lines to a Don*]

20 You find when you are giving up the ghost, / That those who loved you best despised you most. [Quoted in Sagittarius and George, *The Perpetual Pessimist*]

21 The Servile State [Title of a book]

22 Child! do not throw this book about! / Refrain from the unholy pleasure / Of cutting all the pictures out! [*Dedication on the Gift of a Book to a Child*]

23 Birds in their little nests agree / With Chinamen, but not with me. [*New Cautionary Tales*, 'On Food']

24 The Moral is (I think, at least) / That Man is an UNGRATEFUL BEAST. [*Ib*. 'A Reproof of Gluttony']

25 For *deliberate* and *intentional* boring you must have a man of some ability to practise it well, as you must to practise

any art well. [*A Conversation with a Cat*, 'A Guide to Boring']

1 In further letters to Mrs Asquith he compared faith to 'the knowledge of the real coloured visible world to a man half blind'. [Quoted in Robert Speaight, *Life of Hilaire Belloc*, Ch. 17]

2 I always like to associate with a lot of priests because it makes me understand anti-clerical things so well. [Letter to E. S. P. Haynes, 9 Nov. 1909, quoted in *ib.*]

3 The poor darlings [the Jews], I'm awfully fond of them and I'm awfully sorry for them, but it's their own silly fault – they ought to have let God alone. [Letter to R. Speaight, quoted in *ib.* 19]

SAUL BELLOW

4 I thought myself a bum and had my reasons, the main reason being that I behaved like a bum. [*Henderson the Rain King*, Ch. 1]

5 America is so big, and everyone is working, making, digging, bulldozing, trucking, loading, and so on, and I guess the sufferers suffer at the same rate. [*Ib.* 3]

6 A man may say, 'From now on I'm going to speak the truth.' But the truth hears him and runs away and hides before he's even done speaking. [*Herzog*]

7 Don't kid yourself, kings are the most sublime sick. Manic Depressive heroes pull Mankind into their cycles and carry everybody away. [*Humboldt's Gift*]

8 I said to her, if a tear was an intellectual thing how much more intellectual pure love was. It needed no cognitive additives. [*Ib.*]

9 We were on one of the most glamorous corners of Chicago ... Man had overcome the emptiness of his land. But the emptiness had given him a few good licks in return ... And there we sat amid the flatteries of wealth and power with pretty maidens and booze and tailored suits, and the men wearing jewels and using scent. [*Ib.*]

10 They [two lawyers who 'belonged to the club'] inspired me with an unusual

thought. This was that History had created something new in the USA, namely crookedness with self-respect or duplicity with honour. [*Ib.*]

11 The only real distinction at this dangerous moment in human history and cosmic development has nothing to do with medals and ribbons. Not to fall asleep is distinguished. Everything else is mere popcorn. [*Ib.*]

12 At the centre of the beholder there must be space for the whole, and this nothing-space is not an empty nothing but a nothing reserved for everything ... You can feel this nothing-everything capacity with ecstasy. [*Ib.*]

13 As though to be Jewish weren't trouble enough, the poor woman was German too. [*Mr Sammler's Planet*, Ch. 1]

14 I am more stupid about some things than about others; not equally stupid in all directions; I am not a well-rounded person. [*Ib.* 2]

15 Conquered people tend to be witty. [*Ib.*]

16 And the clergy? Beating swords into ploughshares? No, rather converting dog collars into G-strings. [*Ib.* 3]

17 I think that New York is not the cultural centre of America, but the business and administrative centre of American culture. [Radio interview, *Listener*, 22 May 1969]

18 After all these years wallowing in low seriousness – low seriousness, you understand, is high seriousness that's failed. [Interview in the *Sunday Times*, 12 Jan. 1975]

L. BEMELMANS

19 An American woman, a tourist, a refugee from a conducted tour of the Châteaux de la Loire, dismissed the historic safari with the words: 'Nothing but thick walls and running comment.' [*How to Travel Incognito*, Ch. 1]

ROBERT BENCHLEY

20 Even nowadays a man can't step up and kill a woman without feeling just a bit unchivalrous. [*Chips off the Old Benchley*, 'Down in Front']

35

1 I had just dozed off into a stupor when I heard what I thought was myself talking to myself. I didn't pay much attention to it, as I knew practically everything I would have to say to myself, and wasn't particularly interested. [*Ib.* 'The First Pigeon of Spring']

2 My only solution for the problem of habitual accidents . . . is for everybody to stay in bed all day. Even then, there is always the chance that you will fall out. [*Ib.* 'Good Luck']

3 A great many people have come up to me and asked how I manage to get so much work done and still keep looking so dissipated. [*Ib.* 'How to Get Things Done']

4 The biggest obstacle to professional writing today is the necessity for changing a typewriter ribbon. [*Ib.* 'Learn to Write']

5 I have been told by hospital authorities that more copies of my works are left behind by departing patients than those of any other author. [*Ib.* 'Why Does Nobody Collect Me?']

6 I haven't been abroad in so long that I almost speak English without an accent. [*Inside Benchley*, 'The Old Sea Rover Speaks']

7 Often Daddy sat up very late working on a case of Scotch. [*Editha's Christmas Burglar*]

8 The wise man thinks once before he speaks twice. [*Maxims from the Chinese*]

9 I think that I am violating no confidence when I say that Nature holds many mysteries which we humans have not fathomed as yet. Some of them may not even be worth fathoming. [*Mysteries from the Sky*]

10 The surest way to make a monkey of a man is to quote him. [*Quick Quotations*]

11 Show me a Sunday paper which has been left in a condition fit only for kite flying, and I will show you an anti-social and dangerous character who has left it that way. [*The Wreck of the Sunday Paper*]

12 [When asked by Scott Fitzgerald: 'Don't you know drinking is a slow death?'] So who's in a hurry? [Quoted in review of Sheilah Graham's *The Garden of Allah* in the *Sunday Times*, 20 Jun. 1971]

13 STREETS FULL OF WATER. PLEASE ADVISE. [Telegram on arriving in Venice]

14 As for me, except for an occasional heart attack . . . I feel as young as I ever did. [Letter to the *New Yorker* magazine. Quoted in Groucho Marx, *The Groucho Letters*]

ÉDUARD BENEŠ

15 *Sécurité collective* – collective security. [Words written on a typed draft put before the League of Nations, 1932. A French delegate is said to have protested – '*Impossible; ce n'est pas français.*' – 'Impossible; it's not French.' Quoted in G. M. Young, *Stanley Baldwin*, Ch. 17]

16 *Détruisez l'Autriche-Hongrie!* – Destroy Austria-Hungary. [Slogan in First World War]

RICHARD BENNER

17 Canada is a country so square that even the female impersonators are women. [In film, *Outrageous*. Quoted in the *Guardian*, 21 Sep. 1978]

ALAN BENNETT

18 Life is rather like a tin of sardines – we're all of us looking for the key. [*Beyond the Fringe*]

19 We roll back the lid of the sardine tin of life, we reveal the sardines, the riches of life therein, and we get them out, we enjoy them. But, you know, there's always a little piece in the corner you can't get out. I wonder – I wonder, is there a little piece in the corner of your life? I know there is in mine. [*Ib.*]

20 I have never understood this liking for war. It panders to instincts already catered for within the scope of any respectable domestic establishment. [*Forty Years On*, Act I]

21 Speaking fluent Sanskrit he [T. E. Lawrence] and his Arab body servant,

an unmade Bedouin of great beauty . . . [*Ib.*]

1 [BERTRAND] RUSSELL: But then I have led a very sheltered life. I had no contact with my own body until the spring of 1887, when I suddenly found my feet. I deduced the rest logically. [*Ib.*]

2 In our crass-builded, glass-boated, green-belted world Sunday is for washing the car, tinned peaches and carnation milk. [*Ib.* II]

3 Were we closer to the ground as children or is the grass emptier now? [*Ib.*]

4 [Of dogs] It's the one species I wouldn't mind seeing vanish from the face of the earth. I wish they were like the White Rhino – six of them left in the Serengeti National Park, and all males. [*Getting On*, Act I]

5 When does it happen? When did I turn into this? This sagging cistern, lagged with an overcoat of flesh that gets thicker and thicker every year. The skin sags, the veins break down, more and more galleries are sealed off. And you never notice. There is no pain. No warning shots. No bell rings back at base to indicate that another section of the front line has collapsed . . . I dump it, this body, with less and less enthusiasm on someone else's body. [*Ib.*]

6 I had a good education but it never went to my head, somehow. It should be a journey ending up with you at a different place. It didn't take with me. My degree was a kind of inoculation. I got just enough education to make me immune from it for the rest of my life. [*Ib.*]

7 I thought life was going to be like Brahms, do you know? Instead it's, well it's been Eric Coates. And very nice, too. But not Brahms. [*Ib.* II]

8 Quite candidly I've never seen the point of the sea. Except where it meets the land. The shore has point, the sea none. Of course when you say you miss the sea that's what you mean: you miss the shore. [*The Old Country*, Act I]

9 They are the most embarrassed people in the world, the English. You cannot look each other in the face . . . Is there anyone not embarrassed in England? The Queen perhaps. She is not embarrassed. With the rest it's 'I won't make you feel bad as long as you don't make me feel bad'. That is the social contract. Society is making each other feel better. [*Ib.*]

10 One of the few lessons I have learned in life is that there is invariably something odd about women who wear ankle socks. [*Ib.*]

11 Your whole life is on the other side of the glass. And there is nobody watching. [*Ib.*]

12 We're en route for the millennium. Not that we'll see it. The millennium's a place to go to not arrive at. [*Ib.*]

13 The good is better than the best, else what does society mean? [*Ib.* II]

14 We were put to Dickens as children but it never quite took. That unremitting humanity soon had me cheesed off. [*Ib.*]

15 There are more microbes *per person* than the entire population of the world. Imagine that. Per person. This means that if the time scale is diminished in proportion to that of space it would be quite possible for the whole story of Greece and Rome to be played out between farts. [*Ib.*]

16 It's all very well never to do what's expected of you, but what do you do when the unexpected is what people have come to expect? [*Ib.*]

ARNOLD BENNETT

17 'What great cause is he identified with?' 'He's identified . . . with the great cause of cheering us all up.' [Last words of *The Card*]

18 The people who live in the past must yield to the people who live in the future. Otherwise the world would begin to turn the other way round. [*Milestones*]

19 A man accustomed to think in millions – other people's millions. [*Journal*, Jun. 1929]

20 Every Briton is at heart a Tory – especially every British Liberal. [*Ib.* Dec. 1929]

1 Mr Lloyd George ... spoke for a hundred and seventeen minutes, in which period he was detected only once in the use of an argument. [*Things that have Interested Me*, 'After the March Offensive']

2 Hang Eddie Marsh! He's a miserable fellow. He enjoys everything. [Quoted in James Agate, *Ego*, Bk I, Ch. 7]

3 Between thirty and forty a man may have reached the height of discretion without having tumbled over the top into the feather-bed of correctitude. [*Evening Standard Years*, 29 May 1930]

4 Good taste is better than bad taste, but bad taste is better than no taste. [*Observer*, 'Sayings of the Week', 24 Aug. 1930]

BILLY BENNETT

5 It was Christmas Day in the cookhouse. / The troops had all gone to bed. / None of them had any Christmas pudding / 'Cause the sergeant had done what they said. [*Christmas Day in the Cookhouse*. A parody of George R. Sims's ballad, *Christmas Day in the Workhouse*, used as comic recitation in music-hall act]

6 There was a young fellow called Gandhi / Went into a pub for a shandy. / He used his loincloth / To wipe the froth off, / And the barmaid said, 'Blimey, that's 'andy.' [Limerick used in music-hall act]

JACK BENNY

7 Cannibal – A guy who goes into a restaurant and orders the waiter. [Quoted in A. K. Adams, *Cassell's Book of Humorous Quotations*]

8 [On accepting an award] I don't deserve this, but I have arthritis, and I don't deserve that either. [Quoted in Peter and Josie Holton, *Quote and Unquote*]

A. C. BENSON

9 I believe in instinct, not in reason. When reason is right, nine times out of ten it is impotent, and when it prevails, nine times out of ten it is wrong! [Letter quoted in C. Hassall, *Edward Marsh*, Ch. 7]

STELLA BENSON

10 Edward had no capacity for being comfortable. He lived in a small room in a cheap hotel in San Francisco, and in that room there was no trace of Edward except Edward himself. [*The Poor Man*, Ch. 2]

11 Young brother Cliff was a child of nature, a child, as it were, of suburban nature. He had no reticences. [*Ib.* 5]

NICOLAS BENTLEY

12 He who enjoys a good neighbour, said the Greeks, has a precious possession. Same goes for the neighbour's wife. [Quoted in E. Esar and N. Bentley, *The Treasury of Humorous Quotations*]

13 His was the sort of career that made the Recording Angel think seriously about taking up shorthand. [Quoted in *ib.*]

BERNARD BERENSON

14 In figure painting, the type of all painting, I have endeavoured to set forth that the principal if not sole source of life enchantments are Tactile Values, Movement and Space Composition. [*The Decline of Art*]

15 We define genius as the capacity for productive reaction against one's training. [*Ib.*]

16 History is an art which must not neglect the known facts. [Attr.]

ELISABETH BERESFORD

17 Make Good Use of Bad Rubbish. [*The Wombles*, Ch. 1]

18 Human Beings are an untidy lot. They'd lose their arms and legs if they weren't joined on right. [*Ib.*]

JOHN BERGER

19 [On Titian] The genius bears the full weight of what is common and exists hundreds and thousands of times over. [*A Painter of Our Time*]

20 Animals do not admire each other. A horse does not admire its companions. It is not that they will not race against

each other, but this is of no consequence, for, back in the stable, the one who is heavier and clumsier does not on that account give up his oats to the other, as men want others to do to them. With animals virtue is its own reward. [*G.*, Pt II, Ch. 2]

1 The five senses within whose pentagon each man is alone. [*Ib*. III. 5]

2 If we could all live a thousand years ... we would each, at least once during that period, be considered a genius. Not because of our great age, but because one of our gifts or aptitudes, however slight in itself, would coincide with what people at that particular moment took to be the mark of genius. [*Ib*. III. 6]

3 Von Hartmann was a man who had eliminated all his possible selves. All that remained from his past were obsolete versions of the same self. He was like a man engraved on a postage stamp. [*Ib*. IV. 8]

4 The spectacle creates an eternal present of immediate expectation; memory ceases to be necessary or desirable. With the loss of memory the continuities of meaning and judgement are also lost to us. The camera relieves us of the burden of memory. [Article in *New Society*, 17 Aug. 1978]

5 Peasants are the most observant class in the world. They notice and read more coded signs every day than an intelligence agent does in a week. This makes them brilliant tacticians. But they have seldom been in a position to be strategists, and their philosophy has been opposed to it. [*Ib*. 17 May 1979]

JOHN BERGER et al.

6 You are receiving images which are arranged. I hope you will consider what I have arranged and be sceptical of it. [*Ways of Seeing*]

7 The social presence of a woman is different in kind from that of a man ... A man's presence suggests what he is capable of doing to you or for you ... A woman's presence ... defines what can and cannot be done to her. [*Ib*.]

8 To be naked is to be oneself. To be nude is to be seen naked by others, and yet

not recognized for oneself ... Nudity is a form of dress. [*Ib*.]

DR BERGLER

9 Every writer, without exception, is a masochist, a sadist, a peeping Tom, an exhibitionist, a narcissist, an 'injustice collector' and a 'depressed person constantly haunted by fear of unproductivity'. [Quoted in Kenneth Tynan, *Tynan Right & Left*, Foreword]

IRVING BERLIN

10 Come on and hear, come on and hear, Alexander's Ragtime Band. [Song: *Alexander's Ragtime Band*]

11 Doin' What Comes Natur'lly. [Title of song in musical, *Annie Get Your Gun*, Act I]

12 There's No Business Like Show Business. [Title of song in *ib*.]

13 They say falling in love is wonderful, / It's wonderful, so they say. [Song: *Falling in Love*, in *ib*.]

14 Anything You Can Do, I Can Do Better. [Title of song in *ib*. II]

15 The Hostess with the Mostes' on the Ball. [Title of song in musical *Call Me Madam*, Act I]

16 This is the army, Mr Jones, / No private baths and telephones. [Song: *This Is the Army*]

17 We joined the Navy to see the world, / And what did we see? We saw the sea. [Song: *We Saw the Sea*]

18 I'm dreaming of a white Christmas, / Just like the ones I used to know. [Song: *White Christmas*, in musical, *Holiday Inn*]

19 The song is ended / But the melody lingers on. [Song: *The Song is Ended*, in musical, *Ziegfeld Follies*]

SIR ISAIAH BERLIN

20 Rousseau was the first militant lowbrow. [Quoted in *Observer*, 'Sayings of the Week', 9 Nov. 1952]

21 Society moves by some degree of parricide, by which the children, on the

whole, kill, if not their fathers, at least the beliefs of their fathers, and arrive at new beliefs. This is what progress is. [BBC TV programme, *Men of Ideas*, 19 Jan. 1978]

ENRICO BERLINGUER

1 A new historic compromise. [Describing pact between Italian Communists and Christian Democrats. Article in *Rináscita*, 12 Oct. 1973]

J. D. BERNAL

2 The full area of ignorance is not mapped: we are at present only exploring its fringes. [Quoted in Sagittarius and George, *The Perpetual Pessimist*]

GEORGE BERNANOS

3 The wish to pray is a prayer in itself. [*The Diary of a Country Priest*, Ch. 4]

ERIC BERNE

4 ... Human life is mainly a process of filling in time until the arrival of death, or Santa Claus, with very little choice, if any, of what kind of business one is going to transact during the long wait. [*Games People Play*, Ch. 18]

JOHN BERRYMAN

5 Blossomed Sarah, and I / blossom. Is that thing alive? I hear a famisht / howl. [*Homage to Mistress Bradstreet*, 21]

6 The moon came up late and the night was cold, / Many men died – although we know the fate / Of none, nor of anyone, and the war / Goes on, and the moon in the breast of man is cold. [*The Moon and the Night and the Men*]

7 I see the dragon of years is almost done, / Its claws loosen, its eyes / Crust now with tears, lust and a scale of lies. [*New Year's Eve*]

8 The statue, tolerant through years of weather, / Spares the untidy Sunday throng its look. [*The Statue*]

9 News of one day, one afternoon, one time. / If it were possible to take these things / Quite seriously, I believe they might / Curry disorders in the strongest brain, / Immobilize the most resilient will, / Stop trains, break up the city's food supply, / And perfectly demoralize the nation. [*World-Telegram*]

10 The artist is extremely lucky who is presented with the worst possible ordeal which will not actually kill him. [Interview in *Paris Review*, Winter 1972]

JOHN BETJEMAN

11 One bottle more of fizzy lemonade. [*An Archaeological Picnic*]

12 Spirits of well-shot woodcock, partridge, snipe / Flutter and bear him up the Norfolk sky. [*Death of King George V*]

13 As beefy ATS / Without their hats / Come shooting through the bridge, / And 'cheerioh' and 'cheeri-bye' / Across the waste of waters die. [*Henley-on-Thames*]

14 Pam, I adore you, Pam, you great big mountainous sports girl / Whizzing them over the net, full of the strength of five. [*Pot Pourri from a Surrey Garden*]

15 Licensed now for embracement, / Pam and I, as the organ / Thunders over you all. [*Ib.*]

16 The gas was on in the Institute, / The flare was up in the gym. [*A Shropshire Lad*]

17 Come, friendly bombs, and fall on Slough. / It isn't fit for humans now. [*Slough*]

18 Miss J. Hunter Dunn, Miss J. Hunter Dunn, / Furnish'd and burnish'd by Aldershot sun. [*A Subaltern's Love-song*]

19 As I struggle with double-end evening tie, / For we dance at the Golf Club, my victor and I. [*Ib.*]

20 Childhood is measured out by sounds and smells / And sights, before the dark of reason grows. [*Summoned by Bells*, IV]

21 The dread of beatings! Dread of being late! / And, greatest dread of all, the dread of games! [*Ib.* VII]

1 'By the boys, *for* the boys. The boys know best. / Leave it to them to pick the rotters out / With that rough justice decent schoolboys know.' [*Ib.*]

2 Aunt Elsie, aunt of normal Scottish boys, / Adopted aunt of lone abnormal me. [*Ib.* VIII]

3 Spiritually I was at Eton, John. [*Ib.* IX]

4 For, while we ate Virginia hams / Contemporaries passed exams. [*Ib.*]

5 And is it true? And is it true, / This most tremendous tale of all, / Seen in a stained-glass window hue, / A baby in an ox's stall? [*Christmas*]

6 Rumbling under blackened girders, Midland, bound for Cricklewood, / Puffed its sulphur to the sunset where that Land of Laundries stood. [*Parliament Hill Fields*]

7 But I'm dying now and done for, / What on earth was all the fun for? / For I'm old and ill and terrified and tight. [*Sun and Fun*]

8 Broad of Church and broad of mind, / Broad before and broad behind, / A keen ecclesiologist, / A rather dirty Wykehamist. [*The Wykehamist*]

9 I can speak only for myself, I would like to be a stationmaster on a small country branch line (single track). [Said when asked to name 'a most suitable second employment' by the *Horizon* questionnaire, 1946]

10 Bournemouth is one of the few English towns that one can safely call 'her'. [*First and Last Loves*]

11 History must not be written with bias, and both sides must be given, even if there is only one side. [*Ib.*]

12 Foot and note disease. [Attr.]

ANEURIN BEVAN

13 The language of priorities is the religion of Socialism. [Quoted in Vincent Brome, *Aneurin Bevan*, Ch. 1]

14 He [Churchill] is a man suffering from petrified adolescence. [Quoted in *Ib.* 11]

15 Its relationship to democratic institutions is that of the death watch beetle – it [the Communist Party] is not a Party,

it is a conspiracy. [Quoted from *Tribune*, in *Ib.* 13]

16 This island is almost made of coal and surrounded by fish. Only an organizing genius could produce a shortage of coal and fish in Great Britain at the same time. [Speech at Blackpool, 18 May 1945]

17 No attempt at ethical or social seduction can eradicate from my heart a deep burning hatred for the Tory Party ... So far as I am concerned they are lower than vermin. [Speech at Manchester, 4 Jul. 1949]

18 If you carry this resolution and follow out all its implications and do not run away from it, you will send a Foreign Secretary, whoever he may be, naked into the conference chamber. [On unilateral disarmament at Labour Party Conference, 2 Oct. 1957]

19 There is no reason to attack the monkey [Selwyn Lloyd] when the organ-grinder [Harold Macmillan] is present. [Speech in House of Commons. Quoted in L. Harris, *The Fine Art of Political Wit*, Ch. 9]

20 We know what happens to people who stay in the middle of the road. They get run over. [*Observer*, 'Sayings of the Week', 9 Dec. 1953]

21 I read the newspaper avidly. It is my one form of continuous fiction. [*Observer*, 'Sayings of the Week', 3 Apr. 1960]

22 Fascism is not in itself a new order of society. It is the future refusing to be born. [Quoted in A. Andrews, *Quotations for Speakers and Writers*]

23 [Of Hugh Gaitskell] A desiccated calculating machine. [Quoted in W. T. Rodgers (ed.), *Hugh Gaitskell*]

24 [Of a Labour colleague during the Bevanite rebellion against the party] Oh, he wants both the thirty pieces of silver and the crown of thorns. [Attr.]

EDWYN BEVAN

25 Argument, generally speaking in religion, can do no more than clear the track; it cannot make the engine move. [*Hellenism and Christianity*]

LORD BEVERIDGE

1 The trouble in modern democracy is that men do not approach to leadership until they have lost the desire to lead anyone. [*Observer*, 'Sayings of the Week', 15 Apr. 1934]

2 Scratch a pessimist, and you find often a defender of privilege. [*Observer*, 'Sayings of the Week', 17 Dec. 1943]

ERNEST BEVIN

3 I didn't ought never to have done it. It was you, Willie, what put me up to it. [To Lord Strang, after recognizing Communist China. Quoted in C. Parrott, *The Serpent and the Nightingale*]

4 [When asked his opinion of Anthony Eden's speeches] Clitch, clitch, clitch. [Attr. See also 77:19]

GEORGES BIDAULT

5 The weak have one weapon: the errors of those who think they are strong. [*Observer*, 'Sayings of the Week', 15 Jul. 1962]

AMBROSE BIERCE

6 *Altar*, n. They stood before the altar and supplied / The fire themselves in which their fat was fried. [*The Devil's Dictionary*]

7 When Eve saw her reflection in a pool, she sought Adam and accused him of infidelity. [*Ib.*]

8 Applause is the echo of a platitude. [*Ib.*]

9 *Bore*, n. A person who talks when you wish him to listen. [*Ib.*]

10 *Brain*, n. An apparatus with which we think that we think. [*Ib.*]

11 *Calamity*, n. Calamities are of two kinds: misfortune to ourselves, and good fortune to others. [*Ib.*]

12 *Cannon*, n. An instrument employed in the rectification of national boundaries. [*Ib.*]

13 *Debauchee*, n. One who has so earnestly pursued pleasure that he has had the misfortune to overtake it. [*Ib.*]

14 *Egotist*, n. A person of low taste, more interested in himself than in me. [*Ib.*]

15 *Faith*, n. Belief without evidence in what is told by one who speaks without knowledge, of things without parallel. [*Ib.*]

16 *Future*, n. That period of time in which our affairs prosper, our friends are true and our happiness is assured. [*Ib.*]

17 *Garter*, n. An elastic band intended to keep a woman from coming out of her stockings and desolating the country. [*Ib.*]

18 *Genealogy*, n. An account of one's descent from a man who did not particularly care to trace his own. [*Ib.*]

19 *Hand*, n. A singular instrument worn at the end of a human arm and commonly thrust into somebody's pocket. [*Ib.*]

20 *Marriage*, n. The state or condition of a community consisting of a master, a mistress and two slaves, making in all two. [*Ib.*]

21 *Patience*, n. A minor form of despair, disguised as a virtue. [*Ib.*]

22 *Peace*, n. In international affairs, a period of cheating between two periods of fighting. [*Ib.*]

23 *Philanthropist*, n. A rich (and usually bald) old gentleman who has trained himself to grin while his conscience is picking his pocket. [*Ib.*]

24 *Prejudice*, n. A vagrant opinion without visible means of support. [*Ib.*]

25 *Riot*, n. A popular entertainment given to the military by innocent bystanders. [*Ib.*]

26 Mark how my fame rings out from zone to zone: / A thousand critics shouting, 'He's unknown!' [*Couplet*]

27 All are lunatics, but he who can analyse his delusion is a philosopher. [Quoted in H. L. Mencken, *A New Dictionary of Quotations*]

28 The gambling known as business looks with austere disfavour upon the business known as gambling. [Quoted in *ib.*]

29 When your friend holds you affectionately by both hands you are safe,

for you can watch both his. [Quoted in *ib.*]

F. E. SMITH, EARL OF BIRKENHEAD

1 JUDGE: I have read your case, Mr Smith, and I am no wiser now than I was when I started.
F. E. S.: Possibly not, My Lord, but far better informed. [Quoted in *Life of F. E. Smith* by his son, the second Earl of Birkenhead, Ch. 9]

2 JUDGE: You are offensive, sir.
F. E. S.: We both are; the difference is that I'm trying to be and you can't help it. [C. E. Bechofer Roberts ('Ephesian'), *Lord Birkenhead*, Ch. 3]

3 WOODROW WILSON: And what, in your opinion, is the trend of the modern English undergraduate?
F. E. S.: Steadily towards women and drink, Mr President. [Quoted in G. M. Young, *Stanley Baldwin*, Ch. 27]

4 MR JUSTICE DARLING: And who is George Robey?
F. E. S.: Mr George Robey is the Darling of the music-halls, m'lud. [Quoted in A. E. Wilson, *The Prime Minister of Mirth*, Ch. 1]

5 Votes are to swords exactly what banknotes are to gold – the one is effective only because the other is believed to lie behind it. [Said of Women's Suffrage in 1910. Quoted in the *Guardian*, 4 May 1978]

LORD BIRKETT

6 I do not object to people looking at their watches when I am speaking. But I strongly object when they start shaking them to make sure they are still going. [Quoted in A. Andrews, *Quotations for Speakers and Writers*]

AUGUSTINE BIRRELL

7 [Reply to the Speaker when called to order in the House of Commons] I'm sorry, sir, that you did not call me to order before. I have now said all the disorderly things that I wanted to. [Attr.]

MORRIS BISHOP

8 'I cannot hear a single word; / Yell if you like,' said Dr Slade. / He patted his Unhearing Aid. [*Free from Speech*]

9 There I stood and humbly scanned / The miracle that sense appals, / And I watched the tourists stand / Spitting in Niagara Falls. [*Public Aid for Niagara Falls*]

10 The lights burn low in the barber-shop / And the shades are drawn with care / To hide the haughty barbers / Cutting each other's hair. [*The Tales the Barbers Tell*]

11 We all know Mumsy was vague and clumsy, / Dithering, drunken and dumb. [*There's Money in Mother and Father*]

JUDGE BLAGDEN

12 A witness cannot give evidence of his age unless he can remember being born. [*Observer*, 'Sayings of the Week', 29 Jan. 1950]

COLIN BLAKEMORE

13 If the cells and fibre in one human brain were all stretched out end to end, they would certainly reach to the moon and back. Yet the fact that they are not arranged end to end enabled man to go there himself. The astonishing tangle within our heads makes us what we are. [In the BBC Reith Lectures for 1976. Lecture reprinted in the *Listener*, 25 Nov. 1976]

14 The biological (if not the aesthetic) value of remembering is not that it allows one to reminisce about the past but that it permits one to calculate coldly about the unknown future. [*Ib.* Lecture reprinted in the *Listener*, 2 Dec. 1976]

GENERAL TASKER BLISS

15 We ought to get out of Europe, horse, foot and dragoons. [Letter quoted in John dos Passos, *Mr Wilson's War*, Ch. 22]

KAREN BLIXEN

See Dinesen, Isak

ALEXANDER BLOK

1 The right words in the right order. [Of poetry. Quoted in D. Burg and G. Feifer, *Solzhenitsyn*]

EDMUND BLUNDEN

2 Old farm-houses with their white faces / Fly, and their ghosts have taken their places; / Even the signposts like grim liars / Point to trapping brakes and briars. [*Evening Mystery*]

3 Can she who shines so calm be fear? / What poison pours she in slumber's ear? [*Ib.*]

4 And nigh this toppling reed, still as the dead / The great pike lies, the murderous patriarch, / Watching the water-pit shelving and dark / Where through the plash his lithe bright vassals tread. [*The Pike*]

5 The field and wood, all bone-fed loam, / Shot up a roaring harvest-home. [*Rural Economy*]

6 A country god to every childish eye. [*The Shepherd*]

7 I saw the sunlit vale, and the pastoral fairy-tale; / The sweet and bitter scent of the may drifted by; / But it looked like a lie, / Like a kindly meant lie. [*The Sunlit Vale*]

WILFRID BLUNT

8 The drawing is on the level of that of an untaught child of seven or eight years old, the sense of colour that of a tea-tray painter, the method that of a schoolboy who wipes his fingers on a slate after spitting on them. [Of the Post-Impressionist Exhibition, Diary: 15 Nov. 1910]

RONALD BLYTHE

9 Constant tact from others had had the effect of making him [the future George VI] far too modest and he had quite lost sight of his own merits, if he ever knew them. He was, in fact, ideally suited for the British Throne. [*The Age of Illusion*, Ch. 11]

10 As for the British churchman, he goes to church as he goes to the bathroom, with the minimum of fuss and no explanation if he can help it. [*Ib.* 12]

11 An industrial worker would sooner have a £5 note but a countryman must have praise. [*Akenfield*, Ch. 5, 'Christopher Falconer']

12 Bugger Sunday, I say, and praise God when you can. [*Ib.* 6, 'Gregory Gladwell']

13 The man with money to spend on a village house in England has got to have everything quaint and curly. [*Ib.*]

HUMPHREY BOGART

14 Play it, Sam. Play 'As Time Goes By'. [In film, *Casablanca*. Script by J. J. Epstein, P. G. Epstein and H. Koch. Usually misquoted as, 'Play it again, Sam']

15 Here's looking at you, kid. [In *ib.*]

16 You know how to whistle, don't you, Steve? You just put your lips together and blow. [In film, *To Have and Have Not*. Script by Jules Furthman and William Faulkner]

NIELS BOHR

17 ... Two sorts of truth: trivialities, where opposites are obviously absurd, and profound truths, recognized by the fact that the opposite is also a profound truth. [Quoted in S. Rozental, *Niels Bohr: his life and work*]

18 An expert is a man who has made all the mistakes, which can be made, in a very narrow field. [Quoted in A. L. Mackay, *The Harvest of a Quiet Eye*]

ROBERT BOLT

19 ROPER: I'd cut down every law in England to do that.
MORE: Oh? And when the last law was down, and the Devil turned round on you – where would you hide, Roper, the laws being flat? This country's planted thick with laws from coast to coast – Man's laws, not God's – and if you cut them down – and you're just the man to do it – d'you really think you could stand upright in the winds that would

blow then? [*A Man for All Seasons*, Act I]

1 The nobility of England, my lord, would have snored through the Sermon on the Mount. [*Ib*. II]

2 I think Lenin was an admirable man, possessed by a terribly wrong idea. It was terribly wrong because it was only partly right. And it was so absolutely punitive that it needed to be absolutely right. [*State of Revolution*, Introduction]

ANDREW BONAR LAW

3 If I am a great man, then a good many of the great men of history are frauds. [Said to Sir Max Aitken, afterwards Lord Beaverbrook, during the Ulster crisis]

4 We have heard of people being thrown to the wolves, but never before have we heard of a man being thrown to the wolves with a bargain on the part of the wolves that they would not eat him. [Speech in House of Commons on Colonel Seely's proffered resignation as War Minister, Mar. 1914]

5 Look at that man's [Mussolini's] eyes. You will hear more of him later. [Said to a secretary, 1922]

6 I must follow them; I am their leader. [Quoted in E. T. Raymond, *Mr Balfour*, Ch. 15]

7 He [Lord Birkenhead] would sooner keep hot coals in his mouth than a witticism. [Attr.]

EDWARD BOND

8 I write about violence as naturally as Jane Austen wrote about manners. Violence shapes and obsesses our society, and if we do not stop being violent we have no future. [*Lear*, Author's Preface]

9 An unjust society causes and defines crime; and an aggressive social structure which is unjust and must create aggressive social disruption, receives the moral sanction of being 'law and order'. Law and order is one of the steps taken to maintain injustice. [*Ib*.]

10 If a God had made the world, might would always be right, that would be so wise, we'd be spared so much suffering. But we made the world out of our smallness and weakness. Our lives are awkward and fragile and we have only one thing to keep us sane: pity, and the man without pity is mad. [*Ib*. Act III, sc. iii]

11 Of course, that's only a symbol, but we need symbols to protect us from ourselves. [*Narrow Road to the Deep North*, Pt I, sc. iv]

12 The English sent all their bores abroad, and acquired the empire as a punishment. [*Ib*. Pt II, sc. i]

JAMES BONE

13 He makes righteousness readable. [Of C. P. Scott, editor of the *Manchester Guardian*. Quoted in A. K. Adams, *Cassell's Book of Humorous Quotations*]

KYRIL BONFIGLIOLI

14 But in the Lower Sixth we all got either religion or Communism – it goes with acne you know. Vanishes as soon as you have proper sexual intercourse. [*Don't Point that Thing at Me*, Ch. 6]

15 Ornithology used to be an arcane hobby for embittered schoolmasters, dotty spinsters and lonely little boys but now it is as normal a weekend occupation as rug-making or wife-swapping. [*Ib*. 18]

LADY VIOLET BONHAM CARTER

16 Tories are not always wrong, but they are always wrong at the right moment. [*Observer*, 'Sayings of the Week', 26 Apr. 1964]

DIETRICH BONHOEFFER

17 Man has learned to cope with all questions of importance without recourse to God as a working hypothesis. [*Letters and Papers from Prison*, Letter, 8 Jun. 1944]

18 I should like to speak of God not on the borders of life but at its centre . . . God is the 'beyond' in the midst of our life. [*Ib*. Letter, 30 Jun. 1944]

45

1 Now that it has come of age, the world is more godless, and perhaps it is for that very reason nearer to God than ever before. [*Ib*. Letter, 18 Jul. 1944]

2 It is the characteristic excellence of the strong man that he can bring momentous issues to the fore and make a decision about them. The weak are always forced to decide between alternatives they have not chosen themselves. [*Ib*. 'Miscellaneous Thoughts']

3 A God who let us prove his existence would be an idol. [*No Rusty Swords*]

4 The man for others [Jesus Christ]. [Quoted in John A. T. Robinson, *Honest to God*, Ch. 4]

EDWARD DE BONO

5 A memory is what is left when something happens and does not completely unhappen. [*The Mechanism of Mind*]

6 A myth is a fixed way of looking at the world which cannot be destroyed because, looked at through the myth, all evidence supports that myth. [*PO, Beyond Yes and No*]

7 Unhappiness is best defined as the difference between our talents and our expectations. [*Observer*, 'Sayings of the Week', 12 Jun. 1977]

DANIEL BOORSTIN

8 We expect to be inspired by mediocre appeals for 'excellence', to be made literate by illiterate appeals for literacy. [*The Image*, Ch. 1]

9 The celebrity is a person who is known for his well-knownness. [*Ib*. 2]

10 Shakespeare, in the familiar lines, divided great men into three classes: those born great, those who achieve greatness, and those who have greatness thrust upon them. It never occurred to him to mention those who hire public relations experts and press secretaries to make themselves look great. [*Ib*.]

11 In the twentieth century our highest praise is to call the Bible 'the World's Best-Seller'. And it has come to be more and more difficult to say whether we think it is a best-seller because it is great, or vice versa. [*Ib*. 4]

12 A best-seller was a book which somehow sold well simply because it was selling well. [*Ib*.]

JORGE LUIS BORGES

13 Writing is nothing more than a guided dream. [*Doctor Brodie's Report*, Preface]

14 I have known uncertainty: a state unknown to the Greeks. [*Ficciones*, 'The Babylonian Lottery']

15 The visible universe was an illusion or, more precisely, a sophism. Mirrors and fatherhood are abominable because they multiply it and extend it. [*Ib*. 'Tlön, Uqbar, Orbis, Tertius']

16 Like every writer, he measured the virtues of other writers by their performances, and asked that they measure him by what he conjectured or planned. [*The Secret Miracle*]

17 We have stopped believing in progress. What progress that is! [Quoted in Ibarra, *Borges et Borges*]

JORGE LUIS BORGES and ADOLFO BIOY CASARES

18 A good actor does not make his entry before the theatre is built. [*Seis problemas para don Isidro Parodi*, written under the pseudonym, 'H. Bustos Domecq']

HORATIO BOTTOMLEY

19 I haven't made a study of the question, but I certainly think it is high time Brighton was relieved. [When questioned on the Jewish National Home, Dec. 1918. Quoted in Julian Symons, *Horatio Bottomley*]

20 VISITOR: Ah, Bottomley, sewing? BOTTOMLEY: No, reaping. [When discovered sewing mail bags by a prison visitor. Quoted in *ib*.]

21 I HAVE PAID, BUT – [Headline to his story of his life in prison, printed in *Weekly Dispatch* after his release. Quoted in *ib*.]

ELIZABETH BOWEN

1 Experience isn't interesting till it begins to repeat itself – in fact, till it does that, it hardly *is* experience. [*The Death of the Heart*, Pt I, Ch. 1]

2 The heart may think it knows better: the senses know that absence blots people out. We have really no absent friends. [*Ib*. II. 2]

3 She had to confess inexperience; her personality was still too much for her, like a punt-pole. [*Friends and Relations*, Pt I, Ch. 1]

4 Today proved to be one of those weekdays, vacant, utterly without character, when some moral fort of a lifetime is abandoned calmly, almost idly, without the slightest assault from circumstance. So religions are changed, celibacy relinquished, marriages broken up, or there occurs a first large breach with personal honour. [*Ib*. II. 3]

5 Proximity was their support; like walls after an earthquake they could fall no further for they had fallen against each other. [*Ib*. II. 7]

6 She was anxious to be someone, and, no one ever having voiced a prejudice in her hearing without impressing her, had come to associate prejudice with identity. You could not be a someone without disliking things. [*The House in Paris*, Pt I, Ch. 1]

7 Meetings that do not come off keep a character of their own. They stay as they were projected. [*Ib*. II. 2]

8 Jealousy is no more than feeling alone among smiling enemies. [*Ib*. II. 8]

9 To talk of books is, for oppressed shut-in lovers, no way out of themselves; what was written is rather dull or too near the heart. But to walk into history is to be free at once, to be at large among people. [*Ib*.]

10 At her confirmation classes they had worked through the Commandments: at the seventh, an evening had been devoted to impure curiosity. [*To the North*, Ch. 5]

11 'But all my friends now are so very respectable: they take me to see girls'

schools.' 'Dear me,' said her aunt, 'are they widowers?' 'No, they have nieces.' [*Ib*. 11]

12 No never forget! ... Never forget any moment; they are too few. [*Ib*. 28]

LORD BOWEN

13 Lord Morley once quoted as the Minister's main function Lord Bowen's famous definition of hard work – 'Answering yes or no, on imperfect information'. [Quoted in Austen Chamberlain, *Politics From Inside*]

SIR MAURICE BOWRA

14 I'm a man / More dined against than dining. [Attr. by J. Betjeman, *Summoned by Bells*, IX]

15 Any amusing deaths lately? [Frequently in conversation]

E. BOYD-JONES and PAUL A. RICHARDS

16 Tell Me Pretty Maiden, Are There Any More At Home Like You? [Title of song in musical, *Floradora*, Act II]

ANDREW BOYLE

17 'Au contraire,' as the Frenchman once said on the storm-tossed ship when asked if he had dined. [*Punch*, 27 Nov. 1974]

GENERAL BRABAZON

18 Of the stationmaster at Aldershot he inquired on one occasion in later years: 'Where is the London twain?' 'It has gone, Colonel.' 'Gone! Bwing another!' [Quoted in Winston Churchill, *My Early Life*, Ch. 5]

LORD BRABAZON

19 Space beckons us to the three brass balls of the pawnbroker. [Speech in House of Lords, Nov. 1962]

20 I take the view, and always have done, that if you cannot say what you have to say in twenty minutes, you should go away and write a book about it. [Reported in press, Jun. 1955]

CHARLES BRACKETT and BILLY WILDER

1 He was five foot three! I went to a judge. A woman needs a man not a radiator cap. [Film, *Hold Back the Dawn*]

BRENDAN BRACKEN

2 It's a good deed to forget a poor joke. [*Observer*, 'Sayings of the Week', 17 Oct. 1943]

MALCOLM BRADBURY

3 His generation was the one between the wars; the thirties were his stamping ground, and his predominant emotion was a puzzled frustration in the face of the fact that all the passions he had held then almost but not quite fitted the situation of the present time. [*Eating People is Wrong*, Ch. 1]

4 'In India,' said the nun ... 'the work of Mr Eliot is very much respected; he is translated; and many people have written his thesis for his doctorate on inclinations of his work.' [*Ib*. 2]

5 Sympathy – for all these people, for being foreigners – lay over the gathering like a woolly blanket; and no one was enjoying it at all. [*Ib*.]

6 He's sexually unpleasant, Stuart. I call him The Solitary Raper. He's like a walking phallic symbol. [*Ib*. 5]

7 It had always seemed to Louis that a fundamental desire to take postal courses was being sublimated by other people into sexual activity. [*Ib*.]

8 I like the English. They have the most rigid code of immorality in the world. [*Ib*.]

9 It amuses me, you know, the way you seem to see women. You think of them as sort of loose-fitting men. [*Ib*. 6]

10 'It's one of these knee-stroking novels,' said Oliver. 'What are they?' asked Treece. 'Oh you know, all pale young working-class men reading Shelley to one another and saying, "Art thou pale for weariness?" and girls who softly stroke their own knees and say, "You know, you're a very strange person."' [*Ib*. 7]

11 'Are you married, Mr Willoughby?' asked the wife of the Vice-Chancellor ... 'I don't suppose he believes in it,' said the Vice-Chancellor in disgruntled tones. 'Well, why buy the cow,' asked Willoughby reasonably, 'when you can steal milk through the fence?' [*Ib*. 8]

12 You're what I call flabby genteel. [*Ib*.]

13 The towers of high-rise council flats, superficially similar, stacked, like a social worker's handbook, with separated wives, unmarried mothers, latchkey children. [*The History Man*, Ch. 1]

14 'We stay together, but we distrust one another.' 'Ah, yes ... but isn't that a definition of marriage?' [*Ib*. 3]

15 I've noticed your hostility towards him ... I ought to have guessed you were friends. [*Ib*. 7]

16 'The only thing that matters to me is attachment to other knowable people, and the gentleness of relationship.' 'Well, that's what we all want, isn't it?' asks Howard, 'sweetness and light and plenty of Mozart.' [*Ib*. 10]

17 Of course, as Henry James says, the house of fiction has many windows. Your trouble is you seem to have stood in front of most of them. [*Ib*. 12]

18 Only the old are innocent. That is what the Victorians understood, and the Christians. Original sin is the property of the young. The old grow beyond corruption very quickly. [*Stepping Westward*, Bk 1, Ch. 1]

19 Reading someone else's newspaper is like sleeping with someone else's wife. Nothing seems to be precisely in the right place, and when you find what you are looking for, it is not clear then how to respond to it. [*Ib*.]

20 My experience of ships is that on them one makes an interesting discovery about the world. One finds one can do without it completely. [*Ib*. I. 2]

21 Oh, I'm a great believer in behaving right. All I ask is for the world to help me along a little. [*Ib*.]

22 There was something craggy and hard about their [the English] personalities that discouraged access ... They don't

spend themselves in relationships until they know what the odds are; long hours spent as babies lying in the rain outside greengrocers' shops have made them tough. [*Ib*. II. 4]

1 English history is all about men liking their fathers, and American history is all about men hating their fathers and trying to burn down everything they ever did. [*Ib*. II. 5]

2 The English are polite by telling lies. The Americans are polite by telling the truth. [*Ib*.]

3 Character is not a fashionable concept. Now we think we act because our family situation was so, because our historical location is so, because we are sailing with the tide of history, or because it has abandoned us as reactionary deviants. Today all our actions are really performed by our grandfathers; we take no responsibility, like the owners of umbrella stands in hotels. [*Ib*. IV. 6]

4 If God had meant us to have group sex, I guess he'd have given us all more organs. [*Who Do You Think You Are?*, 'A Very Hospitable Person']

MALCOM BRADBURY and CHRISTOPHER BIGSBY

5 You Liberals think that goats are just sheep from broken homes. [TV play, *After Dinner Game*]

6 He's the sort of man who thinks euthanasia is the logical extension of the aspirin. [*Ib*.]

7 If God had been a Liberal there wouldn't have been ten commandments, there would have been ten suggestions. [*Ib*.]

RAY BRADBURY

8 The Day It Rained Forever. [Title of book]

ROBERT BRADBURY

9 After all, what is a pedestrian? He is a man who has two cars – one being driven by his wife, the other by one of his children. [*New York Times*, 5 Sep. 1962]

GENERAL OMAR BRADLEY

10 The wrong war, at the wrong place, at the wrong time, and with the wrong enemy. [At the Senate inquiry over General MacArthur's proposal to carry the Korean conflict into China, May 1951]

11 The way to win an atomic war is to make certain it never starts. [*Observer*, 'Sayings of the Week', 20 Apr. 1952]

SIR WILLIAM BRAGG

12 We use the classical theory on Mondays, Wednesdays and Fridays, and the quantum theory on Tuesdays, Thursdays and Saturdays. [Quoted in Whetham, *History of Science*]

CARYL BRAHMS and S. J. SIMON

13 Art, thought Lord Buttonhooke with a clarity of perception that belongs to the slightly drunk alone, is art. [*Castno for Sale*, Ch. 4]

14 'And how,' demanded Mr Brandibal, spearing a kidney, 'was the new Ibsen?' 'Bricks without Shaw,' said Mr Gloom, dissecting a kipper. [*Ib*.]

15 The Prince of Esterhazy is entering his coach ... his Hungarian costume so covered with diamonds and jewels that he looks as if he has been caught in a rain of them and come in dripping. [*Ib*.]

16 Downstairs a billiard saloon, upstairs a brothel – what more can a villain want? [*Ib*.]

17 Uncle Clarence has mistrusted Orientals ever since his ticket failed to win the Calcutta Sweep. [*Ib*.]

18 For ten pounds Beaumont and Fletcher will give you any one of a dozen plays – each indistinguishable from the other. [*No Bed For Bacon*, Ch. 1]

19 'Ale money,' said Burbage. He laughed bitterly. 'Alms for oblivion.' 'By God!' said Shakespeare. 'That's good. That's genius.' [*Ib*. 8]

20 Shakespeare sprang to his feet. 'Master Bacon,' he demanded passionately, 'do I write my plays or do you?' Bacon looked at him. He shrugged. [*Ib*. 13]

1 'Christ Almighty – another letter from my father!' said the Earl of Chesterfield's son. [*No Nightingales*, Ch. 15]

2 Inside the cab Sarah Siddons tried to find a more comfortable portion of herself to sit upon. [*Ib.* 23]

3 The suffragettes were triumphant. Woman's place was in the gaol. [*Ib.* 37]

4 If there are cat-calls . . . you are sure at least that the audience is still there. [*Six Curtains for Stroganova*, Ch. 13]

5 Stroganoff gazed at her with the hurt reproach of a hooked mackerel betrayed by its faithful sprat. [*Ib.* 17]

6 'And is this my fault?' he demanded, a truculent camel refusing to break its back with someone else's last straw. [*Ib.* 18]

H. N. BRAILSFORD

7 One knows what a war is about only when it is over. [*The Levellers and the English Revolution*, Ch. 1]

JOHN BRAINE

8 Room At the Top. [Title of book]

ERNEST BRAMAH (E. B. SMITH)

9 It is proverbial that from a hungry tiger and an affectionate woman there is no escape. [*Kai Lung Unrolls His Mat*, 'The Difficult Progression']

10 Even a goat and an ox must keep in step if they are going to plough together. [*Ib.* 'The Further Continuance']

11 He is capable of any crime, from reviling the Classics to diverting water-courses. [*Ib.* 'The Meeting by the Way with the Warrior of Chi-u']

12 Beware of jealousy . . . Remember it is written, 'Not everyone who comes down your street enters by your door.' [*Ib.*]

13 He who can predict winning numbers has no need to let off crackers. [*Ib.* 'How Kai Lung Sought to Discourage']

14 May bats defile his Ancestral Tablets and goats propagate within his neglected tomb! . . . May the sinews of his hams snap in moments of achievement! [*Kai Lung's Golden Hours*, 'The Timely Intervention of the Mandarin Shan Tien's Lucky Day']

15 How is it possible to suspend topaz in one cup of the balance and weigh it against amethyst in the other; or who in a single language can compare the tranquillizing grace of a maiden with the invigorating pleasure of witnessing a well-contested rat-fight? [*Ib.* 'The Incredible Obtuseness of those who had opposed the Virtuous Kai Lung']

16 Those who walk into an earthquake while imploring heaven for a sign are unworthy of consideration. [*Ib.* 'The Out-passing into a State of Assured Felicity']

17 When struck by a thunderbolt it is unnecessary to consult the Book of Dates as to the precise meaning of the omen. [*The Wallet of Kai Lung*, 'The Transmutation of Ling']

18 I am overwhelmed that I should be the cause of such an engaging display of polished agitation. [*Ib.*]

19 Should a person in returning from the city discover his house to be in flames, let him examine well the change which he has received from the chair-carrier, before it is too late; for evil never travels alone. [*Ib.* 'The Charitable Quen-ki-tong']

20 To what degree do the class and position of her entirely unnecessary parents affect the question? [*Ib.*]

CONSTANTIN BRANCUSI

21 Sculpture is not for young men. [Quoted in Ezra Pound, *ABC of Reading*, 'Treatise on Reading', III]

MARLON BRANDO

22 An actor's a guy who, if you ain't talking about him, ain't listening. [*Observer*, 'Sayings of the Year', Jan. 1956]

G. W. BRANDT

23 Surrounded on all sides, I won the war single-handed. [Quoted in *Cassell's Encyclopaedia of Literature*, 'Plot']

GEORGES BRAQUE

1 I do not believe in things: I believe in relationships. [Quoted in J. Culler, *Saussure*, Ch. 4]

2 Art is meant to disturb. Science reassures. [*Pensées sur l'art*]

WERNHER VON BRAUN

3 [Of the first V2 to fall on London during the Second World War] It was very successful, but it fell on the wrong planet. [Quoted on BBC radio after his death, 17 Jun. 1977]

4 Basic research is when I'm doing what I don't know I'm doing. [Quoted in W. H. Auden and L. Kronenberger, *The Faber Book of Aphorisms*]

BERTOLT BRECHT

5 Fearful is the seductive power of goodness. [*The Caucasian Chalk Circle*, Act I, trans. Eric Bentley]

6 A good soldier has his heart and soul in it. When he receives an order, he gets a hard on, and when he drives his lance into the enemy's guts, he comes. [*Ib.* III]

7 I love the people with their simple straightforward minds. It's only that their smell brings on my migraine. [*Ib.* V]

8 You want justice, but do you want to pay for it, hm? When you go to a butcher you know you have to pay, but you people go to a judge as if you were off to a funeral supper. [*Ib.*]

9 Take note of what men of old concluded: / That what there is shall go to those who are good for it, / Children to the motherly, that they prosper, / Carts to good drivers, that they be driven well, / The valley to the waterers, that it yield fruit. [*Ib.*]

10 Unhappy the land that is in need of heroes. [*Galileo*, sc. xiii]

11 Science knows only one commandment: contribute to science. [*Ib.* xiv]

12 It was never decreed that a god mustn't pay hotel bills. [*The Good Woman of Setzuan*, Prologue, trans. Eric Bentley]

13 You can only help one of your luckless brothers / By trampling down a dozen others. [*Ib.* Act IVa]

14 A real superior man is like a bell. If you ring it, it rings, and if you don't, it don't, as the saying is. [*Ib.* VIII]

15 It isn't important to come out on top, what matters is to be the one who comes out alive. [*Jungle of the Cities*, sc. x]

16 What they could do with round here is a good war. What else can you expect with peace running wild all over the place? You know what the trouble with peace is? No organization. [*Mother Courage*, Act I, trans. Eric Bentley]

17 When he told men to love their neighbour, their bellies were full. Nowadays things are different. [*Ib.* II]

18 In a good country virtues wouldn't be necessary. Everybody could be quite ordinary, middling, and for all I care, cowards. [*Ib.*]

19 I don't trust him. We're friends. [*Ib.* III]

20 Kattrin, beware of thin men! [*Ib.*]

21 When a soldier sees a clean face, there's one more whore in the world. [*Ib.*]

22 THE CHAPLAIN: We're in God's hands now!
MOTHER C.: I hope we're not as desperate as that, but it *is* hard to sleep at night. [*Ib.*]

23 And don't you stand around like Jesus in Gethsemane. [*Ib.*]

24 The finest plans have always been spoiled by the littleness of them that should carry them out. Even emperors can't do it all by themselves. [*Ib.* VI]

25 I say, you can't be sure the war will ever end. Of course it may have to pause occasionally – for breath as it were – it can even meet with an accident – nothing on this earth is perfect – a war of which we could say it left nothing to be desired will probably never exist. [*Ib.*]

26 What happens to the hole when the cheese is gone? [*Ib.*]

27 War is like love, it always finds a way. [*Ib.*]

28 She's not so pretty anyone would want to ruin her. [*Ib.*]

51

1 Don't tell me peace has broken out. [*Ib.* VIII]

2 THE COOK [*to the Chaplain*]: As a grown man, you should know better than to go round advising people. [*Ib.*]

3 Which Adolf was this? I know two Adolfs. One of them's in a lunatic asylum; the other's Adolf Kokoschka, who collects manure. He's in a concentration camp, because he said you couldn't beat an English thoroughbred for really first-class fertilizer. [*Schweyk in the Second World War*, 1]

4 As the old Czech proverb has it, 'Sweaty feet seldom come singly.' [*Ib.* II]

5 A man who sees another man on the street corner with only a stump for an arm will be so shocked the first time he'll give him sixpence. But the second time it'll only be a threepenny bit. And if he sees him a third time, he'll have him cold-bloodedly handed over to the police. [*The Threepenny Opera*, trans. Desmond I. Vesey and Eric Bentley, Act I, sc. i]

6 The wickedness of the world is so great you have to run your legs off to avoid having them stolen from under you. [*Ib.* I. iii]

7 Grub first, then ethics. [*Ib.* II. i]

8 What is robbing a bank compared to founding one? [*Ib.* III. i]

9 Oh the shark has pretty teeth, dear, / And he shows them pearly white. / Just a jack-knife has Macheath / And he keeps it out of sight. [*Ib.*]

10 What does a man live by? By resolutely / Ill-treating, beating, cheating, eating some other bloke! / A man can only live by absolutely / Forgetting he's a man like other folk. [*Ib.* II. iii]

11 The truth is concrete. [Attr.]

12 The question: Is he then living? Answer: He is lived. [*Diaries 1920–1922* (ed. H. Ramthun, trans. J. Willett) quoted in the *Guardian*, 15 Mar. 1979]

GERALD BRENAN

13 Intellectuals are people who believe that ideas are of more importance than values. That is to say, their own ideas and other people's values. [*Thoughts in a Dry Season*, 'Life']

14 Most of our personal opinions lie on the board like iron filings. But pass the magnet of a strong emotion over them and they will change overnight and point in the opposite direction. [*Ib.*]

15 Everyone is a bore to someone. That is unimportant. The thing to avoid is being a bore to oneself. [*Ib.*]

16 Old age takes away from us what we have inherited and gives us what we have earned. [*Ib.*]

17 Some girls only fall in love with ugly men. These are the girls who when they were children preferred golliwogs to dolls. [*Ib.* 'Love']

18 In a happy marriage it is the wife who provides the climate, the husband the landscape. [*Ib.* 'Marriage']

19 When we attend the funerals of our friends we grieve for them, but when we go to those of other people it is chiefly our own deaths that we mourn for. [*Ib.* 'Death']

20 Religions are kept alive by heresies, which are really sudden explosions of faith. Dead religions do not produce them. [*Ib.* 'Religion']

21 My need has made me a fellow traveller of the religious, though I shall get out of their bus several stations before the end. [*Ib.*]

22 In more select galleries pictures stand back and watch the passers-by. Like Victorian ladies in a street they bow only to those who recognize them. [*Ib.* 'Art and Architecture']

23 For Gothic, which is Germanic in spirit although modified by French order and clarity, is all revolt and aspiration. [*Ib.*]

24 The cliché is dead poetry. English, being the language of an imaginative race, abounds in clichés, so that English literature is always in danger of being poisoned by its own secretions. [*Ib.* 'Literature']

25 [Henry] Miller is not really a writer but a non-stop talker to whom someone has given a typewriter. [*Ib.*]

1 When I write a page that reads badly I know that it is myself who has written it. When it reads well it has come through from somewhere else. [*Ib.* 'Writing']

2 Poets and painters are outside the class system, or rather they constitute a special class of their own, like the circus people and the gipsies. For the sake of their moral health they should be relatively poor and should mix mainly with their own kind. When they are short of money it is better for them to practise shop-lifting than to give lectures. [*Ib.*]

3 Every Spaniard is like a man-of-war, armed cap-à-pie to defend himself. That is why so much restraint and good manners are necessary. One man-of-war must reassure the other man-of-war that its guns will not be wanted. [*Ib.* 'People and Places']

ALFRED BRENDEL

4 Schubert sonatas happen. [Remark quoted by Edward Greenfield in the *Guardian*, 25 Nov. 1975]

JIMMY BRESLIN

5 [President] Nixon is a purposeless man, but I have great faith in his cowardice. [Quoted in the *Observer*, 16 Nov. 1969]

ARISTIDE BRIAND

6 People think too historically. They are always living half in a cemetery. [Quoted in H. L. Mencken, *A New Dictionary of Quotations*]

JAMES BRIDIE

7 Macbeth is not sufficient proof that a nervous bloke should not commit a murder. Hamlet, a much more neuropathic gent, should have done it in Act I and lived happy ever after. [Letter of 7 Oct. 1933. Quoted in J. Agate, *Ego*, Bk 2]

ALAN BRIEN

8 My theory is that mature woman is physically polygamous but emotionally monogamous, while mature man is emotionally polygamous but physically monogamous. [*New Statesman*, 6 Dec. 1968]

9 I have done almost every human activity inside a taxi which does not require main drainage. [*Punch*, 5 Jul. 1972]

10 I once met a man who claimed to have elevated his status, without perpetrating a falsehood, by entering in the profession or title space 'Elector of Marylebone', after the fashion of 'Elector of Hanover'. [*Punch*, 9 Oct. 1974]

RAYMOND BRIGGS

11 Fungus inspects his trousers which have been marinading overnight. [*Fungus the Bogeyman*]

12 Bogeys are, by nature, libidinous (lusting after books) and almost all are libertines – (those who habitually disregard the law and borrow more books than they have tickets for). [*Ib.*]

COLM BROGAN

13 There is only one word for aid that is genuinely without strings, and that word is blackmail. [Attr.]

D. W. BROGAN

14 The combination of a profound hatred of war and militarism with an innocent delight in playing soldiers is one of these apparent contradictions of American life that one has to accept. [*The American Character*, Pt I. Ch. 5]

J. BRONOWSKI

15 Among the multitude of animals which scamper, fly, burrow and swim around us, man is the only one who is not locked into his environment. His imagination, his reason, his emotional subtlety and toughness, make it possible for him not to accept the environment but to change it. And that series of inventions, by which man from age to age has remade his environment, is a different kind of evolution – not biological, but cultural evolution. I call that brilliant sequence

53

of cultural peaks *The Ascent of Man*. [*The Ascent of Man*, Ch. 1]

1 He [man] has what no other animal possesses, a jig-saw of faculties which alone, over three thousand million years of life, make him creative. Every animal leaves traces of what it was; man alone leaves traces of what he created. [*Ib*.]

2 There are many gifts that are unique in man; but at the centre of them all, the root from which all knowledge grows, lies the ability to draw conclusions from what we see to what we do not see, to move our minds through space and time, and to recognize ourselves in the past on the steps to the present. [*Ib*.]

3 We have to understand the world can only be grasped by action, not by contemplation. The hand is more important than the eye ... The hand is the cutting edge of the mind. [*Ib*. 3]

4 That is the essence of science: ask an impertinent question, and you are on the way to the pertinent answer. [*Ib*. 4]

5 Revolutions are not made by fate but by men. [*Ib*. 8]

6 Physics becomes in those years [at the turn of the century, after J. J. Thomson's discovery of the electron] the greatest collective work of science – no, more than that, the great collective work of art of the twentieth century. [*Ib*. 10]

7 There is no absolute knowledge. And those who claim it, whether they are scientists or dogmatists, open the door to tragedy. All information is imperfect. We have to treat it with humility. [*Ib*. 11]

8 It is not the business of science to inherit the earth, but to inherit the moral imagination; because without that man and beliefs and science will perish together. [*Ib*. 13]

9 [Of John von Neumann] And he was a genius, in the sense that a genius is a man who has *two* great ideas. [*Ib*.]

10 We are all afraid – for our confidence, for the future, for the world. That is the nature of the human imagination. Yet every man, every civilization, has gone forward because of its engagement with what it has set itself to do. [*Ib*.]

11 The wish to hurt, the momentary intoxication with pain, is the loophole through which the pervert climbs into the minds of ordinary men. [*The Face of Violence*, Ch. 5]

12 The world is made of people who never quite get into the first team and who just miss the prizes at the flower show. [*Ib*. 6]

13 Therapy has become what I think of as the tenth American muse. [Quoted in *Radio Times*]

PETER BROOK

14 I don't particularly mind waste, but I think it's a pity not to know what one is wasting. Some old ladies use pound notes as bookmarks: this is silly only if it is absent-minded. [*The Empty Space*, Ch. 1]

15 It is not the fault of the holy that it has become a middle-class weapon to keep children good. [*Ib*. 2]

LOUISE BROOKS
(Star of silent films)

16 I can't once remember him [Charlie Chaplin] still. He was always standing up as he sat down, and going out as he came in. [Quoted in Kenneth Tynan, 'The Girl who was Lulu', *Observer Magazine*. 11 Nov. 1979]

17 The great art of films does not consist of descriptive movement of face and body but in the movements of thought and soul, transmitted in a kind of intense isolation. [*Ib*.]

18 I never gave away anything without wishing I had kept it; nor kept it without wishing I had given it away. [Her own epitaph, quoted in *ib*.]

MEL BROOKS

19 That's it, baby, if you've got it, flaunt it. [Film, *The Producers*]

20 Tragedy is if I cut my finger. Comedy is if I walk into an open sewer and die. [Quoted in profile by Kenneth Tynan, *New Yorker*, 30 Oct. 1978]

VAN WYCK BROOKS

1 His wife not only edited his works but edited him. [*The Ordeal of Mark Twain*, Ch. 5]

'BIG BILL BROONZY'

2 I guess all songs is folk songs. I never heard no horse sing 'em. [Quoted in C. Keil, *Urban Blues*]

BRIGID BROPHY

3 History is in the shit sense. You have left it behind you. Fiction is piss: a stream of past events but not behind you, because they never really happened. [*In Transit*, Sect. I. 1]

4 An airport is a free-range womb. [*Ib.* I. 4]

5 We Irish had the right word on the tip of our tongue, but the imperialist got at that. What should trip off it we trip over. [*Ib.* I. 6]

6 The thriller is the cardinal twentieth-century form. All it, like the twentieth century, wants to know is: Who's Guilty? [*Ib.* I. 11]

HEYWOOD BROUN

7 The best newspaperman who has ever been President of the United States. [Said of Franklin D. Roosevelt. Quoted in D. Boorstin, *The Image*, Ch. 1]

8 The man who has cured himself of B.O. and halitosis, has learned French to surprise the waiter, and the saxophone to amuse the company, may find that people still avoid him because they do not like him. [Quoted in D. W. Brogan, *The American Character*, Pt I, sect. 6]

CLARENCE BROWN

9 Excellent books are slippery things. They slip through the fingers of police-men who want to prevent them being published, and once they are in print, they slip out of the categories into which tidy-minded critics long to fix them. [Introduction to Nadezhda Mandel-stam, *Hope Against Hope*]

ERNEST BROWN

10 I like a nap. The man who cannot sleep ought not to be in the Cabinet. [*Observer*, 'Sayings of the Week', 16 Apr. 1939]

GENERAL GEORGE BROWN
(Chairman of U S Joint Chiefs of Staff)

11 Britain is no longer a world power – all they have got are generals and admirals and bands. [Quoted in the *Guardian Weekly*, 31 Oct. 1976]

JOHN MASON BROWN

12 To many people dramatic criticism must seem like an attempt to tattoo soap bubbles. [Quoted in Frank Muir, *The Frank Muir Book*]

13 Some television programmes are so much chewing gum for the eyes. [Interview, 28 Jul. 1955]

LEW BROWN

14 Climb upon my knee, Sonny Boy; / Though you're only three, Sonny Boy. [Song, *Sonny Boy*. Sung by Al Jolson]

15 Life is Just a Bowl of Cherries. [Title of song in musical, *Scandals*. Music by Henderson. Sung by Ethel Merman]

LEW BROWN, CHARLIE TOBIAS and SAM H. STEPT

16 Don't Sit Under the Apple Tree with Anyone Else but Me. [Title of song]

OLIVER BROWN

17 A shiver ran through the Scottish MPs, frantically looking for a spine to run up. [*The Extended Tongue*]

W. J. BROWN

18 We have not yet lost this war, but we are overdrawn on the Bank of Miracles. [*Observer*, 'Sayings of the Week', 16 Aug. 1942]

LENNY BRUCE

1 People should be taught what is, not what should be. All my humour is based on destruction and despair. If the whole world were tranquil, without disease and violence, I'd be standing in the breadline – right back of J. Edgar Hoover. [Epigraph to J. Cohen (ed.), *The Essential Lenny Bruce*]

2 Every day people are straying away from the church and going back to God. Really. [*Ib.* 'Religions Inc.']

3 That fact is that you and I have had such bad early toilet training, that the worst sound in the world to all of us is when that toilet-flush noise finishes before you do. [*Ib.* 'The Dirty Word Concept']

4 [Of his drug-taking] I'll die young, but it's like kissing God. [Quoted in R. Neville, *Playpower*]

5 It [the Crucifixion] was just one of those parties which got out of hand. [Quoted in the *Guardian*, 10 May 1979]

JEROME BRUNER

6 Any subject can be effectively taught in some intellectually honest form to any child at any stage of development. [*The Process of Education*, Ch. 3]

JOHN BRUNNER

7 POPULATION EXPLOSION Unique in human experience, an event which happened yesterday but which everyone swears won't happen until tomorrow. [*Stand on Zanzibar*, 'The Hipcrime Vocab']

'BASIL BRUSH'

8 Boom! Boom! [Running gag in TV comedy act. Script by George Martin]

MARTIN BUBER

9 I And Thou. [Title of book]

10 The real struggle is not between East and West, or capitalism and communism, but between education and propaganda. [Quoted in A. Hodes, *Encounter with Martin Buber*]

JOHN BUCHAN
LORD TWEEDSMUIR

11 But for the bold experiment of Fascism the decade has not been fruitful in constructive statesmanship. [*Morning Post*, 31 Dec. 1929]

12 An atheist is a man who has no invisible means of support. [Quoted in A. Andrews, *Quotations for Speakers and Writers*, but also credited to H. E. Fosdick]

JOHN BUCHAN, 2nd LORD TWEEDSMUIR

13 You have to know a man awfully well in Canada to know his surname. [*Observer*, 'Sayings of the Week', 21 May 1950]

FRANK BUCHMAN

14 Suppose everybody cared enough, everybody shared enough? There is enough in the world for everyone's need but not for everyone's greed. [*Remaking the World*]

15 I thank heaven for a man like Adolf Hitler, who built a front line of defence against the anti-Christ of Communism. [Interview quoted in *New York World-Telegram*, 25 Aug. 1936]

ART BUCHWALD

16 Ascot is so exclusive that it is the only racecourse in the world where the horses own the people. [*I choose Caviar*, 'Ordeal at Ascot']

17 I explained to him I had simple tastes and didn't want anything ostentatious, no matter what it cost me. [*Ib.* 'A New Lease on Texas']

18 I always wanted to get into politics, but I was never light enough to make the team. ['Fan Letter to Nixon'. Quoted in H. Thompson, *Fear and Loathing on the Campaign Trail, '72*]

NIKOLAI A. BUKHANIN

19 We might have a two-party system, but one of the two parties would be in office and the other in prison. [Attr. to him

by Isaac Deutscher in *The Prophet Armed, Trotsky: 1879–1921*]

VLADIMIR BUKOVSKY

1 Society already understands that the criminal is not he who washes our dirty linen in public, but he who dirties the linen. [Said on 5 Jan. 1972. Quoted in *Radio Times*, 19 Sep. 1977]

2 The pessimist is the man who believes things couldn't possibly be worse, to which the optimist replies: 'Oh yes they could!' [Quoted in the *Guardian Weekly*, 10 Jul. 1977]

ALAN BULLOCK

3 The people Hitler never understood, and whose actions continued to exasperate him to the end of his life, were the British. [*Hitler*, Ch. 8, sect. v]

4 Hitler showed surprising loyalty to Mussolini, but it never extended to trusting him. [*Ib.* 11. iii]

IVOR BULMER-THOMAS

5 If ever he [Harold Wilson] went to school without any boots it was because he was too big for them. [Said at annual Conservative Conference, 1949]

H. K. BUNNER

6 Shake was a dramatist of note; / He lived by writing things to quote. [*Shake, Mulleary and Go-ethe*]

'BUGS BUNNY'

7 What's up Doc? [Movie cartoon catch phrase]

BASIL BUNTING

8 Name and date / split in soft slate / a few months obliterate. [*Briggflatts*, 1]

9 It looks well enough on the page, but never / well enough. [*Ib.* 2]

10 It is time to consider how Domenico Scarlatti / condensed so much music into so few bars. [*Ib.* 4]

11 Who / swinging his axe / to fell kings, guesses / where we go? [*Ib.* 'Coda']

LUIS BUÑUEL

12 I am an atheist still, thank God. [Quoted in Ado Kyrou, *Luis Buñuel: an Introduction*]

ANTHONY BURGESS

13 O my brothers ... [*The Clockwork Orange, passim*]

14 You were not put on this earth just to get in touch with God. That sort of thing could sap all the strength and the goodness out of a chelloveck. [*Ib.* Pt. 1, Ch. 1].

15 Who ever heard of a clockwork orange? ... The attempt to impose upon man, a creature of growth and capable of sweetness, to ooze juicily at the last round the bearded lips of God, to attempt to impose, I say, laws and conditions appropriate to a mechanical creation, against this I raise my sword-pen. [*Ib.* Ch. 2]

16 Not a future. At least not in Europe. America's different, of course, but America's really only a kind of Russia. You've no idea how pleasant it is not to have any future. It's like having a totally efficient contraceptive. [*Honey for the Bears*, Pt II, Ch. 6]

17 He said it was artificial respiration, but now I find I am to have his child. [*Inside Mr Enderby*, Pt I, Ch. 4, ii]

18 Five days shalt thou labour, as the Bible says. The seventh day is the Lord thy God's. The sixth day is for football and spreading the word and punishing and suchlike. [*Ib.* I. 5. ii]

19 Bath twice a day to be really clean, once a day to be passably clean, once a week to avoid being a public menace. [*Ib.* I. 2. i]

20 *Pax Romana.* Where they made a desolation they called it a peace. What absolute nonsense! It was a nasty, vulgar sort of civilization, only dignified by being hidden and under a lot of declensions. [*Ib*].

1 Would you try it for, say, six months, a
poem every week? Preferably set in the
form of prose, so as not to offend anyone. [*Ib.* I. 3. ii]

2 Rome's just a city like anywhere else.
A vastly overrated city, I'd say. It trades
on belief just as Stratford trades on
Shakespeare. [*Ib.* II. 2. i]

3 The best thing to do, when you've got
a dead body and it's your husband's on
the kitchen floor and you don't know
what to do about it, is to make yourself
a good strong cup of tea. [*One Hand
Clapping*, Ch. 26]

4 A sure sign of an amateur is too much
detail to compensate for too little life.
[Quoted in *The Times Literary Supplement*, 18 Jun. 1971]

JOHNNY BURKE

5 Don't you know each cloud contains /
Pennies from Heaven? [Song: *Pennies
from Heaven*. Music by A. Johnston]

JOHNNY BURKE
and JIMMY VAN HEUSEN

6 Or would you like to swing on a star,/
Carry moonbeams home in a jar,/
And be better off than you are,/Or
would you rather be a fish? [Song:
Swinging on a Star]

FRANCES HODGSON
BURNETT

7 Children's as good as 'rithmetic to set
you findin' out things. [*The Secret
Garden*, Ch. 9]

EDGAR RICE BURROUGHS

8 Me Tarzan, you Jane. [*Tarzan of the
Apes*]

WILLIAM BURROUGHS

9 No one owns life, but anyone who can
pick up a frying pan owns death.
[Quoted in Adrian Henri, *Adrian
Henri's Last Will and Testament*]

DR DOUGLAS BUSCH

10 Behavioural psychology is the science of
pulling habits out of rats. [Quoted in
Laurence J. Peter, *Peter's Quotations*]

MONTAGU BUTLER

11 Would you, my dear young friends, like
to be inside with the five wise virgins, or
outside, alone and in the dark with the
five foolish ones? [Sermon in Trinity
chapel. Quoted in Edward Marsh,
Ambrosia and Small Beer, Ch. 4]

R. A. BUTLER
(later LORD BUTLER)

12 QUESTION: Mr Butler, would you say
that this is the best Prime Minister we
have?
ANSWER: Yes. [In interview about Mr
Macmillan's premiership, London Airport, Dec. 1955]

13 I admire Mr X enormously, he is almost
a great man; but what I think, don't
you, has so far held him up has been
quite simply lack of intelligence?
[Quoted in Charles Ritchie, *The Siren
Years*]

14 Politics is the art of the possible. [Epi-
graph to his autobiography, *The Art of
the Possible*]

SAMUEL BUTLER

15 When you have told anyone you have
left him a legacy the only decent thing
to do is to die at once. [Quoted in
Festing Jones, *Samuel Butler: A
Memoir*, Vol. 2]

MAX BYGRAVES

16 Good idea – son! [Running catch
phrase in variety act, late 1950s and
early 1960s]

17 I've arrived – and to prove it, I'm here.
[Running catch phrase in BBC radio
comedy series, *Educating Archie*, 1950–
53]

DOUGLAS BYNG

1 I'm Millie, a messy old mermaid. [Song]

2 I'm one of the Queens of England / But I can't remember which. [Song: *I'm One of the Queens of England*]

ROBERT BYRON

3 Various incidents enlivened the days. There was the shock of discovering that *chota hasri*, which I had always believed to be a form of suicide, in fact denoted early morning tea. [*First Russia, Then Tibet*, Pt II, Ch. 2]

C

JAMES BRANCH CABELL

1 I shall marry in haste and repeat at leisure. [*Jurgen*, Ch. 16]

JOHN CAGE

2 I have nothing to say, I am saying it, and that is poetry. [Quoted by Cyril Connolly in the *Sunday Times*, 10 Sep. 1972]

HARRY CAHN

3 Love and marriage, love and marriage, / Go together like a horse and carriage. [Song: *Love and Marriage*, from the musical, *Our Town*]

JAMES CALLAGHAN

4 Either back us or sack us. [Speech to Labour Party Conference at Brighton, 5 Oct. 1977]

5 A lie can be half-way round the world before the truth has got its boots on. [Speech, 1 Nov. 1976]

6 If Labour is dead in Scotland then, from now on, I shall believe in life in the hereafter. [At a Glasgow rally, quoted in the *Guardian*, 6 Sep. 1977]

MARIA CALLAS

7 That is the difference between good teachers and great teachers: good teachers make the best of a pupil's means: great teachers foresee a pupil's ends. [Kenneth Harris, *Kenneth Harris Talking To:* 'Maria Callas']

JAMES CAMERON

8 It's like asking a patient, 'Would you like your appendix put back in?' [On the Common Market Referendum in Britain, June 1975. Quoted in the *Sunday Times*, 15 Jun. 1975]

NORMAN CAMERON

9 Forgive me, Sire, for cheating your intent, / That I, who should command a regiment, / Do amble amiably here, O God, / One of the neat ones in your awkward squad. [*Forgive me Sire*]

10 When you confess your sins before a parson, / You find it no great effort to disclose / Your crimes of murder, bigamy and arson, / But can you tell him that you pick your nose? [*Punishment Enough*]

11 These two hated each other at half sight. [*Rimbaud and Verlaine*]

HERBERT CAMPBELL

12 What I liked about that party was / We was all *so refined*. [Chorus of music-hall song. Quoted in George Robey, *Looking Back on Life*, Ch. 14]

JOSEPH CAMPBELL

13 As a white candle / In a holy place, / So is the beauty / Of an aged face. [*The Old Woman*]

14 Her brood gone from her / And her thoughts as still / As the water / Under a ruined mill. [*Ib.*]

PATRICK CAMPBELL

15 The word 'charade' is derived from the Spanish *charrada*, the chatter of clowns. Beyond that, charades have no connection with any kind of entertainment, living or dead. [*A Short Trot with a Cultured Mind*, 'The Chatter of Clowns']

16 Magda was foreign – so foreign, indeed, that it was only possible to place her low down in the Balkans. [*Ib.* 'The Crime in the Cloakroom']

MRS PATRICK CAMPBELL

1 It doesn't matter what you do in the bedroom as long as you don't do it in the street and frighten the horses. [Quoted in Daphne Fielding, *The Duchess of Jermyn Street*, Ch. 2]

2 Marriage is the result of the longing for the deep, deep bliss of the double-bed after the hurly-burly of the chaise-longue. [Quoted in A. Andrews, *Quotations of Speakers and Writers*]

ROY CAMPBELL

3 Translations (like wives) are seldom faithful if they are in the least attractive. [*Poetry Review*, Jun./Jul. 1949]

4 I hate 'Humanity' and all such abstracts: but I love *people*. Lovers of 'Humanity' generally hate *people and children*, and keep parrots or puppy dogs. [*Light on a Dark Horse*, Ch. 13]

5 Who forced the Muse to this alliance? / A Man of more degrees than parts – / The jilted Bachelor of Science / And Widower of Arts. [*On Professor Drenan's Verse*]

6 Or like a poet woo the moon, / Riding an arm-chair for my steed, / And with a flashing pen harpoon / Terrific metaphors of speed. [*The Festivals of Flight*]

7 The English Muse her annual theme rehearses / To tell us birds are singing in the sky . . . / Only the poet slams the door and curses, / And all the little sparrows wonder why! [*Georgian Spring*]

8 Where, having torn the land with shot and shell, / Our sturdy pioneers as farmers dwell, / And, 'twixt the hours of strenuous sleep, relax / To shear the fleeces or to fleece the blacks. [*The Wayzgoose, I*]

9 Feed them on Kipling, nourish them on 'Punch' – / And in their works the World will wrap its lunch! [*Ib.*]

10 . . . burn, with Athens and with Rome, / A sacred city of the mind. [*Toledo, July 1936*]

ALBERT CAMUS

11 I am well aware that an addiction to silk underwear does not necessarily imply that one's feet are dirty. None the less, style, like sheer silk, too often hides eczema. [*The Fall*]

12 A single sentence will suffice for modern man: he fornicated and read the papers. [*Ib.*]

13 How many crimes committed merely because their authors could not endure being wrong! [*Ib.*]

14 You know what charm is: a way of getting the answer yes without having asked any clear question. [*Ib.*]

15 Alas, after a certain age every man is responsible for his face. [*Ib.*]

16 I conceived at least one great love in my life, of which I was always the object. [*Ib.*]

17 It hurts me to confess it, but I'd have given ten conversations with Einstein for a first meeting with a pretty chorus-girl. [*Ib.*]

18 Men are never convinced of your reasons, of your sincerity, of the seriousness of your sufferings, except by your death. [*Ib.*]

19 Bourgeois marriage has put our country into slippers and will soon lead it to the gates of death. [*Ib.*]

20 Don't wait for the Last Judgement. It takes place every day. [*Ib.*]

21 Too many people have decided to do without generosity in order to practise charity. [*Ib.*]

22 A person I knew used to divide human beings into three categories: those who prefer having nothing to hide rather than being obliged to lie, those who prefer lying to having nothing to hide, and finally those who like both lying and the hidden. [*Ib.*]

23 I chose justice . . . in order to remain faithful to the earth. I still believe that this world has no higher meaning, but I know that there is in it something that has meaning, that is man, for he is the only being who demands to have it. [*Letters to a German Friend*, Letter 4]

61

1 The absurd is born of this confrontation between the human need and the unreasonable silence of the world. [*The Myth of Sisyphus*, 'Absurd Walls', trans. J. O'Brien]

2 The absurd has meaning only in so far as it is not agreed to. [*Ib*. 'Philosophical Suicide']

3 The absurd is sin without God. [*Ib*.]

4 The struggle itself towards the heights is enough to fill a man's heart. One must imagine Sisyphus happy. [*Ib*. Title essay]

5 The aim is to live lucidly in a world where dispersion is the rule. [*The Notebooks*]

6 The secret of my universe: just imagine God without man's immortality. [*Ib*.]

7 I am not made for politics because I am incapable of wishing for or accepting the death of my adversary. [*Ib*.]

8 He who despairs over an event is a coward, but he who holds hopes for the human condition is a fool. [*Ib*.]

9 Every fulfilment is slavery. It drives us to a higher fulfilment. [*Ib*.]

10 An intellectual is someone whose mind watches itself. [*Notebooks, 1935–42*]

11 I know of only one duty, and that is to love. [*Ib*.]

12 Mother died today. Or, maybe, yesterday: I can't be sure. [*The Outsider*, Pt I, Ch. 1, trans. Stuart Gilbert]

13 All normal people, I added, as an afterthought, had more or less desired the death of those they loved, at some time or another. [*Ib*. II.1]

14 I laid my heart open to the benign indifference of the universe. [*Ib*. II.5]

15 Since the order of the world is shaped by death, mightn't it be better for God if we refuse to believe in Him and struggle with all our might against death. without raising our eyes towards the heaven where He sits in silence? [*The Plague*, Pt II, Ch. 7, trans. Stuart Gilbert]

16 The evil that is in the world almost always comes of ignorance, and good intentions may do as much harm as malevolence, if they lack understanding. On the whole men are more good than bad; that, however, isn't the real point. But they are more or less ignorant, and it is that we call vice or virtue; the most incorrigible vice being that of an ignorance which fancies it knows everything and therefore claims for itself the right to kill. The soul of a murderer is blind; and there can be no true goodness nor true love without the utmost clear-sightedness. [*Ib*. II.8]

17 All I maintain is that ... there are pestilences and there are victims; no more than that. If, by making that statement, I, too, become a carrier of the plague-germ, at least I don't do it wilfully. I try, in short, to be an innocent murderer. [*Ib*. IV.6]

18 Following the dictates of his heart, he [the author] has deliberately taken the victims' side and tried to share with his fellow-citizens the only certitudes they had in common – love, exile and suffering. [*Ib*. V.5]

19 If one denies that there are grounds for suicide one cannot claim them for murder. One cannot be a part-time nihilist. [*The Rebel*, Introduction]

20 What is a rebel? A man who says no. [*Ib*. Ch. 1]

21 The threat of mortality that hangs over us sterilizes everything. Only the cry of anguish can bring us to life; exaltation takes the place of truth. [*Ib*. 2]

22 Every act of rebelling expresses a nostalgia for innocence and an appeal to the essence of being. [*Ib*. 3]

23 From the moment that the free-thinkers began to question the existence of God, the problem of justice became of primary importance. [*Ib*.]

24 Freedom, 'that terrible word inscribed on the chariot of the storm', is the motivating principle of all revolutions. Without it justice seems inconceivable to the rebel's mind. There comes a time, however, when justice demands the suspension of freedom. Then terror, on a grand or a small scale, makes its appearance to consummate the revolution. [*Ib*.]

1 Martyrs do not build churches; they are the mortar, or the alibi. They are followed by priests and bigots. [*Ib.*]

2 All modern revolutions have ended in a reinforcement of the power of the State. [*Ib.*]

3 The first attempt to found a Church on nothingness was paid for by complete annihilation [*Ib.*]

4 What . . . is a novel but a universe in which action is endowed with form, where final words are pronounced, where people possess one another completely and where life assumes the aspect of destiny? [*Ib.* 4]

5 In art, rebellion is consummated and perpetuated in the act of real creation, not in criticism or commentary. [*Ib.*]

6 To lose the touch of flowers and women's hands is the supreme separation. [Quoted in the *Guardian*, 30 Sep. 1974]

ELIAS CANETTI

7 If a mother could be content to be nothing but a mother; but where would you find one who would be satisfied with that part alone? [*Auto da Fé*, Pt I, Ch. 1]

8 You have but to know an object by its proper name for it to lose its dangerous magic. [*Ib.* III. 2]

9 To circumvent death, to evade it, is one of the oldest and strongest desires of rulers. [*Crowds and Power*, The Crowd in History']

10 A speaker can insult and threaten an assemblage of people in the most terrible way, and they will still love him if, by doing so, he succeeds in forming them into a crowd. [*Ib.* 'The Command']

HUGHIE CANNON

11 Won't you come home Bill Bailey, won't you come home? [Song: *Bill Bailey, Won't You Please Come Home?*]

ROBERT CAPA

12 The war correspondent has his stake – his life – in his own hands, and he can put it on this horse or that horse, or he can put it back in his pocket at the very last minute. [Quoted in *Images of War*]

MORTIMER CAPLAN

13 There is one difference between a tax collector and a taxidermist – the taxidermist leaves the hide. [*Time* magazine, 1 Feb. 1963]

JOHN CAPLES

14 They laughed when I sat down at the piano. But when I started to play! [Advertisement for U S school of music. Quoted in Nat Shapiro, *An Encyclopedia of Quotations about Music*]

AL CAPONE

15 I've been accused of every death except the casualty list of the World War. [Quoted in Kenneth Allsop, *The Bootleggers*, Ch. 11]

16 This [suburban Chicago] is virgin territory for whorehouses. [Quoted in *ib.* 16]

TRUMAN CAPOTE

17 Other Voices, Other Rooms. [Title of book]

18 [On Jack Kerouac] That's not writing, that's typing. [Quoted in A. K. Adams, *Cassell's Book of Humorous Quotations*]

19 Venice is like eating an entire box of chocolate liqueurs at one go. [*Observer*, 'Sayings of the Week', 26 Nov. 1961]

ERNESTO CARDENAL

20 *Señor quienquiera que haya sido el que ella iba a llamar | y no llamó (y tal vez no era nadie | o era Alguién cuyo número no está en el Directorio de Los Ángeles) | contesta Tú el teléfono!* – Lord, whoever it was that she was going to call up, she did not call (perhaps it was no one, perhaps it was Somebody whose name is not in the Los Angeles telephone directory) answer Thou the telephone! [*Oración por Marilyn Monroe*]

SIR NEVILLE CARDUS

1 I've never consciously written for a public or even for an editor. I write for my own enjoyment and self-enlightenment. A writer has to struggle with himself: you write to satisfy the critic who stares at you from the back of your mind. [*Conversations with Cardus*, ed. R. Daniels, Ch. 14]

2 He [Yehudi Menuhin] never *performs*; he communicates to us, through his fiddle, often in spite of his fiddle, the divinely given best of him. [*Full Score*, 'Menuhin']

3 At Trent Bridge it is always four o'clock in the afternoon and 300 for 2. [Attr. Untraced cricket article]

STOKELEY CARMICHAEL

4 Violence is as American as cherry pie. [Attr.]

J. L. CARR

5 If you want to stay free from bother and calm in mind, read nothing except food-tin labels and your rent-book. [*The Harpole Report*, Ch. 9]

6 *You* have not had thirty years' experience . . . *You* have had one year's experience 30 times. [*Ib.* 21]

7 It is because I am not an Expert. Experts invent themselves. Whereas I was born *with my mind made up.* [*How Steeple Sinderby Wanderers Won the FA Cup*]

SANTIAGO CARRILLO

8 For years, Moscow . . . was our Rome. We spoke of the Great October Socialist Revolution as if it were our Christmas. That was the period of our infancy. Today we have grown up. [Speech at East Berlin Conference of European Communist and Workers' Parties, 29 Jun. 1976]

ANTHONY CARSON

9 The civil guard are a secret hard-hatted race like ghosts with rifles who are really longing to be human. [*On to Timbuctoo*, Ch. 2]

10 Pigeons, those dull, unmysterious city unemployables, dressed in their grey, secondhand suits. [*Ib.* 12]

11 She was a blonde nearly-young American woman of such dynamism that the tideless waves struggled to get farther up the beach. [*A Rose by Any Other Name*, Ch. 10]

12 The gull colony returned from the seaside. They had sad little faces with tiny black spectacles. [*Ib.* 20]

13 The apples fell and the swallows crossed off the days. [*Ib.* 21]

14 There is never any doubt, then, that one has arrived in Spain . . . There is a faint sound of drums, a smell of crude olive-oil, and current of strong, leaking electricity. [*A Train to Tarragona*, Pt I, Ch. 2]

SIR EDWARD CARSON

15 [Cross-examining an Irish witness.]
CARSON: Are ye a teetotaller?
WITNESS: No, I'm not.
CARSON: Are ye a modtherate dhrinker?
No answer.
CARSON: Should I be roite if I called ye a heavy dhrinker?
WITNESS: That's my business.
CARSON: Have ye any *other* business? [H. Montgomery Hyde, *Carson*, Ch. 7, sect. ii]

16 My only great qualification for being put in charge of the Navy is that I am very much at sea. [Said to senior Admiralty staff on formation of Coalition, 1916. Quoted in *Ib.* 2. i]

MARCO CARSON

17 And by my grave you'd pray to have me back, / So I could see how well you looked in black. [*To Any Woman*]

RACHEL CARSON

18 For all at last return to the sea – to Oceanus, the ocean river, like the ever-flowing stream of time, the beginning and the end. [*The Sea Around Us*, final words]

'MIZ' LILLIAN CARTER
(Mother of President Jimmy Carter)

1 I love all my children, but some of them I don't like. [Quoted in *Woman*, 9 Apr. 1977]

SYDNEY CARTER

2 Dance, then, wherever you may be; / I am the Lord of the Dance, said he, / And I'll lead you all, wherever you may be, / And I'll lead you all in the Dance, said he. [Gospel song: *Lord of the Dance*. Music adapted from the traditional Shaker hymn tune, *The Gift To Be Simple*]

JOYCE CARY

3 She had a mannish manner of mind and face, able to feel hot and think cold. [*Herself Surprised*, Ch. 7]

4 To abuse a man is a lover-like thing and gives him rights. [*Ib.* 35]

5 The sky was like washed-out Jap silk and there were just a few little clouds coming out of it like down feathers out of an old cushion. [*Ib.* 36]

6 Sun in a mist. Like an orange in a fried fish shop. [*The Horse's Mouth*, Ch. 1]

7 I never pass an empty telephone box without going in to press button B. Button B has often been kind to me. [*Ib.* 2]

8 Sara could commit adultery at one end and weep for her sins at the other, and enjoy both operations at once. [*Ib.* 8]

9 He has a face like what Cardinal Newman's would have been if he had gone into the army instead of the Church, grown an Old Bill moustache, lost most of his teeth, and only shaved on Saturdays, before preaching. [*Ib.* 11]

10 Remember I'm an artist. And you know what that means in a court of law. Next worst to an actress. [*Ib.* 14]

11 Anarchists who love God always fall for Spinoza because he tells them that God doesn't love them. This is just what they need. A poke in the eye. To a real anarchist a poke in the eye is better than a bunch of flowers. It makes him see stars. [*Ib.* 16]

12 Usual modern collection. Wilson Steer, water in water-colour; Matthew Smith, victim of the crime in slaughtercolour; Utrillo, whitewashed wall in mortarcolour; Matisse, odalisque in scortacolour; Picasso, spatchcock horse in tortacolour . . . Rouault, perishing Saint in thoughtacolour; Epstein, Leah waiting for Jacob in squawtacolour. [*Ib.* 22]

13 Hell is paved with good intentions, but heaven goes in for something more dependable. Solid gold. [*Ib.*]

14 Rich people are like royalty. They can't afford to be touchy. Richesse oblige. [*Ib.*]

15 The Professor looked like a choir-boy when the paid tenor comes in wrong. Bursting out of his collar with joy. [*Ib.* 27]

16 A little more of the abstract and we'd both have gone potty. What is there to bite on in the abstract? You might as well eat triangles and go to bed with a sewing machine. [*Ib.* 31]

17 The only good government . . . is a bad one in a hell of a fright. [*Ib.* 32]

18 It was as dark as the inside of a Cabinet Minister. [*Ib.* 33]

19 Of course, I always liked big women. I suppose I was meant to be a sculptor or architect. [*Ib.* 38]

20 It is very pleasant to be written up, even by a writer. [*Ib.* 41]

21 It was a swing door. You can't bang a pub door. The pubs know a lot, almost as much as the churches. They've got a tradition. [*Ib.* 42]

22 I ain't complaining – it's a duty laid down upon us by God – but the Pax Britannia takes a bit of keeping up – with 'arf the world full of savages and 'arf the other 'arf just getting in the way. [*Mister Johnson*]

23 It is the misfortune of an old man that though he can put things out of his head he can't put them out of his feelings. [*To be a Pilgrim*, Ch. 8]

24 Julie had the power, belonging to all those who stand outside convention, of making common moral ideas seem

65

ridiculous or artificial. So a wild tree growing through a Roman imperial pavement makes it seem faded and paltry. [*Ib.* 63]

1 The will is never free – it is always attached to an object, a purpose. It is simply the engine in the car – it can't steer. [*Writers at Work: First Series*]

'CASSANDRA' (Sir William Connor)

2 What a genius the Labour Party has for cutting itself in half and letting the two parts writhe in public. [Quoted in A. Andrews, *Quotations for Speakers and Writers*]

3 To have been alive with him [Sir Winston Churchill] was to have dined at the table of history. [Quoted in *ib.*]

4 I suppose nobody has ever been struck a direct blow by a rabbit. At least, not deliberately. [Quoted in *ib.*]

SIR HUGH CASSON

5 The British love permanence more than they love beauty. [*Observer*, 'Sayings of the Week', 14 Jun. 1964]

STANLEY CASSON

6 In France there are politicians of merit who began life as professors. But in England politicians seem to have been politicians from birth, with Personal Advancement as their fairy godmother. [*Progress and Catastrophe*]

FIDEL CASTRO

7 [Of the unsuccessful assault on the Moncada Barracks] *La Historia me absolverá* – History will absolve me. [Said on 26 Jul. 1953]

CHARLES CAUSLEY

8 Who is the smiling stranger / With hair as white as gin, / What is he doing with the children / And who could have let him in? [*Innocent's Song*]

9 You must keep your fingers / To yourself / And your lollipop eye / From another man's shelf. [*Johnny Alleluia*]

10 Ears like bombs and teeth like splinters: / A blitz of a boy is Timothy Winters. [*Timothy Winters*]

11 Don't send me a parcel at Christmas time / Of socks and nutty and wine / And don't depend on a long weekend / By the Great Western railway line. [*Song of the Dying Gunner A.A.1*]

12 You must take off your clothes for the doctor / And stand as straight as a pin, / His hand of stone on your white breastbone / Where the bullets all go in. [*Recruiting Drive*]

LORD DAVID CECIL

13 It does not matter that Dickens' world is not life-like; it is alive. [*Early Victorian Novelists*]

BENNETT CERF

14 The Atomic Age is here to stay – but are we? [*Observer*, 'Sayings of the Week', 12 Feb. 1950]

HENRY CHADWICK

15 One thing about the Arian controversy which is universally agreed is that everyone behaved very badly. [Birkbeck lecture on Athanasius and the Arian controversy]

OWEN CHADWICK

16 If you are going to have religion at all, it is better to have it tough – blood and nails and vinegar. [Quoted in A. Andrews, *Quotations for Speakers and Writers*]

MARC CHAGALL

17 When I am finishing a picture I hold some God-made object up to it – a rock, a flower, the branch of a tree or my hand – as a kind of final test. If the painting stands up beside a thing man cannot make, the painting is authentic. If there's a clash between the two, it is bad art. [Quoted in Laurence J. Peter, *Peter's Quotations*]

18 One cannot be precise and still be pure. [*Observer*, 'Sayings of the Week', 3 May 1964]

NEVILLE CHAMBERLAIN

1 I wonder what you thought of the Honours List. I have never ceased to congratulate myself that I did not figure among the rabble. [Letter, 12 Jan. 1918. Quoted in K. Feiling, *Life of Neville Chamberlain*, 7]

2 What a day! Two salmon this morning, and the offer of the Exchequer this afternoon. [Letter declining office, May 1923. Quoted in *ib.* 9]

3 Though I never shout at Labour members or insult them, I cannot understand the psychology of some of our men who walked across . . . and endeavoured to reason with them . . . I think this sloppy sentimentality is quite as bad as H.'s rudeness. [Quoted in *ib.*]

4 Stanley [Baldwin] begged me to remember that I was addressing a meeting of gentlemen. I always gave him the impression, he said, when I spoke in the House of Commons, that I looked on the Labour party as dirt. [Diary, 19 Jun. 1927]

5 How horrible, fantastic, incredible it is that we should be digging trenches and trying on gas-masks here because of a quarrel in a far-away country between people of whom we know nothing! [Broadcast of 27 Sep. 1938]

6 One can see already how this war twilight is trying people's nerves. [Letter, 23 Sep. 1939. Quoted in *ib.* 33]

7 Whatever may be the reason – whether it was that Hitler thought he might get away with what he had got without fighting for it, or whether it was that after all the preparations were not sufficiently complete – however, one thing is certain: he missed the bus. [Speech to Conservative and Unionist Associations, 4 Apr. 1940]

8 The peace offensive. [Phrase attr. in Winston Churchill, *The Gathering Storm*, Ch. 24]

RAYMOND CHANDLER

9 The General spoke again, slowly, using his strength as carefully as an out-of-work showgirl uses her last good pair of stockings. [*The Big Sleep*, Ch. 2]

10 It was a blonde. A blonde to make a bishop kick a hole in a stained-glass window. [*Farewell, My Lovely*, Ch. 13]

11 The house itself was not so much. It was smaller than Buckingham Palace, rather grey for California, and probably had fewer windows than the Chrysler Building. [*Ib.* 18]

12 She gave me a smile I could feel in my hip pocket. [*Ib.*]

13 Why, the thing stands out so far you could break off a yard of it and still have enough left for a baseball bat. [*Ib.* 28]

14 Down these mean streets a man must go who is not himself mean. [*Pearls Are a Nuisance*, 'The Simple Art of Murder']

15 What Hollywood seems to want is a writer who is ready to commit suicide in every story conference. What it actually gets is the fellow who screams like a stallion in heat and then cuts his throat with a banana. [*Letters*. Quoted in *Guardian* review, 17 Jun. 1976]

16 Any man who can write a page of living prose adds something to our life, and the man who can, as I can, is surely the last to resent someone who can do it even better. An artist cannot deny art, nor would he want to. If you believe in an ideal, you don't own you, it owns you. [Quoted in F. MacShane, *The Life of Raymond Chandler*]

17 If my books had been any worse I should not have been invited to Hollywood, and if they had been any better I should not have come. [Quoted in *ib.*]

18 Would you convey my compliments to the purist who reads your proofs and tell him or her that I write in a sort of broken-down patois which is something like the way a Swiss waiter talks, and that when I split an infinitive, God damn it, I split it so it will stay split. [Letter to Edward Weeks, editor of the *Atlantic*, quoted in *ib.*]

19 What greater prestige can a man like me (not too greatly gifted but very understanding) have than to have taken a cheap, shoddy, and utterly lost kind of writing, and have made of it something that intellectuals claw each other about. [Letter to Charles Norton. Quoted in *ib.*]

1 [Of Los Angeles] A city with all the personality of a paper cup. [Quoted in Leslie Halliwell, *The Filmgoer's Book of Quotes*]

SIR CHARLES CHAPLIN

2 I am for people, I can't help it. [*Observer*, 'Sayings of the Week', 28 Sep. 1952]

3 All I need to make a comedy is a park, a policeman and a pretty girl. [*My Autobiography*, Ch. 10]

4 I remain just one thing, and one thing only – and that is a clown. It places me on a far higher plane than any politician. [*Observer*, 'Sayings of the Week', 17 Jun. 1960]

5 Life is a tragedy when seen in close-up, but a comedy in long-shot. [Quoted in obituary, *Guardian*, 28 Dec. 1977]

SID CHAPLIN

6 Education is a sieve as well as a lift. [*The Day of the Sardine*, Ch. 2]

M. P. CHARLESWORTH

7 I refuse to consider any theory based on an emendation. [Remark to G. M. Lee]

DAVE CHASEN

8 Bogart's a helluva nice guy till 11.30 p.m. After that he thinks he's Bogart. [Quoted in Leslie Halliwell, *The Filmgoer's Book of Quotes*]

JOHN CHEEVER

9 We travel by plane, oftener than not, and yet the spirit of our country seems to have remained a country of railroads. [*Bullet Park*, Pt I, Ch. 1]

APSLEY CHERRY-GARRARD

10 Polar exploration is at once the cleanest and most isolated way of having a bad time which has been devised. [*The Worst Journey in the World*, Introduction]

11 Take it all in all, I do not believe anybody on earth has a worse time than an Emperor penguin. [*Ib.*]

CHARLIE CHESTER

12 Down in the jungle / Living in a tent, / Better than a prefab – / No rent! [From BBC radio comedy series, *Stand Easy*]

G. K. CHESTERTON

13 I tell you naught for your comfort, / Yea, naught for your desire, / Save that the sky grows darker yet / And the sea rises higher. [*The Ballad of the White Horse*, 1]

14 When all philosophies shall fail, / This word alone shall fit; / That a sage feels too small for life, / And a fool too large for it. [*Ib.* 8]

15 The wine they drink in Paradise / They make in Haute Lorraine. [*A Cider Song*]

16 The road from heaven to Hereford / Where the apple wood of Hereford / Goes all the way to Wales. [*Ib.*]

17 The men that worked for England / They have their graves at home. [*Elegy in a Country Churchyard*]

18 And they that rule in England, / In stately conclave met, / Alas, alas for England / They have no graves as yet. [*Ib.*]

19 St George he was for England, / And before he killed the dragon / He drank a pint of English ale / Out of an English flagon. [*The Englishman*]

20 Merrily taking twopenny ale and cheese with a pocket knife; / But these were luxuries not for him who went for the Simple Life. [*The Good Rich Man*]

21 You will find me drinking gin / In the lowest kind of inn, / Because I am a rigid Vegetarian. [*The Logical Vegetarian*]

22 From all that terror teaches, / From lies of tongue and pen, / From all the easy speeches / That comfort cruel men, / From sale and profanation / Of honour and the sword, / Deliver us, good Lord! [*O God of Earth and Altar*]

23 You have weighed the stars in the balance, and grasped the skies in a span: / Take, if you must have answer, the word of a common man. [*The Pessimist*]

1 'What of vile dust?' the preacher said. / Methought the whole world woke. [*The Praise of Dust*]

2 But who hath seen the Grocer / Treat housemaids to his teas / Or crack a bottle of fish sauce / Or stand a man a cheese? [*The Song against Grocers*]

3 Earth will grow worse till men redeem it, / And wars more evil, ere all wars cease. [*A Song of Defeat*]

4 For the men no lords can buy or sell, / They sit not easy when all goes well. [*Ib.*]

5 The Nothing scrawled on a five-foot page. [*Ib.*]

6 But Higgins is a Heathen, / And to lecture rooms is forced, / Where his aunts, who are not married, / Demand to be divorced. [*The Song of the Strange Ascetic*]

7 I remember my mother, the day that we met, / A thing I shall never entirely forget; / And I toy with the fancy that, young as I am, / I should know her again if we met in a tram. [*Songs of Education*, 3 'For the Crèche']

8 Invoke the philologic pen / To show you that a Citizen / Means Something in the City. [*Ib.* 4 'Citizenship']

9 And the Cock I used to know, / Where all good fellows were my friends / A little while ago. [*When I came back to Fleet Street*]

10 The villas and the chapels where / I learned with little labour / The way to love my fellow-man / And hate my next-door neighbour. [*The World State*]

11 No psychoanalyst has knocked / The bottom out of Bottom's dream. [*The Apology of Bottom the Weaver*]

12 The man who does not look at his change is no true poet. [*The Apostle and the Wild Ducks*, ed. Dorothy E. Collins]

13 'My country, right or wrong', is a thing no patriot would think of saying except in a desperate case. It is like saying, 'My mother, drunk or sober'. [*The Defendant*]

14 To be clever enough to get all that money, one must be stupid enough to want it. [*The Innocence of Father Brown*, 'The Paradise of Thieves']

15 Where does a wise man kick a pebble? On the beach. Where does a wise man hide a leaf? In the forest. [*Ib.* 'The Broken Sword']

16 Every work of art has one indispensable mark . . . the centre of it is simple, however much the fulfilment may be complicated. [*Ib.* 'The Queer Feet']

17 Journalism largely consists in saying 'Lord Jones Dead' to people who never knew Lord Jones was alive. [*The Wisdom of Father Brown*, 'The Purple Wig']

18 An artist will betray himself by some sort of sincerity. [*The Incredulity of Father Brown*, 'The Dagger with Wings']

19 If you convey to a woman that something ought to be done, there is always a dreadful danger that she will suddenly do it. [*The Secret of Father Brown*, 'The Song of the Flying Fish']

20 When we apply it, you call it anarchy; and when you apply it, I call it exploitation. [*The Scandal of Father Brown*, 'The Crime of the Communist']

21 It isn't that they can't see the solution. It is that they can't see the problem. [*Ib.* 'The Point of a Pin']

22 There is a great man who makes every man feel small. But the real great man is the man who makes every man feel great. [*Charles Dickens*]

23 Circumstances break men's bones; it has never been shown that they break men's optimism. [*Ib.*]

24 America has a new delicacy, a coarse, rank refinement. [*Ib.*]

25 A man looking at a hippopotamus may sometimes be tempted to regard a hippopotamus as an enormous mistake; but he is also bound to confess that a fortunate inferiority prevents him personally from making such mistakes. [*Ib.*]

26 A sober man may become a drunkard through being a coward. A brave man may become a coward through being a drunkard. [*Ib.*]

69

1 When some English moralists write about the importance of having character, they appear to mean only the importance of having a dull character. [*Ib.*]

2 Either criticism is no good at all (a very defensible position) or else criticism means saying about an author the very things that would have made him jump out of his boots. [*Ib.*]

3 I am afraid of the Patchwork Peril, which is all colours and none; I am afraid of bits of Bolshevism and bits of insane individualism and bits of independence in the wrong place, floating hither and thither and colliding with they know not what. [*All I Survey*, 'On Dependence and Independence']

4 It is arguable that we ought to put the State in order before there can really be such a thing as a State school. [*Ib.* 'On Education']

5 Unfortunately humanitarianism has been the mark of an inhuman time. [*Ib.* 'On Industrialism']

6 A great deal of contemporary criticism reads to me like a man saying: 'Of course I do not like green cheese: I am very fond of brown sherry.' [*Ib.* 'On Jonathan Swift']

7 The modern world seems to have no notion of preserving different things side by side, of allowing its proper and proportionate place to each, of saving the whole varied heritage of culture. It has no notion except that of simplifying something by destroying nearly everything. [*Ib.* 'On Love']

8 He set out seriously to describe the indescribable. That is the whole business of literature, and it is a hard row to hoe. [*Ib.* 'On Literary Cliques']

9 No animal ever invented anything so bad as drunkenness – or so good as drink. [*All Things Considered*, 'Wine When it is Red']

10 The rich are the scum of the earth in every country. [*The Flying Inn*]

11 Every politician is emphatically a promising politician. [*The Red Moon of Meru*]

12 The word 'orthodoxy' not only no longer means being right; it practically means being wrong. [*Heretics*, Ch. 1]

13 A man's opinion on tramcars matters; his opinion on Botticelli matters; his opinion on all things does not matter. [*Ib.*]

14 As enunciated today, 'progress' is simply a comparative of which we have not settled the superlative. [*Ib.* 2]

15 There is no such thing on earth as an uninteresting subject; the only thing that can exist is an uninterested person. [*Ib.* 3]

16 We ought to see far enough into a hypocrite to see even his sincerity. [*Ib.* 5]

17 Happiness is a mystery like religion, and should never be rationalized. [*Ib.* 7]

18 Every man speaks of public opinion, and means by public opinion, public opinion minus his opinion. [*Ib.* 8]

19 The obvious truth is that the moment any matter has passed through the human mind it is finally and for ever spoilt for all purposes of science. It has become a thing incurably mysterious and infinite; this mortal has put on mortality. [*Ib.* 11]

20 Charity is the power of defending that which we know to be indefensible. Hope is the power of being cheerful in circumstances which we know to be desperate. [*Ib.* 12]

21 Carlyle said that men were mostly fools. Christianity, with a surer and more reverend realism, says that they are all fools. [*Ib.*]

22 Science in the modern world has many uses; its chief use, however, is to provide long words to cover the errors of the rich. The word 'kleptomania' is a vulgar example of what I mean. [*Ib.* 13]

23 Honour is a luxury for aristocrats, but it is a necessity for hall-porters. [*Ib.*]

24 It is quite proper that a British diplomatist should seek the society of Japanese generals if what he wants is Japanese generals. But if what he wants is people different from himself, he had much better stop at home and discuss religion with the housemaid. [*Ib.* 14]

1 To be born into this earth is to be born into uncongenial surroundings, hence to be born into a romance. [*Ib.*]

2 A good novel tells us the truth about its hero; but a bad novel tells us the truth about its author. [*Ib.* 15]

3 The oligarchic character of the modern English commonwealth does not rest, like many oligarchies, on the cruelty of the rich to the poor. It does not even rest on the kindness of the rich to the poor. It rests on the perennial and unfailing kindness of the poor to the rich. [*Ib.*]

4 A third-class carriage is a community, while a first-class carriage is a place of wild hermits. [*Ib.*]

5 The artistic temperament is a disease that afflicts amateurs. [*Ib.* 17]

6 The old are always fond of new things. Young men read chronicles, but old men read newspapers. [*Ib.* 18]

7 When we want any art tolerably brisk and bold we have to go to the doctrinaires. [*Ib.* 20]

8 Bigotry may be roughly defined as the anger of men who have no opinions. [*Ib.*]

9 The modern world is filled with men who hold dogmas so strongly that they do not even know that they are dogmas. [*Ib*]

10 He was solidly dazed by Westminster Abbey, which is not unnatural since that church became the lumber-room of the larger and less successful statuary of the eighteenth century. [*The Man Who Knew Too Much*, 'The Soul of the Schoolboy']

11 Squire Vane was an elderly schoolboy of English education and Irish extraction. His English education, at one of the great public schools, had preserved his intellect perfectly and permanently at the stage of boyhood. But his Irish extraction subconsciously upset in him the proper solemnity of an old boy, and sometimes gave him back the brighter outlook of a naughty boy. [*Ib.* 'The Trees of Pride']

12 He was himself a robust rationalist, but he went to church to set his tenants an example. Of what, it would have puzzled him to say. [*Ib.*]

13 The human race, to which so many of my readers belong, has been playing at children's games from the beginning, and will probably do it till the end, which is a nuisance for the few people who grow up. [*The Napoleon of Notting Hill*]

14 And Mr Mick not only became a vegetarian, but at length declared vegetarianism doomed ('shedding,' as he called it finely, 'the green blood of the silent animals') and predicted that men in a better age would live on nothing but salt. [*Ib.*]

15 When the chord of monotony is stretched most tight, then it breaks with a sound like a song. [*Ib.*]

16 I never in my life said anything merely because I thought it funny; though, of course, I have an ordinary human vainglory, and may have thought it funny because I had said it. [*Orthodoxy*, Ch. 1]

17 The men who really believe in themselves are all in lunatic asylums. [*Ib.* 2]

18 Poets do not go mad; but chess-players do. [*Ib.*]

19 The madman is not the man who has lost his reason. The madman is the man who has lost everything except his reason. [*Ib.*]

20 The cosmos is about the smallest hole that a man can hide his head in. [*Ib.*]

21 Reason is itself a matter of faith. It is an act of faith to assert that our thoughts have any relation to reality at all. [*Ib.* 3]

22 Thinking means connecting things, and stops if they cannot be connected. [*Ib.*]

23 Mr Shaw is (I suspect) the only man on earth who has never written any poetry. [*Ib.*]

24 Every man who will not have softening of the heart must at last have softening of the brain. [*Ib.*]

25 I came to the conclusion that the optimist thought everything good except the pessimist, and that the pessimist thought everything bad, except himself. [*Ib.* 5]

1 A man's friend likes him but leaves him as he is: his wife loves him and is always trying to turn him into somebody else. [*Ib.*]

2 Courage is almost a contradiction in terms. It means a strong desire to live taking the form of a readiness to die. [*Ib.* 6]

3 All conservatism is based upon the idea that if you leave things alone you leave them as they are. But you do not. If you leave a thing alone you leave it to a torrent of change. [*Ib.* 7]

4 Angels can fly because they take themselves lightly. [*Ib.*]

5 The *rules* of a club are occasionally in favour of the poor member. The drift of a club is always in favour of the rich one. [*Ib.* 9]

6 The primary paradox of Christianity is that the ordinary condition of man is not his sane or sensible condition; that the normal itself is an abnormality. [*Ib.* 11]

7 Lying in bed would be an altogether perfect and supreme experience if only one had a coloured pencil long enough to draw on the ceiling. [*Tremendous Trifles*]

8 A debt to Virgil is like a debt to Nature. [*Victorian Literature*]

9 The English statesman is bribed not to be bribed. He is born with a silver spoon in his mouth, so that he may never afterwards be found with the silver spoons in his pocket. [*What's Wrong with the World*]

10 The machinery of science must be individualistic and isolated. A mob can shout round a palace; but a mob cannot shout down a telephone. The specialist appears, and democracy is half spoilt at a stroke. [*Ib.*]

11 Compromise used to mean that half a loaf was better than no bread. Among modern statesmen it really seems to mean that half a loaf is better than a whole loaf. [*Ib.*]

12 The meanest man is immortal and the mightiest movement is temporal, not to say temporary. [*Blackfriars*, Jan. 1923]

13 Blasphemy itself could not survive religion; if anyone doubts that, let him try to blaspheme Odin. [*Daily News*, 24 Jun. 1904]

14 When you break the big laws, you do not get liberty; you do not even get anarchy. You get the small laws. [*Ib.* 29 Jul. 1905]

15 A dying monarchy is always one that has too much power, not too little; a dying religion always interferes more than it ought, not less. [*Ib.* 11 Mar. 1911]

16 Mankind is not a tribe of animals to which we owe compassion. Mankind is a club to which we owe our subscription. [*Ib.* 10 Apr. 1906]

17 Democracy means government by the uneducated, while aristocracy means government by the badly educated. [*New York Times*, 1 Feb. 1931]

18 A puritan's a person who pours righteous indignation into the wrong things. [Attr.]

19 New roads: new ruts. [Attr.]

20 [The Victorians] were lame giants; the strongest of them walked on one leg a little shorter than the other. [Quoted in W. H. Auden and L. Kronenberger, *The Faber Book of Aphorisms*]

21 Tradition may be defined as an extension of the franchise. Tradition means giving votes to the most obscure of all classes, our ancestors. It is the democracy of the dead. [Quoted by D. J. Boorstin in the *Listener*, 11 Dec. 1975]

22 Education is simply the soul of a society as it passes from one generation to another. [*Observer*, 'Sayings of the Week', 6 Jul. 1924]

23 The wildest hope of a healthy person is to get back to his first Christmas party, and be shy enough to be happy. [*Observer*, 'Sayings of the Week', 10 Feb. 1929]

24 Hitlerism is almost entirely of Jewish origin. [*Observer*, 'Sayings of the Week' 23 Jul. 1933]

25 It seems a pity that psychology should have destroyed all our knowledge of human nature. [*Observer*, 'Sayings of the Week', 9 Dec. 1934]

1 It's not the world that's got so much worse but the news coverage that's got so much better. [Attr.]

NOAM CHOMSKY

2 Colourless green ideas sleep furiously. [Sentence to illustrate grammatical structure as independent of meaning. Quoted by C. Blakemore in the BBC Reith Lectures for 1976. Lecture reprinted in the *Listener*, 9 Dec. 1976]

AGATHA CHRISTIE

3 The happy people are failures because they are on such good terms with themselves that they don't give a damn. [*Sparkling Cyanide*]

4 An archaeologist is the best husband any woman can have: the older she gets, the more interested he is in her. [News report, 9 Mar. 1954]

RANDOLPH CHURCHILL

5 I expect you know my friend Evelyn Waugh, who, like you, your Holiness, is a Roman Catholic. [Said in an audience with the Pope]

WINSTON S. CHURCHILL

6 The wars of the peoples will be more terrible than those of kings. [Speech in House of Commons on Army Estimates, 1901. Quoted in *Maxims and Reflections*, sect. v]

7 Men will forgive a man anything except bad prose. [Election speech at Manchester, 1906. Quoted in R. Speaight, *Hilaire Belloc*, Ch. 10, sect. ii]

8 *The Times* is speechless [over Irish Home Rule] and takes three columns to express its speechlessness. [Speech at Dundee, 14 May 1908]

9 He [Lord Charles Beresford] is one of those orators of whom it was well said, 'Before they get up they do not know what they are going to say; when they are speaking, they do not know what they are saying; and when they sit down they do not know what they have said.' [Speech in House of Commons, 20 Dec. 1912]

10 The grass grows green on the battlefield, but never on the scaffold. [Attr. remark on Irish Rebellion, 1916]

11 Labour is not fit to govern. [Speech at 1920 election]

12 Frightfulness is not a remedy known to the British pharmacopoeia. [Speech in House of Commons, 8 Jul. 1920]

13 They [the British] are the only people who like to be told how bad things are – who like to be told the worst. [Speech in 1921, quoted in *Observer*, 'Churchilliana']

14 You cannot ask us to take sides against arithmetic. You cannot ask us to take sides against the obvious facts of the situation. [Speech in House of Commons, 31 Aug. 1926]

15 A hopeful disposition is not the sole qualification to be a prophet. [Speech in House of Commons, 30 Apr. 1927]

16 I have waited fifty years to see the Boneless Wonder [Ramsay MacDonald] sitting on the Treasury Bench. [*Ib*. 28 Jan. 1931]

17 We know that he [Ramsay MacDonald] has, more than any other man, the gift of compressing the largest amount of words into the smallest amount of thought. [*Ib*. 23 Mar. 1933]

18 India is a geographical term. It is no more a united nation than the Equator. [Speech in Royal Albert Hall, 18 Mar. 1931]

19 So they [the Government] go on in strange paradox, decided only to be undecided, resolved to be irresolute, adamant for drift, solid for fluidity, all-powerful for impotence. [*Ib*. 12 Nov. 1936]

20 We have sustained a defeat without a war. [Describing Munich. Speech in House of Commons, 5 Oct. 1938]

21 I cannot forecast to you the action of Russia. It is a riddle wrapped in a mystery inside an enigma; but perhaps there is a key. That key is Russian national interest. [Speech in London, 1 Oct. 1939]

22 You ask: 'What is our aim?' I can answer in one word: 'Victory!' Victory at

all costs, victory in spite of all terror, victory however long and hard the road may be: for without victory there is no survival. [First speech as Prime Minister in House of Commons, 13 May 1940]

1 Learn to get used to it [bombing]. Eels get used to skinning. [Notes for speech, 20 Jun. 1940]

2 You [Hitler] do your worst, and we will do our best. [Speech at Civil Defence Services' Luncheon, 14 Jul. 1941]

3 In my country, as in yours, public men are proud to be servants of the state and would be ashamed to be its masters. [Speech to U S Congress, 26 Dec. 1941]

4 I have not become the King's First Minister in order to preside over the liquidation of the British Empire. [Speech at Mansion House, 10 Nov. 1942]

5 The Almighty in His infinite wisdom did not see fit to create Frenchmen in the image of Englishmen. [Speech in House of Commons, 10 Dec. 1942]

6 The empires of the future are the empires of the mind. [Speech at Harvard University, 16 Sep. 1943]

7 A splendid moment in our great history and in our small lives. [On the unconditional surrender of Germany, 1945]

8 There are few virtues which the Poles do not possess and there are few errors they have ever avoided. [Speech in House of Commons after Potsdam Conference, 1945]

9 We must build a kind of United States of Europe. [Speech in Zürich, 19 Sep. 1946]

10 No one pretends that democracy is perfect or all-wise. Indeed, it has been said that democracy is the worst form of government except all those other forms that have been tried from time to time. [Speech in House of Commons, 11 Nov. 1947]

11 The English never draw a line without blurring it. [*Ib.* 16 Nov. 1948]

12 The whole prospect and outlook of mankind grew immeasurably larger, and the multiplication of ideas also proceeded at an incredible rate. This vast expansion was unhappily not accompanied by any noticeable advance in the stature of man either in his mental faculties or his moral character. His brain got no better; but it buzzed more. [Address in Massachusetts, 31 Mar. 1949]

13 The reason for having diplomatic relations is not to confer a compliment, but to secure a convenience. [Speech in House of Commons, 17 Nov. 1949]

14 Perhaps it is better to be irresponsible and right than to be responsible and wrong. [Party Political Broadcast, London, 26 Aug. 1950]

15 Mr Attlee combines a limited outlook with strong qualities of resistance. [Speech in Royal Albert Hall, 27 Apr. 1951]

16 Personally I like short words and vulgar fractions. [Speech in Margate, 10 Oct. 1953]

17 We should have the art [of making bombs] rather than the article [the bombs themselves]. [Said to Lord Cherwell, Nov. 1951]

18 This bright, nimble, fierce, and comprehending being – Jack Frost dancing bespangled in the sunshine. [On Bernard Shaw. *Great Contemporaries*]

19 I wrote my name at the top of the page, I wrote down the number of the question '1'. After much reflection, I put a bracket round it thus '(1)'. But thereafter I could not think of anything connected with it that was either relevant or true . . . It was from these slender indications of scholarship that Mr Weldon drew the conclusion that I was worthy to pass into Harrow. It is very much to his credit. [*My Early Life*, Ch. 2]

20 Thus I got into my bones the essential structure of the ordinary British sentence – which is a noble thing. [*Ib.*]

21 So they told me how Mr Gladstone read Homer for fun, which I thought served him right. [*Ib.*]

22 Headmasters have powers at their disposal with which Prime Ministers have never yet been invested. [*Ib.*]

1 Which brings me to my conclusion upon Free Will and Predestination, namely let the reader mark it – that they are identical. [*Ib.* 3]

2 Certainly the prolonged education indispensable to the progress of society is not natural to mankind. [*Ib.*]

3 And here I say to parents, especially wealthy parents, 'Don't give your son money. As far as you can afford it, give him horses.' [*Ib.* 4]

4 I had no idea in those days of the enormous and unquestionably helpful part that humbug plays in the social life of great peoples dwelling in a state of democratic freedom. [*Ib.*]

5 I was never tired of listening to his wisdom or imparting my own. [*Ib.* 7]

6 It is a good thing for an uneducated man to read books of quotations. [Of himself. *Ib.* 9]

7 One voyage to India is enough; the others are merely repletion. [*Ib.* 10]

8 Just as the sentence contains one idea in all its fullness, so the paragraph should embrace a distinct episode; and as sentences should follow one another in harmonious sequence, so paragraphs must fit onto one another like the automatic couplings of railway carriages. [*Ib.* 16]

9 Everyone threw the blame on me I have noticed that they nearly always do. I suppose it is because they think I shall be able to bear it best. [*Ib.* 17]

10 Buller was a characteristic British personality. He looked stolid. He said little, and what he said was obscure. [*Ib.* 18]

11 I have always been against the Pacifists during the quarrel, and against the Jingoes at its close. [*Ib.* 26]

12 Those who can win a war well can rarely make a good peace and those who could make a good peace would never have won the war. [*Ib.*]

13 In those days we had a real political democracy led by a hierarchy of statesmen and not a fluid mass distracted by newspapers. [*Ib.* 28]

14 One day President Roosevelt told me that he was asking publicly for suggestions about what the war should be called. I said at once 'the Unnecessary War'. [*The Second World War*, Vol. I: *The Gathering Storm*, Preface]

15 The redress of the grievances of the vanquished should precede the disarmament of the victors. [*Ib.* Ch. 3]

16 No country is so vulnerable, and no country would better repay pillage than our own ... With our enormous metropolis here, the greatest target in the world, a kind of tremendous, fat, valuable cow tied up to attract the beast of prey, we are in a position in which we have never been before. [Speech in House of Commons, 1934. Quoted in *Ib.* 7]

17 Neither of them [Baldwin and Neville Chamberlain] had any wish to work with me except in the last resort. [*Ib.* 12]

18 I have never seen a human being who more perfectly represented the modern conception of a robot. [Comment on Molotov. *Ib.* 20]

19 'Winston is back' [Signal of Board of Admiralty to the Fleet on his return to the Admiralty, 1939. *Ib.* 22]

20 I felt as if I were walking with destiny, and that all my past life had been but a preparation for this hour and this trial ... My warnings over the last six years had been so numerous, so detailed, and were now so terribly vindicated, that no one could gainsay me ... I was sure I should not fail. Therefore, although impatient for the morning, I slept soundly and had no need for cheering dreams. Facts are better than dreams. [*Ib.* 38, closing words]

21 The road across these five years was long, hard and perilous. Those who perished upon it did not give their lives in vain. Those who marched forward to the end will always be proud to have trodden it with honour. [*Ib.* Vol. II: *Their Finest Hour*, Ch. 1]

22 The Mosquito Armada as a whole was unsinkable. In the midst of our defeat glory came to the Island people, united and unconquerable; and the tale of the Dunkirk beaches will shine in whatever records are preserved of our affairs. [*Ib.* 5]

1 We must be very careful not to assign to this deliverance [Dunkirk] the attributes of a victory. Wars are not won by evacuations. [*Ib.*]

2 I longed for more Regular troops with which to rebuild and expand the Army. Wars are not won by heroic militias. [*Ib.* 8]

3 Any chortling by officials who have been slothful in pushing this bomb, over the fact that at present it has not succeeded, will be viewed with great disfavour by me. [Said to General Ismay. *Ib.*]

4 I have often wondered what would have happened if two hundred thousand German storm troops had actually established themselves ashore. The massacre would have been on both sides grim and great . . . I intended to use the slogan 'You can always take one with you.' [*Ib.* 13]

5 High in the air soared the fighter pilots, or waited serene at a moment's notice around their excellent machines. This was a time when it was equally good to live or die. [*Ib.*]

6 There was some talk in Parliament after the danger had passed away of the 'invasion scare'. Certainly those who knew most were the least scared. [*Ib.* 14]

7 I doubt whether any of the Dictators had as much effective power throughout his whole nation as the British War Cabinet. When we expressed our desires we were sustained by the people's representatives and cheerfully obeyed by all. [*Ib.* 17]

8 When I look back on all these worries I remember the story of the old man who said on his deathbed that he had had a lot of trouble in his life, most of which had never happened. [*Ib.* 23]

9 The Battle of Britain was won. The Battle of the Atlantic had now to be fought. [*Ib.* 31]

10 It is dangerous to meddle with Admirals when they say they can't do things. They have always got the weather or fuel or something to argue about. [*Ib.* 35]

11 In my experience . . . officers with high athletic qualifications are not usually successful in the higher ranks. [*Ib.* Appendix C, 4 Feb. 1941]

12 So far as strategy, policy, foresight, competence are arbiters Stalin and his commissars showed themselves at this moment [Hitler's invasion of Russia] the most completely outwitted bunglers of the Second World War. [*Ib.* Vol. III: *The Grand Alliance*, Ch. 20]

13 I have only one purpose, the destruction of Hitler, and my life is much simplified thereby. If Hitler invaded Hell I would make at least a favourable reference to the Devil in the House of Commons. [*Ib.*]

14 Before Alamein we never had a victory. After Alamein we never had a defeat. [*Ib.* Vol. IV: *The Hinge of Fate*, Ch. 33]

15 Tell them from me they are unloading history. [Telegram to the Port Commandant at Tripoli. *Ib.* 40]

16 Well, the principle seems the same. The water still keeps falling over. [When asked whether the Niagara Falls looked the same as when he first saw them. *Ib.* Vol. V: *Closing the Ring*, Ch. 5]

17 I said that the world must be made safe for at least fifty years. If it was only for fifteen to twenty years then we should have betrayed our soldiers. [*Ib.* 20]

18 I then demonstrated with the help of three matches my idea of Poland moving westwards. [*Ib.*]

19 We must have a better word than 'prefabricated'. Why not 'ready-made'? [*Ib.* Appendix C, 2 Apr. 1944]

20 'What is your party?' I asked one group. 'We are the Christian Communists,' their chief replied. I could not help saying, 'It must be very inspiring to your party, having the Catacombs so handy.' [*Ib.* Vol. VI: *Triumph and Tragedy*, Ch. 7]

21 As I was the host at luncheon I . . . said to the interpreter that if it was the religion of His Majesty [Ibn Saud] to deprive himself of smoking and alcohol I must point out that my rule of life prescribed as an absolutely sacred rite smoking cigars and also the drinking of alcohol before, after, and if need be during all meals and in the intervals between them. [*Ib.* 23]

1 Peace with Germany and Japan on our terms will not bring much rest . . . As I observed last time, when the war of the giants is over the wars of the pygmies will begin. [*Ib.* 25]

2 In Franklin Roosevelt there died the greatest American friend we have ever known and the greatest champion of freedom who has ever brought help and comfort from the New World to the Old. [*Ib.* 28]

3 He [Lenin] alone could have led Russia into the enchanted quagmire, he alone could have found the way back to the causeway. He saw; he turned; he perished . . . The Russian people were left floundering in the bog. Their worst misfortune was his birth, their next worst – his death. [*The World Crisis*, Ch. 4, 'Aftermath']

4 You must not underrate England. She is a curious country, and few foreigners can understand her mind . . . She is very clever. If you plunge us into another Great War she will bring the whole world against you, like last time. [To Herr von Ribbentrop, 1936]

5 He is a sheep in wolf's clothing. [Of Clement Attlee. Quoted in A. Andrews, *Quotations for Speakers and Writers*]

6 He's a modest little man with much to be modest about. [Remark on Clement Attlee's becoming Prime Minister. Attr. in Michael Foot, *Aneurin Bevan*]

7 There, but for the grace of God, goes God. [Of Sir Stafford Cripps. Quoted in L. Kronenberger, *The Cutting Edge*, but see also H. J. Mankiewicz on Orson Welles, 221:2]

8 In defeat unbeatable; in victory unbearable. [On Viscount Montgomery. Quoted in Edward Marsh, *Ambrosia and Small Beer*, Ch. 5, sect. ii]

9 The difference between him [Mr Asquith] and Arthur [Balfour] is that Arthur is wicked and moral, Asquith is good and immoral. [Quoted in E. T. Raymond, *Mr Balfour*, Ch. 13]

10 You and I must take care not to lose the next war. [To Lord Ismay, apropos the Nuremberg trials. Quoted by A. J. P. Taylor in BBC TV programme, *The Warlords*, 6 Sep. 1976]

11 I decline to be impartial as between the fire brigade and the fire. [*Observer*, 'Sayings of the Week', 11 Jul. 1926]

12 Jellicoe was the only man on either side who could lose the war in an afternoon. [*Observer*, 'Sayings of the Week', 13 Feb. 1927]

13 Already in 1900 I could boast I had written as many books as Moses. [*Observer*, 'Sayings of the Week', 9 Jul. 1950]

14 Everybody has a right to pronounce foreign names as he chooses. [*Observer*, 'Sayings of the Week', 5 Aug. 1951]

15 It is always wise to look ahead, but difficult to look farther than you can see. [*Observer*, 'Sayings of the Week', 27 Jul. 1952]

16 Personally I'm always ready to learn, although I do not always like being taught. [*Observer*, 'Sayings of the Week', 9 Nov. 1952]

17 Feed a grub on royal jelly and it may become a queen. [On Clement Attlee. Attr.]

18 It is a fine thing to be honest but it is also very important to be right. [Of Mr Baldwin. Attr.]

19 They consist entirely of clichés – clichés old and new – everything from 'God is Love' to 'Please adjust your dress before leaving'. [Of Anthony Eden's speeches. Attr. See also Ernest Bevin, 42:4]

20 It was a case of dislike before first sight. [Describing Kitchener's reaction to him. Attr.]

21 EDWARD MARSH: I'm in favour of kissing him [Roosevelt] on both cheeks. WSC: Yes, but not on all four. [Attr.]

22 Moral of the Work. In war: resolution. In defeat: defiance. In victory: magnanimity. In peace: goodwill. [Attr.]

23 I am myself an English-speaking union. [Attr.]

24 The nation had the lion's heart. I had the luck to give the roar. [Attr. remark on his 80th birthday]

JOHN CIARDI

1 One look at the rush-hour jam in the subway and you know why no one rides it any more. ['Manner of Speaking', *Saturday Review*, 8 Aug. 1964]

KENNETH CLARK (Lord Clark)

2 I cannot distinguish between thought and feeling, and I am convinced that a combination of words and music, colour and movement can extend human experience in a way that words alone cannot do. [*Civilisation*, Foreword]

3 Medieval marriages were entirely a matter of property, and, as everyone knows, marriage without love means love without marriage. [*Ib*. Ch. 3]

4 It's a curious fact that the all-male religions have produced no religious imagery – in most cases have positively forbidden it. The great religious art of the world is deeply involved with the female principle. [*Ib*. 7]

5 I wonder if a single thought that has helped forward the human spirit has ever been conceived or written down in an enormous room: except, perhaps, in the reading room of the British Museum. [*Ib*.]

6 Opera, next to Gothic architecture, is one of the strangest inventions of Western man. It could not have been foreseen by any logical process. [*Ib*. 9]

7 This gives French Classical architecture a certain inhumanity. It was the work not of craftsmen, but of wonderfully gifted civil servants. [*Ib*.]

8 Rococo even spread to England, although the native good sense of a fox-hunting society prevented its more extravagant flights. [*Ib*.]

9 Television is a form of soliloquy. [Quoted in the *Guardian*, 26 Nov. 1977]

MANNING CLARK

10 All those who have something to say are deeply divided, and therefore tormented men or women – that is, they are both innocent children and devils. [*A Discovery of Australia*, 'Being an Historian']

ARTHUR C. CLARKE

11 Overhead without any fuss the stars were going out. [Last words of *The Nine Billion Names of God*]

12 It is three thousand light years from the Vatican. [First line of *The Star*]

13 Open the pod door, Hal. [Film: *2001: A Space Odyssey*. Script by Stanley Kubrick and Arthur C. Clarke]

GRANT CLARKE
and EDGAR LESLIE

14 And then he'd have to get under, / Get out and get under, / And fix up his automobile. [Song: *He'd Have to Get Under*]

PAUL CLAUDEL

15 The poem is not made from these letters that I drive in like nails, but of the white which remains on the paper. [Footnote to *Cinq grandes Odes*, I, 'Les Muses']

16 *Délivrez-moi de moi-même! délivrez l'être de la condition! / Je suis libre, délivrez-moi de la liberté!* – Deliver me from myself! Deliver my being from its condition! I am free, deliver me from liberty! [*Ib*. II, '*L'Esprit et l'Eau*']

17 *Quelqu'un qui soit en moi, plus moi-même que moi.* – Someone who may be in me, more myself than I. [*Vers d'Exil*]

18 *Nous ne naissons pas seuls. Naître, pour tout, c'est connaître. Toute naissance est une connaissance.* – We are not alone. To be born for each man is a getting to know. Every birth is a getting to know. [*Traité de la connaissance du monde*]

GEORGES CLEMENCEAU

19 America is the only nation in history which miraculously has gone directly from barbarism to degeneration without the usual interval of civilization. [Quoted in Laurence J. Peter, *Peter's Quotations*]

20 One is always somebody's reactionary. [Quoted in Ernst Gombrich, the *Listener*, 15 Feb. 1979]

1 War is too important to be left to the generals. [Quoted in Laurence J. Peter, *Peter's Quotations*]

J. STORER CLOUSTON

2 'Are you afraid of having your pockets picked?' 'Alas!' replied Mr Beveridge, 'it would take two men to do that.' 'Huh!' snorted the Emperor, 'you are so damned strong are you?' 'I mean,' answered his *vis-à-vis* with his polite smile, 'that it would take one man to put something in and another to take it out.' [*The Lunatic at Large*, Pt I, Ch. 2]

3 'Then it was false?' 'As an address it was perfectly genuine, only it didn't happen to be mine.' [*Ib*. III. 5]

4 'So many virtues in one room reminds me of the virgins of Gomorrah.' 'I beg your pardon? The what?' asked Mr Duggs with a startled stare. Mr Bunker suspected that he had made a slip in his biblical reminiscences. [*Ib*. IV. 2]

HAROLD CLURMAN

5 He [Thornton Wilder] arranges flowers beautifully, but he does not grow them. [*Lies Like Truth*]

IRVIN COBB

6 The mosaic swimming-pool age – just before the era when they had to have a shin-bone of St Sebastian for a clutch-lever. [Quoted in F. Scott Fitzgerald, *Pat Hobby Himself*]

7 I've just learnt about his illness; let's hope it's nothing trivial. [Quoted in E. Esar and N. Bentley, *Treasury of Humorous Quotations*. Elsewhere attr. to Winston Churchill on Aneurin Bevan]

8 Why should a worm turn? It's probably just the same on the other side. [Quoted in *Ib*.]

CHARLES COBORN

9 'E's all right when you know 'im, / But you've got to know 'im fust. [Song: *'E's all right*]

CLAUD COCKBURN

10 He [Maynard Keynes] was the first Englishman since Horace Walpole to tell The Long Run to go jump into a lake. 'In the long run,' said Maynard Keynes, '. . . we are all dead.' [*Aspects of English History*, 'The Bubble']

11 Lord Rosebery, sometimes called 'Nature's Welfare State'. This is in reference to the fact that by marrying a Rothschild, being Prime Minister and winning the Derby, he demonstrated that it was possible to improve one's financial status and run the Empire without neglecting the study of form. [*Ib*. 'A Good Time Had']

JEAN COCTEAU

12 The essential tact in daring is to know to what extent one can go too far. [*Le Coq et l'Arlequin*]

13 Their [children's] rites are obscure, inexorably secret; calling, we know, for infinite cunning, for ordeal by fear and torture; requiring victims, summary executions, human sacrifices. The particular mysteries are impenetrable, the faithful speak a cryptic tongue; even if we were to chance to overhear unseen, we would be none the wiser. Their trade is all in postage stamps and marbles. [*Les Enfants terribles*, trans. by Rosamond Lehmann]

14 But brawling leads to laryngitis. [*Ib*.]

15 The actual tragedies of life bear no relation to one's preconceived ideas. In the event, one is always bewildered by their simplicity, their grandeur of design, and by that element of the bizarre which seems inherent in them. [*Ib*.]

16 Hugo was a madman who believed he was Hugo. [*Opium*. See also 297:11.]

17 The poet is a liar who always speaks the truth. [Quoted in Laurence J. Peter, *Peter's Quotations*]

18 Picasso insisted everything was miraculous. It was miraculous, he said, 'that one did not melt in one's bath'. [Attr.]

GEORGE M. COHAN

1 We'll be over, we're coming over, / And we won't come back till it's over, over there. [*Over There*, US song of First World War]

LEONARD COHEN

2 Like a bird on a wire, like a drunk in a midnight choir, / I have tried, in my way, to be free. [Song: *Bird on a Wire*]

3 Suzanne takes you down / To her place by the river / And she feeds you tea and oranges / That come all the way from China. / And you want to travel with her / And you want to travel blind. [Song: *Suzanne*]

TERRY COHEN

4 He who laughs last is generally the last to get the joke. [Quoted in P. and J. Holton, *Quote and Unquote*]

DESMOND E. T. COKE

5 His blade struck the water a full second before any other . . . until . . . as the boats began to near the winning-post, his own was dipping into the water twice as often as any other. (Popularly emended to 'All rowed fast but none so fast as stroke'.) [Quoted in A. Andrews, *Quotations for Speakers and Writers*]

F. MOORE COLBY

6 Self-esteem is the most voluble of the emotions. [Quoted in C. Fadiman, *Reading I Have Liked*]

7 One learns little more about a man from the feats of his literary memory than from the feats of his alimentary canal. [Quoted in *ib.*]

TERRY COLEMAN

8 [Of Montagu Norman] Governor of the Bank of England in the days when the Bank of England was as steady as the Bank of England! [*The Liners*]

COLETTE

9 When she raises her eyelids it's as if she were taking off all her clothes. [*Claudine and Annie*]

10 My virtue's still far too small, I don't trot it out and about yet. [*Claudine at School*]

11 It was towards the end of June that incompatibility became established between them like a new season of the year. [*The Cat*]

12 When Camille was alone, she looked very much like the little girl who did not want to say 'how d'you do?' Her face returned to childhood because it wore that expression of inhuman innocence, of angelic hardness which ennobles children's faces. [*Ib.*]

13 Madame Alvarez had taken the name of a Spanish lover now dead, and accordingly had acquired a creamy complexion, an ample bust, and hair lustrous with brilliantine. [*Gigi*]

14 The three great stumbling-blocks in a girl's education, she says, are *homard à l'Américaine*, a boiled egg, and asparagus. Shoddy table manners, she says, have broken up many a happy home. [*Ib.*]

15 Don't ever wear artistic jewellery; it wrecks a woman's reputation. [*Ib.*]

16 Don't eat too many almonds; they add weight to the breasts. [*Ib.*]

17 Jane is rather like one of those refined persons who go out to sew for the rich because they cannot abide contact with the poor. [*The Other One*]

R. G. COLLINGWOOD

18 So, perhaps, I may escape otherwise than by death the last humiliation of an aged scholar, when his juniors conspire to print a volume of essays and offer it to him as a sign that they now consider him senile. [*Autobiography*]

CHAS COLLINS
and FRED W. LEIGH

19 My old man said, 'Follow the van, / Don't dilly dally on the way!' / Off

went the cart with the home packed in it, / I walked behind with my old cock linnet. / But I dillied and dallied, dallied and dillied, / Lost the van and don't know where to roam. [Song: *The Cock Linnet*. Sung by Marie Lloyd]

CHAS COLLINS, E. A. SHEPPARD and FRED TERRY

1 Any Old Iron? [Title of music-hall song. Sung by Harry Champion]

2 You look neat – talk about a treat, / You look dapper from your napper to your feet. [Song: *Any Old Iron?*]

CHAS COLLINS and FRED MURRAY

3 Boiled Beef and Carrots. [Title of music-hall song. Sung by Harry Champion]

CHAS COLLINS and FRED GODFREY

4 Now I Have to Call Him Father. [Title of music-hall song]

MICHAEL COLLINS

5 I am signing my death warrant. [On signing the Irish Treaty, 1921. He was assassinated a few months afterwards. Quoted in Longford, *Peace by Ordeal*, Pt 6, Ch. 1]

NORMAN COLLINS

6 London Belongs To Me. [Title of book]

IVY COMPTON-BURNETT

7 It would be a good plan to remove all sinks and make all rooms into halls . . . It would send up the standard of things. [*A Family and a Fortune*, Ch. 1]

8 'Well, of course, people are only human,' said Dudley to his brother, 'but it really does not seem much for them to be.' [*Ib.* 2]

9 I suppose I shall subscribe to hospitals. That's how people seem to give to the poor. I suppose the poor are always sick. They would be, if you think. [*Ib.* 4]

10 People don't resent having nothing nearly as much as too little. I have only just found that out. I am getting the knowledge of the rich as well as their ways. [*Ib.*]

11 It will be a beautiful family talk, mean and worried and full of sorrow and spite and excitement. I cannot be asked to miss it in my weak state. I should only fret. [*Ib.* 10]

12 Of taking pleasure in any human discomfiture, especially in that of the family he served, he was not ashamed, reserving this feeling for such things as threatened his manhood. [*Men and Wives*, Ch. 1]

13 Of course you are not the one man in the world to me. The world is too full of too many men for that, and I am the one woman of too many. The dear old world! [*Ib.* 24]

14 When I die people will say it is the best thing for me. It is because they know it is the worst. They want to avoid the feeling of pity. As though they were the people most concerned. [*The Mighty and Their Fall*, Ch. 4]

15 There are different kinds of wrong. The people sinned against are not always the best. [*Ib.* 7]

16 I cannot help the low quality of people. They seem to be of a different order from myself. [*Mother and Son*, Ch. 1]

17 Many people misjudge the permanent effect of sorrow and their capacity to live in the past. [*Ib.* 2]

18 It was late that feminine helplessness came into fashion. [*Ib.* 9]

19 We must use words as they are used or stand aside from life. [*Ib.*]

20 Myself and I are on the best of terms. [*Ib.*]

21 There is more difference within the sexes than between them. [*Ib.* 10]

22 There is probably nothing like living together for blinding people to each other. [*Ib.*]

23 Self-deception? I don't think there is such a thing. When people say they do things unconsciously or subconsciously,

I am quite sure they do them consciously . . I think on the whole people know. [In conversation with Kay Dick. Quoted in 'A Civilized Life', *The Times Saturday Review*, 30 Aug. 1969]

1 I would write for a few dozen people; and it sometimes seems that I do so; but I would not write for no one. [Quoted in John Russell Taylor, *Anger and After*, Introduction]

2 Real life seems to have no plots. [Quoted in a review in the *Guardian*, Feb. 1973]

RICHARD CONDON

3 She felt sexual urgings towards Yvonne in the manner that politicians feel an enormous sexual pull toward mirrors. [*Bandicoot*, Ch. 21]

4 No one has been in this much trouble since the American people discovered Richard Nixon. [*Ib.* 28]

5 Power isn't what seems to make things happen but the voice that ordered those things to happen. [*Death of a Politician*, '10 Aug. 1964, Charles Coffey']

6 He was an unzipped fly caught in forever amber. [*The Ecstasy Business*, Ch. 1]

7 I am you and you are me and what have we done to each other? [The *Manchurian Candidate*, epigraph, 'The Keener's Manual']

8 New York, New York! It's a wonderful town! The west side of the island was rich in façades not unlike the possibilities of a fairy princess with syphilis. [*Ib.* Ch. 11]

9 Broadway was controlled by strange-looking pedestrians, people who had grabbed the wrong face in the dark when someone had shouted 'Fire!' and were now out roaming the streets, desperate to find their own. [*Ib.*]

10 Cheese. The adult form of milk. [*A Talent for Loving*, Bk I, Ch. 2]

11 In Mexico the gods ruled, the priests interpreted and interposed, and the people obeyed. In Spain, the priests ruled, the king interpreted and interposed, and the gods obeyed. A nuance in an ideological difference is a wide chasm. [*Ib.* I.6]

12 More time has been spent in the attics of memory than in the contemplation of the mirrors of the present. The world is an army marching backward in martial array, following back-stepping leaders who have convinced them that they are going forward. [*Ib.* II.6]

13 He was in unique voice. It seemed to be shot through with marzipan or silvered with the dandruff of the gods. [*Ib.* III.17]

MARC CONNELLY

14 GOD: I'll just r'ar back an' pass a miracle. [*The Green Pastures*]

15 Even bein' Gawd ain't a bed of roses. [*Ib.*]

BILLY CONNOLLY

16 Your breath's like a badger's bum, an' that. [*The Afternoon After the Morning After the Night Before*]

17 In the unlikely event of this plane crashing into a mountain and bursting into flames, there's a life jacket under your seat. Put it on. Come back to life. No problem. [*The Parachutist*]

18 We used to take the ashes down to the midden in a brief-case. [*What's in a Name*]

19 Marriage is a wonderful invention; but, then again, so is a bicycle repair kit. [Quoted in Duncan Campbell, *Billy Connolly, the Authorized Version*, 'Music']

CYRIL CONNOLLY

20 It is closing time in the gardens of the West and from now on an artist will be judged only by the resonance of his solitude or the quality of his despair. [*The Condemned Playground*]

21 When I write after dark the shades of evening scatter their purple through my prose. [*Enemies of Promise*, Ch. 1]

22 A great writer creates a world of his own and his readers are proud to live in it. A lesser writer may entice them in for

a moment, but soon he will watch them filing out. [*Ib.*]

1 Contemporary books do not keep. The quality in them which makes for their success is the first to go; they turn overnight. [*Ib.* 2]

2 I shall christen this style the Mandarin, since it is beloved by literary pundits. It is the style of all those writers whose tendency is to make their language convey more than they mean or more than they feel, it is the style of most artists and all humbugs. [*Ib.*]

3 The ape-like virtues without which no one can enjoy a public school. [*Ib.*]

4 An author arrives at a good style when his language performs what is required of it without shyness. [*Ib.* 3]

5 Literature is the art of writing something that will be read twice; journalism what will be grasped at once. [*Ib.*]

6 Pater, calling an art-for-art's sake muezzin to the faithful from the topmost turret of the ivory tower. [*Ib.* 5]

7 Puritanism in other people we admire is austerity in ourselves. [*Ib.* 9]

8 For most good talkers, when they have run down, are miserable; they know that they have betrayed themselves, that they have taken material which should have a life of its own to dispense it in noises upon the air. [*Ib.* 13]

9 Whom the gods wish to destroy they first call promising. [*Ib.*]

10 If, as Dr Johnson said. a man who is not married is only half a man, so a man who is very much married is only half a writer. [*Ib.* 14]

11 There is no more sombre enemy of good art than the pram in the hall. [*Ib.*]

12 I should like to see the custom introduced of readers who are pleased with a book sending the author some small cash token: anything between half-a-crown and a hundred pounds . . . Not more than a hundred pounds – that would be bad for my character – not less than half-a-crown – that would do no good to yours. [*Ib.*]

13 The best that can happen for a writer is to be taken up very late or very early, when either old enough to take its measure, or so young that when dropped by society he has all his life before him. [*Ib.* 15]

14 No one can make us hate ourselves like an admirer [*Ib.*]

15 Humorists are not happy men. Like Beachcomber or Saki or Thurber they burn while Rome fiddles. [*Ib.* 16]

16 A poet, with the exception of mysterious water-fluent tea-drinking Auden, must be a highly-conscious technical expert. [*Ib.*]

17 The health of a writer should not be too good, and perfect only in those periods of convalescence when he is not writing. [*Ib.*]

18 All charming people have something to conceal, usually their total dependence on the appreciation of others. [*Ib.*]

19 I have always disliked myself at any given moment; the total of such moments is my life. [*Ib.* 18]

20 A private school has all the faults of a public school without any of its compensations. [*Ib.* 19]

21 Tall, pale, with his flaccid cheeks, large spatulate fingers and supercilious voice, he was one of those boys who seem born old. [George Orwell at prep school. *Ib.*]

22 The art of getting on at school depends on a mixture of enthusiasm with moral cowardice and social sense. The enthusiasm is for personalities and gossip about them, for a schoolboy is a novelist too busy to write. [*Ib.* 21]

23 Boys do not grow up gradually. They move forward in spurts like the hands of clocks in railway stations. [*Ib.*]

24 In the eighteenth century he would have become Prime Minister before he was thirty; as it was he appeared honourably ineligible for the struggle of life. [On Sir Alec Douglas-Home as a schoolboy. *Ib.* 23]

25 For the first time I was aware of that layer of blubber which encases an English peer, the sediment of permanent adulation. [*Ib.*]

CONNOLLY

1 Were I to deduce any system from my feelings on leaving Eton, it might be called *The Theory of Permanent Adolescence*. [*Ib.* 24]

2 Even the Jews in England are boyish, like Disraeli, and not the creators of adult philosophies, like Marx or Freud. [*Ib.*]

3 If he is to enjoy leisure and privacy, marry, buy books, travel and entertain his friends, a writer needs upwards of five pounds a day net. If he is prepared to die young of syphilis for the sake of an adjective, he can do on under. [Answer to a *Horizon* questionnaire. Quoted in *Ideas and Places*]

4 One of those warm stoves round which expatriates rally. [Of Alma Mahler Werfel]

5 'Pushing up theses', that is the euphemism which men of letters use for being dead; a long littleness of dons lies ahead of us, unless we have been afflicted with the curse of lucidity. [*Previous Convictions*, 'Dylan Thomas']

6 Like many artists he was mildly snobbish and thus fortunately aware of the magical and sombre poetry of the Fall of the most haunted of all houses of Usher, the aristocratic civilization built up by the English over two hundred years of plenty. [*Ib.* 'Denton Welch']

7 I refuse to be famous for a book on Wordsworth, although after all it was all Wordsworth was famous for. [*A Romantic Friendship, Letters to Noel Blakiston*, Letter, 27 Aug. 1962]

8 I came to America tourist Third with a cheque for ten pounds and I leave plus five hundred, a wife, a mandarin coat, a set of diamond studs, a state room and a bath, and a decent box for the ferret. That's what everybody comes to America to do and I don't think I've managed badly for a beginner. [*Ib.* 2 Apr. 1930]

9 The more books we read, the clearer it becomes that the true function of a writer is to produce a masterpiece and that no other task is of any consequence. [*The Unquiet Grave*, Ch. 1]

10 'Dry again?' said the Crab to the Rock-Pool. 'So would you be,' replied the Rock-Pool, 'if you had to satisfy, twice a day, the insatiable sea.' [*Ib.*]

11 And yet Original Sin, what rubbish! The Expulsion from Eden is an act of vindictive womanish spite; the Fall of Man. as recounted in the Bible, comes nearer to the Fall of God. [*Ib.*]

12 It is better to be the lichen on a rock than the President's carnation. Only by avoiding the beginning of things can we escape their ending. [*Ib.*]

13 There is no fury like an ex-wife searching for a new lover. [*Ib.*]

14 A comfortable person can seldom follow up an original idea any further than a London pigeon can fly. [*Ib.*]

15 Life is a maze in which we take the wrong turning before we have learnt to walk. [*Ib.*]

16 No city should be too large for a man to walk out of in a morning. [*Ib.*]

17 Everything is a dangerous drug to me except reality, which is unendurable. [*Ib.*]

18 Civilization is an active deposit which is formed by the combustion of the Present with the Past. Neither in countries without a Present nor in those without a Past is it to be encountered. [*Ib.* 2]

19 The civilization of one epoch becomes the manure of the next. Everything over-ripens in the same way. The disasters of the world are due to its inhabitants not being able to grow old simultaneously. [*Ib.*]

20 Imprisoned in every fat man a thin one is wildly signalling to be let out. [*Ib.* See also 14:10; 254:14; 347:13]

21 The true index of a man's character is the health of his wife. [*Ib.*]

22 We are all serving a life-sentence in the dungeon of self. [*Ib.*]

23 Others merely live; I vegetate. [*Ib.*]

24 Our memories are card-indexes consulted and then returned in disorder by authorities whom we do not control. [*Ib.* 3]

84

1 Better to write for yourself and have no public, than write for the public and have no self. [Quoted in *Turnstile One*, ed. V. S. Pritchett]

2 The man who is master of his passions is Reason's slave. [Quoted in *ib.*]

3 Perfect fear casteth out love. [Said to Philip Toynbee during the Blitz. Quoted by Toynbee in obituary, *Observer*, 1 Dec. 1974]

SIR WILLIAM CONNOR
See 'Cassandra'

WILLIS CONOVER

4 Jazz is a language It is people living in sound. Jazz is people talking, laughing, crying, building, painting, mathematicizing, abstracting, extracting, giving to, taking from, making of. In other words, living. [Quoted in L. Feather, *The Book of Jazz*]

JOSEPH CONRAD

5 A work that aspires, however humbly, to the condition of art should carry its justification in every line. [*The Nigger of the 'Narcissus'*, Preface]

SHIRLEY CONRAN

6 Our motto: Life is too short to stuff a mushroom. [*Superwoman*, epigraph]

7 I make no secret of the fact that I would rather lie on a sofa than sweep beneath it. But you have to be efficient if you're going to be lazy. [*Ib.* 'The Reason Why']

8 First things first, second things never [*Ib.* 'How to be a working wife and mother']

9 You cannot have everything and certainly cannot dust everything. To cite Conran's Law of Housework – it expands to fill the time available plus half an hour: so obviously it is never finished . . . Keep housework in its place, which, you will remember, is underfoot. [*Superwoman 2*, quoted in *Telegraph Sunday Magazine*, 30 Oct. 1977]

CONSERVATIVE PARTY PRESS RELEASE

10 This would, at a stroke, reduce the rise in prices, increase productivity and reduce unemployment. [Distributed at Press Conference, 16 Jun. 1960. Wrongly attr. to Edward Heath at the conference, according to D. Butler and A. Sloman, *British Political Facts 1900–1975*]

A. J. COOK

11 Not a penny off the pay; not a minute on the day. [Slogan of Coal Strike, 1925]

PETER COOK

12 You know, I go to the theatre to be entertained . . . I don't want to see plays about rape, sodomy and drug addiction . . . I can get all that at home. [Caption to cartoon by Roger Law, *Observer*, 8 Jul. 1962]

13 We exchanged many frank words in our respective languages. [*Beyond the Fringe*]

14 I am very interested in the Universe – I am specializing in the universe and all that surrounds it. [*Ib.*]

ALISTAIR COOKE

15 Very little is dependable in the politics of a going democracy except the people's conviction that one world-saver at a time is enough. [*America*, Ch. 10]

16 [Of Roosevelt] Not since Lincoln had there been such an artful manipulator of the good, the bad, and the bewildered in between. I believe he saved the capitalist system by deliberately forgetting to balance the books, by transferring the gorgeous resources of credit from the bankers to the government. [*Ib.*]

17 The most damning epitaph you can compose about Edward [VIII] – as a prince, as a king, as a man - is one that all comfortable people should cower from deserving: he was at his best only when the going was good. [*Six Men*, Pt II]

18 Trust the French to touch the nerve of the national spirit, or, as they prefer to

85

say about any country but their own, the problem. [*Talk About America*, Ch. 14]

CALVIN COOLIDGE

1 One with the law is a majority. [Speech of Acceptance, 27 Jul. 1920]

2 The business of America is business. [Speech in Washington, 17 Jan. 1925]

CHESTER COOPER

3 The last crusade. [Of America's war in Vietnam. Quoted in the *Daily Telegraph*, 4 Apr. 1975]

GILES COOPER

4 There was the Reformation and the Civil War and the Repeal of the Corn Laws and the Zeppelin and the Americans, but none of them made much difference, except the Zeppelin, which knocked down an oak tree that the Vikings were supposed to have planted. [*The Forgotten Rotten Borough*, radio drama]

5 Went off to fight the foreigners because they fired their guns at Lowestoft, where he had a day's holiday on the Saturday after he got married. [*Ib.*]

6 Sudanese, called himself a dervish, swallowed a fish-hook, cut himself open, took it out again. If an uneducated savage can do that, you can cut your own hair. [*Mathry Beacon*, radio drama]

7 Plato ... the only five-lettered philosopher ending in o. [*Ib.*]

8 QUENTIN: Have you got the room with the toadstools on the ceiling?
GEORGE: There is a patch or two of damp.
QUENTIN: They glow in the dark with a dim phosphorescent light, which is just as well, considering there's no bulb upstairs of more than twenty watts. [*The Return of General Forefinger*]

9 All schools are hell, nor are we out of them. In a moment you will hear the sound of the second circle: unrestricted boy. [*Unman, Wittering and Zigo*, radio drama]

10 I'm a connoisseur of failure. I can smell it, roll it round my mouth, tell you the vintage and the side of the hill that grew it. [*Ib.*]

11 He was a delayed failure with quite a strong flavour of success about him. Even I did not recognize it until he had been here a year or two. But then I noticed the way he kept looking at the top of other people's heads to see whether they were getting as bald as he was. [*Ib.*]

JILLY COOPER

12 Sex is only the liquid centre of the great Newberry Fruit of friendship. [*SuperJilly*, jacket]

13 If I were a grouse I'd appeal to the Brace Relations Board. [Quoted in the *Guardian*, 28 Dec. 1978]

TOMMY COOPER

14 Last night I dreamt I ate a ten-pound marshmallow. When I woke up the pillow was gone [Gag in variety act. Quoted in John Fisher, *Funny Way To Be a Hero*, 'Just a Wolf in Sheep's Clothing']

WILLIAM COOPER

15 Bolshaw approved of Hitler in so much as he approved of the principle of the Führer's function while feeling that he could fulfil it better himself. [*Scenes from Provincial Life*, Pt I, Ch. 3]

16 If girls aren't ignorant, they're cultured ... You can't avoid suffering. [*Ib.* III. 2]

17 The trouble about finding a husband for one's mistress, is that no other man seems quite good enough. [*Ib.* III. 5]

18 As an absurdity it was so colossal that it took on the air of a great truth. [*Ib.* IV. 4]

AARON COPLAND

19 If a literary man puts together two words about music, one of them will be wrong. [Quoted in Frank Muir, *The Frank Muir Book*]

86

A. E. COPPARD

1 I am able to declare that thus far my autobiography has no more pure fiction in it than my fiction has pure autobiography. [*It's Me, O Lord!*]

ALAN COREN

2 No visit to Dove Cottage, Grasmere, is complete without examining the outhouse where Hazlitt's father, a Unitarian minister of strong liberal views, attempted to put his hand up Dorothy Wordsworth's skirt. [*All Except the Bastard*, 'Bohemia']

3 An infuriating irritant, like the chap you knew before you were married who is now a bachelor supported by beautiful women and constantly drops in to see you on the way to the airport. [*Ib.* 'The Still Centre']

4 It [his book] also concerns the three most perennially popular subjects currently to be found on the bedside tables of the reading public, viz. golf, cats, and the Third Reich. [*Golfing for Cats*, Foreword]

5 The Act of God designation on all insurance policies; which means, roughly, that you cannot be insured for the accidents that are most likely to happen to you. If your ox kicks a hole in your neighbour's Maserati, however, indemnity is instantaneous. [*The Lady from Stalingrad Mansions*, 'A Short History of Insurance']

6 'Golden hands he's got,' said his father gloomily. 'A pianist's hands. Or a surgeon's hands.' 'Both,' said his mother. She blew her nose fiercely 'He could have been both. Operating by day, by night playing Bach.' [*The Sanity Inspector*, 'Wholesale War']

7 The cuckoo clock, in fact, may be said to be the quintessential souvenir, in that it exists purely to be bought, sold, wrapped, carried home, unwrapped, and put in lofts. [*Ib.* 'And Though They Do Their Best']

8 Since both its [Switzerland's] national products, snow and chocolate, melt, the cuckoo clock was invented solely in order to give tourists something solid to remember it by. [*Ib.*]

9 They [the French] are short, bluevested people who carry their own onions when cycling abroad, and have a yard which is 3·37 inches longer than other people's. [*Ib.* 'All You Need to Know about Europe']

10 Like the Germans, the Dutch fall into two quite distinct physical types: the small, corpulent, red-faced Edams, and the thinner, paler, larger Goudas. [*Ib.*]

11 Apart from cheese and tulips, the main product of the country is advocaat, a drink made from lawyers. [*Ib.*]

12 'It's your audience for ten a.m., Your Holiness,' murmured the secretary. 'One man?' said the Pope. 'You call that an audience?' [*Ib.* 'Believe Me']

13 As anyone who has ever forked out for a quarter-pound of mixed metaphors will testify, once a bastion falls, the flood-gates open and before you know where you are you're up to the neck in wrung withers. [*Punch*, 16 Feb. 1972]

14 Democracy consists of choosing your dictators, after they've told you what you think it is you want to hear. [*Daily Mail*, 22 Aug. 1975]

15 People who live in large houses shouldn't know Jones. [On BBC radio, 4 Sep. 1977]

16 A suburb without the urb. [Describing Salisbury, Rhodesia. Quoted in the *Sunday Times Magazine*, 27 Nov. 1977]

17 Cornwall, where it is always 1790 and rotten weather, the sea pounding the rocks and the wind pounding the trees and all the inhabitants pounding doors in the small hours; Cornwall, where not a vital remains unstapped, nor a tush unpished. [Review of BBC TV serial, *Poldark*]

18 There is nothing to be pitied in a dumb animal; its dumbness is its salvation, whereas poor man carries the terrible burden of intelligence, and it will surely wipe him out in the not too distant end. The cats and guppies will have the last laugh over the last corpse of the last man: 'If you're so smart, how come you're extinct.' [In *The Times*]

1 Television is more interesting than people. If it were not, we should have people standing in the corners of our rooms. [*Ib.*]

BERNARD CORNFELD

2 A beautiful woman with a brain is like a beautiful woman with a club foot. [*Daily Telegraph Magazine*, 6 Dec. 1974]

F. M. CORNFORD

3 Propaganda is that branch of the art of lying which consists in nearly deceiving your friends without quite deceiving your enemies. [Quoted in the *New Statesman*, 15 Sep. 1978]

JOHN CORNFORD

4 Only in constant action was his constant certainty found. / He will throw a longer shadow as time recedes. [In *John Cornford, A Memoir*, ed. Pat Sloan, Pt 2, sect. vii: 'Sergei Mironovich Kirov']

BILLY COTTON

5 Wakey-wakey! Rise and shine! [In broadcasts, with his band]

R. COULSON

6 Marriage is not all bed and breakfast. [*Reflections*]

NOËL COWARD

7 Though we all disguise our feelings pretty well, / What we mean by 'Very good' is 'Go to hell'. [*Bitter Sweet*, Act I, sc. ii]

8 I believe that since my life began / The most I've had is just / A talent to amuse. [*Ib.* II. i]

9 Never mind, dear, we're all made the same, though some more than others. [*Collected Sketches and Lyrics*, 'The Café de la Paix']

10 Whatever your Uncle Bob's failings were, he never tucked his serviette into his dickey. [*Ib.*]

11 You always ought to 'ave tom cats arranged, you know – it makes 'em so much more companionable. [*Ib.* 'Cat's Cradle']

12 There's sand in the porridge and sand in the bed, / And if this is pleasure we'd rather be dead. [*Ib.* 'The English Lido']

13 When it's raspberry time in Runcorn, / In Runcorn, in Runcorn, / The air is like a draught of wine, / The undertaker cleans his sign, / The Hull express goes off the line, / When it's raspberry time in Runcorn. [*Ib.* 'Fête Galante']

14 I don't know what London's coming to – the higher the buildings the lower the morals. [*Ib.* 'Law and Order']

15 Sunburn is very becoming – but only when it is even – one must be careful not to look like a mixed grill. [*Ib.* 'The Lido Beach']

16 I've over-educated myself in all the things I shouldn't have known at all. [*Ib.* 'Mild Oats']

17 There are bad times just around the corner, / We can all look forward to despair. / It's as clear as crystal / From Birmingham to Bristol / That we can't save democracy, and we don't much care. [*There Are Bad Times*]

18 We have no reliable guarantee that the afterlife will be any less exasperating than this one, have we? [*Blithe Spirit*, Act I]

19 Considering all the time you took forming yourself, Elsie, I'm surprised you're not a nicer little girl than you are. [*Fumed Oak*, Act II, sc. ii]

20 I belong to a generation of men, most of which aren't here any more, and we all did the same thing for the same reason, no matter what we thought about politics. [*This Happy Breed*, Act I, sc. iii]

21 Not only people in other countries who want to do us in because they're sick of us ruling the roost – and you can't blame them at that! but people here in England. People who let 'emselves get soft and afraid. People who go on a lot about peace and good will and the ideals they believe in but somehow don't seem to believe in 'em enough to think they're worth fighting for. [*Ib.* III. iii]

1 Miss Erikson looked more peculiar than ever this morning. Is her spiritualism getting worse? [*Present Laughter*, Act I]

2 But why, oh why, do the wrong people travel, / When the right people stay at home? [*Sail Away*]

3 Everybody was up to something, especially, of course, those who were up to nothing. [*Future Indefinite*, Pt II, 3]

4 There was a saying, much quoted in the war years, that if an Englishman told you he was a secret agent it was a lie, and that if an American told you the same it was true. [*Ib*. IV. 2]

5 A gentle austerity was the keynote of breakfast at Government House. There was a copy of the *Malta Times* for everyone present, but Lord Gort, rightly, was the only one who had a sort of lectern on which to prop it. [*Ib*. IV. 15]

6 Divorced couples hob-nobbed with each other, and with each other's co-respondents. [*Present Indicative*]

7 Dear 338171 (May I call you 338?) [Opening of letter to T. E. Lawrence. *Letters to T. E. Lawrence*]

8 Dance, dance, dance little lady, / Leave tomorrow behind. [*This Year of Grace*]

9 The sun never sets on Government House. [*Words and Music*]

10 Mad about the boy. [*Ib*.]

11 Whatever crimes the Proletariat commits / It can't be beastly to the Children of the Ritz. [*Ib*.]

12 Work is much more fun than fun. [*Observer*, 'Sayings of the Week', 21 Jun. 1963]

13 He had just one illusion about them and that was that they were no good. [Of Somerset Maugham's boast that he had no illusions about his fellow men. Quoted in Frederick Raphael, *Somerset Maugham and his World*]

14 Learn the lines and don't bump into the furniture. [Advice to a young actor. Attr.]

HARVEY COX

15 The Secular City [Title of book]

TOM CRABTREE

16 Some people are born in circumstances which resemble being saddled in the enclosure at Epsom when the race is at Ripon. [In the *Guardian*, 8 Sep. 1977]

SIR EDWARD GORDON CRAIG

17 Farce is the essential theatre. Farce refined becomes high comedy: farce brutalized becomes tragedy. But at the roots of all drama farce is to be found. [*Index to the Story of My Days*]

18 Never take a bit of notice of traffic and it'll never do you any harm. Like wasps. Let them know who's master. [Quoted in M. Swan, *A Small Part of Time*]

HART CRANE

19 Thin squeaks of radio static, / The captured fume of space foams in our ears. [*The Bridge*, 'Cape Hatteras']

20 Stars scribble on our eyes the frosty sagas, / The gleaming cantos of unvanquished space. [*Ib*.]

21 Our Meistersinger, thou set breath in steel; / And it was thou who on the boldest heel / Stood up and flung the span on even wing / Of that great Bridge, our Myth, whereof I sing. [Ref. to Walt Whitman and Brooklyn Bridge. *Ib*.]

22 You are your father's father, and the stream / A liquid theme that floating niggers swell. [*Ib*. 'The River']

23 The River lifts itself from its long bed, / Poised wholly on its dream. [*Ib*.]

24 And hurry along, Van Winkle – it's getting late. [*Ib*. 'Van Winkle']

25 The phonographs of hades in the brain / Are tunnels that re-wind themselves, and love / A burnt match skating in a urinal. [*Ib*. 'The Tunnel']

26 . . . why do I often meet your visage here, / Your eyes like agate lanterns – on and on / Below the toothpaste and the dandruff ads? [Ref. to Walt Whitman. *Ib*.]

27 The bell-rope that gathers God at dawn / Dispatches me as though I dropped

down the knell / Of a spent day. [*The Broken Tower*]

1 The Cross alone has flown the wave. / But since the Cross sank, much that's warped and cracked / Has followed in its name, has heaped its grave. [*The Mermen*]

2 And onwards, as bells off San Salvador / Salute the crocus lustres of the stars, / In these poinsettia meadows of her tides. [*Voyages*, II]

JAMES CREELMAN and RUTH ROSE

3 Oh no, it wasn't the aeroplanes. It was Beauty killed the Beast. [Final words of film, *King Kong* (1933 version)]

BISHOP CREIGHTON

4 The one real object of education is to leave a man in the condition of continually asking questions. [Quoted in C. A. Alington, *Things Ancient and Modern*, Ch. 9]

5 Oxford men think they rule the world, and Cambridge men don't care a cent who does. [Attr.]

QUENTIN CRISP

6 Keeping up with the Joneses was a full-time job with my mother and father. It was not until many years later when I lived alone that I realized how much cheaper it was to drag the Joneses down to my level. [*The Naked Civil Servant*, Ch. 1]

7 In an expanding universe, time is on the side of the outcast. Those who inhabited the suburbs of human contempt find that without changing their address they eventually live in the metropolis. [*Ib.*]

8 As soon as I stepped out of my mother's womb on to dry land, I realized that I had made a mistake – that I shouldn't have come, but the trouble with children is that they are not returnable. [*Ib.*]

9 Then my hostess said, 'Oh, Denis (as my name was before I dyed it) never plays the part of a man.' [*Ib.* 2]

10 Tears were to me what glass beads are to African traders. [*Ib.*]

11 This school was on top of a hill so that God could see everything that went on. It looked like a cross between a prison and a church and it was. [*Ib.*]

12 Vice is its own reward. [*Ib.*]

13 This woman did not fly to extremes; she lived there. [*Ib.* 3]

14 I don't hold with abroad and think that foreigners speak English when our backs are turned. [*Ib.* 4]

15 My mother protected me from the world and my father threatened me with it. [*Ib.* 5]

16 If one is not going to take the necessary precautions to avoid having parents, one must undertake to bring them up. [*Ib.*]

17 The . . . problem which confronts homosexuals is that they set out to win the love of a 'real' man. If they succeed, they fail. A man who 'goes with' other men is not what they would call a real man. The conundrum is incapable of resolution, but that does not make homosexuals give it up. [*Ib.* 9]

18 Is not the whole world a vast house of assignation of which the filing system has been lost? [*Ib.* 11]

19 I started to shed the monstrous aesthetic affectation of my youth so as to make room for the monstrous philistine postures of my middle age, but it was still some years before I was bold enough to decline an invitation to *Hamlet* on the grounds that I already knew who won. [*Ib.* 12]

20 There was no need to do any housework at all. After the first four years the dirt doesn't get any worse. [*Ib.* 15]

21 . . . God, from whose territory I had withdrawn my ambassadors at the age of fifteen. It had become obvious that he was never going to do a thing I said. [*Ib.* 16]

22 Life was a funny thing that happened to me on the way to the grave. [*Ib.* 18]

23 I became one of the stately homos of England. [*Ib.* 24]

1 Sadly I explained that . . . the conditions in which anyone could be a famous model had vanished long ago. Those few of us who were still in the racket had dwindled into naked Civil Servants. [*Ib.* 29]

2 An autobiography is an obituary in serial form with the last instalment missing. [*Ib.*]

3 In England, failure is all the rage. England is a sort of home for incorrigibles. [Quoted in *The Sayings of Quentin Crisp*]

4 For flavour, Instant Sex will never supersede the stuff you had to peel and cook. [*Ib.*]

5 [On God's susceptibility to prayer at Christmas] The idea that He would take his attention away from the universe in order to give me a bicycle with three speeds is just so unlikely I can't go along with it. [Quoted in the *Sunday Times*, 18 Dec. 1977]

6 I have come to represent a sad person's view of a gay person. [In *An Evening with Quentin Crisp*, his one-man show at the Duke of York's Theatre, London. Quoted in the *Guardian*, 1 Feb. 1978]

BENEDETTO CROCE

7 Philosophy removes from religion all reason for existing . . . As the science of the spirit, it looks upon religion as a phenomenon, a transitory historical fact, a psychic condition that can be surpassed. [*Esthetic*, Ch. 8]

RICHMAL CROMPTON

8 Violet Elizabeth [Bott] dried her tears. She saw that they were useless and she did not believe in wasting her effects. 'All right,' she said calmly, 'I'll thcream then. I'll thcream, an' thcream, an' thcream till I'm thick.' [*Just William*]

BING CROSBY

9 Where the blue of the night / Meets the gold of the day, / Someone waits for me. [Song: *Where the Blue of the Night . . .* Words and music by Crosby, Roy Turk and Fred Ahlert]

10 There is nothing in the world I wouldn't do for Hope, and there is nothing he wouldn't do for me . . . We spend our lives doing nothing for each other. [*Observer*, 'Sayings of the Week', 7 May 1950]

11 I think popular music in this country is one of the few things in the twentieth century that have made giant strides in reverse. [*This Week* magazine. Quoted in Frank Muir, *The Frank Muir Book*]

12 Most of them think: 'Well he [Bing himself] sings about like I do, you know, when I'm in the bathroom, or in the shower, and feel good and wake up with a gay feeling.' Why they think I'm one of the fellas. [Quoted as epigraph in C. Thompson *Bing*]

13 When Irving Berlin sings you have to hug him to hear him. [In a BBC TV interview with Michael Parkinson, 1975]

14 Oh – I listen a lot and talk less. You can't learn anything when you're talking. [In *ib.*]

BING CROSBY and BOB HOPE

15 Like Webster's Dictionary, we're Morocco bound. [Film: *The Road to Morocco*. Song written by Johnny Burke]

LORD CROWTHER

16 It has been said that there are two aspects of education, both necessary. One regards the individual human mind as a vessel, of varying capacity, into which is to be poured as much as it will hold of the knowledge and experience by which human society lives and moves. This is the Martha of education – and we shall have plenty of these tasks to perform. But the Mary regards the human mind more as a fire that has to be set alight and blown with the divine afflatus. That also we take as our ambition. [Inaugural speech as Chancellor of the Open University, 1969]

E. E. CUMMINGS

1 what i want to know is / how do you like your blueeyed boy / Mister Death. [*Collected Poems* (1938), 31]

2 the flyspecked abdominous female / indubitably tellurian / strolls / emitting minute grins [*Ib*. 68]

3 hurries / elsewhere; to blow / incredible wampum. [*Ib*.]

4 bodies lopped / of every / prettiness, / you hew form truly. [*Ib*. 103]

5 Humanity i love you / because you would rather black the boots of / success than enquire whose soul dangles from his / watch-chain which would be embarrassing for both / parties and because you / unflinchingly applaud all / songs containing the words country home and / mother when sung at the old howard [*Ib*. 107]

6 a pretty girl who naked is / is worth a million statues [*Ib*. 133]

7 in every language even deafanddumb / thy sons acclaim your glorious name by gorry / by jingo by gee by gosh by gum [*Ib*. 147]

8 'then shall the voices of liberty be mute?' / He spoke. And drank rapidly a glass of water [*Ib*.]

9 (dreaming, / et / cetera, of / Your smile / eyes knees and of your Etcetera) [*Ib*. 148]

10 how do you find the sun, ladies? / (graduallyverygradually) 'there is not enough / of it' their hands / minutely / answered [*Ib*. 158]

11 when i contemplate her uneyes safely ensconced in thick glass / you try if we are a gentleman not to think of (sh) [*Ib*. 201]

12 and the duckbilled platitude lays & lays / and Lays aytash unee [*Ib*. 203]

13 responds, without getting annoyed / 'I will not kiss your f.ing flag.' [*Ib*. 204]

14 Olaf (upon what were once knees) / does almost ceaselessly repeat / 'there is some shit I will not eat' [*Ib*.]

15 unless statistics lie he was / more brave than me: more blond than you. [*Ib*.]

16 lady will you come with me into / the extremely little house of / my mind. [*Ib*. 230]

17 squeeze your nuts and open your face [*Ib*. 246]

18 he sang his didn't he danced his did [*50 Poems*, xxix]

19 for whatever we lose (like a you or a me) / it's always ourselves we find in the sea [*Poems 95*, 'maggie and milly and molly and may']

20 who knows if the moon's / a balloon, coming out of a keen city / in the sky – filled with pretty people? [Epigraph to David Niven, *The Moon's a Balloon*]

WILL CUPPY

21 To give him his due, Louis XIV brought the technique of dressing and undressing in public to a perfection it never reached before or since. [*The Decline and Fall of Practically Everybody*, IV 'Louis XIV']

22 Unfortunately, this world is full of people who are ready to think the worst when they see a man sneaking out of the wrong bedroom in the middle of the night. [*Ib*. 'Catherine the Great']

23 Henry I . . . is on lots of family trees. He was very good at it. He had twenty illegitimate children before he was married, and nobody counted them afterwards. [*Ib*. V, 'William the Conqueror']

24 Catherine Parr didn't matter. She never committed even low treason. [*Ib*. 'Henry VIII']

25 It's easy to see the faults in people I know; it's hardest to see the good. Especially when the good isn't there. [Attr.]

MICHAEL CURTIZ

26 Nobody should try to play comedy unless they have a circus going on inside. [Quoted in David Niven, *The Moon's a Balloon*, Ch. 11]

27 Bring on the empty horses! [Attr. remark during the filming of *The Charge*

of the Light Brigade, 1936; used by
David Niven as the title of one of his
volumes of autobiography]

EARL CURZON OF
KEDLESTON

1 I am almost astounded at the coolness,
I might even say the effrontery, with
which the British government is in the
habit of parcelling out the territory of
Powers whose independence and integrity it assures them at the same time
it has no other intention than to preserve. [Quoted in Ronaldshay, *Life of
Lord Curzon*, Vol. III, Ch. 2]

2 I never knew the lower classes had such
white skins. [Attr.]

3 Not even a public figure. A man of no
experience. And of the utmost insignificance. [Of Stanley Baldwin's appointment as Prime Minister. Quoted in
Harold Nicolson, *Curzon: The Last
Phase*]

4 In Lord Salisbury's time there stood
here [at the Minister's desk in the
Foreign Office] an ink-stand of alabaster
– what is this contraption of gläss and
bräss? [Lewis Broad, *Sir Anthony Eden*,
Ch. 22. A different version is given in
Ronaldshay, op. cit., III. 12]

5 Better send them a Papal Bull. [Margi-
nal comment on misprint in Foreign
Office document: '... even the monks of
Mount Athos were violating their
cows.' Quoted in *ib*. III. 15]

D

ROALD DAHL

1 'Oh, my sainted aunt!' cried Mr Wonka. 'Don't mention that disgusting stuff in front of me! Do you *know* what breakfast cereal is made of? It's made of all those little curly wooden shavings you find in pencil sharpeners!' [Charlie and the Chocolate Factory, Ch. 27]

DAILY MIRROR

2 Whose finger on the trigger? [Front-page headline, on eve of election, Oct. 1951. See also 218:18]

SALVADOR DALI

3 Do you believe that since the earth is round, you will find landscapes everywhere? Does a round face have several noses? There are very few landscapes. They all converge here. Catalonia is the nose of the earth. [Introduction to Descharnes and Prevost, *Gaudí, the Visionary*]

Sergeant DAN DALY, US Marines

4 Come on, you sons of bitches! Do you want to live for ever? [Attr. at the battle of Belleau Wood, Jun. 1918]

SIDNEY DARK

5 Shaw was, of course, the more Christian of the two. [Comparing G. B. Shaw and Dean Inge. Attr. in conversation]

MR JUSTICE DARLING

6 The Law of England is a very strange one; it cannot compel anyone to tell the truth . . . But what the Law can do is to give you seven years for not telling the truth. [Quoted in D. Walker-Smith, *Lord Darling*, Ch. 27]

7 The law-courts of England are open to all men, like the doors of the Ritz Hotel. [Wrongfully (?) attr. See 323:2]

CLARENCE DARROW

8 When I was a boy I was told that anybody could become President; I'm beginning to believe it. [Quoted in E. Esar and N. Bentley, *Treasury of Humorous Quotations*]

CHARLES GALTON DARWIN

9 Life in the crowded conditions of cities has many unattractive features, but in the long run these may be overcome, not so much by altering them, but simply by changing the human race into liking them. [*The Next Million Years*, Ch. 5]

10 The evolution of the human race will not be accomplished in the ten thousand years of tame animals, but in the million years of wild animals, because man is and will always be a wild animal. [*Ib.* 7]

WALTER DAVENPORT

11 An editor: a person who knows precisely what he wants – but isn't quite sure. [Quoted by Bennett Cerf in *Saturday Review Reader*, No. 2]

LIONEL DAVIDSON

12 For six days, following an old tradition, this labour continued, and on the seventh ceased. [On the Six-Day War. *Smith's Gazelle*, Ch. 10, sect. i]

W. H. DAVIES

13 And hear the pleasant cuckoo, loud and long – / The simple bird that thinks two notes a song. [*April's Charms*]

1 When butterflies will make side-leaps, / As though escaped from Nature's hand / Ere perfect quite. [*Days too Short*]

2 It was the Rainbow gave thee birth, / And left thee all her lovely hues. [*The Kingfisher*]

3 Live with proud Peacocks in green parks. [*Ib.*]

4 A lonely pool, and let a tree / Sigh with her bosom over me. [*Ib.*]

5 I love thee for a heart that's kind – / Not for the knowledge in thy mind. [*Sweet Stay-at-Home*]

BETTE DAVIS

6 I see – she's the original good time that was had by all. [Of a starlet. Quoted in Leslie Halliwell, *The Filmgoer's Book of Quotes*]

7 Pray to God and say the lines. [Advice to actress Celeste Holm, as quoted by latter]

See also 221:7 *et seq.*

SAMMY DAVIS JR

8 Being a star has made it possible for me to get insulted in places where the average Negro could never hope to get insulted. [*Yes I Can*]

9 I'm a coloured, one-eyed Jew – do I need anything else? [*Ib.*]

CLARENCE DAY

10 I meant to be prompt, but it never occurred to me that I had better try to be early. [*Life With Father*, 'Father teaches me to be prompt']

11 Apparently, now that he knew he was in trouble, his thoughts had turned to his God. 'Have mercy!' they heard him shouting indignantly. 'I say have mercy, damn it!' [*Ib.* 'Father is firm ...']

12 Imagine the Lord talking French! Aside from a few odd words in Hebrew, I took it completely for granted that God had never spoken anything but the most dignified English. [*Ib.* 'Father interferes'. See also 114:16]

13 Father said he wouldn't mind if people died only once in a while as they used to. [*Ib.* 'Father plans']

14 'If you don't go to other men's funerals,' he told Father stiffly, 'they won't go to yours.' [*Ib.*]

15 Father declared he was going to buy a new plot in the cemetery, a plot all for himself. 'And I'll buy one on a corner,' he added triumphantly, 'where I can get out.' Mother looked at him, startled but admiring, and whispered to me, 'I almost believe he could do it.' [*Ib.* final words of book]

16 Books! Bottled chatter! Things that some other simian has formerly said. [*This Simian World*]

C. DAY LEWIS

17 Is it birthday weather for you, dear soul? / Is it fine your way, / With tall moon-daisies alight, and the mole / Busy, and elegant hares at play ...? [*Birthday Poem for Thomas Hardy*]

18 All is yet the same as when I roved the heather / Chained to a demon through the shrinking night. [*Emily Brontë*]

19 It is the logic of our times, / No subject for immortal verse – / That we who lived by honest dreams / Defend the bad against the worse. [*Where are the War Poets?*]

20 Then I'll hit the trail for that promising land; / May catch up with Wystan and Rex my friend, / Go mad in good company, find a good country, / Make a clean sweep or make a clean end. [*The Magnetic Mountain*, 4]

MOSHE DAYAN

21 If we lose this war, I'll start another in my wife's name. [Attr.]

22 Whenever you accept our views we shall be in full agreement with you. [Welcoming Cyrus Vance to Israel, in course of Arab-Israeli negotiations. *Observer*, 'Sayings of the Week', 14 Aug. 1977]

ANTHONY C. DEANE

23 When some visitor commented to a verger on a remarkable reading of a

lesson he had heard from Dalton, the verger replied: 'Ah, sir, but you should hear him throw down Jezebel!' [*Time Remembered*]

ARCHBISHOP JOOST DE BLANK

1 Christ in this country [South Africa] would quite likely have been arrested under the Suppression of Communism Act. [*Observer*, 'Sayings of the Week', 27 Oct. 1963]

2 I suffer from an incurable disease – colour blindness. [Attr.]

RÉGIS DEBRAY

3 Revolution in the Revolution? [Book title]

4 We are never completely contemporaneous with our present. History advances in disguise; it appears on stage wearing the mask of the preceding scene, and we tend to lose the meaning of the play. [*Revolution in the Revolution?*, Ch. 1]

MICHEL DEBRÉ

5 *Europe des patries*. – Europe of the fatherlands. [Speech on taking office as Prime Minister of France, 15 Jan. 1959. Often falsely ascribed to General de Gaulle]

CLAUDE DEBUSSY

6 Music is the arithmetic of sounds as optics is the geometry of light. [Quoted in N. Shapiro, *An Encyclopedia of Quotations about Music*]

SYLVIA DEE

7 They try to tell us we're too young / Too young to really be in love. [Song: *Too Young*. Music by Sid Lippman]

WALTER DE LA MARE

8 Our dreams are tales / Told in dim Eden / By Eve's nightingales. [*All That's Past*]

9 Has anybody seen my Mopser? – / A comely dog is he, / With hair the colour of a Charles the Fifth, / And teeth like ships at sea. [*The Bandog*]

10 In search of a Fairy, / Whose Rozez he knowzez / Were not honeyed for he. [*The Bees' Song*]

11 Only with beauty wake wild memories – / Sorrow for where you are, for where you would be. [*The Cage*]

12 What can a tired heart say, / Which the wise of the world have made dumb? / Save to the lonely dreams of a child, / 'Return again, come!' [*Dreams*]

13 So, when with fickle heart / I joyed in the passing day, / A presence my mood estranged / Went grieved away. [*Estranged*]

14 God in His pity knows / Why, in her bodice stuck, / Reeks a mock rose. [*The Fat Woman*]

15 He is the Ancient Tapster of this Hostel, / To him at length even we all keys must resign. [*Hospital*]

16 I can't abear a Butcher, / I can't abide his meat. [*I Can't Abear*]

17 The world's grimed thumb, / Now hooked securely in his matted hair. [*In the Dock*]

18 And out of her cold cottage never answered Mrs Gill / The Fairy mimbling mambling in the garden. [*The Mocking Fairy*]

19 When music sounds, all that I was I am / Ere to this haunt of brooding dust I came. [*Music*]

20 Ere unto Z / My pen drew nigh; / Leviathan told, / And the honey-fly. [*The Scribe*]

21 Did not those night-hung houses, / Of quiet, starlit stone, / Breathe not a whisper – 'Stay, / Thou unhappy one; / Whither so secret away?' [*The Suicide*]

22 I was that man – in a dream: / And each world's night in vain / I patient wait on sleep to unveil / Those vivid hills again. [*The Three Strangers*]

23 Too tired to yawn. too tired to sleep: / Poor tired Tim! It's sad for him. [*Tired Tim*]

1 Flee into some forgotten night and be /
Of all dark long my moon-bright
company; / Beyond the rumour even of
Paradise come, / There, out of all
remembrance, make our home. [*The
Tryst*]

2 Somewhere there nothing is; and there
lost Man / Shall win what changeless
vague of peace he can. [*Ib.*]

3 Until we learn the use of living words
we shall continue to be waxworks inhabited by gramophones. [*Observer*,
'Sayings of the Week', 12 May 1929]

SHELAGH DELANEY

4 I'm not frightened of the darkness outside. It's the darkness inside houses I
don't like. [*A Taste of Honey*, Act I,
sc. i]

5 Women never have young minds. They
are born three thousand years old. [*Ib.*]

6 Do you like me more than you don't
like me or don't you like me more than
you do? [*Ib.* II. ii]

7 The cinema has become more and more
like the theatre, it's all mauling and
muttering. [*Ib.*]

FREDERICK DELIUS

8 Admirable, but what language was he
singing in? [After a recital of his own
songs. Quoted in Sir Thomas Beecham,
A Mingled Chime, Ch. 19]

CECIL B. DE MILLE

9 What I have crossed out I didn't like.
What I haven't crossed out I'm dissatisfied with. [Attr. comment on a
script. Quoted in Leslie Halliwell, *The
Filmgoer's Book of Quotes*]

NIGEL DENNIS

10 Most acts of assent require far more
courage than most acts of protest, since
courage is clearly a readiness to risk
self-humiliation. [*Boys and Girls Come
Out to Play*]

LUDWELL DENNY

11 We shall not make Britain's mistake.
Too wise to try to govern the world, we
shall merely own it. Nothing can stop
us. [Written in 1930. *America Con-
quers Britain*]

DR ALAN DENT

12 JAMES AGATE: Can ghosts be angry?
ALAN DENT: What else is there to do
in the shades except take umbrage?
[Quoted in James Agate, *Ego*, 11,
10 Mar. 1934]

DUKE OF DEVONSHIRE

13 [On hearing Baldwin's attack on the
press barons (see 26:17)] Good God,
that's done it. He's lost us the tarts'
vote. [N. Rees, *Quote ... Unquote*,
cites Harold Macmillan, the duke's
son-in-law, as a witness to the two remarks being made in 1931 at a by-
election meeting]

PETER DE VRIES

14 Our church is, I believe, the first split-
level church in America. It has five
rooms and two baths downstairs ...
There is a small worship area at one
end. [*The Mackerel Plaza*, Ch. 1]

15 It is the final proof of God's omni-
potence that he need not exist in order
to save us. [*Ib.* 2]

16 We know the human brain is a device to
keep the ears from grating on one
another. [*Comfort Me with Apples*, Ch.
1]

17 I think I can say my childhood was as
unhappy as the next braggart's. [*Ib.*]

18 They had lived originally in a dinette
apartment in town but had begun to
drift apart and needed more room. [*Ib.*]

19 He believed that the art of conversation
was dead. His own small talk, at any
rate, was bigger than most people's
large. [*Ib.*]

20 'There is no death,' she said. 'No, my
dear lady, but there are funerals.' [*Ib.* 8]

1 ... The inscription *Gott Mit Uns*. I must ceaselessly resolve this legend as a declaration that one had gloves. [*Ib*. 15]

2 Gluttony is an emotional escape, a sign something is eating us. [*Ib*.]

3 Probably a fear we have of facing up to the real issues. Could you say we were guilty of Noel Cowardice? [*Ib*.]

4 This person was a deluge of words and a drizzle of thought. [*Ib*. 17]

5 I wished now that I had gone to the restaurant across the street where the food had at least the merit of being tasteless. [*Ib*. 18]

6 Or look at it this way. Psychoanalysis is a permanent fad. [*Forever Panting*, opening words]

7 We must love one another, yes, yes, that's all true enough, but nothing says we have to like each other. [*The Glory of the Hummingbird*, Ch. 1]

8 Anyone informed that the universe is expanding and contracting in pulsations of eighty billion years has a right to ask, 'What's in it for me?' [*Ib*.]

9 There are times when parenthood seems nothing but feeding the mouth that bites you. [*Tunnel of Love*, Ch. 5]

10 And when I can no longer bear to think of the victims of broken homes, I begin to think of the victims of intact ones. [*Ib*. 8]

11 The value of marriage is not that adults produce children but that children produce adults. [*Ib*. 8]

12 I was thinking that we all learn by experience, but some of us have to go to summer school. [*Ib*. 14]

13 Everybody hates me because I'm so universally liked. [*The Vale of Laughter*, Pt 1, Ch. 1]

14 I am not impressed by the Ivy League establishments. Of course they graduate the best – it's all they'll take, leaving to others the problem of educating the country. They will give you an education the way the banks will give you money – provided you can prove to their satisfaction that you don't need it. [*Ib*. I. 4]

LORD DEWAR

15 There are two classes of pedestrians in these days of reckless motor traffic: the quick and the dead. [Quoted in George Robey, *Looking Back on Life*, Ch. 28]

SERGEI DIAGHILEV

16 Exactly what I wanted. [After the stormy reception of Stravinsky's *Sacre du Printemps*. Quoted in Igor Stravinsky and Robert Craft, *Conversations*]

NEIL DIAMOND

17 Be as a page that aches for a word / Which speaks on a theme that is timeless. [Song: *Be*]

MARLENE DIETRICH

18 Once a woman has forgiven her man, she must not reheat his sins for breakfast. [*Marlene Dietrich's ABC*]

19 Detectives are only policemen with smaller feet. [In Hitchcock film, *Stage Fright*. Script by Whitfield Crok from S. Jepson's *Man Running*]

20 Most women set out to try to change a man, and when they have changed him they do not like him. [Quoted in A. Andrews, *Quotations for Speakers and Writers*]

HOWARD DIETZ

21 That's Entertainment. [Title of song from musical, *The Band Wagon*]

**ISAK DINESEN
(KAREN BLIXEN)**

22 It is a good thing to have a great sorrow. Or should human beings allow Christ to have died on the Cross for the sake of their toothaches? [*Last Tales*, 'Of Hidden Thoughts and Heaven']

23 I wonder if it is really possible to be absolutely truthful when you are alone. Truth, like time, is an idea arising from, and dependent upon, human intercourse. What is the truth about a mountain in Africa that has no name and not even a footpath across it?

[*Seven Gothic Tales*, 'The Roads Round Pisa']

1 What is man, when you come to think upon him, but a minutely set, ingenious machine for turning, with infinite artfulness, the red wine of Shiraz into urine? [*Ib.* 'The Dreamers']

2 She could only hear the things which could be talked about very loudly, and finished her life in an atmosphere of high-shrieked platitudes. [*Ib.*]

3 I pray thee, good Lord, that I may not be married. But if I am to be married, that I may not be a cuckold. But if I am to be a cuckold, that I may not know. But if I am to know, that I may not mind. [*Ib.* 'The Poet'. A saying described as 'the bachelors' prayer']

4 Man and woman are two locked caskets, of which each contains the key to the other. [*Winter Tales*, 'A Consolatory Tale']

5 Pride is faith in the idea that God had, when he made us. A proud man is conscious of the idea, and aspires to realize it. [*Out of Africa* (published under her real name, Karen Blixen)]

WALT DISNEY

6 Supercalifragilisticexpialidocious. [Song from musical film, *Mary Poppins*. Words by Richard M. and Robert B. Sherman]

7 When You Wish Upon a Star. [Title of song in cartoon film *Pinocchio*. Lyric by Ned Washington]

8 Who's Afraid of the Big Bad Wolf? [Title of song in cartoon film, *Silly Symphony*. Lyric and music by Frank E. Churchill and Ann Ronell]

9 Some Day My Prince Will Come. [Title of song in cartoon film, *Snow White*. Lyric by Larry Morey]

10 Whistle While You Work. [Title of song in *ib.* Lyric by Larry Morey]

11 Heigh ho, heigh ho! / It's off to work we go. [Song in *ib.*]

12 There is a natural hootchy-kootchy to a goldfish. [Attr.]

DOM GREGORY DIX

13 It is no accident that the symbol of a bishop is a crook, and the sign of an archbishop is a double-cross. [Quoted by Francis Bown in a letter to *The Times*, 3 Dec. 1977]

MORT DIXON

14 I'm looking over a four-leaf clover / That I overlooked before. [Song: *I'm Looking Over . . .*]

MILOVAN DJILAS

15 The Party line is that there is no Party line. [Quoted in Fitzroy Maclean, *Disputed Barricade*]

16 The New Class. [Title of book]

BONAMY DOBRÉE

17 It is difficult to be humble. Even if you aim at humility, there is no guarantee that when you have attained the state you will not be proud of the feat. [*John Wesley*, opening sentences, Ch. 1]

KEN DODD

18 The trouble with Freud is that he never played the Glasgow Empire Saturday night. [Interview in ATV programme, 'The Laughter Makers'. Quoted in *The Times*, 7 Aug. 1965]

19 How tickled I am! [Running gag in comedy act]

20 What a beautiful day for putting on a kilt, standing upside down in the middle of the road, and saying 'How's that for a table lamp?' [Running gag with many variants. Quoted in John Fisher, *Funny Way to Be a Hero*, 'How Tickled I Am!']

21 My grandad goes to the Darby and Joan club. I don't know what he does there, but he's got three notches on his walking stick. [Quoted in *ib.*]

22 It's ten years since I went out of my mind. I'd never go back. [Quoted in M. Billington, *How Tickled I Am*, Ch. 4]

23 Men's legs have a terribly lonely life – standing in the dark in your trousers all day. [Quoted in the *Guardian*, 7 Apr. 1973]

SIR GERALD DODSON
(Recorder of London)

1 Sometimes people commit bigamy to please the landlady. [*Observer*, 'Sayings of the Week', 18 Oct. 1942]

J. P. DONLEAVY

2 I got disappointed in human nature as well and gave it up because I found it too much like my own. [*Fairy Tales of New York*, 2]

3 I'm all for Christianity but insolence must be put down. [*The Ginger Man*, Ch. 4]

4 But Jesus, when you don't have any money, the problem is food. When you have money, it's sex. When you have both it's health, you worry about getting ruptured or something. If everything is simply jake then you're frightened of death. [*Ib.* 5]

5 When I die I want to decompose in a barrel of porter and have it served in all the pubs in Dublin. I wonder would they know it was me? [*Ib.* 31]

CHARLES DONNELLY

6 There's a valley in Spain called Jarama / It's a place that we all know too well, / For 'tis there that we wasted our manhood / And most of our old age as well. [Sung to the tune of 'Red River Valley' by the International Brigades. Quoted in Hugh Thomas, *The Spanish Civil War*, Ch. 47. Donnelly fell at the Battle of Jarama]

JOHN DOS PASSOS

7 Rumours of peace talks worried him [Pershing]. Peace would ruin his plans for an American army. [*Mr Wilson's War*, Ch. 21]

JAMES DOUGLAS

8 I would rather put a phial of prussic acid in the hands of a healthy boy or girl than the book in question. [Reviewing Radclyffe Hall's *The Well of Loneliness* in the *Sunday Express*]

9 If only men could love each other like dogs, the world would be a paradise.

[From *Sunday Express*. Quoted in M. Bateman, *This England*, selections from the *New Statesman*, Pt I]

NORMAN DOUGLAS

10 It is the drawback of all sea-side places that half the landscape is unavailable for purposes of human locomotion, being covered by useless water. [*Alone*, 'Mentone']

11 Education is a state-controlled manufactory of echoes. [*How about Europe?*]

12 Roman Catholics have shaken off the nightmare of monotheism. Their Trinity is broken up, the Holy Ghost having evaporated in the course of years, as spirits often do. [*Ib.*]

13 There is a beauty in fitness which no art can enhance. [*Siren Land*, 'The Cove of Crapolla']

14 Bouillabaisse is only good because cooked by the French, who, if they cared to try, could produce an excellent and nutritious substitute out of cigar stumps and empty matchboxes. [*Ib.* 'Rain on the Hills']

15 I am what we call a 'Returned Empty'. It is a phrase we apply in England to Colonial bishops who come back from their dioceses. [*South Wind*, Ch. 1]

16 Don Francesco was a fisher of men, and of women. He fished *ad maiorem Dei gloriam*, and for the fun of the thing. It was his way of taking exercise. [*Ib.* 2]

17 You can tell the ideals of a nation by its advertisements. [*Ib.* 6]

18 ... Impoverished them to such an extent that for three consecutive months they could barely afford the most unnecessary luxuries of life. [*Ib.* 20]

SIR ALEC DOUGLAS-HOME
(Earl of Home)

19 As far as the 14th Earl is concerned, I suppose Mr Wilson, when you come to think of it, is the 14th Mr Wilson. [In TV interview, 21 Oct. 1963. See also 359:2]

20 There are two problems in my life. The political ones are insoluble and the

economic ones are incomprehensible. [Speech, Jan. 1964]

LADY CAROLINE DOUGLAS-HOME

1 He is used to dealing with estate workers. I cannot see how anyone can say he is out of touch. [On her father's becoming Prime Minister. Reported by Jon Akass, *Daily Herald*, 21 Oct. 1963]

SIR ARTHUR CONAN DOYLE

2 It is an old maxim of mine that when you have excluded the impossible, whatever remains, however improbable, must be the truth. [*The Beryl Coronet*]

3 You know my method. It is founded upon the observance of trifles. [*The Boscombe Valley Mystery*]

4 Depend upon it, there is nothing so unnatural as the commonplace. [*A Case of Identity*]

5 I can never bring you to realize the importance of sleeves, the suggestiveness of thumb-nails, or the great issues that may hang from a bootlace. [*Ib.*]

6 Crime is common. Logic is rare. Therefore it is upon the logic rather than upon the crime that you should dwell. [*The Copper Beeches*]

7 A man should keep his little brain attic stocked with all the furniture that he is likely to use, and the rest he can put away in the lumber-room of his library, where he can get it if he wants it. [*Five Orange Pips*]

8 I shall be my own police. When I have spun the web they may take the flies, but not before. [*Ib.*]

9 A study of family portraits is enough to convert a man to the doctrine of reincarnation. [*The Hound of the Baskervilles*]

10 A cast of your skull, sir, until the original is available, would be an ornament to any anthropological museum. [*Ib.*]

11 I read nothing except the criminal news and the agony column. The latter is always instructive. [*The Noble Bachelor*]

12 A bicycle certainly, but not *the* bicycle. I am familiar with forty-two impressions left by tyres. [*The Priory School*]

13 My life is spent in one long effort to escape from the commonplaces of existence. [*The Red-Headed League*]

14 Now, Watson, the fair sex is your department. [*The Second Stain*]

15 In an experience of women that extends over many nations and three separate continents, I have never looked upon a face which gave a clearer promise of a refined and sensitive nature. [Dr Watson in *The Sign of Four*]

16 The most winning woman I ever knew was hanged for poisoning three little children for their insurance money. [*Ib.*]

17 I never make exceptions. An exception disproves the rule. [*Ib.*]

18 The unofficial force – the Baker Street irregulars. [*Ib.*]

19 Rather an irregular proceeding ... However the whole thing is irregular, and I suppose we must wink at it. [*Ib.*]

20 When a doctor does go wrong he is the first of criminals. He has nerve and he has knowledge. [*The Speckled Band*]

21 Where there is no imagination there is no horror. [*A Study in Scarlet*]

22 The giant rat of Sumatra, a story for which the world is not yet prepared. [*The Sussex Vampire*]

23 'I am inclined to think –' said I. 'I should do so,' Sherlock Holmes remarked impatiently. [*The Valley of Fear*]

MARGARET DRABBLE

24 Time ... is not consequential; it occurs simultaneously, and distributed through it in meaningless chronology are spots of sorrow, spots of joy. We combine them as we will, as we can best bear them. We make our own ordering. An undue concentration of sorrows is due to bad selection or undue fortitude. [*The Ice Age*, Pt 3]

25 Lord knows what incommunicable small terrors infants go through, unknown to all. We disregard them, we

say they forget, because they have not the words to make us remember ... By the time they learn to speak they have forgotten the details of their complaints, and so we never know. They forget so quickly, we say, because we cannot contemplate the fact that they never forget. [*The Millstone*]

1 Perhaps the rare and simple pleasure of being seen for what one is compensates for the misery of being it. [*A Summer Bird-Cage*, Ch. 7]

RUTH DRAPER

2 Number seven ... What's it meant to be, dear? ... A 'Study'? ... It doesn't say what of? ... Well, that's an easy way out for an artist. [*At an Art Exhibition in Boston*]

3 Aren't the artists brave to go out and paint a sea as rough as that? ... I don't see how he kept his canvas dry. [*Ib.*]

4 Well, perhaps nobody wanted to come – perhaps they'd *all* like to go – but they're *not* going ... Because they're going to behave – and that's what we *all* have to learn in life – we *have* to learn to *behave*! [*The Children's Party*]

5 Now listen, Christopher, you must not cry, darling – just because a lady kicks you ... You *mustn't* cry ... Because in one way or another everybody gets kicked ... Certainly – we *all* get kicked. Daddy gets kicked and *he* doesn't cry ... No – I don't kick him ... But somebody else may. [*Ib.*]

6 Sometimes I think I'll not send him to school – but just let his individuality develop. [*Ib.*]

7 Green bloomers? – Oh, no – green is a lovely shade Any shade that is near to nature is dear to me. [*A Class in Greek Poise*]

8 And when you lie down, your bodies will take beautiful, sinuous curves, relaxed as if on clouds – like the famous Fates on the Parthenon frieze. [*Ib.*]

9 What is one of the lowest forms of life? ... The earth-worm – exactly! And what does he teach us? ... *To stretch – precisely!* ... He's probably the greatest stretcher in the world! [*Ib.*]

10 Do I believe in Platonic friendship? I certainly *do*. I think it's the most *wonderful* relation between a man and a girl ... I mean, to begin with ... I mean, you know where *you* are – and I like knowing where *I* am. [*A Débutante at a Dance*]

11 You see – he's got a perfectly new idea. He never sees his patients. He's not interested in individuals, he prefers to treat a crowd. And he's organized these mass cures ... And he cures thirty thousand people every Thursday. [*Doctors and Diets*]

12 'In the middle of the road.' That's not very poetical. In English I don't think one *could* begin a poem with 'in the middle of the road'. [*The Italian Lesson*]

13 Of course he was a genius, wasn't he – like Shakespeare? ... He and Dante seem to have known *everything* ... known what would always be true ... I imagine we're going to find this *full* of quotations! [*Ib.*]

14 As a matter of fact, you know I am rather sorry you should see the garden now, because, alas! it is not looking at its best. Oh, it doesn't *compare* to what it was last year. [*Showing the Garden*]

15 And as for my poor *Glubjullas*, they never came up at all! ... I can't think why, because I generally have great luck with my *Glubjullas*. [*Ib.*]

16 It's going to give me a little *vista*, which will be rather exciting, I think! I shall see more sky – which is always desirable. I hope I shall see the horizon – which would be *very* jolly! ... Then, I shall have a sense of space – of distance ... A little glimpse into the beyond, as it were. [*Ib.*]

HUGH DRUMMOND

17 Ladies and Gentlemen I give you a toast. It is 'Absinthe makes the tart grow fonder.' [Quoted in Seymour Hicks, *Vintage Years*]

ALEXANDER DUBČEK

18 Socialism with a Human Face. [Motto of the Prague Spring of 1968]

AL DUBIN

1 Tiptoe through the tulips with me. [Song: *Tiptoe Through the Tulips* from the musical, *Gold Diggers of Broadway*]

2 You may not be an angel / 'Cause angels are so few, / But until the day that one comes along / I'll string along with you. [*Twenty Million Sweethearts*]

GEORGES DUHAMEL

3 Courtesy is not dead – it has merely taken refuge in Great Britain. [*Observer*, 'Sayings of Our Times', 31 May 1953]

JOHN FOSTER DULLES

4 If E D C [European Defence Community] should fail, the United States might be compelled to make an 'agonizing reappraisal' of its basic policy. [Speech at North Atlantic Council in Paris, 14 Dec. 1953]

5 If you are scared to go to the brink, you are lost. [Quoted in *Life* magazine, 16 Jan. 1956]

6 An obsolete conception, and except under very exceptional circumstances it is an immoral and short-sighted conception. [On neutralism, speech at Iowa State College, 9 Jun. 1956]

7 The world is divided into two groups of people: the Christian anti-Communists, and the others. [Attr.]

DAPHNE DU MAURIER

8 Last night I dreamt I went to Manderley again. [*Rebecca*, Ch. 1]

9 It ... was full of dry rot. An unkind visitor said the only reason Menabilly still stood was that the woodworm obligingly held hands. [In an interview]

AMERIGO DUMINI

10 My name is Dumini, twelve assassinations. [Quoted in George Seldes, *Sawdust Caesar*]

ELAINE DUNDY

11 I was merely a disinterested spectator at the Banquet of Life. [*The Dud Avocado*, Ch. 1]

12 I hate champagne more than anything in the world next to Seven-up. [*Ib.*]

13 I find I always have to write SOMETHING on a steamed mirror. [*Ib.*]

14 It was one of those nights when the air is blood temperature and it's impossible to tell where you leave off and it begins. [*Ib. 9*]

15 I mean, the question actors most often get asked is how they can bear saying the same things over and over again night after night, but God knows the answer to *that* is, don't we all *anyway*; might as well get paid for it. [*Ib.*]

DOUGLAS DUNN

16 A dilettante is a product of where wealth and literature meet. [Review in the *Listener*, 3 Feb. 1977]

FINLEY PETER DUNNE

17 Vice ... is a creature of such heejus mien ... that the more ye see it th' better ye like it. [*The Crusade Against Vice*]

JAMES DUNNE

18 The English and the Irish are very much alike, except that the Irish are more so. [In conversation, during the Irish Troubles]

19 The quiet Irishman is about as harmless as a powder magazine built over a match factory. [*Ib.*]

T. E. DUNVILLE

20 A little boy; / a pair of skates; / broken ice; / Heaven's gates! [Droll music-hall song. Quoted in John Fisher, *Funny Way To Be a Hero*, 'The Little Dog Laughed ...']

WILL DURANT

21 The finger that turns the dial rules the air. [*What is Civilization?*]

LEO DUROCHER
(Manager of Brooklyn baseball team, 1951–54)

1 Nice guys finish last. [Attr. by Denis Brogan, *Observer*, 16 May 1965]

LAURENCE DURRELL

2 O men of the Marmion class, sons of the free. [*Mythology*]

3 The city, half-imagined (yet wholly real), begins and ends in us, lodged in our memory. [*Balthazar*, Pt I]

4 I love to feel events overlapping each other, crawling over one another like wet crabs in a basket. [*Ib.*]

5 No one can go on being a rebel too long without turning into an autocrat. [*Ib.* II]

6 BRITAIN TO BUY SERBIAN TIT-PROPS [*Esprit de Corps*, 'Flying the Flag']

7 Somewhere between Calabria and Corfu, the blue really begins. [*Prospero's Cell*, Ch. 1]

8 Poggio's, where people go to watch each other watch each other. [*Tunc*, Ch. 1]

9 No more about sex, it's too boring. Everyone's got one. Nastiness is a real stimulant though – but poor honest sex, like dying, should be a private matter. [*Ib.*]

10 I have always tried to arrange my poems for balanced readability – like one does a vase of flowers. How silly it would be to arrange the flowers in the order of their picking. [On the chronology of his poems. *Selected Poems*, Introduction]

11 History is the endless repetition of the wrong way of living, and it'll start again tomorrow, if it's moved from here today. [In the *Listener*, 20 Apr. 1978]

12 Our cathedrals are like abandoned computers now, but they used to be prayer factories once. [*Ib.*]

13 A poem is what happens when an anxiety meets a technique. [Reported remark]

ELENORA DUSE

14 To save the Theatre, the Theatre must be destroyed, the actors and actresses all die of the Plague ... they make art impossible. [Quoted in A. Symons, *Studies in Seven Arts*]

MRS DYKSTRA

15 He [Thomas E. Dewey] is just about the nastiest little man I've ever known. He struts sitting down. [Quoted in J. T. Patterson, *Mr Republican*]

BOB DYLAN

16 But to love outside the law, you must be honest. [Song: *Absolutely Sweet Marie*]

17 Beware of bathroom walls that've not been written on. [Song: *Advice for Geraldine on Her Miscellaneous Birthday*. See also 103:13]

18 'There must be some way out of here,' said the joker to the thief, / 'There's too much confusion, I can't get no relief.' [Song: *All Along the Watchtower*]

19 How many roads must a man walk down / Before you call him a man? [Song: *Blowin' in the Wind*]

20 Yes, 'n' how many years can some people exist / Before they're allowed to be free? / Yes, 'n' how many times can a man turn his head, / Pretending he just doesn't see? / The answer, my friend, is blowin' in the wind. [*Ib.*]

21 A Hard Rain's A-Gonna Fall. [Title of song]

22 Oh God said to Abraham, 'Kill me a son.' / Abe says, 'Man, you must be puttin' me on.' [Song: *Highway 61 Revisited*]

23 He not busy being born / Is busy dying. [Song: *It's Alright, Ma (I'm Only Bleeding)*]

24 But even the president of the United States / Sometimes must have / To stand naked. [*Ib.*]

25 Money doesn't talk, it swears. [*Ib.*]

26 She takes just like a woman, yes, she does / She makes love just like a woman,

yes, she does / And she aches just like a woman / But she breaks just like a girl. [Song: *Just Like a Woman*]

1 How does it feel / To be without a home / Like a complete unknown / Like a rolling stone? [Song: *Like a Rolling Stone*]

2 Love Is Just a Four-letter Word. [Title of song]

3 She knows there's no success like failure / And that failure's no success at all. [Song: *Love Minus Zero/No Limit*]

4 Hey! Mr Tambourine Man, play a song for me. / I'm not sleepy and there is no place I'm going to. [Song: *Mr Tambourine Man*]

5 Ah, but I was so much older then, / I'm younger than that now. [Song: *My Back Pages*. See also 333:2]

6 Keep a clean nose / Watch the plain clothes / You don't need a weatherman / To know which way the wind blows. [Song: *Subterranean Homesick Blues*]

7 Twenty years of schoolin' / And they put you on the day shift. [*Ib.*]

8 I'll let you be in my dreams if I can be in yours. [Song: *Talkin' World War III Blues*]

9 Come mothers and fathers / Throughout the land / And don't criticize / What you can't understand. [Song: *The Times They Are A-Changin*]

10 I don't call myself a poet, because I don't like the word. I'm a trapeze artist. [Quoted in J. Green, *The Book of Rock Quotes*]

11 [When asked whether he knew what his songs were about] Yeah, some of them are about ten minutes long, others five or six. [In interview, *c.* 1965]

E

CHARLES EAMES

1 You wouldn't say an axe handle has style to it. It has beauty, and appropriateness of form, and a 'this-is-how-it-should-be-ness'. But it has no style because it has no mistakes. Style reflects one's idiosyncrasies. Your personality is apt to show more to the degree that you did not solve the problem than to the degree that you did. [Quoted in Laurence J. Peter, *Peter's Quotations*]

MAX EASTMAN

2 I don't know why it is that we are in such a hurry to get up when we fall down. You might think we would lie there and rest awhile. [*The Enjoyment of Laughter*]

RICHARD EBERHART

3 Then the eighty-year-old lady with a sparkle, / A Cambridge lady, hearing of the latest / Suicide, said to her friend, turning off / TV for tea, 'Well, my dear, doesn't it seem / A little like going where you haven't been invited?' [*How It Is*]

LORD ECCLES

4 A small acquaintance with history shows that all Governments are selfish and the French Governments more selfish than most. [*Observer*, 'Sayings of the Year', 29 Dec. 1962]

SIR ARTHUR EDDINGTON

5 Electrical force is defined as something which causes motion of electrical charge; an electrical charge is something which exerts electric force. [*The Nature of the Physical World*]

6 Matter is what Mr X knows. [*Science and the Unseen World*]

7 When Dr Watson watches rats in mazes, what he knows, apart from difficult inferences, are certain events in himself. [*Ib.*]

8 We used to think that if we knew one, we knew two, because one and one are two. We are finding that we must learn a great deal more about 'and'. [Quoted in A. L. Mackay, *The Harvest of a Quiet Eye*]

SIR ANTHONY EDEN

9 I am wondering whether there is anything more I could have done to prevent this. [After Chamberlain's broadcast in Sep. 1939 announcing that war had been declared. Quoted in Lewis Broad, *Sir Anthony Eden*, Ch. 13]

10 We are living in slightly exceptional times. [1944. *Observer*, 'Sayings of Our Times', 31 May 1953]

11 REPORTER: If Mr Stalin dies, what will be the effect on international affairs? A.E.: That is a good question for you to ask, not a wise question for me to answer. [*Ib.* Conversation on board *Queen Elizabeth*, 4 Mar. 1953]

12 Everybody is always in favour of general economy and particular expenditure. [*Observer*, 'Sayings of the Week', 17 Jun. 1956]

13 We are not at war with Egypt. We are in an armed conflict. [Speech in House of Commons, 4 Nov. 1956]

LADY CLARISSA EDEN

14 During the last few weeks I have felt that the Suez Canal was flowing through my drawing room. [At time of Suez crisis, 1956]

DUKE OF EDINBURGH

1 I include 'pidgin-English' ... even though I am referred to in that splendid language as 'Fella belong Mrs Queen'. [Speech to English-Speaking Union Conference at Ottawa, 29 Oct. 1958]

2 There are many things which we do which don't seem to have any particular point or tangible result. Take today; a lot of time and energy has been spent on arranging for you to listen to me take a long time to declare open a building which everybody knows is open already. [Speech at Opening of Chesterfield College of Technology, 21 Nov. 1958]

3 Just at this moment we are suffering a national defeat comparable to any lost military campaign, and what is more it is self-inflicted ... I think it is about time we pulled our finger out. [Speech to businessmen, 17 Oct. 1961]

4 The rest of the world most certainly does not owe us a living. [Ib.]

5 I never see any home cooking. All I get is fancy stuff. [Observer, 'Sayings of the Week', Dec. 1962]

6 All money nowadays seems to be produced with a natural homing instinct for the Treasury. [Observer, 'Sayings of the Week', 26 May 1963]

7 The biggest waste of water in the country by far. You spend half a pint and flush two gallons. [Attr. in Speech, 1965]

THOMAS EDISON

8 They say Wilson has blundered. Perhaps he has but I notice he usually blunders forward. [Quoted in John dos Passos, Mr Wilson's War, Ch. 2, sect. x]

IRWIN EDMAN

9 Education is the process of casting false pearls before real swine. [Quoted in Frank Muir, The Frank Muir Book]

KING EDWARD VII

10 You can tell when you have crossed the frontier into Germany because of the badness of the coffee. [Quoted in Lord Haldane, Autobiography]

11 Let me introduce you to the last king of England. [To Lord Haldane on introducing him to the Prince of Wales – afterwards George V. Quoted in Dudley Sommer, Haldane of Cloan, Ch. 15]

KING EDWARD VIII

12 There is no central machinery to provide a substitute for the good neighbour. [1932. Observer, 'Sayings of Our Times', 31 May 1953]

13 Something must be done. [Said during tour of unemployment areas in South Wales]

14 But you must believe me when I tell you that I have found it impossible to carry the heavy burden of responsibility and to discharge my duties as King as I would wish to do, without the help and support of the woman I love. [Abdication speech, 11 Dec. 1936]

ILYA EHRENBURG

15 The Thaw. [Title of book]

ALBERT EINSTEIN

16 Science without religion is lame, religion without science is blind. [Out of My Later Years]

17 Nationalism is an infantile disease. It is the measles of mankind. [The World As I See It]

18 If you want to find out anything from the theoretical physicists about the methods they use, I advise you to stick closely to one principle: Don't listen to their words fix your attention on their deeds. [Ib.]

19 I know why there are so many people who love chopping wood. In this activity one immediately sees the results. [Quoted in Carl Seelig, Albert Einstein, Ch. 4]

20 I don't believe in mathematics. [Said to Gustave Ferrière. Quoted in ib. 5]

21 God is subtle but he is not malicious. [Quip carved above the fireplace of Fine Hall, the Mathematical Institute of Princeton University. Ib. 8]

1 I can, if the worst comes to the worst, still realize that the good Lord may have created a world in which there are no natural laws. In short, a chaos. But that there should be statistical laws with definite solutions, i.e. laws that compel the good Lord to throw the dice in each individual case, I find highly disagreeable. [To James Franck. Quoted in *ib*]

2 The release of atom power has changed everything except our way of thinking, and thus we are being driven unarmed towards a catastrophe . . . The solution of this problem lies in the heart of humankind. [Speech to National Commission of Nuclear Scientists, May 1946. Quoted in *ib.*]

3 If only I had known, I should have become a watchmaker. [Of his making the atom bomb possible. Quoted in *New Statesman*, 16 Apr. 1965]

4 I cannot believe that God plays dice with the cosmos. [*Observer*, 'Sayings of the Week', 5 Apr. 1953]

5 You have got the impression that contemporary physics is based on concepts somewhat analogous to the smile of the absent cat. [Comment on Viscount Samuel, *Essay in Physics*. Quoted in John Bowle, *Viscount Samuel*, Ch. 19]

6 As far as the laws of mathematics refer to reality, they are not certain, and as far as they are certain, they do not refer to reality. [Quoted in F. Capra, *The Tao of Physics*, Ch. 2]

7 Art is the expression of the profoundest thoughts in the simplest way. [Quoted in W. Neil, *Concise Dictionary of Religious Quotations*]

8 The process of scientific discovery is, in effect, a continuous flight from wonder. [Quoted in Laurence J. Peter, *Peter's Quotations*]

9 Everything should be made as simple as possible, but not simpler. [Quoted in *Reader's Digest*, Oct. 1977]

10 Common sense is the collection of prejudices acquired by age eighteen. [Quoted in *Scientific American*, Feb. 1976]

11 A theory can be proved by experiment; but no path leads from experiment to the birth of a theory. [Quoted in the *Sunday Times*, 18 Jul. 1976]

LOREN EISELEY

12 Every man contains within himself a ghost continent – a place circled as warily as Antarctica was circled two hundred years ago by Captain James Cook. [*The Unexpected Universe*, Ch. 1]

PRESIDENT EISENHOWER

13 There is one thing about being President – nobody can tell you when to sit down. [*Observer*, 'Sayings of the Week', 9 Aug. 1953]

14 Whatever America hopes to bring to pass in this world must first come to pass in the heart of America. [Inaugural Address, 1953]

15 The military-industrial complex. [Farewell address as President, 1959]

16 A bigger bang for a buck. [Quoted in D. Halberstam, *The Best and the Brightest*]

SIR EDWARD ELGAR

17 Music is in the air – you simply take as much of it as you want. [Attr.]

MIRCEA ELIADE

18 To be, or rather, to become, a man means to be 'religious' . . . The 'total man' is never completely desacralized, and one even doubts that this is possible . . . no living, normal man can be reduced to his conscious, rational activity. [*The Quest*, Preface]

T. S. ELIOT

19 The red-eyed scavengers are creeping / From Kentish Town and Golder's Green. [*A Cooking Egg*]

20 Over buttered scones and crumpets / Weeping, weeping multitudes / Droop in a hundred A.B.C.s [*Ib.*]

21 Here I am, an old man in a dry month, / Being read to by a boy. [*Gerontion*]

22 In the juvescence of the year / Came Christ the tiger. [*Ib.*]

1 An old man in a draughty house /
Under a windy knob. [*Ib.*]

2 After such knowledge, what forgiveness? Think now / History has many
cunning passages, contrived corridors /
And issues. [*Ib.*]

3 Unnatural vices / are fathered by our
heroism. [*Ib.*]

4 Tenants of the house, / Thoughts of a
dry brain in a dry season. [*Ib.*]

5 The hippopotamus's day / Is passed in
sleep; at night he hunts; / God works in
a mysterious way – / The Church can
feed and sleep at once. [*The Hippopotamus*]

6 To hear the latest Pole / transmit the
Preludes, through his hair and finger-
tips. [*Portrait of a Lady*]

7 Discuss the late events, / Correct our
watches by the public clocks. / Then sit
for half an hour and drink our bocks.
[*Ib.*]

8 Yet with these April sunsets, that somehow recall / My buried life, and Paris in
the Spring, / I feel immeasurably at
peace, and find the world / To be
wonderful and youthful, after all. [*Ib.*]

9 You will see me any morning in the park
/ Reading the comics and the sporting
page. / Particularly I remark / An English countess goes upon the stage. [*Ib*]

10 My smile falls heavily among the *bric-
à-brac*. [*Ib.*]

11 The worlds revolve like ancient women/
Gathering fuel in vacant lots. [*Preludes*]

12 Midnight shakes the memory / As a
madman shakes a dead geranium.
[*Rhapsody on a Windy Night*]

13 'Put your shoes at the door, sleep, prepare for life.' / The last twist of the
knife. [*Ib.*]

14 The host with someone indistinct /
Converses at the door apart, / The
nightingales are singing near / The
Convent of the Sacred Heart. [*Sweeney
among the Nightingales*]

15 Uncorseted, her friendly bust / Gives
promise of pneumatic bliss. [*Whispers
of Immortality*]

16 And the wind shall say 'Here were
decent godless people; / Their only
monument the asphalt road / And a
thousand lost golf balls.' [*The Rock*,
Pt. 1]

17 All cases are unique, and very similar to
others. [*The Cocktail Party*, Act II]

18 Yet we have gone on living, / Living and
partly living. [*Murder in the Cathedral*,
Pt I]

19 Only / the fool, fixed in his folly, may
think / He can turn the wheel on which
he turns. [*Ib.*]

20 Clear the air! clean the sky! wash the
wind! take stone from stone and wash
them. [*ib.* II]

21 We like to appear in the newspapers, /
So long as we are in the right column.
[*The Family Reunion*, Act I]

22 He [Hardy] wrote sometimes over-
poweringly well, but always very carelessly; at times his style touches
sublimity without ever having passed
through the stage of being good. [*After
Strange Gods*, quoted in *Dictionary of
Biographical Quotation*, ed. J. Wintle
and R. Kenin]

23 We can say of Shakespeare, that never
has a man turned so little knowledge to
such great account. [*The Classics and
the Man of Letters*, lecture]

24 I do not wish to be accused of inventing
a new heresy to the effect that salvation
depends on getting a first in classics.
[*Ib.*]

25 A good deal of confusion could be
avoided, if we refrained from setting
before the group, what can be the aim
only of the individual; and before
society as a whole, what can be the aim
only of a group. [*Mass Civilization and
Minority Culture*]

26 [Wit] involves, probably, a recognition,
implicit in the expression of every experience, of other kinds of experience
that are possible. [*Selected Essays*,
'Andrew Marvell']

27 It is our business, as readers of literature, to know what we like. It is our
business as Christians, as *well* as readers
of literature, to know what we ought to

109

like. It is our business as honest men not to assume that what we like is what we ought to like. [*Ib*. 'Charles Whibley']

1 The majority of poems one outgrows and outlives, as one outgrows and outlives the majority of human passions. Dante's is one of those that one can only just hope to grow up to at the end of life. [*Ib*. 'Dante']

2 Dryden is distinguished, principally, by his *poetic* ability. [*Ib*. 'John Dryden']

3 No poet, no artist of any sort, has his complete meaning alone. His significance, his appreciation is the appreciation of his relation to the dead poets and artists. [*Ib*. 'Tradition and the Individual Talent']

4 We can only say that it appears likely that poets in our civilization, as it exists at present, must be *difficult*. [*Ib*. 'The Metaphysical Poets']

5 The majority of people live below the level of belief or doubt. It takes application and a kind of genius to believe anything, and to believe anything . . . will probably become more and more difficult as time goes on. [*The Enemy*, Jan. 1927]

6 I confess that I am seldom interested in what he [Ezra Pound] is saying, but only in the way he says it. ['Isolated Superiority', article in *The Dial*, Jan. 1928]

7 The more perfect the artist, the more completely separate in him will be the man who suffers and the mind which creates. [Quoted in 'Palinurus' (Cyril Connolly), *The Unquiet Grave*]

QUEEN ELIZABETH, THE QUEEN MOTHER

8 My favourite programme is 'Mrs Dale's Diary'. I try never to miss it because it is the only way of knowing what goes on in a middle-class family. [From the *Evening News*. Quoted in M. Bateman, *This England*, selections from the *New Statesman*, Pt IV]

9 [When the National Anthem was played at a televised Cup Final] Oh, do turn it off, it's so embarrassing unless one is there – like hearing the Lord's

Prayer when playing canasta. [Quoted in A. Andrews, *Quotations for Speakers and Writers*]

ALF ELLERTON

10 Belgium Put the Kibosh on the Kaiser. [Title of song. Music by Mark Sheridan]

DUKE ELLINGTON

11 Saddest tale told on land or sea / Is the tale they told / When they told the truth on me. [*Saddest Tale*]

MAXINE ELLIOTT

12 I would not marry God. [Cable when her engagement was rumoured. Quoted in D. Forbes Robertson, *Maxine*]

HENRY HAVELOCK ELLIS

13 What we call progress is the exchange of one nuisance for another nuisance. [Quoted in Sagittarius and George, *The Perpetual Pessimist*]

EDWARD ELLSWORTH

14 Force one day was served to him. / Since then they've called him Sunny Jim. [Advertisement for Force, a breakfast cereal]

G. R. ELTON

15 The future is dark, the present burdensome, only the past, dead and buried, bears contemplation. [*The Practice of History*, Preface]

PAUL ÉLUARD

16 *Adieu tristesse / Bonjour tristesse / Tu es inscrite dans les lignes du plafond.* – Farewell sadness, / good day sadness. / You are written in the lines on the ceiling. [*La Vie immédiate*]

17 *Qui n'a pas vu les ruines du ghetto / Ne connaît pas le destin de son corps.* – Anyone who has not seen the ruins of the ghetto does not know the destiny of his body. [*Varsovie la ville fantastique*]

WILLIAM EMPSON

1 Johnson could see no bicycle would go; / 'You bear yourself and the machine as well.' [*Invitation to June*]

2 Slowly the poison the whole blood stream fills. / The waste remains, the waste remains and kills. [*Missing Dates*]

3 But Alice showed her pup Ulysses' bough / Well from behind a thistle, wise with dread. [*The Scales*]

4 There was a period of the cult of Pure Sound when infants were read passages from Homer, and then questioned as to their impressions, not unlike Darwin playing the trombone to his French beans. [*Seven Types of Ambiguity*, Ch. 1]

D. J. ENRIGHT

5 What odds / Whether the couples walk on the campus and look at / The moon or walk on the moon and look at the earth? / Just so long as there's somewhere left to walk, to sit, to cycle, / And something left to look at. [*Addictions*]

SUSAN ERTZ

6 Millions long for immortality who do not know what to do with themselves on a rainy Sunday afternoon. [Quoted in A. Andrews, *Quotations for Speakers and Writers*. See also 166:12]

SENATOR SAM ERVIN

7 That is not executive privilege. It is executive poppycock. [During the Watergate hearings, 1973. Quoted in McCrystal *et al.*, *Watergate: the Full Inside Story*]

SERGEY ESENIN

8 It is no new thing in this world to die, and no newer, of course, to live. [Quoted in K. Paustovsky, *The Restless Years*]

RENÉ ETIEMBLE

9 Parlez-vous Franglais? [Title of book]

SIR ARTHUR EVANS

10 I come back every fifty years [On revisiting the prison of Ragusa in old age. Quoted in Joan Evans, *Time and Chance*, Ch. 20]

DAME EDITH EVANS

11 When a woman behaves like a man, why doesn't she behave like a nice man? [*Observer*, 'Sayings of the Week', 30 Sep. 1956]

12 I may never have been very pretty but I was jolly larky and that's what counts in the theatre. [Quoted in *Radio Times*, 14–20 Aug. 1976]

13 Death is my neighbour now. [In a BBC radio interview, a week before her death, 14 Oct. 1976]

EVENING STANDARD

14 My own personal reaction is that most ballets would be quite delightful if it were not for the dancing. [Quoted in M. Bateman, *This England*, selections from the *New Statesman*, Pt. I]

KURT EWALD

15 Our family is not yet so good as to be degenerating. [*My Little Boy*]

F

FRANTZ FANON

1 However painful it may be for me to accept this conclusion, I am obliged to state it: for the black man there is only one destiny. And it is white. [*Black Skin, White Masks*, Introduction]

2 When people like me, they tell me it is in spite of my colour. When they dislike me, they point out that it is not because of my colour. Either way, I am locked into the infernal circle. [*Ib.* Ch. 1]

3 All forms of exploitation are identical because all of them are applied against the same 'object': man. [*Ib.* 3]

4 The dreams of the native are always of muscular prowess ... During the period of colonization, the native never stops achieving his freedom from nine in the evening until six in the morning. [*The Wretched of the Earth*, Ch. 1]

5 The *fellah*, the unemployed man, the starving native, does not lay a claim to the truth; they do not *say* that they represent the truth, for they *are* the truth. [*Ib.*]

6 In guerrilla war the struggle no longer concerns the place where you are, but the place where you are going. Each fighter carries his warring country between his toes. [*Ib.* 2]

7 The native intellectual, who takes up arms to defend his nation's legitimacy and who wants to bring proofs to bear out that legitimacy, who is willing to strip himself naked to study the history of his body, is obliged to dissect the heart of his body. [*Ib.* 4]

8 When I search for Man in the technique and the style of Europe, I see only a succession of negations of man, and an avalanche of murders. [*Ib.* 6]

ELEANOR FARJEON

9 The night will never stay, / The night will still go by, / Though with a million stars / You pin it to the sky; / Though you bind it with the blowing wind / And buckle it with the moon, / The night will slip away / Like sorrow or a tune. [*The Night Will Never Stay*]

HERBERT FARJEON

10 I've danced with a man, who's danced with a girl, who's danced with the Prince of Wales. [*Picnic*]

KING FAROUK

11 There will soon be only five kings left – the Kings of England, Diamonds, Hearts, Spades and Clubs. [Said to Lord Boyd-Orr, 1951]

ROBERT FARQUHARSON

12 Look at her! A moth entirely surrounded by candles. [Of BBC actress amidst admiring males.]

J. G. FARRELL

13 The Magistrate ... had the red hair and ginger whiskers of the born atheist. [*The Siege of Krishnapur*, Pt I, Ch. 1]

WILLIAM FAULKNER

14 The Swiss who are not a people so much as a neat clean quite solvent business. [*Intruder in the Dust*, Ch. 7]

15 No man can cause more grief than that one clinging blindly to the vices of his ancestors. [*Ib.*, Ch. 3]

16 Between grief and nothing I will take grief. [*The Wild Palms*]

17 Maybe the only thing worse than having to give gratitude constantly all the time,

is having to accept it. [*Requiem For a Nun*, Act II, sc. i]

1 If a writer has to rob his mother, he will not hesitate; the 'Ode to a Grecian Urn' is worth any number of old ladies. [Quoted in A. Andrews, *Quotations for Speakers and Writers*]

JEAN FAYARD

2 If the French were to play cricket they would all want to be 'batsmen' – the cynosure of all eyes at the same time, just as nearly all of them want to be Prime Minister. [In A. Synge (ed.), *Strangers' Gallery*]

VIC FEATHER (Lord Feather)

3 Industrial relations are like sexual relations. It's better between two consenting parties. [Quoted in the *Guardian Weekly*, 8 Aug. 1976]

JULES FEIFFER

4 Writing, I explained, was mainly an attempt to out-argue one's past; to present events in such a light that battles lost in life were either won on paper or held to a draw. [*Ackroyd*, '1964, May 7']

5 No one walks into a party without having a far better party going on inside his head. Every party is going to be that party until we get there. So the key to the boredom and tension at parties is that no one wants to be at the party he's at, he wants to be at the party he's missing. [*Ib*. '1965, February 15']

6 Artists can colour the sky red because they *know* it's blue. Those of us who aren't artists must colour things the way they really are or people might think we're stupid. [*Crawling Arnold*]

7 I know she's alive. I saw her lip curl. [*Sick, Sick, Sick*]

8 There *are* no more policemen. Only police dogs. We've eliminated the middle man. [*Observer*, 7 Jul. 1963]

9 At sixteen I was stupid, confused, insecure and indecisive. At twenty-five I was wise, self-confident, prepossessing and assertive. At forty-five I am stupid, confused, insecure and indecisive. Who would have supposed that maturity is only a short break in adolescence? [Caption to drawing, *Observer*, 3 Feb. 1974]

10 Christ died for our sins. Dare we make his martyrdom meaningless by not committing them? [Quoted in Laurence J. Peter, *Peter's Quotations*]

MARTY FELDMAN

11 Comedy, like sodomy, is an unnatural act. [Quoted in *The Times*, 9 Jun. 1969]

EDNA FERBER

12 Being an old maid is like death by drowning, a really delightful sensation after you cease to struggle. [Quoted in R. E. Drennan, *Wit's End*, 'Completing the Circle']

RACHEL FERGUSON

13 The kind of actress Agate would call husky and orchidaceous [*A Child in the Theatre*. Quoted in James Agate, *Ego 1*, 2, 1933]

LAWRENCE FERLINGHETTI

14 And he is the mad eye of the fourth person singular / of which no body speaks. [*He*]

KATHLEEN FERRIER

15 Now I'll have *eine kleine Pause*. [Quoted in Gerald Moore, *Am I Too Loud?*, as the last words he heard her speak, not long before her death]

'MICHAEL FIELD'
(Katherine Bradley and Edith Cooper)

16 His [George Moore's] smile is like sunshine on putty. [*Journals*]

GABRIEL FIELDING

17 It's not what men fight for. They fight in the last resort to impress their mothers. [*The Birthday King*, Ch. 3]

113

GRACIE FIELDS

1 Wish Me Luck as You Wave Me Good-bye. [Title of song; words by Phil Park]

2 What Can You Give a Nudist On His Birthday? [Title of song]

3 We're going to string old Hitler / From the very highest bough / Of the biggest aspidistra in the world. [Song: *The Biggest Aspidistra*]

W. C. FIELDS

4 It's a funny old world – a man's lucky if he gets out of it alive. [In film, *You're Telling Me*]

5 I must have a drink of breakfast. [Quoted in Leslie Halliwell, *The Film-goer's Book of Quotes*]

6 If at first you don't succeed, try again. Then quit. No use being a damn fool about it. [Quoted in *ib.*]

7 [When asked why he never drank water] Fish fuck in it. [Quoted in *ib.*]

8 We lived for days on nothing but food and water. [Quoted in Laurence J. Peter, *Peter's Quotations*]

9 I was in love with a beautiful blonde once – she drove me to drink – 'tis the one thing I'm indebted to her for. [Quoted in A. Spiegelman and B. Schneider, *Whole Grains*]

10 Women are like elephants to me; I like to look at them, but I wouldn't want to own one. [Quoted in *ib.*]

11 On the whole I would rather be in Philadelphia. [Tombstone epitaph]

12 Anybody who hates children and dogs can't be all bad. [Quoted in *Radio Times*, 12 Aug. 1965, but Leo Rosten claimed to have said it to Fields at Hollywood banquet, 1938]

13 Never Give a Sucker an Even Break. [Film title]

EDWARD A. FILENE

14 Why shouldn't the American people take half my money from me? I took all of it from them. [Quoted in A. M. Schlesinger Jr, *The Coming of the New Deal*, Pt 7, Ch. 2, sect. iv]

RONALD FIRBANK

15 'O God, help me, Dear,' she prayed, 'this little once, O Lord. For Thou knowest my rights.' [*Caprice*, III]

16 'I hear it's the Hebrew in Heaven, sir – Spanish is seldom spoken,' he exclaimed seraphically. [*The Eccentricities of Cardinal Pirelli*, Ch. 8. See also 95:12]

17 She made a ravishing corpse. [*Ib.*]

18 'I've never travelled,' Dona Consolation blandly confessed, 'but I dare say, dear, you can't judge Egypt by Aïda.' [*Ib.* 9]

19 'She reads at such a pace,' she complained, 'and when I asked her where she had learnt to read so quickly she replied "On the screens at cinemas."' [*The Flower Beneath the Foot*, Ch. 1]

20 His Weariness the Prince entered the room in all his tinted Orders. [*Ib.*]

21 Beneath the strain of expectation even the little iced sugar cakes upon the tea-table looked green with worry. [*Ib.* 3]

22 Mrs Barleymoon's position, as a captain's widow with means, unquestionably came before Mrs Montgomery's, who drew a salary and hadn't often an h. [*Ib.* 4]

23 I feel his books are all written in hotels with the bed unmade at the back of the chair. [*Ib.*]

24 I remember the average curate at home was something between a eunuch and a snigger. [*Ib.*]

25 'Basta!' his master replied with all the brilliant glibness of the Berlitz-school. [*Ib.* 5]

26 But I'm so sensitive . . . I seem to *know* when I talk to a man the colour of his braces . . . ! I say to myself: 'Yours are violet . . .' [*Ib.*]

27 She looks at other women as though she would inhale them. [*Ib.*]

28 It is said, I believe, that to behold the Englishman at his *best* one should watch him play tip-and-run. [*Ib.* 14]

29 I always like to be on the right side of my profile! [*Prancing Nigger*, Ch. 10]

30 To be sympathetic without discrimination is so very debilitating. [*Vainglory*, Ch. 7]

1 All millionaires love a baked apple. [*Ib.* 13]

2 Valmouth, with its ancient bridge and great stone church, that from the country had the scheming look of an ex-cathedral. [*Valmouth*, Ch. I]

3 She stands, I fear, poor thing, now, for something younger than she looks. [*Ib.*]

4 Love in the East, Mrs Yaj, I presume, is *only* feasible indoors? [*Ib.* 3]

5 'I know of no joy,' she airily began, 'greater than a cool white dress after the sweetness of confession.' [*Ib.* 4]

6 And *so* poorly and *so* run down. She says her blood is nothing but rose-water. [*Ib.*]

7 There was really no joy in pouring out one's sins while he sat assiduously picking his nose. [*Ib.* 6]

8 'Heaven help me,' she prayed, 'to be decorative and to do right.' [Quoted in W. H. Auden, *A Certain World*]

LOUIS FISCHER

9 But you can burn your fingers on your own chestnuts. [Comment on Stalin's 'burning chestnuts' speech, *The Nation*, 6 Jan. 1940]

H. A. L. FISHER

10 Men wiser and more learned than I have discerned in history a plot, a rhythm, a predetermined pattern. These harmonies are concealed from me. I can see only one emergency following on another. [*A History of Europe*, Preface]

11 W.C. [Winston Churchill] is a bigger danger than the Germans by a long way in what is just now imminent in the Dardanelles. [Letter to Bonar Law, May 1915. Quoted in Robert Blake, *The Unknown Prime Minister*]

CLYDE FITCH

12 The Woman in the Case [Title of play]

ALBERT H. FITZ

13 You are my honey, honeysuckle, I am the bee. [Song: *The Honeysuckle and the Bee*. Music by W. H. Penn]

F. SCOTT FITZGERALD

14 She had once been a Catholic, but discovering that priests were infinitely more attentive when she was in process of losing or regaining faith in Mother Church, she maintained an enchantingly wavering attitude. [*This Side of Paradise*, Bk I, Ch. 1]

15 Monsignor was forty-four then, and bustling – a trifle too stout for symmetry, with hair the colour of spun gold, and a brilliant, enveloping personality. When he came into a room clad in his full purple regalia from thatch to toe, he resembled a Turner sunset. [*Ib.*]

16 Mother always feels the girl is safe if she's with me . . . If I start to hold somebody's hand they laugh at me, and *let* me, just as if it wasn't part of them. As soon as I get hold of a hand they sort of disconnect it from the rest of them. [*Ib.*]

17 He differed from the healthy type that was essentially middle-class – he never seemed to perspire. [*Ib.* I. 2]

18 Life was a damned muddle . . . a football game with everyone off-side and the referee gotten rid of – everyone claiming the referee would have been on his side. [*Ib.* II. 5]

19 Beware of the artist who's an intellectual also. The artist who doesn't fit. [*Ib.*]

20 The idea that to make a man work you've got to hold gold in front of his eyes is a growth, not an axiom. We've done that for so long that we've forgotten there's any other way. [*Ib.*]

21 One thing I know. If living isn't a seeking for the grail it may be a damned amusing game. [*Ib.*]

22 'I know myself,' he cried, 'but that is all.' [*Ib.*]

23 A big man has no time really to do anything but just sit and be big. [*Ib.* III. 2]

24 One of those men who reach such an acute limited excellence at twenty-one that everything afterward savours of anti-climax. [*The Great Gatsby*, Ch. 1]

25 She told me with pride that her husband had photographed her a hundred and twenty-seven times since they had been married. [*Ib.* 2]

115

1 I was so excited that when I got into a taxi with him I didn't hardly know I wasn't getting into a subway train. [*Ib.*]

2 I was one of the few guests who had actually been invited. People were not invited – they went there. [*Ib.* 3]

3 I've been drunk for about a week now, and I thought it might sober me up to sit in a library. [*Ib.*]

4 Everyone suspects himself of at least one of the cardinal virtues, and this is mine: I am one of the few honest people that I have ever known. [*Ib.*]

5 There are only the pursued, the pursuing, the busy, and the tired. [*Ib.* 4]

6 If you want to kiss me any time during the evening, Nick, just let me know and I'll be glad to arrange it for you. Just mention my name. [*Ib.* 6]

7 'What'll we do with ourselves this afternoon?' cried Daisy, 'and the day after" that, and the next thirty years?' [*Ib.* 7]

8 Her voice is full of money. [*Ib.*]

9 When I was a young man it was different – if a friend of mine died, no matter how, I stuck with them to the end. [*Ib.* 9]

10 Gatsby believed in the green light, the orgastic future that year by year recedes before us. It eluded us then, but that's no matter – tomorrow we will run faster, stretch out our arms further . . . And one fine morning – So we beat on, boats against the current, borne back ceaselessly into the past. [*Ib.*]

11 Three British nannies sat knitting the slow pattern of Victorian England, the pattern of the forties, the sixties, and the eighties, into sweaters and socks, to the tune of gossip as formalized as incantation. [*Tender is the Night*, Bk I, Ch. 1]

12 In a real dark night of the soul it is always three o'clock in the morning, day after day. [*The Crack Up*]

13 Though the Jazz Age continued, it became less and less an affair of youth. The sequel was like a children's party taken over by the elders. [*Ib.* 'Echoes of the Jazz Age']

14 The less sought-after girls who had become resigned to sublimating a probable celibacy came across Freud and Jung in seeking their intellectual recompense and came tearing back into the fray. [*Ib.*]

15 It's not a slam at *you* when people are rude – it's a slam at the people they've met before. [*The Last Tycoon*, Ch. 1]

16 Writers aren't exactly people. Or, if they're any good, they're a whole *lot* of people trying so hard to be one person. [*Ib.*]

17 I like people and I like them to like me, but I wear my heart where God put it – on the inside. [*Ib.*]

18 There are no second acts in American lives. [*Ib.* Notes]

19 His life was a sort of dream, as are most lives with the mainspring left out. [*Notebooks*, C]

20 A man says to another man: 'I'd certainly like to steal your girl.' Second man: 'I'd give her to you, but she's part of a set.' [*Ib.* E]

21 Show me a hero and I will write you a tragedy. [*Ib.*]

22 Switzerland is a country where very few things begin, but many things end. [*Ib.*]

23 Hospitality is a wonderful thing. If people really want you, they'll have you even if the cook has just died in the house of small-pox. [*Ib.*]

24 She was one of those people who would just as soon starve in a garret with a man – if she didn't have to. [*Ib.*]

25 She's got to be a loyal, frank person if she's got to bitch everyone in the world to do it. [*Ib.*]

26 'What kind of man was he?' 'Well, he was one of those men who come in a door and make any woman with them look guilty.' [*Ib.*]

27 When he buys his ties he has to ask if gin will make them run. [*Ib.*]

28 S.F.: The rich are different from us. ERNEST HEMINGWAY: Yes, they have more money. [Conversation, reported in *ib.*]

1 He was not the frock-coated and impressive type of millionaire which has become so frequent since the war. He was rather the 1910 model – a sort of cross between Henry VIII and 'our Mr Jones will be in Minneapolis on Friday'. [*Ib*. H]

2 I entertained on a cruising trip that was so much fun that I had to sink my yacht to make my guests go home. [*Ib*. K]

3 Once tried to get up a ship's party on a ferry boat. [*Ib*.]

4 When he urinated, it sounded like night prayer. [*Ib*. M]

5 Listen, little Elia, draw your chair up close to the edge of the precipice and I'll tell you a story. [*Ib*. N]

6 A great social success is a pretty girl who plays her cards as carefully as if she were plain. [From an undated letter to Frances Scott Fitzgerald]

7 All good writing is *swimming under water* and holding your breath. [*Ib*.]

8 Often I think writing is a sheer paring away of oneself leaving always something thinner, barer, more meagre. [Letter to Frances Scott Fitzgerald, 27 Apr. 1940]

9 First you take a drink, then the drink takes a drink, then the drink takes you. [Quoted in Jules Feiffer, *Ackroyd*, '1964, May 7']

10 An author ought to write for the youth of his own generation, the critics of the next, and the schoolmasters of ever afterwards. [Quoted in the *Guardian*, 13 Nov. 1964]

BOB FITZSIMMONS

11 The bigger they come the harder they fall. [Pugilist's boast]

BUD FLANAGAN

12 Underneath the arches / We dream our dreams away. [Song: *Underneath the Arches*]

13 Run, Rabbit [Title of song; words by Noël Gay]

MICHAEL FLANDERS

14 Eating people is wrong [Song: *The Reluctant Cannibal*]

15 Have Some Madeira, M'Dear. [Title of song]

JAMES ELROY FLECKER

16 Plunge not the finger of enquiry into the pie of impertinence, O my uncle. [*Hassan*, Act I, sc. ii]

17 Since when did a door of good reputation open on to this street, my masters? [*Ib*.]

18 Shall I then drop the needle of insinuation and pick up the club of statement? [*Ib*. II. i]

19 You have left the Garden of Art for the Palace of Action. [*Ib*. V. i]

20 Why should the dead be wiser than the living? The dead know only this – that it was better to be alive. [*Ib*.]

21 We are the Pilgrims, master; we shall go / Always a little further; it may be / Beyond that last blue mountain barred with snow / Across that angry or that glimmering sea. [*Ib*. V. ii]

22 What would ye, ladies? It was ever thus. / Men are unwise and curiously planned. [*Ib*.]

NEVILLE FLEESON

23 Say It With Flowers. [Title of song. Music by A. von Tilzer. See also 10:22]

IAN FLEMING

24 Dangerous at both ends and uncomfortable in the middle. [Attr. description of the horse. Quoted in *Sunday Times*, 9 Oct. 1966]

CYRIL FLETCHER

25 Dreaming of thee, dreaming of thee, / Dreaming oh my darling love of thee. [Refrain which became this comedian's catch-phrase from a comic recitation of a serious ode by Edgar Wallace. He has written various parodies on it]

1 Pin back your lug-'oles. Odd Ode No. 1 coming up. [Routine in variety and radio comedy act to introduce a recitation of one of his 'Odd Odes']

2 This is the tale of Margery Spicer / Who leant against a bacon slicer. / And as she jumped back murmured 'Coo, / I think I've lost a slice or two.' ... / When she got home again she found / The errand boy had called around. / A bag and grocer's bill she saw, / For '5 back rashers one and four'. / She said 'This 'ere ain't half a caution, / They've sent me back my missing portion.' ['Odd Ode': *Margery Spicer*]

3 In her bath poor Sheila Clock / Froze into a solid block, / And there with ice floes all around her / Was where her loving Mother found her. ['Odd Ode': *Sheila Clock*]

4 A fool and his money are soon parted. What I want to know is how they got together in the first place. [In BBC radio programme, 28 May 1969]

5 There is a compensation for being over forty ... I now do my crossword puzzles in ink. [In BBC radio programme, *Does the Team Think?* See also 307:1]

ERROL FLYNN

6 My problem lies in reconciling my gross habits with my net income. [Quoted in Jane Mercer, *Great Lovers of the Movies*]

7 If there's anyone listening to whom I owe *money*. I'm prepared to forget it if you are. [In a broadcast in Australia. Quoted in Leslie Halliwell, *The Filmgoer's Book of Quotes*]

MARSHAL FOCH

8 *Victoire, c'est la Volonté!* – The will to conquer is the first condition of victory. [Quoted in Tuchman, *The Guns of August*]

MICHAEL FOOT

9 A Royal Commission is a broody hen sitting on a china egg. [Speech in the House of Commons, 1964]

FORD MADOX FORD

16 You cannot be absolutely dumb when you live with a person unless you are an inhabitant of the North of England or the State of Maine. [*The Good Soldier*, Pt III, Ch. 4]

GERALD FORD

10 I am a Ford, not a Lincoln ... I am proud – very proud – to be one of 200 million Americans. [On becoming Vice-President, 6 Dec. 1973]

11 I guess it just proves that in America anyone can be President. [On becoming President. Quoted in Richard Reeves, *A Ford Not a Lincoln*, Ch. 4]

HENRY FORD

12 I did not say it [history] *was* bunk. It was bunk to *me* ... I did not need it very bad. [Quoted in Allan Nevins, *Ford: Expansion and Challenge*]

13 What we call evil is simply ignorance bumping its head in the dark. [*Observer*, 'Sayings of the Week', 16 Mar. 1930]

14 Exercise is bunk. If you are healthy, you don't need it: if you are sick, you shouldn't take it. [Attr.]

15 Any colour, so long as it's black. [Of choice of colour available for Model-T Ford car. Attr.]

GEORGE FORMBY

17 I'm leaning on a lamp-post at the corner of the street, / In case a certain little lady walks by. [Song: *Leaning on a Lamp-post*. Words and music by Noël Gay. Sung in film, *Feather Your Nest*]

18 I'll climb this blinking ladder till I get right to the top. / The blushing bride she looks divine, / The bridegroom he is doing fine, / I'd rather have his job than mine, / When I'm cleaning windows. [Song: *When I'm Cleaning Windows*. Words and music by H. Gifford, F. E. Cliffe and G. Formby. Original version in film, *Keep Your Seats Please*]

19 With my little stick of Blackpool rock, / Along the Promenade I stroll. / It may

be sticky but I never complain, / It's nice to have a nibble at it now and again. [Song: *With My Little Stick of Blackpool Rock*. Words and music by H. Gifford and F. E. Cliffe]

E. M. FORSTER

1 What the world most needs today are negative virtues – not minding people, not being huffy, touchy, irritable or revengeful. Positive ideals are becoming a curse, for they can seldom be achieved without someone being killed, or maimed or interned. [*Picture Post*, 'Tolerance', July 1939]

2 American women shoot the hippopotamus with eyebrows made of platinum. [Quoted in James Thurber, *Alarms and Diversions*]

3 Only connect! [*Howards End*, Epigraph]

4 They [railway termini] are our gates to the glorious and the unknown. Through them we pass out into adventure and sunshine, and to them, alas! we return. [*Ib*. Ch. 2]

5 Brahms, for all his grumbling and grizzling, had never guessed what it felt like to be suspected of stealing an umbrella. [*Ib*. 5]

6 We are not concerned with the very poor. They are unthinkable, and only to be approached by the statistician or the poet. [*Ib*. 6]

7 He believed in sudden conversion, a belief which may be right, but which is peculiarly attractive to the half-baked mind. [*Ib*.]

8 To speak against London is no longer fashionable. The Earth as an artistic cult has had its day. [*Ib*. 13]

9 Give Mr Bast money and don't worry about his ideals. He'll pick up those for himself. [*Ib*. 15]

10 There is much to be said for apathy in education. [*Maurice*, Ch. 1]

11 Religion is far more acute than science, and if it only added judgement to insight, would be the greatest thing in the world. [*Ib*. 44]

12 Ronny approved of religion as long as it endorsed the National Anthem, but he objected when it attempted to influence his life. [*A Passage to India*, Ch. 5]

13 She felt increasingly ... that, though people are important, the relations between them are not. [*Ib*. 13]

14 'Can you always tell whether a stranger is your friend?' 'Yes.' 'Then you are an Oriental.' [*Ib*. 36]

15 The historian must have ... some conception of how men who are not historians behave. Otherwise he will move in a world of the dead. [*Abinger Harvest*, 'Captain Edward Gibbon']

16 It is pleasant to be transferred from an office where one is afraid of a sergeant-major into an office where one can intimidate generals, and perhaps this is why History is so attractive to the more timid among us. We can recover self-confidence by snubbing the dead. [*Ib*. 'The Consolations of History']

17 It is not that the Englishman can't feel – it is that he is afraid to feel. He has been taught at his public school that feeling is bad form. He must not express great joy or sorrow, or even open his mouth too wide when he tales – his pipe might fall out if he did. [*Ib*. 'Notes on the English Character']

18 How rare, how precious is frivolity! How few writers can prostitute all their powers! They are always implying 'I am capable of higher things.' [*Ib*. 'Ronald Firbank']

19 Yes – oh dear, yes – the novel tells a story. [*Aspects of the Novel*, Ch. 2]

20 *Ulysses* ... is a dogged attempt to cover the universe with mud. [*Ib*. 6]

21 Look at them [the Jews] in the railway carriage now. Their faces are anxious and eloquent of past rebuffs. But they are travelling First. [*Pharos and Pharillon*, 'Philo's Little Trip']

22 If I had to choose between betraying my *country* and betraying my *friend*, I hope I should have the guts to betray my *country*. [*Two Cheers for Democracy*, 'What I Believe']

FORSYTH · FOWLES

1 In no book have I got down more than the people I like, the person I think I am, and the people who irritate me. This puts me among the large body of authors who are not really novelists, and have to get on as best they can with these three categories. [Quoted in Malcolm Cowley (ed.), *Writers at Work*]

2 Spoon feeding in the long run teaches us nothing but the shape of the spoon. [*Observer*, 'Sayings of the Week', 7 Oct. 1951]

3 One has two duties – to be worried and not to be worried. [*Observer*, 'Sayings of the Week', 4 Jan. 1959]

4 There are writers like Cyril Connolly who give pleasure a bad name. [Attr. Quoted by Geoffrey Grigson in a book review in the *Guardian*, 30 Sep. 1976]

BRUCE FORSYTH

5 Didn't he (or she) do well! [Catchphrase on TV programme, *The Generation Game*]

FREDERICK FORSYTH

6 Everyone seems to remember with great clarity what they were doing on November 22nd, 1963, at the precise moment they heard President Kennedy was dead. [*The Odessa File*, opening words]

H. E. FOSDICK

7 An atheist is a man who has no invisible means of support. [Attr. also to John Buchan. See 56:12]

S. C. FOSTER

8 The sun shines bright in the old Kentucky home. [Song: *My Old Kentucky Home*]

MICHEL FOUCAULT

9 One thing in any case is certain: man is neither the oldest nor the most constant problem that has been posed for human knowledge. [*The Order of Things*, Ch. 10, sect. vi]

10 As an archaeology of our thought easily shows, man is an invention of recent date. And one perhaps nearing its end. [*Ib.*]

JOHN FOWLES

11 We [the English] have evolved a language that always means more than it says, both emotionally and imaginatively. With Americans it is the reverse: they mean and feel far less than they have the habit of saying . . . The outward cynic may live in the States but the fundamental ones, the true quietists, live in Britain. [*Daniel Martin*, Ch. 6]

12 The more abhorrent a news item the more comforting it was to be the recipient since the fact that it had happened elsewhere proved that it had not happened here, was not happening here, and would therefore never happen here. [*The Ebony Tower*, 'Poor Koko']

13 The only reason the crime rate was so low in rural areas such as this was the close-knit social structure. When everyone knew everyone else, crime was either difficult or desperate. [*Ib.*]

14 In essence the Renaissance was simply the green end of one of civilization's hardest winters. [*The French Lieutenant's Woman*, Ch. 10]

15 We all write poems; it is simply that poets are the ones who write in words. [*Ib.* 19]

16 All perfect republics are perfect nonsense. The craving to risk death is our last great perversion. We come from night, we go into night. Why live in night? [*The Magus*, rev. edn, Ch. 19]

17 It is not only species of animal that die out, but whole species of feeling. And if you are wise you will never pity the past for what it did not know, but pity yourself for what it did. [*Ib.* 24]

18 There are three types of intelligent person: the first so intelligent that being called very intelligent must seem natural and obvious; the second sufficiently intelligent to see that he is being flattered, not described; the third so little intelligent that he will believe anything. [*Ib.* 36]

19 That is the great distinction between the sexes. Men see objects, women see the

relationship between objects. Whether the objects need each other, love each other, match each other. It is an extra dimension of feeling we men are without and one that makes war abhorrent to all real women – and absurd. [*Ib.* 52]

1 An answer is always a form of death. [*Ib.* 75]

2 There are many reasons why novelists write, but they all have one thing in common – a need to create an alternative world. [*Interview* in the *Sunday Times Magazine*, 2 Oct. 1977]

W. T. B. FOX

3 *The Super Powers.* [Title of book (1944), coining the phrase; subtitled *Their Responsibility for Peace*]

LEO FRAIN

4 A completely planned economy ensures that when no bacon is delivered, no eggs are delivered at the same time. [*Sunday Telegraph*, Jan. 1965]

ANATOLE FRANCE

5 In every well-governed state wealth is a sacred thing; in democracies it is the only sacred thing. [*Penguin Island*]

GENERAL FRANCO

6 The destiny of history has united you with myself and the Duce in an indissoluble way. [Letter to Adolf Hitler]

HANS FRANK

7 Our Constitution is the will of the Führer. [Quoted in A. Bullock, *Hitler*, Ch. 7, sect. vi]

LORD FRANKS

8 The Pentagon, that immense monument to modern man's subservience to the desk. [*Observer*, 'Sayings of the Week', 30 Nov. 1952]

9 It is a secret in the Oxford sense: you may tell it to only one person at a time. [Quoted by K. Rose in the *Sunday Telegraph*, 30 Jan. 1977]

GEORGE MACDONALD FRASER

10 I have observed, in the course of a dishonest life, that when a rogue is outlining a treacherous plan, he works harder to convince himself than to move his hearers. [*Flashman*]

MICHAEL FRAYN

11 There is something about a blurb-writer paying his respects to a funny book which puts one in mind of a short-sighted lord mayor raising his hat to a hippopotamus. [Introduction to *The Best of Beachcomber*]

12 What deeply affects every aspect of a man's experience of the world is his perception that *things could be otherwise*. [*Constructions*]

13 Ah, *now*! That odd time – the oddest time of all times; the time it always is ... by the time we've reached the 'w' of 'now' the 'n' is ancient history. [*Ib.*]

14 I can't help feeling sceptical about the Bible's claim that God made man in his own image. What? Two solemn little Jehovahs to gaze back at him with fathomless wisdom and benevolence? What would have been the fun in that? He could have achieved *that* simply by creating a couple of mirrors, or a closed-circuit television. [*Ib.*]

15 Each man in his time plays many parts. And not just for long runs as Shakespeare seems to suggest, but in repertory – one part on Monday night, another on Tuesday, and a third at the Wednesday matinée. [*Ib*].

16 The Euroglise will be staffed by a carefully chosen team of Divine Relations Officers, and the services will be conducted in Basic Eurish. [*Shouts and Murmurs*, 'Us Poor Blighters in Public Relations']

17 'Wouldn't it be terrible to be bad?' he says to her right hip. 'You'd never know what a relief it was to stop being good.' [*Sweet Dreams*]

18 You can create a good impression on yourself by being right, he realizes, but for creating a good impression on

others there's nothing to beat being totally and catastrophically wrong. [*Ib.*]

1 He recognizes that there is a real divergence of expert opinion between those that believe that men are happy because they are miserable, and those that believe that men are miserable because they are happy; and wisely arrives at a synthesis of both views. [*Ib.*]

2 There is a painful difference, often obscured by popular prejudice, between reporting something and making it up. [*Clouds*, Act I, sc. i]

3 The Government has made small slips before, of course. It has made minor errors of economic policy. It has occasionally deported the wrong people. It has gambled on the wrong defence system. It invaded the wrong country. All these peccadilloes could be forgiven . . . But now a member of the Government has *slept with the wrong woman*, and as a consequence severely strained this country's newsprint resources. [Comment on Profumo case in *Observer*, 1963]

4 To be absolutely honest, what I feel really bad about is that I don't feel worse. There's the ineffectual liberal's problem in a nutshell. [*Observer*, 8 Aug. 1965]

ARTHUR FREED

5 I'm singing in the rain, just singing in the rain; / What a wonderful feeling, I'm happy again. [Song: *Singing in the Rain*, from musical, *Hollywood Revue of 1929*. Music by Nacio Herb Brown]

R. M. FREEMAN

6 Let us have the numbers [of casualties] made instantly public; however large they be they shall never approach the figures arrived at by the reckless arithmetic of rumour. [*Pepys and Wife Go to It*]

PAULO FREIRE

7 True generosity consists precisely in fighting to destroy the causes which nourish false charity. [*Pedagogy of the Oppressed*, Ch. 1]

8 The oppressors do not perceive their monopoly of *having more* as a privilege which dehumanizes others and themselves. [*Ib.*]

9 Liberation, a human phenomenon, cannot be achieved by semi-humans. [*Ib.*]

WILLIAM PERCIVAL FRENCH

10 Where the mountains of Mourne sweep down to the sea. [Song: *The Mountains of Mourne*]

CLEMENT FREUD

11 If you resolve to give up smoking, drinking and loving, you don't actually live longer; it just seems longer. [Attr. to 'a third-rate comedian in Sloane Square'. *Observer*, 27 Dec. 1964]

12 [When asked what he thought of New Zealand] I find it hard to say, because when I was there it seemed to be shut. [Quoted on BBC radio programme, *Quote . . . Unquote*, 12 Apr. 1978]

SIGMUND FREUD

13 We are so made that we can derive intense enjoyment from a contrast and very little from a state of things. [*Civilization and Its Discontents*, Ch. 2]

14 The myth of King Oedipus, who killed his father and took his mother to wife, reveals, with little modification, the infantile wish, which is later opposed and repudiated by the *barrier against incest*. Shakespeare's *Hamlet* is equally rooted in the soil of the incest-complex, but under a better disguise. [*Five Lectures on Psycho-Analysis*, IV]

15 A culture which leaves unsatisfied and drives to rebelliousness so large a number of its members neither has a prospect of continued existence nor deserves it. [*The Future of an Illusion*]

16 We believe that civilization has been built up, *under the pressure of the struggle for existence*, by sacrifices in gratifica-

tion of the primitive impulses. [*Intro-ductory Lectures*]

1 I do not think our successes can compete with those of Lourdes. There are so many more people who believe in the miracles of the Blessed Virgin than in the existence of the unconscious. [*New Introductory Lectures*, Lecture XXXIV]

2 I repeatedly addressed my patient as Mrs Smith ... when her real name is Mrs James. My attention having been called to it, I soon discovered that I had another patient called Mrs James, who refused to pay for her treatment. Mrs Smith was also my patient and paid her bills promptly. [*Psychopathology of Everyday Life*, 5]

3 Two women stopped in front of a drug-store, and one said to her companion, 'If you will wait a few moments I'll soon be back,' but she said *movements* instead. She was on her way to buy some castor-oil for her child. [*Ib.*]

4 A woman who is very anxious to get children always reads *storks* instead of *stocks*. [*Ib.* 6]

5 I wished to make merry with an intimate friend over a statement made by my wife only a few hours earlier, but I found myself hindered by the noteworthy fact that I had entirely forgotten the statement. I had first to beg my wife to recall it to me. [*Ib.* 7]

6 Occasionally I have had to admit to myself that the annoying, awkward stepping aside on the street, whereby for some seconds one steps here and there, yet always in the same direction as the other person, until finally both stop facing each other ... conceals erotic purposes under the mask of awkwardness. [*Ib.* 8]

7 When a member of my family complains that he or she has bitten his tongue, bruised her finger, and so on, instead of the expected sympathy I put the question, 'Why did you do that?' [*Ib.*]

8 Due to unknown motives, Jones left a letter for several days on his desk, forgetting each time to post it. He ultimately posted it, but it was returned to him from the Dead-letter Office because he forgot to address it. After addressing it and posting it a second time, it was again returned to him, this time without a stamp. He was then forced to recognize the unconscious opposition to the sending of the letter. [*Ib.* 11]

9 Psycho-analysis has revealed to us that the totem-animal is really a substitute for the father, and this really explains to us the contradiction that it is usually forbidden to kill the totem animal, that the killing of it results in a holiday, and that the animal is killed and yet mourned. [*Totem and Taboo*, Ch. 4, sect. v.]

MAX FRISCH

10 Technology ... the knack of so arranging the world that we don't have to experience it. [Quoted in D. J. Boorstin, *The Image*, title-page epigraph]

11 Travel is atavistic, the day will come when there will be no more traffic at all and only newlyweds will travel. [Quoted in *Ib.* Ch. 3]

ERICH FROMM

12 *The affirmation of one's own life, happiness, growth, freedom is rooted in one's captivity to love*, i.e. in care, respect, responsibility, and knowledge. If an individual is able to love productively, he loves himself too; if he can love *only* others, he cannot love at all. [*The Art of Loving*, Ch. 2, sect. 3d]

13 Modern man lives under the illusion that he knows what he wants, while he actually wants what he is supposed to want. [*Escape from Freedom*, Pt X, Ch. 7]

14 The aim of sadism is to transform a man into a thing, something animate into something inanimate, since by complete and absolute control the living loses one essential quality of life – freedom. [*The Heart of Man*]

15 Man always dies before he is fully born. [*Man for Himself*, Ch. 3]

16 Man's main task in life is to give *birth* to himself. [*Ib.* 4]

17 In the nineteenth century the problem was that God is dead; in the twentieth

123

century the problem is that man is dead. [*The Sane Society*, Ch. 9]

1 Man has achieved *freedom from* – without yet having *freedom to* – to be himself, to be productive, to be fully awake. [Quoted in Laurence J. Peter, *Peter's Quotations*]

DAVID FROST

2 Hello, good evening, and welcome. [Catch-phrase, opening lines of TV series, *The Frost Programme*]

ROBERT FROST

3 Earth's the right place for love; / I don't know where it's likely to go better. [*Birches*]

4 One could do worse than be a swinger of birches. [*Ib.*]

5 Part of the moon was falling down the west / Dragging the whole sky with it to the hills. [*The Death of the Hired Man*]

6 'Home is the place where, when you have to go there, / They have to take you in.' / 'I should have called it / Something you somehow haven't to deserve.' [*Ib.*]

7 I would have written of me on my stone: / I had a lover's quarrel with the world. [*Epitaph*]

8 Why make so much of fragmentary blue / In here and there a bird, or butterfly, / Or flower, or wearing-stone, or open eye, / When heaven presents in sheets the solid hue? [*Fragmentary Blue*]

9 The land was ours before we were the land's. / She was our land more than a hundred years / Before we were her people. / Such as we were we gave ourselves outright / (The deed of gift was many deeds of war) / To the land vaguely realizing westward, / But still unstoried, artless, unenhanced, / Such as she was, such as she has become. [*The Gift Outright*]

10 Keep cold, young orchard. Goodbye and keep cold. / Dread fifty above more than fifty below. [*Goodbye and Keep Cold*]

11 Friends make pretence of following to the grave, / But before one is in it, their minds are turned / And making the best of their way back to life / And living people, and things they understand. [*Home Burial*]

12 This as it will be seen is other far / Than with brooks taken otherwhere in song. / We love the things we love for what they are. [*Hyla Brook*]

13 For them there was really nothing sad. / But though they rejoiced in the nest they kept, / One had to be versed in country things / Not to believe the phoebes wept. [*The Need of Being Versed in Country Things*]

14 I met a Californian who would / Talk California – a state so blessed, / He said, in climate, none had ever died there / A natural death. [*New Hampshire*]

15 No wonder poets sometimes have to *seem* / So much more business-like than business men. / Their wares are so much harder to get rid of. [*Ib.*]

16 I knew a man who failing as a farmer / Burned down his farmhouse for the fire insurance, / And spent the proceeds on a telescope / To satisfy a life-long curiosity / About our place among the infinities. / And how was that for other-worldliness? [*Ib.*]

17 The bird would cease and be as other birds / But that he knows in singing not to sing. / The question that he frames in all but words / Is what to make of a diminished thing. [*The Oven Bird*]

18 I never dared be radical when young / For fear it would make me conservative when old. [*Precaution*]

19 Pressed into service means pressed out of shape. [*The Self-Seeker*]

20 The best way out is always through. [*A Servant to Servants*]

21 Never tell me that not one star of all / That slip from heaven at night and softly fall / Has been picked up with stones to build a wall. [*A Star in a Stone-Boat*]

22 So near to paradise all pairing ends: / Here loveless birds now flock as winter

friends, / Content with bud-inspecting. [*A Winter Eden*]

1 People are inexterminable – like flies and bed-bugs. There will always be some that survive in cracks and crevices – that's us. [*Observer*, 'Sayings of the Week', 29 Mar. 1959]

2 [On writing 'free verse'] I'd just as soon play tennis with the net down. [Quoted in *Newsweek*, 30 Jan. 1956]

3 I have never started a poem yet whose end I knew. Writing a poem is discovering. [Quoted in the *New York Times*, 7 Nov. 1955]

4 Poetry is a way of taking life by the throat. [Quoted in *Vogue*, 15 Mar. 1963]

5 Lord forgive all the little tricks I play on you, and I'll forgive the great big one you played on me. [Attr.]

CHRISTOPHER FRY

6 If every man gave up women in God's name, / Where in God's name would be the men / To give up women in a generation's time? [*Curtmantle*, Act I]

7 Time walks by your side, ma'am, unwilling to pass. [*Ib.* II]

8 What a man knows he has by experience, / But what a man is precedes experience. [*Ib.*]

9 I apologize / For boasting, but once you know my qualities / I can drop back into a quite brilliant / Humility. [*The Lady's Not for Burning*, Act I]

10 Or Alexander, wearing / His imperial cobwebs and breastplate of shining worms / Wakens and looks for his glasses, to find the empire / Which he knows he put beside his bed. [*Ib.*]

11 Your innocence is on at such a rakish angle / It gives you quite an air of iniquity. [*Ib.*]

12 What after all / Is a halo? It's only one more thing to keep clean. [*Ib.*]

13 When it [the Day of Judgement] comes it will come in the autumn. / Heaven, I am quite sure, wouldn't disappoint / The bulbs. [*Ib.*]

14 Too unusual / Not to be corrupt. [*Ib.* II]

15 Always fornicate / Between clean sheets and spit on a well-scrubbed floor. [*Ib.*]

16 And I'll live too, if it kills me. [*Ib.*]

17 The moon is nothing / But a circumambulating aphrodisiac / Divinely subsidized to provoke the world / Into a rising birth-rate. [*Ib.* III]

18 I know tears when I see them, / My wife has them. [*Ib.*]

19 But life and death / Is cat and dog in this double-bed of a world. [*A Phoenix Too Frequent*]

20 He was so punctual, you could regulate / The sun by him. [*Ib.*]

21 Death's a new interest in life. [*Ib.*]

22 When you belong / To an upper class, the nether world might come strange. / Now I was born nether, madam, though not / As nether as some. [*Ib.*]

23 But how I longed / As a boy for the groves and grooves of Academe. [*Venus Observed*, Act I]

24 You mustn't / Drift into Gothic when your physique is so / Stubbornly Norman. [*Ib.*]

25 A spade is never so merely a spade as the word / Spade would imply. [*Ib.* II]

26 I know an undesirable character / When I see one; I've been one myself for years. [*Ib.*]

27 The patter of tiny criticism. [Attr.]

ROGER FRY

28 Manet and the Post-Impressionists. [Name of exhibition 'struck out in talk with a journalist'. Virginia Woolf, *Roger Fry*, Ch. 7]

29 There has been nothing like this outbreak of militant Philistinism since Whistler's day. [Letter to his mother, on Post-Impressionist exhibition. Quoted in *ib.*]

125

1 We make buildings for our need, and then, sacrificing our pockets to art, cover them with a mass of purely nonsensical forms which we hope may turn them into fine architecture. [Letter to *The Times*, 1912. Quoted in *ib.* 8]

2 Art is significant deformity. [Quoted in *ib.*]

3 No bombardment [of Rheims Cathedral] can do anything like the damage that the last restoration did. [Quoted in *ib.* 9]

4 I've found a perfect description of mysticism – it's the attempt to get rid of mystery. [Quoted in *ib.* 11]

5 Bach almost persuades me to be a Christian. [Quoted in *ib.*]

R. BUCKMINSTER FULLER

6 I am a passenger on the spaceship, Earth. [*Operating Manual for Spaceship Earth*]

7 The most important fact about Spaceship Earth: an instruction book didn't come with it. [Quoted in Laurence J. Peter, *Peter's Quotations*]

ROY FULLER

8 As horrible thoughts, / Loud fluttering aircraft slope above his head / At dusk. The ridiculous empires break like biscuits. [*The Middle of a War*]

9 It [the news] half convinces me that some great faculty, / Like hands, has been eternally lost and all / Our virtues now are the high and horrible / Ones of a streaming wound which heals in evil. [*October 1942*]

10 Anyone happy in this age and place / is daft or corrupt. Better to abdicate / From a material and spiritual terrain / Fit only for barbarians. [*Translation*]

11 Tonight I'd like to bring / The poets from their safe and paper beds, / Show them my comrades and the silver pall / Over the airfield, ask them what they'd sing. [*A Wry Smile*]

12 The poets get a quizzical ahem. / They reflect time, I am the very ticking. [*Ib.*]

DOUGLAS FURBER

13 Any time you're Lambeth way, / Any evening, any day, / You'll find us all doin' the Lambeth walk. [Song: *Doin' the Lambeth Walk*]

G

CLARK GABLE

1 Frankly, my dear, I don't give a damn. [Rhett Butler to Scarlett O'Hara in film, *Gone With the Wind*. Script by Sidney Howard from Margaret Mitchell's novel]

ZSA ZSA GABOR

2 I never hated a man enough to give him diamonds back. [*Observer*, 'Sayings of the Week', 28 Aug. 1957]

HUGH GAITSKELL

3 Surely the right course is to test the Russians, not the bombs. [*Observer*, 'Sayings of the Week', 23 Jun. 1957]

4 There are some of us, Mr Chairman, who will fight and fight and fight again to save the party we love. [Speech at Labour Party Conference, Scarborough, 3 Oct. 1960]

5 All terrorists, at the invitation of the Government, end up with drinks at the Dorchester. [Quoted by Dora Gaitskell in a letter to the *Guardian*, 23 Aug. 1977]

J. K. GALBRAITH

6 Wealth is not without its advantages, and the case to the contrary, although it has often been made, has never proved widely persuasive. [*The Affluent Society*, Ch. 1, sect. i]

7 One of the best ways of avoiding necessary and even urgent tasks is to seem to be busily employed on things that are already done. [*Ib.* 1. ii]

8 Wealth has never been a sufficient source of honour in itself. It must be advertised, and the normal medium is obtrusively expensive goods. [*Ib.* 7. v]

9 It is easy to overlook the absence of appreciable advance in an industry. Inventions that are not made, like babies that are not born, are rarely missed. [*Ib.* 9. iii]

10 Consumer wants can have bizarre, frivolous, or even immoral origins, and an admirable case can still be made for a society that seeks to satisfy them. But the case cannot stand if it is the process of satisfying wants that creates the wants. [*Ib.* 11. ii]

11 It is a far, far better thing to have a firm anchor in nonsense than to put out on the troubled seas of thought. [*Ib.* 11. iv]

12 In a community where public services have failed to keep abreast of private consumption things are very different. Here in an atmosphere of private opulence and public squalor, the private goods have full sway. [*Ib.* 18. ii]

13 In the world of minor lunacy the behaviour of both the utterly rational and the totally insane seems equally odd. [*Ib.* 20. ii]

14 All races have produced notable economists, with the exception of the Irish who doubtless can protest their devotion to higher arts. [*The Age of Uncertainty*, Ch. 1]

15 Much of the world's work, it has been said, is done by men who do not feel quite well. Marx is a case in point. [*Ib.* 3]

16 All successful revolutions are the kicking in of a rotten door. The violence of revolutions is the violence of men who charge into a vacuum. [*Ib.*]

17 These men of the technostructure are the new and universal priesthood. Their religion is business success; their test of virtue is growth and profit.

Their bible is the computer printout; their communion bench is the committee room. The sales force carries their message to the world, and a message is what it is often called. [*Ib.* 9]

1 ... We have been looking at the hard cases – the dark side of the moon. This is in the established tradition of social study. Only the man who finds everything wrong and expects it to get worse is thought to have a clear brain. [*Ib.* 10]

2 Perhaps it is a sense of history that divides good economics from bad. [*Ib.* Broadcast version, 2nd programme]

3 Money is a singular thing. It ranks with love as man's greatest source of joy. And with death as his greatest source of anxiety. Money differs from an automobile, a mistress or cancer in being equally important to those who have it and those who do not. [*Ib.* Broadcast version, 6th programme]

ADOLF GALLAND

4 It felt as if angels were pushing. [On his first flight in a jet aircraft, the Messerschmitt 262, May 1943. *The First and the Last*]

JOHN GALSWORTHY

5 When a Forsyte died – but no Forsyte had as yet died – death being contrary to their principles, they took precautions against it. [*The Forsyte Saga: The Man of Property*, Pt I, Ch. 1]

6 'Very haughty!' he said, 'the wild Buccaneer.' [*Ib.*]

7 He would be setting up as a man of property next, with a place in the country. [*Ib.*]

8 Keep faith! We've all done that. It's not enough. [*Loyalties*, Act III]

9 What is it that gets loose when you begin to fight, and makes you what you think you're not?... Begin as you may, it ends in this – skin game. [*The Skin Game*, Act III]

10 When we began this fight, we had clean hands – are they clean now? What's gentility worth if it can't stand fire? [*Ib.*]

128

MAHATMA GANDHI

11 [When asked by an interviewer what he thought of Western civilization] I think it would be a good idea. [Attr.]

ARCHBISHOP C. GARBETT

12 Any fool can criticize, and many of them do. [Attr.]

GRETA GARBO

13 [When sheltering under a table in the rain] 'Why *did* you give up the movies?' I asked. She considered her answer so carefully that I wondered if she had decided to ignore my personal question. At last, almost to herself, she said, 'I had made enough faces.' [Quoted in David Niven, *Bring on the Empty Horses*]

14 I want to be alone. [Attr.]

FEDERICO GARCÍA LORCA

15 *Cuando sale la luna / de cien rostros iguales, / la moneda de plata / solloza en el bolsillo.* – When the moon of a hundred identical faces comes out, the silver coins sob in the pocket. [*La luna asoma*]

16 *Ni un solo momento, viejo hermoso Walt Whitman, / he dejado de ver tu barba llena de mariposas.* – Not for a moment, beautiful aged Walt Whitman, have I failed to see your beard full of butterflies. [*Oda a Walt Whitman*]

17 *Con el alma de charol / vienen por la carrera.* – With their patent-leather souls, they [the Civil Guards] come along the road. [*Romance de la Guardia civil española*]

18 *El jinete se acercaba / tocando el tambor del llano. / Dentro de la fragua el niño / tiene los ojos cerrados.* – Drumming the plain, the horseman is coming. Inside the smithy the child has closed his eyes. [*Romance de la luna, luna*]

19 *Verde que te quiero verde. / Verde viento. Verde ramas. / El barco sobre el mar / y el caballo en la montaña.* – Green how I love you green. Green wind. Green boughs. The ship on the sea and the horse on the mountain. [*Romance sonambulo*]

JOSÉ GARCÍA OLIVER

[Anarchist Minister of Justice during the Civil War]

1 Justice, I firmly believe, is so subtle a thing that to interpret it one has only need of a heart. [Quoted in Hugh Thomas, *The Spanish Civil War*, Ch. 43]

LEON GARFIELD

2 Long ago, the Englishman's castle was his home; then that went, and his home became his castle. Now his castle is the nation's and his home is the bank's. [*Children's Literature in Education*, Ch. 2]

3 But I do think practising what one preaches is an overrated virtue. Generally it means that he who zealously practises what he preaches is guilty of listening a little too carefully to himself. [*Ib.*]

4 Nature herself had created them to be storesmen. They had the very air of having been not so much born as indented for. [*The Drummer Boy*, Ch. 6]

5 The lady of the house was everyone's neighbour, and knew about half as much as God; and whatever had escaped her she made up out of a fund of experience, gleaned from the purchase and sale of buttons. [*The Pleasure Garden*, Ch. 9]

6 Mirrors are the windows of the devil, overlooking nothing but a landscape of lies! [*The Prisoners of September*, Ch. 2]

7 Everything had a back door. There was always a way in. The corporal was peculiarly experienced in back doors. All his life had been spent in approaching them. He was confident that, when the time came, he would enter Heaven by a back door. [*Ib.* 14]

8 ... Lady Bullock, who had been at death's door for so long now that one might have been pardoned for mistaking her for its knocker. [*Ib.* 29]

JUDY GARLAND

9 I was born at the age of twelve on a Metro-Goldwyn-Mayer lot. [*Observer*, 'Sayings of the Week', 18 Feb. 1951]

ALAN GARNER

10 'There,' he said. 'You'll remember this day, my girl. For the rest of your life.' 'I already have,' said Mary. [*The Stone Book*]

J. L. GARVIN

11 Dear Mr Lansbury stands for our happy exposure to perfect annihilation. With broad amiability he is ready any day for the Gadarene gallop on the back of his own whole hog. [*Observer*, 1937]

GENERAL DE GAULLE

12 *Toute ma vie je me suis fait une certaine idée de la France.* – All my life I have thought of France in a certain way. [*War Memoirs*, Vol. I: *The Call to Honour*, Ch. 1]

13 *Délibérer est le fait de plusieurs. Agir est le fait d'un seul.* – Deliberation is the work of many men. Action, of one alone. [*Ib.* Vol. 2: *Unity*, Ch. 5]

14 As for me, I have never, in any one of my speeches, spoken of *l'Europe des patries* although it is always claimed that I have. [At a press conference, 15 May 1962. See also 96:5]

15 France has lost the battle but she has not lost the war. [In 1940]

16 I myself have become a Gaullist only little by little. [*Observer*, 'Sayings of the Year', 29 Dec. 1963]

17 I have come to the conclusion that politics are too serious a matter to be left to the politicians. [Attr. See also 79:1]

18 The graveyards are full of indispensable men. [Attr.]

19 Events have made me the guide of the nation. [Attr.]

JEAN GENET

20 What we need is hatred. From it are our ideas born. [*The Negroes*, epigraph]

KING GEORGE V

21 I can't understand it. I'm really quite an ordinary sort of chap. [Attr. remark at his Jubilee in 1935]

129

1 Is it possible that my people live in such awful conditions? ... I tell you, Mr Wheatley, that if I had to live in conditions like that I would be a revolutionary myself. [On hearing Mr Wheatley's life story. Quoted in L. MacNeill Weir, *The Tragedy of Ramsay MacDonald*, Ch. 16]

2 Bugger Bognor! [Attr. dying words when told by his physician he would soon be convalescing in Bognor. For official version, see *Penguin Dictionary of Quotations*, 167:2]

KING GEORGE VI

3 Abroad is bloody. [Attr. Quoted in W. H. Auden, *A Certain World*]

DANIEL GEORGE
and 'SAGITTARIUS'

4 O Freedom, what liberties are taken in thy name! [*The Perpetual Pessimist*]

PETER GEORGE,
STANLEY KUBRICK
and TERRY SOUTHERN

5 Gentlemen, you can't fight in here. This is the War Room. [In the film, *Dr Strangelove*. Quoted in Alexander Walker, *Stanley Kubrick Directs*]

6 If you want to know what I think, I think you're some kind of a deviated prevert. [*Ib.* Quoted in *ib.*]

WILLIAM GERHARDIE

7 None of them [the Russians on the train] could understand the Admiral's interpretation of No. They had all grown up with the idea that No meant Yes after an adequate amount of pressure and insistence. [*Futility*, Pt III, Ch. 4]

8 She even sighed offensively ... as if she meant to charge me with the necessity of doing so. [*Ib.* 5]

9 There are as many fools at a university as elsewhere ... But their folly, I admit, has a certain stamp – the stamp of university training, if you like. It is trained folly. [*The Polyglots*, Ch. 7]

10 We are like icebergs in the ocean: one-eighth part consciousness and the rest submerged beneath the surface of articulate apprehension. [*Ib.* 14]

IRA GERSHWIN

11 I got rhythm, / I got music. [Song: *I Got Music*, from musical, *Girl Crazy*. Music by George Gershwin]

12 Oh, I got plenty o' nuthin', / An' nuthin's plenty fo' me. [Song: *I Got Plenty o' Nuthin'*, from musical, *Porgy and Bess*. Music by George Gershwin]

13 It ain't necessarily so, / It ain't necessarily so – / De t'ings dat yo' li'ble / To read in de Bible – / It ain't necessarily so. [Song: *It Ain't Necessarily So*, from *ib.*]

14 Lady, Be Good! [Title of musical. Music by George Gershwin]

15 Nice work if you can get it, / And you can get it – if you try. [Song: *Nice Work If You Can Get It*, from musical, *A Damsel in Distress*. Music by George Gershwin]

16 You'd better dance, little lady! / Dance, little man! / Dance whenever you can! [Song: *Shall We Dance?*, from film of the same title. Music by George Gershwin]

PAUL GETTY

17 The meek shall inherit the earth, but not the mineral rights. [Attr.]

18 If you can actually count your money then you are not a really rich man. [Quoted in Bernard Levin, *The Pendulum Years*, Ch. 1]

PIETER GEYL

19 The man who has made up his mind for all contingencies will often be too quick for one who tries to understand. [*Debates with Historians*, 'Ranke in the Light of the Catastrophe']

ALAIN GHEERBRANT

20 Freedom to Starve. [Title of English trans. of book]

WILLA GIBBS

1 The three kinds of services you generally find in the Episcopal churches. I call them either low-and-lazy, broad-and-hazy, or high-and-crazy. [*The Dean*]

KAHLIL GIBRAN

2 Forget not that modesty is for a shield against the eye of the unclean. And when the unclean shall be no more, what were modesty but a fetter and a fouling of the mind? [*The Prophet*, 'Of Clothes']

3 If he [a teacher] is indeed wise he does not bid you enter the house of his wisdom, but rather leads you to the threshold of your own mind. [*Ib.* 'Of Teaching']

4 Your children are not your children. They are the sons and daughters of Life's longing for itself ... you may strive to be like them, but seek not to make them like you. [*Ib.* 'Of Children']

5 You were born together, and together you shall be for evermore ... but let there be spaces in your togetherness. And let the winds of the heavens dance between you. [*Ib.* 'Of Marriage']

6 I discovered the secret of the sea in meditation upon the dewdrop. [*Spiritual Sayings*]

7 It is slavery to live in the mind unless it has become part of the body. [*Ib.*]

8 The fear of hell is hell itself, and the longing for paradise is paradise itself. [*Ib.*]

W. W. GIBSON

9 But we, how shall we turn to little things / And listen to the birds and winds and streams / Made holy by their dreams, / Nor feel the heart-break in the heart of things? [*A Lament*]

ANDRÉ GIDE

10 The true hypocrite is the one who ceases to perceive his deception, the one who lies with sincerity. [*Journal of 'The Counterfeiters'*, Second Notebook, Aug. 1921]

11 [When asked to name the greatest French poet] Hugo – alas! [In a letter to Paul Valéry, quoted *Oxford Dictionary of Quotations* (new edition)]

12 I call journalism everything that will interest less tomorrow than it does today. [Attr.]

L. WOLFE GILBERT

13 Waitin' for the *Robert E. Lee*. [Title of song. Music by Lewis F. Muir]

W. S. GILBERT

14 Sir, I view the proposal to hold an international exhibition at San Francisco with an equanimity bordering on indifference. [Quoted in Hesketh Pearson, *Gilbert, His Life and Strife*, Ch. 19]

15 [In a letter of complaint to the Stationmaster at Baker Street on the Metropolitan line] Sir, Sunday morning, although recurring at regular and well foreseen intervals, always seems to take this railway by surprise. [Quoted in John Julius Norwich, *A Christmas Cracker*]

16 Funny without being vulgar. [Attr. remark on Irving's *Hamlet*]

GILES

17 Fred's just heard the first cuckoo – and GOT it. [Caption of cartoon. Quoted in Colin MacInnes, *England, Half English*, 'The Express Families']

BRENDAN GILL

18 One day he [E. J. Kahn, Jr] happened to describe his usual procedure on rising. 'I get out of bed,' he said, 'and throw up and take a shower and shave and have breakfast ...' 'You throw up every morning?' 'Of course,' Kahn said. 'Doesn't everyone?' [*Here at the New Yorker*, Ch. 12]

ERIC GILL

19 Man cannot live on the human plane, he must be either above or below it. [*Autobiography*, Conclusion]

20 The artist is not a special kind of man but every man a special kind of artist.

131

[Quoted on BBC TV programme, *Spirit of the Age*]

PETER GILL

1 In this country the only real link between Buckingham Palace, Downing Street and the people is philistinism. [Interview in the *Sunday Times Magazine*, 26 Nov. 1978]

STRICKLAND GILLILAN

2 Adam / Had 'em. [*On the Antiquity of Microbes*]

HERMIONE GINGOLD

3 What we at home call draught, Americans refer to as cross-ventilation. [*Observer*, 'Sayings of the Week', 8 Nov. 1953]

4 There are too many men in politics and not enough elsewhere. [*Observer*, 'Sayings of the Week', 2 Oct. 1958]

ALLEN GINSBERG

5 America I'm putting my queer shoulder to the wheel. [*America*]

6 I saw the best minds of my generation destroyed by madness, starving hysterical naked. [*Howl*]

YEVGENIA GINSBURG

7 All ideologies are relative; the only absolute is the torment that men inflict on each other. [Quoted in Eric de Mauny, *Russian Prospect*]

NORMAN GINSBURY

8 If it weren't for his good manners, Leopold could easily pass for an Englishman. [*The First Gentleman*, II. i]

9 I never snub anybody accidentally. [*Viceroy Sarah*, I. ii]

JEAN GIRAUDOUX

10 Beauty is always the first to hear about the sins of the world. [*Duel of Angels*, Act I]

11 Limousin, the country which has bred more popes and fewer lovers than any other in the world. [*Ib.*]

12 I said that virtue was the weakness of strong generals, and the strength of weak magistrates. [*Ib.*]

13 You spit with great charm, like a shocked schoolgirl. [*Ib.*]

14 Heroes are men who glorify a life which they can't bear any longer. [*Ib.* III]

15 You know women as well as I do. They are only willing when you compel them, but after that they're as enthusiastic as you are. [*Tiger at the Gates*, Act I]

16 On horseback, in the usual style of seducers, leaving a heap of horse manure under the windows. [*Ib.*]

17 Ask any soldier. To kill a man is to merit a woman. [*Ib.*]

18 A man has only one way of being immortal on this earth: he has to forget he is mortal. [*Ib.*]

19 It's odd how people waiting for you stand out far less clearly than people you are waiting for. [*Ib.*]

20 Often I don't recognize faces, but I always recognize the jewellery. [*Ib.*]

21 As soon as war is declared it will be impossible to hold the poets back. Rhyme is still the most effective drum. [*Ib.*]

22 But the annihilation of a people doesn't alter in the least their superior moral position. [*Ib.*]

23 There's no better way of exercising the imagination than the study of law. No poet ever interpreted nature as freely as a lawyer interprets truth. [*Ib.*]

24 The life of a wife and husband who love each other is never at rest. Whether the marriage is true or false, the marriage portion is the same: elemental discord. [*Ib.* II]

25 I forgot they were talking about me. They sound so wonderfully convincing. [*Ib.*]

26 One of the privileges of the great is to witness catastrophes from a terrace. [*Ib.*]

1 Nations, like men, die by imperceptible disorders. We recognize a doomed people by the way they sneeze or pare their nails. [*Ib.*]

2 One way to recognize error is the fact that it's universal. [*Ib.*]

ALEX GLASGOW

3 Close the coalhouse door, lad. / There's blood inside. [Song: *Close the Coalhouse Door*]

MONTAGUE GLASS

4 She was a singer who had to take any note above A with her eyebrows. [Quoted in Frank Muir, *The Frank Muir Book*]

JOHN GLOAG

5 Our Georgian forerunners had faculties that we have lost ... they ignored the natural smells of sweat and dung and dirt, as we ignore the artificial smells of petrol fumes and industrial effluents, but they rejoiced in an unimpaired sense of sight. [*Georgian Grace*, Ch. 1]

6 England is a living guide-book to over two thousand years of civilization. [*2,000 Years of England*, Ch. 1]

7 Architecture cannot lie, and buildings, although inanimate, are to that extent morally superior to men. [*The Significance of Historical Research in Architectural and Industrial Design*, a paper read to the Royal Society of Arts, 20 Mar. 1963]

8 Since the early nineteenth century we have depended almost exclusively on what used to be called book learning, so much so that we have become visually illiterate. [*Ib.*]

MAX GLUCKMAN

9 A science is any discipline in which the fool of this generation can go beyond the point reached by the genius of the last generation. [*Politics, Law and Ritual*]

JEAN-LUC GODARD

10 Photography is truth. And cinema is truth twenty-four times a second. [Film, *Le Petit Soldat*]

11 To me style is just the outside of content, and content the inside of style, like the outside and inside of the human body – both go together, they can't be separated. [Quoted in Richard Roud, *Godard*, Introduction]

12 If I had to define myself, I'd say I am 'a painter of letters' as one would say that there are 'men of letters'. [Quoted in Jay Leyda, *Voices of Film Experience*]

13 I like a film to have a beginning, a middle and an end, but not necessarily in that order. [Attr.]

CHARLES GODFREY

14 When we go to meet the foe, / It's the English speaking race against the world. [Song: *We're Brothers of the Selfsame Race*]

FRED GODFREY and MARK SHERIDAN

15 Who were you with last night? / Out in the pale moonlight. [Song: *Who Were You with Last Night?*]

JOSEF GOEBBELS

16 Our Government of gentlemen ... [*Observer*, 'Sayings of the Week', 22 Oct. 1933]

17 The Iron Curtain. [*Das Reich*]

18 This was the Angel of History! We felt its wings flutter through the room. Was that not the fortune we awaited so anxiously? [On hearing of Roosevelt's death. *Diary*]

HERMANN GOERING

19 They [the British] entered the war to prevent us from going into the East, not to have the East come to the Atlantic. [On the possibilities of splitting the Grand Alliance. Quoted in G. M. Gilbert, *Nuremberg Diary*]

1 I herewith commission you to carry out all preparations with regard to ... a *total solution* of the Jewish question in those territories of Europe which are under German influence. [Instructions to Heydrich, 31 Jul. 1941. Quoted in W. L. Shirer, *The Rise and Fall of the Third Reich*, Bk V, Ch. 27]

OLIVER ST JOHN GOGARTY

2 In spite of his faith in one medicine for many unseen and unknown diseases, he [the Englishman] cannot accept miracles; he burks at the infallibility of the Pope, but unquestioningly accepts the infallibility of the pill. 'Just as much as will fit on a threepenny-piece' instead of as many angels as will stand on the point of a needle. [*As I was Going Down Sackville Street*, Ch. 3]

RUBE GOLDBERG

3 No matter how thin you slice it, it's still baloney. [Quoted in B. Gill, *Here at the New Yorker*, Ch. 13. But Eric Partridge, *A Dictionary of Catch-phrases*, judges it to be a US catch-phrase of the late 1930s]

WILLIAM GOLDING

4 Philip is a living example of natural selection. He was as fitted to survive in this modern world as a tapeworm in an intestine. [*Free Fall*, Ch. 2]

5 I kept my drinking from Beatrice because she thought of pubs as only one degree less damned than the Church of England. [*Ib.* 4]

6 Life is like nothing, because it is everything. [*Free Fall*. Quoted by himself in *The Hot Gates*, 'Tolstoy's Mountain']

7 Ralph wept for the end of innocence, the darkness of man's heart, and the fall through the air of the true, wise friend called Piggy. [*Lord of the Flies*, Ch. 12]

8 What is wrong with a revolution is that it is natural. It is as natural as natural selection, as devastating as natural selection, and as horrible. [*Observer*, 'Sayings of the Year', 29 Dec. 1974]

9 Sleep is when all the unsorted stuff comes flying out as from a dustbin upset in a high wind. [*Pincher Martin*, Ch. 6]

BARRY GOLDWATER

10 I would remind you that extremism in the defence of liberty is no vice. And let me remind you also that moderation in the pursuit of justice is no virtue! [Speech on accepting Republican nomination, San Francisco, 17 Jul. 1964]

11 You've got to forget about this civilian. Whenever you drop bombs, you're going to hit civilians. [Speech in New York, 23 Jan. 1967]

12 A government that is big enough to give you all you want is big enough to take it all away. [Quoted in M. Ivens and R. Dunstan, *Bachman's Book of Freedom Quotations*]

SAMUEL GOLDWYN

13 Too caustic? To hell with cost; we'll make the picture anyway. [Quoted in A. K. Adams, *Cassell's Book of Humorous Quotations*]

14 We're overpaying him but he's worth it. [Quoted in *ib.*]

15 Chaplin is no business man – all he knows is that he can't take anything less. [Quoted in Charles Chaplin, *My Autobiography*, Ch. 19]

16 Include me out. [Attr. Quoted in Philip French, *The Movie Moguls*, Ch. 4]

17 I read part of it all the way through. [Attr. Quoted in *ib.*]

18 We have all passed a lot of water since then. [In discussion with Ezra Goodman. Quoted in *ib.* 9]

19 What we want is a story that starts with an earthquake and works its way up to a climax. [Quoted in Leslie Halliwell, *The Filmgoer's Book of Quotes*]

20 My *Toujours* Lautrec! [Quoted in Lillian Ross, *Picture*, 'Throw the Little Old Lady Down the Stairs!']

21 How'm I gonna do decent pictures when all my good writers are in jail? ... Don't misunderstand me, they all ought to be hung. [Quoted by Dorothy Parker

in Malcolm Cowley (ed.), *Writers at Work, First Series*]

1 Let's have some new clichés. [*Observer*, 'Sayings of the Week', 24 Oct. 1948]

2 Why should people go out and pay money to see bad films when they can stay at home and see bad television for nothing? [*Observer*, 'Sayings of the Week', 9 Sep. 1956]

3 A wide screen just makes a bad film twice as bad. [Said on 9 Sep. 1956]

4 Anybody who goes to see a psychiatrist ought to have his head examined. [Attr.]

5 Every director bites the hand that lays the golden egg. [Attr.]

6 If Roosevelt were alive he'd turn in his grave. [Attr.]

7 I'll give you a definite maybe. [Attr.]

8 It's more than magnificent – it's mediocre. [Attr.]

9 A verbal contract isn't worth the paper it's written on. [Attr.]

10 'Why only twelve?' 'That's the original number.' 'Well, go out and get thousands.' [During the filming of *The Last Supper*. Attr.]

11 [To a man who said, 'What beautiful hands your wife has'] Yes, I'm going to have a bust made of them. [Attr.]

12 You ought to take the bull between the teeth. [Attr.]

13 Tell me, how did you love my picture? [Attr. in J. R. Colombo, *Colombo's Hollywood*]

ERNST GOMBRICH

14 For the historian, as distinct from the critic of art, the chocolate-box is one of the most significant products of our age, precisely because of its role as a catalyst. [*Listener*, 15 Feb. 1979]

DR I. J. GOOD

15 When I hear the word 'gun' I reach for my culture. [*The Scientist Speculates*]

16 I have had so many deadlines to keep, it is a wonder I am still alive. [In conversation]

JOE GOODWIN and LARRY SHAY

17 When you're smiling the whole world smiles with you. [Song: *When You're Smiling*, music by Mark Fisher]

RICHARD GORDON

18 The birds on the Liver building, that are unfairly supposed by Liverpool seafarers to flap their wings when passed by a woman of untarnished virtue, wept ceaselessly on to the bleak pierhead. [*Doctor at Sea*, Ch. 1]

19 She was a girl called Wendy, a blonde, but of the arid sort, like the stubble in a wheatfield after a hot harvest. [*Ib.* 2]

20 I began to suffer an attack of *terror celibans*, or bachelor's panic. [*Ib.*]

21 The established English custom of dropping the national mantle of self-consciousness at Christmastime and revealing the horrible likeness of the charade underneath. [*Doctor in the House*, Ch. 10]

BISHOP GORE

22 Can you lend me a Bible? I remembered my pipe but have forgotten my Bible. [To an ultra-pious vicar and curate before preaching in their church. G. L. Prestige, *Life of Bishop Gore*, Ch. 16, sect. ii]

23 An octave is something idolatrous and wicked and smells of incense and witchcraft. [To a lady puzzled on a point of ritual. Quoted in John Gore, *Charles Gore*, Ch. 5]

24 If there *is* to be a resurrection, we must hold on to our toasting forks. [In delirium. Quoted in C. A. Alington, *Things Ancient and Modern*, Ch. 5]

25 I am increasingly convinced that the *Church Times* is now edited by the Devil in person. [Quoted in *ib*.]

26 But for the miracles I should consider Nero the ideal man. [Attr.]

MAXIM GORKY

27 Everyone knows that it is much harder to turn word into deed than deed into

word. ['On Plays', quoted in *U.S.S.R. in Construction*, Apr. 1937]

1 You must write for children in the same way as you do for adults, only better. [Attr.]

EDMUND GOSSE

2 We were as nearly bored as enthusiasm would permit. [On a Swinburne play. Quoted in Christopher Hassall, *Edward Marsh*, Ch. 6]

3 Gosse amused him one day by pointing to an advertisement in a newspaper: Messrs Gunter send their celebrated Invalid Turtle to all parts of the Kingdom, remarking, 'I conceive of it travelling with a lacklustre eye'. [Quoted in *ib.*]

4 There always seemed to me a worm slumbering at the root of his talent. [On Flecker's death. Letter to Edward Marsh, Jan. 1915]

RICHARD GOTT

5 Development in the Third World usually means the over-development of objects and the underdevelopment of people. [*Guardian*, 30 Nov. 1976]

GERALD GOULD

6 The telephone directory is, because of its rigorous selection and repression, a work of art compared to the waste-paper basket. And [James Joyce's] *Ulysses* is a wastepaper basket. [*The English Novel*]

ANA ANGARIKA GOVINDA

7 A Guru is far more than a teacher in the ordinary sense of the word. A teacher gives knowledge, but a Guru gives himself. [*The Way of the White Clouds*, 6]

SIR ERNEST GOWERS

8 Our use of gentleman, like that of esquire, is being affected by our progress towards a classless society, but in the opposite way: we are all esquires now, and we are none of us gentlemen any more. [*Fowler's Dictionary of Modern English Usage*, 2nd edition]

LORD GRADE

9 All my shows are great. Some of them are bad. But they are all great. [*Observer*, 'Sayings of the Week', 14 Sep. 1975]

10 [On being told that the actor playing Christ in TV series was not married to the girl he was living with] What about it? Do you want to crucify the boy? [Attr.]

GRAFFITI

11 Amnesia rules er – ? – ? [Noted in a pub in London W1]

12 Blow your mind – smoke gunpowder. [Quoted in Robert Reisner, *Graffiti*]

13 A cop sleeps within each of us, he must be killed. [Censier, Paris, May 1968. Quoted in *ib.*, 'French Graffiti']

14 Death is the greatest kick of all, that's why they save it for last. [Quoted in *ib.* 'Death']

15 Dyslexia Rules – K.O.? [Noted in a Birmingham lavatory]

16 Fighting for peace is like fucking for chastity. [Quoted in *Knave* magazine, Mar. 1977]

17 God is dead – Nietzsche.
Nietzsche is dead – God. [Noted in a New York subway]

18 God is not Dead but Alive and Well and working on a Much Less Ambitious Project. [Noted in a Greenwich pub. Quoted in the *Guardian*, 'London Letter', 27 Nov. 1975]

19 Heisenberg probably rules OK.

20 Hey, hey, L.B.J., how many kids did you kill today? [At period of Vietnam War. Quoted in Robert Reisner, *Graffiti*]

21 I'd give my right hand to be ambidextrous. [Noted in a pub in Camden, London, but Robert Reisner gives a US version in *Graffiti*]

22 Incest – a game the whole family can play. [Quoted in Robert Reisner, *Graffiti*, 'Sex']

23 Is there intelligent life on earth?
Yes, but I'm only visiting. [Noted in

Cambridge. Quoted by Norman Shrapnel in the *Guardian*, 17 Oct. 1970]

1 *Je suis Marxiste, tendance Groucho.* [Noted in Paris, 1968]

2 Life is like a rainbow: you get all the colours of the rectum.

3 Man is preceded by forest, followed by desert. [Noted in France during the student revolt, 1968]

4 My mother made me a Lesbian.
Get her to knit one for me, too. [Noted on the campus at Sussex University]

5 No Pope here.
Lucky Pope. [Noted in Londonderry, 1977]

6 Nostalgia isn't what it used to be.

7 Nudists are people who wear one-button suits. [Quoted in Robert Reisner, *Graffiti*, 'Water Closet Etiquette']

8 One hundred thousand lemmings can't be wrong. [Noted at Balliol College, Oxford. Quoted in the *Guardian*, 6 Dec. 1975]

9 One orgasm in the bush is worth two in the hand. [Quoted in Robert Reisner, *Graffiti*, 'Masturbation']

10 Red brothers, go back to your reservations. [Noted in Prague during 1968 uprising. Quoted in *Studies in Comparative Communism*, Jul. 1968]

11 Russian circus in town. Do not feed the animals. [Noted in Czechoslovakia, 1968. Quoted in Robert Reisner, *Graffiti*]

12 Take a cannibal to lunch. [Quoted in Robert Reisner, *Graffiti*, as pseudo-graffito]

13 Today is the first day of the rest of your life. [Quoted in G. Bellamy, *The Secret Lemonade Drinker*]

14 To do is to be – Rousseau.
To be is to do – Sartre.
Doobedoobedoobedoo – Sinatra.
[Quoted by Ronald Fletcher on BBC radio programme, *Quote ... Unquote*, 5 Apr. 1978]

15 Two persons in every one in Woolwich are schizophrenic. [Noted in a lavatory

in a theatre at Woolwich. Quoted in *The Times*, 3 May 1978]

16 The water closet like the harp is essentially – a solo instrument. [Noted in the ladies' room at the Blind Lemon pub, Berkeley, California. Quoted in Robert Reisner, *Graffiti*, 'Water Closet Etiquette']

17 We aim to please. You aim too please. [Inscription in the gentlemen's lavatory of a New York restaurant]

18 We are the writing on your wall. [At 144 Piccadilly, London, when taken over by squatters]

19 When God created man, she was only experimenting. I always thought men were a phallusy. [Noted in a ladies' lavatory]

20 Why does free love cost so much? [Button slogan. Quoted in Robert Reisner, *Graffiti*, 'Love']

21 A woman without a man is like a fish without a bicycle. [Noted on the campus at Birmingham University and elsewhere. Quoted in N. Rees, *Quote ... Unquote*]

W. S. GRAHAM

22 So here we are, you and I, / Thought up out of silence for an instant here / Under the ancient hardware of the sky. [*In Memoriam: Burns Singer*]

KENNETH GRAHAME

23 'But we don't want to teach 'em,' replied the Badger. 'We want to learn 'em ...' [*Wind in the Willows*, Ch. 11]

PERCY GRAINGER

24 Salvation Army Booth objected to the devil having all the good tunes. I object to jazz and vaudeville having all the best instruments! [Preface to *Spoon River*. Quoted in John Bird, *Percy Grainger*, Appendix C]

ANTONIO GRAMSCI

25 All men are intellectuals ...; but all men do not have the function of intellectuals in society. [*Prison Notebooks*, 'The Intellectuals']

1 To wait until one has grown to half the voters plus one is the programme of cowardly souls who wait for socialism by a royal decree countersigned by two ministers. [Quoted in A. Pozzolini: *Antonio Gramsci: an Introduction to His Thought*, Ch. 2]

2 It [sociology] is therefore an attempt to define 'experimentally' the laws of evolution of human society in such a way as to 'predict' that the oak tree will develop out of the acorn. Vulgar evolution is at the root of sociology; and sociology cannot know the dialectical principle with its passage from quantity to quality. [*Prison Notebooks*, quoted James Joll, *Gramsci*, Ch. 8]

3 Pessimism of the spirit; optimism of the will. [Attr.]

CARY GRANT

4 Telegram to C.G.'s agent: 'How old Cary Grant?' C.G.'s reply: 'Old Cary Grant fine. How you?' [Quoted in Leslie Halliwell, *The Filmgoer's Book of Quotes*]

GÜNTER GRASS

5 In a devious way I am uncomplicated. [*From the Diary of a Snail*]

6 You can begin a story in the middle and create confusion by striking out boldly, backward and forward. You can be modern, put aside all mention of time and distance and, when the whole thing is done, proclaim, or let someone else proclaim, that you have finally, at the last moment, solved the space–time problem. Or you can declare at the very start that it's impossible to write a novel nowadays, but then, behind your back, so to speak, give birth to a whopper, a novel to end all novels. [*The Tin Drum*, Bk I, 'The Wide Skirt']

7 What novel – or what else in the world – can have the epic scope of a photograph album? May our Father in Heaven, the untiring amateur who each Sunday snaps us from above, at an unfortunate angle that makes for hideous foreshortening, and pastes our pictures, properly exposed or not, in his album, guide me safely through this album of mine. [*Ib.* 'The Photograph Album']

8 Even bad books are books and therefore sacred. [*Ib.* 'Rasputin and the Alphabet']

ROBERT GRAVES

9 We spurred our parents to the kiss, / Though doubtfully they shrank from this. [*Children of Darkness*]

10 Children are dumb to say how hot the day is, / How hot the scent is of the summer rose. [*The Cool Web*]

11 Counting the beats, / Counting the slow heart beats, / The bleeding to death of time in slow heart beats, / Wakeful they lie. [*Counting the Beats*]

12 A gaping silken dragon, / Puffed by the wind, suffices us for God. [*The Cuirassiers of the Frontier*]

13 Yet love survives, the word carved on the sill / Under antique dread of the headsman's axe. [*End of Play*]

14 How not terrible / When the event outran the alarm / And suddenly we were free. [*The Fallen Tower of Siloam*]

15 I dung on my grandfather's doorstep, / Which is a reasonable and loving due / To hold no taint of spite or vassalage / And understood only by him and me. [*Front Door Soliloquy*]

16 This house is jealous of its nastiness. [*Ib.*]

17 To be mad is not easy, / Will earn him no money, / But a niche in the news. [*The Halls of Bedlam*]

18 These dusty-featured Lollocks / Have their nativity in all disordered / Backs of cupboard drawers. [*Lollocks*]

19 Is it not the height of silent humour / To cause an unknown change in the earth's climate? [*The Meeting*]

20 Stirring suddenly from long hibernation, / I knew myself once more a poet / Guarded by timeless principalities / Against the worm of death. [*Mid-Winter Waking*]

21 The thundering text, the snivelling commentary. [*Ogres and Pygmies*]

1 Any honest housewife would sort them out, / Having a nose for fish, an eye for apples. [*The Poets*]

2 What, then, was war? No mere discord of flags / But an infection of the common sky / That sagged ominously upon the earth / Even when the season was the airiest May? [*Recalling War*]

3 Fortune enrolled me among the second-fated / Who have read their own obituaries in *The Times*. [*The Second-Fated*]

4 Take your delight in momentariness, / Walk between dark and dark – a shining space / With the grave's narrowness, though not its peace. [*Sick Love*]

5 Why have such scores of lovely, gifted girls / Married impossible men? [*A Slice of Wedding Cake*]

6 Love is a universal migraine / A bright stain on the vision / Blotting out reason. [*Symptoms of Love*]

7 They carry / Time looped so river-wise about their house / There's no way in by history's road / To name or number them. [*Through Nightmare*]

8 To bring the dead to life / Is no great magic. / Few are wholly dead: / Blow on a dead man's embers / And a live flame will start. [*To Bring the Dead to Life*]

9 Subdue your pen to his handwriting / Until it prove as natural / To sign his name as yours. [*Ib.*]

10 To evoke posterity / Is to weep on your own grave, / Ventriloquizing for the unborn. [*To Evoke Posterity*]

11 It's an old story – f's for s's – / But good enough for them, the suckers. [*Wm. Brazier*]

12 Goodbye to All That. [Title of book]

13 Nowadays, to curse effectively one cannot rely merely on breaches of religious or semi-religious taboos; a reality or at least a plausibility must be invoked. [*Occupation: Writer*, 'Lars Porsena']

14 Among the working classes one of the unforgivable words of abuse is 'bastard' – because they take bastardy seriously. [*Ib.*]

15 For a woman to have a *liaison* is almost always pardonable, and occasionally, when the lover chosen is sufficiently distinguished, even admirable; but in love as in sport, the amateur status must be strictly maintained. [*Ib.*]

16 As for the Freudian, it is a very low, Central European sort of humour. [*Ib.* 'Mrs Fisher']

17 The poet is the unsatisfied child who dares to ask the difficult question which arises from the schoolmaster's answer to his simple question, and then the still more difficult question which arises from that. [*The White Goddess*, Ch. 6]

18 Nine-tenths of English poetic literature is the result either of vulgar careerism, or of a poet trying to keep his hand in. Most poets are dead by their late twenties. [Quoted in *Observer*, 11 Nov. 1962]

19 To be a poet is a condition rather than a profession. [In *Horizon* questionnaire, 1946]

20 The remarkable thing about Shakespeare is that he is really very good – in spite of all the people who say he is very good. [*Observer*, 'Sayings of the Week', 6 Dec. 1964]

21 I should define a good poem as one that makes complete sense; and says all it has to say memorably and economically, and has been written for no other than poetic reasons. [*Steps*, 'Talk on the Legitimate Criticism of Poetry']

ROBERT GRAVES and ALAN HODGE

22 When greeted by his Bishop on Easter morning with the ancient salutation 'Christ is Risen', he had boorishly withheld the expected response, 'He is Risen indeed,' and said instead: 'Yes, Sir!' [*The Long Week End*, Ch. 7]

23 At the superior nudist camps, a nice class distinction was made: the butlers and maids who brought along the refreshments were forced to admit their lower social standing by wearing loincloths and aprons respectively. [*Ib.* 16]

HAROLD GRAY

1 Little Orphan Annie [Title of American comic strip serial, 1925. Derived from song by J. W. Riley]

SIMON GRAY

2 Sixth-form teachers are something like firemen called in to quench flames that are already out. [*Butley*, Act II]

3 REG: Just one of those historical romances where the hero shoves his sword into assorted villains and his cock into assorted ladies. It won't get the reviews but it'll make us money.
BEN: If he did it the other way round you might get both. [*Ib.*]

4 STEPHEN: What have you got against having children?
SIMON: Well Steve, in the first place there isn't enough room. In the second place they seem to start by mucking up their parents' lives, and then go on in the third place to muck up their own. In the fourth place it doesn't seem right to bring them into a world like this in the fifth place and in the sixth place I don't like them very much in the first place. O.K.? [*Otherwise Engaged*, Act II]

5 In my experience, the worst thing you can do to an important problem is discuss it. [*Ib.*]

CELIA GREEN

6 The way to do research is to attack the facts at the point of greatest astonishment. [*The Decline and Fall of Science*, 'Aphorisms']

7 The remarkable thing about the human mind is its range of limitations. [*Ib.*]

8 In an autocracy, one person has his way; in an aristocracy, a few people have their way; in a democracy, no one has his way. [*Ib.*]

MICHAEL GREEN

9 Coarse sailing is not mucking around in boats, but boating around in muck. [*The Art of Coarse Sailing*, blurb]

GRAHAM GREENE

10 At one with the One, it didn't mean a thing beside a glass of Guinness on a sunny day. [*Brighton Rock*, Pt I, Ch. 1]

11 'Of course there's Hell. Flames and damnation,' he said ... 'torments.' [*Ib.* II. 1]

12 He trailed the clouds of his own glory after him; hell lay about him in his infancy. He was ready for more deaths. [*Ib.* II. 2]

13 Those who marry God ... can become domesticated too – it's just as humdrum a marriage as all the others. [*A Burnt-Out Case*, Ch. 1]

14 His slang ... was always a little out of date as though he had studied in a dictionary of popular usage, but not in the latest edition. [*The Comedians*, Pt I, Ch. 1, sect. i]

15 'One never knows ...' The phrase represented, I think, his deepest research into the meaning of life. [*Ib.* I. 1. iii]

16 Cynicism is cheap – you can buy it at any Monoprix store – it's built into all poor-quality goods. [*Ib.*]

17 However great a man's fear of life ... suicide remains the courageous act, the clear-headed act of a mathematician. The suicide has judged by the laws of chance – so many odds against one, that to live will be more miserable than to die. His sense of mathematics is greater than his sense of survival. [*Ib.* I. 4. i]

18 I have often noticed that a bribe ... has that effect – it changes a relation. The man who offers a bribe gives away a little of his own importance; the bribe once accepted, he becomes the inferior, like a man who has paid for a woman. [*Ib.* I. 4. iii]

19 We mustn't complain too much of being comedians – it's an honourable profession. If only we could be good ones the world might gain at least a sense of style. We have failed – that's all. We are bad comedians, we aren't bad men. [*Ib.* II. 5. ii]

20 Catholics and Communists have committed great crimes, but at least they

have not stood aside, like an established society, and been indifferent. I would rather have blood on my hands than water like Pilate. [*Ib.* III. 4. iv]

1 To me comfort is like the wrong memory at the wrong place or time: if one is lonely one prefers discomfort. [*The End of the Affair*, Pt I, Ch. 1]

2 'I see you were at the old place ... Those were the days, eh? ... I don't suppose you'd remember old Tester (six months for indecent assault). I try to keep up with them. Whose house were you?' [*England Made Me*, Pt II]

3 He spoke with the faintest foreign accent and it was difficult to determine whether he was Jewish or of an ancient English family. He gave the impression that very many cities had rubbed him smooth. [*A Gun for Sale*, Ch. 4, sect. iii]

4 Happiness is never really so welcome as changelessness. [*The Heart of the Matter*, Pt III, Ch. 3]

5 Hail Mary, quite contrary! [*Our Man in Havana*, Pt. I, Ch. 2]

6 Insanity is a kind of innocence. [*The Quiet American*, Pt III, Ch. 2, ii]

7 I had very good dentures once. Some very magnificent gold work. It's the only form of jewellery a man can wear that women fully appreciate. Dear things, they like to put their lips on gold. [*Travels With My Aunt*, Pt II, Ch. 7]

8 All of us at one time or another must have found ourselves in some deplorable and banal situation, haunted by literary parallels, and have discovered how actual life provides the untraditional twist: the untimely hiccups; the laugh in the wrong place. [*Observer*, 'Sayings of the Week', 12 Jun. 1938]

9 Sentimentality – that's what we call the sentiment we don't share. [Quoted in A. Andrews, *Quotations for Speakers and Writers*]

10 Fame is a powerful aphrodisiac. [Quoted in *Radio Times*, 10 Sep. 1964]

GERMAINE GREER

11 Man is jealous because of his *amour propre*; woman is jealous because of her lack of it. [*The Female Eunuch*, 'Egotism']

12 Women have very little idea of how much men hate them. [*Ib.* 'Loathing and Disgust']

13 Women are reputed never to be disgusted. The sad fact is that they often are, but not with men, they are most often disgusted with themselves. [*Ib.*]

JOYCE GRENFELL

14 George – don't do that. [*Passim* in 'Nursery Sketches', quoted in her book of same title]

15 Nikolas, you can manage a big crown, can't you? You've just the ears for it. I think if you pull your ears down a bit that will hold it up. [*George – Don't Do That*, 'Nativity Play']

16 All right, you shall be a cauliflower – only be it *gently*. [*Ib.* 'Flowers']

JULIAN GRENFELL

17 And he is dead who will not fight; / And who dies fighting has increase. [*Into Battle*]

W. GRENFELL

18 When one comes to think of it, it's odd that there should be so much admiration for prowess in drinking, which after all is merely a domestic virtue. [Quoted in Christopher Hassall, *Edward Marsh*, Ch. 8]

CLIFFORD GREY

19 If you were the only girl in the world / And I were the only boy. [Song from musical, *The Bing Boys*. Music by Nat Ayer]

SIR EDWARD GREY

20 The United States is like a gigantic boiler. Once the fire is lighted under it there is no limit to the power it can generate. [Quoted in Winston S. Churchill, *Their Finest Hour*, Ch. 32]

D. W. GRIFFITH

1 Viewed as drama, the [Great] War is somewhat disappointing. [Quoted in Leslie Halliwell, *The Filmgoer's Book of Quotes*]

MERVYN GRIFFITH-JONES

2 Would you allow your wife or your servant to read this book? [Presenting the case for the prosecution of *Lady Chatterley's Lover*, 1960]

TREVOR GRIFFITHS

3 It's the sort of suit you walk into a tailor's in and ask for the cheapest suit in the shop and he says you're wearing it. [*The Comedians*, Act I]

4 Cough and the world coughs with you. Fart and you stand alone. [*Ib.*]

5 We've got to make people laugh till they cry. Cry till they find their pain and their beauty. Comedy is medicine. Not coloured sweeties to rot their teeth with. [*Ib.*]

6 Had a look at the alligators. Just floating handbags, really. [*Ib.* II]

7 The intellectual's problem is not vision, it's commitment. You enjoy biting the hand that feeds you, but you'll never bite it off. [*The Party*, Act I]

8 There's nowt'll replace the formative intellectual matrices of a really well-run Sunday school. By Christ. [*Ib.* II]

JOHN GRIGG
(formerly **Lord Altrincham**)

9 Autobiography is now as common as adultery, and hardly less reprehensible. [In the *Sunday Times*, 28 Feb. 1962]

10 Lloyd George would have a better rating in British mythology if he had shared the fate of Abraham Lincoln. [*Observer*, 'Sayings of the Week', 7 Apr. 1963]

JO GRIMOND

11 He had a mind like a beautiful Clapham Junction, through which lines slid off at every sort of tangent. [Of an Oxford

friend killed in the war. Contribution to book, *My Oxford*]

GEORG GRODDECK

12 Whatever you blame, that you have done yourself. [Quoted in 'Palinurus' (Cyril Connolly), *The Unquiet Grave*, Pt III]

GEORGE GROSSMITH
(The Younger)

13 Yip-i-addy-addy-i-ay, i-ay, yip-i-addy-i-ay! [Song]

MAYOR LA GUARDIA

14 When I make a mistake, it's a beaut. [Quoted in *The Times*, 12 Oct. 1977]

GIOVANNI GUARESCHI

15 I had to do everything to stay alive and succeeded almost completely by dedicating myself to a precise programme which is summarized in my slogan 'I will not die even if they kill me.' [*The Little World of Don Camillo*, 'How I Got Like This']

PHILIP GUEDALLA

16 The cheerful clatter of Sir James Barrie's cans as he went round with the milk of human kindness. [*Some Critics*]

17 No picture of life in Calais was too ludicrous to be believed in Dover; that is one of the advantages of being an Island Race. [*Supers and Supermen*]

18 An Englishman is a man who lives on an island in the North Sea governed by Scotsmen. [*Ib.*]

19 Biography is a very definite region bounded on the north by history, on the south by fiction, on the east by obituary, and on the west by tedium. [*Observer*, 'Sayings of the Week', 3 Mar. 1929]

20 History repeats itself; historians repeat each other. [Quoted in A. Andrews, *Quotations for Speakers and Writers*]

21 The twentieth century is only the nineteenth speaking with a slight American accent. [Attr.]

TEXAS GUINAN

1 Hello, sucker! [Said to night-club customers]

ARTHUR GUITERMAN

2 Don't tell your friends about your indigestion: / 'How are you!' is a greeting, not a question. [*A Poet's Proverbs*, 'Of Tact'. See also 326:6]

SACHA GUITRY

3 If a playwright is funny, the English look for the serious message, and if he is serious they look for the joke. [*Observer*, 'Sayings of the Week', 19 Apr. 1957]

THOM GUNN

4 The group's name on the left, The Knights, / And on the right the slogan Born to Lose. [*Black Jackets*]

5 I saw that lack of love contaminates. / You know I know you know I know you know. [*Carnal Knowledge*]

6 We stand on a white terrace and confer; / This is the last camp of experience. [*From the Highest Camp*]

7 One is always nearer by not keeping still. [*On the Move*]

JOHN GUNTHER

8 Ours is the only country deliberately founded on a good idea. [*Inside America*]

GEORGE GURDJIEFF

9 [Man] is a machine, everything with him *happens* ... He lives in a subjective world ... He does not see the real world. The real world is hidden from him by the wall of imagination. *He lives in sleep*. [Quoted in P. D. Ouspensky, *In Search of the Miraculous*]

10 There is a war going on at the present moment. What does it signify? It signifies that several millions of sleeping people are trying to destroy several millions of other sleeping people. They would not do this, of course, if they were to wake up. [Quoted in *ib.*]

11 He can be called a remarkable man who stands out from those around him by the resourcefulness of his mind, and who knows how to be restrained in the manifestations which proceed from his nature, at the same time conducting himself justly and tolerantly towards the weaknesses of others. [*Meetings with Remarkable Men*, Introduction]

DAVID BEN GURION

12 It doesn't matter what the goyim say, what matters is what the Jews do. [Attr.]

ARLO GUTHRIE

13 I don't know, but I've been told / That the streets of heaven have all been sold. [Song. Quoted in J. Green, *A Book of Rock Quotes*]

WOODY GUTHRIE

14 Some men rob you with a six gun, / Some with a fountain pen. [*Pretty Boy Floyd*]

15 So Long, It's Been Good to Know Yuh. [Title of song]

H

EARL HAIG

1 FOCH: Are the men in good heart?
HAIG: They never were in better heart,
and are longing for a fight. [*Diaries*, 12
Sep. 1915]

EMPEROR HAILE SELASSIE OF ABYSSINIA

2 We have finished the job, what shall we
do with the tools? [Telegram in 1941 to
Winston Churchill, echoing his 'Give
us the tools, and we will finish the
job'. Quoted in Edward Marsh,
Ambrosia and Small Beer, Ch. 4]

LORD HAILSHAM

3 The Conservatives do not believe it
necessary, and, even if it were, we should
oppose it. [Reported in the *Oxford Mail*.
Quoted in M. Bateman, *This England*,
selections from the *New Statesman*, Pt
III]

4 [On the Profumo affair] A great party
is not to be brought down because of a
scandal by a woman of easy virtue and
a proved liar. [In BBC TV interview,
13 Jun. 1963. Quoted in Bernard Levin,
The Pendulum Years, Ch. 3]

5 If the British public falls for this
[Labour policies], I say it will be stark,
staring bonkers. [At press conference at
Conservative Central Office before
general election, 12 Oct. 1964]

J. B. S. HALDANE

6 Einstein – the greatest Jew since Jesus.
I have no doubt that Einstein's name
will still be remembered and revered
when Lloyd George, Foch and William
Hohenzollern share with Charlie Chaplin that ineluctable oblivion which
awaits the uncreative mind. [*Daedalus
or Science and the Future*]

7 Bad as our urban conditions often are,
there is not a slum in the country which
has a third of the infantile death-rate of
the royal family in the middle ages. [*Ib.*]

8 Shelley and Keats were the last English
poets who were at all up to date in their
chemical knowledge. [*Ib.*]

9 The conservative has but little to fear
from the man whose reason is the
servant of his passions, but let him beware of him in whom reason has become
the greatest and most terrible of passions. [*Ib.*]

10 If human beings could be propagated
by cutting, like apple trees, aristocracy
would be biologically sound. [*The
Inequality of Man*, title essay]

11 Christian Science is so often therapeutically successful because it lays stress
on the patient's believing in his or her
own health rather than in Noah's Ark
or the Ascension. [*Possible Worlds*,
'The Duty of Doubt']

12 An angel whose muscles developed no
more power weight for weight than
those of an eagle or a pigeon would
require a breast projecting for about
four feet to house the muscles engaged
in working its wings, while to economize in weight its legs would have to be
reduced to mere stilts. [*Ib.* 'On Being
the Right Size']

13 My own suspicion is that the universe
is not only queerer than we suppose,
but queerer than we can suppose. [*Ib.*
Quoted K. Clark, *Civilization*, Ch. 13.]

J. S. HALDANE

14 The conclusion forced upon me in the
course of a life devoted to natural
science is that the universe as it is assumed to be in physical science is a
spiritual universe in which spiritual

values count for everything. [*The Sciences and Philosophy*]

VISCOUNT HALDANE

1 I was a little exhausted when I arrived [at the War Office] . . . and asked the tall ex-Guards soldier in attendance for a glass of water. 'Certainly, sir: Irish or Scotch?' [Letter quoted in Dudley Sommer, *Haldane of Cloan*, Ch. 8]

2 Yes, I consider Lötze's classroom was my spiritual home. [Remark at Mrs Humphry Ward's, later distorted by Professor Oncken, so that it referred to Germany. *Ib*. 22]

3 The trouble with Lloyd George is that he thinks in images, not in concepts. [Said during the Victory election, 1919. *Ib*. 26]

GENERAL FRANZ HALDER

4 It is hardly too much to say that the campaign against Russia has been won in fourteen days. [Diary note, 3 Jul. 1941. Quoted in W. L. Shirer, *The Rise and Fall of the Third Reich*, Ch. 23]

ÉLIE HALÉVY

5 The Socialists believe in two things which are absolutely different and perhaps even contradictory: freedom and organization. [Quoted in W. R. Inge, *The End of an Age*]

PETER HALL

6 I don't regard Brecht as a man of iron-grey purpose and intellect, I think he is a theatrical whore of the first quality. [Quoted in Frank Muir, *The Frank Muir Book*]

WALTER HALLSTEIN

7 Anyone who does not believe in miracles in European affairs is no realist. [*On the Common Market*]

8 [Of the Common Market] We are not in business, we are in politics. [Quoted in R. Pryce, *The Political Future of the European Community*]

MARGARET HALSEY

9 Englishwomen's shoes look as if they had been made by someone who had often heard shoes described, but had never seen any. [*With Malice Toward Some*]

GENERAL SIR IAN HAMILTON

10 Dig, dig, dig! [Instructions at Gallipoli]

PATRICK HAMILTON

11 Sleep is gross, a form of abandonment, and it is impossible for anyone to awake and observe its sordid consequences save with a faint sense of recent dissipation, of minute personal disquiet and remorse. [*Slaves of Solitude*]

WILLIE HAMILTON

12 The tourists who come to our island take in the Monarchy along with feeding the pigeons in Trafalgar Square. [*My Queen and I*, Ch. 9]

13 Britain is not a country that is easily rocked by revolution . . . In Britain our institutions evolve. We are a Fabian Society writ large. [*Ib*.]

DAG HAMMARSKJÖLD

14 Pray that your loneliness may spur you into finding something to live for, great enough to die for. [*Diaries, 1951*]

15 In our era the road to holiness necessarily passes through the world of action. [*Ib*. 1955]

16 In the last analysis, it is our conception of death which decides our answers to all the questions that life puts to us. [*Ib*. 1958]

17 I don't know Who – or what – put the question, I don't know when it was put. I don't even remember answering. But at some moment I did answer *Yes* to Someone – or Something – and from that hour I was certain that existence is meaningful and that, therefore, my life, in self-surrender, had a goal. [*Markings*, 'Whitsunday 1961']

145

OSCAR HAMMERSTEIN II

1 I Whistle a Happy Tune. [Title of song from musical, *The King and I*, Act I. Music by Richard Rodgers]

2 Hello, Young Lovers, Wherever You Are. [Title of song from *ib.*]

3 Oh, what a beautiful morning! / Oh, what a beautiful day! [Song: *Oh, What a Beautiful Morning*, from musical, *Oklahoma*, Act I. Music by Richard Rodgers]

4 The corn is as high as an elephant's eye. [*Ib.*]

5 Ol' man river, dat ol' man river, / He must know sumpin', but don't say nothin', / He just keeps rollin', he keeps on rollin' along. [Song: *Ol' Man River* from musical *Show Boat*, Act I. Music by Jerome Kern]

6 Tired of living, / And scared of dying. [*Ib.*]

7 The hills are alive with the sound of music / With the songs they have sung / For a thousand years. [Title song from the musical, *The Sound of Music*. Music by Richard Rodgers]

8 Some enchanted evening, / you may see a stranger / 'Cross a crowded room. [Song: *Some Enchanted Evening*, from musical, *South Pacific*, Act I. Music by Richard Rodgers]

9 I'm Gonna Wash That Man Right Out of My Hair. [Title of song in *ib.*]

CHRISTOPHER HAMPTON

10 You know very well that unless you're a scientist, it's much more important for a theory to be shapely, than for it to be true. [*The Philanthropist*, sc. i]

11 You see, I always divide people into two groups. Those who live by what they know to be a lie, and those who live by what they believe, falsely, to be the truth. [*Ib.* vi]

12 If I had to give a definition of capitalism I would say: the process whereby American girls turn into American women. [*Savages*, sc. xvi]

13 It's possible to disagree with someone about the ethics of non-violence with-out wanting to kick his face in. [*Treats*, sc. iv]

14 You have wants the way other people have toothache. Kind of dull and general. [*Ib.* vi]

15 Asking a working writer what he thinks about critics is like asking a lamp-post how it feels about dogs. [Quoted in the *Sunday Times Magazine*, 16 Oct. 1977]

TONY HANCOCK

16 It's red hot, mate. I hate to think of this sort of book getting into the wrong hands. As soon as I've finished this, I shall recommend they ban it. [BBC TV comedy series, *Hancock's Half Hour*, 'The Missing Page'. Scripts by Ray Galton and Alan Simpson]

17 I'm having a little reunion of my old army pals. The Third East Cheam Light Horse. Three of the heaviest drinkers who ever set foot inside a pair of army boots. [*Ib.* 'The Reunion Party']

18 He was the only man I knew who came back from Dunkirk with two women . . . Well it's too far for one to row, isn't it? [*Ib.*]

19 And when I'm finally called, by the Great Architect, and he says 'What did you do?' I shall just bring me book out and say, 'Here you are, add that lot up.' [*Ib.* 'The Blood Donor']

20 I came in here in all good faith to help my country. I don't mind giving a reasonable amount [of blood], but a pint . . . why that's very nearly an armful. I'm sorry. I'm not walking around with an empty arm for anybody. [*Ib.*]

21 Flippin' kids! [Catch-phrase in BBC radio comedy series, *Educating Archie*.]

IRENE HANDL

22 They are silly. They asked me if I'd mind having a slight moustache in this film – and I've got one anyhow. [Quoted in Edward Marsh, *Ambrosia and Small Beer*, Ch. 3]

TERRY HANDS

23 English actresses are mistresses and French ones clever daughters. [Attr.

Quoted in the *Sunday Times Magazine*, 26 Nov. 1978]

JAMES HANLEY

1 That is the art of living that your price shall suit everybody. [*Drift*. Ch. 2]

2 You talk about walking in the wilderness, but what else *is* the world but that, and besides, aren't we all walking in one kind of wilderness or another, since only we can make them. [*A Walk in the Wilderness*, title story]

OTTO HARBACH and FRANK MANDEL

3 Tea for Two, and Two for Tea. [Title of song from musical, *No, No, Nanette*, Act II. Music by Vincent Youmans]

MAJOR-GENERAL HARBORD

4 I met the great little man [Colonel House], the man who can be silent in several languages. [John Dos Passos, *Mr Wilson's War*, Ch. 3, sect. xv]

E. Y. HARBURG

5 Brother, Can You Spare a Dime? [Title of song from musical, *New Americana*. Music by Jay Gorney]

6 Say, it's only a paper moon, / Sailing over a cardboard sea. [Song: *Paper Moon*, from musical, *Take A Chance*]

7 Someday I'll wish upon a star. [Song: *Over the Rainbow* from film, *The Wizard of Oz*. Music by Harold Arlen]

8 Somewhere over the rainbow, / Way up high: / There's a land that I heard of / Once in a lullaby. [*Ib.*]

GILBERT HARDING

9 I would like to quote what a judge said not long ago – that all his experience both as Counsel and Judge had been spent in sorting out the difficulties of people who, upon the recommendation of people they did not know, signed documents which they did not read, to buy goods they did not need, with money they had not got. [Television answer to question on subject of hire purchase. Quoted in *Gilbert Harding and His Friends*]

10 I've never consciously striven for worldly success. But once I was aware I had it I must say that I'm terrified of losing it. [*Ib.*]

11 WYNFORD VAUGHAN THOMAS: Try and seem full of the milk of human kindness.
G.H.: I am full of the stuff, damn it. My trouble is that it gets clotted so easily. [*Ib.*]

12 [To Mae West's manager, who had asked, 'Can't you sound a bit more sexy when you interview her'] If, sir, I possessed the power of conveying unlimited sexual attraction through the potency of my voice, I would not be reduced to accepting a miserable pittance from the BBC for interviewing a faded female in a damp basement. [*Ib.*]

THOMAS HARDY

13 Where once we danced, where once we sang, Gentlemen, / The floors are shrunken, cobwebs hang. [*An Ancient to Ancients*]

14 Yet hear – no doubt to your surprise – / I am grieving, for his sake, / That I have escaped the sacrifice / I was distressed to make! [*Cross-currents*]

15 Smile out; but still suffer: / The paths of love are rougher / Than thoroughfares of stones. [*The End of the Episode*]

16 She chose her bearers before she died / From her fancy-men. [*Julie-Jane*]

17 There's not a modest maiden elf / But dreads the final Trumpet, / Lest half of her should rise herself, / And half some sturdy strumpet! [*The Levelled Churchyard*]

18 'Well, though it seems / Beyond our dreams,' / Said Liddell to Scott, / 'We've really got / To the very end.' [*Liddell and Scott*]

19 Queer are the ways of a man I know. [*The Phantom Horsewoman*]

20 The Roman Road runs straight and bare / As the pale parting-line in hair. [*The Roman Road*]

1 There was Life – pale and hoar; / And slow it said to me, / 'Twice-over cannot be!' [*A Second Attempt*]

2 You were the sort that men forget; / Though I – not yet! – / Perhaps not ever. [*You Were the Sort That Men Forget*]

3 Oh, but I admire the *Iliad* greatly. Why, it's in the *Marmion* class! [Said to T. E. Lawrence. Quoted in Robert Graves, *Good-bye to All That*]

DAVID HARE

4 The theatre is the best way of showing the gap between what is said and what is seen to be done, and that is why, ragged and gap-toothed as it is, it has still a far healthier potential than some poorer, abandoned arts. [*Sunday Times Magazine*, 26 Nov. 1978, 'The Playwright as Historian']

WILLIAM HARGREAVES

5 P.C. 49 [Title of music-hall song]

J. P. HARRINGTON

6 Be Good. If You Can't Be Good, Be Careful! [Title of Song. Music by Tate]

7 Everything in the Garden's Lovely! [Title of music-hall song, sung by Marie Lloyd]

8 Now your country calls you far across the sea, / To do a soldier's duty / For England, home and beauty. [Song: *The Girls You Leave Behind You*]

LORENZ HART

9 Bewitched, Bothered and Bewildered. [Title of song in musical, *Babes in Arms*]

10 That's Why the Lady Is a Tramp. [Title of song in *ib.*]

L. P. HARTLEY

11 The past is a foreign country: they do things differently there. [*The Go-between*, opening words]

MINNIE HASKINS

12 And I said to the man who stood at the gate of the year: 'Give me a light that I may tread safely into the unknown.' And he replied: 'Go out into the darkness and put your hand into the hand of God. That shall be to you better than light and safer than a known way.' [*The Desert*, Introduction. Quoted by King George VI in his Christmas Broadcast, 1939]

CHRISTOPHER HASSALL

13 Some Day My Heart Will Awake. [Title of song from operetta, *King's Rhapsody*, Act I. Music by Ivor Novello]

14 She's genuinely bogus. [Attr. remark on Dame Edith Sitwell]

CAPTAIN GEORGE HASWELL

15 Gentlemen, before the barrage lifts! [Toast before the Battle of the Somme, 1916. Quoted in E. Bush, *Salute the Soldier*]

IAN HAY

16 There is nothing so thoroughly enthuses the feminine mind as an imaginary injustice perpetrated upon someone unknown to her and under circumstances of which she knows nothing. [*The Knight on Wheels*]

WILL HAY

17 MASTER: They split the atom by firing particles at it, at 5,500 miles a second. BOY: Good heavens. And they only split it? [*Passim* in music-hall and radio comedy sketches, *The Fourth Form at St Michael's*]

18 MASTER: Well, who *was* Noah's wife? BOY: Joan of Arc. [*Ib.*]

J. MILTON HAYES

19 There's a one-eyed yellow idol to the north of Khatmandu, / There's a little marble cross below the town, / There's a broken-hearted woman tends the grave of Mad Carew, / And the Yellow God forever gazes down. [*The Green Eye of the Yellow God*]

ARTHUR GARFIELD HAYS

1 When there's a rift in the lute, the business of the lawyer is to widen the rift and gather the loot. [Quoted in A. Andrews, *Quotations for Speakers and Writers*]

JOHN HAYWARD

2 ... A French master at Eton who, after teaching there for 30 years, brought out a little book of instructional dialogues, the first of which began: 'One of the boys in our house has three balls.' 'Has he? Hurrah!' The book had to be re-recalled, and another first page substituted. [Quoted in Edward Marsh, *Ambrosia and Small Beer*, Ch. 5, sect. ii]

DENIS HEALEY

3 Their [the Conservatives'] Europeanism is nothing but imperialism with an inferiority complex. [*Observer*, 'Sayings of the Week', 7 Oct. 1962]

4 Like being savaged by a dead sheep. [On being attacked in a parliamentary debate by Geoffrey Howe over his Budget proposals. Quoted in the *Listener*, 21 Dec. 1978]

TIM HEALY, K.C.

5 Gentlemen, we have witnessed today the greatest miracle since Moses struck the rock: tears from my learned friend. [When Mr Campbell, later Lord Glenavy, wept at the close of a divorce action in which he represented the plaintiff. Quoted in O. St John Gogarty, *As I was Going Down Sackville Street*, Ch. 7]

SEAMUS HEANEY

6 Keep your eye clear / as the blob of the icicle, / trust the feel of what nubbed treasure / your hands have known. [*North*, title poem]

7 Good writing, like good smithy work, is a compound of energy and artifice. [*Observer*, 'Sayings of the Week', 8 Feb. 1970]

W. R. HEARST

8 Stop running those dogs on your page. I wouldn't have them peeing on my cheapest rug. [Comment to editor who was publishing Thurber's drawings. Quoted in James Thurber, *The Years with Ross*]

EDWARD HEATH

9 It is the unpleasant and unacceptable face of capitalism. [Of the Lonrho Affair. Said in the House of Commons, 15 May 1973]

FRED HEATHERTON

10 I've got a loverly bunch of cocoanuts, / There they are a-standing in a row, / Big ones, small ones, some as big as your head. [Song: *I've Got a Lovely Bunch of Cocoanuts*]

11 Singing roll or bowl a ball, a penny a pitch. [*Ib.*]

BEN HECHT

12 The hand of God, reaching down into the mire, couldn't elevate one of them to the depths of degradation. [Film, *Nothing Sacred*]

13 [Of New York] A city where wise guys peddle gold bricks to each other and Truth, crushed down to earth, rises again as phoney as a glass eye. [*Ib.*]

14 To me Pound remains the exquisite showman minus the show. [*Pounding Ezra*]

ERIC HEFFER

15 They are nothing else but a load of kippers, two-faced with no guts. [Of the Conservative Party. Said in the House of Commons, n.d.]

MARTIN HEIDEGGER

16 Only when we turn thoughtfully toward what has already been thought, will we be turned to use for what must still be thought. [*Identity and Difference*]

149

1 We are too late for the gods, too early for Being. [Quoted in review, *Times Literary Supplement*, 1 Jul. 1965]

ROBERT HEINLEIN

2 Stranger in a Strange Land. [Title of novel]

WERNER HEISENBERG

3 An expert is someone who knows some of the worst mistakes that can be made in his subject, and how to avoid them. [*Physics and Beyond*]

4 Natural science does not simply describe and explain nature, it is part of the interplay between nature and ourselves. [*Physics and Philosophy*]

5 Every word or concept, clear as it may seem to be, has only a limited range of applicability. [*Ib.*]

JOSEPH HELLER

6 It was truly a splendid structure, and Yossarian throbbed with a mighty sense of accomplishment each time he gazed at it and reflected that none of the work that had gone into it was his. [*Catch-22*, Ch. 2]

7 'You're crazy,' Clevinger shouted vehemently, his eyes filling with tears. 'You've got a Jehovah complex.' [*Ib.*]

8 He was a self-made man who owed his lack of success to nobody. [*Ib.* 3]

9 He had decided to live for ever or die in the attempt. [*Ib.*]

10 He had opposed his daughter's marriage to Colonel Moodus because he disliked attending weddings. [*Ib.* 4]

11 He disapproved of Adolf Hitler, who had done such a great job of combating un-American activities in Germany. [*Ib.*]

12 Even when he cheated he couldn't win, because the people he cheated against were always better at cheating too. [*Ib.*]

13 I've got these rubber models in my office with all the reproductive organs of both sexes, that I keep locked up in separate cabinets to avoid a scandal. [*Ib.* 5]

14 He could barely read or write and had been assigned to Captain Black as assistant intelligence officer. [*Ib.*]

15 There was only one catch and that was Catch-22, which specified that a concern for one's own safety in the face of dangers that were real and immediate was the process of a rational mind. [*Ib.*]

16 So convincing were these dreams of lying awake that he awoke from them each morning in complete exhaustion and fell right back to sleep. [*Ib.* 6]

17 He knew everything about literature except how to enjoy it. [*Ib.* 8]

18 There was little she hadn't tried and less she wouldn't. [*Ib.*]

19 She was a crazy mathematics major from the Wharton School of Business who could not count to twenty-eight each month without getting into trouble. [*Ib.*]

20 Some men are born mediocre, some men achieve mediocrity. and some men have mediocrity thrust upon them. With Major Major it had been all three. [*Ib.* 9]

21 Hungry Joe collected lists of fatal diseases and arranged them in alphabetical order so that he could put his finger without delay on any one he wanted to worry about. [*Ib.* 17]

22 Good God, how much reverence can you have for a Supreme Being who finds it necessary to include such phenomena as phlegm and tooth-decay in His divine system of Creation? [*Ib.* 18]

23 Frankly, I'd like to see the government get out of war altogether and leave the whole field to private industry. [*Ib.* 24]

24 I want those letters to be sincere letters. I want them filled up with lots of personal details so there'll be no doubt I mean every word you say. [*Ib.* 25]

25 General Peckem liked listening to himself talk, liked most of all listening to himself talk about himself. [*Ib.* 29]

26 Prostitution gives her an opportunity to meet people. It provides fresh air and wholesome exercise, and it keeps her out of trouble. [*Ib.* 33]

LILLIAN HELLMAN

1 It is a mark of many famous people that they cannot part with their brightest hour. [*Pentimento*, 'Theatre']

2 For anybody of my generation, so eager for the neurosis, yours if you could manage it, if desperate somebody else's . . . [*Ib.*]

3 The English don't raise their voices, Arthur, although they may have other vulgarities. [*Ib.* 'Arthur W. A. Cowan']

4 I am suspicious of guilt in myself and in other people: it is usually a way of not thinking, or of announcing one's own fine sensibilities the better to be rid of them fast. [*Scoundrel Time*]

5 I cannot and will not cut my conscience to fit this year's fashions. [Letter to House Committee of un-American Activities, 19 May 1952, quoted in *ib.*]

ROBERT HELPMAN

6 I'm going to introduce sex into *Romeo and Juliet*. [*Observer*, 'Sayings of the Year', Jan. 1957]

ERNEST HEMINGWAY

7 If you are lucky enough to have lived in Paris as a young man, then wherever you go for the rest of your life, it stays with you, for Paris is a moveable feast. [*A Moveable Feast*, epigraph]

8 A man can be destroyed but not defeated. [*The Old Man and the Sea*]

9 A serious writer is not to be confounded with a solemn writer. A serious writer may be a hawk or a buzzard or even a popinjay, but a solemn writer is always a bloody owl. [Quoted in Cyril Connolly, *Enemies of Promise*, Ch. 8]

10 I started out very quiet and I beat Mr Turgenev. Then I trained hard and I beat Mr de Maupassant. I've fought two draws with Mr Stendhal, and I think I had an edge in the last one. But nobody's going to get me in any ring with Mr Tolstoy unless I'm crazy or I keep getting better. [Quoted in Lillian Ross, *Portrait of Hemingway*]

11 An analyst once wrote me, What did I learn from psychoanalysts. I answered, Very little but hope they had learned as much as they were able from my published works. [Quoted in *ib.*]

12 All good books are alike in that they are truer than if they had really happened. [Quoted in A. Andrews, *Quotations for Speakers and Writers*]

13 [Describing William Faulkner] Old Corndrinking Mellifluous. [Quoted in Carlos Baker, *Ernest Hemingway, A Life Story*]

14 Grace under pressure. [Definition of courage. Quoted in J. F. Kennedy, *Profiles in Courage*, Ch. 1]

15 If people bring so much courage to this world, the world has to kill them . . . It kills the very good and very gentle and the very brave impartially. [Quoted in Arthur M. Schlesinger Jr, *A Thousand Days*]

LEON HENDERSON

16 I got my job by hollering, and no day passes but what I holler about something. [Arthur Schlesinger Jr, *The Coming of the New Deal*, Pt II, Ch. 10, sect. iv]

SIR NEVILLE HENDERSON

17 He [Goering] may be a blackguard, but not a dirty blackguard. [Speech at Sleaford, reported in *News Chronicle*. Quoted in M. Bateman, *This England*, selections from the *New Statesman*, Pt II]

ADRIAN HENRI

18 Love is a fanclub with only two fans. [*Love Is . . .*]

O. HENRY (W. S. PORTER)

19 I guess I must have had New England ancestors away back and inherited some of their staunch and rugged fear of the police. [*Conscience in Art*]

20 Esau, that swapped his copyright for a partridge. [*Cupid à la Carte*]

21 There was always something in her voice that made you think of lorgnettes,

of accounts at Tiffany's, of sledges smoothly gliding on the trail from Dawson to Forty Mile, of the tinkling of pendant prisms on your grandmother's chandeliers, of snow lying on a convent roof; of a police sergeant refusing bail. [*The Defeat of the City*]

1 The road lay curling around wood and dale like a ribbon lost from the robe of a careless summer. [*Ib.*]

2 Busy as a one-armed man with the nettlerash pasting on wall-paper. [*The Ethics of Pig*]

3 The true adventurer goes forth aimless and uncalculating to meet and greet unknown fate. A fine example was the Prodigal Son – when he started back home. [*The Green Door*]

4 About the only job left that a woman can beat a man in is female impersonator in vaudeville. [*The Hand that Rules the World*]

5 Men to whom life had appeared as a reversible coat – seamy on both sides. [*The Hiding of Black Bill*]

6 Of course there was nothing the matter with me, but I was very ill. I couldn't work, sleep, eat or bowl. The only way I could get any sympathy was to go without shaving for four days. [*Let Me Feel Your Pulse*]

7 The bride sat in the rocker with her feet resting upon the world. She was wrapt in rosy dreams and a kimono of the same hue. [*Little Speck in Garnered Fruit*]

8 Bagdad-on-the-Subway. [Said of New York in *A Madison Square Arabian Night*, also in other stories]

9 A burglar who respects his art always takes his time before taking anything else. [*Makes the Whole World Kin*]

10 He had the artistic metempsychosis which is half drunk when sober and looks down on airships when stimulated. [*A Midsummer Masquerade*]

11 Satan . . . is a hard boss to work for . . . When other people are having their vacation is when he keeps you the busiest. As old Dr Watts or St Paul or some other diagnostician says: 'He always finds somebody for idle hands to do.' [*Ib.*]

12 A kind of mixture of fools and angels – they rush in and fear to tread at the same time. [*The Moment of Victory*]

13 He was brought up with the idea that to be beautiful was to make good. [*Next to Reading Matter*]

14 She would have made a splendid wife, for crying only made her eyes more bright. [*No Story*]

15 Whenever he saw a dollar in another man's hands he took it as a personal grudge, if he couldn't take it any other way. [*The Octopus Marooned*]

16 There are two times when you never can tell what is going to happen. One is when a man takes his first drink; and the other is when a woman takes her latest. [*Ib.*]

17 He was outwardly decent and managed to preserve his aquarium, but inside he was impromptu and full of unexpectedness. [*Ib.*]

18 The room was about full of curly-headed Cubans and South-American brunettes of different shades and the atmosphere was international with cigarette smoke, lit up by diamond rings, and edged off with a whisper of garlic. [*On Behalf of the Management*]

19 Ready to melt in the crucible of her ire a little more gold plating from the wrought steel chains of matrimony. [*The Pendulum*]

20 He wrote love stories, a thing I have always kept free from, holding the belief that the well-known and popular sentiment is not properly a matter for publication, but something to be privately handled by the alienists and the florists. [*The Plutonian Fire*]

21 There is always hope for a man who, when sober, will not concede or acknowledge that he was ever drunk. [*The Rubaiyat of a Scotch Highball*]

22 A straw vote only shows which way the hot air blows. [*A Ruler of Men*]

23 The best grafts in the world are built up on copybook maxims and psalms and proverbs and Esau's fables. They seem

to kind of hit off human nature. [*A Tempered Wind*]

1 There was too much scenery and fresh air. What I need is a steam-heated flat with no ventilation or exercise. [Letter, 15 April 1910]

2 Turn up the lights; I don't want to go home in the dark. [Last words. Quoted in W. Neil, *Concise Dictionary of Religious Quotations*]

A. P. HERBERT

3 Bring porridge, bring sausage, bring fish for a start, / Bring kidneys and mushrooms and partridges' legs, / But let the foundation be bacon and eggs. [*A Book of Ballads*, 'Bacon and Eggs']

4 Don't let's go to the dogs tonight, / For mother will be there. [*Ib.* 'Don't let's go']

5 For Kings and governments may err / But never Mr Baedeker. [*Ib.* 'Mr Baedeker, or Britons Abroad']

6 Other people's babies – / That's my life! / Mother to dozens, / And nobody's wife. [*Ib.* 'Other People's Babies']

7 Nothing is wasted, nothing is in vain: / The seas roll over but the rocks remain. [*Tough at the Top*]

8 And when the film was finished quite / It made my bosom swell / To find that by electric light / I loved her just as well. [*Ib.* ''Twas at the Pictures, Child, We Met']

9 For I should be a perfect dear / On fifty thousand pounds a year. [*Come to the Ball*, an adaptation of *Die Fledermaus*]

10 The Treasury are never happy; even in Paradise they will be worried about excessive imports. [*Observer*, 'Sayings of the Week', 19 Apr. 1964]

11 The critical period in matrimony is breakfast time. [Attr.]

OLIVER HERFORD

12 She has a whim of iron. [Quoted in F. Crowninshield, *A Wit with a Whim of Iron*]

13 Only the young die good. [Quoted in A. Andrews, *Quotations for Speakers and Writers*]

14 Diplomacy – lying in state. [Quoted in Laurence J. Peter, *Peter's Quotations*]

ÉDOUARD HERRIOT

15 When it's a question of peace one must talk to the Devil himself. [*Observer*, 'Sayings of the Week', 21 Sep. 1953]

WERNER HERZOG

16 Film is not the art of scholars but of illiterates. Film culture is not analysis but agitation of the mind. [Quoted by D. Malcolm in the *Guardian*, 8 Sep. 1977]

HERMANN HESSE

17 If you hate a person, you hate something in him that is part of yourself. What isn't part of ourselves doesn't disturb us. [*Demian*, Ch. 6]

18 The man of power is ruined by power, the man of money by money, the submissive man by subservience, the pleasure seeker by pleasure. [*Steppenwolf*, 'Treatise on the Steppenwolf']

19 The bourgeois is consequently by nature a creature of weak impulses, anxious, fearful of giving himself away and easy to rule. Therefore, he has substituted majority for power, law for force, and the polling booth for responsibility. [*Ib.*]

20 As a body everyone is single, as a soul never. [*Ib.*]

21 I believe that the struggle against death, the unconditional and self-willed determination to live, is the motive power behind the lives and activities of all outstanding men. [*Ib.*]

22 The war against death ... is always a beautiful, noble and wonderful and glorious thing, and so, it follows, is the war against war. But it is always hopeless and quixotic too. [*Ib.*]

LORD HEWART

1 A long line of cases shows that it is not merely of some importance, but it is of fundamental importance, that justice should not only be done, but should manifestly and undoubtedly be seen to be done. [R. Jackson, *The Chief*]

DUBOSE HEYWARD

2 Summertime, and the living is easy. [Song: *Summertime*, from musical, *Porgy and Bess*. Music by George Gershwin]

SEYMOUR HICKS

3 You will recognize, my boy, the first sign of age: it is when you go out into the streets of London and realize for the first time how young the policemen look. [Quoted in Pulling, *They Were Singing*, Ch. 7]

CHRISTOPHER HILL

4 Only very slowly and late have men come to realize that unless freedom is universal it is only extended privilege. [*The Century of Revolution*, Ch. 20]

GEOFFREY HILL

5 He considers the lilies, the rewards. / There is no substitute for a rich man. [*To the (Supposed) Patron*]

JOE HILL

6 You'll get pie in the sky when you die. [Quoted in Alan Lomax, *Folk Songs of North America*, No. 222]

7 Don't mourn, organize. [Before being shot by firing squad, Utah State Penitentiary, 19 Nov. 1915]

SIR EDMUND HILLARY

8 There is precious little in civilization to appeal to a Yeti. [*Observer*, 'Sayings of the Week', 3 Jun. 1960]

HEINRICH HIMMLER

9 We shall never be rough and heartless when it is not necessary, that is clear.

We Germans, who are the only people in the world who have a decent attitude towards animals, will also assume a decent attitude towards these human animals. [Speech, 4 Oct. 1943]

PAUL HINDEMITH

10 Today unexplored regions of the stringed instruments' fingerboard are non-existent; even the arctic zones of the eternal rosin (near the bridge) have become a habitable abode for fearless climbers. [*A Composer's World*, Ch. 7, sect. ii]

EMPEROR HIROHITO OF JAPAN

11 We have resolved to endure the unendurable and suffer what is insufferable. [After the dropping of the atomic bomb on Hiroshima, Aug. 1945. Quoted by A. J. P. Taylor, in the *Listener*, 9 Sep. 1976]

12 You can't imagine the extra work I had when I was a god. [On visit to London, as band played 'God Save the Queen']

ALFRED HITCHCOCK

13 Actors are cattle. [Attr. remark. Quoted in Leslie Halliwell, *The Filmgoer's Book of Quotes*]

14 For me the cinema is not a slice of life, but a piece of cake. [Quoted in the *Sunday Times Magazine*, 6 Mar. 1977]

RAYMOND HITCHCOCK

15 All dressed up and nowhere to go. [From song. Quoted in Eric Partridge, *A Dictionary of Catch-Phrases*]

ADOLF HITLER

16 With a suitcase full of clothes and underwear in my hand and an indomitable will in my heart, I set out for Vienna . . . I too hoped to become 'something'. [*Mein Kampf*, Ch. 1]

17 All those who are not racially pure are mere chaff. [*Ib.* 2]

18 The broad masses of the people can be moved only by the power of speech. All

154

great movements are popular movements, volcanic eruptions of human passions and emotional sentiments, stirred either by the cruel Goddess of Distress or by the firebrand of the word hurled among the masses. [*Ib.* 3]

1 The art of leadership ... consists in consolidating the attention of the people against a single adversary and taking care that nothing will split up that attention. [*Ib.*]

2 Only constant repetition will finally succeed in imprinting an idea on the memory of the crowd. [*Ib.* 6]

3 The great masses of the people ... will more easily fall victims to a big lie than to a small one. [*Ib.* 10]

4 I have never delivered a firebrand speech. [In 1933. *Observer*, 'Sayings of Our Times', 31 May 1953]

5 The victor will not be asked afterwards whether he told the truth or not. In starting and waging a war it is not right that matters, but victory. [Quoted in W. L. Shirer, *The Rise and Fall of the Third Reich*, Ch. 16]

6 I can see no reason why this war must go on. [Speech after the fall of France, quoted in *ib.* 21]

7 When Barbarossa [the invasion of Russia] commences, the world will hold its breath and make no comment. [To Gen. Halder, quoted in *ib.* 23]

8 The essential thing is the formation of the political will of the nation: that is the starting point for political action. [Speech at Düsseldorf, 27 Jan. 1932. Quoted in Alan Bullock, *Hitler*, Pt I, Ch. 4]

9 According to the English there are two countries in the world today which are led by adventurers: Germany and Italy. But England, too, was led by adventurers when she built her Empire. Today she is ruled merely by incompetents. [Remarks to Ciano. Quoted in *ib.* VI. 6]

10 I go the way that Providence dictates with the assurance of a sleepwalker. [Quoted in *ib.* VII. 1]

11 It almost causes me pain to think that I should have been selected by Fate to deal the final blow to the structure which these men [the British government] have already set tottering ... Mr Churchill ought, perhaps, for once to believe me when I prophesy that a great Empire will be destroyed which it was never my intention to destroy or even to harm. [Speech to the Reichstag, 19 Jul. 1940. Quoted in *ib.* X. 3]

12 I can only be grateful to Providence that it entrusted me with the leadership in this historic struggle, which, for the next five hundred or a thousand years, will be described as decisive, not only for the history of Germany but for the whole of Europe and indeed the whole world. A historical revision on a unique scale has been imposed on us by the Creator. [Speech on declaring war on the USA. Quoted in *ib.* XII. 2]

13 The little affair of operational command is something that anybody can do. [To General Halder. Quoted in *ib.*]

14 We have mastered a destiny which broke another man [Napoleon] a hundred and thirty years ago [Speech to the Reichstag, 26 Apr. 1942. Quoted in *ib.* XII. 3]

15 The man should have shot himself ... What hurts me most, personally, is that I promoted him to Field-Marshal ... That's the last Field-Marshal I shall appoint in this war. [On von Paulus's surrender at Stalingrad. Quoted in *ib.* XII. 4]

16 On land I am a hero, but on water I am a coward. [Words to von Runstedt. Quoted in Shulman, *Defeat in the West*]

17 I don't see much future for the Americans ... Everything about the behaviour of American society reveals that it's half judaized, and the other half negrified. How can one expect a state like that to hold together? [*Hitler's Secret Conversation*]

18 We cannot tolerate any more the tutelage of governesses. [Ref. to Great Britain after Munich. Quoted in Winston S. Churchill, *The Gathering Storm*, Ch. 18]

19 Rather than go through it [his meeting with Franco] again, ... I would prefer to have three or four of my teeth out.

[To Mussolini. Quoted from Ciano's *Diplomatic Papers* in Winston S. Churchill, *Their Finest Hour*, Ch. 26]

1 I am not annoyed with Hungary, but she has missed the bus. [Conversation with Darányi, quoted in A. J. P. Taylor, *The Origins of the Second World War*, Ch. 9]

2 GOERING: It is time to stop this *va banque*.
HITLER: It is the only call I ever make. [Conversation of 29 Aug. 1939. Quoted from Weizsäcker in *ib.* 11]

3 Is Paris burning? [On the liberation of Paris, 1944]

4 Who says I am not under the special protection of God? [Attr. After attempt on his life, 20 Jul. 1944]

5 Well, he [Chamberlain] seemed such a nice old gentleman, I thought I would give him my autograph as a souvenir. [After Munich. Attr.]

RUSSELL HOBAN

6 If the past cannot teach the present and the father cannot teach the son, then history need not have bothered to go on, and the world has wasted a great deal of time. [*The Lion of Boaz-Jachin and Jachin-Boaz*, Ch. 1]

7 Everything that is found is always lost again, and nothing that is found is ever lost again. [*Ib.* 2]

8 When you suffer an attack of nerves you're being attacked by the nervous system. What chance has a man got against a system? [*Ib.* 13]

9 There were times when it seemed to him that the different parts of him were not all under the same management. [*Ib.* 15]

10 A map is the dead body of where you've been. A map is the unborn baby of where you're going. There are no maps. Maps are pictures of what isn't. [*Ib.* 22]

11 After all, when you come right down to it, how many people speak the same language even when they speak the same language? [*Ib.* 27]

12 'Cheers,' said Jachin-Boaz, making an upward gesture with two fingers. 'You do it the other way for victory,' said the doctor. 'When I see a victory I'll do it that way,' said Jachin-Boaz. [*Ib.* 28]

13 Sometimes there's nothing but Sundays for weeks on end. Why can't they move Sunday to the middle of the week so you could put it in the OUT tray on your desk. [*Ib.* 32]

14 'Who can know anybody?' said the bookshop owner. 'Every person is like thousands of books. New, reprinting, in stock, out of stock, fiction, non-fiction, poetry, rubbish. The lot. Different every day. One's lucky to be able to put his hand on the one that's wanted, let alone know it.' [*Ib.*]

15 'NIGHT BATTLE ON MEADOW BORDER RESULTS IN ...' He paused and flew lower, in some confusion as to who had won and who had lost. 'VICTORY!' he concluded ... [*The Mouse and his Child*, Ch. 3]

16 His eyes look as if he's pawned his real ones and is wearing paste. [*Turtle Diary*, Ch. 2]

17 The sign said: 'The Green Turtle, *Chelonia mydas*, is the source of turtle soup ...' I am the source of William G. soup if it comes to that. Everyone is the source of his or her kind of soup. In a town as big as London that's a lot of soup walking about. [*Ib.* 3]

18 But when I don't smoke I scarcely feel as if I'm living. I don't feel as if I'm living unless I'm killing myself. [*Ib.* 7]

19 Me, what's that after all? An arbitrary limitation of being bounded by the people before and after and on either side. Where they leave off I begin, and vice versa. [*Ib.* 11]

20 Only a certain number of things can happen and whatever can happen *will* happen. The differences in scale and costume do not alter the event. Oedipus went to Thebes, Peter Rabbit into Mr McGregor's garden, but the story is essentially the same: life points only towards the terror. [*Ib.* 12]

21 He went out with his telephoto lens thrusting before him like a three-foot optical erection. If the authorities ever twig what cameras are about they'll make old men stop flashing their telephotos. [*Ib.* 13]

1 And now it seems she's on my wavelength. That's all I need. My mind isn't much of a comfort to me but at least I thought it was private. [*Ib.* 21]

2 In all the photographs I've seen of him Stravinsky looks to me like a man who was potty-trained too early and that music proves it as far as I'm concerned. [*Ib.* 25]

3 Nothing to be done really about animals. Anything you do looks foolish. The answer isn't in us. It's almost as if we're put here on earth to show how silly they aren't. [*Ib.* 42]

4 I'd always assumed I was the central character in my own story but now it occurred to me I might in fact be only a minor character in someone else's. [*Ib.* 51]

5 Explorers have to be ready to die lost. [Interview in *The Times*, 1975]

HAROLD HOBSON

6 The United States, I believe, are under the impression that they are twenty years in advance of this country; whilst, as a matter of actual verifiable fact, of course, they are just about six hours behind it. [*The Devil in Woodford Wells*, Ch. 8]

ROLF HOCHHUTH

7 Cursed are the peacemakers. [*The Representative*, Act I, sc. i]

M. J. C. HODGART

8 A critic is a haunter of unquiet graves. He tries to evoke the presence of a living art, but usually succeeds only in disturbing the peace of the dead. [*The Ballads*, Ch. 1]

RUDOLF HOESS
(Commandant of Auschwitz)

9 Another improvement that we made . . . was that we built our gas-chambers to accommodate two thousand people at one time. [Affidavit. Quoted in Alan Bullock, *Hitler*, Ch. 12]

SAMUEL HOFFENSTEIN

10 The stars, like measles, fade at last. [*The Mimic Muse*, V]

11 Though women tempt you more than plenty, / Your rate is half a girl in twenty. / In short, from grace you never fell yet – / And what do you get? On all sides hell yet! [*Poems in Praise of Practically Nothing*, First Series]

12 You buy some flowers for your table; / You tend them tenderly as you're able; / You fetch them water from hither and thither – / What thanks do you get for it all? They wither. [*Ib.* Second Series]

13 I think of all the corpses / Worm-eaten in the shade; / I cannot chew my peanuts / Or drink my lemonade: / Good God, I am afraid! [*The Shropshire Lad's Cousin*]

14 Babies haven't any hair; / Old men's heads are just as bare; – / Between the cradle and the grave / Lies a haircut and a shave. [*Songs of Faith in the Year after Next*, VIII]

15 [Of Hollywood people] We are the croupiers in a crooked gambling house. [Quoted in Lillian Ross, *Picture*, 'Throw the Little Old Lady Down the Stairs!'. See also 279:8]

COLONEL MAX HOFFMAN

16 LUDENDORFF: The English soldiers fight like lions.
HOFFMAN: True. But don't we know that they are lions led by donkeys. [Of 1915 battles. Quoted in A. Clark, *The Donkeys*]

LANCELOT HOGBEN

17 This is not the age of pamphleteers. It is the age of engineers. The spark-gap is mightier than the pen. Democracy will not be salvaged by men who talk fluently, debate forcefully and quote aptly. [*Science for the Citizen*]

RICHARD HOGGART

18 The Uses of Literacy. [Title of book]

19 If we felt in our heart of hearts that we were *always* doctoring our experiences,

our attempts to reach others would all be at bottom forms of salesmanship, not attempts to tell things as we think they really are. [In the BBC Reith Lectures for 1971. Lecture reprinted in the *Listener*, Dec. 1971]

SIR WILLIAM (LORD) HOLFORD

1 Large buildings in London and elsewhere today are too often designed in the lift going down to lunch. [*Observer*, 'Sayings of the Week', 5 Jun. 1960]

GUSTAV HOLST

2 Never compose anything unless the not composing of it becomes a positive nuisance to you. [Letter to W. G. Whittaker. Quoted in Nat Shapiro, *An Encyclopedia of Quotations about Music*]

WINIFRED HOLTBY

3 God give me work while I may live and life till my work is done. [Inscription on her grave]

MIROSLAV HOLUB

4 I believe / that only what cannot be trimmed / is a head. / There is much promise / in the circumstance / that so many people have heads. [*A Boy's Head*]

5 But above all / we have / the ability / to sort peas, / to cup water in our hands, / to seek / the right screw / under the sofa / for hours. / This / gives us / wings. [*Wings*, trans. Ian Milner and George Theiner]

BOB HOPE

6 They are doing things on the screen these days that the French don't even put on postcards. [Quoted in Leslie Halliwell, *The Filmgoer's Book of Quotes*]

7 Money is paper blood. [Attr.]

GERARD HOPKINS

8 Why do people lament their follies for which their friends adore them. [Quoted

in V. S. Pritchett, *Great Turnstile*, under initials G.H.]

ALISTAIR HORNE

9 To sum up on Joffre, it might be said that the war was very nearly lost with him, but that it would almost certainly have been lost without him. [*The Price of Glory*, Ch. 2]

KENNETH HORNE and RICHARD MURDOCH

10 Oh, jolly D.! [Dudley Davenport in *Much Binding in the Marsh*, BBC radio comedy series, *passim*]

11 Good morning sir – was there something? [Sam Costa in *ib.*]

12 Not a word to Bessie about this! [Running gag spoken by K.H. in *ib.*]

13 When I was in Sidi Barrani . . . [Running gag spoken by K.H. in *ib.*]

DONALD HORNIG

14 Aside from being tremendous it was one of the most aesthetically beautiful things I have ever seen. [On first atomic test. *The Decision to Drop the Bomb*]

SIR BRIAN HORROCKS

15 I have always regarded the forward edge of the battlefield as the most exclusive club in the world. [*A Full Life*]

ZILPHIA HORTON

16 We Shall Overcome. [Title of Song, original version. Later additions by Pete Seeger, Frank Hamilton, Guy Carawan. See also: 18:15]

COLONEL EDWARD HOUSE

17 My ambition has been so great it has never seemed to me worth while to try to satisfy it. [John Dos Passos, *Mr Wilson's War*, Ch. 1, sect. ii]

18 Saturday was a remarkable day . . . We actually got down to work at half past ten and finished remaking the map of the world as we would have it, at half

past twelve o'clock. [Diary note. Quoted in *ib*. 4. xvi]

GEOFFREY HOUSEHOLD

1 I have noticed that what cats most appreciate in a human being is not the ability to produce food which they take for granted – but his or her entertainment value. [*Rogue Male*]

2 It's easy to make a man confess the lies he tells to himself; it's far harder to make him confess the truth. [*Ib*.]

A. E. HOUSMAN

3 About the woodlands I will go / To see the cherry hung with snow. [*A Shropshire Lad*, II]

4 Lie down, lie down, young yeoman; / The sun moves always west; / The road one treads to labour / Will lead one home to rest, / And that will be the best. [*Ib*. VII]

5 White in the moon the long road lies. [*Ib*. XXXVI]

6 Into my heart an air that kills / From yon far country blows: / What are those blue remembered hills, / What spires, what farms are those? [*Ib*. XL]

7 The Queen of air and darkness / Begins to shrill and cry, / 'O young man, O my slayer, / To-morrow you shall die.' [*Last Poems*, III]

8 May will be fine next year as like as not: / Oh ay, but then we shall be twenty-four. [*Ib*. IX]

9 For so the game is ended / That should not have begun. / My father and my mother / They had a likely son, / And I have none. [*Ib*. XIV]

10 Until from grass and clover / The upshot beam would fade, / And England over / Advanced the lofty shade. [*Ib*. XLI]

11 If you want to get poetry out of me you must be either a relative or a duchess, and you are neither. [When asked to contribute to *Georgian Poetry*. Quoted in Christopher Hassall, *Edward Marsh*, Ch. 9]

12 This University, which once saw Wordsworth drunk and Porson sober, will now see a better scholar than Wordsworth and a better poet than Porson betwixt and between. [Inaugural lecture in the Chair of Latin at Cambridge]

13 I just stand up and spout. [When asked what he did in his lectures. Attr.]

14 I find Cambridge an asylum, in every sense of the word. [On coming from Oxford. Attr.]

15 I'll tell that story on the golden floor. [On being told a joke when he was dying. Attr. by the late Rev. J Plowden-Wardlaw, Vicar of St Edward the Great, Cambridge]

REV. P. F. HOW

16 Yes, that's the worst of living, you get older every day. [Sermon at Runnell Hospital, 1946]

FRANKIE HOWERD

17 Nowadays you can't be filthy unless you've got a degree. [BBC TV programme, *That Was the Week That Was*, 6 Apr. 1963]

18 I was *amazed*! [Catch-phrase in variety act]

ELBERT HUBBARD

19 One machine can do the work of fifty ordinary men. No machine can do the work of one extraordinary man. [*Roycroft Dictionary and Book of Epigrams*]

20 Little minds are interested in the extraordinary; great minds in the commonplace. [*Ib*.]

21 You had better be a round peg in a square hole than a square peg in a square hole. The latter is in for life, while the first is only an indeterminate sentence. [Quoted in W. H. Auden and L. Kronenberger, *The Faber Book of Aphorisms*]

BARON VON HÜGEL

22 I myself have been on excellent terms with matter as long as I can remember

and I am quite contented. [Quoted by E. H. W. Meyerstein in a letter, 12 Jun. 1911]

RICHARD HUGHES

1 Nature is as wasteful of promising young men as she is of fish-spawn. It's not just getting them killed in wars: mere middle age snuffs out ten times more talent than ever wars and sudden death do. [*The Fox in the Attic*, Bk I, Ch. 18]

2 Ju-jitsu (or Judo), being the art of using unbearable pain for the conquest of brute force, has an irresistible attraction for young imaginations, boys' almost as much as girls'. [*Ib*. II. 3]

3 For a politician rises on the backs of his friends (that's probably all they're good for), but it's through his enemies he'll have to govern afterwards. [*Ib*. II. 20]

4 History has to use second-hand timber when she builds a new edifice – like those awkward post-war chickenhouses people build out of bits of army huts and old ammo-boxes, with 'W.D.' stamped all over them and costly enigmatical fittings too much trouble to unscrew. [*Ib*. III. 31]

TED HUGHES

5 The world rolls under the long thrust of his heel. / Over the cage floor the horizons come. [*The Jaguar*]

6 It took the whole of Creation / To produce my foot, my each feather: / Now I hold creation in my foot. [*Hawk Roosting*]

7 But Oedipus he had the luck / For when he hit the ground / He bounced up like a jackinabox / And knocked his Daddy down. [*Crow*, 'Song for a Phallus']

JOSEPHINE HULL

8 Playing Shakespeare is very tiring. You never get to sit down, unless you're a King. [Quoted in Frank Muir, *The Frank Muir Book*]

BARRY HUMPHRIES

9 At Sunday School I was always in demand, especially for our annual Passion Play and Pageant, and I was always given the *meatier* rolls. [*Dame Edna's Coffee Table Book*, 'My Wonderful Career']

10 Buckingham Palace, the Queen's delightful home in the London suburb of Westminster. Although she has no front garden (it's cemented over so they can change the guard on it) her back yard is enormous, with a high wall round it for privacy's sake. Naturally the Queen's rotary hoist is her own affair. [*Ib*. 'My Wondrous World']

11 I hope I don't sound corny. / I hope I don't sound trite. / But when I eat lobster mornay / I pray with all my might / That far away in India / Where Mrs Gandhi's subjects dwell / A million little tinted folk / Are gobbling one as well. [*Ib*. 'What I'm Into']

HERMAN HUPFELD

12 You must remember this; / A kiss is just a kiss, / A sigh is just a sigh – / The fundamental things apply / As time goes by. [Song: *As Time Goes By*. Used in film, *Casablanca*]

JOHN HUSTON

13 A left-handed form of human endeavour. [Definition of crime in film *The Asphalt Jungle*. Quoted in Lillian Ross, *Picture*]

ALDOUS HUXLEY

14 It is very difficult to flagellate yourself with a cane in a room so small that any violent gesture imperils the bric-à-brac. [*Limbo*, 'Farcical History of Richard Greenow']

15 The process of balancing the horoscopes of two elevens one against the other was a very delicate and difficult one. A match between the Spurs and the Villa entailed a conflict in the heavens so vast and so complicated that it was not to be wondered at if she sometimes made a mistake about the outcome. [*Crome Yellow*, Ch. 2]

1 'Which of the contemporary poets do you like best?' 'Blight, Mildew, and Smut,' he replied, with the laconism of one who is absolutely certain of his own mind. [*Ib.* 10]

2 Carminative: for me the word was as rich in content as some tremendous, elaborate work of art; it was a complete landscape with figures. [*Ib.* 20]

3 'But I should like to come,' Miss Spence protested, throwing a rapid Gioconda at him. [*Mortal Coils*, 'The Gioconda Smile', i]

4 She was a machine-gun riddling her hostess with sympathy. [*Ib.* ii]

5 It's a pity they should have chosen the day of the Eton and Harrow match for the funeral. [*Ib*, iii]

6 Miss Penny laughed, and rattled the miniature gallows of her ears. [*Ib.* 'Nuns at Luncheon']

7 She was one of those indispensables of whom one makes the discovery, when they are gone, that one can get on quite as well without them. [*Ib.*]

8 What I glory in is the civilized, middle way between stink and asepsis. [*Antic Hay*, Ch. 4]

9 There are few who would not rather be taken in adultery than in provincialism. [*Ib.* 10]

10 On the other side of the party-wall ... a teeming family of Jews led their dark, compact, Jewish lives with a prodigious intensity. At this moment they were all passionately quarrelling. [*Ib.* 11]

11 Mr Mercaptan went on to preach a brilliant sermon on that melancholy sexual perversion known as continence. [*Ib.* 18]

12 Lady Capricorn, he understood, was still keeping open bed. [*Ib.* 21]

13 I don't know which direction civilization marches – whether north towards Kilburn and Golder's Green, or over the river to the Elephant and Clapham and Sydenham and all those other mysterious places. [*Ib.*]

14 The picture-papers are more than half-filled with photographs of bathing nymphs – photographs that make one understand the ease with which St Anthony rebuffed his temptations. [*On the Margin*, 'Beauty in 1920']

15 She pictured to herself a Calamy who was one of Nature's Guardsmen, touched, as Guardsmen sometimes are, with that awed and simple reverence for the mysteries of art. [*Those Barren Leaves*, Pt I, Ch. 1]

16 I'm afraid of losing my obscurity. Genuineness only thrives in the dark. Like celery. [*Ib.*]

17 At thirty-three ... Lilian Aldwinkle appealed to all the instinctive bigamist in one. She was eighteen in the attics and widow Dido on the floors below. [*Ib.* I. 2]

18 'The Rabbit Fanciers' Gazette' with which, as every schoolboy knows, is incorporated 'The Mouse Breeders' Record'. [*Ib.* II. 2]

19 I always notice that the most grave and awful denunciations of obscenity in literature are to be found precisely in those periodicals whose directors are most notoriously alcoholic. [*Ib.* III. 2]

20 It's the great dead language of the future. If Etruscan didn't exist, it would be necessary to invent it. [*Ib.* IV. 5]

21 If we wrote it ourselves, we might find Etruscan literature interesting. Etruscan literature composed by Etruscans would be as boring as any other ancient literature. [*Ib.*]

22 'It's like the question of the authorship of the *Iliad*,' said Mr Cardan. 'The author of that poem is either Homer or, if not Homer, somebody else of the same name.' [*Ib.* V. 4]

23 Compare the music of *The Beggar's Opera* with the music of a contemporary revue. They differ as life in the garden of Eden differed from life in the artistic quarter of Gomorrah. [*Along the Road*, 'Popular Music']

24 Gazing at the pianist as St Theresa might have gazed at the uplifted Host. [*Two or Three Graces*, title story]

25 In the eighteenth century, when logic and science were the fashion, women

tried to talk like the men. The twentieth century has reversed the process. [*Ib.*]

1 ... Forgetting that several excuses are always less convincing than one. [*Point Counter Point*, Ch. 1]

2 Is it illusion or the revelation of profoundest truth? Who knows? Pongileoni blew, the fiddlers drew their resined horsehair across the stretched intestines of lambs; through the long Sarabande the poet slowly meditated his lovely and consoling certitude. [*Ib.* 2]

3 He had cured her, he remembered, of a passion for Burne-Jones, but never, alas, of her prejudice in favour of virtue. [*Ib.* 4]

4 A correspondence course of passion was, for her, the perfect and ideal relationship with a man [*Ib.* 5]

5 A good housewife, she knew how to hash up the conversational remains of last night's dinner to furnish out this morning's lunch. [*Ib.* 7]

6 It takes two to make a murder. There are born victims, born to have their throats cut, as the cut-throats are born to be hanged. You can see it in their faces. [*Ib.* 12]

7 He had such a pure, childlike and platonic way of going to bed with women, that neither they nor he ever considered that the process really counted as going to bed. [*Ib.* 13]

8 Work gives them the comfortable illusion of existing, even of being important. If they stopped working, they'd realize they simply weren't there at all, most of them. Just holes in the air, that's all. [*Ib.* 17]

9 Brought up in an epoch when ladies apparently rolled along on wheels, Mr Quarles was peculiarly susceptible to calves. [*Ib.* 20]

10 The instinct of acquisitiveness has more perverts, I believe, than the instinct of sex. At any rate, people seem to me odder about money than about even their amours. [*Ib.* 22]

11 Happiness is like coke – something you get as a by-product in the process of making something else. [*Ib.* 30]

12 If Don Juans and Don Juanesses only obeyed their desires, they'd have very few affairs. They have to tickle themselves up imaginatively before they can start being casually promiscuous. [*Ib.* 34]

13 Judd remained for him the Oldest Friend whom one definitely dislikes. [*Brief Candles*, 'After the Fireworks']

14 I've lived most of my life posthumously ...; in reflections and conversations after the fact. [*Ib.* 'Chawdron']

15 You never see animals going through the absurd and often horrible fooleries of magic and religion ... Only man behaves with such gratuitous folly. It is the price he has to pay for being intelligent but not, as yet, quite intelligent enough. [*Texts and Pretexts*, 'Amor Fati']

16 The fact that the Matthew Passion, for example, the Hammerklavier Sonata, had had human authors was a source of hope. It was just conceivable that humanity might some day and somehow be made a little more John-Sebastian-like. [*Eyeless in Gaza*, Ch. 22]

17 People will insist ... on treating the *mons Veneris* as though it were Mount Everest. [*Ib.* 30]

18 Death ... It's the only thing we haven't succeeded in completely vulgarizing. [*Ib.* 31]

19 For Lawrence, existence was one continuous convalescence; it was as though he were newly reborn from a mortal illness every day of his life. What these convalescent eyes saw, his most casual speech would reveal. [*The Olive Tree*, 'D. H. Lawrence']

20 Good is that which makes for unity; Evil is that which makes for separateness. [*Ends and Means*]

21 Why should human females become sterile in the forties, while female crocodiles continued to lay eggs into their third century? [*After Many a Summer*, Pt I, Ch. 5]

22 Christianity accepted as given a metaphysical system derived from several existing and mutually incompatible systems. [*Grey Eminence*, Ch. 3]

1 The quality of moral behaviour varies in inverse ratio to the number of human beings involved. [*Ib.* 10]

2 Think of the inexpugnable retreats for microbes prepared by Michelangelo in the curls of Moses' beard! [*Time Must Have a Stop*, Ch. 3]

3 All that good money going on a mere picture, when it might have been spent on something really useful, like a drinking fountain or a public lavatory. [*Ib.* 4]

4 How appallingly thorough these Germans always managed to be, how emphatic! In sex no less than in war – in scholarship, in science. Diving deeper than anyone else and coming up muddier. [*Ib.* 6]

5 There's only one corner of the universe you can be certain of improving, and that's your own self. [*Ib.* 7]

6 It [champagne] had the taste, he thought, of an apple peeled with a steel knife. [*Ib.* 12]

7 Give me Catholicism every time. Father Cheeryble with his thurible; Father Chatterjee with his liturgy. What fun they have with all their charades and conundrums. If it weren't for the Christianity they insist on mixing with it, I'd be converted tomorrow. [*Ib.*]

8 Only one more indispensable massacre of Capitalists or Communists or Fascists or Christians or Heretics, and there we are – there we are in the Golden Future. [*Ib.*]

9 You mean what everybody means nowadays ... Ignore death up to the last moment; then, when it can't be ignored any longer, have yourself squirted full of morphia and shuffle off in a coma. [*Ib.* 26]

10 Knowledge is proportionate to being ... You know in virtue of what you are. [*Ib.*]

11 In a place where even the king goes on foot – *enfin*, the toilet cabinet. [*Ib.* 27]

12 There isn't any formula or method. You learn to love by loving – by paying attention and doing what one thereby discovers has to be done. [*Ib.* 30]

13 In medieval and early modern Christendom the situation of sorcerers and their clients was almost precisely analogous to that of Jews under Hitler, capitalists under Stalin, Communists and fellow travellers in the United States. [*The Devils of Loudun*, Ch. 5]

14 Few people now believe in the devil; but very many enjoy behaving as their ancestors behaved when the Fiend was a reality as unquestionable as his Opposite Number. [*Ib.*]

15 We participate in a tragedy; at a comedy we only look. [*Ib.* 11]

16 I was seeing what Adam had seen on the morning of his creation – the miracle, moment by moment, of naked existence. [*The Doors of Perception*]

17 'Bed,' as the Italian proverb succinctly puts it, 'is the poor man's opera.' [*Heaven and Hell*]

18 Consistency is contrary to nature, contrary to life. The only completely consistent people are the dead. [*Do What you Will*, 'Wordsworth in the Tropics']

19 He [T. S. Eliot] likes to look on the bile when it's black. [Quoted in Edward Marsh, *Ambrosia and Small Beer*, Ch. 5, sect. i]

20 He [T. E. Lawrence] is one of those great men for whom one feels intensely sorry, because he was nothing but a great man. [Letter to V. Ocampo, 1946. Quoted in J. Wintle and R. Kenin. *Dictionary of Biographical Quotation*]

21 Armaments, universal debt and planned obsolescence – those are the three pillars of Western prosperity. [*Island*, Ch. 9]

JULIAN HUXLEY

22 We all know how the size of sums of money appears to vary in a remarkable way according as they are being paid in or paid out. [*Essays of a Biologist*, Ch. V]

23 The change in our conception of God necessitates the stressing of religious experience as such, as against belief in

particular dogma, or in the efficacy of special ritual. [*Ib.* VI]

1 Sooner or later, false thinking brings wrong conduct. [*Ib.* VII]

2 Operationally, God is beginning to resemble not a ruler but the last fading smile of a cosmic Cheshire cat. [*Religion without Revelation*]

EDWARD HYAMS

3 The consequences of acquiring knowledge are always incalculable and seldom beneficial. [*William Medium*]

4 Assassination . . . should be used as the vote should ideally be used, that is, bearing in mind only the public good and regardless of personal interest. [*Killing No Murder*, Ch. 10]

I

DOLORES IBARRURI ('LA PASIONARIA')

1 It is better to die on your feet than to live on your knees! [Republican slogan broadcast in the Spanish Civil War, but coined by Emiliano Zapata in Mexico in 1910. Quoted in Hugh Thomas, *The Spanish Civil War*, Ch. 16]

HAROLD L. ICKES

2 I am against government by crony. [On resigning as US Secretary of the Interior, Feb. 1946]

3 The trouble with Senator Long is that he is suffering from halitosis of the intellect. That's presuming Emperor Long has an intellect. [Quoted in A. M. Schlesinger Jr, *The Politics of Upheaval*, Pt II, Ch. 14, sect. v]

IVAN D. ILLICH

4 Our hope of salvation lies in our being surprised by the Other. Let us learn always to receive further surprises. [*Celebration of Awareness*, Ch. 9]

5 The more the citizen is trained in the consumption of packaged goods and services, the less effective he seems to become in shaping his environment. [*Ib*. 11]

6 In both rich and poor nations consumption is polarized while expectation is equalized. [*Ib*. 12]

7 Children appeared in Europe along with the pocket watch and the Christian moneylenders of the Renaissance. Before our century neither the poor nor the rich knew of children's dress, children's games or the child's immunity from the law. Children belonged to the bourgeoisie. [*Deschooling Society*, Ch. 2]

8 Any attempt to reform the university without attending to the system of which it is an integral part is like trying to do urban renewal in New York City from the twelfth storey up. [*Ib*. 3]

9 As Max Weber traced the social effects of the belief that salvation belonged to those who accumulated wealth, we can now observe that grace is reserved for those who accumulate years in school. [*Ib*.]

10 Man must choose whether to be rich in things or in the freedom to use them. *Ib*. 4]

11 We must rediscover the distinction between hope and expectation. [*Ib*. 7]

W. R. INGE (Dean of St Paul's)

12 What we know of the past is mostly not worth knowing. What is worth knowing is mostly uncertain. Events in the past may roughly be divided into those which probably never happened and those which do not matter. [*Assessments and Anticipations*, 'Prognostications']

13 To predict the future . . . is not only the most important part of the work of an historian; it is the most scientific and least imaginative part of his duties. Our chief interest in the past is as a guide to the future. [*Ib*.]

14 When our first parents were driven out of Paradise, Adam is believed to have remarked to Eve: 'My dear, we live in an age of transition.' [*Ib*. 'Work']

15 I called democracy a superstition and a fetish: and I repeat that it is plainly both. [*The Church and the Age*, Preface]

16 I confess that any hopefulness for the future of civilization is based on the reasonable expectation that humanity is still only beginning its course. [*Ib*.]

1 I have found myself dubbed 'the gloomy dean', in contrast with certain more popular ecclesiastics who, because they can always conscientiously shout with the largest crowd, are naturally cheerful deans. [*Ib.* Ch. 2]

2 The aim of education is the knowledge not of fact but of values. [*The Church in the World*, Oct. 1932]

3 The proper time to influence the character of a child is about a hundred years before he is born. [*Observer*, 21 Jul. 1929]

4 A nation is a society united by a delusion about its ancestry and by a common hatred of its neighbours. [Quoted in Sagittarius and George, *The Perpetual Pessimist*]

5 Universal suffrage almost inevitably leads to government by mass bribery, an auction of the worldly goods of the unrepresented minority. [*The End of an Age*, Ch. 1]

6 The Lutheran separation of public and private morals is utterly false and pernicious. [*Ib.* 2]

7 The operation of flogging a dead horse is always popular and is very congenial to rhetoricians. Dickens was careful to castigate abuses which were being reformed. [*Ib.*]

8 Man is an amphibious animal. He lives partly in a world of concrete facts, and partly in a world of timeless values, which are not all connected with religion, for mathematics ignores time. [*Ib.*]

9 Hatred and the feeling of solidarity pay a high psychological dividend. The statistics of suicide show that, for non-combatants at least, life is more interesting in war than in peace. [*Ib.* 3]

10 The enemies of Freedom do not argue; they shout and they shoot. [*Ib.* 4]

11 There are many crowd movements which we are unable to explain, since possession by good or evil spirits is now considered unscientific. [*Ib.* 5]

12 Most of us, though we are bidden to look forward to an eternity of calm fruition, cannot spend an evening with-

out trying to escape from a gentleman whom we know slightly and find, it seems, an intolerable bore – ourselves. [*Ib.* 6. See also 111:6]

13 The effect of boredom on a large scale in history is underestimated. It is a main cause of revolutions, and would soon bring to an end all the static Utopias and the farmyard civilization of the Fabians. [*Ib.*]

14 Revivals are shallow things, since they aim at reproducing what never existed or what has perished with the age that gave it birth. [*Ib.*]

15 The distinction between literature and journalism is becoming blurred; but journalism gains as much as literature loses. [*England*]

16 The command 'Be fruitful and multiply' [was] promulgated according to our authorities, when the population of the world consisted of two persons. [*More Lay Thoughts of a Dean*, Pt I, Ch. 6]

17 The vulgar mind always mistakes the exceptional for the important. [*Ib.* Pt III, Ch. 1, 'Private Notebooks']

18 Many people believe that they are attracted by God or by Nature, when they are only repelled by man. [*Ib.*]

19 If ... an outbreak of cholera might be caused either by an infected water supply or by the blasphemies of an infidel mayor, medical research would be in confusion. [*Outspoken Essays*, Second Series, I. i, 'Confessio Fidei']

20 To become a popular religion, it is only necessary for a superstition to enslave a philosophy. [*Ib.* II. iii, 'The Idea of Progress']

21 It is ... an unproved assumption that the domination of the planet by our own species is a desirable thing, which must give satisfaction to its creator. [*Ib.*]

22 Christianity promises to make men free; it never promises to make them independent. [*The Philosophy of Plotinus*]

23 I prudently brought in a book, but the boredom of the six hours in the Abbey

was extreme. [On the coronation of George V. Diary entry]

1 Our day of political pride is over. A great race we are and shall remain; a great power we have been and are no longer. [Ib. Sep. 1914]

2 The world is a much worse place than I ever thought it. [Ib. 7 Jul. 1917]

3 When Arthur Balfour launched his scheme for peopling Palestine with Jewish immigrants, I am credibly informed that he did not know there were Arabs in the country. [From Evening Standard, quoted in M. Bateman, This England, selections from the New Statesman, Pt I]

4 I think middle age is the best time, if we can escape the fatty degeneration of the conscience which often sets in at about fifty. [Observer, 'Saying of the Week', 8 Jun. 1930]

5 Worry is the interest paid on trouble before it falls due. [Observer, 'Sayings of the Week', 14 Feb. 1932]

6 Christ says, 'Judge not,' but we must judge. [Attr.]

7 Religion is a way of walking, not a way of talking. [Attr.]

8 We tolerate shapes in human beings that would horrify us if we saw them in a horse. [Attr.]

RICHARD INGRAMS

9 I have come to regard the law courts [in the Strand] not as a cathedral but rather as a casino. [Guardian, 30 Jul. 1977]

10 When a judge begins to sum up at the end of a case, it is for me as if someone has twirled a roulette and we look anxiously to see if the ball will fall in red or black. [Ib.]

11 When lawyers talk about the law the normal human being begins to think about something else. [Ib.]

12 [As editor of Private Eye] My own motto is publish and be sued. [BBC radio programme, 4 May 1977]

RICHARD INGRAMS and JOHN WELLS

13 [Harold Wilson] remains calm, puffing at his pipe in bed and studying an old book by Mr J. J. Rousseau called The Social Contract. I think it is something to do with bridge. [Mrs Wilson's Diary, 20 Mar. 1974]

14 So we set off, on a lovely May morning, with Mr Haines at the wheel of his Mini, and myself, Harold and Lady Fork-bender in the back. [Ib. 30 May 1975]

SIR THOMAS INSKIP

15 The years that the locust hath eaten. [Applying Joel 2:25 to wasted years, 1931–5; said 1939. Quoted in W. S. Churchill, The Gathering Storm, Ch. 5]

EUGÈNE IONESCO

16 He made the best-looking corpse in Great Britain! And he never looked his age. Poor old Bobby! He'd been dead for four years and he was still warm. A living corpse if ever there was one. [The Bald Prima Donna, Act I]

17 It's a useless but absolutely vital precaution. [Ib.]

18 Describe a circle, stroke its back and it turns vicious. [Ib. II]

19 We haven't the time to take our time. [Exit the King]

20 Many people have delusions of grandeur but you're deluded by triviality. [Ib.]

21 There's an idiotic cloud that can't restrain itself. Like an old man, weak in the bladder. [Ib.]

22 Just because she's our only daughter it doesn't mean she's sterile. [The Future is in Eggs]

23 It's our own mediocrity that makes us let go of love, makes us renounce it. True Love doesn't know the meaning of renunciation, is not even aware of that problem, never resigns itself; resignation is for beaten people, as beaten paths are for beaten men. [The Hermit, trans. Richard Seaver]

1 Once, in a large country town, in the middle of the street, during the summer, I saw a young shepherd, about three o'clock in the afternoon, who was embracing a chameleon . . . It was such a touching scene I decided to turn it into a tragic farce. [*Improvisation*]

2 As you're not a scholar, you've no right to have ideas. [*Ib.*]

3 Autocriticism does honour to the writer, dishonour to the critic. [*Ib.*]

4 Only the ephemeral is of lasting value. [*Ib.*]

5 You've always made the mistake of being yourself. [*Ib.*]

6 The critic should describe, and not prescribe. [*Ib.*]

7 Look at yourself with one eye, listen to yourself with the other! [*Ib.*]

8 I'm going into the next room to pack my bags and you'll never see me again, except at mealtimes and at odd moments during the day and night for a cup of tea and a bun. [*Jacques or Obedience*]

9 A civil servant doesn't make jokes. [*The Killer*, Act I]

10 Yes, the rich are probably as poor as us, if there's any left these days. [*Ib.* II]

11 GIRL ADMIRER: But . . . but . . . the leader hasn't got a head!
ANNOUNCER: What's he need a head for when he's got genius? [*The Leader*]

12 You'll probably say that progress can be good or bad, like Jews or Germans or films! . . . [*Maid to Marry*]

13 A nose that can see is worth two that sniff. [*The Motor Show*]

14 Life is an abnormal business. [*Rhinoceros*, Act I]

15 There are more dead people than living. And their numbers are increasing. The living are getting rarer. [*Ib.* II]

16 But you'll never become a rhinoceros, really you won't . . . you haven't got the vocation! [*Ib.* III]

17 You can only predict things after they've happened. [*Ib.*]

CHRISTOPHER ISHERWOOD

18 I am a camera with its shutter open, quite passive, recording, not thinking. [*A Berlin Diary*. First four words are title of a drama based on Isherwood's Berlin stories by John van Druten.]

J

'JOE' JACOBS
(US boxing manager)

1 I should of stood [have stayed] in bed.
[At World Baseball Series 1935. Quoted
in Jay Lardner, *Strong Cigars and
Lovely Women*]

W. W. JACOBS

2 'Dealing with a man,' said the night-
watchman thoughtfully, 'is as easy as a
teetotaller walking along a nice wide
pavement; dealing with a woman is like
the same teetotaller, arter four or five
whiskies, trying to get up a step that
ain't there.' [*Deep Water*, 'Husbandry']

3 A nice, quiet gal she was, and there
wasn't much went on that she didn't
hear. I've known 'er to cry for hours
with the ear-ache, pore gal. [*Odd Craft*,
'Dixon's Return']

4 Mr Joseph Gibbs finished his half-pint
. . . with the slowness of a man unable
to see where the next was coming from.
[*Ship's Company*, 'Friends in Need']

5 When I told my missis once I should
never dream of being jealous of *her*,
instead of up and thanking me for it,
she spoilt the best frying-pan we ever
had. [*Ib.* 'Good Intentions']

MICK JAGGER

6 We all need someone we can bleed on.
[Song: *Let It Bleed*]

7 It's all right letting yourself go, as long
as you can let yourself back. [Quoted in
J. Green, *The Book of Rock Quotes*]

HENRY JAMES

8 His lordship had been a person . . . in
connexion with whom there was almost
nothing but the pure monotony of his
success to mention. [*The Abasement of
the Northmores*]

9 Strether had at this very moment to
recognize the truth that wherever one
paused in Paris the imagination reacted
before one could stop it. [*The Ambassadors*, Bk II, Ch. 2]

10 'Decent men don't go to Cannes with
the – well with the kind of ladies you
mean.' 'Don't they?' Strether asked
with an interest in decent men that
amused her. 'No: elsewhere, but not to
Cannes. Cannes is different.' [*Ib.* III. 2]

11 She seemed, with little cries and protests
and quick recognitions, movements like
the darts of some fine high-feathered
free-pecking bird, to stand before life as
before some full shop window. You
could fairly hear, as she selected and
pointed, the tap of her tortoise-shell
against the glass. [*Ib.* V. 1]

12 One of those types who don't keep you
explaining – minds with doors as
numerous as the many-tongued cluster
of confessionals at St Peter's. You
might confess to her with confidence in
Roumelian, and even Roumelian sins.
[*Ib.* V. 3]

13 She made him, as under the breath of
some vague western whiff, homesick
and freshly restless; he could really for
the time have imagined himself stranded
with her on a far shore, during an
ominous calm, in a quaint community
of shipwreck. Their little interview was
like a picnic on a coral strand; they
passed each other with melancholy
smiles and looks sufficiently allusive,
such cupfuls of water as they had saved.
[*Ib.* IX. 3]

14 'You mean the youngsters are – unfortunate?' 'No, they're only, like all
the modern young, I think, mysteries,
terrible little baffling mysteries.' [*The
Awkward Age*, Bk I, Ch. 1]

15 London doesn't love the latent or the
lurking, has neither time, nor taste, nor

sense for anything less discernible than the red flag in front of the steam-roller. It wants cash over the counter and letters ten feet high. [*Ib*. I. 2]

1 Little Aggie presented, up and down, an arrangement of dress exactly in the key of her age, her complexion, her emphasized virginity. [*Ib*. II. 8]

2 Experience was to be taken as showing that one might get a five-pound note as one got a light for a cigarette; but one had to check the friendly impulse to ask for it in the same way. [*Ib*. IV. 13]

3 He had not supposed at the moment – in the fifties and the sixties – that he passed for old-fashioned, but life couldn't have left him so far in the rear had the start between them originally been fair. [*Ib*. V. 17]

4 Little Aggie differed from any young person he had ever met in that she had been deliberately prepared for consumption and in that furthermore the gentleness of her spirit had immensely helped the preparation. [*Ib*. V. 18]

5 The men, the young and the clever ones, find it a house . . . with intellectual elbow-room, with freedom of talk. Most English talk is a quadrille in a sentry-box. [*Ib*. V. 19]

6 People talk about the conscience, but it seems to me one must just bring it up to a certain point and leave it there. You can let your conscience alone if you're nice to the second housemaid. [*Ib*. VI. 23]

7 What could the thing that was to happen to him be, after all, but just this thing that had begun to happen? Her dying, her death, his consequent solitude – *that* was what he had figured as the beast in the jungle. [*The Beast in the Jungle*]

8 She had indeed no sense of humour and, with her pretty way of holding her head on one side, was one of those persons whom you want, as the phrase is, to shake, but who have learnt Hungarian by themselves. [*The Figure in the Carpet*]

9 He lacked . . . the light hand with which Corvick had gilded the gingerbread – he laid on the tinsel in splotches. [*Ib*.]

10 The Prince's notion of a recompense to women – similar in this to his notion of an appeal – was more or less to make love to them. [*The Golden Bowl*, Bk I, Pt i, Ch. 1]

11 She would have liked for instance . . . to marry; and nothing in general is more ridiculous, even when it has been pathetic, than a woman who has tried and has not been able. [*Ib*. ii, 10]

12 In her position – that of a young person spending, in framed and wired confinement, the life of a guinea-pig or a magpie. [*In the Cage*, Ch. 1]

13 During the three months . . . after their consent, she had often asked herself what it was that marriage would be able to add to a familiarity so final. [*Ib*.]

14 Nothing could equal the frequency and variety of his communications to her ladyship but their extraordinary, their abysmal propriety. [*Ib*. 4]

15 She managed just the accent they had at Paddington when they stared like dead fish. [*Ib*. 23]

16 The flowers at Waterbath would probably go wrong in colour and the nightingales sing out of tune; but she remembered to have heard the place described as possessing those advantages that are usually spoken of as natural. [*The Spoils of Poynton*, Ch. 1]

17 He might have been a fine young man with a bad toothache, with the first even of his life. What ailed him, above all, she felt, was that trouble was new to him. [*Ib*. 8]

18 The point at which the soft declivity of Hampstead had at that time to confess in broken accents to St John's Wood. [*The Tree of Knowledge*]

19 He was so particularly the English gentleman and the fortunate settled normal person. Seen at a foreign table-d'hôte, he suggested but one thing: 'In what perfection England produces them!' He had kind safe eyes and a voice which, for all its clean fullness, told the quiet tale of its having never had once to raise itself. [*The Wings of the Dove*, Bk I, Ch. 1]

1 He was young for the House of Commons, he was loose for the Army. He was refined, as might have been said, for the City and, quite apart from the cut of his cloth, sceptical, it might have been felt, for the Church. [*Ib.* II. 1]

2 It was an oddity of Mrs Lowder's that her face in speech was like a lighted window at night, but that silence immediately drew the curtain. [*Ib.* II. 2]

3 She was all for scenery – yes; but she wanted it human and personal, and all she could say was that there would be in London – wouldn't there? – more of that kind than anywhere else. [*Ib.* III. 2]

4 He was for ever carrying one well-kept Italian hand to his heart and plunging the other straight into her pocket, which, as she had instantly observed him to recognize, fitted it like a glove. [*Ib.* VII. 3]

5 For a man in whom the vision of her money should be intense, in whom it should be most of the ground for 'making up' to her, any prospective failure on her part to be long for this world might easily count as a positive attraction. [*Ib.* VII. 4]

6 Summer afternoon – summer afternoon; to me those have always been the two most beautiful words in the English language. [Quoted in Edith Wharton, *A Backward Glance*, Ch. 10]

7 So here it is at last, the distinguished thing! [Said by a 'voice' heard as he suffered his first stroke, often wrongly described as his last words. Quoted in *ib.*]

8 Dearest Alice, I could come back to America (could be carried back on a stretcher) to die – but never, never to live. [Letter to his sister-in-law, Alice James. *The Letters of Henry James*, sel. and ed. by Percy Lubbock, Vol. 2]

9 Kidd, turn off the light to spare my blushes. [Said to the maid after Edmund Gosse had told him he had been awarded the O.M. Quoted in James S. Bain, *A Bookseller Looks Back*]

10 It is art that *makes* life, makes interest, makes importance, for our consideration and application of these things, and I know of no substitute whatever for the force and beauty of its process. [Letter to H. G. Wells. Quoted in H. Montgomery Hyde, *Henry James at Home*, Ch. 7, sect. iii]

11 Tell the boys to follow, to be faithful, to take me seriously. [Last recorded words, said to Alice James. Quoted in *ib.* 7. iv]

12 However British you may be, I am more British still. [Said to two English friends in 1914. Quoted in *ib.* 7. v]

13 Splendid Rupert [Brooke] to be the soldier that could beget them on the Muse! and lucky Muse, not less, which could have an affair with a soldier and yet feel herself not guilty of the least deviation. [Letter about *Soldier Sonnets*, 28 Mar. 1915]

14 But then I'm a battered old novelist and it's my business to comprehend. [Letter to Edward Marsh, 1915]

15 A man gives what he has: the rest belongs to the madness of art. [Quoted in Manning Clark, *A Discovery of Australia*, Introduction]

16 It was like morning prayers in a workhouse. [On a would-be Elizabethan production of *Hamlet*. Attr.]

WILLIAM JAMES

17 I think you will practically recognize the two types of mental make-up that I mean if I head the columns by the titles 'tender-minded' and 'tough-minded' respectively. [*Pragmatism*]

18 Waking consciousness, as we call it, is but one special type of consciousness, whilst all about it, parted from it by the flimsiest of screens, there lie potential forms of consciousness entirely different. [*Varieties of Religious Experience*]

19 The moral flabbiness born of the bitch-goddess Success. [Letter to H. G. Wells, 11 Sep. 1906]

20 A great many people think they are thinking when they are merely rearranging their prejudices. [Quoted in A. Andrews, *Quotations for Speakers and Writers*]

21 [James] was being teased by a theological colleague who said to him: 'A

philosopher is like a blind man in a dark cellar, looking for a black cat that isn't there.' 'Yes,' said William James, 'and the difference between philosophy and theology is that theology finds the cat.' [Quoted in A. J. Ayer, *On Making Philosophy Intelligible*]

1 [Environment is] a big, booming, buzzing confusion. [Quoted in Peter F. Smith, *The Dynamics of Urbanism*, Ch. 2]

2 Whenever two people meet there are really six people present. There is each man as he sees himself, each man as the other person sees him, and each man as he really is. [Quoted in Laurence J. Peter, *Peter's Quotations*]

3 The human as distinct from the German mind. [Attr.]

4 The perfection of rottenness. [Comment on a book by Santayana. Attr.]

STORM JAMESON

5 She did not so much cook as assassinate food. [Attr.]

RANDALL JARRELL

6 President Robbins was so well adjusted to his environment that sometimes you could not tell which was the environment and which was President Robbins. [*Pictures from an Institution*, Pt I, Ch. 4]

7 To Americans English manners are far more frightening than none at all. [*Ib.* I. 5]

8 For her there were two species: writers and people; and the writers were really people, and the people weren't. [*Ib.* I. 9]

9 She looked at me the way you'd look at a chessman if it made its own move. [*Ib.* II. 1]

10 She was so thin you could have recognized her skeleton. [*Ib.* II. 3]

11 The people I'm used to just have more marriages and more Matisses than the people you're used to. [*Ib.* III. 6]

12 It is better to entertain an idea than to take it home to live with you for the rest of your life. [*Ib.* IV. 9]

13 I decided that Europeans and Americans are like men and women: they understand each other worse, and it matters less, than either of them suppose. [*Ib.* IV. 10]

14 You Americans do not rear children, you *incite* them; you give them food and shelter and applause. [*Ib.*]

15 In the United States, there one feels free . . . Except from the Americans – but every pearl has its oyster. [*Ib.*]

16 Is an institution always a man's shadow shortened in the sun, the lowest common denominator of everybody in it? [*Ib.* V. 9]

17 It was the speech a vain average would make to an audience of means. [*Ib.* VI. 4]

18 A poem written on a typewriter by a typewriter. [Attr. in *Guardian* book review, 4 Oct. 1974]

ALFRED JARRY

19 By my green candle, shit, madam, certainly I'm satisfied with the way things are. After all, aren't I Captain of the Dragoons, confidential adviser to King Wenceslas, decorated with the order of the Red Eagle of Poland, and ex-King of Aragon – what more do you want? [*King Ubu*, Act 1, sc. i, trans. M. Benedikt and G. E. Wellwarth]

PETER JAY

20 As the Prime Minister [James Callaghan] put it to me . . . he saw his role as being that of Moses. [Quoted in the *Guardian Weekly*, 18 Sep. 1977]

SIR JAMES JEANS

21 Life exists in the universe only because the carbon atom possesses certain exceptional properties. [*The Mysterious Universe*. Ch. 1]

22 One tiny corner at least, and possibly several tiny corners, of this universe of atoms had chanced to become conscious for a time, but was destined in the end, still under the action of blind

mechanical forces, to be frozen out and again leave a lifeless world. [*Ib.* 5]

1 The universe begins to look more like a great thought than a great machine. [*Ib.*]

2 The universe shows evidence of a designing or controlling power that has . . . the tendency to think in the way which, for want of a better word, we describe as mathematical. [*Ib.*]

3 Science should leave off making pronouncements: the river of knowledge has too often turned back on itself. [*Ib.*]

REV. EDWARD JEFFREY

4 People expect the clergy to have the grace of a swan, the friendliness of a sparrow, the strength of an eagle and the night hours of an owl – and some people expect such a bird to live on the food of a canary. [*Observer*, 'Sayings of the Week', 14 Jun. 1964]

LENA JEGER

5 It is a sad woman who buys her own perfume. [*Observer*, 'Sayings of the Week', 20 Nov. 1955]

ANN JELLICOE

6 That white horse you see in the park could be a zebra synchronized with the railings. [*The Knack*, Act III]

VISCOUNT JELLICOE

7 I had always to remember that I could have lost the war in an afternoon. [On battle of Jutland]

ROY JENKINS

8 There are always great dangers in letting the best be the enemy of the good. [In his maiden speech as Home Secretary in the House of Commons. Quoted in the *Sunday Times*, 8 Jun. 1975]

ELIZABETH JENNINGS

9 Now deep in my bed / I turn and the world turns on the other side. [*In the Night*]

PAUL JENNINGS

10 So, cousins all, / A fortnight hence we bid you all to Wales / To tell sad tories of the death of things. ['History of Harold and the Common Market', reprinted in *Shouts and Murmurs* from the *Observer*]

11 In this concept of Activated Sludge two perfectly opposite forces are held in perfect equilibrium, like all those electrons, mesons, neutrons, protons and morons in the atom. [*The Jenguin Pennings*, 'Activated Sludge']

12 *Fernsprechbeamtin* has already provoked a vision of a placid, fair-haired, semi-mythical Teutonic figure, a kind of Telephone Queen, deep in some German forest – the Far-Speaking Beaming One. [*Ib.* 'Far Speaking']

13 Ventre offers us a grand vision of the Universe as One Thing – the Ultimate Thing (Dernière Chose). And it is against us. [*Ib.* 'Report on Resistentialism']

14 Of all musicians, flautists are most obviously the ones who know something we don't know. [*Ib.* 'Flautists Flaunt Afflatus']

15 They have collective farms, why not the collective unconscious? [*Ib.* 'Intourist on Capital']

16 Wembley, adj. Suffering from a vague *malaise*. 'I feel a bit w. this morning.' [*Ib.* 'Ware, Wye, Watford']

17 It is difficult to decide whether translators are heroes or fools. They must surely know that the Afrikaans for 'Hamlet, I am thy father's ghost' sounds something like 'Omlet, ek is de papa spook.' [*Observer*, 'On Beatrix Potter Translated'. Quoted in Stephen Potter, *The Sense of Humour*, Ch. 3]

ARTHUR JENSEN

18 The orthodox environmental theories have been accepted not because they have stood up under proper scientific investigations, but because they harmonize so well with our democratic belief in human equality. [Quoted in Laurence J. Peter, *Peter's Quotations*]

173

JEROME K. JEROME

1 I want a house that has got over all its troubles; I don't want to spend the rest of my life bringing up a young and inexperienced house. [*They and I*]

2 I never read a patent medicine advertisement without being impelled to the conclusion that I am suffering from the particular disease therein dealt with in its most virulent form. [*Three Men in a Boat*, Ch. 1]

3 It is a curious fact, but nobody ever is sea-sick – on land. [*Ib.*]

4 You never saw such a commotion, up and down a house, in all your life, as when my Uncle Podger undertook to do a job. [*Ib.* 3]

5 Nothing satisfies us on Christmas Eve but to hear each other tell authentic anecdotes about spectres. It is a genial, festive season, and we love to muse upon graves, and dead bodies, and murder, and blood. [*Told after Supper*]

C. E. M. JOAD

6 It all depends what you mean by . . . [In *The Brains Trust*, B B C radio series, *passim*]

7 Conscience was the barmaid of the Victorian soul. Recognizing that human beings were fallible and that their failings, though regrettable, must be humoured, conscience would permit, rather ungraciously perhaps, the indulgence of a number of carefully selected desires. Once the appointed limit was reached, conscience would rap on the bar of the soul. 'Time's up, gentlemen,' she would say, 'we close at ten-thirty.' [*Under the Fifth Rib*, Ch. 9]

8 I have come to the conclusion that the degree of my difference from most people exceeds the average of most people's difference from one another; or, to put it more briefly, that my reactions to many things don't conform to popular patterns. [*A Year More or Less*, 3 May 1947]

9 Whenever I look inside myself I am afraid. [*Observer*, 'Sayings of the Week', 8 Nov. 1942]

10 I've not had a new idea for the last twenty years. [*Ib.* 31 Oct. 1943]

11 My life is spent in a perpetual alternation between two rhythms, the rhythm of attracting people for fear I may be lonely and the rhythm of trying to get rid of them because I know that I am bored. [*Ib.* 12 Dec. 1948]

12 There was never an age in which useless knowledge was more important than in our own. [*Ib.* 30 Sep. 1951]

13 It will be said of this generation that it found England a land of beauty and left it a land of beauty spots. [*Observer*, 'Sayings of Our Times', 31 May 1953]

POPE JOHN XXIII

14 I offer my life as a sacrifice for the successful outcome of the Ecumenical Council and for peace among men. [Words to his confessor. Reported in the *Guardian*, 31 May 1963]

15 Men are like wine. Some turn to vinegar, but the best improve with age. [Quoted in Gerald Brenan, *Thoughts in a Dry Season*, 'Life']

16 It often happens that I wake at night and begin to think about a serious problem and decide I must tell the Pope about it. Then I wake up completely and remember I am the Pope. [Quoted in H. Fesquet, *Wit and Wisdom of Good Pope John*]

17 Anybody can be Pope; the proof of this is that I have become one. [Quoted in Laurence J. Peter, *Peter's Quotations*]

18 [To himself when waking up unwell] Who is ruling the Church, John, you or the Holy Ghost? [Attr. Quoted in *The Times*, Sep. 1977]

19 I am able to follow my own death step by step. Now I move softly towards the end. [Said two days before his death. Reported in the *Guardian*, 3 Jun. 1963]

POPE JOHN PAUL I

20 Bishops vary just as much as books. Some are like eagles, soaring high above us, bearing important messages; others are nightingales who sing God's praises in a marvellous way; and others are

174

poor wrens, who simply squawk away on the lowest branch of the ecclesiastical tree, trying to express the odd thought on some great subject. ['Letter to Mark Twain', *Observer*, 8 Oct. 1978]

AUGUSTUS JOHN

1 W. R. RODGERS: What do you think of life?
A.J.: There's nothing more terrifying. [*Sunday Times*, 1 Dec. 1963]

GLYNIS JOHNS

2 I think the Swiss have sublimated their sense of time into clock-making. [Attr.]

ALVA JOHNSON

3 Anyone who extends to him [Mayor La Guardia] the right hand of fellowship is in danger of losing a couple of fingers. [Arthur Schlesinger Jr, *The Politics of Upheaval*, Pt I, Ch. 8, sect. iii]

B. S. JOHNSON

4 Sustaining, cocoa is, they give it you inside to help you suffer. [*Albert Angelo*, 'Prologue']

SENATOR HIRAM JOHNSON

5 The first casualty when war comes is truth. [Epigraph to Phillip Knightley, *The First Casualty*]

LYNDON B. JOHNSON

6 In short, we must be constantly prepared for the worst and constantly acting for the best – strong enough to win a war and wise enough to prevent one. [State of the Union Message, 8 Jan. 1964]

7 [On being asked why he kept J. Edgar Hoover at the FBI] I'd much rather have that fellow inside my tent pissing out, than outside my tent pissing in. [Quoted by J. K. Galbraith in the *Guardian Weekly*, 18 Dec. 1971]

8 When someone asked him [L.B.J.] later why he had not involved the public more in the question of Vietnam, he was told: 'If you have a mother-in-law with only one eye and she has it in the centre of her forehead, you don't keep her in the living room.' [Quoted in D. Halberstam, *The Best and the Brightest*]

9 If you're in politics and you can't tell when you walk into a room who's for you and who's against you, then you're in the wrong line of work. [Quoted in B. Mooney, *The Lyndon Johnson Story*]

10 Jerry Ford is so dumb that he can't fart and chew gum at the same time. [Quoted in R. Reeves, *A Ford, Not a Lincoln*, Ch. 1]

11 Every man has a right to a Saturday night bath. [*Observer*, 'Sayings of the Week', 13 Mar. 1960]

12 For the first time in our history it is possible to conquer poverty. [*Ib.* 22 Mar. 1964]

13 I am going to build the kind of nation that President Roosevelt hoped for, President Truman worked for and President Kennedy died for. [Quoted in the *Sunday Times*, 27 Dec. 1964]

PAUL JOHNSON

14 For me this is a vital litmus test: no intellectual society can flourish where a Jew feels even slightly uneasy. [*Sunday Times Magazine*, 6 Feb. 1977]

HANNS JOHST

15 When I hear anyone talk of culture I reach for my revolver. [Quoted in *Observer*, 10 Jun. 1934. Usually attr. H. Goering. See *Penguin Dictionary of Quotations*, 171:2]

AL JOLSON

16 Wait a minute, wait a minute, you ain't heard nothin' yet, folks. [Film, *The Jazz Singer* (the first talkie). Script by Al Cohn]

HENRY ARTHUR JONES and HENRY HERMAN

17 I backed the right horse, and then the wrong horse went and won. [*The Silver King*, 1]

L. E. JONES

1 The sheer babyhood of the human race against the background of incalculable time makes anything but a questing agnosticism absurdly presumptuous. [*I Forgot to Tell You*]

RICHARD JONES

2 The sun's gonna shine in my back do' some day. [Song: *Troubled in Mind*. Alan Lomax, *Folk Songs of North America*, No. 313]

R. V. JONES

3 I sometimes think that strategy is nothing but tactics talked through a brass hat. [*The Most Secret War*]

ERICA JONG

4 The zipless fuck is absolutely pure. It is free of ulterior motives. There is no power game. The man is not 'taking' and the woman is not 'giving'. No one is attempting to cuckold a husband or humiliate a wife. No one is trying to prove anything or get anything out of anyone. The zipless fuck is the purest thing there is. And it is rarer than the unicorn. And I have never had one. [*Fear of Flying*, Ch. 1]

JANIS JOPLIN

5 She [Bessie Smith] showed me the air and taught me how to fill it. [Quoted in C. Albertson, *Bessie*]

SIR KEITH JOSEPH

6 We need inequality in order to eliminate poverty. [Quoted in Audrey Hilton, *This England*, 74–78, 'Political Persuasion']

7 The cycle of deprivation . . . [Quoted in M. Kellmer Pringle, *The Needs of Children*, Foreword]

MICHAEL JOSEPH

8 Authors are easy enough to get on with – if you are fond of children. [*Observer*, 'Sayings of the Week', 29 May 1949]

JAMES JOYCE

9 Ireland is the old sow that eats her farrow. [*Portrait of the Artist as a Young Man*]

10 The snotgreen sea. The scrotumtightening sea. [*Ulysses* (Bodley Head, 1937), p. 3]

11 When I makes tea I makes tea, as old mother Grogan said. And when I makes water I makes water. [*Ib*. p. 10]

12 The Roman, like the Englishman who follows in his footsteps, brought to every new shore on which he set his foot (on our shore he never set it) only his cloacal obsession. He gazed about him in his toga and he said: It is meet to be here. Let us construct a water-closet. [*Ib*. p. 122]

13 As we read in the first chapter of Guinness's. [*Ib*. p. 122]

14 I caught a cold in the park. The gate was open. [*Ib*. p. 126]

15 We call it D.B.C. because they have damn bad cakes. [*Ib*. p. 235]

16 Saint Thomas – writing of incest from a standpoint different from that of the new Viennese school. [*Ib*. p. 309]

17 A face on him as long as a late breakfast. [*Ib*. p. 309]

18 They believe in rod, the scourger almighty, creator of hell upon earth and in Jacky Tar, the son of a gun, who was conceived of unholy boast, born of the fighting navy, suffered under rump and dozen, was sacrificed flayed and curried, yelled like bloody hell, the third day he arose again from the bed, steered into haven, sitteth on his beamend till further orders whence he shall come to drudge for a living and be paid. [*Ib*. p. 313]

19 There's a bloody sight more pox than pax about that boyo. [Of Edward VII. *Ib*. p. 315]

20 I dream of wellfilled hose. [*Ib*. p. 351]

21 There have been cases of shipwreck and somnambulism in my client's family. [*Ib*. p. 442]

22 I belong to the *faubourg Saint-Patrice* called Ireland for short [*Ib*. p. 606]

1 riverrun, past Eve and Adam's, from swerve of shore to bend of bay, brings us by a commodius vicus of recirculation back to Howth Castle and Environs. [*Finnegans Wake* (1939), Pt I, p. 1]

2 the redaction known as the Sayings Attributive to H. C. Earwicker, prize on schillings, postlots free. [*Ib.* p. 36]

3 Have you heard of one Humpty Dumpty / How he fell with a roll and a rumble / And curled up like Lord Olofa Crumble / By the butt of the Magazine Wall, / (Chorus) Of the Magazine Wall, / Hump helmet and all? [*Ib.* 'The Ballad of Persse O'Reilly', p. 45]

4 He was fafafather of all schemes to bother us / Slow coaches and immaculate contraceptives for the populace. [*Ib.*]

5 Like the bumping bull of the Cassidys / All your butter is in your horns. [*Ib.*]

6 Mind my duvetyne dress above all! It's golded silvy, the newest sextones with princess effect. For Rutland blue's got out of passion. [*Ib.* p. 148]

7 The Mookse and the Gripes. Gentes and laitymen, fullstoppers and semicolonials, hybreds and lubberds! Eins within a space and a wearywide space it wast ere wohned a Mookse. [*Ib.* p. 152]

8 Nuvoletta in her lightdress, spunn of sixteen shimmers, was looking down on them, leaning over the bannistars and listening all she childishly could. [*Ib.* p. 157]

9 Shem is as short for Shemus as Jem is joky for Jacob. [*Ib.* p. 169]

10 Shem was a sham and a low sham and his lowness creeped out first via foodstuffs. [*Ib.* p. 170]

11 O / tell me all about / Anna Livia! I want to hear all / about Anna Livia. Well, you know Anna Livia? Yes, of course, we all know Anna Livia. Tell me all. Tell me now. [*Ib.* p. 196]

12 Can't hear with the waters of. The chittering waters of. Flittering bats, fieldmice bawk talk. Ho! Are you not gone ahome? [*Ib.* p. 215]

13 Dark hawks near us. Night! Night! My ho head halls. I feel as heavy as yonder stone. [*Ib.*]

14 Beside the rivering waters of, hitherandthithering waters of. Night! [*Ib.* p. 216]

15 Voyaging after maidens, belly jonah hunting the polly joans. [*Ib.* II, p. 323]

16 Reefer was a wenchman. One can smell off his westments how he is coming from a beach of promisck. [*Ib.*]

17 The Gracehoper was always jigging a jog, hoppy on akkant of his joyicity. [*Ib.* III, p. 414]

18 *The thing pleased him andt, and andt, / He larved ond he larved on he merd such a nauses / The Gracehoper feared he would mixplace his fauces.* [*Ib.* p. 418]

19 Write it, damn you, write it! What else are you good for? [*Giacomo Joyce*]

20 Envoy: Love me, love my umbrella. [*Ib.*]

21 The devil mostly speaks a language called Bellsybabble which he makes up himself as he goes along but when he is very angry he can speak quite bad French very well though some who have heard him say that he has a strong Dublin accent. [*The Cat and the Devil*]

C. G. JUNG

22 A more or less superficial layer of the unconscious is undoubtedly personal. I call it the personal unconscious. But this personal unconscious rests upon a deeper layer, which does not derive from personal experience and is not a personal acquisition but is inborn. The deeper layer I call the collective unconscious . . . it has contents and modes of behaviour that are more or less the same everywhere and in all individuals. [*Archetypes and the Collective Unconscious*]

23 Nowadays we can see as never before that the peril which threatens all of us comes not from nature, but from man, from the psyches of the individual and the mass . . . If certain persons lose their heads nowadays, a hydrogen bomb will go off. [*Memories, Dreams, Reflections*, Ch. 4]

1 Encounters with people of so many different kinds and on so many different psychological levels have been for me incomparably more important than fragmentary conversations with celebrities. The finest and most significant conversations of my life were anonymous. [*Ib.* 4]

2 The pendulum of the mind oscillates between sense and nonsense, not between right and wrong. [*Ib.* 5]

3 I was never able to agree with Freud that the dream is a 'façade' behind which its meaning lies hidden – a meaning already known but maliciously, so to speak, withheld from consciousness. To me dreams are a part of nature, which harbours no intention to deceive but expresses something as best it can, just as a plant grows or an animal seeks its food as best it can. [*Ib.*]

4 All the eagles and other predatory creatures that adorn our coats of arms seem to me to be apt psychological representations of our true nature. [*Ib.* 9. ii]

5 A man who has not passed through the inferno of his passions has never overcome them. [*Ib.* 9. iv]

6 As far as we can discern, the sole purpose of human existence is to kindle a light in the darkness of mere being. [*Ib.* 11]

7 Every form of addiction is bad, no matter whether the narcotic be alcohol or morphine or idealism. [*Ib.* 12]

8 Among all my patients in the second half of life – that is to say over thirty-five – there has not been one whose problem in the last resort was not that of finding a religious outlook on life. [*Modern Man in Search of His Soul*]

9 Solitude is for me a fount of healing which makes my life worth living. Talking is often a torment for me and I need many days of silence to recover from the futility of words. [*Letters*, Vol. 2, 1951–61]

10 Show me a sane man and I will cure him for you. [Quoted by Vincent Brome in the *Observer*, 19 Jul. 1975]

11 The true leader is always led. [Quoted in the *Guardian Weekly*, 30 Oct. 1976]

12 [When asked if he believed in God] I do not believe . . . I know. [Quoted in Laurens van der Post, *Jung and the Story of Our Time*]

13 We need more understanding of human nature, because the only real danger that exists is man himself . . . We know nothing of man, far too little. His psyche should be studied because we are the origin of all coming evil. [In BBC television 'Face to Face' interview with John Freeman]

ERNST JÜNGER

14 Evolution is far more important than living. [Quoted in Albert Camus, *The Rebel*, Ch. 3]

NORTON JUSTER

15 'Isn't that lovely?' she sighed. 'It's my favourite programme – fifteen minutes of silence – and after that there's a half hour of quiet and then an interlude of lull.' [*The Phantom Tollbooth*, Ch. 12]

16 . . . Did you know that if a beaver two feet long with a tail a foot and a half long can build a dam twelve feet high and six feet wide in two days, all you would need to build the Kariba Dam is a beaver sixty-eight feet long with a fifty-one-foot tail? [*Ib.* 14]

17 . . . As long as the answer is right, who cares if the question is wrong? [*Ib.* 14]

18 Infinity is a dreadfully poor place. They can never manage to make ends meet. [*Ib.* 16]

K

PAULINE KAEL

1 When I see those ads with the quote 'You'll have to see this picture twice', I know it's the kind of picture I don't want to see once. [*Deeper Into Movies*, 'Waiting for Orgy']

2 [Of Barbra Streisand in *What's Up, Doc?*] She's playing herself – and it's awfully soon for that. [*Ib.* 'Collaboration and Resistance']

3 It's the tragedy of TV that instead of drawing upon new experience and fresh sources of comedy it cannibalizes old pop culture. When movies do the same now, they aren't even imitating movies, they're imitating TV. The result is too infantile to be called decadent; it's pop culture for those with bad memories for pop culture, or so young they have no memories. [*Ib.*]

FRANZ KAFKA

4 You've been taken on as Land Surveyor, as you say, but, unfortunately, we have no need of a Land Surveyor. There wouldn't be the least use for one here. The frontiers of our little state are marked out and all officially recorded. [*The Castle*, Ch. 5]

5 It's a working principle of the Head Bureau that the very possibility of error must be ruled out of account. The ground principle is justified by the consummate organization of the whole authority. [*Ib.*]

6 There's no fixed connection with the Castle, no central exchange which transmits our calls further. When anybody calls up the Castle from here the instruments in all the subordinate departments ring, or rather they would ring if practically all the departments ... didn't leave their receivers off. [*Ib.*]

7 Officials are highly educated, but one-sided; in his own department an official can grasp whole trains of thought from a single word, but let him have something from another department explained to him by the hour, he may nod politely, but he won't understand a word of it. [*Ib.* 15, 'Petitions']

8 If you have the right eye for these things, you can see that accused men are often attractive. It's a remarkable phenomenon, almost a natural law. [*The Trial*, Ch. 8]

9 It's often safer to be in chains than to be free. [*Ib.*]

10 Let me remind you of the old maxim: people under suspicion are better moving than at rest, since at rest they may be sitting in the balance without knowing it, being weighed together with their sins. [*Ib.*]

11 If the French were German in their essence, then how the Germans would admire them! [*The Diaries of Franz Kafka*, 17 Dec. 1910]

12 Don't despair, not even over the fact that you don't despair. [*Ib.* 21 Jul. 1913]

13 If there is a transmigration of souls, then I am not yet on the bottom rung. My life is a hesitation before birth. [*Ib.* 24 Jan. 1922]

14 Every revolution evaporates, leaving behind only the slime of a new bureaucracy. [Attr.]

GUS KAHN

15 All God's Chillun Got Rhythm. [Title of song]

16 Yes sir, That's my Baby; / No sir, Don't mean maybe; / Yes sir, That's my Baby now. [Song: *Yes Sir, That's My Baby*. Music by Walter Donaldson]

WALTER KANE

1 Hughes was the only man I ever knew who had to die to prove he had been alive. [Quoted in J. Phelan, *Howard Hughes, The Hidden Years*]

ERICH KÄSTNER

2 *Kennst Du das Land, wo die Kanonen blühn? Du kennst es nicht? Du wirst es kennen lernen.* – Do you know the land where the cannon flower grew? You don't? But you will. [*Bei Durchsicht meiner Bücher*, '*Kennst Du das Land, wo die Kanonen blühn?*']

3 *Da hat mir kürzlich und mitten im Bett eine Studentin der Jurisprudenz erklärt: Jungfernschaft sei, möglicherweise, ganz nett, besäss aber kaum noch Sammlerwert.* – Recently and in the middle of bed, a girl student of law informed me that virginity might possibly be quite nice, but had now hardly any collector's value. [*Ib.* '*Moralische Anatomie*']

4 *Wo sonst die Linie 56 hält | war eine Art von Urwald aufgestellt. | Und Orang Utans hingen in den Zweigen.* – Where once the number 2 bus used to stop / They'd set a kind of pristine jungle up / And apes – orang-outangs – hung on the trees. [*Doktor Erich Kästners Lyrische Hausapotheke*, '*Gefährliches Lokal*', trans. Michael Hamburger]

5 *Weil man mich dann zum Telephone rief | (ein Kunde wollte mich geschäftlich sprechen), war ich genötigt, plötzlich aufzubrechen. | Als ich zurückkam, sah ich, dass ich schlief . . .* – Because they called me to the phone (old Deeping, / My senior clerk, to tell me he was sick) / I was obliged to make my exit quick. / When I came back I saw that I was sleeping. [*Ib.*]

6 *Wenn Frauen Fehler machen wollen, | dann soll man ihnen nicht in Wege stehen.* – When women want to make mistakes, one should not prevent them. [*Ib.* '*Hotelsolo für eine Männerstimme*']

7 *Nun bin ich beinah 40 Jahre | und habe eine kleine Versfabrik.* – Now I am almost 40 and have a little verse-factory. [*Ib.* '*Kurzgefasster Lebenslauf*']

8 Password *Emil.* [*Emil and the Detectives*, Ch. 9]

GEORGE S. KAUFMAN

9 One man's Mede is another man's Persian. [Quoted in R. E. Drennan, *Wit's End*]

10 Satire is something that closes on Saturday night. [Quoted in *ib.*]

11 [On Raoul Fleischmann's saying he was fourteen before he knew he was a Jew] That's nothing. I was sixteen before I knew I was a boy. [Quoted in *ib.*]

12 A poor bridge partner once inquired: 'How should I have played that hand?' 'Under an assumed name,' Kaufman replied. [Quoted in Scott Meredith, *George S. Kaufman and the Algonquin Round Table*]

PRESIDENT KAUNDA OF ZAMBIA

13 Inability of those in power to still the voices of their own consciences is the great force leading to desired changes. [*Observer*, 'Sayings of the Week', 27 Jul. 1965]

P. J. KAVANAGH

14 Mary lived by wondering what lay round the corner. I lived by knowing there was no corner. [*A Happy Man*, Ch. 12]

15 I sometimes think that whenever men want to cool down their lives women instinctively want to hot them up, and vice versa. [*Ib.* 13]

16 Recently I had to make arrangements for my gravestone. This came about in a certain way, the result of things that had gone before, and I felt a need to write down some of those things before it was too late – after all anyone's gravestone is an understatement. And it seemed best to begin at the beginning I knew most about, in other words my own. [*The Perfect Stranger*, opening words]

17 He [Charlie Parker] always filled me with a kind of despair, because he played the way I would have liked to

write, and this wasn't possible for me or anyone else. He made poetry seem word-bound. [*Ib.* 5]

1 You had to follow the clues inside yourself, even if they led to incoherence, to craziness, and people happened to you on the way. You didn't collect them like stamps. [*Ib.*]

2 Try not to despise yourself too much – it's only conceit. [*A Song and Dance*, Ch. 6]

3 But long ago he had decided never to be afraid of the deafeningly obvious, it is always news to somebody. [*Ib.*]

TED KAVANAGH

4 'After you, Claude.' / 'No, after you, Cecil.' [*Itma*, BBC radio comedy series]

5 Boss, boss! Something terrible's happened. [*Ib.*]

6 Dan! Dan! You dilatory old man. [And variations. *Ib.*]

7 Down, Upsey! [*Ib.*]

8 Excuse please, mister. You buy saucy savings stamps – very grimy – oh blimey! [And variations. *Ib.*]

9 I go – I come back. [*Ib.*]

10 It's being so cheerful as keeps me going. [Mona Lott. *Ib.*]

11 'The Mater would be most distressed' [or variations]. 'What – Crafty Clara . . . ?' [*Ib.*]

12 My pappa [Chief Bigga Banga], he say . . . [*Ib.*]

13 Now, now – come-come – that'll do – don't dilly-dally! [*Ib.*]

14 Poppy Poopah's outside. [And variations. *Ib.*]

15 Sir Short Supply of the Ministry of Food. [*Ib.*]

16 T.T.F.N. [Ta-ta for now. *Ib.*]

NIKOS KAZANTZAKIS

17 The doors of heaven and hell are adjacent and identical: both green, both beautiful. [*The Last Temptation*, Ch. 18]

TOM KEATING

18 The feeling came upon me, and I . . . did sixteen [Samuel] Palmers in a weekend. [*The Fake's Progress: Tom Keating's Story*, as told to Frank and Geraldine Norman]

JOHN KEATS

19 The automobile changed our dress, manners, social customs, vacation habits, the shape of our cities, consumer purchasing patterns, common tastes and positions in intercourse. [*The Insolent Chariots*, Ch. 1]

20 If Detroit is right . . . there is little wrong with the American car that is not wrong with the American public. [*Ib.*]

21 The automobile did not put the adventure of travel within reach of the common man. Instead, *it first gave him the opportunity to make himself more and more common.* [*Ib.* 7]

PRESIDENT JOHN F. KENNEDY

22 We stand today on the edge of a new frontier. [Speech on his adoption as Democratic presidential candidate, 15 Jul. 1960]

23 Ask not what your country can do for you; ask what you can do for your country. [Inaugural address as President, 20 Jan. 1961]

24 Let the word go forth from this time and place, to friend and foe alike, that the torch has been passed to a new generation of Americans – born in this century, tempered by war, disciplined by a hard and bitter peace. [*Ib.*]

25 In the past, those who foolishly sought power by riding on the back of the tiger ended up inside. [*Ib.*]

26 Let us never negotiate out of fear. But let us never fear to negotiate. [*Ib.*]

27 We must use time as a tool not as a couch. [*Observer*, 'Sayings of the Week', 10 Dec. 1961]

28 I think it's the most extraordinary collection of talent, of human knowledge, that has ever been gathered together at

the White House – with the possible exception of when Thomas Jefferson dined alone. [At a dinner for Nobel Prizewinners, 29 Apr. 1962]

1 The war against hunger is truly mankind's war of liberation. [Speech at opening of World Food Congress, 4 Jun. 1963]

2 The United States has to move very fast to even stand still. [*Observer*, 'Sayings of the Week', 21 Jul. 1963]

3 When power narrows the areas of man's concern, poetry reminds him of the richness and diversity of his existence. When power corrupts, poetry cleanses. [Address at Dedication of the Robert Frost Library, Amherst College, Mass., 26 Oct. 1963]

4 In free society art is not a weapon . . . Artists are not engineers of the soul. [*Ib.*]

5 If we cannot now end our differences, at least we can help make the world safe for diversity. [Address, American University, Washington, D.C., 10 Jun. 1963]

6 I believe in an America that is on the march. ['Ideas, Attitudes, Purposes from His Speeches and Writings', *Saturday Review*, 7 Dec. 1963]

7 The people of the world respect a nation that can see beyond its own image. [*Ib.*]

8 Mr Khrushchev made one point which I wish to pass on . . . It is easy to dismiss as Communist-inspired every anti-government or anti-American riot, every overthrow of a corrupt régime or every mass protest against misery and despair. [*Ib.*]

9 The basic problems facing the world today are not susceptible to a military solution. [*Ib.*]

10 Our purpose is not to buy friends or hire allies. Our purpose is to defeat poverty . . . Our goal is to again influence history instead of merely observing it. [*Ib.*]

11 Do you realize the responsibility I carry? I'm the only person standing between Nixon and the White House. [Said on 13 Oct. 1960 to Arthur M. Schlesinger. Quoted in Arthur M. Schlesinger, Jr, *A Thousand Days*]

12 It was involuntary. They sank my boat. [Remark when asked how he became a war hero. Quoted in *ib.* 4]

13 Victory has a thousand fathers but defeat is an orphan. [Attr.]

ROBERT KENNEDY

14 One fifth of the people are against everything all the time. [*Observer*, 'Sayings of the Week', 10 May 1964]

HUGH E. KEOUGH

15 The race is not always to the swift, but that is where to look. [Quoted by F. P. Adams in *Atlantic Monthly*, Aug. 1942]

JACK KEROUAC

16 We tiptoed around each other like heart-breaking new friends. [*On the Road*, Pt I, Ch. 1]

17 You can't teach the old maestro a new tune. [*Ib.*]

18 We're really all of us bottomly broke. I haven't had time to work in weeks. [*Ib.* I. 7]

19 Do you know you can go to jail for putting the American flag upside down on a government pole? [*Ib.* I. 11]

20 I had nothing to offer anybody except my own confusion. [*Ib.* II. 3]

JEAN KERR

21 If you can keep your head when all about you are losing theirs, it's just possible you haven't grasped the situation. [*Please Don't Eat the Daisies*, Introduction]

SENATOR KERR of Oklahoma

22 Eisenhower is the only living unknown soldier. [Quoted in Groucho Marx, *The Groucho Letters*, letter to Goodman Ace, 19 Jul. 1960]

GERALD KERSH

23 Prem . . . remembered the woman as a superb brunette, with a contralto voice like hot, damp fur. [*An Ape, a Dog and a Serpent*]

1 His pale and insipid soul was dotted with silly little prejudices and principles as feeble as the vestigial seeds of a banana. [*Neither Man nor Dog*, 'The Conqueror Worm']

2 The habitual liar always imagines that his lie rings true. No miracle of belief can equal his childlike faith in the credulity of the people who listen to him; and so it comes to pass that he fools nobody as completely as he fools himself. [*Night and the City*]

3 Her lips moved, and her eyes became blank; flat and empty, like holes punched in a magazine-cover, with specks of sky visible through them. [*Ib.*]

4 They Died With Their Boots Clean. [Title of book]

KEN KESEY

5 But it's the truth even if it didn't happen. [*One Flew over the Cuckoo's Nest*, Pt I]

J. MAYNARD KEYNES

6 He [Clemenceau] had only one illusion – France; and only one disillusion – mankind. [Quoted in Robert L. Heilbroner, *The Worldly Philosophers*, Ch. 9]

7 Like Odysseus, he [Woodrow Wilson] looked wiser when seated. [Quoted in *ib.*]

8 Whenever you save 5s. you put a man out of work for a day. [In 1931. *Observer*, 'Sayings of Our Times', 31 May 1953]

9 'Sound' finance may be right psychologically; but economically it is a depressing influence. [1932. *Ib.*]

10 The recent gyrations of the dollar have looked to me more like a gold standard on the booze than the ideal managed currency which I hope for. [1933. *Ib.*]

11 Does that mean that because Americans won't listen to sense, you intend to talk nonsense to them? [Remark to Treasury official on the way to international money conference, 1944 or 1945]

12 It is Enterprise which builds and improves the world's possessions ... If Enterprise is afoot, wealth accumulates whatever may be happening to Thrift; and if Enterprise is asleep, Wealth decays, whatever Thrift may be doing. [*Treatise on Money*]

13 If the Treasury were to fill old bottles with banknotes, bury them at suitable depths in disused coalmines which are then filled up to the surface with town rubbish, and leave it to private enterprise on well-tried principles of *laissez-faire* to dig the notes up again ... there need be no more unemployment and, with the help of the repercussions, the real income of the community ... would probably become a good deal larger than it actually is. [*General Theory of Employment*, Bk. III, Ch. 10]

14 Worldly wisdom teaches that it is better for the reputation to fail conventionally than to succeed unconventionally. [*Ib.* IV. 12]

15 It is better that a man should tyrannize over his bank balance than over his fellow citizens. [*Ib.* VI. 24]

16 The ideas of economists and political philosophers, both when they are right and when they are wrong, are more powerful than is commonly understood. Indeed the world is ruled by little else. Practical men, who believe themselves to be quite exempt from any intellectual influences, are usually the slaves of some defunct economist. [*Ib.*]

17 The Economic Problem, as one may call it for short, the problem of want and poverty and the economic struggle between classes and nations, is nothing but a frightful muddle, a transitory and *unnecessary* muddle. [*Essays in Persuasion*, Preface]

18 I work for a Government I despise for ends I think criminal. [When working at the Treasury. In letter to Duncan Grant, Dec. 1917. Quoted in J. Wintle and R. Kenin, *Dictionary of Biographical Quotation*]

19 In the long run ... we are all dead. [Attr. by Professor A. C. Pigou. See also 79:10]

20 It's a good thing to make mistakes so long as you're found out quickly. [Attr.]

1 No, I don't know his telephone number. But it was up in the high numbers. [Attr.]

VELIMIR KHLEBNIKOV

2 What a great thing is a police-station! The place where I have my rendezvous with the State. [Remark quoted in Nadezhda Mandelstam, *Hope against Hope*, Ch. 2]

NIKITA S. KHRUSHCHEV

3 Every year humanity takes a step towards Communism. Maybe not you, but at all events your grandson will surely be a Communist. [In conversation with Sir William Hayter, Jun. 1956]

4 We will bury you. [Statement at Kremlin reception, 26 Nov. 1956]

5 Politicians are the same all over. They promise to build a bridge even where there's no river. [Comment to reporters in US, Oct. 1960]

6 The Americans have become too liberal to fight. [Said in 1962. Quoted in T. W. Wolfe, *Soviet Power and Europe, 1945–70*]

7 They talk about who won and who lost. Human reason won. Mankind won. [On the Cuban crisis. Quoted in *Observer*, 11 Nov. 1962]

8 When you are skinning your customers, you should leave some skin on to grow so that you can skin them again. [Addressing British businessmen. Quoted in *Observer*, 'Sayings of the Week', 28 May 1961]

9 If you start throwing hedgehogs under me, I shall throw two porcupines under you. [Quoted in *Observer*, 'Sayings of the Week', 10 Nov. 1963]

10 We had no use for the policy of the Gospels: if someone slaps you, just turn the other cheek. We had shown that anyone who slapped us on our cheek would get his head kicked off. [*Khrushchev Remembers*, Vol. 2]

11 If you feed people just with revolutionary slogans they will listen today, they will listen tomorrow, they will listen the day after tomorrow, but on the fourth day they will say 'To hell with you!' [Attr.]

DR MARTIN LUTHER KING

12 I want to be the white man's brother, not his brother-in-law. [Quoted in *New York Journal-American*, 10 Sep. 1962]

13 I have a dream today. [On Civil Rights march on Washington, D.C., 1963]

14 Riots are the language of the unheard. [*Observer*, 'Sayings of the Week', 9 Jul. 1969]

15 We shall have to repent in this generation, not so much for the evil deeds of the wicked people, but for the appalling silence of the good people. [Quoted in W. Neil, *Concise Dictionary of Religious Quotations*]

HUGH KINGSMILL

16 What still alive at twenty-two, / A clean, upstanding chap like you! / Sure, if your throat is hard to slit, / Slit your girl's and swing for it. [Parody on Housman. Quoted in H. Pearson and M. Muggeridge, *About Kingsmill*]

17 But bacon's not the only thing / That's cured by hanging from a string. [Parody on Housman. Quoted in *ib.*]

18 Friends are God's apology for relations. [*The Best of Hugh Kingsmill*, ed. Michael Holroyd, Introduction]

19 A gentleman has all the qualities of a saint except saintliness. [Quoted in Michael Holroyd, *Hugh Kingsmill*]

20 Society is based on the assumption that everyone is alike and no one is alive. [Quoted in *ib.*]

RUDYARD KIPLING

21 Seven men from all the world back to town again, / *Rollin' down the Ratcliffe Road drunk and raising Cain.* [*The Ballad of the 'Bolivar'*]

22 It was not preached to the crowd, / It was not taught by the State. / No man spoke it aloud, / When the English began to hate. [*The Beginnings*]

23 There's a little red-faced man, / Which is Bobs. / Rides the tallest 'orse 'e can – / *Our* Bobs. [*Bobs* – Lord Roberts]

1 We have fed our sea for a thousand years / And she calls us, still unfed, / Though there's never a wave of all her waves / But marks our English dead. [*The Coastwise Lights*]

2 Until thy feet have trod the Road / Advise not wayside folk. [*The Comforters*]

3 O they're hangin' Danny Deever in the mornin'! [*Danny Deever*]

4 The 'eathen in 'is blindness must end where 'e began, / But the backbone of the Army is the Non-commissioned Man! [*The 'Eathen*]

5 Who are neither children nor Gods, but men in a world of men! [*England's Answer*]

6 They are lifting their heads in the stillness to yelp at the English Flag! [*The English Flag*]

7 Because to force my ramparts your nutshell navies came. [*Ib.*]

8 Cock the gun that is not loaded, cook the frozen dynamite – / But oh, beware my Country, when my Country grows polite! [*Et Dona Ferentes*]

9 Buy my English posies! / Kent and Surrey may – / Violets of the Undercliff / Wet with Channel spray. [*The Flowers*]

10 God help us, for we knew the worst too young! [*Gentlemen-Rankers*]

11 But when it comes to slaughter / You will do your work on water, / An' you'll lick the bloomin' boots of 'im that's got it. [*Gunga Din*]

12 So I'll meet 'im later on / At the place where 'e is gone – / Where it's always double drill and no canteen. / 'E'll be squattin' on the coals / Givin' drink to poor damned souls, / An' I'll get a swig in hell from Gunga Din! [*Ib.*]

13 Ere yet we loose the legions – / Ere yet we draw the blade, / Jehovah of the Thunders, / Lord God of Battles aid! [*Hymn before Action*]

14 No doubt but ye are the People – your throne is above the King's. / *Whoso speaks in your presence must say acceptable things.* [*The Islanders*]

15 There's times when you'll think that you mightn't, / There's times when you know that you might; / *But the things you will learn from the Yellow and Brown, / They'll 'elp you a lot with the White!* [*The Ladies*]

16 I've taken my fun where I've found it / An' now I must pay for my fun. [*Ib.*]

17 Have it *jest* as you've a mind to, but I've proved it time on time, / If you want to change her nature you have *got* to give her lime. [*The Land*]

18 'Ilev it jest as you've a mind to, *but* – and so he takes command. / For whoever pays the taxes old Mus' Hobden owns the land. [*Ib.*]

19 Thus said the Lord in the Vault above the Cherubim / Calling to the Angels and the Souls in their degree. [*The Last Chantey*]

20 Then said the Soul of the Angel of the Off-shore Wind: / (He that bits the thunder when the bull-mouthed breakers flee). [*Ib.*]

21 And Ye take mine honour from me if Ye take away the sea! [*Ib.*]

22 Then cried the soul of the stout Apostle Paul to God. [*Ib.*]

23 Loud sang the souls of the jolly, jolly mariners, / Plucking at their harps, and they plucked unhandily. [*Ib.*]

24 Then stooped the Lord, and he called the good sea up to Him, / And 'stablishèd its borders unto all eternity. [*Ib.*]

25 *And the ships shall go abroad / To the Glory of the Lord / Who heard the silly sailor-folk and gave them back their sea!* [*Ib.*]

26 There be triple ways to take, of the eagle or the snake, / Or the way of a man with a maid. [*The Long Trail*]

27 Though Thy Power brings / All skill to naught, Ye'll understand a man must think o' things. [*McAndrew's Hymn*]

28 Lord, send a man like Robbie Burns to sing the Song o' Steam! [*Ib.*]

29 And I'm learnin' 'ere in London what the ten-year soldier tells: / 'If you've 'eard the East a-callin', you won't never 'eed naught else.' [*Mandalay*]

185

1 Ten thousand men on the pay-roll, and forty freighters at sea! [*The 'Mary Gloster'*]

2 'Not least of our merchant princes.' Dickie, that's me, your dad! [*Ib.*]

3 Weak, a liar, and idle, and mean as a collier's whelp / Nosing for scraps in the galley. [*Ib.*]

4 King Solomon drew merchantmen, / Because of his desire / For peacocks, apes and ivory, / From Tarshish unto Tyre. [*The Merchantmen*]

5 Here, when they heard the horse-bells ring, / The ancient Britons dressed and rode / To watch the dark Phoenicians bring / Their goods along the Western Road. [*Just So Stories*, 'Merrow Down']

6 I will out and batter the family priest, / Because my Gods have afflicted me! [*Natural Theology*]

7 To my own Gods I go. / It may be they shall give me greater ease / Than your cold Christ and tangled Trinities. [*Plain Tales from the Hills*, 'Lisbeth', chapter heading]

8 ... King over all the children of pride / Is the Press – the Press – the Press! [*The Press*]

9 Gawd, 'oo knows all I cannot say, / Look after me in Thamesfontein [London]. [*The Return*]

10 There's never a law of God or man runs north of Fifty-three. [*The Rhyme of the Three Sealers*]

11 *Brother, thy tail hangs down behind!* [*Road-Song of the 'Bandar-Log'*]

12 Grey gun-'orses in the lando, / An' a rogue is married to a whore. [*The Sergeant's Weddin'*]

13 Shillin' a day, / Bloomin' good pay – / Lucky to touch it, a shillin' a day. [*Shillin' a Day*]

14 The God of Fair Beginnings / Hath prospered here my hand – [*The Song of Diego Valdez*]

15 Hold ye the Faith – the Faith our Fathers sealèd us; / Whoring not with visions – overwise and overstale. [*A Song of the English*]

16 Keep ye the Law – be swift in all obedience – / Clear the land of evil, drive the road and bridge the ford. [*Ib.*]

17 Through the Jungle very softly flits a shadow and a sigh – / He is Fear, O Little Hunter, he is Fear! [*The Song of the Little Hunter*]

18 To these from birth is Belief forbidden; from these till death is Relief afar. / They are concerned with matters hidden – under the earth-line their altars are. [*The Sons of Martha*]

19 Our blunt, bow-headed, whale-backed Downs. [*Sussex*]

20 The sheep-bells and the ship-bells ring / Along the hidden beach. [*Ib.*]

21 Here through the strong and shadeless days / The tinkling silence thrills; / Or little, lost, Down churches praise / The Lord who made the hills. [*Ib.*]

22 And the Long Man of Wilmington / Looks naked towards the shires. [*Ib.*]

23 And ... the faith that ye share with Berkeley Square uphold you, Tomlinson! [*Tomlinson*]

24 Once I ha' laughed at the power of Love and twice at the grip of the Grave, / And thrice I ha' patted my God on the head that men might call me brave. [*Ib.*]

25 The Devil he blew upon his nails, and the little devils ran, / And he said: 'Go husk this whimpering thief that comes in the guise of a man.' [*Ib.*]

26 'Ye have scarce the soul of a louse,' he said, / 'But the roots of sin are there.' [*Ib.*]

27 For it's Tommy this, an' Tommy that, an' 'Chuck him out, the brute!' / But it's 'Saviour of 'is country' when the guns begin to shoot. [*Tommy*]

28 There are whose study is of smells, / And to attentive schools rehearse / How something mixed with something else / Makes something worse. [*A Translation, Horace*, Bk V, Ode 3]

29 England shall bide till Judgment Tide / By Oak, and Ash, and Thorn! [*A Tree Song*]

30 Each in his place, by right, not grace, / Shall rule his heritage – / The men who

simply do the work / For which they draw the wage. [*The Wage-Slaves*]

1 And no one shall work for money, and no one shall work for fame, / But each for the joy of working. [*When Earth's Last Picture is Painted*]

2 When 'Omer smote 'is bloomin' lyre, / He'd 'eard men sing by land an' sea; / An' what he thought 'e might require, / 'E went an' took – the same as me! [*When 'Omer Smote*]

3 By all ye cry or whisper, / By all ye leave or do, / The silent, sullen peoples / Shall weigh your Gods and you. [*The White Man's Burden*]

4 Hands off o' the sons o' the Widow, / Hands off o' the goods in 'er shop. [*The Widow at Windsor*]

5 And you can't refuse when you get the card, / And the Widow gives the party. [*The Widow's Party*]

6 They rest awhile in Zion, / Sit down and smile in Zion; / Ay, even jest in Zion; / In Zion, at their ease. [*Zion, 1914-18*]

7 The Waddy is an infectious disease. [*Wee Willie Winkie*, 'A Second-Rate Woman']

8 A man-cub is a man-cub, and he must learn *all* the Law of the Jungle. [*The Jungle Book*, 'Kaa's Hunting']

9 What the *Bandar-log* think now the jungle will think later. [*Ib.*]

10 Nothing but foolish words, and little picking thievish hands. [*Ib.*]

11 'We be of one blood, thou and I,' Mowgli answered, '. . . my kill shall be thy kill if ever thou art hungry.' [*Ib.*]

12 The Russian is a delightful person till he tucks in his shirt. As an Oriental he is charming. It is only when he insists on being treated as the most easterly of western peoples instead of the most westerly of easterns that he becomes a racial anomaly extremely difficult to handle. [*Life's Handicap*, 'The Man Who Was']

13 Under the rules of the R-royal Humane Society, ye must give me hot whisky and water. [*Many Inventions*, 'Brugglesmith']

14 The two men seemed to agree about everything, but when grown-ups agree they interrupt each other almost as much as if they were quarrelling. [*Rewards and Fairies*, 'The Wrong Thing']

15 'How are you, sir?' 'Loungin' round and sufferin', my son.' [*Debits and Credits*, 'The United Idolaters']

16 He was confined to heavings and shruggin's and copious *Mong Jews!* The French are very badly fitted with relief-valves. [*A Diversity of Creatures*, 'The Horse Marines']

17 He was in a highly malleable condition and full o' *juice de spree*. [*Ib.*]

18 When our combination has finished with Sir Thomas Ingell, Bart, M.P. . . . Sodom and Gomorrah will be a winsome bit of Merrie England beside 'em. [*Ib.* 'The Village that Voted the Earth was Flat']

19 Then he left, in a good deal of astrachan collar and nickel-plated limousine, and the place felt less crowded. [*Ib.*]

20 He spoke and wrote trade-English – a toothsome amalgam of Americanisms and epigrams. [*Ib.*]

21 Politics are not my concern . . . They impressed me as a dog's life without a dog's decencies. [*Ib.*]

22 The Law of the Jungle – which is by far the oldest law in the world. [*The Second Jungle Book*, 'How Fear Came to the Jungle']

23 What matter? I have killed Fear. [*Ib.*]

24 He was without form and void, so far as I remember, but desperately earnest. [*Stalky and Co.*, 'The Flag of Their Country']

25 We've got him – got him on the Caudine Toasting-fork! [*Ib.* 'In Ambush']

26 We ain't goin' to have any beastly Erickin'. [*Ib.* 'The Moral Reformers']

27 'Twiggez-vous?' 'Nous twiggons.' [*Ib.* 'Slaves of the Lamp']

28 The God who Looks after Small Things had caused the visitor that day to receive two weeks' delayed mails in one. [*Traffics and Discoveries*, 'The Captive']

187

1 I despise exaggeration – 'tain't American or scientific. [*Ib.*]

2 He laughed one of those thick, big-ended British laughs that don't lead anywhere. [*Ib.*]

JAMES KIRKWOOD

3 I want out of the freak show and into the main tent. [*P.S. Your Cat is Dead*]

4 With all this horse shit – there must be a pony! [On cover of his novel, *There Must Be a Pony*]

HENRY KISSINGER

5 The conventional army loses if it does not win. The guerrilla wins if he does not lose. ['The Vietnam Negotiations', *Foreign Affairs*, XIII, Jan. 1969]

6 We are all the President's men. [Said in 1970 of the invasion of Cambodia. Quoted in the *Sunday Times Magazine*, 4 May 1975]

7 Power is the ultimate aphrodisiac. [Quoted in the *Guardian*, 28 Nov. 1976]

8 Even a paranoid can have enemies. [Quoted in *Time* magazine, 24 Jan. 1977]

9 There cannot be a crisis next week. My schedule is already full. [Quoted in *ib.*]

10 The superpowers often behave like two heavily-armed blind men feeling their way around a room, each believing himself in mortal peril from the other, whom he assumes to have perfect vision. [*Observer*, 'Sayings of the Week', 30 Sep. 1979]

A. I. KITAIGORODSKII

11 A first-rate theory predicts; a second-rate theory forbids; and a third-rate theory explains after the event. [Lecture given to IUC, Amsterdam, Aug. 1975. Quoted in A. L. Mackay, *The Harvest of a Quiet Eye*]

FRED KITCHEN

12 We're in, Meredith, we're in! [Ascribed to a music-hall sketch in Eric Partridge, *A Dictionary of Catch-Phrases*]

LORD KITCHENER

13 I don't mind your being killed, but I object to your being taken prisoner. [To the Prince of Wales, on his asking to go to the Front. Quoted in Viscount Esher, *Journal*, 18 Dec. 1914]

ANDREW KITT

14 When Mr Malenkov made a botch of the Soviet economy, he was fired as Prime Minister and sent off to run a power station in Kazakstan. [Comment on the prime minister, Edward Heath's, handling of the power crisis, in the *Guardian*, 10 Jan. 1974]

PAUL KLEE

15 An *active* line on a walk, moving freely, without goal. A walk for a walk's sake. [*Pedagogical Sketchbook*, I. 1]

16 The purest mobile form, the cosmic one . . . is only created through the liquidation of gravity (through elimination of material ties). [*Ib.* IV. 35]

17 The father of the arrow is the thought: how do I expand my reach? [*Ib.* IV. 37]

18 I cannot be grasped in this world, for I am as much at home with the dead as with the yet unborn – a little closer to the heart of creation as is usual, if still not close enough. [Extract from *Diary*, inscribed on his grave as an epitaph]

19 Art does not reproduce what we see. It makes us see. [*Creative Credo*]

B. KLIBAN

20 Cat: one Hell of a nice animal, frequently mistaken for a meatloaf. [*Cat*]

JOHN KNAPPSWOOD

21 Commit no thesis. [Inscription for a poet's tomb]

FLETCHER KNEBEL

22 It is now proved beyond doubt that smoking is one of the leading causes of statistics. [Quoted in *Reader's Digest*, Dec. 1961]

CHARLES KNIGHT
and KENNETH LYLE

1 Here We Are! Here We Are!! Here We Are Again!!! [Title of song. Music by Mark Sheridan]

E. V. KNOX

2 I never knew what Life nor Art meant, / I wrote 'Reserved' on my compartment, / And once (I was a guilty man) / I swapped the labels in the guard's van. [*The Everlasting Percy*]

GENERAL KNOX

3 What is wanted is the Cossacks. This people needs the whip! A dictatorship – that is just what it needs. [Quoted in Leon Trotsky, *History of the Russian Revolution*, Pt II, Ch. 9]

RONALD KNOX

4 The baby doesn't understand English and the Devil knows Latin. [When asked to perform a baptism in English. Quoted in Evelyn Waugh, *Ronald Knox*, Pt I, Ch. 5]

5 We love the windows bright / With red and yellow paints / Presenting to our sight / The better class of Saints. [Hymn parody. Quoted in *ib.*]

6 It is so stupid of modern civilization to have given up believing in the devil when he is the only explanation of it. [*Let Dons Delight*]

7 Greet him like Etonians without a single word, / Absolutely silent and indefinitely bored. [*On the Right Method of Greeting a New Headmaster*]

8 A loud noise at one end and no sense of responsibility at the other. [Definition of a baby. Quoted by C. Blakemore in the BBC Reith Lectures for 1976. Lecture reprinted in the *Listener*, 9 Dec. 1976]

9 [On his avoidance of Rome] A bad sailor keeps clear of the engine room. [Quoted by Archbishop Roberts in a *Guardian* review, 8 Mar. 1973]

ARTHUR KOESTLER

10 One may not regard the world as a sort of metaphysical brothel for emotions. [*Darkness at Noon*, 'The Second Hearing', Ch. 7]

11 The definition of the individual was: a multitude of one million divided by one million. [*Ib.* 'The Grammatical Fiction', Ch. 2]

12 Two half-truths do not make a truth, and two half-cultures do not make a culture. [On the 'Two Cultures', *The Ghost in the Machine*, Preface]

13 Behaviourism is indeed a kind of flat-earth view of the mind. Or, to change the metaphor: it has replaced the anthropomorphic fallacy – ascribing to animals human faculties and sentiments – with the opposite fallacy: denying man faculties not found in lower animals; it has substituted for the erstwhile anthropomorphic view of the rat, a ratomorphic view of man. [*Ib.*, Ch. 1]

14 God seems to have left the receiver off the hook, and time is running out. [*Ib.* 18]

15 Just as one could not feel the pull of a magnet with one's skin, so one could not hope to grasp in cognate terms the nature of ultimate reality. It was a text written in invisible ink; and though one could not read it, the knowledge that it existed was sufficient to alter the texture of one's existence. [*The Invisible Writing*, Ch. 33]

16 The most persistent sound which reverberates through men's history is the beating of war drums. [*Janus: A Summing Up*, Prologue]

17 A writer's ambition should be to trade a hundred contemporary readers for ten readers in ten years' time and for one reader in a hundred years' time. [Interview with Harvey Breit in the *New York Times Book Review*, 1 Apr. 1951]

18 If the creator had a purpose in equipping us with a neck, he surely meant us to stick it out. [In *Encounter*, May 1970]

19 Hitherto man had to live with the idea of death as an individual; from now onward mankind will have to live with the

189

idea of its death as a species. [On the atom bomb. Quoted in Laurence J. Peter, *Peter's Quotations*]

ALEXANDRA KOLLONTAI

1 [To Lenin] I regard sex like a glass of water, from which I drink when I am thirsty.
LENIN: But who wants to drink a glass of dirty water? [Quoted in Georgie Anne Geyer, *The Young Russians*, Ch. 15]

BERNARD KOPS

2 We must set the example but that doesn't mean we must follow it. [*Enter Solly Gold*, sc. iii]

ALFRED KORZYBSKI

3 The map is not the territory. [Slogan. Quoted in Fritjof Capra, *The Tao of Physics*, Ch. 2]

ERNIE KOVACS

4 A medium, so called because it is neither rare nor well done. [Of television. Quoted in Leslie Halliwell, *The Filmgoer's Book of Quotes*. See also 9:3]

KARL KRAUS

5 Journalists write because they have nothing to say, and they have nothing to say because they write. [Quoted in W. H. Auden, *A Certain World*]

6 Science is spectrum analysis. Art is photosynthesis. [Quoted in *ib.*]

V. K. KRISHNA MENON

7 That expression 'positive neutrality' is a contradiction in terms. There can be no more positive neutrality than there can be a vegetarian tiger. [*New York Times*, 18 Oct. 1960]

KRISHNAMURTI

8 As long as you are trying to be something other than what you actually are,

your mind merely wears itself out. But if you say, 'This is what I am, it is a fact that I am going to investigate, understand,' then you can go beyond. [*The Penguin Krishnamurti Reader*, 'Questions and Answers']

9 If we can really understand the problem, the answer will come out of it, because the answer is not separate from the problem. [*Ib.*]

10 Happiness comes uninvited; and the moment you are conscious that you are happy, you are no longer happy. [*Ib.*]

11 We all want to be famous people and the moment we want to *be* something, we are no longer free. [*Ib.* 'For the Young']

12 Constantly to seek the purpose of life is one of the odd escapes of man. If he finds what he seeks it will not be worth that pebble on the path. [*The Second Penguin Krishnamurti Reader*, Ch. 14]

13 There is nothing sacred about tradition ... The brain carries the memory of yesterday, which is tradition, and is frightened to let go, because it cannot face something new. Tradition becomes our security; and when the mind is secure, it is in decay. [*Ib.*]

14 The constant assertion of belief is an indication of fear. [*Ib.*]

15 Meditation is not a means to an end. It is both the means and the end. [*Ib.*]

16 The silence of the mind is the true religious mind, and the silence of the gods is the silence of the earth. The meditative mind flows in this silence, and love is the way of this mind. [*Ib.*]

17 Love is always new, and the remembrance of love is the death of love. [*Ib.* 16]

18 Religion is the frozen thought of men out of which they build temples. [*Observer*, 'Sayings of the Week', 22 Apr. 1928]

KRIS KRISTOFFERSON

19 Freedom's just another word for nothing left to lose. [Song: *Me and Bobby McGee*]

PRESIDENT PAULUS KRUGER

1 They have asked for my trousers, and I have given them; for my coat, I have given that also; now they want my life, and that I cannot give. [Of the British. Speech in Raad, 7 Sep. 1899]

STANLEY KUBRICK

2 The great nations have always acted like gangsters, and the small nations like prostitutes. [Quoted in the *Guardian*, 5 Jun. 1963]

L

LABOUR PARTY

1 Yesterday's Men. [Of the Conservatives. 1970 Election slogan]

R. D. LAING

2 Freud was a hero. He descended to the 'Underworld' and met there stark terrors. He carried with him his theory as a Medusa's head which turned these terrors to stone. [*The Divided Self*, Ch. 1]

3 Schizophrenia cannot be understood without understanding despair. [*Ib.* 2]

4 Few books today are forgivable. [*The Politics of Experience*, Introduction]

5 We are born into a world where alienation awaits us. [*Ib.*]

6 Before we can ask such an optimistic question as 'What is a personal relationship?', we have to ask if a personal relationship is possible, or, *are persons possible* in our present situation? [*Ib.* Ch. 1]

7 Children do not give up their innate imagination, curiosity, dreaminess easily. You have to love them to get them to do that. [*Ib.* 3]

8 We are effectively destroying ourselves by violence masquerading as love. [*Ib.* 4]

9 It seems to us that *without exception* the experience and behaviour that gets labelled schizophrenic is *a special strategy that a person invents in order to live in an unlivable situation.* [*Ib.* 5]

10 Madness need not be all breakdown. It may also be break-through. It is potential liberation and renewal as well as enslavement and existential death. [*Ib.* 6]

11 True guilt is guilt at the obligation one owes to oneself to be oneself. False guilt is guilt felt at not being what other people feel one ought to be or assume that one is. [*Self and Others*, Ch. 10]

OSBERT LANCASTER

12 The resulting style, known as Bankers Georgian, always preserves something of the air of a Metro-Goldwyn-Mayer production of *The School for Scandal*. [*Pillar to Post*, 'Bankers Georgian']

13 'Fan vaulting' . . . an architectural device which arouses enormous enthusiasm on account of the difficulties it has all too obviously involved but which from an aesthetic standpoint frequently belongs to the 'Last-supper-carved-on-a-peach-stone' class of masterpiece. [*Ib.* 'Perpendicular']

14 In attitudes of acute discomfort nymphs and tribal deities of excessive female physique and alarming size balanced precariously on broken pediments, threatening the passer-by with a shower of stone fruit from the cavernous interiors of their inevitable cornucopia. [*Ib.* 'Edwardian Baroque']

15 A hundred and fifty accurate reproductions of Anne Hathaway's cottage, each complete with central heating and garage. [*Ib.* 'Stockbrokers Tudor']

ELSA LANCHESTER

16 She looked as though butter wouldn't melt in her mouth – or anywhere else. [Of Maureen O'Hara. Quoted in Leslie Halliwell, *The Filmgoer's Book of Quotes*]

ANDREW LANG

17 Miracles do not happen? It's a miracle if they don't. [Quoted by Basil Willey in paper on *Robert Elsmere*, read before the English Association]

1 He uses statistics as a drunken man uses lamp-posts – for support rather than illumination. [Quoted in A. L. Mackay, *The Harvest of a Quiet Eye*]

JULIA LANG

2 Are you sitting comfortably? Then I'll begin. [*passim. Listen With Mother*, BBC radio programme]

HALVARD LANGE

3 We do not regard Englishmen as foreigners. We look on them only as rather mad Norwegians. [*Observer*, 'Sayings of the Week', 9 Mar. 1957]

DAVID LARDNER

4 The plot was designed in a light vein that somehow became varicose. [Quoted in Bennett Cerf, *Try and Stop Me*]

RING LARDNER, JR

5 I have known what it was like to be hungry, but I always went right to a restaurant. [*The Lardners: My Family Remembered*]

6 He [President Taft] looked at me as if I was a side dish he hadn't ordered. [Quoted in A. K. Adams, *The Home Book of Humorous Quotations*]

7 You know you've had a few too many when you come home and find cold scrambled eggs on top of last night's lamb chops. [Quoted in R. E. Drennan, *Wit's End*]

8 Frenchmen drink wine just like we used to drink water before Prohibition. [Quoted in *ib.*]

PHILIP LARKIN

9 So life was never better than in nineteen sixty-three / – But just too late for me – / Between the end of the Chatterley ban / And the Beatles' first LP. [*Annus Mirabilis*]

10 Hatless, I take off / My cycle-clips in awkward reverence. [*Church-going*]

11 A serious house on serious earth it is. [*Ib.*]

12 Marrying left your maiden name disused. [*Maiden Name*]

13 Clearly money has something to do with life. / In fact they have much in common if you inquire. / You can't put off being young till you retire. [*Money*]

14 Perhaps being old / Is having lighted rooms inside your head / And people in them acting, people you know / Yet can't quite name. [*The Old Fools*]

15 In this way I spent youth, / Tracing the trite untransferable / Truss-advertisement, truth. [*Send No Money*]

16 Here's to the whitest man I know, / Though white is not my favourite colour. [*Sympathy in White Major*]

17 They fuck you up, your mum and dad. / They may not mean to, but they do. / They fill you up with the faults they had / And add some extra, just for you. [*This be the Verse*]

18 Man hands on misery to man, / It deepens like a coastal shelf. / Get out as early as you can, / And don't have any kids yourself. [*Ib.*]

19 Why should I let the toad *work* / Squat on my life? [*Toads*]

20 To prove / Our almost-instinct almost true: / What will survive of us is love. [*An Arundel Tomb*]

21 Get stewed: / Books are a load of crap. [*A Study of Reading Habits*]

22 I thought of London spread out in the sun, / Its postal districts packed like squares of wheat. [*The Whitsun Weddings*]

23 [Of modern novels] Many of them have a beginning, a muddle, and an end. [On presenting the Booker Prize, Nov. 1977. Quoted in the *Bookseller*]

HAROLD LASKI

24 Men think differently who live differently. [Quoted in Dorothy Pickles, *Introduction to Politics*]

25 The meek do not inherit the earth unless they are prepared to fight for their meekness. [Attr.]

26 De mortuis nil nisi bunkum. [Attr.]

HAROLD LASSWELL

1 Politics: Who Gets What, When, How. [Title of book]

CHARLES LAUGHTON

2 I had to throw too many of his kind out of our hotel when I was sixteen. [On refusing to play Falstaff. Quoted in James Agate, *Ego 1*, 1933]

PIERRE LAVAL

3 If peace is a chimaera, I am happy to have caressed her. [1935. *Observer*, 'Sayings of Our Times', 31 May 1953]

D. H. LAWRENCE

4 Creatures that hang themselves up like an old rag, to sleep; / And disgustingly upside down. / Hanging upside down like rows of disgusting old rags / And grinning in their sleep. / Bats! [*Bats*]

5 And so, I missed my chance with one of the lords / Of life. / And I have something to expiate; / A pettiness. [*Snake*]

6 Me or the Mexican who comes to chop wood / All the same, / All humanity is jam to you. [*Bibbles*]

7 You must always be a-waggle with LOVE. [*Ib.*]

8 Is it the secret of the long-nosed Etruscans? / The long-nosed, sensitive footed, subtly-smiling Etruscans, / Who made so little noise outside the cypress groves? [*Cypresses*]

9 Evil, what is evil? / There is only one evil, to deny life / As Rome denied Etruria / And mechanical America Montezuma still. [*Ib.*]

10 Don't be sucked in by the su-superior, / don't swallow the culture-bait. [*Don'ts*]

11 O pity the dead that are dead, but cannot make / the journey, still they moan and beat / against the silvery adamant walls of life's exclusive city. [*The Houseless Dead*]

12 Thought is not a trick, or an exercise, or a set of dodges. / Thought is a man in his wholeness wholly attending. [*Thought*]

13 Cuckoos, like noise falling in drops off the leaves. [*Fantasia of the Unconscious*, Ch. 4]

14 The Romans and Greeks found everything human. Everything had a face, and a human voice. Men spoke, and their fountains piped an answer. [*Ib.*]

15 The refined punishments of the spiritual mode are usually much more indecent and dangerous than a good smack. [*Ib.*]

16 Morality which is based on ideas, or on an ideal, is an unmitigated evil. [*Ib.* 7]

17 We think that love and benevolence will cure anything. Whereas love and benevolence are our poison, poison to the giver, and still more poison to the receiver. [*Ib.*]

18 When Eve ate this particular apple, she became aware of her own womanhood, mentally. And mentally she began to experiment with it. She has been experimenting ever since. So has man. To the rage and horror of both of them. [*Ib.*]

19 Every race which has become self-conscious and idea-bound in the past has perished. [*Ib.*]

20 To make the mind an absolute ruler is as good as making a Cook's tourist-interpreter a king and a god, because he can speak several languages and make an Arab understand that an Englishman wants fish for supper. [*Ib.* 11]

21 Death is the only pure, beautiful conclusion of a great passion. [*Ib.* 15]

22 Better passion and death than any more of these 'isms'. No more of the old purpose done up in aspic. Better passion and death. [*Ib.*]

23 We have all lost the war. All Europe. [*The Ladybird*, title story]

24 And all lying mysteriously within the Australian underdark, that peculiar, lost weary aloofness of Australia. There was the vast town of Sydney. And it didn't seem to be real, it seemed to be sprinkled on the surface of a darkness into which it never penetrated. [*Kangaroo*, Ch. 1]

25 You may be the most liberal Liberal Englishman, and yet you cannot fail to see the categorical difference between

the responsible and the irresponsible classes. [*Ib.*]

1 But Somers was of the people himself, and he had that alert *instinct* of the common people, the instinctive knowledge of what his neighbour was wanting and thinking, and the instinctive necessity to answer. [*Ib.* 2]

2 'We don't like to have anybody overhead here,' said Kangaroo. 'We don't even care to go upstairs, because then we're one storey higher than our true, groundfloor selves.' [*Ib.* 6]

3 The very best that is in the Jewish blood: a faculty for pure disinterestedness, and warm, physically warm love, that seems to make the corpuscles of the blood glow. [*Ib.*]

4 What do the facts we know *about* a man amount to? Only two things we can know of him, and this by pure soul-intuition: we can know if he is true to the flame of life and love which is inside his heart, or if he is false to it. [*Ib.* 7]

5 They were over-ripe; they had been in the sun of prosperity too long, and all their tissues were soft and sweetish. How could they react with any sharpness to any appeal on earth? [*Ib.* 8]

6 The indifference - the fern-dark indifference of this remote golden Australia. Not to care - from the bottom of one's soul, not to care. [*Ib.* 10]

7 Man lives according to his own idea of himself. When circumstances begin really to run counter to his idea of himself, he damns circumstances. When the running-counter persists, he damns the nature of things. And when it *still* persists, he becomes a fatalist. A fatalist or an opportunist - anything of that sort. [*Ib.* 13]

8 The spontaneous soul must extricate itself from the *almost* automatic white octopus of the human ideal, the octopus of humanity. [*Ib.*]

9 Life makes no absolute statement. It is all Call and Answer. [*Ib.*]

10 The highest function of *mind* is its function of messenger. [*Ib.* 16]

11 Man's ultimate love for man? Yes, yes, but only in the separate darkness of

man's love for the present, unknowable God. [*Ib.* 17]

12 He daren't quite bite. Not that he was really afraid of the others. He was afraid of himself, once he let himself go. [*St Mawr*]

13 It always seemed to me that men wore their beards, like they wear their neckties, for show. I shall always remember Lewis for saying his beard was part of him. [*Ib.*]

14 Clever men are mostly such unpleasant *animals*. [*Ib.*]

15 The modern pantheist not only sees the god in everything, he takes photographs of it. [*Ib.*]

16 It was one of those places where the spirit of aboriginal England still lingers, the old savage England, whose last blood flows still in a few Englishmen, Welshmen, Cornishmen. [*Ib.*]

17 Ideal mankind would abolish death, multiply itself million upon million, rear up city upon city, save every parasite alive, until the accumulation of mere existence is swollen to a horror. [*Ib.*]

18 Judas is the last god, and, by heaven, the most potent. [*Ib.*]

19 And suddenly she craved again for the more absolute silence of America. English stillness was so soft, like an inaudible murmur of voices, of presences. [*Ib.*]

20 You may have my husband, but not my horse. My husband won't need emasculating, and my horse I won't have you meddle with. I'll preserve one last male thing in the museum of this world, if I can. [*Ib.*]

21 Her own peculiar dynamic force was stronger than the force of Mind. She could make Mind kiss her hand. [*Ib.*]

22 There's nothing so artificial as sinning nowadays. I suppose it once was real. [*Ib.*]

23 'It [Mexico] is a country where men despise sex, and live for it,' said Ramón. 'Which is suicide.' [*The Plumed Serpent*, Ch. 25]

1 The young Cambridge group, the group that stood for 'freedom' and flannel trousers and flannel shirts open at the neck, and a well-bred sort of emotional anarchy, and a whispering, murmuring sort of voice, and an ultra-sensitive sort of manner. [*Lady Chatterley's Lover*, Ch. 1]

2 It's all this cold-hearted fucking that is death and idiocy. [*Ib.* 14]

3 This is John Thomas marryin' Lady Jane. [*Ib.* 15]

4 A man's most dangerous moment . . . is when he's getting into his shirt. Then he puts his head in a bag. [*Ib.*]

5 But tha mun dress thysen, an' go back to thy stately homes of England, how beautiful they stand. Time's up! Time's up for Sir John, an' for little Lady Jane! Put thy shimmy on, Lady Chatterley! [*Ib.*]

6 No absolute is going to make the lion lie down with the lamb unless the lamb is inside. [*The Later D. H. Lawrence*]

7 Be a good animal, true to your animal instincts. [*The White Peacock*, Pt II, Ch. 2]

8 The identifying ourselves with the visual image of ourselves has become an instinct; the habit is already old. The picture of me, the me that is *seen*, is me. [*Phoenix*, 'Art and Morality']

9 You can't *invent* a design. You recognize it, in the fourth dimension. That is, with your blood and your bones, as well as with your eyes. [*Ib.*]

10 This is the agony of our human existence, that we can only feel things in conventional feeling-patterns. [*Ib.* 'The Good Man']

11 Neither can you expect a revolution, because there is no new baby in the womb of our society. Russia is a collapse, not a revolution. [*Ib.*]

12 Sentimentalism is the working off on yourself of feelings you haven't really got. [*Ib.* 'John Galsworthy']

13 Pornography is the attempt to insult sex, to do dirt on it. [*Ib.* 'Pornography and Obscenity']

14 Russia will certainly inherit the future. What we already call the greatness of Russia is only her pre-natal struggling. [*Ib.* Preface to Leo Shestov, *All Things are Possible*]

15 Away with all ideals. Let each individual act spontaneously from the for ever incalculable prompting of the creative well-head within him. There is no universal law. [*Ib.*]

16 No matter how much of a shabby animal you may be, you can learn from Dostoyevsky and Chekhov, etc., how to have the most tender, unique, coruscating soul on earth. [*Ib.* 'Preface to Mastro-don Gesualdo']

17 It is no good casting out devils. They belong to us, we must accept them and be at peace with them. [*Ib.* 'The Reality of Peace']

18 We know these new English Catholics. They are the last words in Protest. They are Protestants protesting against Protestantism. [*Ib.* Review of Eric Gill, *Art Nonsense*]

19 I am a man, and alive . . . For this reason I am a novelist. And being a novelist, I consider myself superior to the saint, the scientist, the philosopher, and the poet, who are all great masters of different bits of man alive, but never get the whole hog. [*Ib.* 'Why the Novel Matters']

20 Only in the novel are *all* things given full play. [*Ib.*]

21 My destiny has been cast among cocksure women. Perhaps when man begins to doubt himself, woman, who should be nice and peacefully hen-sure, becomes instead insistently cocksure. She develops convictions, or she catches them. And then woe betide everybody. [*Ib.* 'Women are so Cocksure']

22 To every man who struggles with his own soul in mystery, a book that is a book flowers once, and seeds, and is gone. [*Ib.* 'A Bibliography of D.H.L.']

23 One realizes with horror, that the race of men is almost extinct in Europe. Only Christ-like heroes and woman-worshipping Don Juans, and rabid equality-mongrels. [*Sea and Sardinia*, Ch. 3]

1 To the Puritan all things are impure. [*Etruscan Places*]

2 [On Gerhardie's praising the suppleness and pliability of Bertrand Russell's mind] He sniffed. 'Have you seen him in a bathing-dress?' he asked. 'Poor Bertie Russell! He is all Disembodied Mind.' [Quoted in William Gerhardie, *Memoirs of a Polyglot*]

3 Whatever the sun may be, it is certainly not a ball of flaming gas. [Quoted in Ogden and Richards, *Meaning of Meaning*]

4 I think more of a bird with broad wings flying and lapsing through the air, than anything, when I think of metre. [Letter to Edward Marsh, Nov. 1913]

5 I like to write when I feel spiteful: it's like having a good sneeze. [Letter to Lady Cynthia Asquith, Nov. 1913]

6 The ordinary novel would trace the history of the diamond – but I say, 'Diamond, what! This is carbon.' And my diamond may be coal or soot and my theme is carbon. [Letter to Edward Garnett, 5 Jun. 1914]

7 I cannot get any sense of an enemy – only of a disaster. [Letter to Edward Marsh, Autumn 1914]

8 Individuals do not *vitally* concern me any more. Only a *purpose* vitally concerns me. [Letter to Lady Ottoline Morrell, 29 Jul. 1915]

9 Nothing is more painful than to be plunged back into the world of the past, when that past is irrevocably gone by, and a new thing far away is struggling to come to life in one. [Letter to Lady Cynthia Asquith, 24 Dec. 1915]

10 They are great parables, the novels [Dostoyevsky's], but false art. They are only parables. All the people are *fallen angels* – even the dirtiest scrubs. This I cannot stomach. People are not fallen angels, they are merely people. [Letter to J. Middleton Murry and Katherine Mansfield, 17 Feb. 1916]

11 Now it is time for us to leave our Christian-democratic epoch, as it was time for Europe in Michael Angelo's day to leave the Christian-aristocratic epoch. But we cannot leap away, we slip back. [Letter to Lady Ottoline Morrell, 7 Apr. 1916]

12 I am only half there when I am ill, and so there is only half a man to suffer. To suffer in one's whole self is so great a violation, that it is not to be endured. [Letter to Catherine Carswell, 16 Apr. 1916]

13 One has a certain order inviolable in one's soul. There one sits, as in a crow's nest, out of it all . . . Life mustn't be taken seriously any more, at least the outer, social life. The social being I am has become a spectator at a knockabout dangerous farce. [Letter to Lady Cynthia Asquith, 26 Apr. 1916]

14 I think people ought to fulfil sacredly their desires. And this means fulfilling the deepest desire, which is a desire to live unhampered by things that are extraneous, a desire for pure relationships and living truth. [Letter to Catherine Carswell, 16 Jul. 1916]

15 I'm not sure if a mental relation with a woman doesn't make it impossible to love her. To know the *mind* of a woman is to end in hating her. Love means the pre-cognitive flow . . . it is the honest state before the apple. [Letter to Dr Trigant Burrow, 3 Aug. 1927]

16 I am tired of being told there is no such animal by animals who are merely different. [Letter to J. Middleton Murry, 20 May 1929]

JEROME LAWRENCE

17 A neurotic is the man who builds a castle in the air. A psychotic is the man who lives in it. A psychiatrist is the man who collects the rent. [Quoted in Laurence J. Peter, *Peter's Quotations*]

T. E. LAWRENCE

18 All men dream: but not equally. Those who dream by night in the dusty recesses of their minds wake in the day to find that it was vanity: but the dreamers of the day are dangerous men, for they may act their dream with open eyes, to make it possible. [*Seven Pillars of Wisdom*, Ch. 1]

197

1 We were a self-centred army without parade or gesture, devoted to freedom, the second of man's creeds, a purpose so ravenous that it devoured all our strength, a hope so transcendent that our earlier ambitions faded in its glare. [*Ib.*]

2 Before me lay a vista of responsibility and command, which disgusted my thought-riddled nature. I felt mean to fill the place of a man of action; for my standards of value were a wilful reaction against theirs, and I despised their happiness. [*Ib.* 48]

3 Many men would take the death-sentence without a whimper to escape the life-sentence which fate carries in her other hand. [*The Mint*, Pt I, Ch. 4]

4 The trumpets came out brazenly with the last post ... Our eyes smarted against our wills. A man hates to be moved to folly by a noise. [*Ib.* Pt III, Ch. 9]

5 I meant once to write a book on the background of Christ ... Galilee and Syria, social, intellectual and artistic of 40 B.C. It would make an interesting book. As good as Renan's *Life of Jesus* should have been, if only he had had the wit to leave out the central figure. [Letter to Sir Herbert Baker, 20 Jan. 1928]

6 I fancy, for myself, that they are rather out of touch with reality; by reality I mean shops like Selfridges, and motor buses, and the *Daily Express*. [Of James Joyce and fellow expatriate authors in Paris. Letter to W. Hurley, 1 Apr. 1929]

7 I'm re-reading it [*Lady Chatterley's Lover*] with a slow deliberate carelessness. [Letter to Edward Marsh, 18 Apr. 1929]

8 In some ways it's a horrible little book. Like over-brewed tea. [*Ib.* Of *The Mint*]

EDMUND LEACH

9 Far from being the basis of the good society, the family, with its narrow privacy and tawdry secrets, is the source of all our discontents. [In the BBC Reith Lectures for 1967. Lecture reprinted in the *Listener*]

STEPHEN LEACOCK

10 The classics are only primitive literature. They belong in the same class as primitive machinery and primitive music and primitive medicine. [*Homer and Humbug*]

11 A single room is that which has no parts and no magnitude. [*Literary Lapses*, 'Boarding-House Geometry']

12 Any two meals at a boarding-house are together less than two square meals. [*Ib.*]

13 The pleasure of getting out of a cold bed and creeping into a hot bath beats a cold plunge to death. [*Ib.* 'How to Live to be 200']

14 Get your room full of good air, then shut up the windows and keep it. It will keep for years. Anyway, don't keep using your lungs all the time. Let them rest. [*Ib.*]

15 The more we mix together the better I like the things we mix. [*Ib.* 'How to Make a Million Dollars']

16 I detest life-insurance agents; they always argue that I shall some day die, which is not so. [*Ib.* 'Insurance Up to Date']

17 The great man ... walks across his century and leaves the marks of his feet all over it, ripping out the dates on his goloshes as he passes. [*Ib.* 'The Life of John Smith']

18 Astronomy teaches the correct use of the sun and the planets. [*Ib.* 'A Manual of Education']

19 There are no handles to a horse, but the 1910 model has a string to each side of its face for turning its head when there is anything you want it to see. [*Ib.* 'Reflections on Riding']

20 It takes a good deal of physical courage to ride a horse. This, however, I have. I get it at about forty cents a flask, and take it as required. [*Ib.*]

21 Broad, comfortable waistcoats, a yard and a half round the equator. [*Ib.* 'Self-Made Men']

22 Advertising may be described as the science of arresting the human in-

telligence long enough to get money from it. [Quoted in Laurence J. Peter, *Peter's Quotations*]

TIMOTHY LEARY

1 If you take the game of life seriously, if you take your nervous system seriously, if you take your sense organs seriously, if you take the energy process seriously, you must turn on, tune in, and drop out. [*The Politics of Ecstasy*, Ch. 21]

F. R. LEAVIS

2 The only way to escape misrepresentation is never to commit oneself to any critical judgement that makes an impact – that is, never *say* anything. [*The Great Tradition*, Ch. 1]

3 Poetry can communicate the actual quality of experience with a subtlety and precision unapproachable by any other means. But if the poetry and the intelligence of the age lose touch with each other, poetry will cease to matter much and the age will be lacking in finer awareness. [*New Bearings in English Poetry*, Ch. 1]

4 He [Rupert Brooke] energized the Garden-Suburb ethos with a certain original talent and the vigour of a prolonged adolescence. His verse exhibits ... something that is rather like Keats's vulgarity with a Public School accent. [*Ib.* 2]

5 The Sitwells belong to the history of publicity rather than of poetry. [*Ib.*]

6 The question 'This is so, isn't it?' expecting the answer 'Yes, but –' [*Lectures, passim*]

FRAN LEBOWITZ

7 Never judge a cover by its book. [*Metropolitan Life*]

8 Everyone in Milan works and if it rains in Milan they blame it on Rome ... Nobody in Rome works and if it rains in Rome *and* they happen to notice it they blame it on Milan. [*Ib.* 'A World View']

9 Food is an important part of a balanced diet [*Ib.* 'Food for Thought and Vice Versa']

10 Being a woman is of special interest only to aspiring male transsexuals. To actual women, it is simply a good excuse not to play football. [*Ib.* 'Letters']

11 Your child is a writer if ... you have morning sickness at night because the fetus finds it too distracting to work during the day. [*Ib.* 'Writing: A Life Sentence']

12 I am not personally a parent. But I do have two godchildren and am expecting a third. I am naturally concerned for their future. If I ruled the world you could bet your boots that none of them would ever set their eyes on any such contraptions as digital clocks and pocket calculators. But alas, I do not rule the world and that, I am afraid, is the story of my life – always a godmother, never a God. [*Ib.* 'Digital Clocks and Pocket Calculators']

STANISLAW LEC

13 Is it progress if a cannibal uses knife and fork? [*Unkempt Thoughts*]

14 In a war of ideas it is people who get killed. [Quoted in W. H. Auden and L. Kronenberger, *The Faber Book of Aphorisms*]

JOHN LE CARRÉ

15 A committee is an animal with four back legs. [*Tinker Tailor Soldier Spy*, Pt III, Ch. 34]

GYPSY ROSE LEE

16 God is love but get it in writing. [Attr. Quoted in the *Guardian*, 24 Jun. 1975]

17 Royalties are nice and all but shaking the beads brings in money quicker. [Quoted in L. L. Levinson, *Bartlett's Unfamiliar Quotations*, 'Authorship']

HARPER LEE

18 Being Southerners, it was a source of shame to some members of the family

199

that we had no recorded ancestors on either side of the Battle of Hastings. [*To Kill a Mockingbird*, Pt I, Ch. 1]

1 Shoot all the bluejays you want, if you can hit 'em, but remember it's a sin to kill a mockingbird. [*Ib.* II. 10]

LAURIE LEE

2 Effie M. was a monster. Six foot high and as strong as a farm horse. No sooner had she decided that she wanted Uncle Tom than she knocked him off his bicycle and told him. [*Cider with Rosie*, 'The Uncles']

TRYGVE LEE
(UN Secretary)

3 Now we are in a period which I can characterize as a period of cold peace. [*Observer*, 'Sayings of the Week', 21 Aug. 1949]

THÉO LEFÈVRE
(Belgium Prime Minister)

4 In Western Europe there are now only small countries – those that know it and those that don't know it yet. [*Observer*, 'Sayings of the Year', 1963]

ERNEST LEHMAN

5 Sweet Smell of Success. [Title of novel and film]

ROSAMOND LEHMANN

6 The trouble with Ian [Fleming] is that he gets off with women because he can't get on with them. [Quoted in J. Pearson, *The Life of Ian Fleming*]

TOM LEHRER

7 I hold your hand in mine, dear, / I press it to my lips. – / I take a healthy bite / From your dainty finger tips. [Song: *I Hold Your Hand in Mine*]

8 Once all the Germans were warlike and mean. / But that couldn't happen again. / We taught them a lesson in 1918 / And they've hardly bothered us since. [Song: *Sleep, Baby, Sleep*]

9 Life is like a sewer. What you get out of it depends on what you put in. [Preamble to song: *We Will All Go Together When We Go*]

10 [During a recital] I regard the piano as an 88-string guitar. [Quoted by Edward Greenfield in the *Guardian*, 16 Dec. 1975]

11 It is sobering to consider that when Mozart was my age he had already been dead for a year. [Quoted in N. Shapiro, *An Encyclopedia of Quotations about Music*]

FRED W. LEIGH

12 Tiddley-om-Pom! [Title of music-hall song]

13 There was I, waiting at the church, / Waiting at the church, waiting at the church, / When I found he'd left me in the lurch, / Lor', how it did upset me! ... / Can't get away to marry you today – / My wife won't let me. [Song: *Waiting at the Church*. Music by Henry E. Peter. Sung by Vesta Victoria]

SIR FREDERICK LEITH-ROSS

14 Inflation is like sin; every government denounces it and every government practises it. [*Observer*, 'Sayings of the Week', 30 Jun. 1957]

C. A. LEJEUNE

15 Me no leica. [In review of film, *I am a Camera*]

VLADIMIR I. LENIN

16 If it were necessary to give the briefest possible definition of imperialism we should have to say that imperialism is the monopoly stage of capitalism. [*Imperialism, the Highest Stage of Capitalism*, Ch. 7]

17 We can (and must) begin to build up Socialism, not with the fantastic human material especially created by our imagination, but with the material bequeathed us by Capitalism. ['*Left-Wing*' Communism, Ch. 6]

1 History generally, and the history of revolutions in particular, is always richer in content, more varied, more many-sided, more lively and more 'subtle' than even the best parties and the most class-conscious vanguards of the most advanced classes imagine. [*Ib.* 10]

2 One step forward, two steps back ... It happens in the lives of individuals, and it happens in the history of nations and in the development of parties. [*One Step Forward, Two Steps Back*]

3 In its struggle for power the proletariat has no other weapon but organization. [*Ib.*]

4 Democracy is a *state* which recognizes the subordination of the minority to the majority, i.e. an organization for the systematic use of force by one class against another, by one section of the population against another. [*The State and Revolution*, Ch. 4, sect. vi]

5 Under capitalism we have a state in the proper sense of the word, that is, a special machine for the suppression of one class by another. [*Ib.* 5. ii]

6 So long as the state exists there is no freedom. When there is freedom there will be no state. [*Ib.* 5. iv]

7 Under socialism *all* will govern in turn and will soon become accustomed to no one governing. [*Ib.* 6. iii]

8 A bourgeois revolution is *absolutely* necessary in the interests of the proletariat. The more complete, determined and consistent the bourgeois revolution, the more assured will be the proletarian struggle against the bourgeoisie for Socialism. [*Two Tactics of Social-Democracy*, Ch. 6]

9 'A decisive victory of the revolution over tsarism' is the *revolutionary-democratic dictatorship of the proletariat and the peasantry*. [*Ib.*]

10 A Social-Democrat must never forget that the proletariat will inevitably have to wage a class struggle for Socialism even against the most democratic and republican bourgeoisie and petty bourgeoisie. [*Ib.* 10]

11 Revolutionary Social-Democracy always included, and now includes, the fight for reforms in its activities. But it utilizes 'economic' agitation for the purpose of presenting to the government, not only demands for all sorts of measures, but also (and primarily) the demand that it cease to be an autocratic government. [*What is to be Done?*, Ch. 3, sect. A]

12 We must have a committee of professional *revolutionaries*. [*Ib.* 4. C]

13 We are passing from the sphere of history to the sphere of the present and partly to the sphere of the future. [*Ib.* 'Conclusions']

14 To proclaim in advance the dying away of the state will be a violation of historical perspective. [Said at 7th Party Congress, Mar. 1918]

15 Communism is Soviet power plus the electrification of the whole country. [Slogan promoting the electrification programme, 1920]

16 Who, whom? We or they? [Quoted in Fitzroy Maclean, *Disputed Barricade*]

17 Any cook should be able to run the country. [Quoted in Alexander Solzhenitsyn, *The First Circle*]

18 A good man fallen among Fabians. [Attr. remark about Bernard Shaw]

JOHN LENNON

19 It was strange for a man whom have everything and a wife to boot. [*In His Own Write*, 'A Sad Michael']

20 A typical quimmty old hag who spread these vile ruperts was Mrs Weatherby – a widow by her first husbands. [*Ib.* 'Victor Triumphs']

21 Yea, though I wart through the valet of thy shadowy hut I will feed no norman. [*Ib.* 'No Flies on Frank']

22 His wife, a former beauty queer, regarded him with a strange but burly look. [*Ib.*]

23 For the past 17 years the fabled fibe had been forming into adventures on varicose islands and secrete vallets with their famous ill bred dog. [*Ib.* 'The Famous Five']

1 'Belay there me 'earty scabs,' says Large John Saliver entering. [*Ib*. 'Treasure Ivan']

2 That seems to be the crutch of the matter. [*Ib*. 'The Fingeltoad Resort']

3 It was something special, a day amongst days . . . a red lettuce day. [*Ib*. 'Nicely Nicely Clive']

4 Jumble Jim, whom shall remain nameless, was slowly but slowly asking his way through the underpants. [*Ib*. 'On Safairy']

5 Those in the cheaper seats clap. The rest of you rattle your jewellery. [At Royal Variety Performance, 15 Nov. 1963]

6 We're more popular than Jesus Christ now. I don't know which will go first. Rock and roll or Christianity. [*The Beatles Illustrated Lyrics*]

JOHN LENNON and PAUL McCARTNEY

7 All You Need Is Love. [Title of song]

8 How does it feel to be one of the beautiful people, now that that you know who you are? [Song: *Baby You're A Rich Man*]

9 For I don't care too much for money, / For money can't buy me love. [Song: *Can't Buy Me Love*]

10 Eight days a week I love you. [Song: *Eight Days a Week*]

11 Waits at the window, wearing the face that she keeps in a jar by the door / Who is it for? All the lonely people, where do they all come from? / All the lonely people, where do they all belong? [Song: *Eleanor Rigby*]

12 I'm fixing a hole where the rain gets in and stops my mind from wandering where it will go. [Song: *Fixing a Hole*]

13 If there's anything that you want, / If there's anything I can do, / Just call on me, / And I'll send it along with love from me to you. [Song: *From Me to You*]

14 I've got to admit it's getting better. / It's a little better all the time. [Song: *Getting Better*]

15 Happiness is a Warm Gun. [Title of song]

16 It's been a hard day's night. [Song: *A Hard Day's Night* (and film title)]

17 Oh, one day you'll find that I have gone, / But tomorrow may rain, so I'll follow the sun. [Song: *I'll Follow the Sun*]

18 When I caught a glimpse of Rita, / Filling in a ticket in her little white book. / In a cap she looked much older, / And the bag across her shoulder, made her look a little like a milit'ry man. / Lovely Rita, Meter Maid. [Song: *Lovely Rita*]

19 Picture yourself in a boat on a river with tangerine trees and marmalade skies. / Somebody calls you, you answer quite slowly a girl with kaleidoscope eyes. [Song: *Lucy in the Sky with Diamonds*]

20 Bang! Bang! Maxwell's Silver Hammer came down upon her head. / Clang! Clang! Maxwell's Silver Hammer made sure that she was dead. [Song: *Maxwell's Silver Hammer*]

21 He's a real Nowhere Man, / Sitting in his Nowhere Land, / Making all his nowhere plans for nobody. / Doesn't have a point of view, / Knows not where he's going to, / Isn't he a bit like you and me? [Song: *Nowhere Man*]

22 Dear Sir or Madam will you read my book? / It took me years to write, will you take a look? / Based on a novel by a man named Lear and I need a job so I want to be a paperback writer. [Song: *Paperback Writer*]

23 Her name was Magill, she called herself Lil, / But ev'ryone knew her as Nancy. [Song: *Rocky Raccoon*]

24 She's leaving home after living alone for so many years. [Song: *She's Leaving Home*]

25 She loves you, yeh, yeh, yeh, / And with a love like that you know you should be glad. [Song: *She Loves You*]

26 Sergeant Pepper's Lonely Hearts Club Band. [Title of song]

27 It's certainly a thrill, you're such a lovely audience, / We'd like to take you

home with us. [Song: *Sergeant Pepper's Lonely Hearts Club Band*]

1 She's got a ticket to ride, but she don't care. [Song: *Ticket to Ride*]

2 When I get older losing my hair many years from now. / Will you still be sending me a Valentine, birthday greetings, bottle of wine? / If I'd been out till quarter to three would you lock the door? / Will you still need me, will you still feed me, / When I'm sixty-four? [Song: *When I'm Sixty-four*]

3 I get by with a little help from my friends. [Song: *With a Little Help from My Friends*]

4 We all live in a yellow submarine, yellow submarine, yellow submarine. [Song: *Yellow Submarine* (and film title)]

DAN LENO

5 I see the world as a football, kicked about by the higher powers, with me clinging on by my teeth and toenails to the laces. [Quoted in Desmond MacCarthy, *Theatre*]

6 For five and twenty years I've had my eye on Jim, / And if he won't marry me, I'll marry him. [Song: *I'll Marry Him*]

7 Ah what is man? Wherefore does he why? Whence did he whence? Whither is he withering? [Quoted in the *Sunday Times*, 12 Jun. 1977]

HUGH LEONARD

8 In seventy years the one surviving fragment of my knowledge, the only indisputable poor particle of certainty in my entire life is that in a public house lavatory incoming traffic has the right of way. [*Da*]

9 The problem with Ireland is that it's a country full of genius, but with absolutely no talent. [Interview in *The Times*, Aug. 1977]

10 I'm very fascinated by the emergence of a kind of suburban, affluent society in Ireland. People who still believe that a rich man can no more go to heaven than he can get through the eye of a needle, but who have enough money to build

bigger needles. [Quoted in the *Guardian*, 13 Jan. 1979]

ALAN JAY LERNER

11 An Englishman's way of speaking absolutely classifies him / The moment he talks he makes some other Englishman despise him. [*My Fair Lady*, Act I, sc. i]

12 All I want is a room somewhere, / Far away from the cold night air; / With one enormous chair . . . / Oh, wouldn't it be loverly? [*Ib.*]

13 They're always throwin' goodness at you / But with a little bit of luck / A man can duck! [*Ib.* I. ii]

14 I'd be equally as willing / For a dentist to be drilling / Than to ever let a woman in my life. [*Ib.*]

15 There he was, that hairy hound / From Budapest. / Never leaving us alone, / Never have I ever known / A ruder pest. [*Ib.* II. i]

16 Oozing charm from every pore, / He oiled his way around the floor. [*Ib.*]

17 Don't talk of June! / Don't talk of fall! / Don't talk at all! / Show me! [*Ib.* II. ii]

18 I'm getting married in the morning! / Ding dong! the bells are gonna chime. / Pull out the stopper! / Let's have a whopper! / But get me to the church on time! [*Ib.* II. iii]

19 Why can't a woman be more like a man? / Men are so honest, so thoroughly square; / Eternally noble, historically fair. [*Ib.* II. iv]

20 I've grown accustomed to the trace / Of something in the air, / Accustomed to her face. [*Ib.* II. vi]

DORIS LESSING

21 When old settlers say 'One has to understand the country,' what they mean is, 'You have to get used to our ideas about the native.' They are saying, in effect, 'Learn our ideas, or otherwise get out; we don't want you.' [*The Grass is Singing*, Ch. 1]

22 When a white man in Africa by accident looks into the eyes of a native and sees

the human being (which it is his chief preoccupation to avoid), his sense of guilt, which he denies, fumes up in resentment and he brings down the whip. [*Ib.* 8]

ALFRED LESTER

1 Call out the Boys of the Old Brigade, / Who made Old England free – / Call out my Mother, my Sister and my Brother, / But for God's sake don't send me! [*Conscientious Objector's Lament*]

W. R. LETHABY

2 Art is not a special sauce applied to ordinary cooking; it is the cooking itself if it is good. [*Form in Civilization*, 'Art and Workmanship']

3 Art is thoughtful workmanship. [*Ib.*]

OSCAR LEVANT

4 Strip the phoney tinsel off Hollywood and you'll find the real tinsel underneath. [Quoted in Leslie Halliwell, *The Filmgoer's Book of Quotes*]

5 [Of Zsa-Zsa Gabor] She not only worships the Golden Calf, she barbecues it for lunch. [Attr.]

ADA LEVERSON

6 It is an infallible sign of the second-rate in nature and intellect to make use of everything and everyone. [*The Limit*]

7 People were not charmed with Eglantine because she herself was charming, but because she was charmed. [*Love at Second Sight*]

8 You don't know a woman until you have had a letter from her. [*Tenterhooks*]

9 'No hurry, no hurry,' said Sir James, with that air of self-denial that conveys the urgent necessity of intense speed. [*The Twelfth Hour*, Ch. 2]

10 Before he left, Aunt William pressed a sovereign into his hand, as if it were conscience money. He, on his side, took it as though it were a doctor's fee, and both ignored the transaction. [*Ib.* 4]

11 He had a triangular face, the details of which were vague though the outline was clear, like a negative that had been left too long in the sun. [*Ib.* 5]

12 Ridokanaki looked at the clock. It immediately struck ten, tactfully, in a clear subdued tone. [*Ib.* 9]

13 [When told by Wilde that a devoted *apache* used to follow him about Paris with a knife in his hand] I'm sure he had a fork in the other. [Attr.]

14 Thou canst not serve both cod and salmon. [On being offered a choice of fish at a dinner party. Quoted in *The Times*, 7 Nov. 1970]

CLAUDE LÉVI-STRAUSS

15 The anthropologist respects history, but he does not accord it a special value. He conceives it as a study complementary to his own: one of them unfurls the range of human societies in time, the other in space. [*The Savage Mind*]

16 Our own society is the only one which we can transform and yet not destroy, since the changes which we should introduce would come from within. [*World on the Wane*]

BERNARD LEVIN

17 Jehovah's Witnesses, awaiting the Last Day with the quiet kind of satisfaction that a man gets in the dry season when he knows his neighbour's house is not insured against fire ... [*The Pendulum Years*, Ch. I]

18 Paul Getty, who had always been vastly, immeasurably wealthy, and yet went about looking like a man who cannot quite remember whether he remembered to turn the gas off before leaving home. [*Ib.*]

19 It is a fact of history that in every age of transition men are never so firmly bound to one way of life as when they are about to abandon it, so that fanaticism and intolerance reach their most intense forms just before tolerance and mutual acceptance come to be the natural order of things. [*Ib.* 4]

1 Although if everybody brings an orange-box to view the procession none will see it, it is impossible to convince those who are first on the pavement with their orange-boxes of the truth of this. [*Ib.* 9]

2 [Wedgwood] Benn flung himself into the Sixties technology with the enthusiasm (not to say language) of a newly enrolled Boy Scout demonstrating knot-tying to his indulgent parents. [*Ib.* 11]

3 One [of the Harolds, Macmillan and Wilson] played the part of the last aristocrat ... advancing through life with a paralysed shuffle, an assortment of facial tics, a voice which was the distilled essence of all the confidence-tricksters who ever went home and entertained the children after the day's work was done. The role assumed by the other was that of the purposive, technologically-equipped, full twentieth-century citizen, leaning forward when he walked, like a man trying not to fall over if the bus starts with a jerk, his voice the ingratiating wheedle of the toucher who wants yet another fiver to tide him over to pay-day, and will do anything to get it. [*Ib.* 12]

4 Only one man took the full measure of this astonishing truth, and that man the one who knew what Macmillan was made of for the best of all reasons; Harold Wilson was made of the same stuff. Between them, then, Walrus and Carpenter, they divided up the Sixties. [*Ib.*]

5 Inflation in the Sixties was a nuisance to be endured, like varicose veins or French foreign policy. [*Ib.* 'Epilogue']

6 Like the slag-heap calling the polar bear black. [Review of second volume of Lord Hill's autobiography in the *Observer*, Sep. 1974]

7 The silence went straight from rapt to fraught without pausing at pregnant. [*The Times*, 17 Oct. 1974]

8 Once, when a British Prime Minister sneezed, men half a world away would blow their noses. Now when a British Prime Minister sneezes nobody else will even say 'Bless You'. [*The Times*, 8 Jun. 1976]

9 It [a production of Brecht's *The Days of the Commune*] has the depth of a cracker-motto, the drama of a dial-a-recipe service and the eloquence of a conversation between a speak-your-weight machine and a whoopee-cushion. [*Sunday Times*, 6 Nov. 1977]

EUGEN LEVINÉ

10 We Communists are dead men on leave. [At his trial. Quoted in R. Leviné-Meyer, *Leviné: the Life of a revolutionary*, Ch. 3]

C. S. LEWIS

11 There is wishful thinking in Hell as well as on earth. [*The Screwtape Letters*, Preface]

12 I have known a human defended from strong temptations to social ambition by a still stronger taste for tripe and onions. [*Ib.* 13]

13 Gratitude looks to the past and love to the present; fear, avarice, lust and ambition look ahead. [*Ib.* 15]

14 [Of God] He's vulgar, Wormwood. He has a vulgar mind. [*Ib.* 22]

15 The Future is something which everyone reaches at the rate of sixty minutes an hour, whatever he does, whoever he is. [*Ib.* 25]

16 If people knew how much ill-feeling Unselfishness occasions, it would not be so often recommended from the pulpit. [*Ib.* 26]

17 She's the sort of woman who lives for others – you can always tell the others by their hunted expression. [*Ib.*]

18 The long, dull, monotonous years of middle-aged prosperity or middle-aged adversity are excellent campaigning weather [for the Devil]. [*Ib.* 27]

19 Fatigue makes women talk more and men less. [*Ib.* 30]

20 Humanity does not pass through phases as a train passes through stations: being alive, it has the privilege of always moving yet never leaving anything behind. [*The Allegory of Love*, Ch. 1]

21 We can never know that a piece of writing is bad unless we have begun by

trying to read it as if it was very good and ended by discovering that we were paying the author an undeserved compliment. [*An Experiment in Criticism*, Ch. 4]

1 Friendship is unnecessary, like philosophy, like art ... It has no survival value; rather it is one of those things that give value to survival. [*The Four Loves*, 'Friendship']

2 The coarse joke proclaims that we have here an animal which finds its own animality either objectionable or funny. [*Miracles*]

3 Shall we perhaps, in Purgatory, see our own faces and hear our own voices as they really were? [*Reflections on the Psalms*, Ch. 1]

4 This extraordinary pride in being exempt from temptation that you have not yet risen to the level of. Eunuchs boasting of their chastity. [Quoted in Brian Aldiss and Kingsley Amis, *Spectrum IV*]

5 Leavis demands moral earnestness; I prefer morality ... I mean I'd sooner live among people who don't cheat at cards than among people who are earnest about not cheating at cards. [Quoted in *ib.*]

6 The only trouble is that Golding writes so well. In one of his novels, *The Inheritors*, the detail of every sensuous impression ... was so good that you couldn't find out what was happening ... All those little details you only notice in real life if you've got a high temperature. You couldn't see the wood for the leaves. [Quoted in *ib.*]

7 Courage is not simply *one* of the virtues but the form of every virtue at the testing point, which means at the point of highest reality. [Quoted in Cyril Connolly, *The Unquiet Grave*, Ch. 3]

SIR GEORGE CORNEWALL LEWIS

8 Life would be tolerable, were it not for its amusements. [Quoted in Sagittarius and George, *The Perpetual Pessimist*]

JOHN LEWIS Partnership

9 We are never knowingly undersold. [Shop slogan]

JOHN L. LEWIS

10 I'm not interested in classes ... Far be it from me to foster inferiority complexes among the workers by trying to make them think they belong to some special class. That has happened in Europe but it hasn't happened here yet. [Quoted in A. M. Schlesinger Jr, *The Coming of the New Deal*, Pt 7, Ch. 25, sect. viii]

ROSA LEWIS

11 I knew him before he was born. [Quoted in D. Fielding, *The Duchess of Jermyn Street*, Ch. 9]

SINCLAIR LEWIS

12 He was nimble in the calling of selling houses for more than people could afford to pay. [*Babbitt*, Ch. 1]

13 In fact there was but one thing wrong with the Babbitt house; it was not a home. [*Ib.* 2]

14 To George F. Babbitt ... his motor-car was poetry and tragedy, love and heroism. The office was his pirate ship, but the car his perilous excursion ashore. [*Ib.* 3]

15 A thing called Ethics, whose nature was confusing, but if you had it you were a High-class Realtor, and if you hadn't you were a shyster, a piker, and a fly-by-night. [*Ib.* 4]

16 In other countries, art and literature are left to a lot of shabby bums living in attics and feeding on booze and spaghetti, but in America the successful writer or picture-painter is indistinguishable from any other decent business man. [*Ib.* 14]

17 She did her work with the thoroughness of a mind that reveres details and never quite understands them. [*Ib.* 18]

18 Our American professors like their literature clear and cold and pure and very dead. [Address on *The American*

Fear of Literature, given in Stockholm on receiving the Nobel Prize, 12 Dec. 1930]

D. B. WYNDHAM LEWIS

1 Now welcomed, now expelled with angry shrieks, / Plied with champagne, or gnawed by wayward Pekes: / Be this their guerdon in a glorious cause – / They loved the Rich, whom all the world abhors. [Paean]

2 I am one of those unfortunates to whom death is less hideous than explanations. [Welcome to All This]

PERCY WYNDHAM LEWIS

3 The Vorticist does not suck up to Life. He lets Life know its place in a Vorticist universe. [Blast, 'Vorticist Manifesto']

4 The revolutionary simpleton is every-where. [Time and Western Man, Bk I, Ch. 6]

5 People are so overwhelmed with the prestige of their instruments that they consider their personal judgement of hardly any account. [Ib. Bk II, Pt I, Ch. 1]

6 If you want to know what is actually occurring inside, underneath, at the centre, at any given moment, art is a truer guide than 'politics', more often than not. [Ib. Appendix]

7 I ... believe ... that people should be compelled to be freer and more 'in-dividualistic' than they naturally desire to be ... I believe they could with advantage be compelled to remain absolutely alone for several hours every day; and a week's solitary confinement ... every two months, would be an excellent provision. [Ib.]

8 You persisted for a certain number of years like a stammer. You were a stammer, if you like, of Space-Time. [The Human Age, Bk I: The Childermass]

9 If you must go nowhere, step out. [Ib. closing words]

10 It is to what I have called the Apes of God that I am drawing your attention – those prosperous mountebanks who alter-nately imitate and mock at and traduce those figures they at once admire and hate. [The Apes of God, Pt. III]

11 The soul started at the knee-cap and ended at the navel. [Ib. XII]

12 Oh yes Colonel – do tell us how you were killed at Colenso again! [Ib.]

13 I said (and I always say these things with the same voice) / 'Say it with locomotives . . .' [One-Way Song]

14 I am rather like what Mr Shaw would have been like if he had been an artist. ... (He said he was a finer fellow than Shakespeare. I merely prefer myself to Mr Shaw.) [Blasting and Bombardiering]

15 The revolutionary state of mind is then, today, instinctive: the all that is is bad, and to be superseded by a better attitude. [The Art of Being Ruled, Pt I, Ch. 1]

16 'Dying for an idea,' again, sounds well enough, but why not let the idea die instead of you? [Ib.]

17 The delusion of impersonality could best be defined as the mistake by virtue of which persons are enabled to masquerade as things. [Ib. I. 6]

18 I believe that (in one form or another) castration may be the solution. And the feminization of the white European and American is already far advanced, com-ing in the wake of the war. [Ib. II. 2]

19 Sadistic excess attempts to reach roughly and by harshness what art reaches by fineness. [Ib. II. 4]

20 Absence of responsibility, an automatic and stereotyped rhythm, is what men most desire for themselves. All struggle has for its end relief or repose. [Ib. V. 2]

21 The refusal to grow up of Peter Pan was the specific found by the narquois mind of the Zeitgeist for the increasing difficulties connected with growing up. [Ib. VI. 4]

22 The 'homo' is the legitimate child of the 'suffragette'. [Ib. VIII. 4]

23 Try as women will to engarçonner them-selves, to 'reduce' and 'reduce' till they can pass as a diminutive male adoles-cent, they cannot entirely banish the reflection, in those for whom they perform these feats, that they are

nature's agents imitating their betters by a sleight of hand. [*Ib.* IX. 1]

1 There was a Greek proverb to the effect that *it was easier to hide five elephants under one's arm than one pathic.* [*Ib.* IX. 7]

2 The goitrous torpid and squinting husks provided by Matisse in his sculpture are worthless except as tactful decorations for a mental home. [*Ib.* XII. 7]

MAX LIEBERMANN

3 [To a portrait-painter who complained that he could not draw von Hindenburg's features] I can piss the old boy in the snow. [Quoted in Igor Stravinsky and Robert Craft, *Conversations with Stravinsky*]

KARL LIEBNECHT

4 We are fighting for the gates of heaven. [In the abortive German revolution, 1918–19. Quoted in Albert Camus. *The Rebel*, Ch. 3]

N. VACHEL LINDSAY

5 It is portentous, and a thing of state / That here at midnight, in our little town / A mourning figure walks, and will not rest, / Near the old courthouse pacing up and down. [*Abraham Lincoln Walks at Midnight*]

6 And who will bring white peace / That he may sleep upon his hill again? [*Ib.*]

7 Fat black bucks in a wine-barrel room, / Barrel-house kings with feet unstable, / Sagged and reeled and pounded on the table. [*The Congo*]

8 Booth died blind and still by faith he trod, / Eyes still dazzled by the ways of God. [*General William Booth Enters Heaven*]

ERIC LINKLATER

9 With a heavy step Sir Matthew left the room and spent the morning designing mausoleums for his enemies. [*Juan in America*, Prologue]

10 It is notorious that we speak no more than half-truths in our ordinary conversation, and even a soliloquy is likely to be affected by the apprehension that walls have ears. [*Ib.* II. 4]

11 I've been married six months. She looks like a million dollars, but she only knows a hundred and twenty words and she's only got two ideas in her head. The other one's hats. [*Ib.* II. 5]

12 I hear other professional men complaining, but I assure you there is no sign of depression among us morticians. Our parlours, I'm thankful to say, are never empty. [*Ib.* V. 1]

13 'There won't be any revolution in America,' said Isadore. Nikitin agreed. 'The people are too clean. They spend all their time changing their shirts and washing themselves. You can't feel fierce and revolutionary in a bathroom.' [*Ib.* V. 3]

14 'I dislike burdens,' said Juan, 'and at my back I often hear Time's winged chariot changing gear.' [*Juan in China*]

15 All I've got against it [golf] is that it takes you so far from the club house. [*Poet's Pub*, Ch. 3]

16 He had all the confidence which an American motorist in England naturally has, and which comes from the knowledge that England is only a little island where one cannot go seriously out of one's way. [*Ib.* 22]

17 Authors and uncaptured criminals . . . are the only people free from routine. [*Ib.* 23]

MAGNUS LINKLATER

18 Teenage sex-change priest in mercy dash to Palace. [The newspaper editor's dream headline. Quoted on BBC radio programme, 18 Sep. 1976]

LIN YUTANG

19 The German philosophers are the most frivolous of all – they count truths like lovers but seldom propose to marry them. [Attr.]

20 Herbert Spencer, a few days before he died, had the eighteen volumes of *The Synthetic Philosophy* piled on his lap and, as he felt their weight, wondered if he would not have done better could

he have had a grandchild instead. [Attr.]

WALTER LIPPMAN

1 In a free society the state does not administer the affairs of men. It administers justice among men who conduct their own affairs. [*An Enquiry into the Principles of a Good Society*]

HAROLD LLOYD

2 I am just turning forty and taking my time about it. [When asked his age at over seventy. Quoted in *The Times*, 23 Sep. 1970]

LORD LLOYD

3 There never has been a British refugee. [1939. *Observer*, 'Sayings of Our Times', 31 May 1953]

DAVID, EARL LLOYD GEORGE

4 You cannot feed the hungry on statistics. [Speech, 1904, on Tariff Reform. Quoted in Malcolm Thomson, *David Lloyd George*, Ch. 8]

5 Mr Balfour's Poodle. [Description of House of Lords, in reply to a claim that the Lords were 'the watchdog of the nation', House of Commons, 26 Jun. 1907]

6 A fully equipped Duke costs as much to keep up as two Dreadnoughts, and Dukes are just as great a terror, and they last longer. [Speech on the Budget of 1909]

7 You cannot trust the interests of any class entirely to another class; and you cannot trust the interests of any sex entirely to another sex. [Speech on Women's Suffrage, 1911. Quoted in Thomson, op. cit., 9]

8 Every man has a House of Lords in his own head. Fears, prejudices, misconceptions – those are the peers, and they are hereditary. [Speech at Cambridge, 1927]

9 The world is becoming like a lunatic asylum run by lunatics. [1933. *Observer*, 'Sayings of Our Times', 31 May 1953]

10 Winston [Churchill] would go up to his Creator and say that he would very much like to meet His Son, about Whom he had heard a great deal and, if possible, would like to call on the Holy Ghost. Winston *loved* meeting people. [Quoted in A. J. Sylvester, *Diary*, 2 Jan. 1937]

11 He [Ramsay MacDonald] had sufficient conscience to bother him, but not sufficient to keep him straight. [Quoted in *ib*. 29 Aug. 1938]

12 If we are going in without the help of Russia we are walking into a trap. [Speech in House of Commons, 3 Apr. 1939]

13 Without Russia these three guarantees to Poland, to Roumania and to Greece are the most reckless commitments that any country has ever entered. [Speech, May 1939]

14 Poor Bonar can't bear being called a liar. Now I don't mind. [Quoted in G. M. Young, *Stanley Baldwin*]

15 He [Neville Chamberlain] saw foreign policy through the wrong end of a municipal drainpipe. [Quoted in Harris, *The Fine Art of Political Wit*, Ch. 6]

16 The Right Hon. gentleman [Sir John Simon] has sat so long on the fence that the iron has entered his soul. [Attr. in speech in House of Commons]

17 Doctrinaires are the vultures of principle. They feed upon principle after it is dead. [Quoted by Dingle Foot in the *Guardian*, 17 Jan. 1963]

18 I am opposed to Titanic seamanship in politics and as an old mariner I would not drive the ship on to the ice floes that have drifted into our seas from the frozen wastes of the Tory past. [Quoted in *ib*.]

19 May I ask of Protestants and Catholics alike that in these days of rejoicing [Christmas] we shall not forget the pitiful Madonna of the Slums with her pallid children. [Speech in London, 18 Dec. 1925]

20 When they circumcized Herbert Samuel they threw away the wrong bit. [Quoted by John Grigg in the *Listener*, 7 Sep. 1978]

1 [Of Lord Derby] Like a cushion, he always bore the impress of the last man who sat on him. [Quoted in *ib*. Though in J. Wintle and R. Kenin, *Dictionary of Biographical Quotation*, this description is credited to Earl Haig]

2 [Of Field-Marshal Lord Haig] He was brilliant to the top of his army boots. [Quoted in *ib*.]

DAVID LODGE

3 Literature is mostly about having sex and not much about having children; life is the other way round. [*The British Museum is Falling Down*, Ch. 4]

4 Rummidge ... had never been an institution of more than middling size and reputation, and it had lately suffered the mortifying fate of most English universities of its type (civic redbrick): having competed strenuously for fifty years with two universities chiefly valued for being old, it was, at the moment of drawing level, rudely over-taken in popularity and prestige by a batch of universities chiefly valued for being new. Its mood was therefore disgruntled and discouraged, rather as would be the mood of the middle class in a society that never had a bourgeois revolution, but had passed directly from aristocratic to proletarian con-trol. [*Changing Places*, Ch. 1]

5 Four times, under our educational rules, the human pack is shuffled and cut – at eleven-plus, sixteen-plus, eighteen-plus and twenty-plus – and happy is he who comes top of the deck on each occasion, but especially the last. This is called Finals, the very name of which implies that nothing of importance can happen after it. The British postgraduate student is a lonely forlorn soul ... for whom nothing has been real since the Big Push. [*Ib*.]

6 The British, he thought, must be glut-tons for satire: even the weather forecast seemed to be some kind of spoof, predicting every possible combination of weather for the next twenty-four hours without actually committing itself to anything specific. [*Ib*. 2]

7 O'Shea is what you might call an avant-gardener. He believes in ran-domness. His yard is a wilderness of weeds and heaps of coal and broken play equipment and wheelless prams and cabbages, silted-up bird baths and great gloomy trees slowly dying of some unspecified disease. I know how they must feel. [*Ib*. 3]

8 Walt Whitman who laid end to end words never seen in each other's company before outside of a dictionary. [*Ib*. 5]

SIR OLIVER LODGE

9 This Universe must not fail. [Attr.]

FRANK LOESSER

10 I'd like to get you / On a slow boat to China. [Song: *Slow Boat to China*]

11 See what the boys in the back room will have, / And tell them I'll have the same. [Song in film, *Destry Rides Again*. Sung by Marlene Dietrich]

CHRISTOPHER LOGUE

12 For example, he [Brecht] composed / Plays that staged by us promote / All the values he opposed. [*Christopher Logue's ABC*, 'B']

13 Said Marx: 'Don't be snobbish, we seek to abolish / The 3rd Class, not the 1st.' [*Ib*. 'M']

GINA LOLLOBRIGIDA

14 Glamour is when a man knows a woman is a woman. [*Observer*, 'Sayings of the Week', 15 Jul. 1956]

JACK LONDON

15 The certain weak and delicate prettiness which characterizes the cockney lasses, a prettiness which is no more than a promise with no grip on time, and doomed to fade quickly away like the colour from a sunset sky. [*The People of the Abyss*, Ch. 2]

16 In an English ship, they say, it is poor grub, poor pay, and easy work; in an American ship, good grub, good pay,

and hard work. And this is applicable to the working populations of both countries. [*Ib.* 20]

HUEY LONG

1 I looked around at the little fishes present, and said 'I'm the Kingfish.' [Quoted in A. M. Schlesinger Jr, *The Politics of Upheaval*, Bk I, Ch. 4, sect. v]

LORD LONGFORD

2 The male sex still constitute in many ways the most obstinate vested interest one can find. [Speech in House of Lords, 23 Jun. 1963]

3 On the whole I would not say that our Press is obscene. I would say that it trembles on the brink of obscenity. [*Observer*, 'Sayings of the Year', 1963]

4 No sex without responsibility. [*Observer*, 'Sayings of the Week', 3 May 1954]

ANITA LOOS

5 Gentlemen always seem to remember blondes. [*Gentlemen Prefer Blondes*, Ch. 1]

6 So this gentleman said a girl with brains ought to do something else with them besides think. [*Ib.*]

7 Paris is devine. I mean Dorothy and I got to Paris yesterday, and it really is devine. Because the French are devine. [*Ib.*]

8 Any girl who was a lady would not even think of having such a good time that she did not remember to hang on to her jewelry. [*Ib.* 4]

9 The Eyefull Tower is devine. [*Ib.*]

10 Kissing your hand may make you feel very good but a diamond and safire bracelet lasts forever. [*Ib.*]

11 So then Dr Froyd said all I needed was to cultivate a few inhibitions and get some sleep. [*Ib.* 5]

12 I think money is on the way out. [*Observer*, 'Sayings of the Week', 24 Jun. 1956]

13 I'm furious about the Women's Liberationists. They keep getting up on soapboxes and proclaiming that women are brighter than men. That's true, but it should be kept very quiet or it ruins the whole racket. [*Observer*, 'Sayings of the Year', 30 Dec. 1973]

LYDIA LOPOKOVA
[LADY KEYNES]

14 I dislike being in the country in August, because my legs get so bitten by barristers. [Attr. Quoted in Robert L. Heilbroner, *The Worldly Philosophers* Ch. 9]

LORCA. See GARCÍA LORCA

KONRAD LORENZ

15 It is a good morning exercise for a research scientist to discard a pet hypothesis every day before breakfast. It keeps him young. [*On Aggression*, Ch. 2]

LORD LOTHIAN

16 After all they are only going into their own back garden. [Comment on Hitler's military reoccupation of the Rhineland, 1936. Quoted in Winston S. Churchill, *The Gathering Storm*, Ch. 11]

DAVID LOW

17 I do not know whether he [Walt Disney] draws a line himself. I hear that at his studio he employs hundreds of artists to do the work. But I assume that his is the direction, the constant aiming after improvement in the new expression . . . it is the direction of a real artist. It makes Disney, not as a draughtsman but as an artist who uses his brains, the most significant figure in graphic art since Leonardo. [Quoted in R. Schickel, *Walt Disney*, Ch. 20]

ROBERT LOWELL

18 Yours the lawlessness / of something simple that has lost its law. [*Caligula*]

211

1 If we see light at the end of the tunnel, / It's the light of the oncoming train. [*Day by Day*]

2 The man is killing time – there's nothing else. [*The Drinker*]

3 Terrible that old life of decency / without unseemly intimacy / or quarrels, when the unemancipated woman / still had her Freudian papa and maids! [*During Fever*]

4 The monument sticks like a fishbone / in the city's throat. [*For the Union Dead*]

5 Disloyal still, / I doodle handlebar / moustaches on the last Russian Czar. [*Grandparents*]

6 This is death / To die and know it. This is the Black Widow, death. [*Mr Edwards and the Spider*]

7 They died / When time was open-eyed, / Wooden and childish; only bones abide / There, in the nowhere, where their boats were tossed / Sky-high, where mariners had fabled news / of is, the whited monster. [*The Quaker Graveyard in Nantucket*]

8 The Lord survives the rainbow of His will. [*Ib.*]

9 But I suppose even God was born / too late to trust the old religion – / all those setting out / that never left the ground, / beginning in wisdom, dying in doubt. [*Tenth Muse*]

10 Gored by the climacteric of his want, / he stalls above me like an elephant. [*To Speak of the Woe that is in Marriage*]

MALCOLM LOWRY

11 Where are the children I might have had? You may suppose I might have wanted them. Drowned to the accompaniment of the rattling of a thousand douche bags. [*Under the Volcano*, Ch. 10]

12 How alike are the groans of love to those of the dying. [*Ib.* 12]

SUZANNE LOWRY

13 Keeping body and soul together is never as difficult as trying to keep them separate. [On prostitution. *Guardian*, 24 May 1974]

ARTHUR LUCAN
('Old Mother Riley')

14 Good evening blagards, bodyguards, coalyards and fireguards. It's me, Mother Riley, just blown in for a breath of fresh air. [Opening patter to music-hall routine. Quoted in John Fisher, *Funny Way To Be a Hero*, 'Old Mother Riley and Her Daughter Kitty']

F. L. LUCAS

15 Human temperaments are too diverse; we can never agree how drunk we like our art to be. [*Literature and Psychology*, Ch. 10]

16 In some modern literature there has appeared a tendency to replace communication by a private maundering to oneself which shall inspire one's audience to maunder privately to *themselves* – rather as if the author handed round a box of drugged cigarettes. [*Style*, Ch. 2]

GEORGE LUCAS

17 May the Force be with you. [Running phrase in film, *Star Wars*]

DOCTOR KARL LUEGER
(Mayor of Vienna)

18 Science is what one Jew copies from another. [Quoted in the *Sunday Times*, 12 Jun. 1966]

19 I decide who is a Jew. [Quoted in Alan Bullock, *Hitler*, Ch. 1, sect. i. Sometimes wrongly attr. to Goering]

SIR EDWIN LUTYENS

20 Slogan – Learn to make bricks. [Quoted in Elisabeth Lutyens, *A Goldfish Bowl*, Ch. 2]

21 [When asked at a committee what should be done with the Crystal Palace] Put it under a glass case. [Quoted in *ib.*]

1 The answer is in the plural and they bounce. [Before a Royal Commission. Attr.]

2 This piece of cod passes all understanding. [Quoted in R. Lutyens, *Sir Edwin Lutyens*]

ELISABETH LUTYENS

3 All living artists compete with the towering dead with their nightingales and psalms. [*A Goldfish Bowl*, Ch. 2]

ROSA LUXEMBURG

4 Freedom is always and exclusively freedom for the one who thinks differently. [Quoted in H. Shukman, *Lenin and the Russian Revolution*]

LADY LYTTON

5 The first time you meet Winston [Churchill] you see all his faults and the rest of your life you spend in discovering his virtues. [Quoted in Christopher Hassall, *Edward Marsh*, Ch. 7]

M

GENERAL MacARTHUR

1 I shall return. [On leaving the Philippines, 11 Mar. 1942]

ROSE MACAULAY

2 Poem me no poems. [*Poetry Review*, Autumn 1963]

3 Here is one of the points about this planet which should be remembered; into every penetrable corner of it, and into most of the impenetrable corners, the English will penetrate. [*Crewe Train*, Pt I, Ch. 1]

4 Gentlemen know that fresh air should be kept in its proper place – out of doors – and that, God having given us indoors and out-of-doors, we should not attempt to do away with this distinction. [*Ib*. I. 5]

5 Aunt Evelyn's cheek was colossal. She probably laboured under the common delusion that you made things better by talking about them. [*Ib*. I. 12]

6 The great and recurrent question about abroad is, is it worth getting there? [Attr.]

7 She [Ethel M. Dell] rode the trash-horse hell-for-leather. [Attr.]

A. C. McAULIFFE

8 Nuts! [Reply to German demand to surrender Bastogne, 22 Dec. 1944]

GEORGE MacBETH

9 To leave great themes unfinished is / Perhaps the most satisfying exercise / Of power. [*The Spider's Nest*]

DESMOND MacCARTHY

10 When I meet those remarkable people whose company is coveted, I often wish they would show off a little more. [*Theatre*, 'Good Talk']

11 You understand *Epipsychidion* best when you are in love; *Don Juan* when anger is subsiding into indifference. Why not Strindberg when you have a temperature? [*Ib*. 'Miss Julie and the Pariah']

12 The whole of art is an appeal to a reality which is not without us but in our minds. [*Ib*. 'Modern Drama']

13 It [Post-Impressionist painting] may . . . appear ridiculous to those who do not recall the fact that a good rocking-horse has often more of the true horse about it than an instantaneous photograph of a Derby winner. [Introduction to exhibition, *Manet and His Contemporaries*, 1910]

JOSEPH McCARTHY

14 In my sweet little Alice blue gown, / When I first wandered out in the town. [Song: *Alice Blue Gown*, from musical *Irene*, Act I. Music by Harry Tierney]

SENATOR JOSEPH R. McCARTHY

15 McCarthyism is Americanism with its sleeves rolled. [In a speech in 1952. Quoted R. Rovere, *Senator Joe McCarthy*]

MARY McCARTHY

16 God is less like air in the lungs, in Graham Greene, than like a depressing smog that hangs over an industrial city . . . He soaks up the smell of his surroundings – bad cooking and mildew and dirty sheets and stale alcohol. [*Nights and Spectacles*, 'Sheep in Wolves' Clothing']

1 Stepping into his new Buick convertible he [the American] knows that he would gladly do without it, but imagines that to his neighbour, who is just backing *his* out of the driveway, this car is the motor of life. [*On the Contrary*, 'America the Beautiful']

2 Who are these advertising men kidding, besides the European tourist? Between the tired, sad, gentle faces of the subway riders and the grinning Holy Families of the Ad-Mass, there exists no possibility of even a wishful identification. [*Ib.*]

3 When an American heiress wants to buy a man, she at once crosses the Atlantic. The only really materialistic people I have ever met have been Europeans. [*Ib.*]

4 American life, in large cities at any rate, is a perpetual assault on the senses and the nerves; it is out of asceticism, out of unworldliness, precisely, that we bear it. [*Ib.*]

5 The American character looks always as if it had just had a rather bad haircut, which gives it, in our eyes at any rate, a greater humanity than the European, which even among its beggars has an all too professional air. [*Ib.*]

6 The immense popularity of American movies abroad demonstrates that Europe is the unfinished negative of which America is the proof. [*Ib.*]

7 An interviewer asked me what book I thought best represented the modern American woman. All I could think of to answer was: *Madame Bovary*. [*Ib.* 'Characters in Fiction']

8 There are no new truths, but only truths that have not been recognized by those who have perceived them without noticing. A truth is something that everyone can be shown to know and to have known, as people say, all along. [*Ib.* 'The *Vita activa*']

9 It really takes a hero to live any kind of spiritual life without religious belief. [In the *Observer*, 14 Oct. 1979]

10 And I don't feel the attraction of the Kennedys at all ... I don't think they are Christians; they may be Catholics but they are not Christians, in my belief anyway. [*Ib.*]

PAUL McCARTNEY

11 You cannot reheat a soufflé. [When asked if the Beatles were to be reunited. Quoted in J. Green, *The Book of Rock Quotes*]

W. D. H. McCULLOUGH and 'FOUGASSE'

12 A professor of anatomy once declared that there are only fourteen types of women – young women, women who are really wonderful all things considered, and the twelve most famous women in history – and the same applies to Bridge partners. Over and above this, they are usually either so good that you lose all your self-confidence, or so bad that you lose all your money. [*Aces Made Easy*]

13 '... that driving by the people through the people and over the people may shortly perish from the earth' – '*Straight-Eight*' *Lincoln* [Epigraph to *You Have Been Warned*]

HUGH MacDIARMID

14 Honour forever to the International Brigade! / They are a song in the blood of all true men. [*The International Brigade*]

15 It is very rarely that a man loves / And when he does it is nearly always fatal. [*Ib.*]

16 Pedology may tell us *why* a soil / Behaves as it does, / But only a rustic knows exactly *when*. [*In Berwickshire Again*]

17 Killing / Is the ultimate simplification of life. [*England's Double Knavery*]

18 (Though England prefers victims who begin by being restive, / They taste better afterwards – like birds / Cooked while their blood is still warm.) [*Ib.*]

19 Our principal writers have nearly all been fortunate in escaping regular education. [*Observer*, 'Sayings of the Week', 29 Mar. 1953]

BETTY MacDONALD

20 I can feel for her because, although I have never been an Alaskan prostitute

dancing on the bar in a spangled dress, I still get very bored with washing and ironing and dishwashing and cooking day after relentless day. [*The Egg and I*, Ch. 1]

1 In high school and college my sister Mary was very popular with the boys, but I had braces on my teeth and got high marks. [*Ib.* 2]

2 The days slipped down like junket, leaving no taste on the tongue. [*Ib.* 4]

3 A woman wants her friends to be perfect. She sets a pattern, usually a reasonable facsimile of herself, lays a friend out on this pattern and worries and prods at any little qualities which do not coincide with her own image. [*Ib.* 16]

RAMSAY MacDONALD

4 [On forming the National Government] Tomorrow every Duchess in London will be wanting to kiss me! [Quoted in Viscount Snowden, *Autobiography*]

5 Society goes on and on and on. It is the same with ideas. [Speech, 1935. Quoted in Robert Graves and Alan Hodge, *The Long Weekend*]

6 Let them [France and Germany] especially put their demands in such a way that Great Britain could say that she supported both sides. [Quoted in A. J. P. Taylor, *The Origins of the Second World War*, Ch. 3]

WILLIAM C. MacDONALD

7 It took God longer to write the Bible than it has taken Him to build the British Empire. [*Modern Evangelism*]

J. P. McEVOY

8 I've been in too many taxis not to know that a girl is lots safer with an orchestra between her and the tired business man, who don't act nearly as tired as you'd think. [*Show Girl*, Ch. 1]

9 It's been so long since he read anything except the *Graphic* that he can't even dial his own telephone numbers now. We're going to have little pictures put there instead of figures. [*Ib.*]

10 Say, for the last six weeks I've been busier than a one-legged man in a forest fire. [*Ib.* 9]

ARTHUR MacEWEN

11 News is anything that makes a reader say 'Gee whiz!' . . . News is whatever a good editor chooses to print. [Quoted in Daniel Boorstin, *The Image*, Ch. 1]

PHYLLIS McGINLEY

12 I'm happy the great ones are thriving, / But what puzzles my head / Is the thought that they need reviving. / I had never been told they were dead. [*On the Prevalence of Literary Revivals*]

FELIX McGLENNON

13 They may build their ships, my lads, and think they know the game, / But they can't build boys of the bulldog breed / Who made old England's name. [*Sons of the Sea*]

ROGER McGOUGH

14 You will put on a dress of guilt / and shoes with broken high ideals. [*Comeclose and Sleepnow*]

15 Let me die a youngman's death / not a clean & inbetween / the sheets holywater death / not a famous-last-words / peaceful out of breath death. [*Let Me Die a Youngman's Death*]

16 When I'm 73 / & in constant good tumour / may I be mown down at dawn / by a bright red sports car / on my way home / from an allnight party. [*Ib.*]

17 Or when I'm 91 / with silver hair / & sitting in a barber's chair / may rival gangsters / with hamfisted tommyguns bust in / & give me a short back & insides. [*Ib.*]

COLIN MacINNES

18 In England, pop art and fine art stand resolutely back to back. [*England, Half English*, 'Pop Songs and Teenagers']

19 England is, and always has been, a country infested with people who love

216

to tell us what to do, but who very rarely seem to know what's going on. [*Ib.*]

1 The decorations are like those of the embassy of a nation about to go into voluntary liquidation. [*Ib.* 'See you at Mabel's']

2 A coloured man can tell, in five seconds dead, whether a white man likes him or not. If the white man *says* he does, he is instantly – and usually quite rightly – mistrusted. [*Ib.* 'A Short Guide for Jumbles']

DENIS MACKAIL

3 A first night was notoriously distracting owing to the large number of people who stand about looking famous. [*How Amusing*]

SIR COMPTON MACKENZIE

4 Women do not find it difficult nowadays to behave like men; but they often find it extremely difficult to behave like gentlemen. [*On Moral Courage*]

5 Everybody boasted aloud that they fed you really well on the *Murmania*, and hoped silently that perhaps the sense of being imprisoned in a decaying hot-water-bottle . . . would pass away in the fresh Atlantic breezes. [*Poor Relations, Ch. 1*]

6 The houses . . . looked like an over-crowded row of tall thin men watching a football-match on a cold day; each red-faced house had a tree in front of it like an umbrella and trim white steps like spats. [*Ib.* 8]

7 The present school is not fit for children at all . . . 'How many water-closets have you?' one of these wise men from the East . . . was asking me at the last meeting . . . 'How many water-closets, General? The whole island is a water-closet,' I said. [*Whisky Galore*, Ch. 3]

H. S. MACKINTOSH

8 Give me that song of Picardy: / 'He has been duped – the station-master!' [*Ballades and Other Verse*, 'Il est cocu – le chef de gare!']

FITZROY MACLEAN

9 They [the Soviets] are Communists just as the Victorians were Christians. They attend CP meetings and lectures on Marxism-Leninism at regular intervals in exactly the same way as the Victorians attended church on Sunday. They believe in world revolution just as implicitly as the Victorians believed in the Second Coming. And they apply the principles of Marxism in their private lives to just about the same extent as the Victorians applied the principles of the Sermon on the Mount. Neither more nor less. [*Back to Bokhara*]

ARCHIBALD MACLEISH

10 We have learned the answers, all the answers: / It is the question that we do not know. [*The Hamlet of A. Macleish*]

11 History, like a badly constructed concert hall, has occasional dead spots where the music can't be heard. [*Observer*, 'Sayings of the Week', 12 Feb. 1967]

IAIN MACLEOD

12 History is too serious to be left to historians. [*Observer*, 'Sayings of the Week', 16 Jul. 1961]

MARSHALL McLUHAN

13 The new electronic interdependence re-creates the world in the image of a global village. [*The Gutenberg Galaxy*]

14 The world in which Advertisement dwells is a one-day world . . . The average man is invited to slice his life into a series of one-day lives, regulated by the clock of fashion. The human being is no longer the unit. He becomes the containing frame for a generation or sequence of ephemerids, roughly organized into what he calls his personality. [*The Mechanical Bride*]

15 'Real life' often appears, at least, to be an imitation of art. Today, it is poster art. [*Ib.* 'Cokes and Cheesecake']

16 For tribal man space was the uncontrollable mystery. For technological man it is time that occupies the same role. [*Ib.* 'Magic that Changes Mood']

217

1 If the nineteenth century was the age of the editorial chair, ours is the century of the psychiatrist's couch. [*Understanding Media*, Introduction]

2 The medium is the message. This is merely to say that the personal and social consequences of any medium . . . result from the new scale that is introduced into our affairs by each extension of ourselves or by any new technology. [*Ib.* Ch. 1]

3 There is a basic principle that distinguishes a hot medium like radio from a cool one like the telephone, or a hot medium like the movie from a cool one like TV. A hot medium is one that extends one single sense in 'high definition'. High definition is the state of being well filled with data. A photograph is, visually, 'high definition'. A cartoon is low definition simply because very little visual information is provided. Telephone is a cool medium, or one of low definition, because the ear is given a meagre amount of information. Hot media are, therefore, low in participation, and cool media are high in participation or completion by the audience. [*Ib.* 2]

4 The village had institutionalized all human functions in forms of low intensity . . . Participation was high and organization was low. This is the formula for stability. [*Ib.* 10]

5 Work . . . does not exist in a nonliterate world . . . Where the whole man is involved there is no work. Work begins with the division of labour. [*Ib.* 14]

6 The car has become the carapace, the protective and aggressive shell, of urban and suburban man. [*Ib.* 22]

7 Ads push the principle of noise all the way to the plateau of persuasion. They are quite in accord with the procedures of brain-washing. [*Ib.* 23]

8 The young people who have experienced a decade of TV have naturally imbibed an urge toward involvement in depth that makes all the remote visualized goals of usual culture seem not only unreal but irrelevant, not only irrelevant but anaemic. It is the total involvement in all-inclusive *nowness* that occurs in young lives via TV's mosaic image. [*Ib.* 31]

9 The principal aspect of the electric age is that it establishes a global network that has much of the character of our central nervous system. [*Ib.* 33]

10 Television brought the brutality of war into the comfort of the living room. Vietnam was lost in the living rooms of America – not on the battlefields of Vietnam. [Quoted in the *Montreal Gazette*, 16 May 1975]

11 Gutenberg made everybody a reader. Xerox makes everybody a publisher. [Interview with the *Washington Post*. Quoted in the *Guardian Weekly*, 12 Jun. 1977]

12 North Americans have a peculiar bias. They go outside to be alone and they go home to be social. [*Sunday Times Magazine*, 26 Mar. 1978]

HAROLD MACMILLAN

13 You've never had it so good. [Speech on financial situation, 20 Jul. 1957 (originally US presidential election slogan, 1952)]

14 I thought the best thing to do was to settle up these little local difficulties, and then turn to the wider vision of the Commonwealth. [Said at London Airport, 7 Jan. 1958, referring to resignation of Treasury Ministers]

15 Jaw-jaw is better than war-war. [Said at Canberra, 30 Jan. 1958, echoing Churchill's 'Talking jaw to jaw is better than going to war' at a White House lunch, 26 Jun. 1954]

16 When you're abroad you're a statesman: when you're at home you're just a politician. [Speech, 1958. Quoted in the *Observer*, 28 Jul. 1963]

17 The wind of change is blowing through this Continent, and whether we like it or not, this growth of national consciousness is a political fact. [Speech, Cape Town, 3 Feb. 1960]

18 Fifteen fingers on the safety catch. [Speech in the House of Commons, 31 May 1960, on breakdown of summit conference on nuclear disarmament]

1 It is the duty of Her Majesty's government . . . neither to flap nor to falter. [*Observer*, 'Sayings of the Week', 19 Nov. 1961]

2 I have never found in a long experienc of politics, that criticism is ever inhibited by ignorance. [*Observer*, 'Sayings of the Year', 29 Dec. 1963]

JOHN MACMURRAY

3 He [Jesus] is not an idealist – for the same reason that he is not a materialist – because the distinction between the ideal and the material does not arise for him. [*The Clue to History*]

LOUIS MacNEICE

4 Conferences, adjournments, ultimatums, / Flights in the air, castles in the air, / The autopsy of treaties, dynamite under the bridges, / The end of *laissez faire*. [*Autumn Journal*, VII]

5 And we who have been brought up to think of 'Gallant Belgium' / As so much blague / Are now prepared again to essay good through evil / For the sake of Prague. [*Ib.*]

6 A howling radio for our paraclete. [*Ib.*]

7 It's no go the picture palace, it's no go the stadium, / It's no go the country cot with a pot of pink geraniums, / It's no go the Government grants, it's no go the elections, / Sit on your arse for fifty years and hang your hat on a pension. [*Bagpipe Music*]

8 Ordinary men . . . / Put up a barrage of common sense to baulk / Intimacy but by mistake interpolate / Swear-words like roses in their talk. [*Conversation*]

9 Crumbling between the fingers, under the feet, / Crumbling behind the eyes, / Their world gives way and dies / And something twangs and breaks at the end of the street. [*Débâcle*]

10 Time was away and somewhere else, / There were two glasses and two chairs / And two people with one pulse. [*Meeting Point*]

11 In the beginning and in the end the only decent / Definition is tautology: man is

man, / Woman woman, and tree tree. [*Plain Speaking*]

12 He can discover / A selfish motive for anything – and collect / His royalties as recording angel. [*The Satirist*]

SALVADOR DE MADARIAGA

13 Considering how bad men are, it is wonderful how well they behave. [*Morning without Noon*]

14 It is not armaments that cause war, but wars that cause armaments. [*Ib.*]

15 A professor said, 'People are not interested in freedom but in ham and eggs.' To which I retorted, 'Ten years in prison with only ham and eggs for breakfast would cure that.' [BBC TV programme, *Viewpoint*, 14 Oct. 1969]

16 First the sweetheart of the nation, then the aunt, woman governs America because America is a land of boys who refuse to grow up. [Quoted in Sagittarius and George, *The Perpetual Pessimist*]

17 In politics, as in grammar, one should be able to tell the substantives from adjectives. Hitler was a substantive; Mussolini only an adjective. Hitler was a nuisance; Mussolini was bloody. Together a bloody nuisance. [Attr.]

HERB MAGIDSON

18 Music, Maestro, Please. [Title of song]

MAHARISHI MAHESH YOGI

19 Nature will not allow humanity to be deprived of the vision of Reality for very long. [*Bhagavadgita, a New Translation and Commentary*, Preface]

20 Because the self is of unmanifested nature, and because man's life is always in the field of the manifested, it is not to be wondered at if some people hear about it with great surprise, and others are not able to understand it at all. [*Ib.* on Ch. 29]

GUSTAV MAHLER

21 [On visiting Niagara] At last, fortissimo! [Quoted in K. Blankopf, *Mahler*, Ch. 8]

NORMAN MAILER

1 And she gave me a sisterly kiss. Older sister. [*The Deer Park*]

2 Ultimately a hero is a man who would argue with the Gods, and awakens devils to contest his vision. [*Presidential Papers*, Special Preface]

BERNARD MALAMUD

3 Levin wanted friendship and got friendliness; he wanted steak and they offered spam. [*A New Life*, sect. vi]

4 There comes a time in a man's life when to get where he has to go – if there are no doors or windows he walks through a wall. [*Rembrandt's Hat*, 'Man in the Drawer']

GEORGE MALLABY

5 Never descend to the ways of those above you. [*From My Level*]

G. H. L. MALLORY

6 Because it's there. [When asked why he wanted to climb Everest. Quoted in John Hunt, *The Ascent of Everes'*, Ch. 1]

MAE MALOO

7 There's one thing to be said for inviting trouble: it generally accepts. [Quoted in *Reader's Digest*, Sep. 1976]

ANDRÉ MALRAUX

8 A revolution only remains victorious through methods which are alien to those that made it. And sometimes even through sentiments which are similarly alien. [In *L'Espoir*. Quoted in Fitzroy Maclean, *Back to Bokhara*]

MANCHESTER GUARDIAN

9 If Mr Eliot had been pleased to write in demotic Eeglish *The Waste Land* might not have been, as it just is to all but anthropologists and literati, so much wastepaper. [Quoted in Virginia Woolf, *The Common Reader* (First Series), 'How it Strikes a Contemporary']

LORD MANCROFT

10 Happy is the man with a wife to tell him what to do and a secretary to do it. [*Observer*, 'Sayings of the Week', 18 Dec. 1966]

11 If [your wife] happens to be travelling anywhere without you and you want her back in a hurry, send her a copy of your local newspaper with a little paragraph cut out. [*Punch*, 27 Jan. 1971]

OSIP MANDELSTAM

12 No, I am no one's contemporary – ever. / That would have been above my station ... / How I loathe that other with my name. / He certainly never was me. [*Poems*, No. 141, trans. Clarence Brown and W. S. Merwin]

13 Star-salt is melting in the barrel, / icy water is turning blacker, / death's growing purer, misfortune saltier, / the earth's moving nearer to truth and to dread. [*Ib.* No. 216]

14 But whenever there's a snatch of talk / it turns to the Kremlin mountaineer, / the ten thick worms his fingers, / his words like measures of weight, / the huge laughing cockroaches on his top lip, / The glitter of his boot-rims. [*Ib.* No. 286, *Stalin Epigram*]

15 The people need poetry that will be their own secret / To keep them awake forever, / And bathe them in the bright-haired wave / Of its breathing. [*Ib.* No. 287]

16 Now I'm dead in the grave with my lips moving / And every schoolboy repeating my words by heart. [*Ib.* No. 306]

17 You took away the oceans and all the room. / You gave me my shoe-size in earth and bars around it. [*Ib.* No. 307]

RUBY MANIKAN
(Indian Church Leader)

18 If you educate a man you educate a person, but if you educate a woman you educate a family. [*Observer*, 'Sayings of the Week', 30 Mar. 1947]

HERMAN J. MANKIEWICZ

1 You know it's hard to hear what a bearded man is saying. He can't speak above a whisker. [Quoted in R. E. Drennan, *Wit's End*]

2 [Of Orson Welles] There, but for the Grace of God, goes God. [During the making of the film, *Citizen Kane*. Quoted in *The Citizen Kane Book*. But attr. also to Churchill on Stafford Cripps, see 77:7]

3 People never sat at his [Charlie Chaplin's] feet. He went to where people were sitting and stood in front of them. [Quoted in Kenneth Tynan, 'The Girl who was Lulu', *Observer Magazine*, 11 Nov. 1979]

4 That man [a fellow scriptwriter] is so bad he shouldn't be left alone in a room with a typewriter. [Attr.]

HERMAN J. MANKIEWICZ and ORSON WELLES

5 It [death] is the only disease you don't look forward to being cured of. [In film, *Citizen Kane*]

6 I guess Rosebud is just a piece in a jigsaw puzzle – a missing piece. [Final words of *ib.*]

JOSEPH L. MANKIEWICZ

7 [Said by Bette Davis] Fasten your safety belts; it's going to be a bumpy night. [In film, *All About Eve*]

8 It is about time the piano realized it has not written the concerto. [*Ib.*]

9 I admit I may have seen better days, but I am still not to be had for the price of a cocktail – like a salted peanut. [*Ib.*]

10 All playwrights should be dead for three hundred years. [*Ib.*]

11 Eve would ask Abbott to give her Costello. [*Ib.*]

12 The best friend of a boy is his mother, of a man his horse; only it's not clear when the transition takes place. [Quoted in A. Andrews, *Quotations for Speakers and Writers*]

THOMAS MANN

13 Our capacity for disgust, let me observe, is in proportion to our desires; that is in proportion to the intensity of our attachment to the things of this world. [*The Confessions of Felix Krull*, Pt I, Ch. 5]

14 Every intellectual attitude is latently political. [Quoted in the *Observer*, 11 Aug. 1974]

KATHERINE MANSFIELD

15 If there was one thing he hated more than another it was the way she had of waking him in the morning ... It was her way of establishing her grievance for the day. [*Bliss*, 'Mr Reginald Peacock's Day']

16 He stands, smiling encouragement, like a clumsy dentist. [*The Garden Party*, 'Bank Holiday']

17 That evening for the first time in his life ... old Mr Neave felt he was too old for the spring. [*Ib.* 'An Ideal Family']

18 Nothing made little Lennie put it on. Taking him to the cemetery, even, never gave him a colour; a nice shake-up in the bus never improved his appetite. [*Ib.* 'Life of Ma Parker']

19 She couldn't possibly go back to the gentleman's flat; she had no right to cry in strangers' houses. [*Ib.*]

20 E. M. Forster never gets any further than warming the teapot. He's a rare fine hand at that. Feel this teapot. Is it not beautifully warm? Yes, but there ain't going to be no tea. [*Journal*, May 1917]

21 Whenever I prepare for a journey I prepare as though for death. Should I never return, all is in order. This is what life has taught me. [*Ib.* 1922]

MAO TSE-TUNG

22 We should support whatever the enemy opposes and oppose whatever the enemy supports. [*Quotations from Chairman Mao Tse-Tung*, Ch. 2]

23 'War is the continuation of politics.' In this sense war is politics and war itself is a political action. [*Ib.* 5]

1 Every Communist must grasp the truth,
'Political power grows out of the barrel
of a gun.' [*Ib.*]

2 We are advocates of the abolition of
war, we do not want war; but war can
only be abolished through war, and in
order to get rid of the gun it is necessary
to take up the gun. [*Ib.*]

3 All reactionaries are paper tigers. [*Ib.* 6]

4 If you want knowledge, you must take
part in the practice of changing reality.
If you want to know the taste of a pear,
you must change the pear by eating it
yourself. [*Ib.* 22]

5 Letting a hundred flowers blossom and
a hundred schools of thought contend
is the policy for promoting the progress
of the arts and the sciences. [*Ib.* 32]

6 The atom bomb is a paper tiger which
the United States reactionaries use to
scare people. [Interview, Aug. 1946]

7 For the sake of the achievement of a
specific political goal. it is possible to
sacrifice half mankind. [Speech at
meeting in Moscow, Nov. 1957.
Quoted in *Pravda*, 26 Aug. 1973]

8 To read too many books is harmful.
[Quoted in the *New Yorker*, 7 Mar.
1977]

9 The enemy advances, we retreat; the
enemy camps, we harass; the enemy
tires, we attack; the enemy retreats, we
pursue. [Quoted in Evans, *Short History
of Guerrilla Warfare*]

10 The peaceful population is the sea in
which the guerrilla swims like a fish.
[Quoted in R. Taber, *The War of the
Flea*]

11 The government burns down whole
cities while the people are forbidden to
light lamps. [Attr.]

GEORGE MARKSTEIN
and DAVID TOMBLIN

12 I am not a number – I am a free man!
[Used regularly in ATV series, *The
Prisoner*, by political prisoner Number
Six]

222

DON MARQUIS

13 but wotthehell wotthehell / oh i should
worry and fret / death and I will co-
quette / there's a dance in the old dame
yet / toujours gai toujours gai [*archy and
mehitabel*, III, 'the song of mehitabel']

14 a / whole scuttleful of chef douvres
what / you mean is hors douvres
mehitabel i / told her what i mean is
grub [*Ib.* XI, 'why mehitabel jumped']

15 live so that you / can stick out your
tongue / at the insurance / doctor [*Ib.*
XII, 'certain maxims of archy']

16 procrastination is the / art of keeping /
up with yesterday [*Ib.*]

17 i do not care / what a dogs / pedigree
may be ... / millionaires and / bums
taste / about alike to me [*Ib.*]

18 its cheerio / my deario that / pulls a
lady through [*Ib.* XXIV, 'cheerio my
deario']

19 always being / misunderstood by some /
strait laced / prune faced bunch / of
prissy mouthed / sisters of uncharity
[*Ib.*]

20 archy she told me / it is merely a
plutonic / attachment / and the thing
can be / believed for the tom / looks
like one of pluto's demons [*Ib.* XXX,
'the old trouper']

21 the stage is not what it / used to be
tom says / they don't have it any more /
they don't have it here / the old
troupers are gone [*Ib.*]

22 he had a voice / that used to shake /
the ferryboats / on the north river [*Ib.*]

23 you want to know / whether i believe in
ghosts / of course i do not believe in
them / if you had known / as many of
them as i have / you would not / believe
in them either [*Ib.* XXXIII, 'ghosts']

24 one of the most pathetic / sights however / is to see the ghost of queen /
victoria going out every / evening with
the ghost / of a sceptre in her hand /
to find mr lytton strachey / and bean
him [*Ib.* XLIII, 'archy goes abroad']

25 jamais triste archy jamais triste / that
is my motto [*Ib.* XLVI, 'mehitabel sees
paris']

1 there is always / a comforting thought / in time of trouble when / it is not our trouble. [*archy does his part*]

2 To stroke a platitude until it purrs like an epigram. [*New York Sun:* 'The Sun Dial']

3 An idea isn't responsible for the people who believe in it. [*Ib.*]

4 Poetry is what Milton saw when he went blind. [*Ib.*]

MOORE MARRIOTT

5 Next train's gone! [In film, *Oh, Mr Porter!* Screenplay by J. O. C. Orton, Val Guest and Marriott Edgar]

EDWARD MARSH

6 How I dislike 'Technicolor', which suffuses everything with stale mustard. [*Ambrosia and Small Beer*, Ch. 3]

7 *Dialogue between an M. O. and a recruit:*
M. O. : How are your bowels working?
R. : Haven't been issued with any, sir.
M. O. : I mean, are you constipated?
R. : No sir, I volunteered.
M. O. : Heavens man, don't you know the King's English?
R. : No sir, is he? [*Ib.* 4]

8 Why is it that the sudden mention of an aunt is so deflating to a poem? [*Ib.* 5]

9 If you call Le Gallienne a minor poet you might just as well call a street lamp a minor planet. [Letter. Quoted in Christopher Hassall, *Edward Marsh*, Ch. 6]

10 He told me his object in life is to influence people for good, but he can't make up his mind whether to spread out his influence thin over 'millions' or give it in strong doses to a small circle of intimates. [*Ib.* 7]

11 Dear Roger Fry whom I love as a man but detest as a movement. [Quoted in *ib.* 11]

12 Praise of one's friends is always more unmixed pleasure than of oneself, because there isn't the slightest discomfort of doubting inwardly whether it is deserved. [Letter to Henry James, Spring 1915]

ARTHUR MARSHALL

13 Luncheon will be congealing on the table with Irene still staring, her eyes popping from her head, trying to discover just who it was who garotted Mademoiselle, set fire to the chapel and tarred and feathered Miss Parkinson's bust. ['Books for Girls', reprinted in V. S. Pritchett (ed.), *Turnstile One*]

SYBIL MARSHALL

14 Education must have an end in view, for it is not an end in itself. [*An Experiment in Education*, Ch. 4]

KINGSLEY MARTIN

15 I should always prefer influence to power. [*Father Figures*]

CHICO MARX

16 GROUCHO: We're going to have an auction.
CHICO: I came over here on the Atlantic auction. [In film. *The Cocoanuts.* Script by George S. Kaufman and M. Ryskind]

17 Mustard's no good without roast beef. [In film, *Monkey Business*. Script by S. J. Perelman, Will B. Johnstone and Arthur Sheekman]

18 You can't fool me, there ain't no Sanity Clause. [In film, *A Night at the Opera.* Script by George S. Kaufman, M. Ryskind and A. Boasberg]

19 [When caught by his wife, kissing a chorus girl] I wasn't kissing her. I was whispering in her mouth. [Quoted in N. Rees, *Quote . . . Unquote*]

GROUCHO MARX

20 My name is Captain Spalding, / The African explorer – / Did anyone say *schnorrer*? [In film, *Animal Crackers.* Script by Bert Kalmar]

21 Didn't I tell you not to go over Australia? / Didn't I tell you Australia was up? [*Ib.*]

22 What's a thousand dollars? Mere chicken feed. A poultry matter. [In

film, *The Cocoanuts.* Script by George S. Kaufman and M. Ryskind]

1 [As auctioneer]: Now, here's a lot! Oh, I know it doesn't look very big on top, but it goes down as far as you want to go. [*Ib.*]

2 JUDY: May I have one of your pictures?
GROUCHO: Why ... I haven't got one. I could give you my foot prints, but they're upstairs in my socks. [In film, *A Day at the Races.* Screenplay by Robert Pirosh, George Seaton and George Oppenheimer]

3 [Feeling patient's pulse] Either he's dead, or my watch has stopped. [*Ib.*]

4 [On throwing his watch into the hand-basin before carrying out an operation] Better rusty than missin'. [*Ib.*]

5 Send two dozen roses to Room 424 and put 'Emily, I love you' on the back of the bill. [*Ib.*]

6 [Putting his arms around Emily] If I hold you any closer, I'll be in back of you. [*Ib.*]

7 Emily, I've a little confession to make. I really am a horse doctor. But marry me, and I'll never look at any other horse. [*Ib.*]

8 If you can't leave in a taxi you can leave in a huff. If that's too soon, you can leave in a minute and a huff. [In film, *Duck Soup.* Script by Bert Kalmar, Harry Ruby, Arthur Sheekman and Nat Perrin]

9 You know you haven't stopped talking since I came here? You must have been vaccinated with a phonograph needle. [*Ib.*]

10 Why, a four-year-old child could understand this report. Run out and find me a four-year-old child. I can't make head or tail out of it. [*Ib.*]

11 MRS TEASDALE: He's had a change of heart.
FIREFLY [Groucho]: A lot of good that'll do him. He's still got the same face. [*Ib.*]

12 Dig trenches? With our men being killed off like flies? There isn't time to

dig trenches. We'll have to buy them ready made. [*Ib.*]

13 Remember, men, we're fighting for this woman's honour; which is probably more than she ever did. [*Ib.*]

14 In my day a college widow stood for something. She stood for plenty. [In film, *Horse Feathers.* Script by Bert Kalmar, Harry Ruby, S. J. Perelman and Will B. Johnstone]

15 I'll bet your father spent the first year of your life throwing rocks at the stork. [In film, *The Marx Brothers at the Circus.* Script by Irving Brecher]

16 Do you suppose I could buy back my introduction to you? [In film, *Monkey Business.* Script by S. J. Perelman, Will B. Johnstone and Arthur Sheekman]

17 LUCILLE: ... But from the time he got the marriage licence I've led a dog's life.
GROUCHO: Are you sure he didn't get a dog's licence? [*Ib.*]

18 I've worked myself up from nothing to a state of extreme poverty. [*Ib.*]

19 Be back next Thursday and bring a specimen of your money. [*Ib.*]

20 The strains of Verdi will come back to you tonight, and Mrs Claypool's cheque will come back to you in the morning. [In film, *A Night at the Opera.* Script by George S. Kaufman, M. R. Ryskind and A. Boasberg]

21 Time wounds all heels. [Quoted in the *Sunday Telegraph*, 21 Aug. 1977]

22 I only cite these annoyances to show you that it isn't necessary to have relatives in Kansas City to be unhappy. [*The Groucho Letters*, letter to Goodman Ace, 18 Jan. 1951]

23 I've been around so long I can remember Doris Day before she was a virgin. [Quoted in Leslie Halliwell, *The Filmgoer's Book of Quotes*]

24 I didn't like the play, but then I saw it under adverse conditions – the curtain was up. [Quoted in Laurence J. Peter, *Peter's Quotations*]

25 I was so long writing my review that I never got around to reading the book. [Quoted in *ib.*]

1 Military intelligence is a contradiction in terms. [Quoted in A. Spiegelman and B. Schneider, *Whole Grains*]

2 Do you know what this country needs today? A seven-cent nickel ... if it works out, next year we could have an eight-cent nickel ... You could go to the newsstand, buy a three-cent newspaper and get the same nickel back again. One nickel carefully used would last a family a lifetime. [Quoted in *ib.*]

3 Any man who says he can see through a woman is missing a lot. [Quoted in P. and J. Holton, *Quote and Unquote*]

4 I never forget a face, but I'll make an exception in your case. [Quoted in the *Guardian*, 18 Jun. 1965]

5 [When excluded from a smart Californian beach club on racial grounds] Since my daughter is only half-Jewish, could she go in the water up to her knees? [Quoted in obituary by Philip French, *Observer*, 21 Aug. 1977]

6 A man is as young as the woman he feels. [Quoted in *ib.*]

7 No, Groucho is not my real name. I'm breaking it in for a friend. [Attr.]

8 Please accept my resignation. I don't want to belong to any club that will accept me as a member. [Attr. telegram]

HARPO MARX

9 If you see me in the station at Moscow tomorrow morning, remind me I'm alive. [After having some trouble with Russian customs officials. Quoted in Kyle Crichton, *The Marx Brothers*, Ch. 22]

ZEPPO MARX

10 You ever see me act? You could give me every good line since Chaucer, and I'd ruin it. [Quoted in Kyle Crichton, *The Marx Brothers*, Ch. 22]

ERIC MASCHWITZ

11 A Nightingale Sang in Berkeley Square. [Title of song]

JOHN MASEFIELD

12 How still this quiet cornfield is to-night! / By an intenser glow the evening falls, / Bringing, not darkness, but a deeper light. [*August, 1914*]

13 The moonlight runs / Over the grasses of the ancient way / Rutted this morning by the passing guns. [*Ib.*]

14 Best trust the happy moments. What they gave / Makes man less fearful of the certain grave, / And gives his work compassion and new eyes. / The days that make us happy make us wise. [*Biography*]

15 O grave, keep shut lest I be shamed. [*C.L.M.*]

16 Out into street I ran uproarious, / The devil dancing in me glorious. [*The Everlasting Mercy*]

17 'Saul Kane', she said, 'when next you drink, / Do me the gentleness to think / That every drop of drink accursed / Makes Christ within you die of thirst, / That every dirty word you say / Is one more flint upon His way.' [*Ib.*]

18 I did not shrink, I did not strive, / The deep peace burnt my me alive. [*Ib.*]

19 Life's battle is a conquest for the strong; / The meaning shows in the defeated thing. [*The 'Wanderer'*]

20 From the Gallows Hill to the Tineton Copse / There were ten ploughed fields, like ten full-stops. [*Reynard the Fox*]

21 The stars grew bright in the winter sky, / The wind came keen with a tang of frost, / The brook was troubled for new things lost, / The copse was happy for old things found, / The fox came home and he went to ground. [*Ib.*]

22 What am I, Life? A thing of watery salt / Held in cohesion by unresting cells, / Which work they know not why, which never halt, / Myself unwitting where their master dwells? [*Lollingdon Downs*, Sonnet 37]

23 He was one of those born neither to obey nor to command, but to be evil to the commander and the obeyer alike. Perhaps there was nothing in life that he had much wanted to do, except to shoot rabbits and hit his father on the jaw,

225

and both these things he had done. [*The Bird of Dawning*]

1 In those days, as a little child, I was living in Paradise, and had no need of the arts, that at best are only a shadow of Paradise. [*So Long to Learn*]

2 The Fifth-Act-Actor, my friend explained, is one who can be charming, attractive, startling and surprising through the fortunes of four acts, and yet be shattering and triumphant in the fifth. [*Ib.*]

JOHN MASTERS

3 Join a Highland regiment, me boy. The kilt is an unrivalled garment for fornication and diarrhoea. [A major of Highlanders. Quoted in *Bugles and a Tiger*]

GEORGE MATHEW

4 We cannot help the birds of sadness flying over our heads, / But we need not let them build their nests in our hair. [Alleged Chinese saying. Quoted in James Agate, *Ego 1*, 1933]

TOM MATHEWS

5 Why did you keep me on tiptoe so long if you weren't going to kiss me? [When Henry Luce eventually decided against a British Edition of *Time*. Quoted in the *Observer*, 19 May 1963]

HENRI MATISSE

6 I don't know whether I believe in God or not. I think, really, I'm some sort of Buddhist. But the essential thing is to put oneself in a frame of mind which is close to that of prayer. [Quoted in Françoise Gilot and Carlton Lake, *Life with Picasso*, Part VI]

7 Exactitude is not truth. [Essay title quoted in J. D. Flam (ed.), *Matisse on Art*]

BRANDER MATTHEWS

8 A gentleman need not know Latin, but he should at least have forgotten it. [Advice to Dr Joseph Shipley]

REGINALD MAUDLING

9 There comes a time in every man's life when he must make way for an older man. [Remark made in the Smoking Room of the House of Commons on being dropped from Mrs Thatcher's Shadow Cabinet and replaced by a man older than himself. Quoted in the *Guardian*, 20 Nov. 1976]

W. SOMERSET MAUGHAM

10 People are always rather bored with their parents. That's human nature. [*The Bread-Winner*, Act II]

11 I don't think you want too much sincerity in society. It would be like an iron girder in a house of cards. [*The Circle*, Act I]

12 You can't learn too soon that the most useful thing about a principle is that it can always be sacrificed to expediency. [*Ib.* III]

13 I was brought up by a very strict mother to believe that men were naturally wicked. [*The Constant Wife*, Act I]

14 It's not the seven deadly virtues that make a man a good husband, but the three hundred pleasing amiabilities. [*Ib.*]

15 She's too crafty a woman to invent a new lie when an old one will serve. [*Ib.* II]

16 The only places John likes on the Continent are those in which it's only by an effort of the imagination that you can tell you're not in England. [*Ib.* III]

17 Some women can't see a telephone without taking the receiver off. [*Ib.*]

18 We have long passed the Victorian Era when asterisks were followed after a certain interval by a baby. [*Ib.*]

19 JOHN: Do you think I can't be a lover as well as a husband?
CONSTANCE: My dear, no one can make yesterday's cold mutton into tomorrow's lamb cutlets. [*Ib.*]

20 The right people are rude. They can afford to be. [*Our Betters*, Act II]

21 It was such a lovely day I thought it was a pity to get up. [*Ib.*]

1 My dear, she's been my greatest friend for fifteen years. I know her through and through, and I tell you that she hasn't got a single redeeming quality. [*Ib. III*]

2 She felt vaguely the pity of that child deprived of the only love in the world [parental] that is quite unselfish. [*Of Human Bondage*, Ch. 2]

3 Like all weak men he laid an exaggerated stress on not changing one's mind. [*Ib.* 37]

4 Money is like a sixth sense, without which you cannot make a complete use of the other five. [*Ib.* 51]

5 The aesthetic sense . . . is akin to the sexual instinct, and shares its barbarity. [*The Moon and Sixpence*, Ch. 1]

6 I forget who it was that recommended men for their soul's good to do each day two things they disliked . . . it is a precept that I have followed scrupulously; for every day I have got up and I have gone to bed. [*Ib.* 2]

7 It is not true that suffering ennobles the character; happiness does that sometimes, but suffering, for the most part, makes men petty and vindictive. [*Ib.* 17]

8 A woman can forgive a man for the harm he does her . . . but she can never forgive him for the sacrifices he makes on her account. [*Ib.* 41]

9 Because women can do nothing except love, they've given it a ridiculous importance. [*Ib.*]

10 She could not help saying beastly things about even her intimate friends, but she did this because she was a stupid woman and knew no other way to make herself interesting. [*The Razor's Edge*, Pt V, Ch. 7]

11 I could think of no one among my contemporaries who had achieved so considerable a position on so little talent. [*Cakes and Ale*, Ch. 1]

12 Hypocrisy is the most difficult and nerve-racking vice that any man can pursue; it needs an unceasing vigilance and a rare detachment of spirit. It cannot, like adultery or gluttony, be practised at spare moments; it is a whole-time job. [*Ib.*]

13 The Americans who are the most efficient people on earth . . . have invented so wide a range of pithy and hackneyed phrases that they can carry on an amusing and animated conversation without giving a moment's reflection to what they are saying and so leave their minds free to consider the more important matters of big business and fornication. [*Ib.* 2]

14 Poor Henry [James], he's spending eternity wandering round and round a stately park and the fence is just too high for him to peep over and they're having tea just too far away for him to hear what the Countess is saying. [*Ib.* 9]

15 'But I can do nothing unless I am in complete possession of the facts.' 'Obviously you can't cook them unless you have them.' [*Ib.*]

16 From the earliest times the old have rubbed it into the young that they are wiser than they, and before the young had discovered what nonsense this was they were old too, and it profited them to carry on the imposture. [*Ib.*]

17 For to write good prose is an affair of good manners. It is, unlike verse, a civil art . . . Poetry is baroque. [*The Summing Up*, Ch. 12]

18 Most people have a furious itch to talk about themselves and are restrained only by the disinclination of others to listen. Reserve is an artificial quality that is developed in most of us as the result of innumerable rebuffs. [*Ib.* 19]

19 It is dangerous to let the public behind the scenes. They are easily disillusioned and then they are angry with you, for it was the illusion they loved. [*Ib.* 23]

20 I thought to myself: Thank God, I can look at a sunset now without having to think how to describe it. I meant then never to write another book. [*Ib.* 33]

21 How can you write a play of which the ideas are so significant that they will make the critic of *The Times* sit up in his stall and at the same time induce the shop-girl in the gallery to forget the young man who is holding her hand? [*Ib.* 37]

1 Women will write novels to while away their pregnancies; bored noblemen, axed officers, retired civil servants fly to the pen as one might fly to the bottle. There is an impression abroad that everyone has it in him to write one book; but if by this is implied a good book the impression is false. [*Ib.* 47]

2 I'll give you my opinion of the human race in a nutshell ... Their heart's in the right place, but their head is a thoroughly inefficient organ. [*Ib.* 55]

3 The artist's egoism is outrageous; it must be; he is by nature a solipsist and the world exists only for him to exercise upon it his powers of creation. [*Ib.* 61]

4 It is a great nuisance that knowledge can only be acquired by hard work. It would be fine if we could swallow the powder of profitable information made palatable by the jam of fiction. [*10 Novels and Their Authors*, Ch. 1, sect. i]

5 Casting my mind's eye over the whole of fiction, the only absolutely original creation I can think of is Don Quixote. [*Ib.*]

6 American women expect to find in their husbands a perfection that English women only hope to find in their butlers. [Quoted in A. Andrews, *Quotations for Speakers and Writers*]

7 I've always been interested in people, but I've never liked them. [*Observer*, 'Sayings of the Week', 28 Aug. 1949]

8 The trouble with our younger authors is that they are all in the sixties. [*Observer*, 'Sayings of the Week', 14 Oct. 1951]

9 I am sick of this way of life. The weariness and sadness of old age make it intolerable. I have walked with death in hand, and death's own hand is warmer than my own. I don't wish to live any longer. [Remarks to the Press on his ninetieth birthday. Quoted in M. B. Strauss, *Familiar Medical Quotations*]

'BILL' MAULDIN

10 'He's right, Joe, when we ain't fightin' we should act like sojers.' [*Up Front*, cartoon caption]

ANDRÉ MAUROIS

11 In England there is only silence or scandal. [Attr.]

JAMES MAXTON

12 Sit down, man. You're a bloody tragedy. [To Ramsay MacDonald on the occasion of the last speech he made in the House of Commons. Attr.]

ELAINE MAY

13 I like a moral issue so much more than a real issue. [Quoted by Gore Vidal in an article in the *New Statesman*, 4 May 1973]

VLADIMIR MAYAKOVSKY

14 Oh for just / one / more conference / regarding the eradication of all conferences! [*In re Conferences*, trans. Herbert Marshall]

15 Always to shine, / and everywhere to shine, / and, to the very last, / to shine, – / thus runs / my motto / and the sun's. [*A Most Extraordinary Adventure*, trans. *ib.*]

16 Our planet / is poorly equipped / for delight / One must snatch / gladness / from the days that are. / In this life / it's not difficult to die. / To make life / is more difficult by far. [*Sergei Yessenin*, trans. *ib.*]

17 Art is not a mirror to reflect the world, but a hammer with which to shape it. [Quoted in the *Guardian*, 11 Dec. 1974]

LOUIS B. MAYER

18 The number one book of the ages was written by a committee, and it was called The Bible. [Said to writers who complained of changes made to their work. Quoted by Leslie Halliwell, *The Filmgoer's Book of Quotes*]

19 Throw the little old lady down the stairs! Throw the mother's good, homemade chicken soup in the mother's face! *Step* on the mother! *Kick* her! That is *art*, they say. Art! [Quoted in Lillian Ross, *Picture*, 'Throw the Little Old Lady Down the Stairs!']

WILLIAM J. MAYO

1 Specialist – A man who knows more and more about less and less. [Ascribed in A. K. Adams, *Cassell's Book of Humorous Quotations*. but *Oxford Dictionary of Quotations* (New edition) attr. to Nicholas Butler]

SIR PETER MEDAWAR

2 If politics is the art of the possible, research is surely the art of the soluble. [*The Art of the Soluble*]

3 The greater part of it [Teilhard de Chardin's *The Phenomenon of Man*], I shall show, is nonsense tricked out with a variety of tedious metaphysical conceits, and its author can be excused of dishonesty only on the grounds that before deceiving others he has taken great pains to deceive himself. [*Ib.*]

4 Scientific discovery is a private event, and the delight that accompanies it, or the despair of finding it illusory does not travel. [*Hypothesis and Imagination*]

GOLDA MEIR

5 Pessimism is a luxury that a Jew never can allow himself. [*Observer*, 'Sayings of the Year', 29 Dec. 1974]

ANDREW MELLON

6 A nation is not in danger of financial disaster merely because it owes itself money. [1933. *Observer*, 'Sayings of Our Times', 31 May 1953]

H. L. MENCKEN

7 I can't remember a single masculine figure created by a woman who is not, at bottom, a booby. [*In Defence of Women*, Ch. 1, sect. i]

8 The average male gets his living by such depressing devices that boredom becomes a sort of natural state to him. [*Ib.* 3. xxviii]

9 We must respect the other fellow's religion, but only in the sense and to the extent that we respect his theory that his wife is beautiful and his children smart. [Notebooks, *Minority Report*, 1]

10 Men always try to make virtues of their weaknesses. Fear of death and fear of life both become piety. [*Ib.* 54]

11 It is now quite lawful for a Catholic woman to avoid pregnancy by a resort to mathematics, though she is still forbidden to resort to physics and chemistry. [*Ib.* 62]

12 The capacity of human beings to bore one another seems to be vastly greater than that of any other animals. Some of their most esteemed inventions have no other apparent purpose, for example, the dinner party of more than two, the epic poem, and the science of metaphysics. [*Ib.* 67]

13 Men are the only animals who devote themselves assiduously to making one another unhappy. It is, I suppose, one of their godlike qualities. Jahweh, as the Old Testament shows, spends a large part of His time trying to ruin the business and comfort of all other gods. [*Ib.* 98]

14 A show of altruism is respected in the world chiefly for selfish motives ... Everyone figures himself profiting by it tomorrow. [*Ib.* 126]

15 War will never cease until babies begin to come into the world with larger cerebrums and smaller adrenal glands. [*Ib.* 164]

16 A nun, at best, is only half a woman, just as a priest is only half a man. [*Ib.* 221]

17 Whenever one comes to close grips with so-called idealism, as in war time, one is shocked by its rascality. [*Ib.* 223]

18 One of the things that makes a Negro unpleasant to white folk is the fact that he suffers from their injustice. He is thus a standing rebuke to them. [*Ib.* 272]

19 Why assume so glibly that the God who presumably created the universe is still running it? It is certainly perfectly conceivable that He may have finished it and then turned it over to lesser gods to operate. [*Ib.* 298]

20 The chief contribution of Protestantism to human thought is its massive proof that God is a bore. [*Ib.* 309]

229

1 The worst government is the most moral. One composed of cynics is often very tolerant and humane. But when fanatics are on top there is no limit to oppression. [*Ib*. 327]

2 Science, at bottom, is really anti-intellectual. It always distrusts pure reason, and demands the production of objective fact. [*Ib*. 412]

3 The great artists of the world are never Puritans, and seldom even ordinarily respectable. [*Prejudices*, First Series, 16]

4 To sum up: 1. The cosmos is a gigantic fly-wheel making 10,000 revolutions a minute. 2. Man is a sick fly taking a dizzy ride on it. 3. Religion is the theory that the wheel was designed and set spinning to give him the ride. [*Prejudices*, Third Series, '*Ad Imaginem dei creavit illum*', Coda]

5 Poetry is a comforting piece of fiction set to more or less lascivious music. [*Ib*. 'The Poet and his Art']

6 Faith may be defined briefly as an illogical belief in the occurrence of the improbable. [*Ib*. 'Types of Men']

7 Hygiene is the corruption of medicine by morality. It is impossible to find a hygienist who does not debase his theory of the healthful with a theory of the virtuous. [*Ib*.]

8 He [the businessman] is the only man who is for ever apologizing for his occupation. [*Ib*.]

9 The man who boasts that he habitually tells the truth is simply a man with no respect for it. It is not a thing to be thrown about loosely, like small change; it is something to be cherished and hoarded, and disbursed only when absolutely necessary. [*Ib*.]

10 Every man sees in his relatives, and especially in his cousins, a series of grotesque caricatures of himself. [*Ib*.]

11 No healthy male ever really thinks or talks of anything save himself. [*Prejudices*, Fourth Series, 'Reflections on Monogamy', 8]

12 No man is genuinely happy, married, who has to drink worse gin than he used to drink when he was single. [*Ib*. 14]

13 Ah, that the eugenists would breed a woman as capable of laughter as the girl of twenty and as adept at knowing when not to laugh as the woman of thirty-nine! [*Ib*. 15]

14 In one of his books he [Bertrand Russell] speaks very favourably of adultery, but he does so in the scientific way in which one might say a word for the method of least squares, the hook-worm or a respectable volcano. [Quoted in J. Wintle and R. Kenin, *Dictionary of Biographical Quotation*]

15 Opera in English, is, in the main, just about as sensible as baseball in Italian. [Quoted in Frank Muir, *The Frank Muir Book*]

PIERRE MENDÈS-FRANCE

16 To govern is to choose. [Attr.]

KARL MENNINGER

17 Illness is in part what the world has done to a victim, but in a larger part it is what the victim has done with his world, and with himself. [Quoted in Susan Sontag, *Illness as Metaphor*, Ch. 6]

YEHUDI MENUHIN

18 Music creates order out of chaos; for rhythm imposes unanimity upon the divergent, melody imposes continuity upon the disjointed, and harmony imposes compatibility upon the incongruous. [Quoted by Anthony Storr in the *Sunday Times*, 10 Oct. 1976]

19 Holding a violin is like holding a young bird. It is vibrating under your touch and you must hold it without squeezing it . . . It is a good thing to cultivate the feeling of those sympathetic vibrations in dealing with people. [Quoted in the *Daily Mail*, 15 Mar. 1977]

JOHNNY MERCER

20 Ma Moma done tol' me, / When I was in knee pants. [Song: *Blues in the Night*]

21 Days of wine and roses laugh and run away, / Like a child at play. [Song: *Days of Wine and Roses*]

1 I'm an old cow-hand / From the Rio Grande. [Song: *I'm an Old Cow-hand*]

2 Jeepers Creepers – where you get them peepers? [Song: *Jeepers Creepers*]

3 Strange as a will-o'-the-wisp, / Crazy as a loon, / Sad as a gypsy, / Serenading the moon. [Song: *Skylark*]

4 That old black magic has me in its spell. [Song: *That Old Black Magic*]

5 You must have been a beautiful baby, / 'Cos baby just look at you now. [Song: *You Must Have Been a Beautiful Baby*]

BOB MERRILL

6 People who need people are the luckiest people in the world. [Song: *People Who Need People*, from the musical, *Funny Girl*]

E. H. W. MEYERSTEIN

7 It [the last movement of Beethoven's Ninth Symphony] is the song of the angels sung by earth spirits. [Letter to his mother, 21 Oct. 1908]

8 It is pre-Whitman, and therefore pre-Pound and pre-Eliot, but not pre-possessing. [Describing poem by Clough, to R. N. Green-Armitage, 2 Sep. 1940]

SIR FRANCIS MEYNELL

9 So conscious he how short time was / For all he planned to do within it / He nothing did at all, alas, / Save note the hour – and file the minute. [*For a Functionary*]

10 What woman has this old cat's graces? / What boy can sing as the thrush sings? [*Man and Beast*]

JAMES MICHIE

11 Up in the heavenly saloon / Sheriff sun and rustler moon / Gamble, stuck in the sheriff's mouth / The fag end of an afternoon. [*Arizona Nature Myth*]

LUDWIG MIES VAN DER ROHE

12 Less is more. [Quoted in obituary, *The Times*, 19 Aug. 1969]

GEORGE MIKES

13 One of the most popular American entertainments is kissing. Young men and young girls pull up on the highways and kiss each other between 6.30 and 10.30 p.m. This kind of amusement is considered perfectly decent, probably because it keeps you from going to a cinema. [*Down with Everybody*]

14 The Swiss managed to build a lovely country around their hotels. [*Ib.*]

15 The trouble with tea is that originally it was quite a good drink. [*How to be an Alien*]

16 In England it is bad manners to be clever, to assert something confidently. It may be your personal view that two and two make four, but you must not state it in a self-assured way, because this is a democratic country and others may be of a different opinion. [*Ib.*]

17 To employ an English charwoman is a compromise between having a dirty house and cleaning it yourself. [*Ib.*]

18 Taxis are ... a Christian institution. They are here to teach drivers modesty and humility. They teach us never to be over-confident. [*Ib.*]

19 It was twenty-one years ago that England and I first set foot on each other. I came for a fortnight; I have stayed ever since. [*How to be Inimitable*]

20 The New Poor of yester-year are fighting a losing battle. To remain poor needs the utmost skill and ingenuity. [*Ib.*]

21 The one class you do *not* belong to and are not proud of at all is the lower-middle class. No one ever describes himself as belonging to the lower-middle class. [*Ib.*]

22 The place of the upstart is being taken by the downstart. I know people who secretly visit evening elocution classes in order to pick up a cockney accent. [*Ib.*]

23 A man in a queue is as much the image of a true Briton as a man in a bull-ring is the image of a Spaniard or a man with a two-foot cigar of an American. [*Ib.*]

231

1 All English shop assistants are Miltonists. A Miltonist firmly believes that 'they also serve who only stand and wait'. [*Ib.*]

2 Continental people have sex life; the English have hot-water bottles. [Quoted in A. Andrews, *Quotations for Speakers and Writers*]

3 Simply by not owning three medium-sized castles in Tuscany I have saved enough money in the last forty years *on insurance premiums alone* to buy a medium-sized castle in Tuscany. [*Punch*, 29 May 1974]

GENERAL MILLÁN ASTRAY

4 Long live death! Down with intelligence! [Slogan in Spanish Civil War]

EDNA ST VINCENT MILLAY

5 Euclid alone / Has looked on Beauty bare, Fortunate they / Who, though once only and then but far away, / Have heard her massive sandal set on stone. [*Euclid alone has looked on Beauty bare*]

6 I came upon no wine / So wonderful as thirst. [*Feast*]

7 Blessed be death that cuts in marble / What would have sunk in dust. [*Keen*]

8 Who builds her a house with love for timber, / Builds her a house of foam; / And I'd rather be bride to a lad gone down / Than widow to one safe home. [*Ib.*]

9 [Capping Elbert Hubbard. See *Penguin Dictionary of Quotations* 200:18] It is not true that life is one damn thing after another – it is one damn thing over and over. [*Letters of Edna St Vincent Millay*]

ALICE DUER MILLER

10 In a world where England is finished and dead; / I do not wish to live. [*The White Cliffs*]

ARTHUR MILLER

11 The word 'now' is like a bomb through the window, and it ticks. [*After the Fall*, Act I]

12 A suicide kills two people, Maggie, that's what it's for! [*Ib.* II]

13 All organization is and must be grounded on the idea of exclusion and prohibition just as two objects cannot occupy the same space. [*The Crucible*, Act I]

14 There are many who stay away from church these days because you hardly ever mention God any more. [*Ib.*]

15 The concept of unity, in which positive and negative are attributes of the same force, in which good and evil are relative, ever-changing and always joined to the same phenomenon – such a concept is still reserved to the physical sciences and to the few who have grasped the history of ideas. [*Ib.*]

16 I have not moved from there to there without I think to please you, and still an everlasting funeral marches round your heart [*Ib.* II]

17 Oh, Elizabeth, your justice would freeze beer! [*Ib.*]

18 He's liked, but he's not well liked. [*Death of a Salesman*, Act I]

19 The world is an oyster, but you don't crack it open on a mattress. [*Ib.*]

20 Never fight fair with a stranger, boy. You'll never get out of the jungle that way. [*Ib.*]

21 I still feel – kind of temporary about myself. [*Ib.*]

22 Willy Loman never made a lot of money. His name was never in the paper. He's not the finest character that ever lived. But he's a human being, and a terrible thing is happening to him. So attention must be paid. [*Ib.*]

23 A small man can be just as exhausted as a great man. [*Ib.*]

24 Everybody likes a kidder, but nobody lends him money. [*Ib.*]

25 I only wish during the war they'd a took me in the Army. I coulda been dead by now. [*Ib.* II]

26 He's a man way out there in the blue, riding on a smile and a shoeshine. And when they start not smiling back – that's an earthquake . . . A salesman is got to

dream, boy. It comes with the territory. [*Ib*. Death Requiem]

1 The car, the furniture, the wife, the children – everything has to be disposable. Because you see the main thing today is – shopping. Years ago a person, he was unhappy, didn't know what to do with himself – he'd go to church, start a revolution – *something*. Today you're unhappy? Can't figure it out? What is the salvation? Go shopping. [*The Price*, Act I]

2 I am inclined to notice the ruin in things, perhaps because I was born in Italy. [*A View from the Bridge*, Act I]

3 A man comes into a great hotel and says, I am a messenger. Who is this man? He disappears walking, there is no noise, nothing. Maybe he will never come back, maybe he will never deliver the message. But a man who rides up on a great machine, this man exists. He will be given messages. [*Ib*.]

4 A good newspaper, I suppose, is a nation talking to itself. [*Observer*, 'Sayings of the Week', 26 Nov. 1961]

5 Why should I go [to Marilyn Monroe's funeral]? She won't be there. [Attr.]

HENRY MILLER

6 The world does seem to become one, however much its component elements may resist. Indeed, the stronger the resistance the more certain is the outcome. *We resist only what is inevitable.* [*Big Sur and the Oranges of Hieronymus Bosch*]

7 Sex is one of the nine reasons for reincarnation ... The other eight are unimportant. [*Ib*.]

8 Napoleon is nothing to me in comparison with Eddie Carney who gave me my first black eye. [*Black Spring*, 'The 14th Ward']

9 All my good reading, you might say, was done in the toilet ... There are passages of *Ulysses* which can be read only in the toilet – if one wants to extract the full flavour of their content. [*Ib*. 'Paris and its Suburbs']

10 Though I've never read a line of Homer I believe the Greek of today is essentially unchanged. If anything he is more Greek than he ever was. [*The Colossus of Maroussi*, Ch. 1]

11 In this life I am God, and like God / I am indifferent to my own fate. [*The Cosmological Eye*]

12 Every man with a belly full of the classics is an enemy of the human race. [*Tropic of Cancer*, 'Dijon']

HENRY MILLER
(Songwriter)

13 A Boy's Best Friend is His Mother [Title of song]

JONATHAN MILLER

14 I'm not really a Jew; just Jew-ish, not the whole hog. [*Beyond the Fringe*]

15 They do those little personal things people sometimes do when they think they are alone in railway carriages; things like smelling their own armpits. [*Ib*.]

16 Language in fact bears the same relationship to the concept of mind that legislation bears to the concept of parliament: it is a competence forever bodying itself forth in a series of concrete performances. [*McLuhan*, Ch. 5]

17 The human body is private property. We have to have a search warrant to look inside, and even then an investigator is confined to a few experimental tappings here and there, some gropings on the party wall, a torch flashed rather hesitantly into some of the dark corners. [BBC TV programme, *The Body in Question*, 'Perishable Goods', reprinted in the *Listener*, 15 Feb. 1979]

MAX MILLER

18 That's what I like about you, you're quick, aren't you? [Running gag in variety act]

19 I like the girls who do, / I like the girls who don't; / I hate the girl who says she will / And then she says she won't. / But the girl that I like best of all / And I think you'll say I'm right – / Is the

233

one who says she never has / But looks as though she ... / 'Ere, listen ... [Song: *The Girls Who Do*. Quoted in *The Max Miller Blue Book*]

1 Jack and Jill went up the hill / Just like two cock linnets, / Jill came down with half a crown – / She wasn't up there two minutes! [Quoted in *ib.*]

2 There was a little girl / Who had a little curl / Right in the middle of her forehead, / When she was good she was very very good / And when she was bad she was very very popular. [Quoted in *ib.*]

WALTER M. MILLER JNR

3 Someone was smiling. It was only a small smile but in the midst of a sea of grave faces it stood out like a dead fly in a bowl of cream. [*A Canticle for Leibowitz*, '*Fiat Voluntas Tua*']

SPIKE MILLIGAN

4 It was Battery Sergeant-Major 'Jumbo' Day. His hair was so shorn his neck seemed to go straight up the back of his hat. [*Adolf Hitler – My Part in his Downfall*, 'I Join the Regiment']

5 Some people are always late, like the late King George V. [*The Bald Twit Lion*]

6 A baby Sardine / Saw her first submarine: / She was scared and watched through a peephole. / 'Oh, come, come, come,' / Said the Sardine's mum, / 'It's only a tin full of people.' [*A Book of Milliganimals*, 'Sardines']

7 Tigers travel stealthily / Using first, legs one and three. / They alternate with two and four; / And, after that, there are no more. [*Ib.* 'Tiger, Tiger Burning etc.']

8 I said to the First Officer, 'Gad, that sun's hot,' to which he replied, 'Well, you shouldn't touch it.' [*A Dustbin of Milligan*, 'Letters to Harry Secombe', I]

9 I shook hands with a friendly Arab ... I still have my right hand to prove it. [*Ib.*]

10 At dinner a gentleman's shirt front exploded when he saw a lady in a low-cut evening gown. Mind you, her front looked as if it had exploded earlier with a wider area of devastation. [*Ib.* II]

11 He told me he had the sea in his blood, and believe me you can see where it gets in. [*Ib.*]

12 What a beautiful morning it's been out on deck ... Only on the third class tourist class passengers' deck was it a sultry overcast dull morning, but then if you do things on the cheap you must expect these things. [*Ib.*]

13 I have for instance among my purchases ... several original Mona Lisas and all painted (according to the Signature) by the great artist Kodak. [*Ib.* III]

14 By Midday in Colombo, the heat is so unbearable that the streets are empty save for thousands of Englishmen taking mad dogs for walks. [*Ib.*]

15 Nowadays, the old prison has been turned into a first-class hotel with a service that any Michelin guide would be only too pleased to condemn. [*Ib.* V]

16 He walked with a pronounced limp. L-I-M-P, pronounced 'limp'. [*Ib.* 'The Great Man']

17 His thoughts, few that they were, lay silent in the privacy of his head. [*Puckoon*, Ch. 1]

18 Tank heaven the ground broke me fall. [*Ib.* 2]

19 I'm a hero wid coward's legs, I'm a hero from the waist up. [*Ib.*]

20 When she saw the sign 'Members only' she thought of him. [*Ib.* 3]

21 Money can't buy friends, but you can get a better class of enemy. [*Ib.* 6]

22 A thousand hairy savages / Sitting down for lunch / Gobble gobble glup glup / Munch munch munch. [*Silly Verse for Kids*]

23 PETER SELLERS: In South America. HARRY SECOMBE: That's abroad, isn't it? P.S.: It all depends on where you're standing. [BBC radio comedy series, *The Goon Show*, 'The Affair of the Lone Banana']

1 Not so loud, you fool – remember – even people have ears. [*Ib.* 'The Marie Celeste']

2 H. S.: Gad, Bloodnok, I admire your guts.
BLOODNOK: What, are they showing? [*Ib.* Variations in other instalments]

3 Ohhh – my nut – oh – I have been nutted on my bonce – oh I have been nutted! [*Ib.* Variations in other instalments]

4 The court will now stand for Judge Schnorrer – and if you'll stand for him you'll stand for anything. [*Ib.* 'Dishonoured']

5 MORIARTY: How are you at Mathematics?
H. S.: I speak it like a native. [*Ib.*]

6 You silly twisted boy! [*Ib.* and other instalments]

7 BLUEBOTTLE: Enter Bluebottle – where's the sausinges? [*Ib.* and other instalments]

8 Points cardboard finger at thousands of savage naughty men with Indian-type bare chests. [*Ib.* Variations in other instalments]

9 BLUEBOTTLE: What do you want, my Capitain – as if I didn't know! [*Ib.* 'The Great Bank of England Robbery', and repeated elsewhere]

10 Are you going to come quietly or do I have to use earplugs? [*Ib.* 'The Great Mustard and Cress Shortage']

11 I'm walking backwards for Christmas. [Remark by any character in *The Goon Show*]

12 He's fallen in the water. [Running gag in *The Goon Show*]

13 Contraceptives should be used on every conceivable occasion. [*The Last Goon Show of All*]

14 And then the monsoons came, and they couldn't have come at a worse time, bang in the middle of the rainy season. [Quoted in the *Telegraph Sunday Magazine*, 26 Jun. 1977]

15 One day the don't-knows will get in, and then where will we be? [On results of a pre-election poll. Attr.]

16 Don't you think it's going to be rather wet for the horses? [On having the Boat Race course described to him. Attr.]

SPIKE MILLIGAN and ERIC SYKES

17 A floor so cunningly laid that no matter where you stood it was always under your feet. [BBC radio comedy series, *The Goon Show*, 'The China Story']

18 To conserve energy we marched lying down and only stood up to sleep. [*Ib.* 'The Siege of Fort Night']

19 It's only 80 miles as the crow flies – and our crow is a sick man. [*Ib.*]

A. J. MILLS, FRED GODFREY and BENNETT SCOTT

20 Take me back to dear old Blighty, / Put me on the train to London Town. [Song: *Take Me Back to Dear Old Blighty*]

HUGH MILLS

21 Nothing unites the English like war. Nothing divides them like Picasso. [*Prudence and the Pill*, Ch. 4]

A. A. MILNE

22 The average man finds life very uninteresting as it is. And I think that the reason why ... is that he is always waiting for something to happen to him instead of setting to work to make things happen. For one person who dreams of making fifty thousand pounds, a hundred people dream of being left fifty thousand pounds. [*If I May*, 'The Future']

23 It is only the very young girl at her first dinner-party whom it is difficult to entertain. At her second dinner-party, and thereafter, she knows the whole art of being amusing. All she has to do is to listen; all we men have to do is to tell her about ourselves. [*Ib.* 'Going out to Dinner']

24 If I walk through any of the big stores with a parcel in my hand I expect to hear a voice whispering in my ear, 'The manager would like to see you quietly in his office' ... When I settle a bill by

cheque, my 'face-of-a-man-whose-account-is-already-overdrawn' can be read across the whole length of the shop as soon as I enter the door. [*Ib.* 'Not Guilty']

1 Two inches to the north-west is written a word full of meaning – the most purposeful word that can be written on a map. 'Inn'. [*Ib.* 'An Ordnance Map']

2 I wrote somewhere once that the third rate mind was only happy when it was thinking with the majority, the second rate mind was only happy when it was thinking with the minority, and the first rate mind was only happy when it was thinking. [*War with Honour*]

3 I am old enough to be – in fact am – your mother. [*Belinda*]

4 'Well, I sort of made it up,' said Pooh, ... 'it comes to me sometimes.' 'Ah!' said Rabbit, who never let things come to him, but always went and fetched them. [*The House at Pooh Corner*, Ch. 5]

5 He respects Owl, because you can't help respecting anybody who can spell TUESDAY, even if he doesn't spell it right. [*Ib.*]

6 When you are a Bear of Very Little Brain, and you Think of Things, you find sometimes that a Thing which seemed very Thingish inside you is quite different when it gets out into the open and has other people looking at it. [*Ib.* 6]

7 When Rabbit said, 'Honey or condensed milk with your bread?' he was so excited that he said, 'Both,' and then, so as not to seem greedy, he added, 'But don't bother about the bread, please.' [*Winnie-the-Pooh*, Ch. 2]

8 I'm giving him a Useful Pot to Keep Things In. [*Ib.* 6]

9 If the English language had been properly organized ... then there would be a word which meant both 'he' and 'she', and I could write, 'If John or Mary comes, heesh will want to play tennis,' which would save a lot of trouble. [*The Christopher Robin Birthday Book*]

10 And some of the bigger bears try to pretend / That they came round the corner to look for a friend; / And they'll try to pretend that nobody cares / Whether you walk on the lines or the squares. [*When We Were Young*, 'Lines and Squares']

EWART MILNE

11 I ween it is between those twain / That once is seen: that twice is not seen! [*Once More to Tourney*, 'Grandmer's Busy Day']

LORD MILNER

12 If we believe a thing to be bad, and if we have a right to prevent it, it is our duty to try to prevent it and to damn the consequences. [Speech in Glasgow, 26 Nov. 1909]

D. MIRSKY

13 Freud has been accepted as the consecration of all desires and all lusts, a sort of free pass to every kind of freedom or looseness, a complete liberation from all discipline. He has become the Bible of this intelligentsia. [*The Intelligentsia of Great Britain*, Ch. 1, sect. 5]

ADRIAN MITCHELL

14 The man who believes in giraffes would swallow anything. [*Loose Leaf Poem*]

15 I want to be a movement / But there's no one on my side. [*Ib.*]

16 A sinking pool for learning to drown. [*Ib.*]

17 Finally I was given the Chair of Comparative Ambiguity / At Armpit University, Java. [*The Oxford Hysteria of English Poetry*]

18 He gets the odd villain. / A couple of revolutionaries / Whose graves keep catching fire / But mostly they're a decent mob, the dead. [*Please keep off the Dead*]

19 Britain the mixed infant, / its mouth sullen as it enters its second millennium / Of pot-training. [*To Nye Bevan Despite His Change of Heart*]

20 Poetry is an extra hand. It can caress or tickle. It can clench and fight. The hand is hot. Take it or leave it. ['Poetry Lives',

article in the *Sunday Times*, 13 Feb. 1972]

JONI MITCHELL

1 I've looked at life from both sides now / From win and lose and still somehow / It's life's illusions I recall / I really don't know life at all. [Song: *Both Sides Now*]

2 My old man / He's a singer in the park / He's a walker in the rain / He's a dancer in the dark. [Song: *My Old Man*]

3 But when he's gone / Me and them lonesome blues collide. / The bed's too big. / The frying pan's too wide. [*Ib.*]

JULIAN MITCHELL

4 Freud is all nonsense; the secret of neurosis is to be found in the family battle of wills to see who can refuse longest to help with the dishes. The sink is the great symbol of the bloodiness of family life. All life is bad, but family life is worse. [*As Far as You Can Go*, Pt I, Ch. 1]

5 At Oxford he had been deliberately Byronic, and the Don Juan attitude was still there in emergencies. An enemy had once told him to his face that he needed more buckle and less swash. [*Ib.* I. 2]

6 Helen Gallagher was a short girl, and her shortness was emphasized by curly brown hair that looked ... like a mop with a permanent wave. [*Ib.* I. 3]

7 It has been said that a careful reading of *Anna Karenina*, if it teaches you nothing else, will teach you how to make strawberry jam. [*Radio Times*, 30 Oct. 1976]

SUSAN MITCHELL

8 Some men kiss and do not tell, some kiss and tell; but George Moore told and did not kiss. [Quoted in O. St John Gogarty, *As I Was Going Down Sackville Street*, Ch. 5]

JESSICA MITFORD

9 Knowing few children of my own age, I envied the children of literature to whom interesting things were always

happening: 'Oliver Twist was so *lucky* to live in a fascinating orphanage!' [*Hons and Rebels*, Ch. 3]

10 I have nothing against undertakers personally. It's just that I wouldn't want one to bury my sister. [Attr. *Saturday Review*, 1 Feb. 1964]

NANCY MITFORD

11 Aunt Sadie ... so much disliked hearing about health that people often took her for a Christian Scientist, which, indeed, she might have become had she not disliked hearing about religion even more. [*The Pursuit of Love*, Ch. 4]

12 I was always led to suppose that no educated person ever spoke of notepaper. [*Ib.*]

13 I have only read one book in my life, and that is *White Fang*. It's so frightfully good I've never bothered to read another. [*Ib.*]

14 The high spirits, which ... he had seemed to possess, must have been due to youth, drink and good health. Now that he was grown up and married he put all three resolutely behind him. [*Ib.* 10]

15 English women are elegant until they are ten years old, and perfect on grand occasions. [Quoted in L. and M. Cowan, *The Wit of Women*]

DIMITRI MITROPOULOS

16 I never used a score when conducting my orchestra ... Does a lion tamer enter a cage with a book on how to tame a lion? [22 Jan. 1961. Quoted in Nat Shapiro, *An Encyclopedia of Quotations about Music*]

WILSON MIZNER

17 A fellow who is always declaring he's no fool usually has his suspicions. [Quoted in A. Andrews, *Quotations for Speakers and Writers*]

18 Be nice to people on your way up because you'll meet 'em on your way down. [Quoted in Eric Partridge, *A Dictionary of Catch-Phrases*. Also attr. to Jimmy Durante]

237

1 Working for Warner Bros is like fucking a porcupine: it's a hundred pricks against one. [Quoted in David Niven, *Bring on the Empty Horses*]

2 [Of Hollywood] A trip through a sewer in a glass-bottomed boat. [Quoted in A. Johnston, *Legend of a Sport; the New Yorker*]

HENRY MOAT

3 Poor Sir George, he really is an hero for his bed. I have known him often being *tired* of laying in bed, get up to have a rest, and after he had rested get back again into bed like a martyr. [Quoted in Sir Osbert Sitwell, *The Scarlet Tree*, Bk 3, Ch. 3]

GENERAL SIR JOHN MONASH

4 I don't care a damn for your loyal service when you think I am right; when I really want it most is when you think I am *wrong*. [Attr. in Colin MacInnes, *England, Half English*, 'Joshua Reborn']

HAROLD MONRO

5 That star-enchanted song falls through the air / From lawn to lawn down terraces of sound, / Darts in white arrows on the shadowed ground; / While all the night you sing. [*The Nightingale near the House*]

6 Now is your voice a marble high and white, / Then like a mist in fields of paradise; / Now is a raging fire, then is like ice, / Then breaks and it is dawn. [*Ib.*]

MARILYN MONROE

7 JOURNALIST: Didn't you have anything on?
M. M.: I had the radio on. [Quoted in Leslie Halliwell, *The Filmgoer's Book of Quotes*]

8 [On having matzo balls for dinner for the third time at Arthur Miller's parents] Isn't there any other part of a matzo you can eat? [Quoted by Sir Laurence Olivier on a BBC TV programme]

THOMAS L. MONSON

9 Our very business in life is not to get ahead of others, but to get ahead of ourselves. [Attr.]

C. E. MONTAGUE

10 War hath no fury like a non-combatant. [*Disenchantment*, Ch. 15]

11 A gifted small girl has explained that pins are a great means of saving life, 'by not swallowing them'. [*Dramatic Values*]

VISCOUNT MONTGOMERY

12 This sort of thing may be tolerated by the French, but we are British – thank God. [On Homosexuality Bill. Quoted in the *Daily Mail*, 27 May 1965]

HENRI DE MONTHERLANT

13 The man who marries always makes the woman a present because she needs marriage and he does not . . . Woman is made for man, man is made for life. [*Young Girls*]

MONTY PYTHON'S FLYING CIRCUS

14 [Ferndean School Report on God] Progress and Conduct: I'm afraid that I am severely disappointed in God's works. All three of Him have shown no tendency to improve and He merely sits at the back of the class talking to himselves. He has shown no interest in Rugger, asked to be excused Prayers, and moves in a mysterious way. [*The Brand New Monty Python Book*]

15 I'm a lumberjack / And I'm OK / I sleep all night / And I work all day. [*Monty Python's Big Red Book*]

16 It's not pining, it's passed on. This parrot is no more. It's ceased to be. It's expired. It's gone to meet its maker. This is a late parrot. It's a stiff. Bereft of life it rests in peace. It would be pushing up the daisies if you hadn't nailed it to the perch. It's rung down the curtain and joined the choir invisible. It's an ex-parrot. [BBC TV comedy series, programme of 14 Dec. 1969]

1 Nudge, nudge, wink, wink. Know what I mean? [*Passim* in BBC TV comedy series, with variants]

2 And now for something completely different. [*Passim* in *ib.*]

DORIS LANGLEY MOORE

3 The Churches grow old but do not grow up. [*The Vulgar Heart*, Ch. 2]

GEORGE MOORE

4 The best prose is usually written by poets – Shakespeare wrote the best seventeenth century, and Shelley the best nineteenth; and I don't think I'm going too far when I say that Mr Hardy has written the worst. [*Conversations in Ebury Street*, Ch. 5]

5 Mr Conrad has paid us a pretty compliment by learning to write the English language correctly, and the journalists are so pleased that they have assigned him a place in our literature. [*Ib.* 19]

6 I had to keep you waiting till the strain of composition had worn off my face. [Quoted in O. St John Gogarty, *As I Was Going Down Sackville Street*, Ch. 17]

7 To be aristocratic in Art one must avoid polite society. [Quoted in Cyril Connolly, *Enemies of Promise*, Ch. 15]

GERALD MOORE

8 Am I Too Loud? [Title of autobiography]

MARIANNE MOORE

9 Openly, yes, / with the naturalness / of the hippopotamus or the alligator / when it climbs out on the bank to / experience the / sun, I do these / things which I do, which please / no one but myself. [*Black Earth*]

10 My father used to say, / 'Superior people never make long visits.' [*Silence*]

11 Nor was he insincere in saying, 'Make my house / your inn.' / Inns are not residences. [*Ib.*]

12 If 'compression is the first grace of style,' / you have it. [*To a Snail*]

T. STURGE MOORE

13 Two buttocks of one bum. [Of Belloc and Chesterton. Quoted in Stephen Potter, *The Sense of Humour*, Ch. 1]

FRANK MOORHOUSE

14 My venturesome remark about Marshall McLuhan which I considered had attack had fallen noiselessly through the conversation to the floor. To retrieve it would be like searching for a cent on a crowded bus – on a wet day – on crutches. [*The American Poet's Visit*, Ch. 6]

POP MORAND

15 Keeping Up With the Joneses. [Title of cartoon strip which first appeared in 1914 and ran till 1958]

ALBERTO MORAVIA

16 The ratio of literacy to illiteracy is constant, but nowadays the illiterates can read and write. [Quoted by Mary McCarthy in the *Observer*, 14 Oct. 1979]

ERIC MORECAMBE and ERNIE WISE

17 VANESSA REDGRAVE: He is crying again. I wish he wouldn't cry. The tears roll down his legs and make them shrink. I do love him. When he kisses me I can feel his heart beating against my knee-caps. [*The Best of Morecambe and Wise*, 'Napoleon and Josephine'. Scripts by Eddie Braben]

18 Q: What do you think of the show so far?
A: Rubbish. [Running gag in TV show, *The Morecambe and Wise Show*. Scripts by Eddie Braben]

CHRISTIAN MORGENSTERN

19 Ein Knie geht einsam durch die Welt. Es ist ein Knie, sonst nichts. – There wanders through the world a knee, / A knee and nothing more. [*Galgenlieder*, ' Das Knie', trans. R. F. C. Hull]

20 Im Winkel König Fahrenheit / hat still sein Mus gegessen. / – 'Ach Gott, sie war

doch schön, die Zeit, | da man nach mir gemessen!' – In the corner King Fahrenheit | quietly ate his pap. | 'Oh God, those were fine times | when they measured by me.' [*Ib. 'Kronprätendenten'*]

1 *Es war einmal ein Lattenzaun, | mit Zwischenraum, hindurchzuschaun. | Ein Architekt, der dieses sah, | stand eines Abends plötzlich da – | und nahm den Zwischenraum heraus | und baute draus ein grosses Haus.* – There was a fence with spaces you | Could look through if you wanted to. | An architect who saw this thing | Stood there one summer evening, | Took out the spaces with great care | And built a castle in the air. [*Ib. 'Der Lattenzaun'*]

2 *Die Möwen sehen alle aus | als ob sie Emma hiessen.* – The seagulls all look | as if they were called Emma. [*Ib. 'Möwenlied'*]

3 *Wenn ich sitze, will ich nicht | sitzen, wie mein Sitz-Fleisch möchte, | sondern wie mein Sitz-Geist sich, | sässe er, den Stuhl sich flöchte.* – When I sit I don't like to | sit the way my fleshy bottom wants to, | but in the way that my spiritual bottom would, if it sat, | intertwine itself with the chair. [*Der Gingganz, 'Der Aesthet'*]

4 *Es gibt ein Gespenst | das frisst Taschentücher; | es begleitet dich | auf deiner Reise.* – There is a ghost | That eats handkerchiefs; | It keeps you company | On all your travels. [*Ib. 'Gespenst'*]

5 *Korf erwidert darauf kurz und rund: | 'Einer hohen Direktion | stellt sich, laut persönlichen Befund, | untig angefertigte Person | als nichtexistent im Eigen-Sinn | bürgerlicher Konvention | vor und aus.'* – Korf sent an answer mild and bland: | 'Your letter of the 10th to hand. | The undersigned herewith presents | His most obsequious compliments. | But would apprise you of the fact | That, in the strict sense of the Act | As touching personal matters, he | Is a complete nonentity.' [*Palmström, 'Die Behörde'*]

6 *Palmström baut sich eine Geruchs-Orgel | und spielt darauf v. Korfs Nieswurz-Sonate.* – Palmström builds himself a Smell-organ | and plays von Korf's sneeze-wort [hellebore] sonata on it. [*Ib. 'Die Geruchs-Orgel'*]

7 *Zwar ein Werk, wie allerwärts, | doch zugleich ein Werk – mit Herz.* – Though clockwork in its outward part | It hides within – a tender heart. [*Ib.*]

8 *Und er kommt zu dem Ergebnis: | 'Nur ein Traum war das Erlebnis. | Weil,' so schliesst er messerscharf, | 'nicht sein kann, was nicht sein darf.'* – And so he comes to the conclusion | The whole affair was an illusion. | 'For look,' he cries triumphantly, | 'What's not permitted CANNOT be!' [*Ib. 'Die unmögliche Tatsache'*]

CHRISTOPHER MORLEY

9 There are three ingredients in the good life: learning, earning, and yearning. [*Parnassus on Wheels*, Ch. 10]

10 A human being: an ingenious assembly of portable plumbing. [*Human Being*, Ch. 11]

11 He is too experienced a parent ever to make positive promises. [*Thunder on the Left*, Ch. 5]

12 Life is a foreign language: all men mispronounce it. [*Ib.* 14]

13 Prophets were twice stoned – first in anger; then, after their death, with a handsome slab in the graveyard. [*Where the Blue Begins*, Ch. 11]

14 My theology, briefly, is that the universe was dictated but not signed. [Quoted in A. Andrews, *Quotations for Speakers and Writers*]

15 Why do they put the Gideon Bibles only in the bedrooms [of hotels], where it's usually too late? [Quoted in *ib.*]

ROBERT MORLEY

16 The British tourist is always happy abroad so long as the natives are waiters. [*Observer*, 'Sayings of the Week', 20 Apr. 1958]

17 Beware of the conversationalist who adds 'in other words'. He is merely starting afresh. [*Observer*, 'Sayings of the Week', 6 Dec. 1964]

18 There's no such thing in Communist countries as a load of old cod's wallop, the cod's wallop is always fresh made. [*Punch*, 20 Feb. 1974]

1 Music was the one gift denied me, I'm afraid. [Said on BBC TV programme, *Parkinson*, 1 Oct. 1977]

J. E. MORPURGO

2 Every Englishman has to survive one insult the moment he lands on foreign soil: he is called an 'alien'. [*American Excursion*]

3 God would not have invented the automobile if he had intended me to walk. [*The Road to Athens*]

4 Austria is Switzerland, speaking pure German and with history added. [*Ib.*]

DESMOND MORRIS

5 There are one hundred and ninety-three living species of monkeys and apes. One hundred and ninety-two of them are covered with hair. The exception is a naked ape self-named *Homo sapiens*. [*The Naked Ape*, Introduction]

6 He [*Homo sapiens*] is proud that he has the biggest brain of all the primates, but attempts to conceal the fact that he also has the biggest penis. [*Ib.*]

7 Clearly, then, the city is not a concrete jungle, it is a human zoo. [*The Human Zoo*, Introduction]

JAMES MORRIS

8 The master illusion of Spain is the conviction that the Spaniards are a people different, when they are only a people separate. [*The Presence of Spain*]

JIM MORRISON

9 The old get old, the young get younger, / They got the guns but we got the numbers. [Song: *Five to One*]

JOHN MORTIMER

10 And what've I achieved? Three women in my life and one of *them* turned out to be a chartered accountant over thirty! [*Two Stars for Comfort*, Act I. sc. ii]

11 Eddy was a tremendously tolerant person, but he wouldn't put up with the Welsh. He always said, surely there's enough English to go round. [*Ib.*]

12 When I was a boy at school I never minded the lessons. I just resented having to work terribly hard at playing. [*A Voyage Round My Father*, Act I]

13 No brilliance is needed in the law. Nothing but common sense, and relatively clean finger nails. [*Ib.*]

14 The immortality of the soul! What a boring conception! Can't think of anything worse than living for infinity in a great transcendental hotel, with nothing to do in the evenings. [*Ib.* II]

J. B. MORTON ('BEACHCOMBER')

15 Dr Strabismus (Whom God Preserve) of Utrecht is carrying out research work with a view to crossing salmon with mosquitoes. He says it will mean a bite every time for fishermen. [*By the Way*, January Tail-piece]

16 Vegetarians have wicked, shifty eyes, and laugh in a cold and calculating manner. They pinch little children, steal stamps, drink water, favour beards ... wheeze, squeak, drawl and maunder. [*Ib.* 4 June]

17 Ilion is safe, and Agamemnon's fleet / Lies beached: Achilles yawns upon his bed, / Paris lies dreaming at Oenone's feet; / Helen is shingled, and the epic's dead. [*Ib.* June, Tail-piece]

18 I used to be able to shoot the rind off an apple stored in a loft at the top of a cast-iron lighthouse. [*Ib.* 13 August, 'On the Moors: Social Jottings']

19 One disadvantage of being a hog is that at any moment some blundering fool may try to make a silk purse out of your wife's ear. [*Ib.* September, Tail-piece]

20 Hush, hush, / Nobody cares! / Christopher Robin / Has / Fallen / Down- / Stairs. [*Ib.* 18 December, 'Now We are Sick']

21 A Mrs Tasker is accused of continually ringing the doorbell of a Mrs Renton, and then, when the door is opened, pushing a dozen red-bearded dwarfs into the hall and leaving them there. [*The Best of Beachcomber*, 1, 'The Case of the Twelve Red-bearded Dwarfs']

1 The Doctor is said to have invented an extraordinary weapon which will make war less brutal. It is described as a very powerful liquid which rots braces at a distance of a mile. [*Ib.* 5, 'Bracerot']

2 He [Dr Smart-Allick of Narkover] said it was not always the timid fellow, with four conventional aces in his hand, who won the highest honours. 'It is often,' he said, 'the fifth ace that makes all the difference between success and failure.' [*Ib.* 8, 'The Drama at Badger's Earth']

3 She has a Rolls body and a Balham mind. [*Ib.* 9, 'A Foul Innuendo']

4 KEEPING THEIR END UP
Not many of our old families can boast that a Savile Row tailor calls four times a year at their country estate to measure the scarecrows in the fields for new suits. [*Ib.*]

5 He got the OBE later for wearing an opera hat during a night attack on a mutinous tribe. [*Ib.*]

6 Behind every beetle you will find a good mother-beetle. [*Ib.* 10, 'Open Letter to Sir James Barrie']

7 I shall never forget my mother's horror and my father's cry of joy when, for the first time in my life, I said angrily to my father, 'That's not the hand I dealt you, Dad.' [*Ib.* 11, 'The Life and Times of Captain de Courcy Foulenough']

8 To fairy flutes, / As the light advances, / In square black boots / The cabman dances. [*Ib.* 12, 'The Saga of the Saucy Mrs Flobster: The Dancing Cabman']

9 SIXTY HORSES WEDGED IN A CHIMNEY
The story to fit this sensational headline has not turned up yet. [*Ib.* 13, 'Mr Justice Cocklecarrot: Home Life']

10 'Does it occur to you,' asked a voice, 'that the absence of a dead body from a room does not necessarily prove that someone is dead? Your dead body is not in the kitchen, but you are not dead.' [*Ib.* 15, 'Dead Man's Alibi']

11 All over England loving hands are packing trunks for the young gentlemen of Narkover, who reassemble today. [*Ib.* 16, 'The New Boy at Narkover']

12 Doctor Smart-Allick replied gravely, assuring the widow that an unarmed baby could carry the Crown Jewels openly down the High Street without being molested by anyone except the boys and masters. [*Ib.*]

13 Miss Boubou Flaring's reading of Agatha, the wronged rocking-horse maker's daughter, left nothing to be desired except death. [*Ib.* 17, 'If so be That']

14 Last night Cocklecarrot exclaimed, with his customary lucidity, that if a cow with handlebars is a bicycle, within the meaning of the Act, then a bicycle with four legs instead of two wheels is a cow. [*Ib.*]

15 Iron Nostril Balzarotti, the man who tried to stuff the Severn Tunnel with sage and onions. [Richard Ingrams (ed.), *Beachcomber: The Works of J. B. Morton*]

16 ROLAND MILK, the limp-wristed poet: Before I die I want to do something big and clean in the world.
LADY CABSTANLEIGH: Go and wash an elephant. [*Ib.*]

17 Gone to that country from whose Bourne no Hollingsworth returns. [Quoted in N. Rees, *Quote . . . Unquote*]

18 Wagner is the Puccini of music. [Attr.]

LEONARD MOSLEY

19 In parliamentary life, he [Curzon] was to be one who stayed to get his feet wet before deciding that a ship was sinking. [*The Glorious Fault*]

SIR OSWALD MOSLEY

20 'Can't' will be the epitaph of the British Empire – unless we wake up in time. [Speech at Manchester, 9 Dec. 1937]

21 The opponents of our people are the money lords and the press lords who control the old parties. Britain is now ruled by King Bunk and King Bank. [Speech, 5 Mar. 1956]

22 I am not, and never have been, a man of the right. My position was on the left and is now in the centre of politics. [Letter to *The Times*, 26 Apr. 1968]

1 Before the organization of the Black-shirt movement free speech did not exist in this country. [Quoted in M. Bateman, selections from the *New Statesman, This England*, Pt I]

HOWARD MOSS

2 There are no rocks / At Rockaway, / There are no sheep / At Sheepshead Bay, / There's nothing new / In New-foundland, / And silent is / Long Island Sound. [*Geography: A Song*]

STIRLING MOSS

3 It has taken thirty-three years and a bang on the head to get my values right. [*Observer*, 'Sayings of the Week', 23 Sep. 1962]

ROBERT MOTHERWELL

4 Perhaps – I say perhaps because I do not know how to reflect except by opening my mind like a glass-bottomed boat so that I can watch what is swimming below – painting becomes sublime when the artist transcends his personal anguish, when he projects in the midst of a shrieking world an expression of living and its end that is silent and ordered. [*A Tour of the Sublime* (*The Ides of Art*), 'Tiger's Eye', 1 Dec. 1948]

5 Having a retrospective is making a will. [Quoted in F. O'Hara, *Robert Mother-well*]

KITTY MUGGERIDGE

6 [Of David Frost] He rose without trace. [Quoted in N. Rees, *Quote . . . Unquote*]

MALCOLM MUGGERIDGE

7 An orgy looks particularly alluring seen through the mists of righteous indigna-tion. [*The Most of Malcolm Muggeridge*: 'Dolce Vita in a Cold Climate']

8 The orgasm has replaced the Cross as the focus of longing and the image of fulfilment. [*Ib.* 'Down with Sex']

9 Macmillan seemed, in his very person, to embody the national decay he sup-posed himself to be confuting. He exuded a flavour of moth-balls. [*Tread Softly For You Tread on My Jokes*, 'England, whose England']

10 He [Sir Anthony Eden] is not only a bore but he bores for England. ['Boring for England', reprinted in Edward Hyams, *Newstatesmanship*]

11 They asked for a leader and were given a public relations officer; here is the news, and this is Anthony Eden reading it. [*Ib.*]

12 Never forget that only dead fish swim with the stream. [Reported as said to him in Manchester, *Radio Times*, 9 Jul. 1964]

13 Writing about travels is nearly always tedious, travelling being, like war and fornication, exciting but not interesting. [Reviewing *The Diaries of Evelyn Waugh* in the *Observer*, 5 Sep. 1976]

EDWIN MUIR

14 Yet they waited, / Stubborn and shy, as if they had been sent / By an old com-mand to find our whereabouts / And that long-lost archaic companionship. / In the first moment we had never a thought / That they were creatures to be owned and used. [*The Horses*]

15 These words rang in their ears as if they had said, / 'There was another road you did not see.' [*The Road*]

16 The House with the Seven Gables is gone, consumed by fire, / And in the evenings businessmen from Boston / Sit in the beautiful houses, mobbed by cars. [*Salem, Massachusetts*]

FRANK MUIR

17 Were you aware that Strip-Tease was named after the man who imported it into this country at the fag-end of the last century, Phineas Stripp? Well, it was. It had no name in France but when Phineas imported the idea he hired a theatre in London in between the matinée and the evening performance and served tea while the ladies divested. These became known as Stripp Teas, and the name stuck. [In Frank Muir and Denis Norden, *You Can't Have*

Your Kayak and Heat It, 'So he passed over . . .']

1 Dogs, like horses, are quadrupeds. That is to say, they have four rupeds, one at each corner, on which they walk. [In *ib.* 'Ta-ra-ra-boom-de-ay!']

**FRANK MUIR
and DENIS NORDEN**

2 It has been said that a bride's attitude towards her betrothed can be summed up in three words: Aisle. Altar. Hymn. [Frank Muir and Denis Norden, *Upon My Word!*, 'A jug of wine']

3 PSYCHIATRIST: I've examined your son's head, Mr Glum, and there's nothing there. [BBC radio comedy series, *Take It from Here*, 1957]

4 What are you – a sorcerer? / Only at home. In company I drink out of the cup. [*Ib.* Programme No. 216]

KEN MULLEN
(Leo Burnett Advertising Agency)

5 No pomp, just the circumstances. [Poster in advertising campaign for *The Times*, 1973–4]

6 Our readers are blessed with fine features. [Advertisement for *The Times*]

7 Even if it's grim, we'll bare it. [Advertisement for *The Times*]

8 Our sages know their onions. [Advertisement for *The Times*]

9 We take no pride in prejudice. [Advertisement for *The Times*]

HERBERT J. MULLER

10 Few have heard of Fra Luca Parioli, the inventor of double-entry book-keeping; but he has probably had much more influence on human life than has Dante or Michelangelo. [*The Uses of the Past*, Ch. 8]

LEWIS MUMFORD

11 Today, the notion of progress in a single line without goal or limit seems perhaps the most parochial notion of a very parochial century. [*Technics and Civilization*, Ch. 8. sect. xii]

12 However far modern science and technics have fallen short of their inherent possibilities, they have taught mankind at least one lesson: Nothing is impossible. [*Ib.* 8. xiii]

13 In the city time becomes visible. [Quoted in L. L. Levinson, *Bartlett's Unusual Quotations*]

H. H. MUNRO
See 'Saki'

IRIS MURDOCH

14 All art deals with the absurd and aims at the simple. Good art speaks truth, indeed *is* truth, perhaps the only truth. [*The Black Prince*, 'Bradley Pearson's Foreword']

15 Writing is like getting married. One should never commit oneself until one is amazed at one's luck. [*Ib.*]

16 'We aren't getting anywhere. You know that as well as I do.' 'One doesn't have to get anywhere in a marriage. It's not a public conveyance.' [*A Severed Head*, Ch. 3]

RUPERT MURDOCH

17 The Third World never sold a newspaper. [Quoted in the *Observer*, 1 Jan. 1978]

**C. W. MURPHY
and WILL LETTERS**

18 Has anybody here seen Kelly? / Kelly from the Isle of Man? [Song: *Has Anybody Here Seen Kelly?* Sung by Florrie Forde]

DAVID MURRAY

19 A reporter is a man who has renounced everything in life but the world, the flesh, and the devil. [*Observer*, 'Sayings of the Week', 5 Jul. 1931]

FRED MURRAY

20 When she play'd for Mister Gee, / She could always find the key, / Tho' she'd

never had a lesson in her life. [*Song: She'd Never Had a Lesson* ...]

FRED MURRAY and GEO EVERARD

1 And it's all right in the summer time, / In the summer time it's lovely! / While my old man's painting hard, / I'm posing in the old back yard. / But oh, oh! In the winter-time / It's another thing you know, / With a little red nose, / And very little clothes, / And the stormy winds do blow. [Song: *It's All Right in the Summer Time*]

FRED MURRAY and R. P. WESTON

2 I'm Henery the Eighth, I am ... / I got married to the widder next door. / She's been married seven times before, / Hevery one was a Henery, / She wouldn't have a Willy or a Sam. [Song: *I'm Henery the Eighth.* Sung by Harry Champion]

GILBERT MURRAY

3 Experience dulls the edges of all our dogmas. [Attr.]

LES A. MURRAY

4 Where two or three / are gathered together, that / is about enough. [*Company*]

ROBERT MUSIL

5 Progress would be wonderful – if only it would stop. [Attr.]

BENITO MUSSOLINI

6 CURZON: What is your foreign programme?
MUSSOLINI: My foreign policy is 'Nothing for Nothing'. [Quoted in George Seldes, *Sawdust Caesar*, Ch. 12]

7 Fascism is a religion; the twentieth century will be known in history as the century of Fascism. [On Hitler's seizure of power. Quoted in *ib.* 24]

8 Fascism is not an article for export. [German press report, 1932. Quoted in *ib.* 24]

9 Between 1935 and 1940 we shall have reached a point that I should call crucial in European history. [Speech, May 1927]

10 I should be pleased, I suppose, that Hitler has carried out a revolution on our lines. But they are Germans. So they will end by ruining our idea. [Quoted in Christopher Hibbert, *Benito Mussolini*, Pt II, Ch. 1]

11 Yes, I have a tremendous admiration for Caesar. Still ... I myself belong rather to the class of the Bismarcks. [*Conversations with Emil Ludwig*]

12 Believe! Obey! Fight! [Fascist slogan]

13 The Italians will laugh at me; every time Hitler occupies a country he sends me a message. [Remark to Ciano. Quoted in Alan Bullock, *Hitler*, Ch. 8, sect. xii]

14 We cannot change our policy now. After all, we are not political whores. [Quoted in *ib.*]

F. W. H. MYERS

15 If our first clear facts about the Unseen World seem small and trivial, should that deter us from the quest? As well might Columbus have sailed home again, with America in the offing, on the ground that it was not worth while to discover a continent which manifested itself only by dead logs. [*Human Personality*]

16 Do you mean to tell me that you seriously believe in the possibility of the Lesbian vice between the ghost of a governess and a little girl of six? [Of *The Turn of the Screw.* Quoted in Christopher Hassall, *Edward Marsh*]

N

VLADIMIR NABOKOV

1 Don't forget that the whole of Russian literature is the literature of one century and, after the most lenient eliminations, takes up no more than three to three and a half thousand printed sheets, and scarcely one-half of this is worthy of the bookshelf, to say nothing of the bedside table. With such quantitative scantiness we must resign ourselves to the fact that our Pegasus is piebald, and that not everything about a bad writer is bad, and not all about a good one good. [*The Gift*, Ch. 1]

2 There are aphorisms that, like airplanes, stay up only while they are in motion. [*Ib.*]

3 Lolita, light of my life, fire of my loins. My sin, my soul. Lo-lee-ta: the tip of the tongue taking a trip of three steps down the palate to tap, at three, on the teeth. Lo. Lee. Ta. [Opening sentences of *Lolita*]

4 I am sufficiently proud of my knowing something to be modest about my not knowing all. [*Ib.*]

5 As to the rest, I am no more guilty of imitating 'real life' than 'real life' is responsible for plagiarizing me. [*Nabokov's Dozen*, Bibliographical Note]

6 Like so many ageing college people, Pnin had long ceased to notice the existence of students on the campus. [*Pnin*, Ch. 3, sect. vi]

7 Sterile instructors successfully endeavoured to 'produce' by reviewing the books of more fertile colleagues. [*Ib.* 6. i]

8 Discussion in class, which means letting twenty young blockheads and two cocky neurotics discuss something that neither their teacher nor they know. [*Ib.* 6. x]

9 Poor Knight! he really had two periods, the first – a dull man writing broken English, the second – a broken man writing dull English. [*The Real Life of Sebastian Knight*, Ch. 1]

10 Spring and summer did happen in Cambridge almost every year. [*Ib.* 5]

11 I think like a genius, I write like a distinguished author, and I speak like a child. [*Strong Opinions*, Foreword]

12 My desires are modest. Portraits of the heads of the government should not exceed a postage stamp in size. No torture and no executions. No music except coming through earphones or played in theatres. [*Ib.* Ch. 3]

13 [When asked if he believed in God] I know more than I can express in words, and the little I can express would not have been expressed, had I not known more. [*Ib.*]

14 Satire is a lesson, parody is a game. [*Ib.* 6]

15 One of those 'Two Cultures' is really nothing but utilitarian technology; the other is B-grade novels, ideological fiction, popular art. Who cares if there exists a gap between such 'physics' and such 'humanities'? Those Eggheads are terrible Philistines. A real good head is not oval but round. [*Ib.*]

16 A good laugh is the best pesticide. [*Ib.* 9]

17 A novelist is, like all mortals, more fully at home on the surface of the present than in the ooze of the past. [*Ib.* 20]

18 Literature and butterflies are the two sweetest passions known to man. [Quoted in *Radio Times*, Oct. 1962]

19 Actually I always loathed the Viennese quack. I used to stalk him down dark alleys of thought, and now we shall never forget the sight of old, flustered

Freud seeking to unlock his door with the point of his umbrella. [Said in a TV interview, reprinted in the *Listener*, 24 Mar. 1977]

V. S. NAIPAUL

1 'But the man is a BA!' 'And LLB. I know. I wouldn't trust an Aryan with my great-grandmother.' [*A House for Mr Biswas*, Ch. 3]

2 I think, then, that we should pass a resolution to the effect that peaceful persuasion should be followed by militant conversion. All right? [*Ib.*]

3 They say there's good and bad everywhere. There's no good and bad here. They're just Africans. [*In a Free State*, Ch. 6]

FRIDTJOF NANSEN

4 The difficult is what takes a little time; the impossible is what takes a little longer. [Attr. Variant form was motto placarded at South-East Asia HQ in the Second World War. See also 348:14]

OGDEN NASH

5 Women would rather be right than reasonable. [*Frailty, Thy Name Is a Misnomer*]

6 Oh, what a tangled web do parents weave / When they think that their children are naïve. [*Baby, What Makes the Sky Blue?*]

7 Sophisticated parents live agog in a world that to them is enchanted; / Ingenuous children just naïvely take it for granted. [*Ib.*]

8 The camel has a single hump; / The dromedary, two; / Or else the other way around. / I'm never sure. Are you? [*The Camel*]

9 The cow is of the bovine ilk; / One end is moo, the other, milk. [*The Cow*]

10 Another difference between me and Samuel Taylor Coleridge is more massive in design: / People used to interrupt him while he was dreaming his dreams, but they interrupt me while I am recounting mine. [*I Can Hardly Wait for the Sandman*]

11 The trouble with a kitten is / THAT / Eventually it becomes a / CAT. [*The Kitten*]

12 Beneath this slab / John Brown is stowed. / He watched the ads, / And not the road. [*Lather as You Go*]

13 Do you think my mind is maturing late, / Or simply rotted early? [*Lines on Facing Forty*]

14 Do you know my friend Mr Betts? / I wish I could remember as accurately as he forgets. [*Mr Betts's Mind a Kingdom Is*]

15 Tell me, O Octopus, I begs, / Is those things arms, or is they legs? / I marvel at thee, Octopus; / If I were thou, I'd call me Us. [*The Octopus*]

16 I prefer to forget both pairs of glasses and pass my declining years saluting strange women and grandfather clocks. [*Peekaboo, I Almost See You*]

17 He tells you when you've got on / too much lipstick, / And helps you with your girdle / when your hips stick. [*The Perfect Husband*]

18 She left stuff to be posted or expressed, / Hecate Hopper, the Polterguest. [*Polterguest, My Polterguest*]

19 The only incurable troubles of the rich are the troubles that money can't cure, / Which is a kind of trouble which is even more troublesome if you are poor. [*The Terrible People*]

20 The turtle lives 'twixt plated decks / Which practically conceal its sex. / I think it clever of the turtle / In such a fix to be so fertile. [*The Turtle*]

21 Gently my eyelids close; / I'd rather be good than clever; / And I'd rather have my facts all wrong / Than have no facts whatever. [*Who Did Which?*]

22 Life is not having been told that the man has just waxed the floor. [*You and Me and P. B. Shelley*]

23 Plus ça change, plus c'est la memsahib. [Attr.]

TERRY NATION

24 We will exterminate ... [Daleks' chorus in BBC TV series, *Dr Who*]

GRANNI NAZZANO

1 My only hobby is laziness, which naturally rules out all the others. [Attr.]

JOSEPH NEEDHAM

2 *Laboratorium est oratorium.* The place where we do our scientific work is a place of prayer. [Quoted in A. L. Mackay, *The Harvest of a Quiet Eye*]

PABLO NERUDA

3 *Lo que tengo en mí está en medio de las olas. | Un rayo de agua, un día para mí, un fondo férreo.* – What I have in myself is in the midst of the waves. / A flash of water, a day to myself, a depth of iron. [*Vals*]

W. D. NESBIT

4 Let's Keep the Glow in Old Glory and the Free in Freedom Too. [Title of song]

RICHARD NEVILLE

5 Is marijuana addictive? Yes, in the sense that most of the really pleasant things in life are worth endlessly repeating. [*Playpower*]

H. W. NEVINSON

6 He [H. Scott Holland] used to run as if the Holy Grail were just round the corner, and he might catch it if only he could run fast enough. [*In the Dark Backward*]

ANTHONY NEWLEY and LESLIE BRICUSSE

7 Stop the World, I Want to Get Off. [Title of Musical]

BERNARD NEWMAN

8 Surely this is not cricket, even in Bulgaria. [When, told to ride straight on, he rode into the Danube. Attr.]

ERNEST NEWMAN

9 I sometimes wonder which would be nicer – an opera without an interval, or an interval without an opera. [*Berlioz, Romantic and Classic*, essays ed. by Peter Heyworth]

10 My dear boy, you may help a lame dog over a stile but he is still a lame dog on the other side. [Said to Heyworth in answer to the suggestion that Newman should do something to encourage young composers. Quoted in *ib.*]

11 The higher the voice the smaller the intellect. [Attr. by Heyworth in *ib.*]

NEWS OF THE WORLD

12 All human life is here. [Newspaper's slogan]

13 'I have no doubt that this man deliberately took poison and he appears to have done so in a most cold-blooded and heartless way,' the coroner remarked in summing up. [Quoted in *New Statesman*, 'This England', 1937]

SIR JOHN NEWSOM

14 *All* education is, in a sense, vocational, vocational for living. ['The Education Women Need', *Observer*, 6 Sep. 1964]

BEVERLEY NICHOLS

15 It is only to the gardener that time is a friend, giving each year more than he steals. [*Merry Hall*, Feb. 1957]

16 Herr Hitler has one of the endearing characteristics of Ferdinand the Bull. Just when the crowds expect him to be most violent he stops and smells the flowers. I have a feeling, and I hope I am right, that for the next month or so Herr Hitler is going to take things a little easier and smell the flowers and listen to the nightingales. [From the *Sunday Graphic*. Quoted in M. Bateman, *This England*, selections from the *New Statesman*, Pt I]

ROBERT NICHOLS

17 The sound of my own voice. [When asked what music he liked best. Quoted in Edward Marsh, *Ambrosia and Small Beer*, Ch. 5, sect. i)

248

BASIL NICHOLSON

1 There's enough acid in your stomach to burn a hole in the carpet. [Advertisement headline for digestive tablet]

BASIL NICHOLSON (or another member of the firm of J. Walter Thompson)

2 Horlicks guards against Night Starvation. [Advertising slogan]

VIVIAN NICHOLSON

3 Spend, spend, spend. [When asked what she was going to do with record football pools win. Also used as title of her autobiography]

HAROLD NICOLSON

4 He [T. S. Eliot] is without pose and full of poise. He makes one feel that all cleverness is an excuse for thinking hard. [*Diaries and Letters, 1930-1939*, 2 Mar. 1932]

5 I do not consider that efficiency need be mated to extreme delicacy or precision of touch . . . It should possess a sweeping gesture – even if that gesture may at moments sweep the ornaments from the mantelpiece. [*Small Talk*, 'On Being Efficient']

REINHOLD NIEBUHR

6 God grant me the serenity to accept things I cannot change, courage to change things I can, and wisdom to know the difference. [Quoted in W. Neil, *Concise Dictionary of Religious Quotations*]

7 Man's capacity for evil makes democracy necessary and man's capacity for good makes democracy possible. [Quoted by Anthony Wedgwood Benn in *The Times*, 18 Jul. 1977]

MARTIN NIEMÖLLER

8 In Germany, the Nazis came for the Communists and I didn't speak up because I was not a Communist. Then they came for the Jews and I didn't speak up because I was not a Jew. Then they came for the trade unionists and I didn't speak up because I was not a trade unionist. Then they came for the Catholics and I was a Protestant so I didn't speak up. Then they came for me . . . By that time there was no one to speak up for anyone. [Quoted in W. Neil, *Concise Dictionary of Religious Quotations*]

ANAÏS NIN

9 The sculptor must himself feel that he is not so much inventing or shaping the curve of a breast or shoulder as delivering the image from its prison. [*The Journals of Anaïs Nin*, Vol. 5, Spring 1948]

DAVID NIVEN

10 George [Sanders], a giant grizzly of a man, had a face, even in his twenties, which looked as though he had rented it on a long lease and had lived in it so long he didn't want to move out. [*Bring on the Empty Horses*, Ch. 2]

LARRY NIVEN

11 [When asked at a science-fiction convention 'What is the best advice you have ever been given?'] On my twenty-first birthday my father said, 'Son, here's a million dollars. Don't lose it.' [Attr.]

PRESIDENT RICHARD NIXON

12 You won't have Nixon to kick around any more, gentlemen. This is my last Press Conference. [Press conference for governorship of California, 2 Nov. 1962]

13 Let us begin by committing ourselves to the truth, to see it like it is and to tell it like it is, to find the truth, to speak the truth and live with the truth. That's what we'll do. [Nomination acceptance speech, Miami, 8 Aug. 1968]

14 You can say that this Administration will have the first complete, far-reaching attack on the problem of hunger in history. Use all the rhetoric, so long as it doesn't cost money. [From

official minutes of White House meeting 17 Mar. 1969]

1 This is the greatest week in the history of the world since the creation. [Of man's first moon-landing, said on board the *Hornet*, 24 Jul. 1969]

2 It is time for the great silent majority of Americans to stand up and be counted. [Election speech, Oct. 1970]

3 There can be no whitewash at the White House. [TV address on the Watergate crisis, 30 Apr. 1973. Quoted in C. Bernstein and B. Woodward, *All the President's Men*]

4 If some of my judgements were wrong, and some were wrong, they were made in what I believed at the time to be the best interest of the nation. [In his resignation speech, 8 Aug. 1974]

5 I let down my friends, I let down my country. I let down our system of government. [*Observer*, 'Sayings of the Week', 8 May 1977]

6 When the President does it, that means it is not illegal. [In TV interview with David Frost, 20 May 1977]

DAVID NOBBS

7 'This one's going to be a real winner,' said C. J. 'I didn't get where I am today without knowing a real winner when I see one.' [*The Fall and Rise of Reginald Perrin*, 'Thursday']

DENIS NORDEN

8 Another fact of life that will not have escaped you is that, in this country, the twenty-four-hour strike is like the twenty-four-hour flu. You have to reckon on it lasting at least five days. [In Frank Muir and Denis Norden, *You Can't Have Your Kayak and Heat It*, 'Great Expectations']

9 It's a funny kind of month, October. For the really keen cricket fan it's when you discover that your wife left you in May. [In *She* magazine, Oct. 1977]

10 The snows of yesterday can't be re-freezed. [In BBC radio programme, *My Word*, 5 Oct. 1977]

11 If all the world's a stage, and all the men and women merely players, where do all the audiences come from? [In *ib.*, 30 Nov. 1977]

FRANK NORMAN

12 Fings Ain't Wot They Used T'Be. [Title of play]

LORD NORTHCLIFFE

13 It is hard news that catches readers. Features hold them. [Quoted in T. Clarke, *My Northcliffe Diary*]

14 [To Stewart Hamilton] I'm sure you must be a Jew; you've got such a Scotch name. [Quoted in Hamilton Fyfe, *Northcliffe, an Intimate Biography*, Ch. 10]

15 Six hundred years ago, there was near the site of *The Times* office a monastery, the home of the Blackfriars, recluses who lived remote from the world. The same kind of men inhabit Printing House Square today. [Quoted in *ib.* 14]

16 Never put on the table of Demos what you would not have on your own table. [Quoted by Claud Cockburn in BBC TV programme, '*Read All About It*', 28 Jul. 1975]

17 They are only ten. [Said to have been written up in his offices to remind the staff of their public's mental age]

18 When I want a peerage, I shall buy one like an honest man. [Attr.]

MARY NORTON

19 We don't talk fancy grammar and eat anchovy toast. But to live under the kitchen doesn't say we aren't educated. [*The Borrowers*, Ch. 5]

20 If you're born in India, you're bilingual. And if you're bilingual, you can't read. Not so well. [*Ib.* 9]

21 But we *are* Borrowers . . . like you're a – a Human Bean or whatever it's called. [*Ib.* 10]

GILBERT NORWOOD

22 It would be an uplifting sight when some grey-haired fanatic passed into

the Beyond crying, 'Long live "Butter-flies of North-East Bucks".' [*Too Many Books*]

JACK NORWORTH

1 Oh! shine on, shine on, harvest moon / Up in the sky. / I ain't had no lovin' / Since April, January, June or July. [Song: *Shine On, Harvest Moon*. Music by Nora Bayes-Norworth]

MAX NOTTINGHAM

2 Assuming the recent speculation in your columns about God being a Tory is correct, might I suggest that Christ was not 'sent', he left home because of parental incompatibility. [*Spectator*, 18 Apr. 1969]

IVOR NOVELLO

3 There's something Vichy about the French. [Quoted in Edward Marsh, *Ambrosia and Small Beer*, Ch. 4]

4 And Her Mother Came Too. [Title of song]

PATRICK NUTTGENS

5 The challenge for the modern architect is the same as the challenge for all of us in our lives: to make out of the ordinary something out-of-the-ordinary. [BBC TV programme, *Architecture for Everyman*, reprinted in the *Listener*, 1 Mar. 1979]

O

JOHN OATES

1 I am just going outside, and may be some time. [Last words, 16 Mar. 1912. Quoted in Scott's diary, *Scott's Last Expedition*]

JOYCE CAROL OATES

2 Some of the characters in this novel are entirely fictional, a good number of the events are fictional, and all the settings – especially Lockport, New York; Ann Arbor, Michigan; and Toronto, Ontario – are fictional. Any resemblance to reality is accidental and should be resisted. [*Wonderland*, Author's Note]

CONOR CRUISE O'BRIEN

3 It [Dublin] is a city where you can see a sparrow fall to the ground, and God watching it. [Attr.]

EDNA O'BRIEN

4 To Crystal, hair was the most important thing on earth. She would never get married because you couldn't wear curlers in bed. [*Winter's Tales*, 8, 'Come into the Drawing Room, Doris']

5 The vote, I thought, means nothing to women. We should be armed. [Quoted as epigraph to Erica Jong, *Fear of Flying*, Ch. 16]

FLANN O'BRIEN (MYLES NA GOPALEEN)

6 The conclusion of your syllogism, I said lightly, is fallacious, being based upon licensed premises. [*At Swim-Two-Birds*, Ch. 1]

7 [On the perennial youthfulness of policemen] A thing of duty is a boy for ever. [Quoted in the *Listener*, 24 Feb. 1977]

SEAN O'CASEY

8 I killin' meself workin', an' he sthruttin' about from mornin' till night like a paycock! [*Juno and the Paycock*, Act I]

9 He's an oul' butty o' mine – oh, he's a darlin' man, a daarlin' man. [*Ib.*]

10 It's only a little cold I have; there's nothing derogatory wrong with me. [*The Plough and the Stars*, Act I]

11 There's no reason to bring religion into it. I think we ought to have as great a regard for religion as we can, so as to keep it out of as many things as possible. [*Ib.*]

12 I've something else to do besides shinannickin' after Judies! [*Ib.* II]

13 English literature's performing flea. [Of P. G. Wodehouse. Quoted in P. G. Wodehouse, *Performing Flea*]

CLIFFORD ODETS

14 Go out and fight so life shouldn't be printed on dollar bills. [*Awake and Sing*, Act I]

DAVID OGG

15 In the nineteenth century the average length of life for clergymen was eighty-one years, for politicians seventy-seven years and for atheists and sceptics sixty-four years. [Quoted from his book *Europe of the Ancien Régime*, in Gerald Brenan, *Thoughts in a Dry Season*, 'Religion'. Brenan comments: 'So it paid then to believe in God.']

DAVID OGILVY

16 At 60 miles an hour the loudest noise in this new Rolls-Royce comes from the electric clock. [Advertisement]

17 Every soldier carries a marshal's baton in his pack [Napoleon]. Yes, but don't

let it stick out. [*Confessions of an Advertising Man*, Ch. 10]

GEOFFREY O'HARA

1 K-K-Katy, beautiful Katy, / You're the only g-g-g-girl that I adore, / When the m-m-m-moon shines over the cow-shed, / I'll be waiting at the k-k-k-kitchen door. [Song: *K-K-Katy*]

OKAKURA KAKUZO

2 He [the average Westerner] was wont to regard Japan as barbarous while she indulged in the gentle arts of peace: he calls her civilized since she began to commit wholesale slaughter on Manchurian battlefields. [*The Book of Tea*, Ch. 1]

SIR LAURENCE OLIVIER

3 Realism doesn't mean copying art back into life. It means making life into art: not just accepting the facts of life but elevating them. [Kenneth Harris, *Kenneth Harris Talking To*: 'Sir Laurence Olivier']

4 Shakespeare – the nearest thing in incarnation to the eye of God. [*Ib.*]

AUSTIN O'MALLEY

5 An Englishman thinks seated; a Frenchman, standing; an American, pacing; an Irishman, afterward. [Quoted in A. Andrews, *Quotations for Speakers and Writers*]

EUGENE O'NEILL

6 For de little stealin' dey gits you in jail soon or late. For de big stealin' dey makes you emperor and puts you in de Hall o' Fame when you croaks. [*The Emperor Jones*]

7 Our lives are merely strange dark interludes in the electric display of God the Father. [*Strange Interlude*, sc. ix]

GEORGE OPPENHEIMER

8 It rolls off my back like a duck. [In parody of Samuel Goldwyn. Quoted in Philip French, *The Movie Moguls*, Ch. 4]

J. ROBERT OPPENHEIMER

9 We knew the world would not be the same. [After first atomic test. *The Decision to Drop the Bomb*]

10 The physicists have known sin; and this is a knowledge which they cannot lose. [Lecture at Massachusetts Institute of Technology, 25 Nov. 1947]

JOSÉ ORTEGA Y GASSET

11 The epoch of the masses is the epoch of the colossal. We are living . . . under the brutal empire of the masses. [*The Revolt of the Masses*, Ch. 2]

12 The uprising of the masses implies a fabulous increase of vital possibilities; quite the contrary of what we hear so often about the decadence of Europe. [*Ib.*]

13 The world is the sum-total of our vital possibilities. [*Ib.* 4]

14 Revolution is not the uprising against pre-existing order, but the setting-up of a new order contradictory to the traditional one. [*Ib.* 6]

15 Civilization consists in the attempt to reduce violence to the *ultima ratio*, the final argument. [*Ib.* 8]

JOE ORTON

16 I'd the upbringing a nun would envy and that's the truth. Until I was fifteen I was more familiar with Africa than my own body. [*Entertaining Mr Sloane*, Act I]

17 Persuade her. Cut her throat but persuade her! [*Ib.* III]

18 It's all any reasonable child can expect if the dad is present at the conception. [*Ib.*]

19 FAY: Have you known him long?
HAL: We shared the same cradle.
FAY: Was that economy or malpractice? [*Loot*, Act I]

20 Every luxury was lavished on you – atheism, breast-feeding, circumcision. I had to make my own way. [*Ib.*]

21 Policemen, like red squirrels, must be protected. [*Ib.*]

1 Reading isn't an occupation we encourage among police officers. We try to keep the paper work down to a minimum. [*Ib*. II]

2 God is a gentleman. He prefers blondes. [*Ib*.]

3 PRENTICE: You did have a father?
GERALDINE: Oh, I'm sure I did. My mother was frugal in her habits, but she'd never economize unwisely. [*What the Butler Saw*, Act I]

4 You were born with your legs apart. They'll send you to the grave in a Y-shaped coffin. [*Ib*.]

5 This is a boy, sir. Not a girl. If you're baffled by the difference it might be as well to approach both with caution. [*Ib*. II]

6 The whole trouble with Western society today is the lack of anything worth concealing. [From his diary. Quoted in J. Lahr, *Prick Up Your Ears*]

GEORGE ORWELL

7 Whatever goes upon two legs is an enemy. Whatever goes upon four legs, or has wings, is a friend. [*Animal Farm*, Ch. 1]

8 War is war. The only good human being is a dead one. [*Ib*. 4]

9 You would often hear one hen remark to another, 'Under the guidance of our Leader, Comrade Napoleon, I have laid five eggs in six days.' [*Ib*. 8]

10 Squealer always spoke of it as a 're-adjustment', never as a 'reduction'. [*Ib*. 9]

11 Napoleon had commanded that once a week there should be held something called a Spontaneous Demonstration. [*Ib*.]

12 He intended, he said, to devote the rest of his life to learning the remaining twenty-two letters of the alphabet. [*Ib*.]

13 In every one of those little stucco boxes there's some poor bastard who's *never* free except when he's fast asleep and dreaming that he's got the boss down the bottom of a well and is bunging lumps of coal at him. [*Coming Up for Air*, Pt I, Ch. 2]

14 I'm fat, but I'm thin inside. Has it ever struck you that there's a thin man inside every fat man, just as they say there's a statue inside every block of stone? [*Ib*. I. 3]

15 Is it gone for ever? I'm not certain. But I tell you it was a good world to live in. I belong to it. So do you. [*Ib*. I. 4]

16 Before the war, and especially before the Boer War, it was summer all the year round. [*Ib*. II. 1]

17 If the war didn't happen to kill you it was bound to start you thinking. After that unspeakable idiotic mess you couldn't go on regarding society as something eternal and unquestionable, like a pyramid. You knew it was just a balls-up. [*Ib*. II. 8]

18 He was an embittered atheist (the sort of atheist who does not so much disbelieve in God as personally dislike Him). [*Down and Out in Paris and London*, Ch. 30]

19 The novel is practically a Protestant form of art; it is a product of the free mind, of the autonomous individual. [*Inside the Whale*, II]

20 Probably the Battle of Waterloo *was* won on the playing-fields of Eton, but the opening battles of all subsequent wars have been lost there. [*The Lion and the Unicorn*, 'England, Your England']

21 Public life in England has never been *openly* scandalous. It has not reached the pitch of disintegration at which humbug can be dropped. [*Ib*. 'The Ruling Class']

22 A family with the wrong members in control – that, perhaps, is as near as one can come to describing England in a phrase. [*Ib*.]

23 Who controls the past controls the future. Who controls the present controls the past. [*1984*]

24 It is brought home to you . . . that it is only because miners sweat their guts out that superior persons can remain superior. [*The Road to Wigan Pier*, Ch. 2]

25 A person of bourgeois origin goes through life with some expectation of

getting what he wants, within reasonable limits. Hence the fact that in times of stress 'educated' people tend to come to the front. [*Ib.* 3]

1 This business of petty inconvenience and indignity, of being kept waiting about, of having to do everything at other people's convenience, is inherent in working-class life. A thousand influences constantly press a working man into a *passive* role. He does not act, he is acted upon. [*Ib.*]

2 I sometimes think that the price of liberty is not so much eternal vigilance as eternal dirt. [*Ib.* 4]

3 We may find in the long run that tinned food is a deadlier weapon than the machine-gun. [*Ib.* 6]

4 Sheffield, I suppose, could justly claim to be called the ugliest town in the Old World: its inhabitants, who want it to be pre-eminent in everything, very likely do make that claim for it. [*Ib.* 7]

5 There can hardly be a town in the South of England where you could throw a brick without hitting the niece of a bishop. [*Ib.*]

6 You can have an affection for a murderer or a sodomite, but you cannot have an affection for a man whose breath stinks – habitually stinks, I mean. [*Ib.* 8]

7 Comrade X, it so happens, is an old Etonian. He would be ready to die on the barricades, in theory anyway, but you notice that he still leaves his bottom waistcoat button undone. [*Ib.*]

8 As with the Christian religion, the worst advertisement for Socialism is its adherents. [*Ib.* 11]

9 The typical socialist ... a prim little man with a white-collar job, usually a secret teetotaller and often with vegetarian leanings. [*Ib.*]

10 To the ordinary working man, the sort you would meet in any pub on Saturday night, Socialism does not mean much more than better wages and shorter hours and nobody bossing you about. [*Ib.*]

11 One of the analogies between Communism and Roman Catholicism is that only the 'educated' are completely orthodox. [*Ib.*]

12 It is only the 'educated' man, especially the literary man, who knows how to be a bigot. And, *mutatis mutandis*, it is the same with Communism. The creed is never found in its pure form in a genuine proletarian. [*Ib.*]

13 The underlying motive of many Socialists, I believe, is simply a hypertrophied sense of order. The present state of affairs offends them not because it causes misery, still less because it makes freedom impossible, but because it is untidy; what they desire, basically, is to reduce the world to something resembling a chessboard. [*Ib.*]

14 Queer that Comrade Mirsky's spiritual brother should be Father — ! The Communist and the Catholic are not saying the same thing, in a sense they are even saying opposite things, and each would gladly boil the other in oil if circumstances permitted; but from the point of view of an outsider they are very much alike. [*Ib.*]

15 The foaming denouncers of the bourgeoisie, and the more-water-in-your-beer reformers of whom Shaw is the prototype, and the astute young social-literary climbers who are Communists now, as they will be Fascists five years hence, because it is all the go. [*Ib.*]

16 The higher-water mark, so to speak, of Socialist literature is W. H. Auden, a sort of gutless Kipling. [*Ib.*]

17 Man is not, as the vulgarer hedonists seem to suppose, a kind of walking stomach; he has also got a hand, an eye, and a brain. Cease to use your hands, and you have lopped off a huge chunk of your consciousness. [*Ib.* 12]

18 It is usual to speak of the Fascist objective as the 'beehive state', which does a grave injustice to bees. A world of rabbits ruled by stoats would be nearer the mark. [*Ib.*]

19 We of the sinking middle class ... may sink without further struggles into the working class where we belong, and probably when we get there it will not

be so dreadful as we feared, for, after all, we have nothing to lose but our aitches. [*Ib.* 13]

1 In reality there is no kind of evidence or argument by which one can show that Shakespeare, or any other writer, is 'good' . . . Ultimately there is no test of literary merit except survival, which is itself an index to majority opinion. [*Selected Essays*, 'Lear, Tolstoy and the Fool']

2 Creeds like pacifism and anarchism, which seem on the surface to imply a complete renunciation of power, rather encourage this habit of mind. For if you have embraced a creed which appears to be free from the ordinary dirtiness of politics – a creed from which you yourself cannot expect to draw any material advantage – surely that proves that you are in the right? And the more you are in the right, the more natural that everyone else should be bullied into thinking likewise. [*Ib.*]

3 Objective consideration of contemporary phenomena compels the conclusion that success or failure in competitive activities exhibits no tendency to be commensurate with innate capacity, but that a considerable element of the unpredictable must invariably be taken into account. Paraphrase of Ecclesiastes, Ch. 9, 11. [*Ib.* in 'Politics and the English Language']

4 The inflated style is itself a kind of euphemism. A mass of Latin words falls upon the facts like soft snow, blurring the outlines and covering up all the details. The great enemy of clear language is insincerity. [*Ib.*]

5 The Catholic and the Communist are alike in assuming that an opponent cannot be both honest and intelligent. [*Ib.* 'The Prevention of Literature']

6 The quickest way of ending a war is to lose it. [*Shooting an Elephant*, 'Second Thoughts on James Burnham']

7 For casual reading – in your bath, for instance, or late at night when you are too tired to go to bed, or in the odd quarter of an hour before lunch – there is nothing to touch a back number of the *Girl's Own Paper*. [In the *Fortnightly Review*, Nov. 1936]

8 He [Conrad] is pretty certain to come back into favour. One of the surest signs of his genius is that women dislike his books. [In *New English Weekly*, 23 Jul. 1936]

R. OSBORN

9 What religion not only promises a better life hereafter, but also organizes a series of five-year plans to realize that better life here and now? [*Freud and Marx*, Ch. 8]

JOHN OSBORNE

10 Never believe in mirrors or newspapers. [*The Hotel in Amsterdam*, Act I]

11 She's like the old line about justice – not only must be done but must be seen to be done. [*Time Present*, Act I]

12 JENNY: What was known as art silk –
TIM: Like art cinema –
JENNY: It wasn't really silk at all. [*Under Plain Cover*]

CARL VON OSSIETSKY
(German pacifist)

13 Nothing that produced this war has been changed by it. [Said in 1919. Quoted in Erwin Leiser, *A Pictorial History of Nazi Germany*]

FRANK OTTER

14 I am of the opinion that had your father spent more of your mother's immoral earnings on your education you would not even then have been a gentleman. [Seymour Hicks, *Vintage Years*]

P. D. OUSPENSKY

15 Truths that become old become decrepit and unreliable; sometimes they may be kept going artifically for a certain time, but there is no life in them . . . Ideas can be too old. [*A New Model of the Universe*, Preface to Second Edition]

16 Man, as he is, is not a genuine article. He is an imitation of something, and a very bad imitation. [*The Psychology of Man's Possible Evolution*, Ch. 2]

1 What would happen to all our life, without negative emotions? What would happen to what we call art, to the theatre, to drama, to most novels? [*Ib.* 4]

2 Osokin looks round, and suddenly an extraordinarily vivid sensation sweeps over him that, if he were not there, everything would be exactly the same. [*Strange Life of Ivan Osokin*]

WILFRED OWEN

3 And in the happy no-time of his sleeping / Death took him by the heart. [*Asleep*]

4 The old Lie: *Dulce et decorum est / Pro patria mori.* [*Dulce et decorum est*]

5 Whatever mourns when many leave these shores; / Whatever shares / The eternal reciprocity of tears. [*Insensibility*]

6 So secretly, like wrongs hushed-up, they went. / They were not ours: / We never heard to which front these were sent. [*The Send-off*]

7 My soul looked down from a vague height with Death, / As unremembering how I rose or why, / And saw a sad land, weak with sweats of dearth. [*The Show*]

P

VANCE PACKARD

1 The Hidden Persuaders. [Title of book]

SATCHEL PAIGE
(Baseball player and sage)

2 Go very light on vices such as carrying on in society. The social ramble ain't restful. [*Six Rules for a Long Life*]

LORD CHIEF JUSTICE PARKER

3 A judge is not supposed to know anything about the facts of life until they have been presented in evidence and explained to him at least three times. [*Observer*, 'Saying of the Week', 12 Mar. 1961]

CHARLIE PARKER

4 Music is your own experience, your thoughts, your wisdom. If you don't live it, it won't come out of your horn. [Quoted in Nat Shapiro and Nat Hentoff, *Hear Me Talkin' to Ya*]

DOROTHY PARKER

5 He's really awfully fond of coloured people. Well, he says himself, he wouldn't have white servants. [*Arrangement in Black and White*]

6 All I say is, nobody has any business to go around looking like a horse and behaving as if it were all right. You don't catch horses going around looking like people, do you? [*Horsie*]

7 I bet you could get into the subway without using anybody's name. [*Just a Little One*]

8 Three highballs, and I think I'm St Francis of Assisi. [*Ib.*]

9 And I'll stay off Verlaine too; he was always chasing Rimbauds. [*The Little Hours*]

10 I really can't be expected to drop everything and start counting sheep at my age. I hate sheep. [*Ib.*]

11 How do people go to sleep? I'm afraid I've lost the knack. I might try busting myself smartly over the temple with the nightlight. I might repeat to myself, slowly and soothingly, a list of quotations beautiful from minds profound; if I can remember any of the damn things. [*Ib.*]

12 I'm never going to be famous. My name will never be writ large on the roster of Those Who Do Things. I don't do anything. Not one single thing. I used to bite my nails, but I don't even do that any more. [*Ib.*]

13 Sorrow is tranquillity remembered in emotion. [*Sentiment*]

14 'Dinner,' she murmured bashfully, as if it were not quite a nice word for a young woman to use, and vanished. [*Too Bad*]

15 How do you do, Mr Jukes? And how is that dear little brother of yours, with the two heads? [*The Waltz*]

16 There was I, trapped. Trapped like a trap in a trap. [*Ib.*]

17 You can lead a whore to culture but you can't make her think. [Speech to American Horticultural Society]

18 If, with the literate, I am / Impelled to try an epigram, / I never seek to take the credit; / We all assume that Oscar said it. [*Oscar Wilde*]

19 You will be frail and musty / With peering, furtive head, / While I am young and lusty / Among the roaring dead. [*Braggart*]

1 Whose love is given over-well / Shall look on Helen's face in hell, / Whilst they whose love is thin and wise / May view John Knox in paradise. [*Partial Comfort*]

2 Here's my strength and my weakness, gents, / I loved them until they loved me. [*Ballade at Thirty-Five*]

3 The sweeter the apple, the blacker the core – / Scratch a lover and find a foe! [*Ballade of a Great Weariness*]

4 His voice was intimate as the rustle of sheets, and he kissed easily. [*Dusk before Fireworks*]

5 He lies below, correct in cypress wood, / And entertains the most exclusive worms. [*Epitaph for a Very Rich Man*]

6 Some men break your heart in two, / Some men fawn and flatter, / Some men never look at you; / And that cleans up the matter. [*Experience*]

7 That thing he wrote, the time the sparrow died – / (Oh, most unpleasant – gloomy, tedious words!) / I called it sweet, and made believe I cried; / The stupid fool! I've always hated birds. [*From a Letter from Lesbia*]

8 Four be the things I'd been better without: / Love, curiosity, freckles, and doubt. [*Inventory*]

9 There was nothing more fun than a man. [*The Little Old Lady in Lavender Silk*]

10 But I, despite expert advice, / Keep doing things I think are nice, / And though to good I never come – / Inseparable my nose and thumb! [*Neither Bloody nor Bowed*]

11 Why is it no one ever sent me yet / One perfect limousine, do you suppose? / Ah no, it's always just my luck to get / One perfect rose. [*One Perfect Rose*]

12 Accursed from their birth they be / Who seek to find monogamy, / Pursuing it from bed to bed – / I think they would be better dead. [*Reuben's Children*]

13 Lady, Lady, should you meet / One whose ways are all discreet, / One who murmurs that his wife / Is the lodestar of his life, / One who keeps assuring you / That he never was untrue, / Never

loved another one ... / Lady, lady, better run! [*Social Note*]

14 'And if he never came,' said she, / 'Now what on earth is that to me? / I wouldn't have him back!' / I hope / Her mother washed her mouth with soap. [*Story*]

15 The man she had was kind and clean / And well enough for every day, / But oh, dear friends, you should have seen / The one that got away! [*Tombstones in the Starlight*, 'The Fisherwoman']

16 By the time you swear you're his, / Shivering and sighing, / And he vows his passion is / Infinite, undying – / Lady, make a note of this: / One of you is lying. [*Unfortunate Coincidence*]

17 I know there was something, something pretty terrible, too. Not just plain terrible. This was fancy terrible; this was terrible with raisins in it. Ah, yes, I have it. This is my birthday. [*The Penguin Dorothy Parker*, 'The Middle or Blue Period']

18 Wit's End. [Nickname for Alexander Woollcott's New York apartment. Quoted in James Thurber, *The Years with Ross*]

19 A list of authors who have made themselves most beloved and therefore, most comfortable financially, shows that it is our national joy to mistake for the first-rate, the fecund rate. [Quoted in R. E. Drennan, *Wit's End*]

20 [When asked whether she had enjoyed a cocktail party] Enjoyed it! One more drink and I'd have been under the host. [Quoted in *ib.*]

21 You can't teach an old dogma new tricks. [Quoted in *ib.*]

22 Why, I never even knew that he was alive. [On being told that ex-President Coolidge had died. Quoted in *ib*. Similar joke ascribed to Wilson Mizner in A Johnston; *Legend of a Sport; the New Yorker*]

23 This is not a novel to be tossed aside lightly. It should be thrown with great force. [Book review, quoted in *ib.*]

24 I was fired from there [her convent school], finally, for a lot of things,

among them my insistence that the Immaculate Conception was spontaneous combustion. [Quoted in Malcolm Cowley, *Writers at Work, First Series*]

1 As artists they're rot, but as providers they're oil wells; they gush ... And there was that poor sucker Flaubert rolling around on his floor for three days looking for the right word. [Quoted in *ib.*]

2 Hollywood money isn't money. It's congealed snow, melts in your hand, and there you are. [Quoted in *ib.*]

3 Seventy-two suburbs in search of a city. [Of Los Angeles, but others are attr. with the description. Quoted in Leslie Halliwell, *The Filmgoer's Book of Quotes*]

4 [Suggested epitaph for her own tombstone] This is on me. [Quoted in J. Keats, *You Might As Well Live*, Pt I, Ch. 5]

5 [On going into hospital to get an abortion] It serves me right for putting all my eggs in one bastard. [Quoted in *ib.* II. 3]

6 [Of her husband on the day their divorce became final] Oh, don't worry about Alan ... Alan will always land on somebody's feet. [Quoted in *ib.* IV. 1]

7 If all the young ladies who attended the Yale promenade dance were laid end to end, no one would be the least surprised. [Quoted in Alexander Woollcott, *While Rome Burns*]

8 The affair between Margot Asquith and Margot Asquith will live as one of the prettiest love stories in all literature. [Reviewing Margot Asquith, *Autobiography*, in *New Yorker*]

9 Congratulations: we all knew you had it in you. [Telegram to friend who retired to the country to have a baby. Attr.]

10 Why, after all, should readers never be harrowed? Surely there is enough happiness in life without having to go to books for it. [Attr.]

TONY PARKER

11 I don't believe in heaven or hell, they're here; you choose which one you're going to be a lodger in. [Quoting a lighthouse keeper describing his life in *Lighthouse*, Ch. 20]

C. NORTHCOTE PARKINSON

12 Work expands so as to fill the time available for its completion. General recognition of this fact is shown in the proverbial phrase 'It is the busiest man who has time to spare.' [*Parkinson's Law*, Ch. 1]

13 The rise in the total of those employed is governed by Parkinson's Law and would be much the same whether the volume of work were to increase, diminish or even disappear. [*Ib.*]

14 For this real or imagined overwork there are, broadly speaking, three possible remedies. He [A] may resign; he may ask to halve the work with a colleague called B; he may demand the assistance of two subordinates, to be called C and D. There is probably no instance in history, however, of A choosing any but the third alternative. [*Ib.*]

15 Seven officials are now doing what one did before. This is where Factor 2 comes into operation. For these seven make so much work for each other that all are fully occupied and A is actually working harder than ever. [*Ib.*]

16 It is not the business of the botanist to eradicate the weeds. Enough for him if he can tell us just how fast they grow. [*Ib.*]

17 The British, being brought up on team games, enter their House of Commons in the spirit of those who would rather be doing something else. If they cannot be playing golf or tennis, they can at least pretend that politics is a game with very similar rules. [*Ib.* 2]

18 It might be termed the Law of Triviality. Briefly stated, it means that the time spent on any item of the agenda will be in inverse proportion to the sum involved. [*Ib.* 3]

1 The defect in the intelligence test is that high marks are gained by those who subsequently prove to be practically illiterate. So much time has been spent in studying the art of being tested that the candidate has rarely had time for anything else. [*Ib.* 5]

2 While the British Empire was mostly acquired at a period when the Colonial Office (in so far as there was one) occupied haphazard premises in Downing Street, a new phase of colonial policy began when the department moved into buildings actually designed for the purpose. This was in 1875 and the structure was well designed as a background for the disasters of the Boer War. [*Ib.* 6]

3 The age of Frustration will not always be the same ... but its symptoms are easy to recognize. The man who is denied the opportunity of taking decisions of importance begins to regard as important the decisions he is allowed to take. He becomes fussy about filing, keen on seeing that pencils are sharpened, eager to ensure that the windows are open (or shut) and apt to use two or three different-coloured inks. [*Ib.* 10]

4 It is now known ... that men enter local politics solely as a result of being unhappily married. [*Ib.*]

BORIS PASTERNAK

5 Gardens, ponds, palings, the creation, / foamed with the purity of tears, / are only categories of passion, / hoarded by the human heart. [*Definition of the Creative Power*, trans. J. M. Cohen]

6 And yet the order of the acts is planned, /The way's end destinate and uncancealed. / Alone. Now is the time of Pharisees. / *To live is not like walking through a field.* [*Hamlet*, trans. Henry Kamen]

7 When the heart dictates the line / it sends a slave on to the stage / and there's an end of art and there's / a breath of earth and destiny. [*Oh, had I known*, trans. J. M. Cohen]

8 No bad man can be a good poet. [Quoted in Ilya Ehrenburg, *Truce*]

9 The whole of life is symbolic because the whole of it has meaning. [Attr.]

KENNETH PATCHEN

10 God must have loved the People in Power, for he made them so very like their own image of him. [Quoted by Adrian Mitchell in the *Guardian*, 1 Feb. 1972]

BRIAN PATTEN

11 And the rightful owner of the music, / tiny and no longer timid, sang, / for the rightful owners of the song. [*Interruption at the Opera House*]

MERVYN PEAKE

12 They saw nothing absurd in themselves, individually, and why should they? ... There is something about a swarm that is damaging to the pride of its individual members. [*Gormenghast*, Ch. 32]

PHILIPPA PEARCE

13 Then, suddenly, when Ben could hardly see, he saw clearly. He saw clearly that you couldn't have impossible things, however much you wanted them. He saw that if you didn't have the possible things, then you had nothing. [*A Dog So Small*, Ch. 19]

WESTBROOK PEGLER

14 He [Edward VIII] will go from resort to resort getting more tanned and more tired. [On the king's abdication. Quoted in Alistair Cooke, *Six Men*, Pt II]

CHARLES PÉGUY

15 The Social Revolution will be moral, or it will not be. [*Basic Verities*]

16 What will God say to us, if some of us go to him without the others? [Quoted in W. Neil, *Concise Dictionary of Religious Quotations*]

17 He who does not bellow the truth when he knows the truth makes himself the accomplice of liars and forgers. [Attr.]

S. J. PERELMAN

1 No country home is complete without a surly figure seated in the kitchen like Rodin's Thinker, wishing she was back in a hot little room under the Third Avenue Elevated. [*Acres and Pains*, Ch. 11]

2 If anyone wants to trade a couple of centrally located, well-cushioned show-girls for an eroded slope ninety minutes from Broadway, I'll be on this corner tomorrow at eleven with my tongue hanging out. [*Ib.* 18]

3 He takes her to a concert, where Tchaikovsky's Fifth Symphony makes them kinspirits, and, swept away by the bassoons, kisses her. [*Cloudland Revisited*, 'Sodom in the Suburbs']

4 Crazy Like a Fox [Title of book]

5 I guess I'm just an old mad scientist at bottom. Give me an underground laboratory, half a dozen atomsmashers, and a beautiful girl in a diaphanous veil waiting to be turned into a chimpanzee, and I care not who writes the nation's laws. [*Crazy Like a Fox*, 'Captain Future, Block that Kick']

6 Take a small boy smeared with honey and lower him between the walls. The bees will fasten themselves to him by the hundreds and can be scraped off when he is pulled up, after which the boy can be thrown away. If no small boy smeared with honey can be found, it may be necessary to take an ordinary small boy and smear him, which should be a pleasure. [*Ib.* 'Beauty and the Bee']

7 A feeling of emulsion swept over me. [*Ib.* 'The Love Decoy']

8 I tried to resist his overtures, but he plied me with symphonies, quartettes, chamber music and cantatas. [*Ib.*]

9 He bit his lip in a manner which immediately awakened my maternal sympathy, and I helped him bite it. [*Ib.*]

10 There had been a heavy fall of talcum several hours before and as far as the ground could see the eye was white. [*Ib.*]

11 Philomène was a dainty thing, built somewhat on the order of Lois de Fee, the lady bouncer. She had the rippling muscles of a panther, the stolidity of a water buffalo, and the lazy insolence of a shoe salesman. [*Ib.* 'Kitchen Bouquet']

12 For years I have let dentists ride roughshod over my teeth; I have been sawed, hacked, chopped, whittled, bewitched, bewildered, tattooed, and signed on again; but this is cuspid's last stand. [*Ib.* 'Nothing but the Tooth']

13 I'll dispose of my teeth as I see fit, and after they've gone, I'll get along. I started off living on gruel, and by God, I can always go back to it again. [*Ib.*]

14 Every now and then, when business slackens up in the bowling alley and the other pin boys are hunched over their game of bezique, I like to exchange my sweat shirt for a crisp white surgical tunic, polish up my optical mirror, and examine the corset advertisements in the New York *Herald Tribune* rotogravure section and the various women's magazines. [*Ib.* 'Sauce for the Gander']

15 You've a sharp tongue in your head, Mr Essick. Look out it doesn't cut your throat. [*The Rising Gorge*, 'All Out . . .']

16 Do young men nowadays still become hopelessly enamoured of married women easily ten years their senior who have mocking, humorous mouths, eyes filled with tender raillery, and indulgent husbands? Back in the twenties, when it was a lot easier for a woman to be ten years my senior than it is now, I was privileged to know one who fitted these specifications. [*Keep It Crisp*, 'The Longer the Lip, the Smoother the Grift']

17 Love is not the dying moan of a distant violin – it's the triumphant twang of a bedspring. [Quoted in A. Andrews, *Quotations for Speakers and Writers*]

SHIMON PERES

18 Most of them [Israeli observers who study overseas systems] are like the lawyer who appeared before the jury and said: 'The following are the conclusions on which I base my facts.' [Attr.]

GABRIEL PÉRI
(French communist)

1 In a few minutes I am going out to shape all the singing tomorrows. [Said before his execution by the Germans in 1942. Quoted in A. Andrews, *Quotations for Speakers and Writers*]

JUAN PERÓN

2 If I had not been born Perón, I would have liked to be Perón. [*Observer*, 'Sayings of the Week', 21 Feb. 1960]

MARSHAL PÉTAIN

3 Nobody was better placed than the President [Poincaré] to be aware that France was neither led nor governed. [On Poincaré's handling of the war. Quoted in Alistair Horne, *The Price of Glory*, Ch. 26]

4 One does not fight with men against material; it is with material served by men that one makes war. [Quoted in *ib.* 27]

5 To make a union with Great Britain would be fusion with a corpse. [On Churchill's proposal for Anglo-French union, 1940. Quoted in Winston S. Churchill, *Their Finest Hour*, Ch. 10]

ZARKO PETAN

6 Cowards' hearts beat faster than heroes', but last longer. [Quoted in *The Times*, 15 Jun. 1977]

7 In the theatre, the director is God – but unfortunately, the actors are atheists. [Quoted in *ib.*]

LAURENCE J. PETER

8 A pessimist is a man who looks both ways before crossing a one-way street. [*Peter's Quotations*]

LAURENCE J. PETER and RAYMOND HULL

9 *The Peter Principle:* In a Hierarchy Every Employee Tends to Rise to his Level of Incompetence. [*The Peter Principle*, Ch. 1]

10 Work is accomplished by those employees who have not yet reached their level of incompetence. [*Ib.*]

11 Competence, like truth, beauty and contact lenses, is in the eye of the beholder. [*Ib.* 3]

12 The watchword for Side-Issue Specialists is *Look after the molehills and the mountains will look after themselves.* [*Ib.* 13]

13 If you don't know where you are going, you will probably end up somewhere else. [*Ib.* 15]

14 *Lateral Arabesque* – a pseudo-promotion consisting of a new title and a new work place. [*Ib.* Glossary]

15 *Papyromania* – compulsive accumulation of papers ...
Papyrophobia – abnormal desire for 'a clean desk'. [*Ib.*]

NIKOLAUS PEVSNER

16 To fight against the shoddy design of those goods by which our fellow-men are surrounded becomes a moral duty. [*Industrial Art in England*]

17 Hearty, robust and revolting. [Of a church. *London, except the Cities of London and Westminster*]

18 No part of the walls is left undecorated. From everywhere the praise of the Lord is drummed into you. [*Ib.*]

PIERRE PFLIMLIN

19 The Channel really is not much wider than the Rhine. [*Observer*, 'Sayings of the Week', 20 Jan. 1963]

BARONESS PHILLIPS

20 On the subject of confused people, I liked the store detective who said he'd seen a lot of people so confused that they'd stolen things, but never one so confused that they'd paid twice. [*Sunday Telegraph*, 14 Aug. 1977]

EDEN PHILPOTTS

21 Beer drinking don't do half the harm of lovemaking. [*The Farmer's Wife*, Ch. 1]

PABLO PICASSO

1 The beautiful doesn't matter to me. [*Attr.* Quoted in Murray Schafer, *British Composers in Interview*]

2 God is really only another artist. He invented the giraffe, the elephant and the cat. He has no real style, He just goes on trying other things. [Quoted in Françoise Gilot and Carlton Lake, *Life with Picasso*, Ch. 1]

3 Every positive value has its price in negative terms, and you never see anything very great which is not, at the same time, horrible in some respect. The genius of Einstein leads to Hiroshima. [Quoted in *ib*. 2]

4 I hate that aesthetic game of the eye and the mind, played by these connoisseurs, these mandarins who 'appreciate' beauty. What *is* beauty, anyway? There's no such thing. I never 'appreciate', any more than I 'like'. I love or I hate. [Quoted in *ib*.]

5 Age only matters when one is ageing. Now that I have arrived at a great age, I might just as well be twenty. [Quoted in John Richardson, 'Picasso in Private', reprinted in *Shouts and Murmurs* from the *Observer*]

6 Painting is a blind man's profession. He paints not what he sees, but what he feels, what he tells himself about what he has seen. [Quoted in Jean Cocteau, *Journals*, 'Childhood']

7 I do not seek, I find. [*Attr.*]

8 You invent something, and then someone else comes along and does it pretty. [*Attr.*]

DR H. R. PICKARD

9 If you give a girl an inch nowadays she will make a dress of it. [*Observer*, 'Sayings of the Week', 7 Oct. 1928; cf. 353:16]

MARY PICKFORD

10 Douglas [Fairbanks] had always faced a situation the only way he knew how, by running away from it. [*Sunshine and Shadow*]

WILFRED PICKLES

11 Are you courting? [*Passim*, in BBC radio programme series, *Have A Go*]

12 Give him the money, Barney. [*Ib.* Addressed to Barney Colehan]

13 In Cornwall it's Saturday before you realize it's Thursday. [In *ib*.]

HAROLD PINTER

14 I got this mate in Shepherd's Bush. In the convenience. Well, he was in the convenience. Run about the best convenience they had. [*The Caretaker*, Act I]

15 I said to this monk, here, I said, . . . you haven't got a pair of shoes, have you, a pair of shoes, I said, enough to keep me on my way . . . Piss off, he said to me. [*Ib.*]

16 If only I could get down to Sidcup! I've been waiting for the weather to break. He's got my papers, this man I left them with, it's got it all down there, I could prove everything. [*Ib.*]

17 Shirts like these don't go far in the winter-time. I mean that's one thing I know for a fact. No, what I need, is a kind of a shirt with stripes, a good solid shirt, with stripes going down. [*Ib.* II]

18 I mean, don't forget the earth's about five thousand million years old, at least. Who can afford to live in the past? [*The Homecoming*, Act II]

19 In other words, apart from the known and the unknown, what else is there? [*Ib.*]

20 He's had more dolly than you've had cream cakes. [*Ib.*]

21 I've been the whole hog plenty of times. Sometimes . . . you can be happy . . . and not go the whole hog. Now and again . . . you can be happy . . . without going any hog. [*Ib.*]

22 In my day nobody changed. A man was. Only religion could alter him, and that at least was a glorious misery. [*No Man's Land*, Act II]

23 'But what would you say your plays were *about*, Mr Pinter?' 'The weasel under the cocktail cabinet.' [Exchange

at a new writers' brains trust. Quoted in J. Russell Taylor, *Anger and After*, Ch. 7]

1 The more acute the experience the less articulate its expression. [Programme note to *The Room* and *The Dumb Waiter*. Quoted in *ib*.]

DAVID PIPER

2 A magnanimous tribute by Imperial England to a gallant if muddle-headed girl. [On the statue of Joan of Arc at Stanhope Gate, Hyde Park. *The Companion Guide to London*]

ROBERT M. PIRSIG

3 The truth knocks on the door and you say, 'Go away, I'm looking for the truth,' and so it goes away. Puzzling. [*Zen and the Art of Motorcycle Maintenance*, Pt 1, Ch. 1]

4 'What's new?' is an interesting and broadening eternal question, but one which, if pursued exclusively, results only in an endless parade of trivia and fashion, the silt of tomorrow. I would like, instead, to be concerned with the question 'What is best?', a question which cuts deeply rather than broadly, a question whose answers tend to move the silt downstream. [*Ib*.]

5 You are never dedicated to something you have complete confidence in. No one is fanatically shouting that the sun is going to rise tomorrow. They *know* it's going to rise tomorrow. When people are fanatically dedicated to political or religious faiths or any other kind of dogmas or goals, it's always because these dogmas or goals are in doubt. [*Ib*. II. 13]

6 Mental reflection is so much more interesting than TV it's a shame more people don't switch over to it. They probably think what they hear is unimportant but it never is. [*Ib*. III. 17]

7 One thing about pioneers that you don't hear mentioned is that they are invariably, by their nature, messmakers. [*Ib*. III. 21]

8 One geometry cannot be more true than another; it can only be more con-

venient. Geometry is not true, it is advantageous. [*Ib*. III. 22. This echoes Henri Poincaré]

9 Traditional scientific method has always been at the very *best*, 20–20 hindsight. It's good for seeing where you've been. [*Ib*. III. 24]

10 We keep passing unseen through little moments of other people's lives. [*Ib*.]

11 Other people can talk about how to expand the destiny of mankind. I just want to talk about how to fix a motorcycle. I think that what I have to say has more lasting value. [*Ib*. III. 25]

12 That's the classical mind at work, runs fine inside but looks dingy on the surface. [*Ib*.]

RUTH PITTER

13 The seldom female in a world of males! [*The Kitten's Eclogue*, IV]

WILLIAM PITTS

14 It is the overtakers who keep the undertakers busy. [*Observer*, 'Saying of the Week', 22 Dec. 1963]

MAX PLANCK

15 I regard consciousness as fundamental. I regard matter as derivative from consciousness. We cannot get behind consciousness. [In an interview with J. W. N. Sullivan. Quoted in Kenneth Walker, *The Circle of Life*, Pt II, Ch. 3]

SYLVIA PLATH

16 A man in black with a Meinkampf look. [*Daddy*]

17 So daddy, I'm finally through. / The black telephone's off at the root, / The voices just can't worm through. [*Ib*.]

18 Love set you going like a fat gold watch. [*Morning Song*]

19 Winter is for women – / The woman still at her knitting, / At the cradle of Spanish walnut, / Her body a bulb in the cold and too dumb to think. [*Wintering*]

265

WILLIAM PLOMER

1 Out of that bungled, unwise war / An alp of unforgiveness grew. [*The Boer War*]

2 A pleasant old buffer, nephew to a lord, / Who believed that the bank was mightier than the sword, / And that an umbrella might pacify barbarians abroad: / Just like an old liberal / Between the wars. [*Father and Son: 1939*]

3 With first-rate sherry flowing into second-rate whores, / And third-rate conversation without one single pause: / Just like a couple / Between the wars. [*Ib.*]

4 Who strolls so late, for mugs a bait, / In the mists of Maida Vale, / Sauntering past a stucco gate / Fallen, but hardly frail? [*French Lisette*]

5 On a sofa upholstered in panther skin / Mona did researches in original sin. [*Mews Flat Mona*]

6 'Look who's here! / Do come and help us fiddle while Rome burns!' [*The Playboy of the Demi-World: 1938*]

7 So never say to D'Arcy, 'Be your age!' – / He'd shrivel up at once or turn to stone. [*Ib.*]

8 It's so utterly out of the world! / So fearfully wide of the mark! / A Robinson Crusoe existence will pall / On that unexplored side of the Park – / Not a soul will be likely to call! [*A Shot in the Park*]

HENRI POINCARÉ

9 Thought is only a flash between two long nights, but this flash is everything. [Quoted in H. L. Mencken, *A New Dictionary of Quotations*]

DEPUTY POLIVANOV

10 I place my trust in the impenetrable spaces, impassable mud, and the mercy of Saint Nicholas Mirlikisky, Protector of Holy Russia. [Speech in the Duma, 4 Aug. 1915. Quoted in Leon Trotsky, *History of the Russian Revolution*, Vol. II]

A. W. POLLARD

11 He is a bad man who does not pay to the future at least as much as he has received from the past. [*Observer*, 'Saying of the Week', 31 Jul. 1927]

QUINTON POLLARD

12 If you can see the French coast, it means that it is going to rain; if you can't see it, then it's already raining. [Attr.]

JACKSON POLLOCK

13 Painting is self-discovery. Every good artist paints what he is. [Quoted in F. V. O'Connor, *Jackson Pollock*]

PRESIDENT POMPIDOU

14 A statesman is a politician who places himself at the service of the nation. A politician is a statesman who places the nation at his service. [*Observer*, 'Sayings of the Year', 30 Dec. 1973]

MICHAEL POPE

15 A fire has destroyed the Chameleon at Strood, / Which makes me exceedingly glad; / For the waitresses there were disgustingly rude / And the food was incredibly bad. [*Capital Levities*, 'Epitaph on a Country Inn Destroyed by Fire']

SIR KARL POPPER

16 Our knowledge can only be finite, while our ignorance must necessarily be infinite. [*Conjectures and Refutations*]

17 Observation is always selective. It needs a chosen object, a definite task, an interest, a point of view, a problem. And its description presupposes a descriptive language, with property words; it presupposes interests, points of view, and problems. [*Ib.*]

18 But I shall certainly admit a system as empirical or scientific only if it is capable of being *tested* by experience. These considerations suggest that not the *verifiability* but the *falsifiability* of a system is to be taken as a criterion of

demarcation . . . *It must be possible for an empirical scientific system to be refuted by experience.* [*The Logic of Scientific Discovery*, Ch. 1, sect. vi]

1 Our civilization . . . has not yet fully recovered from the shock of its birth – the transition from the tribal or 'closed society', with its submission to magical forces, to the 'open society' which sets free the critical powers of man. [*The Open Society and Its Enemies*]

2 There is no history of mankind, there are only many histories of all kinds of aspects of human life. And one of these is the history of political power. This is elevated into the history of the world. [*Ib.*]

3 We must plan for freedom, and not only for security, if for no other reason than that only freedom can make security secure. [*Ib.*]

4 Science must begin with myths, and with the criticism of myths. ['Philosophy of Science: A Personal Report', in C. A. Mace (ed.), *British Philosophy in the Mid-Century*]

5 The fundamental thing about human languages is that they can and should be used to describe something; and this something is, somehow, the world. To be constantly and almost exclusively interested in the medium – in spectacle-cleaning – is a result of a philosophical mistake. [Quoted in Brian Magee, *Modern British Philosophy*]

6 We may become the makers of our fate when we have ceased to pose as its prophets. [Quoted in an editorial in the *Observer*, 28 Dec. 1975]

JACK POPPLEWELL

7 Horses for courses, yes – but not at table if you please. [*Dear Children*]

8 Wife (borrowing mink coat from her husband's mistress), 'We shared the skunk – why not the mink?' [*Every Other Evening*]

COLE PORTER

9 But I'm always true to you, darlin', in my fashion, / Yes, I'm always true to you, darlin', in my way. [Song: *Always True to You in My Fashion*. From the musical, *Kiss Me, Kate*]

10 Now: heaven knows, anything goes. [Song: *Anything Goes*, and title of musical]

11 I Get a Kick Out of You. [Title of song, from musical, *Anything Goes*]

12 And we suddenly know, what heaven we're in, / When they begin the beguine. [Song: *Begin the Beguine*, from musical, *Jubilee*]

13 Don't Fence Me In. [Title of song, from film, *Hollywood Canteen*]

14 I love Paris in the springtime. [Song: *I Love Paris*, from musical, *Can-Can*]

15 It's delightful, / It's delicious, / It's delectable, / It's delirious. [Song: *It's Delovely*, from musical, *Red Hot and Blue*]

16 I've Got You Under My Skin. [Title of song, from musical, *Born to Dance*]

17 If you want to buy my wares, / Follow me and climb the stairs. / Love for sale. [Song: *Love for Sale*, from musical, *The New Yorkers*]

18 It's not 'cause I wouldn't / It's not 'cause I shouldn't / And, Lord knows, it's not 'cause I couldn't, / It's simply because I'm the laziest gal in town. [Song: *The Laziest Gal in Town*, from musical, *Stage Fright*. Sung by Marlene Dietrich]

19 Let's Do It; Let's Fall in Love. [Title of song, from musical, *Paris*]

20 Miss Otis regrets she's unable to lunch today. [Song: *Miss Otis Regrets*, from musical, *Hi Diddle Diddle*]

21 My heart belongs to Daddy / 'Cause my Daddy, he treats me so well. [Song: *My Heart Belongs to Daddy*, from musical, *Leave It to Me*]

22 Night and day you are the one, / Only you beneath the moon and under the sun. [Song: *Night and Day*, from musical, *Gay Divorce*]

23 And his cheques, I fear, / Mean that sex is here / To stay. [Song: *Sex is Here to Stay*]

1 HE: Have you heard it's in the stars / Next July we collide with Mars? / SHE: Well, did you evah! What a swell party this is. [Song: *Well, Did You Evah!*, from film, *High Society*]

2 Who Wants to Be a Millionaire? I don't. [Song: *Who Wants to be a Millionaire?*, in *ib.*]

PETER PORTER

3 London is full of chickens on electric spits, / Cooking in windows where the public pass. / This, say the chickens, is their Auschwitz, / And all poultry eaters are psychopaths. [*Annotations of Auschwitz*]

4 Who would be loved / If he could be feared and hated, yet still / Enjoy his lust, eat well and play the flute? [*Soliloquy at Potsdam*]

5 Some of us may die. / Remember, statistically / It is not likely to be you. / All flags are flying fully dressed / On Government buildings – the sun is shining / Death is the least we have to fear. [*Your Attention Please*]

BEATRIX POTTER

6 I shall tell you a tale of four little rabbits whose names were Flopsy, Mopsy, Cottontail and Peter. [*The Tale of Peter Rabbit*]

7 You may go into the field or down the lane, but don't go into Mr McGregor's garden. [*Ib.*]

8 I am worn to a ravelling. [*The Tailor of Gloucester*]

9 I am undone and worn to a threadpaper for I have NO MORE TWIST. [*Ib.*]

10 It is said that the effect of eating too much lettuce is 'soporific'. [*The Tale of the Flopsy Bunnies*]

GILLIE POTTER

11 Good evening, England. This is Gillie Potter speaking to you in basic English. [*Passim* in BBC radio broadcasts as the 'Squire of Hogsnorton'. Quoted in John Fisher, *Funny Way To Be a Hero*, '. . . To See Such Fun']

STEPHEN POTTER

12 It was only by his *opening remarks*, his power of creating a sense of dis-ease, that one realized, as one used to say of him, that Gattling was *always in play*. [*Lifemanship*, Ch. 1]

13 It is an *important general rule* always to refer to your friend's country establishment as a 'cottage'. [*Ib.* 2]

14 There is no doubt that basic weekendmanship should contain some reference to Important Person Play. [*Ib.*]

15 If you have nothing to say, or, rather, something extremely stupid and obvious, say it, but in a 'plonking' tone of voice – i.e. roundly, but hollowly and dogmatically. [*Ib.* 3]

16 In Newstatesmaning the critic must always be on top of, or better than, the person criticized. [*Ib.* 5]

17 Donsmanship he defines as 'the art of criticizing without actually listening'. [*Ib.* 6]

18 If your man says of some picture, 'Yes, but what does it mean?' ask him, and keep on asking him, what his carpet means, or the circular patterns on his rubber shoe-soles. Make him lift up his foot to look at them. [*One-Upmanship*, Ch. 4]

19 Basic Birdsmanship is of course to have the best pair of field-glasses in any group. [*Ib.* 10]

20 It is WRONG to do what everyone else does – namely, to hold the wine list just out of sight, look for the second cheapest claret on the list, and say, 'Number 22, please'. [*Ib.* 14]

21 A good general rule is to state that the bouquet is better than the taste, and vice versa. [*Ib.*]

EZRA POUND

22 Real education must ultimately be limited to men who insist on knowing; the rest is mere sheep-herding. [*ABC of Reading*]

23 The author's conviction . . . is that music begins to atrophy when it departs

too far from the dance; that poetry begins to atrophy when it gets too far from music. [*Ib.* 'Warning']

1 Any general statement is like a cheque drawn on a bank. Its value depends on what is there to meet it. [*Ib.* Ch. 2]

2 Rhythm is a form cut into TIME, as a design is determined SPACE. [*Ib.* 'Treatise on Reading', I]

3 Great Literature is simply language charged with meaning to the utmost possible degree. [*How to Read*]

4 I once told Fordie [Ford Madox Ford] that if he were placed naked and alone in a room without furniture, I would come back in an hour and find total confusion. [Quoted in V. S. Pritchett, *The Working Novelist*]

5 Observed the elegance of Circe's hair / Rather than the mottoes on sundials. [*Hugh Selwyn Mauberley*, 'E. P. Ode Pour L'Élection de son Sepulcre', I]

6 Caliban casts out Ariel. [*Ib.* III]

7 Walked eye-deep in hell / believing in old men's lies, then unbelieving / came home, home to a lie. [*Ib.* IV]

8 There died a myriad, / And of the best, among them, / For an old bitch gone in the teeth, / For a botched civilization. [*Ib.* V]

9 Dowson found harlots cheaper than hotels. [*Ib.* 'Siena mi fe; disfecemi Maremma']

10 And give up verse, my boy, / there's nothing in it. [*Ib.* 'Mr Nixon']

11 And we have heard the fauns chiding Proteus / in the smell of hay under the olive-trees, / And the frogs singing against the fauns / in the half-light. [*Cantos*, II]

12 And the life goes on, mooning upon bare hills; / Flame leaps from the hand, the rain is listless, / Yet drinks the thirst from our lips, / solid as echo. [*Ib.* VII]

13 Go to hell Apovitch. Chicago aint the whole punkin. [*Ib.* XII]

14 'I am not your fader but your moder,' quod he. / 'Your father was a rich merchant in Stambouli.' [*Ib.*]

15 The blossoms of the apricot / blow from the east to the west, / And I have tried to keep them from / falling. [*Ib.* XIII]

16 And old T.E.H. went to it, / With a lot of books from the library, / London Library, and a shell buried 'em in a dug-out, / And the Library expressed its annoyance. [*Ib.* XVI]

17 To the beat of the measure / From star-up to the half-dark / From half-dark to half-dark / Unceasing the measure. [*Ib.* XXXIX]

18 Said Paterson: / Hath benefit of interest in all / the moneys which it, the bank, creates out of / nothing. [*Ib.* XLVI]

19 Pull down thy vanity / Thou art a beaten dog beneath the hail, / A swollen magpie in a fitful sun, / Half black half white / Nor knowst'ou wing from tail / Pull down thy vanity. [*Ib.* LXXXI]

20 Of all those young women / not one has enquired the cause of the world / Nor the modus of lunar eclipses / Nor whether there be any patch left of us / After we cross the infernal ripples. [*Homage to Sextus Propertius*]

21 She is dying piece-meal / of a sort of emotional anaemia. / And round about there is a rabble / of the filthy, sturdy, unkillable infants / of the very poor. [*Lustra*, 'The Garden']

22 The difference between a gun and a tree is a difference of tempo. The tree explodes every spring. [In *Criterion*, Jul. 1937]

ANTHONY POWELL

23 'He fell in love with himself at first sight and it is a passion to which he has always remained faithful. Self-love seems so often unrequited.' [*The Acceptance World*, Ch. 1]

24 Dinner at the Huntercombes' possessed 'only two dramatic features – the wine was a farce and the food a tragedy'. [*Ib.* 4]

25 Her carriage suggested that she was unable to decide whether she wanted to be taken for a discontented tragedy queen on a holiday or a careless tomboy

caught up through no fault of her own in serious bohemian life. [*Agents and Patients*, Ch. 1]

1 All men are brothers, but, thank God, they aren't all brothers-in-law. [At *Lady Molly's*, Ch. 4]

2 All the same, you know parents – especially step-parents – are sometimes a bit of a disappointment to their children. They don't fulfil the promise of their early years. [*A Buyer's Market*, Ch. 2]

3 There is a strong disposition in youth, from which some individuals never escape, to suppose that everyone else is having a more enjoyable time than we are ourselves. [*Ib.* 4]

4 Fashions of one generation, moral or mystical, are scarcely at all accessible in terms of another. They cannot be properly equated. [*Hearing Secret Harmonies*, Ch. 1]

5 People think that because a novel's invented, it isn't true. Exactly the reverse is the case. Biography and memoirs can never be wholly true, since they cannot include every conceivable circumstance of what happened. The novel can do that. [*Ib.* 3]

6 These arbitrarily accepted conjectures of one's earlier years – to the effect that nothing of the slightest interest happens to people who, for reasons best known to themselves, have chosen to grow old – were not wholly borne out by observation of one's contemporaries. [*Ib.* 4]

7 You knew that château-bottled shit Widmerpool. [*Ib.* 7]

8 He took no pleasure in reading. No doubt that was a wise precaution for a man of action, whose imagination must be rigorously disciplined, if the will is to remain unsapped by daydreams, painting and music being, for some reason, less deleterious than writing in that respect. [*The Kindly Ones*, Ch. 2]

9 It must be generations since anyone but highbrows lived in this cottage . . . I imagine most of the agricultural labourers round here commute from London. [*Ib.*]

10 Erridge, a rebel whose life had been exasperatingly lacking in persecution, had enjoyed independence of parental control, plenty of money, assured social position, early in life. Since leaving school he had been deprived of all the typical grudges within the grasp of most young men. Some of these grudges, it was true, he had later developed with fair success by artificial means. [*Ib.* 4]

11 One of the worst things about life is not how nasty the nasty people are. You know that already. It is how nasty the nice people can be. [*Ib.*]

12 Growing old is like being increasingly penalized for a crime you haven't committed. [*Temporary Kings*, Ch. 1]

13 Borrit . . . once spoke of the Masai tribe holding, as a tenet of faith, that all cows in the world belong to them. Ada, in similar manner, arrogated to herself all the world's gossip, sources other than her own a presumption. [*Ib.* 3]

14 That one's rather a worry too. Young people are nowadays. It's either a Regan or a Goneril. [Bagshaw on his stepdaughters in *ib.* 4]

15 So far as jokes were concerned his [Cheesman's] features proclaimed an intact virginity as to any experience or sense of them, immaculately so. [*Ib.* 4]

ENOCH POWELL

16 As I look ahead, I am filled with foreboding. Like the Roman, I seem to see 'the River Tiber foaming with much blood'. [Speech in Birmingham, 21 Apr. 1968]

ROBERT POWELL

17 People are either escapists or Buddhists in this world. [*Zen and Reality*, 'Thoughts on Life']

SANDY POWELL

18 Can you hear me, mother? [Catchphrase coined in early days of radio comedy. Quoted in *Can You Hear Me, Mother? Sandy Powell's Lifetime of Music-Hall*, Ch. 3]

DAVID POWNALL

1 Doctor Livingstone thought that football was God in the same way as his fellow Glaswegians. All the rules are the same as those of God. Would God allow us to be off-side? Of course not. To molest the unprotected goalkeeper? Never. [*The Raining Tree War*, Ch. 5]

JOHN COWPER POWYS

2 He combined scepticism of everything with credulity about everything . . . and I am convinced this is the true Shakespearean way wherewith to take life. [*Autobiography*]

JACQUES PRÉVERT

3 *La mère fait du tricot / Le fils fait la guerre / Elle trouve ça tout naturel la mère / Et le père qu'est-ce qu'il fait le père?* – The mother is knitting / The son is fighting in the war. / The mother finds this quite natural, and what's the father up to? [*Familiale*]

4 *Notre Père qui êtes aux cieux / Restez-y / Et nous resterons sur la terre / Qui est quelquefois si jolie.* – Our Father that art in heaven, stay there and we will stay on earth which is sometimes so pretty. [*Pater Noster*]

ANDRÉ PREVIN

5 The basic difference between classical music and jazz is that in the former the music is always greater than its performance – whereas the way jazz is performed is always more important than what is being played. [Quoted in Nat Shapiro, *An Encyclopedia of Quotations about Music*]

DORY PREVIN

6 I have flown to star-stained heights / on bent and battered wings / in search of mythical kings, mythical kings. / Sure that everything of worth was in the sky / and not the earth. [Song: *Mythical Kings and Iguanas*]

FRANK PREWETT

7 Alas, no maid shall get him / For all her love, / Where he sleeps a million strong. [*Voices of Women*]

J. B. PRIESTLEY

8 I can't help feeling wary when I hear anything said about the masses. First you take their faces from 'em by calling 'em the masses and then you accuse 'em of not having any faces. [*Saturn Over the Water*, Ch. 2]

9 They [dons] will review a book by a writer much older than themselves as if it were an over-ambitious essay by a second-year student . . . It is the little dons I complain about, like so many corgis trotting up, hoping to nip your ankles. [*Outcries and Asides*]

10 [Of Politicians] A number of anxious dwarfs trying to grill a whale. [*Ib.*]

11 Comedy, we may say, is society protecting itself – with a smile. [*George Meredith*]

12 I never walk into my own tailor's without feeling apologetic. I know I am unworthy of their efforts. It is as if a man without an ear for music should be invited to spend an evening with the Lener Quartet. [*Self-Selected Essays*, 'At the Tailor's']

13 When I first entered adult life I imagined, like the young idiot I then was, that I had complete control of my face . . . As I never saw myself, it was some time before I was disillusioned. [*Ib.* 'Different Inside']

14 If there was a little room somewhere in the British Museum that contained only about twenty exhibits and good lighting, easy chairs, and a notice imploring you to smoke, I believe I should become a museum man. [*Ib.* 'In the British Museum']

15 I fancy that the Hell of Too Many People would occupy a respectable place in the hierarchy of infernal regions. [*Ib.* 'Too Many People']

16 Our great-grandchildren, when they learn how we began this war by snatching glory out of defeat . . . may also

learn how the little holiday steamers made an excursion to hell and came back glorious. [On Dunkirk. Broadcast, 5 Jun. 1940]

1 Our trouble is that we drink too much tea. I see in this the slow revenge of the Orient, which has diverted the Yellow River down our throats. [*Observer*, 'Sayings of the Week', 15 May 1949]

2 It is hard to tell where MCC ends and the Church of England begins. ('Topside Schools', *New Statesman*, 20 Jul. 1962]

3 God can stand being told by Professor Ayer and Marghanita Laski that He doesn't exist. ['The BBC's Duty to Society', *Listener*, 1 Jul. 1965]

V. S. PRITCHETT

4 Dickens was not the first or the last novelist to find virtue more difficult to portray than the wish for it. [*Books in General*, 'Oliver Twist']

5 The detective novel is the art-for-art's-sake of yawning Philistinism. [*Ib*. 'The Roots of Detection']

6 Smollett's temper was, in some respects, a new, frost-bitten bud of civilization, of which sick, divided and impossible men are frequently the growing point. [*Ib*. 'The Unhappy Traveller']

7 Human beings are simply archaic, ivy-covered ruins, preserved by the connoisseur, and they stand out oddly in the new world of the masses. [*New Writing and Daylight*, 'The Future of Fiction']

P. J. PROBY

8 I think God is groovy. He had a great publicity agent. [Quoted in J. Green, *The Book of Rock Quotes*]

MARCEL PROUST

9 The taste was that of the little crumb of madeleine which on Sunday mornings at Combray ..., when I used to say good-day to her in her bedroom, my aunt Léonie used to give me, dipping it first in her own cup of real or of lime-flower tea. [*Remembrance of Things Past*: *Swann's Way*, 'Overture', trans. R. Scott Moncrieff]

10 That was not to say that M. Legrandin was anything but sincere when he inveighed against snobs. He could not (from his own knowledge, at least) be aware that he was one also, since it is only with the passions of others that we are ever really familiar, and what we come to find out about our own can be no more than what other people have shown us. [*Ib*. 'Combray']

11 Swann, who behaved quite simply and was at his ease when with a duchess, would tremble, for fear of being despised, and would instantly begin to pose, were he to meet her grace's maid. [*Ib*. 'Swann in Love']

12 People often say that, by pointing out to a man the faults of his mistress, you succeed only in strengthening his attachment to her, because he does not believe you; yet how much more so if he does! [*Ib*.]

13 To think that I have wasted years of my life, that I have longed for death, that the greatest love that I have ever known has been for a woman who did not please me, who was not in my style! [*Ib*.]

14 In theory one is aware that the earth revolves, but in practice one does not perceive it, the ground upon which one treads seems not to move, and one can live undisturbed. So it is with Time in one's life. [*Ib. Within a Budding Grove*, 'Madame Swann at Home']

15 The man of genius, to shelter himself from the ignorant contempt of the world, may say to himself that, since one's contemporaries are incapable of the necessary detachment, works written for posterity should be read by posterity alone, like certain pictures which one cannot appreciate when one stands too close to them. [*Ib*.]

16 A powerful idea communicates some of its strength to him who challenges it. [*Ib*.]

17 There can be no peace of mind in love, since the advantage one has secured is never anything but a fresh starting-point for further desires. [*Ib*.]

1 As soon as one is unhappy one becomes moral. [*Ib.*]

2 It is our noticing them that puts things in a room, our growing used to them that takes them away again and clears a space for us. [*Ib.* 'Place Names']

3 As to the pretty girls who went past, from the day on which I had first known that their cheeks could be kissed, I had become curious about their souls. [*Ib.*]

4 He strode rapidly across the hotel, seeming to be in pursuit of his monocle, which kept darting away in front of him like a butterfly. [*Ib.*]

5 To strip our pleasures of imagination is to reduce them to their own dimensions, that is to say to nothing. [*Ib.* 'Bloch']

6 The human face is indeed, like the face of the God of some Oriental theogony, a whole cluster of faces, crowded together but on different surfaces so that one does not see them all at once. [*Ib.* 'Elstir']

7 The other person is destroyed when we cease to see him; after which his next appearance means a fresh creation of him, different from that which immediately preceded it, if not from them all. [*Ib.*]

8 She's the sort of woman who does a tremendous lot for her old governesses. [*Ib. The Guermantes Way*, Vol. I]

9 She had one of those faces to which distance – and not necessarily that between stalls and stage, the world being in this respect only a larger theatre – gives form and outline and which, seen close at hand, dissolve back into dust. [*Ib.*]

10 A doctor who doesn't say too many foolish things is a patient half-cured, just as a critic is a poet who has stopped writing verse and a policeman a burglar who has retired from practice. [*Ib.*]

11 All the greatest things we know have come to us from neurotics. It is they and they only who have founded religions and created great works of art. Never will the world be conscious of how much it owes to them, nor above all of what they have suffered in order to bestow their gifts on it. [*Ib.* 'My Grandmother's Illness']

12 Neurosis has an absolute genius for malingering. There is no illness which it cannot counterfeit perfectly ... If it is capable of deceiving the doctor, how should it fail to deceive the patient? [*Ib.*]

13 As soon as he ceased to be mad he became merely stupid. There are maladies we must not seek to cure because they alone protect us from others that are more serious. [*Ib.*]

14 It has been said that the highest praise of God consists in the denial of Him by the atheist, who finds creation so perfect that he can dispense with a creator. [*Ib.* Vol. II, Ch. 2]

15 There was nothing else in the picture, a bundle of asparagus exactly like what you're eating now. But I must say I declined to swallow M. Elstir's asparagus. He asked three hundred francs for them. [*Ib.*]

16 His hatred of snobs was a derivative of his snobbishness, but made the simpletons (in other words, everyone) believe that he was immune from snobbishness. [*Ib.*]

17 I was beginning to learn the exact value of the language, spoken or mute, of aristocratic affability, an affability that is happy to shed balm upon the sense of inferiority in those persons towards whom it is directed, though not to the point of dispelling that sense, for in that case it would no longer have any reason to exist. [*Ib. Cities of the Plain*, Vol. 1 Pt II, Ch. 1]

18 I hope, for his own sake, that he has younger people than me at his disposal if he wishes to ask for bad advice; especially if he means to follow it. [*Ib.*]

19 Good-bye, I've barely said a word to you, it is always like that at parties, we never see the people, we never say the things we should like to say, but it is the same everywhere in this life. Let us hope that when we are dead things will be better arranged. [*Ib.*]

20 I have sometimes regretted living so close to Marie ... because I may be

very fond of her, but I am not quite so fond of her company. [*Ib.*]

1 Illness is the doctor to whom we pay most heed: to kindness, to knowledge we make promises only; pain we obey. [*Ib.*]

2 I have a horror of sunsets, they're so romantic, so operatic. [*Ib.* II. 2]

3 Habit is a second nature which prevents us from knowing the first, of which it has neither the cruelties nor the enchantments. [*Ib.*]

4 Distances are only the relation of space to time and vary with that relation. [*Ib.* II. 3]

5 Albertine never related facts that were capable of injuring her, but always other facts which could be explained only by them, the truth being rather a current which flows from what people say to us and which we apprehend, invisible as it may be, than the actual thing that they say. [*Ib.*]

6 War . . . does not escape the laws of our old Hegel. It is a state of perpetual becoming. [*Ib. Time Regained*, Ch. 2, trans. Stephen Hudson]

7 Mme Verdurin, who suffered from headaches on account of being unable to get *croissants* to dip into her coffee. [*Ib.*]

8 Life deceives us so much that we come to believing that literature has no relation with it and we are astonished to observe that the wonderful ideas books have presented to us are gratuitously exhibited in everyday life, without risk of being spoilt by the writer. [*Ib.*]

9 Happiness is beneficial for the body, but it is grief that develops the powers of the mind. [*Ib.* 3]

10 For all the fruitful altruisms of Nature develop in an egotistical mode; human altruism which is not egoism is sterile, it is that of a writer who interrupts his work to receive a friend who is unhappy, to accept some public function or to write propaganda articles. [*Ib.*]

J. W. PRUITT

11 An' the Devil says, 'Boys, the next stop's Hell' / An' all the passengers yelled with pain / An' begged the Devil to stop the train. [Song, *The Hellbound Train*]

12 You paid the fare with the rest of my load / An' you got to ride to the end of the road. [*Ib.*]

DAVID PRYCE-JONES

13 When you're bored with yourself, marry and be bored with someone else. [*Owls and Satyrs*, Pt. I]

JOHN PUDNEY

14 Do not despair / For Johnny Head-in-Air. / He sleeps as sound / As Johnny Underground. [Lines scribbled on an envelope during an air-raid in 1941. Later used for the film, *The Way to the Stars*]

PUNCH

15 Darling only one more instalment and Baby will be *ours*. [Quoted in Robert Graves and Alan Hodge, *The Long Weekend*, Ch. 11]

COMMANDER PURSEY, M.P.

16 There we were, one foot on a bar of soap and the other in the gutter. [Attr.]

Q

WILLARD QUINE

1 This is the old Platonic riddle of non-being. Nonbeing must in some sense be, otherwise what is it that there is not? This tangled doctrine might be nick-named Plato's beard; historically it has proved tough, frequently dulling the edge of Occam's razor. [*From A Logical Point of View*, 'On What There Is']

R

JOHN RAE

1 A mother has an innate ability for aggravating the wounds of her offspring's pride. This is inevitable since the relationship between mother and child is a most unnatural one; other species have the good sense to banish their young at an early age. [*The Custard Boys*, Ch. 13]

2 War is, after all, the universal perversion. We are all tainted: if we cannot experience our perversion at first hand we spend our time reading war stories, the pornography of war; or seeing war films, the blue films of war; or titillating our senses with the imagination of great deeds, the masturbation of war. [*Ib.*]

ADMIRAL RAEDER

3 The C.-in-C. Navy [Raeder] cannot . . . advocate an invasion of Britain as he did in the case of Norway. [Quoted in W. L. Shirer, *The Rise and Fall of the Third Reich*, Ch. 2]

SIR WALTER RALEIGH

4 On leaving the Exhibition at the Royal Academy in company with his friend Mr Bell, the Author expressed his conviction that it is better, after all, to be a Human Being. Speaking of the writings of William Morris, Olive Schreiner and Andrew Lang, the Author remarked that they were very like the Bible, only sillier. [*Laughter from a Cloud*, 'Remarks']

5 We could not lead a pleasant life, / And 'twould be finished soon, / If peas were eaten with the knife, / And gravy with the spoon. / Eat slowly: only men in rags / And gluttons old in sin / Mistake themselves for carpet bags / And tumble victuals in. [*Ib.* 'Stans puer ad mensam']

6 An anthology is like all the plums and orange peel picked out of a cake. [Letter to Mrs Robert Bridges, 15 Jan. 1915, *Letters*, Vol. II]

7 There is no one thing to be found in books which it is a disgrace not to know. [Attr.]

DAVID RANDOLPH

8 [Of *Parsifal*] The kind of opera that starts at six o'clock and after it has been going three hours, you look at your watch and it says 6:20. [Quoted in Frank Muir, *The Frank Muir Book*]

JOHN CROWE RANSOM

9 And if no Lethe flows beneath your casement, / and when ten years have not brought full effacement, / Philosophy was wrong, and you may meet. [*Parting at Dawn*]

10 Here lies a lady of beauty and high degree. / Of chills and fevers she died, of fever and chills. [*Here lies a Lady*]

ARTHUR RANSOME

11 BETTER DROWNED THAN DUFFERS IF NOT DUFFERS WONT DROWN. [*Swallows and Amazons*, Ch. 1]

FREDERICK RAPHAEL

12 This [Cambridge] is the city of perspiring dreams. [*The Glittering Prizes: An Early Life*, Act III]

13 I come from suburbia, Dan, personally, I don't ever want to go back. It's the one place in the world that's further away than anywhere else. [*Ib. A Sex Life*, Act I, sc. iii]

14 I find it quite remarkable, don't you, how people always take offence when a

conversation ceases to be personal? [*Ih An Academic Life*, Act III, sc. iii]

1 We thought philosophy ought to be patient and unravel people's mental blocks. Trouble with doing that is, once you've unravelled them, their heads fall off. [*Ib. A Double Life*, Act III, sc. ii]

2 Proust saw his friends, in old age, disguised with white hair; I see mine, in their mid-40s, prudent upon their pedestals, just as young as they were, only older. ['25 Years Ago in Cambridge', *Listener*, 5 Feb. 1976]

3 He looked at me with the weary tact of those who have come a long way down the mountain to avoid any appearance of condescension. [*Ib.*]

4 Great restaurants are, of course, nothing but mouth-brothels. There is no point in going to them if one intends to keep one's belt buckled. [*Sunday Times Magazine*, 25 Sep. 1977]

TERENCE RATTIGAN

5 The headmaster said you ruled with a rod of iron. He called you the Himmler of the lower fifth. [*The Browning Version*]

6 She has ideas above her station ... How would you say that in French? ... you can't say au-dessus de sa gare. It isn't that sort of station. [*French without Tears*, Act I]

7 You can be in the Horse Guards and still be common, dear. [*Separate Tables:* 'Table Number Seven']

8 In future I trust that a son of mine will at least show enough sense to come in out of the rain. [*The Winslow Boy*, Act I]

9 A nice, respectable, middle-class, middle-aged maiden lady, with time on her hands and the money to help her pass it ... Let us call her Aunt Edna ... Aunt Edna is universal, and to those who may feel that all the problems of the modern theatre might be solved by her liquidation, let me add that ... she is also immortal. [*Collected Plays*, Vol. II, Preface]

GWEN RAVERAT

10 But she never, never missed the train. I think she felt that it would not have been sporting to start in time; it would not have given the train a fair chance of getting away without her. [*Period Piece*, Ch. 5]

11 I have defined Ladies as people who did not do things themselves. [*Ib.* 7]

HERBERT READ

12 I saw him stab / And stab again / A well-killed Boche. / This is the happy warrior. / This is he ... [*The Happy Warrior*]

PETER REDGROVE

13 He sighs, and the waves are a city of doors slamming; / God's arm engloves this tree and brandishes it. [*The Affianced*]

14 For sixpence he can get drunk / And be a torero, the government, or a saint. [*Malagueño*]

HENRY REED

15 It is, we believe, / Idle to hope that the simple stirrup-pump / Can extinguish hell. [*A Map of Verona*, 'Chard Whitlow' (Mr Eliot's Sunday Evening Postscript)]

16 To-day we have naming of parts. Yesterday / We had daily cleaning. And tomorrow morning, / We shall have what to do after firing. But to-day, / To-day we have naming of parts. [*Ib.* 'Lessons of the War', I]

17 They call it easing the Spring: it is perfectly easy / If you have any strength in your thumb: like the bolt, / And the breech, and the cocking-piece, and the point of balance, / Which in our case we have not got. [*Ib.*]

18 You must never be over-sure. You must say, when reporting: / At five o'clock in the central sector is a dozen / Of what appear to be animals; whatever you do, / Don't call the bleeders *sheep*. [*Ib.*]

19 And the various holds and rolls and throws and breakfalls / Somehow or other I always seemed to put / In the

wrong place. And as for war, my wars /
Were global from the start. [*Ib*. III]

1 I think it may justly be said that English
women in general are very common
diatonic little numbers. They differ
greatly in this from the women of, say,
North Africa. [Radio drama, *Emily
Butter*]

2 Henry has always led what could be
called a sedentary life, if only he'd ever
got as far as actually sitting up. [Radio
drama, *Not a Drum was Heard: The
War Memoirs of General Gland*]

3 It was, I think, a *good* war, one of the
best there have so far been. I've often
advanced the view that it was a war
deserving of better generalship than it
received on either side. [*Ib*.]

4 It's a life-mask of myself wearing an
army respirator. Rather an experimental
piece, of course. I did it myself. [*Ib*.]

5 She's invented a new religion. Called
'Creative Sleep'. [*Ib*.]

6 In a civil war, a general must know –
and I'm afraid it's a thing rather of
instinct than of practice – he must know
exactly when to move over to the other
side. [*Ib*.]

7 GLAND: I would say it's somehow
redolent, and full of vitality.
HILDA: Well, I would say it's got about
as much life in it as a potted shrimp.
GLAND: Well, I think we're probably
both trying to say the same thing in
different words. [Radio drama, *The
Primal Scene, as it were*]

8 Anyone else in my position would have
been riddled with internal persecutors,
riddled with them; but my internal persecutors are all external ones, as you
have only to look around you to see.
[*Ib*.]

9 I dream quite a bit, myself. Only when
I'm asleep, of course. Curious thing is
it's always the same dream ... Not
that I mind, of course, I'm not one to
hanker after change the whole time.
[*Ib*.]

10 If one doesn't get birthday presents it
can remobilize very painfully the
persecutory anxiety which usually
follows birth. [*Ib*.]

11 Richard Sherwin is the only man, alive
or dead, who can ever have been said to
have interfered with ... my basic tone-
row. [Radio drama, *The Private Life of
Hilda Tablet*]

12 The sooner the tea's out of the way, the
sooner we can get out the gin, eh? [*Ib*.]

13 The original idea was that it should take
place in the sixteenth century on a boat
anchored off Rimini; it's Hilda who's
altered it to a mutiny in the bargain
basement of a drapery store. [*Ib*.]

14 Of course, we've all dreamed of reviving
the castrati; but it's needed Hilda to take
the first practical steps towards making
them a reality ... She's drawn up a list
of well-known singers who she thinks
would benefit from ... treatment ...
It's only a question of getting them to
agree. [*Ib*.]

15 BETTY: Modest? My word, no.
Nobody could say that. He was an all-
the-lights-on man, Dicky Sherwin was.
ADELA: And a looking-glass too.
[Radio drama, *A Very Great Man
Indeed*]

16 She's really quite playful sometimes. I
know you wouldn't think it, but really I
have known her pass the whole evening
without mentioning a single book, or *in
fact anything unpleasant* at all. [*Ib*.]

17 It's the last scene from that final exquisite study in the ambiguity that
attends all human relationships, *The
Arse and the Elbow*. [*Ib*.]

JOHN REED

18 Ten Days that Shook the World [Title
of book on Russian Revolution]

REX REED

19 In Hollywood, if you don't have
happiness you send out for it. [Quoted
in J. R. Colombo, *Colombo's Hollywood*,
'Hollywood the Bad']

GEORGE REEDY

20 You know that nobody is strongminded
around a President; ... it is always:
'yes sir,' 'no sir' (the 'no sir' comes
when he asks whether you're dis-

satisfied). [Quoted in R. Gordon Hoxie (ed.), *The White House*]

WILLIAM REEL

1 In highbrow circles, ridiculing Jews is nazism, ridiculing blacks is racism, ridiculing feminists is sexism, but ridiculing Christians is freedom of speech. [Quoted in *The Times*, 23 Jul. 1977]

C. B. REES

2 Beethoven's Fifth Symphony may be Fate – or Kate – knocking at the door. That is up to you. [*Penguin Music Magazine*, 1946]

LEONARD REES

3 Damn it, man, I could cut the Lord's Prayer! [Quoted in James Agate, *Ego 1*]

CHARLES A. REICH

4 The Greening of America. [Title of book]

WILHELM REICH

5 Every kind of destructive action by itself is the reaction of the organism to the denial of the gratification of a vital need, especially the sexual. [*The Function of the Orgasm*]

6 The few bad poems which occasionally are created during abstinence are of no great interest. [*The Sexual Revolution*]

REV. JAMES REID

7 'What's the good?' expresses the most characteristic mood of the modern mind. [1932. *Observer*, 'Sayings of Our Times', 31 May 1953]

GOTTFRIED REINHARDT

8 Hollywood people are afraid to leave Hollywood. Out in the world, they are frightened . . . Sam Hoffenstein used to say we are the croupiers in a crooked gambling house. And it's true. Everyone of us thinks, You know, I really

don't deserve a swimming pool. [Quoted in Lillian Ross, *Picture*, 'Throw the Little Old Lady Down the Stairs!'. Cf. 157:15]

9 You know, there are three kinds of intelligence – the intelligence of man, the intelligence of the animal, and the intelligence of the military. In that order. [Quoted in *ib*. 'Piccolos under Your Name, Strings under Mine'. See also 225:1]

10 Money is good for bribing yourself through the inconveniences of life. [Quoted in *ib*. 'Looks Like We're Still in Business']

LORD REITH

11 [On the best form of government] Despotism tempered by assassination. [Quoted in the *Observer*, 12 Nov. 1972]

12 You can't think rationally on an empty stomach, and a whole lot of people can't do it on a full one either. [Attr.]

M. J. RENDALL

13 Nation shall speak peace unto nation. [Motto of BBC, 1927]

DAVID REUBEN M.D.

14 Everything You've Always Wanted to Know About Sex, But Were Afraid to Ask. [Title of book]

CHARLES REVSON

15 In the factory we make cosmetics. In the store we sell hope. [Quoted in A. Tobias, *Fire and Ice*]

MALVINA REYNOLDS

16 They're all made out of ticky-tacky, and they all look just the same. [Song: *Little Boxes*, about the tract houses in the hills south of San Francisco. Quoted in *The Times* obituary, 7 Apr. 1978. Sung by Pete Seeger]

CECIL RHODES

1 Remember that you are an Englishman, and have consequently won first prize in the lottery of life. [Quoted in Peter Ustinov, *Dear Me*, Ch. 4]

JEAN RHYS

2 The feeling of Sunday is the same everywhere, heavy, melancholy, standing still. Like when they say, 'As it was in the beginning, is now, and ever shall be, world without end.' [*Voyage in the Dark*, Ch. 4]

MANDY RICE-DAVIES

3 I am notorious. I will go down in history as another Lady Hamilton. [Apropos the Profumo scandal, 1963]

FRANK RICHARDS

4 'My esteemed chums,' murmured Hurree Jamset Ram Singh. 'This is not an occasion for looking the gift horse in the mouthfulness.' [*Bunter's Last Fling*, Ch. 5]

I. A. RICHARDS

5 Anything is valuable that will satisfy an appetency without involving the frustration of some equal or *more important* appetency. [*Principles of Literary Criticism*]

6 To be forced by desire into any unwarrantable belief is a calamity. [*Ib.*]

7 It [poetry] is a perfectly possible means of overcoming chaos. [*Science and Poetry*]

SIR RALPH RICHARDSON

8 [Of styles of acting] It's like Edith Evans – she used to open a window to her heart and then slam it shut, so that you'd come back the next night to see more. [Quoted in Kenneth Tynan's profile of him at seventy-five, 'Tynan on Richardson', *Observer Magazine*, 18 Dec. 1977]

9 In music, the punctuation is absolutely strict, the bars and the rests are absolutely defined. But our punctuation cannot be quite strict, because we have to relate it to the audience. In other words, we are continually changing the score. [Quoted in *ib.*]

10 The most precious things in speech are pauses. [Attr. See also 299:15]

WILLIAM J. RICHARDSON

11 Do you want your philosophy straight or with a dash of legerdemain? [*Heidegger*]

MORDECAI RICHLER

12 Remember this, Griffin. The revolution eats its own. Capitalism re-creates itself. [*Cocksure*, Ch. 22]

13 And furthermore did you know that behind the discovery of America there was a Jewish financier? [*Ib.* 24]

14 'I'm world-famous,' Dr Parks said, 'all over Canada.' [*The Incomparable Atuk*, Ch. 4]

EDGELL RICKWORD

15 My soul's a trampled duelling ground where Sade, / the gallant marquis, fences for his life / against the invulnerable retrograde / Masoch, his shade, more constant than a wife. [*Chronique Scandaleuse*]

16 The oldest griefs of summer seem less sad / than drone of mowers on suburban lawns / and girls' thin laughter, to the ears that hear / the soft rain falling of the failing stars. [*Regrets*, II]

W. PETT RIDGE

17 The street in which she lived had started with the idea of going somewhere, but being discouraged had come to a definite stop as at the bottom of a sack. [*Lost Property*, Pt I, Ch. 5]

18 He took her up in his arms in the way of a bachelor who in his time has had amateur experience of the carrying of nieces. [*Ib.* I. 8]

19 Got looped up now with a publican's widow . . . It's a funny thing she can't see a tumbler without wiping it with her handkercher. Still I don't blame her for giving up public life. [*Ib.* II. 20]

1 When you take the bull by the horns . . .
what happens is a toss up. [*Love at
Paddington Green*, Ch. 4]

2 Gertie recommended her to adopt the
habit of not magnifying grievances; if
you wanted to view trouble, you could
take opera-glasses, but you should be
careful to hold them the wrong way
round. [*Ib.*]

3 'How did you think I managed at
dinner, Clarence?' 'Capitally!' 'I had a
knife and two forks left at the end,' she
said regretfully. [*Ib.* 6]

4 Gertie thanked him with a glance that,
at any honestly managed exchange
office, could be converted into bank
notes. [*Ib.* 11]

5 Ballard admitted he was no hand at
giving descriptions; the man was apparently a gentleman and the woman –
well, not exactly a lady, although she
had a very fine flow of language. [*Mrs
Galer's Business*, Ch. 6]

DAVID RIESMAN

6 The Lonely Crowd. [Title of book]

RAINER MARIA RILKE

7 *O Bäume Lebens, o wann winterlich? /
Wir sind nicht einig. Sind nicht wie die
Zug- / vögel verständigt. Überholt und
spät, / so drängen wir uns plötzlich
Winden auf / und fallen ein auf teilnahmslosen Teich.* – O trees of life, when
will it be winter for you? We are not
at one. We are not of one mind like the
migratory birds. Overtaken and late,
we suddenly hurry up-wind and fall on
the indifferent pond. [*Duineser Elegien*,
IV]

8 *Uns aber, wo wir Eines meinen ganz, /
ist schon des andern Aufwand fühlbar.
Feindschaft / ist uns das Nächste.* But we,
when we are entirely intent on one
thing, can feel the pull of another.
Hostility comes easiest to us. [*Ib.*]

9 *Wer zeigt ein Kind, so wie es steht? Wer
stellt / es ins Gestirn und gibt das Mass
des Abstands / ihm in die Hand?* – Who
will show a child, as it really is? Who

will place it in its constellation and put
the measure of distance in its hand?
[*Ib.*]

10 *den ganzen Tod, noch vor dem Leben so /
sanft zu enthalten und nicht bös zu sein, /
ist unbeschreiblich.* – To contain the
whole of death so gently even before
life has begun, and not be angry – this
is beyond description. [*Ib.*]

11 *Plätze, o Platz in Paris, unendlicher
Schauplatz, / wo die Modistin, Madame
Lamort, / die ruhlosen Wege der Erde,
endlose Bänder, / schlingt und windet.* –
Squares, O square in Paris, endless
showplace where the modiste, Madame
Lamort, loops and winds endless
ribbons, the restless roads of the world.
[*Ib.* V]

12 *ihre Türme aus Lust, ihre / längst, wo
Boden nie war, nur aneinander / lehnenden Leitern, bebend.* – Their towers of
pleasure, their ladders that have for so
long now leaned against each other,
where there was no ground, trembling.
[*Ib.*]

13 *Feigenbaum, seit wie lange schon ists mir
bedeutend, / wie du die Blüte beinah ganz
überschlägst / und hinein in die zeitig
entschlossene Frucht, / ungerühmt,
drängst dein reines Geheimnis.* – Figtree, for a long time now I have found
meaning in the way you almost entirely
overleap the stage of blossom and
thrust your pure mystery, unsung, into
the early set fruit. [*Ib.* VI]

14 *Wunderlich nah ist der Held doch den
jugendlich Toten.* – The hero is strangely
akin to those who die young. [*Ib.*]

15 *War er nicht Held schon in dir, O Mutter,
begann nicht / dort schon, in dir, seine
herrische Auswahl?* – Was he not
already a hero inside you, O mother?
Did not his imperious choice already
begin there, in you? [*Ib.*]

16 *abgewendet schon, stand er am Ende der
Lächeln, anders.* – But already withdrawn, he stood at the end of smiles,
different. [*Ib.*]

17 *Unser / Leben geht hin mit Verwandlung.*
– Our life passes in transformation. [*Ib.*
VII]

18 *Wo einmal ein dauerndes Haus war, /
schlägt sich erdachtes Gebild vor, quer,*

zu Erdenklichem | völlig gehörig. – Where once a lasting house was, obliquely an invented picture starts up, which belongs entirely to the imaginary. [*Ib.*]

1 *o Glück der Mücke, die noch innen hüpft, | selbst wenn sie Hochzeit hat: denn Schooss ist alles.* – O joy of the gnat, that still leaps inwards even in the act of wedding; for womb is all! [*Ib.* VIII]

2 *so leben wir und nehmen immer Abschied.* – Thus we live, for ever taking leave. [*Ib.*]

3 *Hier ist des Säglichen Zeit, hier seine Heimat. | Sprich und bekenn.* – Here is the time of the tellable, here is its home. Speak and proclaim. [*Ib.* IX]

4 *Preise dem Engel die Welt, nicht die unsägliche, ihm | kannst du nicht grosstun mit herrlich Erfühltem; im Weltall, | wo er fühlender fühlt, bist du ein Neuling. Drum zeig | ihm das Einfache.* – Praise the world to the angel, not the untellable. You cannot impress him with the splendour you have felt; in the cosmos where he feels with greater feeling you are a novice. So show him the simple thing. [*Ib.*]

5 *beklebt mit Plakaten des 'Todlos', | jenes bitteren Biers, das den Trinkenden süss scheint.* – Stuck with placards for 'Deathless', that bitter beer that tastes sweet to its drinkers. [*Ib.* x]

6 *Das war der Seelen wunderliches Bergwerk.* – That was the wonderful mine of souls. [*Orpheus, Eurydike, Hermes*]

7 *Sie war schon aufgelöst wie langes Haar | und hingegeben wie gefallner Regen | und ausgeteilt wie hundertfacher Vorrat.* – She was already loosened like long hair, given up like fallen rain, and divided like a hundredfold store. [*Ib.*]

8 *Ist er ein Hiesiger? Nein, aus beiden | Reichen erwuchs seine weite Natur.* – Is he a man of this side? No, his broad nature grew from both realms. [*Die Sonette an Orpheus*, I, vi]

9 *Nicht sind die Leiden erkannt, | nicht ist die Liebe gelernt, | und was im Tod uns entfernt, | ist nicht entschleiert.* – Sorrows are not known, love is not learnt, and what removes us in death is not revealed. [*Ib.* xix]

10 *Frühling ist wiedergekommen. Die Erde – ist wie ein Kind, das Gedichte | weiss.* Spring has returned. The earth is like a child that knows poems. [*Ib.* xxi]

11 *Alles das Eilende | wird schon vorüber sein; | denn das Verweilende | erst weiht uns ein.* – All that is hurrying will soon be past; for that which stays gives us our first initiation. [*Ib.* xxiii]

12 *O du verlorener Gott! Du unendliche Spur! | Nur weil dich reissend zuletzt die Feindschaft verteilte, | sind wir die Hörenden jetzt und ein Mund der Natur.* – O thou lost God! O endless trace! Only because hostility finally tore you to pieces are we now the listeners and a mouthpiece of Nature. [*Ib.* xxvi]

13 *O dieses ist das Tier, das es nicht gibt.* – O this is the animal that does not exist. [*Ib.* II. iv]

14 *Alles Erworbene bedroht die Maschine.* – The machine threatens all achievement. [*Ib.* x]

15 *Sei allem Abschied voran, als wäre hinter | dir, wie der Winter der eben geht.* – Be ahead of all farewells, as if they were behind you, like the winter that is just departing. [*Ib.* xiii]

16 *Alle die dich suchen, versuchen dich. | Und die, so dich finden, binden dich | an Bild und Gebärde.* – All who seek you tempt you, and as soon as they find you, bind you to an image and a posture. [*Das Stundenbuch, 'Alle welche dich suchen'*]

17 *Die Könige der Welt sind alt | und werden keine Erben haben.* – The kings of the earth are old and will have no heirs. [*Ib. 'Die Könige der Welt sind alt'*]

18 *Was wirst du tun, Gott, wenn ich sterbe? | Ich bin dein Krug (wenn ich zerscherbe?)* – What will you do, God, if I die? I am your pitcher (if I break?). [*Ib. 'Was wirst du tun, Gott'*]

NIKOLAI RIMSKY-KORSAKOV

19 I have already heard it [Debussy's music]. I had better not go: I will start to get accustomed to it and finally like it. [Quoted in Robert Craft and Igor

Stravinsky, *Conversations with Stravinsky*]

TOM ROBBINS

1 Amnesia is not knowing who one is and wanting desperately to find out. Euphoria is not knowing who one is and not caring. Ecstacy is knowing exactly who one is – and still not caring. [*Another Roadside Attraction*]

2 Among the Haida Indians of the Pacific Northwest, the verb for 'making poetry' is the same as the verb 'to breathe'. [*Ib.*]

3 Human beings were invented by water as a device for transporting itself from one place to another. [*Ib.*]

MICHAEL ROBERTS

4 More often than prose or mathematics, poetry is received in a hostile spirit, as if its publication were an affront to the reader. [*The Faber Book of Modern Verse*, Introduction]

MAX ROBERTSON

5 Here comes Queen Ingrid looking beautiful in an off-the-hat-face. [Attr. during BBC radio commentary on Wimbledon Lawn Tennis Tournament]

GEORGE ROBEY

6 Desist! [Said with raised eyebrows and lifted hand to quell applause. Quoted in A. E. Wilson, *The Prime Minister of Mirth*, Ch. 3]

7 The inmate of a lunatic asylum was writing a letter. A man looked over his shoulder and asked: 'To whom are you writing?' The inmate replied: 'I am writing to myself.' 'What are you saying?' asked the other man. 'Oh, I shan't know till I get it tomorrow,' said the inmate. [Quoted in *ib.* 12]

8 The Prime Minister of Mirth [Sobriquet of unknown origin]

9 I said 'Archibald, certainly not'. [Song refrain]

10 I stopped, I looked and I listened. [Song in *The Bing Boys*. Words by Clifford Grey]

11 The pleasantry of the Music Hall is to show Father bathing the twins, not seducing the typist. [*Looking Back on Life*, Ch. 14]

12 I am satiated with fishing stories – there's no truth in them! The man who caught that fish [stuffed in a glass case] is a blasted liar! [Reported conversation after Piscatorial Society dinner. *Ib.* 26]

13 *Complaints* should be made to the management in writing and placed in the receptacle installed for that purpose at the Entrance, which is cleared twice weekly by the Dustman. [*George Robey's Advertiser*]

LEO ROBIN

14 Thanks For the Memory. [Title of song from musical, *Big Broadcast*]

15 Diamonds Are A Girl's Best Friend. [Title of song from musical, *Gentlemen Prefer Blondes*]

EDWIN ARLINGTON ROBINSON

16 Friends / To borrow my books and set wet glasses on them. [*Captain Craig*, II]

17 I shall have more to say when I am dead. [*John Brown*]

18 Miniver loved the Medici, / Albeit he had never seen one; / He would have sinned incessantly / Could he have been one. [*Miniver Cheevy*]

GEOFFREY ROBINSON

19 They [psychiatrists] have a financial interest in being wrong; the more children they can disturb, the larger their adult clientele. [*Hedingham Harvest*]

JAMES HARVEY ROBINSON

20 Partisanship is our great curse. We too readily assume that everything has two sides and that it is our duty to be on one or the other. [*The Mind in the Making*]

ROBERT ROBINSON

1 Certain people are born with natural false teeth. [BBC radio programme, *Stop the Week*, 1977]

2 The national dish of America is menus. [BBC TV programme, *Robinson's Travels*, Aug. 1977]

ANDRÉ ROCHE

3 Mount Everest is very easy to climb, only just a little too high. [*Observer*, 'Sayings of the Week', 25 Jan. 1953]

JAMES W. RODGERS

4 [When asked if he had any last request before he was shot] Why yes – a bullet proof vest! [Quoted in Jonathon Green, *Famous Last Words*]

JOHN RODKER

5 It [*The Good Soldier*] is the finest French novel in the English language. [Quoted by Ford Madox Ford in a dedicatory letter to the novel]

JOSÉ RODÓ

6 Democratic equality is the most efficacious instrument of spiritual selection. [*Ariel*]

THEODORE ROETHKE

7 Over this damp grave I speak the words of my love: / I, with no rights in this matter, / Neither father nor lover. [*Elegy for Jane*]

8 I wake to sleep, and take my waking slow. / I learn by going where I have to go. [*The Waking*]

WILL ROGERS

9 We know lots of things we used to dident know but we don't know any way to prevent em happening. [In letter to Will Durant, on eve of the New Deal, 1931]

10 A comedian can only last till he either takes himself serious or his audience takes him serious. [Newspaper article 1931]

11 I was born because it was a habit in those days, people dident know anything else. [*Autobiography*, Ch. 1]

12 Communism is like prohibition, it's a good idea but it won't work. [*Ib*. Nov. 1927]

13 I never was much on this Book reading, for it takes em too long to describe the colour of the eyes of all the Characters. [*Ib*. 14]

14 England elects a Labour Government. When a man goes in for politics over here, he has no time to labour, and any man that labours has no time to fool with politics. Over there politics is an obligation; over here it's a business. [*Ib*.]

15 You can't say civilization don't advance, however, for in every war they kill you a new way. [*Ib*.]

16 It's great to be great but it's greater to be human. [*Ib*. 15]

17 Half our life is spent trying to find something to do with the time we have rushed through life trying to save. [*Ib*.]

18 The movies are the only business where you can go out front and applaud yourself. [Quoted in Daniel Boorstin, *The Image*, Ch. 1]

19 See what'll happen to you if you don't stop biting your finger-nails. [On the Venus de Milo. Quoted in Bennett Cerf, *Shake Well Before Using*. Elsewhere ascribed to Noël Coward]

20 Any nation is heathen that ain't strong enough to punch you in the jaw ... Missionaries teach em not only to serve the Lord but run a Ford car ... then the American agent sells em one ... You take religion backed up by Commerce and it's awful hard for a heathen to overcome. [From 'A Rogers Thesaurus', *Saturday Review*, 25 Aug. 1962]

21 Being a hero is about the shortest-lived profession on earth. [*Ib*.]

22 Coolidge is a better example of evolution than either Bryan or Darrow, for he knows when not to talk, which is the biggest asset the monkey possesses over the human. [*Ib*.]

1 I don't make jokes – I just watch the government and report the facts. [*Ib.*]

2 I had just enough white in me to make my honesty questionable. [*Ib.*]

3 It [Income Tax] has made more liars out of the American people than Golf. [*Ib.*]

4 Once you are a showman you are plum ruined for manual labour again. [*Ib.*]

5 The more you read about politics, you got to admit that each party is worse than the other. [*Ib.*]

6 They got him [Pancho Villa] in the morning editions, but the afternoon ones let him get away. [*Ib.*]

7 The United States never lost a war or won a conference. [*Ib.*]

8 Everybody is ignorant, only on different subjects. [*The Illiterate Digest*]

9 Everything is funny as long as it's happening to somebody else. [*Ib.*]

10 My folks didn't come over on the *Mayflower*, but they were there to meet the boat. [Quoted in *Treasury of Humorous Quotations*]

11 Our country has plenty of good five-cent cigars, but the trouble is they charge fifteen cents for them. [Quoted in *ib.*]

12 So live that you wouldn't be ashamed to sell the family parrot to the town gossip. [Quoted in *ib.*]

ROMAIN ROLLAND

13 It's the artist's job to create sunshine when there isn't any. [*Jean Christophe: La Foire sur la Place*]

SIR HUMPHREY ROLLESTON

14 First they [physicians] get *on*, then they get *honour*, then they get *honest*. [Quoted in David Ogilvy, *Confessions of an Advertising Man*]

C. H. ROLPH

15 Queen Victoria and I just missed each other. Between 22 January 1901 when she died at Osborne House, and 23 August in the same year when I was born in what was then called a 'dwelling' on the site of the old Marshalsea Prison, English history presents a disfiguring gap of seven months. [*Living Twice*, Pt I, Ch. 1]

SIGMUND ROMBERG

16 A love song is just a caress set to music. [Quoted in Nat Shapiro, *An Encyclopedia of Quotations about Music*]

ELEANOR ROOSEVELT

17 Remember, no one can make you feel inferior without your consent. [Quoted in Laurence J. Peter, *Peter's Quotations*]

FRANKLIN D. ROOSEVELT

18 This generation of Americans has a rendezvous with destiny [Speech accepting renomination, 27 Jun. 1936]

19 We have always known that heedless self-interest was bad morals; we know now that it is bad economics. [Second Inaugural Address, 20 Jan. 1937]

20 The change in the moral climate of America. [*Ib.*]

21 Quarantine the aggressors. [Speech at Chicago, 5 Oct. 1937]

22 I have told you once and I will tell you again – your boys will not be sent into any foreign wars. [Election Speech, 1940]

23 The trouble is that when you sit around a table with a Britisher he usually gets 80 per cent of the deal and you get what's left. [Quoted in John Morton Blum, *From the Morgenthau Diaries*, Vol. I: *Years of Crisis, 1928–1938*]

24 The best immediate defence of the United States is the success of Great Britain defending itself. [At press conference, 17 Dec. 1940. Quoted in Winston S. Churchill, *Their Finest Hour*, Ch. 28]

25 It is fun to be in the same decade with you. [To Churchill, in answer to congratulations on his 60th birthday. Quoted in Winston S. Churchill, *The Hinge of Fate*, Ch. 4]

1 Stalin hates the guts of all your top people. He thinks he likes me better, and I hope he will continue to do so. [Quoted in *ib*. 11]

2 Defeat of Germany means the defeat of Japan, probably without firing a shot or losing a life. [Quoted in *ib*. 25]

3 Never before have we had so little time in which to do so much. [Radio address, 23 Feb. 1942]

4 The only limit to our realization of to-morrow will be our doubts of today. [Address written for Jefferson Day dinner to have been given 13 Apr. 1945. He died on the 12th]

THEODORE ROOSEVELT

5 I took the Canal Zone and let Congress debate, and while the debate goes on the Canal does too. [Speech, 23 Mar. 1911]

6 One of our defects as a nation is a tendency to use what have been called 'weasel words'. When a weasel sucks eggs the meat is sucked out of the egg. If you use a 'weasel word' after another there is nothing left of the other. [Speech, 1916. Quoted in Lewis C. Henry, *Best Quotations for All Occasions*]

7 There can be no fifty-fifty Americanism in this country. There is room here for only one hundred per cent Americanism. [Speech at Saratoga, 19 Jul. 1918]

8 Kings and such like are just as funny as politicians. [Quoted in John Dos Passos, *Mr Wilson's War*, Ch. 1, sect. 1]

NED ROREM

9 To see itself through, music must have an idea or magic. The best has both. Music with neither dies young, though sometimes rich. [*Pure Contraption*]

BILLY ROSE

10 Does the Spearmint Lose Its Flavour on the Bedpost Overnight? [Title of song]

11 Me and My Shadow [Title of Song. Music by Al Jolson and Dave Dreyer]

BERNARD ROSENBERG

12 Radical: A person whose left hand does not know what his other left hand is doing. [Quoted in Laurence J. Peter, *Peter's Quotations*]

ISAAC ROSENBERG

13 The darkness crumbles away – / It is the same old druid Time as ever. [*Break of Day in the Trenches*]

14 Droll rat, they would shoot you if they knew / Your cosmopolitan sympathies / (And God knows what antipathies). [*Ib*]

15 Earth has waited for them, / All the time of their growth / Fretting for their decay: / Now she has them at last. [*Dead Man's Dump*]

16 Death could drop from the dark / As easily as song. [*Returning, We hear the Larks*]

JULIUS ROSENBERG

17 We are innocent. That is the whole truth. To forsake this truth is to pay too high a price even for the priceless gift of life. For life thus purchased we could not live out in dignity. [In his mercy petition to President Eisenhower, 1953, quoted in Jonathon Green, *Famous Last Words*]

EUGEN ROSENSTOCK-HUESSY

18 He who believes in nothing still needs a girl to believe in him. [Quoted in W. H. Auden, *A Certain World*]

MRS ANNA ROSS (AMANDA ROS)

19 I don't believe in publishers who wish to butter their bannocks on both sides while they'll hardly allow an author to smell treacle. I consider they are too grabby together and like Methodists they love to keep the Sabbath and everything else they can lay their hands on. [Letter to Lord Ponsonby, 1910]

HAROLD W. ROSS

20 You can exclude noise by soundproofing your mind. [Quoted in James Thurber, *The Years with Ross*]

1 Is Moby Dick the whale or the man? [Quoted in *ib.*]

2 I don't want you to think I'm not incoherent. [Quoted in *ib.*]

3 Thurber is the greatest unlistener I know. [Quoted in *ib.*]

4 WOMAN AT ZOO: Is that a male or a female hippopotamus? KEEPER: Madam, I don't see how that could interest anybody except another hippopotamus. [Tale of unknown origin, told by H. R., quoted in *ib.*]

5 I understand the hero keeps getting in bed with women, and the war wasn't fought that way. [Comment on Hemingway's *A Farewell to Arms*. Quoted in *ib.*]

6 I've never been in there [the Louvre] . . . but there are only three things to see, and I've seen colour reproductions of all of them. [Quoted in *ib.*]

LILLIAN ROSS

7 He was almost the only man in Chasen's [restaurant] who was not at that moment looking around at someone other than the person he was talking to. [*Picture*, 'Throw the Little Old Lady Down the Stairs!']

8 'The music isn't right,' he says. 'It's a picture about France,' he said, 'so I want a lot of French horns.' [*Ib.*]

JEAN ROSTAND

9 To be adult is to be alone. [*Thoughts of a Biologist*]

PHILIP ROTH

10 Since I was a little girl I always wanted to be Very Decent to People. Other little girls wanted to be nurses and pianists. They were less dissembling. [*Letting Go*, Pt I, Ch. 1]

11 My first impression of her had been clear and sharp: profession – student; inclinations – neurotic. [*Ib.*]

12 It's the little questions from women about tappets that finally push men over the edge. [*Ib.*]

13 It's a family joke that when I was a tiny child I turned from the window out of which I was watching a snowstorm, and hopefully asked, 'Momma, do we believe in winter?' [*Portnoy's Complaint*]

14 Doctor, my doctor, what do you say – let's put the id back in yid! [*Ib.*]

15 A Jewish man with parents alive is a fifteen-year-old boy, and will remain a fifteen-year-old boy till they die. [*Ib.*]

LORD ROTHERMERE

16 Hats off to France. [Title of article in the *Daily Mail*, 1923, supporting French occupation of the Ruhr]

GEORGES ROUAULT

17 For me, painting is a way to forget life. It is a cry in the night, a strangled laugh. [Quoted in Laurence J. Peter, *Peter's Quotations*]

M. E. ROURKE

18 And when I told them how beautiful you are / They didn't believe me! They didn't believe me! [Song: *They Didn't Believe Me*. Music by Jerome D. Kern]

ROWAN AND MARTIN'S LAUGH-IN

19 Sock it to me. [Running gag in TV comedy series]

EDWARD ROWLAND

20 A mademoiselle from Armenteers, / She hasn't been kissed for forty years, / Hinky, dinky, par-lee-voo. [Song: *Mademoiselle from Armentières*]

RICHARD ROWLAND

21 The lunatics have taken over the asylum. [Comment when United Artists was taken over by Chaplin, Pickford, Fairbanks and Griffith. Quoted in Leslie Halliwell, *The Filmgoer's Book of Quotes*]

287

A. L. ROWSE

1 Burnings of people and (what was more valuable) works of art. [Quoted in H. R. Trevor-Roper, *Historical Essays*]

PAUL RUBENS

2 She was a miller's daughter, / And lived beside the mill; / Yes, there were flies on the water / But she was flier still! [Song from *Three Little Maids*]

3 We Don't Want To Lose You But We Think You Ought To Go. [Title of song]

MICHAEL RUBINSTEIN

4 To be and not to be, that is the answer. [In conversation]

DANNY LA RUE

5 The essence of any blue material is timing. If you sit on it, it becomes vulgar. [Quoted in P. and J. Holton, *Quote and Unquote*]

SIR STEVEN RUNCIMAN

6 Unlike Christianity, which preached a peace that it never achieved, Islam unashamedly came with a sword. [*A History of the Crusades*, 'The First Crusade']

DAMON RUNYON

7 Little Isadore reaches out and spears himself a big hunk of my gefillte fish with his fingers, but I overlook this, as I am using the only knife at the table. [*Furthermore*, 'Butch Minds the Baby']

8 Sonny tells him to be sure and be at the track this day to bet on a certain horse in the fifth race, because it is nothing but a boat race, and everything in it is as stiff as a plank, except this certain horse. [*Ib.* 'The Lemon Drop Kid']

9 Now of course this is strictly the old ackamarackus, as the Lemon Drop Kid cannot even spell arthritis, let alone have it. [*Ib.*]

10 Any time you see him he is generally by himself because being by himself is not apt to cost him anything. [*Ib.* 'Little Miss Marker']

11 If this little doll is sitting in your joint all afternoon ... the best thing to do right now is to throw a feed into her as the chances are her stomach thinks her throat is cut. [*Ib.*]

12 Personally, I consider a taxicab much more convenient and less expensive than an old-fashioned victoria if you wish to get to some place, but of course guys and dolls engaged in a little offhand guzzling never wish to get any place in particular, or at least not soon. [*Ib.* 'Princess O'Hara']

13 The way you give a hot foot is to sneak up behind some guy who is standing around thinking of not much, and stick a paper match in his shoe between the sole and the upper along about where his little toe ought to be, and then light the match. [*Ib.* 'Sense of Humour']

14 My boy ... always try to rub up against money, for if you rub up against money long enough, some of it may rub off on you. [*Ib.* 'A Very Honourable Guy']

15 All she has to do is to walk around and about Georgie White's stage with only a few light bandages on, and everybody considers her very beautiful, especially from the neck down. [*Ib.*]

16 Even Mr Justin Veezee is not so old-fashioned as to believe any doll will go to his apartment just to look at etchings nowadays. [*Ib.* 'What, No Butler?']

17 Charlotte is not such a doll as cares to spend more than one or two years looking at the pictures on the wall. [*More than Somewhat*, 'The Brain Goes Home']

18 Sam the Gonoph is by no means a college guy. In fact, the nearest Sam ever came to college is once when he was passing through the yard belonging to the Princetons, but Sam is on the fly at the time as a gendarme is after him, so he does not really see much of the college. [*Ib.* 'Hold 'em, Yale!']

19 'In fact,' Sam the Gonoph says, 'I long ago came to the conclusion that all life is six to five against.' [*Ib.* 'A Nice Price']

1 Angie the Ox is an importer himself, besides enjoying a splendid trade in other lines, including artichokes and extortion. [*Ib.* 'The Old Doll's House']

2 And you cannot tell by the way a party looks or how he lives in this town, if he has any scratch, because many a party who is around in automobiles, and wearing good clothes, and chucking quite a swell is nothing but a phonus bolonus and does not have any real scratch whatever. [*Ib.* 'The Snatching of Bookie Bob']

3 If I have all the tears that are shed on Broadway by guys in love, I will have enough salt water to start an opposition to the Atlantic and Pacific, with enough left over to run the Great Salt Lake out of business. [*Ib.* 'Tobias the Terrible']

4 I judge from the sound that he gets his kiss, and it is a very large kiss indeed, with the cut-out open. [*Ib.* 'Breach of Promise']

5 She is a smart old broad. It is a pity she is so nefarious. [*Runyon à la carte*, 'Broadway Incident']

6 At such an hour the sinners are still in bed resting up from their sinning of the night before, so they will be in good shape for more sinning a little later on. [*Ib.* 'The Idyll of Miss Sarah Brown']

7 I quietly give Girondel a boff over his pimple with a blackjack and flatten him like a welcome mat. [*Ib.* 'A Light in France']

8 I step over to his table and give him a medium hello, and he looks up and gives me a medium hello right back, for, to tell the truth, Maury and I are never bosom friends. [*Ib.*]

9 If I am interested in the kissing and hugging business, I will most certainly take my business to Marie, especially as she speaks English, and you will not have to waste time with the sign language. [*Ib.*]

10 I remarked that his eyes were open so he must be awake. 'The one on your side is,' said a backer, 'but the one on the other side is closed. He is sleeping one-eyed.' [*Short Takes*, 'Bed-Warmers']

11 I once knew a chap who had a system of just hanging the baby on the clothes line to dry and he was greatly admired by his fellow citizens for having discovered a wonderful innovation on changing a diaper. [*Ib.* 'Diaper Dexterity']

12 A free-loader is a confirmed guest. He is the man who is always willing to come to dinner. [*Ib.* 'Free-Loading Ethics']

13 I do not approve of guys using false pretences on dolls, except, of course, when nothing else will do [*Take it Easy*, 'It comes up Mud']

14 These citizens are always willing to bet that what Nicely-Nicely dies of will be over-feeding and never anything small like pneumonia, for Nicely-Nicely is known far and wide as a character who dearly loves to commit eating. [*Ib.* 'Lonely Heart']

15 He is without strict doubt a Hoorah Henry, and he is generally figured as nothing but a lob as far as doing anything useful in this world is concerned. [*Ib.* 'Tight Shoes']

16 Much as he is opposed to lawbreaking, he is not bigoted about it. [Attr.]

DEAN RUSK

17 I wouldn't make the slightest concession for moral leadership. It's much overrated. [Said in 1962. Quoted in D. Halberstam, *The Best and the Brightest*]

18 We're eyeball to eyeball, and the other fellow just blinked. [On the Cuban missile crisis, Oct. 1962. Quoted in Eric de Mauny, *Russian Prospect*]

BERTRAND RUSSELL

19 I was told that the Chinese said they would bury me by the Western Lake and build a shrine to my memory. I have some slight regret that this did not happen, as I might have become a god, which would have been very *chic* for an atheist. [*The Autobiography of Bertrand Russell*, Vol. II: *1914–1944*, Ch. 3]

20 One of the symptoms of approaching nervous breakdown is the belief that one's work is terribly important. If I

were a medical man, I should prescribe a holiday to any patient who considered his work important. [*Ib.* 5]

1 Of all forms of caution, caution in love is perhaps the most fatal to true happiness. [*Ib.* 12]

2 One of the great drawbacks to self-centred passions is that they afford so little variety in life. The man who loves only himself cannot, it is true, be accused of promiscuity in his affections, but he is bound in the end to suffer intolerable boredom from the inevitable sameness of the object of his devotion. [*Ib.* 17]

3 Man is not a solitary animal, and so long as social life survives, self-realization cannot be the supreme principle of ethics. [*History of Western Philosophy*, 'Romanticism']

4 Mathematics, rightly viewed, possesses not only truth, but supreme beauty – a beauty cold and austere, like that of sculpture. [*Mysticism and Logic*, Ch. 4]

5 The solution of the difficulties which formerly surrounded the mathematical infinite is probably the greatest achievement of which our age can boast. [*Ib.*]

6 Mathematics may be defined as the subject in which we never know what we are talking about, nor whether what we are saying is true. [*Ib.* 4]

7 Pure mathematics consists entirely of assertions to the effect that, if such and such a proposition is true of *anything*, then such and such another proposition is true of that thing. It is essential not to discuss whether the first proposition is really true, and not to mention what the anything is, of which it is supposed to be true. [*Ib.* 5]

8 Organic life, we are told, has developed gradually from the protozoon to the philosopher, and this development, we are assured, is indubitably an advance. Unfortunately it is the philosopher, not the protozoon, who gives us this assurance. [*Ib.* 6]

9 Better the world should perish than that I or any other human being should believe a lie ... that is the religion of thought, in whose scorching flames the dross of the world is being burnt away. [*Ib.* 10]

10 Only on the firm foundation of unyielding despair can the soul's edifice henceforth be built. [Quoted in Sagittarius and George, *The Perpetual Pessimist*]

11 Matter ... a convenient formula for describing what happens where it isn't. [*An Outline of Philosophy*]

12 The megalomaniac differs from the narcissist by the fact that he wishes to be powerful rather than charming, and seeks to be feared rather than loved. To this type belong many lunatics and most of the great men of history. [*The Conquest of Happiness*, Ch. 1]

13 Suspicion of one's own motives is especially necessary for the philanthropist and the executive. [*Ib.* 8]

14 What men really want is not knowledge but certainty. [Quoted by G. M. Carstairs, *Listener*, 30 Jul. 1964]

15 ... the nuns who never take a bath without wearing a bathrobe all the time. When asked why, since no man can see them, they reply 'Oh, but you forget the good God.' [*The Basic Writings*, Pt II, Ch. 7]

16 All intellectuals should suffer a certain amount of persecution as early in life as possible. Not too much. That is bad for them. But a certain amount. [Quoted in Kenneth Harris, *Kenneth Harris Talking To*: Bertrand Russell]

17 People don't seem to realize that it takes time and effort and preparation to think. Statesmen are far too busy making speeches to think. [*Ib.*]

18 There's a Bible on that shelf there. But I keep it next to Voltaire – poison and antidote. [*Ib.*]

19 Hume seems to me to have been the only one of the great philosophers who wanted to get at the truth. The rest all wanted to get at something else, something that would flatter humanity, or suit their prejudices, or refute their enemies. [*Ib.*]

20 Patriots always talk of dying for their country, and never of killing for their country. [Attr.]

1 I think that bad philosophers may have a certain influence, good philosophers, never. [*Observer*, 'Sayings of the Week', 24 Apr. 1955]

2 The collection of prejudices which is called political philosophy is useful provided that it is not called philosophy. [*Observer*, 'Sayings of the Year', 1962]

3 Many people would sooner die than think. In fact they do. [Quoted as epigraph in A. Flew, *Thinking About Thinking*]

4 [Of the nuclear confrontation of the super-powers] You may reasonably expect a man to walk a tightrope safely for ten minutes; it would be unreasonable to do so without accident for two hundred years. [Quoted in D. Bagley, *The Tightrope Men*]

5 The stars are in one's brain. [Quoted in R. D. Laing, *Politics of Experience*, Ch. 1]

6 The average man's opinions are much less foolish than they would be if he thought for himself. [Attr.]

7 Few people can be happy unless they hate some other person, nation or creed. [Attr.]

LORD RUTHERFORD

8 Well, I made the wave, didn't I? [In answer to the jibe: 'Lucky fellow, Rutherford, always on the crest of the wave.' Quoted in C. P. Snow, *The Two Cultures and the Scientific Revolution*]

GILBERT RYLE

9 So too Plato was, in my view, a very unreliable Platonist. He was too much of a philosopher to think that anything he had said was the last word. It was left to his disciples to identify his footmarks with his destination. [*Dilemmas*, Ch. 1]

10 Philosophy is the replacement of category-habits by category-disciplines. [*The Concept of Mind*, Introduction]

11 Many people can talk sense with concepts but cannot talk sense about them; they know by practice how to operate with concepts, anyhow inside their chosen fields, but they cannot state the logical regulations governing their use. They are like people who know their way about their own parish, but cannot construct or read a map of it, much less of the region, or continent in which their parish lies. [*Ib.*]

12 A myth is, of course, not a fairy story. It is the presentation of facts belonging to one category in the idioms appropriate to another. To explode a myth is accordingly not to deny the facts but to re-allocate them. [*Ib.*]

13 The dogma of the Ghost in the Machine. [*Ib.* Ch. 1]

S

VICTORIA SACKVILLE-WEST

1 They had a passion for getting something for nothing. Every blackberry in the hedgerow was an agony to Lavinia until she had bottled it. [*All Passion Spent*, Ch. 1]

2 The country habit has me by the heart, / For he's bewitched for ever who has seen, / Not with his eyes but with his vision, Spring / Flow down the woods and stipple leaves with sun. [*The Land*, 'Winter']

3 Forget not bees in winter, though they sleep, / For winter's big with summer in her womb. [*Ip*. 'Spring']

4 Only the moon shall look behind the hedge, / Confederate of youth. [*Ib.* 'Summer']

5 Birds moult, and in the leafy copses hide, / And summer makes a silence after spring. [*Ib.*]

6 All craftsmen share a knowledge. They have held / Reality down fluttering to a bench. [*Ib.*]

7 I saw the round moon rise above the pines, / One quiet planet prick the greening west, / As goats came leaping up the stony crest / And the crook'd goatherd moved between the rocks. [*Ib.* 'Autumn']

MICHAEL SADLEIR

8 Fanny by Gaslight. [Title of book]

MORT SAHL

9 It is said the President [Kennedy] is willing to laugh at himself. That is fine. But when is he going to extend the privilege to us? [Quoted in V. Lasky, *J.F.K.: The Man and the Myth*]

10 People tell me there are a lot of guys like me, which doesn't explain why I'm lonely. [Quoted in E. Lax, *Woody Allen and his Comedy*, Ch. 12]

11 [Of President Nixon] Would you buy a second-hand car from this man? [Attr.]

ANTOINE DE SAINT-EXUPÉRY

12 Grown-ups never understand anything for themselves, and it is tiresome for children to be always and forever explaining things to them. [*The Little Prince*, Ch. 1]

13 It is such a secret place, the land of tears. [*Ib.* 7]

14 It is much more difficult to judge oneself than to judge others. [*Ib.* 10]

15 It is only with the heart that one can see rightly; what is essential is invisible to the eye. [*Ib.* 21]

16 You become responsible, forever, for what you have tamed. You are responsible for your rose. [*Ib.*]

17 Philosophy is a battle against the bewitchment of our intelligence by means of language. [Attr.]

'SAKI' (H. H. MUNRO)

18 I believe I once considerably scandalized her by declaring that clear soup was a more important factor in life than a clear conscience. [*The Blind Spot*]

19 By insisting on having your bottle pointing to the north when the cork is being drawn, and calling the waiter Max, you may induce an impression on your guests which hours of laboured boasting might be powerless to achieve. For this purpose, however, the guests must be chosen as carefully as the wine. [*The Chaplet*]

20 A little inaccuracy sometimes saves tons of explanation. [*The Comments of Moung Ka*]

1 His hair and forehead furnished a recessional note in a personality that was in all other respects obtrusive and assertive. [*Cousin Teresa*]

2 One of those strapping florid girls that go so well with autumn scenery or Christmas decorations in church. [*Esmé*]

3 Waldo is one of those people who would be enormously improved by death. [*The Feast of Nemesis*]

4 To say that anything was a quotation was an excellent method, in Eleanor's eyes, for withdrawing it from discussion. [*The Jesting of Arlington Stringham*]

5 The censorious said that she slept in a hammock and understood Yeats's poems, but her family denied both stories. [*Ib.*]

6 The people of Crete unfortunately make more history than they can consume locally. [*Ib.*]

7 All decent people live beyond their incomes nowadays, and those who aren't respectable live beyond other people's. A few gifted individuals manage to do both. [*The Match-Maker*]

8 His socks compelled one's attention without losing one's respect. [*Ministers of Grace*]

9 Scandal is merely the compassionate allowance which the gay make to the humdrum. [*Reginald at the Carlton*]

10 The young have aspirations that never come to pass, the old have reminiscences of what never happened. [*Ib.*]

11 There may have been disillusionments in the lives of the medieval saints, but they would scarcely have been better pleased if they could have foreseen that their names would be associated nowadays chiefly with racehorses and the cheaper clarets. [*Ib.*]

12 Every reformation must have its victims. You can't expect the fatted calf to share the enthusiasm of the angels over the prodigal's return. [*Reginald on the Academy*]

13 She took to telling the truth; she said she was forty-two and five months. It may have been pleasing to the angels, but her elder sister was not gratified. [*Reginald on Besetting Sins*]

14 People may say what they like about the decay of Christianity; the religious system that produced green Chartreuse can never really die. [*Reginald on Christmas Presents*]

15 Even the Hooligan was probably invented in China centuries before we thought of him. [*Reginald on House-Parties*]

16 I think she must have been very strictly brought up, she's so desperately anxious to do the wrong thing correctly. [*Reginald on Worries*]

17 Her frocks are built in Paris, but she wears them with a strong English accent. [*Ib.*]

18 I always say beauty is only sin deep. [*Reginald's Choir Treat*]

19 Temptation came to him, in middle age, tentatively and without insistence, like a neglected butcher-boy who asks for a Christmas box in February for no more hopeful reason than that he didn't get one in December. [*The Reticence of Lady Anne*]

20 The aunt of Clovis ... churned away like a Nile steamer, with a long brown ripple of Pekingese spaniel trailing in her wake. [*The Talking-out of Tarrington*]

21 The woman who can sacrifice a clean unspoiled penny stamp is probably unborn. [*The Unbearable Bassington*]

22 To see her standing at the top of an expensively horticultured staircase receiving her husband's guests was rather like watching an animal performing on a music-hall stage. One always tells oneself that the animal likes it, and one always knows that it doesn't. [*Ib.*]

23 The English have a proverb: 'Conscience makes cowboys of us all.' [*Wratislav*]

24 There's nothing in Christianity or Buddhism that quite matches the sympathetic unselfishness of an oyster. [Quoted in L. L. Levinson, *Bartlett's Unfamiliar Quotations*]

'SAKI' (H. H. MUNRO) and CHARLES MAUDE

1 My father believed in smiting sin wherever he found it; what I complained of was that he always seemed to find it in the same place. [*The Watched Pot*, Ch. 1]

2 Woman is a belated survival from a primeval age of struggle and competition; that is why, the world over, you find all the superfluous dust and worry being made by the gentler sex. [*Ib.* 3]

J. D. SALINGER

3 Sex is something I really don't understand too hot. You never know *where* the hell you are. I keep making up these sex rules for myself, and then I break them right away. [*The Catcher in the Rye*, Ch. 9]

4 I was about half in love with her by the time we sat down. That's the thing about girls. Every time they do something pretty, even if they're not much to look at, or even if they're sort of stupid, you fall half in love with them, and then you never know *where* the hell you are. [*Ib.* 10]

5 He looked like the kind of a guy that wouldn't talk to you much unless he wanted something off you. He had a lousy personality. [*Ib.* 11]

6 The thing is, it's really hard to be roommates with people if your suitcases are much better than theirs – if yours are really good ones and theirs aren't. You think if they're intelligent and all, the other person, and have a good sense of humour, that they don't give a damn whose suitcases are better, but they do. [*Ib.* 15]

7 They didn't act like people and they didn't act like actors. It's hard to explain. They acted more like they knew they were celebrities and all. I mean they were good, but they were *too* good. [*Ib.* 17]

8 He was the kind of phoney that have to give themselves *room* when they answer somebody's question. He stepped back, and stepped right on the lady's foot behind him. [*Ib.*]

9 Take most people, they're crazy about cars . . . and if they get a brand-new car already they start thinking about trading it in for one that's even newer. I don't even like *old* cars. I mean they don't even interest me. I'd rather have a goddam horse. A horse is at least *human*, for God's sake. [*Ib.*]

10 The trouble with girls is, if they like a boy, no matter how big a bastard he is, they'll say he has an inferiority complex, and if they *don't* like him, no matter how nice a guy is, or how big an inferiority complex he has, they'll say he's conceited. Even smart girls do it. [*Ib.* 18]

11 Sally said I was a sacrilegious atheist. I probably am. The thing Jesus *really* would've liked would be the guy that plays the kettle drums in the orchestra. [*Ib.*]

12 For Esmé, With Love and Squalor. [Title of story]

13 Poetry, surely, is a crisis, perhaps the only actionable one we can call our own. [*Seymour: An Introduction*]

14 Probably passed on, these many years, of an overdose of garlic, the way all New York barbers eventually go. [*Ib.*]

15 A confessional passage has probably never been written that didn't stink a little bit of the writer's pride in having given up his pride. [*Ib.*]

16 One of the thousand reasons I quit going to the theatre when I was about twenty was that I resented like hell filing out of the theatre just because some playwright was forever slamming down his silly curtain. [*Ib.*]

LORD SALISBURY

17 [Of Iain MacLeod and other young Tories] Too clever by a half. [Attr.]

HARRY SALTZMAN

18 [When Ken Russell told him he would like to make a film on Tchaikovsky] You can't do Tchaikovsky . . . Dimitri Tiomkin's gonna do that, *and he's already writing the music.* [Interview with Russell in J. Baxter, *An Appalling Talent*]

ANTHONY SAMPSON

1 Members rise from CMG (known sometimes in Whitehall as 'Call me God') to the KCMG ('Kindly Call me God') to ... the GCMG ('God Calls me God'). [*Anatomy of Britain*, Ch. 18]

GEORGE SAMPSON

2 The well-meaning people who talk about education as if it were a substance distributable by coupon in large or small quantities never exhibit any understanding of the truth that you cannot teach anybody anything that he does not want to learn. [*Seven Essays*]

LORD SAMUEL

3 To expect us to feel 'humble' in the presence of astronomical dimensions merely because they are big, is a kind of cosmic snobbery ... what is significant is mind. [*Belief and Action*]

4 Democracy is like a hobby-horse: it will carry you nowhere unless you use your own legs. [*Observer*, 'Sayings of the Week', 27 Mar. 1927]

5 Without doubt the greatest injury ... was done by basing morals on myth, for sooner or later myth is recognized for what it is, and disappears. Then morality loses the foundation on which it has been built. [*Romanes Lecture*, 1947]

6 Hansard is history's ear, already listening. [*Observer*, 'Sayings of the Week', 18 Dec. 1949]

7 A library is thought in cold storage. [In his *A Book of Quotations*]

8 A friend in need is a friend to be avoided. [Quoted in *Sunday Telegraph Magazine*, 27 Nov. 1977]

9 A difficulty for every solution. [Of the Civil Service. Attr.]

CARL SANDBURG

10 The people will live on. / The learning and blundering people will live on. / They will be tricked and sold and again sold / And go back to the nourishing earth for rootholds. [*The People, Yes*]

11 Sometime they'll give a war and nobody will come. [*Ib.*]

12 Hog Butcher for the World. [Of Chicago in *Chicago*]

13 Poetry is the achievement of the synthesis of hyacinths and biscuits. ['Poetry Considered', in the *Atlantic Monthly*, Mar. 1923]

14 I am an idealist. I don't know where I'm going but I'm on my way. [Quoted in Laurence J. Peter, *Peter's Quotations*]

GEORGE SANTAYANA

15 The working of great institutions is mainly the result of a vast mass of routine, petty malice, self interest, carelessness, and sheer mistake. Only a residual fraction is thought. [*The Crime of Galileo*]

16 The young man who has not wept is a savage, and the old man who will not laugh is a fool. [*Dialogues in Limbo*, Ch. 3]

17 The barbarian is the man who regards his passions as their own excuse for being; who does not domesticate them either by understanding their cause or by conceiving their ideal goal. [*Egotism in German Philosophy*]

18 As the Latin languages are not composed of two diverse elements, as English is of Latin and German, so the Latin mind does not have two spheres of sentiment, one vulgar and the other sublime. All changes are variations on a single key, which is the key of intelligence. [*Interpretations of Poetry and Religion*]

19 English genius is anti-professional; its affinities are with amateurs. [Quoted in Rayne Kruger, *Good-bye Dolly Gray*, Postscript]

20 Life is not a spectacle or a feast; it is a predicament. [Quoted in Sagittarius and George, *The Perpetual Pessimist*]

21 The truth is cruel, but it can be loved, and it makes free those who have loved it. [Introduction to Spinoza's *Ethics*]

22 Those who do not remember the past are condemned to relive it. [*The Life of Reason*, Vol. I, Ch. 12]

1 Happiness is the only sanction of life; where happiness fails, existence remains a mad lamentable experiment. [*Reason in Common Sense*, Ch. 10]

2 Art supplies constantly to contemplation what nature seldom affords in concrete experience – the union of life and peace. [*Ib.* 4]

3 Trust the man who hesitates in his speech and is quick and steady in action, but beware of long arguments and long beards. [*Soliloquies in England*, 'The British Character']

4 The truth, which is a standard for the naturalist, for the poet is only a stimulus. [*Ib.* 'Ideas']

5 Nothing you can lose by dying is half so precious as the readiness to die, which is man's charter of nobility. [*Ib.* 'Tipperary']

6 My instinct is to go and stand under the cross with the monks and crusaders, far away from these Jews and Protestants who adore the world and who govern it. [*Ib.* 'War Shrines']

7 If all the arts aspire to the condition of music, all the sciences aspire to the condition of mathematics. [*Observer*, 'Sayings of the Week', 4 Mar. 1928]

JEAN-PAUL SARTRE

8 I hate victims who respect their executioners. [*Altona*, Act I]

9 There are two ways of destroying a people. Either condemn them *en bloc* or force them to repudiate the leaders they adopted. The second is the worse. [*Ib.*]

10 When one does nothing, one believes oneself responsible for everything. [*Ib.*]

11 An American is either a Jew, or an anti-Semite, unless he is both at the same time. [*Ib.*]

12 HUGO: Not all means are good.
HOEDERER: All means are good as long as they work. [*Crime Passionnel*, Tableau 5, sc. iii]

13 Human life begins on the other side of despair. [*The Flies*, Act III, sc. ii]

14 Hell is other people. [*Huis clos*, sc. v (English title: *In Camera*)]

15 I don't think the profession of historian fits a man for psychological analysis. In our work, we have to deal only with simple feelings to which we give generic names such as Ambition and Interest. [*Nausea*, Monday, 29 Jan. 1932. Trans. by Robert Baldick]

16 Three o'clock is always too late or too early for anything you want to do. [*Ib.* Friday]

17 I think they do that to pass the time, nothing more. But time is too large, it refuses to let itself be filled up. [*Ib.* 5.30]

18 A man is always a teller of tales, he lives surrounded by his stories and the stories of others, he sees everything that happens to him through them; and he tries to live his life as if he were recounting it. [*Ib.* Saturday, noon]

19 You get the impression that their normal condition is silence and that speech is a slight fever which attacks them now and then. [*Ib.* Sunday]

20 Doctors, priests, magistrates, and officers know men as thoroughly as if they had made them. [*Ib.* Shrove Tuesday]

21 Things are entirely what they appear to be and *behind them* . . . there is nothing. [*Ib.* Monday]

22 My thought is *me*: that is why I can't stop. I exist by what I think . . . and I can't prevent myself from thinking. [*Ib.*]

23 Existence is a repletion which man can never abandon. [*Ib.* Six o'clock in the evening]

24 At the same time, I learnt that you always lose. Only the bastards think they win. [*Ib.* Tuesday at Bouville]

25 They think about Tomorrow, in other words simply about another today; towns have only one day at their disposal which comes back exactly the same every morning. [*Ib.*]

26 I know perfectly well that I don't want to do anything; to do something is to create existence – and there's quite enough existence as it is. [*Ib.* One hour later]

27 If a Jew is fascinated by Christians it is not because of their virtues, which he

values little, but because they represent anonymity, humanity without race. [*Anti-Semite and Jew*]

1 Man is a useless passion. [*Being and Nothingness*]

2 In reality, people read because they want to write. Anyway, reading is a sort of rewriting. [*Between Existentialism and Marxism*, 'The Purposes of Writing']

3 Man is condemned to be free. [*Existentialism is a Humanism*]

4 Life is nothing until it is lived; but it is yours to make sense of, and the value of it is nothing other than the sense you choose. [*Ib.*]

5 The world could get along very well without literature; it could get along even better without man. [*What Is Literature?*]

6 I distrust the incommunicable; it is the source of all violence. [*Ib.*]

7 The writer, a free man addressing free men, has only one subject – freedom. [*Ib.*]

8 These modest yet proud middle-class people considered beauty above their means or below their condition; they allowed it to titled women and prostitutes. [*Words*, Pt 1]

9 Families naturally prefer widows to unmarried mothers, but only just. [*Ib.*]

10 Dying is not everything: you have to die in time. [*Ib.*]

11 In fact, he rather overdid the sublime: he was a nineteenth-century man who, like so many others, including Victor Hugo himself, thought he was Victor Hugo. [*Ib.* See also 79:16]

12 A kiss without a moustache, they said then, is like an egg without salt; I will add to it: and it is like Good without Evil. [*Ib.*]

13 I realized afterwards that it is possible to know everything about our affections except their strength; that is to say, their sincerity. [*Ib.*]

14 I was ready to admit – if only I had been old enough to understand them – all the right-wing truths which an old left-wing man taught me through his actions: that Truth and Myth are one and the same thing, that you have to simulate passion to feel it and that man is a creature of ceremony. [*Ib.*]

15 At the time, a refined family had to include at least one delicate child. I was a perfect subject because I had some thought of dying at birth. [*Ib.*]

16 Polite Society believed in God so that it need not talk of Him. [*Ib.*]

17 She believed in nothing; only her scepticism kept her from being an atheist. [*Ib.*]

18 Like all dreamers, I mistook disenchantment for truth. [*Ib.* 2]

19 Be self-satisfied, and other self-satisfied people will love you, rend your neighbour, the other neighbours will laugh. But if you hurt your own soul, all other souls will cry out. [*Ib.*]

20 Faith, even when profound, is never complete. [*Ib.*]

21 I confused things with their names: that is belief. [*Ib.*]

22 Culture saves nothing and nobody, nor does it justify. But it is a product of man: he projects himself through it and recognizes himself in it; this critical mirror alone shows him his image. [*Ib.*]

23 In whatever circle of hell we live, I think that we are free to break it. And if people do not break it, then they stay there of their own free will. So they put themselves in hell freely. [Quoted in *L'Express*, 11–17 Oct. 1965]

24 I am not fond of the word psychological. There is no such thing as psychological. Let us say that one can improve the biography of the person. [Quoted in R. D. Laing, *The Divided Self*, Ch. 8]

25 In the first days of the revolt you must kill: to shoot down a European is to kill two birds with one stone, to destroy an oppressor and the man he oppresses at the same time: there remain a dead man, and a free man. [Quoted in the Preface to F. Fanon, *The Wretched of the Earth*]

26 Evil is the product of the ability of humans to make abstract that which is

concrete. [Quoted in *New Society*, 31 Dec. 1970]

SIEGFRIED SASSOON

1 If I were fierce and bald and short of breath, / I'd live with scarlet Majors at the Base, / And speed glum heroes up the line to death. [*Base Details*]

2 And there'd be no more jokes in Music-halls / To mock the riddled corpses round Bapaume. [*Blighters*]

3 'He's a cheery old card,' grunted Harry to Jack / As they slogged up to Arras with rifle and pack . . . / But he did for them both by his plan of attack. [*The General*]

4 Here was the world's worst wound. And here with pride / 'Their name liveth for ever,' the Gateway claims. / Was ever an immolation so belied / As these intolerably nameless names? [*On Passing the New Menin Gate*]

5 Safe with his wound, a citizen of life, / He hobbled blithely through the garden gate, / And thought: 'Thank God they had to amputate!' [*The One-Legged Man*]

6 There must be crowds of ghosts among the trees, – / Not people killed in battle – they're in France / But horrible shapes – old men who died – / Slow natural deaths – old men with ugly souls, / Who wore their bodies out with nasty sins. [*Repression of War Experience*]

7 He spoke with homicidal eloquence, keeping the game alive with genial and well-judged jokes . . . Man, it seemed, had been created to jab the life out of Germans. [*Memoirs of an Infantry Officer*, Pt I, Ch. 1]

8 My stretcher was popped into an ambulance which took me to a big hospital at Denmark Hill. At Charing Cross a woman handed me a bunch of flowers and a leaflet by the Bishop of London who earnestly advised me to lead a clean life and attend Holy Communion. [*Ib.* VIII. 4]

9 I am making this statement as a wilful defiance of military authority because I believe that the War is being deliberately prolonged by those who have the power to end it. [Letter quoted in *ib.* X. 3]

VIDAL SASSOON

10 The only place where success comes before work is in a dictionary. [On BBC radio, quoting one of his teachers]

ERIK SATIE

11 My doctor has always told me to smoke. He even explains himself: 'Smoke, my friend. Otherwise someone else will smoke in your place.' [*Mémoires d'un amnésique*]

12 M. Ravel has refused the Légion d'Honneur but all his music accepts it. [Quoted in James Harding, *Erik Satie*, Ch. 21]

13 I came to this world very young at a very old time. [Quoted in Pierre-Daniel Templier, *Erik Satie*, Ch. 1, trans. E. L. and D. S. French]

14 If the dead vanish fast, money, which is no more stupid than anything else, vanishes as fast as they do; and it's a pleasure to see it go, straight ahead, with never a glance behind and proud as a peacock for all that. [Letter to his brother. Quoted in *ib.*]

15 I had the pleasure of meeting myself last Monday at Darius Milhaud's, where I was lunching with Auric. [Quoted in *ib.*]

16 When I was young, I was told: 'You'll see, when you're fifty.' I am fifty and I haven't seen a thing. [Quoted in *ib.* 2]

17 The musician is perhaps the most modest of animals, but he is also the proudest. It is he who invented the sublime art of ruining poetry. [Quoted in *ib.*]

18 I want to compose a piece for dogs, and I already have my décor. The curtain rises on a bone. [Quoted in *ib.* 3]

DOROTHY L. SAYERS

19 I can't see that she could have found anything nastier to say if she'd thought it out with both hands for a fortnight. [*Busman's Holiday*, 'Prothalamion']

1 'Providence,' said the old woman, 'don't you talk to me about Providence. I've had enough of Providence. First he took my husband, and then he took my 'taters, but there's One above as'll teach him to mend his manners, if he don't look out.' [*The Nine Tailors*, Pt II, sect. 1]

HUGH SCANLON

2 Here we are again with both feet firmly planted in the air [On his union's attitude to the Common Market. *Observer*, 'Sayings of the Year', 30 Dec. 1973]

3 Liberty is conforming to the majority. [*Observer*, 'Sayings of the Week', 14 Aug. 1977]

SENATOR SCHALL
(of Minnesota)

4 To hell with Europe! [1935. *Observer*, 'Sayings of Our Times', 31 May 1953]

EGON SCHIELE

5 Man is a rope stretched between the beast and the superhuman: a rope stretched across the abyss. [Quoted in TV film by J.-L. Fournier, 12 Jul. 1977]

FIELD MARSHAL VON SCHLIEFFEN

6 When you march into France, let the last man on the right brush the Channel with his sleeve. [Of the Schlieffen plan. Quoted in B. Tuchman, *The Guns of August*, Ch. 2]

7 Only make the right wing strong. [*Ib.*]

ARTUR SCHNABEL

8 I am attracted only to music which I consider to be better than it can be performed. [*My Life and Music*, Pt II, Ch. 1]

9 It is easier to gain fame than to retain it. [*Ib.* II. 4]

10 I don't think there was ever a piece of music that changed a man's decision on how to vote. [*Ib.* II. 8]

11 Interpretation is a free walk on firm ground. [*Ib.* II. 10]

12 I know two kinds of audience only – one coughing and one not coughing. [*Ib.* See also 11:8]

13 Applause is a receipt, not a bill. [In explanation of his refusal to give encores. Quoted in I. Kolodin, *Musical Life*]

14 The sonatas of Mozart are unique; they are too easy for children, and too difficult for artists. [Quoted in Nat Shapiro, *An Encyclopedia of Quotations about Music*]

15 The notes I handle no better than many pianists. But the pauses between the notes – ah, that is where the art resides. [Quoted in *Chicago Daily News*, 11 Jun. 1958. See also 280:10]

ARNOLD SCHOENBERG

16 Once, in the army, I was asked if I was really the composer Arnold Schoenberg. 'Somebody had to be,' I said. [*Letters*]

17 For whom, then, do they [aesthetic laws] exist? For the critic? He who can distinguish a good fruit from a bad with his palate does not have to be able to express the distinction through a chemical formula and does not need the formula to recognize the distinction. [*The Theory of Harmony*, Ch. 22, trans. Roy Carter]

18 Art should be cold. [Quoted in Artur Schnabel, *My Life and Music*, Pt II, Ch. 9, but elsewhere ascribed to Stravinsky]

19 Very well, I can wait. [Attr. remark when told his violin concerto needed a soloist with six fingers. Quoted in Nat Shapiro, *An Encyclopedia of Quotations about Music*]

B. P. SCHULBERG

20 Czar of all the rushes. [Of Louis B. Mayer, head of M-G-M. Quoted in Leslie Halliwell, *The Filmgoer's Book of Quotes*]

CHARLES M. SCHULZ

21 I love mankind – it's people I can't stand. [*Go Fly a Kite, Charlie Brown*]

1 LINUS: You got sort of nervous when she walked by, didn't you, Charlie Brown?
CHARLIE BROWN: What makes you think I got nervous?
LINUS: You tied your peanut butter sandwich in a knot. ['Peanuts' strip cartoon]

2 That's the only dog I know who can smell someone just *thinking* about food. [*Ib.*]

3 Never try to lick ice-cream off a hot sidewalk. [*Ib.*]

E. F. SCHUMACHER

4 Small is Beautiful. [Title of book, subtitled *A Study of Economics as if People Mattered*]

5 The heart of the matter, as I see it, is the stark fact that world poverty is primarily a problem of two million villages, and thus a problem of two thousand million villagers. [*Ib.* 13]

6 After all, for mankind as a whole there are no exports. We did not start developing by obtaining foreign exchange from Mars or the moon. Mankind is a closed society. [*Ib.* 14]

7 Any intelligent fool can make things bigger, more complex, and more violent. It takes a touch of genius – and a lot of courage – to move in the opposite direction. [Quoted in obituary, the *Guardian*, 6 Sep. 1977]

ALBERT SCHWEITZER

8 I too had thoughts once of being an intellectual, but I found it too difficult. [To an African who refused to perform some humdrum duty on the grounds that he was an intellectual. Attr.]

C. P. SCOTT

9 Comment is free but facts are sacred. [Quoted in A. Andrews, *Quotations for Speakers and Writers*]

10 Television? No good will come of this device. The word is half Greek and half Latin. [Attr.]

CAPTAIN ROBERT SCOTT

11 What lots and lots I could tell you of this journey. How much better has it been than lounging in too great comfort at home. [Extract from letter. Quoted in Apsley Cherry-Garrard, *The Worst Journey in the World*]

RONALD SEARLE

(Original concept; author of stories, D. B. Wyndham Lewis)

12 During her first year at Somerville, a Fellow of Judas, having essayed a private pinch in the Bodleian Lounge, described her as physically a *fausse maigre*. [*The Terror of St Trinian's*, Ch. 3]

13 Though loaded firearms were strictly forbidden at St Trinian's to all but Sixth-Formers ... one or two of them carried automatics acquired in the holidays, generally the gift of some indulgent relative. [*Ib.*]

14 It was at this precise moment that a brilliant idea recurred to Angela Menace. That very night she would set fire to the School. [*Ib.* 6]

15 In the spring ... your lovely Chloë lightly turns to one mass of spots. [*Ib.* 7]

16 His strong red face resembled something terrible out of Easter Island. [*Ib.* 9]

HARRY SECOMBE

17 My advice if you insist on slimming: Eat as much as you like – just don't swallow it. [Quoted in the *Daily Herald*, 5 Oct. 1962]

PETE SEEGER

18 Where have all the flowers gone? / Young girls picked them every one. [Song: *Where Have All the Flowers Gone?*]

ERICH SEGAL

19 Love means never having to say you're sorry. [Film, *Love Story*. See also 10:8]

GEORGE SELDES

1 Sawdust Caesar [Title of biography of Benito Mussolini]

H. GORDON SELFRIDGE

2 The Great Principles on which we will build this Business are as everlasting as the Pyramids. [Preliminary announcement on Selfridge's store]

3 The customer is always right. [Shop slogan]

W. C. SELLAR
and R. J. YEATMAN

4 To confess that you are totally Ignorant about the Horse, is social suicide: you will be despised by everybody, especially the horse. [Horse Nonsense]

5 America became top nation and history came to a full stop. [1066 and All That]

6 For every person wishing to teach there are thirty not wanting to be taught. [And Now All This]

MAURICE SENDAK

7 There must be more to life than having everything! [Higglety Pigglety Pop!, Ch. 1]

MACK SENNETT

8 Anyone who tells you he has discovered something new is a fool, or a liar or both. [Quoted in James Agee, Agee on Film, Vol. I]

ROBERT SERVICE

9 Ah! the clock is always slow; / It is later than you think. [It is Later than You Think]

DR SEUSS

10 Adults are obsolete children. [Quoted in L. L. Levinson, Bartlett's Unfamiliar Quotations]

PETER SHAFFER

11 Rehearsing a play is making the word flesh. Publishing a play is reversing the process. [Equus, A Note on the Text]

12 All my wife has ever taken from the Mediterranean – from that whole vast intuitive culture – are four bottles of Chianti to make into lamps, and two china condiment donkeys labelled Sally and Peppy. [Ib. Act I, sc. xviii]

13 The Normal is the good smile in a child's eyes – all right. It is also the dead stare in a million adults. It both sustains and kills – like a God. It is the Ordinary made beautiful; it is also the Average made lethal. [Ib. I, xix]

14 Can you think of anything worse one can do to anybody than take away their worship? [Ib. II. xxv]

15 Passion, you see, can be destroyed by a doctor. It cannot be created. [Ib. II. xxxv]

THE SHAH OF IRAN

16 My real opposition is myself. [Interview in Le Monde, 1 Oct. 1976]

IDRIES SHAH

17 Quite a common observation is: 'It takes all sorts to make a world.' This may well be true: but if it is – where are they all? [Reflections, 'The Difference Between Saying and Doing']

18 A certain person may have, as you say, a wonderful presence: I do not know. What I do know is that he has a perfectly delightful absence. [Ib. 'Presence and Absence']

TOM SHARPE

19 The South African Police would leave no stone unturned to see that nothing disturbed the even terror of their lives. [Indecent Exposure, Ch. 1]

20 I have yet to meet a liberal who can withstand the attrition of prolonged discussion of the inessentials. [Porterhouse Blue, Ch. 2]

21 Skullion had little use for contraceptives at the best of times. Unnatural, he called them, and placed them in the lower social category of things along with elastic-sided boots and made-up bow ties. Not the sort of attire for a gentleman. [Ib. 9]

1 His had been an intellectual decision founded on his conviction that if a little knowledge was a dangerous thing, a lot was lethal. [*Ib*. 18]

GEORGE BERNARD SHAW

2 Why, how is it that you've just beaten us? Sheer ignorance of the art of war, nothing else. [*Indignantly*] I never saw anything so unprofessional. [*Arms and the Man*, Act I]

3 My father is a very hospitable man: he keeps six hotels. [*Ib*.]

4 Bulgarians of really good standing – people in our position – wash their hands nearly every day. So you see I can appreciate your delicacy. [*Ib*.]

5 A man ought to be able to be fond of his wife without making a fool of himself about her. [*Candida*, Act I]

6 So long as you come here honestly as a self-respecting, thorough, convinced scoundrel, justifying your scoundrelism and proud of it, you are welcome. [*Ib*.]

7 Love is assumed to be the only theme that touches all your audience infallibly ... And yet love is the one subject that the drawing room drama dare not present. [*Three Plays for Puritans*, Preface]

8 I have a technical objection to making sexual infatuation a tragic theme. Expeaience proves that it is only effective in the comic spirit. [*Ib*.]

9 So much for Bardolatry! [*Ib*.]

10 It does not follow ... that the right to criticize Shakespear involves the power of writing better plays. And in fact ... I do not profess to write better plays. [*Ib*.]

11 BETTER THAN SHAKESPEAR? [Of his own work. *Ib*. crossheading]

12 This is Britannus, my secretary. He is an islander from the western end of the world, a day's voyage from Gaul. [*Caesar and Cleopatra*, Act II]

13 He is a barbarian, and thinks that the customs of his tribe and island are the laws of nature. [*Ib*.]

14 When a stupid man is doing something he is ashamed of, he always declares that it is his duty. [*Ib*. III]

15 Give women the vote, and in five years there will be a crushing tax on bachelors. [*Man and Superman*, Preface]

16 Effectiveness of assertion is the alpha and omega of style. [*Ib*.]

17 Beware of the man whose god is in the skies. [*Ib*. 'Maxims for Revolutionists']

18 Do not love your neighbour as yourself. If you are on good terms with yourself it is an impertinence; if on bad, an injury. [*Ib*.]

19 He who slays a king and he who dies for him are alike idolaters. [*Ib*.]

20 The maternal instinct leads a woman to prefer a tenth share in a first rate man to the exclusive possession of a third rate one. [*Ib*.]

21 Titles distinguish the mediocre, embarrass the superior, and are disgraced by the inferior. [*Ib*.]

22 Self-denial is not a virtue; it is only the effect of prudence on rascality. [*Ib*.]

23 The most intolerable pain is produced by prolonging the keenest pleasure. [*Ib*.]

24 She'll commit every crime a respectable woman can; and she'll justify every one of them by saying that it was the wish of her guardians. [*Ib*. Act I]

25 The more things a man is ashamed of, the more respectable he is. [*Ib*.]

26 Vitality in a woman is a blind fury of creation. She sacrifices herself to it. [*Ib*.]

27 Of all human struggles there is none so treacherous and remorseless as that between the artist man and the mother woman. [*Ib*.]

28 Your pious English habit of regarding the world as a moral gymnasium built expressly to strengthen your character in. [*Ib*.]

29 Very nice sort of place, Oxford, I should think, for people that like that sort of place. [*Ib*. II]

30 ... Never noticing the advent of the New Man. Straker's the New Man. [*Ib*.]

31 As a rule there is only one person an English girl hates more than she hates

her eldest sister; and thats her mother. [*Ib.*]

1 Lying hardly describes it. I overdo it. I get carried away in an ecstasy of mendacity. [*Ib.*]

2 ... any port from which we can sail to a Mahometan country where men are protected from women. [*Ib.*]

3 I am a gentleman: I live by robbing the poor. [*Ib.* III]

4 Until a movement shews itself capable of spreading among brigands, it can never hope for a political majority. [*Ib.*]

5 We are dregs and scum, sir: the dregs very filthy, the scum very superior. [*Ib.*]

6 There is plenty of humbug in hell. [*Ib.*]

7 If you go to Heaven without being naturally qualified for it, you will not enjoy yourself there. [*Ib.*]

8 In the arts of peace Man is a bungler. [*Ib.*]

9 As an old soldier I admit the cowardice: it's as universal as sea sickness, and matters just as little. [*Ib.*]

10 What is virtue but the Trade Unionism of the married? [*Ib.*]

11 Marriage is a mantrap baited with simulated accomplishments and delusive idealizations. [*Ib.*]

12 Those who talk most about the blessings of marriage and the constancy of its vows are the very people who declare that if the chain were broken and the prisoners left free to choose, the whole social fabric would fly asunder. You cannot have the argument both ways. If the prisoner is happy, why lock him in? If he is not, why pretend that he is? [*Ib.*]

13 Hot water is the revolutionist's element. You clean men as you clean milk-pails, by scalding them. [*Ib.* IV]

14 We're from Madeira, but perfectly respectable, so far. [*You Never Can Tell*, Act I]

15 Well, sir, you never can tell. That's a principle in life with me, sir, if you'll excuse my having such a thing, sir. [*Ib.* II]

16 To ask him his intentions? What a violation of Twentieth Century principles! [*Ib.* III]

17 He's the very incarnation of intellect. You can hear his mind working. [*Ib.* IV]

18 My speciality is being right when other people are wrong. [*Ib.*]

19 All matches are unwise. It's unwise to be born; it's unwise to be married; it's unwise to live; and it's wise to die. [*Ib.*]

20 My way of joking is to tell the truth. It's the funniest joke in the world. [*John Bull's Other Island*, Act II]

21 He's not an Irishman. He'll never know theyre laughing at him; and while theyre laughing he'll win the seat. [*Ib.* IV]

22 I am somewhat surprised to hear a member of your Church quote so essentially a Protestant document as the Bible. [*Ib.*]

23 We must be thoroughly democratic, and patronize everybody without distinction of class. [*Ib.*]

24 What really flatters a man is that you think him worth flattering. [*Ib.*]

25 You will comfort me with ... the sight of the little children carrying the golf clubs of your tourists as a preparation for the life to come. [*Ib.*]

26 For four wicked centuries the world has dreamed this foolish dream of efficiency; and the end is not yet. [*Ib.*]

27 That is sound Crosstianity. But this Crosstianity has got entangled with something that Barbara calls Christianity and which unexpectedly causes her to refuse to play the hangman's game of Satan casting out Satan. [*Major Barbara*, Preface]

28 Nobody can say a word against Greek: it stamps a man at once as an educated gentleman. [*Major Barbara*, Act I]

29 He is always breaking the law. He broke the law when he was born: his parents were not married. [*Ib.*]

30 I am a sort of collector of religions; and the curious thing is that I find I can believe in them all. [*Ib.* II]

1 The love of the common people may please an earl's granddaughter and a university professor; but I have been a common man and a poor man; and it has no romance for me. [*Ib.*]

2 I cant talk religion to a man with bodily hunger in his eyes. [*Ib.*]

3 Alcohol is a very necessary article ... It enables Parliament to do things at eleven at night that no sane person would do at eleven in the morning. [*Ib.*]

4 CUSINS: Do you call poverty a crime?
UNDERSHAFT: The worst of all crimes. All the other crimes are virtues beside it. [*Ib.* IV]

5 Whatever can blow men up can blow society up. The history of the world is the history of those who had courage enough to embrace this truth. [*Ib.*]

6 Like all young men, you greatly exaggerate the difference between one young woman and another. [*Ib.*]

7 I now want to give the common man weapons against the intellectual man. I love the common people. I want to arm them against the lawyers, the doctors, the priests ... who, once in authority, are more disastrous and tyrannical than all the fools, rascals and impostors. [*Ib.*]

8 It's easier to replace a dead man than a good picture. [*The Doctor's Dilemma*, Act II]

9 Morality consists in suspecting other people of not being legally married. [*Ib.* III]

10 I dont believe in morality. I'm a disciple of Bernard Shaw. [*Ib.*]

11 The injury to the child would be far less if the voluptuary said frankly: 'I beat you because I like beating you; and I shall do it whenever I can contrive an excuse for it.' [*Misalliance*, Preface]

12 Heaven, as conventionally conceived, is a place so inane, so dull, so useless, so miserable, that nobody has ever ventured to describe a whole day in heaven, though plenty of people have described a day at the seaside. [*Ib.*]

13 The secret of being miserable is to have leisure to bother about whether you are happy or not. [*Ib.*]

14 Children must be taught some sort of religion. Secular education is an impossibility. Secular education comes to this: that the only reason for ceasing to do evil and learning to do well is that if you do not you will be caned. This is worse than being taught in a church school that if you become a dissenter you will go to hell; for hell is presented as the instrument of something eternal, divine and inevitable; you cannot evade it the moment the schoolmaster's back is turned. [*Ib.*]

15 Assassination is the extreme form of censorship. [*The Shewing-Up of Blanco Posnet*, 'The Limits of Toleration']

16 John the Baptist may have been a Keir Hardie; but Jesus of Matthew is of the Ruskin–Morris class. [*Androcles and the Lion*, Preface]

17 Years ago I said that the conversion of a savage to Christianity is the conversion of Christianity to savagery. [*Ib.*]

18 When Jesus called Peter from his boat, he spoiled an honest fisherman, and made nothing better out of the wreck than a salvation monger. [*Ib.*]

19 Whether you think Jesus was God or not, you must admit that he was a first-rate political economist. [*Ib.* Preface, 'Jesus as Economist']

20 I dont want to talk grammar. I want to talk like a lady. [*Pygmalion*, Act II]

21 No: I dont want no gold and no diamonds. I'm a good girl, I am. [*Ib.*]

22 My needs is as great as the most deserving widow's that ever got money out of six different charities in one week for the death of the same husband. [*Ib.*]

23 Undeserving poverty is my line. Taking one station in society with another, it's – it's – well, it's the only one that has any ginger in it, to my taste. [*Ib.*]

24 They all thought she was dead; but my father he kept ladling gin down her throat till she came to so sudden that she bit the bowl off the spoon. [*Ib.* III]

25 Gin was mother's milk to her. [*Ib.*]

26 Tied me up and delivered me into the hands of middle class morality. [*Ib.* V]

1 All great truths begin as blasphemies. [*Annajanska*]

2 When I meet a man who makes a hundred thousand a year, I take off my hat to that man ... and call him brother. [*Heartbreak House,* Act I]

3 You want to rest your wounded bosom against a grindstone. Well ... here is the grindstone. [*Ib*. II]

4 The very burglars cant behave naturally in this house. [*Ib.*]

5 Go anywhere in England where there are natural, wholesome, contented, and really nice English people: and what do you always find? That the stables are the real centre of the household. [*Ib*. III]

6 The captain is in his bunk, drinking bottled ditchwater; and the crew is gambling in the forecastle ... Do you think the laws of God will be suspended in favour of England because you were born in it? [*Ib.*]

7 God's trustiest lieutenants often lack official credentials. They may be professed atheists who are also men of honor and high public spirit. [*Back to Methuselah*, Preface]

8 Every genuine scientist must be ... a metaphysician. [*Ib.*]

9 Make me a beautiful word for doing things tomorrow, for that surely is a great and blessed invention. [*Ib.* Pt I, Act I]

10 Well, as the serpent used to say, why not? [*Ib*. I. II]

11 The He-Ancient. [Character in *ib.* Pt V]

12 It is the only remaining fragment of a lost scripture called The Confessions of St Augustin, the English Opium Eater. [*Ib.*]

13 If ever I utter an oath again may my soul be blasted to eternal damnation! [*St Joan*, sc. ii]

14 We were not fairly beaten, my lord. No Englishman is ever fairly beaten. [*Ib.* iv]

15 Take Gateshead and Middlesbrough alone! ... their daily output of chocolate creams totals up to twenty thousand tons. [*The Apple Cart*, Act I]

16 I never resist temptation, because I have found that things that are bad for me do not tempt me. [*Ib*. II]

17 No woman can shake off her mother. There should be no mothers, only women. [*Too Good to be True*]

18 Half the young ladies in London spend their evenings making their father take them to plays that are not fit for elderly people to see. [*Fanny's First Play*, Introduction]

19 It's all that the young can do for the old, to shock them and keep them up to date. [*Ib.*]

20 You don't expect me to know what to say about a play when I don't know who the author is, do you? [*Ib.* Epilogue]

21 All Shaw's characters are himself: mere puppets stuck up to spout Shaw. [*Ib.*]

22 The one point on which all women are in furious secret rebellion against the existing law is the saddling of the right to a child with the obligation to become the servant of a man. [*Getting Married*, Preface]

23 There are couples who dislike one another furiously for several hours at a time; there are couples who dislike one another permanently; and there are couples who never dislike one another; but these last are people who are incapable of disliking anybody. [*Ib.*]

24 In the middle classes, where the segregation of the artificially limited family in its little brick box is horribly complete, bad manners, ugly dresses, awkwardness, cowardice, peevishness and all the petty vices of unsociability flourish like mushrooms in a cellar. [*Ib.*]

25 Physically there is nothing to distinguish human society from the farm-yard except that children are more troublesome and costly than chickens and women are not so completely enslaved as farm stock. [*Ib.*]

26 What God hath joined together no man shall ever put asunder: God will take care of that. [*Getting Married*]

27 Very few books of any nationality are worth reading. People read to kill time;

305

consequently it is no more objection to a book that it is not worth reading than it is to a pack of cards that it does not pile up treasures in heaven. [*Table-Talk of G.B.S.*]

1 It is the sexless novel that should be distinguished: the sex novel is now normal. [*Ib.*]

2 I could not write the words Mr Joyce used: my prudish hand would refuse to form the letters. [*Ib.*]

3 Martyrdom is the only way in which a man can become famous without ability. [Quoted in Preface to 1908 reprint of *Fabian Essays*]

4 Look after the limelight; and the play will look after itself. [Letter to Herbert Samuel on Censorship controversy. Quoted in J. Bowle, *Viscount Samuel*, Ch. 5, sect. ii]

5 No, he isn't dancing. That's the Ethical Movement. [On seeing Dr Stanton Coit dancing. Quoted in C. E. Bechofer Roberts, 'Ephesian', *Philip Snowden*, Ch. 6]

6 LORD NORTHCLIFFE: The trouble with you, Shaw, is that you look as if there were famine in the land.
G.B.S.: The trouble with you, Northcliffe, is that you look as if you were the cause of it. [Attr.]

7 If all economists were laid end to end, they would not reach a conclusion. [Attr.]

8 Like fingerprints, all marriages are different. [Quoted in Pulling, *They Were Singing*, Ch. 5]

9 We are a nation of governesses. [*New Statesman*, 12 Apr. 1913]

10 If he [T. E. Lawrence] hides in a quarry he puts red flags all round. [Quoted in the *Guardian*, 22 Jan. 1963]

11 The trouble, Mr Goldwyn, is that you are only interested in art and I am only interested in money. [When declining to sell Goldwyn the screen rights of his plays. Quoted in Philip French, *The Movie Moguls*, Ch. 4]

306

SIR HARTLEY SHAWCROSS (LORD SHAWCROSS)

12 We are the masters at the moment – and not only for the moment, but for a very long time to come. [Said in the House of Commons in a debate on the trade unions, 2 Apr. 1946]

13 The so-called new morality is too often the old immorality condoned. [*Observer*, 'Sayings of the Week', 17 Nov. 1963]

PATRICK SHAW-STEWART

14 I saw a man this morning / Who did not wish to die: / I ask, and cannot answer, / If otherwise would I. [Quoted in Evelyn Waugh, *Ronald Knox*, Pt I, Ch. 4]

LLOYD SHEARER

15 [David] Selznick gave the impression that he stormed through life demanding to see the manager – and that, when the manager appeared, Selznick would hand him a twenty-page memo announcing his instant banishment to Elba. [Quoted in R. Behlmer, *Memo from David O. Selznick*]

GILBERT SHELTON

16 Dope can see you through times of no money better than money can see you through times of no dope. [Song: *Freewheelin' Franklin*]

SIR JOHN SHEPPARD

17 He knew Greek. [Slight tittering.] Well, some of them don't, you know! [Estimating in a Cambridge lecture the merits of an editor of Aeschylus. Attr.]

ROBERT E. SHERWOOD

18 It is disappointing to report that George Bernard Shaw appearing as George Bernard Shaw is sadly miscast in the part. Satirists should be heard and not seen. [Review of Shaw play]

ROBERT SHIELDS

19 A well-preserved virginity *may* signify a limited capacity for love. [*Observer*, 13 Jun. 1965]

CLEMENT SHORTER

1 The latest definition of an optimist is one who fills up his crossword puzzle in ink. [*Observer*, 'Sayings of the Week', 22 Feb. 1925. See also 118:5]

DIMITRI SHOSTAKOVITCH

2 A Soviet composer's reply to just criticism. [*Epigraph to his Fifth Symphony*]

JEAN SIBELIUS

3 Pay no attention to what the critics say; no statue has ever been put up to a critic. [Quoted in A. Andrews, *Quotations for Speakers and Writers*]

WALTER SICKERT

4 Nothing links man to man like the frequent passage from hand to hand of cash. [Quoted in W. H. Auden, *A Certain World*]

H. R. SIDEY

5 The heights by great men reached and kept / Were not attained without exertion / But they, while their companions worked, / Were contacting the proper person. [*Spectator*, competition, 20 Aug. 1955]

MAURICE SIGLER

6 Little Man, You've Had a Busy Day. [Title of song]

FRANK SILVER
and IRVING COHN

7 Yes, we have no bananas, / We have no bananas today. [Song: *Yes, We Have No Bananas*]

PAUL SIMON

8 Like a bridge over troubled water, / I will ease your mind. [Song: *Bridge Over Troubled Water*]

9 Here's to you, Mrs Robinson, / Jesus loves you more than you will know. [Song: *Mrs Robinson*]

10 People talking without speaking, / People listening without hearing, / People writing songs that voices never shared. / No one dared. [Song: *Sound of Silence*]

11 The words of the prophet are written / On the subway halls and tenement walls. [*Ib.*]

N. F. SIMPSON

12 There's somebody at the door wanting you to form a government. [*A Resounding Tinkle*, Act I, sc. i]

13 If he's a criminal, he's in plain clothes – that's all I can say. [*Ib.*]

14 The small of my back is too big, doctor. [*Ib.*]

15 And suppose we solve all the problems it presents? What happens? We end up with more problems than we started with. Because that's the way problems propagate their species. A problem left to itself dries up or goes rotten. But fertilize a problem with a solution – you'll hatch out dozens. [*Ib.*]

16 We lent him a couple of lampshades Myrtle has grown out of for his little boy. [*Ib.* II]

17 I sometimes envy the man in the street who's never learned to drink for himself at all. [*Ib.*]

18 The best that can be hoped for from the ending is that sooner or later it will arrive. [*Ib.*]

19 I eat merely to put food out of my mind. [*The Hole*]

20 MRS EDO: Sid just had another bad night worrying about being so different from the people he sees round him.
MRS MESO: Has he tried resembling anybody? [*Ib.*]

21 He went to Dr Bunch – he's been going to him for years – and complained about his ribs, and told him they seemed to be giving him claustrophobia. [*Ib.*]

22 He's out of step with it – he's breathing in all the time when he should be breathing out and that puts him out all the way along. He can't get back into phase with it except by breathing in twice running. [*Ib.*]

1 Knocked down a doctor? With an ambulance? How could she? It's a contradiction in terms. [*One-Way Pendulum*, Act I]

2 It'll do him good to lie there unconscious for a bit. Give his brain a rest. [*Ib.*]

3 She said she had a string of pearls in the form of a necklace but she wore it round her waist for the tightness. [*Ib.* II]

4 In sentencing a man for one crime, we may well be putting him beyond the reach of the law in respect of those crimes which he has not yet had an opportunity to commit. The law, however, is not to be cheated in this way. I shall therefore discharge you. [*Ib.*]

ROBERT SIMPSON

5 Let us reserve the term 'advanced' for those [composers] who deserve it – dead these five centuries or alive now. [Talk on BBC radio, 1976]

ISAAC BASHEVIS SINGER

6 Children don't read to find their identity, to free themselves from guilt, to quench the thirst for rebellion or to get rid of alienation. They have no use for psychology. They detest sociology. They still believe in God, the family, angels, devils, witches, goblins, logic, clarity, punctuation, and other such obsolete stuff ... When a book is boring, they yawn openly. They don't expect their writer to redeem humanity, but leave to adults such childish illusions. [Speech on receiving the Nobel Prize for Literature. Quoted in the *Observer*, 17 Dec. 1978]

EDITH SITWELL

7 The fire was furry as a bear. [*Dark Song*]

8 Jumbo asleep! / Grey leaves thick-furred / As his ears, keep / Conversations blurred. [*Lullaby for Jumbo*]

9 Do not take a bath in Jordan, / Gordon, / On the holy Sabbath, on the peaceful day! [*Scotch Rhapsody*]

10 Virginia Woolf, I enjoyed talking to her, but thought *nothing* of her writing. I considered her 'a beautiful little knitter'. [Letter to G. Singleton, 11 Jul. 1955. Quoted in J. Wintle and R. Kenin, *Dictionary of Biographical Quotation*]

11 I have often wished I had time to cultivate modesty ... But I am too busy thinking about myself. [*Observer*, 'Sayings of the Week', 30 Apr. 1950]

SIR OSBERT SITWELL

12 Chrysanthemums, which in their art shades of mauve, and terra-cotta and russet, smell of moths, camphorball, and drowned sailors. [*Essay on Gardening*]

13 Now the nimble fingers are no more nimble, / And the silver thimble lies cold and tarnished black. [*Miss Mew's Window-Box*]

14 In reality, *killing time* / Is only the name for another of the multifarious ways / By which Time kills us. [*Milordo Inglese*]

15 On the coast of Coromandel / Dance they to the tunes of Handel. [*On the Coast of Coromandel*]

16 But He was never, well, / What I call / A Sportsman; / For forty days / He went out into the desert / – And never shot anything. [*Old Fashioned Sportsmen*]

17 Our poverty, then, signified chiefly that we were no longer allowed to throw down pennies, done up in screws of paper, to the conductors of German bands. [*The Scarlet Tree*, Bk III, Ch. 1]

18 When younger he [Sir George Sitwell] had invented many other things; at Eton, for example, a musical toothbrush which played 'Annie Laurie' as you brushed your teeth, and a small revolver for killing wasps. [*Ib.* IV. 1]

19 The artist, like the idiot or clown, sits on the edge of the world, and a push may send him over it. [*Ib.* IV. 2]

20 We attended stables, as we attended church, in our best clothes, thereby no doubt showing the degree of respect due to horses, no less than to the deity. [*Ib.*]

1 The terrible, newly-imported American doctrine that everyone ought to do something. [*Great Morning*, Bk V, Ch. 2]

2 [Sir George Sitwell] would omnisciently reply, with an air of final and absolute authority, and without deeming it necessary to offer proof or divulge the source of such, no doubt, mystical awareness, '*We happen to know*.' [*Ib.*]

3 She belonged to the super-annuated dairy-maid type, and possessed a voice that, like a mill, ground silence into its component parts. [*Ib.*]

4 [Of Dame Ethel Smythe] She would be like Richard Wagner, if only she looked a bit more feminine. [Quoted in Elisabeth Lutyens, *A Goldfish Bowl*, Ch. 2]

5 Education: in the holidays from Eton. [Entry in *Who's Who*]

ROBIN SKELTON

6 A man does not write poems about what he knows, but about what he does not know. [*Teach Yourself Poetry*]

CORNELIA OTIS SKINNER

7 Woman's virtue is man's greatest invention. [Attr.]

PROFESSOR B. F. SKINNER

8 Education is what survives when what has been learnt has been forgotten. [*New Scientist*, 21 May 1964]

9 Indeed one of the ultimate advantages of an education is simply coming to the end of it. [*The Technology of Teaching*]

GEORGE SLOCOMBE

10 He [Woodrow Wilson] was the Messiah of the new age, and his crucifixion was yet to come. [On Wilson's visit to Europe for the Versailles conference. *Mirror to Geneva*]

ELIZABETH SMART

11 By Grand Central Station I Sat Down and Wept. [Title of book]

CYRIL SMITH

12 Parliament is the longest running farce in the West End. [Quoted in *The Times*, 23 Sep. 1977]

GEORGE JOSEPH SMITH
(murderer of the Brides in the Bath)

13 Sir – In answer to your application regarding my parentage, my mother was a bus-horse, my father a cab-driver, my sister a rough-rider over the Arctic regions. My brothers were all gallant sailors on a steam-roller. [Letter to father-in-law produced at trial. Quoted in Edward Marjoribanks, *Life of Sir Edward Marshall Hall*, Ch. 10]

IAN SMITH

14 I don't believe in black majority rule ever in Rhodesia ... not in a thousand years. [Speech in Mar. 1976. Quoted in N. Rees, *Quote . . . Unquote*]

LOGAN PEARSALL SMITH

15 How awful to reflect that what people say of us is true! [*All Trivia*]

16 I might give my life for my friend, but he had better not ask me to do up a parcel. [*Ib.*]

17 I am one of the unpraised, unrewarded millions without whom Statistics would be a bankrupt science. It is we who are born, who marry, who die, in constant ratios. [*Ib.*]

18 I cannot forgive my friends for dying: I do not find these vanishing acts of theirs at all amusing. [*Ib.*]

19 Is it seemly that I, at my age, should be hurled with my books of reference, and bed-clothes, and hot-water bottle, across the sky at the unthinkable rate of nineteen miles a second? As I say, I don't like it at all. [*Ib.*]

20 It is the wretchedness of being rich that you have to live with rich people. [*Ib.*]

21 Solvency is entirely a matter of temperament and not of income. [*Ib.*]

22 That Stonehenge circle of elderly disapproving faces – Faces of the Uncles,

and Schoolmasters and the Tutors who frowned on my youth. [*Ib.*]

1 There is more felicity on the far side of baldness than young men can possibly imagine. [*Ib.*]

2 These pieces of moral prose have been written, dear Reader, by a large Carnivorous Mammal, belonging to that sub-order of the Animal Kingdom which includes also the Orang-outang, the tusked Gorilla, the Baboon with his bright blue and scarlet bottom, and the gentle Chimpanzee. [*Ib.*]

3 The thought that my mind is really nothing but an empty sieve – often this, too, disconcerts me. [*Ib.*]

4 We need two kinds of acquaintances, one to complain to, while we boast to the others. [*Ib.*]

5 What I like in a good author is not what he says, but what he whispers. [*Ib.*]

6 What is more enchanting than the voices of young people, when you can't hear what they say? [*Ib.*]

7 Yes, there it still was, the old External World, still apparently quite unaware of its own non-existence. [*Ib.*]

8 [When asked shortly before his death if he had discovered any meaning in life] There is a meaning, at least for me, there is one thing that matters – to set a chime of words tinkling in the mind of a few fastidious people. [Quoted in an obituary appreciation by Cyril Connolly, *New Statesman*, 9 Mar. 1946]

9 A friend who loved perfection would be the perfect friend, did not that love shut his door on me. [Last words in *Great Turnstile*, ed. V. S. Pritchett]

STEVIE SMITH

10 A Good Time Was Had by All. [Title of book (1937), ascribed as source of phrase in Eric Partridge, *A Dictionary of Catch-Phrases*]

11 'O Charley, Charley, do not go upon the water' / Cries a friendly swan, 'with the Duke's daughter.' [*The Magic Morning*]

12 Shall I tell you the signs of a New Age coming? / It is a sound of drubbing and sobbing / Of people crying, We are old, we are old / And the sun is going down and becoming cold. [*The New Age*]

13 I was much too far out all my life. / And not waving but drowning. [*Not Waving But Drowning*]

14 Oh to become sensible about social advance at seventeen is to be lost. [*Parents*]

15 Private Means is dead, / God rest his soul, / Officers and fellow-rankers said. [*Private Means is Dead*]

16 The crux and Colonel of the whole matter, / (As you can read in the Journal, if it's not tattered) / Lies in the Generals, Collapse, Debility, Panic and Uproar, / Who are too old in any case / To go to War. [*Ib.*]

17 It [my poetry] does as well for telling atom secrets as for knowing whatever Mabel's been up to lately. [Quoted in the *Observer*, 9 Nov. 1969]

18 I do really think that death will be marvellous . . . If there wasn't death, I think you couldn't go on. [Quoted in *ib.*]

THORNE SMITH

19 Stevens' mind was so tolerant that he could have attended a lynching every day without becoming critical. [*The Jovial Ghosts*, Ch. 11]

20 'I find it rather sad. Mrs Hart had a hard life.' 'You mean she led a hard life,' declared Marion. 'She was a trull before she could toddle.' [*Topper Takes a Trip*, Ch. 14]

WALLACE SMITH

21 Mildred's always managed to confuse the duties of matrimony with its pleasures. [*The Captain Hates the Sea*, Ch. 9]

22 'The major probably guessed,' said Mister Layton, 'that you're one of these hot-pants athletes whenever you get shore-leave.' [*Ib.* 20]

C. P. SNOW

23 The Two Cultures. [Title of article in the *New Statesman*, 6 Oct. 1956]

1 Jam today, and men aren't at their most exciting: Jam tomorrow, and one often sees them at their noblest. [*The Two Cultures*, 4]

2 When scientists are faced with an expression of the traditional culture it tends . . . to make their feet ache. [*Ib.*]

3 'I grant you that he's not two-faced,' I said. 'But what's the use of that when the one face he has got is so peculiarly unpleasant?' [*The Affair*, Ch. 4]

4 I like humour dry. Charles's splashes. [*The Search*, Pt III, Ch. 2]

PHILIP SNOWDEN

5 It would be desirable if every Government, when it comes into power, should have its old speeches burned. [Quoted in C. E. Bechofer Roberts, 'Ephesian', *Philip Snowden*, Ch. 12]

VISCOUNTESS SNOWDEN

6 We were behind the 'iron curtain' at last! [*Through Bolshevik Russia* (1920). The phrase was later used by Goebbels and taken up by Winston Churchill in his Fulton speech in 1946. Derived from the safety curtain in a theatre.]

GARY SNYDER

7 Taste all, and hand the knowledge down. [*Turtle Island*, 'Ethnobotany']

ALEXANDER SOLZHENITSYN

8 The whole of his life had prepared Podduyev for living, not for dying. [*Cancer Ward*, Pt I, Ch. 8, trans. N. Bethell and D. Burg]

9 If it were a life sentence, well, I suppose my coffin could be brought back home to Russia, but since it's 'perpetual', it means even that won't be allowed back. I won't be allowed back even after the sun goes out. Perpetuity is longer. [*Ib.* I. 12]

10 The Rusanovs loved the People, their great People. They served the People and were ready to give their lives for the People. But as the years went by they found themselves less and less able to tolerate actual human beings, those obstinate creatures who were always resistant, refusing to do what they were told and, besides, demanding something for themselves. [*Ib.* I. 14]

11 He was not frightened of dying 'one day', he was frightened of dying now. [*Ib.* I. 19]

12 It is not the level of prosperity that makes for happiness but the kinship of heart and the way we look at the world. Both attitudes are within our power, so that a man is happy so long as he chooses to be happy, and no one can stop him. [*Ib.* I. 20]

13 Nowadays we don't think much of a man's love for an animal; we laugh at people who are attached to cats. But if we stop loving animals, aren't we bound to stop loving humans too? [*Ib.*]

14 The camps had taught him that people who say nothing carry something within themselves. [*Ib.* II. 10]

15 Capitalism was doomed ethically before it was doomed economically, a long time ago. [*Ib.*]

16 If decade after decade the truth cannot be told, each person's mind begins to roam irretrievably. One's fellow countrymen become harder to understand than Martians. [*Ib.* II. 11]

17 One of the [zoo] cages had a notice on it: 'White owls do not do well in captivity.' So they know that! And they still lock them up! What sort of degenerate owls, he wondered, did so well in captivity? [*Ib.* II. 14]

18 How can one expect a butcher to be a surgeon? [*The First Circle*, Ch. 5, trans. M. Guybon]

19 To understand the nature of happiness we first have to know what it means to eat one's fill . . . It's not a matter of *how much* you eat, but of the *way* you eat. It's the same with happiness – it doesn't depend on the actual number of blessings we manage to scratch from life, but only our attitude towards them. [*Ib.* 8]

20 You took my freedom away a long time ago and you can't give it back because you haven't got it yourself. [*Ib.* 17]

1 You only have power over people so long as you don't take *everything* away from them. But when you've robbed a man of everything he's no longer in your power – he's free again. [*Ib.*]

2 They don't sell tickets to the past. [*Ib.* 37]

3 Their teacher had advised them not to read Tolstoy's novels, because they were very long and would easily confuse the clear ideas which they had learned from reading critical studies of him. [*Ib.* 40]

4 Generosity is a two-edged virtue for an artist – it nourishes his imagination but has a fatal effect on his routine. [*Ib.* 42]

5 No regime has ever loved great writers, only minor ones. [*Ib.* 57]

6 Unfortunately for us mortals and fortunately for the powers that be, it is in the nature of man that as long as he is alive there is always something which can be taken away from him. [*Ib.* 84]

7 None of us who lived close to her perceived that she was that one righteous person without whom, as the saying goes, no city can stand.
    Nor the world. [*Matryona's House*, final words, trans. M. Glenny]

8 We are always boasting about our equality for women and our kindergartens but we hide the fact that all this is just a substitute for the family we have undermined. Equality for women doesn't mean that they have to occupy *the same number* of factory jobs and office positions as men, but just that all these posts should in principle be equally open to women. [*Letter to Soviet Leaders*, 5, trans. H. Sternberg]

9 This universal, obligatory force-feeding with lies is now the most agonizing aspect of existence in our country – worse than all our material miseries, worse than any lack of civil liberties. [*Ib.* 6]

10 Prayers are like those appeals of ours. Either they don't get through or they're returned with 'rejected' scrawled across 'em. [*One Day in the Life of Ivan Denisovich*, trans. R. Parker]

11 A day without dark cloud. Almost a happy day. [*Ib.*]

12 When truth is discovered by someone else, it loses something of its attractiveness. [*Candle in the Wind*, sc. iii]

13 Forget the outside world. Life has different laws in here. This is Campland, an invisible country. It's not in the geography books, or the psychology books or the history books. This is the famous country where ninety-nine men weep while one laughs. [*The Love-Girl and the Innocent*, Act 1, sc. iii, trans. N. Bethell and D. Burg]

14 If people didn't live in families, no tyrant would be able to stay on his throne. He'd be washed away as if by a flood ... They break our necks and all we do is start families. [*Ib.* III. ii]

15 In our country the lie has become not just a moral category but a pillar of the State. [*Observer*, 'Sayings of the Year', 29 Dec. 1974]

16 For us in Russia, communism is a dead dog, while, for many people in the West, it is still a living lion. [On BBC Russian service, published in the *Listener*, 15 Feb. 1979]

E. Œ. SOMERVILLE and MARTIN ROSS

17 Neither principalities nor powers should force me into the drawing-room, where sat the three unhappy women of my party, being entertained within an inch of their lives by Mrs McRory. [*Further Experiences of an Irish R.M.*, 'Sharper than a Ferret's Tooth']

ANASTASIO SOMOZA
(Dictator of Nicaragua)

18 [To an opponent who accused him of rigging the elections] Indeed, you won the elections, but I won the count. [Quoted by Richard Gott in the *Guardian*, 17 Jun. 1977. See also 319: 12]

STEPHEN SONDHEIM

19 [On airways food] The shiny stuff is tomatoes. / The salad lies in a group. / The curly stuff is potatoes. / The stuff that moves is soup. / Anything that is white is sweet. / Anything that is brown

is meat. / Anything that is grey, don't eat. [Song: *Do I Hear a Waltz?*]

1 Everything's Coming Up Roses. [Song title from musical, *Gypsy*]

2 It's not talk of God / And the decade ahead / That allows you to get through the worst. / It's 'you do' and 'I don't' and 'nobody said that' / And 'who brought the subject up first?' [Song: *It's the Little Things*, from musical, *Company*]

3 One's impossible, two is dreary, / Three is company, safe and cheery. [Song: *Side by Side by Side*, from *ib.*]

4 Send in the Clowns. [Song title from musical, *A Little Night Music*]

SUSAN SONTAG

5 Illness is the night-side of life, a more onerous citizenship. Everyone who is born holds dual citizenship, in the kingdom of the well and in the kingdom of the sick. Although we all prefer to use only the good passport, sooner or later each of us is obliged, at least for a spell, to identify ourselves as citizens of that other place. [*Illness as Metaphor*, opening words]

6 A large part of the popularity and persuasiveness of psychology comes from its being a sublimated spiritualism: a secular, ostensibly scientific way of affirming the primacy of 'spirit' over matter. [*Ib.* Ch. 7]

7 A photograph is not only an image (as a painting is an image), an interpretation of the real; it is also a trace, something directly stencilled off the real, like a footprint or a death mask. [*On Photography*]

CHARLES SORLEY

8 Give them not praise. For, deaf, how should they know / It is not curses heaped on each gashed head? [*When You See Millions of the Mouthless Dead*]

NANCY SPAIN

9 Only a fool would make the bed every day. [Quoted in Quentin Crisp, *The Naked Civil Servant*, Ch. 15]

MURIEL SPARK

10 On another occasion he had said, 'My sympathies are not entirely with Patrick. He may be a good medium, but as a citizen –' 'It is time spiritualism was recognized as a mark of good citizenship,' Marlene said. [*The Bachelors*]

11 She doesn't have anything to do with youth clubs. There are classes within classes in Peckham. [*The Ballad of Peckham Rye*, Ch. 3]

12 A short neck denotes a good mind ... You see, the messages go quicker to the brain because they've shorter to go. [*Ib.* 7]

13 The one certain way for a woman to hold a man is to leave him for religion. [*The Comforters*, Ch. 1]

14 Parents learn a lot from their children about coping with life. [*Ib.* 6]

15 All the nice people were poor; at least, that was a general axiom, the best of the rich being poor in spirit. [*The Girls of Slender Means*, Ch. 1]

16 Every communist has a fascist frown, every fascist a communist smile. [*Ib.* 4]

17 With the impurity of those to whom all things pertaining to themselves are pure. [*The Go-Away Bird*, 'Daisy Overend']

18 Selwyn Macgregor, the nicest boy who ever committed the sin of whisky. [*Ib.* 'A Sad Tale's Best for Winter']

19 If you had been mine when you were seven you would have been the crème de la crème. [*The Prime of Miss Jean Brodie*, Ch. 2]

20 But I did not remove my glasses, for I had not asked for her company in the first place, and there is a limit to what one can listen to with the naked eye. [*Voices at Play*, 'The Dark Glasses']

21 Do you think it pleases a man when he looks into a woman's eyes and sees a reflection of the British Museum Reading Room? [Quoted in L. and M. Cowan, *The Wit of Women*]

FRED SPARKS

22 The man who is always the life of the party will be the death of his wife.

313

[*Saturday Review*, 5 Dec. 1964, 'As it Happens']

JOHN SPARROW

1 Without you, Heaven would be too dull to bear, / And Hell will not be Hell if you are there. [Epitaph on Maurice Bowra. Quoted by John Grigg in *The Times Literary Supplement*, 30 May 1975]

EUGENE SPEICHER

2 A portrait is a picture in which there is something wrong with the mouth. [Quoted in Frank Muir, *The Frank Muir Book*]

JOHNNY SPEIGHT

3 You silly moo. [Catch-phrase from BBC TV comedy series, *Till Death Do Us Part*]

4 They start bloody wars they can't afford ... That old fool Chamberlain that was ... 'Peace in our time' ... Didn't give a thought to the cost of it – didn't enter his head to go into a few figures – get an estimate – soppy old sod. [*Ib.* 'The Bird Fancier']

5 Well, your natives have that. They have *sounds* for things, but it's not language. I mean, a dog barks but it's not language. I mean, yer Jocks an' yer Irish they've got that, they've got sounds. Yer Gaelic ... but it's no good to 'em 'cept for talking among themselves. They wanna talk to other people, they've got to learn English. [*Ib.*]

6 If Her Majesty stood for Parliament – if the Tory Party had any sense and made Her its leader instead of that grammar school twit Heath – us Tories, mate, would win every election we went in for. [*Ib.* 'I Can Give It Up']

7 ALF: That's the one [religion] you got to belong to. No good belonging to any of the others. But who knows which one is His? I mean, that's your problem, annit? 'Cos God ain't said nothing for years, He ain't ...
MIKE: You ought to join all the religions – don't take any chances ... [*Ib.* 'Sex before Marriage']

8 Look, if the Maker had wanted us to wear pyjamas, we'd have been born in 'em. [*Ib.* 'Women's Lib. and Bournemouth']

9 Don't be daft. You don't get any pornography on there, not on the telly. Get filth, that's all. The only place you get pornography is in yer Sunday papers. [*Ib.* 'Royal Variety Performance 1972']

10 'Cos as the Lord Jesus said, it will be easier for a needle to pass through the eye of a camel than for a rich man to enter the Kingdom of Heaven. [*Ib.* 'If We Want a Proper Democracy ...']

11 Have you noticed, the last four strikes we've had, it's pissed down? It wouldn't be a bad idea to check the weather reports before they pull us out next time. [*Ib.*]

CARDINAL SPELLMAN

12 Pray as if everything depended on God, and work as if everything depended upon man. [Quoted in Lewis C. Henry, *Best Quotations for all Occasions*]

STANLEY SPENCER

13 I no more like people personally than I like dogs. When I meet them I am only apprehensive whether they will bite me, which is reasonable and sensible. [Quoted in Maurice Collis, *Stanley Spencer, a Biography*, Ch. 17]

14 Beautifully done. [Last words, to the nurse who had given him his injection. Quoted in *ib.* 19]

STEPHEN SPENDER

15 Different living is not living in different places / But creating in the mind a map. [*Different Living*]

16 But let the wrong cry out as raw as wounds / This Time forgets and never heals, far less transcends. [*In Railway Halls*]

17 Born of the sun, they travelled a short while towards the sun / And left the vivid air signed with their honour. [*I Think Continually*]

18 Our single purpose was to walk through snow / With faces swung to their pro-

digious North / Like compass needles.
[*Polar Exploration*]

1 Pylons, those pillars / Bare like nude
giant girls that have no secret. [*The
Pylons*]

2 Only the lucid friend to aerial raiders /
The brilliant pilot moon, stares down /
Upon this plain she makes a shining
bone. [*Two Armies*]

3 Who live under the shadow of a war, /
What can I do that matters? [*Who live
under the Shadow*]

4 People sometimes divide others into
those you laugh at and those you laugh
with. The young Auden was someone
you could laugh-at-with. [Address at
W. H. Auden's memorial service,
Oxford, 27 Oct. 1973]

HILDE SPIEL

5 Malice is like a game of poker or tennis;
you don't play it with anyone who is
manifestly inferior to you. [*The
Darkened Room*]

MICKEY SPILLANE

6 Don't stand too near the window,
honey, someone might blow you a kiss.
[In film, *Kiss Me Deadly*. Script by
A. I. Bezzerides]

DR BENJAMIN SPOCK

7 You know more than you think you do.
[Opening words of *Baby and Child Care*]

8 How to fold a diaper depends on the
size of the baby and the diaper. [*Ib.*
§ 261]

9 To win in Vietnam, we will have to
exterminate a nation. [*Dr Spock on
Vietnam*, Ch. 7]

VERNON SPROXTON

10 Relics have nothing to do with the truth
... any more than the *truth* of the myth
of the Garden of Eden would be enhanced by the discovery of a fossilized
apple with two bites taken from it!
[Introduction to Fynn, *Mister God, This
Is Anna*]

SIR JOHN SQUIRE

11 But Shelley had a hyper-thyroid face.
[*Ballade of the Glandular Hypothesis*]

12 Full many a vice is born to blush unseen, / Full many a crime the world
does not discuss, / Full many a pervert
lives to reach a green / Replete old age,
and so it was with us. [*If Gray had had
to write his Elegy in the Cemetery of
Spoon River*]

13 To a land where the sky is as red as the
grass / And the sun as green as the rain.
[*Parody of G. K. Chesterton*]

SRI AUROBINDO

14 Nothing to the supernatural sense is
really finite; it is founded on a feeling
of all in each and each in all. [*The
Synthesis of Yoga*]

MR JUSTICE STABLER

15 I cannot imagine a worse cure for
psycho-neurosis than safe-blowing
with gelignite. [*Observer*, 'Sayings of
the Week', 21 Mar. 1954]

16 It would be much better if young women
should stop being raped much earlier in
the proceedings than some of them do.
[*Observer*, 'Sayings of the Week', 8 Jan.
1961]

HENRY DE VERE STACPOOLE

17 In home-sickness you must keep moving
– it is the only disease that does not
require rest. [*The Bourgeois*]

J. V. STALIN

18 The state is an instrument in the hands
of the ruling class for suppressing the
resistance of its class enemies. [On
'Proletarian democracy'. Quoted in
Stalin's Kampf, ed. M. R. Werner]

19 The tasks of the party are ... to be
cautious and not allow our country to
be drawn into conflicts by warmongers
who are accustomed to have others pull
the chestnuts out of the fire for them.
[Speech to the 8th Congress of the Communist Party, 6 Jan. 1941]

315

1 Personnel selection is decisive. People are our most valuable capital. [Quoted in Alexander Solzhenitsyn, *The Love-Girl and the Innocent*]

2 To govern is not to write resolutions and distribute directives; to govern is to control the implementation of the directives. [Quoted in N. McInnes, *The Communist Parties of Western Europe*, Ch. 3]

3 The party is the rallying-point for the best elements of the working class. [Attr.]

OLIVER STANLEY

4 You see, whether we win or lose, it will be the end of everything we stand for. [On 11 Sep. 1938. Quoted in Harold Nicolson, *Diaries and Letters, 1930–39*, ed. Nigel Nicolson]

COL. C. E. STANTON

5 Lafayette, we are here! [At Lafayette's grave, 1917. Attr.]

OLAF STAPLEDON

6 That strange blend of the commercial traveller, the missionary, and the barbarian conqueror, which was the American abroad. [*Last and First Men*, Ch. 3, sect. i]

CHRISTINA STEAD

7 A self-made man is one who believes in luck and sends his son to Oxford. [*House of All Nations*, 'Credo']

8 If all the rich men in the world divided up their money amongst themselves, there wouldn't be enough to go round. [*Ib.*]

WICKHAM STEED

9 The famous 'A.E.I.O.U.' policy – *Austriae est imperare orbi universo* (to Austria belongs universal rule). [*The Hapsburg Monarchy*]

LINCOLN STEFFENS

10 I have seen the future and it works. [Said to Bernard Baruch after a visit to the Soviet Union in 1919. Quoted in *Autobiography*, Ch. 18. See also 332:18.

11 City government is of the people, by the rascals, for the rich. [Quoted in *The Times*, 18 Jul. 1977]

GERTRUDE STEIN

12 Two things are always the same the dance and war. One might say anything is the same but the dance and war are particularly the same because one can see them. That is what they are for. [*Everybody's Autobiography*, Ch. 5]

13 Pigeons on the grass alas. [*Four Saints in Three Acts*, Act III, sc. iii]

14 Ida never sighed, she just rested. When she rested she turned a little and she said, yes dear. She said that very pleasantly. That was all of Ida's life just then. [*Ida*, Pt II]

15 Ida decided that she was just going to talk to herself. Anybody could stand around and listen but as for her she was just going to talk to herself. She no longer even needed a twin. [*Ib.*]

16 It is difficult never to have been younger but Ida almost was she almost never had been younger. [*Ib.*]

17 Ida never spoke, she just said what she pleased. Dear Ida. [*Ib.*]

18 Ida returned more and more to be Ida. She even said she was Ida. [*Ib.*]

19 In the United States there is more space where nobody is than where anybody is. That is what makes America what it is. [*The Geographical History of America*]

20 Disillusionment in living is the finding out nobody agrees with you not those that are fighting for you. Complete disillusionment is when you realize that no one can for they can't change. [*The Making of Americans*]

21 Any one not coming to be a dead one before coming to be an old one comes to be an old one and comes then to be a dead one as any old one comes to be a dead one. [*Ib.*]

22 [Of F. Scott Fitzgerald] The first of the last generation. [Quoted in J. M. Brinnin, *The Third Rose*]

1 [Of Ezra Pound] A village explainer, excellent if you were a village, but if you were not, not. [Quoted in Malcolm Cowley, *Exile's Return*]

2 Anything one is remembering is a repetition, but existing as a human being, that is being, listening and hearing is never repetition. [Quoted in David Lodge, *Changing Places*, Ch. 5]

3 Just before she died she asked, 'What *is* the answer?' No answer came. She laughed and said, 'In that case what is the question?' Then she died. [Last words, recorded by Duncan Sutherland in *G.S.*, *a Biography of her Work*]

JOHN STEINBECK

4 Man, unlike any other thing organic or inorganic in the universe, grows beyond his work, walks up the stairs of his concepts, emerges ahead of his accomplishments. [*The Grapes of Wrath*, Ch. 14]

5 Okie use' to mean you was from Oklahoma. Now it means you're scum. Don't mean nothing itself, it's the way they say it. [*Ib.* 18]

WILHELM STEKEL

6 The mark of the immature man is that he wants to die nobly for a cause, while the mark of the mature man is that he wants to live humbly for one. [Quoted in J. D. Salinger, *The Catcher in the Rye*, Ch. 24]

JAMES STEPHENS

7 Finality is death. Perfection is finality. Nothing is perfect. There are lumps in it. [*The Crock of Gold*]

8 Men come of age at sixty, women at fifteen. [*Observer*, 'Sayings of the Week', 1 Oct. 1944]

ANDREW B. STERLING

9 Meet Me in St Louis, Louis. [Title of song. Music by Kerry Mills]

RICHARD G. STERN

10 Every man has a question which terrifies him, and to the avoidance of which he gives himself with an energy that helps shape his life. [*Golk*, Ch. 1, sect. i]

11 When love gets to be important to someone, it means that he hasn't been able to manage something else. Falling in love seems to me an almost sure sign of failure. Except for the very few who have a real talent for it. [*Ib.* 2. iii]

12 Anybody can shock a baby, or a television audience. But it's too easy, and the effect is disproportionate to the effort. [*Ib.* 4. iii]

WALLACE STEVENS

13 What counted was mythology of self, / Blotched out beyond unblotching. [*The Comedian as the Letter C*, I]

14 The only emperor is the emperor of ice-cream. [*The Emperor of Ice-Cream*]

15 Poetry is the supreme fiction, madame. / Take the moral law and make a nave of it / And from the nave build haunted heaven. [*A High-toned Old Christian Woman*]

16 In the high west there burns a furious star. / It is for fiery boys that star was set / And for sweet-smelling virgins close to them. [*Le Monocle de Mon Oncle*]

17 If sex were all, then every trembling hand / Could make us squeak, like dolls, the wished-for words. [*Ib.*]

18 She bathed in her still garden, while / The red-eyed elders watching, felt / The basses of their beings throb / In witching chords, and their thin blood / Pulse pizzicati of Hosanna. [*Peter Quince at the Clavier*]

19 Beauty is momentary in the mind – / The fitful tracing of a portal; / But in the flesh it is immortal. [*Ib.*]

20 I do not know which to prefer, / The beauty of inflections / Or the beauty of innuendoes, / The blackbird whistling / Or just after. [*Thirteen Ways of Looking at the Blackbird*]

21 I had as lief be embraced by the porter at the hotel / As to get no more from the moonlight / Than your moist hand. [*Two Figures in Dense Violet Night*]

ADLAI STEVENSON

1 A lie is an abomination unto the Lord, and a very present help in trouble. [Speech, Springfield, Ill., Jan. 1951]

2 I offer my opponents a bargain: if they will stop telling falsehoods about us, I will stop telling the truth about them. [During 1952 Presidential Campaign. Quoted in the *Sunday Times*, 8 Jun. 1975, but ascribed to Senator Depew in A. Andrews, *Quotations for Speakers and Writers*]

3 Let's talk sense to the American people. Let's tell them the truth, that there are no gains without pains. [Speech in Chicago, 26 Jul. 1952]

4 Your public servants serve you right. [Speech in Los Angeles, 11 Sep. 1952]

5 There is no evil in the atom; only in men's souls. [Speech in Hartford, Connecticut, 18 Sep. 1952]

6 My definition of a free society is a society where it is safe to be unpopular. [Speech in Detroit, Oct. 1952]

7 God bless mother and daddy, my brother and sister, and save the King. And, oh God, do take care of yourself, because if anything happens to you we're all sunk. [Speech at Harvard Business School, 6 Jun. 1959]

8 Flattery is all right – if you don't inhale. [Speech, 1 Feb. 1961]

9 She [Eleanor Roosevelt] would rather light candles than curse the darkness, and her glow has warmed the world. [Address to the United Nations General Assembly, 9 Nov. 1962]

10 Power corrupts, but lack of power corrupts absolutely. [Quoted in the *Observer*, Jan. 1963]

11 A funny thing happened to me on the way to the White House. [On his defeat in Presidential Election. Quoted in the *Wall Street Journal*, 27 Dec. 1966]

12 They remind me of a very tired rich man who said to his chauffeur 'Drive off that cliff, James, I want to commit suicide.' [Quoted in A. Andrews, *Quotations for Speakers and Writers*]

13 There was a time when a fool and his money were soon parted, but now it happens to everybody. [*The Stevenson Wit*]

14 An editor is one who separates the wheat from the chaff and prints the chaff. [*Ib.*]

15 A politician is a statesman who approaches every question with an open mouth. [Quoted in L. Harris, *The Fine Art of Political Wit*. Also ascribed to Arthur Goldberg describing diplomats]

JOHN STILL

16 The memories of men are too frail a thread to hang history from. [*The Jungle Tide*, Ch. 5]

MARY STOCKS

17 It is clearly absurd that it should be possible for a woman to qualify as a saint with direct access to the Almighty while she may not qualify as a curate. [*Still More Commonplace*]

MERVYN STOCKWOOD, BISHOP OF SOUTHWARK

18 A psychiatrist is a man who goes to the Folies-Bergère and looks at the audience. [*Observer*, 'Sayings of the Week', 15 Oct. 1961, but probably of earlier origin]

I. F. STONE

19 If you live long enough, the venerability factor creeps in; you get accused of things you never did and praised for virtues you never had. [Quoted in Laurence J. Peter, *Peter's Quotations*]

G. M. STONIER
(under pseudonym of FANFARLO)

20 It was on the forty-seventh day of the new razor-blade. Well, one must start somewhere. [*Shaving through the Blitz*, Ch. 1]

21 There it is, the Blitz, all night and half the day, coming and going, sniffing, grunting, throwing up showers of gravel against the windows, as though one had accommodated too big a dog in the garden. [*Ib.*]

318

1 I explain my theory of optimo-pessimism. [*Ib.* 5]

2 I have always felt a faint scepticism, a mild horror, about the country. One goes for quiet; and a gang of rooks is at work murderously tearing at the furrows. [*Ib.* 6]

TOM STOPPARD

3 Why are you bothering to lie to me? You are like a man on a desert island refusing to admit to his only companion that he ate the last coconut. [*Artist Descending a Staircase*]

4 Skill without imagination is craftsmanship and gives us many useful objects such as wickerwork picnic baskets. Imagination without skill gives us modern art. [*Ib.*]

5 That's why he comes over as a sanctimonious busybody with an Energen roll where his balls ought to be. [*Dirty Linen*]

6 *The Times* has published no rumours; it's only reported facts, namely that other, less responsible papers are publishing certain rumours. [*Ib.*]

7 If you took away everything in the world that had to be invented, there'd be nothing left except a lot of people getting rained on. [*Enter a Free Man*, Act I]

8 A circle is the longest distance to the same point. [*Every Good Boy Deserves Favour*]

9 What is known as common sense, whose virtue, uniquely among virtues, is that everybody has it. [*Jumpers*, Act I]

10 To attempt to sustain the attention of rival schools of academics by argument alone is tantamount to constructing a Gothic arch out of junket [*Ib.*]

11 The result was, as I will now demonstrate, that though an arrow is always approaching its target, it never quite gets there, and Saint Sebastian died of fright. [*Ib.*]

12 It's not the voting that's democracy, it's the counting. [*Ib.* See also 312:18]

13 If rationality were the criterion of things being allowed to exist, the world would be a gigantic field of soya beans! [*Ib.*]

14 I can't think of anyone more susceptible to the Rad-Lib philosophy: 'No problem is insoluble given a big enough plastic bag.' [*Ib.*]

15 This is a British murder inquiry and some degree of justice must be seen to be more or less done. [*Ib.* II]

16 Do you think every *sole meunière* comes to you untouched by suffering? [*Ib.*]

17 Do not despair – many are happy much of the time; more eat than starve, more are healthy than sick, more curable than dying; not so many dying as dead; and one of the thieves was saved. Hell's bells and all's well – half the world is at peace with itself, and so is the other half; vast areas are unpolluted; millions of chilren grow up without suffering deprivation, and millions, while deprived, grow up without suffering cruelties, and millions, while deprived and cruelly treated, none the less grow up. No laughter is sad and many tears are joyful. [*Ib.* 'Coda']

18 A foreign correspondent is someone who lives in foreign parts and corresponds, usually in the form of essays containing no new facts. Otherwise he's someone who flies around from hotel to hotel and thinks the most interesting thing about any story is the fact that he has arrived to cover it. [*Night and Day*, Act I]

19 The media. It sounds like a convention of spiritualists. [*Ib.*]

20 A lady, if surprised by melancholy, might go to bed with a chap, once; or a thousand times if consumed by passion. But twice, Wagner, *twice* ... a lady might think she'd be taken for a tart. [*Ib.*]

21 MILNE: No matter how imperfect things are, if you've got a free press everything is correctable, and without it everything is conceivable.
RUTH: I'm with you on the free press. It's the newspapers I can't stand. [*Ib.*]

22 Junk journalism is the evidence of a society that has got at least one thing right, that there should be nobody with

319

the power to dictate where responsible journalism begins. [*Ib.*]

1 MCKENDRICK: You know perfectly well you wouldn't be seen dead in it.
ANDERSON: Even if that were true, my being seen dead in a place has never so far as I know been thought a condition of its excellence. [*Professional Foul*]

2 ANDERSON: Tomorrow is another day, McKendrick.
MCKENDRICK: Tomorrow, in my experience, is usually the same day. [*Ib.*]

3 We do on the stage the things that are supposed to happen off. Which is a kind of integrity, if you look on every exit being an entrance somewhere else. [*Rosencrantz and Guildenstern Are Dead*, Act I]

4 You're familiar with the tragedies of antiquity, are you? The great homicidal classics? [*Ib.*]

5 All your life you live so close to truth, it becomes a permanent blur in the corner of your eye, and when something nudges it into outline it is like being ambushed by a grotesque. [*Ib.*]

6 We have been left so much to our own devices – after a while one welcomes the uncertainty of being left to other people's. [*Ib.* II]

7 A man talking sense to himself is no madder than a man talking nonsense not to himself. [*Ib.*]

8 Eternity's a terrible thought. I mean, where's it going to end? [*Ib.*]

9 The bad end unhappily, the good unluckily. That is what tragedy means. [*Ib.*]

10 We drift down time, clutching at straws. But what good's a brick to a drowning man? [*Ib.* III]

11 Life is a gamble, at terrible odds – if it was a bet, you wouldn't take it. [*Ib.*]

12 An essentially private man who wished his total indifference to public notice to be universally recognized. [*Travesties*, Act I]

13 My art belongs to Dada 'cos Dada / 'e treats me so – well . . . [*Ib.*]

14 What a bloody country [Switzerland], even the cheese has got holes in it! [*Ib.*]

15 War is capitalism with the gloves off and many who go to war know it but they go to war because they don't want to be a hero. [*Ib.*]

16 It is a librarian's duty to distinguish between poetry and a sort of belle-litter. [*Ib.*]

17 Unrelieved truthfulness can give a young girl a reputation for insincerity. I have known plain girls with nothing to hide, captivate the London season purely by discriminate mendacity. [*Ib.*]

18 What is an artist? For every thousand people there's nine hundred doing the work, ninety doing well, nine doing good, and one lucky bastard who's the artist. [*Ib.* Also used with slightly different wording in *Artist Descending a Staircase*]

19 There is no one so radical as a man-servant whose freedom of the champagne bin has been interfered with. [*Ib.* II]

20 I learned three things in Zürich during the war. I wrote them down. Firstly, you're either a revolutionary or you're not, and if you're not you might as well be an artist as anything else. Secondly, if you can't be an artist, you might as well be a revolutionary . . . I forget the third thing. [*Ib.*]

21 The ninth earl sighed. 'I am an island, Mr Moon, and when the bell tolls it tolls for thee.' [*Lord Malquist and Mr Moon*, Pt I, 1]

22 My problem is that I am not frightfully interested in anything, except myself. And of all forms of fiction autobiography is the most gratuitous. [*Ib.* II. 3]

23 Nothing sounds more studied than a repeated spontaneity. [*Ib.*]

24 I agree with everything you say but I would attack to the death your right to say it – Voltaire (the younger). [*Ib.*]

25 Socialists treat their servants with respect and then wonder why they vote Conservative. So unintelligent. [*Ib.* V. 1]

26 The House of Lords, an illusion to which I have never been able to sub-

scribe – responsibility without power, the prerogative of the eunuch throughout the ages. [*Ib*. VI. 1. See also 26:17; 97:13]

1 I do not pretend to understand the universe. It is a great deal bigger than I am. [*Ib*. VI. 2]

2 I write fiction because it's a way of making statements I can disown, and I write plays because dialogue is the most respectable way of contradicting myself. [TV interview, quoted in the *Guardian*, 21 Mar. 1973]

3 A truth is always a compound of two half-truths, and you never reach it, because there is always something more to say. [*Ib*.]

4 I doubt that art needed Ruskin any more than a moving train needs one of its passengers to shove it. [*The Times Literary Supplement*, 3 Jun. 1977]

5 Pinter, Osborne, Arden and Wesker were the four hoarse men of the new apocalypse. [In an interview in the *Telegraph Sunday Magazine*, 26 Jun. 1977]

REX STOUT

6 There are two kinds of statistics, the kind you look up and the kind you make up. [*Death of a Doxy*, Ch. 9]

7 When the last trumpet sounds the *Times* [the *New York Times*] will want to check with Gabriel himself, and for the next edition will try to get it confirmed by even Higher Authority. [*Gambit*, Ch. 3]

8 He was born with the attitude toward all attractive women that a fisherman has toward all the trout in the stream, and has never seen any reason to change it. [*Ib*. 9]

9 Handshakes can be faked and usually are, but smiles can't. It isn't often that a man gets a natural, friendly, straightforward smile from a young woman, with no come on, no catch, and no dare, and the least he can do is return it if he has that kind in stock. [*Homicide Trinity*, 'Death of a Demon']

10 'I'll discuss it with you,' she said, in a voice that could have been used to defrost her refrigerator. [*Three Witnesses*, 'Die like a Dog', III]

11 I like to walk around Manhattan, catching glimpses of its wild life, the pigeons and cats and girls. [*Ib*. 'When a Man Murders']

JACK STRACHEY

12 These Foolish Things Remind Me of You. [Title of song]

JOHN STRACHEY

13 The oldest and greatest monopolist of all, Holy Church herself, the monopolist in God, had to be assailed if the new middle men, the soldiers of the market, were to grow and prosper. [*The Coming Struggle for Power*, Pt I, Ch. 1]

14 While the other arts . . . are the algebra of emotional expression, literature is the arithmetic. Music and the plastic arts seek to express the generalized essence of man's predicament in the universe. Literature, for the most part, attempts to illuminate some particular predicament of a particular man or a particular woman at a given time and place. [*Ib*. III. 10]

15 Becoming an Anglo-Catholic must surely be a sad business – rather like becoming an amateur conjurer. [*Ib*. III. 11]

16 Mr MacDonald has become . . . an actor – and that type of actor which the cruel French call a '*m'as-tu vu?*' 'Have you seen me as the Prime Minister? – My greatest role, I assure you,' Mr MacDonald is anxiously asking the nation. Yes, we have seen him. [*Ib*. V. 17]

17 Fascism means war. [Slogan of the 1930s]

LYTTON STRACHEY

18 First I write one sentence: then I write another. That's how I write. And so I go on. But I have a feeling writing ought to be like running through a field.

[In conversation with Max Beerbohm. Quoted in Virginia Woolf, *A Writer's Diary*, 1 Nov. 1938]

1 I stopped thinking about him [H. G. Wells] when he became a thinker. [In conversation with Hesketh Pearson, May 1921. Quoted in J. Wintle and R. Kenin, *Dictionary of Biographical Quotation*]

2 If this is dying, I don't think much of it. [Dying words. Quoted in Michael Holroyd, *Lytton Strachey*, Pt V, Ch. 17, sect. 8]

EUGENE STRATTON

3 Little Dolly Daydream, pride of Idaho. [Song: *Little Dolly Daydream*]

4 I know she likes me, / 'Cause she says so. [Song: *The Lily of Laguna*]

HENRY G. STRAUSS
(later Lord Conesford)

5 I have every sympathy with the American who was so horrified by what he had read of the effects of smoking that he gave up reading. [Quoted in A. Andrews, *Quotations for Speakers and Writers*]

IGOR STRAVINSKY

6 It is not art that rains down upon us in the song of a bird; but the simplest modulation, correctly executed, is already art. [*Poetics of Music*, Ch. 2]

7 If melody were all of music, what could we prize in the various forces that make up the immense work of Beethoven, in which melody is assuredly the least? [*Ib.*]

8 Poussin said quite correctly that 'the goal of art is delectation'. He did not say that this delectation should be the goal of the artist who must always submit solely to the demands of the work to be done. [*Ib.* 4]

9 A renewal is fruitful only when it goes hand in hand with tradition. [*Ib.* 5]

10 Rachmaninov's immortalizing totality was his scowl. He was a six-and-a-half-foot-tall scowl. [Igor Stravinsky and Robert Craft, *Conversations with Igor Stravinsky*]

11 He [Rachmaninov] was the only pianist I have ever seen who did not grimace. That is a great deal. [*Ib.*]

12 It is interesting to note that conductors' careers are made for the most part with 'romantic' music. 'Classic' music eliminates the conductor; we do not remember him in it. [*Ib.*]

13 Nothing is likely about masterpieces, least of all whether there will be any. [*Ib.* 'The Future of Music']

14 The very people who have done the breaking through are themselves often the first to try to put a scab on their achievement. [*Ib.* 'Advice to Young Composers']

15 Academism results when the reasons for the rule change, but not the rule. [*Ib.* 'Some Musical Questions']

16 A good composer does not imitate; he steals. [Quoted in Peter Yates, *Twentieth Century Music*]

17 Film music should have the same relationship to the film drama that somebody's piano-playing in my living-room has on the book I'm reading. [*Music Digest*, Sep. 1946]

18 My music is best understood by children and animals. [*Observer*, 'Sayings of the Week', 8 Oct. 1961]

19 I had another dream the other day about music critics. They were small and rodent-like with padlocked ears, as if they had stepped out of a painting by Goya. [Quoted in the *Evening Standard*, 29 Oct. 1969]

MR JUSTICE STREATFIELD

20 Facts speak louder than statistics. [*Observer*, 'Sayings of the Week', 19 Mar. 1950]

AUGUST STRINDBERG

21 I loathe people who keep dogs. They are cowards who haven't got the guts to bite people themselves. [*A Madman's Diary*]

REV. G. A. STUDDERT-KENNEDY

1 When Jesus came to Birmingham, they simply passed him by, / They never hurt a hair of him, they only let him die. [Hymn: *When Jesus Came To Birmingham*]

JUDGE STURGESS

2 Justice is open to everybody in the same way as the Ritz Hotel. [*Observer*, 'Sayings of the Week', 22 Jul. 1928. See 94:7]

TERRY SULLIVAN

3 She sells sea-shells on the sea-shore. / The shells she sells are sea-shells, I'm sure. [Song: *She Sells Sea-shells*]

GRAHAM SUTHERLAND

4 [Of portraiture] To 'portray' (used in the best sense) has become synonymous with 'betray'. [Quoted in the *Guardian*, 9 Jun. 1978]

SHINICHI SUZUKI

5 Teaching music is not my main purpose. I want to make good citizens. If a child hears fine music from the day of his birth, and learns to play it himself, he develops sensitivity, discipline and endurance. He gets a beautiful heart. [Quoted in *Reader's Digest*, Nov. 1973]

ITALO SVEVO

6 The really original woman is the one who first imitates a man. [*A Life*, Ch. 8]

7 In a theatre Annetta cared less about the performance on the stage than the audience. She said that she preferred watching people like herself rather than wretched creatures perform with other wretched creatures. [*Ib.* 9]

8 For a long time young Lanucci had ceased struggling against his own laziness, and to spare himself remorse elevated it to a theory. [*Ib.* 13]

9 Whenever I look at a mountain I always expect it to turn into a volcano. [*Confessions of Zeno*]

10 There are three things I always forget. Names, faces, and – the third I can't remember. [Attr.]

B. G. DE SYLVA

11 California, Here I Come. [Title of song]

THOMAS SZASZ

12 A child becomes an adult when he realizes that he has a right not only to be right but also to be wrong. [*The Second Sin*, 'Childhood']

13 Masturbation: the primary sexual activity of mankind. In the nineteenth century it was a disease; in the twentieth, it's a cure. [*Ib.* 'Sex']

14 A teacher should have maximal authority and minimal power. [*Ib.* 'Education']

15 Happiness is an imaginary condition, formerly often attributed by the living to the dead, now usually attributed by adults to children, and by children to adults. [*Ib.* 'Emotions']

16 The proverb warns that, 'You should not bite the hand that feeds you.' But maybe you should, if it prevents you from feeding yourself. [*Ib.* 'Control and Self-control']

17 The stupid neither forgive nor forget; the naïve forgive and forget; the wise forgive but do not forget. [*Ib.* 'Personal Conduct']

18 Two wrongs don't make a right, but they make a good excuse. [*Ib.* 'Social Relations']

19 Psychiatrists classify a person as neurotic if he suffers from his problems in living, and as psychotic if he makes others suffer. [*Ib.* 'Psychiatry']

20 If you talk to God, you are praying; if God talks to you, you have schizophrenia. If the dead talk to you, you are a spiritualist; if God talks to you, you are a schizophrenic. [*Ib.* 'Schizophrenia']

323

1 There is no psychology; there is only biography and autobiography. [*Ib.* 'Psychology']

2 Paternalism: the moral principle that enjoins a person to give another everything but respect. [*Ib.* 'Professionalism']

3 Formerly, when religion was strong and science weak, men mistook magic for medicine; now, when science is strong and religion weak, men mistake medicine for magic. [*Ib.* 'Science and Scientism']

A. SZENT-GYORGYI

4 Discovery consists of seeing what everybody has seen and thinking what nobody has thought. [Quoted in I. J. Good, *The Scientist Speculates*]

T

ROBERT TABER

1 The guerrilla fights the war of the flea, and his military enemy suffers the dog's disadvantages: too much to defend; too small, ubiquitous, and agile an enemy to come to grips with. [*The War of the Flea*, Ch. 2]

JOSEPH TABRAR

2 Daddy wouldn't buy me a bow-wow, bow-wow. / I've got a little cat / And I'm very fond of that. [Song: *Daddy Wouldn't Buy Me A Bow-wow*]

RABINDRANATH TAGORE

3 He who wants to do good knocks at the gate; he who loves finds the door open. [*Stray Birds*, 83]

S. G. TALLENTYRE

4 The crowning blessing of life – to be born with a bias to some pursuit. [*The Friends of Voltaire*]

BOOTH TARKINGTON

5 There are two things that will be believed of any man whatsoever, and one of them is that he has taken to drink. [*Penrod*, Ch. 10]

ALLEN TATE

6 Row upon row with strict impunity / The headstones yield their names to the element. [*Ode to the Confederate Dead*]

7 Autumn is desolation in the plot / Of a thousand acres, where these memories grow / From the inexhaustible bodies that are not / Dead, but feed the grass, row after rich row. [*Ib.*]

8 The brute curiosity of an angel's stare / Turns you like them to stone. [*Ib.*]

9 Those midnight restitutions of the blood. [*Ib.*]

10 Now that the salt of their blood / Stiffens the saltier oblivion of the sea. [*Ib.*]

BERNIE TAUPIN

11 Goodbye Norma Jean / Though I never knew you at all / You had the grace to hold yourself / While those around you crawled. / They crawled out of the woodwork / And they whispered into your brain / Set you on the treadmill / And made you change your name. [Song: *Candle in the Wind*]

R. H. TAWNEY

12 As long as men are men, a poor society cannot be too poor to find a right order of life, nor a rich society too rich to have need to seek it. [*The Acquisitive Society*]

A. J. P. TAYLOR

13 He [Lord Northcliffe] aspired to power instead of influence, and as a result forfeited both. [*English History, 1914–1945*, Ch. 1]

14 History gets thicker as it approaches recent times. [*Ib.* Bibliography]

15 Communism continued to haunt Europe as a spectre – a name men gave to their own fears and blunders. But the crusade against Communism was even more imaginary than the spectre of Communism. [*The Origins of the Second World War*, Ch. 2]

16 Lenin was the first to discover that capitalism 'inevitably' caused war; and he discovered this only when the First World War was already being fought. Of course he was right. Since every great state was capitalist in 1914, capitalism

obviously 'caused' the First World War; but just as obviously it had 'caused' the previous generation of Peace. [*Ib.* 6]

1 A racing tipster who only reached Hitler's level of accuracy would not do well for his clients. [*Ib.* 7]

2 But can dreams really come true? Or do they remain dreams even if men enact them in waking life? [On de Gaulle. *Observer*, 27 Sep. 1959]

3 He [Napoleon III] was what I often think is a dangerous thing for a statesman to be – a student of history; and like most of those who study history, he learned from the mistakes of the past how to make new ones. [*Listener*, 6 Jun. 1963]

4 They say that men become attached even to Widnes. [*Observer*, 15 Sep. 1963]

5 Many historians do not like this suggestion; they like to sort people out into classes. The suggestion that, in the last resort, historical characters are individuals who differ one from another because their individual character differs is very unwelcome to historians, but it is often true. ['The First Modern Revolution', in the *Listener*, 13 Jul. 1978]

BERT LESTON TAYLOR

6 A bore is a man who, when you ask him how he is, tells you. [Quoted in A Andrews, *Quotations for Speakers and Writers*. See also 143:2]

ELIZABETH TAYLOR

7 Life persists in the vulnerable, the sensitive . . . They carry it on. The invulnerable, the too heavily armoured perish. [*A Wreath of Roses*, Ch. 5]

8 He loved himself only as much as self-respect required, and the reason why he saw himself so clearly was that he looked not often, but suddenly, so catching himself unawares. [*Ib.* Ch. 9]

9 It is very strange . . . that the years teach us patience; that the shorter our time, the greater our capacity for waiting. [*Ib.* Ch. 10]

JOHN TAYLOR
(Editor of *Tailor and Cutter*)

10 The only man who really needs a tail coat is a man with a hole in his trousers. [Remark quoted in *Shouts and Murmurs*, from the *Observer*]

PIERRE TEILHARD DE CHARDIN

11 Faith has need of the whole truth. [*The Appearance of Man*]

12 Individual human beings are so subtly developed through the centuries that it is strictly impermissible to compare any two men who are not contemporaries – that is to say are taken from two quite different times. [*Ib.* Ch. 17, sect. ii]

13 The past has revealed to me the structure of the future. [*Letters from a Traveller*]

14 The only universe capable of containing the human person is an irreversibly 'personalizing' universe. [*The Phenomenon of Man*, Bk IV, Ch. 3, sect. iii]

15 From an evolutionary point of view, man has stopped moving, if he ever did move. [*Ib.* Postscript]

WILLIAM TEMPLE, ARCHBISHOP OF CANTERBURY

16 If a man is going to be a villain, in heaven's name let him remain a fool. [*Mens Creatrix*]

17 Personally, I have always looked on cricket as organized loafing. [Remark to parents when Headmaster of Repton School]

18 I am greater than the stars for I know that they are up there and they do not know that I am down here. [Quoted in W. Neil, *Concise Dictionary of Religious Quotations*]

19 It is a mistake to assume that God is interested only, or even chiefly, in religion. [Quoted in *ib.*]

20 It is not the ape, nor the tiger in man that I fear, it is the donkey. [Attr.]

21 The Church exists for the sake of those outside it. [Attr.]

1 I believe in the Church. One Holy, Catholic and Apostolic, and I regret that it is nowhere exists. [Attr.]

2 Unless all existence is a medium of revelation, no particular revelation is possible. [Attr.]

SHERPA TENSING

3 We've done the bugger! [On climbing Everest. Attr.]

ELLEN TERRY

4 How Henry would have loved it! [At Sir Henry Irving's funeral. Quoted in Robert Hitchens, *Yesterdays*]

PAUL THEROUX

5 They say that if the Swiss had designed these mountains [the Alps], they'd be rather flatter. [*The Great Railway Bazaar*, Ch. 2]

6 Extensive travelling induces a feeling of encapsulation, and travel, so broadening at first, contracts the mind. [*Ib.* 21]

7 The Japanese have perfected good manners and made them indistinguishable from rudeness. [*Ib.* 28]

8 The ship follows Soviet custom: it is riddled with class distinctions so subtle, it takes a trained Marxist to appreciate them. [*Ib.* 30]

9 All writing, even the clumsy kind, exposes in its loops and slants a yearning deeper than an intention, the soul of the writer flopping on the clothes-peg of his exclamation mark. [*Saint Jack*, Ch 1]

10 A foreign swear-word is practically inoffensive except to the person who has learnt it early in life and knows its social limits. [*Ib.* 12]

ALLEN D. THOMAS

11 Women add zest to the unlicensed hours. [Remark made in a pub, 1964]

CALVIN THOMAS

12 Living Well is the Best Revenge. [Title of book, quoting old Spanish proverb]

DYLAN THOMAS

13 Her fist of a face died clenched on a round pain; / And sculptured Ann is seventy years of stone. [*After the Funeral*]

14 Before I knocked and flesh let enter, / With liquid hands tapped on the womb, / I who was shapeless as the water / That shaped the Jordan near my home / Was brother to Mnetha's daughter / And sister to the fathering worm. [*Before I Knocked*]

15 I, born of flesh and ghost, was neither / A ghost nor man, but mortal ghost. / And I was struck down by death's feather. [*Ib.*]

16 The conversation of prayers about to be said / Turns on the quick and the dead, and the man on the stairs / Tonight shall find no dying but alive and warm. [*The Conversation of Prayer*]

17 Do not go gentle into that good night. / Rage, rage against the dying of the light. [*Do not go gentle into that good night*]

18 Ears in the turrets hear / Hands grumble on the door, / Eyes in the gables see / The fingers at the locks. [*Ears in the turrets hear*]

19 The hunchback in the park / A solitary mister / Propped between trees and water. [*The Hunchback in the Park*]

20 And the wild boys innocent as strawberries. [*Ib.*]

21 The world is half the devil's and my own, / Daft with the drug that's smoking in a girl / And curling round the bud that forks her eye. [*If I were Tickled by the Rub of Love*]

22 Man be my metaphor. [*Ib.*]

23 And I rose / In the rainy autumn / And Walked abroad in a shower of all my days. [*Poem in October*]

24 ... A child's / Forgotten mornings when he walked with his mother / Through the parables / Of sun light / And the legends of the green chapels. [*Ib.*]

25 It was my thirtieth / Year to heaven stood there then in the summer noon. [*Ib.*]

1 A process in the weather of the heart /
Turns damp to dry; the golden shot /
Storms in the freezing tomb. [*A Process
in the Weather of the Heart*]

2 A process blows the moon into the sun,
/ Pulls down the shabby curtains of the
skin; / And the heart gives up its dead.
[*Ib.*]

3 Deep in the first dead lies London's
daughter, / Robed in the long friends, /
The grains beyond age, the dark veins
of her mother, / Secret by the un-
mourning water / Of the riding Thames.
/ After the first death there is no other.
[*A Refusal to Mourn the Death, by
Fire, of a Child in London*]

4 The ball I threw while playing in the
park / Has not yet reached the ground.
[*Should lanterns shine*]

5 There shall be corals in your beds, /
There shall be serpents in your tides, /
Till all our sea-faiths die. [*Where once
the Waters of your Face*]

6 I read somewhere of a shepherd who,
when asked why he made, from within
fairy rings, ritual observances to the
moon to preserve his flocks, replied:
'I'd be a damn fool if I didn't!' [Note
to *Collected Poems*]

7 I'm Jonah Jarvis, come to a bad end,
very enjoyable. [*Under Milk Wood*]

8 Chasing the naughty couples down the
grassgreen gooseberried double bed of
the wood. [*Ib.*]

9 Every night of her married life she has
been late for school. [*Ib.*]

10 ... kissed her once by the pigsty when
she wasn't looking and never kissed her
again although she was looking all the
time. [*Ib.*]

11 Oh, isn't life a terrible thing, thank
God? [*Ib.*]

12 Oh I'm a martyr to music. [Mrs Organ
Morgan. *Ib.*]

13 I love you until Death do us part and
then we shall be together for ever and
ever. [*Ib.*]

14 ... thinking of a woman soft as Eve and
sharp as sciatica to share his bread-
pudding bed. [*Ib.*]

15 ... his nicotine eggyellow weeping
walrus Victorian moustache worn thick
and long in memory of Doctor Crippen.
[*Ib.*]

16 Portraits of famous bards and preachers,
all fur and wool from the squint to the
kneecaps. [*Ib.*]

17 I missed the chance of a lifetime, too.
Fifty lovelies in the rude and I'd left my
Bunsen burner home. [*Portrait of the
Artist as a Young Dog*, 'One Warm
Saturday']

18 The land of my fathers. My fathers can
have it. [Quoted in John Ackerman,
Dylan Thomas]

19 Too many of the artists of Wales spend
too much time about the position of the
artist of Wales. There is only one
position for an artist anywhere: and
that is, upright. [Quoted by Geoffrey
Grigson in the *New Statesman*, 18 Dec.
1964]

EDWARD THOMAS

20 All are behind, the kind / And the unkind too, no more / To-night than a
dream. The stream / Runs softly and
drowns the Past, / The dark-lit stream
has drowned the Future and the Past.
[*The Bridge*]

21 There is not any book / Or face of
dearest look / That I would not turn
from now / To go into the unknown /
I must enter, and leave, alone, / I know
not how. [*Lights Out*]

22 Its silence I hear and obey / That I
may lose my way / And myself. [*Ib.*]

23 All was foretold me; naught / Could I
foresee; / But I learned how the wind
would sound / After these things should
be. [*The New House*]

24 The green elm with the one great bough
of gold / Lets leaves into the grass slip,
one by one. [*October*]

25 But if this be not happiness – who
knows? / Some day I shall think this a
happy day, / And this mood by the
name of melancholy / Shall no more
blackened and obscurèd be. [*Ib.*]

1 How weak and little is the light, / All the universe of sight, / Love and delight, / Before the might, / If you love it not, of night. [*Out in the Dark*]

2 Merrily / Answered staid drinkers, good bedmen, and all bores: / 'At Mrs Greenland's Hawthorn Bush,' said he / 'I slept.' [*A Private*]

3 Now all roads lead to France / And heavy is the tread / Of the living; but the dead/ Returning lightly dance. [*Roads*]

4 I like the dust on the nettles, never lost / Except to prove the sweetness of a shower. [*Tall Nettles*]

5 Make me content / With some sweetness / From Wales / Whose nightingales / Have no wings. [*Words*]

GWYN THOMAS

6 I wanted a play that would paint the full face of sensuality, rebellion and revivalism. In South Wales these three phenomena have played second fiddle only to the Rugby Union which is a distillation of all three. [Introduction to *Jackie the Jumper, Plays and Players*, 19 Jan. 1963]

7 You are truly God's trumpet, Mr Rees. After a session on you he must feel whacked. [*Jackie the Jumper*, Act II]

8 My life's been a meeting, Dad, one long meeting. Even on the few committees I don't yet belong to, the agenda winks at me when I pass. [*The Keep*, Act I]

9 A bit like God in his last years, the Alderman. [*Ib.*]

10 A man catches a glimpse of what he's shrunk into and he tries to get back to his full height. That's what most of the Sunday papers are about. [*Ib.*]

11 A good voice but too autocratic for oratorio. [*Ib.* II]

12 Her first economic drive will be to replace X-ray by hearsay. [*Ib.*]

13 There are still parts of Wales where the only concession to gaiety is a striped shroud. [*Punch*, 18 Jun. 1958]

IRENE THOMAS

14 Protestant women may take the Pill. Roman Catholic women must keep taking the *Tablet*. [Attr. in conversation]

15 It should be a very happy marriage – they are both so much in love with *him*. [Attr.]

R. S. THOMAS

16 It is too late to start / For destinations not of the heart. / I must stay here with my hurt. [*Here*]

17 Shelley dreamt it. Now the dream decays. / The props crumble. [*Song at the Year's Turning*]

18 ... an impotent people, / Sick with inbreeding, / Worrying the carcase of an old song. [*Welsh Landscape*]

E. P. THOMPSON

19 This 'going into Europe' will not turn out to be the thrilling mutual exchange supposed. It is more like nine middle-aged couples with failing marriages meeting in a darkened bedroom in a Brussels hotel for a Group Grope. [On the Europe debate, *Sunday Times*, 27 Apr. 1975]

H. W. THOMPSON

20 An old man marrying a young girl is like buying a book for some one else to read. [*Body, Boots and Britches*]

21 Never speak loudly to one another unless the house is on fire. [*Ib.*]

LORD THOMSON OF FLEET

22 A stake in commercial television is the equivalent of having a licence to print money. [Quoted in the *Guardian Weekly*, 15 Aug. 1976, but dating back to the start of commercial TV in Britain]

JEREMY THORPE

23 [Of Macmillan's swingeing Cabinet reshuffle in 1962] Greater love hath no man than this, that he lay down his

329

friends for his life. [Quoted in Bernard Levin, *The Pendulum Years*, Ch. 12]

JAMES THURBER

1 She developed a persistent troubled frown which gave her the expression of someone who is trying to repair a watch with his gloves on. [*The Beast in Me and Other Animals*, 'Look Homeward, Jeannie']

2 Grandog. [*The Dogs*, Preface]

3 Charles Vayne, as regular and as futile as a clock in an empty house, showed up once a week. [*Alarms and Diversions*, 'A final note on Chanda Bell']

4 'I think this calls for a drink' has long been one of our national slogans. [*Ib.* 'Merry Christmas']

5 'Joe,' I said, 'was perhaps the first great nonstop literary drinker of the American nineteenth century. He made the indulgences of Coleridge and De Quincey seem like a bit of mischief in the kitchen with the cooking sherry.' [*Ib.* 'The Moribundant Life . . .']

6 I was seized by the stern hand of Compulsion, that dark, unseasonable Urge that impels women to clean house in the middle of the night. [*Ib.* 'There's a Time for Flags']

7 No man . . . who has wrestled with a self-adjusting card table can ever quite be the man he once was. [*Let Your Mind Alone*, 'Sex ex Machina']

8 Old Nat Burge sat on the rusted wreck of an ancient sewing machine in front of Hell Fire, which was what his shack was known as among the neighbours and to the police. He was chewing on a splinter of wood and watching the moon come up lazily out of the old cemetery in which nine of his daughters were lying, and only two of them were dead. [*Ib.* 'Bateman Comes Home']

9 I myself have accomplished nothing of excellence except a remarkable and, to some of my friends, unaccountable expertness in hitting empty ginger ale bottles with small rocks at a distance of thirty paces. [*My Life and Hard Times*, Preface]

10 They [humorists] lead, as a matter of fact, an existence of jumpiness and apprehension. They sit on the edge of the chair of Literature. In the house of Life they have the feeling that they have never taken off their overcoats. [*Ib.*]

11 Q. We have cats the way most people have mice. [Signed] Mrs C. L. FOOT-LOOSE
A. I see you have. I can't tell from your communication whether you wish advice or are just boasting. [*The Owl in the Attic*]

12 'We all have flaws,' he said, 'and mine is being wicked.' [*The 13 Clocks*, Ch. 8]

13 If he knew where he was going, it is not apparent from this distance. He fell down a great deal during this period, because of a trick he had of walking into himself. [On himself as a child. *The Thurber Carnival*, Preface]

14 If you don't pay no mind to diseases, they will go away. [*Ib.* 'Recollections of the Gas Buggy']

15 There is, of course, a certain amount of drudgery in newspaper work, just as there is in teaching classes, tunnelling into a bank, or being President of the United States. I suppose that even the most pleasurable of imaginable occupations, that of batting baseballs through the windows of the RCA Building, would pall a little as the days ran on. [*Ib.* 'Memoirs of a Drudge']

16 You wait here and I'll bring the etchings down. [*Men, Women and Dogs*, cartoon caption]

17 I said the hounds of spring are on winter's traces – but let it pass, let it pass! [*Ib.* Cartoon caption]

18 Why don't you get dressed, then, and go to pieces like a man? [*Alarms and Diversions*, cartoon caption]

19 Ooooo, guesties! [*Ib.* Cartoon caption]

20 All right, have it your way – you heard a seal bark. [*The Seal in the Bedroom*, cartoon caption]

21 You might as well fall flat on your face as lean over too far backward. [*Fables for Our Time*, 'The Bear Who Let It Alone']

330

1 Early to rise and early to bed makes a male healthy and wealthy and dead. [*Ib.*, 'The Shrike and the Chipmunks']

2 It is better to have loafed and lost than never to have loafed at all. [*Ib.* 'The Courtship of Arthur and Al']

3 You can fool too many of the people too much of the time. [*Ib.* 'The Owl Who Was God']

4 Though statisticians in our time have never kept the score, Man wants a great deal here below and Woman even more. [*Further Fables for Our Time*, 'The Godfather and His Godchild']

5 Ashes to ashes, and clay to clay, if the enemy doesn't get you your own folks may. [*Ib.* 'The Peacelike Mongoose']

6 Mosher came out into the reception room, looking like a professor of English literature who has not approved of the writings of anybody since Sir Thomas Browne. [*The Years with Ross*, Ch. 2]

7 [On the advantages of blindness to a writer] You are constantly distracted by the sight of flowers and the buds bursting. I can sit here and I don't get distracted by flying birds or the sight of a pretty girl going by. Of course . . . I can still *hear* a pretty girl go by. [Quoted in Alistair Cooke, *Talk About America*, Ch. 15]

8 It had only one fault. It was kind of lousy. [When asked his opinion of a play. Quoted in P. G. Wodehouse, *Performing Flea*, 1947–52]

9 The difference between our decadence and the Russians' is that while theirs is brutal, ours is apathetic. [*Observer*, 'Sayings of the Week', 5 Feb. 1961]

10 Why do you have to be a nonconformist like everybody else? [Attr. Thurber. Actually cartoon caption by Stan Hunt in *New Yorker*]

THWACKHURST

11 'You have ruined all the graffiti. You can't find anything in a piss-house now but political remarks . . . And just when the spread of popular education was bringing the graffiti lower on the walls.' 'Lower on the walls?' 'Sure. Don't you see the little children were beginning to add their quota, when all this damn politics comes along.' [Quoted in Oliver St John Gogarty, *As I Was Going Down Sackville Street*, Ch. 4]

PAUL TILLICH

12 Faith is the state of being ultimately concerned. [*Dynamics of Faith*, Ch. 1]

13 Life could not continue without throwing the past into the past, liberating the present from its burden. [*The Eternal Now*, Pt. II, Ch. 1]

14 Neurosis is the way of avoiding non-being by avoiding being. [*The Courage to Be*]

15 You must forget everything traditional that you have learned about God, perhaps even that word itself. [*The Shaking of the Foundations*, 'The Depth of Existence']

THE TIMES

16 In my childhood it was said by all: 'A child of ten can go on the road of a town playing with a golden ball in perfect safety under British rule.' [Quoted in *The Times*]

CHARLES TOBIAS
see LEW BROWN

ALVIN TOFFLER

17 Future Shock. [Title of book. Derived from term 'Culture Shock']

PALMIRO TOGLIATTI

18 The experience accomplished in the building of a socialist society in the Soviet Union cannot contain instructions for resolving all the questions which may present themselves to us and to Communists in other countries . . . There is established . . . a polycentric system. [Speech to the central committee of Italian Communist Party, 24 Jun. 1956]

J. R. R. TOLKIEN

1 In a hole in the ground there lived a hobbit. [*The Hobbit*, Ch. 1]

2 One Ring to rule them all, One Ring to find them, / One Ring to bring them all and in the darkness bind them. [*The Lord of the Rings*, Part I: *The Fellowship of the Ring*, Ch. 2]

3 The night was tailing against the morning of which it was bereaved, and the cold was cursing the warmth for which it hungered. [*Ib.* 8]

LEO TOLSTOY

4 Historians are like deaf people who go on answering questions that no one has asked them. [Quoted in Manning Clark, *A Discovery of Australia*, 'Being an Historian']

5 How do peasants die? [Death-bed words, attr. in Kenneth Clark, *Civilisation*, Ch. 13]

NICHOLAS TOMALIN

6 *Tout comprendre, c'est tout pardonner*, and *tout pardonner* makes very dull copy. [Quoted by James Cameron on BBC radio, Nov. 1976]

RUDOLPHE TOMASCHEK

7 Modern Physics is an instrument of [world] Jewry for the destruction of Nordic science. . . . True physics is the creation of the German spirit. [Quoted in W. L. Shirer, *The Rise and Fall of the Third Reich*, Ch. 8]

H. M. TOMLINSON

8 I will never believe again that the sea was ever loved by anyone whose life was married to it. [*The Sea and the Jungle*, Ch. 1]

ARTURO TOSCANINI

9 After I die, I shall return to earth as the doorkeeper of a bordello and I won't let a one of you in. [To his orchestra at rehearsal. Quoted in Nat Shapiro, *An Encyclopedia of Quotations about Music*]

MICHEL TOURNIER

10 Nakedness is a luxury in which a man may only indulge without peril to himself when he is warmly surrounded by the multitude of his fellows. [*Friday or the Other Island*, Ch. 2]

F. H. TOWNSEND

11 O Cuckoo, shall I call thee bird, / Or but a wandering voice? / State the alternative preferred / And reasons for your choice. [Parody of Wordsworth's *To the Cuckoo*]

PETE TOWNSHEND

12 I hope I die before I get old. [Song: *My Generation*]

13 I was born with a plastic spoon in my mouth. [Song: *Substitute*]

ARNOLD TOYNBEE

14 No annihilation without representation. [Pressing for a greater British voice in the affairs of UNO, 1947]

15 America is a large, friendly dog in a very small room. Every time it wags its tail it knocks over a chair. [Broadcast news summary, 14 Jul. 1954]

16 The human race's prospects of survival were considerably better when we were defenceless against tigers than they are today when we have become defenceless against ourselves. [*Observer*, 'Sayings of the Year', 1963]

PHILIP TOYNBEE

17 What I mean by moral progress is an increasing and active recognition of the fact that other human beings are fully as human as oneself. ['Two Cheers for Moral Progress', reprinted in *Shouts and Murmurs* from the *Observer*]

18 [Of America] I have seen the future and it does not work. [*Observer*, 'Pockets of Sanity in a Land of Madness', 27 Jan. 1974. See also 316:10]

19 He [John Middleton Murry] was the type of man who is always trying to live beyond his moral means. [Book review in the *Observer*, 12 Jan. 1975]

SPENCER TRACY

1 [Of his early struggles] There were times my pants were so thin I could sit on a dime and tell if it was heads or tails. [Quoted in L. Swindell, *Spencer Tracy*]

SIR HERBERT BEERBOHM TREE

2 I was born old and get younger every day. At present I am sixty years young. [Quoted in Hesketh Pearson, *Beerbohm Tree*, Ch. 1. See also 105:5]

3 FELLOW-MEMBER [after a scene at the Garrick Club]: When I joined all the members were gentlemen.
TREE: I wonder why they left. [Quoted in *ib.* 5]

4 The only man who wasn't spoilt by being lionized was Daniel. [*Ib.* 12]

5 A whipper-snapper of criticism who quoted dead languages to hide his ignorance of life. [Of A. B. Walkley. Quoted in *ib.*]

6 The national sport of England is obstacle-racing. People fill their rooms with useless and cumbersome furniture, and spend the rest of their lives in trying to dodge it. [*Ib.*]

7 She has kissed her way into society. I don't like her. But don't misunderstand me: my dislike is purely platonic. [Of an actress who was better as a lover than on the stage. Quoted in *ib.*]

8 My poor fellow, why not carry a watch? [To a man who was staggering in the street under the weight of a grandfather clock. Quoted in *ib.*]

9 Oh my God! Remember you're in Egypt. The *skay* is only seen in Kensington. [To a leading lady. Quoted in *ib.* 16]

10 Sirs, I have tested your machine. It adds a new terror to life and makes death a long-felt want. [To a gramophone company who asked for a testimonial. Quoted in *ib.* 19]

11 When I pass my name in such large letters I blush, but at the same time instinctively raise my hat. [Quoted in *ib.*]

12 God is a sort of burglar. As a young man you knock him down; as an old man you try to conciliate him, because he may knock you down. [Quoted in *ib.* 21]

13 His face shining like Moses, his teeth like the Ten Commandments, all broken. [Of Israel Zangwill. Quoted in *ib.*]

14 He is an old bore; even the grave yawns for him. [*Ib.*]

15 TREE [in a post-office]: Do you sell postage-stamps?
GIRL: Yes, sir.
T : Please show me some. [Then pointing to one in the middle of the sheet] I'll have that one, please. [Quoted in George Robey, *Looking Back on Life*, Ch. 27]

16 Ladies, just a little more virginity, if you don't mind. [To a 'collection of damsels that had been dragged into the theatre as ladies in waiting to the queen' in his production of *Henry VIII*. Quoted in Alexander Woollcott, *Shouts and Murmurs*, 'Capsule Criticism']

G. M. TREVELYAN

17 Walpole . . . even when Prime Minister was said to open his gamekeeper's letters first of the batch. [*History of England*, Bk V, Ch. 2]

18 Nelson, born in a fortunate hour for himself and for his country, was always in his element and always on his element. [*Ib.* V. 5]

H. R. TREVOR-ROPER

19 [James I] remained an omniscient umpire whom no one consulted. [*Archbishop Laud*]

LIONEL TRILLING

20 We are all ill: but even a universal sickness implies an idea of health. [*The Liberal Imagination*, 'Art and Neurosis']

21 There is no connexion between the political ideas of our educated class and the deep places of the imagination. [*Ib.* 'The Function of the Little Magazine']

22 It would seem that Americans have a kind of resistance to looking closely at

society. [*Ib.* 'Manners, Morals and the Novel']

TOMMY TRINDER

1 You lucky people! [Catch-phrase used in variety and radio comedy act]

2 KING: Well, Trinder, you've done well since I saw you last.
TRINDER: You haven't done so badly yourself, sir! [In conversation with George VI shortly after the Duke of Windsor's abdication. Quoted in John Fisher, *Funny Way To Be a Hero*, 'You Lucky People']

3 [Of the G.I.s] They're overpaid, overfed, oversexed and over here. [Attr. by Alan Brien in the *Sunday Times*, 4 Jan. 1976]

LEON TROTSKY

4 Revolution by its very nature is sometimes compelled to take in more territory than it is capable of holding. Retreats are possible – when there is territory to retreat from. [*Diary in Exile*, 15 Feb. 1935]

5 Nicholas II inherited from his ancestors not only a giant empire, but also a revolution. And they did not bequeath him one property that would have made him capable of governing an empire or even a province or a county. [*History of the Russian Revolution*, Pt I, Ch. 4]

6 The 23rd of February was International Woman's Day ... It had not occurred to anyone that it might become the first day of the revolution. [*Ib.* I. 7]

7 The revolution does not choose its paths: it made its first steps towards victory under the belly of a Cossack's horse. [*Ib.*]

8 The English and French bourgeoisie created a new society after their own image. The Germans came later, and they were compelled to live for a long time on the pale gruel of philosophy. [*Ib.* I. 10]

9 The most revolutionary party which human history until this time had ever known was nevertheless caught unawares by the events of history. [*Ib.* I. 21]

10 The slanders poured down like Niagara. If you take into consideration the setting – the war and the revolution – and the character of the accused – revolutionary leaders of millions who were conducting their party to the sovereign power – you can say without exaggeration that July 1917 was the month of the most gigantic slander in world history. [*Ib.* II. 5]

11 Revolutions are always verbose. [*Ib.* II. 12]

12 Civilization has made the peasantry its pack animal. [*Ib.* III. 1]

13 A civil war is inevitable. We have only to organize it as painlessly as possible. [Speech quoted in *ib.* III. 5]

14 In practice a reformist party considers unshakable the foundations of that which it intends to reform. [*Ib.*]

15 Insurrection is an art, and like all arts it has its laws. [*Ib.* III. 6]

16 The fundamental premise of a revolution is that the existing social structure has become incapable of solving the urgent problems of development of the nation. [*Ib.*]

17 There is a limit to the application of democratic methods. You can inquire of all the passengers as to what type of car they like to ride in, but it is impossible to question them as to whether to apply the brakes when the train is at full speed and accident threatens. [*Ib.*]

18 From being a patriotic myth, the Russian people have become an awful reality. [*Ib.* III. 7]

19 Armed insurrection stands in the same relation to revolution that revolution as a whole does to evolution. It is the critical point when accumulating quantity turns with an explosion into quality. [*Ib.* III. 9]

20 The historic ascent of humanity, taken as a whole, may be summarized as a succession of victories of consciousness over blind forces – in nature, in society, in man himself. [*Ib.* Conclusion]

21 For us, the tasks of education in socialism were closely integrated with those of fighting. Ideas that enter the

mind under fire remain there securely and for ever. [*My Life*, Ch. 35]

1 Whatever opposition there might be was tested in action, on the very spot . . . If we had had more time for discussion we should probably have made a great many more mistakes. [*Ib.* 36]

2 It was the supreme expression of the mediocrity of the apparatus that Stalin himself rose to his position. [*Ib.* 40]

3 We only die when we fail to take root in others. [Quoted in Trevor Griffiths, *The Party*, Act II]

4 Lenin's method leads to this: the party organization at first substitutes itself for the party as a whole. Then the central committee substitutes itself for the party organization, and finally a single dictator substitutes himself for the central committee. [Written in 1906. Quoted in N. McInnes, *The Communist Parties of Western Europe*, Ch. 3]

5 Patriotism to the Soviet State is a revolutionary duty, whereas patriotism to a bourgeois State is treachery. [Quoted in Fitzroy Maclean, *Disputed Barricade*]

6 The end may justify the means as long as there is something that justifies the end. [Quoted in A. Pozzolini, *Antonio Gramsci: an introduction to his thought*, Preface]

7 I myself took this job [Commissar for Foreign Relations] so I would have more time for Party work. All there is to do is to publish the secret treaties. Then I will close the shop. [Quoted in A. Ulam, *Expansion and Coexistence*]

8 An ally has to be watched just like an enemy. [Quoted in *ib.*]

PRESIDENT HARRY TRUMAN

9 The buck stops here. [Notice on his presidential desk]

10 If we see that Germany is winning the war we ought to help Russia, and if Russia is winning we ought to help Germany, and in that way let them kill as many as possible. [Reported in the *New York Times* on 24 Jul. 1941, the day the Nazis invaded Russia]

11 The President spends most of his time kissing people on the cheek in order to get them to do what they ought to do without getting kissed. [*Observer*, 'Sayings of the Week', 6 Feb. 1949]

12 An eight-ulcer man on a four-ulcer job, and all four ulcers working. [Letter to *Washington Post* on unflattering reviewer of his daughter's song recital, 5 Dec. 1950. Quoted in Frank Muir, *The Frank Muir Book*]

13 It's a recession when your neighbour loses his job; it's a depression when you lose your own. [*Observer*, 'Sayings of the Week', 6 Apr. 1958]

14 A politician is a man who understands government, and it takes a politician to run a government. A statesman is a politician who's been dead ten or fifteen years. [Quoted in the *New York World Telegram and Sun*, 12 Apr. 1958]

15 [On Vice-President Nixon's candidacy for the Presidency] You don't set a fox to watching the chickens just because he has a lot of experience in the hen house. [Speech, 30 Oct. 1960]

16 I didn't fire him [General MacArthur] because he was a dumb son of a bitch, although he was, but that's not against the law for generals. If it was, half to three-quarters of them would be in gaol. [Said in an interview. Quoted in Merle Miller, *Plain Speaking*]

17 I sit here all day trying to persuade people to do the things they ought to have sense enough to do without my persuading them . . . That's all the powers of the President amount to. [Quoted in R. E. Neustadt, *Presidential Power*]

BARBARA W. TUCHMAN

18 Dead battles, like dead generals, hold the military mind in their dead grip. [*The Guns of August*, Ch. 2]

19 No more distressing moment can ever face a British government than that which requires it to come to a hard and fast and specific decision. [Of August 1914. *Ib.* 9]

335

SOPHIE TUCKER

1 The Last of the Red-Hot Mamas. [Description of herself. Quoted in J. Wintle and R. Kenin, *Dictionary of Biographical Quotation*]

2 Life begins at forty. [Quoted in *The Times*, 21 Jan. 1978]

A. W. TUER

3 English as She is Spoke. [Title of book of English-Portuguese conversation]

ROY TURK

4 Walking My Baby Back Home. [Title of song]

CHARLES TURLEY

5 Modesty can be cultivated until it becomes something very like a crime. [*A Band of Brothers*]

W. J. TURNER

6 There is virtue in recognizing that Bach had more intellectual and emotional power than an infinite number of Puccinis and Stravinskys. But Bach a great religious composer! Oh, dear no! [Review reprinted in V. S. Pritchett, *Turnstile One*]

JULIAN TUWIM

7 There are two kinds of blood, the blood that flows in the veins and the blood that flows out of them. [*We, the Polish Jews*]

MARK TWAIN

8 There are three kinds of lies – lies, damned lies and statistics. [*Autobiography*, Pt V, Ch. 1]

9 It is by the goodness of God that we have in our country three unspeakably precious things: freedom of speech, freedom of conscience, and the prudence never to practise either. [Quoted in Sagittarius and George, *The Perpetual Pessimist*]

10 Whoever has lived long enough to find out what life is knows how deep a debt of gratitude we owe to Adam, the first great benefactor of our race. He brought death into the world. [Quoted in *ib.*]

'TWEETY-PIE'

11 I t'ought I saw a puddy-tat . . . [Catchline in the 'Sylvester and Tweety-Pie' cartoon series]

KENNETH TYNAN

12 William Congreve is the only sophisticated playwright England has produced; and like Shaw, Sheridan, and Wilde, his nearest rivals, he was brought up in Ireland. [*Curtains*, 'The Way of the World']

13 A novel is a static thing that one moves through; a play is a dynamic thing that moves past one. [*Ib.* 'Cards of Identity']

14 Forty years ago he [Noël Coward] was Slightly in *Peter Pan*, and you might say he has been wholly in *Peter Pan* ever since. [*Curtains*, 'A Tribute to Mr Coward']

15 If his [Noël Coward's] face suggested an old boot, it was unquestionably hand-made. [*The Sound of Two Hands Clapping*, 'In Memory of Mr Coward']

16 A good drama critic is one who perceives what is happening in the theatre of his time. A great drama critic also perceives what is not happening. [*Tynan Right and Left*, Foreword]

17 What, when drunk, one sees in other women, one sees in Garbo sober. [Quoted in the *Sunday Times*, 25 Aug. 1963]

18 A critic is a man who knows the way but can't drive the car. [Quoted in the *New York Times Magazine*, 9 Jan. 1966]

19 [Of Ralph Richardson's voice] Something between bland and grandiose: blandiose perhaps. [Quoted in *Observer Magazine*, 'Tynan on Richardson', 18 Dec. 1977]

GEORGE TYRRELL

20 I never quite forgave Mahaffy for getting himself suspended from preach-

ing in the College Chapel. Ever since his sermons were discontinued, I suffer from insomnia in church. [Quoted in Oliver St John Gogarty, *As I Was Going Down Sackville Street*, Ch. 25]

1 That's this country [Ireland] all over! Not content with a contradiction in terms, it must go on to an antithesis in ideas. 'Temperance Hotel'! You might as well speak of a celibate kip [brothel]! [Quoted in *ib.*]

2 We do not need to prove religion to men but to prove to them that they are religious. [Attr.]

U

MIGUEL DE UNAMUNO

1 *La vida es duda, | y la fe sin la duda es sólo muerte.* – Life is doubt, and faith without doubt is nothing but death. [*Poesías*, 1907]

2 All right, my lord creator, Don Miguel, you too will die and return to the nothing whence you came. God will cease to dream you! [*Mist*]

3 It is not usually our ideas that make us optimists or pessimists, but it is our optimism or pessimism, of physiological or pathological origin . . . that makes our ideas. [*The Tragic Sense of Life*, Ch. 1]

4 My work . . . is to shatter the faith of men here, there and everywhere, faith in affirmation, faith in negation, and faith in abstention from faith, and this for the sake of faith in faith itself. [*Ib.* Conclusion]

5 May God deny you peace but give you glory! [*Ib.* Closing words]

6 They [the Franco rebels] will conquer, but they will not convince. [Said at the end of his life]

UNESCO

7 Since wars begin in the minds of men, it is in the minds of men that the defence of peace must be constructed. [Constitution]

UNKNOWN JUDGE

8 [Reprimanding prisoner before sentence] You have been found guilty of indulging in unnatural practices under one of London's most *beautiful* bridges. [Traditional at the Bar]

JOHN UPDIKE

9 A healthy male adult bore consumes each year one and a half times his own weight in other people's patience. [*Assorted Prose*, 'Confessions of a Wild Bore']

10 The founding fathers in their wisdom decided that children were an unnatural strain on parents. So they provided jails called schools, equipped with tortures called education. School is where you go between when your parents can't take you and industry can't take you. [*The Centaur*, Ch. 4]

11 In general the churches, visited by me too often on weekdays . . . bore for me the same relation to God that billboards did to Coca-Cola: they promoted thirst without quenching it. [*A Month of Sundays*, Ch. 2]

12 Americans have been conditioned to respect newness, whatever it costs them. [*Ib.* 18]

13 Donald is considerably to the right of our Lord and Saviour Jesus Christ! [*Ib.*]

14 It is hard, of course, to console or advise professional consolers and advisers; rote phrases, professional sympathy, even an emphatic patience are brusquely shunted aside. At a convention of masseurs no one turns his back. [*Ib.* 25]

15 Everybody who tells you how to act has whisky on their breath. [*Rabbit, Run*]

16 The difficulty with humorists is that they will mix what they believe with what they don't; whichever seems likelier to win an effect. [*Ib.*]

17 He is a man of brick. As if he was born as a baby literally of clay and decades of exposure have baked him to the colour and hardness of brick. [*Ib.*]

RICHARD USBORNE

18 There is no suggestion that either clubman or girl would recognize a double

bed except as so much extra sweat to make an apple-pie of. [*Wodehouse at Work*, 'The Short Stories']

1 A monstrous aunt can be funny. A monstrous mother would be tragic. [*Wodehouse at Work to the End*, Ch. 2]

2 Lovely Pamela, who found / One sure way to get around / Goes to bed beneath this stone / Early, sober, and alone. [*Epitaph on a Party Girl*]

3 Definition of a slogan: a form of words for which memorability has been bought. [In letter to editors, 1964]

PETER USTINOV

4 Courage is not a requisite for the loss of life. While it is for an injection, if you're not used to it. There's irony for you. [*The Moment of Truth*, Act I]

5 I prefer our military past. The harm's done and there it is. As for being a General, well at the age of four with paper hats and wooden swords we're all Generals. Only some of us never grow out of it. [*Romanoff and Juliet*, Act I]

6 A diplomat these days is nothing but a head-waiter who's allowed to sit down occasionally. [*Ib.*]

7 This is a free country, madam. We have a right to share your privacy in a public place. [*Ib.*]

8 I began life as a ne'er-do-well, but was discovered cheating at cards, so my career was finished. [*Ib.*]

9 Sometimes I wish I could fall in love. Then at least you know who your opponent is! [*Ib.* II]

10 I was irrevocably betrothed to laughter, the sound of which has always seemed to me the most civilized music in the world. [*Dear Me*, Ch. 3]

11 I have always imagined cricket as a game invented by roughnecks in a moment of idleness by casually throwing an unexploded bomb at one another. The game was observed by some officer with a twisted and ingenious mind who devoted his life to inventing impossible rules for it. [*Ib.* 4]

12 I do not believe that friends are necessarily the people you like best, they are merely the people who got there first. [*Ib.* 5]

13 I sometimes wished he [his father] would realize that he was poor instead of being that most nerve-racking of phenomena, a rich man without money. [*Ib.* 6]

14 Thanks to the movies, gunfire has always sounded unreal to me, even when being fired at. [*Ib.* 7]

15 And here is the lesson I learned in the army. If you want to do a thing badly, you have to work at it as though you want to do it well. [*Ib.* 8]

16 I am an optimist, unrepentant and militant. After all, in order not to be a fool an optimist must know how sad a place the world can be. It is only the pessimist who finds this out anew every day. [*Ib.* 9]

17 The conviction was growing in me that, whereas Shakespeare was admittedly the greatest of our playwrights, there was a general recognition of the fact that Sir Arthur Pinero was the best of them. [*Ib.* 13]

18 Revolutions have never succeeded unless the establishment does three-quarters of the work. [*Ib.* 15]

19 I can take no allegiance to a flag if I don't know who's holding it. [*Ib.* 16]

20 It was Nabokov and his perfumed English, so dense and intense you can hardly read it without taking deep breaths. [*Ib.* 17]

21 There are no old men any more. *Playboy* and *Penthouse* have between them made an ideal of eternal adolescence, sunburnt and saunaed, with the grey dorianed out of it. [*Ib.* 18]

22 It seems to be the habit to elect presidents for their lack of evident vices instead of for their possession of evident virtues. The existence of vices is allowed to become apparent during the incumbency. [*Ib.* 19]

23 I believe that the Jews have made a contribution to the human condition

out of all proportion to their numbers: I believe them to be an immense people. Not only have they supplied the world with two leaders of the stature of Jesus Christ and Karl Marx, but they have even indulged in the luxury of following neither one nor the other. [*Ib.*]

1 In my day, there were things that were done, and things that were not done, and there was even a way of doing things that were not done. [*Photo Finish*, quoted in *ib*. 17]

2 Once we are destined to live out our lives in the prison of our mind, our one duty is to furnish it well. [Quoted in *ib*. 20]

3 Laughter would be bereaved if snobbery died. [*Observer*, 'Sayings of the Week', 13 Mar. 1955]

4 If Botticelli were alive today he'd be working for *Vogue*. [*Observer*, 'Sayings of the Week', 21 Oct. 1962]

5 People at the top of the tree are those without qualifications to detain them at the bottom. [Attr.]

V

HORACE ANNESLEY VACHELL

1 In nature there are no rewards or punishments; there are consequences. [*The Face of Clay*, Ch. 10]

LUDVÍK VACULÍK

2 Assuming that none of us was born to make life easy for his rulers ... the first law of power is its desire to continue. It reproduces itself in ever more faithful copies ... power prefers people of the same inner constitution as itself. But since these are in short supply, it has to make use of other people too and adjust them to its needs. [Quoted in the *Guardian*, 22 Jul. 1976]

3 If you had been awarded a regular doctorate, and had then become a judge in Czechoslovakia, you would today have to sentence many a Czech writer ... to three years' imprisonment for a manuscript captured on his desk. [Letter to Dr Kurt Waldheim, Secretary General of UN, on his receiving an honorary doctorate of law from the Charles University in Prague. Quoted in *ib.*]

AMANDA VAIL

4 Sometimes I think if there was a third sex men wouldn't get so much as a glance from me. [*Love Me Little*, Ch. 6]

5 We talked a lot about life. There was nothing else to talk about. [*Ib.* 8]

6 'Parents are strange,' Amy said, 'for their age.' [*Ib.* 10]

7 'American girls do have regrets,' Amy said. 'That is what distinguishes them from French girls.' [*Ib.*]

PAUL VALÉRY

8 Man is only man at the surface. Remove his skin, dissect, and immediately you come to machinery. [Quoted in W. H. Auden, *A Certain World*]

9 A man is infinitely more complicated than his thoughts. [Quoted in *ib.*]

10 Consciousness reigns but does not govern. [Quoted in *ib.*]

11 A poem is never finished, only abandoned. [Quoted in *ib.*]

VIVIEN VAN DAMM

12 We Never Closed. [Slogan of London's Windmill Theatre during the Second World War, when he was its manager]

LAURENS VAN DER POST

13 Neither Heaven nor Hell are hereafter. Hell is time arrested within and refusing to join in the movement of wind and stars. Heaven is the boulder rock unrolled to let new life out: it is man restored to all four of his seasons rounding for eternity. [*The Seed and the Sower*]

14 'The story is like the wind,' the Bushman prisoner said. 'It comes from a far off place, and we feel it.' [*A Story Like the Wind*]

BARTOLOMEO VANZETTI

15 [On receiving the death sentence] If it had not been for these things, I might have lived out my life talking at street corners to scorning men. I might have died, unmarked, unknown, a failure. Now we [Sacco and himself] are not a failure. This is our career and our triumph. Never in our full life could we hope to do such work for tolerance, for justice, for man's understanding of

man as now we do by accident. Our words – our lives – our pains – nothing! The taking of our lives – lives of a good shoemaker and a poor fish-pedlar – all! That last moment belongs to us – that agony is our triumph. [Quoted in Douglas Hyde, *I Believed*]

'VARIETY'

1 Sticks Nix Hicks Pix. [On Midwestern reaction to films about poor hillbillies. Quoted in Leslie Halliwell, *The Filmgoer's Book of Quotes*]

R. VAUGHAN WILLIAMS

2 I realize now it [his London Symphony] is not as boring as I thought it was. [Quoted by Sir Adrian Boult in a broadcast, 1 Aug. 1965]

3 I don't know whether I like it [his Fourth Symphony], but it is what I meant. [Quoted in *ib.*]

THORSTEN VEBLEN

4 All business sagacity reduces itself in the last analysis to a judicious use of sabotage. [*The Nature of Peace*]

5 The outcome of any serious research can only be to make two questions grow where only one grew before. [*The Place of Science in Modern Civilization*]

6 That was *not* my niece. [Referring to a young lady staying in his house. Quoted in R. Heilbroner, *The Worldly Philosophers*, Ch. 8]

CARL VAN VECHTEN

7 There are, I have discovered, two kinds of people in this world, those who long to be understood and those who long to be misunderstood. It is the irony of life that neither is gratified. [*The Blind Bow-Boy*]

A. W. VERRALL

8 Arthur is a good boy; he doesn't say *them*'s grouses, he says *them*'s grice. [Said of himself as a child standing before a picture of partridges. Prefatory Memoir to *Collected Literary Essays*, ed. M. A. Bayfield]

9 Oh, quite easy! The Septuagint minus the Apostles. [To someone who said that 58 was a difficult number to remember. Attr.]

DR VERWOERD
(Prime Minister of South Africa)

10 We did what God wanted us to do. [*Observer*, 'Sayings of the Week', 26 Mar. 1961]

BORIS VIAN

11 What interests me isn't the happiness of every man, but that of each man. [*L'Écume des Jours*]

'VICKY'

12 Introducing Super-Mac. [Caption to cartoon of Macmillan as Superman, *Evening Standard*, 6 Nov. 1958]

GORE VIDAL

13 A candidate should not mean but be. [*The Best Man*]

14 The novel being dead, there is no point to writing made-up stories. Look at the French who will not and the Americans who cannot. [*Myra Breckinridge*, Ch. 2]

15 A radical theory I had always held but dared not openly formulate: that boredom in the arts can be, under the right circumstances, dull. [*Ib.* 21]

16 Like all analysts Randolph is interested only in himself. In fact, I have often thought that the analyst should pay the patient for allowing himself to be used as a captive looking-glass. [*Ib.* 37]

17 Marietta is a tough in-fighter, and knows all the right questions. Unfortunately she is driven to give wrong answers. She is very effective on television panel programmes. [*Two Sisters*]

18 [To Dwight Macdonald] Don't you realize, Dwight, you have nothing to say, only to add? [*Ib.*]

19 He will lie even when it is inconvenient, the sign of the true artist. [*Ib.*]

1 American writers want to be not good but great; and so are neither. [*Ib.*]

2 The astronauts! ... Rotarians in outer space. [*Ib.*]

3 My attention span is not what it was, since the thoughts of middle age are short thoughts. One grows dreamy, reading, the eye has a tendency to slip from the relentless line of text to the cool white of the margin, and there bathe indefinitely. [*Ib.*]

4 Never have children, only grandchildren. [*Ib.*]

5 Whenever a friend succeeds, a little something in me dies. [Quoted in the *Sunday Times Magazine*, 16 Sep. 1973]

6 I'm all for bringing back the birch, but only between consenting adults. [On a David Frost TV programme about corporal punishment. Quoted in *ib.*]

7 [Commercialism is] doing well that which should not be done at all. [On BBC TV programme, *Success Story*. Quoted in the *Listener*, 7 Aug. 1975]

COMMANDER ALAN VILLIERS

8 Only fools and passengers drink at sea. [*Observer*, 'Sayings of the Week', 28 Apr. 1957]

STEPHEN VIZINCZEY

9 I was told I am a true cosmopolitan: I am unhappy everywhere. [*Guardian*, 7 Mar. 1968]

KURT VONNEGUT

10 One of the main effects of war, after all, is that people are discouraged from being characters. [*Slaughterhouse 5*, Ch. 7]

11 And so it goes ... [Passim in *ib.*]

JOHN VORSTER
(Prime Minister of South Africa)

12 As far as criticism is concerned, we don't resent that unless it is absolutely biased, as it is in most cases. [*Observer*, 'Sayings of the Week', 9 Nov. 1969]

ANDREI VOZNESENSKY

13 it is time / For you to run out of me and I / Out of you. [*Autumn in Sigulda*, trans. W. H. Auden]

14 The art of creation / is older than the art of killing. [*Poem with a Footnote*]

15 Genius is in the planet's blood. / You're either a poet or a Lilliputian. [*Who Are We?*, trans. S. Moss]

DIANA VREELAND

16 Pink is the navy blue of India. [Attr. Quoted in *Rolling Stone*, 11 Aug. 1977]

ANDREI VYSHINSKY

17 Confession is the queen of evidence. [Quoted in D. Burg and G. Feifer, *Solzhenitsyn*]

W

JOHN WAIN

1 The lesson is that dying men must groan; / And poets groan in rhymes that please the ear. / But still it comes expensive, you must own. [*Don't let's spoil it all, I thought we were going to be such good friends*]

2 Poetry is to prose as dancing is to walking. [Talk on BBC radio, 13 Jan. 1976]

ARTHUR WALEY

3 It is not difficult to censor foreign news, / What is hard today is to censor one's own thoughts, – / To sit by and see the blind man / On the sightless horse, riding into the bottomless abyss. [*Censorship*]

4 In the early dusk, down an alley of green moss, / The garden-boy is leading the cranes home. [*The Cranes*, trans. from the Chinese of Po-Chü-I]

5 Keep off your thoughts from things that are past and done; / For thinking of the past wakes regret and pain. [*Resignation*, trans. from the Chinese of Po-Chü-I]

JAMES WALKER

6 Will you love me in December / As you did in May? [Song: *Will You Love Me in December?*]

JAMES J. WALKER

7 A reformer is a guy who rides through a sewer in a glass-bottomed boat. [Speech as Mayor of New York, 1928]

KENNETH WALKER

8 The patient has been so completely taken to pieces that nobody is able to look on him again as a whole being. He is no longer an individual man but a jumble of scientific data. [*The Circle of Life*, Pt I, Ch. 1]

MAX WALL

9 Success! That's it! [Catch-phrase used in BBC radio variety series, *Variety Bandbox*. Quoted in Max Wall with Peter Ford, *The Fool on the Hill*, Ch. 7]

10 Oh *look*. Here's Humphrey, everybody! [Running gag in BBC radio comedy series, *Our Shed*. Quoted in *ib*.]

11 If my life has been a training for being an idiot, perhaps I will succeed at last. [*Ib*. 12]

12 Wall is the name – Max Wall. My father was the Great Wall of China. He was a brick. [Opening patter to variety act]

13 To me Adler will always be Jung. [Telegram to his friend Larry Adler on his sixtieth birthday]

WALL STREET JOURNAL

14 A true gentleman is a man who knows how to play the bagpipes – but doesn't. [Quoted in *Reader's Digest*, Mar. 1976]

EDGAR WALLACE

15 A writer of crook stories ought never to stop seeking new material. [On standing for Parliament. Quoted in Robert Graves and Alan Hodge, *The Long Weekend*]

NELLIE WALLACE

16 Oh what a nippy little bit of goods my sailor was! I can see him now. He used to pull me to him, sit me on his knee, and say, 'Any old port in a storm.' He

hadn't had a storm lately. [From a music-hall sketch. Quoted in John Fisher, *Funny Way To Be a Hero*, 'Are Women Funny?']

JOHN WANAMAKER

1 Half the money I spend on advertising is wasted, and the trouble is I don't know which half. [Paraphrasing the first Lord Leverhulme. Quoted in David Ogilvy, *Confessions of an Advertising Man*, Ch. 3]

WENDY WARD

2 The worst moment for an atheist is when he feels grateful and has no one to thank. [Quoted in P. and J. Holton, *Quote and Unquote*]

GEORGE WARE

3 The boy I love is up in the gallery, / The boy I love is looking now at me. [Song: *The Boy in the Gallery*, sung by Marie Lloyd]

ANDY WARHOL

4 Try the Andy Warhol New York City Diet: when I order in a restaurant, I order everything I don't want, so I have a lot to play around with while everyone else eats. [*From A to B and Back Again*, 'Beauty']

5 An artist is someone who produces things that people don't need to have but that he – for *some reason* – thinks it would be a good idea to give them. [*Ib.* 'Atmosphere']

6 It's the place where my prediction from the sixties finally came true: 'In the future everyone will be famous for fifteen minutes.' [*Andy Warhol's Exposures*, 'Studio 54']

JACK WARNER

7 Mind my bike! [Repeated in *Garrison Theatre*, wartime broadcasts]

8 Evening, all. [*Passim* as Sergeant Dixon in BBC TV series, *Dixon of Dock Green*. Original scripts by Ted (now Lord) Willis]

CHIEF JUSTICE EARL WARREN

9 Many people consider the things which government does for them to be social progress, but they consider the things government does for others as socialism. [Quoted in Laurence J. Peter, *Peter's Quotations*]

JAMES D. WATSON

10 The thought could not be avoided that the best home for a feminist was in another person's lab. [*The Double Helix*, Ch. 2]

11 Already for thirty-five years he [Francis Crick] had not stopped talking and almost nothing of fundamental value had emerged. [*Ib.* 8]

12 I was twenty-five and too old to be unusual. [*Ib.* 29]

G. F. WATTS

13 I was so desirous of getting it right [a drawing] I did it with my shoes off. [Quoted in Chrisopher Hassall, *Edward Marsh*, Ch. 6]

EVELYN WAUGH

14 I expect you'll be becoming a schoolmaster, sir. That's what most of the gentlemen does, sir, that gets sent down for indecent behaviour. [*Decline and Fall*, Prelude]

15 We class schools, you see, into four grades: Leading School, First-rate School, Good School, and School. [*Ib.* I. 1]

16 Meanwhile you will write an essay on 'self-indulgence'. There will be a prize of half a crown for the longest essay, irrespective of any possible merit. [*Ib.* I. 5]

17 I can't quite explain it, but I don't believe one can ever be unhappy for long provided one does just exactly what one wants to and when one wants to. [*Ib.*]

18 For generations the British bourgeoisie have spoken of themselves as gentlemen, and by that they have meant, among other things, a self-respecting scorn of

irregular perquisites. It is the quality that distinguishes the gentleman from both the artist and the aristocrat. [*Ib*. I. 6]

1 There aren't many left like him nowadays, what with education and whisky the price it is. [*Ib*. I. 7]

2 We can trace almost all the disasters of English history to the influence of Wales. [*Ib*. I. 8]

3 Nonconformity and lust stalking hand in hand through the country, wasting and ravaging. [*Ib*.]

4 'The Welsh,' said the Doctor, 'are the only nation in the world that has produced no graphic or plastic art, no architecture, no drama. They just sing,' he said with disgust, 'sing and blow down wind instruments of plated silver.' [*Ib*.]

5 If my brother had been alive he'd have licked all that out of the young cub. It takes a man to bring up a man. [*Ib*.]

6 I have noticed again and again since I have been in the Church that lay interest in ecclesiastical matters is often a prelude to insanity. [*Ib*.]

7 But no man can you ask against his Maker to blaspheme whatever unless him to pay more you were. Three pounds for the music is good and one for blasphemy look you. [*Ib*. I. 9]

8 I have often observed in women of her type a tendency to regard all athletics as inferior forms of fox-hunting. [*Ib*. I. 10]

9 I haven't been to sleep for over a year. That's why I go to bed early. One needs more rest if one doesn't sleep. [*Ib*. II. 3]

10 There is a species of person called a 'Modern Churchman' who draws the full salary of a beneficed clergyman and need not commit himself to any religious belief. [*Ib*. II. 4]

11 'But you married?' 'Yes, mum, but it was in the war, and he was very drunk.' [*Ib*. II. 5]

12 Services are voluntary – that is to say, you must either attend all or none. [*Ib*. III. 1]

13 He stood twice for Parliament, but so diffidently that his candidature passed almost unnoticed. [*Ib*.]

14 I came to the conclusion many years ago that almost all crime is due to the repressed desire for aesthetic expression. [*Ib*.]

15 'How do you do?' said Paul politely. 'Are you here for long?' 'Life,' said the other. 'But it doesn't matter much. I look daily for the Second Coming.' [*Ib*. III. 3]

16 Anyone who has been to an English public school will always feel comparatively at home in prison. It is the people brought up in the gay intimacy of the slums, Paul learned, who find prison so soul-destroying. [*Ib*. III. 4]

17 He was greatly pained at how little he was pained by the events of the afternoon. [*Ib*. III. 4]

18 Instead of this absurd division into sexes they ought to class people as static and dynamic. [*Ib*. III. 7]

19 When the war broke out she took down the signed photograph of the Kaiser and, with some solemnity, hung it in the menservants' lavatory; it was her one combative action. [*Vile Bodies*, Ch. 3]

20 She had heard someone say something about an Independent Labour Party, and was furious that she had not been asked. [*Ib*. 4]

21 All this fuss about sleeping together. For physical pleasure I'd sooner go to my dentist any day. [*Ib*. 6]

22 Assistant masters came and went ... Some liked little boys too little and some too much. [*A Little Learning*]

23 That impersonal insensitive friendliness that takes the place of ceremony in that land [the USA] of waifs and strays. [*The Loved One*]

24 You never find an Englishman among the underdogs – except in England of course. [*Ib*.]

25 Most cemeteries, he says, provide a dog's toilet and a cat's motel. [*Ib*.]

26 I took Art at College as my second subject one semester. I'd have taken it as first subject only Dad lost his money in religion so I had to learn a trade. [*Ib*.]

1 In the dying world I come from quotation is a national vice. It used to be the classics, now it's lyric verse. [*Ib.*]

2 '*The Beast* stands for strong mutually antagonistic governments everywhere,' he said. 'Self-sufficiency at home, self-assertion abroad.' [*Scoop*, Bk I, Ch. 1]

3 Yes, cider and tinned salmon are the staple diet of the agricultural classes. [*Ib.*]

4 Feather-footed through the plashy fen passes the questing vole ... [*Ib.*]

5 Pappenhacker says that every time you are polite to a proletarian you are helping bolster up the capitalist system. [*Ib.*]

6 Personally I can't see that foreign stories are ever news – not *real* news. [*Ib.* I. 5]

7 News is what a chap who doesn't care much about anything wants to read. And it's only news until he's read it. After that it's dead. [*Ib.*]

8 The better sort of Ishmaelites have been Christian for many centuries and will not publicly eat human flesh uncooked in Lent, without special and costly dispensation from their bishop. [*Ib.* II. 1]

9 As there was no form of government common to the peoples thus segregated, nor tie of language, history, habit, or belief, they were called a Republic. [*Ib.*]

10 'I will not stand for being called a woman in my own house,' she said. [*Ib.*]

11 Other nations use 'force'; we Britons alone use 'Might'. [*Ib.* II. 5]

12 Freddy was large, masculine, prematurely bald and superficially cheerful; at heart he was misanthropic and gifted with that sly, sharp instinct for self-preservation that passes for wisdom among the rich; his indolence was qualified with enough basic bad temper to ensure the respect of those about him. [*Put Out More Flags*]

13 Enclosing every thin man, there's a fat man demanding elbow-room. [*Officers and Gentlemen*, Interlude. See also 14:10; 84:20; 254:14]

14 Manners are especially the need of the plain. The pretty can get away with anything. [*Observer*, 'Sayings of the Year', 1962]

15 All fictional characters are flat. A writer can give an illusion of depth by giving an apparently stereoscopic view of a character – seeing him from two vantage points; all a writer can do is give more or less information about a character, not information of a different order. [Interview in *Paris Review*, 1963]

16 No writer before the middle of the 19th century wrote about the working classes other than as grotesques or as pastoral decorations. Then when they were given the vote certain writers started to suck up to them. [*Ib.*]

17 We are all American at puberty; we die French. [*Diaries*, ed. M. Davie, 'Irregular Notes', 18 Jul. 1961]

18 Punctuality is the virtue of the bored. [*Ib.* 26 Mar. 1962]

19 One can write, think and pray exclusively of others; dreams are all egocentric. [*Ib.* 5 Oct. 1962]

20 One forgets words as one forgets names. One's vocabulary needs constant fertilizing or it will die. [*Ib.* 25 Dec. 1962]

21 [On Randolph Churchill's having a lung removed] It was announced that the trouble was not 'malignant' ... I remarked that it was a typical triumph of modern science to find the only part of Randolph that was not malignant and remove it. [*Ib.* Mar. 1964]

22 [On why he didn't vote at elections] I do not aspire to advise my sovereign in her choice of servants. [*A Little Order*, ed. D. Gallagher]

23 No admittance on business. [Notice on his house gate]

24 I put the words down and push them a bit. [Quoted in obituary, *New York Times*, 11 Apr. 1966]

25 [In reply to Graham Greene, who had said that he intended to write a political novel] I wouldn't give up writing about God at this stage, if I was you. It would

be like P. G. Wodehouse dropping Jeeves half-way through the Wooster series. [Quoted in Christopher Sykes, *Evelyn Waugh*]

1 [Of Winston Churchill] Simply a radio personality who outlived his prime. [Quoted in *ib.*]

LORD WAVELL

2 'The best confidential report I ever heard of,' said Lord Wavell, 'was also the shortest. It was by one Horse Gunner of another, and ran, "Personally I would not breed from this officer."' [Quoted in Gilbert Harding, *Treasury of Insult*]

BEATRICE WEBB

3 If I ever felt inclined to be timid as I was going into a room full of people, I would say to myself, 'You're the cleverest member of one of the cleverest families in the cleverest class of the cleverest nation in the world, why should you be frightened?' [Quoted in Bertrand Russell, *Portraits from Memory*, VIII]

SIDNEY and BEATRICE WEBB

4 Old people are always absorbed in something, usually themselves; we prefer to be absorbed in the Soviet Union. [Quoted by Kingsley Martin in *The Webbs and Their Work*, ed. Margaret Cole]

ANTON VON WEBERN

5 Music is natural law as related to the sense of hearing. [*The Path to the New Music*, two lectures trans. by Leo Black]

ANTHONY WEDGWOOD BENN

6 Britain today is suffering from galloping obsolescence. [*Observer*, 'Sayings of the Week', 2 Feb. 1963]

7 I am on the right wing of the middle of the road with a strong radical bias.

[Said in the mid 1950s. Quoted in N. Rees, *Quote . . . Unquote*]

SIMONE WEIL

8 Culture is an instrument wielded by professors to manufacture professors, who when their turn comes will manufacture professors. [*The Need for Roots*]

9 All sins are attempts to fill voids. [Quoted in W. H. Auden, *A Certain World*]

10 What a country calls its vital economic interests are not the things which enable its citizens to live, but the things which enable it to make war. Petrol is more likely than wheat to be a cause of international conflict. [Quoted in *ib.*]

MAX WEINREICH

11 A language is a dialect that has an army and a navy. [Quoted in Leo Rosten, *The Joys of Yiddish*, Preface]

PETER WEISS

12 We invented the Revolution / but we don't know how to run it. [*The Marat/Sade*, sc. xv, trans. G. Skelton and A. Mitchell]

13 When I wrote / I always wrote with action in mind / kept sight of the fact / that writing was just a preparation. [*Ib.* xxviii]

CHAIM WEIZMANN

14 Difficult things take a long time, the impossible takes a little longer. [Quoted in V. Weizmann, *The Impossible Takes Longer*. But also attr. to Nansen, see 247:4]

RAQUEL WELCH

15 The mind can also be an erogenous zone. [Quoted in J. R. Colombo, *Colombo's Hollywood*]

ORSON WELLES

16 In Italy for thirty years under the Borgias they had warfare, terror, murder, bloodshed – they produced

Michelangelo, Leonardo da Vinci and the Renaissance. In Switzerland they had brotherly love, five hundred years of democracy and peace, and what did they produce ...? The cuckoo clock. [Harry Lime's parting speech in film, *The Third Man*. Script by Graham Greene, but *The Oxford Companion to Film* states Welles wrote this speech in himself]

1 I started at the top and worked my way down. [Quoted in Leslie Halliwell, *The Filmgoer's Book of Quotes*]

MME WELLINGTON KOO

2 The air is thick with the wings of birds coming home to roost. [Remark after Munich Crisis. Attr.]

DEE WELLS

3 Maybe show-business people don't share our 20-years-of-Mortgage, 20-years-of-children, and Have-you-put-the-cat-out? view of marriage. [*Daily Herald*, 13 Feb. 1964]

H. G. WELLS

4 Rich men amenable to use are hard to find and often very intractable when found. [*The Autocracy of Mr Parham*]

5 It was a room to eat muffins in. [*Ib.*]

6 The cat is the offspring of a cat and the dog of a dog, but butlers and lady's maids do not reproduce their kind. They have other duties. [*Bealby*, Pt I, Ch. 1]

7 The life of breezy freedom resolves itself in practice chiefly into washing up and an anxious search for permission to camp. [*Ib.* III. 7]

8 He was quite sure that he had been wronged. Not to be wronged is to forgo the first privilege of goodness. [*Ib.* IV. 1]

9 Miss Madeleine Philips was making it very manifest to Captain Douglas that she herself was a career; that a lover with any other career in view need not – as the advertisements say – apply. [*Ib.* V. 5]

10 He began to think the tramp a fine, brotherly, generous fellow. He was also

growing accustomed to something – shall I call it an olfactory bar – that had hitherto kept them apart. [*Ib.* VI. 3]

11 The army ages men sooner than the law and philosophy; it exposes them more freely to germs, which undermine and destroy, and it shelters them more completely from thought, which stimulates and preserves. [*Ib.* VIII. 1]

12 He had one peculiar weakness; he had faced death in many forms but he had never faced a dentist. The thought of dentists gave him just the same sick horror as the thought of Socialism. [*Ib.*]

13 Cossar was a large-bodied man with gaunt inelegant limbs casually placed at convenient corners of his body, and a face like a carving abandoned as altogether too unpromising for completion. [*The Food of the Gods*]

14 Mr Polly went into the National School at six, and he left the private school at fourteen, and by that time his mind was in much the same state that you would be in, dear reader, if you were operated on for appendicitis by a well-meaning, boldly enterprising, but rather overworked and underpaid butcher boy, who was superseded towards the climax of the operation by a left-handed clerk of high principles but intemperate habits – that is to say, it was in a thorough mess. [*The History of Mr Polly*, Pt I, Ch. 2]

15 '*Language*, man!' roared Parsons; 'why, it's LITERATURE!' [*Ib.* I. 3]

16 'Back to the collar, O' Man,' Parsons would say. There is no satisfactory plural to 'O' Man', so he always used it in the singular. [*Ib.* I. 4]

17 'The High Egrugious is fairly on,' he said, and dived down to return by devious subterranean routes to the outfitting department. [*Ib.* II. 2]

18 'Smart Juniors,' said Polly to himself, 'full of Smart Juniosity. The Shoveacious Cult.' [*Ib.* III. 1]

19 'You're a Christian?' 'Church of England,' said Mr Polly. 'Mm,' said the employer, a little checked. 'For good all round business work, I should have preferred a Baptist.' [*Ib.*]

349

WELLS

1 Uncle Penstemon was rather a shock. He was an aged rather than a venerable figure. Time had removed the hair from the top of his head and distributed a small dividend of the plunder in little bunches carelessly and impartially over the rest of his features. [*Ib*. IV. 3]

2 High old jawbacious argument we had, I tell you. [*Ib*. V. 2]

3 'They do say,' said Uncle Penstemon, 'one funeral makes many. This time it's a wedding. But it's all very much of a muchness . . .' [*Ib*. VI. 7]

4 Arson, after all, is an artificial crime . . . A large number of houses deserve to be burnt. [*Ib*. X. 1]

5 Of course he had no desire to place himself on an equality in any way with Ibsen; still the fact remained that his own experience in England and America and the colonies was altogether more extensive than Ibsen could have had. Ibsen had probably never seen 'one decent bar scrap' in his life. [*Kipps*, Bk I, Ch. 4, sect. iv]

6 'It's giving girls names like that [Euphemia],' said Buggins, 'that nine times out of ten makes 'em go wrong. It unsettles 'em. If ever I was to have a girl, if ever I was to have a dozen girls, I'd call 'em all Jane.' [*Ib*. I. 6. ii]

7 It's legitimate. Much more legitimate than the Wild Duck – where there isn't a duck! [*Ib*. II. 1. v]

8 Of course we can Learn even from Novels, Nace Novels that is, but it isn't the same thing as serious reading. [*Ib*. II. 2. i]

9 He felt like some lonely and righteous man dynamited into Bliss. [*Ib*. II. 2. ii]

10 She stamped Kipps so deeply with the hat-raising habit that he would uncover if he found himself in the same railway ticket office with a lady, and so stand ceremoniously until the difficulties of change drove him to an apologetic provisional oblique resumption of his headgear. [*Ib*. II. 5. ii]

11 He found that a fork in his inexperienced hand was an instrument of chase rather than capture. [*Ib*. II. 7. vi]

12 It's 'aving 'ouses built by men, I believe, makes all the work and trouble. [*Ib*. III. 1. ii]

13 Everybody hates house-agents because they have everybody at a disadvantage. All other callings have a certain amount of give and take; the house-agent simply takes. [*Ib*. III. 1. iii]

14 One book's very like another – after all what is it? Something to read and done with. It's not a thing that matters like print dresses or serviettes – where you either like 'em or don't, and people judge you by. [*Ib*. III. 3. iii]

15 Except that it failed, the Associated Booksellers' Trading Union had all the stigmata of success. Its fault perhaps was that it had them all instead of only one or two. [*Ib*. III. 3. iv]

16 Miss Heydinger sat in the room her younger sister called her 'Sanctum'. Her Sanctum was only too evidently an intellectualized bedroom. [*Love and Mr Lewisham*, Ch. 16]

17 The Social Contract is nothing more nor less than a vast conspiracy of human beings to lie to and humbug themselves and one another for the general Good. Lies are the mortar that binds the savage individual man into the social masonry. [*Ib*. 23]

18 Notice the smug suppressions of his face. In his mouth are Lies in the shape of false teeth. [*Ib*.]

19 We were taught as the chief subjects of instruction Latin and Greek. We were taught very badly because the men who taught us did not habitually use either of these languages. [*The New Machiavelli*, Bk I, Ch. 3, sect. v]

20 I sometimes think that if Adam and Eve had been merely engaged, she would not have talked with the serpent; and the world had been saved an infinity of misery. [*Select Conversations with an Uncle*]

21 Now it is on the whole more convenient to keep history and theology apart. [*A Short History of the World*, Ch. 37]

22 Their prose was convulsive, they foamed at the headline . . . Before the week was out they were not so much published as

350

carried screaming into the street. [*The War in the Air*, Ch. 1]

1 To Europe she was America, to America she was the gateway of the earth. But to tell the story of New York would be to write a social history of the world. [*Ib.* 6]

2 The third peculiarity of aerial warfare was that it was at once enormously destructive and entirely indecisive. [*Ib.* 8]

3 The War to End War. [Title of book published in 1914]

4 So why should I not write and forget altogether that visible chill, that inky catarrh of a climate which is snivelling against the window-panes? [*The World of William Clissold*]

5 'I'll call my article', meditated the war correspondent, ' "Mankind *versus* Ironmongery" '.' [*Short Stories*, 'The Land Ironclads']

6 He had the face of a saint, but he had rendered this generally acceptable by growing side-whiskers. [*Ib.* 'The Last Trump']

7 He was an enormous asset in the spiritual life of the metropolis – to give it no harsher name – and his fluent periods had restored faith and courage to many a poor soul hovering on the brink of the dark river of thought. [*Ib.*]

8 Cynicism is humour in ill-health. [*Ib.*]

9 He was a practical electrician but fond of whisky, a heavy red-haired brute with irregular teeth. He doubted the existence of the Deity but accepted Carnot's cycle, and he had read Shakespeare and found him weak in chemistry. [*Ib.* 'The Lord of the Dynamos']

10 At first the miracles worked by Mr Fotheringay were timid little miracles – little things with the cups and parlour fitments, as feeble as the miracles of Theosophists. [*Ib.* 'The Man who Worked Miracles']

11 Bricklayers kick their wives to death, and dukes betray theirs; but it is among the small clerks and shopkeepers nowadays that it comes most often to the cutting of throats. [*Ib.* 'The Purple Pileus']

12 If Max [Beaverbrook] gets to Heaven he won't last long. He will be chucked out for trying to pull off a merger between Heaven and Hell ... after having secured a controlling interest in key subsidiary companies in both places, of course. [Quoted in A. J. P. Taylor, *Beaverbrook*]

13 It seems to me that I am more to the left than you, Mr Stalin. [In an interview with Stalin, *New Statesman*, 27 Oct. 1934]

14 There is no reason whatever to believe that the order of nature has any greater bias in favour of man than it had in favour of the icthyosaur or the pterodactyl. [Quoted in Sagittarius and George, *The Perpetual Pessimist*]

15 ... my epitaph. That, when the time comes, will manifestly have to be: 'I told you so. You *damned* fools.' (The italics are mine.) [1941. Preface to *The War of the Worlds*, originally written 1907]

ARNOLD WESKER

16 You breed babies and you eat chips with everything. [*Chips with Everything*, Act I, sc. ii]

17 Every place I look at I work out the cubic feet, and I say it will make a good warehouse or it won't. Can't help myself. One of the best warehouses I ever saw was the Vatican in Rome. [*Ib.* I. vi]

18 Don't you sit there and sigh gal like you was Lady Nevershit. [*Roots*, Act III]

19 There's nothing more pathetic than the laughter of people who have lost their pet faith. [*I'm Talking about Jerusalem*, Act II, sc. i]

MAE WEST

20 Keep cool and collect. [In film, *Belle of the Nineties*]

21 A man in the house is worth two in the street. [*Ib.*]

22 I'm glad you like my Catherine. I like her too. She ruled thirty million people and had three thousand lovers. I do the best I can in two hours. [Curtain

351

speech after performance of *Catherine Was Great*]

1 'My goodness, those diamonds are lovely!'
M.W.: 'Goodness had nothing whatever to do with it.' [*Diamond Lil*]

2 It ain't no sin to crack a few laws now and then, just so long as you don't break any. [In film, *Every Day's a Holiday*]

3 [Of Delilah] I have a lot of respect for that dame. There's one lady barber that made good. [In film, *Going to Town*]

4 She's the kind of girl who climbed the ladder of success, wrong by wrong. [In film, *I'm no Angel*]

5 Beulah, peel me a grape. [*Ib.*]

6 Between two evils, I always pick the one I never tried before. [In film, *Klondike Annie*]

7 A gold rush is what happens when a line of chorus girls spot a man with a bank roll. [*Ib.*]

8 Come up some time and see me. [In film, *She Done Him Wrong*. Quoted in N. Rees, *Quote ... Unquote*. Usually misquoted as 'Come up and see me sometime']

9 [On being told that ten men were waiting to meet her at home] I'm tired, send one of them home. [Quoted in J. Weintraub, *Peel Me a Grape*]

10 Virtue has its own reward, but no sale at the box office. [Quoted in *ib.*]

11 When I'm good I'm very very good, but when I'm bad I'm better. [Quoted in *ib.*]

12 I used to be Snow White ... but I drifted. [Quoted in *ib.*]

13 You can say what you like about long dresses, but they cover a multitude of shins. [Quoted in *ib.*]

14 Everything. [When asked what she wanted to be remembered for. Quoted in the *Observer Weekend Review*, 30 Nov. 1969]

15 CONNIE HINES: Oh, Miss West, I've heard so much about you.
M.W.: Yeah, honey, but you can't prove a thing. [In TV programme, *Mister Ed*]

16 Is that a pistol in your pocket or are you just glad to see me? [Quoted in the *Guardian*, 13 Nov. 1974. Var. version: 'your sword']

17 She's one of the finest women who ever walked the streets. [Quoted in Leslie Halliwell, *The Filmgoer's Book of Quotes*]

NATHANAEL WEST

18 Are-you-in-trouble? – Do-you-need-advice? – Write-to-Miss-Lonelyhearts-and-she-will-help-you. [*Miss Lonelyhearts*]

19 When they ask for bread don't give them crackers as does the Church, and don't, like the State, tell them to eat cake. Explain that man cannot live by bread alone, and give them stones. [*Ib.* 'Miss Lonelyhearts and the dead pan']

20 He could not go on finding the same joke funny thirty times a day for months on end. And on most days he received more than thirty letters, all of them alike, stamped from the dough of suffering with a heart-shaped cookie knife. [*Ib.* 'In the dismal swamp']

21 Goldsmith ... smiled, bunching his fat cheeks like twin rolls of smooth pink toilet paper. [*Ib.*]

DAME REBECCA WEST

22 Our four uncles [Wells and Bennett, Shaw and Galsworthy. Quoted in Stephen Potter, *The Sense of Humour*, Ch. 1]

23 Margaret Thatcher's great strength seems to be the better people know her, the better they like her. But, of course, she has one great disadvantage – she is a daughter of the people and looks trim, as the daughters of the people desire to be. Shirley Williams has such an advantage over her because she's a member of the upper-middle class and can achieve that kitchen-sink-revolutionary look that one cannot get unless one has been to a really good school. [In interview with Jilly Cooper, *Sunday Times*, 25 Jul. 1976]

24 He is every other inch a gentleman. [Quoted in L. and M. Cowan, *The Wit*

of Women. But J. Wintle and R. Kenin, *Dictionary of Biographical Quotation,* ascribe to Alexander Woollcott on Michael Arlen]

R. P. WESTON

1 Some soldiers send epistles, say they'd sooner sleep in thistles / Than the saucy, soft, short shirts for soldiers, sister Susie sews. [Song: *Sister Susie's Sewing Shirts for Soldiers.* Music by Herman E. Darewski. Sung by Jack Norworth]

R. P. WESTON, F. R. BARNES and MAURICE SCOTT

2 Hush! Here comes a Whizz-Bang! [Title of song]

R. P. WESTON and BERT LEE

3 Good-bye-ee! – good-bye-ee! / Wipe the tear, baby dear, from your eye-ee. / Tho' it's hard to part, I know, / I'll be tickled to death to go. / Don't cry-ee! – don't sigh-ee! – / There's a silver lining in the sky-ee! – / Bonsoir, old thing! cheerio! chin-chin! / Nahpoo! Toodle-oo! Good-bye-ee! [Song: *Good-bye-ee!*]

GENERAL WEYGAND

4 In three weeks England will have her neck wrung like a chicken. [At the fall of France. Quoted in Winston S. Churchill, *Their Finest Hour,* Ch. 10; Churchill answered, 'Some chicken, some neck!']

EDITH WHARTON

5 Blessed are the pure in heart for they have so much more to talk about. [*John O'London's Weekly,* 10 Apr. 1932]

6 An unalterable and unquestioned law of the musical world required that the German text of French operas sung by Swedish artists should be translated into Italian for the clearer understanding of English speaking audiences. (*The Age of Innocence,* Bk I, Ch. 1]

7 She keeps on being Queenly in her own room with the door shut. [*The House of Mirth,* Bk II, Ch. 1]

HUGH WHEELER

8 To lose a lover or even a husband or two during the course of one's life can be vexing. But to lose one's teeth is a catastrophe. [Musical, *A Little Night Music.* Music by Stephen Sondheim]

9 Solitaire is the only thing in life that demands absolute honesty. [*Ib.*]

E. B. WHITE

10 As in the sexual experience, there are never more than two persons present in the act of reading – the writer who is the impregnator, and the reader who is the respondent. [*The Second Tree from the Corner*]

11 The dream of the American male is for a female who has an essential languor which is not laziness, who is unaccompanied except by himself, and who does not let him down. He desires a beautiful, but comprehensible creature who does not destroy a perfect situation by forming a complete sentence. [*Ib.* 'Notes on our Time']

12 To perceive Christmas through its wrapping becomes more difficult with every year. [*Ib.* 'Time Present']

13 All poets who, when reading from their own works, experience a choked feeling, are major. For that matter, all poets who read from their own works are major, whether they choke or not. [*How to Tell a Major Poet from a Minor Poet*]

14 It is easier for a man to be loyal to his club than to his planet; the by-laws are shorter, and he is personally acquainted with the other members. [*One Man's Meat*]

15 MOTHER: It's broccoli, dear.
CHILD: I say it's spinach, and I say the hell with it. [Caption to cartoon by Carl Rose]

E. P. G. WHITE
(Chief Constable of Gloucester)

16 If you give a woman an inch she'll park a car on it. [Quoted in A. Andrews, *Quotations for Speakers and Writers.* See also 264:9]

353

PATRICK WHITE

1 But bombs *are* unbelievable until they actually fall. [*Riders in the Chariot*, Pt I, Ch. 4]

2 It was perhaps doubtful if anyone would ever notice Mrs Poulter or Mrs Dun unless life took its cleaver to them. [*The Solid Mandala*, Ch. 1]

3 'I dunno,' Arthur said. 'I forget what I was taught. I only remember what I've learnt.' [*Ib.* 2]

4 Mrs Armstrong was inclined to apologize for her wealth, and to give freely to charities, without realizing she was the cause of them. [*The Tree of Man*, Ch. 12]

5 He would have liked to sit down and talk with someone about the flat things, as blameless as paper, about which it is necessary to talk. It is not possible with parents, any more than with corkscrews. His mother would bore right in, hoping to draw something out. [*Ib.* 16]

6 Conversation is imperative if gaps are to be filled, and old age, it is the last gap but one. [*Ib.* 22]

7 Few people of attainments take easily to a plan of self-improvement. Some discover very early their perfection cannot endure the insult. Others find their intellectual pleasure lies in the theory, not the practice. Only a few stubborn ones will blunder on, painfully, out of the luxuriant world of their pretensions into the desert of mortification and reward. [*Voss*, Ch. 4]

T. H. WHITE

8 The Victorians had not been anxious to go away for the weekend. The Edwardians, on the contrary were nomadic. [*Farewell Victoria*, Ch. 4]

A. N. WHITEHEAD

9 Life is an offensive, directed against the repetitious mechanism of the Universe. [*Adventures of Ideas*, Pt I, Ch. 5]

10 Language is incomplete and fragmentary, and merely registers a stage in the average advance beyond ape-mentality. But all men enjoy flashes of insight beyond meanings already stabilized in etymology and grammar. [*Ib.* III. 15]

11 It is more important that a proposition be interesting than that it be true. [*Ib.* III. 16]

12 Philosophy is the product of wonder. [*Nature and Life*, Ch. 1]

13 A dead Nature aims at nothing. It is the essence of life that it exists for its own sake, as the intrinsic reaping of value. [*Ib.*]

14 Science can find no individual enjoyment in Nature: science can find no aim in Nature; science can find no creativity in Nature; it finds mere rules of succession. [*Ib.* 2]

15 The fact of the instability of evil is the moral order of the world. [Quoted in Victor Gollancz, *A Year of Grace*]

16 Civilization advances by extending the number of important operations which we can perform without thinking about them. [Quoted in W. H. Auden, *A Certain World*]

17 Scientific reasoning is completely dominated by the pre-supposition that mental functionings are not properly part of nature. [Quoted in *ib.*]

18 A science which hesitates to forget its founders is lost. [Attr.]

19 The history of Western philosophy is, after all, no more than a series of footnotes to Plato's philosophy. [Attr.]

KATHARINE WHITEHORN

20 Hats divide generally into three classes: offensive hats, defensive hats, and shrapnel. [*Shouts and Murmurs*, a selection from the *Observer* 1962–3, 'Hats']

21 I yield to no one in my admiration for the office as a social centre, but it's no place actually to get any work done. [*Sunday Best*, Introduction]

22 Filing is concerned with the past; anything you actually need to see again has to do with the future. [*Ib.* 'Sorting Out']

1 I wouldn't say when you've seen one Western you've seen the lot; but when you've seen the lot you get the feeling you've seen one. [*Ib.* 'Decoding the West']

2 And what would happen to my illusion that I am a force for order in the home if I wasn't married to the only man north of the Tiber who is even untidier than I am? [*Ib.* 'Husband-Swapping']

3 The Life and Soul, the man who will never go home while there is one man, woman or glass of anything not yet drunk. [*Ib.*]

4 They are not quite my friends, but I know them better than many who are; they aren't related to me, but they might as well be. They are the close friends of *my* close friends – my friends-in-law. [*Ib.* 'Best Friend Once Removed']

5 My brother cuts the time it takes to read a newspaper by skipping everything in the future tense; and it's amazing what he doesn't miss. [*Ib.* 'Never-Never Land']

6 It is a pity, as my husband says, that more politicians are not bastards by birth instead of vocation. [*Observer*, 12 Jan. 1964]

7 Have you ever taken anything out of the clothes basket because it had become, relatively, the cleaner thing? ['On Shirts', *Observer*, 1964]

8 In real life, women are always trying to mix something up with sex – religion or babies or hard cash; it is only men who long for sex separated out, without rings or strings. ['Man's Ideal Woman', *Observer*, 20 Dec. 1964]

9 A good listener is not someone who has nothing to say. A good listener is a good talker with a sore throat. [Quoted in Prochnow, *The Public Speaker's Treasure Chest*]

WILLIAM WHITELAW

10 I do not intend to prejudge the past. [On first arrival in Ulster in 1972. Quoted in *The Times*, 3 Dec. 1973]

RICHARD WHITNEY

11 I claim that this country [the USA] has been built by speculation, and further progress must be made in that line. [Quoted in A. M. Schlesinger Jr, *The Coming of the New Deal*, Pt VII, Ch. 29, sect. iv]

L. L. WHYTE

12 Thought is born of failure. [*The Next Development of Man*]

WILLIAM H. WHYTE

13 This book is about the organization man . . . I can think of no other way to describe the people I am talking about. They are not the workers, nor are they the white-collar people in the usual, clerk sense of the word. These people only work for the Organization. The ones I am talking about *belong* to it as well. [*The Organization Man*, Ch. 1]

GEORGE WIGG

14 For Hon. Members opposite the deterrent is a phallic symbol. It convinces them that they are men. [*Observer*, 'Sayings of the Week', 8 Mar. 1964]

BILLY WILDER

15 I've met a lot of hardboiled eggs in my time, but you're twenty minutes. [Film, *Ace in the Hole*. Script by Billy Wilder, Lesser Samuels and Walter Newman]

16 HOLDEN: You used to be in pictures, you used to be big.
SWANSON: I am big. The films got small. [Film, *Sunset Boulevard*. Script by Billy Wilder, Charles Brackett and D. M. Marshman]

17 Why don't you slip out of those wet clothes and into a dry Martini. [Film, *The Major and the Minor*. Script by Billy Wilder and Charles Brackett. Line spoken by Robert Benchley, to whom it is sometimes ascribed]

18 France is a country where the money falls apart in your hands and you can't tear the toilet paper. [Quoted in Leslie Halliwell, *The Filmgoer's Book of Quotes*]

1 You have Van Gogh's ear for music. [Attr. remark to Cliff Osmond]

2 Hindsight is always twenty-twenty. [Quoted in J. R. Colombo, *Colombo's Hollywood*]

THORNTON WILDER

3 For what human ill does not dawn seem to be an alleviation? [*The Bridge of San Luis Rey*, Ch. 3]

4 Most everybody in the world climbs into their graves married. [*Our Town*, Act II]

5 My advice to you is not to inquire why or whither, but just enjoy your ice-cream while it's on your plate, – that's my philosophy. [*The Skin of our Teeth*, Act I]

6 We'll trot down to the movies and see how girls with wax faces live. [*Ib.* III]

7 When you're at war you think about a better life; when you're at peace you think about a more comfortable one. [*Ib.*]

8 A living is made, Mr Kemper, by selling something that everybody needs at least once a year. Yes, sir! And a million is made by producing something that everybody needs every day. You artists produce something that nobody needs at any time. [*The Matchmaker*, Act I]

9 Ninety-nine per cent of the people in the world are fools and the rest of us are in great danger of contagion. [*Ib.*]

10 Marriage is a bribe to make a housekeeper think she's a householder. [*Ib.*]

11 The future is the most expensive luxury in the world. [*Ib.*]

12 The best undertaker in Brooklyn, respected, esteemed. He knew all the best people – knew them well, even before they died. [*Ib.*]

13 The best part of married life is the fights. The rest is merely so-so. [*Ib.* II]

14 AMBROSE: That old man with one foot in the grave!
MRS LEVI: And the other three in the cash box. [*Ib.* III]

15 There's nothing like eavesdropping to show you that the world outside your head is different from the world inside your head. [*Ib.*]

16 That's not a friend, that's an employer I'm trying out for a few days. [*Ib.*]

17 Never support two weaknesses at the same time. It's your combination sinners – your lecherous liars and your miserly drunkards – who dishonour the vices and bring them into bad repute. [*Ib.*]

18 But there comes a moment in everybody's life when he must decide whether he'll live among human beings or not – a fool among fools or a fool alone. [*Ib.* IV]

KAISER WILHELM II

19 I would have liked to go to Ireland, but my grandmother [Queen Victoria] would not let me. Perhaps she thought I wanted to take the little place. [Quoted in H. Montgomery Hyde, *Carson*, Ch. 9, sect. vi]

20 You will be home before the leaves have fallen from the trees. [To troops leaving for the Front, Aug. 1914. Quoted in B. Tuchman, *The Guns of August*, Ch. 9]

21 A contemptible little army. [Description of British Expeditionary Force. [Order at Aix-la-Chapelle H.Q., 19 Aug. 1914]

ELLEN WILKINSON

22 I should like to help Britain to become a Third Programme country. [*Observer*, 'Sayings of the Week', 2 Feb. 1947]

GEOFFREY WILLANS and RONALD SEARLE

23 Lately things are a bit different. The oiks have become v. well dressed certainly beter than pauncefootes pater and their skools are quite remarkable with all those windows to let the sunshine in. [*How to be Topp*, Ch. 2]

24 Cads have always a grandmother who is the DUCHESS of BLANK hem hem. They are inclined to cheat at conkers having baked them for 300 years in the ancestral ovens. [*Ib.* 4]

1 Still xmas is a good time with all those presents and good food and i hope it will never die out or at any rate not until i am grown up and have to pay for it all. [*Ib.* 11]

CHARLES WILLIAMS

2 It is almost impossible to state what one in fact believes, because it is almost impossible to hold a belief and to define it at the same time. [Quoted in W. H. Auden and L. Kronenberger, *The Faber Book of Aphorisms*]

DR ERIC WILLIAMS

3 A small country like ours [Trinidad and Tobago] only has principles. [*Observer*, 'Sayings of the Week', 27 Jun. 1965]

RAYMOND WILLIAMS

4 A very large part of English middle-class education is devoted to the training of servants ... In so far as it is, by definition, the training of upper servants, it includes, of course, the instilling of that kind of confidence which will enable the upper servants to supervise and direct the lower servants. [*Culture and Society*, Ch. 3, Conclusion]

5 The human crisis is always a crisis of understanding: what we genuinely understand we can do. [*Ib.*]

6 The real ruling class could not be put in question, so they are seen as temporarily absent, or as the good old people succeeded by the bad new people – themselves succeeding themselves. We have heard this sad song for many centuries now: a seductive song, turning protest into retrospect, until we die of time. [*The Country and the City*, Ch. 8, sect. iii]

7 When art communicates, a human experience is actively offered and actively received. Below this activity threshold there can be no art. [*The Long Revolution*, Pt I, Ch. 1, sect. vi]

TENNESSEE WILLIAMS

8 Why d'ya call Gooper's kiddies no-neck monsters? [*Cat on a Hot Tin Roof*, Act 1]

9 I'm not living with you. We occupy the same cage. [*Ib.*]

10 [Big Mama points at the bed] When a marriage goes on the rocks, the rocks are *there*, right *there*. [*Ib.*]

11 You can be young without money but you can't be old without it. [*Ib.*]

12 BRICK: Well, they say nature hates a vacuum, Big Daddy.
B. D.: That's what they say, but sometimes I think that a vacuum is a hell of a lot better than some of the stuff that nature replaces it with. [*Ib.* II]

13 That Europe's nothin' on earth but a great big auction, that's all it is. [*Ib.*]

14 It is a terrible thing for an old woman to outlive her dogs. [*Camino Real*, Prologue]

15 The most dangerous word in any human tongue is the word for brother. It's inflammatory. [*Ib.* Block 2]

16 My suit is pale yellow. My nationality is French, and my normality has been often subject to question. [*Ib.* Block 4]

17 Caged birds accept each other but flight is what they long for. [*Ib.* Block 7]

18 *Make voyages! – Attempt them!* there's nothing else. [*Ib.* Block 8]

19 But tenderness, the violets in the mountains – can't break the rocks! [*Ib.* Block 10]

20 We're all of us guinea pigs in the laboratory of God. Humanity is just a work in progress. [*Ib.* Block 12]

21 For time is the longest distance between two places. [*The Glass Menagerie*, sc. vii]

22 Excuse the way I'm – not dressed ... [*The Rose Tattoo*, Act II, sc. i]

23 I can't stand a naked light bulb, any more than I can a rude remark or a vulgar action. [*A Streetcar Named Desire*, Act II, sc. iii]

24 Poker shouldn't be played in a house with women. [*Ib.*]

25 I have always depended on the kindness of strangers. [Blanche's final words in *ib.* xi]

1 If people behaved in the way nations do they would all be put in straitjackets. [In a BBC interview]

WILLIAM CARLOS WILLIAMS

2 Obviously, in a plutocracy / the natural hero / is the man who robs a bank. [*Childe Harold to the Round Tower Came*]

3 Liquor and love / rescue the cloudy sense / banish its despair / give it a home. [*The World Narrowed to a Point*]

4 Minds like beds always made up, / (more stony than a shore) / unwilling or unable. [*Patterson*, I, Preface]

5 Divorce is / the sign of knowledge in our time. [*Ib.*]

6 so much depends / upon / a red wheel / barrow / glazed with rain / water / beside the white / chickens. [*Spring and Fall*, 21, 'The Red Wheelbarrow']

7 This is just to say / I have eaten / the plums / that were in / the icebox / and which / you were probably / saving / for breakfast. / Forgive me / they were delicious / so sweet / and so cold. [*This is just to say*]

WENDELL WILLKIE

8 The constitution does not provide for first and second class citizens. [*An American Programme*, Ch. 2]

9 There exists in the world today a gigantic reservoir of good will toward us, the American people. [*One World*, Ch. 10]

10 Freedom is an indivisible word. If we want to enjoy it, and fight for it, we must be prepared to extend it to everyone, whether they are rich or poor, whether they agree with us or not, no matter what their race or the colour of their skin. [*Ib.* 13]

ANGUS WILSON

11 She was more than ever proud of the position of the bungalow, so almost in the country. [*A Bit Off the Map*, 'A Flat Country Christmas']

12 He would give them his every imitation from 'Eton and Oxford' to the flushing of the lavatory cistern, and so, perhaps, carry the evening through. [*Ib.*]

13 I have no concern for the common man except that he should not be so common. [*No Laughing Matter*]

14 'God knows how you Protestants can be expected to have any sense of direction,' she said. 'It's different with us. I haven't been to mass for years, I've got every mortal sin on my conscience, but I know when I'm doing wrong. I'm still a Catholic.' [*The Wrong Set*, 'Significant Experience']

CHARLES E. WILSON

15 What is good for the country is good for General Motors, and what's good for General Motors is good for the country. [To a Congressional Committee, 1952]

EDMUND WILSON

16 A point of view (I invented this). 'I always give the whores as little as possible: I don't think that prostitution ought to be encouraged.' [*The Twenties*, 'After the War']

17 Of all the great Victorian writers, he [Dickens] was probably the most antagonistic to the Victorian age itself. [*The Wound and the Bow*, 'The Two Scrooges']

18 No two people read the same book. [Quoted by John Russell in the *Sunday Times*, 25 Jul. 1971]

SIR HAROLD WILSON

19 All these financiers, all the little gnomes of Zürich and the other financial centres, about whom we keep on hearing. [Speech in House of Commons, 12 Nov. 1956]

20 This party is a moral crusade, or it is nothing. [At Labour Party Conference, 1962]

21 There is something utterly nauseating about a system of society which pays a harlot 25 times as much as it pays its Prime Minister, 250 times as much as it

pays its Members of Parliament, and 500 times as much as it pays some of its ministers of religion. [On the case of Christine Keeler. Speech in House of Commons, Jun. 1963]

1 We are redefining and we are restating our socialism in terms of the scientific revolution ... the Britain that is going to be forged in the white heat of this revolution will be no place for restrictive practices or out-dated methods on either side of industry. [Speech at Labour Party Conference, 1 Oct. 1963]

2 After half a century of democratic advance, the whole process has ground to a halt with a 14th Earl. [Speech in Manchester, 19 Oct. 1963. For riposte, 21 Oct. 1963, 100: 19]

3 Everybody should have an equal chance – but they shouldn't have a flying start. [*Observer*, 'Sayings of the Year', 1963]

4 A week is a long time in politics. [Probably said in 1964 at parliamentary lobby after sterling crisis. Quoted in N. Rees, *Quote ... Unquote*]

5 It does not mean, of course, that the pound here in Britain in your pocket or purse or in your bank has been devalued. [In prime-ministerial broadcast on TV announcing devaluation, 20 Nov. 1967]

6 I believe the greatest asset a head of state can have is the ability to get a good night's sleep. [In BBC Radio interview, *The World Tonight*, 16 Apr. 1975]

7 The monarchy is a labour-intensive industry. [*Observer*, 'Sayings of the Week', 13 Feb. 1977]

8 Hence the practised performances of latter-day politicians in the game of musical daggers: never be left holding the dagger when the music stops. [*The Governance of Britain*, Ch. 2]

JOSEPH RUGGLES WILSON

9 When you frame a sentence don't do it as if you were loading a shotgun but as if you were loading a rifle. Don't fire in such a way and with such a load that you will hit a lot of things in the neighbourhood besides, but shoot with a single

bullet and hit that one thing alone. [Quoted in John Dos Passos, *Mr Wilson's War*, Ch. 1, sect. ii]

SANDY WILSON

10 She says it's nicer, much nicer in Nice. [*The Boy Friend*, Act II]

11 DULCIE: The modern buildings that you see / Are often most alarming.
LORD B.: But I am sure that you'll agree
DULCIE: A ruin
LORD B.: Can be charming. [*Ib.* III]

12 It's never too late to have a fling / For autumn is just as nice as spring, / And it's never too late to fall in love. [*Ib.*]

PRESIDENT WOODROW WILSON

13 I would never read a book if it were possible to talk half an hour with the man who wrote it. [Advice to his students at Princeton, 1900]

14 Business underlies everything in our national life, including our spiritual life. Witness the fact that in the Lord's Prayer the first petition is for daily bread. No one can worship God or love his neighbour on an empty stomach. [Speech, New York, 1912]

15 It [D. W. Griffith's film *Birth of a Nation*] is like writing history with lightning. [Quoted in Daniel J. Boorstin, *The Image*, Ch. 4]

16 Right is more precious than peace. [Quoted in *Radio Times*, 10 Sep. 1964]

17 Never murder a man who is committing suicide. [Of Governor Hughes's election campaign. Quoted in John Dos Passos, *Mr Wilson's War*, Pt II, Ch. 10, sect. x]

18 Once lead this people into war and they'll forget there ever was such a thing as tolerance. [Quoted in *ib.* III.2 xii]

19 America ... is the prize amateur nation of the world. Germany is the prize professional nation. [Speech to officers of the fleet, Aug. 1917. Quoted in *ib.* Pt III, Ch. 13]

20 People will endure their tyrants for years, but they tear their deliverers to

pieces if a millennium is not created immediately. [Said to George Creel. Quoted in *ib.*, heading to Pt V, Ch. 22]

1 Tell me what's right and I'll fight for it. [To his experts at the Peace Conference. Quoted in *ib.*]

2 The war we have just been through, though it was shot through with terror, is not to be compared with the war we would have to face next time. [Quoted in *ib.*]

ROB WILTON

3 The day war broke out ... [Running gag in comedy act on radio and in variety]

ARTHUR WIMPERIS

4 O Hades! The ladies who leave their wooden huts / For Gilbert, the Filbert, the Col'nel of the Knuts. [Song: *Gilbert the Filbert*]

5 I Don't Want to Be a Soldier. [Title of song]

6 On Sunday I walk out with a soldier, / On Monday I'm taken by a tar, / On Tuesday I'm out with a baby Boy Scout, / On Wednesday an Hussar. [Song: *I'll Make a Man of You*]

7 And on Saturday I'm willing, / If you'll only take the shilling, / To make a man of every one of you. [*Ib.*]

8 My dear fellow a unique evening! I wouldn't have left a turn unstoned. [On a vaudeville show. Quoted in E. Short, *Fifty Years of Vaudeville*]

MARTY WINCH

9 It's better to be wanted for murder than not to be wanted at all. [*Psychology in the Wry*]

DUCHESS OF WINDSOR

10 One can never be too thin or too rich. [Attr.]

GODFREY WINN

11 Praise be to God and to Mr Chamberlain. I find no sacrilege, no bathos, in

360

coupling these two names. [*Daily Express*, Sep. 1938]

12 If you find that your own dog doesn't take to your boy and greet him with affection, you can make up your mind on the spot that there's a yellow streak in that young man's make-up somewhere. [*Woman's Own*, 1937]

JOHN WISDOM

13 ... Another sort of doubt which I venture to call 'philosophical', though I cannot here present all the excuses for stretching the word to cover all doubts of this sort. Examples of this sort are, 'Can a man keep a promise by mistake?', 'Is a zebra without stripes a zebra?'. [*Other Minds*]

LUDWIG WITTGENSTEIN

14 Philosophy, as we use the word, is a fight against the fascination which forms of expression exert upon us. [*The Blue Book*, p. 27]

15 In order to draw a limit to thinking, we should have to be able to think both sides of this limit. [*Tractatus Logico-Philosophicus*, Preface]

16 The world is everything that is the case. [*Ib.* 1.1]

17 All philosophy is 'Critique of language' ... [*Ib.* 4.0031]

18 Philosophy is not a theory but an activity. [*Ib.* 4.112]

19 Everything that can be said can be said clearly. [*Ib.* 4.116]

20 In logic process and result are equivalent. (Therefore no surprises.) [*Ib.* 6. 1261]

21 Whereof one cannot speak, thereof one must be silent. [*Ib.* 7]

22 If there were a verb meaning 'to believe falsely', it would not have any significant first person, present indicative. [Quoted in W. H. Auden, *A Certain World*]

23 Ethics does not treat of the world. Ethics must be a condition of the world, like logic. [Quoted in *ib.*]

WOBURN HOUSE
Seat of committees for relief of German refugees, 1933 onwards)

1 The Bei unsers. [German refugees who complained that in England there was no central heating, etc. From the phrase: *'Bei uns in Berlin . . .'*]

2 Sein Emigranz. [Title for self-important German refugee]

P. G. WODEHOUSE

3 Chumps always make the best husbands. When you marry, Sally, grab a chump. Tap his forehead first, and if it rings solid, don't hesitate. All the unhappy marriages come from the husbands having brains. What good are brains to a man? They only unsettle him. [*The Adventures of Sally*]

4 'What ho!' I said, 'What ho!' said Motty. 'What ho! What ho!' 'What ho! What ho! What ho!' After that it seemed rather difficult to go on with the conversation. [*Carry On Jeeves*, 'Jeeves and the Unbidden Guest']

5 Aunt Agatha, who eats broken bottles and wears barbed wire next to the skin. [*The Code of the Woosters*, Ch. 1]

6 It is no use telling me that there are bad aunts and good aunts. At the core they are all alike. Sooner or later, out pops the cloven hoof. [*Ib*. 2]

7 'Have you ever seen Spode eat asparagus?' 'No.' 'Revolting. It alters one's whole conception of Man as Nature's last word.' [*Ib*. 4]

8 Big chap with a small moustache and the sort of eye that can open an oyster at sixty paces. [*Ib*.]

9 'Oh Bertie,' she said in a low voice like beer trickling out of a jug, 'you ought not to be here!' [*Ib*. 3]

10 He paused, and swallowed convulsively, like a Pekingese taking a pill. [*Ib*.]

11 It was the look which caused her to be known in native bearer and halfcaste circles as 'Mgobi-'Mgumbi, which may be loosely translated as She On Whom It Is Unsafe To Try Any Oompus-Boompus. [*Money in the Bank*, Ch. 2]

12 'That,' I replied cordially, 'is what it doesn't do nothing else but.' [*Ukridge*, Ch. 6]

13 'Alf Todd,' said Ukridge, soaring to an impressive burst of imagery, 'has about as much chance as a one-armed blind man in a dark room trying to shove a pound of melted butter into a wild cat's left ear with a red-hot needle.' [*Ib*.]

14 I can honestly say that I always look on Pauline as one of the nicest girls I was ever engaged to. [*Thank You Jeeves*, Ch. 6]

15 One of the foulest cross-country runs that ever occurred outside Dante's *Inferno*. [*Mike*]

16 The stationmaster's whiskers are of a Victorian bushiness and give the impression of having been grown under glass. [Quoted in Richard Usborne, *Wodehouse at Work to the End*, Ch. 2]

17 Like so many substantial Americans, he had married young and kept on marrying, springing from blonde to blonde like the chamois of the Alps leaping from crag to crag. [Quoted in *ib*. 3]

18 He felt like a man who, chasing rainbows, has had one of them suddenly turn and bite him in the leg. [*Ib*. 4]

19 Unlike the male codfish which, suddenly finding itself the parent of three million five hundred thousand little codfish, cheerfully resolves to love them all, the British aristocracy is apt to look with a somewhat jaundiced eye on its younger sons. [*Ib*. 5]

20 He was either a man of about a hundred and fifty who was rather young for his years or a man of about a hundred and ten who had been aged by trouble. [*Ib*. 6]

21 It is never difficult to distinguish between a Scotsman with a grievance and a ray of sunshine. [*Ib*. 8]

22 The fishy glitter in his eye became intensified. He looked like a halibut which had been asked by another halibut to lend it a quid till next Wednesday. [*Ib*. 10]

23 He groaned slightly and winced, like Prometheus watching his vulture dropping in for lunch. [*Ib*.]

361

1 She went out, breathing flame quietly through her nostrils. [*Ib.* Appendix 1]

2 I turned to Aunt Agatha, whose demeanour was now rather like that of one who, picking daisies on the railway, has just caught the down express in the small of the back. [*The Inimitable Jeeves*, Ch. 4]

3 She had a penetrating sort of laugh. Rather like a train going into a tunnel. [*Ib.* 6]

4 Sir Roderick Glossop ... is always called a nerve specialist, because it sounds better, but everybody knows that he's really a sort of janitor to the looney-bin. [*Ib.* 7]

5 He had a pair of shaggy eyebrows which gave his eyes a piercing look which was not at all the sort of thing a fellow wanted to encounter on an empty stomach. [*Ib.* 8]

6 I trickled out to the Lambs Club, where I had an appointment to feed the Wooster face with a cove of the name of Caffyn. [*Ib.* 9]

7 It was one of those cold, clammy, accusing sort of eyes – the kind that makes you reach up to see if your tie is straight: and he looked at me as I were some sort of unnecessary product which Cuthbert the Cat had brought in after a ramble among the local ash-cans. [*Ib.* 10]

8 Did you notice a fellow standing on my left in our little troupe yesterday? Small, shrivelled chap. Looks like a haddock with lung-trouble. [*Ib.* 11]

9 Jeeves coughed one soft, low, gentle cough like a sheep with a blade of grass stuck in its throat. [*Ib.* 13]

10 I found the proceedings about as scaly as I had expected. It was a warm day, and the hall grounds were a dense, almost liquid mass of peasantry. [*Ib.* 14]

11 Mr Steggles offered to back his nominee in a weight-for-age eating contest against Master Burgess for a pound a side. [*Ib.* 15]

12 Even the Tough Eggs liked it. [*Ib.* 15]

13 I'm not lugged into Family Rows. On the occasions when Aunt is calling to Aunt like mastodons bellowing across primeval swamps and Uncle James's letter about Cousin Mabel's peculiar behaviour is being shot round the family circle ('Please read this carefully and send it on to Jane'), the clan has a tendency to ignore me. [*Ib.* 16]

14 It must have been about one in the afternoon when I woke. I was feeling more or less like something the Pure Food Committee had rejected. [*Ib.*]

15 There's no doubt that Jeeves's pick-me-up will produce immediate results in anything short of an Egyptian mummy. [*Ib.*]

16 It was my Uncle George who discovered that alcohol was a food well in advance of modern medical thought. [*Ib.*]

17 She gave a sort of despairing gesture, like a vicar's daughter who has discovered Erastianism in the village. [*Laughing Gas*, Ch. 9]

18 It is a good rule in life never to apologize. The right sort of people do not want apologies, and the wrong sort take a mean advantage of them. [*The Man Upstairs*, title story]

19 Women with hair and chins like Mary's may be angels most of the time, but when they take off their wings for a bit, they aren't half-hearted about it. [*My Man Jeeves*, 'Absent Treatment']

20 I felt rather like Lot's friends must have done when they dropped in for a quiet chat and their genial host began to criticize the Cities of the Plain. [*Ib.* 'The Aunt and the Sluggard']

21 New York's a small place when it comes to the part of it that wakes up just as the rest is going to bed. [*Ib.*]

22 His ideas of first-aid stopped short at squirting soda-water. [*Ib.* 'Doing Clarence a Bit of Good']

23 I don't owe a penny to a single soul – not counting tradesmen, of course. [*Ib.* 'Jeeves and the Hard-Boiled Egg']

24 Dear old Bicky ... was in many ways one of the most pronounced fatheads that ever pulled on a suit of gent's underwear. [*Ib.*]

1 In this matter of shimmering into rooms the chappie [Jeeves] is rummy to a degree. [*Ib.*]

2 He moves from point to point with as little uproar as a jellyfish. [*Ib.*]

3 A very decent chappie, but rather inclined to collar the conversation and turn it in the direction of his home-town's new water-supply system. [*Ib.*]

4 She fitted into my biggest armchair as if it had been built round her by some-one who knew they were wearing arm-chairs tight about the hips that season. [*Ib.* 'Jeeves and the Unbidden Guest']

5 His eyes bulged, too, but they weren't bright. They were a dull grey with pink rims. His chin gave up the struggle about half-way down, and he didn't appear to have any eyelashes. [*Ib.*]

6 I gave Motty the swift east-to-west. [*Ib.*]

7 What with excellent browsing and sluicing and cheery conversation and what-not, the afternoon passed quite happily. *Ib.*]

8 I've got about a month of New York, and I mean to store up a few happy memories for the long winter evenings. This is my only chance to collect a past, and I'm going to do it. [*Ib.*]

9 And what with brooding on this prospect, and sitting up in the old flat waiting for the familiar footstep, and putting it to bed when it got there, and stealing into the sick-chamber next morning to contemplate the wreckage, I was beginning to lose weight. [*Ib.*]

10 Another slightly *frappé* silence. [*Ib.*]

11 As a rule, from what I've observed, the American captain of industry doesn't do anything out of business hours. When he has put the cat out and locked up the office for the night, he just relapses into a state of coma from which he emerges only to start being a captain of industry again. [*Ib.* 'Leave it to Jeeves']

12 I was so darned sorry for poor old Corky that I hadn't the heart to touch my breakfast. I told Jeeves to drink it himself. [*Ib.*]

13 She was rather like one of those in-nocent-tasting American drinks which

creep imperceptibly into your system so that, before you know what you're doing, you're starting out to reform the world by force if necessary, and pausing on your way to tell the large man in the corner that, if he looks at you like that, you will knock his head off. [*Ib.*]

14 I spent the afternoon musing on Life. If you come to think of it, what a queer thing Life is! So unlike anything else, don't you know, if you see what I mean. [*Ib.* 'Rallying Round Old George']

15 My record speaks for itself. Three times pinched, but never once sentenced under the correct label. [*Right Ho, Jeeves*, Ch. 15]

16 'I may as well inform you that it is not twenty-four hours since she turned me down.' 'Turned you down?' 'Like a bedspread. In this very garden.' [*Ib.*]

17 'How much gin did you put in the jug?' 'A liberal tumblerful, sir.' 'Would that be a normal dose for an adult defeatist, do you think?' [*Ib.* 16]

18 Bingo uttered a stricken woofle like a bull-dog that has been refused cake. [*Very Good, Jeeves!*, 'Jeeves and the Impending Doom']

19 The Right Hon. was a tubby little chap who looked as if he had been poured into his clothes and had forgotten to say 'When!'. [*Ib.*]

20 Aunt Agatha, ... better known as the Pest of Pont Street, the human snap-ping-turtle. [*Ib.* 'Jeeves and the Kid Clementina']

21 I once got engaged to his daughter, Honoria, a ghastly dynamic exhibit who read Nietzsche and had a laugh like waves breaking on a stern and rock-bound coast. [*Ib.* 'Jeeves and the Yule-Tide Spirit']

22 She was as sore as a sunburnt neck be-cause she had had her trip for noth-ing. [*Ib.* 'The Ordeal of Young Tuppy']

23 If I had had to choose between him and a cockroach as a companion for a walking-tour, the cockroach would

have had it by a short head. [*Ib.* 'The Spot of Art']

1 And closing the door with the delicate caution of one brushing flies off a sleeping Venus, he passed out of my life. [*Ib.* 'Jeeves and the Old School Chum']

2 In my Rogues Gallery of repulsive small boys I suppose he would come about third. [*Thank You, Jeeves*, Ch. 3]

3 I did not quite slap him on the back, but I made a sort of back-slapping gesture. [*Ib.* 10]

HUMBERT WOLFE

4 You cannot hope / To bribe or twist / Thank God! The British journalist / But seeing what / That man will do / Unbribed, there's no occasion to. [Contribution to *Punch*]

THOMAS WOLFE

5 Most of the time we think we're sick, it's all in the mind. [*Look Homeward, Angel*, Pt I, Ch. 1]

6 Making the world safe for hypocrisy. [*Ib.* III. 36]

SIR DONALD WOLFIT

7 You are going to let me do what you want done in the way that I want to do it. [To BBC producer. Attr.]

LT-CDR 'TOMMY' WOODROOFE

8 The Fleet's lit up. It is like fairyland; the ships are covered with fairy lights. [Radio commentary at the Coronation Review of the Royal Navy, May 1937. Quoted in *The Times* obituary, 3 Apr. 1978. Also ascribed to John Snagge]

CHARLOTTE WOOLF

9 Women have always been the guardians of wisdom and humanity which makes them natural, but usually secret, rulers. The time has come for them to rule openly, but together with and not against men. [*Bisexuality: A Study*, Ch. 2]

LEONARD WOOLF

10 The grinding of the intellect is for most people as painful as a dentist's drill. [*Observer*, 'Sayings of the Week', 28 Jun. 1959]

VIRGINIA WOOLF

11 Somewhere, everywhere, now hidden, now apparent in whatever is written down, is the form of a human being. If we seek to know him, are we idly occupied? [*The Captain's Death Bed*, 'Reading']

12 The poet gives us his essence, but prose takes the mould of the body and mind entire. [*Ib.*]

13 *Middlemarch*, the magnificent book which with all its imperfections is one of the few English novels for grown up people. [*The Common Reader*, 1st Series, 'George Eliot']

14 She [Charlotte Brontë] does not attempt to solve the problems of human life; she is even unaware that such problems exist; all her force, and it is the more tremendous for being constricted, goes into the assertion, 'I love', 'I hate', 'I suffer'. [*Ib.* 'Jane Eyre']

15 A good essay must have this permanent quality about it; it must draw its curtain round us, but it must be a curtain that shuts us in not out. [*Ib.* 'The Modern Essay']

16 Trivial personalities decomposing in the eternity of print. [*Ib.*]

17 Life is not a series of gig lamps symmetrically arranged; life is a luminous halo, a semi-transparent envelope surrounding us from the beginning of consciousness to the end. [*Ib.* 'Modern Fiction']

18 The interest in life does not lie in what people do, nor even in their relations to each other, but largely in the power to communicate with a third party, antagonistic, enigmatic, yet perhaps persuadable, which one may call life in general. [*Ib.* 'On Not Knowing Greek']

19 At Mudie's corner in Oxford Street all the red and blue beads had run together

on the string. The motor omnibuses were locked. [*Jacob's Room*, Ch. 5]

1 Each had his past shut in him like the leaves of a book known to him by heart; and his friends could only read the title. [*Ib.*]

2 She first washed her head; then ate chocolate creams; then opened Shelley. [*Ib.*]

3 It's not catastrophes, murders, deaths, diseases, that age and kill us; it's the way people look and laugh, and run up the steps of omnibuses. [*Ib.* 6]

4 The lamps of London uphold the dark as upon the points of burning bayonets. [*Ib.* 8]

5 Fraser . . . left his children unbaptized – his wife did it secretly in the washing basin. [*Ib.* 9]

6 There is in the British Museum an enormous mind. Consider that Plato is there cheek by jowl with Aristotle; and Shakespeare with Marlowe. This great mind is hoarded beyond the power of any single mind to possess it. [*Ib.*]

7 'The guns?' said Betty Flanders, half asleep . . . Again, far away, she heard the dull sound, as if nocturnal women were beating great carpets. [*Ib.* 13]

8 Life itself, every moment of it, every drop of it, here, this instant, now, in the sun, in Regent's Park, was enough. Too much, indeed. [*Mrs Dalloway*]

9 Rigid, the skeleton of habit alone upholds the human frame. [*Ib.*]

10 Women have served all these centuries as looking-glasses possessing the magic and delicious power of reflecting the figure of man at twice its natural size. [*A Room of One's Own*]

11 So that is marriage, Lily thought, a man and a woman looking at a girl throwing a ball. [*To the Lighthouse*, Ch. 13]

12 I have lost friends, some by death . . . others through sheer inability to cross the street. [*The Waves*]

13 Let a man get up and say, 'Behold, this is the truth', and instantly I perceive a sandy cat filching a piece of fish in the background. Look, you have forgotten the cat, I say. [*Ib.*]

14 On the outskirts of every agony sits some observant fellow who points. [*Ib.*]

15 [Of Aldous Huxley's *Point Counter Point*] All raw, uncooked, protesting. A descendant, oddly enough, of Mrs [Humphry] Ward: interest in ideas; makes people into ideas. [*A Writer's Diary*, 23 Jan. 1935]

16 A man or woman of thoroughbred intelligence galloping across open country in pursuit of an idea. [Definition of a highbrow. Quoted in Kenneth Tynan, *Curtains*]

ALEXANDER WOOLLCOTT

17 The chair . . . was upholstered in one of those flagrant chintzes, designed, apparently, by the art editor of a seed catalogue. [*While Rome Burns*, 'The Editor's Easy Chair']

18 Subjunctive to the last, he preferred to ask, 'And that, sir, would be the Hippodrome?' [*Ib.* 'Our Mrs Parker']

19 I am in no need of your God-damned sympathy. I ask only to be entertained by some of your grosser reminiscences. [*Letter to a Friend*, 1942]

20 Ross, a man who knew nothing . . . and had contempt for anything he didn't understand, which was practically everything. [Quoted in James Thurber, *The Years with Ross*]

21 A broker is a man who runs your fortune into a shoestring. [Quoted in R. E. Drennan, *Wit's End*]

22 All the things I really like to do are either immoral, illegal, or fattening. [Quoted in *ib.*]

MRS WRIGHT

23 Eh! but it would make a grand Co-op! [Of All Souls College, Oxford. Quoted in E. M. Wright's biography of Prof. J. Wright]

FRANK LLOYD WRIGHT

24 The physician can bury his mistakes, but the architect can only advise his client to plant vines. [*New York Times Magazine*, 4 Oct. 1953]

1 Give me the luxuries of life and I will willingly do without the necessities. [Quoted in obituary, 9 Apr. 1959]

ESME WYNNE-TYSON

2 Scheherazade is the classical example of a woman saving her head by using it. [Attr.]

JON WYNNE-TYSON

3 The wrong sort of people are always in power because they would not be in power if they were not the wrong sort of people. [Book review in *The Times Literary Supplement*]

X

MALCOLM X

1 It's just like when you've got some coffee that's too black, which means it's too strong. What do you do? You integrate it with cream, you make it weak . . . It used to wake you up, now it puts you to sleep. [On Black Power and the Civil Rights movement. *Malcolm X Speaks*, Ch. 14]

Y

ADMIRAL YAMAMOTO

1 I fear we have only awakened a sleeping giant, and his reaction will be terrible. [After Japanese attack on Pearl Harbor, 1941. Quoted by A. J. P. Taylor, in the *Listener*, 9 Sep. 1976]

JUDGE LÉON R. YANKWICH

2 There are no illegitimate children – only illegitimate parents. [Decision in State District Court for the Southern District of California, Jun. 1928]

W. B. YEATS

3 That William Blake / Who beat upon the wall / Till Truth obeyed his call. [*An Acre of Grass*]

4 Nothing can stay my glance / Until that glance run in the world's despite / To where the damned have howled away their hearts, / And where the blessed dance. [*All Souls' Night*]

5 Bring the balloon of the mind / That bellies and drags in the wind / Into its narrow shed. [*The Balloon of the Mind*]

6 That dolphin-torn, that gong-tormented sea. [*Byzantium*]

7 Suddenly I saw the cold and rook-delighting heaven / That seemed as though ice burned and was but the more ice. [*The Cold Heaven*]

8 I would be ignorant as the dawn / That has looked down / On that old queen measuring a town / With the pin of a brooch. [*The Dawn*]

9 Yet always when I look death in the face, / When I clamber to the heights of sleep, / Or when I grow excited with wine, / Suddenly I meet your face. [*A Deep-Sworn Vow*]

10 The fascination of what's difficult / Has dried the sap out of my veins, and rent / Spontaneous joy and natural content / Out of my heart. [*The Fascination of What's Difficult*]

11 I swear before the dawn comes round again / I'll find the stable and pull out the bolt. [*Ib.*]

12 What tumbling cloud did you cleave, / Yellow-eyed hawk of the mind, / Last evening? that I, who had sat / Dumbfounded before a knave, / Should give to my friend / A pretence of wit. [*The Hawk*]

13 Processions that lack high stilts have nothing that catches the eye. [*High Talk*]

14 I have drunk ale from the Country of the Young / And weep because I know all things now. [*He Thinks of his Past Greatness*]

15 I shudder and I sigh to think / That even Cicero / And many-minded Homer were / *Mad as the mist and snow*. [*Mad as the Mist and Snow*]

16 We had fed the hearts on fantasies, / The heart's grown brutal from the fare. [*Meditations in Time of Civil War*, VI]

17 An intellectual hatred is the worst. [*A Prayer for My Daughter*]

18 Soul clap its hands and sing, and louder sing / For every tatter in its mortal dress. [*Sailing to Byzantium*]

19 A Roman Caesar is held down / Under this hump. [*The Saint and the Hunchback*]

20 We have gone round and round / In the narrow theme of love / Like an old horse in a pound. [*Solomon to Sheba*]

21 He that crowed out eternity / Thought to have crowed it in again. [*Solomon and the Witch*]

22 It seems that I must bid the Muse go pack, / Choose Plato and Plotinus for a

friend / Until imagination, ear and eye, / Can be content with argument and deal / In abstract things; or be derided by / A sort of battered kettle at the heel. [*The Tower*, I]

1 Unwearied still, lover by lover, / They paddle in the cold / Companionable streams or climb the air. [*The Wild Swans at Coole*]

2 It is so many years before one can believe enough in what one feels even to know what the feeling is. [*Autobiographies*]

3 Out of the quarrel with others we make rhetoric; out of the quarrel with ourselves we make poetry. [*Essay*]

4 The young men are mad jealous of their leaders for being shot. [Said by old Irish cabinet-maker after Easter Week rising. Reported in letter to Lord Haldane, see D. Sommer, *Haldane of Cloan*, Ch. 23]

5 He [Wilfred Owen] is all blood, dirt and sucked sugar stick. [*Letters on Poetry to Dorothy Wellesley*, Letter, 21 Dec. 1936]

6 People are responsible for their *opinions*, but Providence is responsible for their morals. [Quoted in Christopher Hassall, *Edward Marsh*, Ch. 6]

7 Too true, too sincere. The Muse prefers the liars, the gay and warty lads. [Of James Reeves' *The Natural Need*. Quoted in Robert Graves and Alan Hodge, *The Long Weekend*]

8 It's not a writer's business to hold opinions. [Remark to playwright, Denis Johnston. Quoted in the *Guardian*, 5 May 1977]

9 When I try to put all into a phrase I say 'Man can embody truth, but he cannot know it.' [From a letter just before his death, quoted in Jonathon Green, *Famous Last Words*]

10 o'connor: How are you? w. b. y.: Not very well, I can only write prose today. [Attr.]

JACK YELLEN

11 Happy Days Are Here Again. [Title of song.

YEVGENY YEVTUSHENKO

12 No Jewish blood runs among my blood, / but I am as bitterly and hardly hated / by every anti-semite / as if I were a Jew. By this / I am a Russian. [*Babiy Yar*, trans. R. Milner-Gulland and P. Levi]

13 The hell with it. Who never knew / the price of happiness will not be happy. [*Lies*]

ANDREW YOUNG

14 For still I looked on that same star, / That fitful, fiery Lucifer, / Watching with mind as quiet as moss / Its light nailed to a burning cross. [*The Evening Star*]

15 It was the time of year / Pale lambs leap with thick leggings on / Over small hills that are not there, / That I climbed Eggardon. [*A Prehistoric Camp*]

16 Stars lay like yellow pollen / That from a flower has fallen; / And single stars I saw / Crossing themselves in awe; / Some stars in sudden fear / Fell like a falling tear. [*The Stars*]

17 The Swallows twisting here and there / Round unseen corners of the air / Upstream and down so quickly passed / I wondered that their shadows flew as fast. [*The Swallows*]

MICHAEL YOUNG

18 The Rise of the Meritocracy. [Title of book]

Z

ISRAEL ZANGWILL

1 No Jew was ever fool enough to turn Christian unless he was a clever man. [*Children of the Ghetto*, Ch. I, sect. vii]

2 She was a pale, bent woman, with spectacles, who believed in the mission of Israel, and wrote domestic novels to prove that she had no sense of humour. [*Ib.* 2 i]

3 There she lies, the great Melting Pot – listen! Can't you hear the roaring and the bubbling? . . . Here shall they all unite to build the Republic of Man and the Kingdom of God. [*The Melting Pot*, Ch. 4]

4 The law of dislike for the unlike will always prevail. And whereas the unlike is normally situated at a safe distance, the Jews bring the unlike into the heart of *every milieu*, and must there defend a frontier line as large as the world. [*Speeches, Articles and Letters*, 'The Jewish Race']

DARRYL F. ZANUCK

5 For God's sake don't say yes until I've finished talking. [Quoted in Philip French, *The Movie Moguls*, Ch. 5]

6 If two men on the same job agree all the time, then one is useless. If they disagree all the time, then both are useless. [*Observer*, 'Sayings of the Week', 23 Oct. 1949]

RICHARD ZIEGLER
(Press Secretary to President Nixon)

7 This is an operative statement. The others are inoperative. [Statement to White House press corps, 17 Apr. 1973, admitting the untruth of earlier denials of government involvement in Watergate affair]

LUIS DE ZULUETA

8 The Church complains of persecution when it is not allowed to persecute. [Speech in the Cortes, 1936]

INDEX

... Most probably she'll have it filed under whoever said it, which we don't know, or the occasion he said it upon, which we don't know either. But conceivably she may also or alternatively have it under as it were Corporal Punishment. Or Punishment Corporal. Or Labour Party. Or Parties Labour.

Michael Frayn, *Alphabetical Order*, Act 1

INDEX

References are given thus: '214:15', which means 'page 214, quotation 15'.

Plurals and the third person singular of verbs, where these take only an 's' or 'es', are indexed under the singular or nominative. For example, 'hate' and 'hates' are indexed together, 'hate' being abbreviated to 'h.' and 'hates' to 'h.s'. Plurals which take the 'ies' form (and those where the plural produces a key-word which is naturally independent, e.g. 'sex' and 'sexes') appear separately.

Where a person is the subject of a quotation, without his or her name actually forming part of the quotation, the reference is to the quotation as a whole, e.g. Churchill, Winston: 41:14.

The index includes the key foreign as well as English words. The former are printed in italics.

A

Abbott: ask A. to give her Costello 221:11
A.B.C.: droop in a hundred A.s 108:20
Abnormal: aunt of lone a. me 41:2
About: a. ten minutes long 105:11
Abraham: oh God said to A. 104:22
Abroad: a. is bloody 130:3
  British tourist is happy a. 240:16
  haven't been a. in so long 36:6
  I don't hold with a. 90:14
  recurrent question about a. 214:6
  that's a., isn't it 234:23
Abschied: nehmen immer A. 282:2
  sei allem A. voran 282:15
Absence: a. blots people out 47:2
  he has a perfectly delightful a. 301:18
  shoot me in my a. 33:9
Absinthe: a. makes the tart grow fonder 102:17
Absolve: History will a. me 66:7
Absorbed: old . . . are always a. 348:4
Abstands: gibt das Mass des A. 281:9
Abstinence: bad poems . . . created during a. 279:6
Abstract: ability to make a. that which is concrete 297:26
  deal in a. things 368:22
  what is there to bite on in the a. 65:16
Absurd: a. has meaning only in so far 62:2
  a. is born of this confrontation 62:1

a. is sin without God 62:3
  art deals with the a. 244:14
  saw nothing a. in themselves 261:12
Absurdist: A. plays . . . in No Man's Land 9:11
Absurdity: as an a. it was so colossal 86:18
Abuse: to a. a man is a lover-like thing 65:4
Academe: groves and grooves of A. 125:23
Academic: attention of rival schools of a.s 319:10
Academism: a. results when the reasons 322:15
Accent: a. they had at Paddington 170:15
  with the faintest foreign a. 141:3
Accept: whenever you a. our views we shall be 95:22
Acceptable: must say a. things 185:14
Accident: cannot be insured for the a.s 87:5
  the problem of habitual a.s 36:2
  when . . . a. threatens 334:17
Accomplished: I myself have a. nothing 330:9
Accomplishment: emerges ahead of his a.s 317:4
  mighty sense of a. 150:6
Accountant: chartered a. over thirty 241:10
Accused: a. men are often attractive 179:8
  a. of things you never did 318:19
Accustomed: a. to her face 203:20
Ace: fifth a. 242:2
  on the back of the A. 22:10
Achievement: hams snap in moments of a. 50:14
  the machine threatens all a. 282:14
Acid: enough a. in your stomach 249:1
Ackamarackus: strictly the old a. 288:9
Acquaintance: need two kinds of a.s 310:4
Acquisitiveness: a. has more perverts 162:10
Act: can't a. Can't sing 21:11
  easier to a. than to think 20:1
  everyone who tells you how to a. 338:15
  order of the a.s is planned 261:6
Action: all our a.s . . . grandfathers 49:3
  always wrote with a. in mind 348:13
  man of a. 198:2
  political will . . . for political a. 155:8
  quick and steady in a. 296:3
  road to holiness . . . world of a. 145:15
  true men of a. in our time 23:14
  work of many men. A., of one 129:13
  world . . . grasped by a. 54:3
Activity: every human a. inside a taxi 53:9
  philosophy . . . an a. 360:18

Actor(s): 18:14
a. . . . ain't listening 50:22
a.s . . . all die of the Plague 104:14
a.s are atheists 263:7
a.s are cattle 154:13
Fifth-Act-A. 226:2
good a. does not make his entry 46:18
question a.s most often get asked 103:15
type of a. the French call 321:16
Actress: English a.es are mistresses 146:23
fame of the a. is transitory 28:15
kind of a. Agate would call 113:13
next worst to an a. 65:10
Ad: a.s push the principle of noise 218:7
he watched the a.s 247:12
Adam: A. is believed to have remarked
165:14
A. had 'em 132:2
debt of gratitude . . . to A. 336:10
if A. and Eve . . . engaged 350:20
she sought A. and accused him 42:7
what A. had seen . . . the miracle 163:16
Add: here you are, a. that lot up 146:19
nothing to say, only to a. 342:18
Addiction: every form of a. is bad 178:7
terminal point of a. 23:12
Additive: needed no cognitive a.s 35:8
Address: a. . . . was perfectly genuine 79:3
Adjective: die . . . for the sake of an a. 84:3
Adjusted: agreed that He was very well a.
13:22
so well a. to his environment 172:6
Adler: A. will always be Jung 344:13
Ad-Mass: the Holy-Families of the A. 215:2
Admiral: dangerous to meddle with A.s
76:10
Admire: animals do not a. each other
38:20
Admirer: make us hate ourselves like an a.
83:14
Admittance: no a. on business 347:23
Adolescence: ideal of eternal a. 339:21
maturity . . . a short break in a. 113:9
suffering from petrified a. 41:14
Theory of Permanent A. 84:1
vigour of a prolonged a. 199:4
Adolescent: diminutive male a. 207:23
Adolf: which A. was this 52:3
Adulation: sediment of permanent a. 83:25
Adult: a.s are obsolete children 301:10
but that children produce a.s 98:11
child becomes an a. when 323:12
happiness . . . attributed by a.s 323:15
only between consenting a.s 343:6
to be a. is to be alone 287:9
when I first entered a. life 271:13
Adultery: a. at one end and weep . . . at the
other 65:8
autobiography . . . as common as a. 142:9
rather be taken in a. than in 161:9
speaks very favourably of a. 230:14
Adulthood: if this was a. 14:1
Advance: absence of . . . a. in an industry
127:9
a. beyond ape-mentality 354:10

indubitably an a. 290:8
twenty years in a. of this country 157:6
Advantage: those a.s . . . spoken of as natural
170:16
Adventure: through them we pass into a.
119:4
Adventurer: England . . . was led by a.s 155:9
true a. goes forth aimless 152:3
Adversary: accepting the death of my a. 62:7
people against a single a. 155:1
Advertisement: ideals of a nation by its a.s
100:17
world in which A. dwells 217:14
Advertising: a. may be described 198:22
half the money . . . on a. 345:1
who are these a. men kidding 215:2
Advice: if he wants to ask for bad a. 273:18
what is the best a. 249:11
Advising: know better than to go round a.
52:2
Advocaat: a. . . . made from lawyers 87:11
A.E.I.O.U.: famous 'A.' policy 316:9
Aerial: a. warfare . . . indecisive 351:2
Aesthetic: a. sense is akin 227:5
crime . . . desire for a. 346:14
degree of my a. emotion 34:2
for whom do . . . [a. laws] exist 299:17
Affability: language . . . of aristocratic a.
273:17
Affectation: shed the . . . a. of my youth 90:19
Affection: forbidden to mention . . . a. 28:4
know everything about our a.s 297:13
you cannot have an a. 255:6
Affirmation: a. of one's own life 123:12
Afford: barely a. the . . . luxuries 100:17
Afraid: he was a. of himself 195:12
not that I'm a. to die 13:12
we are all a. 54:10
whenever I look inside myself I am a. 174:9
Africa: white man in A. 203:22
African: they're just A.s 247:3
Afterlife: a. . . . any less exasperating 88:18
fear that there may be no a. 13:13
Afternoon: fag end of an a. 231:11
summer a. . . . most beautiful words 171:6
what to do . . . on a rainy Sunday a.
111:6
Against: a. everything all of the time 182:14
life is six to five a. 288:19
Agate, James: the kind of actress A. would
call 113:13
Age: a. only matters 264:5
'Be your a.!' 266:7
give evidence of his a. 43:12
men . . . the best improve with a. 174:15
mosaic swimming-pool a. 79:6
recognize . . . the first sign of a. 154:3
tell you the signs of a New A. 310:12
Aged: a. rather than . . . venerable 350:1
beauty of an a. face 60:13
Agenda: a. winks at me 329:8
Agent: told you he was a secret a. 89:4
Aggressor: quarantine the a.s 285:21
Agitation: display of polished a. 50:18
film culture . . . a. of the mind 153:16

Agnosticism: anything but a questing a. 176:1
Agony: a. column . . . always instructive
   101:11
   outskirts of every a. 365:14
   that a. is our triumph 341:15
Agree: I a. with everything . . . but 320:24
   if two men . . . a. 370:6
Agreement: our views we shall be in full a.
   95:22
Agricultural: diet of the a. classes 347:3
   fault of the A. . . . Service 18:17
Ahead: always wise to look a. 77:15
   to get a. of ourselves 238:9
Aid: a. . . . is blackmail 53:13
Aïda: you can't judge Egypt by A. 114:18
Aim: you a. too please 137:17
Air: clear the a. I clean the sky 109:20
   feet firmly planted in the a. 299:2
   finger that turns the dial rules the a.
      103:21
   fresh air should be kept 214:4
   full of good a. 198:14
   into my heart an a. that kills 159:6
   nights when the a. is blood temperature
      103:14
   showed me the a. and . . . how to fill it
      176:5
   straw vote only shows . . . the hot a. 152:22
Aircraft: loud fluttering a. slope 126:8
Airport: a. is a free-range womb 55:4
Aisle: A. Altar. Hymn 244:2
Aitches: nothing to lose but our a. 255:19
Alamein: after A. we never had a defeat
   76:14
Alarm: event outran the a. 138:14
Alcohol: a. was a food 362:16
   prescribed . . . the drinking of a. 76:21
Alderman: bit like God . . . the A. 329:9
Ale: a. from the Country of the Young 368:14
   drank a pint of English a. 68:19
   taking twopenny a. and cheese 68:20
Alexander: A. . . . looks for his glasses 125:10
   A.'s Ragtime Band 39:10
Algebra: a. bears to arithmetic 23:23
   what is a. exactly 29:3
Alguién: A. cuyo número no está 63:20
Alice: A. showed her pup Ulysses' bough
   111:3
Alien: he is called an 'a.' 241:2
   methods which are a. 220:8
Alienation: a. awaits us 192:5
Alike: everyone is a. 184:20
   they are very much a. 255:14
Alive: a. . . . out of hospital 30:11
   as long as he is a. there is 312:6
   dead know . . . it was better to be a. 117:20
   die to prove he had been a. 180:1
   know she's a. I saw 113:7
   lucky if he gets out of it a. 114:4
   never even knew that he was a. 259:22
   no one is a. 184:20
   one who comes out a. 51:15
   remind me I'm a. 225:9
Allegiance: can take no a. to a flag 339:19
Alley: down an a. of green moss 344:4

Alliance: forced the Muse to this a. 61:5
Alligator: a.s . . . floating handbags 142:6
All-round: wonderful a. man, but 33:4
Ally: a. has to be watched 335:8
Alma: el a. de charol 128:17
Almond: don't eat too many a.s 80:16
Alms: ale money . . . a. for oblivion 49:19
Alone: bed . . . early, sober and a. 339:2
   I want to be a. 128:14
   living a. for so many years 202:24
   remain a. for several hours 207:7
   they go out to be a. 218:12
   to be . . . truthful when you are a. 98:23
Alphabet: remaining . . . letters of the a.
   254:13
Alps: 327:5
Altar: stood before the a. 42:6
   under the earth-line their a.s are 186:18
Alternative: state the a. preferred 332:11
Altruism: fruitful a.s of Nature 274:10
   show of a. is respected 229:14
Amateur: America . . . is the prize a. nation
   359:19
   artistic temperament . . . afflicts a.s 71:5
   in love as in sport, the a. status 139:15
   its affinities are with a.s 295:19
   sure sign of an a. 58:4
Amazed: I was a. 159:18
Amber: fly caught in forever a. 82:6
Ambidextrous: give my right hand to be a.
   136:21
Ambiguity: a. that attends all . . . relationships
   278:17
   Chair of Comparative A. 236:17
Ambition: generic names such as A. and
   Interest 296:15
   my a. has been so great 158:17
   temptations to social a. 205:12
Ambulance: knocked down a doctor . . . an a.
   308:1
America: 332:18
   absolute silence of A. 195:19
   A. . . . barbarism to degeneration 78:19
   A. became top nation 301:5
   A. . . . dog in a very small room 332:15
   A. has a . . . rank refinement 69:24
   A. is a land of boys 219:16
   A. is so big 35:5
   A. . . . is the prize amateur nation 359:19
   A. is the proof 215:6
   A. that is on the march 182:6
   A.'s . . . a kind of Russia 57:16
   and mechanical A. Montezuma 194:9
   behind the discovery of A., there was a
      Jewish financier 280:13
   business of A. is business 86:2
   I came to A. tourist Third 84:8
   I could come back to A. . . . to die 171:8
   in A. the successful writer 206:16
   living rooms of A. 218:10
   must first come to pass in . . . A. 108:14
   national dish of A. 284:2
   to A. she was the gateway 351:1
   with A. in the offing 245:15
   won't be any revolution in A. 208:13

American: A. captain of industry 363:11
A. character 215:5
A. . . . dismissed the historic safari 35:19
A. doctrine . . . do something 309:1
A. girls do have regrets 341:7
A. history . . . hating their fathers 49:1
A. is either a Jew or an anti-Semite 296:1
A. life in large cities 215:4
A. motorist in England 208:16
A. thinks pacing 253:5
A. woman of such dynamism 64:11
A. women expect to find 228:6
A. women like quiet men 15:9
A. . . . would do without it 215:1
A. writers want to be 343:1
A.s are polite . . . telling the truth 49:2
A.s are the most efficient people 227:13
A.s as if it were commonplace 16:1
A.s dislike only *some* Irish 33:18
A.s do not rear children 172:14
A.s have a perfect right to exist 32:18
A.s have a . . . resistance 333:22
A.s have become too liberal 184:6
A.s . . . kept on marrying 361:17
A.s . . . mean and feel far less 120:11
A.s refer to as cross-ventilation 132:3
A.s . . . respect newness 338:12
A.s who cannot 342:14
A.s won't listen to sense 183:11
business . . . centre of A. culture 35:17
clean-limbed A. boys 15:20
contradictions of A. life 53:14
don't see much future for the A.s 155:17
dream of the A. male 353:11
Europeans and A.s are like men 172:13
good will toward us, the A. people 358:9
greatest A. friend we have 77:2
if an A. told you . . . it was true 89:4
image . . . of an A. 231:23
in an A. ship 210:16
most popular A. entertainments 231:13
new generation of A.s 181:24
no second acts in A. lives 116:18
North A.s have a bias 218:12
our A. professors 206:18
process whereby A. girls turn 146:12
proud . . . one of 200 million A.s 118:10
represented the modern A. woman 215:7
strange blend . . . A. abroad 316:6
therapy . . . the tenth A. muse 54:13
to A.s English manners are far more 172:7
twentieth century . . . A. accent 142:21
violence is as A. as cherry pie 64:4
we are all A. at puberty 347:17
when an A. heiress wants to buy 215:3
wrong with the A. public 181:20
Americanism: McCarthyism is A. 214:15
no fifty-fifty A. 286:7
toothsome amalgam of A.s 187:20
Amnesia: a. is not knowing who one is 283:1
a. rules – er 136:11
Amour: jealous because of his *a. propre*
141:11
Amputate: thank God they had to a. 298:5
Amusement: were it not for its a.s 206:8

Anaemia: a sort of emotional a. 269:21
Analyst: a. should pay the patient 342:16
Anarchist: a.s who love God 65:11
Anarchy: a. in your own heart 28:13
emotional a. 196:1
we apply it, you call it a. 69:20
Ancestor: clinging . . . to the vices of his a.s
112:15
most obscure of all classes . . . a.s 72:21
shame that we had no recorded a.s 199:18
Ancient: as boring as any other a. literature
161:21
And: must learn . . . more about 'a.' 106:8
Angel: A. of the Off-shore Wind 185:20
a. whose muscles developed 144:12
a.s play only Bach 29:13
a.s . . . take themselves lightly 72:4
brute curiosity of an a.'s stare 325:8
calling to the A.s 185:19
felt as if a.s were pushing 128:4
Herald A.s sing, Mrs Simpson 16:8
may have been pleasing to the a. 293:13
mixture of fools and a.s – they rush 152:12
most of an a. . . . inside 15:7
people are not fallen a.s 197:10
Recording A. . . . shorthand 38:13
royalties as recording a. 219:12
women . . . may be a.s 362:19
you may not be an a. 103:2
Anglo-Catholic: becoming an A. . . . sad
321:15
Anglo-Irishman: A. . . . with a horse 33:7
Angry: contain the whole of death and not be
a. 281:10
Anguish: a. can bring us to life 62:21
Animal: a. that does not exist 282:13
a.s do not admire each other 38:20
be a good a. 196:7
every a. leaves traces 54:1
have a decent attitude towards a.s 154:9
if we stop loving a.s 311:13
intelligence of the a. 279:9
man is and will always be a wild a. 94:10
nothing to be done . . . about a.s 157:3
nothing to be pitied in a dumb a. 87:18
one . . . tells oneself the a. likes it 293:22
there is no such a. 197:16
what appear to be a.s 277:18
we have here an a. 206:2
you never see a.s going through 162:15
Animate: transform . . . something a. 123:14
Ann: sculptured A. is seventy 327:13
Anna: we all know A. Livia 177:11
Anna Karenina: 237:7
Annie: Little Orphan A. 140:1
Annihilation: a. of a people doesn't alter
132:22
no a. without representation 332:14
our happy exposure to . . . a. 129:11
paid for by complete a. 63:3
Anonymity: they represent a. 296:27
Answer: a. is always a form of death 121:1
a. is in the plural 213:1
a. is not separate from the problem 190:9
a., my friend, is blowin' 104:20

a.? . . . what is the question 317:3
a. 'Yes, but' 199:6
all Call and A. 195:9
as long as the a. is right 178:17
driven to give wrong a.s 342:17
that is the a. 288:4
we have learned the a.s 217:10
Antarctica: as warily as A. was circled 108:12
Anthem: as long as it endorsed the National A. 119:12
Anthology: a. is like all the plums . . . picked out of a cake 276:6
Anthony: ease with which St A. rebuffed 161:14
Anthropologist: a. respects history 204:15
Anti-clerical: makes me understand a. things 35:2
Anti-Communist: Christian A.s, and the others 103:7
Anti-professional: English genius is a. 295:19
Anti-Semite: either a Jew, or an a. 296:11
hated by every a. 369:12
Anti-social: I will show you an a. 36:11
Antithesis: a. . . . Temperance Hotel 337:1
Anxiety: persecutory a. which . . . follows birth 278:10
poem . . . when an a. meets a technique 104:13
Anything: a. goes 267:10
I don't want to do a. 296:26
Apathetic: ours is a. 331:9
Apathy: much to be said for a. in education 119:10
Ape: a.-like virtues without which 83:3
I have called the A.s of God 207:10
naked a. . . . Homo Sapiens 241:5
Aphorism: there are a.s that . . . stay up 246:2
Aphrodisiac: the ultimate a. 188:7
Apocalypse: four hoarse men of the new a. 321:5
Apologetic: without feeling a. 271:12
Apologize: rule . . . never to a. 362:18
Apostle: A.s . . . kissed everybody 12:15
Appendix: would you like your a. put back 60:8
Appetency: anything . . . that will satisfy an a. 280:5
Appetite: never improved his a. 221:18
Applaud: go out front and a. yourself 284:18
Applause: a. is a receipt 299:13
a. is the echo of a platitude 42:8
Apple: a.s fell 64:13
millionaires love a baked a. 115:1
sweeter the a. 259:3
Under the A. Tree with Anyone Else 55:16
Appreciate: I never 'a.' 264:4
Appreciation: a. of his relation to the dead 110:3
dependence on the a. of others 83:18
Apprentice: to become an a. once more 30:9
Aquarium: managed to preserve his a. 152:17
Arab: A. . . . a Jew on horseback 15:11

he did not know there were A.s 167:3
shook hands with a friendly A. 234:9
Arc, Joan of: 265:2
Archaeologist: a. is the best husband 73:4
Arches: underneath the a. 117:12
Archibald: A., certainly not 283:9
Architect: a. can only advise his client 365:24
a. who saw this thing 240:1
challenge for the modern a. 251:5
finally called, by the Great A. 146:19
Architecture: a. cannot lie 133:7
a. is a sub-division 18:9
French Classical a. . . . gifted 78:7
hope may turn them into . . . a. 126:1
your left leg, it's modern a. 27:18
Arden, John: A. . . . four hoarse men 321:5
Are: Here We A. 189:1
Argument: a. . . . cannot make the engine move 41:25
beware of long a.s 296:3
detected . . . in the use of an a. 38:1
jawbacious a. 350:2
sustain the attention . . . by a. 319:10
Arian: one thing about the A. controversy 66:15
Ariel: Caliban casts out A. 269:6
Aristocracy: a. . . . the badly educated 72:17
a. would be biologically sound 144:10
British a. . . . eye on its younger sons 361:19
Aristocrat: honour is a luxury for a.s 70:23
played the part of the last a. 205:3
Aristocratic: a. civilization built up by . . . plenty 84:6
language . . . of a. affability 273:17
to be a. in Art 239:7
Arithmetic: children's as good as a. 58:7
literature is . . . a. 321:14
reckless a. of rumour 122:6
Arm: is those things a.s 247:15
Armada: Mosquito A. . . . unsinkable 75:22
Armament: a.s . . . pillars of Western prosperity 163:21
it is not a.s that cause war 219:14
Armchair: a.s tight about the hips 363:4
Armies: spring leaf with your a. 12:10
Armpit: smelling their own a.s 233:15
Army: a. ages men sooner 349:11
backbone of the A. 185:4
contemptible little a. 356:21
conventional a. loses 188:5
dialect that has an a. 348:11
ever set foot inside . . . a. boots 146:17
join the A. . . . kill them 17:1
lesson I learned in the a. 339:15
loose for the A. 171:1
this is the a., Mr Jones 39:16
we were a self-centred a. 198:1
Arresting: a. the human intelligence 198:22
Arrived: I've a. – and to prove it 58:17
Arrow: though an a. is always approaching 319:11
Arse: sit on your a. for fifty years 219:7
The Arse and the Elbow 278:17
Arson: a. . . . artificial crime 350:4

Art: all a. deals with the absurd 244:14
all the a.s aspire to the condition of music 296:7
any a. tolerably brisk and bold 71:7
a. and literature are left 206:16
A. and Religion . . . to ecstasy 34:1
a. does not reproduce what we see 188:19
a. . . . expression of the profoundest thoughts 108:7
a. is a truer guide 207:6
a. is an appeal to a reality 214:12
a. is meant to disturb 51:2
a. is not a mirror 228:17
a. is not a special sauce 204:2
a. is not a weapon 182:4
a. is photosynthesis 190:6
a. is significant deformity 126:2
a. is thoughtful workmanship 204:3
a. . . . *makes* life, makes interest 171:10
a. should be cold 299:18
a., thought Lord Buttonhooke 49:13
a.s . . . the algebra of emotional 321:14
aspires . . . to the condition of a. 85:5
boredom in the a.s can be 342:15
burnings of . . . works of a. 288:1
enemy of good a. . . . the pram 83:11
every work of a. . . . is simple 69:15
goal of a. is delectation 322:8
great religious a. of the world 78:4
had no need of the a.s 226:1
have the a. rather than the article 74:17
how drunk we like our a. to be 212:15
I doubt that a. needed Ruskin 321:4
I took A. at College 346:26
if there's a clash . . . it's bad a. 66:17
imagination without skill . . . modern a. 319:4
in a., rebellion is consummated 63:5
it is not a. that rains down 322:6
left the Garden of A. for the Palace 117:19
Mr Goldwyn . . . you are only interested in a. 306:11
my a. belongs to Dada 320:13
neurotics . . . have created great works of a. 273:11
object of a. . . . shape 19:4
physics . . . great collective work of a. 54:6
pop a. and fine a. 216:18
real life . . . an imitation of a. 217:15
realism . . . means making life into a. 253:3
rest belongs to the madness of a. 171:15
telephone directory . . . is a work of a. 136:6
that is *a.*, they say 228:19
three a.s . . . pastry-making 18:9
to be aristocratic in A. 239:7
verbal a. . . . is reflective 23:21
Welsh . . . no graphic or plastic a. 346:4
what a. reaches 207:19
what was known as a. silk 256:12
what we call a. 257:1
when a. communicates 357:7
Widower of A.s 61:5
Arthritis: a., and I don't deserve that 38:8
cannot even spell a. 288:9

Artist: all living a.s compete 213:3
aren't the a.s brave to go out 102:3
a. And you know what that means 65:10
a. cannot deny art 67:16
a. is extremely lucky who 40:10
a. is not a special kind of man 131:17
a. man and the mother woman 302:27
a. . . . must always submit 322:8
a. produces things that people 345:5
a. . . . sits on the edge of the world 308:19
a. transcends his . . . anguish 243:4
a. will betray . . . sincerity 69:18
a.s can colour the sky red 113:6
a.'s egoism is outrageous 228:3
a.s . . . something that nobody needs 356:8
as a.s they're rot 260:1
beware of the a. who's an intellectual 115:19
direction of a real a. 211:17
every good a. paints what he is 266:13
from now on an a. will be judged 82:20
generosity . . . virtue for an a. 312:4
gentleman from . . . the a. 345:18
great a.s of the world 230:3
if he had been an a. 207:14
if you can't be an a. 320:20
it's the a.'s job 285:13
let the a. have just enough to eat 34:4
lie . . . sign of the true a. 342:19
many a.s . . . mildly snobbish 84:6
more perfect the a., the more . . . separate 110:7
one lucky bastard who's the a. 320:18
only one position for an a. 328:19
too difficult for a.s 299:14
Artistic: a. temperament . . . afflicts amateurs 71:5
Aryan: I wouldn't trust an A. 247:1
Ascent: cultural peaks . . . *A. of Man* 53:15
Asceticism: out of a. 215:4
Ascot: A. . . . the horses own the people 56:16
Ashamed: a. . . . threatened his manhood 81:12
more things a man is a. of 302:25
Ash-can: ramble among the local a.s 362:7
Ashes: a. to a. . . . your own folks 331:5
Asleep: not to fall a. is distinguished 35:11
Asparagus: declined to swallow M. Elstir's a. 273:15
Spode eat a. 361:7
Aspidistra: biggest a. in the world 114:3
Aspiration: all revolt and a. 52:23
a.s that never come to pass 293:10
Aspirin: euthanasia . . . extension of the a. 49:6
Asquith, H. H.: A. is good and immoral 77:9
Asquith, Margot: affair between Margot A. 260:8
going to marry Margot A. 27:5
Assassination: a. . . . should be used 164:4
despotism tempered by a. 279:11
Dumini, twelve a.s 103:10
Assent: acts of a. require far more courage 97:10
Assertion: effectiveness of a. is . . . style 302:16

Assignation: world a vast house of a. 90:18
Asterisk: when a.s were followed 226:18
Astronaut: a.s . . . Rotarians 343:2
Astronomical: 'humble' in the presence of a. dimensions 295:3
Astronomy: a. teaches the use of the sun 198:18
Asunder: no man shall ever put a. 305:26
Asylum: Cambridge an a., in every sense 159:14
  inmate of a lunatic a. 283:7
Atheism: a., breast-feeding, circumcision 253:20
Atheist: a. . . . finds creation so perfect 273:14
  a. . . . has no one to thank 345:2
  a. . . . no invisible means of support 56:12, 120:7
  a. still, thank God 57:12
  a. who does not . . . disbelieve in God 254:18
  a.s who are also men of honor 305:7
  average length of life for a.s 252:15
  red hair . . . of a born a. 112:13
  scepticism kept her from being an a. 297:17
  very *chic* for an a. 289:19
Athens: burn, with A. and with Rome 61:10
Athlete: he suffers from a.'s foot 10:19
  you're like . . . a.'s foot 24:5
Athletic: a. qualifications are not . . . successful 76:11
Atlantic: Battle of the A. had now 76:9
  East come to the A. 133:19
  I came here on the A. auction 223:16
Atlas; immense, improbable a. 21:21
Atmosphere: a. was international with . . . smoke 152:18
Atom: no evil in the a. 318:5
  protons and morons in the a. 173:11
  release of a. power has changed everything 108:2
Atom bomb: 108:3, 189:19
  a. is a paper tiger 222:6
Atomic: A. Age is here to stay . . . are we 66:14
  way to win an a. war 49:11
Attached: men become a. even to Widnes 326:4
Attachment: our a. to the things of this world 221:13
  strengthening his a. to her 272:12
Attack: during a night a. 242:5
  his plan of a. 298:3
Attending: man in his wholeness wholly a. 194:12
Attention: a. span is not what it was 343:3
  his socks compelled one's a. 293:8
  learn to love . . . by paying a. 163:12
  so a. must be paid 232:22
Attitude: number of blessings . . . only our a. 311:19
Attlee, Clement: 77:5, 77:6, 77:17
  A. combines a limited outlook 74:15
Attraction: a.s for their coming week 22:18
  failure . . . a positive a. 171:5
Attractive: accused men are often a. 179:8

Auction: Europe's . . . a great big a. 357:13
Auden: W. H. A., a sort of gutless Kipling 255:16
  A. . . . you could laugh-at-with 315:4
  mysterious . . . tea-drinking A. 83:16
Audience: a. is still there 50:4
  a. . . . she preferred watching 323:7
  better understanding of . . . a.s 353:6
  such a lovely a. 202:27
  theme that touches all your a. 302:7
  two kinds of a. only 299:12
  we have to relate it to the a. 280:9
  where do all the a.s come from 250:11
  you call that an a. 87:12
Aufwand: des andern A. fühlbar 281:8
Aunt: A. Elsie, a. of normal Scottish boys 41:2
  A. is calling to A. like mastodons 362:13
  bad a.s and good a.s 361:6
  his a.s, who are not married 69:6
  monstrous a. can be funny 339:1
  sudden mention of an a. 223:8
Auschwitz: this, say the chickens, is their A. 268:3
Austerity: gentle a. was the keynote 89:5
  puritanism . . . is a. 83:7
Australia: didn't I tell you A. was up 223:21
  remote golden A. 195:6
  weary aloofness of A. 194:24
Austria: A. is Switzerland 241:4
  to A. belongs universal rule 316:9
Austria-Hungary: destroy A. 36:16
Auswahl: begann nicht . . . seine herrische A. 281:15
Author: allow an a. to smell treacle 286:19
  a. arrives at a good style 83:4
  a. handed round a box 212:16
  a. ought to write for the youth 117:10
  a.s and uncaptured criminals 208:17
  a.s . . . if you are fond of children 176:8
  a.s who are not really novelists 120:1
  bad novel tells us . . . about its a. 71:2
  I don't know who the a. is 305:20
  I write like a distinguished a. 246:11
  list of a.s . . . most beloved 259:19
  our younger a.s 228:8
  paying the a. a . . . compliment 205:21
  sending the a. some . . . cash 83:12
  transitory as the fame of the a.s 28:15
  what I like in a good a. 310:5
Authority: an air of final and absolute a. 309:2
  confirmed by even Higher A. 321:8
  maximal a. and minimal power 323:14
  no morality . . . founded on a. 24:9
Autobiography: a. . . . as common as adultery 142:9
  a. is an obituary in serial form 91:2
  of all forms of fiction a. 320:22
  my a. has no more . . . fiction 87:1
Autocracy: in an a., one person has his 140:8
Autocrat: rebel . . . turning into an a. 104:5
Autograph: give him my a. as a souvenir 156:5
Automatics: carried a. acquired in the holidays 300:13

Automobile: a. changed our ... positions in
  intercourse 181:19
  a. did not put the adventure of travel
    within reach 181:20
  God would not have invented the a. 241:3
Autumn: a. is desolation in the plot 325:7
  a. is just as nice as spring 359:12
  comes it will come in the a. 125:13
  girls that go so well with a. scenery 293:2
  rose in the rainy a. 327:23
Average: A. made lethal 301:13
  a. man's opinions 291:6
  the speech a vain a. would make 172:17
Aviator: a poor a. lay dying 17:27
Avoid: people still a. him 55:8
Avoiding: ways of a. necessary ... tasks
  127:7
Awake: he must be a. 289:10
Awkward: neat ones in your a. squad 60:9
Axe: dread of the headsman's a. 138:13
  swinging his a. to fell kings 57:11
Ayer, Professor: 272:3

B

BA: the man is a B. 247:1
Babies: b. haven't any hair 157:14
  breed b. and you eat 351:16
  other people's b. 153:6
  so many b. ... bath water 26:5
Baby: and B. will be ours 274:15
  and B. will be ours 274:15
  anybody can shock a b. 317:12
  asterisks were followed by a b. 226:18
  b. doesn't understand English 189:4
  b. in an ox's stall 41:5
  depends on the size of the b. 315:8
  hanging the b. on the clothes line 289:11
  hot b. on a cold slab 17:18
  that's a beautiful b. 17:16
  that's my B. 179:16
  unarmed b. 242:12
  Walking My B. Back Home 336:4
  you must have been a beautiful b. 231:5
Babyhood: sheer b. of the human race 176:1
Bach, J. S.: 162:16
  angels play only B. 29:13
  B. a great religious composer 336:6
  B. almost persuades me 126:5
Bachelor: a b. is a cagey guy 15:14
  b. supported by beautiful women 87:3
  crushing tax on b.s 302:15
  terror celibans or b.'s panic 135:20
  took her up in his arms in the way of a b.
    280:18
Back: either b. us or sack us 60:4
  I'll be in b. of you 224:6
  it rolls off my b. like a duck 253:8
  no one turns his b. 338:14
  small of my b. is too big 307:14
  sort of b.-slapping gesture 364:3

Bacon: b.'s not the only thing 184:17
  leant against a b. slicer 118:2
  let the foundation be b. and eggs 153:3
Bacon, Francis: B. ... do I write my plays
  49:20
Bad: b. end unhappily 320:9
  b. times just around the corner 88:17
  considering how b. men are 219:13
  defend the b. against the worse 95:19
  feel really b. ... that I don't feel worse
    122:4
  he is a b. man 266:11
  no b. man can be a good poet 261:8
  when I'm b. I'm better 352:11
  when she was b. 234:2
  wouldn't it be terrible to be b. 121:17
Badedas: when you take a B. bath 10:24
Badly: if you want to do a thing b. 339:15
Baedeker: may err but never Mr B. 153:5
Bag: no problem ... big enough plastic b.
  319:14
Bagdad: B.-on-the-Subway 152:8
Bagpipe: knows how to play the b.s – but
  344:14
Bailey: Bill B., won't you come home 63:11
Baker Street: B. irregulars 101:18
Balance: like the bolt ... and the point of b.
  277:17
Bald: see whether ... as b. as he was 86:11
Baldness: felicity on the far side of b. 310:1
Baldwin, Stanley: 75:17, 77:18, 93:3, 97:13
  S. begged me to remember 67:4
Balfour, Arthur: 77:9
  B. ... did not know there were Arabs
    167:3
  B. was difficult 21:8
  Mr B.'s Poodle 209:5
Ball: b. I threw while playing 328:4
  one of the boys ... has three b.s 149:2
  roll or bowl a b. 149:11
  Saxons have stolen my b.s 33:11
  where his b.s ought to be 319:5
Ballet: b.s would be quite delightful 111:14
Balloon: bring the b. of the mind: 368:5
Balls-up: you knew it was just a b. 254:17
Baloney: how thin you slice it ... still b.
  134:3
Ban: as soon as I've finished ... b. it 146:16
Banality: b. of evil 19:17
Banana: yes, we have no b.s 307:7
Band: all they have ... admirals and b.s 55:11
Bandar-log: what the B. think now 187:9
Bänder: endlose B., schlingt und windet 281:11
Bang: bigger b. for a buck 108:16
  it has taken ... a b. on the head 243:3
Banish: b. their young at any early age 276:1
Banishment: announcing his instant b. 306:15
  love is b. 31:3
Bank: b. was mightier 266:2
  girls spot a man with a b. roll 352:7
  glance that ... could be converted into b.
    notes 281:4
  man who robs a b. 358:2
  moneys which ... the b. ... creates 269:18
  robbing a b. ... founding one 52:8

tyrannize over his b. balance 183:15
way the b.s will give you money 98:14
when the B. of England was as steady
    80:8
Banknote: fill old bottles with b.s 183:13
    what b.s are to gold 43:5
Banque: time to stop this *va b.* 156:2
Baptist: I should have preferred a B. 349:19
Barba: tu b. llena de mariposas 128:16
Barbarian: b. is the man who regards his
    passions 295:17
    fit only for b.s 126:10
Barbarism: directly from b. to degeneration
    78:19
Barbarossa: when B. commences, the world
    155:7
Barber: hide the haughty b.s 43:10
    one lady b. that made good 352:3
Barco: el b. sobre el mar 128:19
Bard: portraits of famous b.s 328:16
Bardolatry: so much for B. 302:9
Bargain: b. . . . they would not eat him 45:4
Barmaid: b. said 'Blimey, that's 'andy' 38:6
Barrage: before the b. lifts 148:15
Barricade: he would be ready to die on the b.s
    255:7
Barrie, Sir James: B. . . . with the milk of
    human kindness 142:16
Barrister: legs get bitten by b.s 211:14
Baseball: b. in Italian 230:15
    b.s through the windows 330:15
Basement: a mutiny in the bargain b. 278:13
Bastard: b.s by . . . vocation 355:6
    b.s think they win 296:24
    unforgivable words of abuse . . . 'b.' 139:14
Bat: grinning in their sleep. B.s 194:4
Bath: b. twice a day to be really clean 57:19
    creeping into a hot b. 198:13
    every man has a right to a . . . b. 175:11
    no private b.s and telephones 39:16
    so many babies . . . b. water 26:5
Bathed: she b. in her still garden 317:18
Bathroom: b. walls that've not been written on
    104:17
    feel revolutionary in a b. 208:13
Baton: carries a marshal's b. 252:17
Battle: B. of Britain was won 76:9
    B. of Waterloo *was* won 254:20
    b.s . . . hold the military mind 335:18
    b.s lost in life . . . won on paper 113:4
    Lord God of B.s aid 185:13
    lost the b. but . . . not lost the war 129:15
    night b. . . . results in 156:15
Battlefield: edge of the b. . . . exclusive club
    158:15
    grass grows green on the b. 73:10
Bäume: o B. Lebens, o wann winterlich 281:7
Bayonet: b. is a weapon with a worker 15:15
    Orion with your b.s 12:10
    points of burning b.s 365:4
BBC: miserable pittance from the B. 147:12
Be: moment we want to *b.* something 190:11
    to b. and not to b. 288:4
Bead: tears were to me what glass b.s 90:10
Beam: upshot b. would fade 159:10

Beaming: Far-Speaking B. One 173:12
Bean: playing the trombone to his . . . b.s 111:4
Beanz: B. Meanz Heinz 10:10
Bear: B. of Very Little Brain 236:6
    fire was furry as a b. 308:7
    some of the bigger b.s 236:10
Beard: b. full of butterflies 128:16
    wore their b.s . . . like neckties 195:13
Bearded: hard to hear what a b. man is saying
    221:1
Bearer: chose her b.s before she died 147:16
Beast: between the b. and the superhuman
    299:5
    figured as the b. in the jungle 170:7
    it was Beauty killed the B. 90:3
    The B. stands for strong 347:2
Beat: bought a most expensive b. 18:18
    counting the slow heart b.s 138:11
Beaten: no Englishman is ever fairly b. 305:14
Beatles: B.s' first L.P. 193:9
Beaumont, Francis: for ten pounds B. and
    Fletcher 49:18
Beautiful: b. doesn't matter 264:1
    b. woman with a brain 88:2
    black is b. 15:19
    everybody considers her very b. 288:15
    how b. you are 287:18
    one of the b. people 202:8
    one of the most aesthetically b. 158:14
    to be b. was to make good 152:13
Beautifully: b. done 314:14
Beauty: b. above their means or below their
    condition 297:8
    b. and the lust for learning 32:16
    B. . . . first to hear about the sins 132:10
    b. in fitness which no art 100:13
    b. is momentary in the mind 317:19
    b. is only sin deep 293:18
    b. of an aged face 60:13
    British love permanence more than . . . b.
        66:5
    for England, home and b. 148:8
    it was B. killed the Beast 90:3
    left it a land of b. spots 174:13
    not only truth, but . . . b. 290:4
    what *is* b., anyway 264:4
Beaver: b. sixty-eight feet long 178:16
Beaverbrook, Max: 351:12
Becoming: war . . . is a state of perpetual b.
    274:6
Bed: b. . . . is the poor man's opera 163:17
    b's too big 237:3
    deep bliss of the double-b. 61:2
    everybody to stay in b. all day 36:2
    fool would make the b. every day 313:9
    get out of b. . . . throw up 131:18
    getting out of a cold b. 198:13
    go to b. with a sewing machine 65:16
    goes to b. beneath this stone 339:2
    gooseberried double b. of the wood 328:8
    hero for his b. 238:3
    hero keeps getting in b. 287:5
    I have gone to b. 227:6
    I should of stood in b. 169:1
    in hotels with the b. unmade 114:23

Bed – *Contd.*
lying in b. . . . draw on the ceiling 72:7
musical b.s is the faculty sport 12:2
platonic way of going to b. 162:7
pursuing it from b. to b. 259:12
recognize a double b. 338:18
rest is going to b. 362:21
share his bread-pudding b. 328:14
third day he rose again from his b. 176:18
was still keeping open b. 161:12
Bedouin: unmade B. 36:21
Bedroom: comment in the b. 25:6
doesn't matter what you do in the b. 61:1
intellectualized b. 350:16
sneaking out of the wrong b. 92:22
Bedspring: triumphant twang of a b. 262:17
Bee: b.s will fasten themselves 262:2
forget not b.s in winter 292:3
Beef: Boiled B. and Carrots 81:3
Beehive: b. state 255:18
Beer: b. drinking don't do half the harm 263:21
'deathless', that bitter b. 282:5
glorious b. 15:5
religions change; b. . . . remain 12:20
Beethoven, Ludwig van: 231:7
B.'s Fifth Symphony may be Fate . . . knocking 279:2
forces that make up . . . B. 322:7
Beetle: behind every b. you will find 242:6
Beggar's Opera, The: compare the music of *B.* 161:23
Begin: country where very few things b. 116:22
when they b. the beguine 267:12
where they leave off I b. 156:19
Beginner: don't think . . . badly for a b. 84:8
Beginning: b. I knew most about 180:16
God of Fair B.s 186:14
have a b., a middle, and an end 133:13
only by avoiding the b. 84:12
Behave: how well they b. 219:13
Behaved: everyone b. very badly 66:15
Behaviourism: b. is a flat-earth view 189:13
of course, b. 'works' 23:10
Beholder: at the centre of the b. 263:11
in the eye of the b. 35:12
Being: avoiding non-b. by avoiding b. 331:14
knowledge is proportionate to b. 163:10
light in the darkness of mere b. 178:6
we are . . . too early for B. 150:1
Belgium: B. Put the Kibosh on the Kaiser 110:10
'Gallant B.' 219:5
Belief: any unwarrantable b. 280:6
confused things with their names: that is b. 297:21
constant assertion of b. 190:14
impossible to hold a b. 357:2
Rome . . . trades on b. 58:2
to these . . . is B. forbidden 186:18
Believe: b. enough in what one feels 369:2
B.! Obey! Fight! 245:12

better for God if we refuse to b. 62:15
do we b. in winter? 287:13
he who b.s in nothing 286:18
I can b. in them all 303:30
I do not b. . . . I know 178:12
I do not b. in things 51:1
men who really b. in themselves 71:17
mix what they b. with what 338:16
takes application . . . to b. anything 110:5
they didn't b. me 287:18
verb meaning 'to b. falsely' 360:22
Believing: b. in his . . . health rather than 144:11
Bell: as b.s off San Salvador 90:2
sheep-b.s and ship-b.s ring 186:20
superior man is like a b. 51:14
when the b. tolls . . . for thee 320:21
Belle-litter: distinguish . . . poetry and a sort of b. 320:16
Bellies: their b. were full 51:17
Bell-rope: b. that gathers God at dawn 89:27
Belloc, Hilaire: 239:13
Belly: embrace me, b. 23:1
through his wife's b. 12:5
Belt: fasten your safety b.s 221:7
see a b. without hitting below 21:7
Bench: grass is growing on the Front B. 21:14
Benn, A. Wedgwood: 205:2
Bennett, Arnold: 352:22
Bergwerk: der Seelen wunderliches B. 282:6
Berkeley: faith ye share with B. Square 186:23
Berlin, Irving: when B. sings you have to hug him 91:13
Berlitz: all the . . . glibness of the B.-school 114:25
Bernhardt, Sarah: even to please S. 31:23
Bessie: not a word to B. 158:12
Best: dangers in letting the b. be the enemy 173:8
'What is b.?' 265:4
Best-seller: b. . . . somehow sold well 46:12
call the Bible 'the World's B.' 46:11
Bet: if it was a b., you wouldn't 320:11
Betray: have the guts to b. my *country* 119:22
'portray' . . . synonymous with 'b.' 323:4
Better: he can do b. next time 31:4
it's getting b. 202:14
Bewitched: B., Bothered and Bewildered 148:9
Bewitchment: b. of our intelligence 292:17
Bible: B. on that shelf 290:17
B.-ridden, white South 15:6
call the B. 'the World's Best-Seller' 46:11
number one book . . . called the B. 228:18
put the Gideon B.s in the bedrooms 240:15
remembered my pipe . . . forgotten my B. 135:22
so essentially Protestant . . . as the B. 303:22
took God longer to write the B. 216:7
very like the B., only sillier 276:4
Bicycle: a b. certainly, but not *the* 101:12
b. with four legs 242:14
could see no b. would go 111:1
delirious b.s 19:13

Biers: '*Todlos*', *jenes bitteren B.* 282:5
Big: I am b. The films got small 355:16
  just sit and be b. 115:23
Bigamist: appealed to . . . the instinctive b.
  161:17
Bigamy: b. . . . one husband too many 15:18
  b. to please the landlady 100:1
Bigger: any . . . fool can make things b. 300:7
  b. they come the harder they fall 117:11
Bigot: followed by priests and b.s 63:1
Bigoted: not b. about it 289:16
Bigotry: b. . . . men who have no opinions
  71:8
Bike: mind my b. 345:7
Bild: so dich finden, binden dich an D. 282:16
Bile: likes to look on the b. when 163:19
Bilingual: if you're born in India, you're b.
  250:20
Bill: god mustn't pay hotel b.s 51:12
  on the back of the b. 224:5
Billboard: b.s . . . to Coca-Cola 338:11
Billiard: b. saloon . . . a brothel 49:16
Biography: b. . . . can never be wholly true
  270:5
  b. is a very definite region 142:19
  improve the b. of the person 297:24
  no psychology . . . only b. 324:1
Birch: all for bringing back the b. 343:6
Bird: b. on a wire 80:2
  b. would cease and be as other b.s 124:17
  b.s in their little nests agree 34:23
  b.s moult and in the . . . copses hide 292:5
  b.s on the Liver building 135:18
  caged b.s accept each other 357:17
  I've always hated b.s 259:7
  listen to the b.s and winds 131:9
  loveless b.s now flock as . . . friends 124:22
  of one mind like the migratory b.s 281:7
  she was one of the early b.s 30:5
  simple b. that thinks two notes 94:13
  some high-feathered, free-pecking b. 169:11
  tell us b.s are singing 61:7
  wings of b.s coming home 349:2
Birdsmanship: basic B. 268:19
Birkenhead, Lord: 45:6
  B. is very clever 21:9
Birmingham: when Jesus came to B. 323:1
Birth: every b. is a getting to know 78:18
  give *b.* to himself 123:16
  only b. . . . brought a doctor 28:20
  persecutory anxiety which follows b. 278:10
  provoke . . . a rising b.-rate 125:17
Birthday: if one doesn't get b. presents 278:10
  is it b. weather for you 95:17
  this was my b. 259:17
Bishop: be the mother of a b. 33:20
  b.s vary just as much as books 174:20
  colonial b.s who come back 100:15
  symbol of a b. is a crook 99:13
  without hitting the niece of a b. 255:5
Bismarck: the class of the B.s 245:11
Bit: I am afraid of b.s . . . and b.s 70:3
Bitch: got to b. everyone in the world 116:25
  old b. gone in the teeth 269:8
  we are all sons of b.s 26:1

Bite: b. from your finger tips 200:7
  he daren't quite b. 195:12
  I helped him b. it 262:9
  not b. the hand . . . but maybe 323:16
  only apprehensive whether they will b.
    314:13
  turn and b. him in the leg 361:18
Black: any colour, so long as it's b. 118:15
  b. is beautiful 15:19
  b. majority . . . not in a thousand 309:14
  calling the polar bear b. 205:6
  for the b. man . . . only one destiny 112:1
  future is . . . b. 26:6
  or to fleece the b.s 61:8
  see how well you looked in b. 64:17
Blackberry: every b. in the hedgerow 292:1
Blackbird: the b. whistling or just after 317:20
Blackguard: b., but not a dirty b. 151:17
Black Power: 367:1
Blackshirt: organization of the B. movement
  243:1
Blade: ere yet we draw the b. 185:13
Blagard: good evening b.s 212:14
Blake, William: W.B. who beat upon the wall
  368:3
Blame: b. on me . . . able to bear it best 75:9
  whatever you b. . . . have done yourself
    142:12
Bland: between b. and grandiose 336:19
Blasphemies: great truths begin as b. 305:1
Blasphemy: b. . . . could not survive religion
  72:13
  one for b. look you 346:7
Bleak: Wet, Dim, Drip and B. 22:18
Bleed: all need someone we can b. on 169:6
Blessed: where the b. dance 368:4
Blessing: the crowning b. of life 325:4
Blight: contemporary poets . . . B. 161:1
Blighty: dear old B. 235:20
Blind: b. man's profession 264:6
  one-armed b. man in a dark room 361:13
  sit by and see the b. man 344:3
Blinding: nothing like living together for b.
  81:22
Blindness: 331:7
Blinked: other fellow just b. 289:18
Bliss: man dynamited into B. 350:9
  promise of pneumatic b. 109:15
Blitz: there it is, the B. 318:21
Blonde: b., but of the arid sort 135:19
  b. to make a bishop kick 67:10
  gentlemen . . . remember b.s 211:5
  springing from b. to b. 361:17
Blood: 146:20
  b., dirt and sucked sugar 369:5
  b. is b. 18:18
  her b. is nothing but rose-water 115:6
  Jewish b. . . . among my b. 369:12
  midnight restitutions of the b. 325:9
  now that the salt of their b. 325:10
  rather have b. on my hands than water
    140:20
  religion . . . b. and nails and vinegar 66:16
  two kinds of b. 336:7
  we be of one b. 187:11

Bloodiness: the b. of family life 237:4
Blossom: and I b. 40:5
  b.s. of the apricot 269:15
  you . . . overleap the stage of b.
    281:13
Blotched: b. out beyond unblotching
  317:13
Blue: Corfu, the b. really begins 104:7
  make so much of fragmentary b. 124:8
  essence of any b. material 288:5
Bluebottle: enter B. 235:7
Blues: them lonesome b. 237:3
Blunder: he usually b.s forward 107:8
Blurb: b.-writer paying his respects 121:11
Blush: I b., but at the same time 333:11
  turn off the light to spare my b.s
  171:9
Blüte: wie du die B. beinah 281:13
B.O.: man who has cured himself of B. 55:8
Boarding-house: two meals at a b. 198:12
Boasting: b., but once you know my qualities
  125:9
  impression . . . b. might be powerless to
    achieve 292:19
  wish advice or are just b. 330:11
Boat: in a glass-bottomed b. 238:2
  on a b. anchored off Rimini 278:13
Boating: not mucking . . . but b. around
  140:9
Bobs: red-faced man, which is B. 184:23
Boche: a well-killed B. 277:12
Bock: and drink our b.s 109:7
Bodies: b. lopped of every 92:4
  inexhaustible b. that are not 325:7
  wore their b. out 298:6
  your b. will take . . . curves 102:8
Body: as a b. everyone is single 153:20
  happiness is beneficial for the b. 274:9
  human b. is private 233:17
  I dump it, this b. 37:5
  keeping b. and soul together 212:13
  know the destiny of his b. 110:17
  mind unless . . . part of the b. 131:7
  more familiar with Africa than my own b.
    253:16
  naked to study the history of his b.
    112:7
  no contact with my own b. until 37:1
Boer: disasters of the B. War 261:2
Boff: b. over his pimple 289:7
Bogart, Humphrey: 25:2
  after that he thinks he's B. 68:8
Bogey: b.s are . . . libertines 53:12
Bognor: bugger B. 130:2
Bogus: she's genuinely b. 148:14
Bolt: and pull out the b. 368:11
Bomb(s): 74:17
  b.s *are* unbelievable 354:1
  casually throwing . . . b. 339:11
  come, friendly b.s 40:17
  hydrogen b. will go off 177:23
  slothful in pushing this b. 76:3
  test the Russians, not the b.s 127:3
  whenever you drop b.s . . . hit civilians
    134:11

Bonce: nutted on my b. 235:3
Bone: only b.s abide 212:7
Bonkers: it will be stark, staring b. 144:5
Booby: who is not . . . a b. 229:7
Book: acid . . . than the b. in question 100:8
  allow your . . . servant to read this b.
    142:2
  b. getting into the wrong hands 146:16
  b. that is a b. flowers 196:22
  b. . . . was written by a committee 228:18
  b.s are a load of crap 193:21
  b.s . . . things that some other simian 95:16
  b.s . . . truer than if they had really 151:12
  b.s . . . undeservedly remembered 23:18
  bought the b.s for the prison 33:19
  contemporary b.s do not keep 83:1
  do not throw this b. about 34:22
  even bad b.s are b.s and . . . sacred 138:8
  everyone has it in him to write one b.
    228:1
  excellent b.s are slippery 55:9
  feel his b.s are all written in hotels 114:23
  few b.s . . . are worth reading 305:27
  few b.s today are forgivable 192:4
  friend to borrow my b.s 283:16
  had written as many b.s as Moses 77:13
  horrible little b. 198:8
  I meant never to write another b. 227:20
  I would never read a b. 359:13
  if my b.s had been any worse 67:17
  in no b. have I got down more 120:1
  judge a cover by its b. 199:7
  like buying a b. for someone 329:20
  lusting after b.s 53:11
  never got around to reading the b. 224:25
  never much on this b. reading 284:13
  one b.'s very like another 350:14
  people read the same b. 358:18
  person is like thousands of b.s 156:14
  read any good b.s lately 20:15
  read one b. in my life 237:13
  talk of b.s is . . . no way out 47:9
  there is no one thing to be found in b.s
    276:7
  there is not any b. 328:21
  to read too many b.s is harmful 222:8
  what used to be called b. learning 133:8
  when a b. is boring, they yawn 308:6
  without having to go to b.s 260:10
  without mentioning a single b. 278:16
  women dislike his b.s 256:8
  wonderful ideas b.s have presented to us
    274:8
  write a b. about it 47:20
Book-keeping: inventor of double-entry b.
  244:10
Bookseller: B.s' Trading Union had all 350:15
Boom: b.! b. 56:8
Boot: any b.s . . . because he was too big 57:5
  face suggested an old b. 336:15
  lick the bloomin' b.s 185:11
  They Died With Their B.s Clean 183:4
Booth, General: B. died blind 208:8
Bordello: as the doorkeeper of a b. 332:9
Border: 'stablishèd its b.s 185:24

Bore: avoid . . . being a b. to oneself 52:15
b. consumes . . . his own weight 338:9
b.; even the grave yawns 333:14
b. . . . how he is, tells you 326:6
b. right in, hoping to draw 354:5
B. . . . talks when you wish him 42:9
capacity of human beings to b. one another
    229:12
English sent all their b.s abroad 45:12
good bedmen, and all b.s 329:2
he b.s for England 243:10
intolerable b. – ourselves 166:12
Bored: because I know that I am b. 174:11
b. as enthusiasm would permit 136:2
punctuality . . . virtue of the b. 347:18
rather b. with their parents 226:10
silent and indefinitely b. 189:7
when you're b. with yourself 274:13
Boredom: b. becomes a . . . natural state
    229:8
b. from the . . . sameness 290:2
b. in the arts can be 342:15
b. of the six hours in the Abbey 166:23
effect of b. on a large scale 166:13
key to those b. and tension 113:5
Boring: deliberate and intentional b. 34:25
not as b. as I thought 342:2
Born: b. because it was a habit 284:11
b. with a bias to some pursuit 325:4
dies before he is fully b. 123:15
I was b. at the age of twelve 129:9
knew him before he was b. 206:11
to be b. . . . b. into a romance 71:1
unless he can remember being b. 43:12
Borrower: but we are B.s 250:21
Bös: und nicht b. zu sein 281:10
Bosom: wounded b. against a grindstone
    305:3
Boss: got the b. down the bottom of a well
    254:13
hand of the b.'s daughter 26:9
Bossing: nobody b. you about 255:10
Botanist: the business of the b. 260:16
Botticelli, Sandro: B. . . . working for Vogue
    340:4
Bottle: b. pointing north 292:19
who eats broken b.s 360:5
Bottom: b. out of B.'s dream 69:11
my spiritual b. 240:3
their b.s are so gay 18:8
Bounce: they b. 213:1
Bouncer: Lois de Fee, the lady b. 262:11
Boundaries: rectification of national b. 42:12
Bouquet: the b. is better than the taste 268:21
Bourgeois: b. . . . creature of weak impulses
    153:19
person of b. origin 254:25
Bourgeoisie: b. created a new society 334:8
British b. . . . gentlemen 345:18
children belonged to the b. 165:7
foaming denouncers of the b. 255:15
most democratic . . . b. 201:10
Bournemouth: B. . . . can safely call 'her'
    41:10
Bovary, Madame: 215:7

Bowel: how are your b.s working 223:7
Bowra, Maurice: 314:1
Bow-wow: atrocious b. public park manner
    29:4
Daddy wouldn't buy me a b. 325:2
Box: those little stucco b.s 254:13
virtue . . . no sale at the b. office 352:10
Boy: America is a land of b.s 219:16
American b.s have mothers 15:20
best friend of a b. is his mother 221:12
blitz of a b. 66:10
b. does not put his hand 28:21
b. for ever 252:7
b. I love is up in the gallery 345:3
B.'s Best Friend 233:13
b.s do not grow up gradually 83:23
b.s in the back room 210:11
b.s will take you out 10:25
brighter outlook of a naughty b. 71:11
how do you like your blueeyed b. 92:1
if the b.s are still there 29:20
it is for fiery b.s 317:16
liked little b.s too little 346:22
little b. a pair of skates 103:20
one of those b.s . . . born old 83:21
Rogues Gallery of . . . b.s 364:2
sixteen before I knew I was a b. 180:11
take a small b. smeared with honey
    262:6
tell the b.s to follow 171:11
this is a b. 254:5
very popular with the b.s 216:1
wild b.s innocent 327:20
you silly twisted b. 235:6
your b.s will not be sent 285:22
Boyfriend: I had a lovely b. 24:17
Braces: it rots b. 242:1
Brahms, Johannes: B., for all his grumbling
    119-5
life was going to be like B. 37:7
Brain: beautiful woman with a b. 88:2
b. got no better; but it buzzed more 74:12
b. is a device to keep the ears 97:16
b. . . . second favourite organ 13:6
b. . . . we think that we think 42:10
girl with b.s 211:6
he has the biggest b. 241:6
his b.s go to his head 21:9
if . . . human b. were all stretched 43:13
keep his little b. attic stocked 101:7
messages go quicker to the b. 313:12
must . . . have softening of the b. 71:24
procedures of b.-washing 218:7
stars are in one's b. 291:5
what good are b.s 361:3
Brake: whether to apply the b.s 334:17
Brave: more b. than me: more blond 92:15
that men might call me b. 186:24
Brawling: b. leads to laryngitis 79:14
Bread: cannot live by b. . . . stones 352:19
don't bother about the b. 236:7
petition is for daily b. 359:14
Break: Never Give a Sucker an Even B.
    114:13
she b.s just like a girl 104:26

Breakdown: symptoms of approaching
nervous b. 289:20
Breaker: when the bull-mouthed b.s flee 185:20
Breakfast: critical period . . . is b. time 153:11
heart to touch my b. 363:12
probably saving for b. 358:7
Breaking: b. it in for a friend 225:7
people who have done the b. through
322:14
Break-through: it may also be b. 192:10
Breast: almonds . . . add weight to the b.s
80:16
Breath: man whose b. stinks 255:6
your b.'s like a badger's bum 82:16
Breathe: verb to b. 283:2
Breathing: b. in twice running 307:22
Brecht, Bertolt: 205:9, 210:12
B. . . . is a theatrical whore 145:6
Breed: I would not b. from this officer 348:2
Bribe: b. . . . changes a relation 140:18
b. . . . the British journalist 364:4
marriage is a b. 356:10
Bribed: b. not to be b. 72:9
Bric-à-brac: smile falls heavily among the b.
109:10
violent gesture imperils the b. 160:14
Brick: b. to a drowning man 320:10
he is a man of b. 338:17
learn to make b.s 212:20
you could throw a b. 255:5
Bride: all jealousy to the b. 29:7
b. sat in the rocker 152:7
b. to a lad gone down 232:8
b.'s attitude towards her betrothed 244:2
my b. to be he murmered 20:16
Bridge: b. over troubled water 307:8
herd of b.s 19:10
London's most beautiful b.s 338:8
same applies to B. partners 215:12
that great B., our Myth 89:21
they promise to build a b. 184:5
Brigade: Boys of the Old B. 204:1
Honour forever to the International B.
215:14
Brigand: movement . . . capable of spreading
among b.s 303:4
Brighton: high time B. was relieved 46:19
Brilliant: far less b. pen than mine 31:22
he was b. to the top 210:2
other man was less b. 29:8
Brink: if you are scared to go to the b. 103:5
Britain: B. . . . galloping obsolescence 348:6
B. had a savage culture 27:10
B. is not . . . easily rocked 145:13
B. is now ruled by King Bunk 242:21
B. . . . no longer a world power 55:11
B. the mixed infant 236:19
B.'s mistake . . . to govern the world
97:11
cannot . . . advocate an invasion of B. 276:3
help B. to become a Third Programme
356:22
I'm backing B. 16:20
to make a union with Great B. 263:5
Britannus: this is B., . . . an islander 302:13

British: 73:13, 133:19, 155:11
bribe . . . the B. journalist 364:4
B. bourgeoisie . . . gentlemen 345:18
B., brought up on team games 260:17
B. churchman . . . goes to church 44:10
B. Empire was acquired 261:2
B. government . . . habit of parcelling out
93:1
B. love permanence 66:5
B. must be gluttons for satire 210:6
B. tourist is always happy 240:16
characteristic B. . . . looked stolid 75:10
distressing moment . . . a B. government
335:19
epitaph of the B. Empire 242:20
I am more B. still 171:12
Hitler never understood . . . the B. 57:3
never has been a B. refugee 209:3
perfect safety under B. rule 331:16
to build the B. Empire 216:7
we are B. – thank God 238:12
when a B. Prime Minister sneezes 205:8
British Museum: B. an enormous mind 365:6
in the reading room of the B. 78:5
reflection of the B. Reading Room 313:21
Britisher: B. . . . gets 80 per cent 285:23
Briton: ancient B.s dressed and rode 186:5
every B. is at heart a Tory 37:20
image of a true B. 231:23
we B.s . . . use 'Might' 347:11
Broad: B. of Church and b. of mind 41:8
smart old b. 289:5
Broadway: B. was controlled by . . .
pedestrians 82:9
ninety minutes from B. 262:2
tears . . . shed on B. 289:3
Broccoli: it's b. . . . it's spinach 353:15
Broken: b. homes . . . victims of intact ones
98:10
Broker: b. . . . runs your fortune 365:21
Bronchitis: unless he . . . has b. 11:8
Brontë, Charlotte: 364:14
Brooch: with the pin of a b. 368:8
Brood: her b. had gone from her 60:14
Brook: b. was troubled 225:21
b.s taken otherwhere in song 124:12
Brooke, Rupert: 199:4
splendid R. to be the soldier 171:13
Brooklyn: B. . . . heart of the Old World 13:16
Brothel: great restaurants are . . . mouth-b.s
277:4
metaphysical b. for emotions 189:10
played the piano . . . in a b. 15:23
upstairs a b. – what more 49:16
Brother: b.s . . . sailors on a steam-roller 309:12
I take off my hat . . . and call him b. 305:2
O my b.s 57:13
they aren't all b.s-in-law 270:1
word for b. . . . inflammatory 357:15
Brought: strictly b. up 293:16
Browne, Sir Thomas: anybody since B. 331:6
Bubble: attempt to tattoo soap b.s 55:12
Buccaneer: haughty . . . the wild B. 128:6
Buck: b. stops here 335:9
fat black b.s 208:7

Buckingham Palace: B. . . . in the London
  suburb 160:10
link between B. . . . philistinism 132:1
Buckle: more b. and less swash 237:5
Buddhism: nothing in Christianity or B.
  293:24
Buddhist: people are either escapists or B.s
  270:17
Buffer: pleasant old b. 266:2
Bugger: we've done the b. 327:3
Building: b.s . . . morally superior to men
  133:7
  b.s . . . often designed in the lift 158:1
  higher the b.s the lower the morals 88:14
  make b.s for our need, and then 126:1
Bulb: can't stand a naked light b. 357:23
  her body a b. 265:19
  no b. . . . more than twenty watts 86:8
Bulgaria: not cricket . . . even in B. 248:8
Bulgarian: B.s of really good standing . . .
  wash their hands 302:4
Bull: better send them a Papal B. 93:5
  bumping b. of the Cassidys 177:5
  take the b. between the teeth 135:12
  take the b. by the horns 281:1
  taking the b. by both horns 20:16
Bulldog: boys of the b. breed 216:13
  b. . . . refused cake 363:18
Bullet: b.-proof vest 284:4
  shoot with a single b. 359:9
  where the b.s all go in 66:12
Bum: I thought myself a b. 35:4
Bungler: most completely outwitted b.s 76:12
Bunk: I said it was b. to me 118:12
  ruled by King B. 242:21
Bunkum: de mortuis nil nisi b. 193:26
Bureau: working principle of the Head B.
  179:5
Bureaucracy: slime of a new b. 179:14
Burglar: b. who respects his art 152:9
  b.s cant behave naturally 305:4
  God is a sort of b. 333:12
Burgundies: white b. . . . I hate them 14:14
Burne-Jones, Sir Edward: cured . . . of a
  passion for B. 162:3
Burning: b.s of people 288:1
Burns, Robbie : 185:28
Bury: we will b. you 184:4
Bus: Hitler . . . missed the b. 67:7
  Hungary . . . has missed the b. 156:1
  I shall get out of their b. 52:21
  nice shake-up in the b. 221:18
  number 2 b. used to stop 180:4
Busier: b. than a one-legged man 216:10
Busiest: b. man has time to spare 260:12
Business: all b. sagacity reduces 342:4
  any other decent b. man 206:16
  anything out of b. hours 363:11
  b. of America is b. 86:2
  (b. man) is forever apologizing 230:8
  b. underlies everything 359:14
  Chaplin is no b. man 134:15
  for good all round b. work 349:19
  gambling known as b. 42:28
  important matters of big b. 227:13

much more b.-like than b. men 124:15
not a people so much as a . . . b. 112:14
principles on which we will build this B.
  301:2
their religion is b. success 127:17
Businessmen: tired b. who don't act . . . tired
  216:8
  b. from Boston 243:16
Bust: I'm going to have a b. made 135:11
  uncorseted, her friendly b. 109:15
Busy: b. as a one-armed man 152:2
  he not b. being born 104:23
  Little Man, You've Had a B. Day 307:6
  pursuing, the b. and the tired 116:5
Butcher: expect a b. to be a surgeon 311:18
  Hog B. for the World 295:12
  I can't abear a B. 96:16
Butcher-boy: like a neglected b. 293:19
Butler: b.s . . . do not reproduce 349:6
  hope to find in their b.s 228:6
Butter: b. into a wild cat's left ear 361:13
  b. wouldn't melt in her mouth 192:16
Butterflies: "B.s of North-East Bucks" 250:22
  b. will make side-leaps 95:1
  literature and b. 246:18
Butterfly: darting away . . . like a b. 273:4
Buttock: two b.s of one bum 239:13
Buy: b. saucy savings stamps 181:8
Byron, Lord: B. . . . would be all forgotten
  32:26
Byronic: he had been deliberately B. 237:5

C

Cabinet: another to mislead the C. 21:3
  cannot sleep ought not to be in the C. 55:10
  power . . . as the British War C. 76:7
Cabman: c. dances 242:8
Cad: c.s have always a grandmother 356:24
Caesar: Roman C. is held down 368:19
  sawdust C. 301:1
  tremendous admiration for C. 245:11
Cage: we occupy the same c. 357:9
Cain: raising C. 184:21
Cake: c.s . . . looked green with worry 114:21
  State . . . to eat c. 352:19
  than you've had cream c.s 264:20
Calabria: somewhere between C. and Corfu
  104:7
Calais: no picture of life in C. 142:17
Calamities: c. are of two kinds 42:11
Calamity: unwarrantable belief is a c. 280:6
Calculating: a desiccated c. machine 41:23
Calf: c. won't get much sleep 13:11
  worships the Golden C. 204:5
  you can't expect the fatted c. 293:12
Caliban: C. casts out Ariel 269:6
California: C., Here I Come 323:11
  talk C. – a state so blessed 124:14
Call: not a soul will be likely to c. 266:8

Callaghan, James: 172:20
Calm: if you want to stay . . . c. 64:5
Calves: particularly susceptible to c. 162:9
Cambridge: C. an asylum, in every sense 159:14
  C. is the city of perspiring dreams 276:12
  C. lady, hearing of the latest 106:3
  C. men don't care a cent 90:5
  in C. almost every year 246:10
  young C. group 196:1
Camel: c. has a single hump 247:8
  c. refusing to break its back 50:6
Cameo: hardly more affable than a c. 32:11
Camera: c. relieves us of the burden 39:4
  ever twig what c.s are about 156:21
  I am a c. with its shutter 168:18
Camp: search for permission to c. 349:7
  the c.s had taught him 311:14
Campaign: c. against Russia has been won 145:4
Campeur: accoutrement des faux c.s 19:13
Campland: this is C., an invisible country 312:13
Campus: walk on the c. and look at . . . moon 111:5
Canaan: white streams of C. 19:8
Canada: C. is a country so square 36:17
  know a man awfully well in C. 56:13
  world-famous, . . . all over C. 280:14
Canal: I took the C. Zone 286:5
Canasta: Lord's Prayer when playing c. 110:9
Candidate: c. should not mean but be 342:13
Candidature: his c. passed . . . unnoticed 346:13
Candle: by my green c., shit 172:19
  white c. . . . aged face 60:13
Caning: emotional experiences . . . c. 14:15
Cannes: but not to C. C. is different 169:10
Cannibal: C. . . . orders the waiter 38:7
  c. uses knife and fork 199:13
  take a c. to lunch 137:12
Cannon: C. . . . in the rectification 42:12
  kill winter with your c. 12:10
Capacity: commensurate with innate c. 256:3
Capitain: what do you want, my C. 235:9
Capital: people . . . most valuable c. 316:1
Capitalism: c. 'inevitably' caused war 325:16
  C. is the exploitation 18:16
  c. . . . process whereby American girls 146:12
  c. re-creates itself 280:12
  c. was doomed ethically 311:15
  material bequeathed by C. 200:17
  monopoly stage of c. 200:16
  unacceptable face of c. 149:9
  under c. we have a state 201:5
  war is c. with the gloves off 320:15
Capitalist: helping bolster up the c. 347:5
  saved the c. system 85:16
  situation of . . . c.s under Stalin 163:13
Captain: start being a c. of industry 363:11
Captivity: did so well in c. 311:17
Car: buy a second-hand c. 292:11
  c. has become the carapace 218:6

c.s . . . Gothic cathedrals 29:16
  inquire . . . what type of c. 334:17
  little wrong with the American c. 181:20
  mobbed by c.s 243:16
  pedestrian . . . has two c.s 49:9
  this c. is the motor of life 215:1
Car park: c. with a grass roof 24:6
Carbon: only because the c. atom possesses 172:21
  this is c. 197:6
Card: cheery old c. 298:3
  c. refusing to break its back 50:6
Cared: suppose everybody c. enough 56:14
Career: c. that made the Recording Angel 38:13
  having a c. of my own 27:5
  my c. was finished 339:8
  she herself was a c. 349:9
Careerism: poetic literature . . . vulgar c. 139:18
Careful: If You Can't Be Good, Be C. 148:6
Carelessness: slow deliberate c. 198:7
Caress: c. set to music 285:16
Carew: woman tends the grave of Mad C. 148:19
Caricature: a series of c.s of himself 230:10
Carlyle, Thomas: C. said that men were mostly fools 70:21
Carminative: c. . . . the word was as rich 161:2
Carnation: better to be the lichen . . . President's c. 84:12
Carnot, Nicolas: accepted C.'s cycle 351:9
Carpenter: Walrus and C. 205:4
Carpet: women were beating great c.s 365:7
Carpeting: their values . . . God and c. 13:16
Cartoon: a c. is low definition 218:3
Case: world is everything that is the c. 360:16
Cash: London . . . wants c. over the counter 169:15
  nothing links man to man like . . . c. 307:4
  the other three in the c. box 356:14
Casino: regard the law courts . . . as a c. 167:9
Castle: built a c. in the air 240:1
  Englishman's . . . c. is the nation's 129:2
  medium-sized c. in Tuscany 232:3
  no fixed connection with the C. 179:6
Castor-oil: on her way to buy some c. 123:3
Castrati: we've all dreamed of reviving the c. 278:14
Castration: c. may be the solution 207:18
Casualty: first c. . . . is truth 175:5
Cat: analogous to the smile of the absent c. 108:5
  c.: one Hell of a nice animal 188:20
  c.s the way most people have mice 330:11
  Cuthbert the C. had brought in 362:7
  eventually it becomes a C. 247:11
  God . . . smile of a cosmic Cheshire c. 164:2
  ought to 'ave tom c.s arranged 88:11
  perennially popular subjects . . . c.s 87:4
  this old c.'s graces 231:10
  what c.s most appreciate in a human 159:1
  you have forgotten the c. 365:13

Catacombs: having the C. so handy 76:20
Catalonia: C. is the nose of the earth 94:3
Catastrophe: not c.s, murders, deaths 365:3
   witness c.s from a terrace 132:26
Cat-call: c.s ... audience is still there 50:4
Catch: only one c. and that was C.-22 150:15
Cathedral: c.s are like abandoned computers
   104:12
   equivalent of the ... c.s 29:16
Catherine: glad you like my C. 351:22
Catholic: C. and the Communist 256:5
   C. ... isn't chic 19:16
   C. women ... taking 'The Tablet' 329:14
   C.s and Communists have committed
   140:20
   C.s have shaken off ... monotheism 100:12
   Communist and C. are not saying the same
   thing 255:14
   did not attend was C. 14:11
   doing wrong, I'm still a C. 358:14
   lawful for a C. woman 229:11
   like you ... is a Roman C. 73:5
   new English C.s 196:18
   she had once been a C. 115:14
   they may be C.s 215:10
   they opened a C. chapel 33:21
Catholicism: analogies between Communism
   and C. 255:11
   give me C. every time 163:7
Cauliflower: all right, you shall be a c. 141:16
Cause: great c. of cheering us all 37:17
   some c. was just 23:2
   wants to die nobly for a c. 317:6
Caustic: too c.? To hell with cost 134:13
Caution: approach both with c. 254:5
   c. in love 290:21
   c. of one brushing flies 364:1
Celebrities: more important than ... c. 178:1
Celebrity: c. ... known for his well-known-
   ness 46:9
   c. ... works hard all his life 12:18
Celibacy: sublimating a probable c. 116:14
   world c. championships 34:10
Cemeteries: most c. ... a dog's toilet 346:25
Cemetery: always living half in a c. 53:6
   going to buy a new plot in the c. 95:15
   taking him to the c. 221:18
Censor: it is not difficult to c. 344:3
Cereal: do you know what ... c. is made of
   94:1
Cerebrum: larger c.s 229:15
Ceremony: man is a creature of c. 297:14
Certain: laws of mathematics ... not c. 108:6
Certainty: in constant action was his ... c.
   88:4
   not knowledge but c. 290:14
Certitude: the only c.s they had 62:18
Chaff: editor ... prints the c. 318:14
Chain: safer to be in c.s than free 179:9
Challenge: to him who c.s it 272:16
Chamberlain, Neville: 75:17, 156:5, 209:15
   praise be to God and to Mr C. 360:11
   that old fool C. that was 314:4
Chameleon: shepherd ... embracing a c.
   168:1

Champagne: 163:6
   hate c. more than anything 103:12
   whose freedom of the c. hin 320:19
Chance: I missed the c. of a lifetime 328:17
   longing for – a second c. 29:9
Change: accept things I cannot c. 249:6
   c.s are variations on a single key 295:18
   c.s ... come from within 204:16
   leave it to a torrent of c. 72:3
   let him examine well the c. 50:19
   man who does not look at his c. 69:12
   most women ... try to c. a man 98:20
   no better, no worse, no c. 30:17
   not one to hanker after c. 278:9
   plus ça o. 247:23
   we breathe, we c. 30:16
   wind of c. 218:17
Changed: c. everything except our ...
   thinking 108:2
   in my day nobody c. 264:22
Changelessness: so welcome as c. 141:4
Changing: c. the human race into liking them
   94:9
Channel: brush the C. with his sleeve 299:6
   C. really is not much wider 263:19
Chant: avec ses c.s 19:7
   vos c.s sont mis 19:14
Chaos: born to make c. cosmic 32:9
   [poetry] means of overcoming c. 280:7
Chapel: legends of the green c.s 327:24
   set fire to the c. 223:13
Chaplin, Charlie: 54:16, 221:3
   C. is no business man 134:15
Character: about the importance of having c.
   70:1
   bad for my c. ... no good to yours 83:12
   central c. in my own story 157:4
   c. is not ... fashionable 49:3
   children are true judges of c. 22:21
   colour of the eyes of all the c.s 284:13
   discouraged from being c.s 343:10
   moral gymnasium ... to strengthen your c.
   302:28
   proper time to influence ... c. 166:3
   stereoscopic view of a c. 347:15
   true index of a man's c. 84:20
Charade: c.s have no connection with ...
   entertainment 60:15
Chardin, Teilhard de: 229:3
Charities: c. ... was the cause of them 354:4
Charity: causes which nourish false c. 122:7
   c. is the power of defending 70:20
   without generosity ... to practise c. 61:21
Charles I: forbidden to mention ... C. 28:4
Charley: C., C., do not go upon 310:11
Charm: c. ... way of getting the answer yes
   61:14
   issue of their c. depended 22:8
   oozing c. from every pore 203:16
Charmed: because she was c. 204:7
Charming: c. people have something to conceal
   83:18
Chartreuse: system that produced ... C. can
   never really die 293:14
Charwoman: an English c. 231:17

389

Chase: fork ... instrument of c. 350:11
Chastity: like fucking for c. 136:16
Chat: hell must be ... small c. 30:14
Chatter: books! Bottled c. 95:16
Chatterley: end of the C. ban 193:9
Chaucer: every good line since C. 225:10
Cheap: if you do things on the c. 234:12
Cheaper: c. ... to drag the Joneses down 90:6
Cheapest: second c. claret on the list 268:20
Cheat: inclined to c. at conkers 356:24
    people who don't c. 206:5
Cheated: even when he c. he couldn't win 150:12
Cheating: disovered c. at cards 339:8
    forgive me, Sire, for c. 60:9
    Peace ... a period of c. 42:22
Cheek: c.s like ... toilet paper 352:21
    on both c.s ... not on all four 77:21
    slapped us on our c. 184:10
    their c.s could be kissed 273:3
Cheerful: being so c. as keeps me going 181:10
Cheering: great cause of c. us all up 37:17
Cheerio: 'c.' ... across the waste of waters 40:13
    c. my deario 222:18
Cheese: c. the adult form of milk 82:10
    even the c. has got holes 320:14
    to the hole when the c. is gone 51:26
Chef d'oeuvre: a whole scuttleful of c.s 222:14
Chekhov, Anton: you can learn from ... C. 196:16
Chelloveck: all the strength ... of a c. 57:14
Chemical: poets ... up to date in their c. 144:8
Chemistry: resort to physics and c. 229:11
    Shakespeare ... weak in c. 351:9
Cheque: his c.s ... mean that sex is here 267:23
    like a c. drawn on a bank 269:1
    Mrs Claypool's c. will come back 224:20
    settle a bill by c. 235:24
Cherries: Life is Just a Bowl of C. 55:15
Cherry: see the c. hung with snow 159:3
Cherubim: in the Vault above the C. 185:19
Chessboard: reduce the world to ... a c. 255:13
Chessman: a c. if it made its own move 172:9
Chess-player: poets do not go mad ... c.s do 71:18
Chesterfield, Earl of: another letter ... said C.'s son 50:1
Chesterton, G. K.: 239:13
Chestnut: burn your fingers on your own c.s 115:9
    warmongers ... have others pull the c.s 315:19
Chew: c.s the carpet 18:7
Chic: C. is Episcopalian 19:16
Chicago 63:16, 295:12
    C. aint the whole punkin 269:13
    most glamorous corners of C. 35:9
Chick: have been a crowd of c.s 24:13

Chicken: England ... neck wrung like a c. 353:4
    London is full of c.s on ... spits 268:3
Child: a c.'s forgotten mornings 327:24
    any subject ... to any c. 56:6
    as a little c. 226:1
    c. as it really is 281:9
    c. becomes an adult when 323:12
    C.! Do not throw this book 34:22
    c. has closed his eyes 128:18
    c. ... with a golden ball 331:16
    find I am to have his c. 57:17
    four-year-old c. could understand this 224:10
    good smile in a c.'s eyes 301:13
    I speak like a c. 246:11
    law is ... the right to a c. 305:22
    only c. ... one sister 13:17
    that He was ... an only c. 13:22
    time to influence the character of a c. 166:3
Childhood: c. ... inhuman innocence 80:12
    c. is measured out by sounds 40:20
    c. was as unhappy as the next 97:17
Children: 79:13
    attributed by adults to c. 323:15
    beastly to the C. of the Ritz 89:9
    being constantly with c. 25:9
    but that c. produce adults 98:11
    c. appeared in Europe 165:7
    c. are dumb to say how hot 138:10
    c. ... are not returnable 90:8
    c. are true judges 22:21
    c. do not give up imagination 192:7
    c. don't read to find ... identity 308:6
    c. I might have had 212:11
    c. ... set you findin' out things 58:7
    c. to the motherly 51:9
    c. ... unnatural strain 338:10
    closer to the ground as c. 37:3
    do not rear c., you incite them 172:14
    don't you see the little c. 331:11
    I envied the c. of literature 237:9
    ingenuous c. 247:7
    it is tiresome for c. 292:12
    last people ... to have c. 34:8
    left his c. unbaptized 365:5
    love all my c., but some 65:1
    more c. they can disturb 283:19
    my music ... understood by c. 322:18
    neither c. nor Gods 185:5
    never have c. 343:4
    parents learn a lot from their c. 313:14
    started life as c. 14:12
    think their c. are naïve 247:6
    to the farmer's c. you beckon 21:18
    too easy for c. 299:14
    very anxious to get c. 123:4
    weapon to keep c. good 54:15
    what have you got against ... c. 140:4
    what is he doing with the c. 66:8
    when he cried the little c. 22:1
    who hates c. ... can't be all bad 114:12
    write for c. ... as ... for adults 136:1
    your c. are not your c. 131:4

Chill: of c.s and fevers she died 276:10
  that visible c. 351:4
Chillun: All God's C. 179:15
Chin: c. gave up the struggle 363:5
China: Hooligan was probably invented in C.
  293:15
  slow boat to C. 210:10
Chinamen: with C., but not with me 34:23
Chinese: C. said they would bury me 289:19
Chintzes: one of those flagrant c. 365:17
Chips: eat c. with everything 351:16
Chocolate: daily output of c. creams 305:15
  then ate c. creams 365:2
Chocolate-box: c. is . . . the most significant
  135:14
Choice: his imperious c. 281:15
  little c. . . . what kind of business 40:4
  rational and moral c. 23:24
Choir-boy: like a c. when the paid tenor 65:15
Choke: whether they c. or not 353:13
Cholera: if . . . c. might be caused 166:19
Chopin: gap between Dorothy and C. 10:5
Chord: c. of C major twenty times 31:14
Chorus: c. girls spot a man 352:7
  Einstein for . . . a pretty c.-girl 61:18
Christ: allow C. to have died . . . toothaches
  98:22
  background of C. 198:5
  came C. the tiger 108:22
  C. died for our sins. Dare we 113:10
  C. is Risen . . . Yes, Sir 139:22
  C. . . . likely have been arrested 96:1
  C. says, 'Judge not', but we must 167:6
  C. was not 'sent' 251:2
  makes C. within you die of thirst 225:17
  your cold C. 186:7
Christendom: half of C. worships a Jew 16:7
Christian: almost persuades me to be a C.
  126:5
  as C.s . . . to know what we ought 109:27
  as the Victorians were C.s 217:9
  as with the C. religion 255:8
  better sort . . . have been C. 347:8
  C. Science is . . . successful 144:10
  Jew . . . fool enough to turn C. 370:1
  Jew is fascinated by C.s 296:27
  people took her for a C. Scientist 237:11
  Shaw was . . . the more C. 94:5
  they are not C.s 215:10
  we are the C. Communists 76:20
Christianity: C. accepted . . . a metaphysical
  162:22
  C. . . . never promises to make 166:22
  C. . . . preached a peace 288:6
  C. . . . says that they are all fools 70:21
  C. . . . why journalism 27:6
  Crosstianity has got entangled with . . . C.
  303:27
  if it weren't for the C. 163:7
  I'm all for C. but insolence 100:3
  nothing in C. or Buddhism 293:24
  primary paradox of C. 72:6
  say . . . about the decay of C. 293:14
Christmas: 91:5
  C. Day in the cookhouse 38:5

  C. Eve . . . authentic anecdotes 174:4
  I'm dreaming of a white C. 39:18
  perceive C. through its wrapping 353:12
  walking backwards for C. 235:11
Christmastime: national mantle . . . at C.
  135:21
Christopher Robin: C. Has Fallen Downstairs
  241:20
Chrysanthemum: c.s . . . smell of moths
  308:12
Chum: my esteemed c.s 280:4
Chump: c.s always make the best husbands
  361:3
Church: attended stables, as . . . c. 308:20
  away from the c. . . . back to God 56:2
  between a prison and a c. 90:11
  broad of C. and broad of mind 41:8
  C. can feed and sleep at once 109:5
  C. complains of persecution 370:8
  C. exists for . . . those outside 326:21
  c. . . . had the scheming look 115:2
  c. he currently did not attend 14:11
  C. . . . nowhere exists 327:1
  C. Times is now edited by the Devil 135:25
  c.es either low-and-lazy 131:1
  C.es grow old 239:3
  c.es . . . same relation to God 338:11
  crackers as does the C. 352:19
  Down c.es praise 186:21
  first split-level c. in America 97:14
  found a C. on nothingness 63:3
  get me to the c. on time 203:18
  greatest monopolist . . . Holy C. 321:13
  insomnia in c. 336:20
  many who stay away from c. 232:14
  martyrs do not build c.es 63:1
  pubs know . . . as much as the c.es 65:21
  pubs . . . less damned than the C. 134:5
  rationalist, but he went to c. 71:12
  sceptical . . . for the C. 171:1
  to c. as he goes to the bathroom 44:10
  waiting at the c. 200:13
  where the C. of England begins 272:2
  who is ruling the C. 174:18
Churchill, Winston: 41:14, 66:3, 209:10,
  213:5, 218:15, 285:25, 348:1
  C. is a bigger danger 115:11
  C. ought . . . for once to believe me 155:11
  W., if I were married 21:13
  W. is back 75:19
  W. with his hundred-horse-power mind
  26:13
Churchman: species called a 'Modern C.'
  346:10
Cicero: C. and many-minded Homer 368:15
Cider: c. and tinned salmon 347:3
Cigar: good five-cent c.s 285:11
  Queen believed c.s 22:22
  sacred rite smoking c.s 76:21
Cinema: c. is not a slice of life 154:14
  c. is truth twenty-four times 133:10
  c. . . . more like the theatre 97:7
  had learnt to read . . . at c.s 114:19
  like art c. 256:12
Circe: elegance of C.'s hair 269:5

Circle: c. is the longest distance 319:8
　describe a c., stroke its back 167:18
Circumcized: when they c. 209:20
Circumnavigator: the poles' c. 23:7
Circumstance: born in c.s which resemble
　89:16
　c.s break men's bones 69:23
　he damns c.s 195:7
Circus: have a c. going on inside 92:26
Cities: c. . . . by changing the human race
　94:9
　c. had rubbed him smooth 141:3
　criticize the C. of the Plain 362:20
Citizen: first and second class c.s 358:8
City: c. . . . begins and ends in us 104:3
　c. government is of the people 316:11
　c. is a human zoo 241:7
　c. with all the personality 68:1
　in the c. time becomes visible 244:13
　Means Something in the C. 69:8
　no c. should be too large 84:16
　refined . . . for the C. 171:1
　sacred c. of the mind 61:10
　Secular C. 89:15
　without whom . . . no c. can stand 312:7
Civil: architecture . . . gifted c. servants 78:7
　c. servant doesn't make jokes 168:9
　dwindled into naked C. Servants 91:1
　c. war is inevitable 334:13
Civilian: drop bombs, you're going to hit c.s
　134:11
Civilization: 128:11
　c. advances by extending 354:16
　c. consists in the attempt to reduce violence
　253:15
　c. didn't advance 284:15
　c. has been built up . . . by sacrifices 122:16
　c. has made the peasantry 334:12
　c. is an active deposit 84:18
　c. marches – whether north 161:13
　c. of one epoch . . . manure of the next
　84:19
　every c. has gone forward 54:10
　for a botched c. 269:8
　frost-bitten bud of c. 272:6
　little in c. to appeal to a Yeti 154:8
　living guide-book to . . . c. 133:6
　nasty, vulgar sort of c. 57:20
　one of c.'s hardest winters 120:14
　our c. . . . has not yet recovered 267:1
　so stupid of modern c. 189:6
　without the usual interval of c. 78:19
Clan: c. has a tendency to ignore 362:13
Clap: in the cheaper seats c. 202:5
Clapham Junction: mind like a beautiful C.
　142:11
Claret: names associated . . . the cheaper c.s
　293:11
Class: abolish the 3rd C. 210:13
　at . . . nudist camps, a nice c. distinction
　139:23
　c.es within c.es in Peckham 313:11
　discussion in c. 246:8
　I'm not interested in c.es 206:10
　inherent in working-c. life 255:1

like to sort people out into c.es 326:5
lower c.es had such white skins 93:2
lower-middle c. 231:21
mood of the middle c. 210:4
New C. 99:16
on the third c. tourist c. deck 234:12
one c. you do not belong to 231:21
sinking middle c. 255:19
Soviet . . . c. distinctions so subtle 327:8
suppression of one c. 201:5
trust the interests of any c. 209:7
Classic: 'c.' music eliminates 322:12
Classical: difference between c. music and jazz
　271:5
　that's the c. mind at work 265:12
Classics: any crime, from reviling the C. 50:11
　c. are primitive literature 198:10
　it used to be the c. 347:1
　man with a belly full of the c. 233:12
　salvation depends on . . . a first in c. 109:24
Classless: our progress towards a c. society
　136:8
Classroom: Lötze's c. was my spiritual home
　145:1
Claude: after you, C. 181:4
Claustrophobia: ribs . . . giving him c. 307:21
Clean: be c., be tidy 23:9
　impels women to c. house 330:6
Cleaner: relatively, the c. thing 355:7
Clear: c. soup . . . more important . . . than a
　c. conscience 292:18
Cleaver: unless life took its c. 354:2
Clemenceau, Georges: 183:6
Clergy: c. . . . converting dog collars 35:16
　expect the c. to have the grace 173:4
Clergymen: average length of life for c.
　252:15
Clever: bad manners to be c. 231:16
　c. men . . . unpleasant animals 195:14
　I'd rather be good than c. 247:21
　to be c. enough . . . be stupid 69:14
　too c. by half 294:17
Cleverest: you're the c. member 348:3
Cleverness: all c. is an excuse 249:4
Cliché: c., c., c. 42:4
　c. is dead poetry 52:24
　entirely of c.s – c.s old and new 77:19
　let's have some new c.s 135:1
Climacteric: c. of his want 212:10
Climate: inky catarrh of a c. 351:4
　so blessed . . . in c., none had ever 124:14
　unknown change in the . . . c. 138:19
Climax: starts with an earthquake and works
　. . . to a c. 134:19
Clock: cuckoo c. . . . give tourists something
　87:8
　cuckoo c. . . . quintessential souvenir 87:7
　futile as a c. in an empty house 330:3
　looked at the c. 204:12
　saluting . . . grandfather c.s 247:16
　Swiss have sublimated . . . c.-making 174:2
　Switzerland . . . the cuckoo c. 348:16
　wind the c. 23:9
Clockwork: c. in its outward part 240:7
Closed: We Never C. 341:12

Clothes: and very little c. 245:1
  as if she were taking off all her c. 80:9
  hanging the baby on the c. line 289:11
  poured into his c. 363:19
  taken anything out of the c. basket 355:7
  wet c. . . . dry Martini 355:17
Cloud: idiotic c. that can't restrain 167:21
Clover: I'm looking over a four-leaf c. 99:14
Clown: c. . . . higher . . . than any politician
  68:4
  Send in the C.s 313:4
Club: c. . . . in favour of the rich 72:5
  I don't want to belong to any c. 225:8
  loyal to his c. than . . . planet 353:14
  mankind is a c. to which we owe 72:16
Clubman: either c. or girl 338:18
Clue: c.s inside yourself 181:1
CMG: members rise from C. 295:1
Coal: this island is . . . made of c. 41:16
Coalhouse: close the c. door, lad 133:3
Coat: man who really needs a tail c. 326:10
Coates, Eric: it's been C. And very nice, too
  37:7
Coca-Cola: billboards . . . to C. 338:11
Cocaine: c. isn't habit-forming 27:14
Cock: and the C. I used to know 69:9
  his c. into assorted ladies 140:3
Cockney: in order to pick up a c. accent
  231:22
  prettiness which characterizes the c. lasses
  210:15
Cockroach: c. . . . by a short head 363:23
  huge laughing c.s on his lip 220:14
Cocoa: c. . . . to help you suffer 175:4
Cocoanut: I've got a loverly bunch of c.s
  149:10
Cod: load of old c.'s wallop 240:18
  piece of c. passes all understanding 213:2
  serve both c. and salmon 204:14
Codfish: male c. . . . parent of three million
  361:19
Coffee: because of the badness of the c. 107:10
  c. that's too black 367:1
Coffin: it's a kid or a c. 28:20
  Y-shaped c. 254:4
Cognitive: needed no c. additives 35:8
Coin: silver c.s sob in the pocket 128:15
Cold: caught a c. . . . gate was open 176:14
  c. was cursing the warmth 332:3
  keep c., young orchard 124:10
  leapt straight past the common c. 24:16
Cold-blooded: in a most c. way 248:13
Colenso: how you were killed at C. 207:12
Coleridge, Samuel Taylor: difference between
  me and . . . C. 247:10
Colleague: more fertile c.s 246:7
Collect: keep cool and c. 351:20
Collective: c. farms . . . c. unconscious 173:15
  c. security 36:15
College: by no means a c. guy 288:18
  many ageing c. people 246:6
Colonel: crux and C. of the whole matter
  310:16
Colonial: new phase of c. policy began
  261:2

Colonized: wouldn't have c. the Isle of Wight
  34:12
Colour: all the c.s of the rectum 137:2
  any c., so long as it's black 118:15
  incurable disease – c. blindness 96:2
  like me . . . in spite of my c. 112:2
  never gave him a c. 221:18
  seem to know . . . c. of his braces 114:26
Coloured: awfully fond of c. people 258:5
  c. man can tell 217:2
  c., one-eyed Jew . . . anything else 95:9
Columbus: as well might C. have sailed home
  245:15
Coma: shuffle off in a c. 163:9
Combustion: spontaneous c. 259:24
Come: c. up and see me sometime 352:8
  I c. back every fifty years 111:10
Comedian: c. can only last 284:10
  mustn't complain . . . of being c.s 140:19
Comedy: all I need to make a c. 68:3
  at a c. we only look 163:15
  c. is if I . . . die 54:20
  c. is medicine 142:5
  c. . . . is society protecting itself 271:11
  c. is tragedy interrupted 24:8
  c., like sodomy, is . . . unnatural 113:11
  farce refined . . . high c. 89:17
  life is . . . a c. in long-shot 68:5
  play c. unless they have a circus 92:26
Comfort: c. came in with the middle classes
  34:6
  c. is like the wrong memory 141:1
  lounging in too great c. 300:11
  naught for your c. 68:13
Comfortable: c. person can seldom follow
  84:14
  no capacity for being c. 38:10
Comforting: more c. to be the recipient 120:12
Comic: only effective in the c. spirit 302:8
Coming: I look daily for the Second C. 346:15
Command: little affair of operational c. 155:13
  neither to obey nor to c. 225:23
Commandment: had worked through the C.s
  47:10
  like the Ten C.s, all broken 333:13
  science knows only one c. 51:11
  scoffingly of the Ten C.s 21:4
  ten c.s . . . ten suggestions 49:7
Comment: c. is free but facts are sacred 300:9
  thick walls and running c. 35:19
Commentary: thundering text, snivelling c.
  138:21
Commerce: religion backed up by c. 284:20
Commercial: blend of the c. traveller 316:6
Commercialism: 343:7
Commission: Royal C. is a broody hen 118:9
Commit: one should never c. oneself 244:15
Commitment: intellectual's problem . . . c.
  142:7
Committee: c. is an animal 199:15
  c. substitutes itself 335:4
Common: barrage of c. sense 219:8
  c. sense . . . everybody has it 319:9
  c. sense is the collection of prejudices 108:10
  full weight of what is c. 38:19

Common – *Contd.*
no concern for the c. man 358:13
nothing but c. sense 241:13
opportunity to make himself more and more
c. 181:21
word of a c. man 68:23
Common Market: 145:8
Commonplace: English treat the c. 16:1
escape from the c.s of existence 101:13
great minds in the c. 159:20
nothing so unnatural as the c. 101:4
Commons: British . . . enter their House of C.
260:17
young for the House of C. 171:1
Commotion: you never saw such a c. 174:4
Communicate: c. with a third party 364:18
when art c.s 357:7
Communication: tendency to replace c. 212:16
variety of his c.s 170:14
Communion: lead a clean life and attend
Holy C. 298:8
Communism: analogies between C. and
Catholicism 255:11
anti-Christ of C. 56:15
between Capitalism and C. 18:16
C. continued to haunt Europe 325:15
c. is like prohibition 284:12
c. is Soviet power 201:15
C. – it goes with acne 45:14
in Russia, c. is a dead dog 312:16
it is the same with C. 255:12
not between . . . capitalism and c. 56:10
step towards C. 184:3
Communist: another C. is born 9:6
Catholic and the C. 256:5
Catholics and C.s have committed 140:20
climbers who are C.s now 255:15
C. and Catholic are not saying the same
thing 255:14
c. has a fascist frown 313:16
easy to dismiss as C.-inspired 182:8
every C. must grasp the truth 222:1
instructions . . . to C.s 331:18
no such thing in C. countries 240:18
situation of . . . C.s and fellow travellers
163:13
they are C.s 217:9
we are the Christian C.s 76:20
we C.s are dead men 205:10
Communist Party: 41:15
Community: third-class carriage is a c. 71:4
Commute: labourers c. from London 270:9
Companion: cockroach as c. 363:23
Companionship: long-lost archaic c. 243:14
Company: by the c. he kept 14:2
I am not quite so fond of her c. 273:20
Compare: who in a single language can c.
50:15
Compensation: c. for being over forty 118:5
Competence: c. forever bodying itself 233:16
c. . . . is in the eye 263:11
Complaint: c.s should be made . . . in writing
283:13
Complex: military-industrial c. 108:15
you've got a Jehovah c. 150:7

Complicated: man is . . . more c. 341:9
men of good taste have c. me 33:14
Compliment: his most obsequious c.s 240:5
Compose: never c. anything unless 158:2
Composer: asked if I was really the c. 299:16
Bach a great religious c. 336:6
good c. . . . steals 322:16
Soviet c.'s reply 307:2
Composers: 308:5
Composition: the strain of c. 239:6
Comprehend: novelist . . . my business to c.
171:14
Comprehending: this bright . . . and c. being
74:18
Comprehensive: Heaven has gone c. 20:10
Comprendre: tout c. . . . very dull 332:6
Compression: c. is the first grace 239:12
Compromise: c. . . . better than a whole loaf
72:11
c. between having a dirty house 231:17
new historic c. 40:1
Compulsion: the stern hand of C. 330:6
Computer: cathedrals are like abandoned c.s
104:12
Comrade: C. X . . . is an old Etonian 255:7
his c.s were gathered 17:27
Concealing: the lack of anything worth c.
254:6
Conceit: it's only c. 181:2
Concept: c. . . . limited range of applicability
150:5
talk sense with c.s 291:11
walks up the stairs of his c.s 317:4
Conception: Immaculate C. 259:24
immoral and short-sighted c. 103:6
present at the c. 253:18
Concerned: faith . . . being ultimately c.
331:12
Concession: only c. to gaiety 329:13
Conciliate: as an old man you try to c.
333:12
Conclusion: ability to draw c.s 54:2
c.s on which I base 262:18
economists . . . would not reach a c. 306:7
Concrete: ability to make abstract . . . c.
297:26
Condemned: c. to be free 297:3
Condescension: to avoid any appearance of c.
277:3
Condition: crowded c.s . . . may be overcome
94:9
my people live in such awful c.s 130:1
Conduct: false thinking brings wrong c. 164:1
your c. unethical 20:13
Conducting: when c. my orchestra 237:16
Conductor: 'classic' music eliminates the c.
322:12
third-rate foreign c.s 31:18
Confederate: c. of youth 292:4
Conference: just one more c. 228:14
naked into the c. chamber 41:18
never lost a war or won a c. 285:7
Confess: c. the lies he tells himself 159:2
might c. to her . . . in Roumelian 169:12
when you c. your sins 60:10

Confession: after the sweetness of c. 115:5
c. is the queen of evidence 343;17
C.s of . . . the English Opium Eater 305:12
Confessional: c. passage has . . . never been
written 294:15
Confidence: all the c.-tricksters 205:3
something you have . . . c. in 265:5
Confinement: young person . . . in . . . c.
170:12
Confirmation: at her c. classes 47:10
Conflict: not at war . . . in an armed c. 106:13
petrol . . . cause of . . . c. 348:10
Confused: c. things with their names 297:21
so c. that they'd stolen things 263:20
Confusion: big, booming, buzzing c. 172:1
find total c. 269:4
nothing to offer except c. 182:20
too much c. I can't get no relief 104:18
Congreve, William: C. . . . only sophisticated
336:12
Conjecture: arbitrarily accepted c.s 270:6
Conjurer: like becoming an amateur c. 321:15
Connaitre: naitre . . . c'est c. 78:17
Connect: only c. 119:3
Connecting: thinking means c. things 71:22
Connection: no fixed c. with the Castle 179:6
Connoisseur: I'm a c. of failure 86:10
played by these c.s 264:4
Connolly, Cyril: C. . . . give pleasure a bad
name 120:4
Conquer: c., but . . . not convince 338:6
Conquered: c. people tend to be witty 35:15
Conqueror: barbarian c. . . . American abroad
316:6
not that returning c. 23:7
Conquest: a c. for the strong 225:19
Conrad, Joseph: C. is certain to come back
256:8
Mr C. has paid us a compliment 239:5
Conscience: clear soup . . . more important
. . . than a clear c. 292:18
c. makes cowboys of us all 293:23
c. was the barmaid 174:7
cut my c. to fit this year's 151:5
fatty degeneration of the c. 167:4
freedom of c. . . . never to practise 336:9
his c. is picking his pocket 42:23
people talk about the c., but 170:6
still . . . their own c.s 180:13
sufficient c. to bother him 209:11
Consciousness: beginning of c. to the end
364:17
chunk of your c. 255:17
c. . . . does not govern 341:10
c. over blind forces 334:20
I regard c. as fundamental 265:15
meaning . . . withheld from c. 178:3
waking c. . . . is but one 171:18
we are . . . one-eighth part c. 130:10
Consenting: better between two c. 113:3
Consequence: damn the c.s 236:12
in nature . . . there are c.s 341:1
Conservatism: all c. is based upon 72:3
Conservative: c. has but little to fear 144:9
C.s do not believe it necessary 144:2

then wonder why they vote C. 320:25
would make me c. when old 124:18
Conservative Party: 192:1
Conservatives: 149:3
Consistency: c. is contrary to nature 163:18
Consoler: console . . . professional c.s 338:14
Constellation: who will place it in its c. 281:9
Constipated: are you c. 223:7
Constitution: c. does not provide 358:8
C. is the will of the Führer 121:7
Construction: but her c. was faultless 20:6
Consumer: c. wants can have bizarre 127:10
Consumption: citizen is trained in . . . c. 165:5
c. is polarized while expectation 165:6
she has been . . . prepared for c. 170:4
Contacting: were c. the proper person 307:5
Contagion: fools . . . danger of c. 356:9
Contemplation: grasped by action, not by
c. 54:3
Contemporaries: compare any . . . not c.
326:12
c. passed exams 41:4
one's c. are incapable 272:15
Contemporary: c. books do not keep 83:1
I am no one's c. 220:12
Contempt: the suburbs of human c. 90:7
Contemptible: a c. little army 356:21
Content: style is . . . the outside of c. 133:11
Continence: that . . . perversion known as c.
161:11
Continent: every man contains . . . a ghost c.
108:12
not worth while to discover a c. 245:15
only places John likes on the C. 226:16
Contraception: c. . . . she said 'no' 13:18
Contraceptive: best c. is . . . cold water 15:17
c.s should be used 235:13
had ancient use for c.s at the best of times
301:21
immaculate c.s for the populace 177:4
like . . . a totally efficient c. 57:16
Contract: Social C. . . . to do with bridge
167:13
that is the social c. 37:9
verbal c. isn't worth the paper 135:9
Contradiction: it's a c. in terms 308:1
live to the full the c. 29:15
Contraire: au c. . . . if he had dined 47:17
Contrast: enjoyment from a c. and very little
122:13
Control: who c.s the past 254:23
Convalescence: existence . . . continuous c.
162:19
Convenience: about the best c. they had
264:14
at other people's c. 255:1
not . . . a compliment, but to secure a c.
74:13
Convention: all those who stand outside c.
65:24
Conversation: amusing and animated c. 227:13
cheery c. and what-not 363:7
c. is imperative if 354:6
fallen noiselessly through the c. 239:14
inclined to collar the c. 363:3

Conversation – *Contd.*
  most significant c.s ... anonymous 178:1
  that the art of c. was dead 97:19
  third-rate c. 266:3
  TV ... cutting down ... c. 9:3
Conversational: c. remains of ... dinner
  162:5
Conversion: followed by militant c. 247:2
  he believed in sudden c. 119:7
Converted: weren't for the Christianity ...
  I'd be c. 163:7
Conviction: she develops c.s 196:21
Convince: conquer, but ... not c. 338:6
  works harder to c. himself 121:10
Convinced: never c. ... except by your death
  61:18
Convincing: talking about me ... wonderfully
  c. 132:25
Cook: any c. should be able to run the country
  201:17
  even if the c. has just died 116:23
  not so much c. as assassinate food 172:5
Cooked: good because c. by the French 100:14
Cookhouse: Christmas Day in the c. 38:5
Cooking: I never see any home c. 107:5
Cool: men want to c. down their lives 180:15
Coolidge, Calvin: C. is a better example 284:22
Co-op: would make a grand c. 365:23
Cooper, Gary: in a world of C.s 26:11
Cop: c. sleeps within each of us 136:13
Copse: c. was happy 225:21
Copyright: swapped his c. for a partridge
  151:20
Coral: there shall be c.s 328:5
Corfu: somewhere between Calabria and C.
  104:7
Corn: c. is as high as an elephant's eye 146:4
Corner: anyhow in a c. 22:14
  knowing there was no c. 180:14
  little piece in the c. 36:19
Cornfield: how still this quiet c. is 225:12
Cornucopia: their inevitable c. 192:14
Cornwall: C., where it is always 1790 87:17
  in C. it's Saturday 264:13
Coromandel: C. dance they to ... Handel
  308:15
Coronation: 166:23
Corpse: best-looking c. in Great Britain
  167:16
  fusion with a c. 263:5
  good wishes to the c. 29:7
  greeting a c. would give 27:1
  I think of all the c.s 157:13
  mock the riddled c.s 298:2
  she made a ravishing c. 114:17
Correctitude: the feather-bed of c. 38:3
Correspondence: c. course of passion 162:4
Correspondent: foreign c. ... corresponds
  319:18
Corrupt: too unusual not to be c. 125:14
Corruption: old grow beyond c. 48:18
Corset: examine the c. advertisements 262:14
Cosmetic: in the factory we make c.s 279:15
Cosmopolitan: c. ... unhappy everywhere
  343:9

Cosmos: c. is a gigantic fly-wheel 230:4
  c. is ... the smallest hole 71:20
  that God plays dice with the c. 108:4
Cossack: the belly of a C.'s horse 334:7
  what is wanted is the C. 189:3
Cost: not apt to c. him anything 288:10
  she c. me seven and sixpence 28:2
Costume: c. so covered with diamonds 49:15
Cottage: Death ... at the door of the c.
  32:22
  highbrows lived in this c. 270:9
  refer to your friend's ... establishment as a
  'c.' 268:13
Cough: c. and the world c.s with you 142:4
  gentle c. like a sheep 362:9
Count: but I won the c. 312:18
Counted: stand up and be c. 250:2
Countess: English c. goes upon the stage 109:9
Counting: not the voting ... the c. 319:12
Countries: other c. ... sick of us 88:21
  there are only small c. 200:4
Country: being in the country in August
  211:14
  bungalow so almost in the c. 358:11
  c. god to every childish eye 44:6
  c. habit has me by the heart 292:2
  c. like ours only has principles 357:3
  c., right or wrong ... no patriot 69:13
  had to be versed in c. things 124:13
  have the guts to betray my c. 119:22
  I let down my c. 250:5
  in all good faith to help my c. 146:20
  killing for their c. 290:20
  mild horror, about the c. 319:2
  no c. home is complete 262:1
  only c. deliberately founded 143:8
  quarrel in a far-away c. 67:5
  understand the c. 203:21
  what a c. calls its ... interests 348:10
  what is good for the c. 358:15
  what this c. needs today 225:2
  what your c. can do for you 181:23
  when my C. grows polite 185:8
  your c. calls you far across 148:8
  your King and C. need you 19:2
Countryman: c. must have praise 44:11
Couple: chasing the naughty c.s 328:8
  c.s walk on the campus 111:5
  c.s who dislike one another furiously 305:23
Courage: 151:14
  c. is not a requisite 339:4
  c. is not *one* of the virtues 206:7
  c. ... readiness to die 72:2
  c. to change things 249:6
  c. to ride a horse 198:20
  c. ... to risk self-humiliation 97:10
  if people bring so much c. 151:15
Course: desire to take postal c.s 48:7
Courtesy: c. is not dead 103:3
Courting: are you c. 264:11
Courtmartialled: c. in my absence 33:9
Cow: c. is of the bovine ilk 247:9
  c. with handlebars 242:14
  all c.s ... belong to them 270:13
  metropolis ... fat, valuable c. 75:16

ten c.s and we did very well 18:17
why buy the c. 48:11
Coward: become a drunkard through being a
   c. 69:26
c.s' hearts beat faster 263:6
everybody could be ... c.s 51:18
hero, but on water I am a c. 155:16
hero wid c.'s legs 234:19
people who keep dogs ... are c.s 322:21
Coward, Noël: 336:14, 336:15
like a play by Mr C. 20:6
Cowardice: guilty of Noël C. 98:3
soldier I admit the c. 303:9
Cowboys: conscience makes c. of us all
   293:23
Cow-hand: I'm an old c. 231:1
Crab: said the C. to the Rock-Pool 84:10
Crack: c. in the tea-cup opens 22:17
Cradle: we shared the same c. 253:19
Craftsmanship: skill without imagination is
   c. 319:4
Craftsmen: all c. share a knowledge 292:6
Crane: garden-boy is leading the c.s 344:4
Crawled: while those around you c. 325:11
Crazy: C. Like a Fox 262:4
Create: man who suffers ... mind which c.s
   110:7
Creation: cars ... the supreme c. 29:16
closer to the heart of c. 188:18
c. ... older than ... killing 343:14
finds c. so perfect 273:14
fresh c. of him 273:7
gardens, ponds, palings, the c. 261:5
his powers of c. 228:3
I hold c. in my foot 160:6
in real c., not in criticism 63:5
since the c. 250:1
tooth decay in His ... C. 150:22
Creative: faculties ... make [man] c. 54:1
Creator: would go up to his C. 209:10
Creature: they were c.s to be owned 243:14
Credential: lieutenants often lack official c.s
   305:7
Credit: the gorgeous resources of c. 85:16
Credulity: childlike faith in the c. 183:2
c. about everything 271:2
Creed: c. which appears to be free 256:2
Crème: would have been the c. de la c.
   313:19
Crete: people of C. ... make more history
   293:6
Cricket: c. ... invented by roughnecks 339:11
c. ... organized loafing 326:17
if the French were to play c. 113:2
not in support of c. 33:5
really keen c. fan 250:9
Cried: when he c. the little children 22:1
Crime: 160:13
arson ... artificial c. 350:4
Catholics and Communists have committed
   great c.s 140:20
commit every c. a respectable woman can
   302:24
c. ... desire for aesthetic 346:14
c., from reviling the Classics 50:11

c. is common. Logic is rare 101:6
c. the world does not discuss 315:12
c. you haven't committed 270:12
many c.s committed merely because 61:13
those c.s which he has not yet 308:4
unjust society causes ... c. 45:9
when everyone knew everyone else, c. 120:13
Criminal: c. ... he who dirties the linen 57:1
c. ... in plain clothes 307:13
doctor ... the first of c.s 101:20
for ends I think c. 183:18
I wanted to be an arch-c. 13:21
nothing except the c. news 101:11
uncaptured c.s 208:17
Cripps, Sir Stafford: 77:7
Crisis: c. is always a c. of understanding 357:5
there cannot be a c. 188:9
Critic: author ought to write for ... c.s 117:10
autocriticism ... dishonour to the c. 168:3
c. ... can't drive the car 336:18
c. ... from the back of your mind 64:1
c. is a haunter of unquiet graves 157:8
c. is a poet 273:10
c. must always be on top 268:16
c. should describe, not prescribe 168:6
c.s ... with padlocked ears 322:19
function of the c. 34:2
good drama is one 336:16
make the c. of The Times sit up 227:21
no statue ... to a c. 307:3
responsibility of the c. 26:3
tidy-minded c.s long to fix them 55:9
writer what he thinks about c.s 146:15
Critical: learned from reading c. studies 312:3
lynching every day without ... c. 310:19
Criticism: composer's reply to just c. 307:2
c. ... absolutely biased 343:12
c. is inhibited 219:2
c. ... tattoo soap bubbles 55:12
either c. is no good at all 70:2
great deal of contemporary c. 70:6
in real creation, not in c. 63:5
patter of tiny c. 125:27
whipper-snapper of c. 333:5
Criticize: any fool can c., and many ... do
   128:12
c. the Cities of the Plain 362:20
don't c. what you can't understand 105:9
Criticizing: art of c. 268:17
Crocodile: c.s continue to lay eggs 162:21
Croissant: unable to get c.s to dip into her
   coffee 274:7
Crony: against government by c. 165:2
Crook: my forbears were ... c.s 20:7
writer of c. stories 344:15
Crookedness: c. with self-respect 35:10
Cross: C. alone has flown the wave 90:1
light nailed to a burning c. 369:14
orgasm has replaced the C. 243:8
stand under the c. with the monks 296:6
take up your c. and relax 18:6
Crossed: what I haven't c. out I'm dissatisfied
   with 97:9
Crosstianity: C. has got entangled with ...
   Christianity 303:27

Crossword: fills up his c. . . . in ink 307:1
now do my c. . . . in ink 118:5
Crow: our c. is a sick man 235:19
Crowd: flock of sheep . . . a c. of men 32:19
many c. movements which we are unable
166:11
not preached to the c. 184:22
The Lonely C. 281:6
Crowded: place felt less c. 187:19
Crowed: he that c. out eternity 368:21
Crown: can manage a big c., can't you 141:15
Jill came down with half a c. 234:1
succeeds in forming them into a c. 63:10
Crucifixion: 56:5
his c. was yet to come 309:10
Crucify: do you want to c. the boy 136:10
Crumbling: c. between the fingers 219:9
Crusade: c. against Communism . . . imaginary
325:15
last c. 86:3
this party is a moral c. 358:20
Crusoe: Robinson C. existence will pall 266:8
Crutch: c. of the matter 202:2
Cry: c. till they find their pain 142:5
don't c.-ee 353:3
no right to c. in strangers' houses 221:19
Crying: c. only made her eyes more bright
152:14
Crystal Palace: 212:21
how near the C. seems 28:6
Cub: licked . . . out of the young c. 346:5
Cuckold: am to be a c. . . . I may not know
99:3
Cuckoo: and hear the pleasant c. 94:13
c.s, like noise falling in drops 194:13
Fred's just heard the first c. 131:17
O C., shall I call thee 332:11
Culture: business . . . centre of American c.
35:17
c. I reach for my revolver 175:15
c. is an instrument 348:8
c. is no better than its woods 23:8
C. . . . more dangerous than Philistinism
34:5
c. saves nothing and nobody 297:22
c. . . . their feet ache 311:2
c. which . . . drives to rebelliousness 122:15
'gun' I reach for my c. 135:15
it cannibalizes old pop c. 179:3
lead a whore to c. 258:17
one of those 'Two C.s' 246:15
swallow the c.-bait 194:10
that whole vast intuitive c. 301:12
The Two C.s 310:23
two half-c.s do not make a c. 189:12
Cultured: if girls aren't ignorant, they're c.
86:16
Cup: I drink out of the c. 244:7
Curate: c. . . . something between a eunuch
114:24
I feel like a shabby c. 23:13
Cure: he c.s thirty thousand people 102:11
masturbation . . . a c. 323:13
show me a sane man and I will c. him
178:10

Curiosity: devoted to impure c. 47:10
I'd been better without: . . . c. 259:8
masters have . . . the vulgar c. 23:15
Curler: you wouldn't wear c.s in bed 252:4
Currency: ideal managed c. 183:10
Current: truth being . . . a c. 274:5
Curse: how should they know it is not c.s
313:8
to c. effectively one cannot rely 139:13
Curtain: behind the 'iron c.' 311:6
c. that shuts us in 364:15
c. rises on a bone 298:18
c. was up 224:24
forever slamming down his silly c. 294:16
The Iron C. 133:17
Curzon, Lord: 242:19
I met C. 27:1
Cushion: like a c. 210:1
Cuspid: this is c.'s last stand 262:12
Customer: c. is always right 301:3
Cut: I could c. the Lord's Prayer 279:3
Cut-throat: c.s are born to be hanged 162:6
Cycle-clips: I take off my c. 193:9
Cylinder: the c.s out of my brain 18:1
Cynic: one composed of c.s 230:1
outward c. may live in the States 120:11
Cynicism: c. is cheap – you can buy it 140:16
c. is humour in ill-health 351:8
Cyril: nice one, C. 17:21
Czar: c. of all the rushes 299:20
Czechoslovakia: in C., you would . . . sentence
341:3

D

D.: oh, jolly D. 158:10
Dachshund: d. once so long 18:12
Dad: if the d. is present at the conception
253:18
like D., keep Mum 15:16
Dada: my art belongs to D. 320:13
Daddy: and knocked his D. down 160:7
D. wouldn't buy me a bow-wow 325:2
my heart belongs to D. 267:21
Daemon: divine d. is absolute 34:4
Daft: anyone happy . . . is d. or corrupt
126:10
Dagger: never be left holding the d. 359:8
Daily Telegraph: D. is read by the people 11:3
Dainty: Philomène was a d. thing 262:11
Dairy-maid: the super-annuated d. type 309:3
Daisies: picking d. on the railway 362:2
Dalton, Bishop: a remarkable reading . . .
from D. 95:23
Dam: beaver . . . can build a d. 178:16
Damn: my dear, I don't give a d. 127:1
Damnation: addiction . . . called d. 23:12
soul be blasted to eternal d. 305:13
Damned: d. have howled away their hearts
368:4
Damp: toadstools . . . patch or two of d. 86:8
Dan: D! You dilatory old man 181:6

Dance: always the same the d 316:12.
    better d., little lady 130:16
    can d. a little 21:11
    d., d., d. little lady 89:8
    d. in the old dame yet 222:13
    departs too far from the d. 268:23
    I am the Lord of the D. 65:2
Danced: I've d. with a man, who's d. 112:10
    where once we d., where 147:13
Dancer: he's a d. in the dark 237:2
Dancing: d. is a perpendicular 15:21
    delightful if it were not for the d. 111:14
Danger: only real d. . . . is man himself 178:13
Dangerous: d. at both ends and uncomfortable
    117·24
    man's most d. moment: 1964:4
Daniel: spoilt by being lionized D. 333:4
Dante: D. . . . just hope to grow up to 110:1
    D. . . . known everything 102:13
    more influence . . . than has D. 244:10
Dapper: d. from your napper to your feet 81:2
Dardanelles: imminent in the D. 115:11
Dark: don't want to go home in the d. 153:2
Darkness: candles than curse the d. 318:9
    d. crumbles away 286:13
    d. inside houses I don't like 97:4
Darling: he's a d. man 252:9
    Robey is the D. 43:4
Darwin, Charles: D. playing the trombone
    111:4
Data: patient . . . scientific d. 344:8
Daughter: brother to Mnetha's d. 327:14
    d.s are the thing 29:10
    dead lies London's d. 328:3
    just because she's our only d. 167:22
    nine of his d.s were lying 330:8
Dawn: d. . . . an alleviation 356:3
    ignorant as the d. 368:8
    then breaks and it is d. 238:6
    without the hope of d. 11:14
Day: The D. It Rained Forever 49:8
    d. to myself, a depth of iron 248:3
    d. without dark cloud 312:11
    d.s of wine and roses 230:21
    d.s slipped down like junket 216:2
    d.s that make us happy 225:14
    Happy D.s Are Here Again 369:11
    I joyed in the passing d. 96:13
    red lettuce d. 201:3
    Ten D.s that Shook the World 278:18
Day, Doris: 224:23
Daydream: Little Dolly D. 322:3
D.B.C.: call it D. . . . damn bad cakes 176:15
Dead: absence of a d. body 242:10
    among the roaring d. 258:19
    at home with the d. 188:18
    coming to be a d. one before . . . old 316:21
    days when we wished we were d. 30:14
    d. battles, like d. generals 335:18
    d. fish swim with the stream 243:12
    d. returning lightly dance 329:3
    decent mob, the d. 236:18
    democracy of the d. 72:21
    either he's d. 224:3
    few are wholly d. 139:8

he is d. who will not fight 141:17
historian . . . in a world of the d. 119:15
I coulda been d. by now 232:25
in the long run we are all d. 183:19
in the long run . . . we are all d. 79:10
lane to the land of the d. 22:17
marks our English d. 185:1
more d. people than living 168:15
more to say when I am d. 283:17
my being seen d. in a place 320:1
never been told they were d. 216:12
only completely consistent people . . . d.
    163:18
pity the d. that are d. 194:11
wanted to make sure he was d. 17:22
when we are d. things will be better arranged
    273:19
when you've got a d. body 58:3
why should the d. be wiser 117:20
Deadline: so many d.s . . . wonder I am still
    alive 135:16
Deal: 80 per cent of the d. 285:23
Dean: dubbed 'the gloomy d.' 166:1
Dear: I should be a perfect d. 153:9
Death: accepting the d. of my adversary 62:7
    after the first d. there is 328:3
    any amusing d.s lately 47:15
    benefactor . . . brought d. 336:10
    birth or d. brought a doctor 28:20
    blessed be d. 232:7
    can pick up a frying pan owns d. 58:9
    circumvent d. . . . desires of rulers 63:9
    d. and I will coquette 222:13
    d. . . . as easily lying down 13:13
    d. . . . contrary to their principles 128:5
    d. could drop 286:16
    d. . . . decides our answers to all 145:16
    D. do us part and then we shall 328:13
    d. is an acquired trait 13:25
    d. is less hideous 207:2
    d. is my neighbour now 111:13
    d. is the greatest kick of all 136:14
    d. is the least we have to fear 268:5
    d. is the only . . . conclusion 194:21
    d. is the only disease 221:5
    D. knocks . . . at the door 32:22
    D. must take me for someone else 31:7
    d. . . . only thing we haven't succeeded
        162:18
    d. took him by the heart 257:3
    d.'s a new interest in life 125:21
    D.'s artifact 9:2
    d.'s growing purer 220:13
    d.'s own hand is warmer than my own
        228:9
    desired the d. of those they loved 62:13
    faced d. in many forms 349:12
    faith without doubt . . . d. 338:1
    filling in time until . . . d. 40:4
    follow my own d. step by step 174:19
    if there wasn't d. . . . couldn't go on 310:18
    ignore d. up to the last moment 163:9
    had been at d.'s door for so long 129:8
    how do you like . . . Mister D. 92:1
    I am signing my d. warrant 81:5

Death – *Contd.*
I prepare as though for d. 221:21
I've been accused of every d. 63:15
idea of d. as an individual 189:19
ideal mankind would abolish d. 195:17
left nothing to be desired except d. 242:13
let me die a youngman's d. 216:15
life and d. is cat and dog 125:19
like d. by drowning ... delightful 113:12
long live d. 232:4
look d. in the face 368:9
makes d. a long-felt want 333:10
never convinced ... except by your d. 61:18
no d. ... but there are funerals 97:20
none had ever died ... natural d. 124:14
our own d.s that we mourn for 52:19
people who would be ... improved by d. 293:3
slow natural d.s 298:6
speed ... heroes up the line to d. 298:1
struck down by d.'s feather 327:15
struggle against d. ... is the motive 153:21
take the d.-sentence 198:3
then you're frightened of d. 100:4
this is d., to die and know it 212:6
to contain the whole of d. 281:10
vague height with D. 257:7
war against d. ... war against war 153:22
what removes us in d. 282:9
world is shaped by d. 62:15
Deathless: 'd.', that bitter beer 282:5
Death-rate: d. of the royal family 144:7
Death-sentence: one wrote a d. 22:10
Debate: while the d. goes on 286:5
Debauchee: D. ... pursued pleasure 42:13
Decade: in the same d. with you 285:25
Decadence: between our d. and the Russians' 331:9
Decay: fretting for their d. 286:15
Macmillan seemed to embody d. 243:9
Deceive: fail to d. the patient 273:12
Deceiving: nearly d. your friends 88:3
December: love me in D. 344:6
Decency: that old life of d. 212:3
Decent: d. men don't go to Cannes 169:10
d. people live beyond their incomes 293:7
very d. to people 287:10
Decided: d. only to be undecided 73:19
Decision: come to a ... d. 335:19
strong man ... make a d. 46:2
taking d.s of importance 261:3
Declension: under a lot of d.s 57:20
Decorative: to be d. and to do right 115:8
Dedicated: you are never d. to something 265:5
Deed: fix your attention on their d.s 107:18
much harder to turn word into d. 135:27
their d.s are ... speechless 23:14
Deever, Danny: they're hangin' D. 185:3
Defeat: d. comparable to any lost military campaign 107:3
d. is an orphan 182:13
d. of Germany 286:2

in d.: defiance 77:22
snatching glory out of d. 271:16
sustained a d. without a war 73:20
Defence: best immediate d. 285:24
only d. is in offence 26:14
Defenceless: become d. against ourselves 332:16
Defiance: wilful d. of military authority 298:9
Define: to d. things not words 29:17
Defined: electrical force is d. 106:5
Definite: I'll give you a d. maybe 135:7
Definition: high d. is the state 218:3
Deformity: art is significant d. 126:2
Degenerating: not yet so good as to be d. 111:15
Degradation: elevate ... to the depths of d. 149:12
Degree: can't be filthy unless you've got a d. 159:17
man of more d.s than parts 61:5
my d. was ... inoculation 37:6
Deity: doubted the existence of the D. 351:9
Delectation: goal of art is d. 322:8
Deliberation: d. is the work of many men. Action 29:13
Delicacy: I can appreciate your d. 302:4
Delicate: at least one d. child 297:15
Delight: poorly equipped for d. 228:16
Delightful: it's d., it's delicious 267:15
Delilah: 352:3
Deliver: D. us, good Lord 68:22
Deliverance: not to assign to this d. 76:1
Deliverer: tear their d.s to pieces 359:20
Délivrez: d.-moi de moi-même 78:16
Dell, Ethel M.: 214:7
Democracies: wealth ... in d. ... only sacred thing 121:5
Democracy: can't save d., and we don't much care 88:17
d. a superstition and a fetish 165:15
d. ... choosing your dictators 87:14
d. ... government by the uneducated 72:17
d. is a *state* 201:4
d. is like a hobby-horse 295:4
d. is the worst ... government 74:10
d. means government 21:15
d. ... never sinks 14:8
d. will not be salvaged by men who 157:17
dependable in ... a going d. 85:15
five hundred years of d. 348:16
in a d., no one has his way 140:8
makes d. necessary 249:7
not the voting that's d. 319:12
real political d. led by ... statesmen 75:13
specialist appears, and d. is ... spoilt 72:10
trouble in modern d. 42:1
Democratic: half a century of d. advance: 359:2
its relationship to d. institutions 41:15
limit to ... d. methods 334:17
our Christian-d. epoch 197:11
we must be thoroughly d. 303:23
Demon: chained to a d. 95:18
Demonstration: a Spontaneous D. 254:11
Demos: table of D. 250:16

Dental: a d. cripple 10:17
Dentist: had never faced a d. 349:12
    I have let d.s ride rough-shod 262:12
    sooner go to my d. 346:21
Dentures: I had very good d. once 141:7
Depart: d., I say, and let us have done 14:7
Department: in his own d. an official 179:7
    instruments in all the ... d.s 179:6
Depend: it all d.s what you mean by 174:6
Depression: it's a d. when you 335:13
Depressive: Manic D. heroes pull Mankind
    35:7
Deprivation: cycle of d. 176:7
Deprived: d. of all the grudges 270:10
Derby, Lord · 210·1
    winning the D. ... study of form 79:11
Derogatory: nothing d. wrong with me 252:10
Descend: d. to the ways of those above 220:5
Descent: one's d. ... care to trace his own
    42:18
Describe: languages ... should ... d. some-
    thing 267:5
    to d. the indescribable 70:8
Description: its d. presupposes 266:17
Desert: d. sighs in the bed 22:17
    like a man on a d. island 319:3
    man is ... followed by d. 137:3
    out into the d. – And never shot anything
    308:16
Deserve: and I don't d. that either 38:8
    something you ... haven't to d. 124:6
Design: d. is determined SPACE 269:2
    fight against the shoddy d. 263:16
    you can't invent a d. 196:9
Desire: consecration of all d.s 236:13
    fresh starting-point for further d.s 272:17
    horizontal d. 15:21
    people ought to fulfil their d.s 197:14
Desist: d.! 283:6
Desk: abnormal desire for 'a clean d.' 263:15
    man's subservience to the d. 121:8
Despair: banish its d. 358:3
    don't d. 179:12
    filled me with a kind of d. 180:17
    firm foundation of unyielding d. 290:10
    he who d.s ... is a coward 62:8
    humour is based on ... d. 56:1
    on the other side of d. 296:13
    Patience ... form of d. 42:21
    without understanding d. 192:3
Desperate: hope we're not as d. as that
    51:22
Despise: try not to d. yourself 181:2
Despised: loved you best d. you most 34:20
Despotism: d. tempered by assassination
    279:11
Destination: for d.s not of the heart 329:16
Destiny: breath of earth and d. 261:7
    expand the d. of mankind 265:11
    mastered a d. which broke another 155:14
    rendezvous with d. 285:18
    walking with d. 75:20
    where life assumes the aspect of d. 63:4
Destroyed: man can be d. but not defeated
    151:8

Destroying: simplifying something by d. 70:7
    two ways of d. people 296:9
Destructive: d. action ... is the reaction of the
    organism 279:5
Detachment: [Balfour's] formidable d. 21:8
Detail: mind that reveres d.s 206:17
    too much d. ... too little life 58:4
Detective: d. novel is the art-for-art's-sake
    272:5
    d.s ... policemen with smaller feet 98:19
Deterrent: the d. is a phallic symbol 355:14
Devastation: a wider area of d. 234:10
Development: child at any stage of d. 56:6
    d. in the Third World ... means 136:5
Deviant: as reactionary d.s 49:3
Device: our own d.s ... other people's 320:6
Devil: awakens d.s to contest 220:2
    Church Times ... edited by the D. 135:25
    d. dancing in me glorious 225:16
    D. he blew upon his nails 186:25
    d. is the only explanation 189:6
    D. knows Latin 189:4
    d. mostly speaks ... Bellsybabble 177:21
    favourable reference to the D. 76:13
    few people now believe in the d. 163:14
    no good casting out d.s 196:17
    one must talk to the D. himself 153:15
    world is half the d.'s 327:21
Dewey, Thomas E.: 104:15
Dia: un dia para mí 248:3
Dialect: d. that has an army 348:11
Dialectical: sociology cannot know the d.
    138:2
Dialogue: d. ... way of contradicting myself
    321:2
Diamond: covered with d.s ... dripping 49:15
    d. and safire bracelet lasts 211:10
    d.s are a girl's best friend 283:15
    goodness, those d.s are lovely 352:1
    hated a man enough to give d.s back 127:2
Diaper: changing a d. 289:11
    how to fold a d. depends 315:8
Diaries: only good girls keep d. 27:16
Diarrhoea: unrivalled garment for ... d.
    226:3
Diatonic: English women are ... d. little
    numbers 278:1
Dice: cannot believe that God plays d. 108:4
    compel the ... Lord to throw the d. 108:1
Dickens, Charles: 358:17
    D. was careful to castigate 166:7
    D. was not the first ... novelist 272:4
    D.' world ... is alive 66:13
    we were put to D. 37:14
Dictator: democracy ... choosing your d.s
    87:14
    d. substitutes himself 335:4
    D.s had as much ... power 76:7
Dictatorship: d. of the proletariat 201:9
    d. – that is what it needs 189:3
Did: he danced his d. 92:18
Dido: and widow D. on the floors below
    161:17
Die: after I d., I shall return 332:9
    better to d. on your feet 165:1

Die – *Contd.*
could come back to America . . . to d. 171:8
decent thing . . . is to d. at once 58:15
desire to live . . . readiness to d. 72:2
d. tonight I would repent 29:1
don't let me d. in harness 14:13
hope I d. before I get old 332:12
how do peasants d. 332:5
I shall some day d. 198:16
it's not difficult to d. 228:16
my slayer . . . you shall d. 159:7
no hero is mortal till he d.s 23:3
no new thing . . . to d. and no newer 111:8
not that I'm afraid to d. 13:12
only d. when we fail to take root 335:3
sooner d. than think 291:2
those who d. young 281:14
to live . . . more miserable than to d. 140:17
what will you do, God, if I d. 282:18
when d. go sky 16:6
when I d. I want to decompose 100:5
when I d. people will say 81:14
who did not wish to d. 306:14
will not d. even if they kill me 142:15
Died: I might have d., unmarked 341:15
if people d. only once in a while 95:13
They D. With Their Boots Clean 183:4
Diet: staple d. of the agricultural 347:3
Warhol New York City D. 345:4
Difference: degree of my d. from most 174:8
more d. within the sexes 81:21
wisdom to know the d. 249:6
Different: d. living is not living 314:15
now for something completely d. 239:2
worrying about being so d. 307:20
Differently: men think d. who live d. 193:24
one who thinks d. 213:4
Difficult: d. . . . takes a little time 247:4
d. things take a long time 348:14
fascination of what's d. 368:10
poets . . . must be *d.* 110:4
Difficulties: little local d. 218:14
Difficulty: d. for every solution 295:9
Dig: d., d., d. 145:10
Digest: popular philosophical d. 16:24
Dilettante: d. . . . wealth and literature meet 103:16
Dilly-dally: don't d. 181:13
don't d. on the way 80:19
Dime: Brother, Can You Spare a D. 147:5
Dined: au contraire . . . if he had d. 47:17
Dingy: looks d. on the surface 265:12
Dining: more dined against than d. 47:14
Dinner: d. at the Huntercombes' 269:24
d. party of more than two 229:12
'd.,' she murmured bashfully 258:14
I managed at d. 281:3
willing to come to d. 289:12
Diplomacy: d. – lying in state 153:14
Diplomat: d. . . . a head-waiter 339:6
Diplomatic: reason for having d. relations 74:13
Diplomatist: quite proper that a British d. 70:24
Director: d. is God 263:7

Dirt: d. doesn't get any worse 90:20
price of liberty is . . . eternal d. 255:2
Disappointed: d. in human nature as well 100:2
Disarmament: precede the d. of the victors 75:15
Disaster: all the d.s of English history 346:2
d.s of the world are due 84:19
only of a d. 197:7
Discomfiture: taking pleasure in . . . d. 81:12
Discord: marriage . . . elemental d. 132:24
Discovery: d. consists of seeing 324:4
d. is . . . flight from wonder 108:8
scientific d. is a private event 229:4
Discreet: one whose ways are all d. 259:13
Discretion: may have reached the height of d. 38:3
Discrimination: to be sympathetic without d. 114:30
Discuss: worst thing . . . is d. it 140:5
Discussion: d. in class 246:8
d. . . . more mistakes 335:1
government by d. 21:15
withdrawing it from d. 293:4
Disease: death is the only d. 221:5
d. that does not require rest 315:17
don't pay no mind to d.s 330:14
in the last stage of d. 22:21
lists of fatal d.s . . . to worry about 150:21
masturbation . . . was a d. 323:13
Dis-ease: sense of d. 268:12
Disenchantment: mistook d. for truth 197:18
Disgrace: d. stares from every human face 22:6
Disgust: our capacity for d. 221:13
Dish: side d. he hadn't ordered 193:6
Dishonesty: author can be excused of d. 229:3
fury of accumulated d. 28:18
Disillusionment: d. . . . finding out nobody agrees 316:20
d.s in lives of the medieval saints 293:11
Disinterestedness: faculty for pure d. 195:3
Dislike: case of d. before first sight 77:20
friend whom one definitely d.s 162:13
I – don't d. you 24:5
my d. is . . . platonic 333:7
law of d. for the unlike 370:4
Disliked: have always d. myself 83:19
to do each day two things they d. 227:6
Disliking: could not be a someone without d. 47:6
Disney, Walt : 211:17
Disorder: d.s in the strongest brain 40:9
nations . . . die by imperceptible d.s 133:1
Disorderly: have now said all the d. things 43:7
Dispensation: special and costly d. 347:8
Dispersion: world where d. is the rule 62:5
Disposable: everything has to be d. 233:1
Disraeli, Benjamin: boyish, like D. 84:2
Disrespect: there is d. in setting up 31:20
Disruption: create aggressive social d. 45:9
Dissatisfied: haven't crossed out I'm d. with 97:9
Dissembling: they were less d. 287:10
Dissipated: still keep looking so d. 36:3
Dissipation: sleep is gross, . . . d. 145:11

Dissolution: home . . . lingering d. 30:10
Distance: d.s are only the relation of space to
    time 274:4
  longest d. between two places 357:21
  longest d. to the same point 319:8
  measure of d. in its hand 281:9
  to which d. . . . gives form 273:9
Distinction: d. . . . Not to fall asleep 35:11
  to recognize the d. 299:17
Distinguished: here it is . . . the d. thing 171:7
Distracted: d. by the sight of flowers 331:7
Distrust: d. one another . . . marriage 48:14
Disturb: what isn't part of ourselves doesn't d.
    153:17
Diversity: make the world safe for d. 182·5
Divine: team of D. Relations Officers 121:16
Divinely: d. given best of him 64:2
Diving: d. deeper . . . coming up muddier 163:4
Divorce: d. is the sign of knowledge 358:5
Divorced: d. couples hob-nobbed 89:6
  not married, demand to be d. 69:6
Do: Anything You Can D., I Can D. 39:14
  confronted with what they d. 20:4
  d. with ourselves this afternoon 116:7
  doctrine . . . everyone ought to d. 309:1
  it's 'you d.' and 'I don't' 313:2
Doc: never play cards with . . . 'D.' 12:17
  what's up D. 57:6
Doctor: capable of deceiving the d. 273:12
  d. who doesn't say too many foolish things
    273:10
  d.s . . . know men as thoroughly 296:20
  my d. has . . . told me to smoke 298:11
  passion . . . can be destroyed by a d. 301:15
  stick out your tongue at the insurance d.
    222:15
  take off your clothes for the d. 66:12
  when a d. does go wrong 101:20
Doctrinaire: d.s are the vultures 209:17
  we have to go to the d.s 71:7
Document: signed d.s they did not read 147:9
Dog(s): 37:4
  all the d.s of Europe bark 22:5
  America is . . . friendly d. 332:15
  are you sure he didn't get a d.'s licence
    224:17
  beaten d. beneath the hail 269:19
  Blitz . . . too big a d. 318:21
  comely d. is he 96:9
  compose a piece for d.s 298:18
  d. doesn't take to your boy 360:12
  d.s . . . are quadrupeds 244:1
  don't let's go to the d.s tonight 153:4
  hate *people and children* and keep . . . d.s
    61:4
  hates . . . d.s can't be all bad 114:12
  I wish I'd bought a d. 28:2
  if only men could love . . . like d.s 100:9
  old woman to outlive her d.s 357:14
  only d. I know who can smell 300:2
  people who keep d.s . . . cowards 322:21
  politics . . . a d.'s life 187:21
  running those d.s on your page 149:8
  taking mad d.s for walks 234:14
  their famous ill bred d. 201:23

where the d.s go on 22:14
  woman who is . . . kind to d.s 32:15
Dogma: do not even know that they are d.s
    71:9
  experience dulls . . . all our d.s 245:3
  teach an old d. new tricks 259:21
Doing: D. What Comes Natur'lly 39:11
  d. what I don't know I'm d. 51:4
Doll: not such a d. 288:17
  to believe any d. will go 288:16
  using false pretences on d.s 289:13
Dollar: life shouldn't be printed on d. bills
    252:14
  saw a d. in another man's hands 152:15
Dolly: he's had more d. 264:20
Don: it is the little d.s 271:9
  long littleness of d.s 84:5
Don Juan: D. when anger is subsiding 214:11
  if D.s . . . only obeyed their desires 162:12
  woman-worshipping D.s 196:23
Don Quixote: 228:5
Done: didn't ought never to have d. it 42:3
  doing things that were not d. 340:1
  must be seen to be d. 256:11
  something must be d. 107:13
Donkey: English soldiers . . . lions led by d.s
    157:16
  tiger in man . . . the d. 326:20
Donsmanship: D. he defines as 268:17
Don't-know: one day the d.s will get in 235:15
Door: d. of good reputation 117:17
  everything had a back d. 129:7
  Freud seeking to unlock his d. 246:19
  O for d.s to be open 23:4
  who loves finds the d. open 325:3
Doorbell: continually ringing the d. 241:21
Dope: money . . . through times of no d.
    306:16
  your proper share . . . of d. 23:5
Dose: d. for an adult defeatist 363:17
Dostoyevsky, F.: 197:10
  you can learn from D. 196:16
Doubt: because these dogmas . . . are in d.
    265:5
  d. which I venture to call 'philosophical'
    360:13
  dying in d. 212:9
  faith without d. . . . death 338:1
  I'd been better without: . . . d. 259:8
  live below the level of belief or d. 110:5
Douche: thousand d. bags 212:11
Doughnut: a d. and only see the hole 16:10
Douglas-Home, Sir Alec: 83:24, 101:1
Douleur: roi de mes d.s 19:14
Downs: our blunt, bow-headed . . . D. 186:
    19
Dowson, Ernest: 269:9
Drag: she was God in d. 27:17
Dragon: silken d. . . . suffices us for God
    138:12
Drainpipe: wrong end of a municipal d.
    209:17
Drama: as d., the War is . . . disappointing
    142:1
  at the roots of all d. farce 89:17

Drama – *Contd.*
    d. of a dial-a-recipe service 205:9
    good d. critic is one 336:16
    subject . . . drawing room d. dare not present 302:7
Draught: what we at home call d. 132:3
Draw: hoping to d. something out 354:5
    pencil long enough to d. on the ceiling 72:7
Drawing: d. . . . that of an untaught child 44:8
Dread: behind a thistle, wise with d. 111:3
    d. of beatings 40:21
Dreadnought: costs as much . . . as two D.s 209:6
Dream: act their d. with open eyes 197:18
    can d.s really come true 326:2
    city of perspiring d.s 276:12
    d. of being left fifty thousand pounds 235:22
    d.s are all egocentric 347:19
    facts are better than d.s 75:20
    God will cease to d. you 338:2
    his life was a sort of d. 116:19
    I have a d. today 184:13
    I'll let you be in my d.s 105:8
    I was that man – in a d. 96:22
    it's always the same d. 278:9
    now the d. decays 329:17
    our d.s are tales 96:8
    seems beyond our d.s 147:18
    those d.s of lying awake 150:16
    to me d.s are a part of nature 178:3
    to the lonely d.s of a child 96:12
    we who lived by honest d.s 95:19
    while he was dreaming his d.s 247:10
    wrapt in rosy d.s and a kimono 152:7
    writing . . . a guided d. 46:13
Dreamer: d.s of the day 197:18
Dreaming: d. oh my darling love of thee 117:25
Dreamt: last night I d. . . . Manderley 103:8
Dreg: d.s are very filthy 303:5
Dress: cool white d. after the sweetness 115:5
    d. exactly in the key of her age 170:1
    mind my duvetyne d. 177:6
    she will make a d. of it 264:9
Dressed: all d. up and nowhere to go 154:15
    get d. . . . go to pieces 330:18
    OK if you're dressed for it 13:8
    way I'm – not d. 357:22
Dresses: long d. . . . multitude of shins 352:13
Dressing: technique of d. and undressing in public 92:21
Drift: adamant for d. 73:19
    begun to d. apart and needed more room 97:18
Drink: d., then the d. takes a d. 117:9
    drove me to d. . . . I'm indebted 114:9
    every drop of d. accursed 225:17
    I must have a d. of breakfast 114:5
    innocent-tasting American d.s 363:13
    never learned to d. for himself 307:17
    one more d. 259:20
    only fools . . . d. at sea 343:8
    steadily towards women and d. 43:3

tea . . . was quite a good d. 231:15
    this calls for a d. 330:4
    told Jeeves to d. it 363:12
    when a man takes his first d. 152:16
    will be believed . . . taken to d. 325:5
    your proper share . . . d. 23:5
Drinker: first . . . nonstop literary d. 330:5
    heaviest d.s who ever set foot 146:17
    heavy d.? That's my business 64:15
    staid d.s, good bedmen 329:2
Drinking: 36:12
    d. . . . merely a domestic virtue 141:18
    if you . . . give up . . . d. 122:11
Driver: remained in the d.'s seat 30:8
Driving: that d. by the people 215:13
Dromedary: the d., two 247:8
Drop: turn on, tune in, and d. out 199:1
Drown: pool for learning to d. 236:16
Drowned: BETTER D. THAN DUFFERS 276:11
Drowning: not waving but d. 310:13
Drudgery: d. in newspaper work 330:15
Drug: daft with the d. that's smoking 327:21
    everything is a dangerous d. 84:17
    give me . . . a few d.s 23:10
Drunk: belongs to the slightly d. 49:13
    for a sixpence he can get d. 277:14
    he was very d. 346:11
    I've been d. for about a week 116:3
    like a d. in a midnight choir 80:2
    what, when d., one sees 336:17
    will not concede . . . he was ever d. 152:21
    woman or glass . . . not yet d. 355:3
Drunkard: become a d. through being a coward 69:26
Drunkenness: so bad as d. – or so good 70:9
Dryden, John: D. . . . his *poetic* ability 110:2
Dublin: devil . . . has a strong D. accent 177:21
    D. is a city where you can see 252:3
    served in all the pubs in D. 100:5
Duce: history has united you . . . and the D. 121:6
Duchess: at his ease when with a d. 272:11
    D. of Blank hem hem 356:24
    every D. . . . will be wanting to kiss me 216:4
    must be either a relative or a d. 159:11
Duck: Wild D. . . . isn't even a d. 350:7
Duda: la fe sin la d. 338:1
Due: reasonable and loving d. 138:15
Duffer: BETTER DROWNED THAN D.S 276:11
Duke: fully equipped D. 209:6
    wives . . . d.s betray theirs 351:11
Dulce: d. et decorum est 257:4
Dull: d. man writing broken English 246:9
    tout pardonner . . . very d. 332:6
Dumb: d. . . . not against the law 335:16
    you cannot be absolutely d. 118:16
Dumbness: its d. is its salvation 87:18
Dung: I d. on my grandfather's doorstep 138:15
Dunkirk: 76:1
    came back from D. with two women 146:18
    tale of the D. beaches 75:22

Dunn: Miss J. Hunter D. 40:18
Duplicity: d. with honour 35:10
Dust: I like the d. on the nettles 329:4
  this d. will not settle 30:12
  what of vile d. 69:1
  you cannot . . . d. everything 85:9
Dutch: the D. fall into two . . . types 87:10
Duties: two d. – to be worried 120:3
Duty: becomes a moral d. 263:16
  declares that it is his d. 302:14
  it's a d. laid down upon us 65:22
  only one d. . . . to love 62:10
  thing of d. 252:7
Dwarf: anxious d.s trying to grill a whale
  271:10
  dozen red-bearded d.s 241:21
Dying: cannot forgive my friends for d. 309:18
  'd. for an idea' 207:16
  d., I don't think much of it 322:1
  d. is not everything 297:10
  d. men must groan 344:1
  I . . . thought of d. at birth 297:15
  I'm d. now and done for 41:7
  immortality . . . through not d. 13:26
  no d. but alive and warm 327:16
  not busy being born is busy d. 104:23
  not frightened of d. 'one day' 311:11
  nothing you can lose by d. 296:5
  so many ways of us d. 25:15
Dyslexia: D. Rules – K.O. 136:15

E

Eagle: e.s. . . . apt psychological representations
  178:4
Ear: each e. . . . to its hearing 21:17
  e. tends to be lazy 23:17
  e.s in the turrets hear 327:18
  e.s like bombs 66:10
  even people have e.s 235:1
  foams in our e.s 89:19
  if you pull your e.s down 141:15
  miniature gallows of her e.s 161:6
  Van Gogh's e. for music 356:1
Ear-ache: cry for hours with the e. 169:3
Earl: 14th E. . . . 14th Mr Wilson 100:19
  halt with a 14th E. 359:2
Early: be prompt . . . try to be e. 95:10
  e. to rise . . . wealthy and dead 331:1
Earnest: he was . . . desperately e. 187:24
Earnestness: moral e. 206:5
Earnings: your mother's immoral e. 256:14
Earplugs: do I have to use e.s 235:10
Earth: E . . . has had its day 119:8
  e. has waited for them 286:15
  e. is like a child 282:10
  E. will grow worse till men redeem 69:3
  e.'s moving nearer to truth 220:13
  E 's the right place for love 124:3
  go back to the . . . e. for rootholds 295:10
  is there intelligent life on e. 136:23
  not . . . science to inherit the e. 54:8

one is aware that the e. revolves 272:14
  passenger on the spaceship, E. 126:6
  we will stay on e. 271:4
Earthquake: those who walk into an e. 50:16
Earwicker: Sayings Attributive to H. C. E.
  177:2
East: if you've 'eard the E. a-callin' 185:29
  love in the E. . . . only feasible 115:4
  not between E. and West 56:10
  prevent us from going into the E. 133:19
Easter: greeted by his Bishop on E. morning
  139:22
East-to-west: gave . . . the swift e. 363:6
Eat: anything that is grey, don't e. 312:19
  e. slowly 276:5
  e. . . . to put food out of my mind 307:19
  what it means to e. one's fill 311:19
  while everyone else e.s 345:4
Eaten: I have e. the plums 358:7
Eating: e. people is wrong 117:14
  gluttony . . . sign something is e. us 98:2
  loves to commit e. 289:14
  weight-for-age e. contest 362:11
Eavesdropping: nothing like e. 356:15
Ecclesiastes: paraphrase of E. 256:3
Ecclesiastic: e.s . . . naturally cheerful 166:1
Echoes: education . . . manufactory of e.
  100:11
Eclipse: the modus of lunar e.s 269:20
Economic: E. Problem . . . the problem of
  want 183:17
  her first e. drive 329:12
  history . . . divides good e.s from bad
  128:2
  problems . . . e. ones are incomprehensible
  100:20
  self-interest . . . is bad e.s 285:19
  vital e. interests are not 348:10
Economically: doomed ethically before . . . e.
  311:15
Economist: all races have . . . notable e.s
  127:14
  e.s were laid end to end 306:7
  some defunct e. 183:16
Economize: she'd never e. unwisely 254:3
Economy: general e. and particular expenditure
  106:12
  made a botch of the Soviet e. 188:14
  planned e. ensures . . . no bacon 121:4
Ecstasy: e. is not knowing exactly who one is
  283:1
  nothing-everything . . . with e. 35:12
Ecumenical: outcome of the E. Council 174:14
Eden: expulsion from E. is an act of . . . spite
  84:11
  myth of the Garden of E. . . . enhanced
  315:10
Eden, Anthony: 42:4, 77:19, 243:10
  this is Anthony E. reading it 243:11
Edge: artist . . . sits on the e. 308:19
Edited: his wife . . . e. him 55:1
Edition: Pancho Villa in the morning e.s 285:6
Editor: e. . . . but isn't quite sure 94:11
  e. . . . prints the chaff 318:14
  good e. chooses to print 216:11

Editorial: age of the e. chair 218:1
Edna: let us call her Aunt E. 277:9
Educate: if you e. a woman 220:18
Educated: doesn't say we aren't e. 250:19
  'e.' people . . . come to the front 254:25
  no e. person 237:12
  only the 'e.' are orthodox 255:11
  only the 'e.' man . . . knows how to be a
    bigot 255:12
Education: aim of e. is . . . values 166:2
  all e. is . . . vocational 248:14
  between e. and propaganda 56:10
  e. as if it were distributable by coupon
    295:2
  e., at one of the . . . public schools 71:11
  e. . . . coming to the end of it 309:9
  e. . . . false pearls before real swine 107:9
  e.: in the holidays from Eton 309:5
  e. is a sieve as well as a lift 68:6
  e. is what survives 309:8
  e. . . . manufactory of echoes 100:11
  e. must have an end in view 223:14
  e. . . . the soul of a society 72:22
  e. was bringing the graffiti 331:11
  escaping regular e. 215:19
  give you an e. the way the banks 98:14
  good e. but it never went to my head 37:6
  middle class e. . . . training of servants 357:4
  much to be said for apathy in e. 119:10
  object of e. . . . asking questions 90:4
  prolonged e. . . . not natural 75:2
  real e. must be limited 268:22
  spent more . . . on your e. 256:14
  stumbling-blocks in a girl's e. 80:14
  there are two aspects of e. 91:16
  what with e. and whisky 346:1
Educational: under our e. rules 210:5
Edward [VII], King: E. . . . sporting publican
  11:5
Edward VIII: 261:14
  most damning epitaph . . . about E. 85:17
Edwardian: E.s . . . were nomadic 354:8
Eel: e.s get used to skinning 74:1
Effacement: ten years have not brought full e.
  276:9
Efficiency: I do not consider that e. need be
  mated 249:5
  this foolish dream of e. 303:26
Efficient: have to be e. if you're . . . lazy 85:7
  most e. people on earth 227:13
Effrontery: the e., with which the British 93:1
Egg: all my e.s in one bastard 260:5
  go to work on an e. 10:16
  laid five e.s in six days 254:9
  lay one more bloody e. 24:14
  like an e. without salt 297:12
  met a lot of hardboiled e.s 355:15
  only ham and e.s for breakfast 219:15
  Tough E.s liked it 362:12
Eggardon: I climbed E. 369:15
Egghead: those E.s are Philistines 246:15
Ego: Chairman of E., Inc. 23:5
Egocentric: an e. had fallen in love 10:7
Egotist: E. . . . more interested in himself
  42:14

Egrugious: the High E. 349:17
Egypt: remember you're in E. 333:9
  we are not at war with E. 106:13
  you can't judge E. by Aïda 114:18
Eiffel: bergère ô tour E. 19:10
  E. Tower is devine 211:9
Eighteen: she was e. in the attics 161:17
Eighteenth: e. century, when logic 161:25
Eilende: das E. wird schon vorüber sein 282:11
Eines: wo wir E. meinen ganz 281:8
Einfache: drum zeig ihm das E. 282:4
Einstein, Albert: 16:16
  E. . . . greatest Jew since Jesus 144:6
  genius of E. 264:3
  given ten conversations with E. 61:18
Eisenhower, Dwight D.: 182:22
Elder: the red-eyed e.s watching 317:18
Elderly: plays . . . not fit for e. people 305:18
Election: it's no go the e.s 219:7
  loss of the e. . . . more certain 26:15
  win every e. we went in for 314:6
  you won the e.s, but I won 312:18
Elector: 'E. of Marylebone' 53:10
Electric: by e. light I loved her 153:8
  principal aspect of the e. age 218:9
Electrical: e. force is defined 106:5
Electricity: strong, leaking e. 64:14
Electrification: e. of the whole country 201:15
Electronic: new e. interdependence 217:13
Element: always on his e. 333:18
Elephant: e.s . . . seldom lost 11:10
  go and wash an e. 242:16
  hide five e.s 208:1
  stalls above me like an e. 212:10
  women are like e.s to me 114:10
Eleven-plus: human pack is shuffled . . . at e.
  210:5
Elf: not a modest maiden e. 147:17
Eliot, T. S.: 163:19, 220:9, 249:4
  in India . . . E. is very much respected 48:4
Elm: the green e. with the one 328:24
Eloquence: e. of a conversation 205:9
Embarrassed: most e. people in the world
  37:9
Embers: blow on a dead man's e. 139:8
Embracement: licensed now for e. 40:15
Emergency: see only one e. . . . on another
  115:10
Emigranz: Sein E. 361:2
Emil: password E. 180:8
Emma: as if they were called E. 240:2
Emotion: magnet of a strong e. 52:14
  metaphysical brothel for e.s 189:10
  therefore incalculable e.s 28:18
Emperor: dey makes you e. 253:6
  e.s can't do it all by themselves 51:24
  only e. is the e. of ice-cream 317:14
Empire: acquired the e. as a punishment 45:12
  Britain has lost an E. 9:7
  British E. was acquired 261:2
  E. . . . never my intention to destroy 155:11
  e.s of the mind 74:6
  epitaph of the British E. 242:20
  his glasses, to find the e. 125:10
  inherited . . . not only a giant e. 334:5

liquidation of the British E. 74:4
ridiculous e.s break like biscuits 126:8
Employed: e. on things . . . already done 127:7
Employee: every e. tends to rise 263:9
Employer: not a friend, that's an e. 356:16
Emptiness: overcome the e. of his land 35:9
Empty: I am . . . Returned E. 100:15
Emulsion: feeling of e. 262:7
Enamoured: hopelessly e. of married women
    262:16
Encounter: e.s with people . . . important
    178:1
Encouragement: he stands, smiling e. 221:16
End: a bad e., very enjoyable 328:7
    e. may justify the means 335:6
    infinity . . . to make e.s meet 178:18
    thin is not the e. of me 27:19
    whether we win . . . it will be the e. 316:4
Endeavour: left-handed form of . . . e. 160:13
Ending: can we escape their e. 84:12
    e. . . . sooner or later it will arrive 307:18
Endure: resolved to e. the unendurable 154:11
Enemies: alone among smiling e. 47:8
    through his e. . . . have to govern 160:3
Enemy: better class of e. 234:21
    cannot get any sense of an e. 197:7
    e. advances, we retreat 222:9
    if your e. doesn't get you 331:5
    mausoleums for his e.s 208:9
    oppose whatever the e. supports 221:22
    three kinds of e. face 22:20
    watched just like an e. 335:8
    whatever goes upon two legs is an e. 254:7
Energy: good writing . . . e. and artifice 149:7
Engaged: Adam and Eve . . . merely e. 350:20
    girls I was ever e. to 361:14
Engine: assemble the e. again 18:1
    will . . . is simply the e. 66:1
Engineer: artists are not e.s of the soul 182:4
    this is . . . the age of e.s 157:17
England: describing E. in a phrase 254:22
    E. and I first set foot 231:19
    E. is a living guide-book 133:6
    E. is . . . infested with people 216:19
    E. is only a little island 208:16
    E. prefers victims 215:18
    E. shall bide till Judgement 186:29
    E. . . . the native good sense 78:8
    E. . . . was led by adventurers 155:9
    E. will have her neck wrung 353:4
    even the Jews in E. are boyish 84:2
    for E., home and beauty 148:8
    found E. a land of beauty 174:13
    in a world where E. is finished 232:10
    in E., failure is all the rage 91:3
    in E. it is bad manners 231:16
    in E. politicians . . . from birth 66:6
    in E., pop art and fine art 216:18
    in E. there is only silence 228:11
    in what perfection E. produces them 170:19
    last king of E. 107:11
    laws of God . . . suspended in favour of E.
        305:6
    men that worked for E. 68:17
    middle-class woman of E. 28:10

only five kings left . . . E., Diamonds 112:11
public life in E. 254:21
speak for E. 14:6
spirit of aboriginal E. 195:16
St George he was for E. 68:19
who made old E.'s name 216:13
winsome bit of Merrie E. 187:18
you can tell you're not in E. 226:16
you must not underrate E. 77:4
English (the): 48:22, 120:11
    almost speak E. without an accent 36:6
    aristocratic civilization built up by the E.
        84:6
    broken man writing dull E. 246:9
    disasters of E. history 346:2
    E. . . . abounds in clichés 52:24
    E. and the Irish . . . much alike 103:18
    E. are polite by telling lies 49:2
    E. as She is Spoke 336:3
    E. . . . bourgeoisie created 334:8
    E. . . . dislike only some Irish 33:18
    E. don't raise their voices 151:3
    E. . . . dropping the national mantle 135:21
    E. education . . . preserved his intellect 71:11
    E. genius is anti-professional 295:19
    E. habit of regarding the world as a moral
        gymnasium 302:28
    E. have hot-water bottles 232:2
    E. history . . . men liking their fathers 49:1
    E. . . . lions led by donkeys 157:16
    E. look for the serious message 143:3
    E. manners are far more frightening 172:7
    E. may not like music 31:17
    E. never draw a line without blurring 74:11
    E. . . . rigid code of immorality 48:8
    E. sent all their bores abroad 45:12
    E. speaking race against the world 133:14
    E. statesman is bribed 72:9
    E. treat the commonplace 16:1
    E. will penetrate 214:3
    E. women are elegant 237:15
    E. women . . . find in their butlers 228:6
    God had never spoken anything but . . . E.
        95:12
    if the E. language 236:9
    in an E. ship 210:16
    marks our E. dead 185:1
    most embarrassed people . . . the E. 37:9
    most E. talk is a quadrille 170:5
    nothing unites the E. like war 235:21
    oligarchic . . . modern E. commonwealth
        71:3
    speaking to you in basic E. 268:11
    that typically E. characteristic 10:1
    there's enough E. to go round 241:11
    they've got to learn E. 314:5
    when the E. began to hate 184:22
    within these breakwaters E. 21:21
Englishman: 134:2
    behold the E. at his best 114:28
    born an E. and remained one 33:6
    could easily pass for an E. 132:8
    E. . . . his cloacal obsession 176:12
    E. is . . . governed by Scotsmen 142:18
    E. thinks seated 253:5

Englishman – *Contd.*
  E.'s castle was his home . . . that went
    129:2
  E.'s way of speaking 203:11
  every E. has to survive 241:2
  if an E. told you . . . a lie 89:4
  never . . . E. among the underdogs 346:24
  no E. is ever fairly beaten 305:14
  not that the E. can't feel 119:17
  remember that you are an E. 280:1
Englishmen: E. taking mad dogs for walks
    234:14
  Frenchmen in the image of E. 74:5
  if all E. were like him 34:12
  regard E. as foreigners 193:3
English-speaking: I am myself an E. union
    77:23
  understanding of E. audiences 353:6
Englishwomen: E.'s shoes look as if 145:9
Enjoy: miserable fellow . . . e.s everything
    38:2
Enjoyable: having a more e. time than we are
    270:3
Enjoyment: derive . . . e. from a contrast
    122:13
  no . . . e. in Nature 354:14
Enquiry: the finger of e. into the pie 117:16
Enterprise: E. builds and improves 183:12
Entertain: difficult to e. 235:23
Entertained: e. within an inch of their lives
    312:17
Entertainment: cats most appreciate . . . e.
    159:1
  no connection with . . . e. 60:15
  That's E. 98:21
Enthusiasm: bored as e. would permit 136:2
  mixture of e. with . . . cowardice 83:22
Entrance: every exit being an e. 320:3
Environment: 172:1
  effective . . . in shaping his e. 165:5
  man . . . not locked into his e. 53:15
  so well adjusted to his e. 172:6
Environmental: e. theories have been accepted
    173:18
Ephemeral: only the e. is of lasting value 168:4
Epic: the e.'s dead 241:17
Epigram: I am impelled to try an e. 258:18
  until it purrs like an e. 223:2
Epipsychidion: understand *E.* when in love
    214:11
Episcopalian: Chic is E. 19:16
Epitaph: e. of the British Empire 242:20
  my e. . . . I told you so 351:15
Epsom: saddled . . . at E. when the race is at
    Ripon 89:16
Epstein, Jacob: 16:16
  E. . . . squawtacolour 65:12
Equal: everybody should have an e. chance
    359:3
Equality: e. for women doesn't mean 312:8
  e. is the most efficacious instrument 284:6
  our democratic belief in human e. 173:18
Equanimity: e. bordering on indifference
    131:14
Equator: a yard and a half round the e. 198:21

Erastianism: E. in the village 362:17
Erben: die Könige . . . werden keine E. haben
    282:17
Erde: die E. – ist wie ein Kind 282:10
Erection: like a three-foot optical e. 156:21
Erfühltem: nicht grosstun mit herrlich E.
    282:4
Erickin': beastly E. 187:26
Erogenous: mind can also be an e. zone
    348:15
Erotic: conceals e. purposes under the mask
    123:6
Error: Government . . . has made minor e.s
    122:3
  very possibility of e. 179:5
  way to recognize e. . . . it's universal 133:2
Erworbene: alles E. bedroht die Maschine
    282:14
Esau: E. . . . swapped his copyright 151:20
Escape: from a hungry tiger . . . no e. 50:9
  one of the odd e.s of man 190:12
Escapist: people are either e.s or Buddhists
    270:17
Esprit de corps: typically English . . . e. 10:1
Esquire: we are all e.s now 136:8
Essay: conspire to print a volume of e.s 80:18
  e. . . . permanent quality about it 364:15
  longest e., irrespective 345:16
  will review a book . . . an over-ambitious e.
    271:9
Essential: what is e. is invisible 292:15
Establishment: e. does . . . the work 339:18
Estimate: Chamberlain . . . didn't get an e.
    314:4
Etcetera: eyes knees and of your E. 92:9
Etching: I'll bring the e.s down 330:16
  just to look at 288:16
Eté: j'ai bu l'é. 19:15
Eternity: e. of calm fruition 166:12
  e. . . . where's it going to end 320:8
  he that crowed out e. 368:21
  rounding for e. 341:13
Ethical: that's the E. Movement 306:5
Ethically: capitalism was doomed e. 311:15
Ethics: e. does not treat of the world 360:23
  grub first, then e. 52:7
  supreme principle of e. 290:3
  thing called E. 206:15
Eton: education: in the holidays from E. 309:5
  my feelings on leaving E. 84:1
  playing-fields of E. 254:20
  spiritually I was at E. 41:3
Etonian: Comrade X . . . is an old E. 255:7
  greet him like E.s 189:7
Etruscan: if E. didn't exist, 161:20
  long-nosed E.s 194:8
Euclid: E. alone has looked on Beauty 232:5
Eunuch: e.s boasting of chastity 206:4
  prerogative of the e. 320:26
  something between a e. and a snigger 114:24
Euphoria: e. is not knowing who one is 283:1
Euroglise: E. . . . Divine Relations Officers
    121:16
Europe: almost extinct in E. 196:23
  Communism continued to haunt E. 325:15

decadence of E. 253:12
E. des patries 96:5
E. is the unfinished negative 215:6
E.'s . . . a great big auction 357:13
get out of E., horse, foot and dragoons 43:15
in Western E. there are only small countries 200:4
kind of United States of E. 74:9
never . . . spoken of *E. des patries* 129:14
not a future . . . in E. 57:16
search for Man in . . . style of E. 112:8
that has happened in E. 206:10
this 'going into E.' 329:19
to E. she was America 351:1
to hell with E. 299:4
European: believe in miracles in E. affairs 145:7
E.s and Americans are like men 172:13
greater humanity than the E. 215:5
have been E.s 215:3
to shoot down a E. 297:25
Europeanism: their E. is . . . imperialism 149:3
Euthanasia: e. . . . extension of the aspirin 49:6
Evacuation: wars are not won by e.s 76:1
Evans: like Edith E. – . . . to open a window to her heart 280:8
Evasion: the field of e.-technique 15:2
Eve: E. . . . accused him of infidelity 42:7
when E. ate this . . . apple 194:18
Evening: by an intenser glow the e. falls 225:12
e., all 345:8
some enchanted e. 146:8
Event: love to feel e.s overlapping 104:4
rats in mazes . . . e.s in himself 106:7
Ever: did you e. 268:1
Everybody: e. was up to something 89:3
Everything: e. 352:14
knew e. . . . knew other things 28:23
life is like nothing . . . is e. 134:6
responsible for e. 196:10
so long as you don't take e. 312:1
Evidence: confession is the queen of e. 343:17
Evil: banality of e. 19:17
between two e.s I always pick 352:6
clear the land of e. 186:16
don't believe . . . [God] is e. 13:3
E. cannot imagine Good 23:11
e. . . . comes of ignorance 62:16
e. deeds of the wicked 184:15
e. . . . ignorance bumping its head 118:13
e. . . . is misplaced good 12:16
e. is the product . . . of humans 297:26
e. never travels alone 50:19
Good . . . makes for unity; E. 162:20
like Good without E. 297:12
man's capacity for e. 249:7
morality . . . is an unmitigated e. 194:16
no e. in the atom 318:5
speechless E. borrowed 21:19
the instability of e. 354:15
there is only one e. 194:9
to essay good through e. 219:5
we are the origin of all coming e. 178:13

Evolution: better example of e. 284:22
e. . . . more important than living 178:14
e. . . . will not be accomplished 94:10
inventions . . . cultural e. 53:15
vulgar e. . . . root of sociology 138:2
Exactitude: e. is not truth 226:7
Exaggeration: I despise e. 188:1
Exaltation: e. takes the place of truth 62:21
Exam: contemporaries passed e.s 41:4
Example: e. of what, it . . . puzzled him 71:12
we must set the e. 190:2
Excellence: been thought a condition of its e. 320:1
mediocre appeals for 'e.' 46:8
reach such an acute limited e. 115:24
Exception: e. disproves the rule 101:17
Exceptional: living in slightly e. times 106:10
Excess: e. is most exhilarating 19:5
sadistic e. attempts to reach roughly 207:19
Exchequer: offer of the E. this afternoon 67:2
Excited: so e. that when I got into a taxi 116:1
Excrement: de-narcissus-ized . . . e. 22:3
Excuse: two wrongs . . . make a good e. 323:18
several e.s are . . . less convincing 162:1
Executioner: victims who respect their e.s 296:8
Executive: philanthropist and the e. 290:13
Exercise: e. is bunk 118:14
prostitution . . . wholesome e. 150:26
steam-heated flat with no . . . e. 153:1
Exertion: not attained without e. 307:5
Exhausted: just as e. 232:23
Exhibit: e. who read Nietzsche 363:21
Exile: not abrupt e. 22:9
only certitudes . . . love, e. 62:18
Exist: he need not e. in order to save us 97:15
I e. by what I think 296:22
Existence: alter the texture of one's e. 189:15
certain that e. is meaningful 145:17
e. is a repletion 296:23
e. . . . medium of revelation 327:2
e. remains a mad lamentable experiment 296:1
God who let us prove his e. 46:3
quite enough e. as it is 296:26
sole purpose of human e. 178:6
struggle for e. 122:16
Existing: e. . . . never repetition 317:2
Exit: every e. being an entrance 320:3
to make my e. quick 180:5
Expansion: e. was unhappily not accompanied by . . . advance 74:12
Expatriate: stoves round which e.s rally 84:4
Expect: not only e.s the worst 20:8
Expectation: distinction between hope and e. 165:11
while e. is equalized 165:6
Expediency: sacrificed to e. 226:12
Expenditure: general economy and particular e. 106:12
Experience: a lot of e. in the hen house 335:15
e. dulls . . . all our dogmas 245:3

Experience – *Contd.*
e. is actively offered 357:7
e. isn't interesting till 47:1
e. was to be taken as showing 170:2
his own e. . . . more extensive 350:5
last camp of e. 143:6
more acute the e. 265:1
my e. of life has been drawn 32:17
one year's e. 30 times 64:6
other kinds of e. . . . are possible 109:26
really intense emotional e.s 14:15
she made up out of a fund of e. 129:5
that we don't have to e. it 123:10
we were *always* doctoring our e.s 157:19
what a man is precedes e. 125:8
Experiment: from e. to the birth of a theory 108:11
Experimental: e. piece, . . . I did it myself 278:4
Experimenting: God . . . was only e. 137:19
Expert: e. . . . has made all the mistakes 44:18
e. . . . knows some of the worst mistakes 150:3
e.s invent themselves 64:7
Expertness: e. in hitting . . . bottles 330:9
Explainer: a village e. 317:1
Explanation: less hideous than e.s 207:2
Exploitation: all forms of e. are identical 112:3
you apply it, I call it e. 69:20
Explorer: e.s have to be ready to die lost 157:5
Export: article for e. 245:8
for mankind . . . there are no e.s 300:6
Express: e. in the small of the back 362:2
Expression: by their hunted e. 205:17
forms of e. exert upon us 360:14
he projects . . . an e. of living 243:4
less articulate its e. 265:1
Exterminate: we will e. 247:24
we will . . . e. a nation 315:9
External: old E. World, still . . . unaware 310:7
Extinct: if you're so smart, how come you're e. 87:18
Extortion: including artichokes and e. 289:1
Extreme: did not fly to e.s; she lived there 90:13
Extremism: e. . . . is no vice 134:10
Ex-wife: no fury like an e. searching 84:13
Eye: as far as the ground could see the e. was white 262:10
bud that forks her e. 327:21
clammy, accusing sort of e.s 362:7
e. . . . craves the novel 23:17
e. that can open an oyster 361:8
e.s are the windows of the soul 32:13
e.s bulged, too 363:5
e.s in the gables see 327:18
e.s still dazzled 208:8
e.s were filled with woe 18:12
fishy glitter in his e. 361:22
hand is more important than the e. 54:3
he is the mad e. of the fourth 113:14
her e.s became blank 183:3
his e.s were open 289:10

hundred e.s were fixed 32:8
keep your e. clear 149:6
less . . . than meets the e. 27:11
locked and frozen in each e. 22:6
look at yourself with one e. 168:7
looks into a woman's e.s and sees 313:21
mother-in-law with only one e. 175:8
my first black e. 233:8
television . . . chewing gum for the e.s 55:13
your e.s like agate lanterns 89:26
your lollipop e. 66:9
Eyeball: we're e. to e. 289:18
Eyebrow: pair of shaggy e.s 362:5
take any note above A with her e.s 133:4
with e.s made of platinum 119:2
Eyelash: didn't . . . have any e.es 363:5
Eyelid: when she raises her e.s 80:9

F

Fabian: fallen among F.s 201:18
farmyard civilization of the F.s 166:13
we are a F. Society writ large 145:13
Façades: f. . . . princess with syphilis 82:8
Face: all his f.s were designed 15:3
complete control of my f. 271:13
don't recognize f.s, but . . . jewellery 132:20
elderly disapproving f.s 309:22
every man . . . responsible for his f. 61:15
f. like a carving abandoned 349:13
f. like what Cardinal Newman's 65:9
f. . . . long as a late breakfast 176:17
f. of a saint . . . acceptable 351:6
f. resembled something . . . of Easter Island 300:16
f. that she keeps in a jar 202:11
f. which looked as though he had rented it 249:10
f.s . . . eloquent of past rebuffs 119:21
f.s to which distance . . . gives form 273:9
grabbed the wrong f. in the dark 82:9
her f. . . . like a lighted window 171:2
her fist of a f. died 327:13
his f. shining like Moses 333:13
human f. is . . . a cluster of f.s 273:6
I had made enough f.s 128:13
I never forget a f. 225:4
libel action against your f. 16:19
off the-hat f. 283:5
or f. of dearest look 328:21
private f.s in public places 22:11
smug suppressions of his f. 350:18
squeeze your nuts and open your f. 92:17
still got the same f. 224:11
suddenly I meet your f. 368:9
triangular f. 204:11
you take their f.s from 'em 271:8
Fact: attack the f.s at the point 140:6
conclusions on which I base my f.s 262:18
f.s are better than dreams 75:20
f.s are sacred 300:9

f.s . . . louder than statistics 322:20
f.s of life 258:3
I'd rather have my f.s all wrong 247:21
in complete possession of the f.s 227:15
must not neglect . . . f.s 38:16
partly in a world of concrete f.s 166:8
spiritual side of f.s 28:8
when the legend becomes f. 34:9
Faculties: had f. that we have lost 133:5
jig-saw of f. 54:1
Faculty: some great f. . . . eternally lost 126:9
Fad: psychoanalysis is a . . . f. 98:6
Fading: not so much . . . f. away 25:12
Fafafather: f. of all schemes 177:8
Fahrenheit: King F. quietly ate 239:20
Fail: better to f. conventionally 183:14
Failing: f.s . . . he never tucked his serviette
   88:10
f.s . . . must be humoured 174:7
Failure: difference between success and f.
   242:2
f. is all the rage 91:3
f.'s no success at all 105:3
falling in love . . . sign of f. 317:11
happy people are f.s 73:3
he was a delayed f. 86:11
I'm a connoisseur of f. 86:10
I might have died . . . a f. 341:15
thought is born of f. 355:12
Fairbanks, Douglas: 264:10
Fairy: F. mimbling mambling 96:18
in search of a F. 96:10
myth is . . . not a f. story 291:12
Fairy-tale: the pastoral f. 44:7
Faith: act of f. to assert that our thoughts 71:21
dedicated to political or religious f.s 265:5
f. . . . being ultimately concerned 331:12
f. has need of the whole truth 326:11
f. . . . is never complete 297:20
f. . . . knowledge of the real 35:1
f. may be defined as an illogical belief
   230:6
F. our Fathers sealèd us 186:15
F. . . . things without parallel 42:15
f. without doubt is . . . death 338:1
f. ye share with Berkeley Square 186:23
fluent periods had restored f. 351:7
heresies . . . explosions of f. 52:20
in process of losing or regaining f. 115:14
keep f. . . . it's not enough 128:8
my work . . . to shatter the f. 338:4
people who have lost their pet f. 351:19
Faithful: seldom f. if . . . attractive 61:3
to follow, to be f. 171:11
Fall: F. of Man . . . F. of God 84:11
how did you f., sir 22:2
hurry to get up when we f. 106:2
might as well f. . . . as lean 330:21
they could f. no further 47:5
Fallacy: Pathetic F. less fallacious 11:7
Fallen: f., but hardly frail 266:4
Falling: tried to keep them from f. 269:15
False: among the f. fronts 17:20
Falsehood: if they will stop telling f.s 318:2
Falsifiability: f. of a system 266:18

Falstaff, Sir John: 194:2
Fame: easier to gain f. than to retain it 299:9
f. is a powerful aphrodisiac 141:10
f. is rot: daughters 29:10
f. of the actress is transitory 28:15
how my f. rings out 42:26
no one shall work for f. 187:1
Familiarity: marriage would . . . add to a f.
   170:13
Families: f. . . . prefer widows to unmarried
   mothers 297:9
grinning Holy F. 215:2
if people didn't live in f. 312:14
Family: beautiful f. talk 81:11
bur f. life will out 239:4
f. is . . . source of all discontents 198:9
f. we have undermined 312:8
f. with the wrong members 254:22
is on lots of f. trees 92:23
our f. is not yet so good 111:15
shot round the f. circle 362:13
you educate a f. 220:18
Famine: as if there were f. 306:6
Famous: f. . . . cannot part with their brightest
   hour 151:1
I'm never going to be f. 258:12
I'm world-f. 280:14
stand about looking f. 217:3
Fan: 'f. vaulting' . . . an architectural device
   192:13
Fanatic: some grey-haired f. 250:22
when f.s are on top 230:1
Fanaticism: f. and intolerance 204:19
Fanny: F. by Gaslight 292:8
Fantasies: fed the heart on f. 368:16
Far-away: quarrel in a f. country 67:5
Farce: decided to turn it into a tragic f. 168:1
f. is the essential theatre 89:17
history repeats . . . as f. 19:1
Fare: you paid the f. 274:12
Farewell: A F. to Arms 287:5
Farmer: sturdy pioneers as f.s 61:8
Farm-house: f.s with their white faces 44:2
Farm-yard: human society from the f. 305:25
Fart: f. and you stand alone 142:4
whole story . . . played out between f.s
   37:15
Fascism: bold experiment of F. 56:11
F. . . . future refusing to be born 41:22
F. is a religion 245:7
F. is not an article for export 245:8
f. means war 321:7
Fascist: every f. a communist smile 313:16
F. objective 255:18
will be F.s five years hence 255:15
Fashion: f.s of one generation 270:4
true to you in my f. 267:9
[Victoria] not . . . a f. leader 9:15
Fastidious: the mind of a few f. people 310:8
Fat: imprisoned in every f. man a thin one
   84:20
in which their f. was fried 42:6
outside every f. man 14:10
there's a f. man demanding 347:13
thin man inside every f. man 254:14

Fatal: it is nearly always f. 215:15
Fate: F. – or Kate – knocking at your door 279:2
  know the f. of none 40:6
  we may become the makers of our f. 267:6
Fathead: one of the most pronounced f.s 362:24
Father: animal . . . substitute for the f. 123:9
  are your f.'s f. 89:22
  children . . . kill, if not their f.s 39:21
  hit his f. on the jaw 225:23
  land of my f.s. My f.s can 328:18
  my f.'s cry of joy 242:7
  Now I Have to Call Him F. 81:4
  our F. that art in heaven 271:4
  problem in finding a lost f. 29:14
  what's the f. up to 271:3
  you did have a f. 254:3
  your f. was a rich merchant 269:14
Fatherhood: f. . . . abominable 46:15
Fatigue: f. makes women talk 205:19
Fattening: immoral, illegal, or f. 365:22
Faubourg: f. Saint-Patrice . . . Ireland 176:22
Fauces: *mixplace his f.* 177:18
Faulkner, William: 151:13
Fault: easy to see the f.s in people 92:25
  f.s of his mistress 272:12
  fill you up with the f.s they had 193:17
  my f.s, but changing my tune 31:9
  only one f. . . . lousy 331:8
  you see all his f.s 213:5
Faun: we have heard the f.s 269:11
Fe: la f. sin la duda 338:1
Fear: F. and the Muse stand watch 11:14
  f.s . . . are hereditary 209:8
  he is F., Ó Little Hunter 186:17
  I have killed F. 187:23
  indication of f. 190:14
  never negotiate out of f. 181:26
  perfect f. casteth out love 85:3
  she who shines so calm be f. 44:3
Feared: if he could be f. 268:4
Feast: Paris is a moveable f. 151:7
  f.s hold them 250:13
Fecund: f. rate 259:19
Feed: f. the Wooster face 362:6
  hand that f.s you . . . prevents you 323:16
  throw a f. to her 288:11
Feel: able to f. hot and think cold 65:3
  believe enough in what one f.s 369:2
  he paints . . . what he f.s 264:6
  we can only f. things 196:10
Feeling: all disguise our f.s pretty well 88:7
  can't put them out of his f.s 65:23
  deal only with simple f.s 296:15
  die out, but whole species of f. 120:17
  distinguish between thought and f. 78:2
  f.s you haven't really got 196:12
  taught . . . that f. is bad form 119:17
Feet: f. firmly planted in the air 299:2
  land on somebody's f. 260:6
  stayed to get his f. wet 242:19
  sweaty f. seldom come singly 52:4
Fehler: wenn Frauen F. machen wollen 180:6

Feigenbaum: F., seit wie lange schon 281:13
Feindschaft: F. ist uns das Nächste 281:8
  zuletzt die F. verteilte 282:12
Felicity: more f. . . . than young men can 310:1
Fell: he f. down a great deal 330:13
Fellah: f. . . . does not lay a claim 112:5
Fellow: f. countrymen become harder to understand 311:16
  f. traveller of the religious 52:21
Fellow-man: way to love my f. 69:10
Fellowship: hand of f. . . . losing . . . fingers 175:3
Female: art . . . involved with the f. 78:4
  flyspecked abdominous f. 92:2
  for a f. who has . . . languor 353:11
  seldom f. in a world of males 265:13
  why should human f.s become sterile 162:21
Feminine: f. helplessness came into fashion 81:18
  if only she looked a bit more f. 309:4
  nothing so . . . enthuses the f. mind 148:16
Feminist: best home for a f. 345:10
Feminization: f. of the white European 207:18
Fen: through the plashy f. 347:4
Fence: Don't F. Me In 267:13
  f. is just too high for him 227:14
  has sat so long on the f. 209:16
  sit on a f. and yet keep 17:26
Ferdinand: characteristics of F. the Bull 248:16
Ferret: decent box for the f. 84:8
Ferryboat: voice that used to shake the f.s 222:22
Fertile: in such a fix to be so f. 247:20
Fetched: always went and f. them 236:4
Fiction: autobiography has no more . . . f. 87:1
  f. . . . I can disown 321:2
  f. is piss 55:3
  house of f. has many windows 48:17
  jam of f. 228:4
  newspaper . . . continuous f. 41:21
  over the whole of f. 228:5
Fictional: all f. characters are flat 347:15
  some of the characters are f. 252:2
Fictitious: what is f. in a novel 11:15
Fiddle: f. while Rome burns 266:6
Field: f. and wood, all bone-fed loam 44:5
  ten ploughed f.s, like ten full-stops 225:20
Field-glasses: best pair of f. 268:19
Field-Marshal: last F. I shall appoint 155:15
Fifteen: f.-year-old boy 287:15
Fifty: I am f. and I haven't seen a thing 298:16
Fight: and are longing for a f. 144:1
  best part of married life is the f.s 356:13
  can't f. in here. This is the War Room 130:5
  Ebenezer thought it wrong to f. 34:17
  f. and f. and f. again to save 127:4
  f. . . . to impress their mothers 113:17
  go out and f. 252:14
  one does not f. with men 263:4
  right and I'll f. for it 360:1

what . . . gets loose when you begin to f. 128:9
when we began this f., we had clean 128:10
Fighter: f. carries his warring country 112:6
Fighting: period of cheating between . . . f. 42:22
we are f. for the gates 208:4
Figtree: f., for a long time now 281:13
Figure: leave out the central f. 198:5
Filing: f. is concerned with the past 354:22
Film: f. is not the art of scholars 153:16
f. music should have 322:17
great art of f.s 54:17
I am big. The f.s got small 355:16
I like a f. to have a beginning 133:13
see bad f.s when they can stay at home 135:2
when the f. was finished quite 153:8
Fils: le f. fait la guerre 271:3
Filthy: nowadays you can't be f. unless 159:17
Finality: f. is death 317:7
Finals: this is called F. 210:5
Finance: sound f. may be right 183:9
Financial Times: F. is read by the people 11:3
Financier: f.s . . . gnomes of Zürich 358:19
Find: I do not seek, I f. 264:7
Finden: so dich f., binden dich an Bild 282:16
Finger: burn your f.s on your own chestnuts 115:9
fifteen f.s on the safety catch 218:18
f. that turns the dial rules 103:21
keep your f.s to yourself 66:9
nimble f.s are no more nimble 308:13
points cardboard f. 235:8
ten thick worms his f.s 220.14
time we pulled our f. out 107:3
upward gesture with two f.s 156:12
Finger-nail: stop biting your f.s 284:19
Fings: F. Ain't Wot They Used T'Be 250:12
Finite: nothing . . . is really f. 315:14
Fire: f. was furry as a bear 308:7
ideas they enter . . . under f. 334:21
impartial as between the f. brigade 77:11
she would set f. to the School 300:14
unless the house is on f. 329:21
Firearms: loaded f. were . . . forbidden 300:13
Firemen: teachers are something like f. 140:2
First: anxious . . . But they are travelling F. 119:21
f. things f., second things never 85:8
First-aid: f. stopped short 362:22
First-rate: mistake for the f. 259:19
Fish: f. fuck in it 114:7
. . . hunk of my gefilte f. 288:7
man who caught that f. 283:12
nose for f., an eye for apples 139:1
only dead f. swim with the stream 243:12
this island is . . . surrounded by f. 41:16
would you rather be a f. 58:6
Fisher: was a f. of men, and of women 100:16
Fishermen: bite every time for f. 241:15
Fitness: a beauty in f. which no art 100:13
Fitzgerald, F. Scott: 316:22
Five: introspection . . . in the F. Towns 32:6
Five-cent: plenty of good f. cigars 285:11

Flag: f. if I don't know who's holding 339:19
I will not kiss your f.ing f. 92:13
less discernible than the red f. 169:15
putting the American f. upside down 182:19
[T. E. Lawrence] . . . puts red f.s all around 306:10
to yelp at the English F. 185:6
Flagellate: very difficult to f. yourself 160:14
Flame: breathing f. quietly 362:1
f. leaps from the hand 269:12
Flap: neither to f. nor to falter 219:1
Flash: thought is only a f. 266:9
Flat: towers of high-rise council f.s 48:13
Flatter: some men fawn and f. 259:6
what really f.s a man 303:24
Flattery: f. is all right — if you don't inhale 318:8
Flaubert: that poor sucker F. 260:1
Flaunt: if you've got it, f. it 54:19
Flautist: f.s . . . know something we don't 173:14
Flaw: we all have f.s 330:12
Flea: literature's performing f. 252:13
Flecker, James Elroy: 136:4
Fleece: to shear the f.s or to f. 61:8
Fleet: F.'s lit up 364:8
Fleming, Ian: 200:6
Flesh: I, born of f. and ghost 327:15
in the f. it is immortal 317:19
knocked and f. let enter 327:14
overcoat of f. that gets thicker 37:5
will not publicly eat human f. 347:8
Fleur: le démenti des f.s 19:13
Flier: she was a f. still 288:2
Flight: f. is what they long for 357:17
Fling: too late to have a f. 359:12
Floor: f. so cunningly laid 235:17
f.s are shrunken 147:13
Flopsy: whose names were F., Mopsy, Cottontail and Peter 268:6
Flower: arrange my poems . . . a vase of f.s 104:10
arranges f.s . . . does not grow them 79:5
buy some f.s for your table 157:12
f.s . . . go wrong in colour 170:16
he stops and smells the f.s 248:16
letting a hundred f.s blossom 222:5
only the dusty f.s 11:13
say it with f.s 10:22, 117:23
to lose the touch of f.s 63:6
where have all the f.s gone 300:18
Flu: like the twenty-four-hour f. 250:8
Flush: spend half a pint and f. two gallons 107:7
Flute: eat well and play the f. 268:4
what was once a Magic F. 16:21
Fly: unzipped f. caught in . . . amber 82:6
Folies-Bergère: F. and looks at the audience 318:18
Folk: all songs are f. songs 55:2
my f.s didn't come over on the Mayflower 285:10
Folk-dancing: everything once, except . . . f. 30:1
Follies: f. for which their friends adore 158:8
Follow: I must f. . . . I am their leader 45:6

Folly: he knew human f. 22:1
    their f. . . . is trained f. 130:9
Fond: I may be very f. of her 273:20
Food: don't have any money, the problem is f.
    100:4
    eat . . . to put f. out of my mind 307:19
    f. in this place 13:2
    f. is an important part 199:9
    f. was a tragedy 269:24
    f. was incredibly bad 266:15
    just *thinking* abut f. 300:2
    lived for days on nothing but f. 114:8
    Pure F. Committee had rejected 362:14
    sweet sticky f. 24:15
    where the f. had at least the merit 98:5
Fool: always declaring he's no f. 237:17
    any f. can criticize, and many . . . do 128:12
    any . . . f. can make things bigger 300:7
    f., a liar or both 301:8
    f. among f.s or a f. alone 356:18
    f. and his money . . . how they got together
        118:4
    f., fixed in his folly 109:19
    f. of this generation . . . genius 133:9
    f. too large for it 68:14
    f. too many of the people 331:3
    he f.s nobody as completely as himself 183:2
    I'd be a damn f. if I didn't 328:6
    making a f. of himself 302:5
    man who will not laugh is a f. 295:16
    mixture of f.s and angels 152:12
    ninety-nine per cent . . . are f.s 356:9
    only a f. would make the bed 313:9
    only f.s . . . drink at sea 343:8
    says that they are all f.s 70:21
    there was a time when a f. 318:13
    villain . . . let him remain a f. 326:16
Foolish: These F. Things 321:12
Foot: I could give you my f. prints 224:2
    one f. on a bar of soap 274:16
    produce my f., my each feather 160:6
Football: good excuse not to play f. 199:10
    I see the world as a f. 203:5
    life was . . . a f. game 115:18
    sixth day is for f. 57:18
    thought f. was God 271:1
Footnote: philosophy . . . f.s to Plato 354:19
Footstep: waiting for the familiar f. 363:9
Forbear: my f.s were . . . crooks 20:7
Forbidden: hinting at the f. 21:18
Force: f. of Mind 195:21
    F. one day was served to him 110:14
    may the F. be with you 212:17
    other nations use 'f.' 347:11
    use of f. by one class 201:4
Ford, Ford Madox: 269:4
Ford, Gerald: F. . . . can't fart and chew gum
    175:10
    F. was unknown 18:20
Foreboding: I am filled with f. 270:16
Foreign: f. correspondent . . . lives in f. parts
    319:18
    f. – so f., indeed 60:16
    f. stories . . . not *real* news 347:6
    f. swear-word 327:10

my f. policy is 'Nothing . . .' 245:6
    pronounce f. names as he chooses 77:14
Foreigner: due to him being a f. 25:14
    few f.s can understand 77:4
    f.s speak English when our backs 90:14
    regard Englishmen as f.s 193:3
    sympathy . . . for being f.s 48:5
    went off to fight the f.s 86:5
Foretold: all was f. me; naught 328:23
Forget: as accurately as he f.s 247:14
    f. everything . . . about God 331:15
    f. what I was taught 354:3
    f.s words as one f.s names 347:20
    naïve forgive and f. 323:17
    never f. any moment 47:11
    painting is a way to f. life 287:17
    terrors infants . . . never f. 101:25
    three things I always f. 323:10
    you were the sort that men f. 148:2
Forgive: f. . . anything except bad prose 73:7
    f. but do not forget 323:17
Forgiven: once a woman has f. her man 98:18
Forgiveness: such knowledge, what f. 109:2
Forgotten: books . . . undeservedly f. 23:18
    I had entirely f. the statement 123:5
Fork: f. in the other 204:13
    f. . . . instrument of chase 350:11
    we've got him on the Caudine Toasting-f.
        187:25
Forkbender: myself, Harold and Lady F.
    167:14
Form: purest mobile f. 188:16
    'significant f.' . . . reality 33:22
Forming: all the time you took f. yourself
    88:19
Formula: does not need the f. to recognize
    299:17
Fornicate: always f. between clean sheets
    125:15
Fornicated: f. and read the papers 61:12
Fornication: big business and f. 227:13
    like war and f. 243:13
    unrivalled garment for f. 226:3
Forster, E. M.: 221:20
Forsyte: no F. had as yet died 128:5
Forties: human females become sterile in the f.
    162:21
Fortissimo: at last, f. 219:21
Fortune: calamities . . . good f. to others
    42:11
    F. enrolled me among the second fated
        139:3
    f. into a shoestring 365:21
    f. we awaited so anxiously 133:18
Forty: compensation for being over f. 118:5
    just turning f. 209:2
    life begins at f. 336:2
Found: nothing that is f. is ever 156:7
Foundation: f.s . . . intends to reform 334:14
Founder: hesitates to forget its f.s 354:18
Fountain: f.s piped an answer 194:14
Four: it is always f. o'clock 64:3
Fox: don't set a f. to . . . chickens 335:15
    f. came home 225:21
Fraction: like short words and vulgar f.s 74:16

Fragile: we are essentially f. 25:15
Fragment: carry his f.s away 17:27
France: 216:6
  F. has lost the battle but she 129:15
  F. is a country where 355:18
  F. was neither led nor governed 263:3
  hats off to F. 287:16
  have thought of F. in a certain way 129:12
  in F. there are politicians 66:6
  now all roads lead to F. 329:3
  only one illusion – F. 183:6
Francis: I think I'm St F. 258:8
Franco, General F.: 155:19
Franglais: Parlez-vous F. 111:9
Frankie: F. and Johnnie were lovers 16:4
Fraud: the great men of history are f.s 45:3
Frauen: wenn F. Fehler machen wollen 180:6
Freak: want out of the f. show 188:3
Freckles: I'd been better without: . . . f.
  259:8
Free: before they're allowed to be f. 104:20
  condemned to be f. 297:3
  dead man, and a f. man 297:5
  feels f. . . . Except from the Americans
  172:15
  f. country . . . share your privacy 339:7
  f. society . . . safe to be unpopular 318:6
  in a f. society 209:1
  some poor bastard who's never f. 254:13
  there is no f. lunch 18:10
  tried, in my way, to be f. 80:2
  truth . . . makes f. those who have loved it
  295:21
  truth that makes men f. 11:4
  we are no longer f. 190:11
  when you've robbed a man . . . he's f. 312:1
Freedom: believe in . . . f. and organization
  145:5
  enemies of F. . . . shout and they shoot
  166:10
  Free in F. Too 248:4
  f. for some, but not this peace 23:6
  f. for the one who thinks differently 213:4
  f. from – without . . . f. to 124:1
  f. is an indivisible world 358:10
  f. of speech, f. of conscience 336:9
  f. . . . terrible word 62:24
  f., the second of man's creeds 198:1
  F. to Starve 130:20
  F., what liberties . . . in thy name 130:4
  f.'s just another word 190:19
  greatest champion of f. 77:2
  group that stood for 'f.' 196:1
  life of breezy f. 349:7
  native never stops achieving his f. 112:4
  one essential quality of life – f. 123:14
  only one subject – f. 297:7
  people are not interested in f. 219:15
  rich in things or in the f. 165:10
  ridiculing Christians is f. of speech 279:1
  unless f. is universal it is only 154:4
  we must plan for f. 267:3
  when there is f. 201:6
  you took my f. away 311:20
Free-loader: f. is a confirmed guest 289:12

Freely: they put themselves in hell f. 297:23
Freemasonry: a kind of bitter f. 32:14
Free verse: 125:2
Freighter: forty f.s at sea 186:1
French: 87:9
  devil . . . can speak quite bad F. 177:21
  doing things . . . the F. don't even 158:6
  finest F. novel in the English language
  284:5
  F. are badly fitted 187:16
  F. are devine 211:7
  F. bourgeoisie created 334:8
  F. Classical architecture . . . gifted 78:7
  F. foreign policy 205:5
  F. ones clever daughters 146:23
  F. who will not 342:14
  good because cooked by the F. 100:14
  I want a lot of F. horns 287:8
  if the F. were German 179:11
  if the F. were to play cricket 113:2
  imagine the Lord talking F. 95:12
  may be tolerated by the F. 238:12
  modified by F. order and clarity 52:23
  my nationality is F. 357:16
  selfish . . . F. Governments more than most
  106:4
  something Vichy about the F. 251:3
  trust the F. to touch the nerve 85:18
  we die F. 347:17
  you can see the F. coast 266:12
Frenchman: F. thinks standing 253:5
Frenchmen: create F. in the image of Englishmen 74:5
  F. drink wine 193:8
Freud, Sigmund: 211:11
  came across F. . . . and came tearing back
  116:14
  F. has been accepted 236:13
  F. is all nonsense 237:4
  F. seeking to unlock his door 246:19
  F. was a hero 192:2
  never able to agree with F. 178:3
  trouble with F. is that he never played . . .
  Glasgow Empire 99:18
Freudian: F. papa and maids 212:3
  F. . . . very low, Central European 139:16
Friend: all good fellows were my f.s 69:9
  close f.s of my close f.s 355:4
  follies for which their f.s adore them 158:8
  f. in need is a f. to be avoided 295:8
  f. . . . leaves him as he is 72:1
  f.s are God's apology 184:18
  f.s could only read the title 365:1
  f.s . . . got there first 339:12
  f.s make pretence of following 124:11
  f.s now are so very respectable 47:11
  f.s to borrow my books 283:16
  funerals of our f.s 52:19
  give up my life for my f., but 309:16
  guessed you were f.s 48:15
  had to choose . . . betraying my f. 119:22
  heart-breaking new f.s 182:16
  I don't trust him. We're f.s 51:19
  I have lost f.s 365:12
  if a f. of mine died, no matter 116:9

Friend – *Contd.*
lay down his f.s for his life 329:23
little help from my f.s 203:3
never bosom f.s 289:8
Oldest F. whom one definitely 162:13
praise of one's f.s 223:12
Proust saw his f.s 277:2
rises on the backs of his f.s 160:3
we have really no absent f.s 47:2
when your f. holds ... both hands 42:29
whenever a f. succeeds 343:5
woman wants her f.s 216:3
would be the perfect f. 310:9
your best f.s won't tell you 10:14
Friendliness: impersonal insensitive f. 346:23
Friendship: do I believe in Platonic f. 102:10
f. is unnecessary 206:1
great Newberry Fruit of f. 86:12
wanted f. and got friendliness 220:3
Frightened: not f. of dying 'one day'
311:11
Frightfulness: f. is not a remedy 73:12
Frivolity: how precious is f. 119:18
Frock: her f.s are built in Paris 293:17
Frog: f.s singing against the fauns 269:11
Front: her f. looked as if it had exploded
234:10
to which f. these were sent 257:6
Frontier: f.s of our little state 179:4
new f. 181:22
Frost: Jack F. dancing bespangled 74:18
Frost, David: 243:6
Frown: persistent troubled f. 330:1
Froze: Sheila Clock f. into a ... block 118:3
Frucht: hinein in die zeitig entschlossene F.
281:13
Frühling: F. ist wiedergekommen 282:10
Frustration: age of F. 261:3
puzzled f. 48:3
Fry: dear Roger F. whom I love as a man
223:11
Fuchsia: f. drenched with rain 11:9
Fuck: they f. you up 193:17
zipless f. is ... pure 176:4
Fucking: cold-hearted f. 196:2
Führer: Constitution is the will of the F.
121:7
principle of the F.'s function 86:15
purer F. 15:10
Fulfilment: every f. is slavery 62:9
image of f. 243:8
Fume: captured f. of space 89:19
Fun: most f. I ever had 12:22
nothing more f. than a man 259:9
taken my f. where I've found it 185:16
work ... much more f. than f. 89:12
Funeral: day of the ... match for the f.
161:5
f. ... make sure he was dead 17:22
f.s of our friends 52:19
if you don't go to other men's f.s 95:14
no death ... but there are f.s 97:20
one f. makes many 350:3
weddings is sadder than f.s 33:16
Fungus: F. inspects his trousers 53:11

Funny: everything is f. 285:9
f. because I had said it 71:16
f. without being vulgar 131:16
monstrous aunt can be f. 339:1
Furniture: and don't bump into the f. 89:14
f. ... trying to dodge it 333:6
Further: it's f. ... away than anywhere else
276:13
Future: any hopefulness for the f. 165:16
calculate coldly about the ... f. 43:14
controls the f. 254:23
drowned the F. and the Past 328:20
f. and it does not work 332:18
f. and it works 316:10
F. ... happiness is assured 42:16
f. is ... black 26:6
f. is dark, the present burdensome 110:15
F. is something everyone reaches 205:15
f. is the most expensive luxury 356:11
f. ... not what it was 16:3
f. refusing to be born 41:22
F. Shock 331:17
orgastic f. that ... recedes 116:10
past has revealed ... the f. 326:13
pay to the f. 266:11
pleasant ... not to have any f. 57:16
Russia will inherit the f. 196:14
skipping everything in the f. 355:5
sphere of the f. 201:13
there we are in the Golden F. 163:8
Fuyez: f. les bois 19:14

G

Gabor, Zsa-Zsa: 204:5
Gabriel: want to check with G. himself 321:7
Gadarene: G. gallop on the ... whole hog
129:11
Gai: toujours g. 222:13
Gain: there are no g.s without pains 318:3
Gaitskell, Hugh: 41:23
Galleries: in more select g. 52:22
Gallery: boy I love is up in the g. 345:3
Gallienne: if you call Le G. a minor poet 223:9
Galsworthy, John: 352:22
Gamble: life is a g., at terrible odds 320:11
Gambling: business known as g. 42:28
croupiers in a crooked g. house 157:15
Game: dread of g.s 40:21
human race ... playing at children's g.s
71:13
may be a damned amusing g. 115:21
so the g. is ended 159:9
Gamekeeper: his g.'s letters first 333:17
Gandhi, Mahatma: a young fellow called G.
38:6
Gangster: great nations acted like g.s 191:2
Gaol: woman's place ... in the g. 50:3
Gap: old age ... last g. but one 354:6
Garbo, Greta: sees in G. sober 336:17
Garden: closing time in the g.s of the West
82:20

Everything in the G.'s Lovely 148:7
g. . . . doesn't *compare* to what it was
    102:14
g.s, ponds, palings 261:5
no front g. . . . cemented over 160:10
their own back g. 211:16
weed the g., wind the clock 23:9
Garden-boy: g. is leading the cranes 344:4
Gardener: only to the g. 248:15
you might call an avant-g. 210:7
Garden-Suburb: G. ethos 199:4
Gare: ideas . . . au-dessus de sa g. 277:6
Gargoyle: g. hewn by a drunken stonemason
    33:1
Garlic: edged off with a whisper of g. 152:18
Garter: G. . . . desolating the country 42:17
Gas: turn off the g. 204:18
Gas-chamber: we built our g.s to accommo-
    date two thousand 157:9
Gate: to do good knocks at the g. 325:3
Gathered: where two or three are g. 245:4
Gaulle, Charles de: 326:2
Gaullist: I myself have become a G. 129:16
Gave: never g. away anything 54:18
Gay: allowance . . . the g. make to the hum-
    drum 293:9
    sad person's view of a g. person 91:6
    their bottoms are so g. 18:8
    we're g. and we're proud 18:4
Gazette: Rabbit Fanciers' G.
    161:18
Gazing: g. . . . as St Theresa might have
    161:24
Gebild: schlägt sich erdachtes G. von 281:18
Geheimnis: drängst dein reines G. 281:13
Gelignite: cure . . . safe-blowing with g.
    315:15
Gendarme: g. is after him 288:18
Genealogy: G. . . . care to trace his own 42:18
General: all they have got are g.s 55:11
    at the age of four . . . all G.s 339:5
    lies in the G.s, Collapse 310:16
    not against the law for g.s 335:16
    office where one can intimidate g.s 119:16
    too important to be left to the g.s 79:1
General Motors: good for G. 358:15
Generalship: a war deserving of better g.
    278:3
Generation: as it passes from one g. 72:22
    fashions of one g. 270:4
    first of the last g. 316:22
    his g. was . . . between the wars 48:3
    I belong to a g. of men 88:20
    new g. of Americans 181:24
    this g. of Americans 285:18
    youth of his own g. 117:10
Generosity: do without g. . . . to practise
    charity 61:21
    g. consists . . . in fighting to destroy 122:7
    g. is a two-edged virtue 312:4
Genius: country full of g. 203:9
    each . . . be considered a g. 39:2
    fool of this generation . . . g. of the last
    133:9
    g. bears . . . weight of what is common 38:19

g. . . . has *two* great ideas 54:9
g. is in the planet's 343:15
g. . . . reaction against one's training 38:15
g. which does what it must 28:3
g.-worship . . . an uncreative age 34:3
g.es are the luckiest 23:20
I think like a g. 246:11
man of g. 272:15
need a head . . . when he's got g. 168:11
signs of his g. 256:8
Genteel: flabby g. 48:12
Gentility: what's g. worth if it can't stand fire
    128:10
Gentle: do not go g. 327:17
Gentleman: between a g. and a gent 27:3
    distinguishes the g. 345:18
    every other inch a g. 352:24
    g. has the qualities of a saint 184:19
    g. . . . knows how 344:14
    g. need not know Latin 226:8
    g. stays eagerly awake 24:7
    g. . . . wouldn't hit a woman 12:19
    God is a g. 254:2
    Greek: it stamps a man . . . as an educated
    g. 303:28
    I am a g. 303:3
    if we are a g. not to think 92:11
    man was apparantly a g. 281:5
    not the sort of attire for a g. 301:21
    so particularly the English g. 170:19
    whether I be . . . quite a g. 32:21
    you would not . . . have been a g. 256:14
Gentlemen: all the members were g. 333:3
    difficult to behave like g. 217:4
    g. . . . remember blondes 211:5
    our Government of g. 133:16
    we are none of us g. any more 136:8
Gentleness: g. of her spirit had immensely
    170:4
Genuine: g., only it didn't happen to be mine
    79:3
Genuineness: g. only thrives in the dark
    161:16
Geometry: one g. cannot be more true 265:8
George: G. – don't do that 141:14
George VI: 44:9, 334:1
Georgian: our G. forerunners had faculties
    133:5
    style known as Bankers G. 192:12
German: all the G.s were warlike 200:8
    appallingly thorough these G.s 163:4
    bigger danger than the G.s 115:11
    but they are G.s 245:10
    G. philosophers 208:19
    G.s came later 334:8
    G.s would admire them 179:11
    human as distinct from the G. mind 172:3
    if . . . G. storm troops had actually 76:4
    jab the life out of the G.s 298:7
    poor woman was G. too 35:13
    true physics . . . the G. spirit 332:7
    we G.s, who are the only people 154:9
Germany: 216:6
    defeat of G. 286:2
    G. is the prize professional nation 359:19

Germany – *Contd.*
we ought to help G. 335:10
you can tell when ... into G. 107:10
Gespenst: es gibt ein G. 240:4
Gestirn: wer stellt es ins G. 281:9
Gesture: possess a sweeping g. 249:5
Get: it was a pity to g. up 226:21
Getty, Paul: 204:18
Ghetto: vu les ruines du g. 110:17
Ghost: can g.s be angry ... what else 97:12
crowds of g.s among the trees 298:6
g. in the machine 291:13
g. nor man, but mortal g. 327:15
g. of a governess 245:16
g. that eats handkerchiefs 240:4
like g.s with rifles 64:9
ruling the Church ... the Holy G. 174:18
when you are giving up the g. 34:20
whether i believe in g.s 222:23
Giant: awakened a sleeping g. 368:1
[the Victorians] lame g.s 72:20
Gift: deed of g. was many deeds of war 124:9
God's g. ... take her back 28:22
love ... the g. of oneself 19:3
many g.s ... unique to man 54:2
one of our g.s ... would coincide 39:2
Gifted: not ... g. but very understanding
67:19
Gilbert: G., the Filbert 360:4
Gill: never answered Mrs G. 96:18
Gin: ask if the g. will make them run 116:27
g. in the lowest kind of inn 68:21
has to drink worse g. 230:12
how much g. ... in the jug 363:17
little drops of g. 17:4
Gingerbread: light hand ... gilded the g.
170:9
Gioconda: throwing a rapid G. at him 161:3
Giraffe: man who believes in g.s 236:14
Girder: iron g. in a house of cards 226:11
Girdle: helps you with your g. 247:17
Girl: bare like nude giant g.s 315:1
beautiful g. in a diaphanous veil 262:5
big mountainous sports g. 40:14
breaks just like a g. 104:26
can still *hear* a pretty g. 331:7
drug that's smoking in a g. 327:21
florid g.s that go ... well with autumn
293:2
gifted g.s married impossible men 139:5
g. is lots safer 216:8
g. is safe if she's with me 115:16
g. ... part of a set 116:20
g. with brains 211:6
G.'s Own Paper 256:7
g.s do have regrets 341:7
g.s ... fall in love with ugly men 52:17
g.s, I'd call 'em all Jane 350:6
g.s I was ever engaged to 361:14
good story about a bad g. 16:13
how g.s with wax faces live 356:6
I like the g.s who do 233:19
if g.s aren't ignorant, they're cultured 86:16
if you were the only g. in the world 141:19
less sought-after g.s 116:14

needs a g. to believe in him 286:18
nice, quiet g. she was 169:3
not a g. 254:5
one person an English g. hates more 302:31
pretty g. who naked is 92:6
process whereby American g.s turn 146:12
there was a little g. 234:2
young g.s picked them every one 300:18
your rate is half a g. in twenty 157:11
G.I.s: 334:3
Give: man g.s what he has: the rest 171:15
Glacier: g. knocks in the cupboard 22:17
Gladstone, W. E.: G. read Homer for fun
74:21
Glamour: g. is when a man 210:14
Glance: nothing can stay my g. 368:4
thanked him with a g. 281:4
Gland: smaller adrenal g.s 229:15
Glass: whiskers ... grown under glass 361:16
Glasses: forget both pairs of g. 247:16
I did not remove my g. 313:20
Glimpse: little g. into the beyond 102:16
Global: g. network 218:9
g. village 217:13
Glory: deny you peace but give you g. 338:5
Keep the Glow in Old G. 248:4
trailed the clouds of his own g. 140:12
Glove: *Gott Mit Uns* ... had g.s 98:1
Glow: her g. has warmed the world 318:9
Glubjullas: luck with my *G.* 102:15
Glutton: and g.s old in sin 276:5
Gluttony: g. ... sign something is eating us
98:2
Glyn, Elinor: figure in an E.G. novel 16:11
Mrs G. achieved the paradox 30:3
Gnat: o joy of the g. 282:1
Gnome: little g.s of Zürich 358:19
Go: I g. – I come back 181:9
in the name of God, *g.* 14:7
to get where he has to g. 220:4
Goat: as g.s came leaping up 292:7
g. and an ox must keep in step 50:10
g.s propagate within his ... tomb 50:14
g.s ... sheep from broken homes 49:5
Gobble: g. g. glup glup 234:22
God: 91:5, 178:12
about G. being a Tory 251:2
absurd is sin without G. 62:3
an atheist still, thank G. 57:12
and G. watching it 252:3
asked if he believed in G. 246:13
away from the church ... back to G. 56:2
bein' G. ain't a bed of roses 82:15
believe that they are attracted by G. 166:18
better for G. if we refuse to believe 62:15
but for the grace of G., goes G. 77:7, 221:2
cannot believe that G. plays dice 108:4
change in our conception of G. 163:23
churches ... same relation to G. 338:11
die young, but it's ... kissing G. 56:4
does not ... disbelieve in G. 254:18
even G. was born too late 212:9
extra work ... when I was a g. 154:12
eye of G. 253:4
forget everything ... about G. 331:15

give up writing about G. 347:25
G. ain't said nothing for years 314:7
G. ... an under-achiever 13:3
G. can stand being told 272:3
G., do take care of yourself 318:7
G. don't come when you want Him 16:5
G., from whose territory I had withdrawn 90:21
G. had never spoken anything but ... English 95:12
G., help me ... this little once 114:15
G. in His pity knows 96:14
G. is a gentleman 254:2
G. is a sort of burglar 333:12
G. in dead – Nietzsche 136:17
G. Is groovy 272:8
G. is interested ... in religion 326:19
G. is ... like a depressing smog 214:16
G. is love but get it in writing 199:16
G. is not Dead but Alive and Well 136:18
G. is only another artist 264:2
G. is subtle but ... not malicious 107:21
G. must have loved the People 261:10
g. mustn't pay hotel bills 51:12
G. ... need not exist in order to save 97:15
G. not on the borders of life 45:18
G. of some Oriental theogony 273:6
G. seems to have left the receiver off 189:14
G. ... smile of a cosmic Cheshire cat 164:2
G. who created the universe 229:19
G. who let us prove his existence 46:3
G. who Looks after Small Things 187:28
G. will cease to dream you 338:2
G. without man's immortality 62:6
G. works in a mysterious way – 109:5
G.'s trustiest lieutenants often lack 305:7
g.s ruled ... the g.s obeyed 82:11
g.s wish to destroy ... call promising 83:9
guinea pigs in the laboratory of G. 357:20
highest praise of G. 273:14
his thoughts had turned to his G. 95:11
hold some G.-made object up to it 66:17
I am disappointed in G.'s works 238:14
I don't know whether I believe in G. 226:6
I would not marry G. 110:12
idea that G. had, when he made us 99:5
if a g. had made the world 45:10
if G. cannot do this 26:8
if G. had been a Liberal 49:7
in G.'s hands ... hard to sleep 51:22
in the name of G., go 14:7
in this life I am G. 233:11
it paid then to believe in G. 252:15
Judas is the last g. 195:18
just to get in touch with G. 57:14
like G. in his last years 329:9
man whose g. is in the skies 302:17
my G.s have afflicted me 186:6
not only is there no G. 13:9
o thou lost G. 282:12
observed by yours faithfully, G. 15:22
ought to have left G. alone 35:3
polite Society believed in G. 297:16

praise G. when you can 44:12
pray as if everything depended on G. 314:12
present, unknowable G. 195:11
problem was that G. is dead 123:17
proof that G. is a bore 229:20
question the existence of G. 62:23
recourse to G. as a ... hypothesis 45:17
ruin the business ... of all other g.s 229:13
sceptical ... that G. made man 121:14
shall weigh your G.s and you 187:3
she was G. in drag 27:17
so that G. could see everything 90:11
tells them that G. doesn't love them 65:11
their values ... G. and carpeting 13:16
those who marry G. ... domesticated 140:13
thought football was G. 271:1
truly G.'s trumpet, Mr Rees 329:7
ways of G. 208:8
we are too late for the g.s 150:1
we did what G. wanted 342:10
what ... G. thinks of money 28:5
what is the prose for G. 28:14
what will G. say to us 261:16
when G. created man, she was 137:19
who would argue with the G.s 220:2
world ... nearer to G. than ever 46:1
Yellow G. forever gazes down 148:19
you forget the good G. 290:15
you hardly ever mention G. 232:14
Godiva: if she were cast as Lady G. 16:17
God-men: G. say when die 16:6
Godmother: always a g. 199:12
Godot: we're waiting for G. 30:19
Goering, H. W.: 151:17
Goes: and so it g. 343:11
Going: at his best only when the g. was good 85:17
if you don't know where you are g. 263:13
Gold: g. rush ... line of chorus girls 352:7
g. standard on the booze 183:10
like to put their lips on g. 141:7
to hold g. in front of his eyes 115:20
what banknotes are to g. 43:5
Goldfish: natural hootchy-kootchy to a g. 99:12
Golding, William: G. writes so well 206:6
Goldwyn, Sam: Mr G. ... you are only interested in art: 306:11
Golf: 208:15
carrying the g. clubs of your tourists 303:25
earnest protest against g. 33:5
made more liars ... than g. 285:3
perennially popular subjects ... g. 87:4
thousand lost g. balls 109:16
we dance at the G. Club 40:19
Golliwog: who ... preferred g.s to dolls 52:17
Gomorrah: Eden differed from ... G. 161:23
of the virgins of G. 79:4
Good: bad end unhappily, the g. unluckily 320:9
borrowed the language of G. 21:19
especially when the g. isn't there 92:25
extending our knowledge of g. 23:24

Good – *Contd.*
G. can imagine Evil 23:11
g. is better than the best 37:13
G. . . . makes for unity 162:20
g. will toward us, the American people 358:9
he who wants to do g. 325:3
men have never been g. 29:12
obtrusively expensive g.s 127:8
only g. girls keep diaries 27:16
there's no g. and bad here 247:3
to buy g.s they did not need 148:9
to influence people for g. 223:10
what a relief . . . to stop being g. 121:17
what we like is not necessarily g. 34:6
what's the g. 279:7
when I'm g. . . . I'm better 352:11
you've never had it so g. 218:13
Goodbye: g.-ee . . . wipe the tear 353:3
G. to All That 139:12
Goodness: forgo the . . . privilege of g. 349:8
g. had nothing . . . to do with it 352:1
seductive power of g. 51:5
true g. . . . clear-sightedness 62:16
Good Soldier: G. is the finest French novel 284:5
Gospel: no use for the policy of the G.s 184:10
Gossip: all the world's g. 270:13
g. as formalized as incantation 116:11
parrot to the town g. 285:12
Gothic: G. . . . all revolt and aspiration 52:23
G. architecture . . . one of the strangest 78:6
you mustn't drift into G. 125:24
Gott: G. Mit Uns . . . had gloves 98:1
o du verlorener G. 282:12
Govern: *all* will g. in turn 201:7
consciousness . . . does not g. 341:10
g. is to control the implementation 316:2
g. is to choose 230:16
too wise to try to g. the world 97:11
Governess: does a tremendous lot for her old g.es 273:8
nation of g.es 306:9
tutelage of g.es 155:18
Government: against g. by crony 165:2
all G.s are selfish and the French 106:4
duty of Her Majesty's g. 219:1
every g. . . . a health warning 16:2
g. . . . big enough to give you all 134:12
g. burns down cities 222:11
g. by mass bribery 166:5
G. has made small slips 122:3
g. . . . requires it to come 335:19
G. . . . should have its old speeches 311:5
I just watch the g. 285:1
I work for a G. I despise 183:18
like to see the g. get out of war 150:23
mutually antagonistic g.s 347:2
no form of g. common to 347:9
only good g. . . . is a bad one 65:17
our G. of gentlemen 133:16
politician . . . understands g. 335:14
things which g. does for them 345:9

wanting you to form a g. 307:12
worst g. is the most moral 230:1
Government House: austerity . . . at G. 89:5
House: sun never sets on G. 89:9
Gown: my sweet little Alice blue g. 214:14
Goyim: doesn't matter what the g. say 143:12
Grabby: they are too g. 286:19
Grace: g. under pressure 151:14
you had the g. to hold 325:11
Gracehoper: G. was always jigging a jog 177:17
Gradient: an altered g. 22:9
Graduate: of course they g. the best 98:14
Graffiti: education . . . g. lower 331:11
Grail: as if the Holy G. were just round the corner 248:6
do with the G. when they found it 33:3
if living isn't a seeking for the g. 115:21
Grammar: we don't talk fancy g. 250:19
Grandad: G. . . . got three notches 99:21
Grandchild: had a g. instead 208:20
Grandchildren: never have children, only g. 343:4
Grandeur: delusions of g., but you're deluded 167:20
Grandog: g. 330:2
Grandson: your g. will be a Communist 184:3
Grape: peel me a g. 352:5
refused to eat g.s 13:7
Graphic: read anything except the G. 216:9
significant figure in g. art 211:17
Grasmere: no visit to . . . G. is complete 87:2
Grass: car park with a g. roof 24:6
g. grows green on the battlefield 73:10
g. . . . on the Front Bench 21:14
is the g. emptier now 37:3
Gratification: denial of the g. of a vital need 279:5
Gratitude: debt of g. . . . to Adam 336:10
g. looks to the past 205:13
only thing worse than . . . g. 112:17
Grave: between the cradle and the g. lies 157:14
bore; even the g. yawns 333:14
by my g. you'd pray to have me back 64:17
climbs into their g.s married 356:4
fearful of the certain g. 225:14
festive season and we . . . muse upon g.s 174:5
foot in the g. . . . the other three 356:14
funny thing that happened . . . to the g. 90:22
g.'s narrowness, though not its peace 139:4
grip of the G. 186:24
have their g.s at home 68:17
now I'm dead in the g. 220:16
O g., keep shut 225:15
over this damp g. 284:7
pretence of following to the g. 124:11
were alive he'd turn in his g. 135:6
Gravestone: make arrangements for my g. 180:16
Graveyard: handsome slab in the g. 240:13
no bone to pick with g.s 31-2
Gravity: liquidation of g. 188:16

Great: g. men of history are frauds 45:3
g. man . . . makes every man feel g. 69:22
g. man walks across his century 198:17
g. men of history 290:12
g. . . . witness catastrophes from a terrace 132:26
he was nothing but a g. man 163:20
it's g. to be g. 284:16
not good but g. . . . neither 343:1
secretaries to make themselves look g. 46:10
some . . . bad. But they are all g. 136:9
Great Britain: B. could say she supported 216:6
B. defending itself 285:24
B. has lost an Empire 9:7
courtesy . . . taken refuge in B. 103:3
Greater: I am g. than the stars 326:18
Greece: whole story of G. and Rome 37:15
Greed: need but not for everyone's g. 56:14
Greek: G. . . . taught very badly 350:19
G.s found everything human 194:14
G.s Had a Word For It 10:6
he is more G. than . . . ever 233:10
he knew G. 306:17
nobody can say a word against G. 303:28
uncertainty . . . unknown to the G.s 46:14
Green: g. bloomers . . . g. is a lovely shade 102:7
g. how I love you g. 128:19
Greene, Graham: 214:16, 347:25
Greening: The G. of America 279:4
Greeting: 'how are you' is a g., not 143:2
Grey: the g. dorianed out of it 339:21
Grief: between g. and nothing . . . take g. 112:16
g. develops the powers of the mind 274:9
king of my g.s 19:14
no man can cause more g. 112:15
oldest g.s of summer 280:16
Grievance: habit of not magnifying g.s 281:2
her g. for the day 221:15
Grieving: I am g., for his sake 147:14
Griffith, D. W.: 359:15
Grill: careful not to look like a mixed g. 88:15
Grim: even if it's g., we'll bare it 244:7
Grin: emitting minute g.s 92:2
Grindstone: wounded bosom against a g. 305:3
Gripe: Mookse and the G.s 177:7
Groan: g.s of love 212:12
poets g. in rhymes 344:1
Grocer: who hath seen the G. 69:2
Grotesque: like being ambushed by a g. 320:5
working classes . . . as g.s 347:14
Ground: g. broke me fall 234:18
Group: setting before the g. . . the individual 109:25
Grouse: if I were a g. I'd appeal 86:13
g.s . . . them's grice 342:8
Grow: do not g. up gradually 83:23
generals . . . never g. out of it 339:5
Grown: lampshades Myrtle has g. out of 307:16

Grown-up: g. and have to pay for it 357:1
g.s never understand 292:12
novels for g. people 364:13
when g.s agree 187:14
Grub: g. first, then ethics 52:7
g. . . . may become a queen 77:17
poor g., poor pay 210:16
what i mean is g. 222:14
Grudge: all the typical g.s 270:10
Gruel: I started living on g. 262:13
G-strings: converting dog collars into G. 35:16
Guarantee: these three g.s 209:13
Guard: be in the Horse G.s and still be common 277.7
Guard, Civil: 128:17
civil g. . . . secret hard-hatted race 64:9
Guardian: G. is read by the people 11:3
Guardsmen: touched, as G. sometimes are 161:15
Guerre: que la g. est jolie 19:7
Guerrilla: g. fights the war of the flea 325:1
g. swims like a fish 222:10
g. wins 188:5
in g. war the struggle 112:6
Guest: few g.s who had . . . been invited 116:2
g.s must be chosen as carefully as the wine 292:19
receiving her husband's g.s 293:22
sink my yacht to make my g.s go 117:2
Guesties: Oooo, g. 330:19
Guide: made me the g. of the nation 129:19
Guilt: put on a dress of g. 216:14
suspicious of g. in myself 151:4
true g. is g. at the obligation 192:11
Guilty: make any woman with them look g. 116:26
wants to know . . . Who's G. 55:6
Guinea: g. pigs in the laboratory of God 357:20
Guinness: 10:20
beside a glass of G. on a sunny day 140:10
read in the first chapter of G.'es 176:13
Gull: g. colony . . . tiny black spectacles 64:12
Gum: can't fart and chew g. at the same time 175:10
Gun: cock the g. that is not loaded 185:8
difference between a g. and a tree 269:22
fired their g.s at Lowestoft 86:5
grows out of the barrel of a g. 222:1
'G.s?' said Betty Flanders 365:7
ironic g.s 19:13
rutted . . . by the passing g.s 225:13
some men rob you with a six g. 143:14
they got the g.s 241:9
to get rid of the g. 222:2
when I hear the word 'g.' 135:15
Gunfire: g. has always sounded unreal 339:14
Gunga Din: 185:12
Gunpowder: blow your mind – smoke g. 136:12
Guru: G. gives himself 136:7
Guts: I admire your g. 235:2
Gutter: other foot in the g. 274:16

Guy: g.s and dolls engaged in . . . guzzling 288:12
  g.s using false pretences 289:13
Guzzling: little offhand g. 288:12
Gym: flare was up in the g. 40:16
Gypsy: sad as a g. 231:3

H

Haar: schon aufgelöst wie langes H. 282:7
Habit: cocaine isn't h.-forming 27:14
  h. alone upholds 365:9
  h. is a second nature 274:3
  pulling h.s out of rats 58:10
  reconciling my gross h.s with my net 118:6
Haddock: h. with lung-trouble 362:8
Hades: phonographs of h. in the brain 89:25
Haig, Earl: 30:7, 210:2
Hair: babies haven't any h. 157:14
  cutting each other's h. 43:10
  everyone grew their h. 25:10
  h. and forehead furnished a recessional note 293:1
  h. was the most important thing 252:4
  loosened like long h. 282:7
  time had removed the h. 380:1
  you can cut your own h. 86:6
Haircut: lies a h. and a shave 157:14
Half-pint: finished his h. . . . with the 169:4
Halibut: another h. to lend it a quid 361:22
Halo: h. . . . one more thing to keep clean 125:12
  life is a luminous h. 364:17
Hamilton: another Lady H. 280:3
Hamlet: Afrikaans for 'H., I am' 173:17
  decline an invitation to *H.* . . . knew who won 90:19
  H. is . . . rooted in . . . incest-complex 122:14
  H. . . . should have done it 53:7
Hammer: art is . . . a hammer 228:17
  Maxwell's Silver H. 202:20
Hammock: she slept in a h. 293:5
Hampstead: H. had . . . to confess 170:18
Hand: always finds somebody for idle h.s 152:11
  bites the h. that lays the golden egg 135:5
  cease to use your h.s 255:17
  enjoy biting the h. that feeds 142:7
  golden h.s he's got 87:6
  H. . . . a singular instrument 42:19
  h. . . . cutting edge of the mind 54:3
  h.s grumble on the door 327:18
  I hold your h. in mine 200:7
  I still have my right h. 234:9
  if I start to hold somebody's h. 115:16
  moonlight than your moist h. 317:21
  picking thievish h.s 187:10
  put your h. into the h. of God 148:12
  that's not the h. I dealt you 242:7
  their h.s minutely answered 92:10
  when your friend holds . . . both h.s 42:29

Handel, G. F.: Coromandel dance . . . H. 308:15
Handshake: h.s can be faked 321:9
Hang-gliding: 18:11
Hanging: cured by h. from a string 184:17
  they're h. Danny Deever 185:3
Hansard: H. is history's ear 295:6
Happen: h.s and does not . . . unhappen 46:5
  the thing that was to h. 170:7
  whatever can h. *will* h. 156:20
Happened: the fact that it had h. elsewhere 120:12
Happening: worrying . . . what's h. now 25:3
Happiness: but if this be not h. 328:25
  fatal to true h. 290:1
  h. . . . . *captivity to love* 123:12
  h. comes uninvited 190:10
  h. . . . imaginary condition 323:15
  h. is . . . a by-product 162:11
  h. is a mystery like religion 70:17
  H. is a Warm Gun 202:15
  h. is beneficial for the body 274:9
  h. is never really so welcome 141:4
  h. is the only sanction of life 296:1
  h. of every man . . . each man 342:11
  if you don't have h. 278:19
  never knew the price of h. 369:13
  there is enough h. in life 260:10
  to understand the nature of h. 311:19
Happy: almost a h. day 312:11
  anyone h. in this age 126:10
  few people can be h. 291:7
  h. people are failures 73:3
  h. so long as he chooses to be h. 311:12
  many are h. much of the time 319:17
  men are h. because they are miserable 122:1
  must imagine Sisyphus h. 62:4
  never h. unless . . . miserable 17:24
  the days that make us h. 225:14
Hard: h. question is simple 22:23
  you mean she led a h. life 310:20
Hardy, Thomas: 109:22
  Mr H. has written the worst 239:4
Hare: elegant h.s at play 95:17
Harlot: found h.s cheaper than hotels 269:9
  prerogative of the h. 26:17
  society which pays a h. 358:21
Harlow, Jean: *t* is silent as in H. 21:10
Harmony: h. imposes compatibility 230:18
Harp: plucking at their h.s 185:23
Harpsichord: h. resembles . . . a bird-cage 31:19
Harrow: worthy to pass into H. 74:19
Harvest-home: shot up a roaring h. 44:5
Hat: going without a h. 25:10
  h.s divide generally 354:20
  instinctively raise my h. 333:11
  other one's h.s 208:10
  stamped . . . with the h.-raising habit 350:10
Hate: anybody who h.s children and dogs 114:12
  each sequestered in its h. 22:5
  everybody h.s me because I'm . . . liked 98:13
  h. some other person . . . or creed 291:7

how much men h. them 141:12
when the English began to h. 184:22
you h. . . . part of yourself 153:17
Hated: I never h. a man enough to give 127:2
Hathaway: Anne H.'s cottage 192:15
Hatred: deep burning h. for the Tory Party
  41:17
  h. . . . high psychological dividend 166:9
  intellectual h. is the worst 368:17
  united by . . . h. of its neighbours 166:4
  what we need is h. 129:20
Haunt: this h. of brooding dust 96:19
Haus: wo einmal ein dauerndes H. war 281:18
Hawk: dark h.s near us 177:13
  yellow-eyed h. of the mind 368:12
Hawthorn: at Mrs Greenland's H. Bush
  329:2
He: word which meant both 'h.' and 'she'
  236:9
Head: a real good h. is . . . round 246:15
  astonishing tangle within our h.s 43:13
  how many times can a man turn his h.
    104:20
  I've examined your son's h. 244:4
  keep your h. 182:21
  need a h. . . . when he's got genius 168:11
  [people's] h.s fall off 277:1
  that so many people have h.s 158:4
  their h. is . . . inefficient 228:2
  with the two h.s 258:15
  woman saving her h. 366:2
Headache: Mme Verdurin . . . suffered from
  h.s 274:7
Headline: story to fit this sensational h. 242:9
  they foamed at the h. 350:22
Headmaster: h.s have powers 74:22
Headmistress: headmaster . . . was a h. 27:17
Headstone: the h.s yield their names 325:6
Health: disliked hearing about h. 237:11
  h. of a writer should not be too good
    83:17
  h., you worry about 100:4
  universal sickness . . . idea of h. 333:20
Healthy: h. and wealthy and dead 331:1
He-ancient: the h. 305:1
Hear: can still *h.* a pretty girl 331:7
  can you h. me, mother 270:18
Heard: I have already h. it 282:19
  you ain't h. nothin' yet 175:16
Hearing: h., so none hear 21:17
Heart: darkness of man's h. 134:7
  Edith Evans – . . . open a window to her h.
    280:8
  except for an occasional h. attack 36:14
  . . . funeral marches round your h. 232:16
  he gets a beautiful h. 323:5
  half as many h.s lost to her 32:8
  he's had a change of h. 224:11
  h.-break in the h. of things 131:8
  h. gives up its dead 328:2
  h. may think it knows better 47:2
  h.'s grown brutal 368:16
  h.s that we broke long ago 22:28
  I can feel his h. beating 239:17
  it hides within – a tender h. 240:7

kinship of h. to h. 311:12
love thee for a h. that's kind 95:5
my h. belongs to Daddy 267:21
no iron can stab the h. 25:1
one has only need of a h. 129:1
one well-kept hand . . . to his h. 171:4
only with the H. that one can see 292:14
process in the weather of the h. 328:1
solution . . . lies in the h. of humankind
  108:2
Some Day My H. Will Awake 148:13
some men break your h. in two 259:6
their h.'s in the right place 228:2
they never were in better h. 144:1
way to a man's h. 12:5
wear my h. where God put it 116:17
what can a tired h. say 96:12
when the h. dictates the line 261:7
will not have softening of the h. 71:24
Heartless: never . . . h. when it is not necessary
  154:9
Heat: white h. of this revolution 359:1
Heath, Edward: 188:14
Heathen: hard for a h. to overcome 284:20
  h. in 'is blindness 185:4
Higgins is a H. 69:6
Heather: the same as when I roved the h.
  95:18
Heaven: cold and rook-delighting h. 368:7
  doors of h. and hell 181:17
  enter H. by a back door 129:7
  from the nave build haunted h. 317:15
  gates of h. 208:4
  go to H. without being . . . qualified 303:7
  h. goes in for something more dependable
    65:13
  H. has gone comprehensive 20:10
  H. he won't last long 351:12
  H. is the . . . rock unrolled 341:13
  h. presents in sheets the . . . hue 124:8
  I don't believe in h. or hell 260:11
  it's the Hebrew in H. 114:16
  road from h. to Hereford 68:16
  streets of h. have all been sold 143:13
  without you, H. would be too dull 314:1
Heaving: he was confined to h.s 187:16
Hebrew: it's the H. in Heaven 114:16
Hedgehog: throwing h.s under me 184:9
Hefner, Hugh: 16:24
Hegel, G. F. W.: laws of our old H. 274:6
Height: h.s by great men reached 307:5
  I have flown to star-stained h.s 271:6
Heineken: H. Refreshes the parts 10:18
Heinz: Beanz Meanz H. 10:10
Heir: kings . . . will have no h.s 282:17
Heiress: an American h. 215:3
Heisenberg: H. probably rules O.K. 136:19
Held: war er nicht H. schon in dir 281:15
  wunderlich nah ist der H. 281:14
Helen: H. is shingled 241:17
Hell: all schools are h., nor are we out 86:9
  creator of h. upon earth 176:18
  done away with H. 20:10
  doors of heaven and h. 181:17
  fear of h. is h. itself 131:8

Hell – *Contd.*
h. ... good intentions, but heaven 65:13
H. is other people 296:14
H. is time arrested 341:13
h. lay about him in his infancy 140:12
h. must be ... small chat 30:14
H. of Too Many People 271:15
H. will not be H. if you are there 314:1
H.'s full at last 17:11
if Hitler invaded H. 76:13
made an excursion to h. 271:16
mean by 'Very good' is 'Go to h.' 88:7
merger between Heaven and H. 351:12
next stop's H. 274:11
of course there's H. 140:11
sat ... in front of H. Fire 330:8
shall look on Helen's face in h. 259:1
stirrup pump can extinguish h. 277:15
they put themselves in h. 297:23
they were mad about h. 14:15
walked eye-deep in h. 269:7
wishful thinking in H. 205:11
Hello: gives me a medium h. 289:8
Help: lie ... very present h. 318:1
little h. from my friends 203:3
only h. one of your luckless brothers 51:13
Helpful: h. as throwing ... both ends 25:5
Helplessness: feminine h. came into fashion
81:18
He-man: be a real h. 10:9
Hen: might have been a farmyard h. 24:13
Henry I: H. ... on lots of family trees 92:23
Henry VIII: a sort of cross between H. 117:1
I'm H. I am 245:2
Hereford: where the apple wood of H. 68:16
Heresies: religions are kept alive by h. 52:20
Heritage: shall rule his h. 186:30
whole varied h. of culture 70:7
Hermit: first-class carriage is a place of ...
h.s 71:4
Hero: being a h. is the shortest-lived 284:21
h. inside you 281:15
h. is strangely akin 281:14
h. keeps getting in bed 287:5
H. ... who robs a bank 358:2
h. ... would argue with the Gods 220:2
I'm a h. from the waist up 234:19
no h. is mortal till he dies 23:3
on land I am a h., but on water 155:16
show me a h. and I will write 116:21
they don't want to be a h. 320:15
Heroes: h. ... glorify a life which they 132:14
speed ... h. up the line to death 298:1
unhappy the land ... in need of h. 51:10
Heroism: vices ... fathered by our h. 109:3
Hibernation: stirring ... from long h. 138:20
Hick: Sticks Nix H.s Pix 342:1
Hidden: like both lying and the h. 61:22
Hide: prefer lying to having nothing to h.
61:22
Hiesiger: ist er ein H. 282:8
Highball: three h.s and I think I'm St Francis
258:8
Highbrow: 365:16
h.s lived in this cottage 270:9

Highland: join a H. regiment 226:3
Hill: h.s are alive with the sound 146:7
sleep on his h. again 208:6
those blue remembered h.s 159:6
Himmler, Heinrich: H. of the lower fifth 277:5
Himself: being by h. 288:10
Hindenburg, General von: draw von H.'s
features 208:3
Hindsight: h. is always twenty-twenty 356:2
scientific method has ... been ... 20-20 h.
265:9
Hip: when your h.s stick 247:17
Hippopotamus: American women shoot the
h. 119:2
anybody except another h. 287:4
h. ... an enormous mistake 69:25
h.'s day is passed in sleep 109:5
naturalness of the h. 239:9
Hire purchase: 147:9
Hiroshima: genius of Einstein leads to H.
264:3
Historian: for the h. ... the chocolate-box
135:14
h.s are like deaf people 332:4
history repeats ... h.s repeat 142:20
how men who are not h.s behave 119:15
profession of h. fits a man 296:15
to predict ... the work of an h. 165:13
unwelcome to h.s, but ... true 326:5
Historically: people think too h. 53:6
History: 118:12
anthropologist respects h. 204:15
caught unawares by ... h. 334:9
crucial in European h. 245:9
English h. is all about men 49:1
have discerned in h. a plot 115:10
h. advances in disguise 96:4
H. had created something new 35:10
H. has many cunning passages 109:2
h. ... has occasional dead spots 217:11
h. has to use second-hand timber 160:4
h. has united you ... and the Duce 121:6
h. is in the shit sense 55:3
H. is so attractive to the ... timid 119:16
h. is the endless repetition 104:11
h. is to be free at once 47:9
h. is too serious 217:12
H. must not be written with bias 41:11
h. need not have bothered 156:6
H. ... not neglect the known facts 38:16
h. of revolutions 201:1
h. presents a ... gap 285:15
h. repeats itself ... farce 19:1
h. ... thicker as it approaches 325:14
H. will absolve me 66:7
in h. lie like bones 24:1
keep h. and theology apart 350:21
like most of those who study h. 326:3
man is a h.-making creature 23:16
memories ... thread to hang h. from 318:16
more h. than they can consume locally
293:6
New York ... h. of the world 351:1
our goal is to again influence h. 182:10
sailing with the tide of h. 49:3

sense of h. .... divides good economics
  128:2
sphere of h. 201:13
splendid moment in our great h. 74:7
there is no h. of mankind 267:2
they are unloading h. 76:15
this was the Angel of H. 133:18
to have dined at the table of h. 66:3
writing h. with lightning 359:15
Hit: h. a woman with his hat on 12:19
  h. that one thing alone 359:9
Hitler, Adolf: 18:7, 121:6
  approved of H. in so much 86:15
  every time H. occupies a country 245:13
  going to string old H. 114:3
  Herr H. has one of the ... characteristics
    248:16
  H. has carried out a revolution 245:10
  H. ... missed the bus 67:7
  H. never understood ... the British 57:3
  H. showed ... loyalty to Mussolini 57:4
  H. has a substantive 219:17
  H., who had done such a great job 150:11
  I thank heaven for ... H. 56:15
  tipster who only reached H.'s level of
    acuracy 326:1
Hitlerism: H. is ... of Jewish origin 72:24
Hobbit: there lived a h. 332:1
Hobby: my only h. is laziness 248:1
  ornithology ... an arcane h. 45:15
Hobby-horse: democracy is like a h. 295:4
Hog: been the whole h. 264:21
  on the back of his own whole h. 129:11
  one disadvantage of being a h. 241:19
Holds: various h. and rolls and throws 277:19
Hole: smallest h. ... hide his head in 71:20
  square peg in a square h. 159:21
  what happens to the h. 51:26
Holiday: I should prescribe a h. 289:20
Holiness: road to h. .... through the world
  145:15
  your H., is a Roman Catholic 73:5
Holland, H. Scott: 248:6
Holler: no day passes but ... I h. 151:16
Hollingsworth: from whose Bourne no H.
  returns 242:17
Hollywood: 30:3, 157:15, 238:2
  H. buys a good story 16:13
  H. is like being nowhere 19:6
  H. money isn't money 260:2
  H. people are afraid to leave 279:8
  H. seems to want a writer who 67:15
  H. .... the false fronts 17:20
  in H., if you don't have happiness 278:19
  invited to H. .... should not have come
    67:17
  strip the tinsel off H. 204:4
Holy: H. Ghost having evaporated 100:12
  not the fault of the h. 54:15
Home: came h., h. to a lie 269:7
  Englishman's ... h. is the bank's 129:2
  feel to be without a h. 105:1
  h. .... they have to take you in 124:6
  it was not a h. 206:13
  out of all remembrance, make our h. 97:1

rape, sodomy ... can get all that at h.
  85:12
she's leaving h. 202:24
thy stately h.s of England 196:5
won't you come h. Bill Bailey 63:11
you will be h. before the leaves 356:20
Homer: Cicero and many-minded H. 368:15
  either H. or ... of the same name 161:22
  Gladstone read H. .... served him right
    74:21
  I've never read a line of H. 233:10
  when H. smote 'is ... lyre 187:2
Homesick: some vague western whiff, h. 169:13
Home-sickness: in h. you must keep moving
  315:17
Homicidal: great h. classics 320:4
  spoke with h. eloquence 298:7
Homo: ape self-named H. sapiens 241:5
  'h.' is the ... child 207:22
  one of the stately h.s 90:21
Homosexual: problem which confronts h.s
  90:17
Homosexuality: 238:12
Honest: h. to the verge of simplicity 26:12
  I am one of the few h. people 116:4
  it is a fine thing to be h. but 77:18
  then they get h. 285:14
  to love outside the law ... be h. 104:16
Honesty: make my h. questionable 285:2
  only thing ... that demands h. 353:9
Honey: small boy smeared with h. 262:6
  h. or condensed milk 236:7
Honeysuckle: you are my honey, h. 115:13
Honour: have trodden it with h. 75:21
  h. .... necessity for hall-porters 70:23
  H.s List ... the rabble 67:1
  vivid air signed with their h. 314:17
  we're fighting for this woman's h. 224:13
  ye take mine h. from me 185:21
Hoof: out pops the cloven h. 361:6
Hooligan: H. was probably invented in China
  293:15
Hoorah Henry: without ... doubt a H. 289:15
Hoover, J. Edgar: 175:7
Hope: distinction between h. and expectation
  165:11
  he who holds h.s ... is a fool 62:8
  h. is the power of being cheerful 70:20
  h. so transcendent 198:1
  in the store we sell h. 279:15
  wildest h. of a healthy person 72:23
Hope, Bob: nothing ... I wouldn't to for H.
  91:10
Hopeful: h. disposition is not the sole 73:15
Hörenden: sind wir die H. jetzt 282:12
Horizon: over the cage floor the h.s 160:5
Horizontal: none but the h. one 21:20
Horlicks: H. guards against Night Starvation
  249:2
Horn: all your butter is in your h.s 177:5
  it won't come out of your h. 258:4
Horoscope: balancing the h.s of two elevens
  160:15
Horrible: no wonder ... were so h. 14:12
  not, at the same time, h. 264:3

425

Horror: no imagination there is no h. 101:21
Horse: 117:24
    Ascot . . . the h.s own the people 56:16
    backed the right h. . . . the wrong 175:17
    bring on the empty h.s 92:27
    don't . . . frighten the h.s 61:1
    don't give your son . . . give him h.s 75:3
    good rocking-h. 214:13
    grey gun-h.s in the lando 186:12
    h. would steal the act 16:17
    h.s for courses 267:7
    I'll never look at any other h. 224:7
    ignorant about the H. 301:4
    it takes courage to ride a h. 198:20
    like an old h. in a pound 368:20
    looking like a h. 258:6
    looking the gift h. in the mouthfulness
        280:4
    my husband, but not my h. 195:20
    names associated with race h.s 293:11
    no handles to a h. 198:19
    of a man his h. 221:12
    rather wet for the h.s 235:16
    SIXTY H.S WEDGED IN A CHIMNEY
        242:9
    to bet on a certain h. 288:7
    white h. . . . could be a zebra 173:6
Horseman: drumming the plain, the h. is
    coming 128:18
Horsepower: h. . . . only horses had it 16:14
Hosanna: pulse pizzicati of H. 317:18
Hose: dream of wellfilled h. 176:20
Hospitable: father is a very h. man 302:3
Hospital: alive . . . and out of h. 30:11
    big h. at Denmark Hill 298:8
    I shall subscribe to h.s 81:9
Hospitality: h. is a wonderful thing 116:23
Host: h. with someone indistinct 109:14
    I'd have been under the h. 259:20
Hostess: The H. with the Mostes' 39:15
Hostility: h. comes easiest to us 281:8
    h. finally tore you 282:12
    noticed your h. towards him 48:15
Hot: English have h.-water bottles 232:2
    imprisoned in a h.-water bottle 217:5
    you give a h. foot 288:13
Hotel: country around their h.s 231:14
    he keeps six h.s 302:3
    written in h.s with the bed unmade 114:23
Hot-pants: one of these h. athletes 310:22
Hound: H. that caught the Pubic Hare 33:8
House: 'aving h.s built by men 350:12
    bringing up a young . . . h. 174:1
    darkness inside h.s I don't like 97:4
    discover his h. to be in flames 50:19
    h. . . . smaller than Buckingham Palace
        67:11
    h. . . . with intellectual elbow-room 170:5
    H. with the Seven Gables 243:16
    h.s . . . looked like a . . . row 217:6
    man in the h. is worth 351:21
    old man in a draughty h. 109:1
    people who live in large h.s shouldn't
        87:15
    this h. is jealous of its nastiness 138:16

    those night-hung h.s 96:21
    whose h. were you 141:2
House, Colonel E.: 147:4
House-agent: the h. simply takes 350:13
Household: stables . . . real centre of the h.
    305:5
Housekeeper: make a h. think she's 356:10
Housemaid: if you're nice to the . . . h. 170:6
Housewife: any honest h. would sort 139:1
    good h. . . . knew how to hash 162:5
Housework: h. . . . expands to fill the time
    85:9
    no need to do any h. 90:20
Howe, Sir Geoffrey: 149:4
Howl: I hear a famisht h. 40:5
Howth: back to H. Castle 177:1
Hubris: H. clobbered by Nemesis 12:11
Hue: left thee all her lovely h.s 95:2
Huff: you can leave in a h. 224:8
Hughes, Howard: 180:1
Hugo, Victor: H. – alas 131:11
    H. was a madman 79:16
    man who . . . thought he was H. 297:11
Human: all h. life is here 248:12
    any h. being should believe 290:9
    bound to stop loving h.s too 311:13
    but he's a h. being 232:22
    decent attitude towards . . . h. animals 154:9
    had had h. authors was a source of hope
        162:16
    hopes for the h. condition is a fool 62:8
    H. Bean 250:21
    h. being: an ingenious assembly 240:10
    h. being is no longer the unit 217:14
    H. Beings are an untidy lot 38:18
    h. beings are simply archaic 272:7
    h. beings, those obstinate creatures 311:10
    h. beings were invented 283:3
    h. nature . . . too much like my own 100:2
    h. society from the farm-yard 305:25
    inverse ratio to the number of h. beings 163:1
    it is better to be a H. Being 276:4
    not injure a h. being 20:17
    only good h. being is a dead one 254:8
    other h. beings . . . as h. as oneself 332:17
    poetry must be h. 12:14
    somewhere . . . is the form of a h. being
        364:11
    whether he'll live among h. beings 356:18
Humanitarianism: h. . . . mark of an inhuman
    time 70:5
Humanity: all h. is jam to you 194:6
    greater h. than the European 215:5
    hate 'H.' . . . but I love people 61:4
    historic ascent of h. 334:20
    h. . . . a work in progress 357:20
    h. does not pass 205:20
    H. i love you 92:5
    h. is . . . only beginning its course 165:16
    h. might . . . somehow be made 162:16
    octopus of h. 195:8
    that unremitting h. 37:14
Humble: feel 'h.' in the presence 295:3
Humbug: helpful part that h. plays 75:4
    h. themselves and one another 350:17

pitch ... at which h. can be dropped 254:21
plenty of h. in hell 303:6
Humdrum: allowance ... the gay make to the
   h. 293:9
Hume, David: H. ... wanted to get at the
   truth 290:19
Humility: aim at h., there is no guarantee
   99:17
   quite brilliant h. 125:9
   teach drivers modesty and h. 231:18
   treat [information] with h. 54:7
Humorist(s): 330:10
   difficulty with h.s 338:16
   h.s are not happy men 83:15
Humour: cynicism is h. in ill-health 351:8
   height of silent h. 138:19
   h. ... based on destruction 56:1
   h. undiluted ... most depressing 32:3
   I like h. dry 311:4
   prove ... no sense of h. 370:2
   ridiculous, but no sense of h. 12:4
   very low ... sort of h. 139:16
Hump: Roman Caesar ... under this h.
   368:19
Humphrey: here's H., everybody 344:10
Humpty Dumpty: H. ... fell with a roll 177:3
Hunchback: the h. in the park 327:19
Hundred: man of about a h. and fifty 361:20
Hunger: attack on the problem of h. 249:14
   war against h. 182:1
Hungry: known what it was like to be h. 193:5
Hurled: h. with my books ... across the sky
   309:19
Hurly-burly: the h. of the chaise-longue 61:2
Hurrying: all that is h. will soon be past
   282:11
Hurt: must stay here with my h. 329:16
Husband: chumps always make the best h.s
   360:3
   expect to find in their h.s 228:6
   finding a h. for one's mistress 86:17
   h. the landscape 52:18
   make a man a good h. 226:14
   one h. too many 15:18
   sneaking a look at her h. 17:20
   you may have my h. 195:20
Huxley, Aldous: 365:15
Hyde Park: H.'s not country 24:6
Hygiene: h. is the corruption of medicine 230:7
Hypocrisy: h. is the most difficult ... vice
   227:12
   world safe for h. 364:6
Hypocrite: to see far enough into a h. 70:16
   true h. ... ceases to perceive 131:10
Hypothesis: discard a pet h. 211:15

I

I: great love ... I was always the object
   61:17
   I am you ... what have we done 82:7
Ibsen, Henrik: I.? Bricks without Shaw 49:14
   I. had probably never seen 350:5

Ice: as though i. burned 368:7
   broken i.; Heaven's gates 103:20
   i. is breaking up 34:16
   there with i. floes all around her 118:3
Iceberg: we are like i.s 130:10
Ice-cream: emperor of i. 317:14
   never try to lick i. 300:3
Icthyosaur: in favour of the i. 351:14
Id: i. by the odd 17:19
   put the i. back in yid 287:14
Ida: I. never sighed 316:14
   more and more to be I. 316:18
Idea: better to entertain an i. than 172:12
   can seldom follow up an original i. 84:14
   country ... founded on a good i. 143.8
   genius ... has two great i.s 54:9
   good i. – son 58:16
   green i.s sleep furiously 73:2
   hatred. From it our i.s are born 129:20
   his own i. of himself 195:7
   i. isn't responsible 223:3
   i.s can be too old 256:15
   i.s ... importance than values 52:13
   i.s that enter the mind under fire 334:21
   in pursuit of an i. 365:16
   it is the same with i.s 216:5
   it would be a good i. to give 345:5
   let the i. die instead 207:16
   makes people into i.s 365:15
   morality which is based on i.s 194:16
   not had a new i. for ... twenty years
      174:10
   not usually our i.s that make 338:3
   only put i.s into your head 21:4
   powerful i. communicates 272:16
   she's only got two i.s in her head 208:11
   terribly wrong i. 45:2
   war of i.s 199:14
   we lose ... our i.s 30:16
Ideal: i. ... owns you 67:16
   i.s. He'll pick up those 119:9
   shoes with broken high i.s 216:14
   tell the i.s ... by its advertisements 100:17
Idealism: close grips with so-called i. 229:17
   whether the narcotic be ... or i. 178:7
Idealist: I am an i. 295:14
   Jesus is not an i. 219:3
Idée: une certaine i. de la France 129:12
Identification: even a wishful i. 215:2
Ideological: nuance in an i. difference 82:11
Ideologies: all i. are relative 132:7
Idiocy: death and i. 196:2
Idiosyncrasies: style reflects one's i. 106:1
Idiot: training for being an i. 344:11
Idol: one-eyed yellow i. 148:19
   would be an i. 46:3
Idolator: he who slays a king and he who dies
   ... i.s 302:19
Ignorance: dead languages ... i. of life 333:5
   evil ... comes of i. 62:16
   evil ... i. bumping its head 118:13
   full area of i. 40:2
   i. of the art of war 301:2
   inhibited by i. 219:2
   our i. must ... be infinite 266:16

Ignorant: everybody is i. 285:8
if girls aren't i., they're cultured 86:16
Iliad: I. . . . it's in the *Marmion* class 148:3
question of the authorship of the *I.* 161:22
Ilion: I. is safe 241:17
Ill: for what human i. does not dawn 356:3
only half there when I am i. 197:12
very i. I couldn't work, sleep 152:6
we are all i. 333:20
Illegal: that means it is not i. 250:6
Illegitimate: there are no i. children 368:2
twenty i. children before he married 92:23
Illiterate: film is . . . art of . . . i.s 153:16
i.s can read 239:16
Illness: his i. . . . hope it's nothing trivial 79:7
i. is the doctor 274:1
i. is the night-side of life 313:5
i. is what the world has done 230:17
Ill-treating: i., beating, cheating 52:10
Illumination: support rather than i. 193:1
Illusion: is it i. or the revelation 162:1
it was the i. they loved 227:19
it's life's i.s I recall 237:1
just one i. . . . no good 89:13
whole affair was an i. 240:8
work gives . . . i. of existing 162:8
Image: culture . . . shows man his i. 297:22
delivering the i. from its prison 249:9
receiving i.s which are arranged 39:6
see beyond its own i. 182:7
they . . . bind you to an image 282:16
thinks in i.s, not in concepts 145:3
visual i. of ourselves 196:8
Imaginary: which belongs entirely to the i.
281:18
Imagination: deep places of the i. 333:21
generosity . . . nourishes his i. 312:4
give up their innate i. 192:7
hidden . . . by the wall of i. 143:9
his i., his reason 53:15
i. must be . . . disciplined 270:8
i. without skill . . . modern art 319:4
in Paris the i. reacted 169:9
nature of the human i. 54:10
to inherit the moral i. 54:8
to strip our pleasures of i. 273:5
until i., ear and eye 368:22
where there is no i. 101:21
Imagine: Evil cannot i. Good 23:11
Imitate: original woman . . . i.s a man 323:6
Imitation: give them his every i. 358:12
man . . . is an i. 256:16
Immature: i. man . . . wants to die nobly 317:6
Immolation: was ever an i. so belied 298:4
Immoral: i., illegal, or fattening 365:22
worse than i., it's a mistake 9:8
Immorality: most rigid code of i. 48:8
Immortal: i. . . . has to forget he is mortal
132:18
meanest man is i. 72:12
Immortality: imagine God without man's i.
62:6
i. of the soul 241:14
i. . . . through not dying 13:26
millions long for i. who do not know 111:6

Impartial: i. as between the fire brigade
77:11
Imperialism: Europeanism . . . i. with an
inferiority complex 149:3
i. is the monopoly stage 200:16
Impersonality: delusion of i. 207:17
Impersonator: even the female i.s are women
36:17
woman can beat a man . . . female i. 152:4
Impertinence: into the pie of i. 117:16
love your neighbour . . . is an i. 302:18
Implementation: to control the i. 316:2
Import: even in Paradise . . . excessive i.s
153:10
Importance: gives away a little of his own i.
140:18
Important: I. Person Play 268:14
I . . . the most i. figure 14:9
mistakes the exceptional for the i. 166:17
not i. enough, why bother 30:2
Importer: an i. himself 289:1
Impossible: i. takes a little longer 348:14
i. . . . takes . . . longer 247:4
nothing is i. 244:12
when you have excluded the i. 101:2
you couldn't have i. things 261:13
Imposture: carry on the i. 227:16
Impoverished: i. them to such an extent
100:18
Impression: can create a good i. on yourself
121:18
Improbable: belief in the occurrence of the i.
230:6
however i., must be the truth 101:2
Impromptu: inside he was i. 152:17
Improved: people who would be i. by death
293:3
Improving: corner of the universe . . . certain
of i. 163:5
Impulse: friendly i. to ask for it 170:2
gratification of . . . primitive i.s 122:16
Impurity: i. of those to whom all things
313:17
In: we all knew you had it i. you 260:9
Inaccuracy: little i. . . . saves explanation
292:20
Incest: everything once except i. 30:1
i. . . . the whole family can play 136:22
opposed . . . by the *barrier against i.* 122:14
writing of i. from a standpoint 176:16
Inch: every other i. a gentleman 352:24
give a girl an i. nowadays 264:9
give a woman an i. and she'll park 353:16
Include: i. me out 134:16
Incoherent: I'm not i. 287:2
Income: decent people live beyond their i.s
293:7
my gross habits with my net i. 118:6
real i. of the community 183:13
Incommunicable: distrust the i. 297:6
Incompatibility: because of parental i. 251:2
i. became established 80:11
Incompetence: his Level of I. 263:9
Incompetent: England . . . ruled merely by i.s
155:9

Inconveniences: bribing yourself through the i. 279:10
Increase: who dies fighting has i. 141:17
Incurable: i. yet to be stricken 28:18
Indecencies: so much sculpture . . . missed the i. 9:9
Indecent: sent down for i. behaviour 345:14
Indemnity: if your ox . . . i. is instantaneous 87:5
India: in I. . . . Eliot is very much respected 48:4
  in I. where Mrs Gandhi's 160:11
  I. . . . no more a united nation 73:18
  one voyage to I. is enough 75:7
  pink is the navy blue of I. 343:16
Indian: you are the I. 26:11
Indifference: benign i. of the universe 62:14
  equanimity bordering on i. 131:14
  fern-dark i. 195:6
Indigestion: don't tell your friends about your i. 143:2
Indignation: mists of righteous i. 243:7
Indispensable: graveyards are full of i. men 129:18
  she was one of those i.s 161:7
Individual: autonomous i. 254:19
  definition of the i. 189:11
  historical characters are i.s 326:5
  i.s do not . . . concern me 197:8
  let each i. act spontaneously 196:15
  no longer an i. 344:8
  not interested in i.s 102:11
  setting before the group . . . the i. 109:25
Individualistic: compelled to be . . . 'i.' 207:7
Individuality: just let his i. develop 102:6
Indivisible: freedom is an i. word 358:10
Indolence: his i. was qualified 317:12
Indoors: God having given us i. 214:4
Indulgence: craving your i. 24:12
  made the i.s of Coleridge 330:5
Industrial: i. relations are like sexual 113:3
Industry: American captain of i. 363:11
  i. can't take you 338:10
  monarchy is a labour-intensive i. 359:7
Inequality: need i. . . . to eliminate poverty 176:6
Inexperience: she had to confess i. 47:3
Infallibility: i. of the pill 134:2
Infant: i.s were read passages from Homer 111:4
  unkillable i.s of the very poor 269:21
  what . . . terrors i.s go through 101:25
  wish I'd been a mixed i. 33:10
Infatuation: making sexual i. a tragic theme 302:8
Infection: an i. of the common sky 139:2
Inferior: make you feel i. 285:17
Inferiority: fortunate i. prevents him 69:25
  shed balm upon the sense of i. 273:17
Inferno: runs . . . outside Dante's I. 361:15
Infidelity: sought Adam and accused him of i. 42:7
Infinite: mathematical i. 290:5
Infinities: our place among the i. 124:16

Infinity: i. is a dreadfully poor place 178:18
  living for i. 241:14
Inflation: i. in the Sixties 205:5
  i. is like sin 200:14
Inflection: the beauty of i.s 317:20
Influence: aspired to power instead of i. 325:13
  I . . . prefer i. to power 223:15
  whether to spread his i. thin 223:10
Information: all i. is imperfect 54:7
  powder of profitable i. 228:4
  yes or no, on imperfect i. 47:13
Informed: no wiser . . . but far better i. 43:1
Inge, Dean: 94:5
Ingenuity: to remain poor needs . . . i. 231:20
Inhibition: cultivate a few i.s 211:11
Iniquity: gives you quite an air of i. 125:11
Injection: courage . . . for an i. 339:4
Injustice: acts of i. done 24:1
  he suffers from their i. 229:18
  imaginary i. perpetrated 148:16
  law and order . . . maintain i. 45:9
Ink: text written in invisible i. 189:15
Ink-stand: an i. of alabaster 93:4
Inn: i.s are not residences 239:11
  written on a map, 'I.' 236:1
Innocence: end of i., the darkness of man's heart 134:7
  i. is on at such a rakish angle 125:11
  rebelling . . . nostalgia for i. 62:22
Innocent: boys i. as strawberries 327:20
  try . . . to be an i. murderer 62:17
  we are i. 286:17
Innuendoes: or the beauty of i. 317:20
Inoculation: my degree was a kind of i. 37:6
Inoperative: others are i. 370:7
Inquire: not to i. why or whither 356:5
Insanity: i. is a kind of innocence 141:6
  often a prelude to i. 346:6
Insides: short back & i. 216:17
Insight: all men enjoy flashes of i. 354:10
Insignificance: man . . . of the utmost i. 93:3
Insincerity: enemy of clear language is i. 256:4
  truthfulness . . . reputation for i. 320:17
Insinuation: drop the needle of i. 117:18
Insolence: i. must be put down 100:3
Insomnia: i. in church 336:20
Instability: fact of the i. of evil 354:15
Instalment: only one more i. 274:15
Instinct: alert i. of the common people 195:1
  believe in i., not reason 38:9
  i.s already catered for 36:20
Institute: gas was on in the I. 40:16
Institution: is an i. always a man's shadow 172:16
  working of great i.s 295:15
Instruction: Earth: an i. book 126:7
Instrument: jazz . . . having all the best i.s 137:24
  prestige of their i.s 207:5
  unexplored regions of the stringed i.s 154:10
  wind i.s of plated silver 346:4
Insurance: Act of God . . . all i. policies 87:5
  burned down . . . for the fire i. 124:16
  I detest life-i. agents 198:16

Insured: his hands are i. 10:19
  not i. against fire 204:17
Insurrection: i. is an art 334:15
  i. . . . relation to revolution 334:19
Integrity: i. was not enough 22:24
Intellect: grinding of the i. 364:10
  halitosis of the i. 165:3
  i. deteriorates 29:21
  smaller the i. 248:11
  very incarnation of i. 303:17
Intellectual: all i.s suffer . . . persecution
    290:16
  all men are i.s 137:25
  beware of the artist who's an i. 115:19
  every i. attitude 221:14
  had thought once of being an i. 300:8
  i. is the same as . . . a gent 27:3
  i. . . . someone whose mind watches itself
    62:10
  'I.' suggests straight away 22:15
  i.'s problem . . . commitment 142:7
  i.s . . . believe that ideas 52:13
  native i., who takes up arms 112:7
  that i.s claw each other about 67:19
Intelligence: assigned . . . as assistant i. 150:14
  defect in the i. test 261:1
  down with i. 232:4
  i. galloping across open country 365:16
  i. of man 279:9
  i. is directly reflected 14:4
  key of i. 295:18
  military i. is a contradiction 225:1
  quite simply lack of i. 58:13
Intelligent: price . . . for being i. but not
    162:15
  three types of i. person 120:18
Intelligentsia: Bible of this i. 236:13
Intent: entirely i. on one thing 281:8
Intercourse: vanishes as soon as you have . . . i.
    45:14
Interest: i. in life does not lie 364:18
Interested: I've always been i. in people 228:7
Interesting: that a proposition be i. 354:11
Interlude: merely strange dark i.s 253:7
Interpretation: i. is a free walk 299:11
Interpreter: i. can do no more 31:15
Interrupt: people used to i. him 247:10
Interval: i. without an opera 248:9
Interview: their little i. was like a picnic
    169:13
Interviewing: for i. a faded female 147:12
Intractable: rich men . . . i. 349:4
Introduction: buy back my i. to you 224:16
Introspection: how much i. there is 32:6
Invasion: cannot . . . advocate an i. 276:3
  'i. scare' 76:6
Invent: you i. something 264:8
Invented: took away everything . . . i. 319:7
Invention: i.s . . . kind of evolution 53:15
  i.s that are not made 127:9
Investigator: an i. is confined 233:17
Invite: i. with gilded edges 23:4
Invited: going where you haven't been i.
    106:3
  not i. – they went there 116:2

Involuntary: it was i. 182:12
Ire: to melt in the crucible of her i. 152:19
Ireland: 337:1
  affluent society in I. 203:10
  faubourg Saint-Patrice . . . I. 176:22
  I. . . . sow that eats her farrow 176:9
  problem with I. 203:9
  sophisticated playwright . . . in I. 336:12
  would have liked to go to I. 356:19
Irish: I. are more so 103:18
  I. don't know what they want 16:22
  I. extraction subconsciously upset 71:11
  I. . . . have a psychosis 33:17
  I. that the I. themselves detest 33:18
  I. . . . their devotion to higher arts 127:14
  we I. had the right word 55:5
Irishman: he's not an I. 303:21
  I. thinks afterward 253:5
  quiet I. is about as harmless 103:19
Iron: Any Old I. 81:1
  i. has entered his s. 209:16
Ironmongery: Mankind *versus* I. 351:5
Irony: it is the i. of life 342:7
  there's i. for you 339:4
Irregular: Baker Street i.s 101:18
  whole thing is i. 101:19
Irresponsible: better to be i. and right 74:13
Irritant: an infuriating i. 87:3
Irving, Henry: 15:12, 32:1, 131:16, 327:4
Islam: I. . . . came with a sword 288:6
Island: advantages of being an I. Race 142:17
  glory came to the I. people 75:22
  I am an i. 320:21
  whole i. a water closet 217:7
Islander: i. from the western end of the world
    302:13
Isness: i. of things 31:13
Isolation: transmitted in . . . i. 54:17
Israel: believed in the mission of I. 370:2
Issue: i.s that may hang from a bootlace 101:5
  to discuss i.s civilly 14:5
It: she coined the word 'I.' 30:3
Italian: I.s will laugh at me 245:13
Italy: because I was born in I. 233:2
  in I. . . . they had warfare 348:16
Ivory: topmost turret of the i. tower 83:6
Ivy: not impressed by the I. League 98:14

                    J

Jack: J. and Jill went up the hill 234:1
Jahweh: J. spends a large part of His time
    229:13
Jam: how to make strawberry j. 237:7
  j. tomorrow, and one often 311:1
James I: 333:19
James, Henry: 32:5, 227:14
  as J. says, the house of fiction 48:17
  J. . . . this is his defect 23:15
Jane: I'd call 'em all J. 350:6
Japan: defeat of J. 286:2
  wont to regard J. 253:2

Japanese; J. have perfected . . . manners 327:7
Jarama; a valley in Spain called J. 100:6
Jaw; j.-j. is better than war-war 218:15
Jawbacious: high old j. argument 350:2
Jazz: J. Age . . . less an affair of youth 116:13
   j. is a language 85:4
   j. . . . having all the best instruments 137:24
   way J. is performed 271:5
Jealous: never dream of being j. of *her* 169:5
   young men are mad j. 369:4
Jealousy: beware of j. 50:12
   j. . . . among smiling enemies 47:8
Jean: goodbye Norma J. 325:11
Jeepers: J. Creepers 231:2
Jeeves: J. coughed . . . like a sheep 362:9
   like . . . Wodehouse dropping J. 347:23
Jefferson, Thomas : 181:28
Jehovah: J. of the Thunders 185:13
   J.'s Witnesses 204:17
   two solemn little J.s 121:14
   you've got a J. complex 150:7
Jellicoe, Earl: J. . . . could lose the war 77:12
Jellyfish: little uproar as a j. 363:2
Jem: J. is joky for Jacob 177:9
Jesus: 46:4, 219:3
   as good as Renan's *Life of J.* 198:5
   J. . . . detached from the goods 20:5
   Mrs Robinson, J. loves you 307:9
   stand around like J. in Gethsemane 51:23
   supplied the world with . . . J. Christ
     339:23
   to the right of . . . J. Christ 338:13
   we're more popular than J. Christ 202:6
   when J. came to Birmingham 323:1
Jew(s): 35:3, 119:21
   Arab . . . a J. on horseback 15:11
   coloured, one-eyed J. . . . anything else 95:9
   Einstein . . . greatest J. since Jesus 144:6
   even the J.s in England are boyish 86:2
   fourteen before he knew he was a J. 180:11
   half of Christendom worships a J. 16:7
   I decide who is a J. 212:19
   if a J. is fascinated by Christians 296:27
   I'm not really a J.; just J.-ish 233:14
   I'm sure you must be a J. 250:14
   J. . . . fool enough to turn Christian 370:1
   J.s . . . an immense people 339:23
   J.s bring the unlike into the heart 370:4
   J.s have a psychosis 33:17
   luxury that a J. never can allow 229:5
   no . . . society can flourish where a J. 175:14
   one J. copies from another 212:18
   situation of . . . J.s under Hitler 163:13
   what matters is what the J.s do 143:12
Jewellery: don't recognize faces, but . . . j.
     132:20
   hang on to her j. 211:8
   j. . . . wrecks a woman's reputation 80:15
   rattle your j. 202:5
Jewess: other half [worships] a J. 16:7
Jewish: J. man with parents 287:15
   best that is in the J. blood 195:3
   Hitlerism is . . . of J. origin 72:24
   J. isn't chic 19:16
   led their dark . . . J. lives 161:10

my daughter is only half-J. 225:5
no J. blood runs 369:12
to be J. weren't trouble enough 35:13
Jewry: Physics . . . instrument of J. 332:7
Jezebel: you should hear him throw down J.
   95:23
Jim: they've called him Sunny J. 110:14
Jinete: el j. se acercaba 128:18
Jingo: by j. by gee 92:7
Jingoes: against the J. at its close 75:11
Job: eight-ulcer man on a four-ulcer j. 335:12
   Thou hast a good j. 13:10
   Uncle Podger undertook to do a j. 174:4
   we have finished the j., what 144:2
   J. . . . cried to the Lord 13:10
Joffre, J. J.! J. . . . lost without him 158:9
John XXIII, Pope: 17:23
Johnny: do not despair for J. Head-in-Air
   274:14
Johnson, L. B.: Hey, hey, L.B.J., how many
   136:20
Joined: what God hath j. 305:26
Joke: civil servant doesn't make j.s 168:9
   coarse j. proclaims . . . an animal 206:2
   good deed to forget a poor j. 48:1
   I don't make j.s 285:1
   j. with a double meaning 28:16
   same j. . . . thirty times 352:20
   so far as j.s were concerned 270:15
Joker: said the j. to the thief 104:18
Joking: my way of j. is to tell the truth
   303:20
Jonah: belly j. hunting 177:15
Jones: large houses shouldn't know J. 87:15
Joneses: Keeping Up With the J. 239:15
   much cheaper . . . to drag the J. down 90:6
Jordan: shaped the J. near my home 327:14
   take a bath in J., Gordon 308:9
Journalism: between literature and j. 166:15
   but why j. 27:6
   j. . . . saying 'Lord Jones Dead' 69:17
   j. . . . will be grasped at once 83:5
   j. . . . will interest less tomorrow
     131:12
   junk j. is the evidence 319:22
Journalist: bribe . . . the British j. 364:4
   j.s write because they have nothing to say
     190:5
   responsibility as a j. 26:3
Journey: lots I could tell you of this j. 300:11
   whenever I prepare for a j. 221:21
Joy: bursting out of his collar with j. 65:15
   money . . . man's greatest source of j. 128:3
   spontaneous j. and natural content 368:10
Joyce, James: 198:6
   not write the words Mr J. used 306:2
Judaized: American society . . . half j. 155:17
Judas: J. is the last god 195:18
Judge: go to a j. as if . . . to a funeral 51:8
   if you had . . . become a j. 341:3
   j. is not supposed to know 258:3
   'j. not', *but we must j.* 167:6
   more difficult to j. oneself 292:14
   when a j. begins to sum up 167:10
   you can't j. Egypt by *Aïda* 114:18

Judgement: if it only added j. to insight 119:11
Last J. . . . every day 61:20
never commit oneself to any j. 199:2
some of my j.s were wrong 250:4
Day of J. 125:13
Judies: besides shinannickin' after J. 252:12
Judo: J. . . . has an irresistible attraction 160:2
Juice: full o' *j. de spree* 187:17
Jumbo: J. asleep! Grey leaves 308:8
June: J. that was stabbed 19:12
Jung: Adler will always be J. 344:13
Jungfernschaft: J. sei, möglicherweise 180:3
Jungle: down in the j. living 68:12
j. will think later 187:9
Law of the J. 187:22
learn *all* the Law of the J. 187:8
never get out of the j. 232:20
set a kind of pristine j. up 180:4
through the J. very softly 186:17
Junior: smart J.s . . . Juniosity 349:18
Junket: Gothic arch out of j. 319:10
slipped down like j. 216:2
Justice: administers j. among men 209:1
I chose j. . . . to remain faithful 61:23
j. became of primary importance 62:23
j. demands the suspension of freedom 62:24
j. is open . . . as the Ritz 323:2
J. . . . is so subtle a thing 129:1
j. should not only be done, but 154:1
military j. is to j. 17:12
some degree of j. must be seen 319:15
want j., but do you want to pay 51:7
your j. would freeze beer 232:17
Justification: should carry its j. in every line 85:5
Justifies: something that j. the end 335:6
Juvescence: in the j. of the year 108:22

K

Kaiser: Belgium Put the Kibosh on the K. 110:10
took down the . . . photograph of the K. 346:19
Kaleidoscope: k. eyes 202:19
Kanonen: das Land, wo die K. blühn 180:2
Kariba: to build the K. Dam is a beaver 178:16
Katy: K-K-K., beautiful K. 253:1
Keats, John: rather like K.'s vulgarity 199:4
Shelley and K. were the last 144:8
Kelly: has anybody here seen K. 244:18
Kennedy: attraction of the K.s 215-10
Kennedy, John F.: 292:9
kind of nation . . . K. died for 175:13
moment they heard K. was dead 120:6
Kensington: *skay* is only seen in K. 333:9
Kentucky: in the old K. home 120:8
Kept: without wishing I had k. it 54:18
Kerouac, Jack: 63:18

Kettle: battered k. at the heel 368:22
Key: all of us looking for the k. 36:18
even we all k.s must resign 96:15
she could always find the k. 244:20
to throw away the k. 22:9
Keynes, J. M.: 'in the long run,' said K. 79:10
Khatmandu: yellow idol to the north of K. 148:19
Khrushchev, Nikita: 182:8
Kick: I Get a K. Out of You 267:11
Kicked: we *all* get k. 102:5
Kid: don't have any k.s yourself 193:18
flippin' k.s 146:21
it's a k. or a coffin 28:20
Kidder: everybody likes a k. 232:24
Kidnapped: k. . . . rent out my room 13:23
Kill: ignorance . . . the right to k. 62:16
k. me a son 104:22
k. more women and children 26:14
let them k. as many 335:10
meet interesting people and k. them 17:1
my k. shall be thy k. 187:11
step up and k. a woman 35:20
to k. a man is to merit a woman 132:17
Killed: Bill (who k. him) thought it right 34:17
I don't mind your being k. 188:13
Killing: k. is the ultimate simplification 215:17
k. time . . . Time kills us 308:14
older than the art of k. 343:14
Kilt: k. is an unrivalled garment 226:3
putting on a k., standing upside down 99:20
Kind: all are behind, the k. 328:20
Kind: wer zeigt ein K. 281:9
Kindness: clatter . . . with the milk of human k. 142:16
depended on the k. of strangers 357:25
k. of the poor to the rich 71:3
milk of human k. . . . gets clotted 147:11
King: barrel-house k.s 208:7
duties as K. as I would wish 107:14
five k.s left . . . England, Diamonds 112:11
in search of mythical k.s 271:6
introduce you to the last k. of England 107:11
K.s and governments may err 153:5
k.s . . . are just as funny 286:8
k.s are the most sublime sick 35:7
k.s of the earth are old 282:17
Mrs Simpson's pinched our k. 16:8
Northcliffe has sent for the K. 16:9
sit down, unless you're a K. 160:8
wars . . . more terrible than those of k.s 73:6
where even the k. goes on foot 163:11
your K. and Country need you 19:2
Kingdom: Thine is the k. . . . Don't blow it 13:10
Kingfish: I'm the K. 211:1
Kinspirit: Tchaikovsky . . . makes them k.s 262:3
Kipling, Rudyard: Feed them on K. 61:9
Kipper: k.s, two-faced with no guts 149:15
Kiss: if you want to k. me 116:6
if you weren't going to k. me 226:5

k. is just a k. 160:12
k. without a moustache 297:12
sisterly k. Older sister 220:1
some men k. and do not tell 237:8
someone might blow you a k. 315:6
very large k. indeed 289:4
Kissed: he k. easily 259:4
he k. her violently 20:16
k. her . . . she wasn't looking 328:10
k. her way into society 333:7
she hasn't been k. for forty years 287:20
some . . . want to be k. 28:7
Kissing: accuse Rasputin of k. 12:15
I wasn't k. her 223:19
I Wonder Who's K. Her Now 9:13
k. and hugging business 289:9
k. him on both cheeks 77:21
k. your hand 211:10
one of the most popular . . . is k. 231:12
President . . . k. people 335:11
Kitchen: k.-sink-revolutionary look 352:23
Kitchener, Earl: 77:20
Kitten: trouble with a k. 247:11
Knave: dumbfounded before a k. 368:12
Knee: k. and nothing more 239:19
let man's hands stay off my k.s 24:12
Knew: if we k. one, we k. two 106:8
k. everything . . . k. other things 28:23
Knight: group's name on the left, The K.s
143:4
Knife: using the only k. 288:7
Knit: k. one, purl one 24:17
Knitter: Virginia Woolf . . . little k. 308:10
Knocker: at death's door . . . its k. 129:8
Know: awareness . . . happen to k. 309:2
'e's all right when you k. 'im 79:9
illusion that he k.s what he wants 123:13
k. myself . . . but that is all 115:22
k.s the way but can't drive 336:18
never k.s . . . his deepest research
140:15
So Long, It's Been Good to K. You 143:15
we k. lots of things 284:9
you k. I k. you k. I k. 143:5
you k. more than you think 315:7
Knowing: men who insist on k. 268:22
modest about my not k. all 246:4
Knowledge: acquiring k. . . . seldom beneficial
164:3
divorce is the sign of k. 358:5
if a little k. was a dangerous thing 302:1
if you want k. 222:4
impress anyone with as much k. 16:24
k. can only be acquired 228:4
k. is proportionate to being 163:10
k. not of facts but of values 166:2
love thee . . . not for the k. 95:5
not k. but certainty 290:4
never an age in which useless k. 174:12
our k. can only be finite 266:16
problem . . . for human k. 120:9
river of k. has too often turned 173:3
so little k. to such great account 109:23
such k., what forgiveness 109:2
taste all, and hand the k. down 311:7

there is no absolute k. 54:7
to k., we make promises 274:1
Known: apart from the k. and the unknown
264:19
k. for his well-knownness 46:9
Kodak: the great artist K. 234:13
Könige: die K. der Welt sind alt 282:17
Kremlin: talk . . . turns to the K. mountaineer
220:14
Krug: ich bin dein K. 282:18

L

Lab: best home . . another person's l. 345:10
Laboratorium: l. est oratorium 248:2
Laboratory: give me an underground l. 262:5
Labour: consider the history of l. 26:9
division of l. 218:5
England elects a L. Government 284:14
I never shout at L. members 67:3
if L. is dead in Scotland 60:6
L. . . . cutting itself in half 66:2
L. is not fit to govern 73:11
L. Party . . . she had not been asked 346:20
l. songs but no work songs 20:2
looked on the L. party as dirt 67:4
shalt thou l., as the Bible says 57:18
Labourer: agricultural l.s commute 270:9
Lächeln: stand er am Ende der L. 281:16
Ladder: I'll climb this blinking l. 118:18
l. of success, wrong by wrong 352:4
Ladies: l. in London spend their evenings
305:18
if all the young l. 260:7
when l. apparently rolled along 162:9
worth any number of old l. 113:1
Lady: any girl who was a l. 211:8
here lies a l. of beauty 276:10
in case a certain little l. 118:17
L., Be Good 130:14
l. . . . might go to bed with a chap 319:20
L., L., should you meet 259:13
That's Why the L. Is a Tramp 148:10
throw the little old l. down the stairs 228:19
well, not exactly a l. 281:5
Lady Chatterley's Lover: 198:7
Lafayette, General: L., we are here 316:5
La Guardia, Mayor: 175:3
Laid: were l. end to end 260:7
Laissez faire: end of l. 219:4
principles of l. 183:13
Lamb: l.s leap with thick leggings 369:15
unless the l. is inside 196:6
Lambeth: doin' the L. walk 126:13
Lame: he is still a l. dog 248:10
Lamort: Madame L. . . . winds endless ribbons
281:11
Lamp: call a street l. a minor planet 223:9
how's that for a table l. 99:20
l.s of London uphold 365:4
Lamp-post: I'm leaning on a l. 118:17
Lampshade: lent him a couple of l.s 307:16

Land: and saw a sad l. 257:7
l. laid waste 22:8
l. ... my fathers can have it 328:18
l. was ours before we were 124:9
l. where the cannon flower grew 180:2
Mus' Hobden owns the l. 185:18
Landlady: commit bigamy to please the l.
  100:1
Landscape: half the l. is unavailable 100:10
there are very few l.s 94:3
Language: bewitchment of our intelligence by
  ... l. 292:17
can be silent in several l.s 147:4
did not habitually use ... l.s 350:19
enemy of clear l. 256:4
fine flow of l. 281:5
frank words in our respective l.s 85:13
fundamental thing about human l.s 267:5
great dead l. of the future 161:20
his l. performs ... without shyness 83:4
how many people speak the same l.
  156:11
l. bears the same relationship 233:16
l. charged with meaning 269:3
l. is a dialect 348:11
l. is incomplete 354:10
l. ... it's literature 349:15
l. that always means more 120:11
life is a foreign l. 240:12
philosophy is 'Critique of L.' 360:17
sounds ... but it's not l. 314:5
Languor: l. which is not laziness 353:11
Lansbury, George: L. stands for our happy
  129:11
Larky: was jolly l. and that's what counts
  111:12
Larved: l. ond he l. 177:18
Laryngitis: brawling leads to l. 79:14
Laski, Marghanita: 272:3
Last: nice guys finish l. 104:1
Last Supper: L.-carved-on-a-peach-stone
  192:13
Late: never too l. to fall in love 359:12
some people are always l. 234:5
Later: l. than you think 301:9
Lateral: L. Arabesque 263:14
Latin: gentleman need not know L. 226:8
  L. languages are not composed of two
    elements 295:18
  L. quarter of Cowley 17:3
  L. ... taught very badly 350:19
  that weary L. 29:2
Lattenzaun: es war einmal ein L. 240:1
Laugh: British l.s that don't lead anywhere
  188:2
good l. is the best pesticide 246:16
he who l.s ... last to get the joke 80:4
l. in the wrong place 141:8
l. like waves breaking 363:21
make people l. till they cry 142:5
ninety-nine men weep while one l.s 312:13
penetrating sort of l. 362:3
someone you could l.-at-with 315:4
way people look and l. 365:3
willing to l. at himself 292:9

Laughed: few women care to be l. at 24:3
l., and rattled the miniature gallows 161:6
when he l., respectable 22:1
Laughing: while they're l., he'll win the seat
  303:21
Laughter: capable of l. 230:13
irrevocably betrothed to l. 339:10
l. of people who have lost 351:19
l. would be bereaved if 340:3
no l. is sad 319:17
Laundries: that Land of L. stood 41:6
Lautrec: My Toujours L. 134:20
Lava: buried in l. and not turn a hair 31:4
Lavatory: public house l. 203:8
useful, like ... a public l. 163:3
Law: crack a few l.s now and then 352:2
exercising the imagination ... study of l.
  132:23
has lost its l. 211:18
he broke the l. when he was born 303:29
I'd cut down every l. 44:19
insurrection ... has its l.s 334:15
keep ye the L. 186:16
l. and order ... maintain injustice 45:9
L. ... cannot compel anyone to tell the
  truth 94:6
l. ... not to be cheated in this way 308:4
L. of the Jungle 187:22
l.s ... Negro lady once taught 12:17
l.s of God will be suspended 305:6
music is natural l. 348:5
no brilliance is needed in the l. 241:13
rebellion against the existing l. 305:22
regard the l. courts ... as a casino 167:9
there's never a l. of God or man 186:10
when you break the big l.s 72:14
world in which there are no natural l.s
  108:1
Law, Andrew Bonar: 209:14
L. ... honest to the verge 26:12
Lawbreaking: opposed to l. 289:16
Law-court: l.s of England are open to all
  94:7
Lawrence, D. H.: for L., existence was ...
  convalescence 162:19
Lawrence, T. E.: 36:21, 89:7, 163:20, 306:10
Lawyer: business of the l. is to widen 149:1
when l.s talk about the law 167:11
Lay: l. interest in ecclesiastical 346:6
Laziest: I'm the l. gal in town 267:18
Laziness: my only hobby is l. 248:1
struggling against his own l. 323:8
Lazy: be efficient if you're ... l. 85:7
Leader: following back-stepping l.s 82:12
I must follow ... I am their l. 45:6
jealous of their l.s for being shot 369:4
repudiate the l.s they adopted 296:9
they asked for a l. 243:11
true l. is always led 178:11
under the guidance of our L. 254:9
Leadership: approach to l. until they have lost
  42:1
art of l. ... consolidating 155:1
l. in this historic struggle 155:12
Lean: as l. over too far backward 330:21

Leap: it isn't the wild ecstatic l. 16:23
Learn: always ready to l. although 77:16
  anything he does not want to l. 295:2
  we all l. by experience, but some 98:12
  we *have* to l. to *behave* 102:4
  we must l. . . . more about 'and' 106:8
  we want to l. 'em 137:23
Learning: beauty and the lust for l. 32:16
  devote the rest of his life to l. 254:12
  l., earning and yearning 240:9
  sleep – and l. of a sort 34:19
Learnt: but who have l. Hungarian by
  themselves 170:8
  only remember what I've l. 354:3
Leave: for ever taking l. 282:2
Leaves: grey l. thick furred 308:8
  home before the l. 356:20
Leavis, F. R.: 206:5
Leben: L. geht hin mit Verwandlung 281:17
  so l. wir 282:2
Lecture: better . . . shop-lifting than to give
  l.s 53:2
Led: France was neither l. nor governed
  263:3
Left: more to the l. than . . . Stalin 351:13
  my position was on the l. 242:22
Left-handed: l. form of . . . endeavour 160:13
Leg: born with your l.s apart 254:4
  l.s . . . stolen from under you 52:6
  men's l.s have a . . . lonely life 99:23
  using first, l.s one and three 234:7
  whatever goes upon two l.s 254:7
Legacy: have left him a l. . . . die at once
  58:15
Legend: l. becomes fact, print the l. 34:9
  l.s . . . the spiritual side of facts 28:8
Legion: ere yet we loose the l.s 185:13
Légion: refused the L. d'Honneur 298:12
Legislation: that l. bears 233:16
Legitimacy: to defend his nation's l. 112:7
Legitimate: more l. than the Wild D. 350:7
Leica: me no l. 200:15
Leiden: nicht sind die L. erkannt 282:9
Leisure: work has become a l. 9:1
Leitern: nur aneinander lehnenden L. 281:12
Lemming: hundred thousand l.s can't be wrong
  137:8
Lemonade: one bottle more of fizzy l. 40:11
Lenin, Vladimir I.: 77:3
  L. was the first to discover 325:16
  L. was . . . terribly wrong 45:2
  L.'s method leads to this 335:4
Lens: with his telephoto l. thrusting 156:21
Leonardo: in graphic art since L. 211:17
Lesbian: l.s are mighty fine 18:4
  my mother made me a L. 137:4
  possibility of the L. vice 245:16
Less: l. is more 231:12
Lesson: I never minded the l.s 241:12
  she'd never had a l. in her life 244:20
  taught mankind at least one l. 244:12
Let: I l. down my friends 250:5
Lethal: little knowledge was . . . dangerous, a
  lot was l. 302:1
Lethe: and if no L. flows 276:9

Letter: another l. from my father 50:1
  answered your l. sooner 9:4
  left a l. for several days 123:8
  until you have had a l. from her 204:8
Letting: it's all right l. yourself go 169:7
Lettuce: eating too much l. 268:10
Leviathan: L. told and the honey-fly 96:20
Liaison: for a woman to have a *l.* 139:15
Liar: accomplice of l.s and forgers 261:17
  being called a l. 209:14
  habitual l. always imagines 183:2
  fool, a l. or both 301:8
  poet is a l. 79:17
  scandal by . . . a proved l. 144:4
  [lax] has made more l.s 285:3
  that fish . . . is a blasted l. 283:12
  weak, a l., and idle 186:3
Liberal: just like an old l. 266:2
  if God had been a L. 49:7
  l.'s problem in a nutshell 122:4
  L.s think that goats are just sheep 49:5
  most l. L. Englishman 194:25
  too l. to fight 184:6
  Tory – especially every . . . L. 37:20
Liberation: l. . . . cannot be achieved by semi-
  humans 122:9
  l. from all discipline 236:13
  madness is potential l. 192:10
  mankind's war of l. 182:1
Liberationist: Women's L.s 211:13
Liberties: worse than any lack of . . . l. 312:9
Libertine: l.s . . . disregard the law 53:12
Liberty: deliver me from l. 78:16
  extremism in the defence of l. 134:10
  l. is conforming to the majority 299:3
  price of l. 255:2
  shall the voices of l. be mute 92:8
  there can be no effective l. 34:7
  when you break . . . laws, you do not get l.
  72:14
Librarian: l.'s duty to distinguish 320:16
Library: books from the . . . London L.
  269:16
  l. is thought in cold storage 295:7
  might sober me up to sit in a l. 116:3
Lice: I've l. in my tunic 22:26
Licence: a l. to print money 329:22
Lichen: better to be the l. on a rock 84:12
Liddell: said L. to Scott 147:18
Lie: believing in old men's l.s 269:7
  from l.s of tongue and pen 68:22
  invent a new l. 226:15
  kinds of l.s . . . statistics 336:8
  l. . . . a very present help 318:1
  l. can be half-way round the world 60:5
  l. has become . . . pillar of the State 312:15
  l.s are the mortar 350:17
  l.s in the shape of false teeth 350:18
  like a kindly meant l. 44:7
  live by what they know to be a l. 146:11
  lust and a scale of l.s 40:7
  more easily fall victims to a big l. 155:3
  old L.: *Dulce et decorum est* 257:4
  one who l.s with sincerity 131:10
  overlooking a landscape of l.s 129:6

Lie – *Contd.*
that I . . . should believe a l. 290:9
universal . . . force-feeding with l.s 312:9
why are you bothering to l. to me 319:3
will l. even when . . . inconvenient 342:19
Liebe: nicht ist die L. gelernt 282:9
Lieder: singing l. is like putting 26:2
Life: about as much l. . . . as a potted shrimp 278:7
actual l. provides the untraditional 141:8
advised me to lead a clean l. 298:8
all l. is six to five against 288:19
all the questions that l. puts to us 145:16
art . . . give l. a shape 19:4
art . . . *makes* l., makes interest 171:10
at war you think about a better l. 356:7
average length of l. for clergymen 252:15
average man finds l. very uninteresting 235:22
before l. as . . . some full shop window 169:11
citizen of l. 298:5
courage . . . for the loss of l. 339:4
each time of l. has . . . rewards 13:13
give me . . . l. till my work is done 158:3
glorify a l. . . . they can't bear 132:14
God not on the borders of l. 45:18
guilty of imitating 'real l.' 246:5
how I feel about l. 13:2
I never knew what L. . . . meant 189:2
I really don't know l. at all 237:1
I shall believe in l. in the hereafter 60:6
if it were a l. sentence 311:9
in the house of L. they have 330:10
it is the same everywhere in this l. 273:19
l. . . . a comedy in long-shot 68:5
l. a terrible thing, thank God 328:11
l. and death is cat and dog 125:19
L. and Soul . . . will never go 355:3
l. begins at forty 336:2
l. begins on the other side 296:13
l. couldn't have left him so far 170:3
l. deceives us 274:8
l. exists in the universe only because 182:21
l. had appeared as a reversible coat 152:5
l. is a foreign language 240:12
l. is a hesitation before birth 179:13
l. is a luminous halo 364:17
l. is an abnormal business 168:14
l. is an offensive 354:9
l. is doubt 338:1
l. is . . . filling in time 40:4
l. is like a rainbow 137:2
l. is like a sewer 200:9
l. is like nothing . . . is everything 134:6
l. is not a spectacle 295:2
l. is not having been told 247:22
l. is nothing until it is lived 297:4
l. . . . is one damn thing over and over 232:9
l. is the other way round 210:3
l. is too short to stuff a mushroom 85:6
L. is Just a Bowl of Cherries 55:15
l. is on the other side of the glass 37:11
l. itself, every moment of it 365:8
l. jacket . . . Come back to l. 82:17

l. makes no absolute statement 195:9
l. mustn't be taken seriously 197:13
l. persists in the vulnerable 326:7
l. seems to have no plots 82:2
l. to come . . . was always that 30:15
l. was a funny thing that happened 90:22
l. would be tolerable 206:8
l.'s exclusive city 194:11
live his l. as if . . . recounting it 296:18
lived most of my l. posthumously 162:14
more to l. than having everything 301:7
my experience . . . drawn from l. itself 32:17
no one owns l. 58:9
not the party of l. 25:6
now they want my l. 191:1
only one evil, to deny l. 194:9
priceless gift of l. 286:17
our l. passes in transformation 281:17
'real l.' appears to be an imitation 217:15
slice his l. into a series 217:14
talked a lot about l. 341:5
there was L. – pale and hoar 148:1
three ingredients in the good l. 240:9
too much detail . . . too little l. 58:4
unless l. took its cleaver 354:2
what a queer thing L. is 363:14
would give my l. for my friend, but 309:16
Life-like: not l.; it is alive 66:13
Life-mask: l. of myself wearing an army respirator 278:4
Life-sentence: l. in the dungeon of self 84:22
to escape the l. 198:3
Light: against the dying of the l. 327:17
all-the-l.s-on man 278:15
believed in the green l. 116:10
how weak and little is the l. 329:1
l. at the end of the tunnel 212:1
to kindle a l. in the darkness 178:6
turn up the l.s I don't want 153:2
Lightning: writing history with l. 359:15
Like: don't know whether I l. it 342:3
friends . . . people you l. 339:12
it is our business . . . to know what we l. 109:27
l. me more than you don't l. me 97:6
l. people and I l. them to l. me 116:17
l.s me, 'cause she says so 322:4
love all my children, but some . . . don't l. 65:1
my work . . . I don't l. it 25:4
no more l. people . . . than I l. dogs 314:13
nothing says . . . l. each other 98:7
people still . . . do not l. him 55:8
seek not to make them l. you 131:3
Liked: hates me because I'm so . . . l. 98:13
he's l., but he's not well l. 232:18
Lilies: considers the l., the rewards 154:5
Lilliputian: a poet or a L. 343:15
Limb: inelegant l.s casually placed 349:13
Lime: you have *got* to give her l. 185:17
Limelight: look after the l. 306:4
Limestone: see a l. landscape 22:7
Limit: think both sides of this l. 360:15
Limitation: human mind . . . range of l.s 140:7

Limousin: L. . . . more popes and fewer lovers 132:11
Limousine: one perfect l. 259:11
Limp: L-I-M-P pronounced 'l.' 234:16
Lincoln: Ford, not a L. 118:10
 if he had shared the fate of Abraham L. 142:10
Line: *active* l. on a walk 188:15
 learn the l.s and don't bump 89:14
 pray to God and say the l.s 95:7
 walk on the l.s or the squares 236:10
Linen: criminal is . . . he who dirties the l. 57:1
Linnet: with my old cock l. 80:19
Lion: does a l. tamer enter a cage 237:16
 English soldiers . . . l.s led by donkeys 157:16
 l. and the calf shall lie 13:11
 make the l. lie down with the lamb 196:6
 nation had the l.'s heart 77:24
Lionized: wasn't spoilt by being l. 333:4
Lip: he bit his l. 262:9
 if his l.s move, he's lying 34:14
 lying . . . his l.s are moving 16:15
 my l.s are not yet unsealed 26:16
Lipstick: finding l. on a café cup 34:13
 got on too much l. 247:17
Liquor: drank our l. straight 22:27
 l. and love rescue 358:3
Listen: all she has to do is to l. 235:23
 can l. . . . with the naked eye 313:20
 I l. a lot and talk less 91:14
Listener: are we now the l.s 282:12
 good l. is a good talker 355:9
Listening: liked l. to himself talk 150:25
 l. . . . too carefully to himself 129:3
Literacy: illiterate appeals for l. 46:8
 ratio of l. to illiteracy 239:16
 The Uses of L. 157:18
Literary: haunted by l. parallels 141:8
 l. man puts together two words 86:19
 no test of l. merit 256:1
Literature: between l. and journalism 166:15
 edge of the chair of L. 330:10
 everything about l. except how to enjoy 150:17
 find Etruscan l. interesting 161:21
 get along very well without l. 297:5
 great L. is . . . language charged with meaning 269:3
 in some modern l. 212:16
 language . . . it's l. 349:15
 l. and butterflies 246:18
 l. clear and cold 206:18
 l. has no relation with life 274:8
 l. is . . . about sex 210:3
 l. is . . . arithmetic 321:14
 l. of one century 246:1
 l. . . . poisoned by its own secretions 52:24
 l. . . . will be read twice 83:5
 our business, as readers of l. 109:27
 place in our l. 239:5
 professor of English l. who 331:6
 that is the whole business of l. 70:8

Live: desire to l. . . . readiness to die 72:2
 determination to l. . . . is the motive 153:21
 do you want to l. for ever 94:4
 I don't wish to l. any longer 228:9
 I'll l. too, if it kills me 125:16
 in order to l. in an unlivable situation 192:9
 it was equally good to l. or die 76:5
 l. for ever or die in the attempt 150:9
 l. so you can stick out your tongue 222:15
 others merely l.; I vegetate 84:23
 something to l. for, great enough 145:14
 thus we l., for ever taking leave 282:2
 to die, and no newer . . . to l. 111:8
 to die . . . than to l. on your knees 165:1
 to l. lucidly in a world 62:5
Liver: birds on the L. building 135:18
Lives: did not give their l. in vain 75:21
 l. with the mainspring left out 116:19
 loose talk can cost l. 17:7
 no second act in . . . l. 116:18
 our l. are merely . . . interludes 253:7
Living: happiness . . . attributed by the l. 323:15
 heavy is the tread of the l. 329:3
 I don't feel . . . l. unless I'm killing 156:18
 l. and partly l. 109:18
 l.? . . . he is lived 52:12
 l. is made . . . by selling 356:8
 L. Well is the Best Revenge 327:12
 nothing like l. together for blinding 81:22
 prepared . . . for living, not 311:8
 repetition of the wrong way of l. 104:11
 tired of l. . . . scared of dying 146:6
 world . . . does not owe us a l. 107:4
Livingstone: Doctor L. thought that football was God 271:1
Lloyd, Selwyn: 41:19
Lloyd George, David: 21:7, 30:8
 L. had said of Bonar Law 26:12
 L. . . . in the use of an argument 38:1
 L. . . . thinks in images 145:3
 L. would have a better rating 142:10
Loaf: half a l. is better than a whole 72:11
Loafed: it is better to have l. 331:2
Lob: nothing but a l. 289:15
Lobby: not a man would go into the L. 26:16
Lock: be tidy, oil the l. 23:9
Locomotive: 'say it with l.s' 207:13
Locust: years that the l. hath eaten 167:15
Logic: crime is common. L. is rare 101:6
 in l. process and result 360:21
 l. is the art of going wrong 17:6
 l. of our times 95:19
 principles of l. . . . are true 24:10
Logically: I deduced the rest l. 37:1
Loin: gird your blue-veined l.s 12:7
 Lolita, . . . fire of my l.s 246:3
Loincloth: l. to wipe the froth off 38:6
Loisir: ses longs l.s 19:7
Lolita: L., light of my life 246:3
Lollock: dusty-featured L.s 138:18
London: dead lies L.'s daughter 328:3
 I thought of L. spread out 193:22
 L. Belongs To Me 81:6

London – *Contd.*
  L. doesn't love the latent 169:15
  don't know what L.'s coming to 88:14
  L. . . . for those who can get out 27:8
  there would be in L. 171:3
  to speak against L. is no longer 119:8
Loneliness: pray that your l. may spur 145:14
Lonely: all the l. people 202:11
  attracting . . . for fear I may be l. 174:11
  if . . . l., one prefers discomfort 141:1
  why I'm l. 292:10
Lonelyhearts: write-to-Miss-L. 352:18
Long: in the l. run . . . we are all dead 79:10
Longer: don't actually live l.; it just seems
    122:11
Look: to l. farther than you can see 77:15
Looking: here's l. at you, kid 44:15
  l. around at someone 287:6
Looking-glass: used as a captive l. 342:16
  women . . . as l.es 365:10
Looney-bin: sort of janitor to the l. 362:4
Loot: widen the rift and gather the l. 149:1
Lord: good L. may have created 108:1
  I am the L. of the Dance 65:2
  neither a L., nor a privy 25:8
  L. forgive all the little tricks 125:5
  L. survives the rainbow 212:8
  one of the l.s of life 194:5
  praise of the L. is drummed into you 263:18
Lords, House of: 209:5
  had taken his seat in the L. 32:12
  L., an illusion to which 320:26
  L. in his own head 209:8
Los Angeles: 68:1, 260:3
  not in the L. telephone directory 63:20
Lose: don't l. it 249:11
  I learnt that you always l. 296:24
  nothing left to l. 190:19
  slogan Born to L. 143:4
  that I may l. my way 328:22
  We Don't Want to L. You 288:3
  whatever we l. (like a you or a me) 92:19
Lost: elephants . . . are seldom l. 11:10
  found is always l. again 156:7
Lot: rather like L.'s friends 362:20
  gathering fuel in vacant l.s 109:11
  now, here's a l. 223:1
Loud: Am I Too L. 239:8
Loudly: never speak l. . . . unless 329:21
Louis XIV: L. . . . dressing and undressing
    92:21
Lourdes: our successes . . . those of L. 123:1
Louse: the soul of a l. 186:26
Lousy: conduct unethical and l. 20:13
  l. but loyal 17:8
  only one fault . . . l. 331:8
Love: All You Need Is L. 202:7
  always ourselves we l. 25:13
  a-waggle with l. 194:7
  both . . . in l. with *him* 329:15
  caution in l. 290:1
  could l. each other like dogs 100:9
  Earth's right place for l. 124:3
  falling in l. . . . sign of failure 317:11
  greater l. . . . lay down his friends 329:23

greatest l. that I have ever known 272:13
groans of l. 212:12
guys in l. 289:3
he fell in l. with himself 269:23
he who l.s finds the door 325:3
how did you l. my picture 135:13
I'd been better without: l. 259:8
'I l.', 'I hate', 'I suffer' 364:14
I l. or I hate 264:4
I'm tired of L. 34:18
I speak the words of my l. 284:7
I wish I could fall in l. 339:9
in l. . . . 'Against whom?' 10:7
in one's captivity to l. 123:12
in the narrow theme of l. 368:20
it is rarely that a man l.s 215:15
laughed at the power of L. 186:24
Let's Fall in L. 267:19
liquor and l. rescue 358:3
l. a burnt match 89:25
L. and marriage . . . and carriage 60:3
l. for sale 267:17
l. in the East . . . *only* feasible 115:4
l. is a fanclub with only two fans 151:18
l. is a universal migraine 139:6
l. is always new 190:17
l. is banishment 31:3
L. Is Just a Four-letter Word 105:2
l. is not learnt 282:9
l. is not the dying moan 262:17
l. is . . . the only theme 302:7
l. levels all, doesn't it 32:25
l. looks to the present 205:13
l. means never having to say you're sorry
    300:19
l. means the pre-cognitive flow 197:15
l. outside the law . . . be honest 104:16
l. set you going 265:18
l. stories . . . have always kept free from
    152:20
l. . . . the gift of oneself 19:3
l. the things we l. for what they are 124:12
l. . . . will cure anything 194:17
make l. not war 17:9
man's ultimate l. for man 195:11
marriage without l. means l. 78:3
money can't buy me l. 202:9
much more intellectual pure l. 35:8
music . . . the breakfast food of l. 11:11
one great l. in my life 61:17
only certitudes . . . l., exile 62:18
only l. . . . that is unselfish 227:2
only one duty . . . that is to l. 62:10
paths of l. are rougher 147:15
perfect fear casteth out l. 85:3
recompense to women . . . make l. to them
    170:10
saw that lack of l. contaminates 143:5
say falling in l. is wonderful 39:13
sex with someone you l. 13:1
she l.s you, yeh 202:25
there can be no peace of mind in l. 272:17
too young to really be in l. 96:7
true l. . . . clear-sightedness 62:16
True L. doesn't know the meaning 167:23

try to imagine a faultless l. 22:7
violence masquerading as l. 192:8
virginity . . . a limited capacity for l. 306:19
we must l. one another . . . but 98:7
what will survive of us is l. 193:20
when he told men to l. their neighbours 51:17
why does free l. cost so much 137:20
will you l. me in December 344:6
win the l. of a 'real' man 90:17
with l. for timber 232:8
with l. from me to you 202:13
whose l. is given over-well 259:1
women can do nothing except l. 227:9
yet l. survives, the word 138:13
you have to l. them 192:7
you learn to l. by loving 163:12
Loved: desired the death of those they l. 62:13
he l. himself only as much 326:8
I l. them until they l. me 259:2
who would be l. 268:4
Lovelies: fifty l. in the rude 328:17
Lovely: wouldn't it be l. 203:12
Lovemaking: half the harm of l. 263:21
Lover: be a l. as well as a husband 226:19
ex-wife searching for a new l. 84:13 ◆
Frankie and Johnnie were l.s 16:4
had three thousand l.s I 351:22
Hello, Young L.s, Wherever 146:2
lose a l. . . . lose one's teeth 353:8
l. with any other career in mind 349:9
oppressed shut-in l.s 47:9
scratch a l. 259:3
to abuse a man is a l.-like thing 65:4
unwearied still, l. by l. 369:1
Loving: I ain't had no l. 251:1
if we stop l. animals 311:13
make us . . . more l. 26:8
Low-brow: first militant l. 39:20
Lowness: his l. creeped out first 177:10
Loyal: lousy but l. 17:8
she's got to be a l., frank person 116:25
to be l. to his club 353:14
your l. service when . . . I am right 238:4
Lucifer: that fitful, fiery L. 369:14
Luck: believes in l. and sends his son 316:7
Wish Me L. as You Wave 114:1
with a little bit of l. 203:13
Lucky: you l. people 334:1
Lug-'ole: pin back your l.s 118:1
Lumberjack: I'm a l. 238:15
Luna: cuando sale la l. 128:15
Lunacy: in the world of minor l. 127:13
Lunatic: all are l.s 42:27
l. asylum run by l.s 209:9
l.s have taken over the asylum 287:21
many l.s and . . . the great men of history 290:12
Lunch: there is no free l. 18:10
unable to l. today 267:20
Lung: don't keep using your l.s 198:14
Lust: nonconformity and l. 346:3
if he could . . . enjoy his l. 268:4
Lust: ihre Türme aus L. 281:12

Lutheran: L. separation of public 166:6
Luxuries: barely afford the . . . l. 100:18
give me the l. of life 366:1
these were l. not for him 68:20
every l. was lavished on you 253:20
future is the most expensive l. 356:11
Lying: diplomacy – l. in state 153:14
he's l. . . . lips are moving 16:15
if his lips move, he's l. 34:14
one of you is l. 259:16
prefer l. to having nothing to hide 61:22
Lyre: when 'Omer smote 'is bloomin' l. 187:2

M

MacArthur, General: 335:16
Macbeth: M. . . . proof that a nervous bloke 53:7
MacCarthyism: M. is Americanism 214:15
MacDonald, Ramsay: 73:16, 73:17, 209:11, 228:12
M. . . . an actor 321:16
McGregor: don't go into Mr M.'s garden 268:7
Macheath: jack-knife has M. 52:9
Machine: I have tested your m. 333:10
m. for turning . . . into urine 99:1
m. threatens all achievement 282:14
man who rides up on a great m. 233:3
no m. can do the work of one 159:19
some great roaring m. 30:12
Machinery: man is . . . m. 341:8
Mackerel: m. betrayed by its . . . sprat 50:5
Macleod, Iain: 294:17
McLuhan, Marshall: my remark about, M. 239:14
Macmillan, Harold: 41:19, 205:3, 205:4, 243:9, 329:23
Mad: all born m. Some remain so 31:1
as soon as he ceased to be m. 273:13
go m. in good company 95:20
m. about the boy 89:10
m. as the mist and snow 368:15
poets do not go m. . . . chess-players do 71:18
to be m. is not easy 138:17
Madeira: from M., but perfectly respectable 303:14
Have Some M., M'Dear 117:15
Madeleine: little crumb of m. 272:9
Mademoiselle: who garotted M. 223:13
m. from Armenteers 287:20
Madman: m. . . . lost everything except his reason 71:19
m. shakes a dead geranium 109:12
Madness: best minds . . . destroyed by m. 132:6
m. need not be breakdown 192:10
Madonna: M. of the Slums 209:19
Maestro: teach the old m. a new tune 182:17
Magazine: butt of the M. Wall 177:3

Magic: men mistook m. for medicine 324:3
  music must have . . . magic 286:9
  that old black m. 231:4
Magistrate: virtue . . . strength of weak m.s
  132:12
Magnet: feel the pull of a m. 189:15
Magnifying: habit of not m. grievances 281:2
Mahler, Alma: 84:4
Mahometan: M. country where men are
  protected 303:2
Mai: M. qui fut sans nuage 19:12
Maid: being an old m. is like . . . drowning
  113:12
  m.s do not reproduce 349:6
  no m. shall get him 271:7
  were he to meet her grace's m. 272:11
Maiden: Pretty M., Are There Any More
  47:16
  tranquillizing grace of a m. 50:15
  voyaging after m.s 177:15
Maigre: physically a *fausse m.* 300:12
Maine: inhabitant of the State of M. 118:16
Mainspring: lives with the m. left out 116:19
Majesty: if Her M. stood for Parliament
  314:6
Majority: bourgeois . . . substituted m. for
  power 153:19
  great silent m. 250:2
  index to m. opinion 256:1
  liberty is conforming to the m. 299:3
  m. to have their way 25:7
  never hope for a political m. 303:4
  one with the law is a m. 86:1
  subordination . . . to the m. 201:4
  thinking with the m. 236:2
Majors: I'd live with scarlet M. 298:1
Maker: against his M. to blaspheme 346:7
  if the M. had wanted . . . pyjamas 314:8
  m.s' lives are spent 22:3
Make-up: streak in that young man's m.
  360:12
Maladies: there are m. we must not seek to
  cure 273:13
Male: all-m. religions 78:4
  average m. gets his living 229:8
  dream of the American m. 353:11
  in a world of m.s 265:13
  m. sex . . . vested interest 211:2
  no healthy m. 230:11
Malice: m. is like a game of poker 315:5
Malicious: God is subtle but . . . not m.
  107:21
Malignant: only part . . . not m. 347:21
Malingering: absolute genius for m. 273:12
Malleable: in a highly m. condition 187:17
Malpractice: was that economy or m. 253:19
Mama: Last of the Red-Hot M.s 336:1
Mammal: written . . . by a large . . . M. 310:2
Man: 143:9
  against the same 'object': m. 112:3
  are only repelled by m. 166:18
  build the Republic of M. 370:3
  dealing with a m. . . . is as easy 169:2
  each m. as he sees himself 172:2
  every man who is high up 29:6

he was her m. 16:4
how many roads must a m. 104:19
if every m. gave up women 125:6
knew a m. by the company 14:2
make a m. by standing a sheep 32:19
make a m. of every one of you 360:7
m. . . . ingenious machine 99:1
m. always dies before he is . . . born 123:15
m. and woman are two locked caskets 99:4
M. as Nature's last word 361:7
m. be my metaphor 327:22
m. can only live . . . Forgetting 52:10
m. cannot live on the human plane 131:19
m. engraved on a postage stamp 39:3
m. . . . grows beyond his work 317:4
m. hands on misery to m. 193:18
m. in his wholeness wholly attending 194:12
m. in the house is worth 351:21
m. is a rope 299:5
m. is a sick fly 230:4
m. is a useless passion 297:1
m. is an amphibious animal 166:8
m. is an invention of recent date 120:10
m. is and will always be a wild animal 94:10
m. is emotionally polygamous 53:8
m. is jealous because of *amour propre*
  141:11
m. is made for life 238:13
m. is neither the oldest nor 120:9
m. is only m. at the surface 341:8
m. is preceded by forest 137:3
m. lives according to his own idea 195:7
m. must think o' things 185:27
m. . . . not locked into his environment
  53:15
m. she had was kind and clean 259:15
M. wants a great deal here below 331:4
m.'s ultimate love for m. 195:11
nature . . . in favour of m. 351:14
no . . . m. can be reduced to his conscious
  108:18
not the one m. in the world 81:13
nothing more fun than a m. 259:9
only m. behaves with such . . . folly 162:15
only real danger . . . is m. himself 178:13
peril . . . not from nature, but from m.
  177:23
problem is that m. is dead 123:17
search for M. in . . . the style of Europe
  112:8
something that has meaning . . . m. 61:23
takes a m. to bring up a m. 346:5
way for a woman to hold a m. 313:13
way of a m. with a maid 185:26
win the love of a 'real' m. 90:17
woman's virtue is m.'s . . . invention 309:7
women . . . reflecting the figure of m. 365:10
women . . . try to change a m. 98:20
world could get along . . . without m. 297:15
Management: parts . . . not . . . same m. 156:9
Manager: demanding to see the m. 306:15
  m. would like to see you 235:24
Man-cub: a m. is a m. 187:8
Mandarin: M. . . . beloved by literary pundits
  83:2

Manderley: dreamt I went to M. 103:8
Manhattan: M. . . . its wild life 321:11
Manhood: there that we wasted our m. 100:6
   things as threatened his m. 81:12
Manifested: the field of the m. 219:20
Manifold: m.s out of my larynx 18:1
Manipulator: artful m. of the good the bad
   85:16
Mankind: I love m. 299:21
   ideal m. would abolish death 195:17
   m. is a closed society 299:6
   m. is a club to which we owe 72:16
   M. versus Ironmongery 351:5
   m. won 184:7
   one giant step for m. 20:12
   only one disillusion – m. 183:6
   there is no history of m. 267:2
Manner: affair of good m.s 227:17
   English m.s are far more frightening 172:7
   good m.s . . . indistinguishable 327:7
   if it weren't for his good m.s 132:8
   m.s . . . the need of the plain 347:14
   shoddy table m.s . . . have broken up 80:14
   why . . . good m.s are necessary 53:3
Mannish: she had a m. manner of mind 65:3
Man-of-war: every Spaniard is like a m.
   53:3
Manservant: m. whose . . . champagne bin
   320:19
Mantrap: marriage is a m. 303:12
Manure: civilization of one epoch . . . m. of
   the next 84:19
Manuscript: m. captured on his desk 341:3
Many: few too m. 193:7
Map: creating in the mind a m. 314:15
   m. . . . dead body of where you've been
   156:10
   m. is not the territory 190:3
Marble: death that cuts in m. 232:7
Marched: we m. lying down 235:18
Margery: some went upstairs with M. 22:27
Margin: cool white of the m. 343:3
Marijuana: is m. addictive 248:5
Mariner: jolly, jolly m.s 185:23
   where m.s had fabled news 212:7
Mark: I got high m.s 216:1
Marmion: Iliad . . . it's in the M. class 148:3
   O men of the M. class 104:2
Marriage: all m.s are different 306:8
   blessings of m. and the constancy of its
   vows 303:12
   distrust . . . a definition of m. 48:14
   from the time he got the m. licence 224:17
   in a happy m., it is the wife 52:18
   just as humdrum a m. 140·13
   Love and M. . . . horse and carriage 60:3
   m. goes on the rocks 357:10
   m. is a bribe 356:10
   m. is a mantrap 303:12
   m. is an attempt to change 17:10
   m. is the result of the longing 61:2
   m. has put . . . into slippers 61:19
   m. is a wonderful invention; but 82:19
   m. is not all bed and breakfast 88:6
   m. . . . man and a woman 365:11

M. . . . master, a mistress and two slaves
   42:20
m. portion . . . elemental discord 132:24
m. without love . . . love without m. 78:3
one doesn't have to get anywhere in a m.
   244:16
opposed his daughter's m. . . . because
   150:10
people . . . just have more m.s 172:11
she needs m. 238:13
should be a very happy m. 329:15
so . . . m.s broken up 47:4
20-years-of-Mortgage . . . m. 349:3
unhappy m.s come from . . . brains 361:3
value of m. is not 98:11
what . . . m. would be able to add 170:13
Married: best part of m. life is the fights
   356:13
   but you m. 346:11
   climbs into their graves m. 356:4
   enamoured of m. women 262:16
   gifted girls m. impossible men 139:5
   going to be m. today 20:14
   I'm getting m. in the morning 203:18
   if I were m. to you 21:13
   m., that I may not be a cuckold 99:3
   m. . . . why buy the cow 48:11
   no man is genuinely happy, m. 230:12
   result of being unhappily m. 260:4
   sea . . . life was m. to it 332:8
   she's been m. seven times 245:2
   Trade Unionism of the m. 303:11
   very much m. is only half a writer 83:10
   writing is like getting m. 244:15
Marry: can't . . . m. you today 200:13
   I'll m. him 203:6
   I would not m. God 110:12
   m. and be bored with someone else 274:13
   m. . . . having a career 27:5
   m. in haste and repeat 60:1
   m. me, and I'll never look at any other
   horse 224:7
   to m.; and nothing . . . is more ridiculous
   170:11
Marrying: Americans . . . kept on m. 361:17
   m. left your maiden name disused 193:12
Mars: next July we collide with M. 268:1
Marsh, Edward: M. . . . enjoys everything
   38:2
Marshmallow: dreamt I ate a ten-pound m.
   86:14
Martini: slip . . . into a dry M. 355:17
Martyr: m.s . . . priests and bigots 63:1
Martyrdom: dare we make his m. meaningless
   113:10
   even the dreadful m. 22:14
   m. . . . become famous without ability 306:3
Marx, Karl: 210:13
   not . . . well. M. is a case 127:15
   supplied the world with . . . M. 339:23
Marxism: principles of M. 217:9
Marxist: takes a trained M. to appreciate
   327:8
   you don't have to be a M. 19:1
Marxiste: M., tendance Groucho 137:1

Mary: hail M., quite contrary 141:5
Masculine: a single m. figure 229:7
Masoch: M., . . . more constant than a wife 280:15
Masochist: every writer . . . is a m. 39:9
Massacre: one more indispensable m. 163:8
Masses: epoch of the m. 253:11
m. . . . easily fall victims to a big lie 155:3
new world of the m. 272:7
uprising of the m. 253:12
when I hear anything said about the m. 271:7
Masseur: at a convention of m.s 338:14
Master: m.s came and went 346:22
Old M.s 22:13
unwitting where their m. dwells 225:22
we are the m.s 306:12
Masterpiece: nothing is likely about m.s 322:13
true function of a writer . . . a m. 84:9
Masturbation: 13:1
m. . . . primary sexual activity 323:13
Mat: flatten him like a welcome m. 289:7
Match: chosen the day of the Eton . . . m. 161:5
m. between the Spurs and the Villa 160:15
paper m. in his shoe 288:13
Matches: all m. are unwise 303:19
Mater: M. would be most distressed 181:11
Material: fight with men against m. 263:4
Materialistic: only really m. people 215:3
Maternal: m. instinct leads a woman to prefer 302:20
Mathematical: tendency to think . . . as m. 173:2
Mathematics: by a resort to m. 229:11
his sense of m. is greater 140:17
how are you at m. 235:5
I don't believe in m. 107:20
laws of m. . . . do not refer to reality 108:6
m. consists . . . of assertions 290:7
m. major . . . who could not count 150:19
m. may be defined 290:6
m. . . . possesses not only truth 290:4
sciences aspire to the condition of m. 296:7
Matisse, Henri: 208:2
M. . . . in scortacolour 65:12
more M.s than . . . the people you're used to 172:11
Martrimony: confuse the duties of m. with its pleasures 310:21
critical period in m. 153:11
steel chains of m. 152:19
Matter: few things m. at all 27:7
I regard m. as derivative 265:15
m. . . . a convenient formula 290:11
M. is what Mr X knows 106:6
on excellent terms with m. 159:22
primacy of 'spirit' over m. 313:6
Matthew Passion: M. . . . had human authors 162:16
Mattress: you don't crack it open on a m. 232:19
Mature: m. man . . . wants to live humbly 317:6

Maturity: m. . . . a short break in adolescence 113:9
Matzo: isn't there any other part of a m. 238:8
Maugham, W. Somerset: 89:13
Maupassant, Guy de: trained hard and I beat . . . M. 151:10
Mausoleum: designing m.s 208:9
Maxim: copybook m.s and psalms 152:23
May: M. will be fine next year 159:8
Maybe: I'll give you a definite m. 135:7
Mayer, Louis B.: 17:22
Mayflower: didn't come over on the M. 285:10
Mayor: short-sighted lord m. raising 121:11
Maze: life is a m. in which we take 84:15
MCC: hard to tell where M. ends 272:2
Me: m. that is seen 196:8
m., what's that after all 156:19
universe . . . what's in it for m. 98:8
Meal: two m.s at a boarding-house 198:12
Mean: don't m. nothing itself 317:5
down these m. streets a man must go 67:14
yes, but what does it m. 268:18
Meaning: double m. . . . mean one thing 28:16
m. shows in the defeated thing 225:19
something that has m. . . . man 61:23
whole of it has m. 261:9
Means: all m. are good 296:12
justify the m. so long as 335:6
Meant: but it is what I m. 342:3
Measles: nationalism . . . m. of mankind 107:17
Measure: m. him by what he conjectured 46:16
to the beat of the m. 269:17
Measured: when they m. by me 239:20
Mechanism: repetitious m. of the Universe 354:9
Mede: one man's M. 180:9
Media: m. . . . sounds like a convention 319:19
Medical: advance of modern m. thought 362:16
m. research would be in confusion 166:19
Medici: Miniver loved the M. 283:18
Medicinal: m. discovery, it moves 24:16
Medicine: in spite of his faith in one m. 134:2
men mistake m. for magic 324:3
never read a patent m. advertisement 174:2
Mediocre: more than magnificent – it's m. 135:8
some men are born m., some 150:20
titles distinguish the m. 302:21
Mediocrity: expression of the m. 335:2
it's our own m. that makes us 167:23
Meditation: m. is both means and end 190:15
secret of the sea in m. 131:6
Meditative: m. mind 190:16
Mediterranean: all my wife has taken from the M. 301:12
Medium: he may be a good m., but 313:10
hot m. 218:3
m., neither rare nor well done 190:4
m. because nothing's well done 9:3
m. is the message 218:2
to be . . . interested in the m. 267:5

442

Meek: m. do not inherit the earth 193:25
    m. shall inherit . . . not the mineral rights
        130:17
Meeting: life's been . . . one long m. 329:8
    m.s that do not come off 47:6
    pleasure of m. myself 298:15
Megalomaniac: the m. differs from the
        narcissist 290:12
Meinkampf: with a M. look 265:16
Meistersinger: Our M., thou set 89:21
Melancholy: mood by the name of m.
        328:25
Mellifluous: Old Corndrinking M. 151:13
Melody: if m. were all of music 322:7
    m. imposes continuity 230:18
    m. lingers on 39:19
Melting: great M. pot 370:3
Member: acquainted with the . . . m.s 353:14
    all the m.s were gentlemen 333:3
    sign 'M.s only' 234:20
Memorability: m. has been *bought* 339:3
Memories: acres, where these m. grow 325:7
    m. are card-indexes . . . in disorder 84:24
    m. are hunting-horns 19:9
    m. for the long winter evenings 363:8
    m. . . . too frail a thread 318:16
    with beauty wake wild m. 96:11
Memory: camera relieves us of . . . m. 39:4
    feats of his literary m. 80:7
    m. is what is left 46:5
    m. of yesterday 190:13
    more time . . . in the attics of m. 82:12
    no thought but a great m. 31:12
    thanks for the m. 283:14
Memsahib: plus c'est la m. 247:23
Men: all we m. have to do 235:23
    American women like quiet m. 15:9
    inquire into what m. think 20:4
    laughed at . . . m. not at all 24:3
    m. . . . a phallusy 137:19
    m. are like wine . . . improve with age
        174:15
    m. are so honest 203:19
    m. are unwise and curiously planned 117:22
    m. come of age at sixty, women 317:8
    m. . . . devote themselves . . . to making
        one another unhappy 229:13
    m. have never been good 29:12
    m. in a world of m. 185:5
    m. . . . long for sex separated 355:8
    m. no lords can buy 69:4
    m. see objects, women see 120:19
    m. wouldn't get . . . a glance 341:4
    race of m. is almost extinct 196:23
    some m. never look at you 259:6
    too many m. in politics and not enough
        132:4
    where m. are protected from women 303:2
Mendacity: atmosphere of accredited m. 9:10
    carried away in an ecstasy of m. 303:1
    has a high m. quotient 34:14
    purely by discriminate m. 320:17
Mental: m. functionings are not . . . nature
        354:17
    m. reflection is much more interesting 265:6

philosophy ought to . . . unravel people's
    m. blocks 277:1
Menuhin, Yehudi: 64:2
Menus: national dish of America is m.
        284:2
Merchant: not least of our m. princes 186:2
    rich m. in Stambouli 269:14
Mère: la m. fait du tricot 271:3
Meredith: we're in, M. 188:12
Merger: pull off a m. between Heaven
        351:12
Meritocracy: The Rise of the M. 369:18
Mess: that unspeakable idiotic m. 254:17
    they are invariably . . . m.-makers 265:7
Message: he will be given m.s 233:3
Messiah: M. of the new age 309:10
Metaphor: man be my m. 327:22
    quarter-pound of mixed m.s 87:13
    terrific m.s of speed 61:6
Metaphysical: m. system derived from several
        162:22
Metaphysician: scientist must be . . . a m.
        305:8
Metaphysics: cheating on the m. exam 13:15
    principles of . . . m. are true 24:10
    science of m. 229:12
Metempsychosis: had the artistic m. 152:10
Metre: when I think of m. 197:4
Metro-Goldwyn-Mayer: born . . . on a M. lot
        129:9
    M. production 192:12
Metropolis: m. . . . fat, valuable cow 75:16
    they eventually live in the m. 90:7
Mexican: M. who comes to chop the wood
        194:6
Mexico: 195:23
    in M. the gods ruled 82:11
Michelangelo: M. in the curls of Moses'
        beard 163:2
    warfare . . . produced M. 348:16
Michelin: any M. guide 234:15
Microbe: m.s . . . in the curls of Moses' beard
        163:2
    more m.s *per person* 37:15
Midden: take the ashes down to the m. 82:18
Middle: happens to . . . the m. of the road
        41:20
    m. age is the best time, if 167:4
    m. age snuffs out . . . more talent 160:1
    m.-aged prosperity 205:18
    temptation came to him in the m. age 293:19
    we've eliminated the m. man 113:8
Middle class: comfort came in with the m.es
        34:6
    healthy type . . . essentially m. 115:17
    member of the upper-m. 352:23
    m. education . . . training of servants 357:4
    m. people considered beauty above their
        means 297:8
    m. weapon to keep children good 54:15
    m.es . . . the artificially limited family 305:24
    mood of the m. 210:4
    not proud of . . . is the lower-m. 231:21
    we of the sinking m. 255:19
    what goes on in a m. family 110:8

Middlemarch: M. . . . for grown up people 364:13
Midland: M., bound for Cricklewood 41:6
Midnight: m. shades the memory 109:12
Might: m. would always be right 45:10
   times when you know that you m. 185:15
   we Britons . . . use 'M.' 347:11
Milan: if it rains in M. 199:8
Military: battles . . . hold the m. mind 335:18
   defiance of m. authority 298:9
   entertainment given to the m. 42:25
   I prefer our m. past 339:5
   intelligence of the m. 279:9
   m.-industrial complex 108:15
   m. intelligence is a contradiction 225:1
   m. justice is to justice 17:12
   susceptible to a m. solution 182:9
Milk: one end is moo, the other, m. 247:9
Milka: drinka pinta m. day 10:13
Milky Way: M., O shining sister 19:8
Millennium: m. is not created immediately 359:20
   m.'s a place to go to 37:12
Miller, Henry: M. is not really a writer 52:25
Miller: she was a m.'s daughter 288:2
Millie: M., a messy old mermaid 59:1
Million: accustomed to think in m.s 37:19
   I am one of the unpraised . . . m.s 309:17
   man who has a m. dollars 21:12
   m. is made by producing 356:8
   multitude of one m. 189:11
   son, here's a m. dollars 249:11
Millionaire: all m.s love a baked apple 115:1
   m.s and bums taste about alike 222:17
   not the . . . impressive type of m. 117:1
   Who Wants to Be a M. 268:2
Milton: what M. saw when he went blind 223:4
Miltonist: M. firmly believes 232:1
Mind: any matter . . . passed through the human m. 70:19
   Balham m. 242:3
   best m.s . . . destroyed by madness 132:6
   born *with my m. made up* 64:7
   bring the balloon of the m. 368:5
   British Museum an enormous m. 365:6
   concept of m. 233:16
   empires of the m. 74:6
   extremely little house of my m. 92:16
   grief develops the powers of the m. 274:9
   he is all Disembodied M. 197:2
   hear his m. working 303:17
   highest function of *m.* 195:10
   his m. . . . in a thorough mess 349:14
   human as distinct from the German m. 172:3
   human m. . . . range of limitations 140:7
   I will ease your m. 307:8
   it's all in the m. 364:5
   keep violence in the m. 12:13
   laid stress on not changing one's m. 227:3
   Latin m. does not have two spheres 295:18
   little m.s are interested in the 159:20
   make M. kiss her hand 195:21
   man who has made up his m. for all 131:12

m. as quiet as moss 369:14
m. can also be an erogenous 348:15
m. . . . fire that has to be set alight 91:16
m. like a beautiful Clapham 142:11
m. merely wears itself out 190:8
m. oscillates between sense 178:2
m. that reveres details 206:17
m. unless . . . part of the body 131:6
m.s like beds always made up 358:4
m.s with doors as numerous 169:12
my m. . . . an empty sieve 310:3
my m. is maturing late 247:13
my m. isn't much of a comfort 157:1
opening my m. like a glass-bottomed boat 243:4
out of my m. I'd never go back 99:22
prison of our m. . . . furnish it 340:2
product of the free m. 254:19
someone whose m. watches itself 62:10
soundproofing your m. 286:20
stops my m. from wandering 202:12
third rate m. 236:2
to make the m. an absolute ruler 194:20
wars begin in the m.s of men 338:7
what is significant is m. 295:3
when the m. is secure, it is in decay 190:13
Mine: wonderful m. of souls 282:6
Miner: because m.s sweat their guts out 254:24
   provoke . . . the m.s 27:4
Mineral: inherit the earth but not the m. rights 130:17
Minister: as dark as the inside of a . . . M. 65:18
   First M. in order to preside 74:4
   this M. is neither a Lord 25:8
Mink: trick of wearing m. 27:9
   why not the m. 267:8
Minority: m. to have their say 25:7
Minute: file the m. 231:9
   leave in a m. and a huff 224:8
   not a m. on the day 85:11
Miracle: believe in m.s in European affairs 145:7
   but for the m.s . . . Nero the ideal 135:26
   cannot accept m.s 134:2
   greatest m. . . . from my learned friend 149:5
   many more . . . believe in the m.s 123:1
   m. . . . of naked existence 163:16
   m. that sense appals 43:9
   m.s do not happen 192:17
   overdrawn on the Bank of M.s 55:18
   r'ar back and pass a m. 82:14
   timid little m.s 351:10
Miraculous: m. . . . did not melt in one's bath 79:18
Mirror: bevelled edge of a sunlit m. 9:2
   m.s . . . are abominable 46:15
   m.s are the windows of the devil 129:6
   sexual pull towards m.s 82:3
   write something on a steamed m. 103:13
Misanthropic: at heart he was m. 347:12
Mischief: m. . . . with the cooking sherry 330:5
Miserable: men are happy because they are m. 122:1

Misery: compensates for the m. of being it
102:1
that . . . was a glorious m. 264:22
Mislead: one to m. the public 21:3
Misrepresentation: only way to escape m.
199:2
Missionaries: m. teach 'em 284:20
Missionary: blend of . . . the m. 316:6
my brother's a slum m. 17:15
Mistake: discussion . . . more m.s 335:1
expert . . . has made all the m.s 44:18
expert . . . knows some of the worst m.s
150:3
good thing to make m.s 183:20
hippopotamus . . . an enormous m. 69:25
made the m. of being yourself 188:3
realized that I had made a m. 90:8
result of routine . . . and sheer m. 295:15
same m.s . . . sooner 27:13
when I make a m., it's a beaut. 142:14
when women want to make m.s 180:6
Mister: hunchback . . . a solitary m. 327:19
Mistress: faults of his m. 272:12
finding a husband for one's m. 86:17
Misunderstood: those who long to be m. 342:7
Mix: I like the things we m. 198:15
Mob: m. cannot shout down a telephone 72:10
Moby Dick: M. the whale or the man 287:1
Mockingbird: to kill a m. 200:1
Model: anyone could be a famous m. 91:1
Moder: not your fader but your m. 269:14
Moderation: m. . . . is no virtue 134:10
Modern: m. world . . . no notion of preserving
70:7
Modest: making him far too m. 44:9
m. about my not knowing all 246:4
M.? . . . Nobody could say that 278:15
with much to be m. about 77:6
Modesty: m. . . . against the eye of the unclean
131:2
m. . . . very like a crime 336:5
wished . . . to cultivate m. 308:11
Modulation: simplest m. . . . already art
322:6
Molehill: *look after the m.s* 263:12
Molested: without being m. 242:12
Molotov, V. M.: 75:18
Mom: never eat at . . . 'M.'s' 12:17
Moma: Ma M. done tol' me 230:20
Momentariness: delight in m. 139:4
Mona Lisa: several original M.s 234:13
Monarchy: dying m. . . . has too much power
72:15
m. . . . a splendid ship 14:8
m. is a labour-intensive industry 359:7
tourists . . . take in the M. 145:12
Monastery: there was . . . a m. 250:15
Moneda: la m. . . . solloza 128:15
Money: beads brings in m. quicker 199:17
bring me a specimen of your m. 224:19
conscience m. 204:10
divided up their m. among themselves
316:8
don't give your son m. 75:3
drop in your m. 24:11

fool and his m. . . . how they got together
118:4
give him the m., Barney 264:12
give . . . money and don't worry 119:9
good m. . . . on a mere picture 163:3
greatest m.-spending machine 28:10
half the m. . . . wasted 345:1
her voice is full of m. 116:8
Hollywood m. isn't m. 260:2
how the m. rolls in 17:15
I am only interested in m. 306:11
I don't care too much for m. 202:9
I have saved enough m. 232:3
if there's anyone . . . to whom I owe m.
118:7
interest in all the m.s 269:18
it owes itself m. 229:6
licence to print m. 329:22
lost his m. in religion 346:26
man in whom the vision of her m. 171:5
man with m. to spend 44:13
m. can't buy friends 234:21
m. doesn't talk, it swears 104:25
m. falls apart in your hands 355:18
m. gives me pleasure all the time 34:18
m. . . . greatest source of joy 128:3
m. has something to do with life 193:13
m. is better than poverty 13:14
m. is good for bribing yourself 279:10
m. is like a sixth sense 227:4
m. is on the way out 211:12
m. is paper blood 158:7
m. lords 242:21
m. nowadays seems to be produced 107:6
m. . . . see you through times of no dope
306:16
m. . . . stupid enough to want it 69:14
m. . . . vanishes as fast 298:14
no one shall work for m. 187:1
nobody lends him m. 232:24
people seem . . . odder about m. 162:10
rich are different . . . they have more m.
116:28
size of sums of m. seems to vary 163:22
so long as it doesn't cost m. 249:14
take half my m. . . . I took all of it 114:14
time when a fool and his m. 318:13
troubles that m. can't cure 247:19
try to rub up against m. 288:14
what . . . God thinks of m. 28:5
when you don't have any m. 100:4
with m. they had not got 147:9
you can be young without m. 357:11
you lose all your m. 215:12
Monk: I said to this m. 264:15
Monkey: attack the m. . . . organ-grinder is
present 41:19
biggest asset the m. possesses 284:22
Monocle: in pursuit of his m. 273:4
Monogamous: man is . . . physically m.
53:8
Monogamy: who seek to find m. 259:12
Monopolist: greatest m. of all . . . Church
321:13
Monopoly: their m. of *having more* 122:8

Monotony: pure m. of his success 169:8
  when the chord of m. is stretched 71:15
Monroe, Marilyn: 63:20, 233:5, 325:11
Mons: the *m. Veneris* as ... Mount Everest
  162:17
Monsignor: M. was forty-four 115:15
Monsoon: then the m.s came 235:14
Monster: Effie M. was a m. 200:2
  IS, the whited m. 212:7
  kiddies no-neck m.s 357:8
Monstrous: m. aunt can be funny 339:1
Montezuma: M.'s revenge 17:13
Montgomery, Viscount B.: 77:8
Month: an old man in a dry m. 108:21
Monument: the m. sticks 212:4
Moo: you silly m. 314:3
Mood: m. of the modern mind 279:7
Mookse: ere wohned a M. 177:7
Moon: blows the m. into the sun 328:2
  brilliant pilot m. 315:2
  if the m.'s a balloon 92:20
  it's only a paper m. 147:6
  m. in the breast of man 40:6
  m. is nothing but 125:17
  m. of a hundred identical faces 128:15
  m. shall look behind the hedge 292:4
  m-m-m-m. shines over the cow-shed 253:1
  only you beneath the m. 267:22
  part of the m. was falling down 124:5
  reach to the m. and back 43:13
  m. rise above the pines 292:7
  shine on, harvest m. 251:1
  walk on the m. and look at the earth 111:5
Moonlight: get no more from the m. 317:21
  m. runs over the grasses 225:13
Moore, George: 113:6
  M. told and did not kiss 237:8
Mop: looked ... like a m. 237:6
Mopser: has anybody seen my M. 96:9
Moral: higher the buildings the lower the m.s
  88:14
  I like a m. issue 228:13
  instability of evil is the m. 354:15
  live beyond his m. means 332:19
  making ... m. ideas seem ridiculous 65:24
  m. behaviour varies in inverse ratio 163:1
  m. gymnasium ... to strengthen your
    character 302:28
  M. is (I think, at least) 34:24
  m. leadership 289:17
  one becomes m. 273:1
  Providence ... responsible for their m.s
    369:6
  self-interest was bad m.s 285:19
  separation of public and private m.s 166:6
  Social Revolution will be m. 261:15
  take the m. law and make a nave 317:15
  what I mean by m. progress 332:17
  wicked and m. ... good and immoral 77:9
  worst government is the most m. 230:1
Moralist: m.s write about ... having character
  70:1
Morality: corruption of medicine by m. 230:7
  I prefer m. 206:5
  m. based on ideas 194:16

m. loses the foundation 295:5
  no m. ... founded on authority 24:9
  so-called new m. 306:13
Mori: pro patria m. 257:4
Morning: if they take you in the m. 26:10
  m. of which it was bereaved 332:3
  oh, what a beautiful m. 146:3
Morning Star: M. is read by the people 11:3
Morocco: like Webster's ... M. bound 91:15
Morris, William: 276:4
  M. was a wonderful all-round man 33:4
Mortality: this mortal has put on m. 70:19
  threat of m. ... sterilizes 62:21
Mortgage: more covered with m.s 10:4
  20-years-of-M. ... marriage 349:3
Mortician: depression among us m.s 208:12
Moscow: M. ... was our Rome 64:8
Moses: had written as many books as Moses
  77:13
  he saw his role as ... M. 172:20
  since M. wrote the Ten Commandments 9:5
Mostest: The Hostess with the M. 39:15
Mote: The M. in the Middle Distance 32:5
Moth: m. entirely surrounded by candles
  112:12
Moth-ball: he exuded a flavour of m.s 243:9
Mother: American boys have m.s 15:20
  And Her M. Came Too 251:4
  be the m. of a bishop 33:20
  best friend of a boy is his m. 221:12
  between the artist man and the m. woman
    302:27
  Boy's Best Friend is His M. 233:13
  come m.s and fathers 105:9
  English girl hates ... her m. 302:31
  God bless m. and daddy 318:7
  if a m. could be content 63:7
  men fight ... to impress their m.s 113:17
  M. died today. Or ... yesterday 62:12
  m. has an innate ability 276:1
  m. is knitting 271:3
  m. protected me ... father threatened 90:15
  m. to dozens ... nobody's wife 153:6
  my m., drunk or sober 69:13
  my m. was a bus-horse 309:13
  old enough to be ... your m. 236:3
  prefer widows to unmarried m.s 297:9
  remember my m., the day that we met
    69:7
  there should be no m.s 305:17
  to the dogs ... m. will be there 153:4
  very strict m. 226:13
  with his m. through the parables 327:24
  wouldn't sleep with my own m. 12:8
Mother-in-law: a m. with only one eye 175:8
Motor-car: his m. was poetry and tragedy
  206:14
Motor-cycle: how to fix a m. 265:11
Motorist: American m. in England 208:16
Motto: rather than the m.s on sundials 269:5
  thus runs my m. 228:15
Mountain: even the nicest m. 22:12
  m.s of Mourne 122:10
  m.s will look after themselves 263:12
    that last blue m. barred with snow 117:21

those who have come a long way down the
m. 277.3
whenever I look at a m. 323:9
Mountebank: *those prosperous m.s* 207:10
Mount Everest: M. is very easy to climb 284:3
Mourn: whatever m.s when many leave 257:5
Mourne: mountains of M. sweep down 122:10
Moustache: his nicotine eggyellow . . . m.
328:15
I doodle handlebar m.s 212:5
slight m. . . . I've got one anyhow 146:22
Mouth: feeding the m. that bites you 98:9
Move: m.s . . . as a jellyfish 363:2
Movement: detest as a m. 223:11
great m.s are popular m.s 154.18
I want to be a m. 236:15
moments . . . she said *m.s* 123:3
mightiest m. is temporal 72:12
m.s of thought and soul 54:17
Movies: m. are the only business 284:18
popularity of American m. 215:6
thanks to the m. 339:14
trot down to the m. and see 356:6
why *did* you give up the m. 128:13
Moving: man has stopped m. 326:15
Möwen: die M. sehen alle 240:2
Mower: drone of m.s on suburban lawns
280:16
Mozart, W. A.: angels . . . play M. 29:13
light and plenty of M. 48:16
sonatas of M. are unique 299:14
when M. was my age 200:11
Mrs: never M. one 15:14
Mücke: o Glück der M. 282:1
Mud: impenetrable spaces, impassable m.
266:10
Muddier: diving deeper . . . coming up m.
163:4
Muddle: beginning, a m., and an end 193:23
life was a damned m. 115:18
transitory and *unnecessary* m. 183:17
Multiply: command 'Be fruitful and m.'
166:16
some guy . . . fruitful and m. 13:20
Multitude: warmly surrounded by the m.
332:10
weeping, weeping m.s 108:20
Mum: like Dad, keep M. 15:16
your m. and dad 193:17
Mummy: results in . . . an Egyptian m. 362:15
Mumsy: all know M. was . . . clumsy 43:11
Munch: m. m. m. 234:22
Murder: avalanche of m.s 112:8
better to be wanted for m. 360:9
cannot claim . . . for m. 62:19
m. a man . . . committing suicide 359:17
nervous . . . should not commit a m. 53:7
takes two to make a m. 162:6
this is a British m. inquiry 319:15
Murderer: affection for a m. 255:6
soul of a m. is blind 62:16
Murdoch, Rupert: M. has found a gap 11:3
Murry, John Middleton: 332:19
Muse: bid the M. go pack 368:22
English M. her annual theme 61:7

Fear and the M. stand watch 11:14
forced the M. to this alliance 61.5
lucky M. . . . affair with a soldier 171:13
M. prefers the liars 369:7
Museum: I should become a m. man 271:14
Mushroom: life is too short to stuff a m. 85:6
Music: alive with the sound of m. 146:7
all his m. accepts it 298:12
arts aspire to the condition of m. 296:7
attracted only to m. 299:8
compare the m. of *The Beggar's* 161:23
difference between classical m. and jazz
271:5
English may not like m. 31:17
film m. should have 322.17
he's already writing the m. 294:18
I'm a martyr to m. 328:12
if melody were all of m. 322:7
in m., the punctuation is . . . strict 280:9
laughter . . . most civilized m. 339:10
military m. is to m. 17:12
m. begins to atrophy 268:23
m. creates order 230:18
m. critics . . . padlocked ears 322:19
m. . . . goes on to become 23:21
m. is . . . digesting time 23:22
m. is in the air – you simply take 108:17
m. is natural law 348:5
m. is the arithmetic of sounds 96:6
m. is your own experience 258:4
M., Maestro, Please 219:18
m. must have an idea 286:9
m. *per se* means nothing 31:15
m. teacher came twice each week 10:5
m. that changed a man's decision 299:10
m. . . . the breakfast food of love 11:11
m. under a microscope 26:2
m. was the one gift denied me 241:1
my m. . . . understood by children 322:18
no m. except through earphones 246:12
popular m. . . . strides in reverse 91:11
rightful owner of the m. 261:11
so much m. into so few bars 57:10
teaching m. is not my main purpose 323:5
that m. proves it 157:2
three pounds for the m. 346:7
two words about m., one of them 86:19
Van Gogh's ear for m. 356:1
when m. sounds, all that I was 96:19
where the m. can't be heard 217:11
Musical: game of m. daggers 359:8
Music-hall: Darling of the m.s 43:4
pleasantry of the m. 283:11
Musician: m. is . . . most modest of animals
298:17
m.s did not like the piece 31:14
Musicologist: m. is a man who can read 31:16
Mussolini, Benito: 45:5, 301:1
Hitler showed . . . loyalty to M. 57:4
M. was only an adjective 219:17
Must: they m. do . . . want to do 23:20
Mustard: m.'s no good without . . . beef
223:17
Musty: you will be frail and m. 258:19
Mutiny: m. in the bargain basement 278:13

Mutton: make yesterday's cold m. 226:19
Myriad: there died a m. 269:8
Myself: more m. than I 78:17
  m. and I are on the best 81:20
  pleasure of meeting m. 298:15
Mysteries: like all the modern young . . . m. 169:14
  m. . . . worth fathoming 36:9
  particular m. . . . impenetrable 79:13
Mysterious: become a thing incurably m. 70:19
Mystery: mysticism . . . attempt to get rid of m. 126:4
  pure m. . . . into early set fruit 281:8
Mysticism: m. . . . to get rid of mystery 126:4
Myth: m. is a fixed way of looking 46:6
  m. is a type of speech 29:17
  m. is not a fairy story 291:12
  m. is recognized for what it is 295:5
  science must begin with m.s 267:4
  Truth and M. are one and the same 297:14
Mythology: what counted was m. of self 317:13

N

Nabokov, Vladimir: N. . . . perfumed English 339:20
Nageur: n.s morts suivrons-nous 19:8
Nail: I used to bite my n.s 258:12
  relatively clean finger n.s 241:13
Naissance: toute n. . . . connaissance 78:17
Naked: must have to stand n. 104:24
  n. into the conference chamber 41:18
  to be n. is to be oneself 39:8
Nakedness: n. is a luxury 332:10
Name: and made you change your n. 325:11
  as my n. was before I dyed it 90:9
  but to know an object by its . . . n. 63:8
  Groucho is not my real n. 225:7
  headstones yield their n.s 325:6
  just mention my n. 116:6
  my n. in such large letters 333:11
  my n. will never be writ large 258:12
  n. and date . . . obliterate 57:8
  n.s associated . . . with racehorses 293:11
  n.s like that . . . makes 'em go wrong 350:6
  sons acclaim your glorious n. 92:7
  that other with my n. 220:12
  these intolerably nameless n.s 298:4
  under an assumed n. 180:12
  when her real n. is Mrs James 123:2
  without using anybody's n. 258:7
  wrote my n. at the top of the page 74:19
  you've got such a Scotch n. 250:14
Nameless: Jim, who shall remain n. 202:4
Naming: today we have n. of parts 277:16
Nancy: ev'ryone knew her as N. 202:23
Nannies: n. sat knitting the slow pattern 116:11
Napoleon Bonaparte: 155:14
  N. is nothing to me 233:8
Napoleon III: 326:3

Narcissist: megalomaniac differs from the n. 290:12
Narcotic: whether the n. be . . . idealism 178:7
Narkover: young gentlemen of N. 242:11
Nastier: anything n. to say 298:19
Nastiness: n. is a real stimulant 104:9
  this house is jealous of its n. 138:16
Nasty: how n. the n. people are 270:11
Nation: America became top n. 301:5
  America . . . is the prize amateur n. 359:19
  at the service of the n. 266:14
  behaved in the way n.s do 358:1
  best interest of the n. 250:4
  great n.s 191:2
  kind of n. . . . Roosevelt hoped 175:13
  living n.s wait 22:5
  n. about to go into . . . liquidation 217:1
  n. had the lion's heart 77:24
  n. is a society united 166:4
  n. is not in danger of . . . disaster 229:6
  n. shall speak peace unto n. 279:13
  n. talking to itself 233:4
  n. that can see beyond its own image 182:7
  n.s . . . die by imperceptible disorders 133:1
  perfectly demoralize the n. 40:9
  places the n. at his service 266:14
Nationalism: n. . . . an infantile disease 107:17
Nationality: other people have a n. 33:17
Native: dreams of the n. are always 112:4
  eyes of a n. 203:22
  our ideas about the n. 203:21
  so long as the n.s are waiters 240:16
  your n.s have . . . sounds 314:5
Natur: aus beiden Reichen erwuchs seine . . . N. 282:8
  ein Mund der N. 282:12
Naturalist: truth, . . . a standard for the n. 296:4
Naturalness: with the n. of the hippopotamus 239:9
Nature: any shade that is near to n. 102:7
  at two with n. 13:19
  escaped from N.'s hand ere perfect 95:1
  habit is a second n. 274:3
  if you want to change her n. 185:17
  in n. . . . there are consequences 341:1
  natural science . . . interplay between n. 150:4
  n. harbours no intention 178:3
  N. holds many mysteries 36:9
  n. . . . wasteful of promising young men 160:1
  N. will not allow humanity to be deprived 219:19
  no . . . enjoyment in N. 354:14
  not properly part of n. 354:17
  order of n. . . . in favour of man 351:14
  representations of our true n. 178:4
  stuff that n. replaces it with 357:12
  thought-riddled n. 198:2
  what n. seldom affords 296:2
Navies: your nutshell n. came 185:7
Navy: charge of the N. . . . much at sea 64:16
  joined the N. to see the world 39:17
  N.'s here 17:17

Nazi: the N.s came for the Communists 249:8
Neat: you look n. 81:2
Necessities: do without the n. 366:1
Necessity: honour . . . n. for hall-porters
  70:23
Neck: comes and wrings our n.s 24:13
  England will have her n. wrung 353:4
  equipping us with a n. 189:18
  especially from the n. down 288:15
  his n. seemed to go straight up 234:4
  short n. denotes a good mind 313:12
Need: between the human n. and . . . silence
  62:1
  friend in n. . . . to be avoided 295:8
  n. but not for everyone's greed 56:14
  selling something that everybody n.s 356:8
  will you still n. me 203:2
Needle: build bigger n.s 203:10
  easier for a n. to pass 314:10
Ne'er-do-well: I began life as a n. 339:8
Nefarious: she is so n. 289:5
Negative: without n. emotions 257:1
  world most needs . . . n. virtues 119:1
Negotiate: let us never n. out of fear 181:26
Negrified: American society . . . half n. 155:17
Negro: insulted in places where the average N.
  95:8
  N. . . . is a standing rebuke 229:18
  N. problem will no longer exist 25:7
Neigh: people expect me to n. 15:8
Neighbour: do not love your n. as yourself
  302:18
  hate my next-door n. 69:10
  imagines that to his n. 215:1
  lady of the house was everyone's n. 129:5
  no one can . . . love his n. 359:14
  no . . . substitute for the good n. 107:12
  same goes for the n.'s wife 38:12
  when he told men to love their n.s 51:17
Nelson, Horatio, Lord: N. . . . on his element
  333:18
Nemesis: Hubris clobbered by N. 12:11
Nero: I should consider N. the ideal man
  135:26
Nerve: he has n. and he has knowledge
  101:20
  n. specialist . . . sounds better 362:4
  when you suffer an attack of n.s 156:8
Nervous: n. when she walked by 300:1
Nest: build their n.s in our hair 226:4
  they rejoiced in the n. they kept 124:13
Nether: not as n. as some 125:22
Neumann, John von: 54:9
Neurosis: imagine a worse cure for psycho-n.
  315:15
  n. . . . avoiding non-being 331:14
  n. has an absolute genius 273:12
  secret of n. 237:4
  so eager for the n. 151:2
Neurotic: n. . . . builds a castle 197:17
  greatest things we know have come to us
  from n.s 273:11
  n. if he suffers 323:19
  inclinations – n. 287:11
Neutralism: 103:6

Neutrality: 'positive n.' is a contradiction
  190:7
Nevershit: like you was Lady N. 351:18
New: advent of the N. Man 302:30
  he has discovered something n. 301:8
  'What's n.?' 265:4
New England: must have had N. ancestors
  151:19
Newfoundland: nothing new in N. 243:2
Newman, John Henry: face like what Cardinal
  N.'s 65:9
Newness: Americans . . . respect n. 338:12
News: foreign stories . . . not real n. 347:6
  hard n. catches readers 250:13
  more abhorrent a n. item 120:12
  n. coverage that's got so much better 73:1
  n. is anything that makes a reader 216:11
  n. of one day, one afternoon 40:9
  only n. until he's read it 347:7
Newspaper: but old men read n.s 71:6
  certain . . . drudgery in n. work 330:15
  fluid mass distracted by n.s 75:13
  good n. . . . is a nation 233:4
  like to appear in the n.s 109:21
  never believe in . . . n.s 256:10
  n. . . . continuous fiction 41:21
  n.s I can't stand 319:21
  reading someone else's n. 48:19
  send her a copy of your local n. 220:11
  time it takes to read a n. 355:5
Newspaperman: best n. who has ever been
  President 55:7
Newsprint: strained this country's n. resources
  122:3
Newstatesmaning: in N. the critic must be on
  top 268:16
New York: 149:13, 152:8
  N. is not the cultural centre 35:17
  N. . . . the west side 82:8
  N.'s a small place 362:21
  to tell the story of N. 351:1
New York Times: 321:7
New Zealand: 122:12
Next: there is no n. time 31:4
Niagara Falls: 219:21
  spitting in N. 43:9
Nice: be n. to people on your way up 237:18
  how nasty the n. people can be 270:11
  keep doing things I think are n. 259:10
  n. guys finish last 104:1
  n. one, Cyril 17:21
  why doesn't she behave like a n. man 111:11
Nice: nicer, much nicer in N. 359:10
Nicely-Nicely: N. is known far and wide
  289:14
Nicholas II: N. inherited . . . revolution
  334:5
Nichtexistent: als n. im Eigen-Sinn 240:5
Nickel: seven-cent n. 225:2
Niece: that was not my n. 342:6
Nietzsche: N. is dead – God 136:17
Night: coming for us that n. 26:10
  each world's n. in vain 96:22
  every n. of her married life 328:9
  first n. was notoriously distracting 217:3

449

Night – *Contd.*
go gently into that good n. 327:17
guards against N. Starvation 249:2
hard day's n. 202:16
if you love it not, of n. 329:1
in a real dark n. of the soul 116:12
into some forgotten n. 97:1
n. and day you are the one 267:22
n. was tailing against 332:3
n. will never stay 112:9
we come from n. . . . Why live in n. 120:16
where the blue of the n. 91:9
who were you with last n. 133:15
Nightdress: the n. in which she became 9:15
Nightingale: N. Sang in Berkeley Square
225:11
n.s are singing in 22:28
n.s are singing near 109:14
n.s sing out of tune 170:16
whose n.s have no wings 329:5
Nihilist: cannot be a part-time n. 62:19
Nineteen: life was never better than in n.
sixty-three 193:9
Nineteenth century: n. . . . age of the editorial
chair 218:1
n. man . . . thought he was Victor Hugo
297:11
Nineties: world was young, in the n. 30:20
Niño: dentro de la fragua el n. 128:18
Nixon, Richard: 292:11, 335:15
in this much trouble since . . . N. 82:4
N. is . . . purposeless 53:5
standing between N. and the White House
182:11
you won't have N. to kick around 249:12
No: idea that N. meant Yes 130:7
rebel . . . man who says n. 62:20
No Man's Land: Absurdist plays . . . in N.
9:11
Noah: who *was* N.'s wife? Joan of Arc 148:18
Nobility: man's charter of n. 296:5
n. . . . snored through the Sermon 45:1
Noise: loud n. at one end 189:8
moved to folly by a n. 198:4
n.s at dawn will bring 23:6
they absolutely love the n. 31:17
you can exclude n. 286:20
Nonbeing: n. must in some sense be 275:1
Non-commissioned: the N. Man 185:4
Nonconformist: a n. like everybody else 331:10
Nonconformity: n. and lust 346:3
Nonentity: a complete n. 240:5
Non-existence: unaware of its own n. 310:7
Non-literate: a n. world 218:5
Non-problem: pseudo-light . . . on n.s 15:1
Nonsense: a firm anchor in n. 127:11
greater part . . . is n. 229:3
man talking n. not to himself 320:7
n. does not pass by 29:21
Non-violence: possible to disagree about . . . n.
146:13
Noon: then in the summer n. 327:25
Normal: n. is the good smile in a child's eyes
301:13
n. itself an abnormality 72:6

Normality: n. . . . . subject to question 357:16
Norman: I will feed no n. 201:21
your physique is so . . . N. 125:24
Norman, Montagu: 80:8
North: inhabitant of the N. of England
118:16
swung to their prodigious N. 314:18
Northcliffe, Lord: 325:13
N. has sent for the King 16:9
trouble with you, N. 306:6
Norway: as he did in the case of N. 276:3
Norwegian: rather mad N.s 193:3
Nose: cannot see beyond his own n. 32:2
keep a clean n. 105:6
n. that can see is worth 168:13
sat assiduously picking his n. 115:7
tell him that you pick your n. 60:10
Nostalgia: n. isn't what it used to be 137:6
Notches: three n. on his walking stick 99:21
Note: foot and n. disease 41:12
n.s . . . no better than many pianists 299:15
Notepaper: ever spoke of n. 237:12
Nothing: behind them . . . there is n. 296:21
doesn't do n. else but 361:12
doing n. for each other 91:10
don't get n. out 24:11
getting something for n. 292:1
I got plenty o' n. 130:12
n. is wasted, n. is in vain 153:7
n. matters very much 27:7
N. for N. 245:6
n. reserved for everything 35:12
n. scrawled on a five-foot page 69:5
n. to be done 30:18
somewhere there n. is 97:2
when one does n. 296:10
Nothingness: eternal n. is OK 13:8
Noticing: it is our n. . . . things 273:2
Notorious: n. . . . another Lady Hamilton
280:3
Novel: 193:23
because a n.'s invented, it isn't 270:5
good n. tells us the truth 71:2
impossible to write a n. nowadays 138:6
knee-stroking n.s 48:9
not a n. to be tossed aside 259:23
n. . . . a universe in which action 63:4
n. being dead 342:14
n. is . . . a Protestant form of art 254:19
n. is a static thing 336:13
n.s for grown up people 364:13
only in the n. 196:20
ordinary n. would trace the history 197:6
sexless n. that should be distinguished 306:1
we can Learn even from N.s 350:8
what is fictitious in a n. 11:15
what n. . . . epic scope of a photograph
138:7
women will write n.s 228:1
wrote domestic n.s 370:2
yes – the n. tells a story 119:19
Novelist: authors who are not really n.s
120:1
I am a n. 196:19
n. . . . my business to comprehend 171:14

n. is ... more at home 246:17
n. ..., the only one alive 23:19
n.s ... create an alternative world 121:2
schoolboy is a n. too busy 83:22
Now: n. ... the 'n' is ancient history 121:13
word 'now' is like a bomb 232:11
Nowhere: if you must go n. 207:9
leading from somewhere to n. 11:13
n. and talking to nobody 19:6
N. Man 202:21
Nowness: all-inclusive n. 218:8
Nuclear: [confrontation] 291:4
Nudge: n., n., wink, wink 239:1
Nudist: at the superior n. camps 139:23
n.s ... wear one-button suits 137:7
What Can You Give a N. 114:2
Nudity: n. is a form of dress 39:8
Nuisance: progress ... the exchange of one
n. 110:13
together a bloody n. 219:17
Number: I am not a n. 222:12
more dead people ... n.s are increasing
168:15
up in the high n.s 184:1
we got the n.s 241:9
Nun: n. is only half a woman 229:16
Nut: n.s 214:8
squeeze your n.s and open 92:17
Nutted: I have been n. 235:3
Nuvoletta: N. in her lightdress 177:8
Nyasaland: bring Stonehenge to N. 27:10
Nymph: n.s and tribal deities 192:14

O

Oak: by O., and Ash, and Thorn 186:29
Oath: if ever I utter an o. again 305:13
you see, I am on o. 20:9
OBE: he got the O. later 242:5
Obey: born neither to o. 225:23
Obituaries: who have read their own o. 139:3
Obituary: autobiography is an o. in serial form
91:2
Obligation: politics is an o. 284:14
Oblivion: o. which awaits the uncreative mind
144:6
stiffens the saltier o. 325:10
Obscene: press is o. 211:3
Obscenity: denunciations of o. in literature
161:19
Obscurity: afraid of losing my o. 161:16
Observance: my method ... o. of trifles
101:3
why he made ... ritual o.s 328:6
Observant: o. fellow who points 365:14
Observation: o. is always selective 266:17
Obsession: brought ... only his cloacal o.
176:12
Obsolescence: galloping o. 348:6
planned o. ... Western prosperity 163:21
Obsolete: o. versions of the same self 39:3
Obstacle: national sport ... o.-racing 333:6
Obvious: deafeningly o. 181:3

Occam, William: dulling the edge of O.'s
razor 275:1
Occupation: most pleasurable ... o.s 330:15
Ocean: for me it is the o. 31:5
you took away the o.s 220:16
Oceanus: all at last return to ... O. 64:18
Octave: o. is something idolatrous 135:23
October: a funny kind of month, O. 250:9
Octopus: tell me, O O. 247:15
Odd: something o. about women 37:10
Ode: 'O. to a Grecian Urn' is worth any
number 113:1
Odour: Body O. 10:11
Oedipus: myth of King O. 122:14
O. he had the luck 160:7
Offence: how people always take o. 276:14
only defence is in o. 26:14
Offend: present state of affairs o.s them 255:13
Offensive: life is an o. 354:9
you are o., sir 43:2
Office: o. ... any work done 354.21
o. was his pirate ship 206:14
Officer: o.s with high athletic qualifications
76:11
would not breed from this o. 348:2
Official: o.s are highly educated 179:7
seven o.s are now doing 260:15
O'Hara, Maureen: 192:16
Oik: o.s have become v. well dressed 356:23
Oiseaux: o. querelleurs 19:14
Oklahoma: use' to mean you was from O.
317:5
Olas: en medio de las o. 248:3
Old: as an o. man you try to conciliate 333:12
astonishing any of us choose o.ᵗage 25.15
being o. is having lighted rooms 193:14
born o. and get younger 333:2
dead ... before coming to be an o. one
316:21
for I'm o. and ill and terrified 41:7
growing o. is like being penalized 270:12
hope I die before I get o. 332:12
how old Cary Grant 138:4
it is the misfortune of an o. man 65:23
longer lease for the o. gang 28:12
my o. man said 80:19
no o. men any more 339:21
o. age ... last gap but one 354:6
o. age ... older than I 29:19
o. age ... what we have earned 52:16
o. ... are always absorbed 348:4
o. are ... fond of new things 71:6
o. enough to take its measure 83:13
o. get o. 241:9
o. have reminiscences 293:10
o. have rubbed it into the young 227:16
o. man in a draughty house 109:1
o. man in a dry month 108:21
o. man marrying a young girl 329:19
o. man who will not laugh 295:16
o. woman to outlive her dogs 357:14
only the o. are innocent 48:18
people who ... have chosen to grow o.
270:6
plural to 'O. Man' 349:16

451

Old – *Contd.*
  too o. for the spring 221:17
  too o. to be unusual 345:12
  universities valued for being o. 210:4
  very young at a very o. time 298:13
  wasted . . . most of our o. age as well 100:6
  weariness and sadness of o. age 228:9
  young can do for the o. 305:19
Older: he must make way for an o. man 226:9
  I was so much o. then 105:5
  o. she gets, the more interested he is 73:4
  worst of living, you get o. 159:16
Old-fashioned: supposed . . . he passed for o.
    170:3
Olfactory: call it an o. bar 349:10
Oligarchies: o. . . . cruelty of the rich 71:3
Omen: as to the precise meaning of the o.
    50:17
Omnibuses: motor o. were locked 364:19
On: this is o. me 260:4
One: o. that got away 259:15
  o.'s impossible, two is dreary 313:3
Oneself: painful to be no longer o. 31:3
Onion: carry their own o.s when cycling 87:9
Oompus-Boompus: Unsafe to Try Any O.
    361:11
Open: o. a building . . . o. already 107:2
  'o. society' 267:1
Opera: bed . . . is the poor man's o. 163:17
  kind of o. that starts at six o'clock 276 8
  o. in English 230:15
  o. . . . one of the strangest inventions 78:6
  o. . . . should be translated 353:6
  o. without an interval 248:9
  what language an o. is sung in 19:11
Operation: o.s . . . can perform without
    thinking 354:16
Opinion: anger of men who have no o.s 71:8
  average man's o.s . . . less foolish 291:6
  means . . . public o. minus his o. 70:18
  now but a climate of o. 22:4
  o. on all things does not matter 70:13
  o. without visible means of support 42:24
  o.s . . . will change overnight 52:14
  people are responsible for their o.s 369:6
  writer's business to hold o.s 369:8
Opium: Confessions of . . . the English O.
    Eater 305:12
Opponent: know who your o. is 339:9
  o. cannot be both honest and intelligent
    256:5
Opportunist: be an o. and float 27:2
Oppose: whatever the enemy o.s 221:22
Opposite: o. is also a profound truth 44:17
Opposition: my real o. is myself 301:16
  o. . . . tested in action 335:1
Oppression: there is no limit to o. 230:1
Oppressor: destroy an o. 297:25
  o.s do not perceive their monopoly 122:8
Optics: o. is the geometry of light 96:6
Optimism: never . . . break men's o. 69:23
  o. of the will 138:3
  our o. . . . makes our ideas 338:3
Optimist: o. . . . fills up his crossword 307:1
  o., unrepentant 339:16

  o. replies 'Oh yes they could' 57:2
  o. thought everything good except 71:25
  pessimist . . . well-informed o. 17:25
Opulence: private o. and public squalor 127:12
Orange: clockwork o. 57:15
  feeds you tea and o.s 80:3
  like an o. in a fried fish shop 65:6
Orange-box: if everybody brings an o. 205:17
Orator: one of those o.s of whom 73:9
Oratorio: too autocratic for o. 329:11
Orchard: keep cold, young o. 124:10
  o.s of our mothers 22:28
Ordeal: with the worst possible o. 40:10
Order: I am a force for o. 355:2
  music creates o. 230:18
  Prince . . . in all his tinted O.s 114:20
  receives an o., he gets a hard on 51:6
  setting up of a new o. 253:14
Ordinary: O. made beautiful 301:13
  make out of the o. something out-of the-o.
    251:5
  quite an o. sort of chap 129:21
Organ: he'd have given us all more o.s 49:4
Organic: o. life has developed 290:8
Organization: all o. is . . . grounded 232:13
  no other weapon but o. 201:3
  o. man 355:13
  o. . . . substitutes itself 335:4
  o. of the whole authority 179:5
  o. was low 218:4
Organize: don't mourn, o. 154:7
Orgasm: one o. in the bush . . . two in the
    hand 137:9
  o. has replaced the Cross 243:8
Orgy: o. looks . . . alluring 243:7
Orient: slow revenge of the O. 272:1
Oriental: as an O. he is charming 187:12
  has mistrusted O.s 49:17
  then you are an O. 119:14
Original: the really o. woman 323:6
Ornament: sweep the o.s from the mantlepiece
    249:5
Ornithology: o. . . . an arcane hobby 45:15
Orthodox: only the 'educated' are o. 255:11
Orthodoxy: o. . . . means being wrong 70:12
Orwell, George: 83:21
Osborne, John: O. . . . four hoarse men 321:5
Ostentatious: anything o., no matter what it
    cost 56:17
Other: if some of us go to him without the
    o.s 261:16
  man for o.s 46:4
  only with the passions of o.s 272:10
  woman who lives for o.s 205:17
  how was that for o.-worldliness 124:16
Otherwise: *things could be o.* 121:12
Otis: Miss O. regrets 267:20
Out: much too far o. all my life 310:13
Outcast: time is on the side of the o. 90:7
Outlook: o. of mankind grew . . . larger 74:12
Outside: I am just going o. 252:1
Over: back till it's o., o. there 80:1
Overcoat: never taken off their o.s 330:10
Overcome: we shall o. 18:15
  We Shall O. 158:16

Over-educated: o. myself in all the things 88:16
Overpaid: o. . . . and over here 334:3
Overpaying: o. him but he's worth it 134:14
Oversexed: o. and over here 334:3
Overtaker: o.s . . . keep the undertakers 265:14
Overture: I tried to resist his o.s 262:8
Overwork: real or imagined o. 260:14
Owe: I don't o. a penny 362:23
Owen, Wilfred: 369:5
Owl: what sort of degenerate o.s 311:17
Own: world, we shall merely o. it 97:11
Ox: goat and an o. must keep in step 50:10
Oxford: 17:3
  notable in debate at O. 29:8
  O. Don: 'I don't feel 22:19
  O. men think they rule the world 90:5
  secret in the O. sense 121:9
  self-made . . . sends his son to O. 316:7
  to exercise that right in O. 32:18
  very nice sort of place, O. 302:29
Oyster: eye that can open an o. 361:8
  sympathetic unselfishness of an o. 293:24
  world is an o. 232:19

P

Pacifist: always been against the P.s 75:11
Pack: going into the next room to p. 168:8
Paddington: accent they had at P. 170:15
Pagan: Martha is the only true p. 12:3
Page: looks well enough on the p. 57:9
  p. that aches for a word 98:17
  p. that reads badly 53:1
Pageant: especially for our annual . . . P. 160:9
Paid: I have p., but 46:21
Pain: clenched on a round p. 327:13
  intoxication with p. 54:11
  most intolerable p. 302:23
  p. we obey 274:1
Pained: p. at how little he was p. 346:17
Painful: p. to be no longer oneself 31:3
Paint: brave to . . . p. a sea as rough 102:3
Painter: colour that of a tea-tray p. 44:8
  I am a 'p. of letters' 133:12
  p.s are outside the class system 53:2
Painting: figure p., the type of all p. 38:14
  if the p. stands up beside a thing 66:17
  my old man's p. hard 245:1
  p. becomes sublime 243:4
  p. . . . being . . . less deleterious 270:8
  p. is a blind man's profession 264:6
  p. is a way to forget life 287:17
  p. is self-discovery 266:13
Pairing: near to paradise all p. ends 124:22
Palace: mercy dash to P. 208:18
Palestine: scheme for peopling P. 167:3
Palmer, Samuel: 181:18
Pam: P., I adore you 40:14
Pan: frying p.'s too wide 237:3
Panic: the wind of p. 19:13

Pantheist: modern p. . . . sees the god in everything 195:15
Pants: p. so thin I could sit on a dime 333:1
Paper: compulsive accumulation of p.s 263:15
  fornicated and read the p.s 61:12
  he's got my p.s 264:16
  less responsible p.s . . . rumours 319:6
  p.s . . . aiming at is power 26:17
  pornography is in . . . Sunday p.s 314:9
  show me a Sunday p. 36:11
  try to keep the p. work down 254:1
  verbal contract isn't worth the p. 135:9
  what . . . Sunday p.s are about 329:10
  white which remains on the p. 78:15
Paperback: I want to be a p. writer 202:22
Pappa: my p., he say 181:12
Parable: great p.s, but false art 197:10
Paradise: beyond the rumour even of P. 97:1
  like dogs, the world would be a p. 100:9
  longing for p. is p. 131:8
  may view John Knox in p. 259:1
  only a shadow of P. 226:1
  wine they drink in P. 68:15
Paragraph: p. should embrace a distinct episode 75:8
Paranoid: even a p. can have enemies 188:8
Parcel: don't send me a p. 66:11
  not ask me to do up a p. 309:16
Pardonner: tout p. . . . very dull 332:6
Parent: bored with their p.s 226:10
  her entirely unnecessary p.s 50:20
  his p.s were not married 303:29
  I am not personally a p. 199:12
  Jewish man with p.s alive 287:15
  mucking up their p.s' lives 140:4
  my p.s . . . rent out my room 13:23
  my p.s . . . very old world 13:16
  not possible with p.s 354:5
  p.s . . . are sometimes a disappointment 270:2
  p.s are strange 341:6
  p.s . . . give him horses 75:3
  p.s learn a lot from their children 313:14
  p.s are the very last people 34:8
  precautions to avoid having p.s 90:16
  sophisticated p.s live agog 247:7
  spurred our p.s to the kiss 138:9
  too experienced a p. 240:11
  tangled web do p.s weave 247:6
  unnatural strain on p.s 338:10
Parentage: application regarding my p. 309:13
Parenthood: p. . . . the mouth that bites you 98:9
Parioli, Fra Luca: few have heard of P. 244:10
Paris: her frocks are built in P. 293:17
  I love P. in the springtime 267:14
  is P. burning 156:3
  O square in P. 281:11
  P. is devine 211:7
  P. is a moveable feast 151:7
  somehow recall . . . P. in the Spring 109:8
  wherever one paused in P. 169:9
Park: inch she'll p. a car on it 353:16
  see me any morning in the p. 109:9

Park – *Contd.*
threw while playing in the p. 328:4
unexplored side of the P. 266:8
Parker, Charlie: 180:17
Parkinson, C. Northcote: P.'s Law 260:13
Parliament: p. . . . longest running farce
   309:12
stood twice for P. 346:13
Parochial: most p. notion 244:11
Parody: p. is a game 246:14
Parr, Catherine: P. didn't matter 92:24
Parricide: society moves by . . . p. 39:21
Parrot: sell the family p. 285:12
this p. is no more 238:16
Parsifal: 276:8
Part: plays many p.s . . . in repertory 121:15
today we have naming of p.s 277:16
Parthenon: famous Fates on the P. frieze
   102:8
Participation: hot media are low in p. 218:3
Parties: it is always like that at p. 273:19
one of the two p. . . . in prison 56:19
p. which got out of hand 56:5
Partisanship: p. is our great curse 283:20
Party: back to his first Christmas p. 72:23
each p. is worse than the other 285:4
far better p. . . . inside his head 113:5
great p. is not to be brought down 144:4
life of the p. . . . death of his wife 313:22
like a children's p. taken over 116:13
not a P. . . . a conspiracy 41:15
not the p. of life 25:6
p. is a moral crusade 358:20
p. is the rallying-point 316:3
organization . . . for the p. 335:4
tasks of the p. are 315:19
P. line . . . there is no P. line 99:15
tried to get up a ship's p. 117:3
Party system: 25:7
Pass: let it p., let it p. 330:17
Passing: we keep p. unseen 265:10
Passion: beautiful conclusion of . . . p. 194:21
better p. and death 194:22
categories of p. 261:5
have to simulate p. to feel it 297:14
man is a useless p. 297:1
master of his p.s is Reason's slave 85:2
passed through the inferno of his p.s 178:5
p. . . . destroyed by a doctor 301:15
p. to which he has remained faithful 269:23
p.s as their own excuse for being 295:17
Past: borne back ceaselessly into the p. 116:10
can neither repeat his p. 23:16
capacity to live in the p. 81:17
chance to collect a p. 363:8
combustion of the Present with the P. 84:18
do not intend to prejudge the p. 355:10
do not remember the p. 295:22
filing is concerned with the p. 354:22
he has received from the p. 266:11
if the p. cannot teach the present 156:6
living in the p. . . . cheaper 17:5
never pity the p. for what it did not 120:17
not . . . to reminisce about the p. 43:14
only the p. . . . bears contemplation 110:15

only thing I regret about my p. 27:13
ooze of the p. 246:17
p. . . . as a guide to the future 165:13
p. has revealed . . . the future 326:13
p. is a foreign country 148:11
p. shut in him 365:1
people who live in the p. 37:18
runs softly and drowns the P. 328:20
something rather absurd about the p. 31:21
they don't sell tickets to the p. 312:2
thinking of the p. wakes 344:5
throwing the p. into the p. 331:13
what we know of the p. 165:12
who can afford to live in the p. 264:18
world of the p. 197:9
writing . . . to out-argue one's p. 113:4
Pastry-making: three arts . . . p. 18:9
Patch: whether there be any p. left of us
   269:20
Patchwork: afraid of the P. Peril 70:3
Patent: their p.-leather souls 128:17
Pater, Walter: P., calling . . . muezzin 83:6
Paternalism: p. . . . everything but respect
   324:2
Patience: bore consumes . . . people's p. 338:9
P. . . . minor form of despair 42:21
strange . . . the years teach us p. 326:9
Patient: analyst should pay the p. 342:16
fail to deceive the p. 273:12
I repeatedly addressed my p. 123:2
never sees his p.s 102:11
p. half-cured 273:10
p. . . . taken to pieces 344:8
p.s in the second half of life 178:8
Patriarch: murderous p. 44:4
Patriot: no p. would think of saying 69:13
p.s talk of dying 290:20
Patriotism: p. to a bourgeois . . . treachery
   335:5
Patronize: p. everybody without distinction
   303:23
Patter: p. of tiny criticism 125:27
Paul: soul of the stout Apostle P. 185:22
most precious things in speech are
   p.s 280:10
Pause: p.s between the notes 299:15
Pause: I'll have *eine kleine* P. 113:15
Pawnbroker: I met with a Gaelic p. 33:11
space beckons us to . . . the p. 47:19
Pax: P. Britannia takes a bit 65:22
P. Romana . . . absolute nonsense 57:20
Pay: good grub, good p. 210:16
p.s a harlot 25 times as much 358:21
Paycock: he shruttin' about . . . like a p.
   252:8
Pay-roll: ten thousand men on the p. 186:1
P.C.: P.C. 49 148:5
Pea: ability to sort p.s 158:5
if p.s were eaten with the knife 276:5
Peace: can rarely make a good p. 75:12
changeless vague of p. he can 97:2
cold p. 200:3
deep p. burnt my me alive 225:18
deny you p. but give you glory 338:5
fighting for p. is like fucking 136:16

half the world is at p. with itself 319:17
hard and bitter p. 181:24
if p. is a chimaera 194:3
in p.: goodwill 77:22
in the arts of p. Man is a bungler 303:8
in the minds . . . p. must be 338:7
made a desolation . . . called it a p. 57:20
muttering the one word P. 12:9
P. . . . a period of cheating 42:22
p. has broken out 52:1
p. no bird can contradict 23:6
p. offensive 67:8
p. running wild all over the place 51:16
p. . . . will not bring much rest 77:1
p. would ruin his plans 100.7
right is more precious than p. 359:16
when it's a question of p. one must 153:15
when you're at p. you think 356:7
who will bring white p. 208:6
Peacemaker: cursed are the p.s 157:7
Peaches: Sunday is for . . . tinned p. 37:2
there is poetry in p. 28:9
Peacock: desire for p.s, apes and ivory 186:4
proud P.s in green parks 95:3
Peanut: like a salted p. 221:9
Pear: you must change the p. 222:4
Pearl: false p.s before real swine 107:9
Pearl Harbor: 368:1
Pearly Gates: through P. where river flow 16:6
Peasant: p.s are the most observant 39:5
Peasantry: almost liquid mass of p. 362:10
civilization has made the p. 334:12
Pebble: kick a p.? On the beach 69:14
Pedestrian: p. . . . man who has two cars 49:9
p.s . . . quick and the dead 98:15
Pedigree: what a dog's p. may be 222:17
Pediment: balanced on broken p.s 192:14
Pee: colour of children's p. 14:14
Peer: blubber which encases an English p.
83:25
Peerage: when I want a p., I shall buy one
250:18
Peg: better be a round p. 159:21
Pekingese: like a P. taking a pill 361:10
Pellet: me spray of p.s 24:14
Pen: some with a fountain p. 143:14
subdue your p. to his handwriting 139:9
with a flashing p. harpoon 61:6
Penguin: has a worse time than . . . p.
68:11
Penis: he also has the biggest p. 241:6
Pennies: P. from Heaven 58:5
throw down p. . . . in screws of paper 308:17
Penny: not a p. off the pay 85:11
Pension: hang your hat on a p. 219:7
Pentagon: P., that immense monument 121:8
People: am for p. I can't help it 68:2
blundering p. will live on 295:10
Hell of Too Many P. 271:15
here were decent godless p. 109:16
horses . . . looking like p. 258:6
I love the p. 51:7
impotent p. sick with inbreeding 329:18
interested in p. 228:7
loved the P., their great P. 311:10

low quality of p. 81:16
makes p. into ideas 365:15
moments of other p.'s lives 265:10
only two kinds of p. 20:3
p. are forbidden to light lamps 222:11
p. are inexterminable 125:1
p. are only human 81:8
p. happened to you on the way 181:1
though p. are important, the relations
119:13
p. in them acting 193:14
p. . . . most valuable capital 316:1
p. who need p. 231:6
silent, sullen p.s 187:3
wars of the p.s will be more terrible 73.6
whenever two p. meet there are . . . six
172:2
writers . . . a whole lot of p. 116:16
writers were really p., and the p. 172:8
ye are the P. 185:14
Pepper: Sergeant P.'s Lonely Hearts 202:26
Percentage: that is a generous p. 31:6
Perception: p. that things could be otherwise
121:12
Père: p. qu'est-ce qu'il fait 271:3
notre P. qui êtes aux cieux 271:4
Perfect: nothing is p. There are lumps 317:7
Perfection: friend who loved p. would be 310:9
some discover . . . their p. 354:7
Performance: cared less about the p. 323:7
Performed: music . . . better than it can be p.
299:8
Perfume: a sad woman who buys her own p.
173:5
Perfumed: p. English, so dense 339:20
Peril: p. . . . not from nature, but from man
177:23
Period: he really had two p.s 246:9
Permanence: British love p. more than . . .
beauty 66:5
Permitted: what's not p. CANNOT be 240:8
Perón, Juan: I would have liked to be P. 263:2
Perpendicular: p. expression of . . . desire
15:21
Perpetuity: p. is longer 311:9
Perquisite: scorn of irregular p.s 345:18
Persecution: Church complains of p. 370:8
intellectuals should suffer . . . p. 290:16
life had been lacking in p. 270:10
Persecutor: my internal p.s are all external
278:8
Pershing, J. J.: 100:7
Persian: another man's P. 180:9
Person: are p.s possible 192:6
capable of containing the human p. 326:14
every p. is like thousands of books 156:14
eye of the fourth p. singular 113:14
p. he was talking to 287:7
most of a p. . . . outside 15:7
other p. is destroyed 273:7
p.s are enabled to masquerade 207:17
to us he is no more a p. 22:4
Personalities: their p. . . . discouraged access
48:22
trivial p. decomposing 364:16

Personality: as a p. he is immortal 32:4
her p. was still too much for her 47:3
p. . . . obtrusive and assertive 293:1
p. who outlived his prime 348:1
what he calls his p. 217:14
your p. is apt to show more 106:1
Personnel: p. selection is decisive 316:1
Perspire: he never seemed to p. 115:17
Persuade: cut her throat but p. her 253:17
trying to p. people to do 335:17
Persuader: The Hidden P.s 258:1
Persuasion: peaceful p. should be followed 247:2
plateau of p. 218:7
Perversion: to risk death . . . last great p. 120:16
war is the universal p. 276:2
Pervert: full many a p. lives to reach 315:12
p. climbs into the minds 54:11
you're some kind of deviated p. 130:6
Pessimism: my theory of optimo-p. 319:1
p. is a luxury 229:5
p. of the spirit; optimism of the will 138:3
Pessimist: he is a real p. 16:10
only the p. who finds this out 339:16
p. . . . defender of privilege 42:2
p. . . . everything bad, except himself 71:25
p. is a man who 17:24
p. is the man who believes 57:2
p. . . . well-informed optimist 17:25
Pest: been a ruder p. 203:15
P. of Pont Street 363:20
Pestilence: there are p.s and . . . victims 62:17
Peter: The P. Principle 263:9
Peter Pan: has been wholly in P. 336:14
refusal to grow up in P. 207:21
Pettiness: something to expiate; a p. 194:5
Petrol: p. . . . cause of . . . conflict 348:10
Phallic: deterrent is a p. symbol 355:14
walking p. symbol 48:6
Pharisee: now is the time of P.s 261:6
Phase: pass through p.s as a train 205:20
Philadelphia: I would rather be in P. 114:11
Philanthropist: p. and the executive 290:13
P. . . . rich (and usually bald) 42:23
Philistine: p. postures of my middle age 90:19
those Eggheads are P.s 246:15
Philistinism: Culture . . . more dangerous than P. 34:5
outbreak of militant P. 125:29
only real link . . . is p. 132:1
yawning P. 272:5
Philosopher: bad p.s may have a certain influence 291:1
five-lettered p. ending in o 86:7
from the protozoon to the p. 290:8
German p.s 208:19
one of the great p.s 290:19
p. is like a blind man 171:21
who can analyse . . . is a p. 42:27
Philosophical: doubt which I venture to call p. 360:13
Philosophies: when all p. shall fail 68:14
Philosophy: do you want your p. straight 280:1

for a superstition to enslave a p. 166:20
pale gruel of p. 334:8
p. . . . a fight against the fascination 360:14
p. . . . footnotes to Plato 354:19
p. is a battle against . . . bewitchment 292:17
p. is 'Critique of language' 360:17
p. is not a theory 360:18
p. is the replacement of category-habits 291:10
p. is . . . wonder 354:12
p. ought to be patient 277:1
p. removes from religion all reason 91:7
P. was wrong 276:9
prejudices . . . called political p. 291:2
susceptible to the Rad-Lib p. 319:14
Phoebe: not to believe the p.s wept 124:13
Phoenicians: watch the dark P. bring 186:5
Phone: they called me to the p. 180:5
Phoney: Truth . . . rises again as p. 149:13
Phonograph: vaccinated with a p. needle 224:9
Phonus: nothing but a p. bolonus 289:2
Photograph: epic scope of a p. album 138:7
he takes p.s of it 195:15
not a p. of me 31:5
p. is 'high definition' 218:3
p. is not only an image 313:7
p.s that make one understand 161:14
p. me through linoleum 27:15
you should see his p. 17:16
Photographed: pride that her husband had p. 115:25
Photography: p. is truth 133:10
Physician: first [p.s] get on 285:14
p. can bury his mistakes 365:24
Physicist: p.s . . . don't listen to their words 107:18
p.s have known sin 253:10
Physics: p. . . . analogous to the smile 108:5
P. . . . instrument of Jewry 332:7
p. . . . great collective work of art 54:6
Pianist: golden hands . . . a p.'s hands 87:6
notes . . . no better than many p.s 299:15
only p. . . . who did not grimace 322:11
Piano: about time the p. realized 221:8
I regard the p. as a . . . guitar 200:10
laughed when I sat down at the p. 63:14
played the p. . . . in a brothel 15:23
Picasso, Pablo: nothing divides them like P. 235:21
P. . . . in tortacolour 65:12
P. insisted . . . miraculous 79:18
Pick-me-up: Jeeves's p. . . . immediate results 362:15
Picture: cutting all the p.s out 34:22
do decent p.s when all my good writers 134:21
every p. tells a story 10:15
good money . . . on a mere p. 163:3
how did you love my p. 135:13
invented p. starts up 281:18
like certain p.s which one cannot appreciate 272:15
looking at the p.s 288:17

456

maps are p.s of what isn't 156:10
no go the p. palace 219:7
p. about France . . . French horns 287:8
p. I don't want to see once 179:1
p. is . . . apprehension of form 33:23
p.s . . . instead of figures 216:9
p.s . . . those who recognize them 52:22
portrait is a p. in which 314:2
there was nothing else in the p. 273:15
you used to be in p.s 355:16
Pidgin: p.-English . . . splendid language
    107:1
Pie: p. in the sky when you die 154:6
Piece: go to p.s like a man 330:18
Piety: both become p. 229.10
Pig: p. . . . taught to play the fiddle 15:12
Pigeon: p.s on the grass alas 316:13
    p.s, those . . . unemployables 64:10
Piggy: wise friend called P. 134:7
Pike: great p. lies 44:4
Pilgrim: We are the P.s, master 117:21
Pill: infallibility of the p. 134:2
Pillow: when I woke up the p. was gone 86:14
Pilot: fighter p.s . . . waited serene 76:5
Pin: p.s are a great means of saving life
    238:11
Pinch: essayed a private p. 300:12
Pinched: p., but never sentenced 363:15
Pinero, Sir Arthur: P. was the best 339:17
Pink: p. is the navy blue of India 343:16
Pinter, Harold: P. . . . four hoarse men 321:5
Pioneer: one thing about p.s 265:7
    our sturdy p.s as farmers 61:8
Pipe: his p. might fall out 119:17
    remembered my p. . . . forgotten my Bible
    135:22
Piss: I can p. the old boy 208:3
    p. off, he said to me 264:15
Pissing: inside my tent p. out than outside
    175:7
Pistol: is that a p. in your pocket 352:16
Piston: p. rods out of my kidneys 18:1
Pitcher: I am your p. 282:18
Pity: man without p. is mad 45:10
    never p. the past . . . p. yourself 120:17
    seas of p. lie 22:6
    they want to avoid . . . p. 81:14
Pius XII, Pope: 17:23
Pix: Sticks Nix Hicks P. 342:1
Place: private faces in public p.s 22:11
Plagiarizing: responsible for p. me 246:5
Plain: manners . . . the need of the p. 347:14
Plan: p.s have always been spoiled 51:24
    a series of five-year p.s 256:9
Plane: travel by p. . . . and yet the spirit 68:9
    unlikely event of this p. crashing 82:17
Planet: domination of our p. by our own
    species 166:21
    it fell on the wrong p. 51:3
    loyal to his club than . . . p. 353:14
    our p. is poorly equipped 228:16
    p. prick the greening west 292:7
    points about this p. 214:3
Platitude: applause is the echo of a p. 42:8
    atmosphere of high-shrieked p.s 99:2

duckbilled p. lays 92:12
    stroke a p. until it purrs 223:2
Plato: choose P. and Plotinus 368:22
    footnotes to P.'s philosophy 354:19
    nicknamed P.'s beard 275:1
    P. . . . cheek by jowl with Aristotle 365:6
    P. . . . the only five-lettered 86:7
Platonic: do I believe in P. friendship 102:10
    P. was . . . unreliable Platonist 281:9
    p. way of going to bed 162:7
Plätze: P., o Platz in Paris 281:11
Play: any one of a dozen p.s 49:18
    Brecht composed p.s 210:12
    but when I started to p. 63:14
    don't want to see p.s about rape 85:12
    Gattling was always in play 268:12
    how can you write a p. 227:21
    I didn't like the p. 224:24
    know what to say about a p. 305:20
    p. is a dynamic thing 336:13
    p. it, Sam 44:14
    p. that would paint . . . sensuality 329:6
    p. will look after itself 306:4
    p.s . . . not fit for elderly people 305:18
    power of writing better p.s 302:10
    rehearsing a p. 301:11
    what would you say your p.s were about
    264:23
    write p s because dialogue 321:2
Playboy: P. . . . eternal adolescence 339:21
Played: Freud . . . never p. the Glasgow Empire
    99:18
Player: all the men and women merely p.s
    250:11
Playful: she's really quite p. 278:16
Playing: having to work . . . hard at p. 241:12
    she's p. herself 179:2
Playmate: hullo p.s 21:1
Playwright: all p.s should be dead 221:10
    if a p. is funny, the English 143:3
    only sophisticated p. England 336:12
    p.s . . . Pinero was the best 339:17
    some p. was forever slamming down 294:16
Pleasant: most of the really p. things in life
    248:5
    we could not lead a p. life 276:5
Pleased: never spoke . . . said what she p.
    316:17
Pleasure: for physical p. I'd sooner 346:21
    if this is p. we'd rather be dead 88:12
    quite happy about p. 22:19
    p. of being seen for what one is 102:1
    prolonging the keenest p. 302:23
    ruined . . . the p. seeker by p. 153:18
    so earnestly pursued p. 42:13
    to strip our p.s of imagination 273:5
    towers of p. 281:12
    writers . . . who give p. a bad name 120:4
Plonking: say it in a 'p.' tone of voice 268:15
Plot: real life seems to have no p.s 82:2
Plum: p.s that were in the icebox 358:7
Plumber: try getting a p. on weekends 13:9
Plumbing: assembly of portable p. 240:10
Plutocracy: in a p. the natural hero 358:2
Plutonic: merely a p. attachment 222:20

Pocket: afraid of having your p.s picked 79:2
his conscience is picking his p. 42:23
his hand into his p. until 28:21
other straight into her p. 171:4
pound . . . in your p. 359:5
thrust into somebody's p. 42:19
Pod: open the p. door, Hal 78:13
Poem: arrange my p.s . . . a vase of flowers
 104:10
bad p.s . . . created during abstinence
 279:6
begin a p. with 'in the middle 102:12
esteemed inventions . . . the epic p. 229:12
good p. . . . makes complete sense 139:21
majority of p.s one outgrows 110:1
p. . . . anxiety meets a technique 104:13
p. . . . in the form of prose 58:1
p. is never finished 341:11
p. is not made from these letters 78:15
p. me no p.s 214:2
p.s . . . about what he does not know
 309:6
so deflating to a p. 223:8
we all write p.s 120:15
writing a p. is discovering 125:3
p. written . . . by a typewriter 172:18
Poet: all p.s who, when reading 353:13
best prose is written by p.s 239:4
better p. than Porson 159:12
by the statistician or the p. 119:6
call Le Gallienne a minor p. 223:9
either a p. or a Lilliputian 343:15
I knew myself once more a p. 138:20
impossible to hold the p.s back 132:21
last English p.s . . . chemical knowledge
 144:8
like a p. woo the moon 61:6
limp-wristed p. 242:16
most p.s are dead by their . . . twenties
 139:18
no bad man can be a good p. 261:8
no p. . . . has his complete meaning alone
 110:3
no wonder p.s . . . have to seem 124:15
not look at his change is no true p. 69:12
only the p. slams the door 61:7
p. . . . condition rather than a profession
 139:19
p. . . . don't like the word 105:10
p. gives us his essence 364:12
p. is the unsatisfied child 139:17
p. . . . liar who always speaks the truth
 79:17
p. . . . technical expert 83:16
p. . . . the only one alive 23:19
p.s . . . are outside the class system 53:2
p.s do not go mad 71:18
p.s from their safe and paper beds 126:11
p.s get a quizzical ahem 126:12
p.s groan in rhymes 344:1
p.s . . . must be *difficult* 110:4
room of the banished p. 11:14
truth . . . for the p. is only a stimulus
 296:4
which . . . p.s do you like . . . Blight 161:1

Poetry: 44:1, 280:7, 310:17
duty to distinguish between p. 320:16
if you want to get p. out of me 159:11
made p. seem word-bound 180:17
nothing to say . . . that is p. 60:2
only man . . . who has never written any p.
 71:23
people need p. 220:15
p. begins to atrophy 268:23
p. can communicate 199:3
p. cannot celebrate them 23:14
p. cleanses 182:3
p. is a . . . piece of fiction 230:5
p. is an extra hand 236:20
p. is baroque 227:17
p. is . . . hyacinths and biscuits 295:13
P. is not concerned 23:24
p. is received in a hostile spirit 283:4
p. is reflective 23:21
p. is . . . taking life by the throat 125:4
p. is the supreme fiction 317:15
p. is to prose 344:2
p. is what Milton saw 223:4
p. must be human 12:14
P. . . . relation to Prose 23:23
publicity rather than p. 199:5
quarrel . . . we make p. 369:3
sublime art of ruining p. 298:17
there is p. in peaches 28:9
verb for 'making p.' 283:2
Poincaré, President: 263:3
Poison: I'd put p. in your coffee 21:13
love and benevolence are our p. 194:17
p. . . . in slumber's ear 44:3
p. the whole blood stream fills 111:2
this man deliberately took p. 248:13
Poisoning: p. three little children 101:16
Poker: p. shouldn't be played in a house
 357:24
Poland: my idea of P. moving westwards
 76:18
Polar: P. exploration . . . having a bad time
 68:10
Pole: few virtues . . . P.s do not possess
 74:8
latest P. transmit the Preludes 109:6
Police: among p. officers 254:1
cold-bloodedly handed over to the p. 52:5
I shall be my own p. 101:8
p. sergeant refusing bail 151:21
South African P. would leave no stone
 301:19
staunch and rugged fear of the p. 151:19
what a great thing is a p.-station 184:2
Policeman: a p. is a burglar who has retired
 273:10
Policemen: detectives . . . p. with smaller feet
 98:19
how young the p. look 153:3
no more p. Only police dogs 113:8
p. . . . must be protected 253:21
p. . . . prevent them being published 55:9
youthfulness of p. 252:7
Polite: English are p. by telling lies 49:2
P. Society believed in God 297:16

Political: every ... attitude is ... p. 221:14
    formation of the p. will 155:8
    history of p. power 267:2
    p. ideas of our educated 333:21
    ideas of p. philosophers 183:16
    p. leader must keep looking 29:20
    problems ... p. ones are insoluble 100:20
    taken a serious p. stand 13:7
    we are not p. whores 245:14
Politician: 271:10
    average length of life for p.s 252:15
    clown ... higher ... than any p. 68:4
    every p. is ... a promising p. 70:11
    have been p.s from birth 66:6
    just as funny as p.s 286:8
    men of action ... not the p.s 23:14
    performances of latter-day p.s 359:8
    pity ... p.s are not bastards 355:6
    p. is a statesman 266:14
    p. is an animal 17:26
    p. rises on the backs of 160:3
    p. ... understands government 335:14
    p. ... with an open mouth 318:15
    p.s are the same all over 184:5
    p.s feel ... pull towards mirrors 82:3
    you're just a p. 218:16
Politics: all this damn p. comes along 331:11
    I always wanted to get into p. 56:18
    I am not made for p. 62:7
    if p. is the art of the possible 229:2
    if you're in p. and you can't tell 175:9
    in p., as in grammar 219:17
    in the centre of p. 242:22
    men enter local p. 261:4
    more you read about p. 285:5
    no matter what we thought about p. 88:20
    not in business, we are in p. 145:8
    ordinary dirtiness of p. 256:2
    p. are not my concern 187:21
    p. is an obligation 284:14
    p. is the art of the possible 58:14
    p. ... too serious a matter to be left 129:17
    some want you to talk p. 28:7
    they ... pretend that p. is a game 260:17
    Titanic seamanship in p. 209:18
    too many men in p. and not enough 132:4
    truer guide than 'p.' 207:6
    war is p. 221:23
    week is a long time in p. 359:4
    P.: Who Gets What, When, How 194:1
Polly: Mr P. went into the National 349:14
Polterguest: Hecate Hopper, the P. 247:18
Polycentric: p. system 331:18
Polygamous: p. but emotionally monogamous
    53:8
Pomp: no p., just the circumstances 244:5
Pond: fall on the indifferent p. 281:7
Pont: troupeau des p.s 19:10
Pony: there must be a p. 188:4
Poodle: Mr Balfour's P. 209:5
Pool: sinking p. 236:16
Poopah: Poppy P.'s outside 181:14
Poor: all the nice people were p. 313:15
    cannot abide contact with the p. 80:17
    infants of the very p. 269:21

kindness of the p. to the rich 71:3
    more troublesome if you are p. 247:19
    New P. 231:20
    not concerned with the very p. 119:6
    poets and painters ... relatively p. 53:2
    p. society cannot be too p. 325:12
    suppose the p. are always sick 81:9
    what fun ... excessively p. 19:5
    would realize he was p. 339:13
Pop: p. culture for those with bad memories
    179:3
Popcorn: everything else is mere p. 35:11
Pope: anybody can be P. 174:17
    bred more p.s and fewer lovers 132:11
    I must tell the P. ... I am the P. 174:16
    P. in the quarter finals 34:10
    No P. here. Lucky P. 137:5
    'One man?' said the P. 87:12
Popular: when she was bad she was very p.
    234:2
Population: peaceful p. is the sea 222:10
    p. explosion ... happened yesterday 56:7
    when the p. of the world consisted 166:16
    working p.s of both countries 210:16
Pornography: p. is the attempt to insult sex
    196:13
    you don't get any p. on there 314:9
Porridge: bring p., bring sausage 153:3
Porson, Richard: saw ... P. sober 159:12
Port: any old p. in a storm 344:16
    compact of ancient tales, and p. 34:19
Portentous: it is p. 208:5
Portion: sent me back my missing p. 118:2
    such small p.s ... life 13:2
Portrait: paint his own p. for the Uffizi
    32:23
    p. ... something wrong with the mouth
    314:2
    p.s of famous bards 328:16
    p.s of the heads of government 246:12
    study of family p.s is enough 101:9
Portray: 'p.' ... synonymous with 'betray'
    323:4
Pose: without p. and full of poise 249:4
    would instantly begin to p. 272:11
Posies: buy my English p. 185:9
Posing: I'm p. in the old back yard 245:1
Positive: every p. value has its price 264:3
    p. ideals are ... a curse 119:1
Possession: tenth share ... to exclusive p.
    302:20
Possible: if you didn't have the p. things
    261:13
    politics is the art of the p. 58:14
Possibilities: our vital p. 253:13
Post: brazenly with the last p. 198:4
Postage-stamp: do you sell p.s 333:15
Postcard: the French don't even put on p.s
    158:6
Posted: she left stuff to be p. 247:18
Posterity: to evoke p. is to weep 139:10
    works written for p. should be read by p.
    272:15
Post-Impressionist: Manet and the P.s 125:28
    P. painting 214:13

Pot: second millennium of p.-training 236:19
    Useful P. to Keep Things In 236:8
Poultry: all p. eaters are psychopaths 268:3
    p. matter 223:22
Pound: on fifty thousand p.s a year 153:9
    p. . . . in your pocket 359:5
    use p. notes as bookmarks 54:14
Pound, Ezra: 110:6, 317:1
    P. . . . showman minus the show 149:14
Poverty: from nothing to a state of extreme p.
    224:18
    it is possible to conquer p. 175:12
    money is better than p. 13:14
    need inequality . . . to eliminate p. 176:6
    our p. . . . signified chiefly 308:17
    p. . . . a problem of two million villages
    300:5
    to defeat p. 182:10
Power: aspired to p. instead of influence
    325:13
    Britain . . . no longer a world p. 55:11
    dying monarchy . . . has too much p. 72:15
    exercise of p. 214:9
    great p. we have been and are no longer
    167:1
    inability of those in p. 180:13
    lack of p. corrupts absolutely 318:10
    man of p. is ruined by p. 153:18
    maximal authority and minimal p. 323:14
    no limit to the p. it can generate 141:20
    people are always in p. 366:3
    People in P. 261:10
    political p. grows out of . . . a gun 222:1
    p. is the ultimate aphrodisiac 188:7
    p. isn't what seems to make things 82:5
    p. . . . its desire to continue 341:2
    p. without responsibility 26:17
    prefer influence to p. 223:15
    renunciation of p. 256:2
    seductive p. of goodness 51:5
    struggle against death . . . the motive p.
    153:21
    those who foolishly sought p. 181:25
    Thy P. brings all skill to naught 185:27
    universe shows evidence of a . . . p. 173:2
    when p. corrupts 182:3
    you only have p. over people 312:1
Powerful: p. rather than charming 290:12
Pox: more p. than pax about that boyo
    176:19
Practical: p. men . . . usually the slaves 183:16
Practise: he who p.s what he preaches is
    guilty 129:3
Prague: for the sake of P. 219:5
Praise: countryman must have p. 44:11
    give them not p. For, deaf 313:8
    p. of one's friends 223:12
Pram: enemy of good art . . . the p. 83:11
Pray: one can . . . p. exclusively 347:19
    p. as if everything depended 314:12
    p. to God and say the lines 95:7
Prayer: cathedrals . . . p. factories once
    104:12
    commonest p. in all languages 29:1
    conversation of p.s about 327:16

frame of mind . . . close to that of p. 226:6
    I could cut the Lord's P. 279:3
    like morning p.s in a workhouse 171:16
    Lord's P. when playing canasta 110:9
    place of p. 248:2
    p.s are like those appeals 312:10
    wish to pray is a p. 40:3
Praying: if you talk to God, you are p.
    323:20
Precaution: p.s to avoid having parents 90:16
    useless but . . . vital p. 167:17
Precipice: draw your chair up . . . to the p.
    117:5
Precise: one cannot be p. and . . . pure 66:18
Predestination: Free Will and P. . . . identical
    75:1
Predicament: life . . . is a p. 295:20
Predict: he who can p. 50:13
    p. things after they've happened 168:17
Prefab: better than a p. – no rent 68:12
Prefabricated: better word than 'p.' 76:19
Pregnancies: to while away their p. 228:1
Pregnancy: to avoid p. 229:11
Prejudge: do not intend to p. the past 355:10
Prejudice: associate p. with identity 47:6
    merely rearranging their p.s 171:20
    P. . . . A vagrant opinion 42:24
    p.s acquired by age eighteen 108:10
    p.s . . . called political philosophy 291:1
    take no pride in p. 244:9
Prelude: transmit the P.s, through his hair
    109:6
Premise: based upon licensed p.s 252:6
Presence: person may have . . . a wonderful p.
    301:18
    social p. of a woman 39:7
Present: eternal p. of . . . expectation 39:4
    liberating the p. 331:13
    never . . . contemporaneous with our p.
    96:4
    on the surface of the p. 246:17
    past on the steps to the p. 54:2
    who controls the p. 254:23
Preserving: p. different things side by side
    70:7
President: being P. – nobody can tell you
    when 108:13
    best newspaperman . . . ever been P. 55:7
    drudgery in . . . being P. 330:15
    even the p. of the United States 104:24
    P. . . . kissing people 335:11
    p.s . . . evident vices 339:22
    proves that in America anyone can be
    P. 118:11
    that's all the powers of the P. 335:17
    told that anybody could become P. 94:8
    we are all the P.'s men 188:6
    when the P. does it 250:6
Press: I'm with you on the free p. 319:21
    King over all . . . is the P. 186:8
    our P. is obscene 211:3
    p. lords . . . control the old parties 242:21
Pressed: p. into service means p. out 124:19
Pretence: using false p.s on dolls 289:13
Prettiness: weak and delicate p. 210:15

Pretty: never have been very p. but 111:12
  not so p. anyone would want to 51:28
  p. can get away with anything 347:14
  p. girl who plays her cards as carefully 117:6
  someone else . . . does it p. 264:8
Prevent: anything more I could have done to p. 106:9
  duty to try to p. it 236:12
Price: never knew the p. of happiness 369:13
  that your p. shall suit everybody 147:1
Prick: hundred p.s against one 238:1
Pride: our day of political p. is over 167:1
  p. is faith in the idea that God 99:5
  this extraordinary p. 206:4
  wounds of her offspring's p. 276:1
Priest: associate with a lot of p.s 35:2
  batter the family p. 186:6
  p. is only half a man 229:16
  p.s . . . know men as thoroughly 296:20
  p.s ruled . . . gods obeyed 82:11
  p.s were infinitely more attentive 115:14
  teenage sex-change p. 208:18
Prime Minister: as much as it pays its P. 358:21
  best P. we have 58:12
  British P. sneezed 205:8
  have you seen me as the P. 321:16
  he was fired as P. 188:14
  he would have become P. 83:24
  headmasters have powers . . . P.s have never 74:22
  no British P. should provoke 27:4
  P. of mirth 283:8
  Unknown P. 21:5
Primitive: classics are p. literature 198:10
Prince: P. of the Empire 34:16
  Some Day My P. Will Come 99:9
  who's danced with the P. of Wales 112:10
Principalities: guarded by timeless p. 138:20
Principle: country like ours only has p.s 357:3
  go to the bottom with my p.s 27:2
  p. . . . can be sacrificed 226:12
  p. . . . if you'll excuse my having such a thing 303:15
  P.s on which we will build 301:2
  violation of Twentieth Century p.s 303:16
  vultures of p. 209:17
Print: decomposing in the eternity of p. 364:16
Printemps: p. dans ses plis 19:12
Priorities: p. . . . the religion of Socialism 41:13
Prison: at home in p. 346:16
  books for the p. by weight 33:19
  cross between a p. 90:11
  old p. has been turned into 234:15
  p. of our mind . . . furnish it 340:2
  ten years in p. 219:15
Prisoner: if the p. is happy 303:12
  your being taken p. 188:13
Privacy: right to share your p. 339:7
Private: at least I thought it was p. 157:1
  p. faces in public places 22:11

p. man . . . universally recognized 320:12
P. Means is dead 310:15
Privilege: freedom . . . only extended p. 154:4
  pessimist . . . a defender of p. 42:2
  p. which dehumanizes others 122:8
  that is not executive p. 111:7
Privy: neither a Lord, nor a p. 25:8
Prize: first p. in the lottery of life 280:1
  who just miss the p.s 54:12
Problem: about any country but their own, the p. 85:18
  answer is not separate from the p. 190:9
  constant p. . . . for human knowledge 120:9
  no p. . . . big enough plastic bag 319:14
  p. . . . finding a religious outlook 178:8
  p. left to itself dries up 307:15
  that you did not solve the p. 106:1
  they can't see the p. 69:21
  two p.s . . . political ones are insoluble 100:20
  worst thing you can do to . . . p. 140:5
Proceeding: p.s about as scaly 362:10
Process: p. and result are equivalent 360:21
  p. blows the moon 328:2
Procession: p.s that lack high stilts 368:13
  to view the p. 205:1
Procrastination: p. is the art of keeping up 222:16
Prodigal: enthusiasm . . . over the p.'s return 293:12
  fine example was the P. Son 152:4
Profanation: from sale and p. 68:22
Professional: all too p. air 215:5
  Germany is the prize p. nation 359:19
Professor: our American p.s 206:18
  p. . . . who has not approved 331:6
  p.s to manufacture p.s 348:8
Profile: be on the right side of my p. 114:29
Programme: my favourite p. is 'Mrs Dale' 110:8
  my favourite p. . . . silence 178:15
Progress: government does . . . social p. 345:9
  have stopped believing in p. 46:17
  notion of p. in a single line 244:11
  p. . . . a comparative of which 70:14
  p. if a cannibal uses knife 199:13
  p. . . . one nuisance for another 110:13
  p. would be wonderful 245:5
  rake that never made any p. 34:15
  say that p. can be good or bad 168:12
  what I mean by moral p. 332:17
  what p. is 39:21
Progressive: one of those p. places 25:11
Prohibition: Communism is like p. 284:12
  drink water before P. 193:8
  idea of exclusion and p. 232:13
Project: God . . . Much Less Ambitious P. 136:18
Proletarian: aristocratic to p. control 210:4
  never found in a genuine p. 255:12
  you are polite to a p. 347:5
Proletariat: dictatorship of the p. 201:9
  in the interests of the p. 201:8
  p. has no other weapon 201:3
  whatever crimes the P. commits 89:11

Prometheus: P. watching his vulture 361:23
Promiscuous: before they can start being . . .
   p. 162:12
Promise: don't fulfil the p. of their early
   years 270:2
   to make positive p.s 240:11
Promising: gods wish to destroy . . . call p.
   83:9
Promoted: p. thirst without quenching 338:11
Promotion: pseudo-p. 263:14
Prompt: meant to be p., but it never 95:10
Pronounce: right to p. . . . as he chooses
   77:14
Prop: buy Serbian tit-p.s 104:6
Propaganda: between education and p. 56:10
   p. is that branch of the art 88:3
   to write p. articles 274:10
Propagated: if human beings could be p.
   144:10
Property: human body is private p. 233:17
   man of p. 128:7
   marriages . . . a matter of p. 78:3
Prophet: ceased to pose as its p.s 267:6
   p.s were twice stoned 240:13
   sole qualification to be a p. 73:15
   words of the p. are written 307:11
Proposition: such a p. is true 290:7
   that a p. be interesting 354:11
Propriety: their abysmal p. 170:14
Prose: best p. is written by poets 239:4
   can only write p. today 369:10
   forgive . . . anything except bad p. 73:7
   hears his own remarks as p. 21:16
   poetry is to p. 344:2
   Poetry . . . relation to P. 23:23
   p. takes the mould 364:12
   their p. was convulsive 350:22
   their purple through my p. 82:21
   these pieces of moral p. 310:2
   to write good p. 227:17
   write a page of living p. 67:16
Prosperity: in the sun of p. too long 195:5
   not . . . p. that makes for happiness 311:12
   three pillars of Western p. 163:21
Prostitute: acted like p.s 191:2
   I have never been an Alaskan p. 215:20
   titled women and p.s 297:8
Prostitution: p. . . . keeps her out of trouble
   150:26
   p. ought to be encouraged 358:16
Protect: we need symbols to p. us 45:11
Protection: I am . . . under the special p. of
   God 156:4
Protest: require far more courage than . . .
   p. 97:10
   turning p. into retrospect 357:6
Protestant: Anglo-Irishman . . . a P. with a
   horse 33:7
   P. document as the Bible 303:22
   P. women may take the Pill 329:14
   P.s . . . any sense of direction 358:14
   P.s protesting 196:18
Protestantism: chief contribution of P. 229:20
Protozoon: from the p. to the philosopher
   290:8

Proud: aim at humility . . . you will not be p.
   99:17
   p. of the position of the bungalow 358:11
Proust, Marcel: P. saw his friends 277:2
Prove: do not need to p. religion 337:2
   heard so much . . . can't p. 352:15
Providence: I go the way that P. dictates 155:10
   I've had enough of P. 299:1
   P. . . . responsible for their morals 369:6
Provider: as p.s they're oil wells 260:1
Provincialism: rather . . . adultery than in p.
   161:9
Prowess: dreams of the native . . . muscular p.
   112:4
Proximity: p. was their support 47:5
Pru: man from the P. 10:21
Prudence: effect of p. on rascality 302:22
Prudent: p. upon their pedestals 277:2
Prudish: p. hand would refuse 306:2
Prussic: rather . . . p. acid in the hands 100:8
Pseudo-light: p. it threw 15:1
Psyche: peril . . . from the p.s 177:23
   p. should be studied 178:13
Psychiatrist: anybody who goes to see a p.
   135:4
   century of the p.'s couch 218:1
   p. . . . collects the rent 197:17
   p. . . . looks at the audience 318:18
   p.s classify a person 323:19
   p.s have a financial interest 283:19
Psychiatry: p. . . . id by the odd 17:19
Psycho-analysis: p. has revealed to us 123:9
   p. is a permanent fad 98:6
Psychoanalyst: no p. has knocked 69:11
   what did I learn from p.s 151:11
Psychological: apt p. representations 178:4
   fits a man for p. analysis 296:15
   no such thing as p. 297:24
Psychology: children . . . have no use for p.
   308:6
   p. . . . destroyed all our knowledge 72:25
   p. . . . pulling habits out of rats 58:10
   p. . . . sublimated spiritualism 313:6
   there is no p. 324:1
Psychosis: Irish and the Jews have a p. 33:17
Psychotic: p. if he makes others 323:19
   p. . . . lives in it 197:17
Pub: p.s know a lot 65:21
   p.s . . . less damned than the Church 134:5
   served in all the p.s in Dublin 100:5
   wasn't a p. open in the city 33:13
Puberty: we are all American at p. 347:17
Public: anyone who has been to . . . p. school
   346:16
   hell . . . like their p. school 14:15
   his indifference to p. notice 320:12
   let the p. behind the scenes 227:19
   means . . . p. opinion minus his 70:18
   no one can enjoy a p. school 83:3
   one to mislead the p. 21:3
   private faces in p. places 22:11
   p. life in England 254:21
   taught at his p. school that feeling 119:17
   were given a p. relations officer 243:11
   write for yourself and have no p. 85:1

Publican: best type of sporting p. 11:5
  looped up with a p.'s widow 280:19
Publication: not properly a matter for p.
  152:20
Publicity: God had a great p. agent 272:8
Publish: motto is p. and be sued 167:12
  to p. the secret treaties 335:7
Publisher: I don't believe in p.s 286:19
  Xerox makes everybody a p. 218:11
Puccini, Giacomo: infinite number of P.s
  336:6
  Wagner is the P. of music 242:18
Puddy-tat: I t'ought I saw a p. 336:11
Pull: feel the p. of another 281:8
Pulse: two people with one p. 219.10
Punch: on Kipling, nourish them on 'P.' 61:9
Punctual: so p., you could regulate 125:20
Punctuality: p. . . . virtue of the bored 347:18
Punctuation: in music, the p. is absolutely
  strict 280:9
Punishing: p. and suchlike 57:18
Punishment: p.s of the spiritual mode 194:15
Punitive: it was so absolutely p. 45:2
Pupil: great teachers foresee a p.'s ends 60:7
Puppet: p.s stuck up to spout Shaw 305:21
Pure: as p. as the driven slush 27:12
  one cannot be precise and . . . p. 66:18
  P. Food Committee had rejected 362:14
  p. in heart . . . more to talk about 353:5
  things pertaining to themselves are p. 313:17
Purgatory: in P., see our own faces 206:3
Purist: p. who reads your proofs 67:18
Puritan: great artists are never P.s 230:3
  p. . . . into the wrong things 72:18
  to the P. all things are impure 197:1
Puritanism: p. in other people we admire 83:7
Purple: scatter their p. through my prose
  82:21
Purpose: only a p. . . . concerns me 197:8
  p. of life 190:12
Pursued: the p., the pursuing 116:5
Pursuit: born with a bias to some p. 325:4
Pygmies: wars of the p. will begin 77:1
Pylon: p.s, those pillars 315:1

Q

Quack: I loathed the Viennese q. 246:19
Quad: always about in the q. 15:22
Quaint: everything q. and curly 44:13
Quaker: timid . . . beaten up by Q.s 13:5
Qualification: without q.s to detain them
  340:5
Quality: help the low q. of people 81:16
  she hasn't got a single redeeming q. 227:1
Quantity: q. turns . . . into quality 334:19
Quantum: q. theory on Tuesdays 49:12
Quarrel: had a lover's q. with the world 124:7
  q. with others . . . rhetoric 369:3
Queen: discontented tragedy q. 269:25
  I'm one of the Q.s of England 59:2
  Q. believed cigars were all one price 22:22

q. measuring a town 368:8
Q. of air and darkness 159:7
Q.'s delightful home 160:10
Queen Victoria: Q. and I just missed each
  other 285:15
Queenly: being Q. in her own room 353:7
Queer: all is not q. that titters 15:13
  q. are the ways of a man I know 147:19
  we're here because we're q. 33:15
Queerer: not only q. than we suppose 144:13
Question: all q.s are open 34:7
  answer? . . . what is the q. 317:3
  ask the hard q. 22:23
  dares to ask the difficult q. 139:17
  every man has a q. 317:10
  I don't know Who . . . put the q. 145:17
  impertinent q. . . . pertinent answer 54:4
  it is the q. we do not know 217:10
  knows all the right q.s 342:17
  little q.s from women 287:12
  make two q.s grow where 342:5
  not a wise q. for me to answer 106:11
  object of education . . . asking q.s 90:4
  q. that he frames in all but words 124:17
  q.s that no one has asked them 332:4
  q.s . . . without recourse to God 45:17
  who cares if the q. is wrong 178:17
  without . . . any clear q. 61:14
Queue: a man in a q. 231:23
Quick: pedestrians . . . the q. and the dead
  98:15
  turns on the q. and the dead 327:16
  you're q., aren't you 233:18
Quiet: women like q. men 15:9
Quietist: true q.s . . . live in Britain 120:11
Quotation: find this full of q.s 102:13
  good . . . to read books of q.s 75:6
  list of q.s beautiful 258:11
  needs no dictionary of q.s 32:13
  q. is a national vice 347:1
  say that anything was a q. 293:4
Quote: by writing things to q. 57:6
  make a monkey of a man . . . q. him 36:10

R

Rabbit: except to shoot r.s 225:23
  r.s ruled by stoats 255:18
Run, R. 117:13
  struck a direct blow by a r. 66:4
  tale of four little r.s 268:6
Race: every r. which has become self-conscious
  194:19
  great r. we are and shall remain 167:1
  humanity without r. 296:27
  r. is not always to the swift 182:15
  r. is r. 18:18
Rachmaninov, Sergei: 322:11
  R.'s immortalizing . . . scowl 322:10
Racially: those who are not r. pure . . . chaff
  154:17
Racism: ridiculing blacks is r. 279:1

Radical: I never dared be r. when young
124:18
  middle of the road with . . . r. 348:7
  no one so r. as a manservant 320:19
  r.: a person whose left hand . . . 286:12
Radio: howling r. for our paraclete 219:6
  I had the r. on 238:7
RAF: R. do not have traditions 18:2
Rage: designed to express r. 15:3
  r., r. against the dying 327:17
Raider: friend to aerial r.s 315:2
Railroad: remained a country of r.s 68:9
Railway: home's a r. carriage 24:18
  take this r. by surprise 131:15
Rain: Hard R.'s A-Gonna Fall 104:21
  I'm singing in the r. 122:5
  it is going to r. 266:12
  r. comes pattering 22:26
  r. is listless 269:12
  sense to come in out of the r. 277:8
Rainbow: like a man . . . chasing r.s 361:18
  R. gave thee birth 95:2
  r. of His will 212:8
  simple blessing of a r. 9:2
  somewhere over the r. 147:8
Rained: lot of people getting r. on 319:7
  The Day It R. Forever 49:8
Rake: the r. that never made any progress
34:15
Raped: young women should stop being r.
315:16
Raper: Solitary R. 48:6
Rascal: government . . . by the r.s 316:11
Rascality: one is shocked by its r. 229:17
Raspberry: it's r. time in Runcorn 88:13
Rasputin: they accuse R. of kissing 12:15
Rat: droll r., they would shoot you 286:14
  r.s in mazes . . . events in himself 106:7
Ratcliffe: rollin' down the R. Road 184:21
Rat-fight: well-contested r. 50:15
Rational: reduced to his . . . r. activity 108:18
  utterly r. and the . . . insane 127:13
Rationalist: r., but he went to church 71:12
Rationality: if r. were the criterion 319:13
Rationalized: happiness . . . should never be r.
70:17
Ratomorphic: r. view of man 189:13
Ravel, Maurice: R. has refused the Légion
d'Honneur 298:12
Ravelling: I am worn to a r. 268:8
Raw: r., uncooked, protesting 365:15
Razor-blade: forty-seventh day of . . . r.
318:20
Reaction: my r.s . . . don't conform 174:8
  r. against one's training 38:15
Reactionary: one is always somebody's r.
78:20
Read: if you're bilingual, you can't r. 250:20
  only news until he's r. it 347:7
  people r. to kill time 305:27
  r. part of it all the way through 134:17
  something to r. and done with 350:14
  to stay . . . calm in mind, r. 64:5
  where she had learnt to r. so quickly
114:19

Reader: Gutenberg made everybody a r.
218:11
  hard news catches r.s 250:13
  his r.s are proud to live in it 82:22
  our r.s are blessed 244:6
  poetry . . . an affront to the r. 283:4
  r. who is the respondent 353:10
  r.s . . . sending the author 83:12
  trade a hundred contemporary r.s 189:17
  why should r.s never be harrowed 260:10
Reading: all my good r. 233:9
  course in speed r. 13:27
  effects of smoking . . . gave up r. 322:5
  for casual r. 256:7
  he took no pleasure in r. 270:8
  isn't the same thing as . . . r. 350:8
  r. is a sort of rewriting 297:2
  r. isn't an occupation we encourage 254:1
Readjustment: always spoke of it as a 'r.'
254:10
Realism: r. doesn't mean copying art 253:3
Reality: any resemblance to r. 252:2
  appeal to a r. 214:12
  by r. I mean shops like Selfridges 198:6
  held r. down fluttering 292:6
  laws of mathematics . . . do not refer to r.
108:6
  nature of ultimate r. 189:15
  practice of changing r. 222:4
  r., which is unendurable 84:17
  vision of R. 219:19
Realm: his . . . nature grew from both r.s
282:8
Reaping: sewing? . . . r. 46:20
Reappraisal: agonizing r. 103:4
Rearm: we must r. 26:15
Reason: before the dark of r. grows 40:20
  human r. won 184:7
  it distrusts pure r. 230:2
  madman . . . lost everything except his r.
71:19
  master of his passions is R.'s slave 85:2
  only r. can convince us 34:7
  r. . . . a matter of faith 71:21
  r. . . . most terrible of passions 144:9
  when r. is right . . . it is impotent 38:9
Reasonable: rather be right than r. 247:5
Rebel: r. . . . says no 62:20
  r. . . . turning into an autocrat 104:5
  r. whose life had been lacking 270:10
Rebelling: r. expresses a nostalgia 62:22
Rebellion: in art, r. is consummated 63:5
  sensuality, r. and revivalism 329:6
Rebelliousness: culture which . . . drives to r.
122:15
Rebuke: standing r. to them 229:18
Receiver: didn't have their r.s off 179:6
  left the r. off the hook 189:14
  without taking the r. off 226:17
Recent: thicker as it approaches r. times
325:14
Recession: r. when your neighbour loses
335:13
Recessional: hair and forehead furnished a r.
note 293:1

Recirculation: vicus of r. 177:1
Recluse: r.s who lived remote 250:15
Recompense: notion of a r. to women 170:10
Red: r. brothers, go back 137:10
Redaction: r. known as the Sayings 177:2
Redbrick: civic r. 210:4
Reefer: R. was a wenchman 177:16
Reeves, James: 369:7
Refined: like one of those r. persons 80:17
   r. family had to include 297:15
   we was all *so* r. 60:12
Refinement: America has a . . . rank r. 69:24
Reform: out to r. the world 363:13
Remark: any more than . . . a rude r. 357:23
Reformation: every r. must have its victims
   293:12
Reformer: more-water-in-your-beer r.s 255:15
   r. . . . rides through a sewer 344:7
Reformist: r. party considers 334:14
Refresh: r.es the parts 10:18
Refrigerator: voice . . . to defrost her r.
   321:10
Refugee: never has been a British r. 209:3
Refuted: *to be r. by experience* 266:18
Regalia: r. from thatch to toe 115:15
Regan: either a R. or a Goneril 270:14
Regime: no r. has ever loved . . . writers
   312:5
Regiment: I, who should command a r. 60:9
Regret: girls do have r.s 341:7
   Miss Otis r.s 267:20
   my one r. in life 13:24
   past wakes r. and pain 344:5
   r. cannot come today 18:3
Regular: as r. and as futile 330:3
Rehearsing: r. a play is making the word flesh
   301:1
Reich: popular subjects , , , the Third R.
   87:4
Reincarnation: convert . . . to the doctrine of
   r. 101:9
   nine reasons for r. 233:7
Rejected: returned with 'r.' scrawled across
   312:10
Relation: God's apology for r.s 184:18
   industrial r.s are like sexual 113:3
   though people are important, the r.s 119:13
Relationship: desire for pure r.s 197:14
   don't spend themselves in r.s 48:22
   gentleness of r. 48:16
   I believe in r.s 51:1
   ideal r. with a man 162:4
   men see objects, women see the r. 120:19
   r. between mother and child 276:1
   what is a personal r. 192:6
Relative: every man sees in his r.s 230:10
Relax: take up your cross and r. 18:6
Relaxing: fallen short . . . frightfully r. 14:17
Relic: r.s have nothing to do with the truth
   315:10
Relief: from these . . . is R. afar 186:18
   I can't get no r. 104:18
Religion: approved of r. as long as it endorsed
   119:12
   argument . . . in r. can do no more 41:25

Art and R. . . . to ecstasy 34:1
blasphemy . . . could not survive r. 72:13
collector of r.s 303:30
discuss r. with the housemaid 70:24
disliked hearing about r. 237:11
do not need to prove r. 337:2
dying r. always interferes 72:15
God is interested . . . in r. 326:19
horrible fooleries of magic and r. 162:15
if it was the r. of His Majesty 76:21
neurotics . . . have founded r.s 273:11
new r. called 'Creative sleep' 278:5
no reason to bring r. into it 252:11
only r. could alter him 264:22
philosophy removes from r, all reason
   91·7
r. backed up by Commerce 284:20
r. . . . better to have it tough 66:16
r. . . . goes with acne 45:14
r. is a way of walking 167:7
r. is far more acute than science 119:11
r. is the frozen thought of men 190:18
r. is the theory that the wheel was designed
   230:4
r. without science is blind 107:16
r.s are kept alive by heresies 52:20
r.s change; beer and wine 12:20
r.s have produced no . . . imagery 78:4
respect the other fellow's r. 229:9
so r.s are changed 47:4
their r. is business success 127:17
to become a popular r., it is only 166:20
to hold a man . . . leave him for r. 313:13
to trust the old r. 212:9
what religion not only promises 256:9
when r. was strong 324:3
you ought to join all the r.s 314:7
Religious: commit himself to any r. belief
   346:10
   fellow traveller of the r. 52:21
   problem . . . finding a r. outlook 178:8
   stressing of r. experience 163:23
   to be . . . a man means to be 'r.' 108:18
   true r. mind 190:16
   without r. belief 215:9
Remarkable: commonplace as if it were r.
   16:1
   r. . . . resourcefulness of his mind 143:11
Remember: I wish I could r. as accurately
   247:14
   if I can r. any of the damn things 258:11
   you'll r. this . . . I already have 129:10
Remembering: anything one is r. 317:2
   r. . . . permits one to calculate 43:14
Remembrance: r. of love is death 190:17
Reminiscence: some of your grosser r.s 365:19
Removal: self-r. to South America 15:2
Renaissance: Christian moneylenders of the
   R. 165:7
   R. was simply the green end 120:14
Renewal: r. is fruitful only 322:9
Repeating: worth endlessly r. 248:5
Repent: to die tonight I would r. 29:1
   we shall have to r. 184:15
Repertory: plays many parts . . . in r. 121:15

Repetition: eye . . . bored by r. 23:17
  only constant r. will . . . succeed 155:2
  remembering is a r. 317:2
  anticipation of a favourable r. 24:12
Report: best confidential r. 348:2
Reporter: r. is a man who has renounced 244:19
Reporting: between r. . . . and making it up 122:2
Representation: annihilation without r. 332:14
Reproduce: butlers . . . do not r. 349:6
Republic: perfect r.s are perfect nonsense 120:16
  they were called a R. 347:9
  up the R. 31:11
Reputation: wrecks a woman's r. 80:15
Research: did r.es in original sin 266:5
  outcome of any serious r. 342:5
  r. . . . attack the facts at the point 140:6
  r. . . . doing what I don't know 51:4
  r. is the art of the soluble 229:2
Resembling: has he tried r. anybody 307:20
Resent: r. someone who can do it better 67:16
Reserve: r. is an artificial quality 227:18
Reserved: I wrote 'R.' on my compartment 189:2
Reservoir: gigantic r. of good will 358:9
Residence: inns are not r.s 239:11
Resignation: r. is for beaten people 167:23
Resist: we r. only what is inevitable 233:6
Respect: give . . . everything but r. 324:2
Respecting: you can't help r. 236:5
Respiration: he said it was artificial r. 57:17
Responsible: r. . . . classes 194:25
  than to be r. and wrong 74:13
Responsibility: absence of r. 207:20
  impossible to carry the . . . r. 107:14
  no r., like . . . umbrella stands 49:3
  no sense of r. 189:8
  power without r. 26:17
  r. without power 320:26
Rest: might . . . lie there and r. awhile 106:2
  needs more r. if one doesn't 346:9
Restaurant: r.s are . . . mouth-brothels 277:4
  went right to a r. 193:5
Restoration: damage that the last r. did
Result: chopping wood . . . sees the r.s 107:19
  don't seem to have . . . tangible r. 107:2
Resurrection: if there is to be a r. 135:24
Reticence: he had no r.s 38:11
Retreat: enemy advances, we r. 222:9
  r.s are possible – when 334:4
Retrospect: turning protest into r. 357:6
Retrospective: having a r. 243:5
Return: I shall r. 214:1
Reunion: little r. of my old army pals 146:17
Revelation: existence . . . medium of r. 327:2
Revenge: Living Well is the Best R. 327:12
Revenue: I warn the R. 11:6
Reverence: how much r. can you have 150:22
  that awed and simple r. 161:15
Review: so long writing my r. 224:25
Reviewer: r.s . . . those who had little to say 32:7

Reviewing: r. the books of . . . colleagues 246:7
Revision: historical r. . . . imposed on us 155:12
Revival: r.s are shallow things 166:14
Revivalism: rebellion and r. . . . in South Wales 329:6
Revolting: hearty, robust and r. 263:17
Revolution: believe in world r. 217:9
  bourgeois r. is necessary 201:8
  boredom . . . cause of r.s 166:13
  Britain is not . . . easily rocked by r. 145:13
  every r. evaporates 179:14
  fundamental premise of a r. 334:16
  history of r.s 201:1
  inherited . . . a r. 334:5
  neither can you expect a r. 196:11
  R. as if it were our Christmas 64:8
  r. as . . . to evolution 334:19
  r. does not choose its paths 334:7
  R. in the R. 96:3
  r. . . . is sometimes compelled 334:4
  r. is . . . the setting up of a new order 253:14
  r. only remains victorious 220:8
  r.s are always verbose 334:10
  r.s are not made by fate 54:5
  r.s have never succeeded 339:18
  r.s . . . kicking in of a rotten door 127:16
  r.s . . . reinforcement of the . . . State 63:2
  Social R. will be moral 261:15
  terror . . . to consummate the r. 62:24
  we invented the R. but 348:12
  what is wrong with a r. 134:8
  white heat of this r. 359:1
  Woman's Day . . . first day of the r. 334:6
  won't be any r. in America 208:13
Revolutionaries: couple of r. 236:18
  professional r.s 201:12
Revolutionary: either a r. or you're not 320:20
  I would be a r. myself 130:1
  most r. party 334:9
  r. simpleton 207:4
  r. state of mind 207:15
Revolver: culture I reach for my r. 175:15
Reward: desert of mortification and r. 354:7
  in nature there are no r.s 341:1
Rhetoric: quarrel we make r. 369:3
  use all the r. 249:14
Rhetorician: very congenial to r.s 166:7
Rhine: not much wider than the R. 263:19
Rhino: wish they were like the . . . R. 37:4
Rhinoceros: you'll never become a r. 168:16
Rhodes, Cecil: wishing Mr R. had not enabled them 32:18
Rhodesia: black majority rule ever in R. 309:14
Rhyme: groan in r.s 344:1
  I'm still more tired of R. 34:18
  r. is still the most effective drum 132:21
Rhythm: All God's Chillun Got R. 179:15
  I got r. 130:11
  r. imposes unanimity 230:18
  r. is a form cut into TIME 269:2

Ribbon: r. lost from . . . careless summer 152:1
Rich: as well off as if he were r. 21:12
  choose whether to be r. in things 165:10
  drift of a club . . . in favour of the r. 72:5
  easier for a needle . . . than for a r. 314:10
  government . . . for the r. 316:11
  if all the r. men . . . divided up 316:8
  kindness of the poor to the r. 71:3
  knowledge of the r. . . . their ways 81:10
  never be too thin or too r. 360:10
  no substitute for a r. man 154:5
  only . . . troubles of the r. 247:19
  r. are different . . . have more money 116:28
  r. are probably as poor as us 168:10
  r. are the scum of the earth 70:10
  r. being poor in spirit 313:15
  r. . . . have to live with r. people 309:20
  r. man without money 339:13
  r. men . . . very intractable 349:4
  r. society too r. to have need 325:12
  r., whom the world abhors 207:1
  then you are not a really r. man 130:18
  to cover the errors of the r. 70:22
  very tired r. man who said 318:12
Richardson, Ralph: 336:19
Richesse: r. oblige 65:14
Riddle: r. wrapped in a mystery 73:21
Ride: you got to ride to the end of the road
  274:12
Ridiculous: fine sense of the r. but 12:4
Right: also very important to be r. 77:18
  attack to the death your r. 320:24
  better to be irresponsible and r. 74:13
  considerably to the r. of our Lord 338:13
  for Thou knowest my r.s 114:15
  good impression on yourself by being r.
  121:18
  great believer in behaving r. 48:21
  man of the r. 242:22
  more you are in the r. 256:2
  r. not only to be r. 323:12
  r. is more precious than peace 359:16
  r. sort . . . do not want apologies 362:18
  r. wing of the middle 348:7
  so desirous of getting it r. 345:13
  tell me what's r. 360:1
  to be decorative and to do r. 115:8
Righteous: that one r. person without whom
  312:7
Righteousness: he makes r. readable 45:13
Riley: Mother R. 212:14
Rimbaud: always chasing R.s 258:9
Ring: One R. to rule them all 332:2
Riot: R. . . . A popular entertainment 42:25
  r.s are the language of the unheard 184:14
Ripple: after we cross the infernal r.s 269:20
Rita: Lovely R., Meter Maid 212:14
Ritz: justice is open . . . as the R. 323:2
  law-courts are open to all men, like the . . .
  R. 94:7
River: ol' man r. 146:5
  r. lifts itself from its long bed 89:23
Riverrun: r., past Eve and Adam's 177:1
Road: and not the r. 247:12
  another r. you did not see 243:15

begin a poem with 'in the middle of the r.'
  102:12
drive the r. 186:16
follow the yellow brick r. 29:22
how many r.s must a man walk down 104:19
r. lay curling around wood 152:1
r. one treads to labour 159:4
r. . . . was long, hard and perilous 75:21
Roman R. runs straight 147:20
until thy feet have trod the R. 185:2
white in the moon the long r. 159:5
Robbing: r. a bank . . . founding one 52:8
Robert E. Lee: Waitin' for the R. 131:13
Robey, George: R. is the Darling 43:4
Robinson: here's to you, Mrs R. 307:9
Robot: perfectly represented . . . a r. 75:18
  r. may not injure 20:17
Rock: marriage goes on the r.s 357:10
  my little stick of Blackpool r. 118:19
  no r.s at Rockaway 243:2
  r. and roll 202:6
  seas roll over but the r.s remain 153:7
  tenderness . . . can't break the r.s 357:19
Rock-Pool: replied the R. 84:10
Rococo: R. even spread to England 78:8
Rod: in r., the scourger almighty 176:18
Rogue: if you're not a r. 16:19
  r. is married to a whore 186:12
  r. . . . works harder to convince himself
  121:10
R.s Gallery of . . . boys 364:2
Rolls: R. body 242:3
Rolls-Royce: loudest noise in this new R.
  252:16
Roman: R. . . . his cloacal obsession 176:12
  R.s . . . found everything human 194:14
  wild tree growing through a R. imperial
  pavement 65:24
Romance: one of those historical r.s 140:3
  to be born into a r. 71:1
Romans: 57:20
Rome: 189:9
  as R. denied Etruria 194:9
  nobody in R. works 199:8
  R.'s just a city 58:2
  they burn while R. fiddles 83:15
Romeo: as R. . . . a pig 15:12
Romeo and Juliet: introduce sex into R. 151:6
Room: all I want is a r. somewhere 203:12
  back in a hot little r. 262:1
  conceived . . . in an enormous r. 78:5
  drift apart and needed more r. 97:18
  got the r. with the toadstools 86:8
  lighted r.s inside your head 193:14
  make all r.s into halls 81:7
  r. to eat muffins in 349:5
Roosevelt, Eleanor: 318:9
Roosevelt, Franklin D.: 55:7, 85:16, 133:18
  if R. were alive 135:6
  kind of nation . . . R. hoped 175:13
  R. . . . asking publicly for suggestions 75:14
  R. . . . greatest champion of freedom 77:2
Roost: birds coming home to r. 349:2
  they're sick of us ruling the r. 88:21
Root: we fail to take r. in others 335:3

Rope: throwing ... both ends of a r. 25:5
Rose: Everything's Coming Up R.s 313:1
  hot the scent is of the summer r. 138:10
  if you gave Ruth a r. 24:4
  les lilas ni les r.s 19:12
  one perfect r. 259:11
  reeks a mock r. 96:14
Rosebery, Earl of: R. ... Nature's Welfare
  State 79:11
Rosebud: R. is just a piece in a jigsaw 221:6
Rose-water: her blood is nothing but r. 115:6
Ross, Harold W.: 365:20
Rossetti, D. G.: when they found it, Mr R.
  33:3
Rotarian: astronauts ... R.s 343:2
Rothschild: by marrying a R. 79:11
Rotted: or simply r. early 247:13
Rottenness: perfection of r. 172:4
Rotter: leave it to them to pick the r.s 41:1
Rouault, Georges: R. ... thoughtacolour
  65:12
Roulette: as if someone has twirled a r.
  167:10
Round: we have gone r. and r. 368:20
Rousseau, J.-J.: R. ... first militant low-brow
  39:20
  to do is to be – R. 137:14
Row: I'm not lugged into Family R.s 362:13
Royalties: r. are nice 199:17
Rubbish: Make Good Use of Bad R. 38:17
Rude: not a slam at *you* when people are r.
  116:15
  right people are r. 226:20
  waitresses there were disgustingly r. 266:15
Rudeness: have perfected ... r. 327:7
Rugby: R. Union ... distillation of all 329:6
Ruin: human beings are ... ivy-covered r.s
  272:7
  r. can be charming 359:11
  not so pretty ... want to r. her 51:28
  seen the r.s of the ghetto 110:17
  to notice the r. in things 233:2
Rule: inventing impossible r.s 339:11
  reasons for the r. change 322:15
  they that r. in England 68:18
  to r. was a pleasure 22:10
Ruler: circumvent death ... desires of r.s 63:9
  to make life easy for his r.s 341:2
Ruling: instrument in the hands of the r.
  315:18
  r. class ... not be put in question 357:6
Rum: if the sergeant steals your r. 16:18
Rumble: he fell with a roll and a r. 177:3
Rummy: [Jeeves] is r. to a degree 363:1
Rumour: reckless arithmetic of r. 122:6
  Times has published no r.s 319:6
Run: for you to r. out of me 343:13
  foulest cross-country r.s 361:15
  lady, lady, better r. 259:13
Runcorn: it's raspberry time in R. 88:13
Running: r. away from it 264:10
Rural: r. life is a mystery 14:16
Rush-hour: one look at the r. jam 78:1
Ruskin, John: doubt that art needed R. 321:4
Russell, Bertrand: 37:1, 197:2, 230:14

Russia: America's ... a kind of R. 57:16
  if R. is winning 335:10
  in R., communism is a dead dog 312:16
  Protector of Holy R. 266:10
  R. has been won in fourteen days 145:4
  R. is a collapse 196:11
  R. ... is a riddle 73:21
  R. will inherit the future 196:14
  War and Peace ... about R. 13:27
  without the help of R. 209:12
  without R. most reckless commitments
    209:13
Russian: by this I am R. 369:12
  our decadence and the R.s' 331:9
  R. circus in town ... animals 137:11
  R. is a delightful person 187:12
  R. people ... awful reality 334:18
  R. people were left floundering 77:3
  test the R.s, not the bombs 127:3
  whole of R. literature 246:1
Russi ns: 130:7
Rustic: why ... go on being a r. 14:16
Rusty: better r. than missin' 224:4
Rut: new roads: new r.s 72:19

S

Sabbath: bath ... on the holy S. 308:9
  trouts bite best on the S. 28:19
Sabotage: business ... use of s. 342:4
Sack: either back us or s. us 60:4
Sacrifice: I have escaped the s. 147:14
  it is possible to s. half mankind 222:7
  my life as a s. for ... peace 174:14
  s.s he makes 227:8
Sacrificed: s. flayed and curried 176:18
Sacrilege: no s., no bathos 360:11
Sadism: aim of s. is to transform 123:14
Sadness: birds of s. 226:4
  farewell s. 110:16
Safe: world must be made s. 76:17
Safer: s. to be in chains 179:9
Safety: concern for one's own s. 150:15
  fingers on the s. catch 218:18
  perfect s. under British rule 331:16
Saga: frosty s.s 89:20
Sage: s. feels too small for life 68:14
  s.s knew their onions 244:8
Said: everything ... s. can be s. clearly 360:19
Sailing: s. ... boating around in muck 140:9
Sailor: bad s. keeps clear 189:9
  nippy ... my s. was 344:16
  who heard the silly s.-folk 185:25
Saint: all the qualities of a s. 184:19
  better class of S.s 189:5
  possible for a woman ... s. 318:17
St George: S. he was for England 68:19
St John's Wood: to confess ... to S. 170:18
St Louis: Meet Me in S. 317:9
St Sebastian: S. died of fright 319:11
Salary: drew a s. and hadn't often 114:22
Salesman: s. is got to dream 232:26

Salesmanship: attempts to reach others . . . s. 157:19
Salisbury, Rhodesia : 87:16
Salmon: cider and tinned s. 347:3
  crossing s. with mosquitoes 241:15
  two s. this morning 67:2
Salt: thing of watery s. 225:22
  would live on nothing but s. 71:14
Salvation: s. depends on getting a first 109:24
  s. lies in our being surprised 165:4
Same: everything would be . . . the s. 257:2
  saying the s. things . . . don't we all 103:15
  they all look just the s. 279:16
  we're all made the s., though some 88:9
Sammlerwert: aber kaum noch S. 180:3
Samuel, Herbert: 209:20
Sanctum: s. . . . intellectualized bedroom 350:16
Sand: there's s. in the porridge 88:12
Sandal: her massive s. set on stone 232:5
Sanders: George S., a giant grizzly 249:10
Sane: only one thing to keep us s. 45:10
  show me a s. man and I will cure him 178:10
Sang: he s. his shirt 92:18
Sanity: there ain't no S. Clause 223:18
Santayana, George: 172:4
Sap: s. out of my veins 368:10
Sarabande: through the long S. 162:2
Sarcasm: s. the condition of truth 29:15
Sardine: baby S. 234:6
  life . . . like a tin of s.s 36:18
Sartre, J.-P.: to be is to do – S. 137:14
Sat: you have s. here too long 14:7
Satan: S. . . . is a hard boss to work for 152:11
Satire: gluttons for s. 210:6
  s. is a lesson 246:14
  s. is something that closes 180:10
Satirist: s.s should be heard 306:18
Satisfaction: quiet kind of s. 204:17
Saturday: it's S. before you realize it . . . 264:13
  on S. I'm willing 360:7
Savage: 'arf the world full of s.s 65:22
  Britain had a s. culture 27:10
  if an uneducated s. can do that 86:6
  thousand hairy s.s 234:22
Saviour: it's 'S. of 'is country' 186:27
Saxon: S.s have stolen my balls 33:11
Say: cannot s. what you have to 47:20
  do not know what they are going to s. 73:9
  interested . . . only in the way he s.s it 110:6
  nothing to s., only to add 342:18
  nothing to s. . . . that is poetry 60:2
  people who s. nothing carry something 311:14
  those who have something to s. 78:10
Scab: me 'earty s.s 202:1
Scaffold: battlefield, but never on the s. 73:10
Scandal: s. by a woman of easy virtue 144:4
  separate cabinets to avoid a s. 150:13
  there is only silence or s. 228:11
Scarecrow: to measure the s.s 242:4
Scarlatti, Domenico: S. condensed so much 57:10

Scavenger: red-eyed s.s are creeping 108:19
Scenery: she was all for s. – yes 171:3
  there was too much s. 153:1
Sceptical: I hope you will . . . be s. 39:6
Scepticism: combined s. of everything 271:2
Scheherazade: S. is the classical example 366:2
Schizophrenia: if God talks to you . . . s. 323:20
  s. cannot be understood 192:3
Schizophrenic: behaviour labelled s. 192:9
  two persons in every one . . . s. 137:15
Schlief: dass ich s. 180:5
Schnorrer: did anyone say s. 223:20
Scholar: as you're not a s., you've no right 168:2
  better s. than Wordsworth 159:12
  last humiliation of an aged s. 80:18
  very fair s. . . . no thought 31:12
Scholarship: these slender indications of s. 74:19
School: all s.s are hell 86:9
  art of getting on at s. 83:22
  before . . . such a thing as a State s. 70:4
  he had been to night s. 10:2
  I think I'll not send him to s. 102:6
  into the National S. at six 349:14
  Leading S. . . . and S. 345:15
  love and the Board s. 32:25
  married life . . . late for s. 328:9
  Parochial s. with a vicar 25:11
  present s. is not fit for children 217:7
  private s. has . . . faults of a public s. 83:20
  s. . . . cross between a prison 90:11
  s. is where you go 338:10
  s. . . . last because there was no profit 33:21
  take me to see girls' s.s 47:11
  their s.s are quite remarkable 356:23
  those who accumulate years in s. 165:9
  unless . . . a really good s. 352:23
Schoolboy: every s. repeating my words 220:16
  justice decent s.s know 41:1
  s. is a novelist 83:22
Schooling: twenty years of s. 105:7
Schoolmaster: author ought to write for . . . s.s 117:10
  you'll be becoming a s. 345:14
Schubert, Franz: S. sonatas happen 53:4
Science: essence of s.: ask . . . question 54:4
  greatest collective work of s. 54:6
  jilted Bachelor of S. 61:5
  now, when s. is strong 324:3
  reserved to the physical s.s 232:15
  s. can find no aim in Nature 354:14
  s. is any discipline 133:9
  s. . . . interplay between nature and ourselves 150:4
  s. is really anti-intellectual 230:2
  s. is spectrum analysis 190:6
  s. is what one Jew copies 212:18
  s. knows only one commandment 51:11
  s. . . . long words to cover the errors 70:22
  s. must be individualistic 72:10
  s. must begin with myths 267:4
  s. reassures 51:2

Science – *Contd.*
  s. should leave . . . pronouncements 173:3
  s. . . . to inherit the moral imagination 54:8
  s. which hesitates to forget 354:18
  s. without religion is lame 107:16
  typical triumph of . . . s. 347:21
  universe . . . in physical s. 144:14
Science fiction: s. is no more . . . for scientists
  12:12
Scientific: *empirical s. system* 266:18
  s. discovery is a private event 229:4
  s. reasoning is . . . dominated 354:17
  traditional s. method 265:9
  where we do our s. work 248:2
Scientist: exercise for a research s. 211:15
  in the company of s.s 23:13
  just an old mad s. at bottom 262:5
  s. must be . . . a metaphysician 305:8
  true men of action . . . the s.s 23:14
  unless you're a s. 146:10
  when s.s are faced with . . . culture 311:2
Scotch: working on a case of S. 36:7
Scotsman: Englishman is . . . governed by S.
  142:18
  S. with a grievance 361:18
Scott, C. P.: 45:13
Scout: out with a baby Boy S. 360:6
Scrap: decent bar s. 350:5
Scratch: if he has any s. 289:2
Scream: s., an' s. till I'm thick 91:8
Screaming: carried s. into the street 350:22
Screen: things on the s. these days 158:6
  wide s. . . . bad film twice as bad 135:3
Screw: right s. under the sofa 158:5
Sculptor: I suppose I was meant to be a s.
  65:19
  s. must himself feel 249:9
Sculpture: s. is not for young men 50:21
  so much s. that I . . . missed 9:9
Scum: s. very superior 303:5
Sea: all at last return to the s. 64:18
  charge of the Navy . . . much at s. 64:16
  fed our s. for a thousand years 185:1
  he called the good s. up 185:24
  he had the s. in his blood 234:11
  if Ye take away the s. 185:21
  never seen the point of the s. 37:8
  only fools . . . drink at s. 343:8
  ourselves we find in the s. 92:19
  satisfy . . . the insatiable s. 84:10
  s. rises higher 68:13
  s. was ever loved by anyone 332:8
  snotgreen s. 176:10
  that gong-tormented s. 368:6
  we saw the s. 39:17
Sea-faith: till all our s.s die 328:5
Seagull: s.s all look as if 240:2
Seal: nor a privy, nor a s. 25:8
  you heard a s. bark 330:20
Seamy: life . . . s. on both sides 152:5
Sea-shell: she sells s.s 323:3
Sea-sick: nobody ever is s. – on land 174:3
Sea-side: drawback of all s. places 100:10
Seat: while they're laughing he'll win the s.
  303:21

Second-rate: sign of the s. 204:6
Secret: as well for telling atom s.s 310:17
  s. in the Oxford sense 121:9
  s. of the sea in . . . dewdrop 131:6
  such a s. place 292:13
Secretary: a s. to do it 220:10
Security: collective s. 36:15
  only freedom can make s. secure 267:3
  tradition becomes our s. 190:13
Sedentary: led . . . a s. life 278:2
Seducer: horseback, in the usual style of s.s
  132:16
See: art does not reproduce what we s.
  188:19
  I s. too deep and too much 28:1
Seeing: s. what everybody has seen 324:4
Seemly: s. that I . . . should be hurled 309:19
Seen: that once is s. 236:11
Sein: nicht s. kann, was nicht s. darf 240:8
Selection: living example of natural s. 134:4
  revolution . . . as natural s. 134:8
Self: certain of improving . . . your own s.
  163:5
  life-sentence in the dungeon of s. 84:22
  s. is of unmanifested nature 219:20
  write for the public and have no s. 85:1
Self-centred: s. passions afford . . . little variety
  290:2
Self-confidence: recover s. by snubbing the
  dead 119:16
  you lose all your s. 215:12
Self-consciousness: national mantle of s.
  135:21
Self-deception: s.? I don't think there is 81:23
Self-denial: s. is not a virtue 302:22
Self-esteem: s. is the most voluble 80:6
Self-improvement: take . . . to a plan of s.
  354:7
Self-indulgence: essay on 's.' 345:16
Self-interest: s. was bad morals 285:19
Selfish: discover a s. motive 219:12
  for s. motives 229:14
Self-made: s. man is one who believes 316:7
Self-preservation: sharp instinct for s. 347:12
Self-realization: s. cannot be the . . . principle
  of ethics 290:3
Self-respect: loved himself only as . . . s.
  326:8
Selfridges: shops like S. 198:6
Self-satisfied: be s., and other s. people will
  love you 297:19
Self-sufficiency: s. at home 347:2
Selling: calling of s. houses 206:12
Selves: eliminated all his possible s. 39:3
  our true, groundfloor s. 195:2
Selznick, David: S. . . . stormed through life
  306:15
Semi-human: liberation . . . cannot be achieved
  by s.s 122:9
Senator: s.s burst with laughter 22:1
Send: don't s. me 204:1
Sensation: vivid s. sweeps over him 257:2
Sense: Americans won't listen to s. 183:11
  assault on the s.s 215:4
  barrage of common s. 219:8

five s.s within whose pentagon 39:1
good poem . . . makes complete s. 139:21
good s. of a fox-hunting society 78:8
man talking . . . to himself 320:7
mind . . . between s. and nonsense 178:2
money is like a sixth s. 227:4
nothing but common s. 241:13
nothing other than the s. you choose 297:4
people can talk s. with concepts 281:11
talk s. to the American people 318:3
Sensible: become s. about social advance 310:14
Sensibilities: announcing one's own fine s.
   151:4
Sensitive: so s. . . . I seem to *know* 114:26
Sensitiveness: s. . . . of the true artist 32:20
Sensuality; lull lace of s. 329:6
Sentence: as the s. contains one idea 75:8
destroy . . . forming a complete s. 353:11
single s. will suffice 61:12
structure of the . . . British s. 74:20
when you frame a s. 359:9
Sentenced: pinched, but never s. 363:15
Sentiment: the well-known and popular s.
   152:20
Sentimentalism: s. is the working off 196:12
Sentimentality: s. . . . sentiment we don't
   share 141:9
sloppy s. is quite as bad 67:3
Sentry: wearily the s. moves 12:9
Septuagint: S. minus the Apostles 342:9
Serenity: s. to accept 249:6
Sergeant: if the s. steals your rum 16:18
s. had done what they said 38:5
Serious: s. house on s. earth 193:11
s. writer is not . . . solemn 151:9
till he . . . takes himself s. 284:10
Seriousness: high s. that's failed 35:18
humour must have . . . s. 32:3
Sermon: brilliant s. on . . . continence 161:11
deliver a s. or wet the bed 16:12
principles of the S. on the Mount 217:9
since his s.s were discontinued 336:20
snored through the S. on the Mount 45:1
Serpent: s. used to say, why not 305:10
shall be s.s in your tides 328:5
Servant: allow your . . . s. to read this book
   142:2
become the s. of a man 305:22
middle class education . . . training of s.s
   357:4
proud to be s.s of the state 74:3
public s.s serve you right 318:4
socialists treat their s.s 320:25
sovereign in her choice of s.s 347:22
who are nice to their s.s 20:3
wouldn't have white s.s 258:5
Service: kinds of s.s . . . in the Episcopal
   churches 130:20
s.s are voluntary 346:12
Serviette: never tucked his s. into his dickey
   88:10
Servile: The S. State 34:21
Seventeen: sensible . . . at s. 310:14
Sewer: s. in a glass-bottomed boat 344:7
trip through a s. 238:2

Sewing: s.? . . . reaping 46:20
Sex: 12:22
attempt to insult s. 196:13
bringing . . . 's. appeal' 30:3
country where men despise s. 195:23
continental people have s. life 232:2
Everything You've Always Wanted to Know
   about S. 279:14
fair s. is your department 101:14
farmyard world of s. 28:11
going to introduce s. into *Romeo* 151:6
had meant us to have group s. 49:4
his S. Life in Ancient Rome face 15:3
if s. ever rears its ugly head 24:2
if s. were all, then every trembling 317:17
if there was a third s. 341:4
Instant S. will never supersede 91:4
is s. dirty? 12:21
literature is about having s. 210:3
no s. without responsibility 211:4
poor honest s. . . . a private matter 104:9
practically conceal its s. 247:20
s. is here to stay 267:23
s. is one of the nine reasons 233:7
s. is only the liquid centre 86:12
s. like a glass of water 190:1
s. novel is now normal 306:1
s. . . . this lasts longer 18:11
s. with someone you love 13:1
trust the interests of any s. 209:7
what to expect of s. 14:17
when you have money . . . s. 100:4
women . . . mix something up with s. 355:8
Sexes: absurd division into s. 346:18
more difference within the s. 81:21
rubber models . . . of both s. 150:13
Sexism: ridiculing feminists is s. 279:1
Sexual: akin to the s. instinct 227:5
enormous s. pull towards mirrors 82:3
gratification of a vital need, especially the s.
   279:5
masturbation . . . primary s. activity
   323:13
nearest I've been to a s. experience 34:13
other people into s. activity 48:7
s. attraction through the . . . voice 147:12
that s. perversion . . . continence 161:11
Shade: advanced the lofty s. 159:10
any s. that is near to nature 102:7
Shadow: Me and My S. 286:11
their s.s flew as fast 369:17
throw a longer s. as time recedes 88:4
Shake: whom you want, as the phrase is, to s.
   170:8
Shakespeare, William: 302:11
genius, wasn't he – like S. 102:13
playing S. is very tiring 160:8
said S. . . . That's genius 49:19
S., in the familiar lines 46:10
S. . . . is really very good 139:20
S. . . . knowledge to such great account
   109:23
S. . . . not to translate him 31:23
S. . . . Pinero was the best 339:17
S. sprang to his feet 49:20

Shakespeare, William – *Contd.*
S. – the nearest thing 253:4
S. . . . weak in chemistry 351:9
S. wrote the best 239:4
S. . . . things to quote 57:6
Shakespearean: true S. way 271:2
Sham: Shem was a s. and a low s. 177:10
Shape: we tolerate s.s in human beings 167:8
Shapeless: I who was s. 327:14
Shark: s. has pretty teeth 52:9
Shaving: get any sympathy . . . go without s. 152:6
Shaw, G. B.: 32:4, 74:18, 201:18, 207:14 352:22
all S.'s characters are himself 305:21
Ibsen? Bricks without S. 49:14
S. appearing as S. 306:18
S. . . . brought up in Ireland 336:12
S. is the prototype 255:15
S. . . . look as if there were famine 306:6
S. . . . never written any poetry 71:23
S. . . . the more Christian 94:5
She: word which meant both 'he' and 's.' 236:9
Sheep: can't . . . start counting s. 258:10
don't call the bleeders s. 277:18
like being savaged by a dead s. 149:4
s. in wolf's clothing 77:5
s. with a blade of grass 362:9
standing a s. on its hind legs 32:19
Sheffield: S. could . . . be called the ugliest town 255:4
Shell: that's S., that was 10:23
Shelley, P. B.: S. best nineteenth 239:4
S. and Keats were the last 144:8
S. dreamt it. Now 329:17
S. had a hyper-thyroid face 315:11
then opened S. 365:2
working-class men reading S. 48:10
Sheltered: s. life . . . no contact with 37:1
Shem: S. is as short for Shemus 177:9
Shepherd: s. . . . embracing a chameleon 168:1
Sheridan, R. B.: S. . . . brought up in Ireland 336:12
Sherry: first-rate s. 266:3
Shift: put you on the day s. 105:7
Shilling: eightpence out of every s. 11:6
if you'll only take the s. 360:7
s. a day 186:13
Shimmering: s. into rooms 363:1
Shimmy: put thy s. on 196:5
Shin: cover a multitude of s.s 352:13
Shine: always to s. 228:15
Ship: s. on the sea and the horse 128:19
s.s . . . discovery about the world 48:20
s.s shall go abroad 185:25
wrong with our bloody s.s 30:4
Shipwreck: cases of s. and somnambulism 176:21
Shire: looks naked towards the s.s 186:22
Shirt: s. with stripes 264:17
s.s . . . sister Susie sews 353:1
when he's getting into his s. 196:4
Shit: château-bottled s. 270:7
some s. I will not eat 92:14
what an utter s. you were 14:15

Shiver: s. . . . looking for a spine 55:17
Shock: anybody can s. a baby 317:12
s. them and keep them up to date 305:19
Shoe: did it with my s.s off 345:13
Englishwomen's s.s look as if 145:9
gave me my s.-size in earth 220:17
like wearing a pair of s.s 25:9
put your s.s at the door, sleep 109:13
you haven't got a pair of s.s, have you 264:15
Shoot: I used to be able to s. 241:18
Shop: all English s. assistants 232:1
hands off o' the goods in 'er s. 187:4
Shop-girl: induce the s. to forget 227:21
Shopping: main thing today is – s. 233:1
Shore: s. has point, the sea none 37:8
Short: discovered I was too s. 13:21
Shortage: produce a s. of coal and fish 41:16
Shot: forty days . . . And never s. 308:16
golden s. storms 328:1
jealous of their leaders for being s. 369:4
man should have s. himself 155:15
Shoveacious: the S. Cult 349:18
Shoulder: I'm putting my queer s. to the wheel 132:5
Show: all my s.s are great 136:9
No Business Like S. Business 39:12
s. me 203:17
what do you think of the s. so far 239:18
wish they would s. off 214:10
Show-business: s. people don't share 349:3
Shower: prove the sweetness of a s. 329:4
s. of all my days 327:23
Showgirl: out-of-work s. uses her last 67:9
trade a couple of s.s 262:2
Showman: exquisite s. minus the show 149:14
once you are a s. 285:4
Shrine: build a s. to my memory 289:19
Shrink: I did not s. 225:18
Shrivel: he'd s. up at once 266:7
Shroud: gaiety . . . a striped s. 329:13
Shrunk: glimpse of what he's s. into 329:10
Shut: when I was there it seemed to be s. 122:12
Shy: be s. enough to be happy 72:23
Shyness: language performs . . . without s. 83:4
Shyster: you were a s. 206:15
Sick: kingdom of the s. 313:5
suppose the poor are always s. 81:9
we think we're s. 364:5
Sickness: if you have morning s. 199:11
Sidcup: if only I could get down to S. 264:16
Siddons, Sarah: S. tried to find 50:2
Side: as a little bit on the s. 24:18
ask us to take s.s against the . . . facts 73:14
even if there is only one s. 41:11
everything has two s.s 283:20
when to move . . . to the other s. 278:6
Sidewalk: ice-cream off a hot s. 200:3
Sidi: when I was in S. Barrani 158:13
Sieve: my mind is . . . an empty s. 310:3
Sighed: never s., she just rested 316:14
she even s. offensively 130:8

Sight: all the universe of s. 329:1
    hated each other at half s. 60:11
    s. of a pretty girl 331:7
    they rejoiced in . . . sense of s. 133:5
Sign: s. his name as yours 139:9
    s. of an archbishop is a double-cross 99:13
    waste time with the s. language 289:9
    while imploring heaven for a s. 50:16
Signpost: s.s like grim liars 44:2
Silence: appalling s. of good people 184:15
    its s. I hear and obey 328:22
    many days of s. to recover 178:9
    my favourite programme . . . s. 178:15
    normal condition is s. 296:19
    s. immediately drew the curtain 171:2
    s. of the mind 190:16
    s. went from rapt 205:7
    slightly frappé s. 363:10
    there is only s. or scandal 228:11
    thought up out of s. 137:22
    tinkling s. thrills 186:21
    unreasonable s. of the world 62:1
Silent: thereof one must be s. 360:20
Silk: like sheer s. . . . hides eczema 61:11
    wasn't really s. at all 256:12
Sillier: very like the Bible, only s. 276:4
Silly: show how s. they aren't 157:3
Silver: the thirty pieces of s. and the crown
    41:24
Simon, Sir John: 209:16
Simple: art . . . aims at the s. 244:14
    as s. as possible, but not simpler 108:9
    every work of art . . . is s. 69:15
    him who went for the S. Life 68:20
    show him the s. thing 282:4
Simplest: expression of . . . thoughts in the s.
    way 108:7
Simplicity: tragedies of life . . . their s. 79:15
Simplification: ultimate s. 215:17
Simpson, Mrs: S.'s pinched our king 16:8
Sin: absurd is s. without God 62:3
    adultery at one end and weep for her s.s
    65:8
    and even Roumelian s.s 169:12
    Beauty . . . first to hear about the s.s 132:10
    beauty is only s. deep 293:18
    Christ died for our s.s. Dare we 113:9
    no joy in pouring out one's s.s 115:7
    original s. is the property of the young
    48:18
    Original S., what rubbish 84:11
    physicists have known s. 253:10
    researches in original s. 266:5
    roots of s. 186:26
    saving young virgins from s. 17:15
    she must not reheat his s.s 98:18
    s. tends to be addictive 23:12
    s.s . . . attempts to fill voids 348:9
    when you confess your s.s 60:10
    weighed together with their s.s 179:10
    wore their bodies out with nasty s.s 298:6
Sinatra, Frank: Rousseau . . . Sartre . . . S.
    137:14
Sincere: I want those letters to be s. 150:24
    too true, too s. 369:7

Sincerity: artist will betray . . . s. 69:18
    never convinced . . . of your s. 61:18
    too much s. in society 226:11
Sing: ask them what they'd s. 126:11
    he s.s about like I do 91:12
    Welsh . . . just s. 346:4
    when . . . s.s you have to hug him 91:13
Singer: he's a s. in the park 237:2
    s. . . . had to take any note above A 133:4
    well-known s.s who would benefit 278:14
Singing: I'm s. in the rain 122:5
    what language was he s. in 97:8
Single: as a body everyone is s. 153:20
    s. room . . . has no parts 198:11
    than he used to drink when he was s. 230:12
Single-handed: I won the war s. 50:23
Sink: democracy . . . never s.s 14:8
    s. is the great symbol 237:4
Sinned: people s. against are not always 81:15
Sinner: s.s are still in bed 289:6
    combination s.s . . . dishonour 356:17
Sinning: nothing so artificial as s. 195:22
Sister: bring a s. for me 13:22
    only child . . . one s. 13:17
    s. a rough-rider over the Arctic 309:13
    sisterly kiss. Older s. 220:1
Sisyphus: must imagine S. happy 62:4
Sit: portion of herself to s. upon 50:2
    when I s. I don't like to s. 240:3
Sitting: are you s. comfortably 193:2
    got as far as . . . s. up 278:2
Situation: you haven't grasped the s. 182:21
Sitwell, Edith: 148:14
    S.s belong to the history 199:5
Sitz-Fleisch: wie mein S. möchte 240:3
Six: for s. days . . . this labour 94:12
Sixpence: we could have saved s. 30:13
Sixties: inflation in the S. 205:5
    S. technology 205:2
    they divided up the S. 205:4
Sixty-four: when I'm s. 203:2
Skeleton: so thin you . . . recognized her s.
    172:10
Skies: grasped the s. in a span 68:23
Skill: s. without imagination 319:4
Skin: ends in this – s. game 128:9
    I've Got You Under My S. 267:16
    leave some s. on to grow 184:8
    lower classes had such white s.s 93:2
    shabby curtains of the s. 328:2
skipping: s. everything in the future 355:5
Skull: cast of your s., sir 101:10
Skunk: we shared the s. 267:8
Sky: bear him up the Norfolk s. 40:12
    everything of worth was in the s. 271:6
    s. grows darker yet 68:13
    s. is as red as the grass 315:13
    s. was like washed-out Jap silk 65:5
    whole s. with it to the hills 124:5
Slain: with all its young men s. 22:8
Slam: not a s. at you when people are rude
    116:15
Slander: most gigantic s. in world history
    334:10
Slang: his s. . . . a little out of date 140:14

Slaughter: when it comes to s. 185:11
Slave: *Marriage* . . . two s.s 42:20
    sends a s. on to the stage 261:7
Slavery: every fulfilment is s. 62:9
    s. to live in the mind unless 131:7
Sleep: get a good night's s. 359:6
    haven't been to s. for 346:9
    he lives in s. 143:9
    he s.s a million strong 271:7
    how do people go to s. 258:11
    I wake to s. 284:8
    insulting to s. with your wife 24:7
    man who cannot s. ought not 55:10
    never s. with anyone whose 12:17
    new religion called 'Creative S.' 278:5
    s. is gross, . . . dissipation 145:11
    s. is when all the unsorted stuff 134:9
    s. with me . . . said 'no' 13:18
    to the heights of s. 368:9
    we only stood up to s. 235:18
    wouldn't s. with my own mother 12:8
Sleeping: fuss about s. together 346:21
    I saw that I was s. 180:5
    in the happy no-time of his s. 257:3
    s. one-eyed 289:10
    s. people are trying to destroy 143:10
Sleepwalker: with the assurance of a s. 155:10
Sleeve: to realize the importance of s.s 101:5
Slept: member . . . has *s. with the wrong*
    122:3
Slice: I think I've lost a s. or two 118:2
    not a s. of life, but a piece of cake 154:14
Slimming: my advice on s. 300:17
Slippers: marriage has put . . . into s. 61:19
Slogan: definition of a s. 339:3
    feed people with revolutionary s.s 184:11
    one of our national s.s 330:4
Slough: and fall on S. 40:17
Sludge: this concept of Activated S. 173:11
Sluicing: excellent browsing and s. 363:7
Slum: gay intimacy of the s.s 346:16
    if you've seen one city s. 11:12
    Madonna of the S.s 209:19
    there is not a s. in the country 144:7
Slush: pure as the driven s. 27:12
Smack: good s. 194:15
Small: makes every man feel s. 69:22
    S. is Beautiful 300:4
    s. of my back is too big 307:14
Smallness: made the world out of our s. 45:10
Smart-Allick: Doctor S. replied gravely 242:12
Smell: builds himself a S.-organ 240:6
    if anyone should have a s. 31:10
    ignored the natural s.s of sweat 133:5
    their s. brings on my migraine 51:7
    those whose study is of s.s 186:28
Smile: handshakes can be faked . . . s.s can't
    321:9
    he stood at the end of s.s 281:16
    his s. is like sunshine on putty 113:16
    it was only a small s. 234:3
    protecting itself – with a s. 271:11
    riding on a s. and a shoeshine 232:26
    s. falls . . . among the *bric-à-brac* 109:10
    s. I could feel in my hip pocket 67:12

s. out; but still suffer 147:15
    s. that children could warm 29:11
    s. was only in the mouth 28:17
Smiling: when you're s. the whole world
    135:17
Smith, Bessie: 176:5
Smoke: s., my friend 298:11
    when I don't s. I scarcely feel 156:18
Smoking: effects of s. . . . gave up reading
    322:5
    if you . . . give up s. 122:11
    s. is one of the leading causes of statistics
    188:22
Smollett, Tobias: S.'s temper 272:6
Smythe Dame Ethel: 309:4
Snapping-turtle: human s. 363:20
Snob: when he inveighed against s.s 272:10
Snobbery: bereaved if s. died 340:3
Snobbish: many artists . . . s. 84:6
Snobbishness: a derivative of his s. 273:16
Snopake: the S. grow on trees 24:12
Snow: it's congealed s. 260:2
    s.s of yesterday 250:10
    was to walk through the s. 314:18
Snow White: used to be S. . . . I drifted
    352:12
Snub: never s. anybody accidentally 132:9
So: it ain't necessarily s. 130:13
Soap: mother washed her mouth with s.
    259:14
Sobbing: sound of drubbing and s. 310:12
Sober: always hope for a man who, when s.
    152:21
    thought it might s. me up 116:2
    which is half drunk when s. 152:10
Social: established tradition of s. study 128:1
    like a s. worker's handbook 48:13
    reason . . . was the close-knit s. structure
    120:13
    S. Contract . . . conspiracy 350:17
    s. ramble 258:2
    so long as s. life survives 290:3
Social-Democracy: revolutionary S. 201:11
Social-Democrat: S. must never forget 201:10
Socialism: build up S. 200:17
    for others . . . s. 345:9
    priorities . . . the religion of S. 41:13
    same sick horror as . . . S. 349:12
    S. does not mean much more 255:10
    s. . . . of the scientific revolution 359:1
    S. with a Human Face 102:18
    souls who wait for s. 138:1
    tasks of education in s. 334:21
    under s. *all* will govern 201:7
    worst advertisement for S. 255:8
Socialist: high-water mark of S. literature
    255:16
    s. society in the Soviet Union 331:18
    S.s believe in two things 145:5
    s.s treat their servants 320:25
    typical s. . . . prim little man 255:9
    underlying motive of many S.s 255:13
Society: affluent s. in Ireland 203:10
    free s. . . . safe to be unpopular 318:6
    mankind is a closed s. 300:6

new s. after their ... image 334:8
no ... s. can flourish where a Jew 175:14
our own s. ... we can transform 204:16
poor s. cannot be too poor 325:12
regarding s. as something eternal 254:17
resistance to looking ... at s. 333:22
s. goes on and on 216:5
s. is making each other feel better 37:9
s. moves by ... parricide 39:21
s. protecting itself 271:11
this great s. is going smash 23:8
tribal or 'closed s.' 267:1
trouble with Western s. 254:6
unjust s. causes ... crime 45:9
violence shapes ... our s. 45:8
what does s. mean 37:13
Sociology: 138:2
Sock: s, it to me 287:19
s.s compelled one's attention 293:8
they're upstairs in my s.s 224:2
women who wear ankle s.s 37:10
Socratic: S. manner is not a game 32:24
Soda-water: first-aid ... squirting s. 362:22
Sodom: S. and Gomorrah 187:18
Sofa: rather lie on a s. than sweep beneath
    85:7
Soil: why a s. behaves as it does 215:16
Sold: they will be tricked and s. 295:10
Soldier: as an old s. I admit the cowardice
    303:9
English s.s ... lions led by donkeys 157:16
good s. has his heart and soul 51:6
I Don't Want to Be a S. 360:5
I'm a Wall s. 22:26
innocent delight in playing s.s 53:14
lucky Muse ... affair with s. 171:13
old s.s ... had never been there 25:12
on Sunday I walk out with a s. 360:6
only living unknown s. 182:22
s.s who passed 12:13
some s.s send epistles 353:1
we should act like s.s 228:10
what the ten-year s. tells 185:29
when a s. sees a clean face 51:21
Sole: s. ... untouched by suffering 319:16
Solemn: s. writer is ... a bloody owl 151:9
Soliloquy: even a s. is likely 208:10
television is a form of s. 78:9
Solitaire: s. is the only thing 353:9
Solitary: man is not a s. animal 290:3
Solitude: by the resonance of his s. 82:20
s. ... a fount of healing 178:9
Solomon: King S. drew merchantmen 186:4
Soluble: art of the s. 229:2
Solution: difficulty for every s. 295:9
fertilize a problem with a s. 307:15
isn't that they can't see the s. 69:21
s. of the difficulties 290:5
total s. of the Jewish question 134:1
Solvency: s. ... a matter of temperament
    309:21
Someone: S. waits for me 91:9
that I am not s. else 13:24
Something: everybody was up to s. 89:3
how s. mixed with s. else 186:28

I too hoped to become 's.' 154:16
was there s. 158:11
Somnambulism: shipwreck and s. 176:21
Son: likely s. ... I have none 159:9
s. is fighting 271:3
thy s.s acclaim your glorious name 92:7
Sonate: v. Korfs Nieswurz-S. 240:6
Song: 105:11
all s.s is folk s.s 55:2
breaks with a sound like a s. 71:15
carcase of an old s. 329:18
love s. is just a caress 285:16
Mr Tambourine Man, play a s. 105:4
rightful owners of the s. 261:11
s. in the blood 215:14
s. is ended 39:19
s. of the angels 231:7
s.s , , . are social 20:2
s.s containing the words country 92:5
that star-enchanted s. 238:5
war ... with its s.s 19:7
your s.s are sent 19:14
Sonny: upon my knee, S. Boy 55:14
Soporific: eating too much lettuce is 's.'
    268:10
Sorcerer: situation of s.s ... that of Jews
    163:13
what are you – a s. 244:4
Sore: s. as a sunburnt neck 363:22
Sorrow: S. for where you are 96:11
good thing to have a great s. 98:22
s. is tranquillity 258:13
misjudge the ... effect of s. 81:17
s.s are not known 282:9
undue concentration of s.s 101:24
Sorry: never having to say you're s. 10:8,
    300:19
Sort: it takes all s.s 301:17
Soufflé: reheat a s. 213:11
Soul: certain order in one's s. 197:13
enquire whose s. dangles 92:5
exposes ... the s. of the writer 327:9
I had become curious about their s.s 273:3
I looked into the s. of another 13:15
if you heat your own s. 297:19
keeping body and s. together 212:13
my s. looked down 257:7
my s.'s a trampled duelling ground 280:15
pale and insipid s. 183:1
s. clap its hands and sing 368:18
s. started at the knee-cap 207:11
spontaneous s. 195:8
tender, unique, coruscating s. 196:16
their patent-leather s.s 128:17
Sound: jazz ... people living in s. 85:4
most persistent s. 189:16
music is the arithmetic of s.s 96:6
music ... sheer s. 31:15
period of the cult of Pure S. 111:4
terraces of s. 238:5
Soup: everyone is the source of ... s. 156:7
stuff that moves is s. 312:19
South: Bible-ridden, white S. 15:6
hardly a town in the S. of England 255:5
South Africa: 96:1

South African: S. Police would leave no stone
 301:19
Southerner: being S.s 199:18
Souvenir: cuckoo clock ... quintessential s.
 87:7
 s.s sont cors 19:9
Sovereign: do not ... advise my s. 347:22
Soviet: absorbed in the S. Union 348:4
 experience ... in the S. Union 331:18
 patriotism to a S. State 335:5
 S. custom ... class distinctions 327:8
 S.s are Communists 217:9
Soya: would be a ... field of s. beans 319:13
Space: cantos of unvanquished s. 89:20
 clears a s. for us 273:2
 design is determined S. 269:2
 Eins within a s. 177:7
 impenetrable s.s 266:10
 let there be s.s in your togetherness 131:5
 more s. where nobody is 316:19
 s. beckons us to ... pawnbroker 47:19
 s. ... between the ears 20:11
 s. was the uncontrollable mystery 217:16
 there must be s. for the whole 35:12
Space–time: you have ... solved the s. problem
 138:6
Spade: s. is never so merely a s. 125:25
Spain: in S. the priests ruled 82:11
 never any doubt ... arrived in S. 64:14
 there's a valley in S. 100:6
Spalding: my name is Captain S. 223:20
Spaniard: image of a S. 231:23
 S. is like a man-of-war 53:3
 S.s are a people different 241:8
Spaniel: Pekingese s. trailing in her wake
 293:20
Spanish: taken the name of a S. lover 80:13
Sparrow: see a s. fall 252:3
 time the s. died 259:7
Speak: there was no one to s. up 249:8
 whereof one cannot s. 360:20
Speaker: s. can insult and threaten 63:10
Speaking: at their watches while I am s. 43:6
 Englishman's way of s. 203:11
Spearmint: Does the S. Lose Its Flavour
 286:10
Specialist: s. – A man who knows more and
 more 229:1
 s. appears, and democracy is ... spoilt 72:10
Species: domination of our planet by our own
 s. 166:21
 idea of death as a s. 189:19
Spectacle: s. creates an eternal present 39:4
Spectator: s. at a knockabout farce 197:13
 s. at the Banquet of Life 103:11
Spectre: authentic anecdotes about s.s 174:5
Speculation: this country ... built by s.
 355:11
Speech: free s. did not exist 243:1
 freedom of s. ... never to practise 336:9
 have its old s.es burned 311:5
 I have never delivered a firebrand s. 155:4
 man who hesitates in his s. 296:3
 masses ... moved only by the power of s.
 154:18

most precious thing in s. are pauses 280:10
s. is a slight fever 296:19
Speechlessness: to express its s. 73:8
Speed: urgent necessity of intense s. 204:9
Spell: anybody who can s. TUESDAY 236:5
Spencer, Herbert: 208:20
Spend: s., s., s. 249:3
Spinach: I say it's s. 353:15
Spine: shiver ... looking for a s. 55:17
Spinoza, Baruch: anarchists ... fall for S.
 65:11
Spirit: Holy Ghost having evaporated ... as
 s.s 100:12
 philosophy ... science of the s. 91:7
 possession by good or evil s.s 166:11
Spiritual: any kind of s. life 215:9
 asset in the s. life 351:7
 s. universe in which s. values 144:14
Spiritualism: is her s. getting worse 89:1
 psychology ... sublimated s. 313:6
 s. ... good citizenship 313:10
Spiritualist: if the dead ... you are a s. 323:20
 media ... sounds like ... s.s 319:19
Spit: s. on a well-scrubbed floor 125:15
 you s. with great charm 132:13
Spiteful: write when I feel s. 197:5
Splendour: s. you have felt 282:4
Split: s. an infinitive ... it will stay s. 67:18
 s. the atom by firing particles 148:17
Spontaneity: more studied than ... s. 320:23
Spontaneous: S. Demonstration 254:11
Spoon: born with a plastic s. 332:13
 silver s.s in his pocket 72:9
 s. feeding ... teaches us nothing 120:2
Sport: musical beds is the faculty s. 12:2
Sporting: not s. to start in time 277:10
Sportsman: never ... what I call a S. 308:16
Spot: turns to one mass of s.s 300:15
Spout: I just stand up and s. 159:13
Spring: I said the hounds of s. 330:17
 s. and summer did happen 246:10
 s. flow down the woods 292:2
 s. has kept in its folds 19:12
 s. has returned 282:10
 they call it easing the s. 277:17
Squalor: private opulence and public s. 127:12
Squeak: Thin s.s of radio static 89:19
Stable: attended s.s, as ... church 308:20
 I'll find the s. 368:11
 s.s ... real centre of the household 305:5
Stage: s. is not what it used to be 222:21
 we do on the s. the things 320:3
Stair: follow me and climb the s.s 267:17
Stalin, J. V.: if Mr S. dies, what will be the
 effect 106:11
 more to the left than ... S. 351:13
 S. and his commissars ... bunglers 76:12
 S. hates the guts of ... top people 286:1
 that S. himself rose 335:2
Stammer: like a s. 207:8
Stand: if you'll s. for him 235:4
 s.s out so far you could break 67:13
Standing: it all depends where you're s. 234:23
Star: being a s. has made it possible 95:8
 did not ... invent the 's.' system 32:1

game between a man and his s.s 31:8
have you heard it's in the s.s 268:1
have weighed the s.s 68:23
I am greater than the s.s 326:18
I looked on that same s. 369:14
never tell me that not one s. 124:21
soft rain . . . of the failing s.s 280:16
someday I'll wish upon a s. 147:7
s.s are in one's brain 291:5
s.s grew bright 225:21
s.s lay like yellow pollen 369:16
s.s, like measles, fade at last 157:10
s.s scribble on our eyes 89:20
s.s were going out 78:11
there burns a furious s. 317:16
When You Wish Upon a S, 99:7
with a million s.s you pin it 112:9
Start: shouldn't have a flying s. 359:3
Starve: just as soon s. . . . if she didn't have
    to 116:24
State: asset a head of s. can have 359:6
dying away of the s. 201:14
lie has become . . . pillar of the S. 312:15
not taught by the S. 184:22
proud to be servants of the s. 74:3
reinforcement of the power of the S. 63:2
s. does not administer 209:1
s. in the proper sense 201:5
s. is an instrument in the hands 315:18
there will be no s. 201:6
we ought to put the S. in order 70:4
Stately: one of the s. homos 90:21
Statement: any general s. is like a cheque 269:1
fiction . . . s.s I can disown 321:2
pick up the club of s. 117:18
Statesman: dangerous thing for a s. 326:3
English s. is bribed 72:9
s. is a politician 266:14
s. . . . politician who's been dead 335:14
when you're abroad you're a s. 218:16
s. . . . with an open mouth 318:15
Statesmen: s. are . . . too busy to think 290:16
democracy led by . . . s. 75:13
Static: class people as s. 346:18
Station: By Grand Central S. I Sat 309:11
ideas above her s. 277:6
Station-master: he has been duped – the s.
    217:8
I would like to be a s. 41:9
Statistician: by the s. or the poet 119:5
Statistics: facts . . . louder than s. 322:20
feed the hungry on s. 209:4
kinds of lies . . . and s. 336:8
leading causes of s. 188:22
S. would be a bankrupt science 309:17
s. . . . you make up 321:6
unless s. lie he was 92:15
uses s. as a drunken man 193:1
Statuary: larger and less successful s. 71:10
Statue: bad s.s familiar to London 31:20
girl . . . is worth a million s.s 92:6
no s. has ever been put up 307:3
s. tolerant through years 40:8
Status: elevated his s., without perpetrating
    53:10

Stealing: for de little s. 253:6
suspected of s. an umbrella 119:5
Steam: sing the Song o' S. 185:28
Steamer: churned away like a Nile s. 293:20
Steel: big shot in s. 10:17
Stein: I don't like the family S. 16:16
Stein, Gertrude: 16:16
Stendhal: fought two draws with Mr S. 151:10
Step: one small s. for a man 20:12
one s. forward 201:2
Stepping: awkward s. aside on the street
    123:6
Sterbe: was wirst du tun, Gott, wenn ich s.
    282:18
Sterile: it doesn't mean she's s. 167:22
s. instructors . . . endeavoured 246:7
Still: always nearer by not keeping s. 143:7
can't once remember him s. 54:16
Stilt: processions that lack high s.s 368:13
Stink: middle way between s. and asepsis
    161:8
Stirrup-pump: s. can extinguish hell 277:15
Stocking: from coming out of her s.s 42:17
Stolen: so confused that they's s. things 263:20
Stomach: can't think . . . on an empty s.
    279:12
encounter on an empty s. 362:5
enough acid in your s. 249:1
love his neighbour on an empty s. 359:14
man is not . . . a walking s. 255:17
s. thinks her throat is cut 288:11
Stone: Ann is seventy years of s. 327:13
as heavy as yonder s. 177:13
bread alone . . . give them s.s 352:19
have written of me on my s. 124:7
like a rolling s. 105:1
s.s to build a wall 124:21
take s. from s. and wash them 109:20
turns you like them to s. 325:8
Stonehenge: brings S. to Nyasaland 27:10
S. circle of . . . faces 309:22
Stop: full s. . . . at the right place 25:1
S. the World 248:7
Stopped: I s., I looked and I listened 283:10
Storesmen: Nature . . . created them to be s.
    129:4
Stories: he lives surrounded by his s. 296:18
no point to . . . made-up s. 342:14
writer of crook s. 344:15
Stork: always reads s.s instead of stocks
    123:4
throwing rocks at the s. 224:15
Story: central character in my own s. 157:4
every picture tells a s. 10:15
fictitious . . . is not so much the s. 11:15
good s. about a bad girl 16:13
I'll tell that s. on the golden floor 159:15
most interesting thing about any s. 319:18
Short S. Conference with God 9:5
s. for which the world is not yet 101:22
s. is essentially the same 156:20
s. is like the wind 341:14
s. that starts with an earthquake 134:19
yes – the novel tells a s. 119:19
you can begin a s. in the middle 138:6

Strabismus: Dr S. (Whom God Preserve) 241:15
Strachey, Lytton: S. . . . imperfect sympathies 33:2
to find mr s. 222:24
Straitjacket: all be put in s.s 358:1
Stranger: depended on the kindness of s.s 357:25
never fight fair with a s. 232:20
right to cry in s.s' houses 221:19
S. in a Strange Land 150:2
tell whether a s. is your friend 119:14
who is the smiling s. 66:8
you may see a s. 146:8
Strategy: s. . . . tactics talked through 176:3
Strauss, Richard: 31:14
Stravinsky, Igor: 98:16
S. looks to me like a man 157:2
Straw: break its back with . . . last s. 50:6
drift down time, clutching at s.s 320:10
Streak: s. in that young man's make-up 360:12
Stream: cold companionable s.s 369:1
murmur of underground s.s 22:7
s. runs softly 328:20
your father's father, and the s. 89:22
Street: breaks at the end of the s. 219:9
down these mean s.s a man must go 67:14
finest . . . ever walked the s.s 352:17
inability to cross the s. 365:12
that took you off the s.s 33:13
s. . . . with the idea of going somewhere 280:17
Streisand, Barbra: 179:2
Strength: communicates some of its s. 272:16
here's my s. and my weakness 259:2
Stress: in times of s. 254:25
Stretcher: greatest s. in the world 102:9
Strike: last four s.s . . . it's pissed down 314:11
twenty-four-hour s. 250:8
Strindberg: S. when you have a temperature 214:11
String: I'll s. along with you 103:2
Strip-Tease: S. was named after the man 243:17
Stroke: at a s., reduce . . . prices 85:10
none so fast as s. 80:5
Strong: characteristic excellence of the s. 46:2
Still Going S. 10:12
those who think they are s. 42:5
Strongminded: nobody is s. around a President 278:20
Structure: existing social s. . . . incapable 334:16
s. of the ordinary . . . sentence 74:20
Struggle: all s. has for its end 207:20
s. itself towards the heights 62:4
s. no longer concerns the place 112:6
Strumpet: half some sturdy s. 147:17
Strut: he s.s sitting down 104:15
Student: British postgraduate s. 210:5
profession – s.; inclinations – neurotic 287:11
to notice the existence of s.s 246:6

Studied: s. . . . a repeated spontaneity 320:23
Study: S. . . . doesn't say what of 102:2
Stuff: tried to s. the Severn Tunnel 242:15
Stump: with only a s. for an arm 52:5
Stupid: because she was a s. woman 227:10
he became merely s. 273:13
not equally s. in all directions 35:13
people might think we're s. 113:6
s. man doing something he is ashamed of 302:14
s. neither forgive nor forget 323:17
Style: alpha and omega of s. 302:16
author arrives at a good s. 83:4
first grace of s. 239:12
God . . . has no real s. 264:2
inflated s. 256:4
s. is . . . the outside of content 133:11
s. . . . often hides eczema 61:11
s. reflects . . . idiosyncrasies 106:1
world might gain . . . a sense of s. 140:19
Subject: who brought the s. up first 313:2
Subjunctive: s. to the last 365:18
Sublime: overdid the s. 297:11
Sublimity: s. without . . . being good 109:22
Submarine: saw her first s. 234:6
yellow s. 203:4
Subordinate: assistance of two s.s 260:14
Subordination: s. of the minority 201:4
Subterfuge: this balancing s. 23:7
Suburb: s. without the urb 87:16
s.s in search of a city 260:3
Suburbia: I come from s. 276:13
Suburban: a child . . . of s. nature 38:11
Subway: get into the s. without using 258:7
s. . . . no one rides it any more 78:1
words of the prophet . . . on the s. 307:11
Succeed: if at first you don't s. . . . quit 114:6
to s. unconventionally 183:14
ugly enough to s. 13:4
whenever a friend s.s 343:5
Succeeding: themselves s. themselves 357:6
Success: all the stigmata of s. 350:15
born of the bitch-goddess, S. 171:19
failure with . . . flavour of s. 86:11
great social s. is a pretty girl 117:6
knows there's no s. like failure 105:3
never consciously striven for . . . s. 147:10
pure monotony of his s. 169:8
self-made man who owed his lack of s. 150:8
s. comes before work 298:10
s. or failure 256:3
s.! That's it 344:9
Sweet Smell of S. 200:5
Sucker: good enough for them, the s.s 139:11
hello, s. 143:1
Never Give a S. an Even Break 114:13
Sued: motto is publish and be s. 167:12
Suez: S. Canal . . . through my drawing room 106:14
Suffer: cocoa . . . to help you s. 175:4
I guess the sufferers s. 35:5
man who s.s and the mind 110:7
neurotic if he s.s 323:19

Suffering: about s. . . . never wrong 22:13
it is not true that s. ennobles 227:7
loungin' round and s. 187:15
only certitudes . . . exile, and s. 62:18
sole . . . untouched by s. 319:16
stamped from the dough of s. 352:20
Suffrage: universal s. almost inevitably 166:5
Suffragette: child of the 's.' 207:22
s.s were triumphant 50:3
Sugar: dirt and sucked s. stick 369:5
Suggestion: ten commandments . . . ten s.s
49:7
Suicide: believed to be a form of s. 59:3
denies . . . grounds for s. 62:19
hearing of the latest s. 106:3
it is s. to be abroad 30:10
James, I want to commit s. 318:12
murder a man . . . committing s. 359:17
statistics of s. show 166:9
s. kills two people 232:12
s. remains . . . courageous 140:17
s. twenty-five years after 30:7
Suit: ask for the cheapest s. in the shop 142:3
s. is pale yellow 357:16
Summer: I drank s. 19:15
it was s. all the year round 254:16
it's all right in the s. time 245:1
s. afternoon . . . most beautiful words
171:6
Summertime: s., and the living 154:2
Sun: born of the s., they travelled 314:17
burnish'd by Aldershot s. 40:18
how do you find the s., ladies 92:10
I'll follow the s. 202:17
parables of s. light 327:24
sheriff s. and rustler moon 231:11
s. as green as the rain 315:13
s. in a mist, Like an orange 65:6
s. is going down and becoming cold 310:12
s. moves always west 159:4
s. never sets on Government House 89:9
S. . . . the oldest gap in the world 11:3
s.'s gonna shine in my back do' 176:2
that s.'s hot 234:8
thus runs my motto and the s.'s 228:15
to experience the s. 239:9
whatever the s. may be 197:3
Sunburn: s. is very becoming – but only 88:15
Sunday: at S. School I was always in demand
160:9
bugger S. 44:12
matrices of a . . . well-run S. school 142:8
nothing but S.s for weeks on end 156:13
on S. I walk out with a soldier 360:6
S. is for washing the car 37:2
S. is the same everywhere 280:2
S. . . . take this railway by surprise 131:15
Sunset: I can look at a s. now 227:20
I have a horror of s.s 274:2
with these April s.s, that somehow 109:8
Sunshine: Scotsman . . . and a ray of s. 361:21
to create s. 285:13
Supercalifragilisticexpialidocious: S. 99:6
Superhuman: between the beast and the s.
299:5

Superior: real s. man is like a bell 51:14
sucked in by the su-s. 194:10
s. people never make 239:10
s. persons can remain s. 254:24
s. to the saint 196:19
titles . . . embarrass the s. 302:21
Superlative: we have not settled the s. 70:14
Super-Mac: Introducing S. 342:12
Superstition: for a s. to enslave a philosophy
166:20
Super-power: The S. 121:3
s.s behave like blind men 188:10
Supply: Sir Short S. 181:15
Support: s. whatever the enemy opposes 221:22
Surface: man is only man at the s. 341:8
Surgeon: or a s.'s hands 87:6
Surgical: crisp white s. tunic 262:14
Surname: awfully well . . . to know his s.
56:13
Surprise: learn always to receive . . . s.s 165:4
Surrounded: s. on all sides, I won 50:23
Surveyor: taken on as Land S. 179:4
Survival: greater than his sense of s. 140:17
no s. value 206:1
no test of literary merit except s. 256:1
prospects of s. were . . . better 332:16
without victory . . . no s. 73:22
Survive: as fitted to s. . . . as a tapeworm
134:4
s. in cracks . . . that's us 125:1
Susie: shirts . . . sister S. sews 353:1
Suspicion: people under s. 179:10
s. of one's own motives 290:13
Suzanne: S. takes you down 80:3
Swallow: just don't s. it 300:17
s.s crossed off the days 64:13
S.s twisting here and there 369:17
Swallowed: s. convulsively, like a Pekingese
361:10
Sympathy: your God-damned s. 365:19
Swarm: there is something about a s. 261:12
Swear: by the time you s. you're his 259:16
Swear-word: foreign s. . . . inoffensive 327:10
s. like roses 219:8
Sweep: a clean s. or make a clean end 95:20
Sweetness: man . . . capable of s. 57:15
Swell: what a s. party this is 268:1
Swift: race is not always to the s. 182:15
Swimmer: like dead s.s 19:8
Swimming: don't deserve a s. pool 279:8
Swine: s. to show . . . the truffles 12:6
Swing: would you like to s. on a star 58:6
Swinger: be a s. of birches 124:4
Swiss: if the S. had designed these 327:5
S. have sublimated . . . clock-making 175:2
S. managed to build 231:14
S. who are not a people so much 112:14
Switzerland: 87:8, 320:14
S. . . . cuckoo clock 348:16
S. . . . many things end 116:22
Sword: beating s.s into ploughshares 35:16
he came bringing a s. 20:5
his s. into assorted villains 140:3
Islam came with a s. 288:16
votes are to s.s 43:5

Syllogism: conclusion of your s. 252:6
Symbol: we need s.s to protect us 45:11
Symbolic: whole of life is s. 261:9
Sympathetic: to be s. without discrimination
 114:30
Sympathies: like the rest of us, imperfect s.
 33:2
 your cosmopolitan s. 286:14
Sympathy: instead of the expected s. 123:7
 only way I could get any s. 152:6
 riddling her hostess with s. 161:4
 s. . . . for being foreigners 48:5
Symphonies: he plied me with s. 262:8
System: attacked by the nervous s. 156:8

T

Table: on your own t. 250:16
 wrestled with a self-adjusting . . . t. 330:7
Tablet: bats defile his . . . T.s 50:14
 women . . . taking 'The T.' 329:14
Tact: essential t. . . . can go too far 79:12
 t. of those who . . . avoid condescension
 277:3
Tactician: peasants are . . . brilliant t.s 39:5
Tactics: t. talked through a brass hat 176:3
Tactile: T. Values 38:14
Taft, President: 193:6
Tail: his little t. went wagging 18:12
 thy t. hangs down behind 186:11
Tailor: Savile Row t. calls 242:4
 walk into my own t.'s 271:12
Take: you can always t. one with you 76:4
Taken: something which can be t. away 312:6
Talcum: a heavy fall of t. 262:10
Tale: most tremendous t. of all 41:5
 saddest t. . . . the t. they told 110:11
Talent: so considerable a position on so little t.
 227:11
 t. to amuse 88:8
 t. which does what it can 28:3
 worm . . . at the root of his t. 136:4
Talk: beautiful family t. 81:11
 English t. . . . quadrille in a sentry-box 170:5
 furious itch to t. about themselves 227:18
 he knows when not to t. 284:22
 it's not t. of God and the decade 313:2
 just going to t. to herself 316:15
 loose t. can cost lives 17:7
 makes women t. more 205:19
 nothing else to t. about 341:5
 pure in heart . . . more to t. about 353:5
 small t. . . . bigger than most people's
 97:19
 t. with someone about the flat things 354:5
 t. . . . . with the man who wrote it 359:13
Talker: good t.s, when they have run down
 83:8
 listener . . . t. with a sore throat 355:9
 non-stop t. . . . given a typewriter 52:25
Talking: ain't t. about him, ain't listening
 50:22

can't learn anything when you're t. 91:14
 he had not stopped t. 345:11
 made things better by t. 214:5
 myself t. to myself 36:1
 people t. without speaking 307:10
 t. is often a torment for me 178:9
 what we are t. about 290:6
Tambourine: Mr T. Man, play a song for me
 105:4
Tamed: responsible for what you have t.
 292:16
Tangerine: t. trees and marmalade skies
 202:19
Tapster: Ancient T. of this Hostel 96:15
Tart: absinthe makes the t. grow fonder 102:17
 he's lost us the t.s' vote 97:13
 Lady Jane became a t. 18:18
 think she'd be taken for a t. 319:20
Tarzan: me T., you Jane 58:8
 wear a T. chest-wig 10:9
Taste: bad t. is better than no t. 38:4
 bouquet is better than the t. 268:21
 simple t.s . . . no matter what it cost 56:17
 t. all, and hand the knowledge 311:7
 t. in us as . . . in clocks 21:8
 t. was that of the little crumb of madeleine
 272:9
Tasteless: had at least the merit of being t.
 98:5
Tatter: t. in its mortal dress 368:18
Taught: any subject can be . . . t. 56:6
 do not always like being t. 77:16
 we were t. very badly 350:19
Tautology: definition is t. 219:11
Tax: difference between a t. collector 63:13
 [t.] has made more liars 285:3
 whoever pays the t.s 185:18
Taxi: every human activity inside a t. 53:9
 I've been in too many t.s 216:8
 t.s are . . . a Christian institution 231:18
Taxicab: consider a t. . . . more convenient
 288:12
Taxidermist: a tax collector and a t. 63:13
Tchaikovsky, Pyotr: 11:9
 you can't do T. 294:18
Tea: denoted early morning t. 59:3
 her own cup of real or of lime-flower t.
 272:9
 make yourself a good . . . cup of t. 58:3
 t.'s out of the way 278:12
 treat housemaids to his t.s 69:2
 T. for Two, and Two for T. 147:3
 trouble with t. 231:15
 we drink too much t. 272:1
 when I makes t. 176:11
Teach: missionaries t. 'em 284:20
 person wishing to t. 301:6
 spoon feeding . . . t.es us nothing 120:2
 t. anybody anything 295:2
Teacher: 131:3
 as a t. . . . . Shaw is no good 32:4
 difference between good t.s and great 60:7
 neither their t. nor they know 246:8
 t. gives knowledge, but a Guru 136:7
 t. should have . . . minimal power 323:14

t.s . . . quench flames that are already 140:2
t.s . . . told to shut up 25:11
Teapot: never gets further than warming the t. 221:20
Tear: all the t.s that are shed 289:3
   eternal reciprocity of t.s 257:5
   foamed with the purity of t.s 261:5
   I know t.s when I see them 125:18
   stars . . . fell like a falling t. 369:16
   t. was an intellectual thing 35:8
   land of t.s 292:13
   t.s from my learned friend 149:5
   t.s roll down his legs 239:17
   t.s were to me what glass beads 90:10
Technicolor: how I dislike 'T.' 223:6
Technics: modern science and t. 244:12
Technique: poem . . . when anxiety meets a t. 104:13
Technological: for t. man 217:16
Technology: any new t. 218:2
   nothing but utilitarian t. 246:15
   Sixties t. 205:2
   t. . . . knack of so arranging 123:10
Technostructure: men of the t. . . . priesthood 127:17
Tedium: biography . . . by t. 142:19
   t. inseparable from the tasks 14:16
Teeth: I had braces on my t. 216:1
   I'll dispose of my t. as I see fit 262:13
   lies in the shape of false t. 350:18
   lose a lover . . . lose one's t. 353:8
   natural false t. 284:1
   prefer to have . . . my t. out 155:19
   ride rough-shod over my t. 262:12
   t. like splinters 66:10
   t. like the Ten Commandments 333:13
   wish I'd looked after me t. 24:15
Teich: fallen ein auf teilnahmslosen T. 281:7
Television: T.? No good will come of this 300:10
Tell: you never can t. 303:15
Tellable: here is the time of the t. 282:3
Teller: t. of tales 296:18
Temptation: t. came to him 293:19
Terror: even t. of their lives 301:19
Teetotaller: are ye a t. 64:15
   secret t. 255:9
   t., arter four or five whiskies 169:2
Teléfono: contesta Tú el t. 63:20
Telephone: answer Thou the t. 63:20
   black t.'s off at the root 265:17
   can't dial his own t. numbers 216:9
   can't see a t. 226:17
   kind of T. Queen 173:12
   never pass an empty t. box 65:7
   t. is a cool medium 218:3
Television: 190:4 (see also T V)
   anybody can shock . . . t. audience 317:12
   effective on t. panel 342:17
   see bad t. for nothing 135:2
   stake in commercial t. 329:22
   t. brought war into the living room 218:10
   t. . . . chewing gum for the eyes 55:13

t. is a form of soliloquy 78:9
   t. is more interesting than people 88:1
Tell: t. it like it is 249:13
Telly: get any pornography . . . on the t. 314:9
Temperament: human t.s are too diverse 212:15
   solvency . . . a matter of t. 309:21
Temperance: antithesis . . . T. Hotel 337:2
Temple: they build t.s 190:18
Temple, Shirley: T. through gauze 27:15
Tempo: difference of t. 269:22
Temporary: I still feel – kind of t. 232:21
Tempt: bad for me do not t. me 305:16
Temptation: exempt from t. 206:4
Ten: they are only t. 250:17
Tenant: t.s of the house, thoughts 109:4
Tender: 't.-minded' and 'tough-minded' 171:17
Tenderness: t. . . . can't break the rocks 357:19
   t. I bear for myself 25:13
Tenement: subway halls and t. walls 307:11
Tennis: play t. with the net down 125:2
Tennyson, Lord: T., remember, thought trains 22:22
Teppichfresser: T. 18:7
Termini (railway): 119:4
Terrible: something t.'s happened 181:5
   this was t. with raisins in it 259:17
Terrifying: life . . . nothing more t. 175:1
Territory: it comes with the t. 232:26
   more t. than it is capable 334:4
   parcelling out the t. of Powers 93:1
Terror: adds a new t. to life 333:10
   all that t. teaches 68:22
   life points only towards the t. 156:20
   met there stark t.s 192:2
   then t. . . . makes its appearance 62:24
   what . . . t.s infants go through 101:25
Terrorist: all t.s . . . end up with drinks 127:5
Testament: discussed the New T. 13:22
Tested: art of being t. 261:1
Teutonic: semi-mythical T. figure 173:12
Text: from the relentless line of t. 343:3
   thundering t. . . . snivelling commentary 138:21
Thamesfontein: look after me in T. 186:9
Thank: atheist . . . has no one to t. 345:2
   ay t. yew 21:2
Thatcher, Margaret: T.'s great strength 352:23
   Mrs T. may be a woman 17:14
Thaw: The T. 107:15
Theatre: entry before the t. is built 46:18
   go to the t. to be entertained 85:12
   in the t., the director is God 263:7
   nobody goes to the t. unless 11:8
   quit going to the t. 294:16
   that's what counts in the t. 111:12
   t. is the best way of showing 148:4
   T. must be destroyed 104:14
Theatrical: Brecht . . . is a t. whore 145:6
Theme: leave great t.s unfinished 214:9

Theology: keep history and t. apart 350:21
  t. finds the cat 171:21
Theory: any t. based on an emendation 68:7
  classical t. on Mondays 49:12
  first-rate t. predicts 188:11
  more important for a t. to be shapely
    146:10
  spare himself . . . elevated it to a t. 323:8
  we respect his t. 229:9
Theosophist: feeble as . . . T.s 351:10
Therapy: t. . . . the tenth American muse
    54:13
There: because it's t. 220:6
Theses: pushing up t. 84:5
Thesis: commit no t. 188:21
  many people have written his t. 48:4
Thief: this whimpering t. 186:25
Thieves: one of the t. was saved 31:6, 319:17
Thimble: t. lies cold and tarnished 308:13
Thin: enclosing every t. man 347:13
  Kattrin, beware of t. men 51:20
  imprisoned in every fat man a t. one 84:20
  never be too t. or too rich 360:10
  no matter how t. you slice it 134:3
  so t. you . . . recognized her skeleton
    172:10
  t. man inside every fat man 254:14
Thing: T. which seemed very T.ish 236:6
  t.s are entirely what they appear 296:21
  t.s happen when you take 10:24
Think: able to feel hot and t. cold 65:3
  can't t. on an empty stomach 279:12
  can't t. without his hat 30:21
  easier to act than to t. 20:1
  Englishman t.s 253:5
  he t.s in images, not in concepts 145:3
  inclined to t. . . . I should 101:23
  men t. differently 193:24
  people t. they are thinking 171:20
  preparation to t. 290:16
  sooner die than t. 291:2
  what men t. . . . they do 20:4
  wise man t.s once 36:8
Thinker: stopped thinking . . . became a t.
    322:1
Thinking: draw a limit to t. 360:15
  false t. brings wrong conduct 164:1
  only happy when it was t. 236:2
  perform without t. 354:16
  t. means connecting 71:22
  t. what nobody has thought 324:4
  wishful t. in Hell 205:11
Third: T. Programme country 356:22
  T. World 26:4
  T. World never sold 244:17
Third-class: t. carriage is a community 71:4
Thirst: no wine so wonderful as t. 232:6
Thirties: t. were his stamping ground 48:3
Thirtieth: it was my t. year 327:25
Thomas: John T. marryin' Lady Jane 196:3
Thorn: silver and the crown of t.s 41:24
Thorough: appallingly t. these Germans 163:4
Thoroughbred: English t. for . . . fertilizer
    52:3
Thou: I and T. 56:9

Thought: archaeology of our t. shows 120:10
  art . . . the profoundest t.s 108:7
  brink of the dark river of t. 351:7
  censor one's own t.s 344:3
  deluge of words . . . drizzle of t. 98:4
  distinguish between t. and feeling 78:2
  father of the arrow is the t. 188:17
  her t.s as still 60:14
  his t.s, few that they were 234:17
  hundred schools of t. contend 222:5
  keep off your t.s 344:5
  library in t. in cold storage 295:7
  man whose second t.s are good 29:5
  more complicated than his t.s 341:9
  my t. is me 296:22
  no t. but a great memory 31:12
  odd t. on some great subject 174:20
  on the troubled seas of t. 127:11
  our t.s have any relation to reality 71:21
  t. . . . in an enormous room 78:5
  t. is born of failure 355:12
  t. is not a trick 194:12
  t. is only a flash 266:9
  t. . . . stimulates and preserves 349:11
  t.s of a dry brain in a dry 109:4
  t.s of middle age are short 343:3
  use for what must still be t. 149:16
  words into the smallest amount of t. 73:17
Thousand: man who makes a hundred t.
    305:2
Three: t. is company, safe and cheery 313:3
  t. o'clock is always too late 296:16
Thrift: whatever T. may be doing 183:12
Thriller: t. is the cardinal . . . form 55:6
Throat: comes . . . to the cutting of t.s 351:11
  her t. is cut 288:11
  if your t. is hard to slit 184:16
  look out it doesn't cut your t. 262:15
Throne: ideally suited for the British T. 44:9
  your t. is above the King's 185:14
Through: so daddy, I'm finally t. 265:17
Throw: you t. up every morning 131:18
Thrown: should be t. with great force 259:23
Thrush: sing as the t. sings 231:10
Thumb: inseparable my nose and t. 259:10
  world's grimed t. 96:17
Thunderbolt: when struck by a t. 50:17
Thurber, James: 149:8
Thyroid: Shelley had a hyper-t. face 315:11
Tiber: River T. foaming with much blood
    270:16
Ticket: t. to ride 203:1
Tickled: how t. I am 99:19
Ticky-tacky: all made out of t. 279:16
Tide: poinsettia meadows of her t.s 90:2
Tiddley: T.-om-Pom 200:12
Tie: see if your t. is straight 362:7
  struggle with . . . evening t. 40:19
  when he buys his t.s he has to ask 116:27
Tier: o dieses ist das T. 282:13
Tiers: T. Monde 26:4
Tiger: from a hungry t. . . . no escape 50:9
  paper t.s 222:3
  riding on the back of the t. 181:25
  t. in man . . . the donkey 326:20

t.s travel stealthily 234:7
vegetarian t. 190:7
we were defenceless against t.s 332:16
Tight: wearing armchairs t. 363:4
Tightness: round her waist for the t. 308:3
Tightrope: walk a t. safely 291:4
Tim: poor tired T. 96:23
Timber: second-hand t. . . . like those
    awkward 160:4
Timbuctoo: Prince of T. 34:16
Time: A Good T. Was Had by All 310:10
as t. goes by 160:12
bleeding to death of t. 138:11
haven't the t. to take our t. 167:19
how short t. was 231:9
man is killing t. 212:2
music is . . . digesting t. 23:22
now . . . the t. it always is 121:13
rhythm is a form cut into T. 269:2
same old druid T. 286:13
she's the original good t. . . . had by all
    95:6
so it is with t. in one's life 272:14
so little t. 286:3
something to do with the t. 284:17
they reflect t. I am the very 126:12
t. becomes visible 244:13
T. forgets and never heals 314:16
t. is a friend 248:15
t. . . . is not consequential 101:24
t. is too large 296:17
t. . . . longest distance between two places
    357:21
T. looped so river-wise 139:7
t. occupies the same role 217:16
t. spent on any item of the agenda 260:18
t. walks by your side . . . unwilling 125:7
t. was away and somewhere else 219:10
t. wounds all heels 224:21
T.'s winged chariot changing gear 208:14
t.'s up, gentlemen . . . we close 174:7
to fill the t. available 260:2
we must use t. as a tool 181:27
Times, The: site of T. office 250:15
T. has published no rumours 319:6
T. is read by the people 11:3
T. is speechless 73:8
very able letters to T. 32:26
Timid: if I ever felt . . . t. 348:3
really a t. person 13:5
Timing: essence . . . is t. 288:5
Tin: only a t. full of people 234:6
Tinned: t. food is a deadlier weapon 255:3
Tinsel: find the real t. underneath 204:4
laid on the t. in splotches 170:9
Tinted: million little t. folk 160:11
Tip-and-run: Englishman . . . watch him play t.
    114:28
Tipster: t. who only reached Hitler's 326:1
Tiptoe: why did you keep me on t. 226:5
Tired: I'm t., send one of them 352:9
more tanned and more t. 261:14
too t. to yawn . . . t. Tim 96:23
Titanic: changing deckchairs on the T. 18:14
Title: t.s distinguish the mediocre 302:21

Tod: was im T. uns entfernt 282:9
den ganzen T . . . zu enthalten 281:10
Today: I didn't get where I am t. 250:7
our doubts of t. 286:4
regret cannot come t. 18:3
t. . . . first day of the rest 137:13
t. is an action replay 34:11
Todlos: des 'T.', Jenes bitteren Biers 282:5
Toffee: t.s I chewed 24:15
Together: we shall be t. for ever 328:13
Togetherness: spaces in your t. 131:5
Toilet: can be read only in the t. 233:9
king goes on foot . . . the t. 163:11
such bad early t. training 56:3
you can't tear the t. paper 355:18
Told: my epitaph . . . I t. you so 351:15
Tolerance: forget . . . such a thing as t.
    359:18
hope to do such work for t. 341:15
t. and acceptance 204:19
Tolerant: so t. . . . attended a lynching 310:19
Tolstoy, Leo: get me in any ring with . . . T.
    151:10
T.'s novels . . . would easily confuse 312:3
Tomatoes: the shiny stuff is t. 312:19
Tomb: storms in the freezing t. 328:1
within his neglected t. 50:14
Tomboy: careless t. 269:25
Tomorrow: all the singing t.s 263:1
beautiful word for doing things t. 305:9
leave t. behind 89:8
our realization of t. 286:4
silt of t. 265:4
swears won't happen until t. 56:7
think about t. 296:25
t. . . . is usually the same day 320:2
Tommy: it's T. this, an' T. that 186:27
Tone: my basic t.-row 278:11
Tongue: right word on the tip of our t. 55:5
you've a sharp t. in your head 262:15
Toni: which Twin has the T. 10:26
Toothache: fine young man with a bad t.
    170:17
Toothbrush: invented . . . a musical t. 308:18
Top: I started at the t. and worked 349:1
isn't important to come out on t. 51:15
people at the t. of the tree 340:5
Room at the T. 50:8
Topaz: suspend t. . . . and weigh it 50:15
Tories: tell sad t. of the death 173:10
T. are not always wrong 45:16
us T., mate, would win 314:6
Torment: only absolute is the t. that men 132:7
Torture: no t. and no execution 246:12
Tory: about God being a T. 251:2
every Briton is at heart a T. 37:20
frozen wastes of the T. past 209:18
T. Party . . . lower than vermin 41:17
Toss-up: what happens is a t. 281:1
Totem: t.-animal . . . substitute for the father
    123:9
Toten: nah is der Held . . . den jugendlich T.
    281:14
Touch: anyone can say he is out of t. 101:1
to lose the t. of flowers 63:6

Tough: long hours ... made them t. 48:22
'tender-minded' and 't.-minded' 171:17
Tourist: and I watched the t.s stand 43:9
  gold clubs of your t.s 303:25
  to give t.s something solid 87:8
  t. ... dismissed the historic safari 35:19
  t.s who come to our island 145:12
Trace: he rose without t. 243:6
  man alone leaves t.s 54:1
  photograph ... is also a t. 313:7
Trade Unionism: T. of the married 303:11
Tradesmen: not counting t. 362:23
Tradition: nothing sacred about t. 190:13
  RAF do not have t.s 18:2
  t. ... extension of the franchise 72:21
Traffic: never take ... notice of t. 89:18
  there will be no more t. 123:11
Tragedies: actual t. of life 79:15
  familiar with the t. of antiquiy 320:4
Tragedy: farce brutalized becomes t. 89:17
  hero and I will write you a t. 116:21
  history repeats ... as t. 19:1
  life is a t. when seen in close-up 68:5
  that is what t. means 320:9
  t. is if I cut my finger 54:20
  we participate in a t. 163:15
  you're a bloody t. 228:12
Tragic: monstrous mother would be t. 339:1
Train: any more than a moving t. 321:4
  begged the Devil to stop the t. 274:11
  laugh ... like a t. 362:3
  never missed the t. 277:10
  next t's gone 223:5
  thought t.s ran in grooves 22:22
  t.s run to time 18:13
  where is the London t. 47:18
Tram: know her again if we met in a t. 69:7
Tramp: began to think the t. 349:10
Trampling: by t. down a dozen others 51:13
Tranquillity: sorrow is t. 258:13
Transformation: life passes in t. 281:17
Transition: age of t. 204:19
  we live in an age of t. 165:14
Translation: t.s (like wives) ... seldom faithful 61:3
Translator: only tribute a French t. 31:23
  whether t.s are heroes or fools 173:17
Transmigration: if there is a t. of souls 179:13
Trap: trapped like a t. in a t. 258:16
Trapeze: I'm a t. artist 105:10
Trash: road the t.-horse 214:7
Traum: nur ein T. war das Erlebnis 240:8
Travel: only newlyweds will t. 123:11
  t. ... contracts the mind 327:6
  why ... do the wrong people t. 89:2
  you want to t. blind 80:3
Travelling: t. being ... exciting but not interesting 243:13
Treachery: patriotism ... is t. 335:5
Tread: they rush in and fear to t. 152:12
Treason: never committed even low t. 92:24
Treasure: feel of what nubbed t. 149:6
Treasury: if the T. were to fill old bottles 183:13
  produced ... for the T. 107:6

provoke ... the T. 27:4
T. are never happy 153:10
Treaties: autopsy of t. 219:4
  to publish the secret t. 335:7
Tree: and that's why the t. 15:22
  God's arm engloves this t. 277:13
  let a t. sigh with her 95:4
  t. explodes every spring 269:22
  t.s of life, when will it be winter 281:7
Tremendous: aside from being t. 158:14
Trench: digging t.es ... because of a quarrel 67:5
  there isn't time to dig t.s 224:12
Trent: at T. Bridge it is always four 64:3
Tribal: for t. man 217:16
Tribute: magnanimous t. by Imperial England 265:2
Trick: forgive all the little t.s 125:5
Tried: I've never t. it 10:20
  there was little she hadn't t. 150:18
Trifle: my method ... observance of t.s 101:3
Trigger: whose finger on the t. 94:2
Trim: t., as the daughters of the people 352:23
Trinities: tangled T. 186:7
Triste: jamais t. archy 222:25
Tristesse: Bonjour t. 110:16
Triumph: this is our ... t. 341:15
Trivialities: t. ... obviously absurd 44:17
Triviality: but you're deluded by t. 167:20
  Law of T. 260:18
Troops: I longed for more ... t. 76:2
Trouble: house that has got over its t.s 174:1
  lot of t. ... never happened 76:8
  man ... aged by t. 361:20
  no one has been in this much t. 82:4
  one thing to be said for inviting t. 220:7
  sleep with anyone whose t.s 12:17
  t. was new to him 170:17
  t.s that money can't cure 247:19
  when it is not our t. 223:1
  worry ... interest paid on t. 167:5
Trouper: old t.s are gone 222:21
Trousers: in the dark in your t. all day 99:23
  they have asked for my t. 191:1
  t. ... have been marinading 53:11
Trout: t.s bite best on the Sabbath 28:19
Trucking: keep on t. 17:2
True: be interesting than that it be t. 354:11
  biography ... can never be wholly true 270:5
  I'm always t. to you, darlin' 267:9
  t. to the flame of life 195:4
  what people say of us is t. 309:15
  what we are saying is t. 290:6
  what we believe is not necessarily t. 34:7
Truer: books ... t. than if they had really 151:12
Trull: t. before she could toddle 310:20
Truman, Harry S.: kind of nation ... T. 175:13
Trumpet: elf ... dreads the final T. 147:17
  when the last t. sounds 321:7
  you are truly God's t. 329:7
Trunk: loving hands are packing t.s 242:11

Trust: I don't t. him. We're friends 51:19
  I wouldn't t. an Aryan 247:1
Truth: Americans ... telling the t. 49:2
  as freely as a lawyer interprets t. 132:23
  before the t. has got its boots on 60:5
  behold, this is the t. 365:13
  boasts that he ... tells the t. 230:9
  cinema is t. twenty-four times 133:10
  committing ourselves to the t. 249:13
  count t.s like lovers 208:19
  exactitude is not t. 226:7
  exaltation takes the place of t. 62:21
  faith has need of the whole t. 326:11
  first casualty ... is t. 175:5
  forsake this t. 286:17
  good art speaks t. 244:14
  harder to make him confess the t. 159:2
  he who does not bellow the t. 261:17
  I will stop telling the t. about them 318:2
  if decade after decade the t. cannot 311:16
  it's the t. even if it didn't happen 183:5
  joking is to tell the t. 303:20
  law ... cannot compel anyone to tell the t.
    94:6
  live by what they believe ... t. 146:11
  man can embody t. 369:9
  mathematics ... possesses not only t. 290:4
  mistook disenchantment for t. 297:18
  opposite is also a profund t. 44:17
  relics have nothing to do with the t. 315:10
  there are no new t.s 215:8
  they are the t. 112:5
  till T. obeyed his call 368:3
  took to telling the t. 293:13
  truss-advertisement, t. 193:15
  t., ... a standard for the naturalist 296:4
  t. acceptable to lying men 22:25
  T. and Myth are one and the same 297:14
  t. being rather a current 274:5
  t. ... dependent upon human intercourse
    98:23
  t. is always a compound 321:3
  t. is concrete 52:11
  t. is cruel 295:21
  t. knocks on the door 265:3
  T. ... rises again as phoney 149:13
  t. ... runs away and hides 35:6
  t. that makes men free 11:4
  t.s begin as blasphemies 305:1
  t.s that become old 256:15
  two half-t.s do not make a t. 189:12
  wanted to get at the t. 290:19
  we speak ... half-t.s 208:10
  whatever remains ... must be the t. 101:2
  when they told the t. on me 110:11
  when t. is discovered by someone else 312:12
Truthfulness: t. can give ... a reputation
  320:17
Try: we t. harder 11:1
  you live so close to t. 320:5
T.T.F.N. 181:16
Tulip: tiptoe through the t.s with me 103:1
Tumour: in constant good t. 216:16
Tune: changing my tune isn't one 31:9
Tunic: crisp white surgical t. 262:14

Tunnel: light at the end of the t. 212:1
  tried to stuff the Severn T. 242:15
Turgenev, I. S.: I beat Mr T. 151:10
Turmoil: t. is but ... the anarchy 28:13
Turn: I t. and the world t.s on the other
  173:9
  left a t. unstoned 360:8
  you must t. on 199:1
Turned: she t. me down 363:16
Turner: J. M. W.: he resembled a T. sunset
  115:15
Turtle: Green T., Chelonia mydas 156:17
  send their celebrated Invalid T. 136:3
  t. lives 'twixt plated decks 247:20
TV (see also Television): decade of T. 218:8
  it's the tragedy of T. 179:3
  reflection is much more interesting than T.
  265:6

  T. – a clever contraction 9:3
Twelve: only t. ..., get thousands 135:10
Twentieth: all ... the t. century wants 55:6
  in the t. century ... man is dead 123:17
  t. century has reversed 161:25
  t. century is ... the nineteenth 142:21
  t. century will be known as the century of
    Fascism 245:7
Twenty-two: what still alive at t. 184:16
Twenty-four: but then we shall be t. 159:8
Twice: t.-over cannot be 148:1
Twiggez: t.-vous 187:27
Twin: no longer even needed a t. 316:15
  which T. has the Toni 10:26
Twist: NO MORE T. 268:9
  Oliver T. was so lucky 237:9
Two: at t. with nature 13:19
Two faced: I grant you that he's not t. 311:3
Typewriter: for changing a t. ribbon 36:4
  great t. in the sky 24:12
  left alone ... with a t. 221:4
  poem written on a t. by a t. 172:18
Tyrannize: t. over his bank balance 183:15
Tyranny: under conditions of t. 20:1
Tyrant: no t. would be able to stay 312:14
  people will endure their t.s 359:20
Tyre: familiar with ... t.s 101:12
  from Tarshish unto T. 186:4

U

Ugliest: u. town in the Old World 255:4
Ugly: girls ... fall in love with u. men 52:17
  u. enough to succeed 13:4
Ulcer: all four u.s working 335:12
Ultimate: U. Thing (Dernière Chose) 173:13
Ultimatum: adjournments, u.s 219:4
Ulysses: showed her pup U.' bough 111:3
  U. can be read only in the toilet 233:9
  U. is a wastepaper basket 136:6
  U. ... to cover the universe with mud
    119:20
Umbrage: to do in the shades except take u.
  97:12

Umbrella: love me, love my u. 177:20
  u. might pacify 266:2
  with the point of his u. 246:19
Umpire: u. . . . no one consulted 333:19
un-American: Hitler . . . combating u. activities
  150:11
Unbaptized: left his children u. 365:5
Uncertain: what is worth knowing is . . . u.
  165:12
Uncertainty: one welcomes the u. 320:6
  u. . . . unknown to the Greeks 46:14
Uncharity: prissy mouthed sisters of u. 222:19
Unchivalrous: kill a woman . . . u. 35:20
Uncle: forbidden like a wicked u. 21:18
  our four u.s 352:22
Unclean: when the u. shall be no more 131:2
Uncomplicated: in a devious way I am u.
  138:5
Unconscious: believe in . . . the u. 123:1
  farms, why not the collective u. 173:15
  forced to recognize the u. 123:8
  good to lie there u. for a bit 308:2
  I call the collective u. 177:22
Unconsciously: people say they do things u.
  81:23
Uncreative: infallible sign of an u. age 34:3
Under: Get out and get u. 78:14
Under-achiever: God . . . an u. 13:3
Underdog: Englishman among the u.s 346:24
Undergraduate: u. . . . women and drink 43:3
Underground: he sleeps as sound as Johnny U.
  274:14
Underpants: through the u. 202:4
Undersold: never knowingly u. 206:9
Understand: contempt for anything he didn't
  u. 365:20
  criticize what you can't u. 105:9
  not pretend to u. the universe 321:1
  one who tries to u. 131:12
  u. each other worse 172:13
Understanding: always a crisis of u. 357:5
  need more u. of human nature 178:13
Understatement: gravestone is an u. 180:16
Understood: those who long to be u. 342:7
Undertaker: best u. in Brooklyn 356:12
  nothing against u.s personally 237:10
  who keep the u.s busy 265:14
Undesirable: u. . . . been one myself 125:26
Uneducated: good thing for an u. man 75:6
  government by the u. 72:17
Unemployment: no more u. 183:13
Unexpected: u. . . . people have come to expect
  37:16
Unfaithful: how fashionable . . . to be u. 25:10
Unforgiveness: alp of u. grew 266:1
Ungrateful: Man is an u. beast 34:24
Unhappily: bad end u. 320:9
Unhappiness: u. . . . talents and our expecta-
  tions 46:7
Unhappy: as soon as one is u. 273:1
  ever be u. for long 345:17
  I am u. everywhere 343:9
  Kansas City to be u. 224:22
  making one another u. 229:13
  u. the land . . . in need of heroes 51:10

Unhearing: patted his U. Aid 43:8
Unimportant: emotionally she was u. 20:6
  think what they hear is u. 265:6
Uninteresting: there is no . . . u. subject 70:15
Union: to make a u. with Great Britain 263:5
  u. of life and peace 296:2
Unique: all cases are u., and very similar
  109:17
United States: best . . . defence of the U.
  285:24
  in the U. . . . one feels free 172:15
  in the U. there is more space 316:19
  U. . . . are under the impression 157:6
  U. . . . gigantic boiler 141:20
  U. has to move fast 182:2
  U. never lost a war 285:7
Unity: concept of u. 232:15
  Good . . . makes for u. 162:20
Universe: benign indifference of the u. 62:14
  God who created the u. 229:19
  irreversibly 'personalizing' u. 326:14
  u. . . . more like a great thought 173:1
  one tiny corner . . . of this u. 172:22
  specializing in the u. 85:14
  this U. must not fail 210:9
  U. as One Thing 173:13
  u. . . . bigger than I am 320:1
  u. . . . is a spiritual u. 144:14
  u. is expanding . . . what's in it 98:8
  u. is not only queerer than we 144:13
  u. shows evidence of a . . . power 173:2
  u. was . . . a sophism 46:15
  u. was dictated 240:14
University: any attempt to reform the u.
  165:8
  as many fools at a u. as elsewhere 130:9
  most English u.s of its type 210:4
  this U., which once saw 159:12
Unknown: apart from the known and the u.
  264:19
  critics shouting, 'He's u.' 42:26
  to go into the u. 328:21
  U. Prime Minister 21:5
  u. throughout the world 18:20
Unlicensed: zest to the u. hours 327:11
Unlike: law of dislike for the u. 370:4
Unlistener: greatest u. 287:2
Unmarried: intense horror of u. girls 32:10
Unnatural: nothing so u. as the commonplace
  101:4
  u. practices under one of 338:8
Unpacker: air of a born u. 32:9
Unpleasant: book, or . . . anything u. 278:16
Unpopular: free society . . . safe to be u.
  318:6
Unpredictable: element of the u. 256:3
Unproductivity: fear of u. 39:9
Unrequited: self-love seems so often u. 269:23
Unsägliche: Preise . . . die Welt, nicht die u.
  282:4
Unselfishness: ill-feeling U. occasions 205:16
Unsers: Bei u. 361:1
Unsociability: petty vices of u. flourish 305:24
Untalent: tapped u. 15:4
Untidier: even u. than I am 355:2

Untidy: Human Beings are an u. lot 38:18
  offends . . . because it is u. 255:13
Untrue: man who's u. to his wife 22:15
  that he never was u. 259:13
Unusual: too old to be u. 345:12
  too u. not to be corrupt 125:14
Unwise: it's u. to be born 303:29
  men are u. and curiously planned 117:22
Upbringing: u. a nun would envy 253:16
Upper: when you belong to an u. class 125:22
Uprising: u. of the masses 253:12
Upsey: down, U. 181:7
Upstairs: we don't care to go u. 195:2
Upstart: place of the u. 231:22
Urban: u. and suburban man 218:6
Urge: that dark, unseasonable U. 330:6
Urinated: u., it sounded like night prayer
  117:4
Urine: red wine of Shiraz into u. 99:1
Urwald: war eine Art von U. aufgestellt 180:4
USA: 346:23, 355:11 (see also United States)
  created something new in the U. 35:10
  God bless the U., so large 22:16
Used: learn to get u. to it 74:1
Useless: then both are u. 370:6
Utopia: end all the static U.s 166:13
Utrillo, Maurice: U. . . . in mortarcolour
  65:12

V

Vacuum: v. is a hell of a lot better 357:12
Valuable: anything is v. 280:5
Value: aim of education is . . . v.s 166:2
  hardly any collector's v. 180:3
  ideas . . . more importance than v.s 52:13
  intrinsic reaping of v. 354:13
  nothing of . . . v. had emerged 345:11
  partly in a world of timeless v.s 166:8
  spiritual v.s count for everything 144:14
  to get my v.s right 243:3
Van Gogh, Vincent: V.'s ear for music 356:1
Vanishing: I do not find these v. acts 309:18
Vanity: pull down thy v. 269:19
  spiritual v. of men 20:5
Vanquished: the grievances of the v. 75:15
Van Winkle: hurry along, V. 89:24
Varicose: vein that became v. 193:4
Vasectomy: v. means not ever having to say
  10:8
  v. of the vocal cords 14:3
Vassal: his lithe bright v.s tread 44:4
Vatican: best warehouses . . . the V. 153:17
  light years from the V. 78:12
  provoke . . . the V. 27:4
Vegetable: without eating her v.s. 14:1
Vegetarian: drinking gin . . . a rigid V. 68:21
  often with v. leanings 255:9
  v.s have wicked eyes 241:16
Vegetarianism: declared v. doomed 71:14
Vegetate: others merely live; I v. 84:23
Vein: blood that flows in the v.s 336:7

Vélo: Aux v.s délirants 19:13
Venceremos: V. 18:15
Vending: I am a cunnin' v. machine 24:11
Venerable: aged rather than . . . v. 350:1
Venerability: v. factor creeps in 318:19
Venice: 36:13
  V. is like eating . . . chocolate 63:19
Ventre: V. offers us a grand vision 173:13
Ventriloquizing: V. for the unborn 139:10
Venus: V. de Milo 284:19
  flies off a sleeping V. 364:1
Verde: V. que te quiero v. 128:19
Verdi, Guiseppe: the strains of V. will come
  back 224:20
Verlaine, Paul: I'll stay off V. 258:9
Vermin: Tory Party . . . lower than v. 41:17
Verse: give up v., my boy 269:10
  little v.-factory 180:7
  v. . . . illness of the ear 22:24
  now it's lyric v. 347:1
Versuchen: alle die dich suchen, v. dich 282:16
Vertical: honour . . . the v. man 21:20
Verwandlung: Leben geht hin mit V. 281:17
Verweilende: das V. erst weiht uns ein 282:11
Vibration: those sympathetic v.s 230:19
Vicar: gesture like a v.'s daughter 362:17
Vice: clinging . . . to the v.s of his ancestors
  112:15
  existence of v.s is allowed 339:22
  full many a v. is born to blush 315:12
  go very light on v.s 258:2
  most difficult and nerve-racking v. 227:12
  most incorrigible v. . . . ignorance 62:16
  quotation is a national v. 347:1
  sinners . . . dishonour the v.s 336:17
  unnatural v.s are fathered 109:3
  v. is its own reward 90:12
  v. . . . the more ye see it th' better 103:17
Vichy: something V. about the French 251:3
Victim: England prefers v.s 215:18
  pestilences and there are v.s 62:17
  there are born v.s 162:6
  v.s who respect their executioners 296:8
  what the v. has done with his world 230:17
Victoria (Queen): 9:15, 356:19
  ghost of queen v. 222:24
Victorian: as the V.s were Christians 217:9
  barmaid of the V. soul 174:7
  [Dickens] antagonistic to the V. age 358:17
  long passed the V. Era 226:18
  slow pattern of V. England 116:11
  V.s had not . . . weekend 354:8
  V.s understood 48:18
Victorians: 72:20
Victories: u. of consciousness 334:20
Victory: before Alamein we never had a v.
  76:14
  in v. unbearable 77:8
  in v.: magnanimity 77:22
  not right that matters, but v. 155:5
  v. has a thousand fathers 182:13
  'V.!' he concluded 156:15
  v. in spite of all terror 73:22
  when I see a v. I'll do it 156:12
  will to conquer . . . condition of v. 118:8

Victuals: and tumble v. in 276:5
Vida: la v. es duda 338:1
Viennese: standpoint different . . . the new V.
     school 176:16
Vietnam: 9:8
  involved the public . . . question of V. 175:8
  to win in V. we will have 315:9
  V. was lost in the living rooms 218:10
View: doesn't have a point of v. 202:21
  points of v. . . . the same topic 14:4
Villa: Pancho V. in the morning editions
     285:6
Village: excellent if you were a v. 317:1
  global v. 217:13
  poverty is . . . a problem of two million v.s
     300:5
  v. had institutionalized 218:4
  v. house in England 44:13
Villain: brothel – what more can a v. 49:16
  if a man is going to be a v. 326:16
Vine: advise his client to plant v.s 365:24
Violation: so great a v. 197:12
Violence: attempt to reduce v. 253:15
  keep v. in the mind 12:13
  source of all v. 297:6
  v. is as American as cherry pie 64:4
  v. masquerading as love 192:8
  v. of revolutions is the v. 127:16
  v. shapes and obsesses 45:8
Violent: expect him to be most v. 248:16
Violet: v.s of the Undercliff 185:9
Violin: holding a v. is like holding a bird
     230:19
Virgil: debt to V. . . . a debt to Nature 72:8
Virgin: be inside with the five wise v.s 58:11
  before she was a v. 224:23
  for sweet-smelling v.s close 317:16
  four v.s wait without 18:5
Virginity: her emphasized v. 170:1
  more v., if you don't mind 333:16
  proclaimed an intact v. 270:15
  v. . . . limited capacity for love 306:19
  v. might possibly be quite nice 180:3
Virtue: drinking . . . a domestic v. 141:18
  form of every v. 206:7
  her prejudice in favour of v. 162:3
  in a good country v.s wouldn't be 51:18
  moderation . . . is no v. 134:10
  my v.'s still far too small 80:10
  our v.s now are the high 126:9
  praised for v.s you never had 318:19
  seven deadly v.s 226:14
  suspects himself of . . . cardinal v.s 116:4
  to find v. more difficult to portray 272:4
  try to make v.s of their weaknesses 229:10
  v. . . . has no sale 352:10
  v. . . . weakness of strong generals 132:12
  with animals, v. . . . its own reward 38:20
  what is v. 303:10
  world most needs . . . negative v.s 119:1
Visage: often meet your v. here 89:26
Vision: whoring not with v.s 186:15
  with his v. 292:2
Visit: never make long v.s 239:10
Vista: going to give me a little *v.* 102:16

Visually: we have become v. illiterate 133:8
Vitality: redolent, and full of v. 278:7
  v. in a woman . . . fury of creation 302:26
Vocabulary: one's v. needs . . . fertilizing
     347:20
Vocal: vasectomy of the v. cords 14:3
Vocational: *all* education is . . . v. 248:14
Vogue: Botticelli . . . working for *V.* 340:4
Voice: attraction through the . . . v. 147:12
  enchanting . . . v.s of young people 310:6
  English don't raise their v.s 151:3
  good voice but too autocratic 329:11
  higher the v. 248:11
  his v. was intimate 259:4
  now is your v. a marble 238:6
  Other V.s, Other Rooms 63:17
  sound of my own v. 248:17
  v. like beer trickling 361:9
  v. like hot, damp fur 182:23
  v. . . . made you think of lorgnettes 151:21
  v. . . . never had once to raise itself 170:19
  v. . . . shot through with marzipan 82:13
  v. that . . . ground silence 309:3
  v. that ordered those things 82:5
  v. that used to shake the ferryboats 222:22
  v. . . . to defrost her refrigerator 321:10
  v. without a face 23:2
  v.s just can't worm through 265:17
Void: sins . . . attempts to fill v.s 348:9
Voie: V. lactée ô sœur 19:8
Volcano: expect it to turn into a v. 323:9
Vole: passes the questing v. 347:4
Volonté: Victoire, c'est la V. 118:8
Voltaire: next to V. 290:17
  V. (the younger) 320:24
Voluntary: v. – that is to say 346:12
Vorticist: V. does not suck up 207:3
Vote: as the v. should ideally be used 164:4
  decision on how to v. 299:10
  give women the v. 302:15
  when they were given the v. 347:16
  lost us the tarts' v. 97:13
  straw v. only shows . . . the hot air 152:22
  v. means nothing to women 252:5
  v.s are to swords 43:5
Voter: half the v.s plus one 138:1
Voting: not the v. . . . it's the counting 319:12
Voyage: make v.s! – Attempt them 357:18
Vulgar: he has a v. mind 205:14
  it becomes v. 288:5
  rude remark or a v. action 357:23
Vulgarizing: haven't succeeded in . . . v. 162:18
Vulnerable: life persists in the v. 326:7
Vulture: v. dropping in for lunch 361:23

W

Waddy: W. is an infectious disease 187:7
Wage: more than better w.s 255:10
Wagner, Richard: W., if only she looked
     309:4
  W. is the Puccini of music 242:18

Waif: that land of w.s and strays 346:23
Waist: necklace . . . round her w. 308:3
Waistcoat: broad, comfortable w.s 198:21
  leaves his bottom w. button undone 255:7
Wait: I can w. 299:19
Waiter: calling the w. Max 292:19
Waiting: being kept w. about 255:1
  greater our capacity for w. 326:9
  people w. for you stand out 132:19
Waitress: w.s there were . . . rude 266:15
Wake: w. up . . . to be married 20:14
  part of it that w.s up 362:21
Wakey-wakey: w. 88:5
Waking: take my w. slow 284:8
  way she had of w. him 221:15
Wales: disasters of English history . . . W.
  346:2
  in South W. these three 329:6
  some sweetness from W. 329:5
  still parts of W. where 329:13
  too many of the artists of W. 328:19
Walk: if he had intended me to w. 241:3
  too large . . . to w. out of 84:16
Walking: trick . . . w. into himself 330:13
Wall: my father was the Great W. 344:12
  no part of the w.s 263:18
Wallace, Henry: 16:12
Wall-paper: one-armed man . . . pasting on w.
  152:2
Walpole, Robert: W. . . . said to open 333:17
Walrus: W. and Carpenter 205:4
Wampum: incredible w. 92:3
Want: actually w.s what he is supposed to w.
  123:13
  satisfying w.s . . . creates the w.s 127:10
  way that I w. to do it 364:7
  what one w.s to all and when 345:17
  you have w.s the way other people 146:14
Wanted: better to be w. for murder 360:9
  exactly what I w. 98:16
War: always the same . . . w. 316:12
  and the w. goes on 40:6
  as drama, the W. is . . . disappointing
  142:1
  beating of w. drums 189:16
  before the w. . . . it was summer 254:16
  boys will not be sent to . . . w.s 285:22
  can't be sure the w. will ever end 51:25
  can't fight in here. This is the W. Room
  130:5
  cold w. 29:18
  could have lost the w. in an afternoon
  173:7
  day w. broke out . . . 360:3
  enable it to make w. 348:10
  give a w. and nobody will come 295:11
  good w., one of the best 278:3
  guerilla fights the w. of the flea 325:1
  hatred of w. . . . playing soldiers 53:14
  how pretty w. is 19:7
  how we began this w. 271:16
  if the w. didn't happen to kill you 254:17
  ignorance of the art of w. 302:2
  in a civil w. a general must know 278:6
  in every w. they kill you 284:15

in . . . w. it is not right that matters 155:5
in w.: resolution 77:22
it is with men . . . that one makes w. 263:4
jaw-jaw is better than w.-w. 218:15
just like a couple between the w.s 266:3
lead this people into w. 359:18
life is more interesting in w. 166:9
like to see the government get out of w.
  150:23
like w. and fornication 243:13
live under the shadow of a w. 315:3
lose the w. in an afternoon 77:12
lose this w., I'll start another 95:21
make love not w. 17:9
my w.s were global 277:19
never lost a w. 285:7
never understood this liking for w. 36:20
no reason why this w. must go on 155:6
not at w. . . . in an armed conflict 106:13
not yet lost this w., but . . . overdrawn
  55:18
nothing that produced this w. 256:13
nothing unites the English like w. 235:21
one of the main effects of w. 343:10
plunge us into another Great W. 77:4
quickest way of ending a w. 256:6
see that Germany is winning the w. 335:10
should be called . . . the Unnecessary W.
  75:14
start bloody w.s they can't afford 314:4
strong enough to win a w. and wise 175:6
take care not to lose the next w. 77:10
that bungled, unwise w. 265:1
The W. to End W. 351:3
this w. twilight is trying 67:6
those who can win a w. well 75:12
w. abhorrent to all real women 120:19
w. against death . . . is the w. against w.
  153:22
w. against hunger 182:1
w. . . . always finds a way 51:27
w. can only be abolished through w. 222:2
w. correspondent has his stake 63:12
w. . . . does not escape the laws 274:6
w. hath no fury 238:10
w. . . . have to face next time 360:2
w. . . . impossible to hold the poets back
  132:21
W. is being deliberately prolonged 298:9
w. is capitalism with the gloves off 320:15
w. is politics 221:23
w. is the universal perversion 276:2
w. is too important to be left 79:1
w. is w. 254:8
w. will never cease 229:15
w. . . . millions of sleeping people 143:10
w. was very nearly lost with him 158:9
w. wasn't fought that way 287:5
w.s are not won by evacuations 76:1
w.s are not won by . . . militias 76:2
w.s begin in the minds 338:7
w.s cause armaments 219:14
w.s more evil, ere all w.s cease 69:3
w.s of the peoples will be more terrible
  73:6

War – *Contd.*
  we have all lost the w. 194:23
  what a w. is about only when 50:7
  what, then, was w. 139:2
  what they could do with . . . a good w.
    51:15
  when the w. broke out she 346:19
  when the w. of the giants is over 77:1
  when you're at w. you think 356:7
  wrong w., at the wrong place 49:10
War and Peace: read *W.* in twenty minutes
    13:27
Ware: if you want to buy my w.s 267:17
Warehouse: will make a good w. 351:17
Warfare: peculiarity of aerial w. 351:2
Warmonger: drawn into conflicts by w.s
    315:18
Warmth: cold was cursing the w. 332:3
Warner: working for W. Bros 238:1
Warring: carries his w. country between his
    toes 112:6
Warrior: this is the happy w. 277:12
Wash: I'm Gonna W. That Man 146:9
  w. their hands nearly every day 302:4
Washing: breezy freedom . . . w. up 349:7
  I get very bored with w. 215:20
Wasp: like w.s. Let them know who's 89:18
  small revolver for . . . w.s 308:18
Waste: I don't particularly mind w. 54:14
  W. Land might not have been w. paper
    220:9
  w. remains and kills 111:2
Watch: like a fat gold w. 265:18
  looking at their w.es . . . shaking them 43:6
  or my w. has stopped 224:3
  our w.es by the public clocks 109:7
  people . . . w. each other w. each other
    104:8
  why not carry a w. 333:8
Watchmaker: had known, I should have
    become a w. 108:3
Water: biggest waste of w. 107:7
  but on w. I am a coward 155:16
  Charley, do not go upon the w. 310:11
  chittering w.s of 177:12
  cold w. . . . instead 15:17
  enough salt w. 289:3
  glass of w. . . Irish or Scotch 145:1
  have passed a lot of w. since then 134:18
  he's fallen in the w. 235:12
  hitherandthithering w.s of 177:14
  invented by w. 283:3
  is now a W. Carrier 16:21
  me squirt of w. 24:14
  nothing but food and w. 114:8
  sea-side . . . by useless water 100:10
  streets full of w. 36:13
  w. in w.-colour 65:12
  w. still keeps falling 76:16
  when I makes w. I makes w. 176:11
Water-closet: let us construct a w. 176:12
  w. . . . a solo instrument 137:16
  whole island is a w. 217:7
Watergate: 370:7
Watneys: wot, no W. 18:19

Waugh, Evelyn: my friend W., who, like you
    73:5
Wave: bright-haired w. of its breathing 220:15
  Cross alone has flown the w. 90:1
  I made the w. 291:8
  in the midst of the w.s 248:3
  never a w. of all her w.s 185:1
  tideless w.s struggled 64:11
  w.s are a city of doors slamming 277:13
Wavelength: it seems she's on my w.
    157:1
Waxed: man has just w. the floor 247:22
Waxworks: w. inhabited by gramophones
    97:3
Way: best w. out is always through 124:20
  there be triple w.s to take 185:26
Wayside: advise not w. folk 185:2
We: referring to himself as 'w.' 14:5
Weak: like all w. men 227:3
  w. are always forced to decide 46:2
  w. have one weapon 42:5
Weakness: make virtues of their w. 229:10
  never support two w.es 356:17
  tolerantly and justly towards the w.es
    143:11
Wealth: dilettante . . . where w. and literature
    103:16
  flatteries of w. and power 35:9
  in every . . . state w. is a sacred thing 121:5
  salvation belonged to . . . w. 165:9
  to apologize for her w. 354:4
  w. accumulates 183:12
  w. is not without . . . advantages 127:6
  w. . . . . must be advertised 127:8
Wealthy: immeasurably w. 204:18
Weapon: deadlier w. than the machine-gun
    255:3
  invented an extraordinary w. 242:1
Weasel: use a 'w. word' 286:6
  w. under the cocktail cabinet 264:23
Weather: check the w. . . . before they pull
    314:11
  w. forecast . . . some kind of spoof 210:6
Weber, Max: as W. traced the social effects
    165:9
Wedding: cried at all his own w.s 25:2
  funeral . . . it's a w. 350:3
  he disliked attending w.s 150:10
  w.s is sadder than funerals 33:16
Weed: to eradicate the w.s 260:16
Week: eight days a w. 202:10
  greatest w. in the history of the world 250:1
  w. is a long time in politics 359:4
Weekday: one of those w.s, vacant 47:4
Weekend: don't depend on a long w. 66:11
  not . . . go away for the w. 354:8
Weekendmanship: basic w. 268:14
Weep: ninety-nine men w. while one laughs
    312:13
  w. because I know all things 368:14
Weight: beginning to lose w. 363:9
Welcome: hello, good evening and w. 124:2
Welfare: Nature's W. State 79:11
Well: didn't he do w. 120:5
  kingdom of the w. 313:5

Welles, Orson: 221:2
Well-rounded: I am not a w. person 35:14
Wells, H. G.: 322:1, 352:22
Welsh: W. . . . just sing 346:4
  wouldn't put up with the W. 241:11
Welt: preise dem Engel die W. 282:4
Wembley: W. . . . a vague malaise 173:16
Wenceslas: confidential adviser to King W.
  172:19
Wenchman: Reefer was a w. 177:16
Wept: By Grand Central Station I . . . W.
  309:11
Werk: doch zugleich ein W. 240:7
Wesker, Arnold: W. . . . four hoarse men
  321:5
West: blow from the east to the w. 269:15
West, Mae: 147:12
Western: most easterly of w. peoples 187:12
  their goods along the W. Road 186:5
  when you've seen one W. 355:1
Westerner: average W. 253:2
Westminster: W. Abbey . . . the lumber-room
  71:10
Whale: trying to grill a w. 271:10
What: 'w. ho!' I said 361:4
Wheel: can turn the w. on which he turns
  109:19
Wheelbarrow: depends upon a red w. 358:6
When: had forgotten to say 'W.' 363:19
  only a rustic knows exactly w. 215:16
Whence: w. did he w. 203:7
Wherefore: w. does he why 203:7
Whim: she has a w. of iron 153:12
Whisker: acceptable by growing side-w.s
  351:6
  can't speak above a w. 221:1
  w.s . . . grown under glass 361:16
Whisky: committed the sin of w. 313:18
  has w. on their breath 338:15
  hot w. and water 187:13
  little nips of w. 17:4
  what with education and w. 346:1
Whisper: good author . . . what he w.s
  310:5
Whispering: I was w. in her mouth 223:19
Whistle: I W. a Happy Tune 146:1
  W. While You Work 99:10
  you know how to w., don't you 44:16
White: one destiny. And it is w. 112:1
  W. people in this country 25:7
  they'll 'elp you a lot with the W. 185:15
  whether a w. man likes him 217:2
  w. is not my favourite colour 193:16
  w. man in Africa 203:22
  w. man's brother 184:12
  whiter than w. 11:1
White Fang: 237:13
Whitehall: known . . . in W. as 'Call me
  God' 295:1
White House: between Nixon and the W.
  182:11
  gathered at the W. 181:28
  no whitewash at the W. 250:3
  on the way to the W. 318:11
Whitewash: no w. at the White House 250:3

Whitman, Walt: 89:21, 89:26, 210:8
  it is pre-W. 231:8
  viejo hermoso W. 128:16
Whizz-Bang: Here Comes a W. 353:2
Who: w., whom 201:16
Whore: flowing into second-rate w.s 266:3
  give the w.s as little as possible 358:16
  one more w. in the world 51:21
  we are not political w.s 245:14
  you can lead a w. to culture 258:17
Whorehouse: virgin territory for w.s 63:16
Why: w. did you do that 123:7
Whyness: w. . . . makes life worth living 31:13
Wicked: flaws . . . mine is being w. 330:12
  to believe that men were naturally w. 226:13
Wickedness: w. of the world is so great 52:6
Widow: Black W., death 212:6
  college w. stood for something 224:14
  position, as a captain's w. with means 114:22
  prefer w.s to unmarried mothers 297:9
  sons o' the W. 187:4
  than w. to one safe home 232:8
  w. by her first husbands 201:20
  W. gives the party 187:5
Wife: all my w. has taken 301:12
  and a w. to boot 201:19
  fond of his w. 302:5
  goes for the neighbour's w. 38:12
  his w., a former beauty queer 201:22
  his w. . . . edited him 55:1
  I'll start another in my w.'s name 95:21
  insulting to sleep with your w. 24:7
  life of the party . . . death of his w. 313:22
  man's character . . . health of his w. 84:21
  over a statement made by my w. 123:5
  silk purse out of your w.'s ear 241:19
  sleeping with someone else's w. 48:19
  w. . . . lets it go at that 29:6
  w. . . . provides the climate 52:18
  w. to tell him what to do 220:10
  w. . . . turn him into somebody else 72:1
  would have made a splendid w. 152:14
  your w. happens to be travelling 220:11
  your w. left you in May 250:9
Wild: Manhattan . . . its w. life 321:11
Wilde, Oscar: 204:13
  assume that O. said it 258:18
  W. . . . brought up in Ireland 336:12
Wilder, Thornton: 79:5
Wilderness: all walking in one kind of w.
  147:2
Will: Free W. and Predestination . . . identical
  75:1
  having a retrospective is making a w. 243:5
  indomitable w. in my heart 154:16
  strange as a w.-o'-the-wisp 231:3
  w. is never free 66:1
Williams, Shirley: W. has such an advantage
  352:23
Willing: only w. when you compel them
  132:15
Wilmington: the Long Man of W. 186:22
Wilson, Harold: 16:15, 57:5, 167:13, 205:3,
  205:4
  14th Mr W. 100:19

Wilson, Woodrow: 183:7, 309:10
W. has blundered 107:8
Win: anyone can w. 10:3
  even when he cheated he couldn't w. 150:12
  whether we w. . . . it will be the end 316:4
Wind: blowin' in the w. 104:20
  know which way the w. blows 105:6
  learned how the w. would sound 328:23
  over the heather the west w. 22:26
  story is like the w. 341:14
  w. came keen 225:21
  w. of change 218:17
  w.s that would blow them 44:19
Winden: so drängen wir uns plötzlich W. auf
  281:7
Window: don't stand too near the w. 315:6
  I'm cleaning w.s 118:18
Wine: chosen as carefully as the w. 292:19
  hold the w. list just out of sight 268:20
  red w. of Shiraz into urine 99:1
  religions change; beer and w. remain 12:20
  w. they drink in Paradise 68:15
  w. was a farce 269:24
Wing: angel . . . in working its w.s 144:12
  make the right w. strong 299:7
  on a W. and a Prayer 9:14
  take off their w.s 362:19
Winner: knowing a real w. 250:7
Winter: do we believe in w. 287:13
  say that they enjoy the w. 9:12
  will it be w. for you 281:7
  w. is for women 265:19
  w.'s big with summer 292:3
  wie der W. der eben geht 282:15
Winters: blitz of a boy is Timothy W. 66:10
Wire: barbed w. next to the skin 361:5
Wisdom: bid you enter the house of his w.
  131:3
  listening to his w. or . . . my own 75:5
  w. to know the difference 249:6
  women . . . the guardians of w. 364:9
Wise: where does a w. man kick a pebble
  69:14
  w. man thinks once 36:8
  w. forgive but do not forget 323:17
  w. of the world have made dumb 96:12
Wiser: looked w. when seated 183:7
  no w. . . . but far better informed 43:1
  they are w. than they 227:16
Wit: 109:26
  give . . . a pretence of w. 368:12
  W.'s End 259:18
Withering: whither is he w. 203:7
Withers: up to the neck in wrung w. 87:13
Witticism: keep hot coals . . . than a w. 45:7
Witty: conquered people tend to be w. 35:15
Wives: bricklayers kick their w. 351:11
  start ploughing pertinent w. 12:5
Wodehouse, P. G.: 252:13
  like W. dropping Jeeves 347:25
Wolf: Who's Afraid of the Big Bad W. 99:8
Wolves: thrown to the w. with a bargain 45:4
Woman: affectionate w. . . . no escape 50:9
  being a w. is of interest 199:10
  breed a w. 230:13

dealing with a w. is like 169:2
every w. knows that 29:6
give a w. an inch she'll park 353:16
he can see through a w. 225:3
knew a w. by the man who 14:2
let a w. in your life 203:14
make any w. with them look guilty 116:26
man and w. are two locked caskets 99:4
man knows a w. is a w. 210:14
Man wants . . . W. even more 331:4
masculine figure created by a w. 229:7
middle-class w. of England 28:10
most winning w. . . . was hanged 101:16
not stand for being called a w. 347:10
once a w. has forgiven her man 98:18
one is not born a w. 30:6
one w. of too many 81:13
only job . . . a w. can beat a man in 152:4
original w. . . . imitates a man 323:6
presence of a w. is different 39:7
takes just like a w., yes 104:26
The W. in the Case 115:12
thinking of a w. soft as Eve 328:14
to know the mind of a w. 197:15
too crafty a w. 226:15
unemancipated w. 212:3
vitality in a w. . . . fury of creation 302:26
way for a w. to hold a man 313:13
when a w. behaves like a man 111:11
when a w. takes her latest 152:16
why can't a w. be more like a man 203:19
without . . . the w. I love 107:14
w., but she isn't a sister 17:14
w. can forgive a man 227:8
w. governs America 219:16
w. he feels 225:6
w. is jealous because of her lack 141:11
w. is made for man 238:13
w. is physically polygamous 53:8
w. . . . may not qualify as a curate 318:17
w. needs a man not a radiator cap 48:2
w. still at her knitting 265:19
w. wants her friends 216:3
w. who can sacrifice 293:21
w. who did not please me 272:13
w. who has tried and not been able 170:11
w. who is . . . anxious to get children 123:4
w. who is . . . kind to dogs 32:15
w. who lives for others 205:17
w. . . . will suddenly do it 69:19
w. without a man is like a fish 137:21
W.'s Day . . . the revolution 334:6
w.'s place . . . in the gaol 50:3
w.'s virtue is man's . . . invention 309:7
you don't know a w. 204:8
Womanhood: became aware of her own w.
  194:18
Womb: w. is all 282:1
Women: boasting about our equality for w.
  312:8
born with the attitude toward . . . w. 321:8
came back from Dunkirk with two w.
  146:18
cocksure w. 196:21
English w. are . . . diatonic 278:1

English w. are elegant 237:15
few w. care to be laughed at 24:3
finest w. who ever walked the streets 352:17
give w. the vote 302:15
he gets off with w. 200:6
I always liked big w. 65:19
if every man gave up w. 125:6
in an experience of w. that extends 101:15
its w. weeping 22:8
lose the touch of . . . w.'s hands 63:6
men come of age at sixty, w. at fifteen
    317:8
men see objects, w. see 120:19
no mothers, only w. 305:17
only fourteen types of w. 215:12
poker . . . in a house with w. 357:24
she looks at other w. as though 114:27
some w. can't see a telephone 226:17
three w. in my life 241:10
try as w. will 207:23
vote means nothing to w. 252:5
when w. want to make mistakes 180:6
w. add zest to the unlicensed 327:11
w. are brighter than men 211:13
w. are in furious secret rebellion 305:22
w. are like elephants to me 114:10
w. are not so completely enslaved 305:25
w. are reputed never to be disgusted 141:3
w. . . . as looking-glasses 365:10
w. can do nothing except love 227:9
w. dislike his books 256:8
w. do not find it difficult 217:4
w. . . . guardians of wisdom 364:9
w. have very little idea of 141:12
w. like quiet men 15:9
w. . . . mix something up with sex 355:8
w. never have young minds 97:5
w. . . . only willing when you compel them
    132:15
w. set out to try to change a man 98:20
w. . . . sort of loose-fitting men 48:9
w. tempt you more than plenty 157:11
w. tried to talk like the men 161:25
w. want to hot them up 180:15
w. who love the same man 32:14
w. who wear ankle socks 37:10
w. will write novels 228:1
w. would rather be right 247:5
Wonder: discovery . . . continuous flight from
    w. 108:8
philosophy is . . . w. 354:12
to see the Boneless W. 73:16
Wood: culture is no better than its w.s 23:8
in the w. . . . a second chance 29:9
see the w. for the leaves 206:6
why . . . people . . . love chopping w. 107:19
Woodcock: spirits of well-shot w. 40:12
Woodland: about the w.s I will go 159:3
Woodworm: w. obligingly held hands 103:9
Woofle: uttered a stricken w. 363:18
Woolf, Virginia: Who's Afraid of W.? 12:1
W., I enjoyed talking 308:10
Wooster, feed the W. face 362:6
Word: better w. than 'prefabricated' 76:19
    compressing the largest amount of w.s 73:17

conversationalist who adds 'in other w.s'
    240:17
dangerous w. . . . w. for brother 357:15
deluge of w.s . . . drizzle of thought 98:4
forgets w.s as one forgets 347:20
had the right w. 55:5
if you use a 'weasel.' 286:6
let the w. go forth 181:24
like short w.s and vulgar fractions 74:16
many frank w.s in our respective 85:13
more than I can express in w.s 246:13
most purposeful w. 236:1
much harder to turn w. into deed 135:27
not quite a nice w. for a young woman
    258·14
nothing but foolish w.s 187:10
page that aches for a w. 98:17
poets are the ones who write in w.s 120:15
provide long w.s to cover the errors 70:22
put the w.s down and push them 347:24
recover from the futility of w.s 178:9
right w.s in the right order 44:1
set a chime of w.s tinkling 310:8
squeak . . . the wished-for w.s 317:17
that w.s alone cannot do 78:2
these w.s rang in their ears 243:15
two most beautiful w.s 171:6
until we learn the use of living w.s 97:3
w. carved on the sill 138:13
w. is half Greek and half Latin 300:10
w. was . . . a complete landscape 161:2
w.s as they are used or stand aside 81:19
w.s never seen 210:8
Wordsworth, William: all W. was famous for
    84:7
once saw W. drunk 159:12
Work: do a thing badly you have to w. 339:15
give me w. while I may live 158:3
I haven't had time to w. 182:18
in their w.s . . . wrap its lunch 61:9
it's off to w. we go 99:11
make so much w. for each other 260:15
man . . . grows beyond his w. 317:4
manage to get so much w. done 36:3
men who simply do the w. 186:30
more . . . of my w.s are left behind 36:5
my w. . . . I don't like it 25:4
nice w. if you can get it 130:15
nine hundred doing the w. 320:17
no place . . . to get any w. done 354:21
none of the w. . . . was his 150:6
one's w. is terribly important 289:20
only be acquired by hard w. 228:4
put a man out of w. 183:8
to make a man w. . . . hold gold 115:20
toad w. 193:19
volume of w. 260:13
w. as if everything depended on man
    314:12
w. begins with the division of labour 218:5
w. . . . done by men who do not feel 127:15
w. expands 260:12
w. gives . . . illusion of existing 162:8
w. has become a leisure activity 9:1
w. is accomplished 263:10

Work – *Contd.*
w. . . . more fun than fun 89:12
w. was like cats 14:13
Worker: I am a sociable w. 33:12
inferiority complexes among the w.s 206:10
no w.s, only candidates 26:9
used to dealing with estate w.s 101:1
weapon with a w. at each end 15:15
w. would sooner have a £5 note 44:11
Working: each for the joy of w. 187:1
inherent in W.-class life 255:1
ordinary w. man 255:10
party . . . best elements of the w. class 316:3
w.-class men reading Shelley 48:10
wrote about the w. classes 347:16
World: all sorts to make a w. 301:17
and again leave a lifeless w. 172:22
development in the Third W. 136:5
English speaking race against the w. 133:14
ethics . . . a condition of the w. 360:23
finished remaking the map of the w. 158:18
I see the w. as a football 203:5
I turn and the w. turns 173:9
if the whole w. were tranquil 56:1
interesting discovery about the w. 48:20
it was a good w. to live in 254:15
most important figure in the w. 14:9
mother protected me from the w. 90:15
not the w. . . . so much worse 73:1
one may not regard the w. 189:10
renounced everything . . . but the w. 244:19
Third W. never sold 244:17
this w. has no higher meaning 61:23
Unseen W. 245:15
when the w. was young 30:20
who adore the w. 296:6
whole w. a vast house of assignation 90:18
w. can only be grasped by action 54:3
w. could get along 297:5
w. does seem to become one 233:6
w. ended yesterday 34:11
w. is a much worse place than I ever 167:2
w. is an army marching backwards 82:12
w. is an oyster 232:19
w. is becoming a lunatic asylum 209:9
w. is everything that is the case 360:16
w. is the sum-total 253:13
w. . . . kills the very good 151:15
w. . . . nearer to God than ever 46:1
w. outside your head is different 356:15
w. rolls under the long thrust 160:5
w. safe for hypocrisy 364:6
w. to help me along 48:21
w. will . . . make no comment 155:7
w. would begin to turn 37:18
w. would not be the same 253:9
w. . . . youthful, after all 109:8
w.s revolve like ancient women 109:11
World-saver: one w. at a time is enough 85:15
Worm: earth-w. . . . what does he teach 102:9
I was one of the w.s 30:5
long w. that has no turning 11:6
most exclusive w.s 259:5
sister to the fathering w. 327:14
why should a w. turn 79:8

Worried: duties – to be w. and not to be w. 120:3
Worry: cakes . . . green with w. 114:21
w. . . . interest paid on trouble 167:5
Worrying: w. . . . what's happening now 25:3
Worship: take away their w. 301:14
Worst: like to be told the w. 73:13
makes the w. of it 20:8
prepared for the worst . . . acting 175:6
think the w. when they see 92:22
your w., and we will do our best 74:2
Would: it's not 'cause I w.n't 267:18
Wound: safe with his w. 298:5
streaming w. which heals 126:9
world's worst w. 298:4
Wrapping: Christmas through its w. 353:12
Wreckage: contemplate the w. 363:9
Wrestled: w. with a self-adjusting . . . table 330:7
Wretchedness: the w. of being rich 309:20
Write: have to w. something on a . . . mirror 103:13
I would not w. for no one 82:1
I w. for . . . self-enlightenment 64:1
I w. in a . . . broken-down patois 67:18
one can w. . . . of others 347:19
when I w. after dark 82:21
w. a page that reads badly 53:1
w. for children . . . as . . . for adults 136:1
w. for yourself and have no public 85:1
w. it, damn you, w. it 177:19
w. when I feel spiteful 197:5
Writer: all my good w.s are in jail 134:21
American w.s want to be 343:1
autocriticism does honour to the w. 168:3
best . . . for a w. is to be taken up 83:13
don't expect their w. to redeem 308:6
every w. . . . is a masochist 39:9
function of a w. . . . produce a masterpiece 84:9
great w. creates a world of his own 82:22
health of a w. should not be too good 83:17
Hollywood seems to want a w. 67:15
how few w.s can prostitute 119:18
if a w. has to rob his mother, he will 113:1
Irish themselves detest . . . w.s 33:18
married . . . only half a w. 83:10
measured the virtues of other w.s 46:16
no regime has ever loved . . . w.s 312:5
not everything about a bad w. is bad 246:1
not really a w. . . . a non-stop talker 52:25
our principal w.s 215:19
pleasant to be written up, even by a w. 65:20
serious w. is not . . . solemn 151:9
Shakespeare, or any other w. 256:1
successful w. 206:16
w., a free man 297:7
w. can give an illusion 347:15
w. . . . imprisonment for a manuscript 341:3
w. much older than themselves 271:9
w. needs . . . five pounds a day 84:3
w. what he thinks about critics 146:15
w. who interrupts his work 274:10

w. who is the impregnator 353:10
w.'s ambition 189:17
w.s aren't exactly people 116:16
w.'s business to hold opinions 369:8
w.s . . . convey more than they mean 83:2
w.s have . . . vulgar curiosity 23:15
w.s started to suck up 347:16
w.s were really people 172:8
your child is a w. 199:11
Writing: all w. . . . a yearning 327:9
cheap, shoddy . . . kind of w. 67:19
don't put anything in w. 30:2
get it in w. 199:16
good w. . . . energy and artifice 149:7
I am w. to myself 283:7
obstacle to professional w. today 36:4
piece of w. is bad 205:21
that's not w., that's typing 63:18
we are the w. on your wall 137:18
w. . . . a guided dream 46:13
w. is like getting married 244:15
w. . . . like running through a field 321:18
w. . . . paring away of oneself 117:8
w. . . . *swimming under water* 117:7
w. . . . to out-argue one's past 113:4
w. was just a preparation 348:13
Wrong: always w. at the right moment 45:16
and he did her w. 16:4
could not endure being w. 61:13
do the w. thing correctly 293:16
financial interest in being w. 283:19
finds everything w. and expects it 128:1
I know when I'm doing w. 358:14
ladder of success, w. by w. 352:4
let the w. cry out as raw 314:16
like w.s hushed-up 257:6
logic is the art of going w. 17:6
nothing to beat being . . . w. 121:18
right . . . to be w. 323:7
there are different kinds of w. 81:15
two w.s . . . make a good excuse 323:18
why . . . do the w. people travel 89:2
w. sort of people 366:3
w. sort take a mean advantage 362:18
w. war, at the w. place 49:10
Wronged: not to be w. is to forgo 349:8
Wykehamist: A rather dirty W. 41:8

X

Xmas: x. is a good time 357:1
X-ray: replace X. by hearsay 329:12

Y

Yacht: sink my y. to make my guests go 117:2
Yard: have a y. which is 3.37 inches 87:9
Year: dragon of y.s is almost done 40:7
light y.s from the Vatican 78:12
man who stood at the gate of the y.
148:12
Yearning: all writing . . . a y. 327:9

Yeats, W. B.: understood Y.'s poems 293:5
Yellow: things you will learn from the Y.
185:15
Yeoman: lie down, young y. 159:4
Yes: always 'y. sir', 'no sir' 278:20
don't say y. until 370:5
I did answer Y. to Someone 145:17
way of getting the answer y. 61:14
y. . . . on imperfect information 47:13
Yesterday: art of keeping up with y. 222:16
Y.'s Men 192:1
Yeti: little in civilization to appeal to a Y.
154:8
Yid: put the id back in y. 287:14
Yip-i-addy-addy-i-ay: Y. 142:13
You: y. are me and what have we done 82:7
Young: ale from the Country of the Y.
368:14
as y. as the woman he feels 225:6
came to this world very y. 298:13
die y., but it's . . . kissing God 56:4
differed from any y. person 170:4
enchanting . . . voices of y. people 310:6
how y. the policemen look 154:3
I am sixty years y. 333:2
I feel as y. as I ever did 36:14
just as y. as they were 277:2
knew the worst too y. 185:10
man . . . rather y. for his years 361:20
nowness that occurs in y. lives 218:8
old man marrying a y. girl 329:20
only the y. die good 153:13
put off being y. till you retire 193:13
so y. . . . his life before him 83:13
try to tell us we're too y. 96:7
while I am y. and lusty 258:19
women never have y. minds 97:5
you can be y. without money 357:11
y. can do for the old 305:19
y. have aspirations 293:10
y. man who has not wept 295:16
y. men read chronicles 71:6
Younger: difficult never to have been y.
316:16
I hope . . . that he has y. people 273:18
I'm y. than that now 105:5
jaundiced eye on its y. sons 361:19
something y. than she looks 115:3
trouble with our y. authors 228:8
Youngman: let me die a y.'s death 216:15
Youngster: letting the y.s in 28:12
y.s are – unfortunate 169:14
Youth: y. would be an ideal 21:6
due to y., drink and good health 237:14
in this way I spent y. 193:15
strong disposition in y. 270:3

Z

Z: unto Z my pen drew nigh 96:20
Zangwill, Israel: 333:13
Zebra: could be a z. synchronized 173:6
is a z. without stripes a z. 360:13

Zeitgeist: mind of the Z. 207:21
Zeppelin: Z. . . . knocked down an oak tree
  86:4
Zion: they rest awhile in Z. 187:6
Zipless: z. fuck is the purest thing 176:4
Zoo: a human z. 241:7

Zürich: learned three things in Z. 320:20
  little gnomes of Z. 358:19
Zwischenraum: nahm den Z. heraus
  240:1
Zugvögel: sind nicht wie die Z. verständigt
  281:7